Microsoft® Office Professional

June Jamrich Parsons
University of the Virgin Islands

Dan Oja
GuildWare, Inc.

Cheryl L. Willis
University of Houston, University Park

Joseph J. Adamski
Grand Valley State University

S. Scott Zimmerman
Brigham Young University

Beverly B. Zimmerman
Brigham Young University

A DIVISION OF COURSE TECHNOLOGY
ONE MAIN STREET, CAMBRIDGE, MA 02142

an International Thomson Publishing company 

Cambridge • Albany • Bonn • Boston • Cincinnati • London • Madrid • Melbourne • Mexico City
New York • Paris • San Francisco • Singapore • Tokyo • Toronto • Washington

Microsoft Office Professional - New Perspectives is published by CTI.

Managing Editor	Mac Mendelsohn
Series Consulting Editor	Susan Solomon
Product Manager	Barbara Clemens
Production Supervisor	Kathryn Dinovo
Text Designer	Sally Steele
Cover Designer	John Gamache

For more information contact:
Course Technology
One Main Street
Cambridge, MA 02142

International Thomson Publishing Europe
Berkshire House 168-173
High Holborn
London WCIV 7AA
England

Thomas Nelson Australia
102 Dodds Street
South Melbourne, 3205
Victoria, Australia

Nelson Canada
1120 Birchmount Road
Scarborough, Ontario
Canada M1K 5G4

International Thomson Editores
Campos Eliseos 385, Piso 7
Col. Polanco
11560 Mexico D.F. Mexico

International Thomson Publishing GmbH
Königswinterer Strasse 418
53227 Bonn
Germany

International Thomson Publishing Asia
211 Henderson Road
#05-10 Henderson Building
Singapore 0315

International Thomson Publishing Japan
Hirakawacho Kyowa Building, 3F
2-2-1 Hirakawacho
Chiyoda-ku, Tokyo 102
Japan

ISBN 0-7600-4664-6

Printed in the United States of America

10 9 8 7 6 5 4 3 2 1

From the Publisher

At Course Technology, we believe that technology will transform the way that people teach and learn. We are very excited about bringing you, college professors and students, the most practical and affordable technology-related products available.

The Course Technology Development Process

Our development process is unparalleled in the higher education publishing industry. Every product we create goes through an exacting process of design, development, review, and testing.

Reviewers give us direction and insight that shape our manuscripts and bring them up to the latest standards. Every manuscript is quality tested. Students whose backgrounds match the intended audience work through every keystroke, carefully checking for clarity, and pointing out errors in logic and sequence. Together with our own technical reviewers, these testers help us ensure that everything that carries our name is error-free and easy to use.

Course Technology Products

We show both *how* and *why* technology is critical to solving problems in college and in whatever field you choose to teach or pursue. Our time-tested, step-by-step instructions provide unparalleled clarity. Examples and applications are chosen and crafted to motivate students.

The Course Technology Team

This book will suit your needs because it was delivered quickly, efficiently, and affordably. In every aspect of business, we rely on a commitment to quality and the use of technology. Every employee contributes to this process. The names of all our employees are listed below.

Diana Armington, Tim Ashe, Debora Barrow, Stephen M. Bayle, Ann Marie Buconjic, Jody Buttafoco, Kerry Cannell, Jei Lee Chong, Jim Chrysikos, Barbara Clemens, Susan Collins, John M. Connolly, Stephanie Crayton, Myrna D'Addario, Lisa D'Alessandro, Jodi Davis, Howard S. Diamond, Kathryn Dinovo, Jennifer Dolan, Joseph B. Dougherty, Patti Dowley, Laurie Duncan, Karen Dwyer, MaryJane Dwyer, Kristen Dyer, Chris Elkhill, Don Fabricant, Jane Fraser, Victor Frengut, Jeff Goding, Laurie Gomes, Eileen Gorham, Catherine Griffin, Jamie Harper, Roslyn Hooley, Marjorie Hunt, Matt Kenslea, Marybeth LaFauci, Susannah Lean, Brian Leussler, Kim Mai, Margaret Makowski, Tammy Marciano, Elizabeth Martinez, Debbie Masi, Don Maynard, Kathleen McCann, Sarah McLean, Jay McNamara, Mac Mendelsohn, Karla Mitchell, Kim Munsell, Michael Ormsby, Debbie Parlee, Kristen Patrick, Charlie Patsios, Darren Perl, Kevin Phaneuf, George J. Pilla, Nicole Jones Pinard, Nancy Ray, Brian Romer, Laura Sacks, Carla Sharpe, Deborah Shute, Roger Skilling, Jennifer Slivinski, Christine Spillett, Audrey Tortolani, Michelle Tucker, David Upton, Jim Valente, Mark Valentine, Karen Wadsworth, Renee Walkup, Donna Whiting, Rob Williams, Janet Wilson, Lisa Yameen.

Preface

Course Technology is proud to present this new book in its Windows series. This book is designed for a first course on Windows and Microsoft Office Professional, which includes Microsoft Word 6.0, Microsoft Excel 5.0, Microsoft Access 2.0, and PowerPoint 4.0. It capitalizes on the energy and enthusiasm students have for the Windows environment and clearly teaches students how to take full advantage of the power of Windows and Microsoft Office.

Organization and Coverage

This book is divided into eight parts:

Essential Computer Concepts
Microsoft Windows 3.1 Tutorials
Introductory Microsoft Office Professional
Introductory Microsoft Word 6.0 for Windows Tutorials
Introductory Microsoft Excel 5.0 for Windows Tutorials
Introducing Microsoft Access 2.0 for Windows Tutorials
Brief Microsoft PowerPoint 4.0 for Windows Tutorials
Integrating Microsoft Office Applications

The first two parts acclimate students to the microcomputer environment. Using the vehicle of reading and interpreting a microcomputer advertisement, **"Essential Computer Concepts"** presents an overview of computer concepts. It includes only those concepts students need before they go into the lab. The two **Microsoft Windows 3.1** tutorials use step-by-step instructions to teach students the essentials skills they need to navigate in the Windows environment—everything from using the mouse, dialog boxes, and menus, to basic file management. "Essential Computer Concepts" and the Windows 3.1 tutorials are unique in their approach, using case scenarios to exemplify the concepts and skills and demonstrating *why* students need to learn them.

The next six parts, **"Introducing Microsoft Office Professional," Microsoft Word 6.0 for Windows** tutorials, **Microsoft Excel 5.0 for Windows** tutorials, **Microsoft Access 2.0 for Windows** tutorials, **Microsoft PowerPoint 4.0 for Windows** tutorials, and **"Integrating Microsoft Office Applications,"** contain hands-on practice and step-by-step instructions on how to use these Windows applications. The **"Introducing Microsoft Office Professional"** section introduces the four Office applications, explains how they work together, and shows students how to use the Office Manager toolbar to switch between applications.

In the four **Microsoft Word 6.0 for Windows** tutorials students learn how to plan, create, edit, format, preview, and print Word documents. By the end of these tutorials, students will have learned how to create multiple-page documents, using tables, styles, headers, and footers, and transfer data between documents.

In the five **Microsoft Excel 5.0 for Windows** tutorials, students learn how to plan, build, test, and document Excel worksheets. In addition to the basics, students will learn how to embed clip art in a chart, use functions, formulas, and absolute references, and create charts.

In the six **Microsoft Access 2.0 for Windows** tutorials, students learn to plan, create, and maintain a database. They learn to retrieve information by creating queries and developing professional-looking reports. Students also learn to create customized forms to access and enter data in a database. The tutorials emphasize the ease-of-use features included in the Access software: toolbar and toolbox buttons, Shortcut menus, graphical relationship tools, graphical query by example (QBE), Cue Cards, and Wizards. After completing the tutorials students will be able to create input masks, import data, create parameter queries, link multiple tables, and create custom forms and reports.

In the four **Microsoft PowerPoint 4.0 for Windows** tutorials, students learn to plan a presentation, create presentations containing text and graphics, and create a slide show.

Approach

This book distinguishes itself from other Windows applications textbooks because of its unique two-pronged approach. First, it motivates students by demonstrating *why* they need to learn the concepts and skills and by teaching with a task-driven, rather than a feature-driven, approach. In working through the tutorials—each motivated by a realistic case—students learn Windows and Windows applications through situations they are likely to encounter in the workplace, rather than learn a list of features one-by-one and out of context. Second, the content, organization, and pedagogy of this book are designed specifically for the graphical user interface. When and how the content is presented capitalize on the power of Windows so students can perform complex modeling tasks earlier and more easily than was possible under DOS. In short, this book does not teach Windows and Windows-based applications as if they were DOS with pictures.

Features

This book is exceptional also because it contains the following features:

- **The CTI WinApps Icon Group** This is an easy-to-install group of computer-aided instruction modules used with the two Microsoft Windows 3.1 tutorials. This icon group includes the following:

  Keyboard Tutorial for student who want more practice using the keyboard.

  Mouse Practice that provides students with an opportunity to use a mouse without disturbing the screen settings.

  Desktop Practice that provides students with a toolbar and a set of windows so they can practice tiling, cascading, and sizing.

  Menu Practice to help students learn how to pull down, close, select options from, and otherwise work with menus.

  Dialog Box Practice that contains command buttons, option buttons, a list box, a drop-down list box, check boxes, a text box, and a spin bar.

  System Information icon that, when clicked, displays information about the configuration of the student's computer system.

  Make Your Student Disk icon that students click to make working copies of the data files that accompany the instructor's copy of the book. There is a separate "Make Your Student Disk" icon for the Windows tutorials, for each Office application, and for the "Integrating Microsoft Office Applications" tutorial.

- **"Read This Before You Begin" Pages** These pages, one before each set of tutorials, are consistent with Course Technology's unequaled commitment to help instructors introduce technology into the classroom. Technical considerations and assumptions about hardware, software, and default settings are listed in one place for each application to help instructors save time and eliminate unnecessary aggravation.

- **Tutorial Case** Each tutorial begins with a business problem that students could reasonably encounter in their first year or two on the job. Thus, the process of solving the problem will be meaningful to students. These cases touch on multicultural, international, and ethical issues—so important in today's curriculum.

- **Step-by-Step Methodology** The unique Course Technology methodology keeps students on track. They click or press keys always within the context of solving the problem posed in the Tutorial Case. The text constantly guides student, letting them know where they are in the process of solving the problem. The numerous screen shots include labels that direct students' attention to what they should look at on the screen.
- **Page Design** Each *full-color* page is designed to help students easily differentiate between what they are to *do* and what they are to *read*. The steps are clearly identified by their color background and numbered bullets. The Windows default colors are used in the screen shots so instructors can more easily ensure that students' screens look like those in the book.
- TROUBLE? TROUBLE? paragraphs anticipate the mistakes that students are likely to make and help them recover from these mistakes. This feature facilitates independent learning and frees the instructor to focus on substantive conceptual issues rather than common procedural errors.
- **Reference Windows and Task Reference** Reference Windows appear throughout the book and provide short, generic summaries of frequently used procedures. The Task References appearing at the end of each application's tutorials summarize how to accomplish tasks using the icons, menus, and keyboard. Both of these features are specially designed and written so students can use the book as a reference manual after completing the course.
- **Questions, Tutorial Assignments, and Case Problems** Each tutorial concludes with meaningful, conceptual Questions that test students' understanding of what they learned in the tutorial. The Questions are followed by Tutorial Assignments, which provide students with additional hands-on practice of the skills they learned in the tutorial. The Tutorial Assignments are followed by three or more complete Case Problems that have approximately the same scope as the Tutorial Case.
- **Exploration Exercises** Unlike DOS, the Windows environment allows students to learn by exploring and discovering what they can do. The Exploration Exercises are Questions, Tutorial Assignments, or Case Problems designated by an E that encourage students to explore the capabilities of the computing environment they are using and to extend their knowledge using the Windows on-line Help facility and other reference materials.

The CTI WinApps Setup Disks

The CTI WinApps Setup Disks, bundled with the instructor's copy of this book, contain an innovative Student Disk generating program designed to save instructors time. Once this software is installed on a network or standalone workstation, students can double-click the "Make (application name) Student Disk" icon for each application in the CTI WinApps group window. Double-clicking this icon on each setup disk transfers all the data files students need to complete the tutorials, Tutorial Assignments, and Case Problems for each application to a high-density disk in drive A or drive B. These files free students from tedious keystroking and allow them to concentrate on mastering the concept or task at hand. Tutorial 1 of each Windows-based application provides complete step-by-step instructions for making the Student Disk.

Adopters of this text are granted the right to install the CTI WinApps icon group on any standalone computer or network used by students who have purchased this text.

For more information on the CTI WinApps Setup Disks, see the "Read This Before You Begin" pages, just before the first tutorial of each application.

The Supplements

- **Instructor's Manual** The Instructor's Manual for each application is written by the authors and is quality-assurance tested. It includes:

- Answers and solutions to all the Questions, Tutorial Assignments, and Case Problems. Suggested solutions are also included for the Exploration Exercises.
- A disk containing solutions to all the Questions, Tutorial Assignments, and Case Problems.
- Tutorial Notes, which contain background information from the authors about the Tutorial Case and the instructional progression of the tutorial.
- Technical Notes, which include troubleshooting tips as well as information on how to customize the students' screens to closely emulate the screen shots in the book.
- Transparency Masters of key concepts.

■ **On-Line Test Manager** This Microsoft Office text features Course Technology's easy-to-use, Windows-based On-Line Test Manager. The Test Manager addresses one of the most time-consuming tasks in an instructor's year: assessment of students' knowledge. The Test Manager provides instructors unprecedented ability to give on-line tests with automatic grading and data export, on-line practice tests with automatic statistics collection, generation of suggestions for additional reading or study, and, of course, printed tests if they prefer. The Test Manager lets instructors

- select questions from a bank of **150 questions for each tutorial**, including true/false, fill-in-the-blank, and essay questions, including questions that ask students to label on-line graphics
- base the test on a **single chapter, multiple chapters**, or the entire text
- include **their own questions** in the form of text or graphics
- **mark any question** as available for any or none of the following: on-line tests, practice tests, printed tests
- use the **computerized calendar** to indicate which sections can take the test, when they can take it, and how long they want the test period to be
- **monitor the practice tests** to find out which students are using them, and how much time they are spending
- **grade tests automatically** on-line, even essay questions

Using the Course On-Line Test Manager frees up instructors to do what they do best: teach.

Acknowledgments

The authors would like to thank the many people who contributed to this book. We thank the reviewers for their insights, constructive criticism, and encouragement: Gary Armstrong of Shippensburg University, Warren Boe of University of Iowa, Sherri Cady of Anoka-Ramsey Community College, Sue Cox of Suffolk Community College, Judy Sunayama Foster of Diablo Valley College, Charles Hommel of University of Puget Sound, Emily Ketcham of Baylor University, Joseph Limmer of Saint Louis Community College of Meramec and Anheuser-Busch, Inc., Dr. Michael Paul of Barry University, Catherine Rathke of College of DuPage, Linda Wise Miller of University of Idaho and Minnie Yen of the University of Alaska at Anchorage.

We also want to thank the dedicated and enthusiastic Course Technology staff including the product development team: Susan Solomon Communications, Marjorie Hunt, Mac Mendelsohn, Barbara Clemens, Nicole Jones Pinard, Kim Crowley, Joan Carey, Kathleen Finnegan, Terry Ann Kremer, Katherine T. Pinard, and Ann Shaffer; the editorial production team; the people at Gex for their care and attention to detail in producing this book; quality-assurance student testers managed by Jeff Goding; and many others too numerous to mention.

Joseph J. Adamski, Dan Oja
June Jamrich Parsons, Cheryl L. Willis
S. Scott Zimmerman and Beverly B. Zimmerman

Brief Contents

Contents

Microsoft Office Professional Tutorial

Introductory Microsoft Word 6.0 for Windows Tutorials

Microsoft Excel 5.0 for Windows Tutorials

TUTORIAL 1

Microsoft Access 2.0 For Windows Tutorials

TUTORIAL 1

TUTORIAL 2

Microsoft Powerpoint 4.0 for Windows Tutorials

Integrating Microsoft Office Applications

Photography Credits

Figure		Credit	Page
1	PC	Courtesy of International Business Machines	EC 4
	Printer	Photo courtesy of Hewlett-Packard Company	EC 4
2		Courtesy of International Business Machines	EC 5
4		Courtesy of International Business Machines	EC 7
5		Preprinted with permission of Compaq Computer Corporation. All rights reserved.	EC 8
6		Courtesy of Toshiba America Information Systems, Inc.	EC 8
7		Courtesy of International Business Machines	EC 8
8		Courtesy of International Business Machines	EC 9
9		Photo by Paul Shambroom, courtesy of Cray Research, Inc.	EC 9
12		Courtesy of Microsoft Corporation	EC 11
13		Courtesy of Intel Corporation	EC 12
18		Courtesy of NEC Technologies, Inc.	EC 16
20		Courtesy of Panasonic Communications Systems Company	EC 16
22		Photo courtesy of Hewlett-Packard Company	EC 17
23		Photo courtesy of Hewlett-Packard Company	EC 17
26		Richard Morgenstein	EC 19
27		Richard Morgenstein	EC 20
28		Photo courtesy of Seagate Technology, Inc.	EC 20
32		Toshiba's SM-3301 Series CD-ROM disc drive	EC 24
35		Courtesy of Microsoft Corporation	EC 29
36		Courtesy of Microsoft Corporation	EC 30
37		Used with permission of Borland International, Inc.	EC 30

Essential Computer Concepts

What is a Computer?

Types of Computers

Computer Hardware

Data Communications

Computer Software

Essential Computer Concepts

OBJECTIVES

In this chapter you will learn:

- The major components of a computer system
- The terms used to specify the capacity and the speed of computer memory, processors, and storage
- How data are represented by the binary number system and the ASCII code
- The common types of network cards and network software
- How peripheral devices are connected to a computer system
- The basic concepts of data communications
- The difference between systems software and applications software

CASE **PR #516859** It is Tenzing Lu's first day in the purchasing department of International ComAir. Her main responsibility is to review purchase requisitions, the paperwork that departmental managers submit to purchase equipment and supplies. Tenzing must find the vendor with the best price and then fill out a purchase order form, which will be sent to the vendor as the official order.

The first purchase requisition, PR #516859, is for a computer system and has a computer ad stapled to it (Figure 1). Tenzing studies the ad for a few minutes and then asks her boss, Pat Kenslea, what the usual procedure is for computer purchases. Pat explains that since prices change so rapidly in the computer industry, it is important to get price quotes from several vendors. She also warns Tenzing that the prices must be for a system with the correct configuration and technical specifications for International ComAir's needs.

After considering this procedure, Tenzing confesses that she doesn't have much technical background in computers and asks if there is some way to pick up the basics quickly. Pat appreciates Tenzing's initiative and pulls out some reference materials and recent computer magazines from her bookshelf. Pat suggests that Tenzing read through the reference materials and then browse through the magazines to get an idea of current prices and features.

If you were a purchasing agent for International ComAir, what would you buy? Does the ad in Figure 1 represent a viable system configuration? How much do you think the system should cost? The information in this chapter will help you answer these questions by developing your understanding of computer technology and terminology.

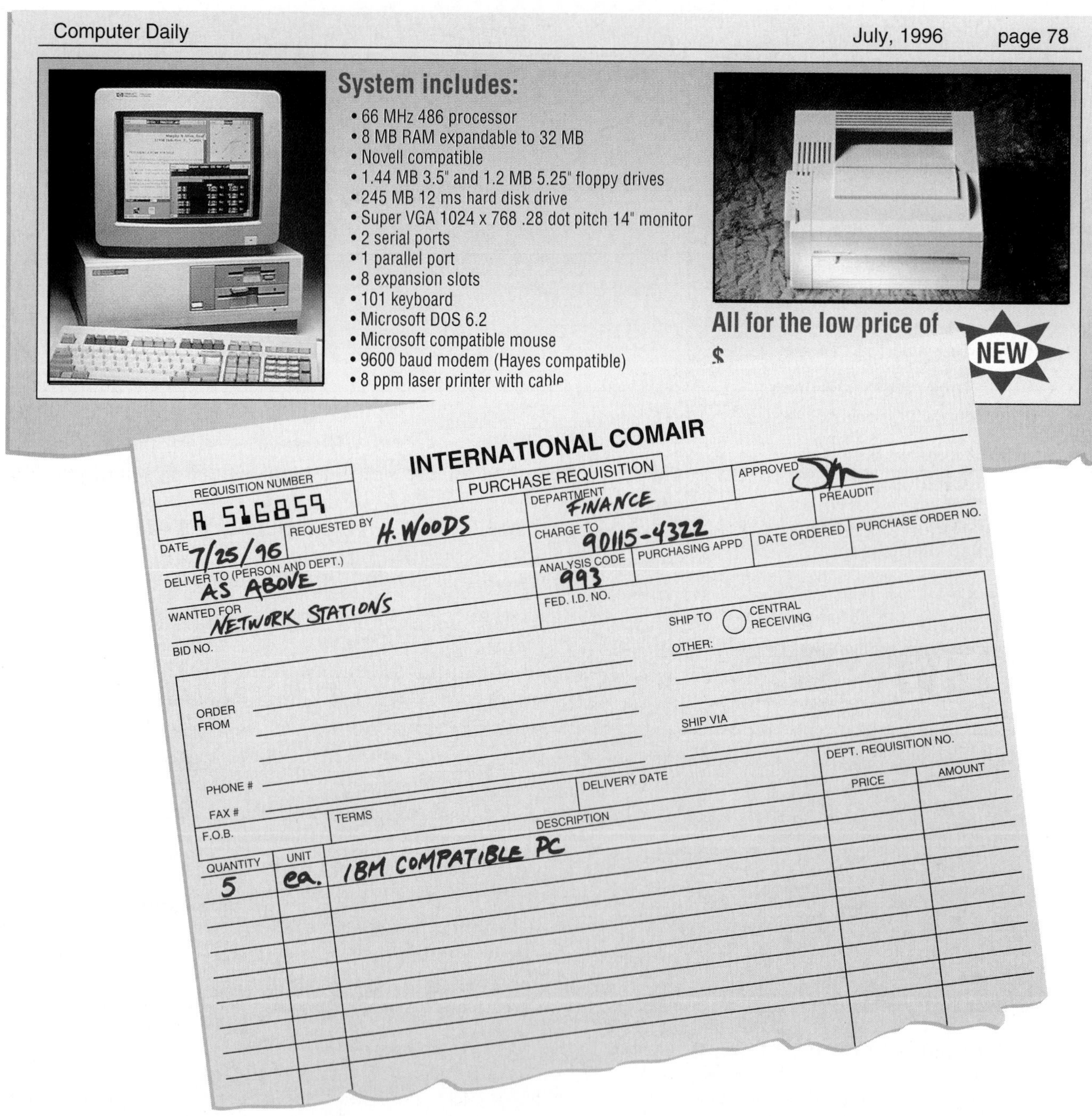

Figure 1: Purchase requisition #516859 and attached computer ad

Figure 2: Office workers at their computers

What Is a Computer?

Computers have become essential tools in almost every type of activity in virtually every type of business (Figure 2). A **computer** can be defined as an electronic device that accepts information, performs arithmetic and logical operations using that information, and then produces the required results. It is a versatile tool with the potential to perform many different tasks.

A **computer system** is composed of a computer and additional devices such as a printer. A computer system can manage financial information, create and manipulate graphs, record day-to-day business transactions, help managers make critical business decisions, maintain inventories, and perform many other tasks to help business personnel be more efficient and productive.

The components of a computer system that you can see and touch are referred to as **hardware**. Keyboards, screens, disk drives, printers, and circuit boards are all examples of hardware. The selection of components that make up a particular computer system is referred to as the **configuration**. The technical details about the speed, the capacity, or the size of each component are called **specifications**. So, a computer system might be *configured* to include a printer, and a *specification* for that printer might be a print speed of eight pages per minute.

Software refers to the components of a computer system, particularly the **programs**, or lists of instructions, that are needed to make the computer perform a specific task. Software is the key to a computer's versatility. When your computer is using word processing software, for example, the Microsoft Word program, you can type memos, letters, and reports. When your computer is using accounting software, such as the DacEasy accounts receivable program, you can maintain information about what your customers owe you.

The hardware and the software of a computer system work together to process **data**—the words, figures, and graphics that describe people, events, things, and ideas.

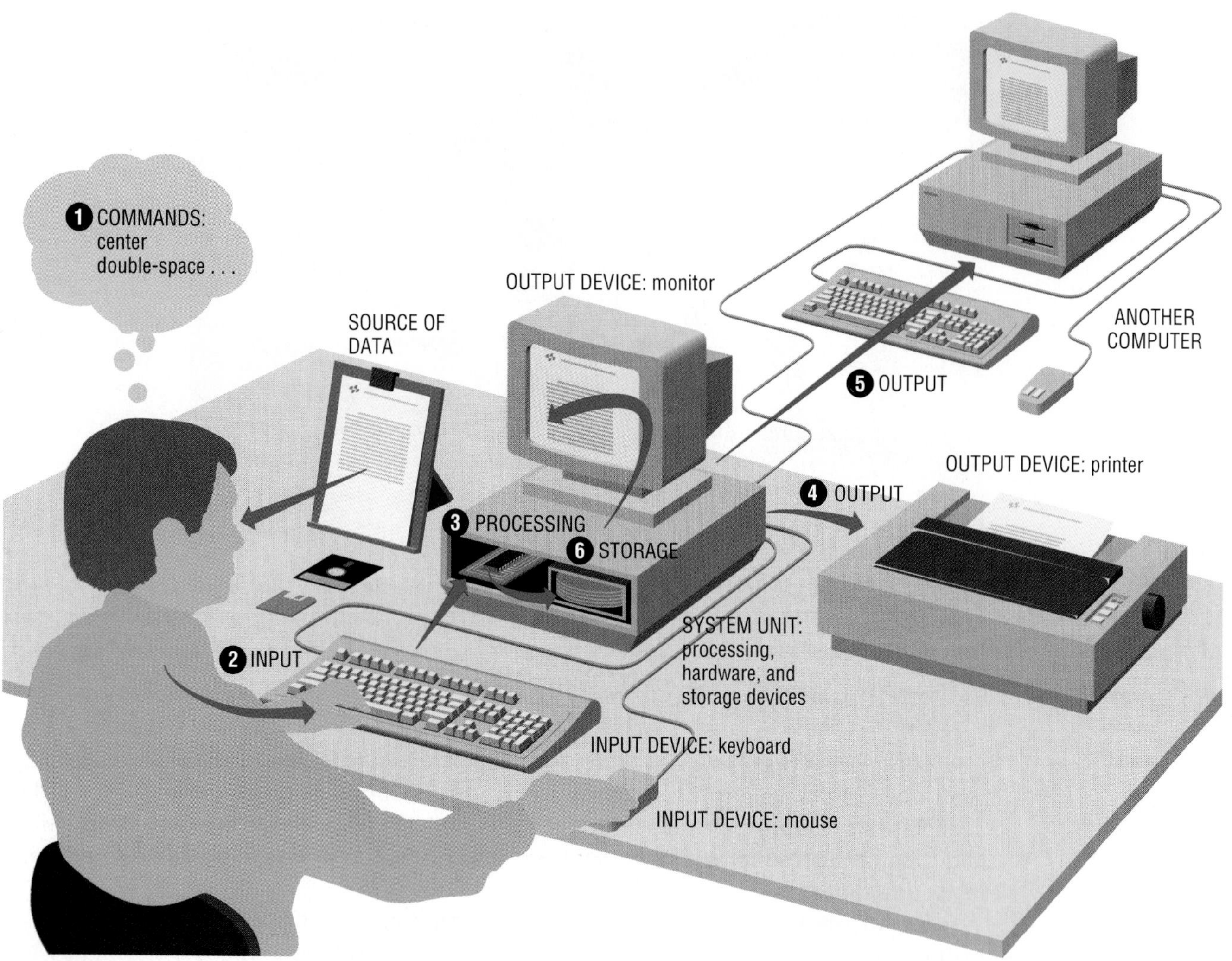

Figure 3: Data are input, processed, stored, and output

Figure 3 shows how you, the computer, the data, and the software interact to get work done. Let's say you want to write a report. First, you would instruct the computer to use the word processing program (1). Once the word processing program has been activated, you would begin to type the text of your report (2). What you type into the computer is called **input**. You might also need to issue commands that tell the computer exactly how to process your input—maybe you want the title to be centered and the text to be double-spaced. You use an **input device**, such as a keyboard or a mouse, to input data and issue commands.

The computer would process the report according to your commands and the instructions contained in the software—the title would be centered and all the text double-spaced. **Processing** changes the data that you have input (3), for example, by moving text, sorting lists, or performing calculations. The processing takes place on the **main circuit board** of the computer, also referred to as the **main board** or the **mother board**, which contains the computer's major electronic components. The electronic components of the main circuit board are referred to as **processing hardware**.

After you have written your report, you might want to print it out (4). The results of computer processing are called **output**. The printers and screens that display output are called **output devices**. Or, instead of dealing with printed output, you might want to send the report electronically (5) so that it gets to a co-worker almost immediately. Sending data from one computer to another is referred to as **data communications**. To send your report to another computer you use a **communications device**.

When you have finished working, you would use a **storage device** (6), such as a disk drive, to save your report on some sort of **storage medium**, such as a disk. The text of your report would be stored on the disk as a **file** under the filename of your choice.

Types of Computers

Computers often are classified by their size, speed, and cost. **Microcomputers**, also called **personal computers (PCs)**, are inexpensive—$500 to $15,000—and small enough to fit on an office desk. Two typical desktop configurations are shown in Figure 4 and Figure 5 (on the following page). Figure 4 shows a standard horizontal system unit. The vertical system unit in Figure 5 is referred to as a **tower case**.

Desktop computers receive their power from a wall outlet, which makes them basically stationary. Notebook microcomputers, such as the one in Figure 6 (on the following page), are transportable. They are smaller and lighter than desktop microcomputers and use rechargeable batteries.

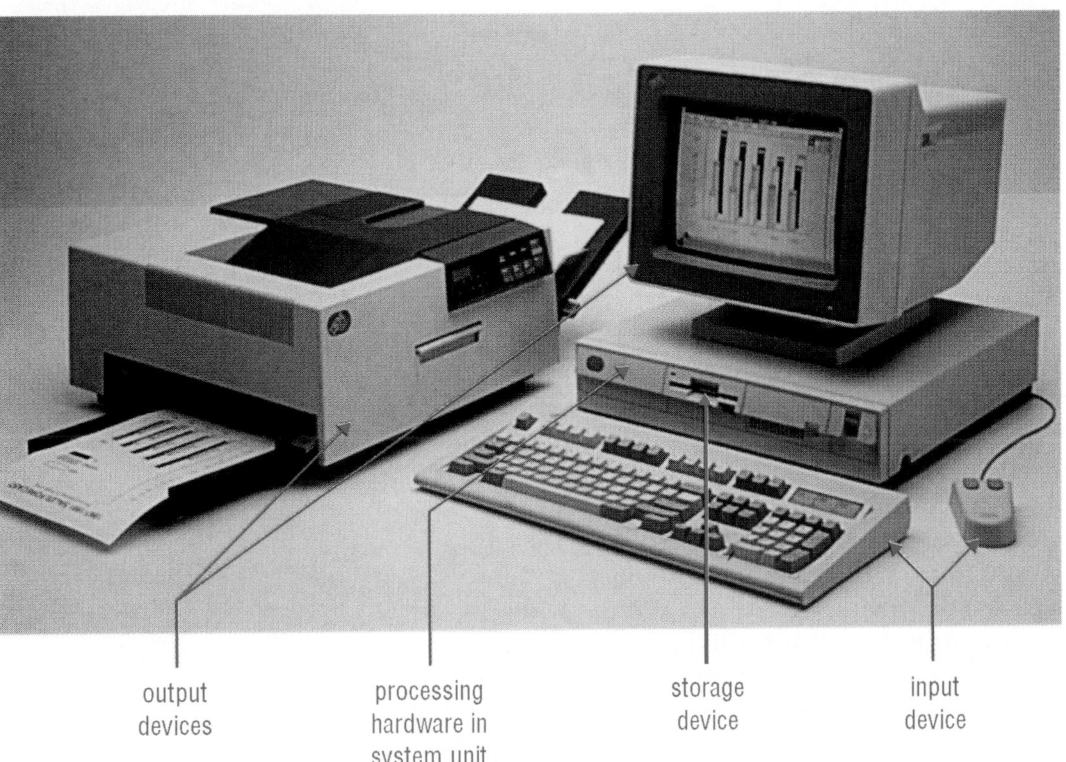

Figure 4: Standard desktop microcomputer system

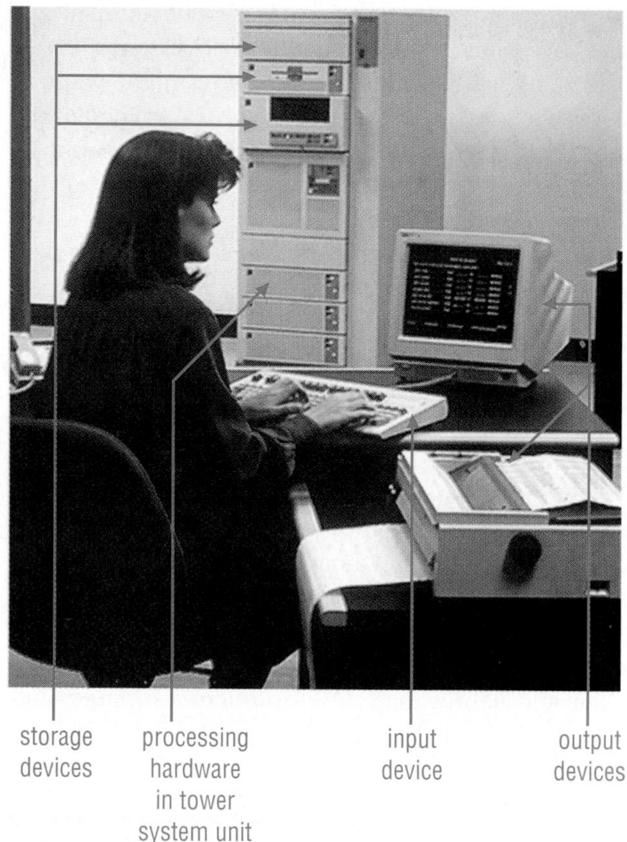

Figure 5: Desktop microcomputer with tower system unit

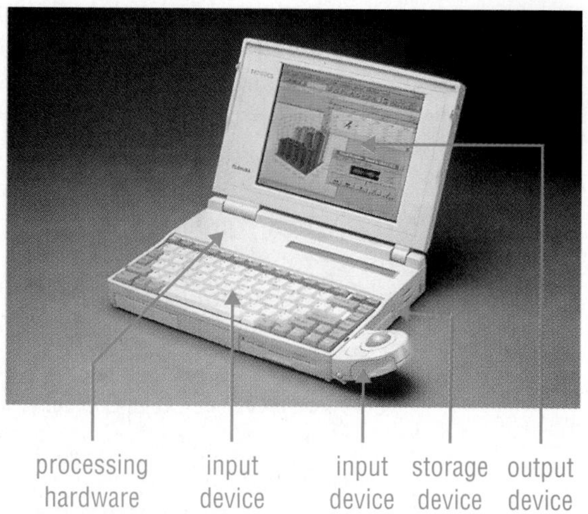

Figure 6: A notebook computer

Figure 7: A minicomputer

Though smaller in size, a notebook computer generally costs more than a desktop computer with equivalent specifications.

Microcomputers are used extensively in small and large businesses. But some businesses, government agencies, and other institutions also use larger and faster types of computers: minicomputers, mainframes, and supercomputers.

Minicomputers, such as the one in Figure 7, are too large and too heavy for desktops. They operate three to 25 times faster than microcomputers and cost anywhere from $15,000 to $500,000. **Mainframe computers**, like the one shown in Figure 8, are larger and more powerful than minicomputers. Mainframes have large capacities for storing and manipulating data, operate 10 to 100 times faster than microcomputers, and cost between $100,000 and $2 million.

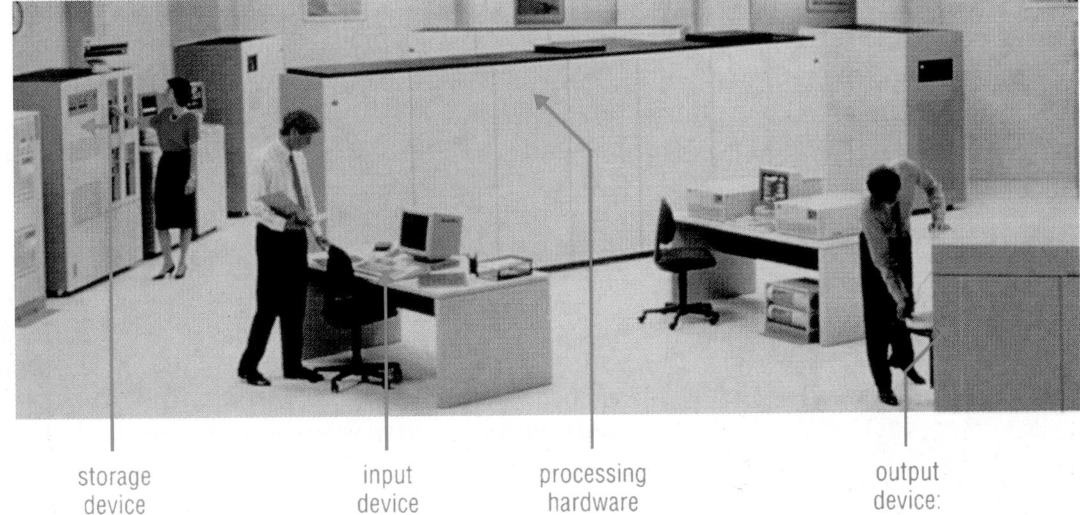

Figure 8:
A mainframe computer

The largest and fastest computers, called **supercomputers**, are so expensive that only the largest companies, government agencies, and universities can afford them. Supercomputers, such as the one shown in Figure 9, operate 50 to 10,000 times faster than microcomputers.

processing hardware

Figure 9: A Cray supercomputer

With the accelerated development of newer and better computers, the guidelines for classifying types of computers have become fuzzy. For example, some recently developed microcomputers operate at higher speeds than some minicomputers.

Now consider the ad attached to PR #516859, the purchase requisition at the beginning of this chapter. How would Tenzing classify the computer in that ad? If your answer is "a desktop microcomputer," you are correct. The computer in that ad fits on a desktop, is not portable, and probably costs $1,000 to $2,000.

The remainder of this chapter will focus on microcomputer hardware and software concepts. These concepts will help you to use successfully the software featured in the tutorial chapters.

Computer Hardware

As you've already learned, computer hardware can be defined as the components of a computer that you can see and touch. Let's now look at the hardware you might use in a typical microcomputer system.

Input Devices

As you have already seen, you can input data and commands by using an input device such as a keyboard or a mouse. The computer can also receive input from a storage device. This section takes a closer look at the input devices you might use. Storage devices are covered in a later section.

Figure 10 shows an 83-key IBM PC-style keyboard; Figure 11 shows an enhanced 101-key IBM PS/2-style keyboard. Both keyboards consist of three major parts: the main keyboard, the numeric keypad, and the function keys. The major difference between the two keyboards is that the enhanced keyboard contains a separate editing keypad. In general these keyboards can do the same things, but the enhanced keyboard makes it easier to do some editing and input tasks. Ask your instructor which keyboard you'll be using.

Your computer also should be equipped with a pointing device such as a **mouse** (Figure 12). As you push or pull the mouse on the surface of your desk, a **pointer** moves on the screen. Using the mouse, you can position the pointer anywhere on the screen,

Figure 10: Standard 83-key keyboard

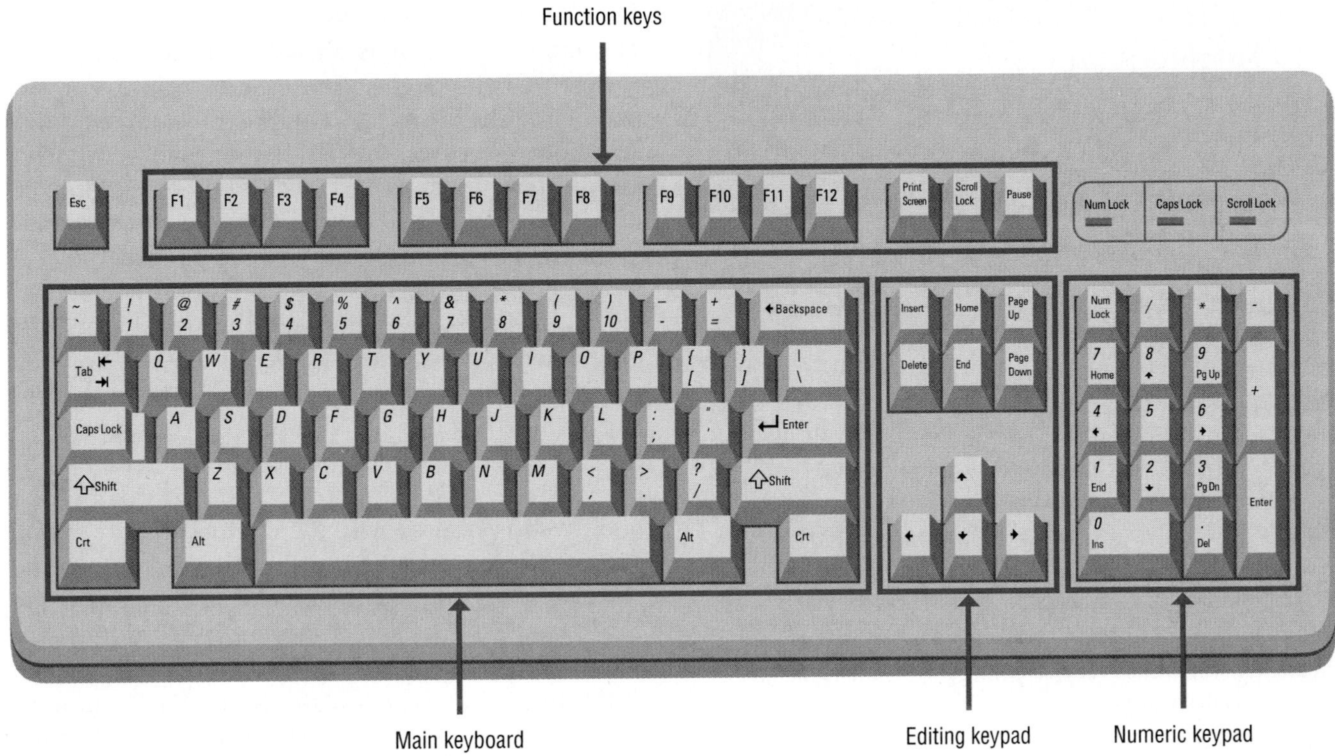

Figure 11: Enhanced 101-key keyboard

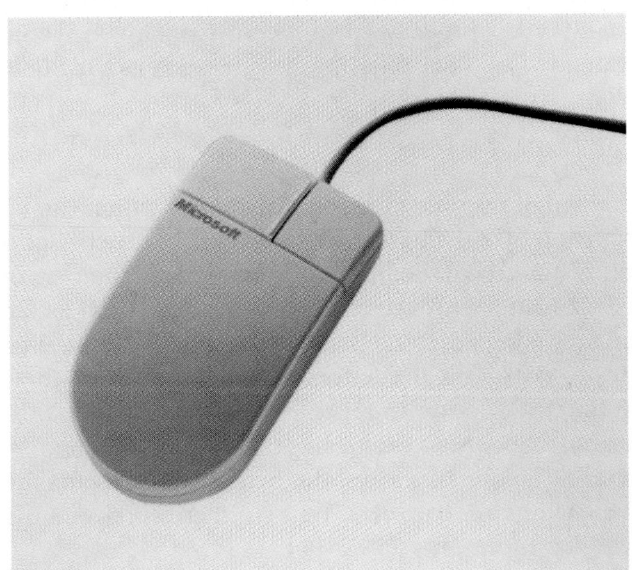

Figure 12: A mouse

manipulate pictorial objects on the screen, and select commands.

Some computer programs, such as Microsoft Windows, are specifically designed to be used with a mouse. If a mouse is not included with your computer system, you can generally add one.

Now that you have read about input devices, refer back to the ad attached to PR #516859 at the beginning of the chapter. Can you list the input devices included with the advertised system? If you said that the system comes with two input devices, a mouse and a keyboard, you are right. You also might have noted that the keyboard is an enhanced 101-key keyboard with a separate editing keypad.

Processing Hardware

The two most important components of microcomputer hardware are the **microprocessor**, sometimes called the **central processing unit (CPU)**, and the **memory**, which stores instructions and data. You should know what type microprocessor is in your computer, and you should know its memory capacity. These factors directly affect the price of a computer and the efficiency of its performance.

Figure 13: An Intel 80486 microprocessor, found in many IBM-compatible computers

THE MICROPROCESSOR

The microprocessor is an **integrated circuit**—an electronic component often called a "chip"—on the main circuit board of the computer. The most popular microprocessors in IBM-compatible computers are the Intel 8088, 8086, 80286, 80386, 80486, and Pentium (Figure 13). The numbers are simply model numbers designated by the manufacturer. Models of more recent processors often are abbreviated 286, 386, and 486. Generally speaking, the higher the model number, the more powerful the microprocessor; this means that the microprocessor can handle larger chunks of data and can process data faster.

The speed of a microprocessor is determined by its clock rate. The computer clock is part of a group of circuits associated with the microprocessor. Think of the **clock rate** as the heartbeat or the pulse of the computer. The higher the clock rate, the faster the computer. Clock rate is measured in millions of cycles per second, or **megahertz (MHz)**. The Intel 8088 microprocessor on the first IBM PC models operated at only 4.77 MHz. The newer Intel Pentium microprocessor typically operates at 90 MHz.

Let's take another look at the ad attached to PR #516859. What is the type and the speed of the microprocessor? Your answer should be that it is an 80486 microprocessor, that can operate at 66 MHz. Since the 486 microprocessor is a recent model, you would expect it to be more costly than computers with older microprocessors such as the 8088, 80286, and 80386.

DATA REPRESENTATION

Within a computer, data is represented by microscopic electronic switches, which can be either off or on. The off switch is designated by a 0 and the on switch by a 1. Each 1 or 0 is called a **binary digit,** or **bit**, for short. Bits are very handy for representing numbers in the binary number system. A series of bits can also represent character data, such as letters and punctuation marks. Each character is represented by a pattern of 1s and 0s, similar to using patterns of dots and dashes to represent the letters of the alphabet in Morse code. Microcomputers commonly use the **ASCII code** to represent character data. ASCII (pronounced "ask-ee") stands for American Standard Code for Information Interchange.

A string of eight bits is called a **byte**. As Figure 14 shows, the byte that represents the integer value 0 is 00000000, with all eight bits set to zero. The byte that represents the integer value 1 is 0000001, and the byte that represents 255 is 11111111.

Each byte can also represent a character such as the letter A or the symbol $. For example, Figure 15 shows that in ASCII code the letter A is represented by the byte 01000001, the letter B by 01000010, and the letter C by 01000011. The symbol $ is represented by 00100100. The phrase "Thank you!" is represented by 10 bytes—each of the eight letters requires one byte, and the space and the exclamation point also require one byte each. To find out how many *bits* are needed to represent the phrase "Thank You!", multiply the number of bytes by eight, since there are eight bits in each byte.

Number	Binary Representation
0	00000000
1	00000001
2	00000010
3	00000011
4	00000100
5	00000101
6	00000110
7	00000111
8	00001000
⋮	⋮
14	00001110
15	00001111
16	00010000
17	00010001
⋮	⋮
253	11111101
254	11111110
255	11111111

Figure 14: Binary representation of the numbers 0 through 255

Character	ASCII
A	01000001
B	01000010
C	01000011
D	01000100
E	01000101
F	01000110
G	01000111
H	01001000
I	01001001
J	01001010
K	01001011
L	01001100
M	01001101
N	01001110
O	01001111
P	01010000
Q	01010001
R	01010010
S	01010011
T	01010100
U	01010101
V	01010110
W	01010111
X	01011000
Y	01011001
Z	01011010
#	00100011
$	00100100
%	00100101
&	00100110

Figure 15: ASCII code representing the letters A to Z and the symbols # $ % &

Byte values can represent not only integers and characters but also other types of data or program instructions. A computer can determine the difference between the various types of data or instructions based on the context of the byte value, just as you can tell, based on context, the difference between the two meanings of the word *hit* in the sentences "He hit me in the arm" and "The movie was a big hit."

As a computer user you don't have to know the binary representations of numbers, characters, and instructions, because the computer handles all the necessary conversions internally. However, because the amount of memory in a computer and the storage capacity of disks are expressed in bytes, you should be aware of how data is represented so you will understand the capacity and the limitations of your computer.

MEMORY

Computer **memory** is a set of storage locations on the main circuit board. Your computer has two types of memory: read-only memory and random-access memory.

Read-only memory (ROM) is the part of memory reserved for a special set of commands that are required for the internal workings of the computer. The microprocessor can read these commands but cannot erase or change them. When you turn off your computer, the commands in ROM remain intact and ready for use when you turn the computer on again.

Random-access memory (RAM) temporarily stores data and program instructions. RAM is measured in kilobytes (K or KB) and megabytes (MB). The prefix *kilo* (pronounced "kee-lo") means one thousand, but for historical and technical reasons a **kilobyte** is actually 1024 bytes. The prefix *mega* usually means one million, but a **megabyte** is precisely 1,024 × 1,024—or 1,048,576—bytes. As shown in Figure 16, each RAM storage location can hold one character of data. Most IBM-compatible microcomputers have a minimum of 640K of RAM. A 640K computer can hold the equivalent of 655,360 (640 × 1,024) characters in RAM.

RAM is one of the most critical elements of a computer system. To use an analogy, we could say that RAM is the major traffic hub of the micro world, where data and instructions wait until it is time to travel elsewhere to be processed or stored. Figure 17 illustrates the flow of data in and out of RAM. When you first switch on your computer, operating system instructions are loaded into an area of RAM, where they remain until you turn the computer off (1). The **operating system** controls many essential internal activities of the computer system. When you want to use an application program, such as a word processor, all or part of the application program is loaded into RAM (2). When you input data from a device such as the keyboard, the data is temporarily stored in RAM (3).

Operating system instructions and program instructions are sent from RAM to the microprocessor for processing (4). Any data needed for the processing indicated by these instructions is fetched from RAM (5). After the data has been processed, the results are sent back into RAM (6). If you want a permanent record of the results, the data is stored (7) or output (8). When you have finished using an application, RAM is freed up for the next program you want to use. When you turn your computer off, all the data in RAM disappears.

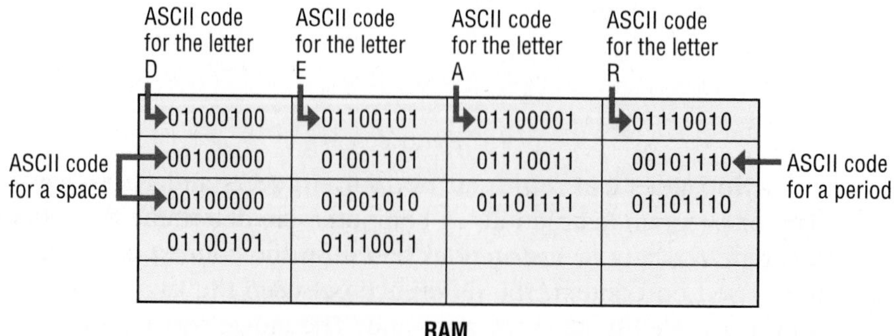

Figure 16: A conceptual model of how data (DEAR[space] MS. [space] JONES) is stored in RAM in ASCII code

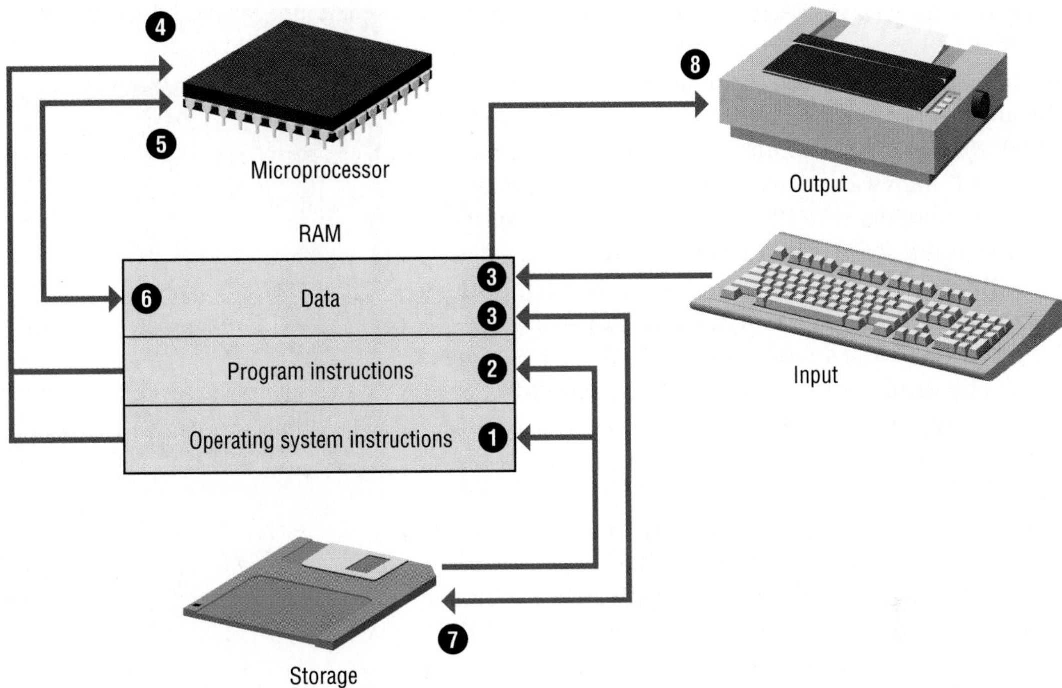

Figure 17: RAM is a temporary storage area for data, programs, and the operating system

Large programs generally require large amounts of RAM. The amount of RAM required for an application program usually is specified on the package or in the program documentation. Computers configured with more RAM typically cost more than those with smaller amounts of RAM. It is usually possible to expand the amount of RAM in a computer up to a specified limit.

Take another look at the ad attached to PR #516859. How much RAM is included with the computer? What is the maximum amount of RAM that can be installed? You are correct if you said that 8MB of RAM are included and that the RAM can be expanded to a maximum of 32MB.

Output Devices

Output is the result of processing data; **output devices** show you those results. The most commonly used output devices are monitors and printers.

A **monitor** is the TV-like video screen that displays the output from a computer (Figure 18 on the following page). Most desktop computer monitors use **cathode ray tube (CRT)** technology, while notebook computers use a flat-panel display technology such as a **liquid crystal display (LCD)**.

Figure 19 (on the following page) shows how text and graphics displayed on computer monitors are created with little dots of light called **pixels**, short for "picture elements." The entire monitor screen is a grid of pixels that combine to create the illusion of a continuous image. A **color graphics adapter (CGA)** monitor has a grid that is 320 pixels across and 200 pixels high. A **video graphics array (VGA)** monitor has a 640 × 480 grid, and a super VGA monitor has a maximum grid size of 800 × 600 or 1024 × 768. As the number of pixels in the grid increases, the **resolution** of the monitor increases. Monitors with higher resolution have displays that are clearer, sharper, and easier to read.

A **display card**—also called a **display adapter**, **video controller**, or **graphics adapter**—connects the monitor to the main circuit board of the computer. The display card must match the monitor. For example, suppose you have purchased a super VGA monitor to add to your current computer system. You need to check the specification sheet that accompanied your old display card to see if it will work with the new monitor. If the specification sheet indicates that the original display card is not compatible with your new monitor, you will need to purchase a new display card.

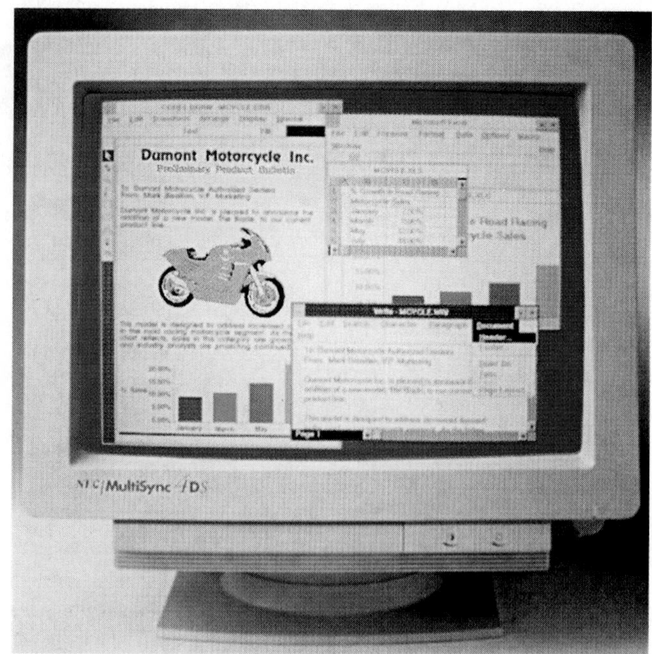

Figure 18: A color monitor

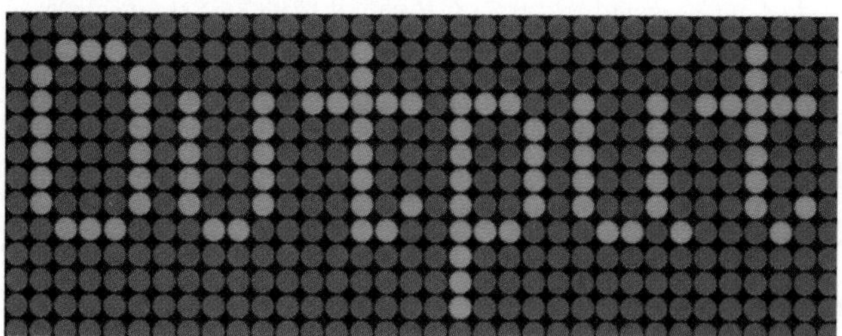

Figure 19: Pixels combining to form the word "output"

Figure 20: A dot-matrix printer

A **printer** produces a paper copy of the text or graphics processed by the computer. A paper copy of computer output is called **hard copy**, because it is more tangible than the electronic or magnetic copies found on a disk, in the computer memory, or on the monitor.

The three most popular types of printers are dot-matrix, ink-jet, and laser printers. **Dot-matrix printers**, like the one shown in Figure 20, form text and graphic images by producing tiny dots of ink on the printer paper. The dots are formed when pins strike an inked ribbon. Less expensive dot-matrix printers have nine pins. More expensive models have 24 pins and produce higher-quality output. Figure 21 shows text that was output in two different modes: draft mode and near-letter-quality mode. **Draft mode** prints very quickly but produces relatively low-quality print, while **near-letter-quality (NLQ) mode** prints more slowly but produces higher-quality print. The speed of a dot-matrix printer usually is measured in characters per second (cps).

Ink-jet printers, like the one in Figure 22, spray tiny dots of ink onto the paper to form text and graphics. Ink-jet printers are quieter than dot-matrix printers and produce graphics of reasonable quality and text of high quality. The speed of an ink-jet printer is comparable to that of a dot-matrix printer.

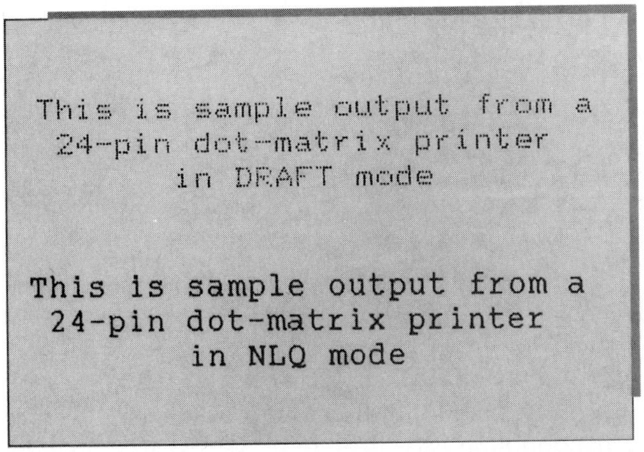

This is sample output from a
24-pin dot-matrix printer
in DRAFT mode

This is sample output from a
24-pin dot-matrix printer
in NLQ mode

Figure 21: Sample output from a dot-matrix printer

Figure 22: An inkjet printer

Laser printers, such as the model in Figure 23, use laser beams to bond a black powdery substance, called **toner**, to the paper. The technology is similar to that used in copy machines. The speed of a laser printer is usually indicated in pages per minute (ppm). Laser printers are quiet and fast and produce the highest-quality printing of any type of printer. For those reasons laser printers are becoming the standard type of printer in the business world.

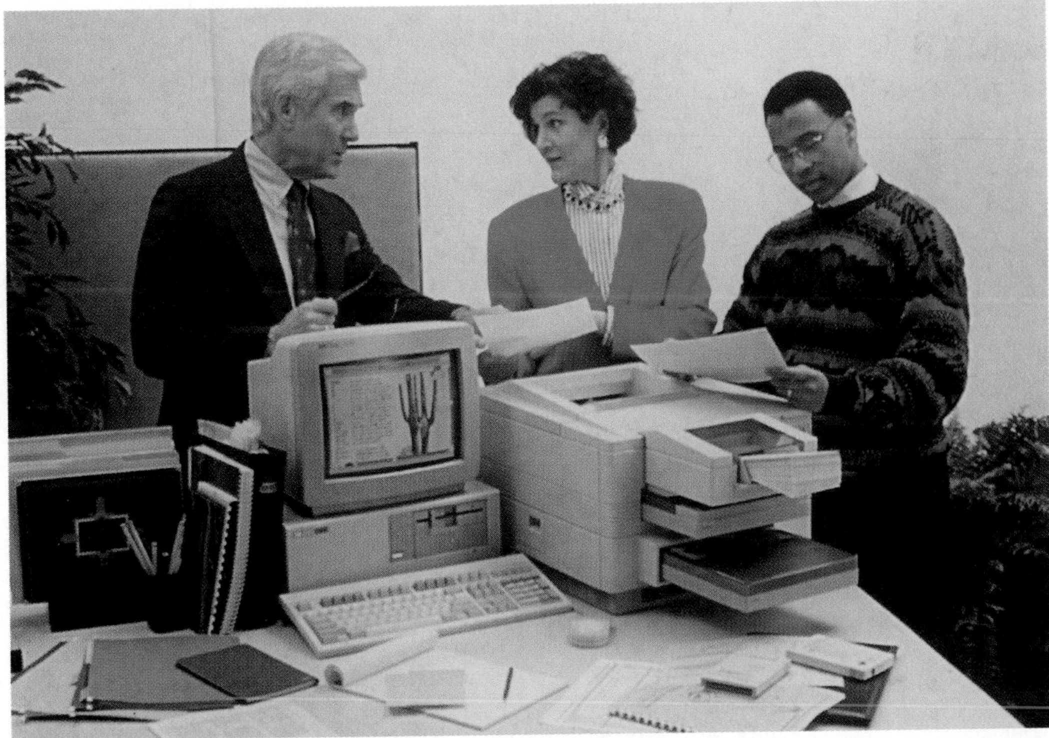

Figure 23: A laser printer

Return to the beginning of the chapter and list the output device(s) included with the computer system in PR #516859. If you listed a monitor and a laser printer, you are correct.

Storage Devices and Media

Because RAM retains data only while the power is on, your computer must have a more permanent storage option. As Figure 24 shows, a **storage device** receives data from RAM and writes it on a storage medium, such as a disk. Later the data can be read and sent back to RAM. So a storage device is used not only to store data but also for data input and output.

There are a variety of microcomputer storage devices, each using a particular storage medium (Figure 25). Hard disk drives store data on hard disks and floppy disk drives store data on floppy disks; tape drives store data on tape cartridges or cassettes; and CD-ROM drives store data on compact discs.

Floppy disks, sometimes called diskettes, are flat circles of oxide-coated plastic enclosed in a square case called a **disk jacket**. The most common sizes of disks for microcomputers are 5.25" and 3.5" (Figure 26). The 5.25" disks have flexible disk jackets and are usually stored in paper sleeves for protection. The 3.5" disks have hard plastic cases and don't require sleeves.

The most common types of disks are double-sided, double-density (DS/DD) and double-sided, high-density (DS/HD). The 5.25" DS/DD disks have a capacity of 360K, and the 3.5" DS/DD disks have a capacity of 720K. The 5.25" DS/HD disks have a capacity of 1.2MB, and the 3.5" DS/HD disks have a capacity of 1.44MB.

Disk drives are also available in double-density and high-density models. A high-density drive can read from both high-density and double-density disks. A double-density drive, on

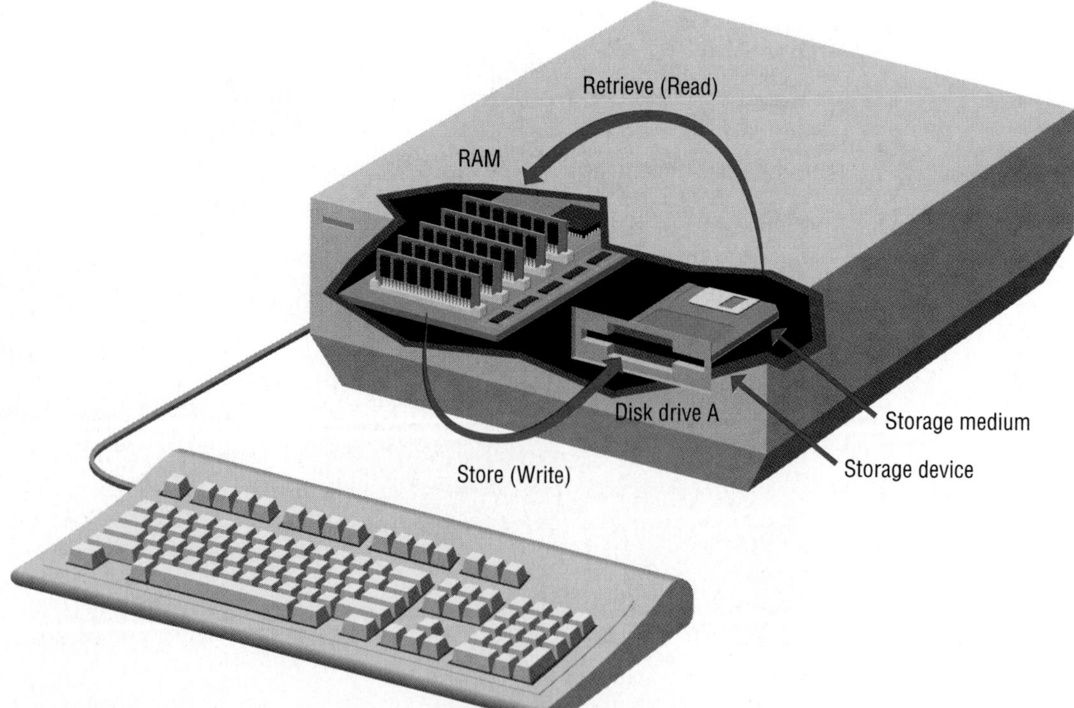

Figure 24: A storage device receives information from RAM, writes it on the storage medium, and reads and sends it back to RAM

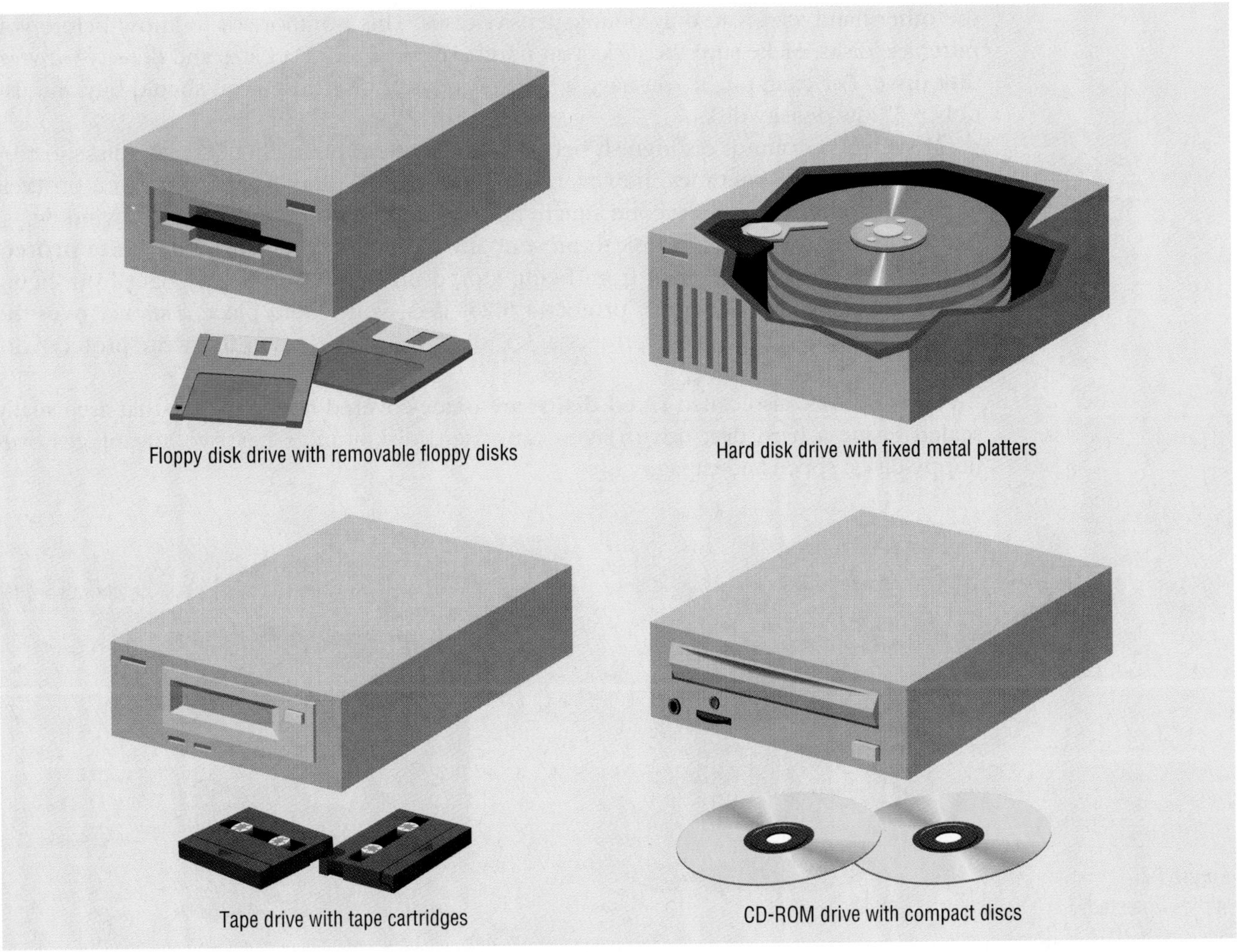

Floppy disk drive with removable floppy disks
Hard disk drive with fixed metal platters
Tape drive with tape cartridges
CD-ROM drive with compact discs

Figure 25: Storage devices and their associated media

write-protect window
write-protect notch
MF2HD
MD2HD

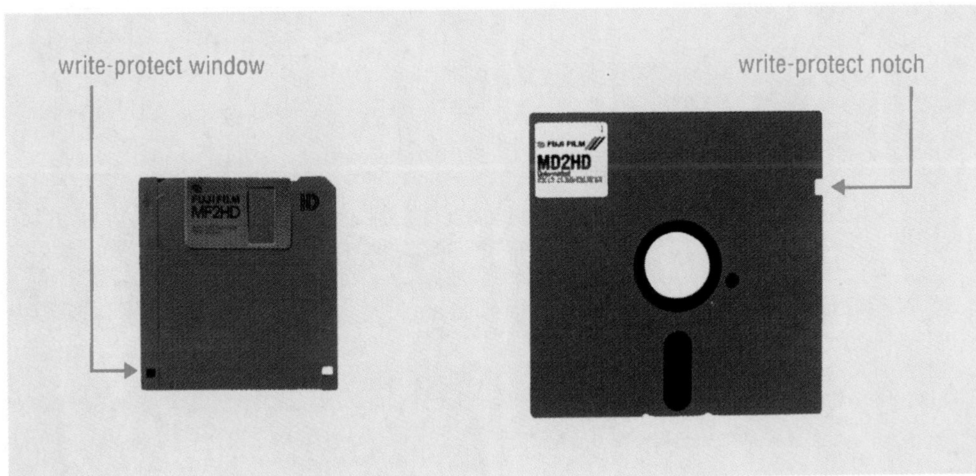

Figure 26: 3.5" disk (*left*) and 5.25" disk (*right*)

the other hand, can read only double-density disks. This is important to know before you purchase disks. Make sure the disks you purchase are the correct size and density for your disk drive. For example, if you have a 3.5" low-density disk drive, you should buy and use only 3.5" low-density disks.

Usually you cannot distinguish between double-density and high-density disks just by looking at them. Sometimes, however, high-density 3.5" disks have HD written on their cases and generally have a second square hole in addition to the write-protect window.

You can write protect a disk to prevent any changes to the data on it. **Write protection** prevents additional data from being stored on the disk, and any data from being erased from the disk. To write protect a 5.25" disk, you would place a sticker over the write-protect notch. To write protect a 3.5" disk, you would open the write-protect window, as shown in Figure 27.

Hard disks, also called **fixed disks**, are oxide-covered metal platters that are usually sealed inside a hard disk drive (Figure 28). Hard disk storage has two advantages over floppy disks: speed and capacity.

Figure 27:
Write-protected 3.5" disk (*left*) and 5.25" disk (*right*)

Figure 28:
A hard disk drive, opened to illustrate internal components

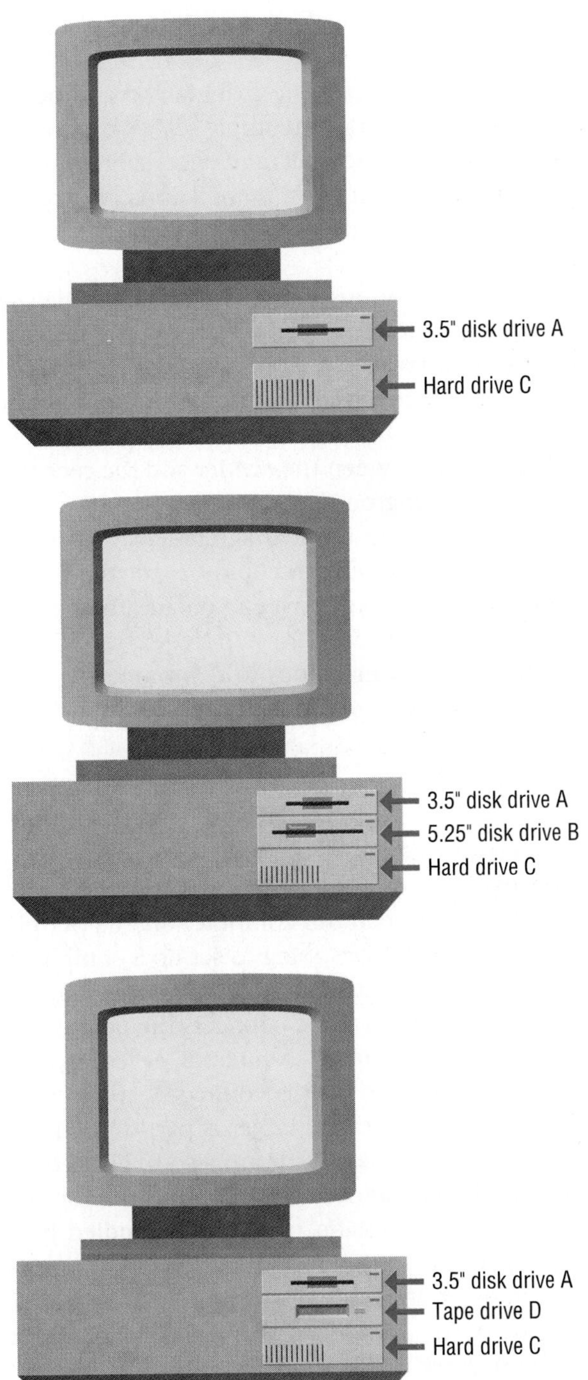

Figure 29: Some common microcomputer storage configurations

The speed of a disk drive is measured by its **access time**, the time required to read or write one record of data. Access time is measured in **milliseconds (ms)**, one-thousandths of a second. A hard disk drive typically has an access time in the range of 10 to 80 ms, the 10-ms access time being the fastest. Floppy disk drives typically have slower access times.

The capacity of microcomputer hard disks is between 20 and 400MB. A small hard disk with a capacity of 20MB can store the equivalent of about 6,500 pages of single-spaced text, compared to only 110 pages on a 360K 5.25" floppy disk. Large hard-disk storage capacity is becoming increasingly important for the new graphics-based computing environments. For example, to install the Microsoft Windows program, you must have a minimum of 6MB of free disk space. The WordPerfect for Windows word processing program needs a minimum of 6MB of disk space.

Optical storage devices use laser technology to read and write data on compact discs (CDs) or laser discs. The advantages of optical storage include reliability and capacity. Unlike data stored on magnetic media, such as floppy disks and hard disks, data stored on optical discs are less susceptible to environmental problems such as dirt, dust, and magnetic fields. Typical storage capacities for optical drives begin at 128MB and can exceed 1 gigabyte (1,000 megabytes). CD-ROM drives are the most common type of optical storage for microcomputers.

Tape drives provide inexpensive archival storage for large quantities of data. Tape storage is much too slow to be used for day-to-day computer tasks; tapes are used to make backup copies of data stored on hard disks. If a hard disk fails, data from the backup tape can be re-loaded on a new hard disk with minimal interruption of operations.

You generally will have a number of storage devices on your computer, each labeled with a letter. Your diskette drive usually will be drive A, and your hard disk drive usually will be drive C. Figure 29 shows some common configurations of storage devices.

Look back at the ad Tenzing is using with PR #516859; how many storage devices are included? How would you describe the type and capacity of each? Your answer should be that the computer comes with three drives: a hard disk drive with 245MB capacity, a 5.25" disk drive with 1.2MB capacity, and a 3.5" disk drive with 1.44 MB capacity.

Data Communications

The transmission of text, numeric, voice, or video data from one machine to another is called **data communications**. This broad-based definition encompasses many critical business activities, such as sending a fax, sending electronic mail, and accessing an information service such as the Dow Jones News/Retrieval. Data communications also refers to the process of sending data between two devices in your computer system, for example, between the computer and the printer.

The four essential components of data communications are a sender, a receiver, a channel, and a protocol. The machine that originates the message is the **sender**. The message is sent over some type of **channel**, such as a twisted-pair phone cable, a coaxial cable, microwaves, or optical fibers. The machine that is designated as the destination for the message is called the **receiver**.

The rules that establish an orderly transfer of data between the sender and the receiver are called **protocols**. For example, when you are talking on the phone, you and the person with whom you are communicating generally have an implied agreement that while one of you is speaking, the other one is listening. This agreement could be called a protocol, because it assists in the orderly exchange of information between you and the person at the other end of the line. Data communication protocols are handled by hardware devices and by software. Usually this means that for two machines to communicate each machine requires a communication device and appropriate communication software.

Peripheral Interfaces

Input and output devices sometimes are referred to as **peripherals**. Communication between your computer and its peripherals is essential. Without it you would not be able to print or to use your mouse. This communication between the computer and its peripheral devices is sometimes referred to as **interfacing**. If you are going to set up a computer, move it, or add peripheral devices, you should have some understanding of interfacing.

Figure 30 shows the components of a device interface. A cable connects the peripheral, in this case, a printer, to the computer. The cable plugs into a connector called a **port**, which usually is located in the back of the system unit. The port is connected to circuitry that controls the transmission of data to the device. This circuitry either is part of the main computer circuit board or is on a **controller card**. Controller cards are also referred to as **interface cards** or **expansion cards.** These cards plug into electrical connectors on the main board called slots or **expansion slots**. The transmission protocol is handled by a **device driver**, a computer program that can establish communication because it contains information about the characteristics of your computer and of the device.

Microcomputers can have several types of ports, including keyboard, video, serial, parallel, MIDI, and SCSI (Figure 31). A **serial port** sends one bit of data at a time. Typically a mouse, a laser printer, a modem, and speech hardware require a serial port. Serial ports are designated COM1, COM2, COM3, and COM4.

A **parallel port** sends more than one bit at a time. Most dot-matrix printers use a parallel port. Parallel ports are designated LPT1 and LPT2.

A **SCSI port** is a variation of the parallel port. **SCSI** (pronounced "scuzzy") stands for small computer system interface. First popularized for Apple Macintosh computers, SCSI has also become established in the IBM-compatible market. Some tape devices, hard disk drives, and CD-ROM drives use a SCSI port. One of the advantages of the SCSI port is that

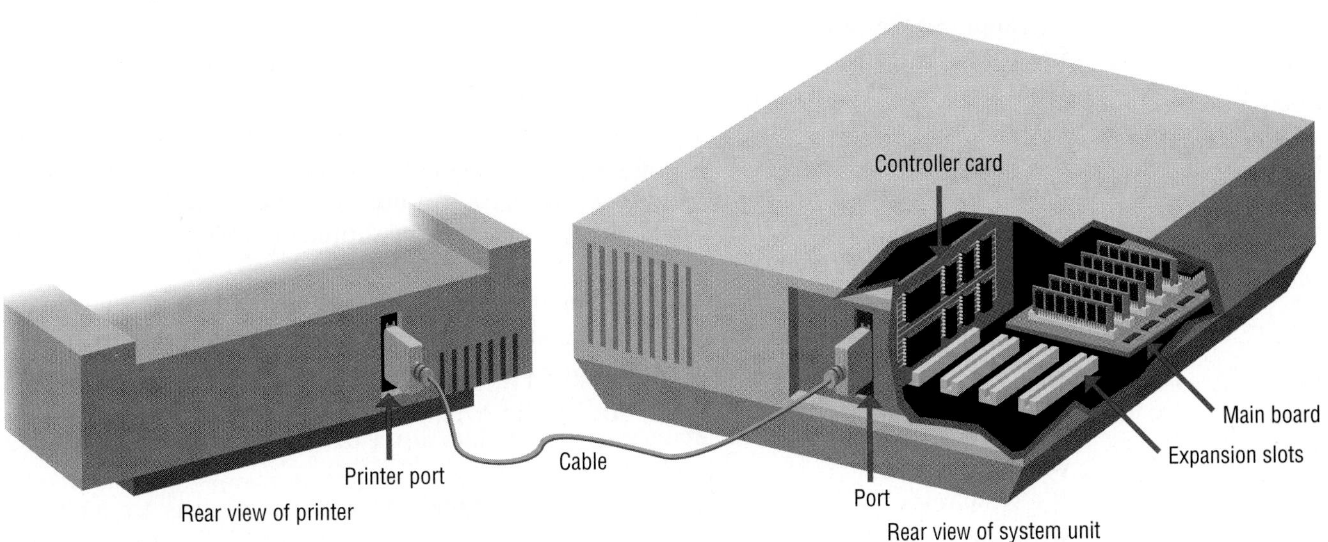

Figure 30: The components necessary to connect a printer to a computer

it has the potential to provide a connection for more than one peripheral device at a time, unlike standard parallel or serial ports, which can provide a connection for only one device at a time.

MIDI ports were originally used in the music industry to send data efficiently between devices that create and play electronic music. MIDI (pronounced "middy") stands for musical instrument digital interface. Now MIDI ports are used to connect computers to electronic instruments and recording devices.

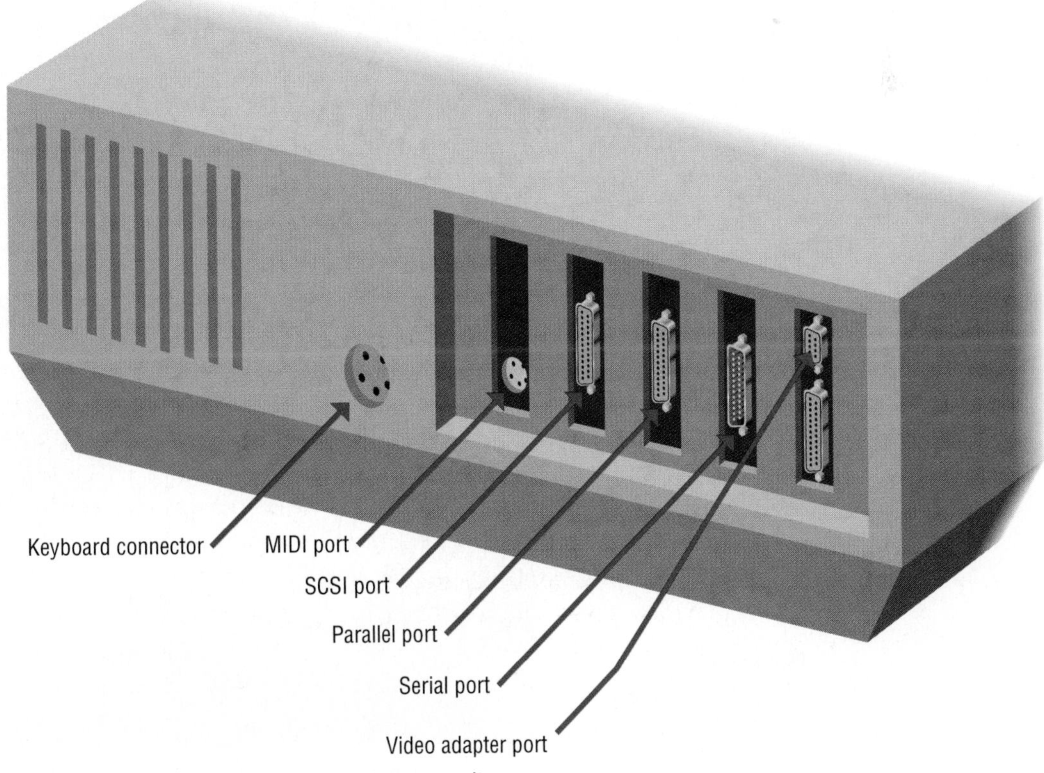

Figure 31: Ports in the back of the system unit

Suppose you want to install a CD-ROM drive, such as the one in Figure 32, so you can use CD-ROM encyclopedias and other reference resources. You need four things: the CD-ROM device, the correct type of cable, the correct port or controller card, and the device driver. Often a device is packaged with all the necessary components. If yours is not, you need to find out what type of port and cable the CD-ROM requires. Usually the packaging or documentation contains this information. If you do not have the correct type of port on your computer or if the port is already in use, you should be able to purchase an expansion card that contains the appropriate port.

This discussion of ports and interfacing may seem a bit technical, but it pertains to an important aspect of computing—expandability. New innovations in computing appear every day, and you probably will want to use some of the new technology without having to purchase a new computer system. Expansion slots make this possible. All other factors being equal, computers with many expansion slots are a better investment than those with only a few.

Now refer back to the ad attached to PR #516859. What types of ports are included with the computer system described in the ad? Is this computer system expandable? How? Your answer is correct if you said that there are two serial ports and one parallel port. The system also appears to have an adequate number of expansion slots. The ad says there are eight but does not indicate if all of them are free. It is likely that some of the slots already are filled with expansion cards for devices such as the modem, the disk drive controller, and the video controller. Tenzing should find out how many of the expansion slots are empty.

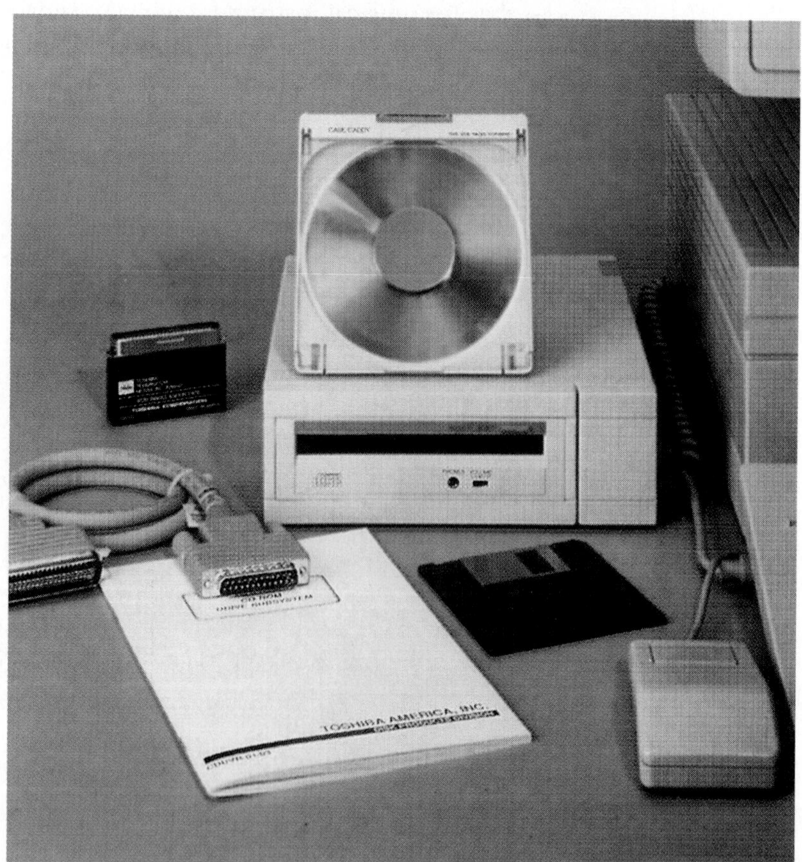

Figure 32:
CD-ROM drive ready for installation

Network Communication

In the business world you usually don't work alone but rather as part of a team. As a team member you'll probably use a computer that is part of a network. A **network** connects your computer to the computers of other team members. It enables you to share data and peripheral devices, such as printers, modems, and fax machines.

There are a variety of networks, too many to discuss thoroughly here. We will focus our discussion on some of the basic concepts pertaining to a local-area network, one of the network types commonly found in businesses.

In a **local-area network (LAN)** computers and peripheral devices are located relatively close to each other, generally in the same building. If you are using a network, it is useful to know three things: the location of the data, the type of network card in your computer, and the software that manages the communications protocols and other network functions.

Many networks have a **file server** (Figure 33), which is a computer that acts as the

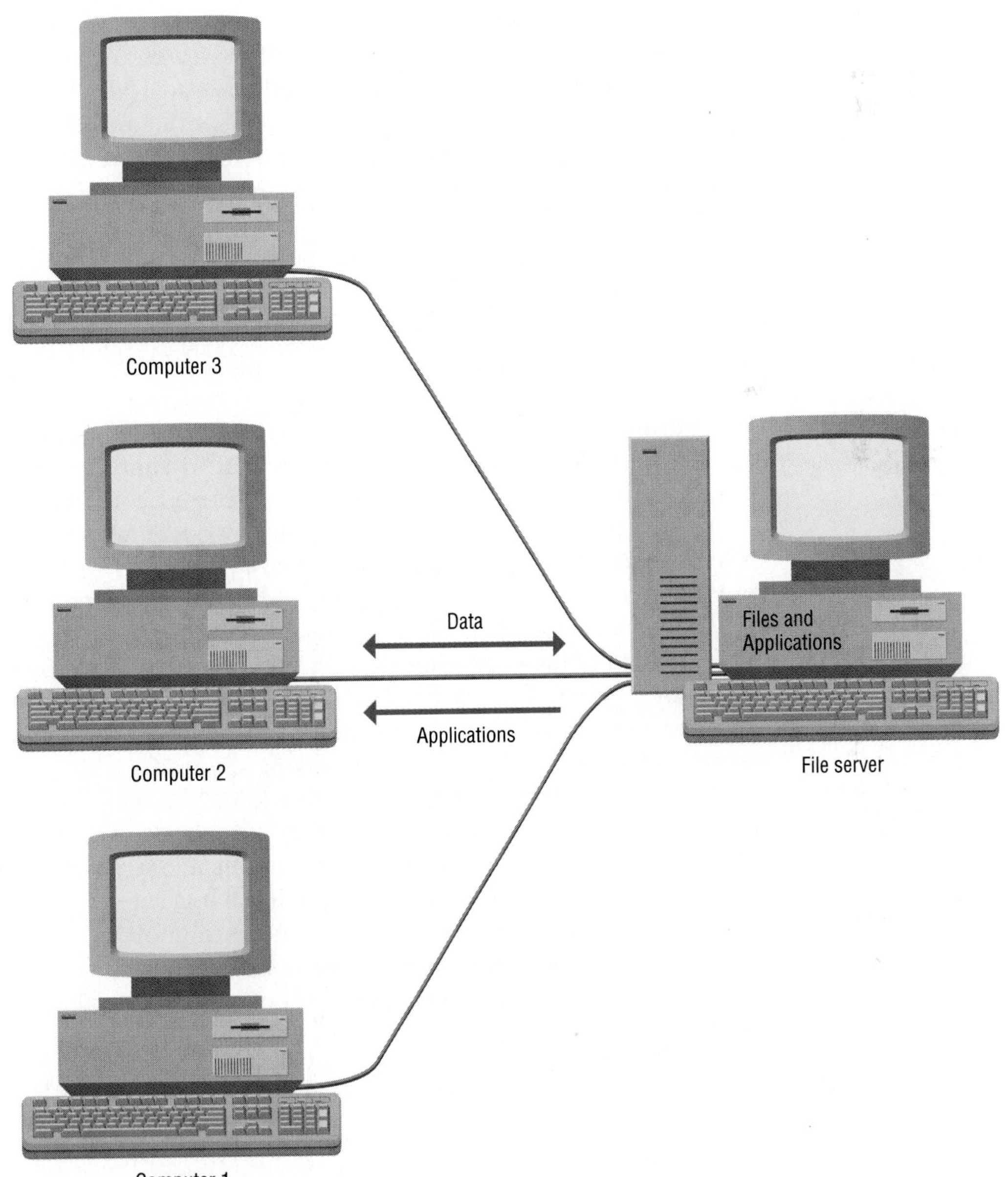

Figure 33:
A file server is the central repository for data and applications programs

central repository for application programs and provides mass storage for most of the data used on the network. A network with a file server is sometimes referred to as a **hierarchical network**. This type of network is dependent on the file server because the file server contains most of the data and software. When a network does not have a file server, all the computers essentially are equal, and the task of storing files and programs is distributed among them. This is called a **peer-to-peer network**.

The type of network card that you have in your computer affects the transmission speed of your data. The network card generally is plugged into one of the expansion slots in your computer. The most common network cards are **Ethernet**, **Arcnet**, and **Token-Ring**.

Network software establishes the communications protocol for the network. Your network software resides on a disk in drive A or on your hard disk drive. Additional network software might be stored on the file server. The most common microcomputer networking software packages include Novell NetWare, Banyan Vines, and Microsoft Windows for Workgroups. Why is it important to know the type of network software you are using? Some software is designed to be used on specific types of networks. If you have a network, before you purchase software, read the packaging or documentation to determine whether the software is designed to work with your network. In addition, some hardware is tested specifically for compatibility with particular networks. The term "Novell compatible," for example, indicates that the hardware should work on a Novell network.

Turn once again to the ad at the beginning of the chapter and think about these questions: Is this computer networked? Can it be networked? Why or why not? Your answer should be that the computer is not currently part of a network and is not shipped with a network card. However, it should be possible to connect this computer to a Novell network with the appropriate network card and software, which would have to be purchased separately.

Telecommunications

Telecommunications means communicating over a long distance. Telecommunications enables you to send data over the phone lines to another computer and to access data stored on computers located in another city, state, or country.

The telecommunications process requires a communications device called a **modem**, which connects your computer to a standard phone jack and converts the **digital** signals your computer uses into **analog** signals, which can traverse the phone lines. An external modem connects to the serial port in the back of the computer, while an internal modem plugs into one of the expansion slots on the computer's main board.

Figure 34 shows the telecommunications process, in which a modem converts digital signals to analog signals at the transmitting site and a second modem converts the analog signals back to digital signals at the receiving site.

To use a modem for telecommunications, you also must have **communications software** to handle the transmission protocols. When you initiate a telecommunications call, you are required to provide specifications about your modem and the destination computer. To do this, you need to know the **baud rate** (speed) of your modem and the port it uses (COM1 or COM2). You also need to know how the destination computer's modem is expecting to receive data: the number of data bits, the number of stop bits, and the parity. To obtain this information, you often need to call the technical support group for the destination computer.

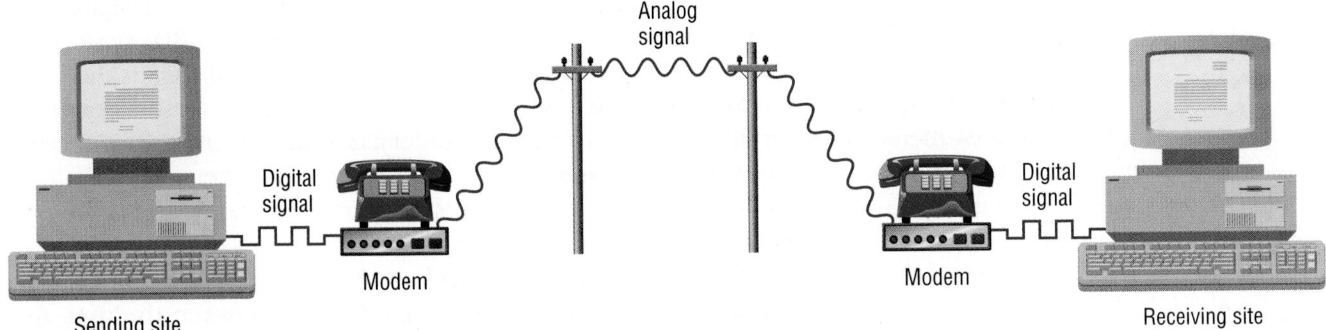

Figure 34: Using modems to send and receive a memo

What about the computer in the ad attached to PR #516859? What do the specifications tell you about its telecommunications capabilities? Your answer should be that the computer system comes with a 9600-baud modem. This is the hardware necessary to connect the computer to the telephone line. However, the ad does not mention communications software, so this may be an additional cost.

Computer Software

Just as a tape recorder or a compact-disc player is worthless without tapes or compact discs, computer hardware is useless without computer software. The types of software that you use determine what you can do with your computer. For example, word processing software enables you to use a computer to prepare documents; graphics software lets you to use a computer to create graphs and illustrations. Software can be divided into two general types: systems software and applications software.

Systems Software

Systems software includes the programs that run the fundamental operations in your computer, such as loading programs and data into memory, executing programs, saving data on a disk, displaying information on the screen, and sending information through a port to a peripheral.

A special type of systems software is the **operating system**, which works like an air-traffic controller to coordinate the activities within the computer. The most popular operating system for IBM-compatible microcomputers is usually referred to as the **disk operating system** or **DOS** (rhymes with "boss"). DOS has been sold under the trade names PC-DOS and MS-DOS. Both systems were developed primarily by Microsoft Corporation, so they are essentially the same.

DOS has gone through several revisions since its introduction in 1981. The original version, numbered 1.0, has been followed by versions 2.0, 3.0, 3.1, 3.3, 4.0, 4.1, 5.0, 6.0, and 6.2. Early versions of DOS lack some of the capabilities of later versions. Consequently, some newer software will not run on computers that use older versions of DOS. You can install newer versions of DOS on your computer if the computer meets certain memory, processor, and storage requirements.

As an operating system, DOS has several drawbacks. It was originally designed for computers with limited amounts of memory and small storage capacities that performed only one task at a time and serviced only one user. Another drawback of DOS is the complexity of commands that you must use to specify tasks. To use most versions of DOS, you must memorize a list of command words and understand the punctuation and spacing rules for constructing valid command "sentences." DOS users often complain that they forget the command words and that typing mistakes or punctuation errors in commands sometimes produce unexpected results.

In response to user complaints, several companies have designed easy-to-use **operating environments**—software that provides a sort of protective layer between the user and DOS. The goal of operating environments such as Microsoft's Windows and Digital Research's GEM is to provide an easier way for users to issue DOS commands. Once the operating environment is installed, you basically can forget that DOS was there.

Microsoft has expanded on the concept of operating environments. With Windows versions 2.0, 3.0, and 3.1 it has tried to make an environment that simplifies the use of any program and provides users with some of the features they need for the newer, more powerful computers.

The first versions of Microsoft Windows were operating environments that supplemented the DOS operating system. More recent versions of Windows, Windows NT and Windows 95, are complete operating systems that do not require DOS. However, these operating systems do allow you to use software written for DOS as well as software written for Windows.

As an alternative to DOS and Windows, IBM has developed an operating system called **OS/2**, which is specifically designed for today's more powerful microcomputer systems with large amounts of RAM and very large disk capacities. To take advantage of the capabilities of OS/2, you must use applications software specifically written to operate in this environment. Since OS/2 is a relative newcomer to the market, the selection of OS/2 applications software is somewhat limited. You can use many of the programs designed for DOS and Windows, but they will function in essentially the same way as on a computer that uses DOS for the operating system.

Applications Software

A wide variety of software exists to help you accomplish many different tasks using your computer. This type of software is called **applications software** because it enables you to apply your computer to accomplish specific goals. Four major types of applications software are word processing, spreadsheet, database management, and graphics.

Word processing software enables you to electronically create, edit, format, and print documents. The advantages of a word processor over a typewriter are numerous. With a word processor you can move paragraphs, check spelling, create tables and columns, modify margins, correct typos, and view how a document will appear before you print it. A wide selection of word processing software is available for the Windows environment, including Microsoft Word for Windows, WordPerfect for Windows, and Lotus Development Corporation's Ami Pro. An example of a screen from a word processing program is shown in Figure 35.

An **electronic spreadsheet** enables you to perform calculations with numbers arranged in a grid of rows and columns on the computer screen. You type numbers into

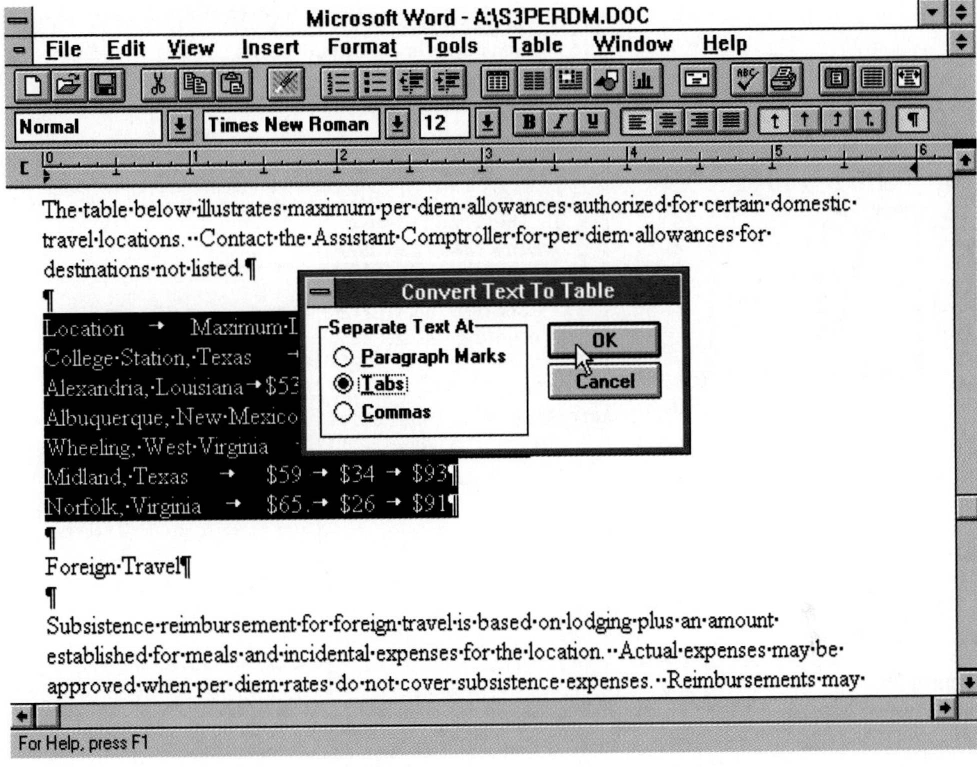

Figure 35: A Microsoft Word for Windows screen

the grid, then create formulas that perform calculations using those numbers. In many ways a spreadsheet is the ultimate calculator—once your numbers are on the screen, you don't have to reenter them when you want to redo a calculation with revised or corrected numbers. As an additional benefit, spreadsheet software provides you with excellent printouts of the raw data or of graphs created from the data.

With the appropriate data and formulas, you can use an electronic spreadsheet to prepare financial reports, analyze investment portfolios, calculate amortization tables, examine alternative bid proposals, and project income, as well as perform many other tasks involved in making informed business decisions. Three of the top-selling spreadsheets for Windows are Microsoft Excel, Borland's Quattro Pro for Windows, and Lotus Development's Lotus 1-2-3 for Windows. An example of a spreadsheet screen is shown in Figure 36 (on the following page).

Database software helps you manage and manipulate information that you previously might have stored in file cabinets or on rolodex cards or index cards. Information about employees, clients, schedules, supplies, and inventory can be managed effectively with a database. Database software lets you easily search, sort, select, delete, and update your file of information. Versatile reporting capabilities also are offered. Borland International's Paradox, Oracle's Card, and Microsoft Corporation's Access are examples of database management software available for the Windows environment. An example of a database screen is shown in Figure 37 (on the following page).

Graphics software makes it possible for you to create illustrations, diagrams, graphs, and charts. Most graphics software provides you with tools to draw lines, boxes, and circles; to fill in or erase areas of your drawing; to enlarge, shrink, or scale a drawing; and to print your finished product. Many graphics programs also provide collections of predrawn pictures, known as **clipart** that you can use as is or incorporate in other drawings. Aldus Corporation's Aldus FreeHand, Corel Systems CorelDRAW, and Adobe Illustrator are three

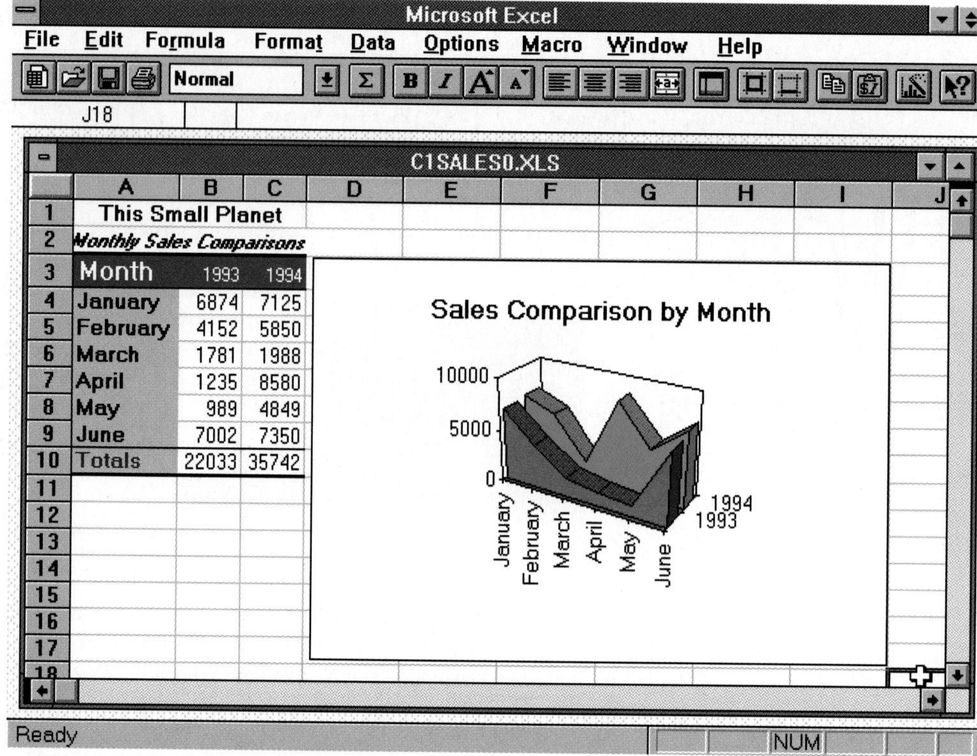

Figure 36:
A Microsoft Excel for Windows screen

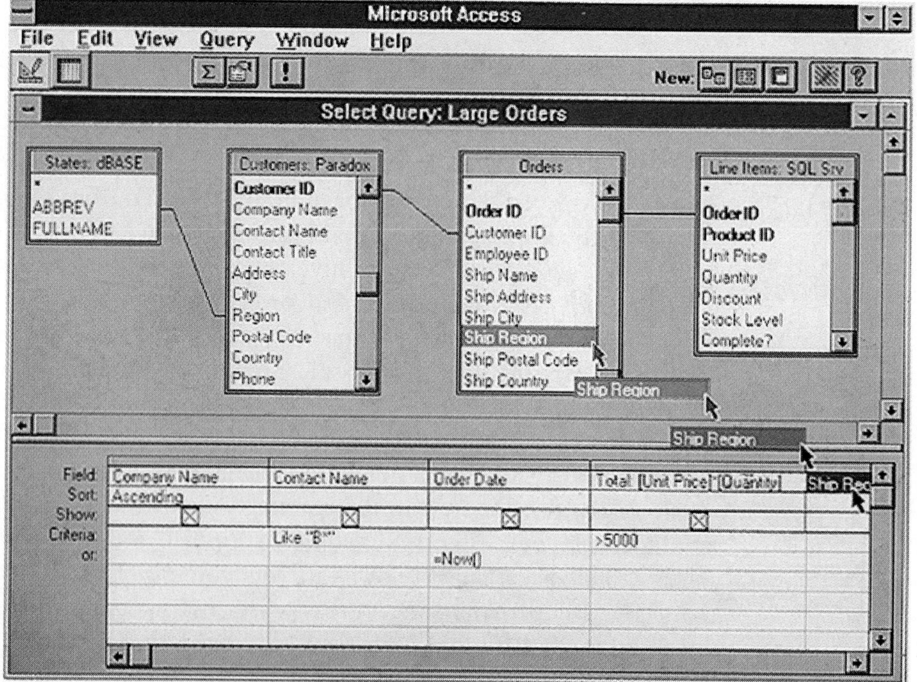

Figure 37:
A Microsoft Access for Windows screen

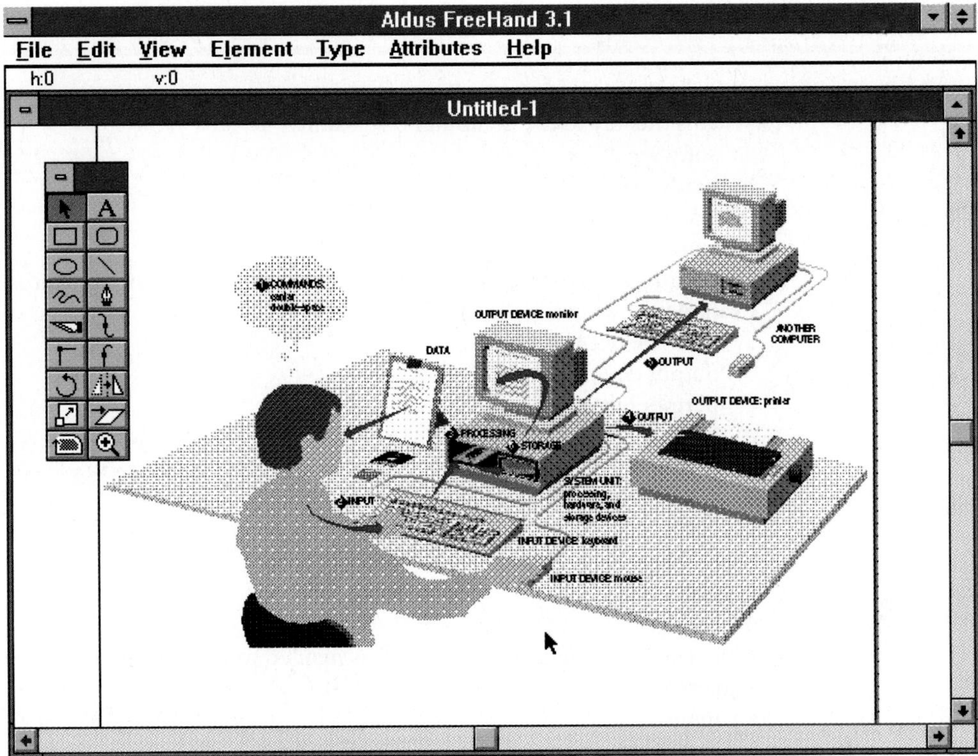

Figure 38: An Aldus Freehand for Windows screen

popular Windows graphics programs. A screen from a popular graphics program is shown in Figure 38.

What types of software are included with the computer described in the ad that accompanied PR #516859? What operating system is provided? Is there an operating environment? Is there any applications software? You are correct if you said that the only software included with the system is the DOS 6.2 operating system. No operating environment or applications software is included.

Now that you have completed this chapter on essential computer concepts, you should have a basic understanding of the hardware and software components of a computer system. You should also be able to understand the terminology in a computer ad, such as the one at the beginning of the chapter. You have seen that the ad attached to PR #516859 includes all the components necessary for a basic computer system, though network hardware and software are not included. Would this be a good system for Tenzing to purchase for International ComAir? To answer that question, you must become familiar with current microcomputer pricing. You will have an opportunity to do some comparison shopping as you work through the questions at the end of this chapter.

■ ■ ■

Questions

1. What is the key to the computer's versatility?
   a. software
   b. hardware
   c. price
   d. super VGA
2. Keyboards, screens, hard disk drives, printers, and main circuit boards are all examples of which of the following?
   a. input devices
   b. output devices
   c. peripherals
   d. hardware
3. Moving text, sorting lists, and performing calculations are examples of which of the following?
   a. input
   b. output
   c. processing
   d. storage
4. What telecommunications hardware is needed to convert digital signals to analog signals?
   a. mouse
   b. device driver
   c. modem
   d. slot
5. What is a collection of data stored on a disk under a name that you assign called?
   a. a file
   b. the operating system
   c. a protocol
   d. a pixel
6. Which one of the following would not be considered a microcomputer?
   a. desktop
   b. notebook
   c. PC
   d. mainframe
7. The selection of components that make up a particular computer system is referred to as
   a. the configuration
   b. the specification
   c. the protocol
   d. the device driver
8. Which of the following maintains data only on a temporary basis?
   a. ROM
   b. a disk
   c. RAM
   d. a hard disk

9. Which one of the following microprocessors is fastest?
   a. 4.77-MHz 8088
   b. 12-MHz 80286
   c. 33-MHz 80386
   d. 50-MHz 80486
10. What is each 1 or 0 used in the representation of data called?
    a. a bit
    b. a byte
    c. an ASCII
    d. a pixel
11. What usually represents one character of data?
    a. a bit
    b. a byte
    c. an integer
    d. a pixel
12. What is a kilobyte?
    a. 100 megabytes
    b. 1,024 bytes
    c. one-half a gigabyte
    d. one million bits
13. Which one of the following would you not expect to find in RAM while the computer is on?
    a. operating system instructions
    b. data the user has entered
    c. application program instructions
    d. write-protect window
14. What connects a monitor to a computer?
    a. a parallel port
    b. a network card
    c. a graphics adapter
    d. near-letter quality mode
15. Which disk has the highest storage capacity?
    a. 5.25" DS/HD
    b. 5.25" DS/DD
    c. 3.5" DS/HD
    d. 3.5" DS/DD
16. Which one of the following statements best defines a peer-to-peer network?
    a. A central file server acts as a repository for all files and applications programs used on the network.
    b. Your messages travel to a mainframe computer and then are routed to their destinations.
    c. The task of storing data and files is distributed among all the computers that are attached to the network.
    d. The messages travel around a ring until they reach their destination.
17. Which one of the following is systems software?
    a. Lotus 1-2-3
    b. DOS 5.0
    c. WordPerfect for Windows
    d. Corel Draw

18. Which one of the following is an operating environment but not an operating system?
    a. DOS 3.3
    b. Windows 3.1
    c. Windows NT
    d. OS/2
19. Computer memory is measured in ____________________.
20. Diskette, hard disk, and tape storage capacity is measured in ____________________.
21. Disk access time is measured in ____________________.
22. The resolution of computer monitors is measured in ____________________.
23. The microprocessor clock rate is measured in ____________________.
24. The transmission of text, numeric, voice, or video data from one computer to another is called __________.
25. Connecting a computer to peripheral devices is called ____________________.
26. List the four essential components of communication.
27. For each of the following data items, indicate how many bits and how many bytes of storage would be required:

Data Item	Bits	Bytes
North		
Scissors		
CEO		
U.S.A.		
General Ledger		
123 N. Main St.		

28. Read the following requirements for using Microsoft Windows 3.1 (taken from the documentation that accompanies the Microsoft Windows 3.1 program). Then turn back to Figure 1 and determine if the computer specifications listed in the ad are sufficient to run Windows 3.1.
    Windows requires:
    - Microsoft MS-DOS version 3.1 or later.
    - For 386 enhanced mode, a personal computer with an 80386 processor (or higher) and 640 kilobytes (K) of conventional memory plus 1024K of extended memory, 8 megabytes (MB) of free disk space (10.0 is recommended), and at least one floppy disk drive.
    - A display adapter that is supported by Windows.
    - A printer that is supported by Windows, if you want to print with Windows.

- A Hayes, Multi-tech, Trail Blazer, or compatible modem, if you want to use Terminal, the Windows communications Application.
- A mouse that is supported by Windows. Though it is not required, a mouse is highly recommended so that you can take full advantage of the easy-to-use Windows graphical interface.

29. Using the Windows specifications in Question 28, look through a recent computer magazine and find the least expensive computer that will run this operating environment. Make a photocopy of the ad showing the specifications, price, and vendor. Write the name of the magazine and the issue date on the top of the ad.
30. Look through the ads in a computer magazine to find a variety of peripheral devices. Note the type of port to which they connect, then add the devices to the appropriate column of the following chart:

Types of Ports and Their Connecting Devices

Type of Port	Device
Serial Port	
Parallel Port	
MIDI Port	
SCSI Port	

Essential Computer Concepts Index

Photography Credits

Figure	Credit	Page
1	Courtesy of Hewlett-Packard Company	EC 4
	Courtesy of Hewlett-Packard Company	EC 4
2	Courtesy of International Business Machines	EC 5
4	Courtesy of International Business Machines	EC 7
5	Courtesy of International Business Machines	EC 8
6	Courtesy of Toshiba American Information Systems, Inc.	EC 8
7	Courtesy of International Business Machines	EC 8
8	Courtesy of International Business Machines	EC 9
9	Photo by Paul Shambroom, courtesy of Cray Research, Inc.	EC 9
12	Courtesy of Microsoft Corporation	EC11
13	Courtesy of Intel Corporation	EC 12
18	Courtesy of NEC Technologies, Inc.	EC 16
20	Courtesy of Panasonic Communications Systems Company	EC 16
22	Photo Courtesy of Hewlett-Packard Company	EC 17
23	Photo Courtesy of Hewlett-Packard Company	EC 17
26	Richard Morgenstein	EC 19
27	Richard Morgenstein	EC 20
28	Photo courtesy of Seagate Technology, Inc.	EC 20
32	Toshiba's XM-3301 Series CD-ROM disc drive	EC 24
35	Courtesy of Microsoft Corporation	EC 29
36	Courtesy of Microsoft Corporation	EC 30
37	Courtesy of Microsoft Corporation	EC 30

Microsoft® Windows™ 3.1 Tutorials

1 **Essential Windows Skills**

2 **Effective File Management**

Read This Before You Begin

To the Student

To use this book, you must have a Student Disk. Your instructor will either provide you with a Student Disk or ask you to make your own by following the instructions in the section called "Preparing Your Student Disk" in Windows Tutorial 2. See your instructor or lab manager for further information.

Using Your Own Computer If you are going to work through this book using your own computer, you need:

- The Student Disk. ***You will not be able to complete the tutorials and exercises in this book using your own computer until you have the Student Disk.*** Ask your instructor or lab manager for details on how to get it.
- A computer system running Microsoft Windows 3.1 and DOS.

To the Instructor

Making the Student Disk To complete the tutorials in this book, your students must have a copy of the Student Disk. To relieve you of having to make multiple Student Disks from a single master copy, we provide you with the CTI WinApps Setup Disk, which contains an automatic Student Disk generating program. Once you install the Setup Disk on a network or standalone workstation, students can easily make their own Student Disks by double clicking on the "Make Win 3.1 Student Disk" icon in the CTI WinApps icon group. Double clicking this icon transfers all the data files students will need to complete the tutorials and Tutorial Assignments to a high-density disk in drive A or B. If some of your students will use their own computers to complete the tutorials and exercises in this book, they must first get the Student Disk. The section called "Preparing Your Student Disk" in Windows Tutorial 2 provides complete instructions on how to make the Student Disk.

If you have disk copying resources available, you might choose to use them for making quantities of the Student Disk. The "Make Win 3.1 Student Disk" provides an easy and fast way to make multiple Student Disks.

Installing the CTI WinApps Setup Disk: To install the CTI WinApps icon group from the Setup Disk, follow the instructions either on the disk label or inside the disk envelope that was bundled with your book. By adopting this book, you are granted a license to install this software on any computer or computer network used by you or your students.

Readme File: A Readme.txt file located on the Setup Disk provides additional technical notes, troubleshooting advice, and tips for using the CTI WinApps software in your school's computer lab. You can view the Readme file using any word processor you choose.

System Requirements for installing the CTI WinApps Disk The minimum software and hardware requirements your computer system needs to install the CTI WinApps icon group are as follows:

- Microsoft Windows version 3.1 on a local hard drive or on a network drive
- A 286 (or higher) processor with a minimum of 2 MB RAM (4 MB RAM or more is strongly recommended).
- A mouse supported by Windows
- A printer that is supported by Windows 3.1
- A VGA 640 x 480 16-color display is recommended; an 800 x 600 or 1024 x 768 SVGA, VGA monochrome, or EGA display is also acceptable
- 1.5 MB of free hard disk space
- Student workstations with at least 1 high-density 3.5 inch-disk drive.
- If you wish to install the CTI WinApps Setup Disk on a network drive, your network must support Microsoft Windows.

T U T O R I A L 1

Essential Windows Skills

Using the Program Manager, CTI WinApps, and Help

OBJECTIVES

In this tutorial you will:

- Start your computer
- Launch and exit Windows
- Use the mouse and the keyboard
- Identify the components of the Windows desktop
- Launch and exit applications
- Organize your screen-based desktop
- Switch tasks in a multi-tasking environment.
- Use Windows menus
- Explore Windows toolbars

CASE

A New Computer, Anywhere, Inc. You're a busy employee without a minute of spare time. But now, to top it all off, a computer technician appears at your office door, introduces himself as Steve Laslow, and begins unpacking your new computer!

You wonder out loud, "How long is it going to take me to learn this?"

Steve explains that your new computer uses Microsoft Windows 3.1 software and that the **interface**—the way you interact with the computer and give it instructions—is very easy to use. He describes the Windows software as a "gooey," a **graphical user interface (GUI)**, which uses pictures of familiar objects such as file folders and documents to represent a desktop on your screen.

Steve unpacks your new computer and begins to connect the components. He talks as he works, commenting on three things he really likes about Microsoft Windows. First, Windows applications have a standard interface, which means that once you learn how to use one Windows application, you are well on your way to understanding how to use others. Second, Windows lets you use more than one application at a time, a capability called **multitasking**, so you can easily switch between applications such as your word processor and your calendar. Third, Windows lets you do more than one task at a time, such as printing a document while you create a pie chart. All in all, Windows makes your computer an effective and easy-to-use productivity tool.

Using the Windows Tutorials Effectively

This tutorial will help you learn about Windows 3.1. Begin by reading the text that explains the concepts. Then when you come to numbered steps on a colored background, follow those steps as you work at your computer. Read each step carefully and completely *before* you try it.

Don't worry if parts of your screen display are different from the figures in the tutorials. The important parts of the screen display are labeled in each figure. Just be sure these parts are on your screen.

Don't worry about making mistakes—that's part of the learning process. TROUBLE? paragraphs identify common problems and explain how to get back on track. Do the steps in the TROUBLE? paragraph *only* if you are having the problem described.

Starting Your Computer and Launching Windows

The process of starting Windows is sometimes referred to as **launching**. If your computer system requires procedures different from those in the steps below, your instructor or technical support person will provide you with step-by-step instructions for turning on your monitor, starting or resetting your computer, logging into a network if you have one, and launching Windows.

To start your computer and launch Windows:

1. Make sure your disk drives are empty.
2. Find the power switch for your monitor and turn it on.
3. Locate the power switch for your computer and turn it on. After a few seconds you should see C:\> or C> on the screen.

   TROUBLE? If your computer displays a "non-system disk" error message, a floppy disk was left in a disk drive at startup. To continue, remove the disk and press [Enter].

4. Type **win** to launch Windows. See Figure 1-1.

Figure 1-1
Launching Windows

❺ Press the key labeled **[Enter]**. Soon the Windows 3.1 title screen appears. Next you might notice an hourglass on the screen. This symbol means your computer is busy with a task and you must wait until it has finished.

After a brief wait, the title screen is replaced by one similar to Figure 1-2. Don't worry if your screen is not exactly the same as Figure 1-2. You are ready to continue the Tutorial when you see the Program Manager title at the top of the screen. If you do not see this title, ask your technical support person for assistance.

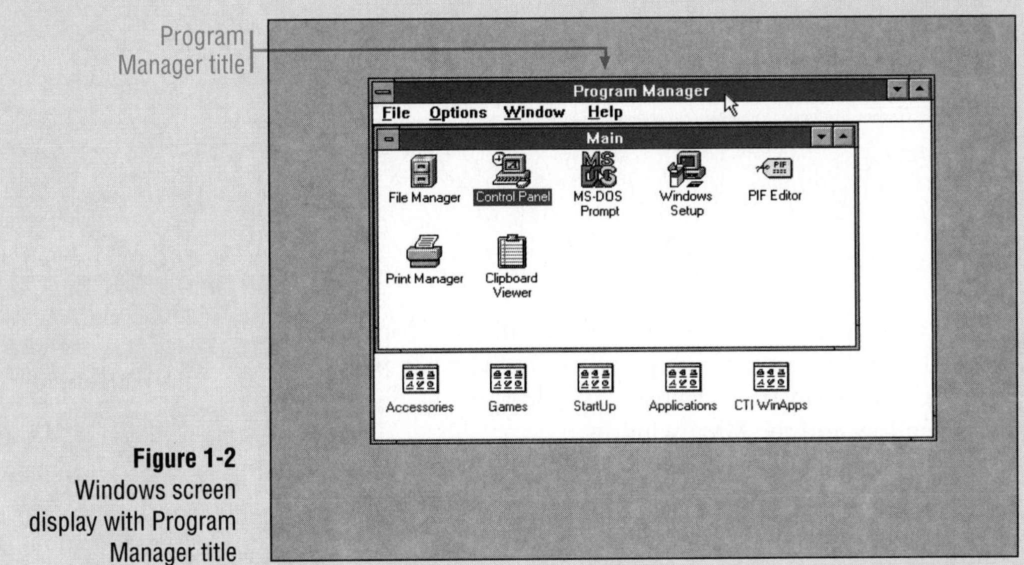

Figure 1-2
Windows screen display with Program Manager title

Basic Windows Controls and Concepts

Windows has a variety of **controls** that enable you to communicate with the computer. In this section you'll learn how to use the basic Windows controls.

The Windows Desktop

Look at your screen display and compare it to Figure 1-3 on the following page. Your screen may not be exactly the same as the illustration. You should, however, be able to locate components on your screen similar to those in Figure 1-3 on the following page.

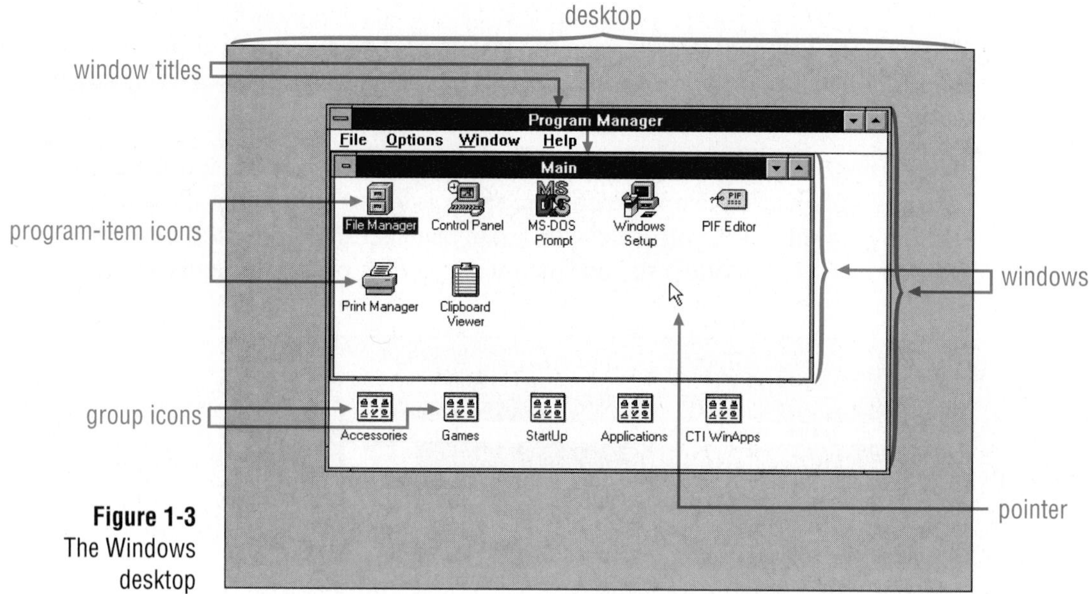

Figure 1-3 The Windows desktop

The screen represents a **desktop**, a workspace for projects and for the tools that are needed to manipulate those projects. Rectangular **windows** (with a lowercase *w*) define work areas on the desktop. The desktop in Figure 1-3 contains the Program Manager window and the Main window.

Icons are small pictures that represent real objects, such as disk drives, software, and documents. Each icon in the Main window represents an **application**, that is, a computer program. These icons are called **program-item icons**.

Each **group icon** at the bottom of the Program Manager window represents a collection of applications. For example, the CTI WinApps icon represents a collection of tutorial and practice applications, which you can use to learn more about Windows. A group icon expands into a group window that contains program-item icons.

The **pointer** helps you manipulate objects on the Windows desktop. The pointer can assume different shapes, depending on what is happening on the desktop. In Figure 1-3 the pointer is shaped like an arrow.

The Program Manager

When you launch Windows, the Program Manager application starts automatically and continues to run as long as you are working with Windows. Think of the Program Manager as a launching pad for other applications. The **Program Manager** displays icons for the applications on your system. To launch an application, you would select its icon.

Using the Mouse

The **mouse** is a pointing device that helps you interact with the screen-based objects in the Windows environment. As you move the mouse on a flat surface, the pointer on the screen moves in the direction corresponding to the movement of the mouse. You can also control the Windows environment from the keyboard; however, the mouse is much more efficient for most operations, so the tutorials in this book assume you are using one.

Find the arrow-shaped pointer on your screen. If you do not see the pointer, move your mouse until the pointer comes into view. You will begin most Windows-based operations by **pointing**.

To position the pointer:

1. Position your right index finger over the left mouse button, as shown in Figure 1-4.

   TROUBLE? If you want to use your mouse with your left hand, ask your technical support person to help you. Be sure you find out how to change back to the right-handed mouse setting, so you can reset the mouse each time you are finished in the lab.

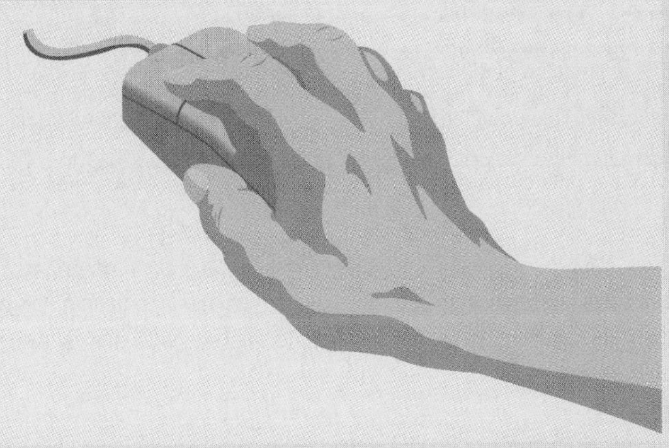

Figure 1-4 How to hold the mouse

2. Locate the arrow-shaped pointer on the screen.
3. Move the mouse and watch the movement of the pointer.
4. Next, move the mouse to each of the four corners of the screen.

   TROUBLE? If your mouse runs out of room, lift it, move it into the middle of a clear area on your desk, and then place it back on the table. The pointer does not move when the mouse is not in contact with the tabletop.

5. Continue experimenting with mouse pointing until you feel comfortable with your "eye-mouse coordination."

Pointing is usually followed by clicking, double-clicking, or dragging. **Clicking** means pressing a mouse button (usually the left button) and then quickly releasing it. Clicking is used to select an object on the desktop. Windows shows you which object is selected by highlighting it.

To click an icon:

1. Locate the Print Manager icon in the Main window. If you cannot see the Print Manager icon, use any other icon for this activity.
2. Position the pointer on the icon.
3. Once the pointer is on the icon, *do not move the mouse*.
4. Press the left mouse button and then quickly release it. Your icon should have a highlighted title like the one in Figure 1-5 on the following page.

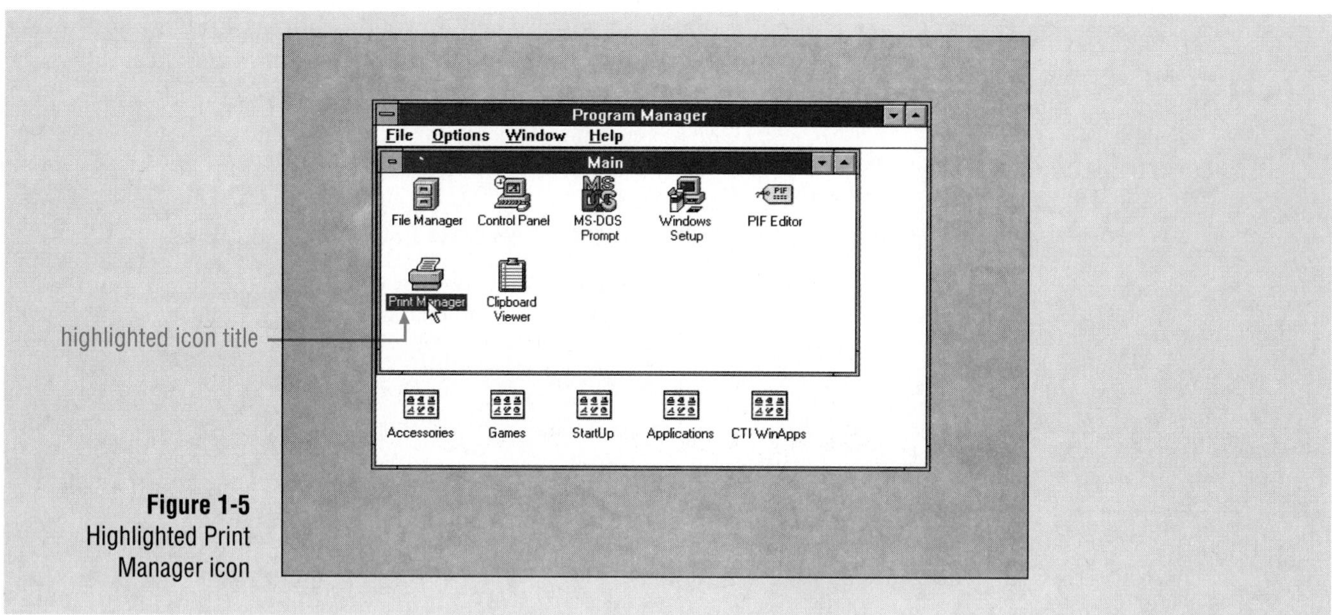

Figure 1-5
Highlighted Print Manager icon

Double-clicking means clicking the mouse button twice in rapid succession. Double-clicking is a shortcut. For example, most Windows users double-click to launch and exit applications.

To double click:

❶ Position the pointer on the Program Manager Control-menu box, as shown in Figure 1-6.

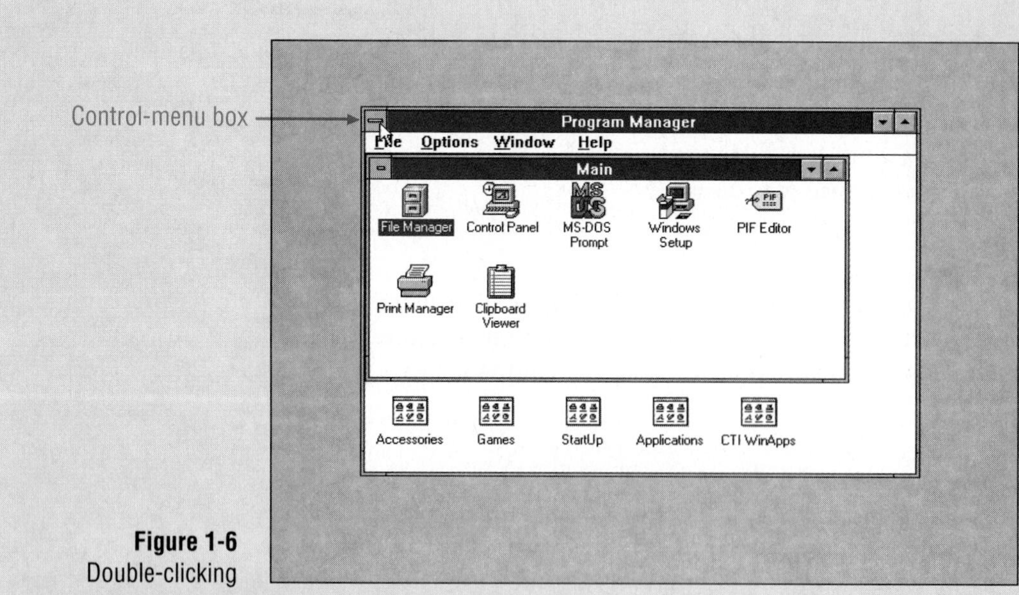

Figure 1-6
Double-clicking

❷ Click the mouse button twice in rapid succession. If your double-clicking is successful, an Exit Windows box appears on your screen.

❸ Now, single-click the **Cancel button**.

Dragging means moving an object to a new location on the desktop. To drag an object, you would position the pointer on the object, then hold the left mouse button down while you move the mouse. Let's drag one of the icons to a new location.

To drag an icon:

1. Position the pointer on any icon on the screen, such as on the Clipboard Viewer icon. Figure 1-7 shows you where to put the pointer and what happens on your screen as you carry out the next step.

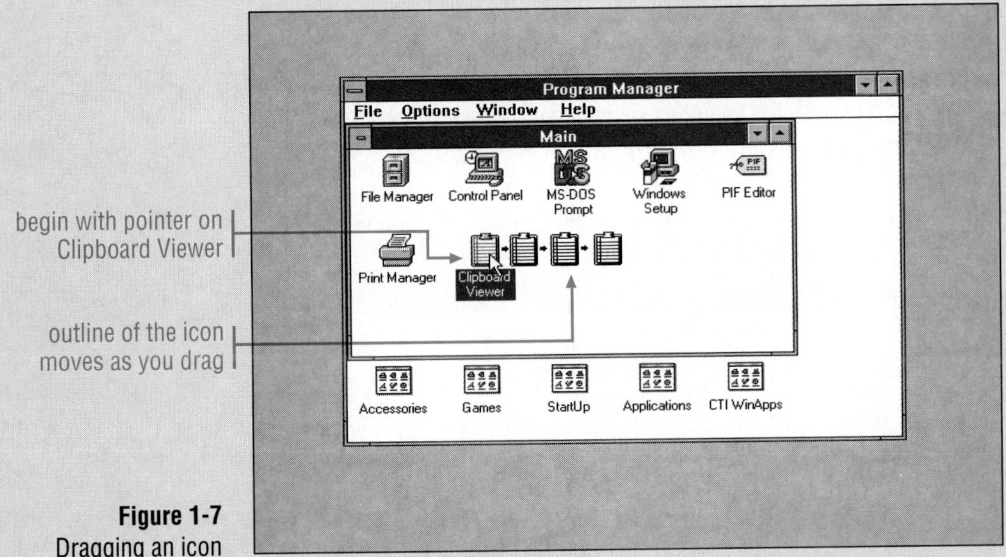

Figure 1-7
Dragging an icon

2. Hold the left mouse button down while you move the mouse to the right. Notice that an outline of the icon moves as you move the mouse.
3. Release the mouse button. Now the icon is in a new location.

   TROUBLE? If the icon snaps back to its original position, don't worry. Your technical support person probably has instructed Windows to do this. If your icon automatically snapped back to its original position, skip Step 4.

4. Drag the icon back to its original location.

Using the Keyboard

You use the keyboard to type documents, enter numbers, and activate some commands. You can use the on-screen CTI Keyboard Tutorial to learn the special features of your computer keyboard. To do this, you need to learn how to launch the Keyboard Tutorial and other applications.

Launching Applications

Earlier in this tutorial you launched Windows. Once you have launched Windows, you can launch other Windows applications such as Microsoft Works. When you launch an application, an application window opens. Later, when you have finished using the application, you close the window to exit.

Launching the CTI Keyboard Tutorial

To launch the CTI Keyboard Tutorial, you need to have the CTI WinApps software installed on your computer. If you are working in a computer lab, these applications should already be installed on your computer system. Look on your screen for a group icon or a window labeled "CTI WinApps."

If you don't have anything labeled "CTI WinApps" on your screen's desktop, ask your technical support person for help. If you are using your own computer, you will need to install the CTI WinApps applications yourself. See your technical support person or your instructor for a copy of the Setup Disk and the Installation Instructions that come with it.

To open the CTI Win Apps group window:

1. Double-click the **CTI WinApps group icon**. Your screen displays a CTI WinApps group window similar to the one in Figure 1-8.

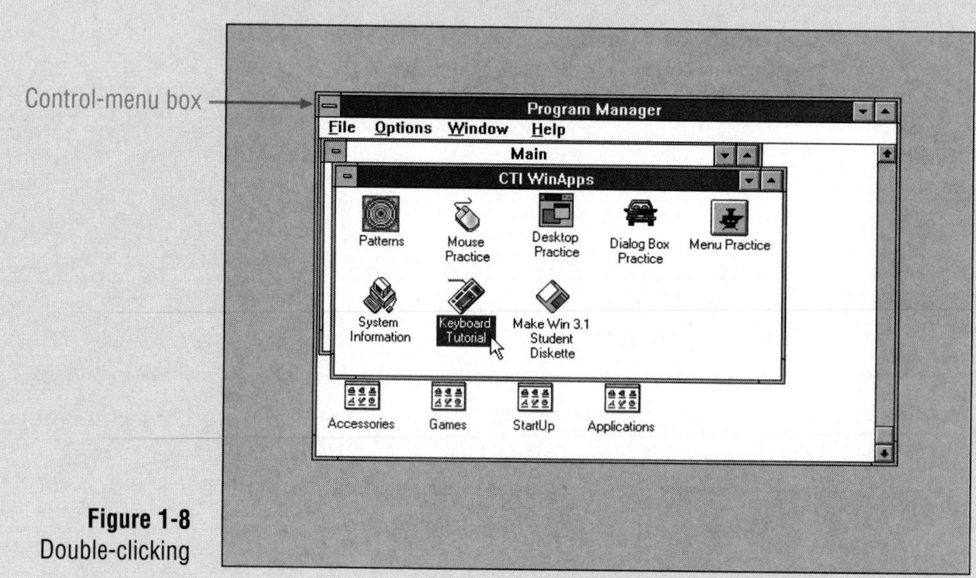

Figure 1-8
Double-clicking

The CTI WinApps group window contains an icon for each application provided with these tutorials. Right now we want to use the Keyboard Tutorial application.

To launch the Keyboard Tutorial:

1. Double-click the **Keyboard Tutorial icon**. Within a few seconds, the tutorial begins.
2. Read the opening screen, then click the **Continue button**. The CTI Keyboard Tutorial window appears. Follow the instructions on your screen to complete the tutorial. See Figure 1-9.

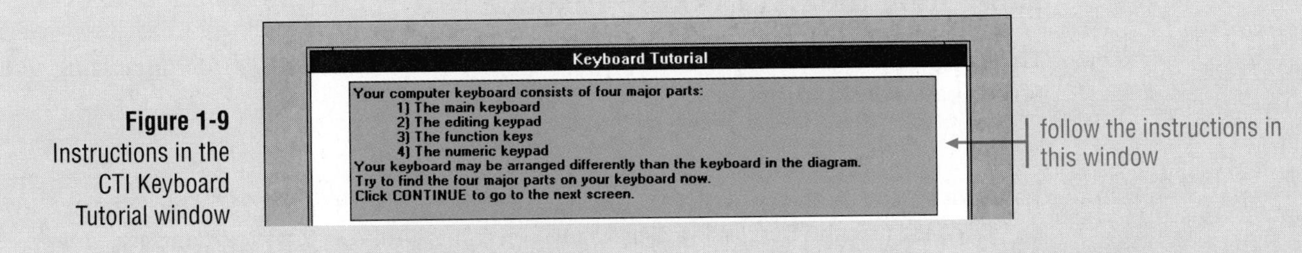

Figure 1-9 Instructions in the CTI Keyboard Tutorial window

TROUBLE? Click the Quit button at any time if you want to exit the Tutorial.

3. When you have completed the Keyboard Tutorial, click the **Quit button**. This takes you back to the Program Manager and CTI WinApps group window.

   TROUBLE? *If you did not have trouble in Step 3, skip this entire paragraph!* If the Program Manager window is not open, look for its icon at the bottom of your screen. Double-click this icon to open the Program Manager window. To prevent this problem from happening again, click the word Options on the Program Manager menu bar, then click Minimize on Use.

Launching the CTI Mouse Practice

To discover how to use the mouse to manipulate Windows controls, you should launch the Mouse Practice.

To launch the Mouse Practice:

1. Make sure the Program Manager and the CTI WinApps windows are open. It is not a problem if you have additional windows open.

   TROUBLE? If the Program Manager window is not open, look for its icon at the bottom of your screen. Double-click this icon to open the Program Manager window. To prevent this problem from happening again, click the word Options that appears near the top of the Program Manager window, then click Minimize.

2. Double-click the **Mouse Practice icon**. The Mouse Practice window opens.

   TROUBLE? If you don't see the Mouse Practice icon, try clicking the scroll bar arrow button or see your technical support person.

3. Click, drag, or double-click the objects on the screen to see what happens. Don't hesitate to experiment.

4. When you have finished using the Mouse Practice, click the **Exit button** to go back to the Program Manager and continue the tutorial steps.

Organizing Application Windows on the Desktop

The Windows desktop provides you with capabilities similar to your desk; it lets you stack many different items on your screen-based desktop and activate the one you want to use.

There is a problem, though. Like your real desk, your screen-based desktop can become cluttered. That's why you need to learn how to organize the applications on your Windows desktop.

Launching the CTI Desktop Practice

The Desktop Practice application will help you learn the controls for organizing your screen-based desktop.

To Launch the Desktop Practice:

1. Double-click the **Desktop Practice icon** to open the Desktop Practice window, shown in Figure 1-10. Your windows might be a different size or in a slightly different position. Don't worry. What's important is that you see a window with the title "Desktop Practice."

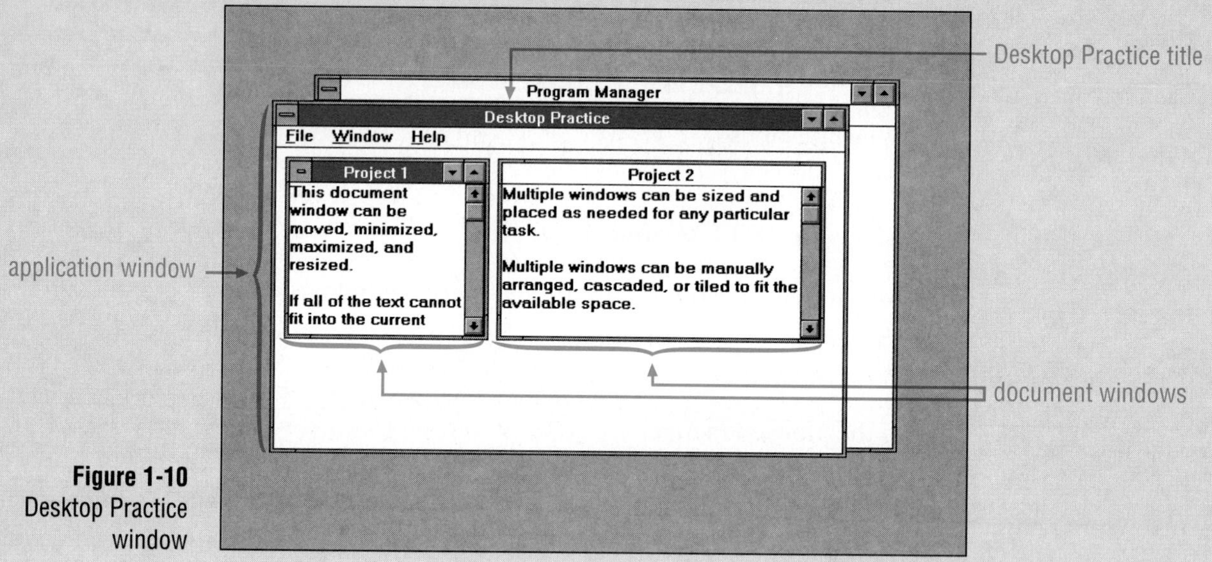

Figure 1-10 Desktop Practice window

Launching the Desktop Practice application opens three new windows on the desktop: Desktop Practice, Project 1, and Project 2. You might be able to see the edges of the Program Manager window "under" the Desktop Practice window. Essentially, you have stacked one project on top of another on your desktop.

The Desktop Practice window is an **application window**, a window that opens when you launch an application. The Project 1 and Project 2 windows are referred to as **document windows**, because they contain the documents, graphs, and lists you create using the application. Document windows are also referred to as **child windows**, because they belong to and are controlled by a "parent" application window.

The ability to have more than one document window open is one of many useful features of the Windows operating environment. Without this capability, you would have to print the documents that aren't being displayed so you could refer to them.

The Anatomy of a Window

Application windows and document windows are similar in many respects. Take a moment to study the Desktop Practice window on your screen and in Figure 1-11 on the following page to familiarize yourself with the terminology. Notice the location of each component but *don't* activate the controls.

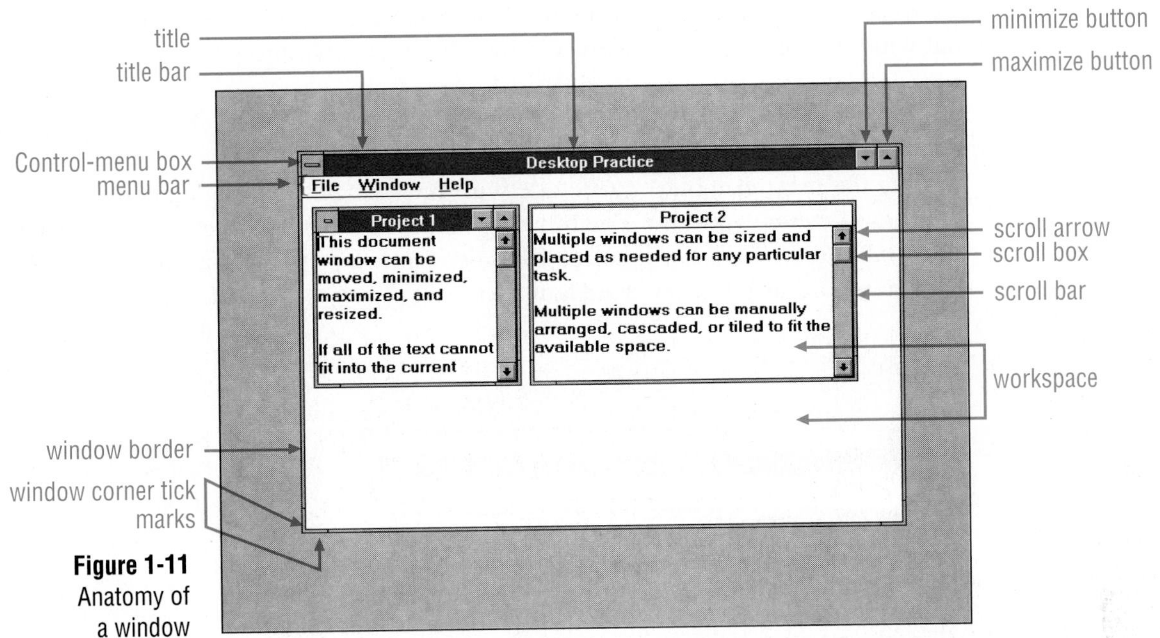

Figure 1-11
Anatomy of a window

At the top of each window is a **title bar**, which contains the window title. A darkened or highlighted title bar indicates that the application window is active. In Figure 1-11, the Desktop Practice application and the Project 1 document windows are active.

In the upper-right of the application window are two buttons used to change the size of a window. The **minimize button**—a square containing a triangle with the point down—is used to shrink the window. The **maximize button**, with the triangle pointing up, is used to enlarge the window so it fills the screen. When a window is maximized, a **restore button** with two triangles replaces the maximize button. Clicking the restore button reduces a maximized window to its previous size.

The **Control-menu box**, located in the upper-left of the Desktop Practice application window, is used to open the **Control menu**, which allows you to switch between application windows.

The **menu bar** is located just below the title bar on application windows. Notice that child windows do not contain menu bars.

The thin line running around the entire perimeter of the window is called the **window border**. The **window corners** are indicated by tick marks on the border.

The gray bar on the right side of each document window is a **scroll bar**, which you use to view window contents that don't initially fit in the window. Both application windows and document windows can contain scroll bars. Scroll bars can appear on the bottom of a window as well as on the side.

The space inside a window where you type text, design graphics, and so forth is called the **workspace**.

Maximizing and Minimizing Windows

The buttons on the right of the title bar are sometimes referred to as **resizing buttons**. You can use the resizing buttons to **minimize** the window so it shrinks down to an icon, **maximize** the window so it fills the screen, or **restore** the window to its previous size.

Because a minimized program is still running, you have quick access to the materials you're using for the project without taking up space on the desktop. You don't need to launch the program when you want to use it again because it continues to run.

A maximized window is useful when you want to focus your attention on the project in that window without being distracted by other windows and projects.

To maximize, restore, and minimize the Desktop Practice window:

1. Locate the maximize button (the one with the triangle pointing up) for the Desktop Practice window. You might see a portion of the Program Manager window behind the Desktop Practice window. Be sure you have found the Desktop Practice maximize button. See Figure 1-12.

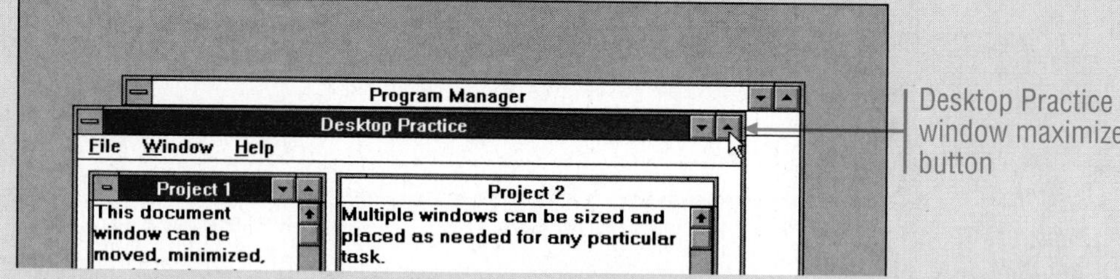

Figure 1-12
Maximizing a window

2. Click the **maximize button** to expand the window to fill the screen. Notice that in place of the maximize button there is now a restore button that contains double triangles.
3. Click the **restore button**. The Desktop Practice window returns to its original size.
4. Next, click the **minimize button** (the one with the triangle pointing down) to shrink the window to an icon.
5. Locate the minimized Desktop Practice icon at the bottom of your screen. See Figure 1-13.

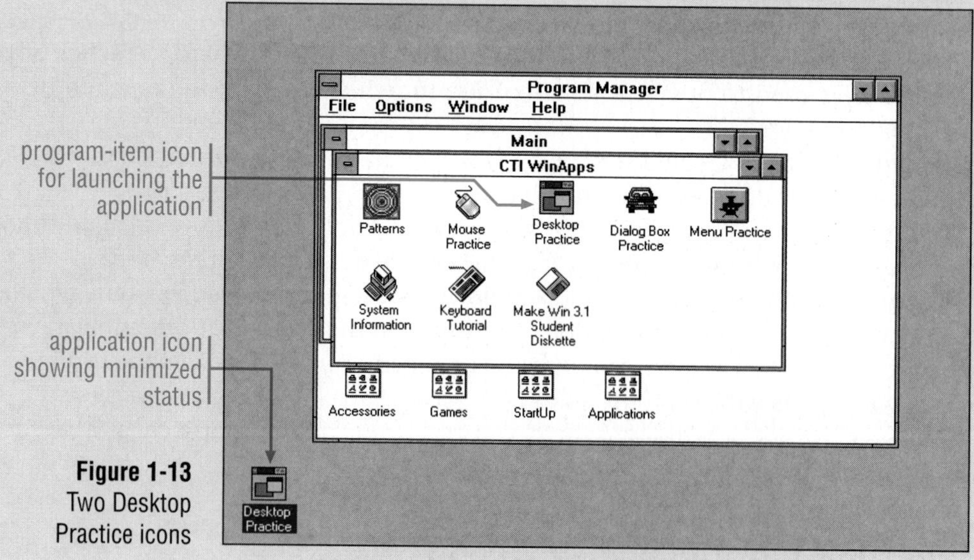

Figure 1-13
Two Desktop Practice icons

TROUBLE? If you cannot locate the Desktop Practice icon at the bottom of your screen, the Program Manager is probably maximized. To remedy this situtation, click the restore button on the Program Manager Window.

When you *close* an application window, you exit the application and it stops running. But when you *minimize* an application, it is still running even though it has been shrunk to an icon. It is important to remember that minimizing a window is not the same as closing it.

The icon for a minimized application is called an **application icon**. As Figure 1-13 illustrates, your screen shows two icons for the Desktop Practice application. The icon at the bottom of your screen is the application icon and represents a program that is currently running even though it is minimized. The other Desktop Practice icon is inside the CTI WinApps window. If you were to double-click this icon, you would launch a second version of the Desktop Practice application. *Don't launch two versions of the same application.* You should restore the Desktop Practice window by double-clicking the minimized icon at the bottom of your screen. Let's do that now.

To restore the Desktop Practice window:

1. Double-click the minimized **Desktop Practice icon** at the bottom of your screen. The Desktop Practice window opens.

Changing the Dimensions of a Window

Changing the dimensions of a window is useful when you want to arrange more than one project on your desktop. Suppose you want to work with the Desktop Practice application and at the same time view the contents of the Program Manager window. To do this, you will need to change the dimensions of both windows so they don't overlap each other.

To change the dimensions of the Desktop Practice window:

1. Move the pointer slowly over the top border of the Desktop Practice window until the pointer changes shape to a double-ended arrow. See Figure 1-14.

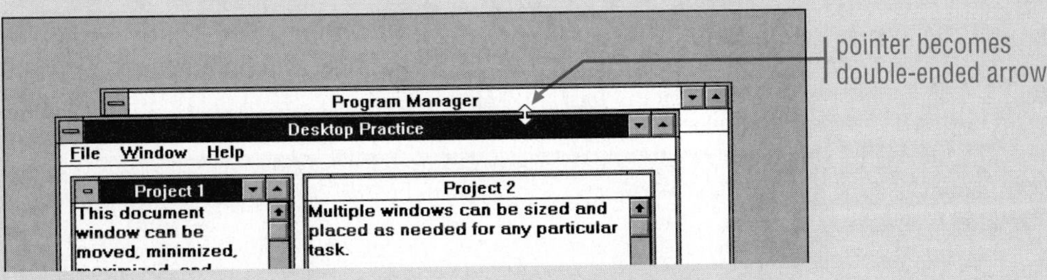

Figure 1-14 Preparing to change the window dimensions

2. Press the left mouse button and hold it down while you drag the border to the top of the screen. Notice how an outline of the border follows your mouse movement.
3. Release the mouse button. As a result the window adjusts to the new border.
4. Drag the left border of the Desktop Practice window to the left edge of the screen.
5. Move the pointer slowly over the lower-right corner of the Desktop Practice window until the pointer changes shape to a double-ended diagonal arrow. Figure 1-15 on the following page shows you how to do this step and the next one.

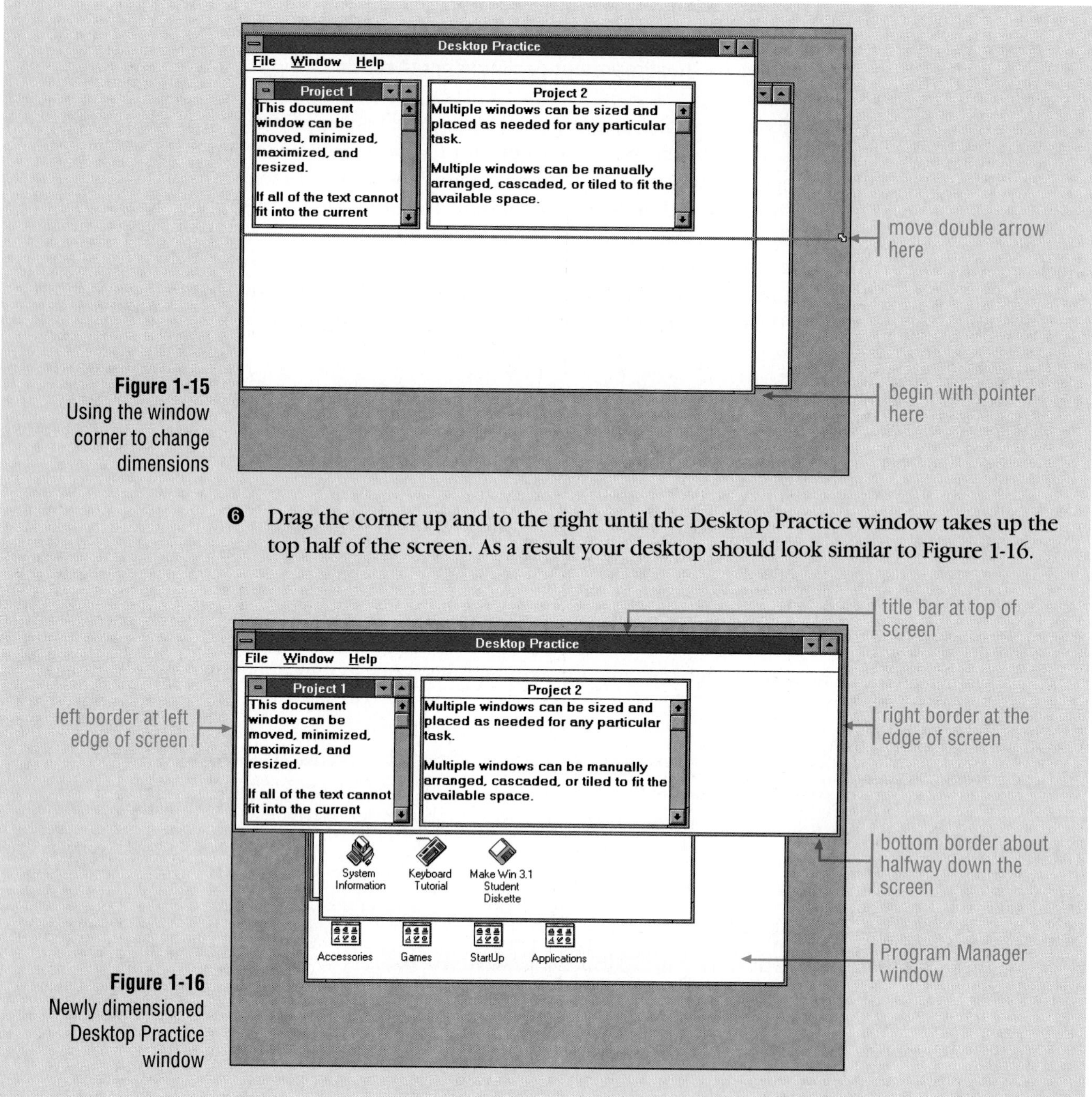

Figure 1-15 Using the window corner to change dimensions

❻ Drag the corner up and to the right until the Desktop Practice window takes up the top half of the screen. As a result your desktop should look similar to Figure 1-16.

Figure 1-16 Newly dimensioned Desktop Practice window

Switching Applications

In the preceding steps you arranged the application windows so they were both visible at the same time. A different approach to organizing windows is to maximize the windows and then switch between them using the **Task List**, which contains a list of all open applications.

Let's maximize the Desktop Practice window. Then, using the Task List, let's switch to the Program Manager window, which will be hidden behind it.

To maximize the Desktop Practice window and then switch to the Program Manager:

1. Click the **maximize button** on the Desktop Practice title bar. As a result the maximized Desktop Practice window hides the Program Manager window.
2. Click the **Control-menu box** on the left side of the Desktop Practice title bar. Figure 1-17 shows you the location of the Control-menu box and also the Control menu, which appears after you click.

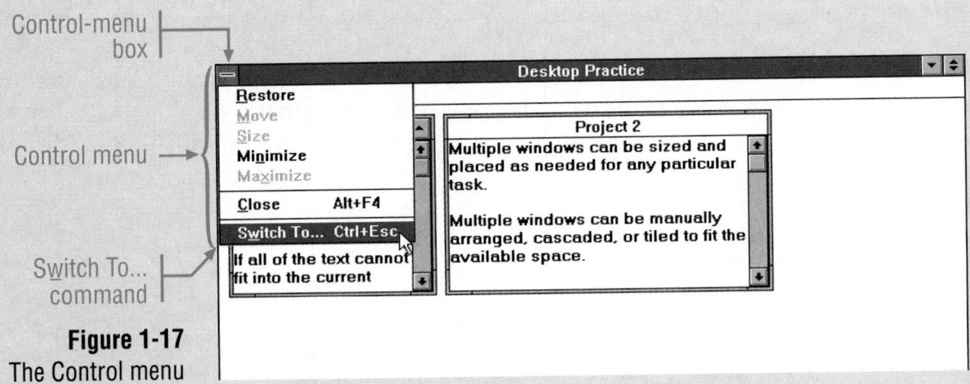

Figure 1-17 The Control menu

3. Click **Switch To...** The Task List box appears, as shown in Figure 1-18.

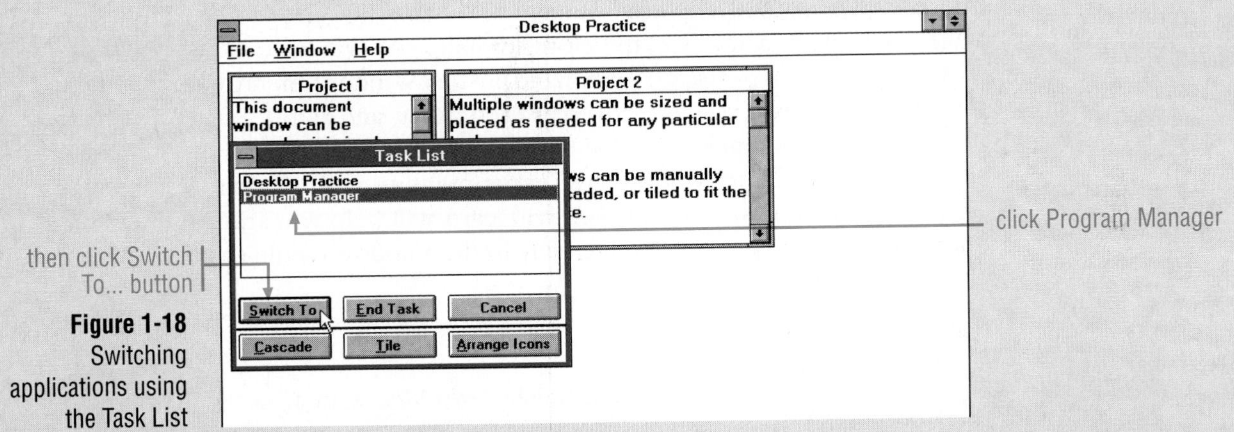

Figure 1-18 Switching applications using the Task List

4. Click the **Program Manager option** from the list, then click the **Switch To button** to select the Program Manager. As a result the Program Manager reappears on the bottom half of your screen.
5. If it is not already maximized, click the **maximize button** on the Program Manager window so both applications (Program Manager and Desktop Practice) are maximized.

The Program Manager window is active and "on top" of the Desktop Practice window. To view the Desktop Practice window, you will need to switch application windows again. You could switch tasks using the mouse, as we did in the last set of steps, or you can use the keyboard to quickly cycle through the tasks and activate the one you want. Let's use the keyboard method for switching windows this time, instead of using the Task List.

To switch to the Desktop Practice window using the keyboard:

1. Hold down **[Alt]** and continue holding it down while you press **[Tab]**. Don't release the Alt key yet! On the screen you should see a small rectangle that says "Desktop Practice."

   TROUBLE? Don't worry if you accidentally let go of the Alt key too soon. Try again. Press [Alt][Tab] until the "Desktop Practice" rectangle reappears.

2. Release the Alt key. Now the maximized Desktop Practice window is open.

When a window is maximized, it is easy to forget what's behind it. If you forget what's on the desktop, call up the Task List using the Control menu or use [Alt][Tab] to cycle through the tasks.

Organizing Document Windows

Think of document windows as subwindows within an application window. Because document windows do not have menu bars, the commands relating to these windows are selected from the menu bar of the application window. For example, you can use the Tile command in the Window menu to arrange windows so they are as large as possible without any overlap. The advantage of tiled windows is that one window won't cover up important information. The disadvantage of tiling is that the more windows you tile, the smaller each tile becomes and the more scrolling you will have to do.

You can use the Cascade command in the Window menu to arrange windows so they are all a standard size, they overlap each other, and all title bars are visible. Cascaded windows are often larger than tiled windows and at least one corner is always accessible so you can activate the window. Try experimenting with tiled and cascading windows. The desktop organizational skills you will learn will help you arrange the applications on your desktop so you can work effectively in the Windows multi-tasking environment.

Closing a Window

You close a window when you have finished working with a document or when you want to exit an application program. The steps you follow to close a document window are the same as those to close an application window. Let's close the Desktop Practice window.

To close the Desktop Practice application window:

1. Click the **Control-menu box** on the Desktop Practice window.
2. Click **Close** as shown in Figure 1-19 on the following page. The Desktop Practice window closes and you see the Program Manager window on the desktop.

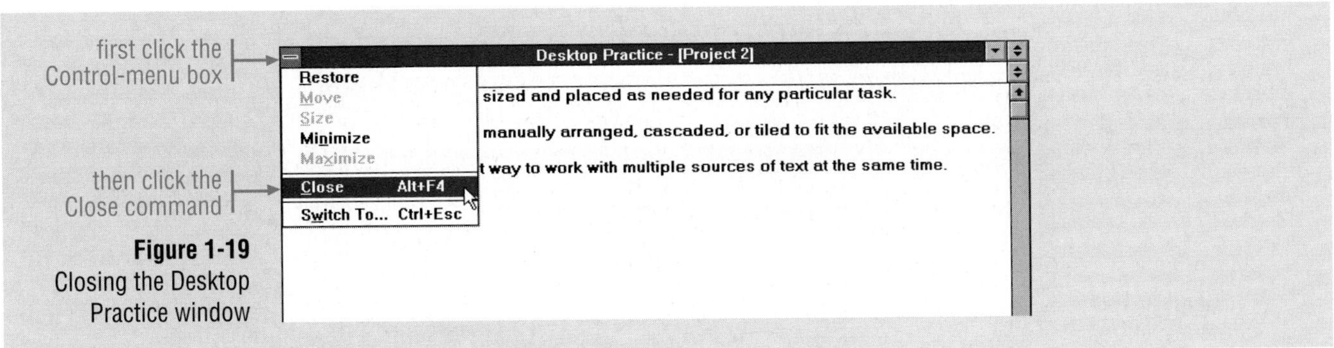

Figure 1-19
Closing the Desktop Practice window

Using Windows to Specify Tasks

In Windows, you issue instructions called **commands** to tell the computer what you want it to do. Windows applications provide you with lists of commands called **menus**. Many applications also have a ribbon of icons called a **toolbar**, which provides you with command shortcuts. Let's launch the Menu Practice application to find out how menus and toolbars work.

To launch the Menu Practice application:

❶ If the CTI WinApps window is not open, double-click its group icon at the bottom of the Program Manager window.

❷ Double-click the **Menu Practice** icon to open the Menu Practice window. See Figure 1-20.

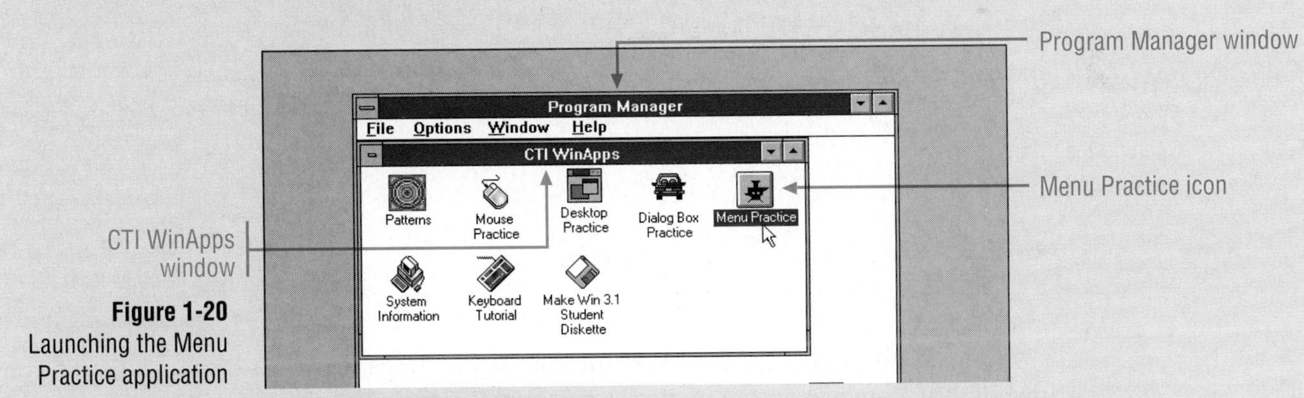

Figure 1-20
Launching the Menu Practice application

❸ Click the **maximize button** (the one with the triangle point up) for the Menu Practice window. The maximized Menu Practice window is shown in Figure 1-21 on the following page.

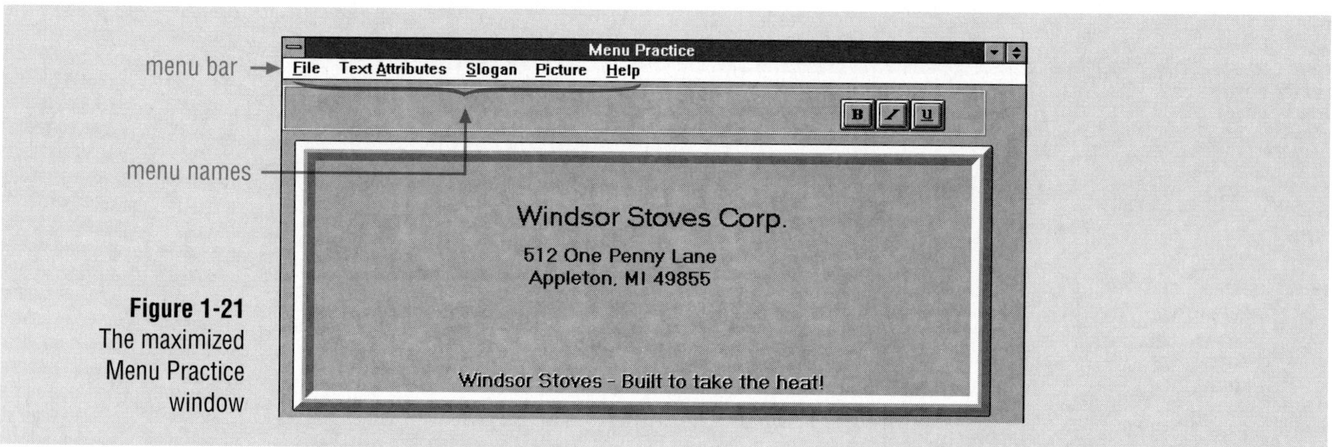

Figure 1-21 The maximized Menu Practice window

Opening and Closing Menus

Application windows, but not document windows, have menu bars such as the one shown in Figure 1-21. The menu bar contains menu names such as File, Text Attributes, Slogan, Picture, and Help. Let's practice opening and closing menus.

To open a menu:

❶ Click **File**. Figure 1-22 shows you where to click and the menu that appears.

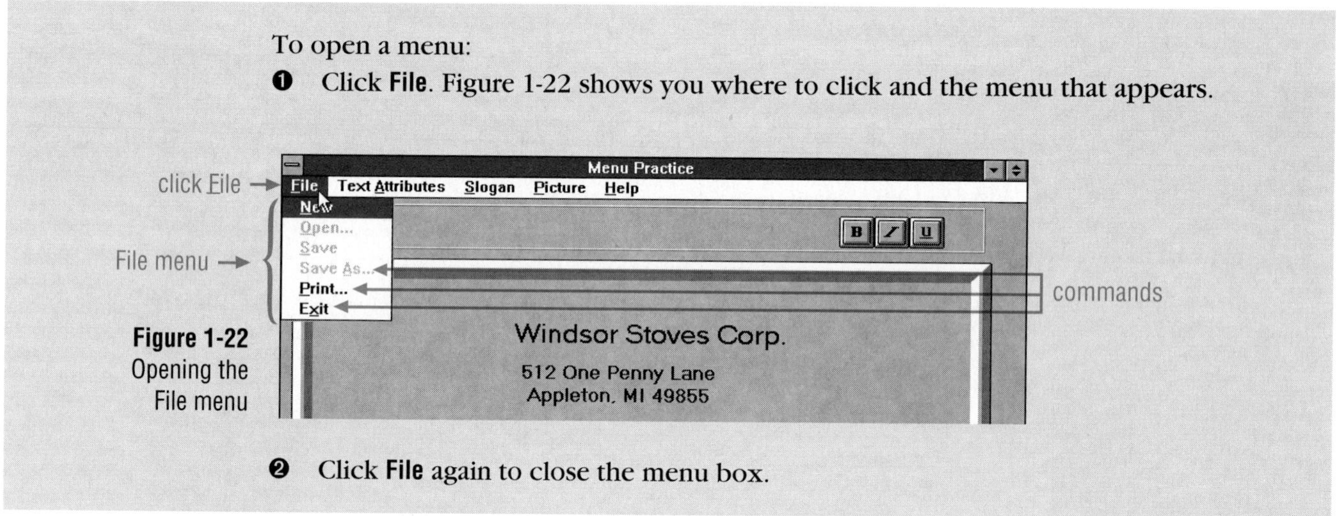

Figure 1-22 Opening the File menu

❷ Click **File** again to close the menu box.

When you click a menu name, the full menu drops down to display a list of commands. The commands on a menu are sometimes referred to as **menu items**.

Menu Conventions

The commands displayed on the Windows menus often include one or more **menu conventions**, such as check marks, ellipses, shortcut keys, and underlined letters. These menu conventions provide you with additional information about each menu command.

A check mark in front of a menu command indicates that the command is in effect. Clicking a checked command will remove the check mark and deactivate the command. For example, the Windsor Stoves logo currently has no graphic because the Show Picture command is not active. Let's add a picture to the logo by activating the Show Picture command.

To add or remove a check mark from the Show Picture command:

1. Click **Picture**. Notice that no check mark appears next to the Show Picture command.
2. Click **Show Picture**. The Picture menu closes, and a picture of a stove appears.
3. Click **Picture** to open the Picture menu again. Notice that a check mark appears next to the Show Picture command because you activated this command in Step 2.
4. Click **Show Picture**. This time clicking Show Picture removes the check mark and removes the picture.

Another menu convention is the use of gray, rather than black, type for commands. Commands displayed in gray type are sometimes referred to as **grayed-out commands**. Gray type indicates that a command is not currently available. The command might become available later, when it can be applied to the task. For example, a command that positions a picture on the right or left side of the logo would not apply to a logo without a picture. Therefore, the command for positioning the picture would be grayed out until a picture was included with the logo. Let's explore how this works.

To explore grayed-out commands:

1. Click **Picture**. Figure 1-23 shows the Picture menu with two grayed-out choices.

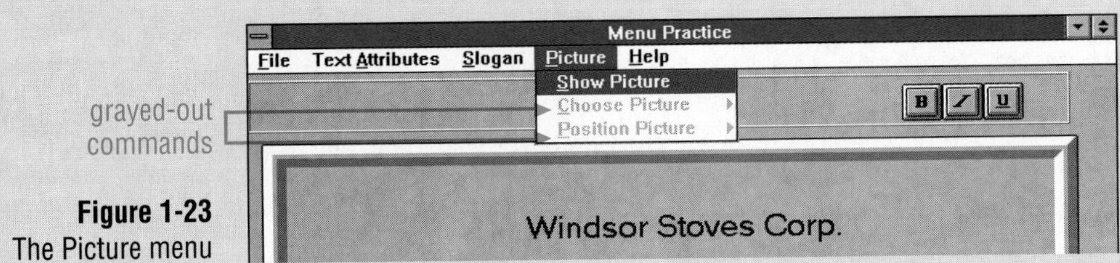

Figure 1-23
The Picture menu

2. Click the grayed-out command **Position Picture**. Although the highlight moves to this command, nothing else happens because the command is not currently available. You cannot position the picture until a picture is displayed.
3. Now click **Show Picture**. The Picture menu closes, and a picture is added to the logo.
4. Click **Picture**. Now that you have opened the Picture menu again, notice that the Choose Picture and Position Picture commands are no longer grayed out.

A **submenu** provides an additional set of command choices. On your screen the Choose Picture and Position Picture commands each have triangles next to them. A triangle is a menu convention that indicates a menu has a submenu. Let's use the submenu of the Position Picture command to move the stove picture to the right of the company name.

To use the position Picture submenu:

1. Click **Position Picture**. A submenu appears with options for left or right. In Figure 1-24 on the following page, the picture is to the left of the company name.

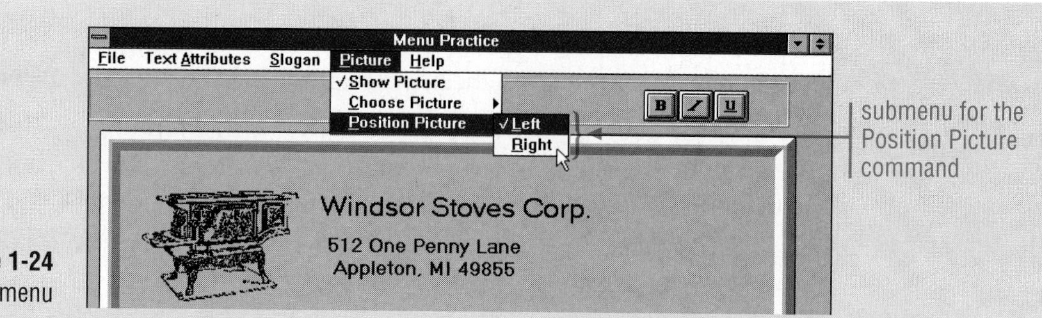

Figure 1-24
Viewing a submenu

2. Click **Right**. Selecting this submenu command moves the picture to the right of the company name.

Some menu conventions allow you to use the menus without a mouse. It is useful to know how to use these conventions because, even if you have a mouse, in some situations it might be faster to use the keyboard.

One keyboard-related menu convention is the underlined letter in each menu name. If you wanted to open a menu using the keyboard, you would hold down the Alt key and then press the underlined letter. Let's open the Text Attributes menu using the keyboard.

To open the Text Attributes menu this way:

1. Look at the menu name for the Text Attributes menu. Notice that the A is underlined.
2. Press **[Alt][A]**. The Text Attributes menu opens.

   TROUBLE? Remember from the Keyboard Tutorial that the [Alt][A] notation means to hold down the Alt key and press A. Don't type the brackets and don't use the Shift key to capitalize the A.

You can also use the keyboard to highlight and activate commands. On your screen the Bold command is highlighted. You use the arrow keys on the keyboard to move the highlight. You activate highlighted commands by pressing [Enter]. Let's use the keyboard to activate the Underline command.

To choose the Underline command using the keyboard:

1. Press [↓] two times to highlight the Underline command.
2. Press **[Enter]** to activate the highlighted command and underline the company name. Now look at the B, I, and U buttons near the upper-right corner of the screen. The U button has been "pressed" or activated. This button is another control for underlining. You'll find out how to use these buttons later.

Previously you used the Alt key in combination with the underlined letter in the menu title to open a menu. You might have noticed that each menu command also has an underlined letter. Once a menu is open, you can activate a command by pressing the underlined letter—there is no need to press the Alt key.

To activate the Italic command using the underlined letter:

1. Press **[Alt][A]**. This key combination opens the Text Attributes menu. Next, notice which letter is underlined in the Italic command.
2. Press **[I]** to activate the Italic command. Now the company name is italicized as well as underlined.

Look at the menu in Figure 1-25. Notice the Ctrl+B to the right of the Bold command. This is the key combination, often called a **shortcut key**, that can be used to activate the Bold command even if the menu is not open. The Windows Ctrl+B notation means the same thing as [Ctrl][B] in these tutorials: hold down the Control key and, while holding it down, press the letter B. When you use shortcut keys, don't type the + sign and don't use the Shift key to capitalize. Let's use a shortcut key to boldface the company name.

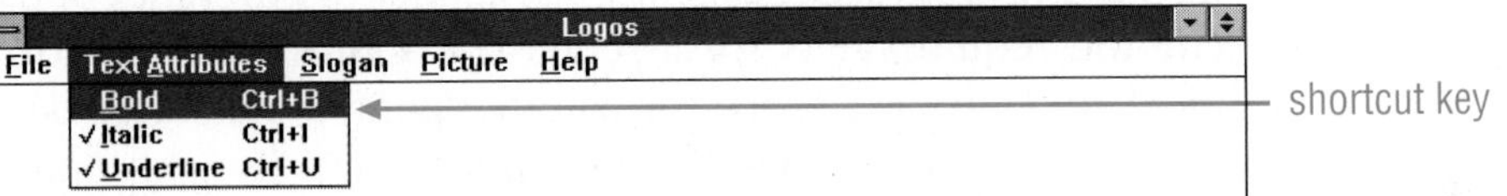

Figure 1-25
The Text Attributes menu

To Boldface the company name using a shortcut key:

1. Press **[Ctrl][B]** and watch the company name appear in boldface type.

The **ellipsis (...)** menu convention means that when you select a command with three dots next to it, a dialog box will appear. A **dialog box** requests additional details about how you want the command carried out. We'll use the dialog box for the Choose Slogan command to change the company slogan.

To use the Choose Slogan dialog box:

1. Click **Slogan**. Notice that the Choose Slogan command is followed by an ellipsis.
2. Click **Choose Slogan...** and study the dialog box that appears. See Figure 1-26. Notice that this dialog box contains four sets of controls: the "Use Slogan" text box, the "Slogan in Bold Letters" check box, the "Slogan 3-D Effects" control buttons, and the OK and Cancel buttons. The "Use Slogan" text box displays the current slogan.

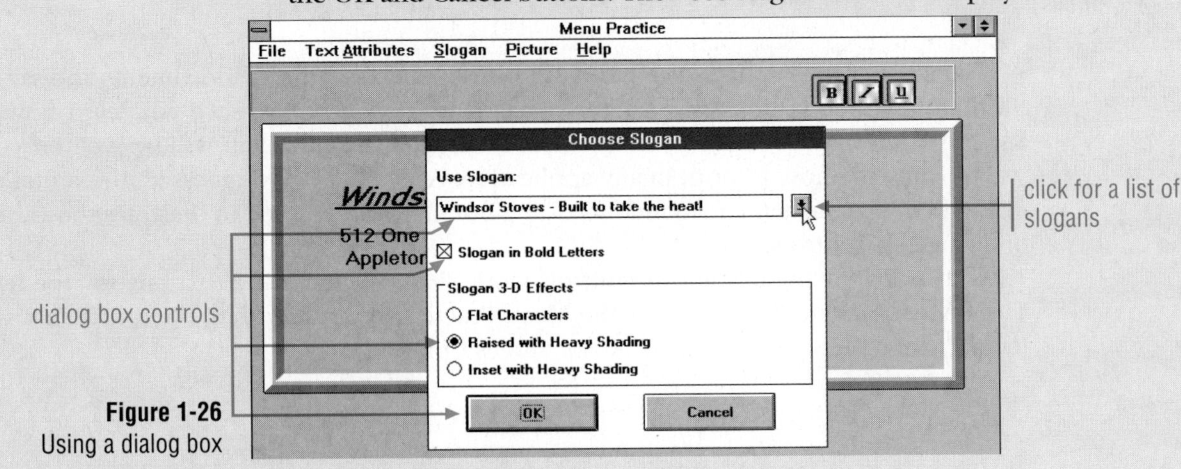

Figure 1-26
Using a dialog box

3. Click the **down arrow button** on the right of the slogan box to display a list of alternative slogans.
4. Click the slogan **Windsor Stoves - Built to last for generations!**
5. Click the **OK button** and watch the new slogan replace the old.

You have used the Menu Practice application to learn how to use Windows menus, and you have learned the meaning of the Windows menu conventions. Next we'll look at dialog box controls.

Dialog Box Controls

Figure 1-27 shows a dialog box with a number of different controls that could be used to specify the requirements for a rental car. **Command buttons** initiate an immediate action. A **text box** is a space for you to type in a command detail. A **list box** displays a list of choices. A drop-down list box appears initially with only one choice; clicking the list box arrow displays additional choices. **Option buttons**, sometimes called radio buttons, allow you to select one option. **Check boxes** allow you to select one or more options. A **spin bar** changes a numeric setting.

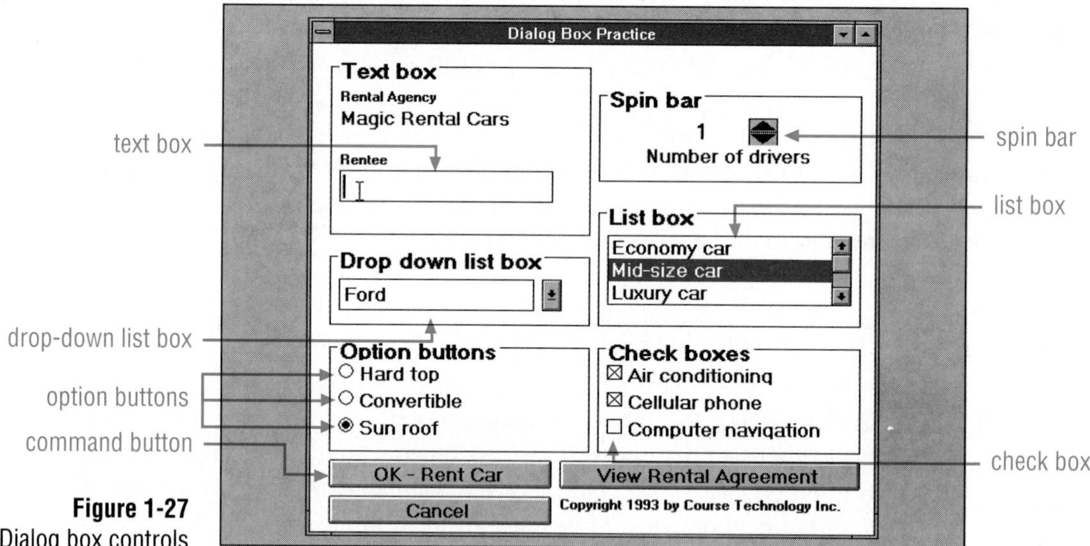

Figure 1-27
Dialog box controls

Windows uses standard dialog boxes for tasks such as printing documents and saving files. Most Windows applications use the standard dialog boxes, so if you learn how to use the Print dialog box for your word processing application, you will be well on your way to knowing how to print in any application. As you may have guessed, the rental car dialog box is not a standard Windows dialog box. It was designed to illustrate the variety of dialog box controls.

Let's see how the dialog box controls work. First, we will use a text box to type text. The Choose Slogan dialog box for the Menu Practice application has a text box that will let us change the slogan on the Windsor Stoves Corp. logo.

To activate the Use Slogan text box:

1. Click **Slogan** to open the Slogan menu.
2. Click **Choose Slogan...** and the Choose Slogan dialog box appears.
3. Move the pointer to the text box and notice that it changes to an **I-bar** shape for text entry. See Figure 1-28.

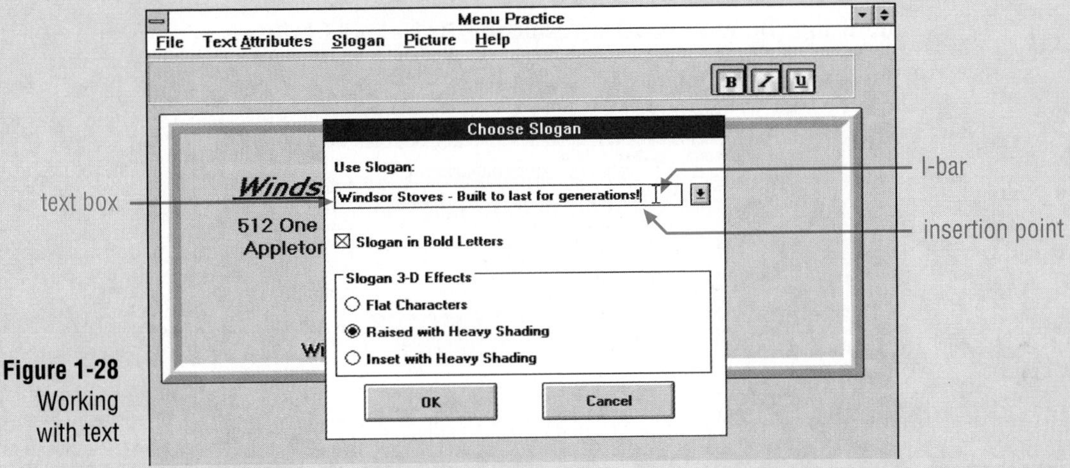

Figure 1-28 Working with text

4. Click the **left mouse button** to activate the text box. A blinking bar called an **Insertion point** indicates that you can type text into the box. Also notice that all the text is highlighted.
5. Press **[Del]** to erase the highlighted text of the old slogan.

When you work with a dialog box, be sure to set all the components the way you want them *before* you press the Enter key or click the OK button. Why? Because the Enter key, like the OK button, tells Windows that you are finished with the entire dialog box. Now let's type a new slogan in the text box and change the slogan 3-D effect.

To type a new slogan in a text box:

1. Type **Quality is our Trademark!** but don't press [Enter], because while this dialog box is open, you are also going to change the slogan 3-D effect.

   TROUBLE? If you make a typing mistake, press [Backspace] to delete the error, then type the correction.

2. Look at the Slogan 3-D Effects list. Notice that the current selection is Raised with Heavy Shading.
3. Click **Inset with Heavy Shading**.
4. Click the **OK button** and then verify that the slogan and the 3-D effect have changed.

   TROUBLE? If you are working on a monochrome system without the ability to display shade of gray, you may not be able to see the 3-D effect.

Using the Toolbar

A **toolbar** is a collection of icons that provides command shortcuts for mouse users. The icons on the toolbar are sometimes referred to as buttons. Generally the options on the toolbar duplicate menu options, but they are more convenient because they can be activated by a single mouse click. The toolbar for the Menu Practice application shown in Figure 1-29 has three buttons that are shortcuts for the Bold, Italic, and Underline commands. In a previous exercise you underlined, boldfaced, and italicized the company name using the menus. As a result the B, U, and I buttons are activated. Let's see what they look like when we deactivate them.

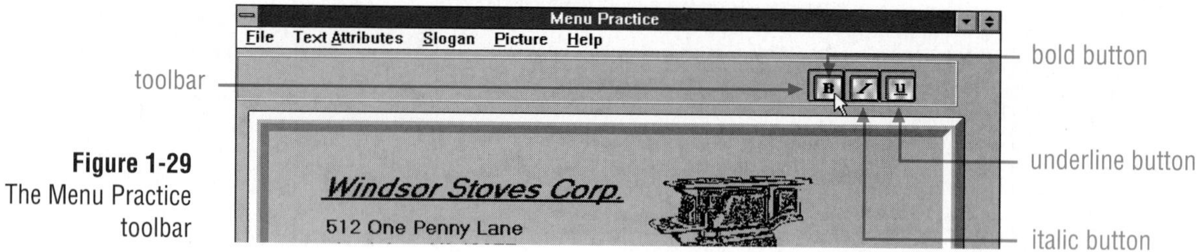

Figure 1-29
The Menu Practice toolbar

To change the type style using the toolbar:

❶ Click B to remove the boldface.

❷ Click I to turn off italics.

❸ Click U to turn off underlining.

❹ Click B to turn on boldface again.

You might want to spend a few minutes experimenting with the Menu Practice program to find the best logo design for Windsor Stoves Corp. When you are finished, close the Menu Practice window.

To close the Menu Practice window:

❶ Click the **Control-menu box**.

❷ Click **Close**. The Menu Practice program closes and returns you to Windows Program Manager.

You have now learned about Windows menus, dialog boxes and toolbars. In the next section, you will survey the Paintbrush application, experiment with tools, and access on-line help.

Using Paintbrush to Develop Your Windows Technique

After you have learned the basic Windows controls, you will find that most Windows *applications* contain similar controls. Let's launch the Paintbrush application and discover how to use it.

To launch the Paintbrush application:

1. Be sure the Program Manager window is open. If it is not open, use the skills you have learned to open it.
2. You should have an Accessories icon or an Accessories window on the desktop. If you have an Accessories group icon on the desktop, double-click it to open the Accessories group window.

   TROUBLE? If you don't see the Accessories icon or window, click the Window menu on the Program Manager menu bar. Look for Accessories in the list. If you find Accessories in this list, click it. If you do not find Accessories, ask your technical support person for help.
3. Double-click the **Paintbrush icon** to launch the Paintbrush application. Your screen will look similar to the one in Figure 1-30.

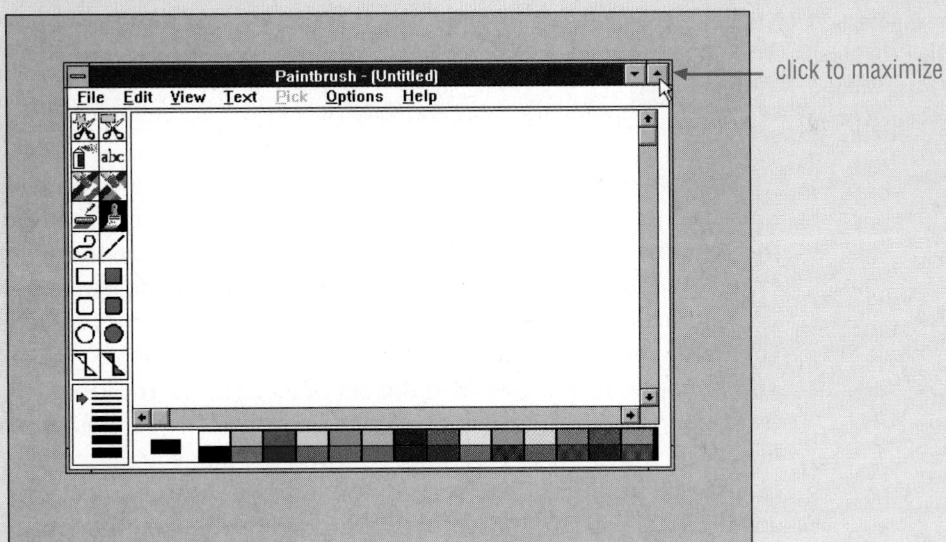

Figure 1-30
The Paintbrush window

4. Click the Paintbrush window **maximize button** so you will have a large drawing area.

Surveying the Paintbrush Application Window

Whether you are using a reference manual or experimenting on your own, your first step in learning a new application is to survey the window and familiarize yourself with its components.

Look at the Paintbrush window on your screen and make a list of the components you can identify. If you have not encountered a particular component before, try to guess what it might be.

Now refer to Figure 1-31 on the following page, which labels the Paintbrush window components.

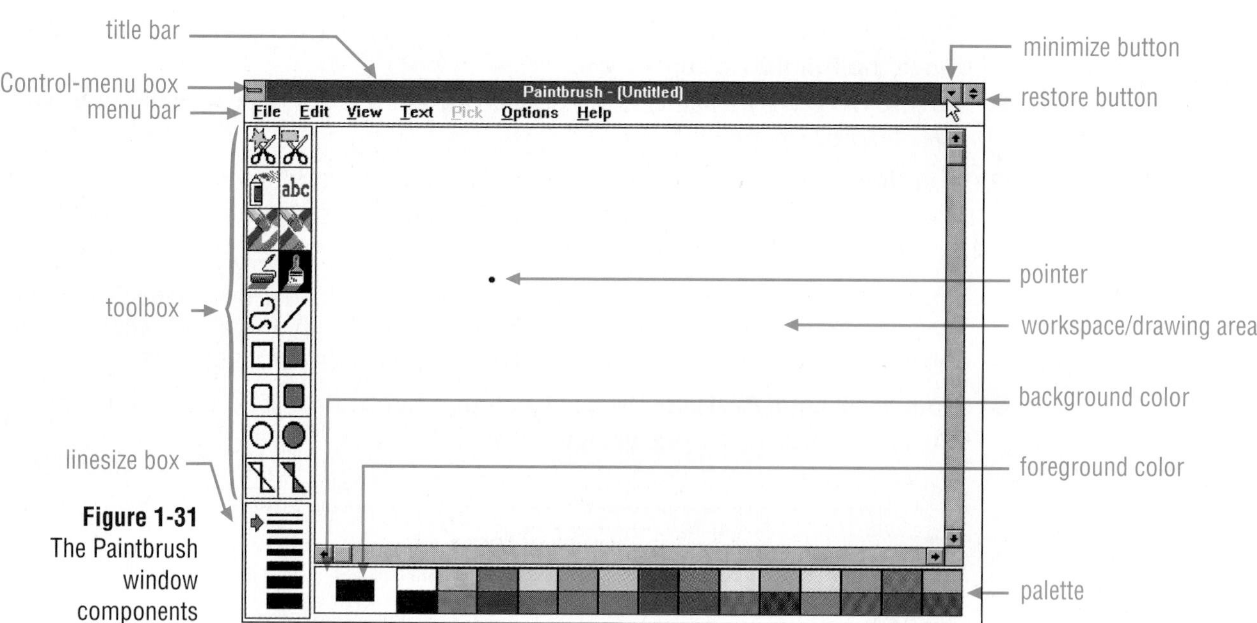

Figure 1-31 The Paintbrush window components

The darkened title bar shows that the Paintbrush window is activated. The resizing buttons are in the upper-right corner, as usual. Because there is a restore button and because the window takes up the entire screen, you know that the window is maximized. The Control-menu box is in the upper-left corner, and a menu bar lists seven menus.

On the left side of the window are a variety of icons. This looks similar to the toolbar you used when you created the logo, only it has more icons, which are arranged vertically. The Windows manual refers to this set of icons as the **toolbox**.

Under the toolbox is a box containing lines of various widths. This is the **linesize box**, which you use to select the width of the line you draw.

At the bottom of the screen is a color **palette**, which you use to select the foreground and background colors. The currently selected colors for the foreground and background are indicated in the box to the left of the palette.

The rectangular space in the middle of the window is the drawing area. When the pointer is in the drawing area, it will assume a variety of shapes, depending on the tool you are using.

Experimenting with Tools

The icons on toolbars might be some of the easiest Windows controls, but many people are a little mystified by the symbols used for some of the tools. Look at the icons in the Paintbrush toolbox and try to guess their use.

You can often make good guesses, when you know what the application does. For example, you probably guessed that the brush tool shown in Figure 1-32 is used for drawing a picture. However, you might not be able to guess how the brush and the roller tools differ.

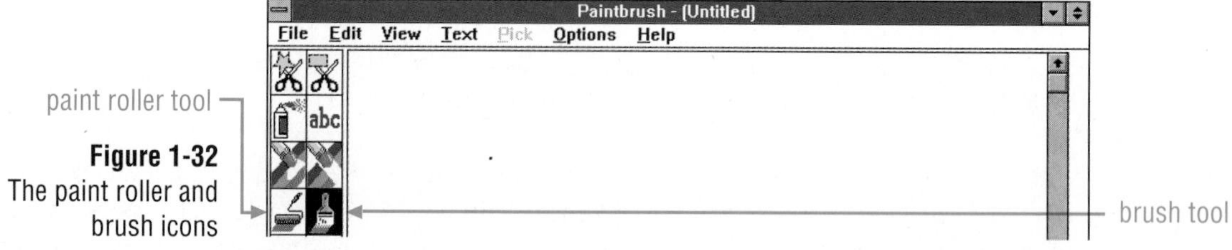

Figure 1-32 The paint roller and brush icons

If you can make some reasonable guess about how a tool works, it's not a bad idea to try it out. Can you write your name using the paintbrush tool? Let's try it.

To use the brush tool:

❶ Locate and click the **brush tool** in the toolbox. The brush tool becomes highlighted, indicating that it is now the selected tool.

❷ Move the pointer to the drawing area. Notice that it changes to a small dot.

❸ Move the pointer to the place where you want to begin writing your name.

When the left mouse button is down, the brush will paint. When you release the mouse button, you can move the pointer without painting.

❹ Use the mouse to control the brush as you write your name. Don't worry if it looks a little rough. Your "John Hancock" might look like the one in Figure 1-33.

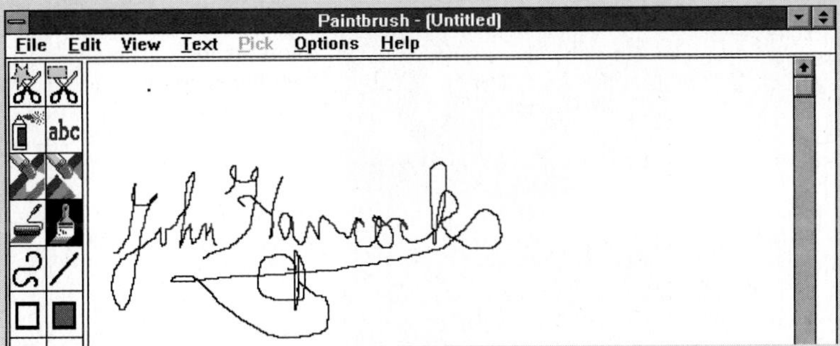

Figure 1-33
Your "John Hancock"

You will recall that we were curious about the difference between the brush and the paint roller. Let's experiment with the paint roller next.

To try the paint roller:

❶ Click the **paint roller** tool.

❷ Position the pointer in the upper-left corner of the drawing area and click. What happened?!

Did you get a strange result? Don't panic. This sort of thing happens when you experiment. Still, we probably should find out a little more about how to control the roller. To do this, we'll use the Paintbrush Help facility.

Using Help

Most Windows applications have an extensive on-line Help facility. A **Help facility** is an electronic reference manual that contains information about an application's menus, tools, and procedures. Some Help facilities also include **tutorials**, which you can use to learn the application.

There are a variety of ways to access Help, so people usually develop their own technique for finding information in it. We'll show you one way that seems to work for many Windows users. Later you can explore on your own and develop your own techniques.

When you use Help, a Help window opens. Usually the Help window overlays your application. If you want to view the problem spot and the Help information at the same time, it is a good idea to organize your desktop so the Help and application windows are side by side.

To access Help and organize the desktop:

❶ Click **Help**. A Help menu lists the Help commands.

❷ Click **Contents** to display a Paintbrush Help window similar to the one in Figure 1-34.

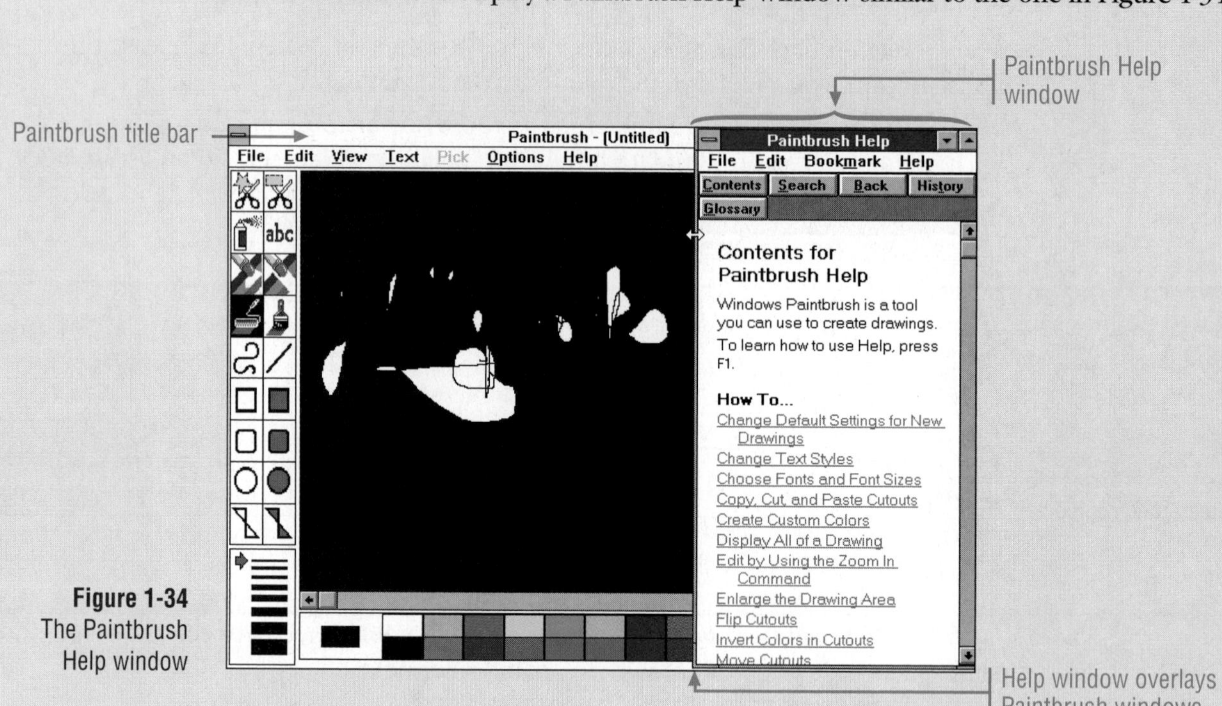

Figure 1-34
The Paintbrush Help window

❸ If the Paintbrush Help window is not the same size and shape as the one in Figure 1-34, drag the corners of the Help window until it looks like the one in the figure.

The Paintbrush application window is partially covered by the Help window. We need to fix that.

❹ Click the **Paintbrush title bar** to activate the Paintbrush window.

❺ Click the **restore button** to display the window borders and corners.

❻ Drag the corners of the Paintbrush application until your screen resembles the one in Figure 1-35 on the following page.

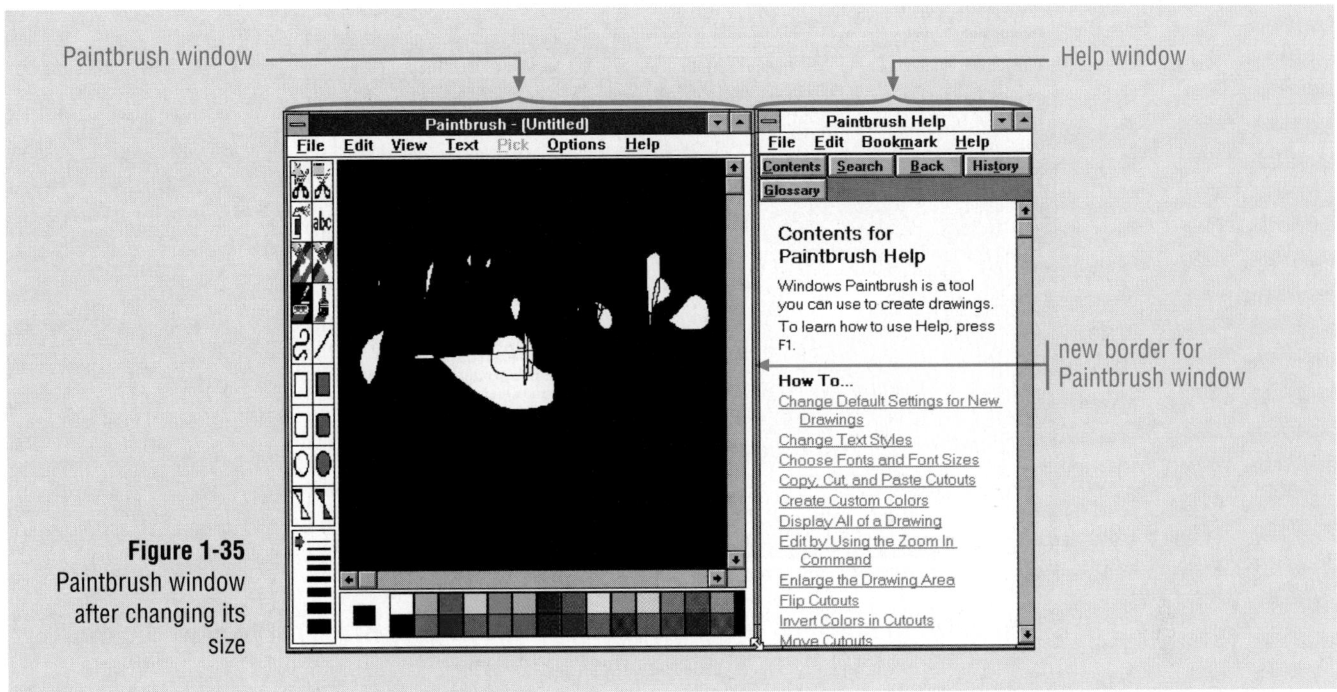

Figure 1-35
Paintbrush window after changing its size

Now that the windows are organized, let's find out about the roller tool. The Paintbrush Help window contains a Table of Contents, which is divided into three sections: How To, Tools, and Commands.

The **How To** section is a list of procedures that are explained in the Help facility. Use this section when you want to find out how to do something. The **Tools** section identifies the toolbar icons and explains how to use them. The **Commands** section provides an explanation of the commands that can be accessed from the menu bar.

To find information about the paint roller tool on the Help facility:

❶ Use the scroll box to scroll down the text in the Help window until you see the Tools section heading.

❷ Continue scrolling until the Paint Roller option comes into view.

❸ Position the pointer on the Paint Roller Option. Notice that the pointer changes to a pointing hand, indicating that Paint Roller is a clickable option.

❹ Click the **left mouse button**. The Help window now contains information about the paint roller, as shown in Figure 1-36 on the following page.

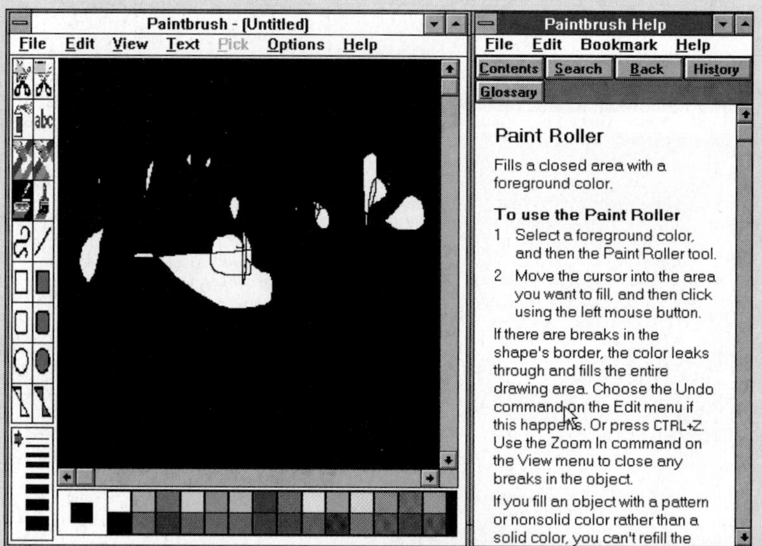

Figure 1-36
Paint Roller Help

❺ Read the information about the Paint Roller, using the scroll bar to view the entire text.

What did you learn about the paint roller? The first item you likely discovered is that the paint roller is used to fill an area. Well, it certainly did that in our experiment. It filled the entire drawing area with the foreground color, black. Next you might have noted that the first step in the procedure for using the paint roller is to select a foreground color. In our experiment, it would have been better if we selected some color other than black for the fill. Let's erase our old experiment so we can try again.

To start a new painting:

❶ Click **File** on the Paintbrush menu bar (not on the Help menu bar) to open the File menu.

❷ Click **New**, because you want to start a new drawing. A dialog box asks, "Do you want to save current changes?"

❸ Click the **No button** to clear the drawing area, because you don't want to save your first experiment.

Now you can paint your name and then use the roller to artistically fill areas. When you have finished experimenting, exit the Paintbrush application.

To exit Paintbrush:

❶ Click the **Control-menu box** and then click **Close**.

❷ In response to the prompt "Do you want to save current changes?" click the **No button**. The Paintbrush window closes, which also automatically closes the Help window.

You've covered a lot of ground. Next, it's time to learn how to exit Windows.

Exiting Windows

You might want to continue directly to the Questions and Tutorial Assignments. If so, stay in Windows until you have completed your work, then follow these instructions for exiting Windows.

To exit Windows:

1. Click the **Control-menu box** in the upper-left of the Program Manager window.
2. Click **Close**.
3. When you see the message "This will end your Windows session," click the **OK button**.

■ ■ ■

Steve congratulates you on your Windows progress. You have learned the terminology associated with the desktop environment and the names of the controls and how to use them. You have developed an understanding about desktop organization and how to arrange the application and document windows so you will use them most effectively. You have also learned to use menus, dialog boxes, toolbars and Help.

Questions

1. GUI is an acronym for __________________.
2. A group window contains which of the following?
   a. application icons
   b. document icons
   c. program-item icons
   d. group icons
3. What is one of the main purposes of the Program Manager?
   a. to organize your diskette
   b. to launch applications
   c. to create documents
   d. to provide the Help facility for applications
4. Which mouse function is used as a shortcut for more lengthy mouse or keyboard procedures?
   a. pointing
   b. clicking
   c. dragging
   d. double-clicking
5. To change the focus to an icon, you ________________ it.
   a. close
   b. select
   c. drag
   d. launch

6. What is another name for document windows?
   a. child windows
   b. parent windows
   c. application windows
   d. group windows
7. In Figure 1-37 each window component is numbered. Write the name of the component that corresponds to the number.

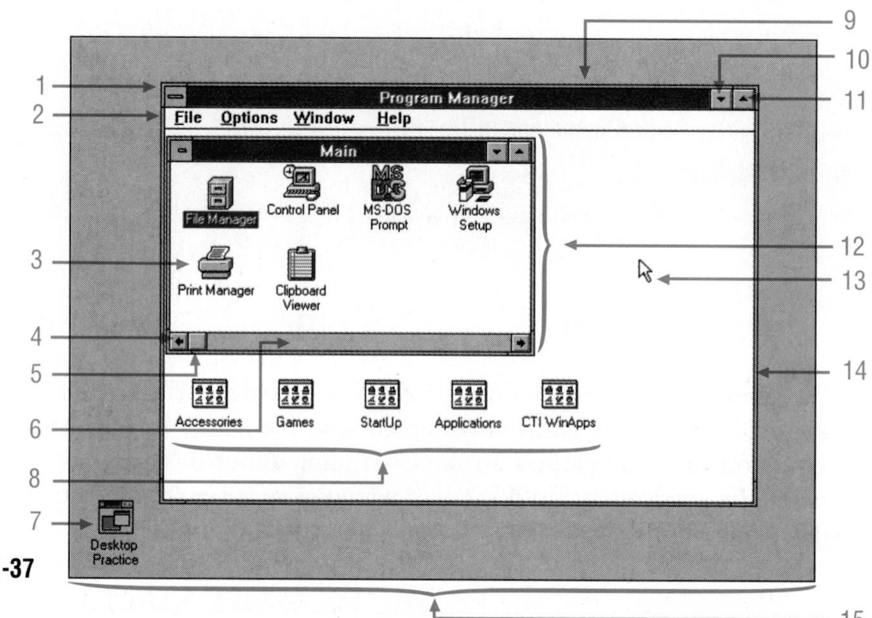

Figure 1-37

8. In Windows terminology you ______________ a window when you want to get it out of the way temporarily but leave the application running.
9. You ______________ a window when you no longer need to have the application running.
10. The ________________ provides you with a way to switch between application windows.
    a. Task List
    b. program-item icon
    c. Window menu
    d. maximize button
11. How would you find out if you had more than one application running on your desktop?
12. ________________ refers to the capability of a computer to run more than one application at the same time.
13. Which menu provides the means to switch from one document to another?
    a. the File menu
    b. the Help menu
    c. the Window menu
    d. the Control menu
14. Describe three menu conventions used in Windows menus.

E 15. The flashing vertical bar that marks the place your typing will appear is ________________.

E 16. If you have access to a Windows reference manual such as the *Microsoft Windows User's Guide*, look for an explanation of the difference between group icons, program-item icons, and application icons. For your instructor's information, write down the name of the reference, the publisher, and the page(s) on which you found this information. If you were writing a textbook for first-time Windows users, how would you describe the difference between these icons?

17. Copy the definition of "metaphor" from any standard dictionary. For your instructor's information, write down the dictionary name, the edition, and the page number. After considering the definition, explain why Windows is said to be a "desktop metaphor."

Tutorial Assignments

If you exited Windows at the end of the tutorial, launch Windows and do Assignments 1 through 15. Write your answers to the questions in Assignments 1, 2, 3, 4, 5, 9, 10, 11, 12, 13, and 15. Also fill out the table in Assignment 7.

1. Close all applications except the Program Manager and shrink all the group windows to icons. What are the names of the group icons on the desktop?
2. Open the Main window. How many program-item icons are in this window?
3. Open the Accessories window. How many program-item icons are in this window?
4. Open, close, and change the dimensions of the windows so your screen looks like Figure 1-38.
   a. How many applications are now on the desktop?
   b. How did you find out how many applications are on the desktop?

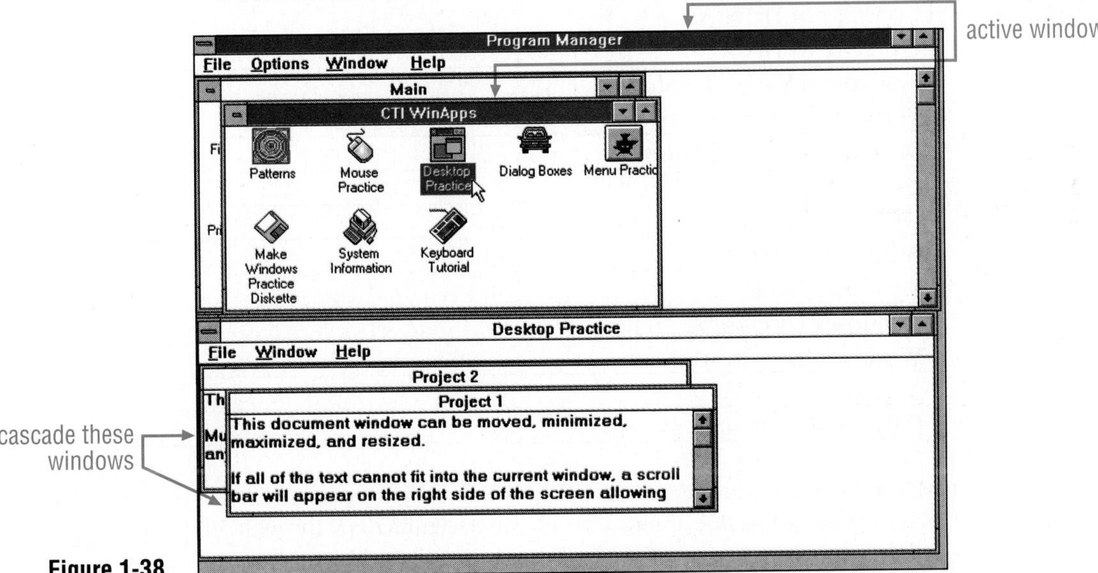

Figure 1-38

5. Open, close, and change the dimensions of the windows so your screen looks like Figure 1-39 on the following page. After you're done, close the Desktop Practice window using the fewest mouse clicks. How did you close the Desktop Practice window?

Open the CTI WinApps window and do Assignments 6 through 8.

Figure 1-39

6. Double-click the System Information icon.
7. Using the information displayed on your screen, fill out the following table:

CPU Type:	
Available Memory:	
Number of Diskette Drives:	
Capacity of Drive A:	
Capacity of Drive B:	
Horizontal Video Resolution:	
Vertical Video Resolution:	
Screen Colors or Shades:	
Network Type:	
DOS Version:	
Windows Version:	
Windows Mode:	
Windows Directory:	
Windows Free Resources:	
Available Drive Letters:	
Hard Drive Capacities:	

8. Click the Exit button to return to the Program Manager.

Launch the Mouse Practice application and do Assignments 9 through 14.

9. What happens when you drag the letter to the file cabinet?
10. What happens when you double-click the mouse icon located in the lower-left corner of the desktop?
11. What happens when you click an empty check box? What happens when you click a check box that contains an "X"?
12. Can you select both option buttons at the same time?
13. What happens when you click "Item Fourteen" from the list?
14. Exit the Mouse Practice.

Launch the Desktop Practice and do Assignments 15 through 17.

15. What is the last sentence of the document in the Project 2 window?
16. Close the Desktop Practice window.
17. Exit Windows.

TUTORIAL 2

Effective File Management

Using the File Manager

OBJECTIVES

In this tutorial you will:

- Open and close the File Manager
- Format and make your student disk containing practice files
- Change the current drive
- Identify the components of the File Manager window
- Create directories
- Change the current directory
- Move, rename, delete, and copy files
- Make a disk backup
- Learn how to protect your data from hardware failures

CASE

A Professional Approach to Computing at Narraganset Shipyard Ruth Sanchez works at the Narraganset Shipyard, a major government defense contractor. On a recent business trip to Washington, DC, Ruth read a magazine article that convinced her she should do a better job of organizing the files on her computer system. The article pointed out that a professional approach to computing includes a plan for maintaining an organized set of disk-based files that can be easily accessed, updated, and secured.

Ruth learns that the Windows File Manager can help to organize her files. Ruth has not used the File Manager very much, so before she begins to make organizational changes to the valuable files on her hard disk, she decides to practice with some sample files on a disk in drive A.

In this Tutorial, you will follow the progress of Ruth's File Manager practice and learn how to use Windows to manage effectively the data stored in your computer.

Files and the File Manager

A **file** is a named collection of data organized for a specific purpose and stored on a floppy disk or a hard disk. The typical computer user has hundreds of files.

The Windows File Manager provides some handy tools for organizing files. Ruth's first step is to launch the File Manager. Let's do the same.

To launch the File Manager:

❶ Launch Windows.

❷ Compare your screen to Figure 2-1. Use the skills you learned in Tutorial 1 to organize your desktop so only the Program Manager window and the Main window are open.

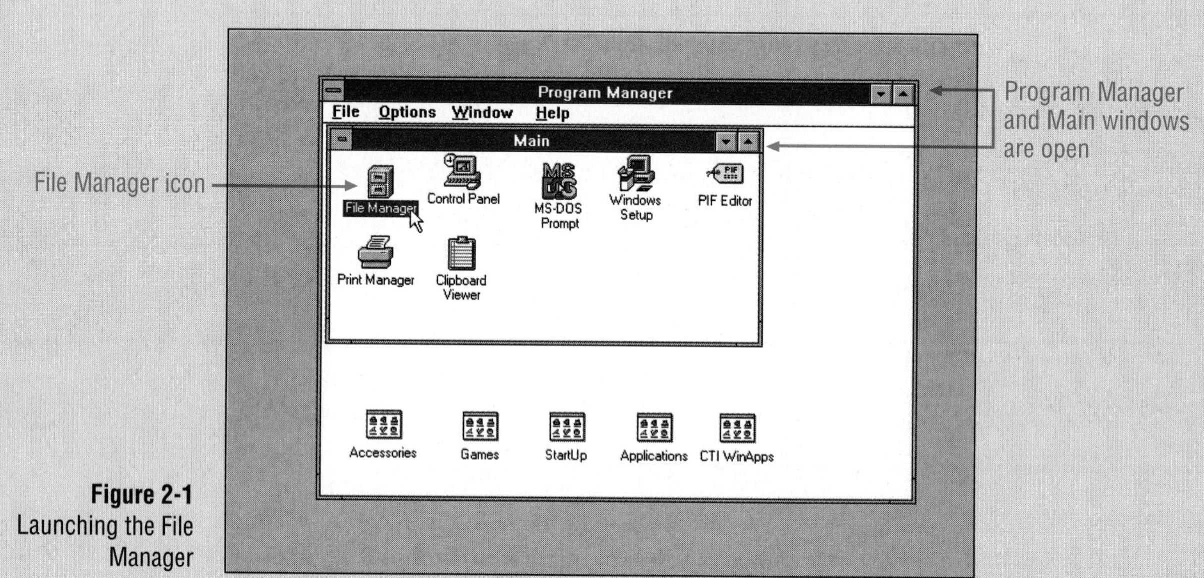

Figure 2-1
Launching the File Manager

❸ Double-click the **File Manager icon** to launch the File Manager program and open the File Manager window.

❹ If the File Manager window is not maximized, click the **maximize button**.

❺ Click **Window**, then click **Tile**. You should now have one child window on the desktop. See Figure 2-2a on the following page. Don't worry if the title of your child window is not the same as the one in the figure.

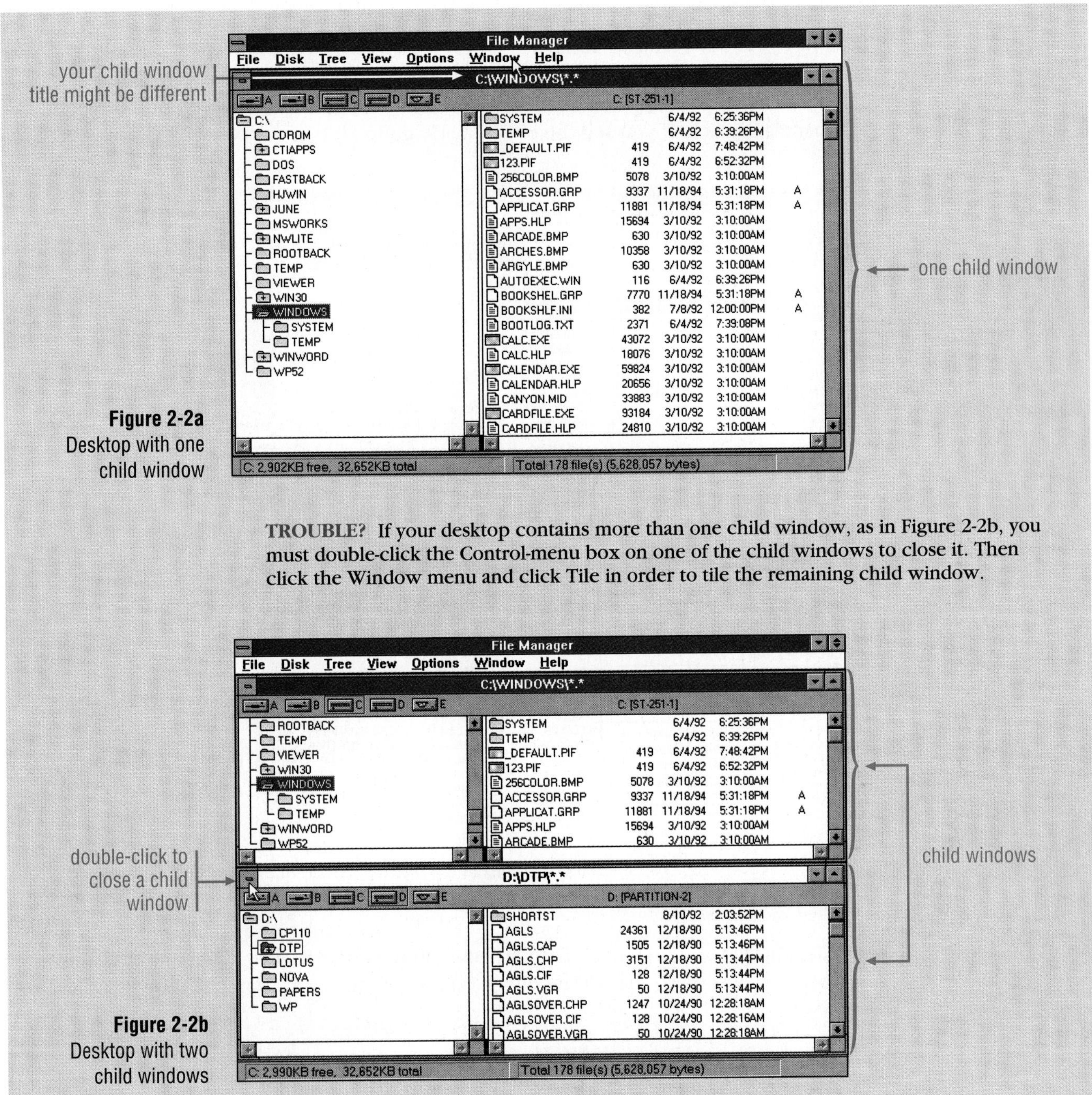

Figure 2-2a Desktop with one child window

TROUBLE? If your desktop contains more than one child window, as in Figure 2-2b, you must double-click the Control-menu box on one of the child windows to close it. Then click the Window menu and click Tile in order to tile the remaining child window.

Figure 2-2b Desktop with two child windows

Ruth decides to check her File Manager settings, which affect the way information is displayed. By adjusting your File Manager settings to match Ruth's, your computer will display screens and prompts similar to those in the Tutorial. *If you do not finish this tutorial in one session, remember to adjust the settings again when you begin your next session.*

To adjust your File Manager settings:

❶ Click **Tree**. Look at the command "Indicate Expandable Branches." See Figure 2-3. If no check mark appears next to this command, position the pointer on the command and click. If you see the check mark, go to Step 2.

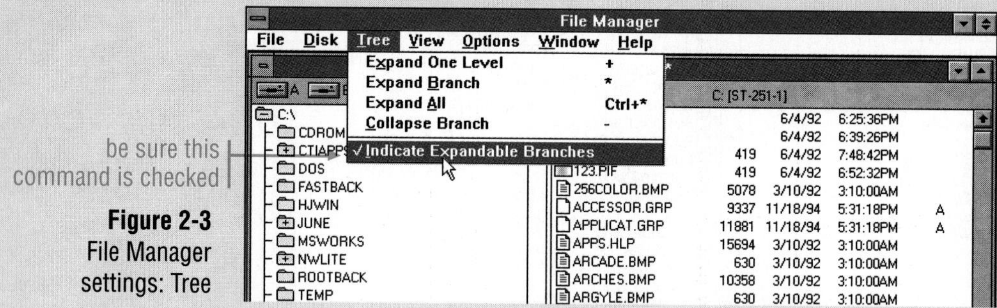

Figure 2-3 File Manager settings: Tree

❷ Click **View**. Make any adjustments necessary so that the settings are the same as those in Figure 2-4.

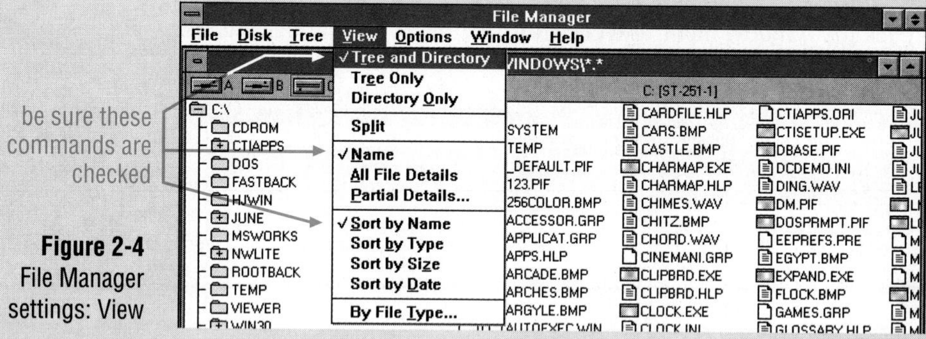

Figure 2-4 File Manager settings: View

TROUBLE? When you click a command to change the check mark, the menu closes. To change another command in the menu or to confirm your changes, you need to click the View menu again.

❸ Click **Options** and then click **Confirmation....** Referring to Figure 2-5, make any adjustments necessary so that all the check boxes contain an X, then click the **OK button**.

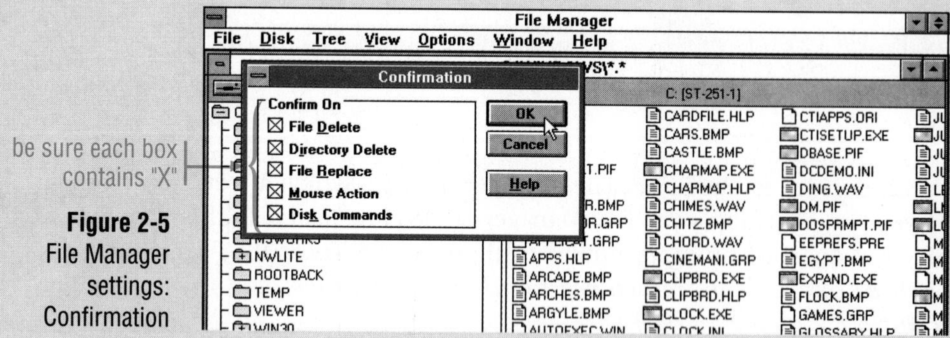

Figure 2-5 File Manager settings: Confirmation

❹ Click **Options** again and then click **Font**. Make any adjustments necessary so your font settings match those in Figure 2-6 on the following page. Click the **OK button** whether or not you changed anything in this dialog box.

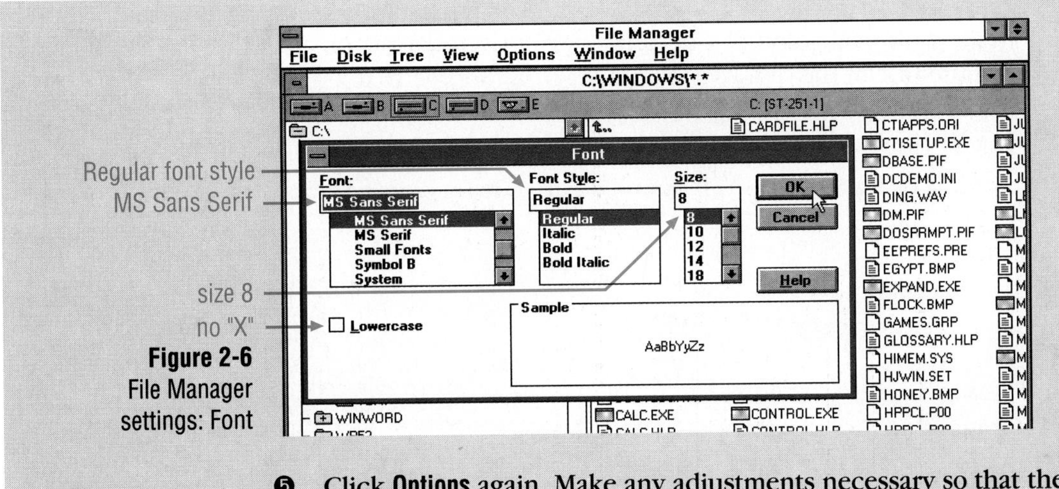

Figure 2-6 File Manager settings: Font

❺ Click **Options** again. Make any adjustments necessary so that the settings are the same as those in Figure 2-7. If no adjustments are necessary, click **Options** again to close the menu.

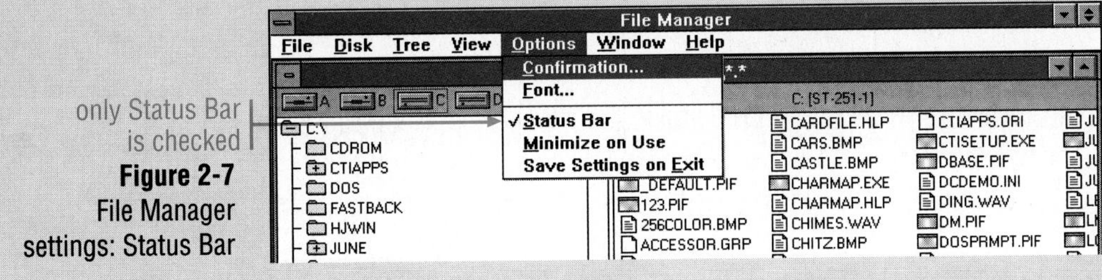

Figure 2-7 File Manager settings: Status Bar

Formatting a Disk

Next, Ruth needs to format the disks she will use for her File Manager practice. Disks must be formatted before they can be used to store data. Formatting arranges the magnetic particles on the disks in preparation for storing data. You need to format a disk when:

- you purchase a new disk
- you want to recycle an old disk that you used on a non-IBM-compatible computer
- you want to erase all the old files from a disk

Pay attention when you are formatting disks. *The formatting process erases all the data on the disk*. If you format a disk that already contains data, you will lose all the data. Fortunately, Windows will not let you format the hard disk or network drives using the Format Disk command.

To complete the steps in this Tutorial you need two disks of the same size and density. You may use blank, unformatted disks or disks that contain data you no longer need. *The following steps assume that you will format the disks in drive A. If you want to use drive B for the formatting process, substitute drive B for drive A* in Steps 3, 4, and 6.

To format the first disk:

❶ Make sure your disk is *not* write-protected. On a 5.25-inch disk the write-protect notch should *not* be covered. On a 3.5-inch disk the hole on the left side of the disk should be *closed.*

2. Write your name, course title, and course meeting time on an adhesive disk label. For the title of the disk, write Student Disk (Source Disk). Apply this label to one of the disks you are going to format. If you are using a 3.5-inch disk, do not stick the label on any of the metal parts.

3. Put this disk into drive A. If your disk drive has a door or a latch, secure it. See Figure 2-8.

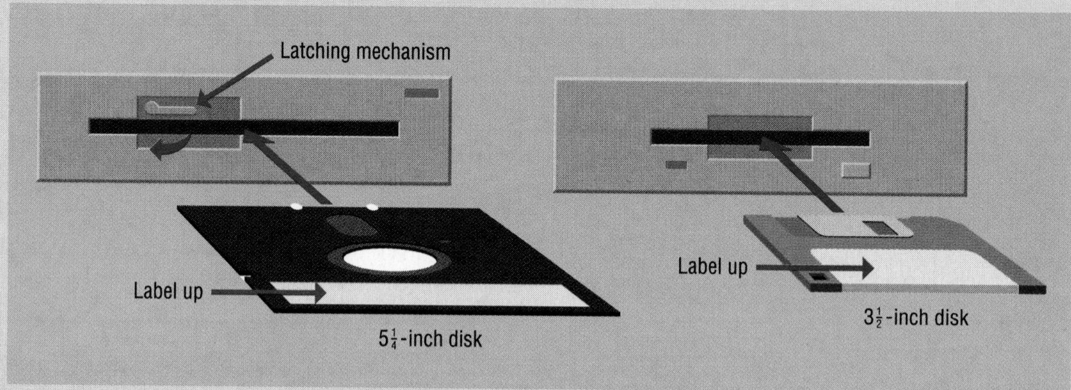

Figure 2-8
Inserting your disk

4. Click **Disk** and then click **Format Disk...**. A Format Disk dialog box appears. See Figure 2-9. If the Disk In box does not indicate Drive A, click the [↓] (down-arrow) button on this box, then click the Drive A option.

be sure these settings are correct

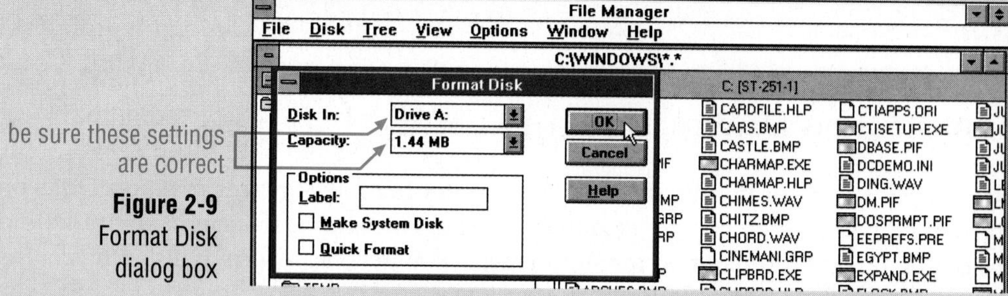

Figure 2-9
Format Disk dialog box

5. Look at the number displayed in the Capacity box. If you are formatting a disk that cannot store the displayed amount of data, click the [↓] (down-arrow) button at the right side of the Capacity box and then click the correct capacity from the list of options provided.

TROUBLE? How can you determine the capacity of your disk? The chart in Figure 2-10 (on the next page) will help you. If you still are not sure after looking at the figure, ask your technical support person.

Diskette size	Diskette density	Diskette capacity
51/4-inch	DD	360K
51/4-inch	HD	1.2MB
31/2-inch	DD	720K
31/2-inch	HD	1.44MB

Figure 2-10
Disk capacities

6. Click the **OK button**. The Confirm Format Disk dialog box appears with a warning. Read it. Look at the drive that is going to carry out the format operation (drive A). Be sure this is the correct drive. Double-check the disk that's in this drive to be sure it is the one you want to format.
7. Click the **Yes button**. The Formatting Disk dialog box keeps you updated on the progress of the format.
8. When the format is complete, the Format Complete dialog box reports the results of the format and asks if you'd like to format another disk. See Figure 2-11.

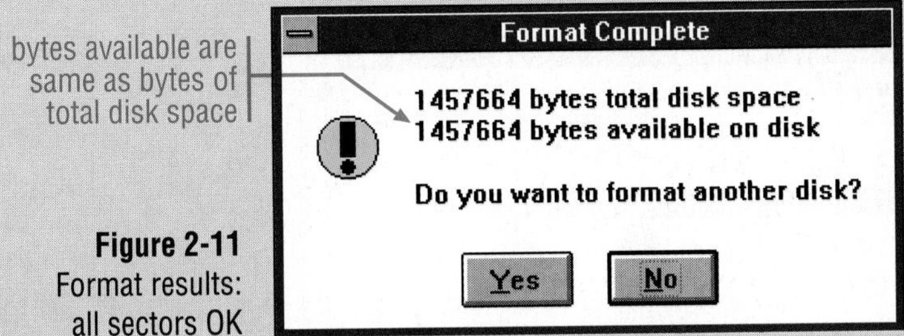

Figure 2-11
Format results: all sectors OK

Let's format your second floppy disk:

1. Click the **Yes button** after you review the formatting results.
2. Remove your Student disk from drive A.
3. Write your name, course title, and course meeting time on the label for the second disk. For the title of this disk write Backup (Destination Disk). Apply this label to your second disk and place this disk in drive A.
4. Be sure the **Disk In box** is set to drive A and the capacity is set to the capacity of your disk. (Remember to substitute B here if you are formatting your disk in drive B.)
5. Click the **OK button** to accept the settings. When you see the Confirm Format Disk dialog box, check to be sure you have the correct disk in the correct drive.
6. Click the **Yes button** to confirm that you want to format the disk. When the format is complete, review the format results.
7. You do not want to format another disk, so click the **No button** when the computer asks if you wish to format another disk.
8. *Remove the backup disk from drive A.* You will not need this backup disk until later.

Preparing Your Student Disk

Now that Ruth has formatted her disks, she is going to put some files on one of them to use for her file management exploration. To follow Ruth's progress, you must have copies of her files. A collection of files has been prepared for this purpose. You need to transfer them to one of your formatted disks.

To transfer files to your Student Disk:

1. Place the disk you labeled Student Disk (Source Disk) in drive A.

The File Manager window is open, but you need to go to the Program Manager window to launch the application that will transfer the files.

❷ Hold down **[Alt]** and continue to press **[Tab]** until Program Manager appears in the box, then release both keys. Program Manager becomes the active window.

❸ If the CTI WinApps window is not open, double-click the **CTI WinApps group icon**. If the CTI WinApps window is open but is not the active window, click it. Your screen should look similar to Figure 2-12.

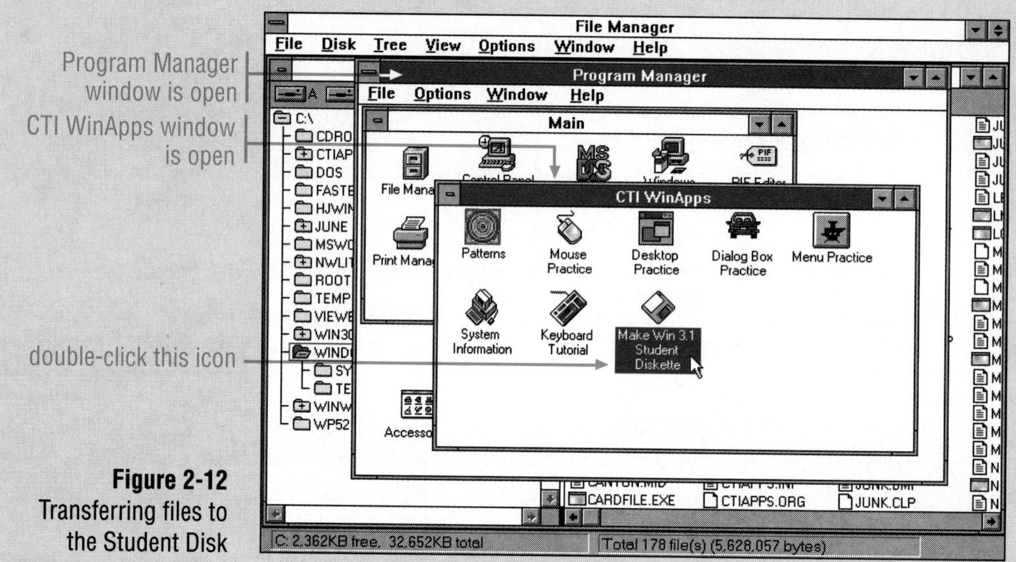

Figure 2-12
Transferring files to the Student Disk

❹ Double-click the **Make Win 3.1 Student Disk icon**. A dialog box appears.

❺ Make sure the drive that is selected in the dialog box corresponds to the drive that contains your disk (drive A or drive B), then click the **OK button**. It will take 30 seconds or so to transfer the files to your disk.

❻ Click the **OK button** when you see the message "24 files copied successfully!"

❼ Double-click on the **CTI WinWorks Apps Control-menu box** to close the window.

Now the data files you need should be on your Student Disk. To continue the Tutorial, you must switch back to the File Manager.

To switch back to the File Manager:

❶ Hold down **[Alt]** and press **[Tab]** until a box with File Manager appears. Then release both keys.

Finding Out What's on Your Disks

Ruth learned from the article that the first step toward effective data management is to find out what's stored on her disks. To see what's on your Student Disk, you will need to be sure your computer is referencing the correct disk drive.

Changing the Current Drive

Each drive on your computer system is represented by a **drive icon** that tells you the drive letter and the drive type. Figure 2-13 shows the drive types represented by these icons.

Floppy Disk

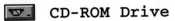

Hard Disk

Network Drive

CD-ROM Drive

Figure 2-13 Drive icons

Near the top of the File Manager window, a **drive icon ribbon** indicates the drives on your computer system. See Figure 2-14. Your screen may be different because the drive icon ribbon on your screen reflects your particular hardware configuration.

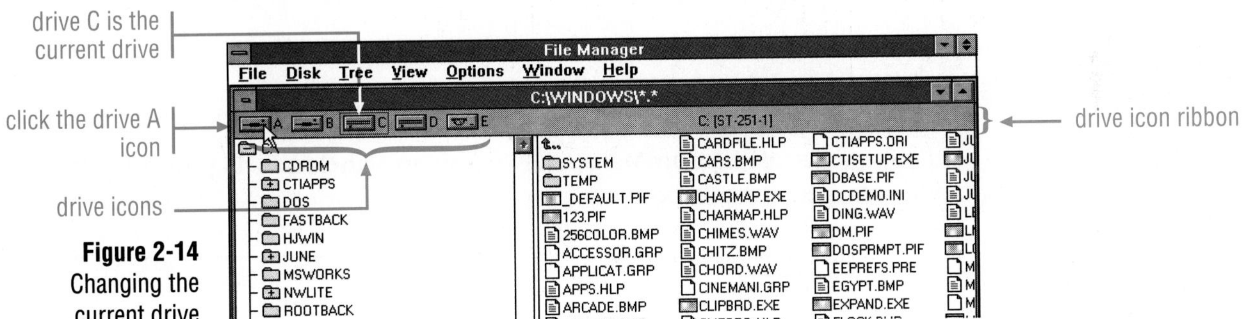

Figure 2-14 Changing the current drive

Your computer is connected to a number of storage drives or devices, but it can work with only one drive at a time. This drive is referred to as the **current drive** or **default drive**. You must change the current drive whenever you want to use files or programs that are stored on a different drive. The drive icon for the current drive is outlined with a rectangle. In Figure 2-14, the current drive is C.

To work with Ruth's files, you must be sure that the current drive is the one in which you have your Student Disk. *For this Tutorial we'll assume that your Student Disk is in drive A. If it is in drive B, substitute "drive B" for "drive A" in the rest of the steps for this Tutorial.*

Follow the next set of steps to change the current drive, if your current drive is not the one containing your Student Disk.

To change the current drive to A:

1. Be sure your Student Disk is in drive A.
2. Click the **drive A icon**. Drive A becomes the current drive. See Figure 2-15 on the following page.

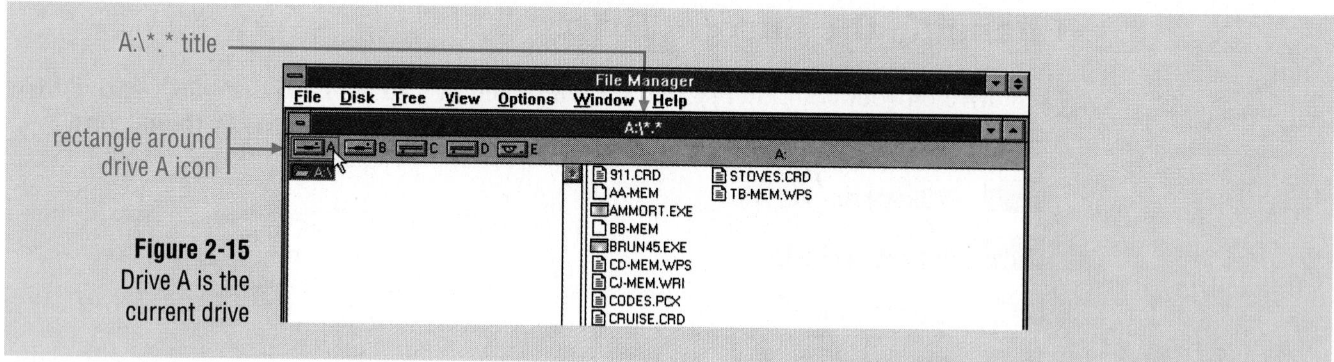

Figure 2-15 Drive A is the current drive

After you make drive A the current drive, your screen should look similar to Figure 2-15. Don't worry if everything is not exactly the same as the figure. Just be sure you see the A:*.* window title and that there is a rectangle around the drive A icon (or the drive B icon if drive B contains your floppy disk).

The File Manager Window

The components of the File Manager window are labeled in Figure 2-16. Your screen should contain similar components.

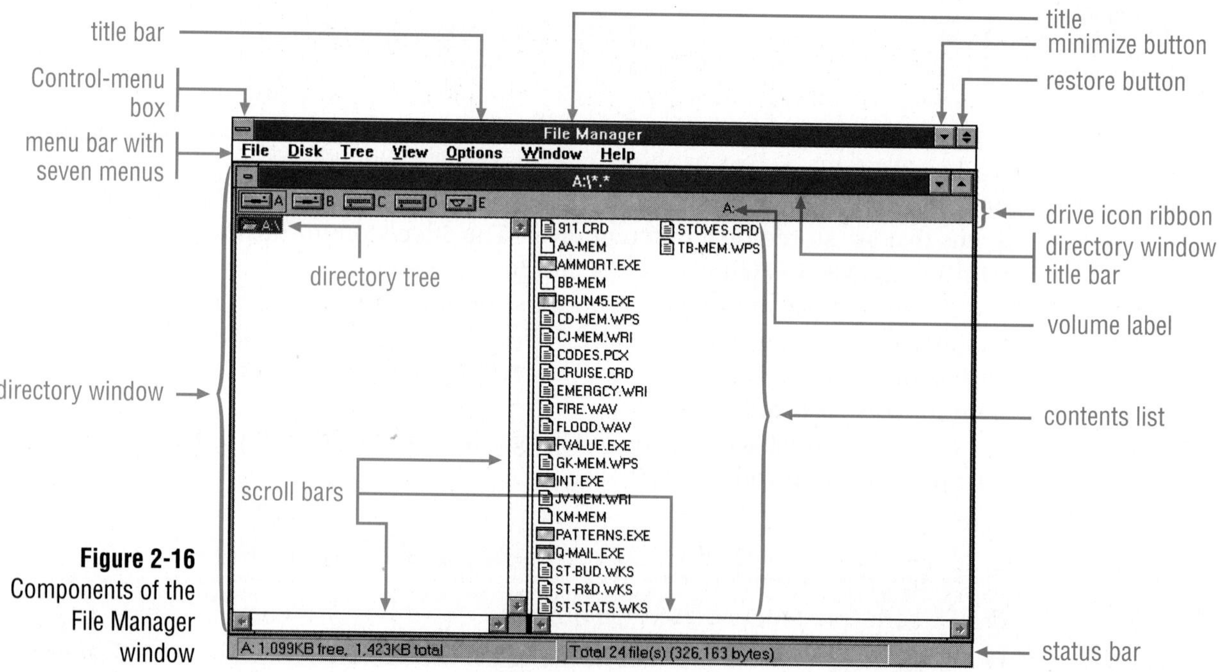

Figure 2-16 Components of the File Manager window

The top line of the File Manager window contains the Control-menu box, the title bar, the title, and the resizing buttons. The File Manager menu bar contains seven menus.

Inside the File Manager window is the **directory window**, which contains information about the current drive. The title bar for this window displays the current drive, in this case, A:*.*. This window has its own Control-menu box and resizing buttons.

Below the directory window title bar is the drive icon ribbon. On this line, the drive letter is followed by a volume label, if there is one. A **volume label** is a name you can assign to your disk during the format process to help you identify the contents of the disk. We did not assign a volume label, so the area after the A: is blank. Why is there a colon after the drive letter? Even though the colon is not displayed on the drive icons, when you type in a drive letter, you must always type a colon after it. The colon is a requirement of the DOS operating system that Windows uses behind the scenes to perform its file management tasks.

At the bottom of the screen, a status bar displays information about disk space. Remember that a byte is one character of data.

Notice that the directory window is split. The left half of the directory window displays the **directory tree**, which illustrates the organization of files on the current drive. The right half of the directory window displays the **contents list**, which lists the files on the current drive. Scroll bars on these windows let you view material that doesn't fit in the current window.

The Directory Tree

A list of files is called a **directory**. Because long lists of files are awkward to work with, directories can be subdivided into smaller lists called **subdirectories**. The organization of these directories and subdirectories is depicted in the directory tree.

Suppose you were using your computer for a small retail business. What information might you have on your disk, and how would it be organized? Figure 2-17 shows the directory tree for a hard disk (drive C) of a typical small business computer system.

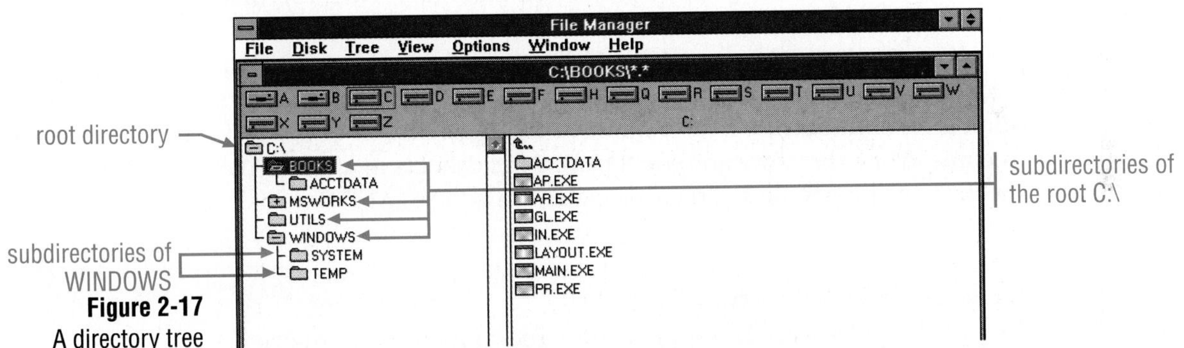

Figure 2-17
A directory tree

At the top of the directory tree is the **root directory**, called C:\ . The root directory is created when you format a disk and is indicated by a backslash after the drive letter and colon. Arranged under the root directory are the subdirectories BOOKS, MSWORKS, UTILS, and WINDOWS.

Directories other than the root directory can have subdirectories. In Figure 2-17 you can see that the BOOKS directory has a subdirectory called ACCTDATA. The WINDOWS directory contains two subdirectories, SYSTEM and TEMP. MSWORKS also has some subdirectories, but they are not listed. You'll find out how to expand the directory tree to display subdirectories later in the this tutorial.

Windows uses directory names to construct a path through the directory tree. For example, the path to ACCTDATA would be C:\BOOKS\ACCTDATA. To trace this path on Figure 2-17, begin at the root directory C:\, follow the line leading to the BOOKS directory, then follow the line leading to the ACCTDATA directory.

Each directory in the directory tree has a **file folder icon**, which can be either open or closed. An open file folder icon indicates the **active** or **current directory**. In Figure 2-17 the current directory is BOOKS. Only one directory can be current on a disk at a time.

Now look at the directory tree on your screen. The root directory of your Student Disk is called A:\. The file folder icon for this directory is open, indicating that this is the current directory. Are there any subdirectories on your disk?

The answer is no. A:\ has no subdirectories because its file folder icon does not contain a plus sign or a minus sign. A plus sign on a folder indicates that the directory can be expanded to show its subdirectories. A minus sign indicates that the subdirectories are currently being displayed. A file folder icon without a plus or a minus sign has no subdirectories.

Organizing Your Files

Ruth's disk, like your Student Disk, contains only one directory, and all her files are in that directory. As is typical of a poorly organized disk, files from different projects and programs are jumbled together. As Ruth's disk accumulates more files, she will have an increasingly difficult time finding the files she wants to use.

Ruth needs to organize her disk. First, she needs to make some new directories so she has a good basic structure for her files.

Creating Directories

When you create a directory, you indicate its location on the directory tree and specify the new directory name. The directory you create becomes a subdirectory of the current directory, which is designated by an open file folder. Directory names can be up to eight characters long.

Your Student Disk contains a collection of memos and spreadsheets that Ruth has created for a project code named "Stealth." Right now, all of these files are in the root directory. Ruth decides that to improve the organization of her disk, she should place her memos in one directory and the Stealth spreadsheets in another directory. To do this, she needs to make two new directories, MEMOS and STEALTH.

To make a new directory called MEMOS:

1. Click the **file folder icon** representing the root directory of drive A. Figure 2-18 shows you where to click. This highlights the root directory A:\, making it the current directory.

click the A:\ file folder

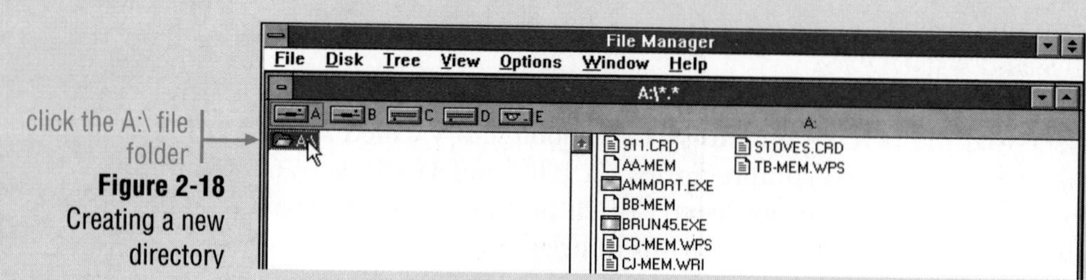

Figure 2-18 Creating a new directory

2. Click **File**, then click **Create Directory...**. The Create Directory dialog box indicates that the current directory is A:\ and displays a text box for the name of the new directory.

3. In the text box, type **MEMOS**, then click the **OK button**. It doesn't matter whether you type the directory name in uppercase or lowercase letters.

As a result, your screen should look like Figure 2-19. A new directory folder labeled MEMOS is now a subdirectory of A:\. The A:\ file folder now displays a minus sign to indicate that it has a subdirectory and that the subdirectory is displayed.

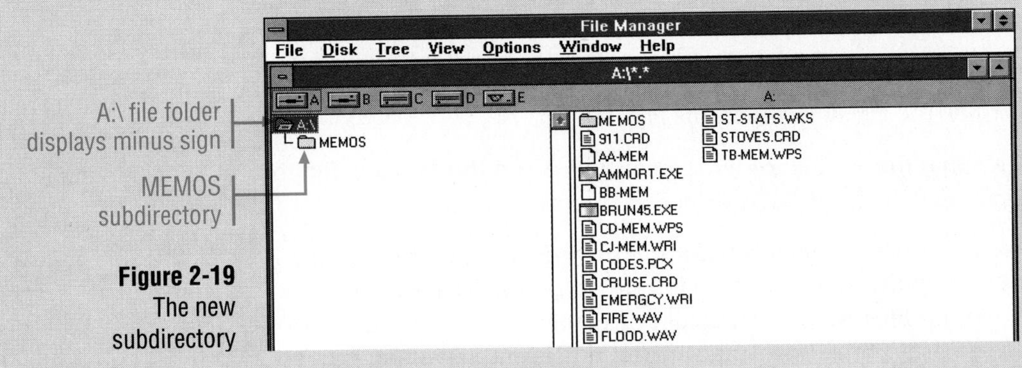

Figure 2-19 The new subdirectory

TROUBLE? If you do not see the minus sign on the A:\ file folder, click Tree, then click Indicate Expandable branches.

Next Ruth will make a directory for the spreadsheets. She wants her directory tree to look like the one in Figure 2-20a, not the one in Figure 2-20b.

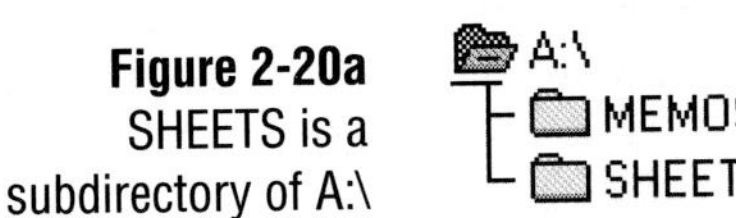

Figure 2-20a SHEETS is a subdirectory of A:\

Figure 2-20b SHEETS is a subdirectory of MEMOS

The spreadsheet directory should be a subdirectory of the root, *not* of MEMOS.

To make a directory for spreadsheets:

1. Click the **directory folder icon for A:**.
2. Click **File**, then click **Create Directory...**.
3. In the text box type **SHEETS**, then click the **OK button**.
4. Make sure that your newly updated directory tree resembles the one in Figure 2-20a. There should be two directories under A:\ — MEMOS and SHEETS.

TROUBLE? If your directory tree is structured like the one in Figure 2-20b, use your mouse to drag the SHEETS directory icon to the A:\ file folder icon.

Now Ruth's disk has a structure she can use to organize her files. It contains three directories: the root A:\, MEMOS, and SHEETS. Each directory can contain a list of files. Ruth is happy with this new structure, but she is not sure what the directories contain. She decides to look in one of the new directories to see what's there.

Changing Directories

When you change directories, you open a different directory folder. If the directory contains files, they will be displayed in the contents list.

First, Ruth wants to look in the MEMOS directory.

To change to the MEMOS directory:

❶ Click the **MEMOS directory file folder icon**.

Notice that the A:\ file folder icon is closed and the MEMOS file folder icon is open, indicating that the MEMOS directory is now current.

Look at the status line at the bottom of your screen. The left side of the status line shows you how much space is left on your disk. The right side of the status line tells you that no files are in the current directory, that is, in the MEMOS directory. This makes sense. You just created the directory, and haven't put anything in it.

❷ Click the **A:\ file folder icon** to change back to the root directory.

Expanding and Collapsing Directories

Notice on your screen that the A:\ file folder icon has a minus sign on it. As you know, the minus sign indicates that A:\ has one or more subdirectories and that those subdirectories are displayed. To look at a simplified directory tree, you would **collapse** the A:\ directory. You would **expand** a directory to redisplay its subdirectories. Ruth wants to practice expanding and collapsing directories.

To expand and then collapse a directory:

❶ Double-click the **A:\ file folder icon** to collapse the directory. As a result the MEMOS and SHEETS branches of the directory tree are removed and a plus sign appears on the A:\ file folder icon.

❷ Double-click the **A:\ file folder icon** again. This time the directory expands, displaying the MEMOS and SHEETS branches. Notice the minus sign on the A:\ file folder icon.

The Contents List

The **contents list** on the right side of the desktop contains the list of files and subdirectories for the current directory. On your screen the directory tree shows that A:\ is the current directory. The status bar shows that this directory contains 26 files and subdirectories. These files are listed in the contents list. Ruth recalls that she had to follow a set of rules when she created the names for these files. Let's find out more about these rules, since you will soon need to create names for your own files.

Filenames and Extensions

A **filename** is a unique set of letters and numbers that identifies a program, document file, directory, or miscellaneous data file. A filename may be followed by an **extension**, which is separated from the filename by a period.

The rules for creating valid filenames are as follows:

- The filename can contain a maximum of eight characters.
- The extension cannot contain more than three characters.
- Use a period only between the filename and the extension.
- Neither the filename nor extension can include any spaces.
- Do not use the following characters: / [ ] ; = " \ : | ,
- Do not use the following names: AUX, COM1, COM2, COM3, COM4, CON, LPT1, LPT2, LPT3, PRN, or NUL.

Ruth used the letters ST at the beginning of her spreadsheet filenames so she could remember that these files contain information on project Stealth. Ruth used the rest of each filename to describe more about the file contents. For example, ST-BUD is the budget for project Stealth, ST-R&D is the research and development cost worksheet for the project, and ST-STATS contains the descriptive statistics for the project. Ruth's memos, on the other hand, begin with the initials of the person who received the memo. She used MEM as part of the filename for all her memos. For example, the file CJMEM.WRI contains a memo to Charles Jackson.

The file extension usually indicates the category of information a file contains. We can divide files into two broad categories, program files and data files. **Program files** contain the programming code for applications and systems software. For example, the computer program that makes your computer run the WordPerfect word processor would be classified as a program file. Program files are sometimes referred to as **executable files** because the computer executes, or performs, the instructions contained in the files. A common filename extension for this type of file is .EXE. Other extensions for program files include .BAT, .SYS, .PIF, and .COM. In the contents list, program files are shown with a **program file icon**, like the one you see next to the file PATTERNS.EXE on your screen and in Figure 2-21.

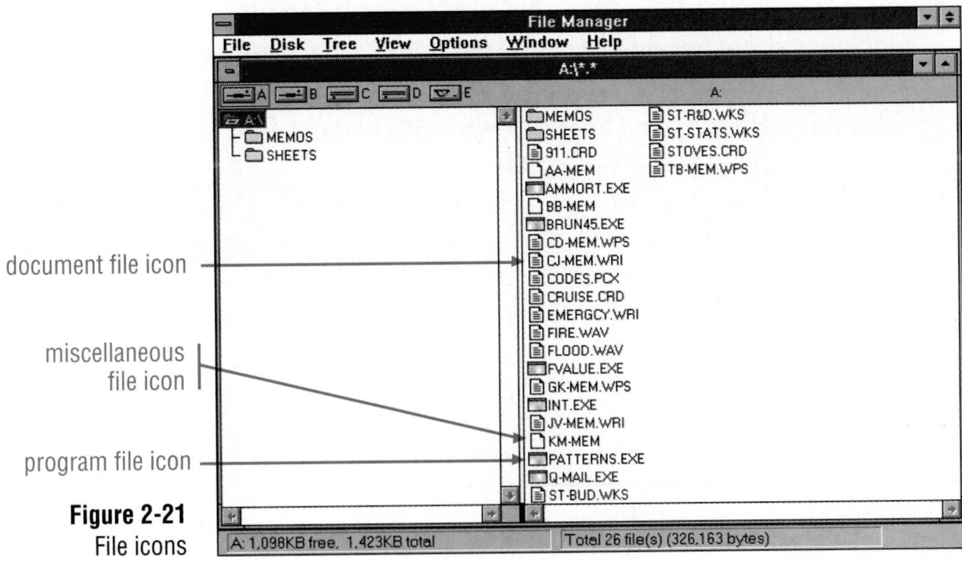

Figure 2-21
File icons

The second file category is data files. **Data files** contain the information with which you work: the memos, spreadsheets, reports, and graphs you create using applications such as word processors and spreadsheets. The filename extension for a data file usually indicates which application was used to create the file. For example, the file CD-MEM.WPS was created using the Microsoft Works word processor, which automatically puts the extension .WPS on any file you create with it. The use of .WPS as the standard extension for Works word processing documents creates an association between the application and the documents you create with it. Later, when you want to make modifications to your documents, Works can find them easily by looking for the .WPS extension.

Data files you create using a Windows application installed on your computer are shown in the contents list with a **document file icon** like the one you see next to CD-MEM.WPS on your screen. Data files you create using a non-Windows application or a Windows application that is not installed on your computer are shown in the contents list with a **miscellaneous file icon** like the one you see next to AA-MEM on your screen. AA-MEM was created using a non-Windows word processor.

Now that you have an idea of the contents for each of Ruth's files, you will be able to help her move them into the appropriate directory.

Moving Files

You can move files from one disk to another. You can also move files from one directory to another. When you move a file, the computer copies the file to its new location, then erases it from the original location. The File Manager lets you move files by dragging them on the screen or by using the File Manager menus.

Now that Ruth has created the MEMOS and SHEETS directories, the next step in organizing her disk is to put files in these directories. She begins by moving one of her memo files from the root directory A:\ to the MEMOS subdirectory. She decides to move JV-MEM.WRI first.

To move the file JV-MEM.WRI from A:\ to the MEMOS subdirectory:

1. Position the pointer on the filename JV-MEM.WRI and click the mouse button to select it. On the left side of the status bar, the message "Selected 1 file(s) (1,408 bytes)" appears.
2. Press the mouse button and hold it down while you drag the file icon to the MEMOS file folder in the directory tree.
3. When the icon arrives at its target location, a box appears around the MEMOS file icon. Release the mouse button. Figure 2-22 on the following page illustrates this procedure.

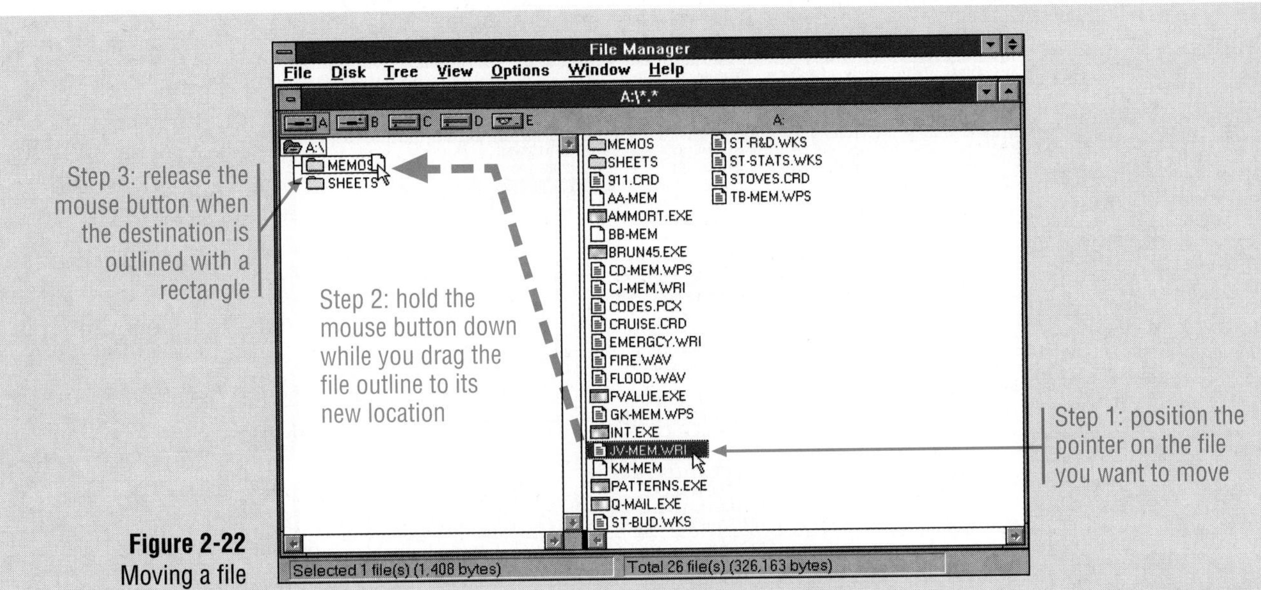

Figure 2-22
Moving a file

❹ Click the **Yes button** in response to the message "Are you sure you want to move the selected files or directories to A:\MEMOS?" A Moving... dialog box may flash briefly on your screen before the file is moved. Look at the contents list on the right side of the screen. The file JV-MEM.WRI is no longer there.

Ruth wants to confirm that the file was moved.

❺ Single click the **MEMOS file folder icon** in the directory tree on the left side of the screen. The file JV-MEM.WRI should be listed in the contents list on the right side of the screen.

TROUBLE? If JV-MEM.WRI is not in the MEMOS subdirectory, you might have moved it inadvertently to the SHEETS directory. You can check this by clicking the SHEETS directory folder. If the file is in SHEETS, drag it to the MEMOS directory folder.

❻ Click the **A:\file folder icon** to display the files in the root directory again.

Ruth sees that several memos are still in the root directory. She could move these memos one at a time to the MEMOS subdirectory, but she knows that it would be more efficient to move them as a group. To do this, she'll first select the files she wants to move. Then, she will drag them to the MEMOS directory.

To select a group of files:

❶ The directory A:\ should be selected on your screen and the files in this directory should be displayed in the right directory window. If this is not the case, click the directory icon for A:\.

❷ Click the filename **CD-MEM.WPS** to select it.

❸ Hold down **[Ctrl]** while you click the next filename you want to add to the group, **CJMEM.WRI**. Now two files should be selected. Ruth wants to select two more files.

❹ Hold down **[Ctrl]** while you click **GK-MEM.WPS**.

❺ Hold down **[Ctrl]** while you click **TB-MEM.WPS**. Release **[Ctrl]**. When you have finished selecting the files, your screen should look similar to Figure 2-23 on the following page. Notice the status bar message, "Selected 4 file(s) (4,590 bytes)."

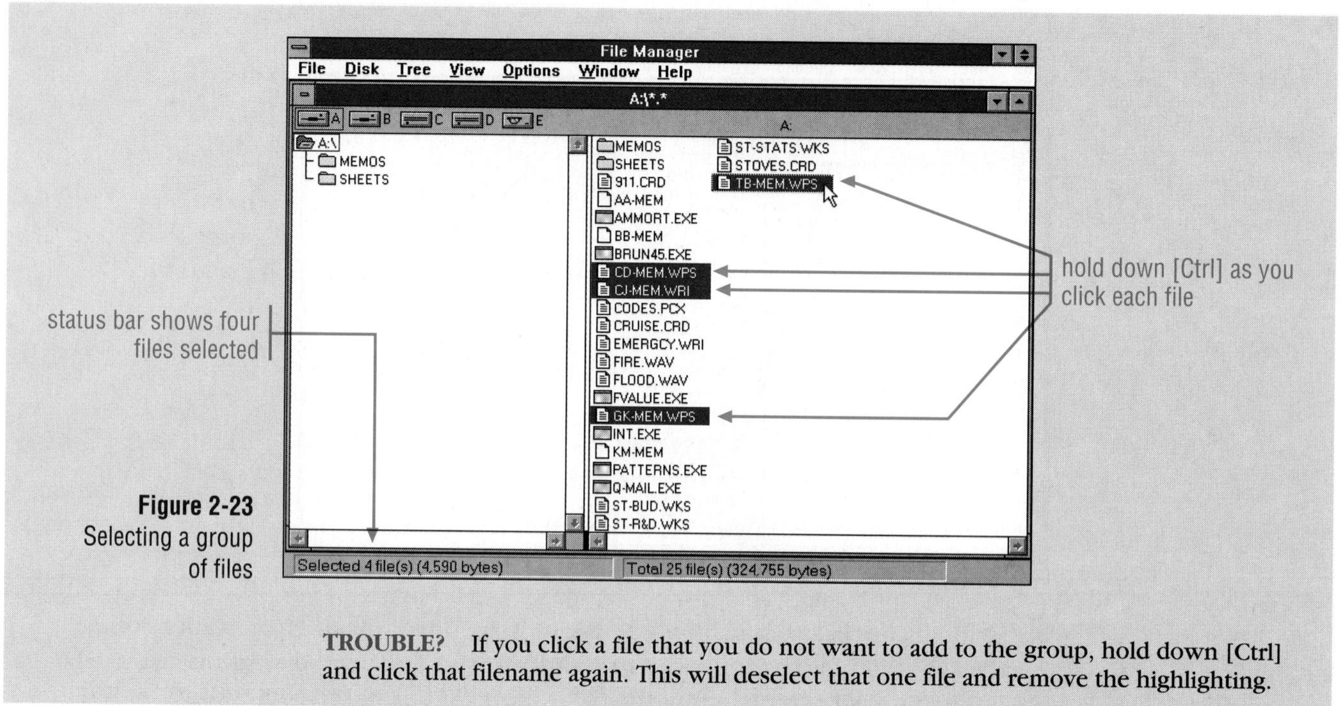

Figure 2-23
Selecting a group of files

TROUBLE? If you click a file that you do not want to add to the group, hold down [Ctrl] and click that filename again. This will deselect that one file and remove the highlighting.

Now that Ruth has selected the files she wants to move, she can drag them to their new location.

To move a group of files:

1. Position the pointer on any one of the highlighted filenames.
2. Press the mouse button and drag the pointer, which now is attached to a multiple file icon, to the MEMOS directory icon. See Figure 2-24.

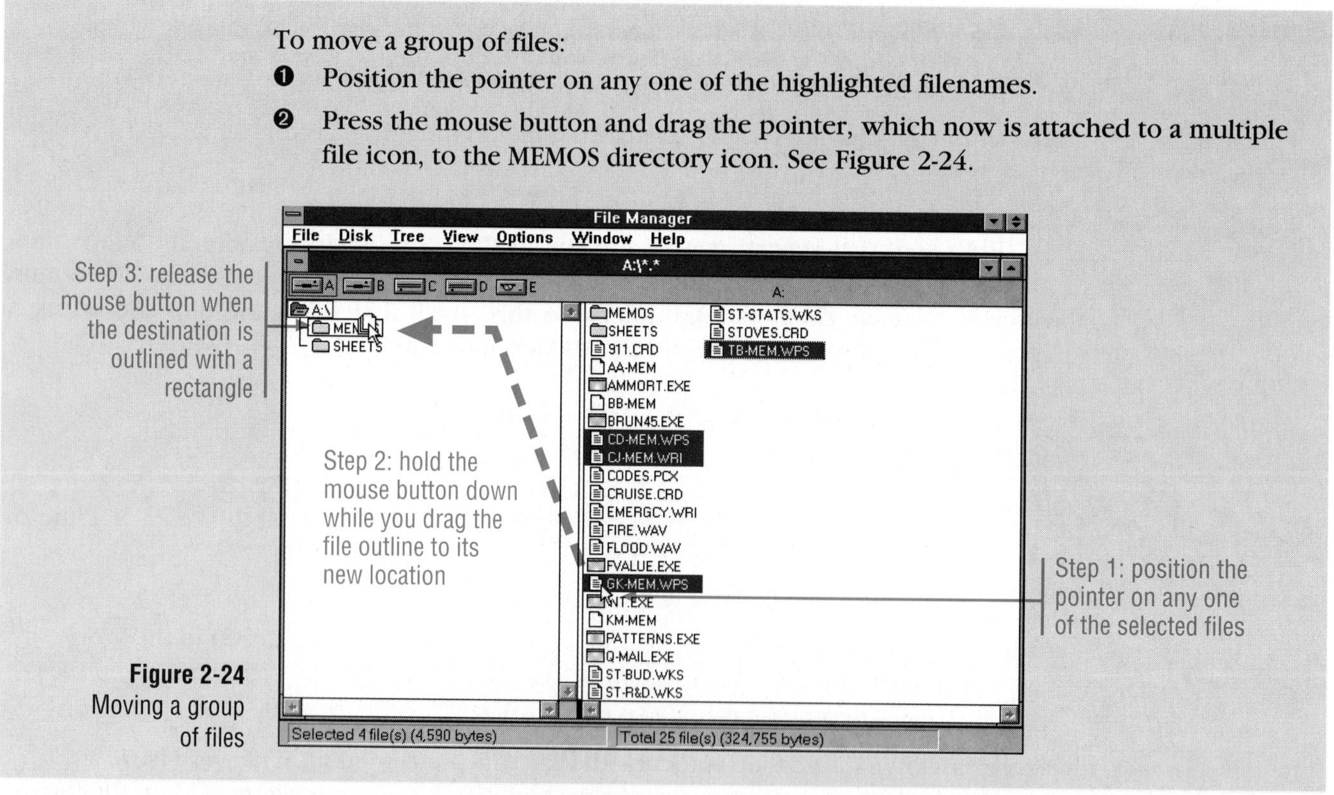

Figure 2-24
Moving a group of files

3. When the you move the file icon onto the MEMOS directory, a box will outline the directory icon. Release the mouse button. The Confirm Mouse Operation dialog box appears.
4. Click the **Yes button** to confirm that you want to move the files. After a brief period of activity on your disk drive, the contents list for the A:\ directory is updated and should no longer include the files you moved.
5. Click the **MEMOS directory icon** to verify that the group of files arrived in the MEMOS directory.
6. Click the **A:\ directory icon** to once again display the contents of the root directory.

Renaming Files

You may find it useful to change the name of a file to make it more descriptive of the file contents. Remember that Windows uses file extensions to associate document files with applications and to identify executable programs, so when you rename a file you should not change the extension.

Ruth looks down the list of files and notices ST-BUD.WKS, which contains the 1994 budget for project Stealth. Ruth knows that next week she will begin work on the 1995 budget. She decides that while she is organizing her files, she will change the name of ST-BUD.WKS to ST-BUD94.WKS. When she creates the budget for 1995, she will call it ST-BUD95.WKS so it will be easy to distinguish between the two budget files.

To change the name of ST-BUD.WKS to ST-BUD94.WKS:

1. Click the filename **ST-BUD.WKS**.
2. Click **File**, then click **Rename**. See Figure 2-25. The Rename dialog box shows you the current directory and the name of the file you are going to rename. Verify that the dialog box on your screen indicates that the current directory is A:\ and that the file you are going to rename is ST-BUD.WKS.

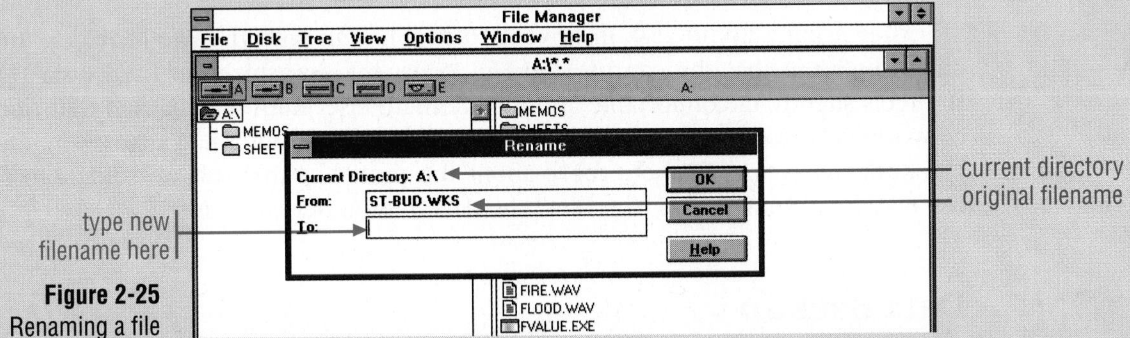

Figure 2-25
Renaming a file

TROUBLE? If the filename is not ST-BUD.WKS, click the Cancel button and go back to Step 1.

3. In the To text box type **ST-BUD94.WKS** (using either uppercase or lowercase letters.
4. Click the **OK button**.
5. Check the file listing for ST-BUD94.WKS to verify that the rename procedure was successful.

Deleting Files

When you no longer need a file, it is good practice to delete it. Deleting a file frees up space on your disk and reduces the size of the directory listing you need to scroll through to find a file. A well-organized disk does not contain files you no longer need.

Ruth decides to delete the ST-STATS.WKS file. Although this file contains some statistics about the Stealth project, Ruth knows by looking at the file's date that those statistics are no longer current. She'll receive a new file from the Statistics department next week.

To delete the file ST-STATS.WKS:

1. Click the filename **ST-STATS.WKS**.
2. Click **File**, then click **Delete**. The Delete dialog box shows you that the file scheduled for deletion is in the A:\ directory and is called ST-STATS.WKS. See Figure 2-26.

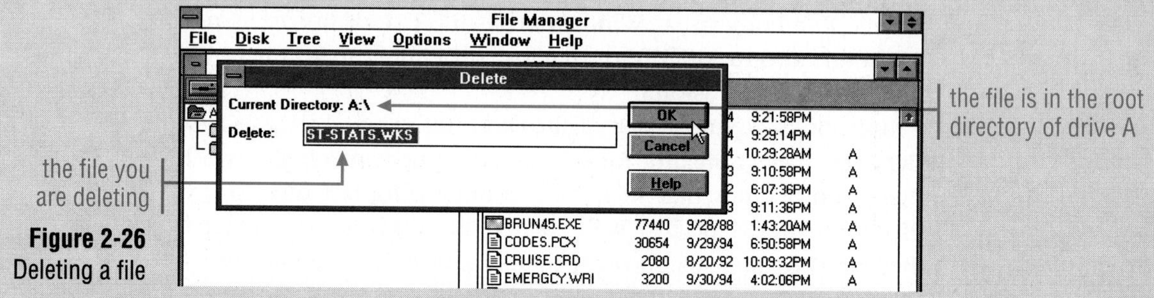

Figure 2-26
Deleting a file

TROUBLE? If the filename ST-STATS.WKS is not displayed in the Delete dialog box, click the Cancel button and go back to Step 1.

3. Click the **OK button**. The Confirm File Delete dialog box appears. This is your last chance to change your mind before the file is deleted.
4. Click the **Yes button** to delete the file. Look at the contents list to verify that the file ST-STATS.WKS has been deleted.

After using a floppy disk in drive A to experiment with the File Manager, Ruth feels more confident that she can use the File Manager to organize her hard disk. However, she feels slightly uncomfortable about something else. Ruth just learned that one of her co-workers lost several days worth of work when his computer had a hardware failure.

Ruth resolves to find out more about the problems that can cause data loss so she can take appropriate steps to protect the data files on her computer.

Data Backup

Ruth's initial research on data loss reveals that there is no totally fail-safe method to protect data from hardware failures, human error, and natural disasters. She does discover, however, some ways to reduce the risk of losing data. Every article Ruth reads emphasizes the importance of regular backups.

A **backup** is a copy of one or more files, made in case the original files are destroyed or become unusable. Ruth learns that Windows provides a Copy command and a Copy Disk command that she can use for data backup. Ruth decides to find out how these commands work, so she refers to the *Microsoft Windows User's Guide* which came with the Microsoft Windows 3.1 software. She quickly discovers that the Copy and Copy Disk commands are in the Windows File Manager.

To prepare the File Manager for data backup:

❶ If you are returning from a break, launch Windows if it is not currently running. Be sure you see the Program Manager window.

❷ Relaunch the File Manager if necessary. Make sure your Student Disk is in drive A.

TROUBLE? If you want to use drive B instead of drive A, substitute "B" for "A" in any steps when drive A is specified.

❸ Click the File Manager **maximize button** if the File Manager is not already maximized.

❹ If necessary, click the **drive A icon** on the drive ribbon to make drive A the default drive.

❺ Click **View** and be sure that a check mark appears next to All File Details.

❻ Click **Window**, then click **Tile**. As a result, your desktop should look similar to Figure 2-27. Don't worry if your list of directories and files is different from the one shown in the figures.

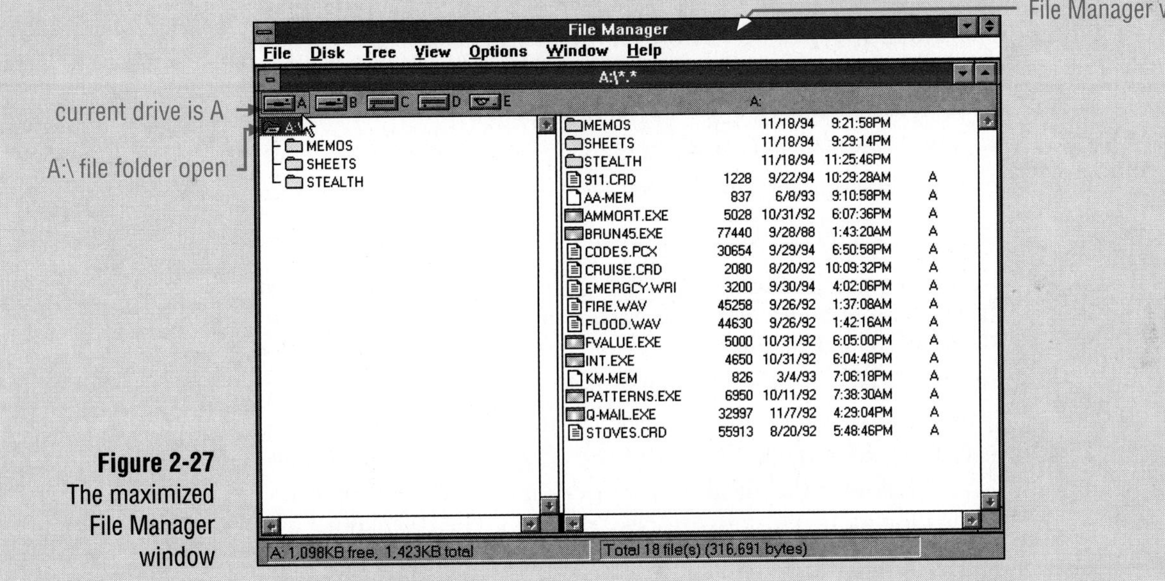

Figure 2-27
The maximized File Manager window

Now that Ruth has the File Manager window set-up, she decides to practice with the Copy command first.

The Copy Command

The Copy command duplicates a file in a new location. When the procedure has been completed, you have two files, your original and the copy. The additional copy of the file is useful for backup in case your original file develops a problem and becomes unusable.

The Copy command is different from the Move command, which you used earlier. The Move command deletes the file from its old location after moving it. When the move is completed, you have only one file.

If you understand the terminology associated with copying files, you will be able to achieve the results you want. The original location of a file is referred to as the **source**. The new location of the file is referred to as the **destination** or **target**.

You can copy one file or you can copy a group of files. In this Tutorial you will practice moving one file at a time. You can also copy files from one directory to another or from one disk to another. The disks you copy to and from do not need to be the same size. For backup purposes you would typically copy files from a hard disk to a disk.

Copying Files Using a Single Disk Drive

Ruth has been working on a spreadsheet called ST-BUD94.WKS for an entire week, and the data on this spreadsheet are critical for a presentation she is making tomorrow. The file is currently on a disk in drive A. Ruth will sleep much better tonight if she has an extra copy of this file. But Ruth has only one floppy disk drive. To make a copy of a file from one floppy disk to another, she must use her hard disk as a temporary storage location.

First, she will copy the file ST-BUD94.WKS to her hard disk. Then she will move the file to another floppy disk. Let's see how this procedure works.

To copy the file ST-BUD94.WKS from the source disk to the hard disk:

1. Make sure your Student Disk is in drive A. Be sure you also have the backup disk you formatted earlier in the tutorial.
2. Find the file ST-BUD94.WKS. It is in the root directory .
3. Click the filename **ST-BUD94.WKS**.
4. Click **File**, then click **Copy**.

   TROUBLE? If you see a message that indicates you cannot copy a file to drive C, click the OK button. Your drive C has been write-protected, and you will not be able to copy ST-BUD94.WKS. Read through the copying procedure and resume doing the steps in the section entitled "Making a Disk Backup."

5. Look at the ribbon of drive icons at the top of your screen. If you have an icon for drive C, type **C:** in the text box of the Copy dialog box. If you do not have an icon for drive C, ask your technical support person which drive you can use for a temporary destination in the file copy process, then type the drive letter.
6. Confirm that the Copy dialog box settings are similar to those in Figure 2-28, then click the **OK button**. The file is copied to the root directory of drive C (or to the directory your technical support person told you to use).

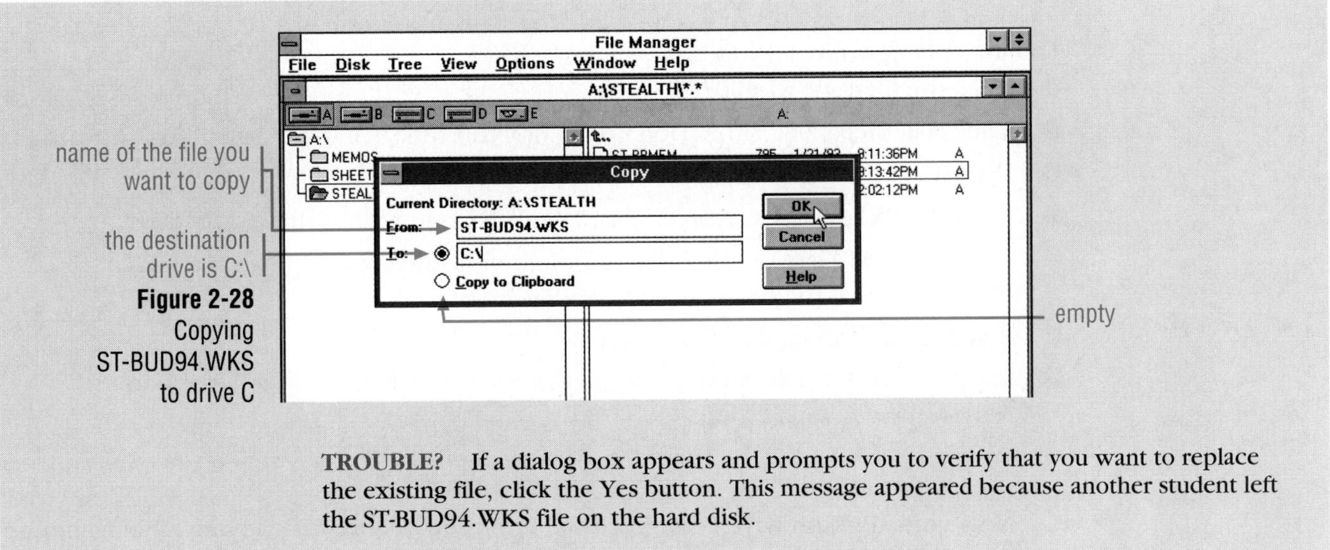

Figure 2-28 Copying ST-BUD94.WKS to drive C

TROUBLE? If a dialog box appears and prompts you to verify that you want to replace the existing file, click the Yes button. This message appeared because another student left the ST-BUD94.WKS file on the hard disk.

After the file has been copied to the hard disk, Ruth needs to switch disks. She will take her original disk out of drive A and replace it with the disk that will receive the copy of the ST-BUD94.WKS file. After Ruth switches disks, she must tell the File Manager to **refresh** the directory tree and the contents list so they show the files and directories for the disk that is now in the drive.

To switch disks and refresh the contents list:

1. Remove your Student Disk from drive A.
2. Put your Backup Disk in drive A.
3. Click the **drive A icon** on the drive ribbon to refresh the contents list. The directory tree will contain only the A:\ folder, because your backup disk does not have the directories you created for your original Student Disk.

Now let's look for the copy of ST-BUD94.WKS that is on drive C.

To locate the new copy of ST-BUD94.WKS:

1. Click the **drive C icon** (or the drive your technical support person told you to use).
2. Click the **C:\ file folder icon** (or the directory your technical support person told you to use).
3. If necessary, use the scroll bar on the side of the content list to find the file ST-BUD94.WKS in the contents list.

Now you need to move the file from the hard disk to the backup disk in drive A. You must use Move instead of Copy so you don't leave the file on your hard disk.

To move the new file copy to drive A:

1. Click the filename **ST-BUD94.WKS**.
2. Click **File**, then click **Move**. (Don't use Copy this time.) A Move dialog box appears.
3. Type **A:** in the text box.
4. Click the **OK button**. As a result, ST-BUD94.WKS is moved to the disk in drive A.
5. Click the **drive A icon** on the drive ribbon to view the contents list for the Backup disk. Verify that the file ST-BUD94.WKS is listed.
6. Remove the Backup disk from drive A.
7. Insert the **Student Disk** in drive A and click the **drive A icon** in the drive ribbon to refresh the contents listing.

Now you and Ruth have completed the entire procedure for copying a file from one disk to another on a single floppy disk system. In her research, Ruth also has discovered a Windows command for copying an entire disk. She wants to practice this command next.

Making a Disk Backup

The Windows Copy Disk command makes an exact duplicate of an entire disk. All the files and all the blank sectors of the disk are copied. If you have files on your destination disk, the Copy Disk command will erase them as it makes the copy so that the destination disk will be an exact duplicate of the original disk.

When you use the Copy Disk command, both disks must have the same storage capacity. For example, if your original disk is a 3.5-inch high-density disk, your destination disk also must be 3.5-inch high-density disk. For this reason, you cannot use the Copy Disk command to copy an entire hard disk to a floppy disk. If your computer does not have two disk drives that are the same size and capacity, the Copy Disk command will work with only one disk drive. When you back up the contents of one disk to another disk using only one disk drive, files are copied from the source disk into the random access memory (RAM) of the computer.

RAM is a temporary storage area on your computer's mother board which usually holds data and instructions for the operating system, application programs, and documents you are using. After the files are copied into RAM, you remove the source disk and replace it with the destination disk. The files in RAM are then copied onto the destination disk. If you don't have enough RAM available to hold the entire contents of the disk, only a portion of the source disk contents are copied during the first stage of the process, and the computer must repeat the process for the remaining contents of the disk.

Ruth wants to practice using the Copy Disk command to make a backup of a disk. She is going to make the copy using only one disk drive because she can use this procedure on both her computer at home, which has one disk drive, and her computer at work, which has two different-sized disk drives.

While Ruth makes a copy of her disk, let's make a backup of your Student Disk. After you learn the procedure, you'll be responsible for making regular backups of the work you do for this course. You should back up your disks at least once a week. If you are working on a particularly critical project, such as a term paper or a thesis, you might want to make backups more often.

To make a backup copy of your Student disk:

1. Be sure your Student Disk is in drive A and that you have the disk you labeled Backup handy. If you want to be very safe, write-protect your source disk before continuing with this procedure. Remember, to write-protect a 5.25-inch disk, you place a tab over the write-protect notch. On a 3.5-inch disk you open the write-protect hole.
2. Click **Disk**, then click **Copy Disk...**. Confirm that the Copy Disk dialog box on your screen looks like the one in Figure 2-29. The dialog box should indicate that "Source In" is A: and "Destination In" is A:. If this is not the case, click the appropriate down-arrow button and select A: from the list. When the dialog box display is correct, click the **OK button**.

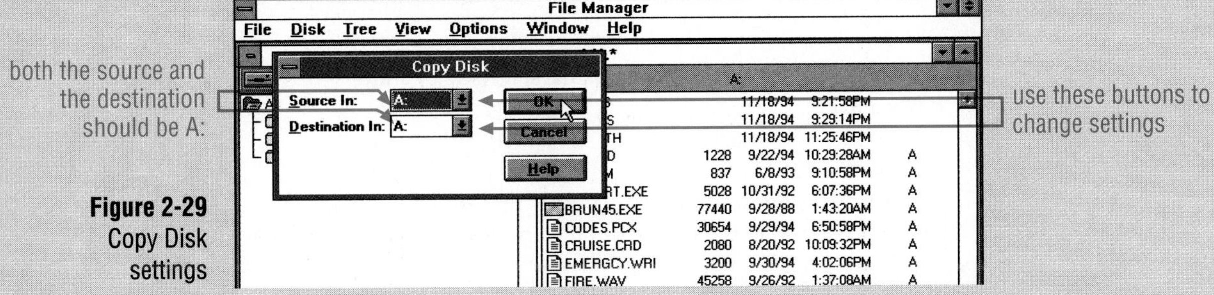

Figure 2-29 Copy Disk settings

3. The Confirm Copy Disk dialog box reminds you that this operation will erase all data from the destination disk. It asks, "Are you sure you want to continue?"
4. Click the **Yes button**. The next dialog box instructs you to "Insert source disk." Your source disk is the Student Disk and it is already in drive A.
5. Click the **OK button**.

After a flurry of activity, the computer begins to copy the data from drive A into RAM. The Copying Disk dialog box keeps you posted on its progress.

6. Eventually another message appears, telling you to "Insert destination disk." Take your Student Disk out of drive A and replace it with the disk you labeled Backup.
7. Click the **OK button**. The computer copies the files from RAM to the destination disk.

Depending on how much internal memory your computer has, you might be prompted to switch disks twice more. Carefully follow the dialog box prompts, remembering that the *source* disk is your Student Disk and the *destination* disk is your Backup disk.

8. When the Copy Disk operation is complete, the Copying Disk dialog box closes. If you write-protected your Student Disk in Step 1, you should unprotect it now; otherwise you won't be able to save data to the disk later.

As a result of the Copy Disk command, your Backup disk should be an exact duplicate of your Student Disk.

Ruth has completed her exploration of file management. Now, Ruth decides to finish for the day. If you are not going to proceed directly to the Tutorial Assignments, you should exit the File Manager.

To exit the File Manager:

1. Click the File Manager **Control-menu box**.
2. Click **Close**.
3. If you want to exit Windows, click the **Program Manager Control-menu box**, then click **Close**, and finally click the **OK button**.

■ ■ ■

Questions

1. Which one of the following is not a characteristic of a file?
   a. It has a name.
   b. It is a collection of data.
   c. It is the smallest unit of data.
   d. It is stored on a device such as a floppy disk or a hard disk.
2. What process arranges the magnetic particles on a disk in preparation for data storage?
3. In which one of the following situations would formatting your disk be the least desirable procedure?
   a. You have purchased a new disk.
   b. You have difficulty doing a spreadsheet assignment, and you want to start over again.
   c. You want to erase all the old files from a disk.
   d. You want to recycle an old disk that was used on a non-IBM-compatible computer.
4. If the label on your 3.5 inch diskette says HD, what is its capacity?
   a. 360K
   b. 720K
   c. 1.2MB
   d. 1.44MB
5. The disk drive that is indicated by a rectangle on the drive ribbon is called the ______________ drive or the ______________ drive.
6. Refer to the File Manager window in Figure 2-30 on the following page. What is the name of each numbered window component?

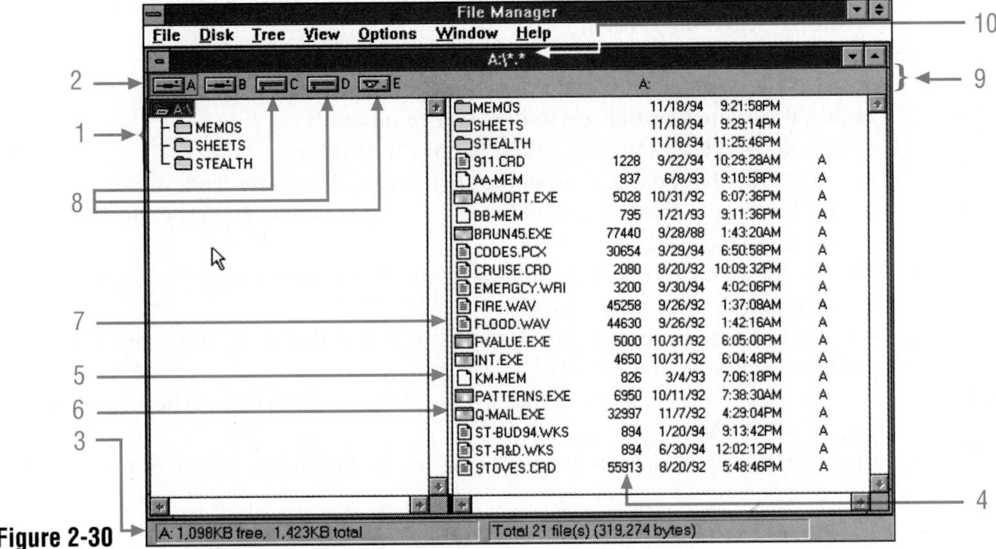

Figure 2-30

7. What is the directory that is automatically created when a disk is formatted?
8. What does a plus sign on a directory file folder icon indicate?
   a. The subdirectories are currently being displayed.
   b. The directory can be expanded.
   c. There are files in the directory.
   d. There are no subdirectories for this directory.
9. Indicate whether each of the following filenames is a valid or not valid Windows filename. If a filename is not valid, explain what is wrong.
   a. EOQ.WKS
   b. STATISTICS.WKS
   c. NUL.DOC
   d. VB-LET.DOC
   e. M
   f. M.M
   g. 92.BUD
   h. LET03/94
   i. CON.BMP
   d. Escape key

Tutorial Assignments

Launch Windows if necessary. Write your answers to Assignments 5, 6, 7, 8, 9, 11, 12, 13, and 14.

1. Move the two Microsoft Works spreadsheet files (.WKS extension) from the root directory to the SHEETS directory of your Student Disk.
2. You have a memo called BB-MEM that is about project Stealth. Now you need to change the filename to reflect the contents of the memo.
   a. Change the name to ST-BBMEM.
   b. Move ST-BBMEM into the MEMOS directory.
3. Create a directory called STEALTH under the root directory of your Student Disk. After you do this, your directory tree should look like Figure 2-30.
4. Now consolidate all the Stealth files.
   a. Move the file ST-BBMEM from the MEMOS directory to the STEALTH directory.

b. Move the files ST-BUD94.WKS and ST-R&D.WKS from the SHEETS directory to the STEALTH directory.

5. After doing Assignment 4, draw a diagram of your directory tree.
6. Make a list of the files that you now have in the MEMOS directory.
7. Make a list of the files that are in the SHEETS directory.
8. Make a list of the files that are in the STEALTH directory.
9. Describe what happens if you double-click the A:\ file folder icon.
10. **E** Click to open the View menu and make sure the All File Details command has a check mark next to it.
11. **E** Use the View menu to sort the files by date. What is the oldest file on your disk? (Be sure to look at all directories!)
12. **E** Use the View menu to sort the files by type. Using this view, name the last file in your root directory contents list.
13. **E** Use the View menu to sort the files by size. What is the name of the largest file on your Student Disk?
14. **E** Change the current drive to C:, or, if you are on a network, to one of the network drives.
    a. Draw a diagram of the directory tree for this disk.
    b. List the filename of any files with .SYS, .COM, or .BAT extensions in the root directory of this disk.
    c. Look at the file icons in the contents list of the root directory. How many of the files are program files? Document files? Miscellaneous data files?
    d. Review the file organization tips that were in the article Ruth read. Write a short paragraph evaluating the organizational structure of your hard disk or network drive.

Windows Tutorials Index

M

O

P

R

S

T

U

V

W

TASK REFERENCE

BRIEF MICROSOFT WINDOWS 3.1

Italicized page numbers indicate the first discussion of each task.

TASK	MOUSE	MENU	KEYBOARD
GENERAL / PROGRAM MANAGER			
Change dimensions of a window *WIN 15*	Drag border or corner	Click [Control-menu box], Size	Alt spacebar, S
Click *WIN 7*	Press mouse button, then release it		
Close a window *WIN 18*	Double-click [Control-menu box]	Click [Control-menu box], Close	Alt spacebar, C or Alt F4
Double-click *WIN 8*	Click left mouse button twice		
Drag *WIN 9*	Hold left mouse button down while moving mouse		
Exit Windows *WIN 33*	Double-click Program Manager [Control-menu box], click OK	Click Program Manager [Control-menu box], Close, OK	Alt spacebar, C, Enter, or Alt F4, Enter
Help *WIN 30*		Click Help	F1 or Alt H
Launch Windows *WIN 4*			Type win and press Enter
Maximize a window *WIN 14*	Click [Maximize button]	Click [Control-menu box], Maximize	Alt spacebar, X
Minimize a window *WIN 14*	Click [Minimize button]	Click [Control-menu box], Minimize	Alt spacebar, N
Open a group window *WIN 10*	Double-click group icon	Click icon, click Restore	Ctrl F6 to group icon, Enter
Restore a window *WIN 14*	Click [Restore button]	Click [Control-menu box], Restore	Alt spacebar, R
Switch applications *WIN 16*		Click [Control-menu box], Switch To...	Alt Tab or Ctrl Esc
Switch documents *WIN 28*	Click the document	Click Window, click name of document	Alt W, press number of document

TASK REFERENCE

BRIEF MICROSOFT WINDOWS 3.1

Italicized page numbers indicate the first discussion of each task.

TASK	MOUSE	MENU	KEYBOARD
FILE MANAGER			
Change current/default drive *WIN 45*	Click [drive icon] on drive icon ribbon	Click Disk, Select Drive...	Alt D, S or Ctrl [drive letter]
Change current/default directory *WIN 50*	Click [folder icon]		Press arrow key to directory
Collapse a directory *WIN 50*	Double-click [folder icon]	Click Tree, Collapse Branch	-
Copy a file *WIN 58*	Hold Ctrl down as you drag the file	Click the filename, click File, Copy	F8
Create a directory *WIN 48*		Click File, Create Directory	Alt F, E
Delete a file *WIN 56*		Click the filename, click File, Delete	Click the filename, press Del, Enter
Diskette copy/backup *WIN 61*		Click Disk, Copy Disk...	Alt D, C
Exit File Manager *WIN 62*	Double-click File Manager [Control menu box]	Click [Control menu box], Close	Alt F4
Expand a directory *WIN 50*	Double-click [folder icon]	Click Tree, Expand Branch	*
Format a diskette *WIN 41*		Click Disk, Format Disk...	Alt D, F
Launch File Manager *WIN 38*	Double-click File Manager	Press arrow key to File Manager then click File, Open	Press arrow key to File Manager then press Enter
Make Student Diskette *WIN 43*	Double-click Make Win 3.1 Student Diskette	Press arrow key to Make Win 3.1 Student Diskette then click File, Open	Press arrow key to Make Win 3.1 Student Diskette then press Enter
Move a file *WIN 52*	Drag file to new directory	Click File, Move	F7
Rename a file *WIN 55*		Click File, Rename	Alt F, N
Select multiple files *WIN 53*	Hold Ctrl down and click filenames	Click File, Select Files...	Alt F, S

TASK REFERENCE

BRIEF MICROSOFT WINDOWS 3.1

Italicized page numbers indicate the first discussion of each task.

TASK	MOUSE	MENU	KEYBOARD
APPLICATIONS			
Exit application *WIN 33*	Double-click application ▬	Click ▬, Close	Alt F4
Launch application *WIN 10*	Double-click application icon	Press arrow key to icon, click File, Open	Press arrow key to icon, Enter

Introduction to Microsoft® Office Professional for Windows 3.1 Tutorials

T U T O R I A L

Introducing Microsoft Office Professional

Streamlining Computer Tasks by Sharing Data

OBJECTIVES

In this tutorial you will:

- Learn what Microsoft Office is and why it is a powerful tool
- Launch Microsoft Office Manager and customize the Office Manager toolbar
- Use the Microsoft Office Manager toolbar to launch, close, and switch applications
- Get Help with Microsoft Office Manager
- Understand the benefits of integrating data among different applications

CASE

Pet Provisions Pet Provisions, started by Manny Cordova in 1991, sells pet food and pet supplies to pet shops around the world. Manny has recently authorized the company's computer analyst, Tami Wells, to purchase and learn Microsoft Office Professional so that the company can more easily maintain and share company data. He asks her to prepare and then present a company-wide training seminar that demonstrates the potential of Microsoft Office to Pet Provisions employees, many of whom are already familiar with Microsoft applications, but none of whom have seen the power of Microsoft Office.

Understanding Microsoft Office

Microsoft Office Professional is a collection of the most popular Microsoft software applications: Word, Excel, Access, and PowerPoint. Microsoft Office is available in two editions: Professional and Standard. Office Professional contains Access, the database application; Office Standard does not. This book assumes you are using Office Professional.

The Office applications are designed to share many features in common, so that once you've learned one, it's easy to learn the others. Further, because these applications are housed and managed under Office, this connection also offers unprecedented data-sharing capabilities, as shown in Figure 1. You can easily access and integrate the same data in all four applications, which will save time and ensure consistent information. In this book, you have the opportunity to learn each Office application, one at a time. The final tutorial of the book, "Integrating Microsoft Office Applications," gives you hands-on experience sharing data among Office applications.

Each Office application provides you with valuable tools to accomplish many tasks, such as writing reports and analyzing data, much more easily and efficiently than if you did these tasks by hand. Using these applications will save you time and allow you to do more professional-looking work. Let's take a quick look now at each of these Office applications.

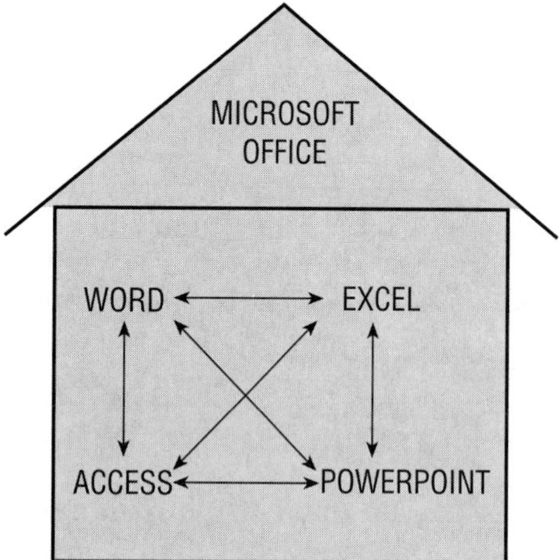

Figure 1
Office and its major applications

Microsoft Word is a word processing application that you use to create text documents. Word offers many special features that help you write and update memos, letters, newsletters, forms, and many other specialized documents—all in an attractive and readable format. You can also create, insert, and position graphics, tables, and other useful objects that enhance your documents. Pet Provisions uses Word to create documents like the business letter shown in Figure 2.

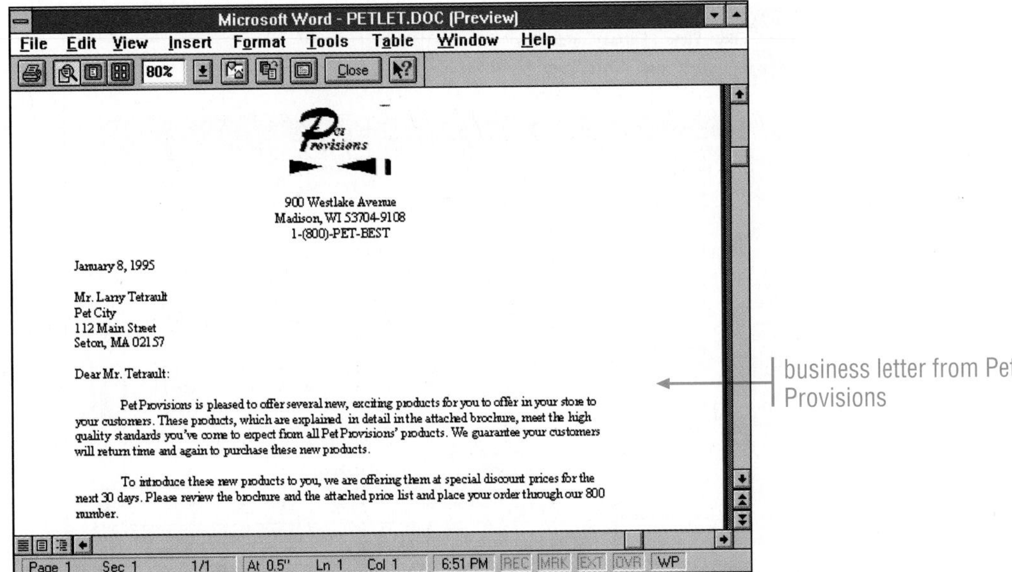

Figure 2
Microsoft Word document

Microsoft Excel is a spreadsheet application that you use to analyze and display numerical information. You can perform calculations easily in Excel. Excel's outstanding graphics capabilities let you visually display your data through, for example, pie charts and bar graphs, to help readers quickly see the significance of the information and the relationships within it. Pet Provisions uses Excel to create spreadsheets like the financial summary spreadsheet shown in Figure 3.

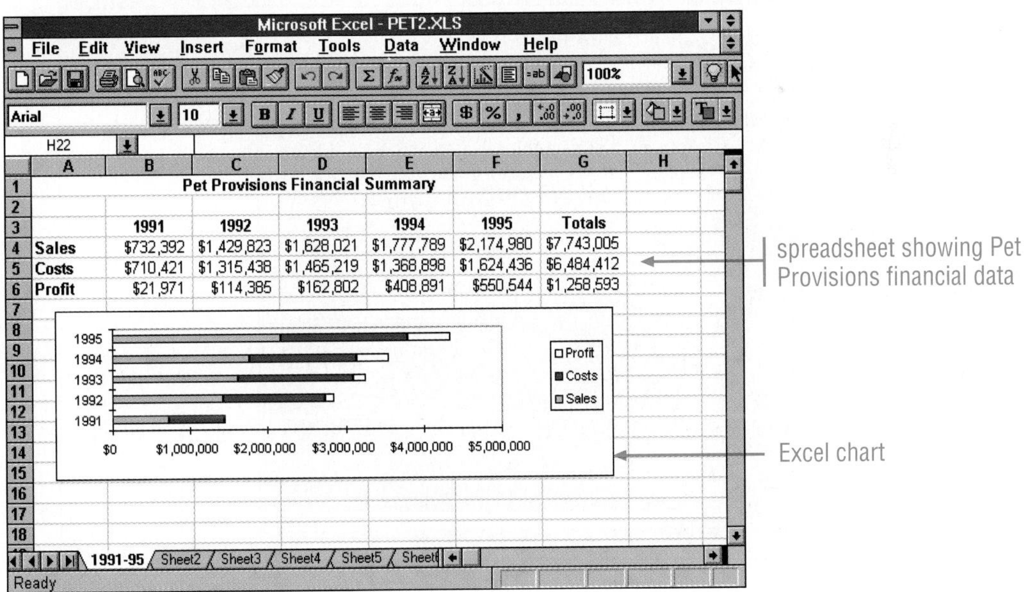

Figure 3
Microsoft Excel spreadsheet

Microsoft Access is a database application that you use to enter, maintain, and retrieve related information. You can create your own entry forms to make data entry easier, change how you organize and retrieve information to fit your needs, and create professional-looking reports to improve the readability of your data. Pet Provisions uses Access to create databases like the client database shown in Figure 4.

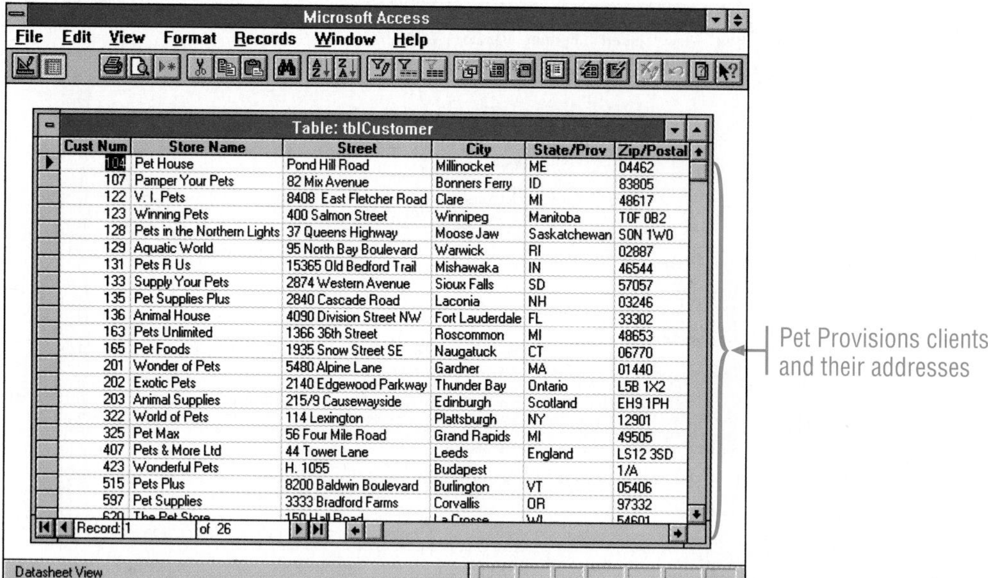

Cust Num	Store Name	Street	City	State/Prov	Zip/Postal
104	Pet House	Pond Hill Road	Millinocket	ME	04462
107	Pamper Your Pets	82 Mix Avenue	Bonners Ferry	ID	83805
122	V. I. Pets	8408 East Fletcher Road	Clare	MI	48617
123	Winning Pets	400 Salmon Street	Winnipeg	Manitoba	T0F 0B2
128	Pets in the Northern Lights	37 Queens Highway	Moose Jaw	Saskatchewan	S0N 1W0
129	Aquatic World	95 North Bay Boulevard	Warwick	RI	02887
131	Pets R Us	15365 Old Bedford Trail	Mishawaka	IN	46544
133	Supply Your Pets	2874 Western Avenue	Sioux Falls	SD	57057
135	Pet Supplies Plus	2840 Cascade Road	Laconia	NH	03246
136	Animal House	4090 Division Street NW	Fort Lauderdale	FL	33302
163	Pets Unlimited	1366 36th Street	Roscommon	MI	48653
165	Pet Foods	1935 Snow Street SE	Naugatuck	CT	06770
201	Wonder of Pets	5480 Alpine Lane	Gardner	MA	01440
202	Exotic Pets	2140 Edgewood Parkway	Thunder Bay	Ontario	L5B 1X2
203	Animal Supplies	215/9 Causewayside	Edinburgh	Scotland	EH9 1PH
322	World of Pets	114 Lexington	Plattsburgh	NY	12901
325	Pet Max	56 Four Mile Road	Grand Rapids	MI	49505
407	Pets & More Ltd	44 Tower Lane	Leeds	England	LS12 3SD
423	Wonderful Pets	H. 1055	Budapest		1/A
515	Pets Plus	8200 Baldwin Boulevard	Burlington	VT	05406
597	Pet Supplies	3333 Bradford Farms	Corvallis	OR	97332

Figure 4
Microsoft Access database

Microsoft PowerPoint is a presentation graphics application that you use to create professional-looking and effective presentations, which you can show either on your computer screen or project onto a screen as a slide show. You can also generate audience handouts, outlines, and speakers' notes. Pet Provisions uses PowerPoint to create slide presentations like the one shown in Figure 5.

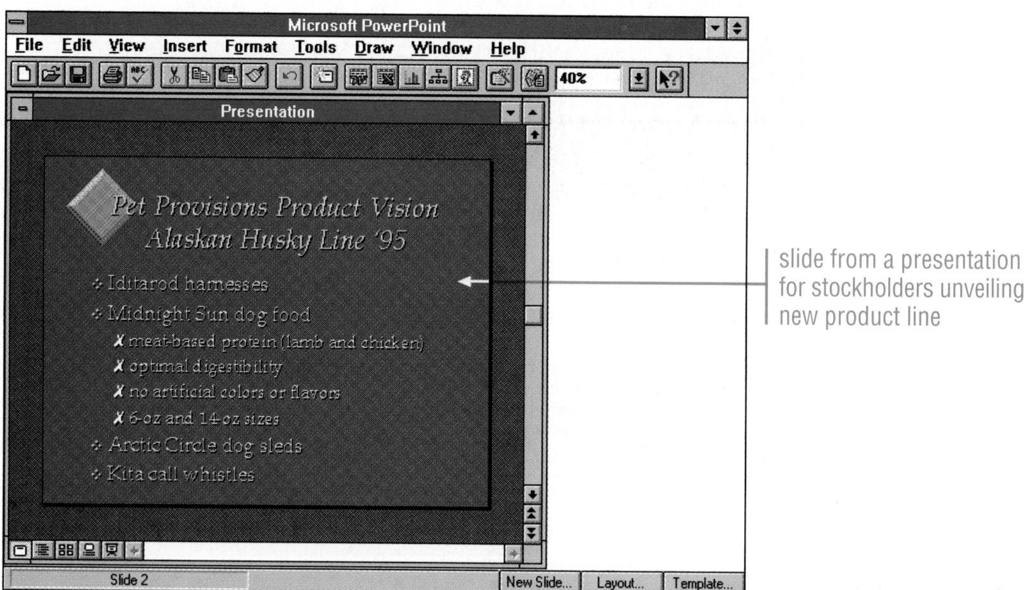

Figure 5
Microsoft PowerPoint slide

Office offers a number of additional tools that you can use within these four applications to create special objects. Figure 6 describes the five primary Office tools, accompanied by an example that Pet Provisions might use.

Office Tool	Example
ClipArt Gallery organizes your clip art conveniently, giving you easy access to the images you need to make your documents interesting. Clip art images are familiar (and fun) illustrations that you can insert into your documents in any size you choose. Office comes with a collection of over 1,000 pieces of clip art. You can also add your own clip art to the Gallery. Pet Provisions might use ClipArt Gallery to create a logo.	 Pet Provisions
Organization Chart lets you create a flowchart showing, for example, the personnel and reporting structure at Pet Provisions.	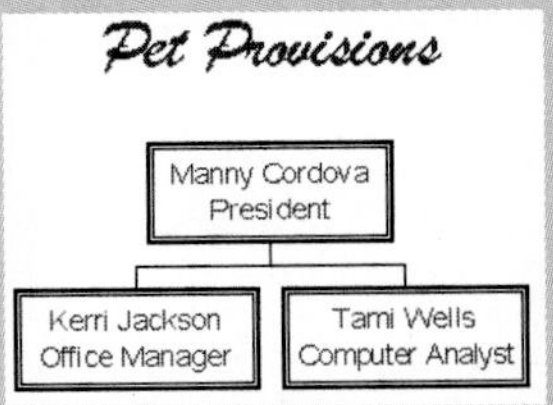 Pet Provisions Manny Cordova President Kerri Jackson Office Manager Tami Wells Computer Analyst
Equation Editor lets you add mathematical symbols and complex equations to a document. The investment officer at Pet Provisions might add an equation like this one to a document about investment maturities.	$\text{Received} = \dfrac{\text{Investment}}{1 - \left(\text{Discount} \times \dfrac{\text{DIM}}{\text{B}}\right)}$
WordArt lets you display and shape text using a variety of special visual effects. You can enhance your text by applying interesting combinations of shading, color, dimension, and rotation. Pet Provisions might use WordArt to design a trademarked company name.	 Pet Provisions
Graph lets you insert charts based on tabular data in a variety of visual displays, like this bar chart showing order status at Pet Provisions.	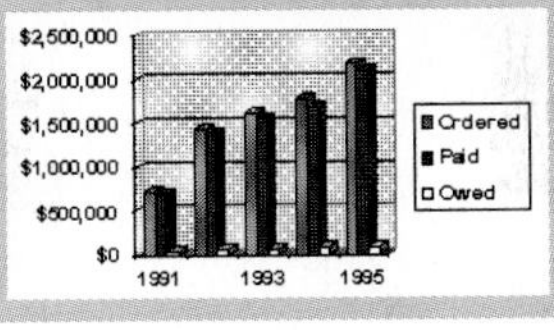 $2,500,000; $2,000,000; $1,500,000; $1,000,000; $500,000; $0 1991 1993 1995 Ordered, Paid, Owed

Figure 6
Office tools

In addition to these helpful tools, Office also includes additional independent applications such as Media Player, PowerPoint Viewer, and Find File, which you may find useful in certain circumstances. Office also includes a license for Microsoft Mail, which entitles you to install and use Microsoft's electronic mail system (which you must order separately). A final Office application is **Microsoft Office Manager**, which lets you quickly launch and navigate applications with a single mouse click. Because this is such an important and time-saving application, let's take a closer look at how Office Manager can make many of your tasks easier and more efficient.

Launching Office Manager

Upon receiving the Office package at Pet Provisions, Tami is eager to start preparing her presentation on the power of Office and its many features. She installs Office and immediately notices that an unfamiliar toolbar now appears at the top of her screen, as shown in Figure 7.

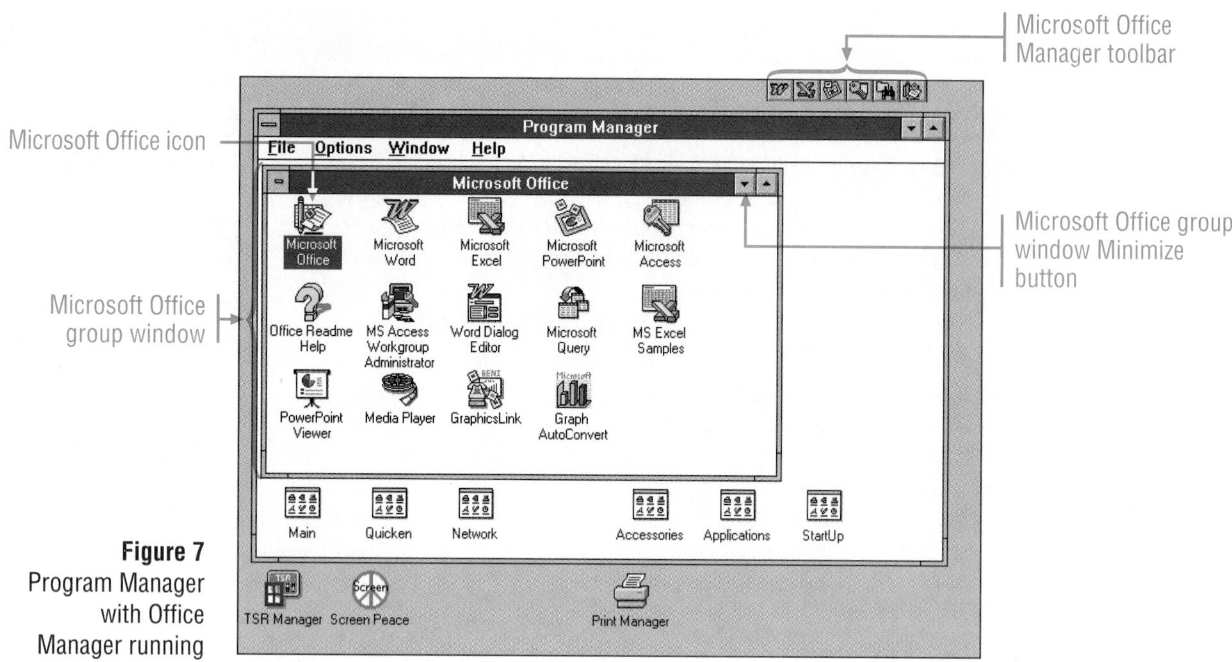

Figure 7
Program Manager with Office Manager running

Tami realizes as she looks over the Office manual that the new toolbar at the top of her screen is the Office Manager toolbar. Office Manager is therefore already running on her computer, and she can get started immediately.

If your computer does not display the toolbar shown in Figure 7 (or one similar to it), either at the upper-right corner of your screen or on top of an active title bar, Office Manager is probably not running. You will need to launch it before you proceed.

To launch Office Manager:

1. Launch Windows and make sure the Program Manager is open.
2. Look for an icon labeled "Microsoft Office" or a window labeled "Microsoft Office" as shown in Figure 7.

   TROUBLE? If you cannot find anything labeled "Microsoft Office," click Window in the Program Manager menu bar, then click Microsoft Office in the menu that opens. If you still can't find anything labeled "Microsoft Office," ask your instructor or technical support person for assistance. If you are using your own computer, make sure you have installed the Office Manager software.
3. If you see an icon labeled "Microsoft Office," double-click it to open the Microsoft Office group window. If the Microsoft Office group window is already open, go to Step 4.
4. Double-click the **Microsoft Office icon** in the Microsoft Office group window.

   The Microsoft Office copyright information appears briefly. When the Office Manager launch is complete, your screen should look similar to Figure 7.
5. Click the **Microsoft Office group window Minimize button**.

   TROUBLE? Don't worry if your screen doesn't look exactly like Figure 7. Your Program Manager window might be maximized and the toolbar might be in the title bar.

The Office Manager Toolbar

After you launch Office Manager, the Office Manager toolbar appears on the screen. The **Office Manager toolbar** has buttons for the four major Office applications: Word, Excel, PowerPoint, and Access (Figure 8). Clicking one of these toolbar buttons quickly launches that application or, if the application is already open, immediately switches to that application. Buttons might also appear for other applications. For example, in Figure 8, there are buttons for Find File and for Microsoft Office.

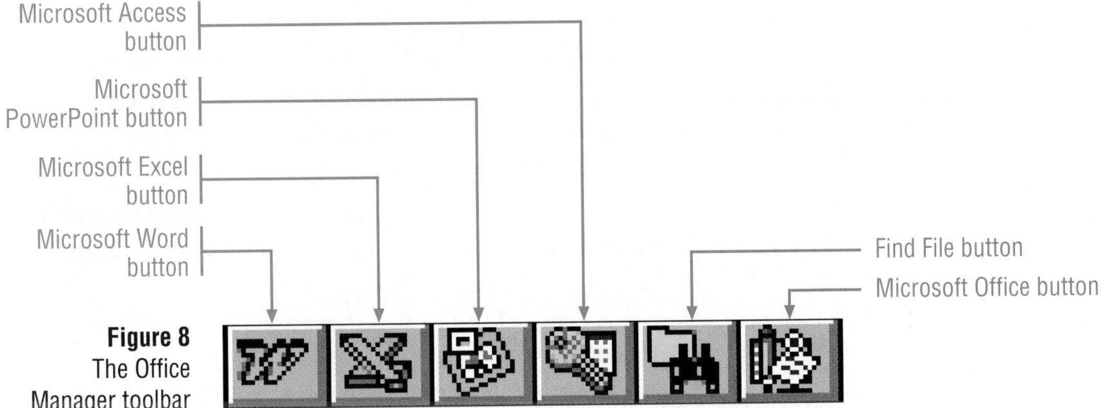

Figure 8 The Office Manager toolbar

Office Manager offers three different toolbar button sizes: small (Figure 8), regular, and large. The regular and large buttons are easier to read, and the toolbar with these buttons can be positioned anywhere on the screen. When the toolbar has small buttons, it resides either on the right side of the title bar of a maximized application window or on the upper-right edge of the screen, as shown in Figure 7. This toolbar position blocks very little of the screen, and **ToolTips** (yellow flags that appear when you leave the mouse pointer on the button for a few seconds) clearly identify the buttons, so you might prefer to display your Office Manager toolbar buttons in their smallest size.

Tami experiments with the button size on the Office Manager toolbar.

To change the Office Manager toolbar button size:

1. Click the **Microsoft Office button** on the Office Manager toolbar, click **Customize...**, then click the **View tab** in the Customize dialog box.
2. Click the **Large Buttons radio button**, then click the **OK button**. Office Manager replaces the small buttons on the toolbar with large buttons and repositions the toolbar.
3. Click , click **Customize...**, click the **Small Buttons radio button**, then click the **OK button**. Office Manager changes back to small buttons and positions the toolbar at the top of the screen.

Launching and Switching Between Applications

You can launch an application by clicking its Office Manager toolbar button. The application opens in a matter of seconds. If you launch two or more applications, you can quickly switch from one to another by clicking the second application's Office Manager toolbar button—another time-saving device. Alternatively, you can launch an application or switch to an open application by clicking the Microsoft Office button on the Office Manager toolbar and then clicking the application's name on the menu.

Tami starts Word, starts Excel, switches back to Word, and then starts File Manager.

To launch Word, Excel, and File Manager, and switch between the applications:

1. Click the **Microsoft Word button** on the Office Manager toolbar to start Word, then click the **Microsoft Word window Maximize button** if the window is not already maximized. The Office Manager toolbar now appears in the Word title bar.
2. Click the **Microsoft Excel button** on the Office Manager toolbar to start Excel. Since Excel is now the active application, the Office Manager toolbar appears in the Excel title bar.

   TROUBLE? If a Quick Preview screen appears when you start Excel, click the Return to Microsoft Excel button in the lower-right corner of the screen.

   Word is still running in the background. Try switching back to Word.
3. Click again to switch to Word from Excel.
4. Click the **Microsoft Office button** on the Office Manager toolbar, then click **File Manager** in the list. The File Manager window opens, while Word and Excel continue running in the background.

Customizing the Office Manager Toolbar

Because the Office Manager toolbar buttons are such an easy, efficient way to do many operations, you might want to add buttons to the Office Manager toolbar to launch other applications. You can also rearrange and delete buttons on the toolbar. To experiment with Office Manager further, Tami adds a button to the Office Manager toolbar for the Calculator accessory (an application that comes with Windows and is usually found in the Accessories group window), rearranges its placement on the toolbar, and then deletes the button.

To add the Calculator button to the Office Manager toolbar:

1. Click the **Microsoft Office button** on the Office Manager toolbar, click **Customize...**, click the **Toolbar tab**, scroll the list box, then click the **Calculator check box** to place an X in the check box. See Figure 9. Your Customize dialog box might look different if you have other applications selected.

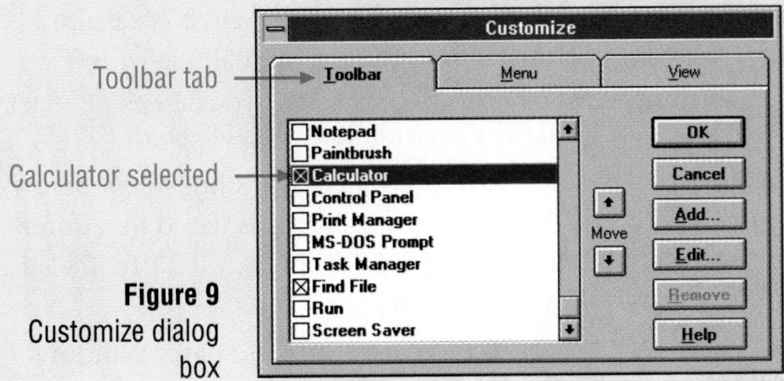

Figure 9
Customize dialog box

TROUBLE? If your Calculator check box is already selected, an icon for Calculator already appears in your Office Manager toolbar. Leave it selected, and continue with Step 2.

2. Click the **OK button**. Office Manager adds the Calculator button to the Office Manager toolbar.

3. Click the **Calculator button** on the Office Manager toolbar to open the Calculator window. See Figure 10. The size and placement of the Calculator and File Manager windows on your screen might differ from Figure 10, and the File Manager window might display different drives and directories.

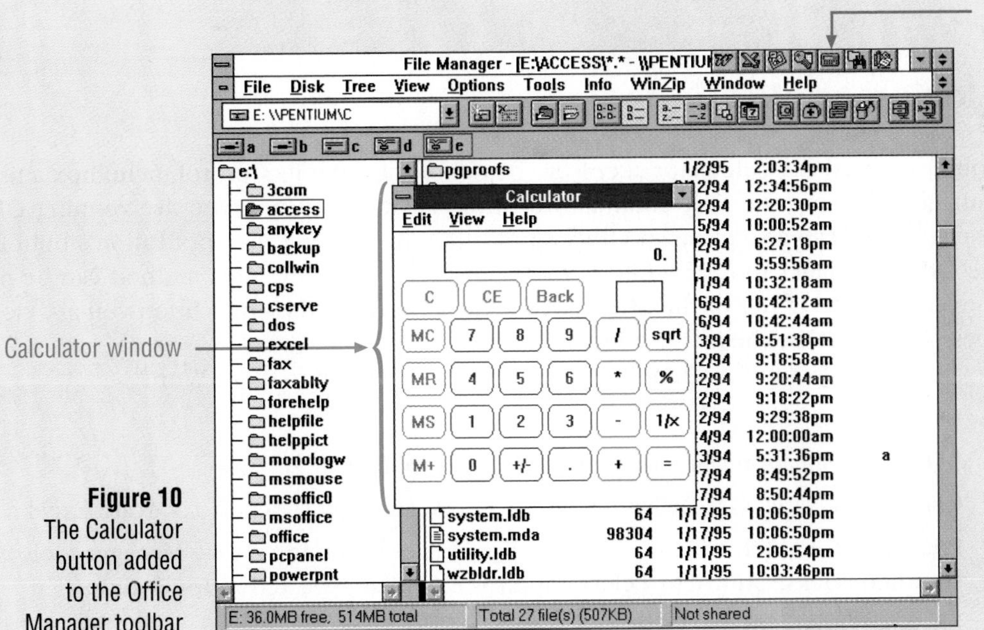

Figure 10
The Calculator button added to the Office Manager toolbar

Now Tami tries moving the Calculator button so that it is to the immediate right of the Find File button, and then she continues to experiment with the Office Manager toolbar by removing the Calculator button.

To move the Calculator button:

1. Click the **Microsoft Office button** on the Office Manager toolbar, click **Customize...**, scroll the list box, then click the name **Calculator** to highlight the calculator line.

   TROUBLE? If you click the Calculator check box instead of the name, you deselect it. Click the check box again to be sure it is selected and the Calculator line is highlighted.
2. Click the **Move down arrow button** five times to move the Calculator check box below Find File in the list box. Your list box might have the applications listed in a different order, so you might need to click a different number of times. Click the **OK button**. The Calculator button moves to the right of the Find File button.
3. Double-click the **Calculator window Control menu box** to close the Calculator window and exit the Calculator application. Now Tami removes the Calculator button from the toolbar.
4. Click , click **Customize...**, scroll the list box, then click the **Calculator check box** to highlight the line and remove the X from the check box.
5. Click the **Move up arrow button** five times to move the Calculator check box back to its initial position in the list box, then click the **OK button**. Office Manager removes the Calculator button from the toolbar. File Manager is active, while Word and Excel run in the background.
6. Click **File** on the File Manager menu bar, then click **Exit** to close File Manager.

Closing Applications

You just closed the Calculator accessory by double-clicking its Control menu box and File Manager by using the Exit command on the File menu. When you are running Office Manager, you can also close an Office application by clicking the application's button on the Office Manager toolbar while holding down the [Alt] key. This method can be more convenient than either of the other two methods because the application you are closing does not have to be the active window.

Tami switches to Excel and then uses this new method to close Word.

To close an application using the Office Manager toolbar:

1. Click the **Microsoft Excel button** on the Office Manager toolbar to activate Excel.
2. Press and hold **[Alt]**, click the **Microsoft Word button** on the Office Manager toolbar, and then release **[Alt]**. Word closes and Excel remains the active application.
3. Press and hold **[Alt]**, click , then release **[Alt]**. Excel closes and returns you to Program Manager.

The tutorials that follow on Word, Excel, Access, and PowerPoint assume Office Manager is not launched, so the Office Manager toolbar does not appear in the figures, and the steps do not suggest using the toolbar as a method of navigating the applications. However, if you keep Office Manager running on your computer, consider using the toolbar to launch, navigate, and close applications whenever necessary. It will speed up your work.

Getting Help

Like the other Microsoft applications, Microsoft Office comes with an on-line Help system. Tami decides to browse through the Help system to see what other Office features she might want to use.

To get help with Microsoft Office:

❶ Click the **Microsoft Office button** on the Office Manager toolbar.

❷ Click **Help...**. The Microsoft Office Help Contents window opens. See Figure 11.

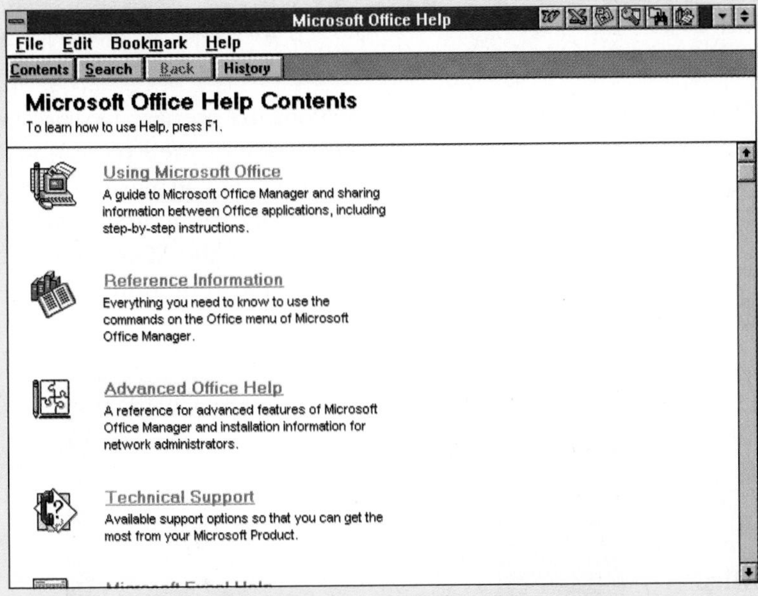

Figure 11
Microsoft Office Help Contents window

❸ Scroll down the Microsoft Office Help Contents window to view the topics available. Tami sees that from this Help window, not only can she get help on Office features, but she can also access the individual Office applications' on-line Help.

❹ Click **File** on Help window menu bar, then click **Exit**. You are back in Program Manager.

Integrating Applications

Tami is already familiar with the four main Office applications—Word, Excel, Access, and PowerPoint—and now that she feels comfortable navigating Office using the toolbar, she begins experimenting with the data-sharing capabilities that Office offers. She can imagine many circumstances in which Pet Provisions would find data sharing useful. For example:

- When preparing a quarterly financial report for stockholders in Word, the Pet Provisions managers can easily insert a table showing profits directly from the Excel spreadsheet that contains the data.
- When the Personnel Department is preparing a slide show in PowerPoint to show to employee recruits, they can insert text from a company handbook prepared in Word that describes the company's profit-sharing plan.
- When creating a mailing promoting a new product to Pet Provisions customers, the Marketing Department can prepare the letter in Word and then use an Access database as the source of the client addresses.

These are all examples of how Office lets you access information from one application and integrate it into another. Integrating information with Office ensures consistent information and saves time because you don't have to re-enter information.

■ ■ ■

Tami, in the meantime, uses PowerPoint to prepare her presentation on how Office will help Pet Provisions improve the efficiency of their operations. Figure 12 shows one of the slides she creates that illustrates how Pet Provisions can create a document in Word and insert a logo from a graphics application called Paintbrush, an address from Access, and a graph from Excel. She integrates the Word document into a PowerPoint Slide that she will show to her colleagues to illustrate how Office can help Pet Provisions operate more effectively.

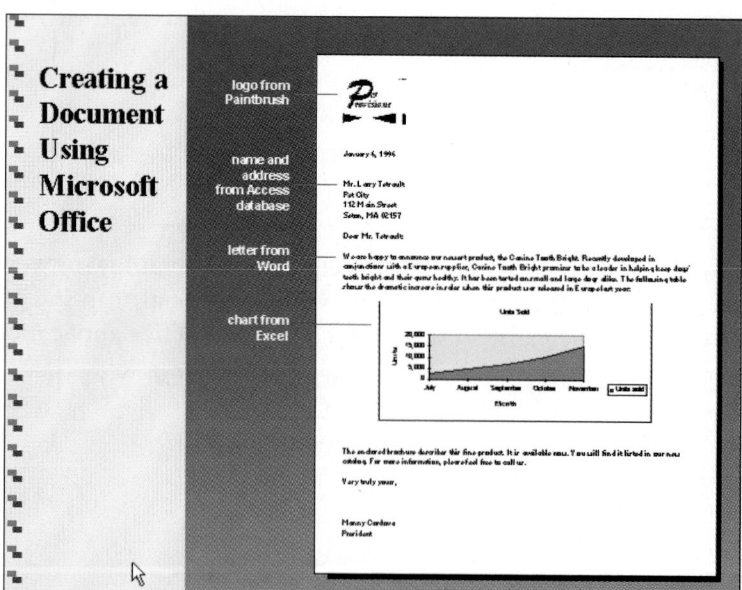

Figure 12 PowerPoint slide showing application integration

You will have an opportunity to learn more about integrating data from one application into another in the "Integrating Microsoft Office Applications" tutorial, after you have learned more about the individual applications themselves.

Questions

1. What are two advantages of using a software package like Microsoft Office?

Match the following software applications to their descriptions.

2. Word — a. Enters, maintains, and retrieves information
3. Excel — b. Analyzes and displays data
4. Access — c. Creates effective presentations
5. PowerPoint — d. Creates a variety of text documents

6. Do you have to have Office Manager running to run Office applications?
7. Under what circumstances does the Office Manager toolbar appear in an application's title bar?
8. If Office Manager isn't running, how do you start it?
9. What are three ways to exit an application if you have Office Manager running?
10. Can you move the Office Manager toolbar when the buttons are set at the small size?
11. If you click the Microsoft Word button on the Office Manager toolbar and Word is not running, what happens?
12. If you click the Microsoft Excel button on the Office Manager toolbar and Excel is running, what happens?
13. **E** Imagine a company that installs swimming pools in the backyards of homeowners. Can you think of three occasions when they might find the integration capabilities of Office useful?

Tutorial Assignments

1. Launch Microsoft Office Manager if it isn't already launched.
2. Change the Office Manager toolbar button size to Regular.
   a. Click the Microsoft Office button on the Office Manager toolbar, then click Customize.
   b. Click the View tab, click the Regular Buttons radio button, then click the OK button.
   c. Drag the Microsoft Office Manager toolbar to the bottom center of your screen.
3. Launch Access by clicking the Microsoft Access button on the Office Manager toolbar (if necessary throughout these steps, activate the Microsoft Office Manager toolbar first by clicking its title bar).
4. Add a button for the Paintbrush accessory that comes with Microsoft Windows to the Office Manager Toolbar.
   a. Click the Microsoft Office button on the Office Manager toolbar, click Customize, then click the Toolbar tab.
   b. Scroll the list box, click the Paintbrush check box to select it, then click the OK button.
   c. Launch Paintbrush by clicking the Paintbrush button you just added.
5. Exit Access by pressing and holding down [Alt] while you click the Microsoft Access button on the Office Manager toolbar, then exit Paintbrush in the same way.

6. Learn more about Office Manager by using the on-line Help system, then printing a Help topic for future reference.
   a. Click the Microsoft Office button on the Office Manager toolbar, then click Help....
   b. Click the first topic, "Using Microsoft Office."
   c. Click the first topic in the Using Microsoft Office window, "Starting Applications and Working with Application Windows."
   d. Click File on the Microsoft Office Help menu bar, then click Print Topic. You now have a printout of how to work with Office applications that you can turn in to your instructor.
   e. Click File on the Microsoft Office Help menu bar, then click Exit.
7. Change the size of the Office Manager toolbar buttons back to Small.
   a. Click the Microsoft Office button on the Office Manager toolbar, then click Customize.
   b. Click the View tab, click the Small Button radio button, then click the OK button.
   c. Exit Office Manager by clicking the Microsoft Office button, then clicking Exit.

Index

Introductory Microsoft® Word 6.0 for Windows™ Tutorials

1 Creating, Editing, Formatting, and Printing a Document

2 Using Page, Paragraph, and Font Formatting Commands

3 Creating a Multiple-Page Document with Tables

4 Creating Reports

Read This Before You Begin

To the Student

To use this book, you must have a Student Disk. Your instructor will either provide you with one or ask you to make your own by following the instructions in the section "Your Student Disk" in Tutorial 1. See your instructor or technical support person for further information. If you are going to work through this book using your own computer, you need a computer system running Microsoft Windows 3.1, Microsoft Word 6.0 for Windows, and a Student Disk. *You will not be able to complete the tutorials and exercises in this book using your own computer until you have a Student Disk.*

Any references to "this book" or to a tutorial (such as "Tutorial 1") refer to the Microsoft Word 6.0 tutorials of *this* Microsoft Office Professional book.

To the Instructor

Making the Student Disk To complete the tutorials in this book, your students must have a copy of the Student Disk. To relieve you of having to make multiple Student Disks from a single master copy, we provide you with the CTI WinApps Setup Disk, which contains an automatic Student Disk generating program. Once you install the Setup Disk on a network or standalone workstation, students can easily make their own Student Disks by double-clicking the "Make Word 6.0 Office Student Disk" icon in the CTI WinApps icon group. Double-clicking this icon transfers all the data files students need to complete the tutorials, Tutorial Assignments, and Case Problems to a high-density disk in drive A or B. If some of your students will use their own computers to complete the tutorials and exercises in this book, they must first get the Student Disk. The section called "Your Student Disk" in Tutorial 1 provides complete instructions on how to make the Student Disk.

Installing the CTI WinApps Setup Disk To install the CTI WinApps icon group from the Setup Disk, follow the instructions on the Setup Disk label. By adopting this book, you are granted a license to install this software on any computer or computer network used by you or your students.

README File A README.TXT file located on the Setup Disk provides complete installation instructions, additional technical notes, troubleshooting advice, and tips for using the CTI WinApps software in your school's computer lab. You can view the README.TXT file using any word processor you choose.

System Requirements

The minimum software and hardware requirements for your computer system are as follows:

- Microsoft Windows version 3.1 or later on a local hard drive or a network drive.
- A 386 or higher processor with a minimum of 4 MB of RAM (6 MB or more is strongly recommended).
- A mouse supported by Windows 3.1.
- A printer supported by Windows 3.1.
- A VGA 640 x 480 16-color display is recommended; an 800 x 600 or 1024 x 768 SVGA, VGA monochrome, or EGA display is also acceptable.
- 20 MB of free hard disk space.
- Student workstations with at least 1 high-density disk drive.
- If you want to install the CTI WinApps Setup Disk on a network drive, your network must support Microsoft Windows.

TUTORIAL 1

Creating, Editing, Formatting, and Printing a Document

Requesting Information from a Supply Source

OBJECTIVES

In this tutorial you will:

- Start and exit Word 6.0 for Windows
- Identify the elements of the Word screen
- Move the insertion point
- Insert and delete text
- Spell check a document
- Select text
- Bold, italicize, and underline text
- Create bulleted lists
- Open, save, and close a document
- Use Word Help
- Print a document and an envelope

Sweet T's, Inc. Denise Hill is assistant director of Research and Development for Sweet T's, Inc. Sweet T's owns and operates seven Sweet Tooth Cafe restaurants in Oklahoma and northern Texas. It has also sold franchises of the Sweet Tooth Cafe to individual licensees who operate another 13 restaurants throughout the southeastern United States. The Sweet Tooth Cafe is known for food that is moderately priced and served in a casual, family dining atmosphere.

Denise works with a staff of three food specialists responsible for creating new menu items for the restaurants. She also has responsibility for finding suppliers for any specialty ingredients required in any menu item. The current supplier of the brownie in Sweet T's famous Deep Fried Brownie is about to go out of business, so Denise must locate a new supply source. Denise calls Doug Stone, a salesperson for a wholesale food distributor, who tells her about Ram Food Purveyors in Dallas, Texas. She decides to write to Ram to inquire if it can produce a brownie that meets Sweet T's specifications.

The technician from Sweet T's Information Services office has just installed Word 6.0 for Windows on Denise's computer. She has learned Windows 3.1 and is anxious to get started learning Word 6.0 for Windows.

In this tutorial you will complete Denise's task. You will also learn an efficient strategy for producing a document, and how to use the features of Word to facilitate the document production process.

Using the Productivity Strategy

A **document** is any written item, such as a letter, memo, or report. Word 6.0 for Windows is a word processing program that allows you to create, edit, format, and print documents. Your ultimate goal in using this powerful tool, however, is to increase your ability to complete high-quality work in a minimal amount of time. To do so, you also need to use a plan for producing your documents efficiently. The plan you will use throughout this book is known as the productivity strategy.

The **productivity strategy** calls for you to approach the production of each document in four separate phases: creating, editing, formatting, and printing. Furthermore, to ensure that you produce the document efficiently, you complete each phase in sequence rather than switching among the four phases.

Using this strategy, first you will create your document. **Creating** a document involves much more than typing text; it begins with planning what you want to communicate to your intended audience. Once you have planned your document, you are ready to enter text. In general, you should not make editing or formatting decisions as you are entering text. In the Sweet T's example, Denise knows that the purpose of her letter is to inquire whether Ram Food Purveyors can supply the right type of brownie. She also knows that she must provide the supplier with the specifications for the brownie and a deadline for receiving the bid proposal.

Editing is the process of inserting, deleting, and moving text. To maintain a high degree of efficiency during this phase of the productivity strategy, you make only editing changes. For example, Denise will read through her document, then insert and delete text to make it clearer. Next, she will spell check her document for spelling errors. Finally, she will proofread her document thoroughly to make sure she has found all her errors.

Next you focus on formatting your document. **Formatting** involves changing your document's appearance to make it more readable and attractive. Use of white space and boldfaced or italicized text and headings are examples of formatting options you can use to make your document easier to read and more appealing to the reader. For her letter, Denise decides to use the standard business format, which includes a date, inside address, salutation, complimentary closing, and writer's name and title. She intends to emphasize several words in the body of her letter, as well as draw attention to the specifications for the brownie.

Printing is the final phase of the productivity strategy. You need a hard copy of your document to give to your reader. You should preview your document, however, before you spend time and resources printing it. Denise intends to use the Word Print Preview feature before printing her document to check its overall appearance. She will then print her letter and an envelope.

Of course, nothing prevents you from retracing your steps. To maximize your efficiency, though, you should concentrate on completing each phase of the productivity strategy in sequence.

In this tutorial you will create the letter and accompanying envelope shown in Figure 1-1. Just as in a real work situation, your document will go through various stages of development before it reaches the final result you see in Figure 1-1. This tutorial also takes you through each phase of the productivity strategy, so that you will learn to use Word 6.0 for Windows to produce professional-looking documents as efficiently as possible.

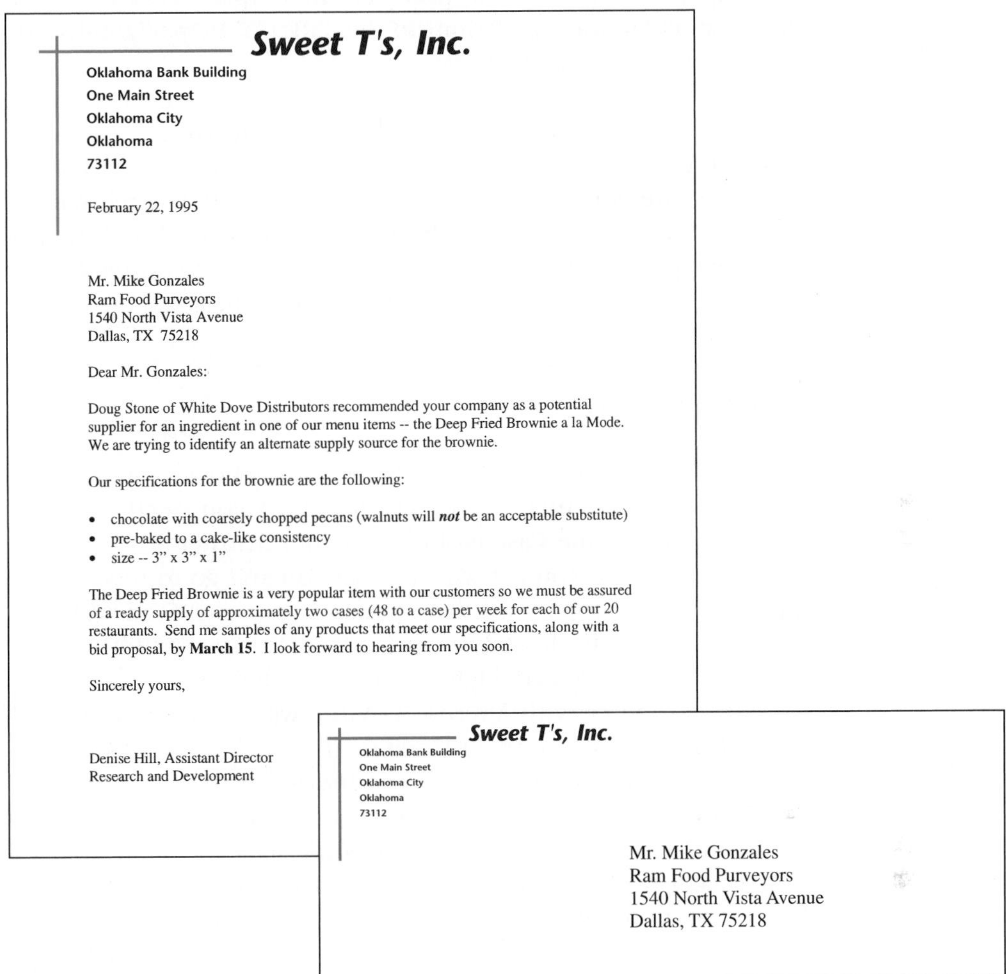

Sweet T's, Inc.

Oklahoma Bank Building
One Main Street
Oklahoma City
Oklahoma
73112

February 22, 1995

Mr. Mike Gonzales
Ram Food Purveyors
1540 North Vista Avenue
Dallas, TX 75218

Dear Mr. Gonzales:

Doug Stone of White Dove Distributors recommended your company as a potential supplier for an ingredient in one of our menu items -- the Deep Fried Brownie a la Mode. We are trying to identify an alternate supply source for the brownie.

Our specifications for the brownie are the following:

- chocolate with coarsely chopped pecans (walnuts will ***not*** be an acceptable substitute)
- pre-baked to a cake-like consistency
- size -- 3" x 3" x 1"

The Deep Fried Brownie is a very popular item with our customers so we must be assured of a ready supply of approximately two cases (48 to a case) per week for each of our 20 restaurants. Send me samples of any products that meet our specifications, along with a bid proposal, by **March 15**. I look forward to hearing from you soon.

Sincerely yours,

Denise Hill, Assistant Director
Research and Development

Sweet T's, Inc.

Oklahoma Bank Building
One Main Street
Oklahoma City
Oklahoma
73112

Mr. Mike Gonzales
Ram Food Purveyors
1540 North Vista Avenue
Dallas, TX 75218

Figure 1-1
Completed letter and envelope

Using the Tutorials Effectively

These tutorials will help you learn about Word 6.0 for Windows. These tutorials assume that you are familiar with the basics of Windows 3.1: how to control windows, how to choose menu commands, how to complete dialog boxes, and how to select directories, drives, and files. If you do not understand these concepts, please consult your instructor.

The tutorials are designed to be used in conjunction with your instructor's discussion of the concepts covered in the tutorials. Begin by reading the tutorial to be discussed by your instructor. After reading the tutorial and listening to your instructor's lecture, complete the numbered steps, which appear on a colored background, as you work at your computer. Read each step carefully and completely before you try it.

As you work, compare your screen with the figures in the tutorial to verify your results. It is relatively easy to change the appearance of Word's screen, so don't worry if parts of your screen are different from the figures. The important parts of the screen display are labeled in each figure. Just be sure these parts are on your screen. If you want to set up the basic Word screen used in this book, follow the procedures in the "Screen Check" section later in this tutorial.

Don't worry about making mistakes—that's part of the learning process. **TROUBLE?** paragraphs identify common problems and explain how to correct them or get back on track. Complete the suggestions in the **TROUBLE?** paragraphs *only* if you are having the specific problem described.

After you have completed a tutorial, you can do the Questions, Tutorial Assignments, and Case Problems found at the end of each tutorial. They are carefully structured so that you will review what you have learned and then apply your knowledge to new situations. When you are doing these exercises, refer to the Reference Window boxes. These boxes, which are found throughout the tutorials, provide short summaries of frequently used procedures. You can also use the Task Reference at the end of the book. It summarizes how to complete tasks using the mouse, the menus, and the keyboard.

Your Student Disk

To complete the tutorials and exercises in this book, you must have a Student Disk. The Student Disk contains all the practice files you need for the tutorials, the Tutorial Assignments, and the Case Problems. If your instructor or lab manager provides you with your Student Disk, you can skip this section and go to the next section entitled "Starting Word." If your instructor asks you to make your own Student Disk, you need to follow the steps in this section. To make your Student Disk, you need:

- A blank, formatted, high-density 3.5-inch disk
- A computer with Microsoft Windows 3.1, Word 6.0 for Windows, and the CTI WinApps icon group installed on it

  If you are using your own computer, the CTI WinApps icon group will not be installed on it. Before you proceed, you must go to your school's computer lab and find a computer with the CTI WinApps icon group installed on it. Once you have made your own Student Disk, you can use it to complete all the tutorials and exercises in this book on any computer you choose.

To make your Word Office Student Disk:

1. Launch Windows and make sure the Program Manager window is open.

   TROUBLE? The exact steps you follow to launch Windows might vary depending on how your computer is set up. On many computer systems, type WIN at the DOS prompt then press [Enter] to launch Windows. If you don't know how to launch Windows, ask your instructor or technical support person.

2. Label your formatted disk "Word 6.0 Office Student Disk" and place it in drive A.

   TROUBLE? If your computer has more than one disk drive, drive A is usually on top. If your Student Disk does not fit into drive A, then place it in drive B and substitute "drive B" whenever you see "drive A" in the steps throughout this book.

3. Look for an icon labeled "CTI WinApps" like the one in Figure 1-2 or a group window labeled "CTI WinApps" like the one in Figure 1-3.

   TROUBLE? If you are running Office Manager, your screen will also include the Office Manager toolbar. This book assumes Office Manager is *not* running.

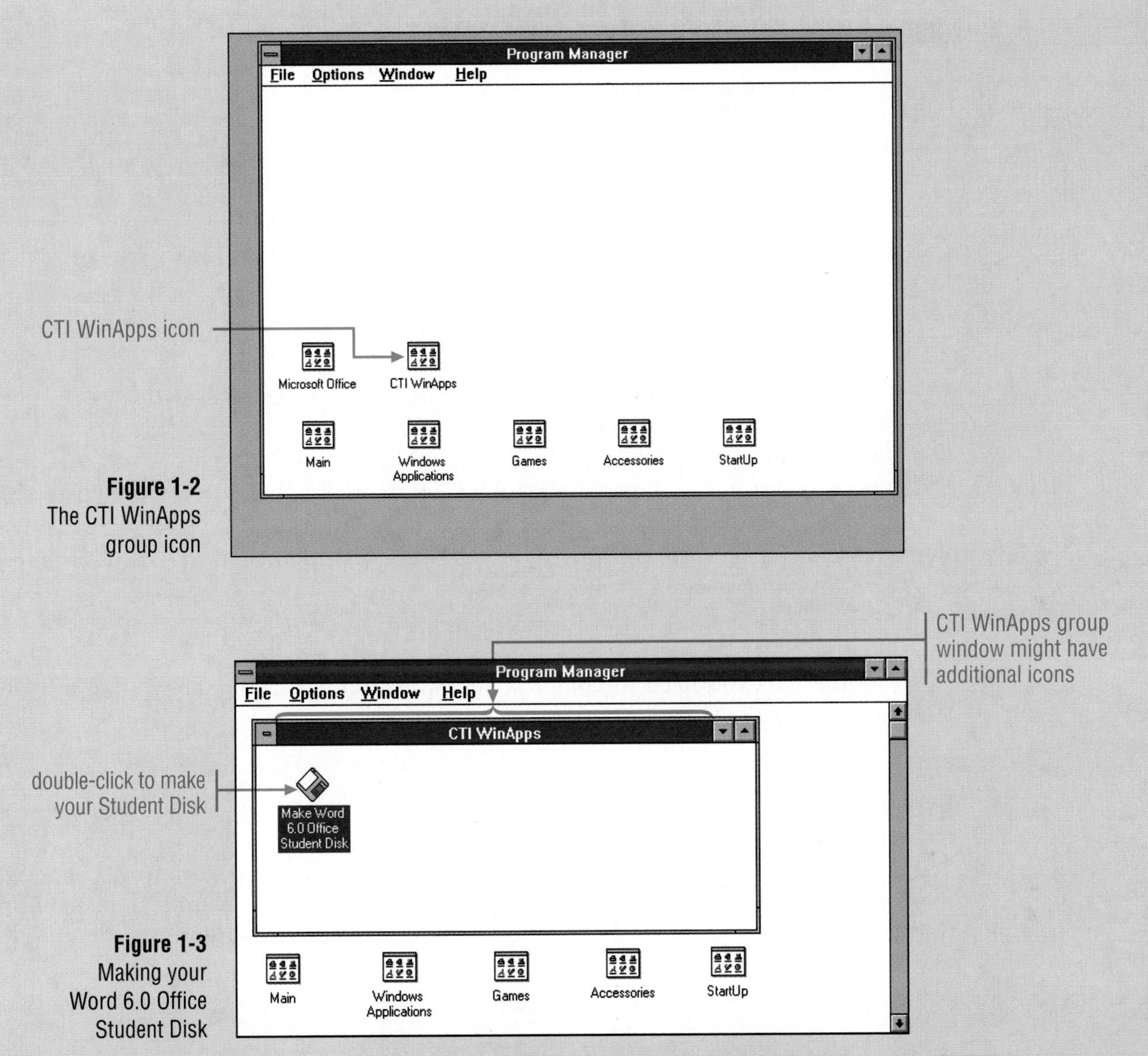

Figure 1-2 The CTI WinApps group icon

Figure 1-3 Making your Word 6.0 Office Student Disk

TROUBLE? If you cannot find anything labeled "CTI WinApps," the CTI software might not be installed on your computer. If you are in a computer lab, ask your instructor or technical support person for assistance. If you are using your own computer, you will not be able to make your Student Disk. To make it you need access to the CTI WinApps icon group, which is, most likely, installed on your school's lab computers. Ask your instructor or technical support person for further information on where to locate the CTI WinApps icon group. Once you create your Student Disk, you can use it to complete all the tutorials and exercises in this book on any computer you choose.

4. If you see an icon labeled "CTI WinApps," double-click it to open the CTI WinApps group window. If the CTI WinApps group window is already open, go to Step 5.
5. Double-click the icon labeled **Make Word 6.0 Office Student Disk**. The Make Word 6.0 Office Student Disk window opens. See Figure 1-4.

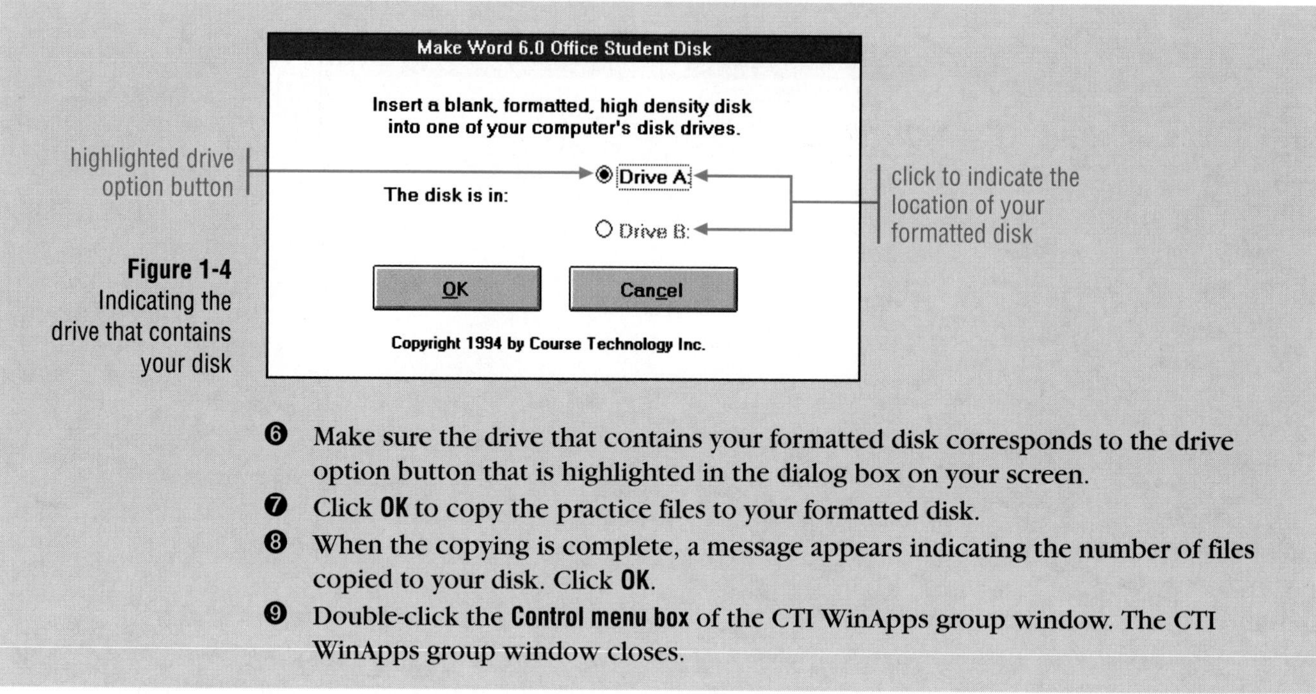

Figure 1-4 Indicating the drive that contains your disk

6. Make sure the drive that contains your formatted disk corresponds to the drive option button that is highlighted in the dialog box on your screen.
7. Click **OK** to copy the practice files to your formatted disk.
8. When the copying is complete, a message appears indicating the number of files copied to your disk. Click **OK**.
9. Double-click the **Control menu box** of the CTI WinApps group window. The CTI WinApps group window closes.

Now the files you need to complete the Word tutorials and exercises are on your Student Disk. Your next step is to start Word.

Starting Word

You are now ready to create Denise's letter, so let's learn how to start Word. Although there are a variety of ways to start Word, this tutorial assumes that Word is launched from the Microsoft Office group window within the Program Manager window.

To start Word:

1. Make sure Windows is launched and the Program Manager window is open. The Microsoft Office group icon should be visible in the Program Manager window.

   TROUBLE? If you don't see the Microsoft Office group icon, ask your instructor or technical support person for help finding the icon. Perhaps Word has not been installed on the computer you are using.

2. Double-click the **Microsoft Office group icon** in the Program Manager window. The Microsoft Office group window opens. See Figure 1-5.

Microsoft Word icon

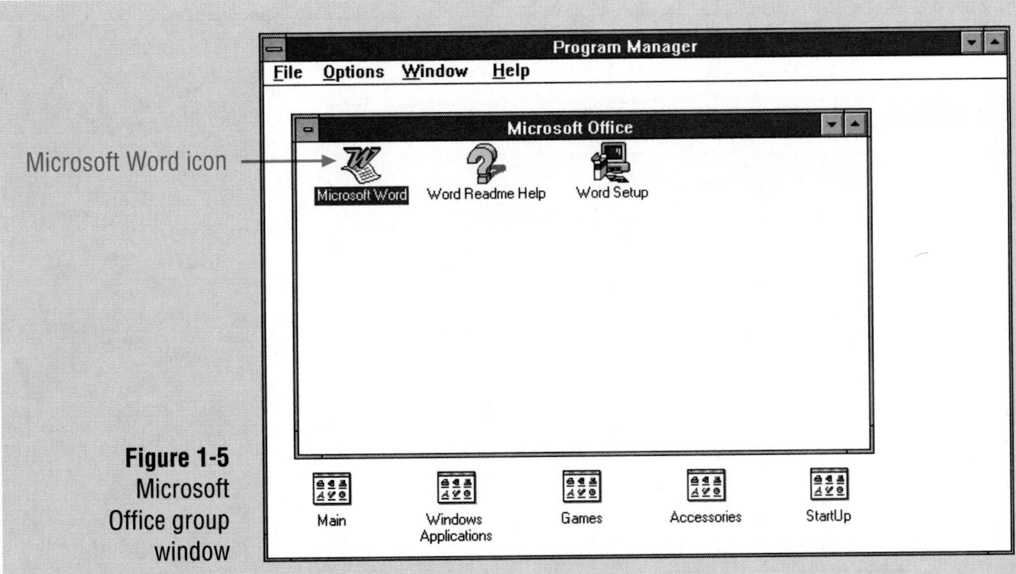

Figure 1-5 Microsoft Office group window

TROUBLE? Don't worry if the Microsoft Office group window contains more program-item icons than shown in Figure 1-5.

❸ Double-click the **Microsoft Word icon** in the Microsoft Office group window.

Word displays a title screen briefly, then the Word screen appears. After starting Word, you might see a Word feature called "Tip of the Day" on your screen. The Tip of the Day provides useful information about different Word features and commands. If you do not see the Tip of the Day, your instructor or technical support person has deactivated this feature.

❹ If the Tip of the Day dialog box appears, read the tip, then click **OK** to close the dialog box. To deactivate this feature, click the **Show Tips at Startup check box** to clear it before clicking OK.

Elements of the Word Screen

Because you are familiar with the Windows screen, or interface, you can already identify several elements of the Word screen: the Word window Control menu box, the title bar, the Word window sizing buttons, the menu bar, the workspace, the mouse pointer, and the scroll bars. These appear as blue labels in Figure 1-6. In addition, you notice a few new elements: the document window Control menu box, the document window Restore button, the Standard toolbar, the Formatting toolbar, the ruler, the insertion point, the end mark, the document view buttons in the horizontal scroll bar, and the status bar. These appear as red labels in Figure 1-6.

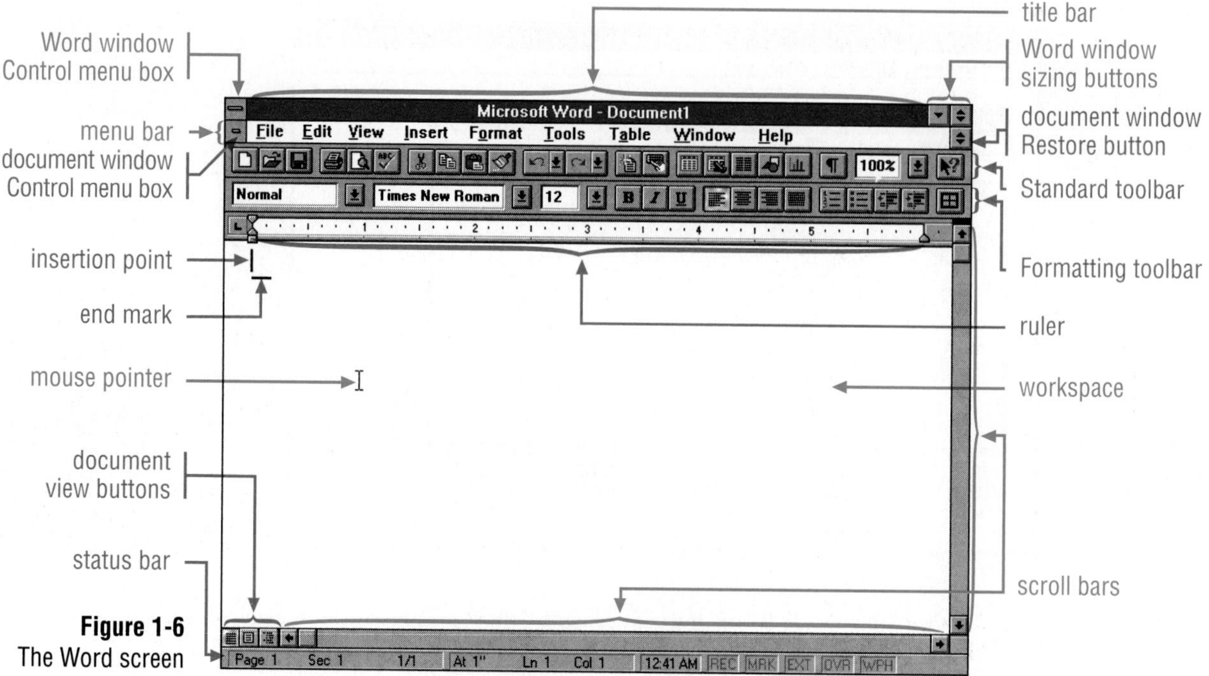

Figure 1-6
The Word screen

If your screen doesn't look like Figure 1-6, going through the next sections of this tutorial should resolve this. Just continue with the tutorial for now.

Figure 1-7 describes the function of each element of the Word screen. You need to become familiar with these elements to take full advantage of Word's features. You will learn to use all of them as you work through the tutorials.

Screen Element	Function
Word window Control menu box	Allows you to size, move, and close the Word window, as well as switch to other applications
Title bar	Identifies the current application (i.e., Word) and the name of the current document
Word window sizing buttons	The Minimize button reduces the Word application to an icon; the Restore button restores the Word window to its standard size
Document window Control menu box	Allows you to size, move, and close the document window
Menu bar	Contains all the Word commands
Document window Restore button	Restores the document window to its standard size
Standard toolbar	Contains buttons that represent some of Word's most often used commands
Formatting toolbar	Contains buttons that represent Word's most often used font and paragraph formatting features
Ruler	Allows you to adjust margins and indents quickly, set tabs, and adjust column widths
Document view buttons	Allow you to view a document in different ways
Scroll bars	Allow you to see different parts of the document
Status bar	Gives information about the location of the insertion point
Workspace	Area where text and graphics are entered
Insertion point	Flashing vertical line that marks the point where characters will be inserted or deleted
End mark	Identifies the end of a document
Mouse pointer	Changes shape depending on its location on the screen

Figure 1-7
Functions of the Word screen elements

If you want, you can take time now to browse through each of Word's menus.

Types of Word Windows

The Word screen is made up of two types of windows: an application window and a document window. Because both windows are maximized and share the same title bar and borders, they appear as one window. The application window, known as the **Word window**, opens automatically when you start Word. The **document window** opens within the Word window and will contain your document.

If you're not sure whether both the Word window and the document window are maximized, compare the shape of your screen's sizing buttons to the right of the title bar (the Word window sizing buttons) and to the right of the menu bar (the document window sizing button) with those in Figure 1-6. If the shapes are different on your screen, the next section gives you the information you need to solve this problem.

Screen Check

The appearance of the Word screen is easily changed. This ability to customize the appearance of the screen is an advantage in the business world, but it can pose problems in the academic world. Business people like Denise usually don't have to share a computer and so don't worry that another user will change the way the Word screen looks. To follow along with the tutorials as easily as possible, conduct a screen check each time you begin a new Word session. This section of the tutorial will help you cope with changes in the appearance of the Word screen from session to session.

Checking the Document View

The document view buttons in the horizontal scroll bar allow you to change the editing view you see on the screen (Figure 1-8). **Normal view** is the default view; you do most of your creating and editing of Word documents in normal view. You use **page layout view** to display your document as it will look when printed. **Outline view** allows you to create a topic outline of your document or to reorganize the sections of your document.

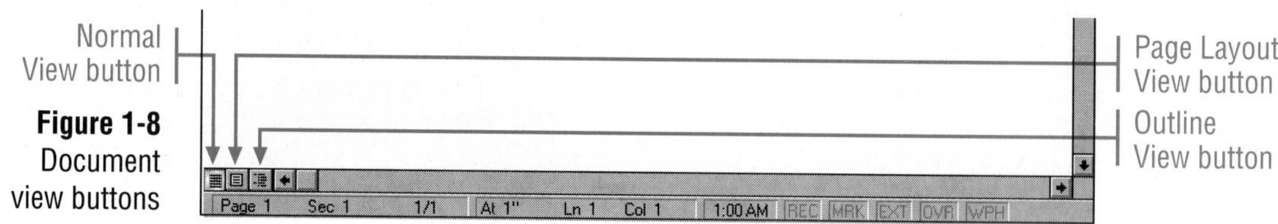

Figure 1-8 Document view buttons

By default, Word displays the document view used by the last person opening Word, so you must know how to switch to normal view before you begin these tutorials. Let's practice that now.

To change document views:

1. Position your pointer on the **Page Layout View button** in the horizontal scroll bar.

   You might notice a Word feature called a "ToolTip" as you move the pointer over the button. The ToolTip feature displays the button name and corresponding status bar message for any button on any toolbar when the pointer is positioned over a button (without clicking).

TROUBLE? If you do not see the ToolTip, the feature has been deactivated. Ask your instructor or technical support person how to activate this feature, if you want to see the ToolTips.

❷ Click ▤. Notice that the Page Layout View button appears lighter to indicate that it is now activated. The document view changes—now a vertical ruler appears on the left side of the screen, and double-headed arrows appear at the bottom of the vertical scroll bar. See Figure 1-9.

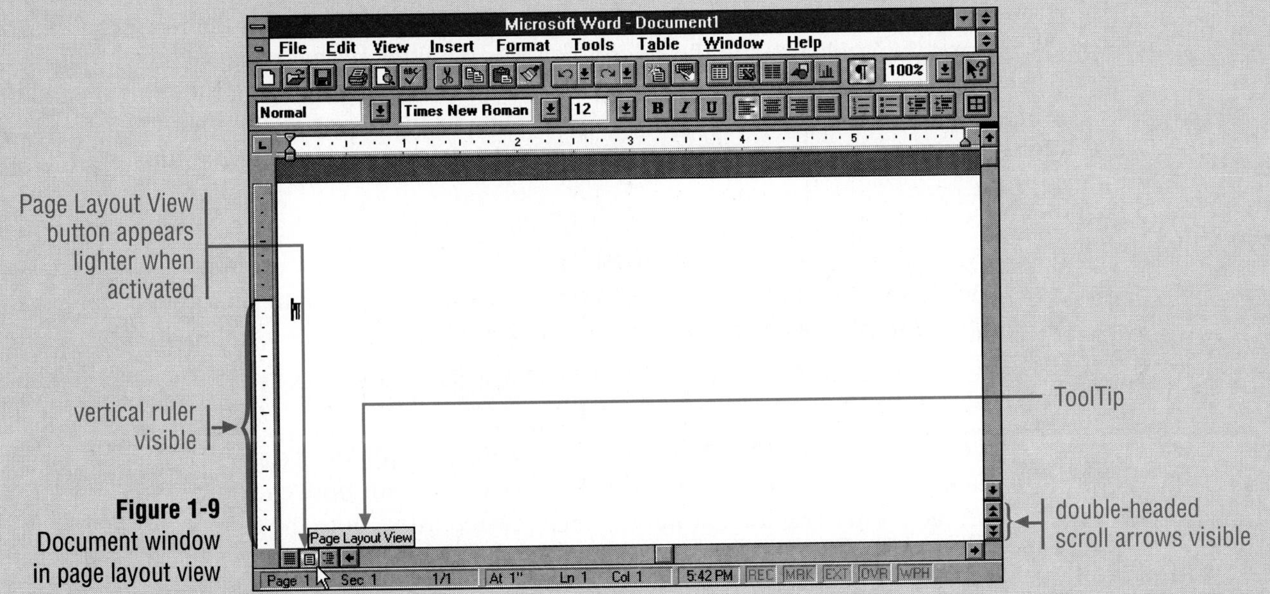

Figure 1-9
Document window in page layout view

❸ Click **View** on the menu bar. Notice that the Page Layout command has a bullet in front of it to indicate that it is activated.

❹ Click **Normal** on the View menu. The vertical ruler and double-headed arrows in the vertical scroll bar disappear. Also notice that the Normal View button in the horizontal scroll bar is lighter to indicate that it is once again activated.

Unless otherwise directed, use normal view when completing these tutorials. If the Normal View button is not selected, you can either click it or choose Normal from the View menu to reset the screen to normal view.

Sizing the Document Window

Unless you are instructed otherwise, the document window you are working in should be maximized. You can use either the document window Restore button or the document window Control menu box to change the size of the document window (see Figure 1-6). Whenever you start a new Word session to work on the tutorials in this book, make sure the document window is maximized.

Sizing the Word Window

The Word window should also be maximized unless otherwise stated. You can use the Word window sizing buttons or the Word window Control menu box to change the size of the Word window. Whenever you start a new session of Word, make sure the Word window is maximized (see Figure 1-6).

Viewing the Toolbars and the Ruler

The procedures in the tutorials instruct you to use the toolbars—the Standard toolbar and the Formatting toolbar—and the ruler whenever possible, because they allow you to speed up your work (Figure 1-6). Because the Word screen is easily changed, the toolbars and the ruler might not always be displayed when you start a Word session. You need to know how to display the toolbars and the ruler in case they have been removed from the screen.

To deactivate and activate the toolbars:

1. Click **View**. The View menu opens. Notice that the Ruler command has a check mark in front of it to indicate that it is activated.

   TROUBLE? If the Ruler command doesn't have a check mark in front of it, click Ruler to display it on the screen, then repeat Step 1.

2. Click **Toolbars...**. The Toolbars dialog box appears with Word's available toolbars listed. See Figure 1-10. Notice that the check boxes for both the Standard toolbar and the Formatting toolbar have been activated. Also, note the Show ToolTips check box. If this box is selected, the ToolTips feature has been activated.

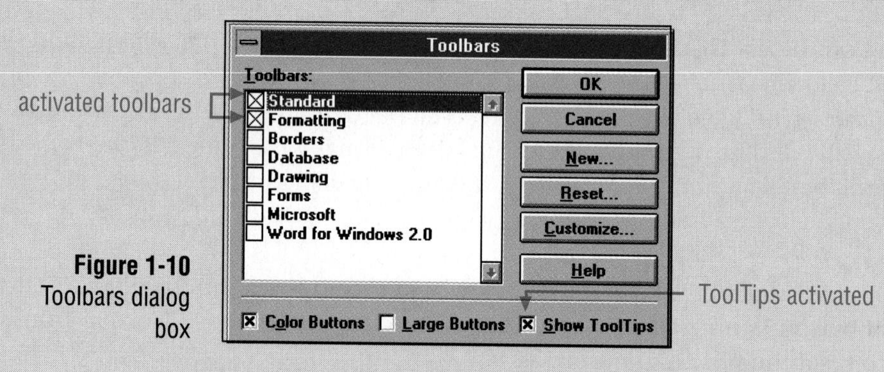

Figure 1-10 Toolbars dialog box

3. Click the **Standard check box** to clear it, then click **OK** or press **[Enter]**. The Standard toolbar disappears from the Word screen, but the Formatting toolbar is still visible.

You can also remove or display toolbars by using the shortcut Toolbar menu. To display the shortcut Toolbar menu, point to any visible toolbar, then click the *right* mouse button. Let's practice activating a toolbar with the shortcut Toolbar menu now.

To use the shortcut Toolbar menu:

1. Point anywhere on the Formatting toolbar, then click the **right mouse button.** A menu appears containing all of Word's available toolbars, with a check mark in front of Formatting to indicate that the Formatting toolbar is displayed. See Figure 1-11.

   TROUBLE? If you do not see the shortcut Toolbar menu, perhaps you did not click the *right* mouse button. Repeat Step 1.

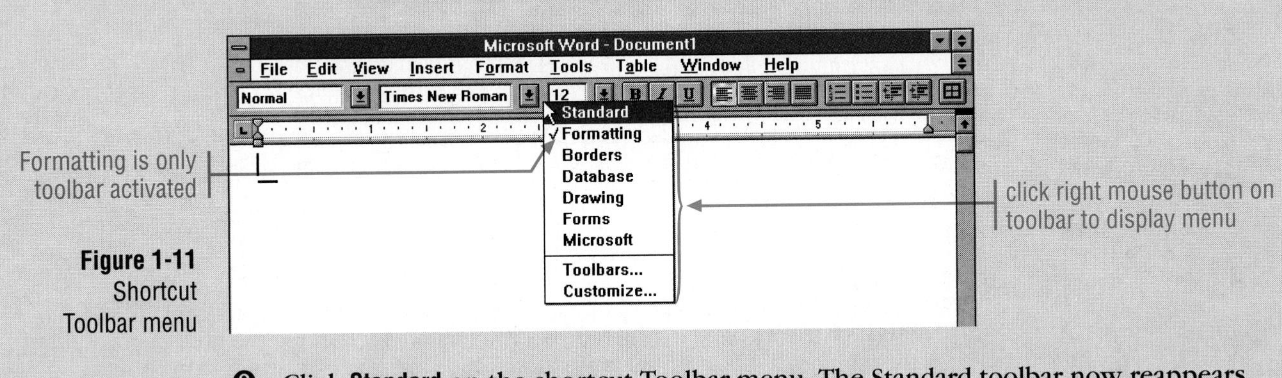

Figure 1-11 Shortcut Toolbar menu

2. Click **Standard** on the shortcut Toolbar menu. The Standard toolbar now reappears.

Now let's practice deactivating and activating the ruler using keyboard commands.

To deactivate and activate the ruler using keyboard commands:

1. Press **[Alt][v]** to display the View menu.
2. Press **[r]** to deactivate the Ruler command. The ruler disappears from the Word screen.
3. Press **[Alt][v]**. The View menu opens again. Notice that the Ruler command does not have a check mark in front of it. The ruler is deactivated.
4. Press **[r]**. The ruler appears once again.

As you complete these tutorials, the Standard and Formatting toolbars should be the only toolbars visible on your screen, unless otherwise instructed. The ruler should also be visible.

Displaying Nonprinting Characters

Word allows you to display paragraph marks, tabs, spaces, and all other nonprinting characters on your screen by activating the Show/Hide ¶ button on the Standard toolbar. To help you recognize the format of your document as you are working in it, and to avoid accidentally deleting one of these characters, work with the Show/Hide ¶ button activated.

To activate the Show/Hide ¶ button:

❶ Click the **Show/Hide ¶ button** on the Standard toolbar. A paragraph mark appears in the workspace of the document. The Show/Hide ¶ button now appears lighter to indicate that the button has been clicked—in other words, that the command is activated. See Figure 1-12.

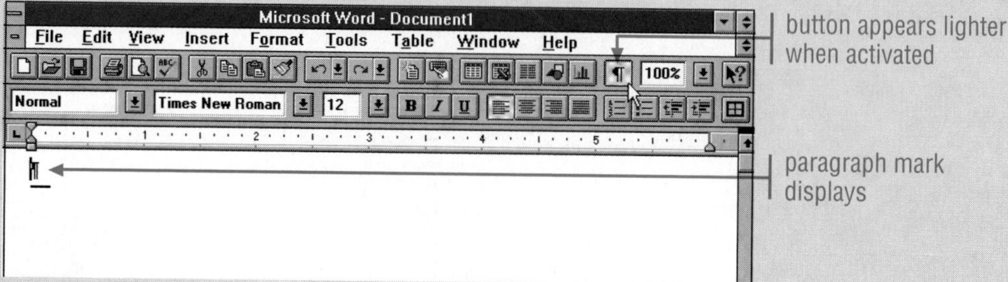

Figure 1-12 Show/Hide ¶ button activated

TROUBLE? If the paragraph mark in your workspace disappeared when you clicked ¶, the Show/Hide ¶ command had already been activated; by clicking the button, you *deactivated* the command. Click ¶ one more time to activate the command.

❷ Press **[Tab]**. A nonprinting character (→) appears to mark the location of the tab inserted into your document.

❸ Type **This is my first Word document.** A nonprinting character (•) appears to mark the location of the spaces inserted into your document. See Figure 1-13.

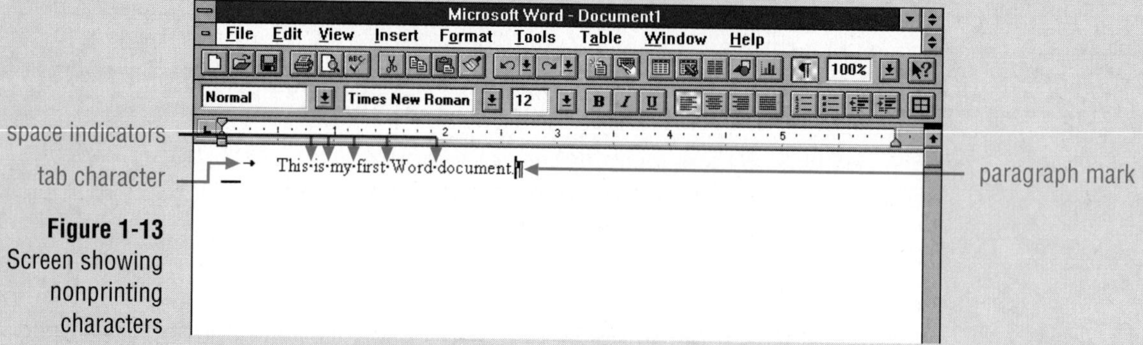

Figure 1-13 Screen showing nonprinting characters

❹ Click ¶ on the Standard toolbar. The nonprinting characters are no longer displayed in the workspace.

You can also activate the nonprinting characters through the Tools Options command.

❺ Click **Tools** then click **Options...**.

❻ Click the **View tab**, if necessary, then click the **All check box** in the Nonprinting Characters section.

❼ Click **OK** or press **[Enter]**. The nonprinting characters appear once again and the Show/Hide ¶ button is activated. Leave the Show/Hide ¶ button activated throughout these tutorials so you can see any special marks you insert.

Checking Font and Point Size Settings

Notice the term "Times New Roman" and the number "12" on the Formatting toolbar. These terms represent the shape (font) and size (point) of the letters used to create the documents shown in the figures throughout the tutorials. If the font or point size settings are different on your screen, ask your instructor or technical support person to adjust these settings for you. (By default, Word uses a 10-point font size in new documents; ask your instructor or technical support person to change the default setting to 12 if your screen shows 10 for the point size.)

In summary, each time you start a new Word session, conduct a screen check by asking yourself the following questions:

- Is the Word window in normal view?
- Is the document window maximized?
- Is the Word window maximized?
- Are only the Standard and Formatting toolbars and the ruler visible?
- Is the Show/Hide ¶ button activated?
- Is the font set to Times New Roman and the point size set to 12?

If you can't answer "yes" to all of these questions, adjust the Word screen appropriately.

Organizing Document Windows

Word makes it easy for you to open more than one document at a time—so easy, in fact, that you might not know it has happened. You need to know how to keep track of your open documents, as well as how to close them.

Opening a New Document

Currently you have one document window open; it is titled Document1. Within that document window, you create your document. You can have as many documents open at one time in Word as your computer's memory will allow. When you open a new document, it is displayed in a new document window. Word automatically assigns the new document a name—the word "Document" followed by a number. The Window menu contains a list of all open or minimized Word documents.

If the document name in your title bar has a different number, you have accidentally created a new document. Don't worry about it now; just continue with the tutorial.

Now let's practice opening two new documents.

To open a new document:

1. Click the **New button** on the Standard toolbar. Notice the change in the title bar. It now reads "Document2." Document1 is still open but is not visible—it is open behind Document2.
2. Type **This is my second Word document.**
3. Click **File** then click **New...**. The New dialog box appears. See Figure 1-14. The Template section contains a listing of Word's predefined document templates. You will learn about document templates later in this book.

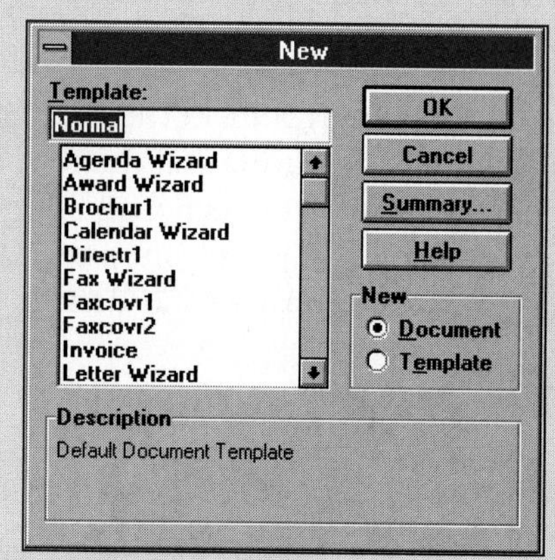

Figure 1-14
New dialog box

4. Click **OK** or press **[Enter]** to open a new document. Notice the change in the title bar. Now it reads "Document3." Document1 and Document2 are still open but not visible.
5. Type **This is my third Word document.**

Switching Between Open Documents

Although you can have many documents open at one time, you can work in only one document at a time. This document is called the **active document.** To work in another open document, you must first make it the active document.

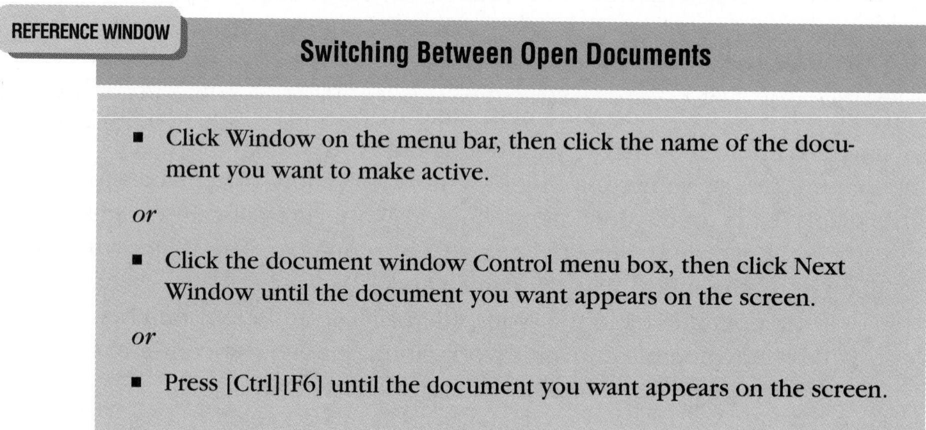

REFERENCE WINDOW

Switching Between Open Documents

- Click Window on the menu bar, then click the name of the document you want to make active.

or

- Click the document window Control menu box, then click Next Window until the document you want appears on the screen.

or

- Press [Ctrl][F6] until the document you want appears on the screen.

Let's practice switching between open documents.

To switch between the open documents:

1. Click **Window** to display the Window menu. Three document names are listed at the bottom of the Window menu, and a check mark is in front of Document3, the active document. See Figure 1-15.

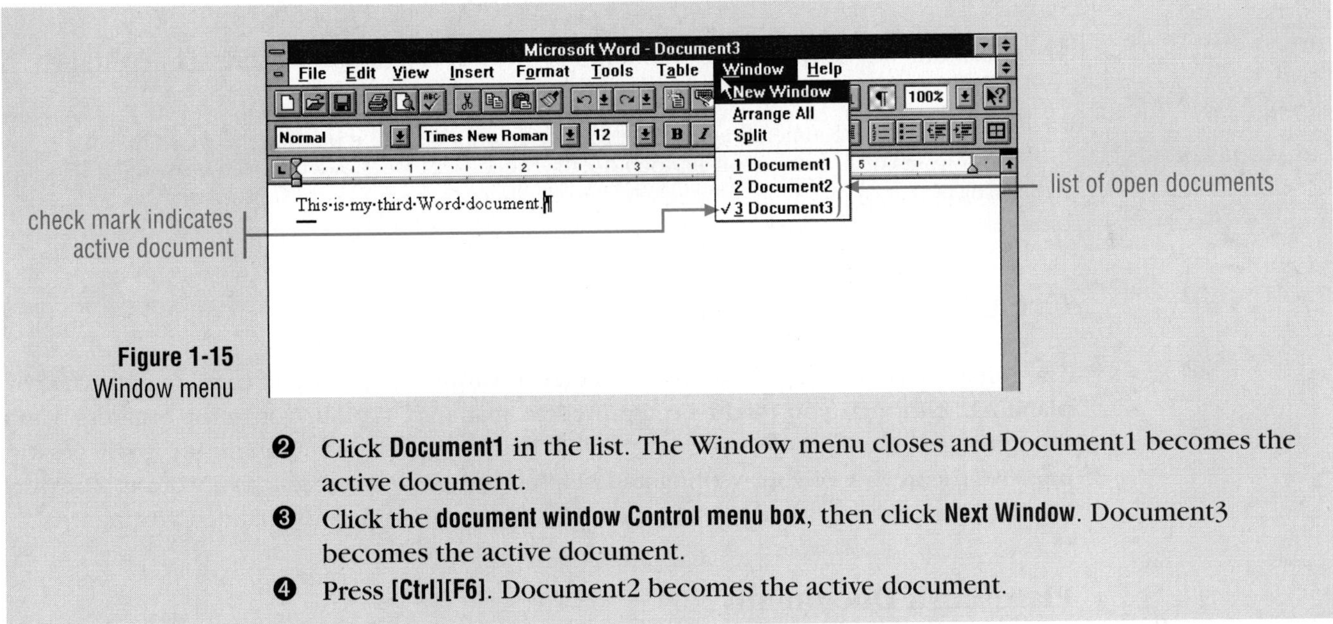

Figure 1-15
Window menu

2. Click **Document1** in the list. The Window menu closes and Document1 becomes the active document.
3. Click the **document window Control menu box**, then click **Next Window**. Document3 becomes the active document.
4. Press **[Ctrl][F6]**. Document2 becomes the active document.

If you ever lose sight of a document you have been working on, open the Window menu to see if your document is listed at the bottom of the menu, or try one of the other techniques to switch between open documents.

Closing a Document

Even though you can have several documents open at one time in Word, you should generally close your documents once you no longer need them. The more windows that are open, the more memory is used and the slower the performance of your computer. When you close a document, you remove that document from your computer's memory.

Let's practice closing a document without saving changes.

To close a document without saving changes:

1. Switch to Document1.
2. Click **File** then click **Close**. The message, "Do you want to save changes to Document1?" appears.
3. Click **No** to indicate that you do not want to save any changes to the document. Document2 is now the active document.
4. Click **Window** in the menu bar. Notice that Document1 is not listed.
5. Close the Window menu by clicking outside the menu.
6. Double-click the **document window Control menu box**. The message, "Do you want to save changes to Document2?" appears.

   TROUBLE? If you mistakenly double-click the Word window Control menu box, click Cancel to return to your document without closing Word. Then repeat Step 6.

7. Click **No**. Document2 closes.
8. Click **Window**. Notice that Document2 is not listed. Document3 is now the active document.

9. Close the Window menu. Document3 is the only document remaining open at this point.

   TROUBLE? If Document3 is not the only document remaining open at this point, use the previous set of steps to close all open documents except Document3 without saving changes.

Creating a Document

The initial phase of the productivity strategy, creating, requires you to do a great deal of planning. Although you might be tempted to just start typing, you must organize your thoughts first. Having a clear picture of what you need to say and how to say it will greatly improve the quality of your writing and help contribute to your success. Word is a powerful word processing program, but it cannot compensate for poorly planned writing.

Planning a Document

Denise decides that she will set the stage for her request in the opening paragraph of her letter, describe the specifications of the brownie in the second paragraph, and close with a request for a bid proposal in the last paragraph. With her writing plan for the body of the letter in mind, she also plans to enter the standard parts of a letter: the date, inside address, salutation, complimentary closing, and her name and title. During this phase of the productivity strategy, Denise is concerned only with typing the text of her letter as she has planned it, and not with editing or formatting the letter.

Entering Text

Each Word document is based on a **document template,** a set of predefined features. Unless you specify otherwise, new documents are assigned the features of the Normal template—8.5 x 11-inch print orientation, single spacing, 1.25-inch left and right margins, 1-inch top and bottom margins, tabs set at every 0.5 inch, and text aligned at the left margin only. These standard features of a document are called **default settings.**

The status bar, located at the bottom of the screen, is an extremely valuable feature when you are entering text because it keeps you informed of the location of the insertion point. Figure 1-16 describes the purpose of each element of the status bar.

This section of the status bar:	Indicates:
Page 1	Page number where the insertion point is located
Sec 1	Section number where the insertion point is located
1/1	Number of pages from the beginning of the document to the insertion point, followed by the total number of pages in the document
At 1"	Position of the insertion point as measured from the top edge of the page
Ln 1	Position of the insertion point as measured from the top margin of the page
Col 1	Position of the insertion point as measured from the left margin of the page
Time	Current time as determined by the computer's clock

Figure 1-16
Status bar elements

Denise doesn't want to change Word's default document settings, but she does want to start the date 2.5 inches from the top edge of the paper to allow room for the company letterhead. The "At" section of the status bar indicates that the insertion point is currently located 1 inch from the top edge of the paper. To insert a blank line in a document, press [Enter]. Each time you press [Enter], a paragraph mark is displayed (if the Show/Hide ¶ button is activated).

Denise must open a new document and then move the insertion point 2.5 inches from the top edge of the paper.

To insert blank lines:

1. Click the **New button** on the Standard toolbar (or click **File**, click **New...**, then click **OK** or press **[Enter]**). A new document titled Document4 appears. Document 3 is still open, just not visible.
2. Make sure the "At" section of the status bar displays 1".

   TROUBLE? If the "At" section does not display 1", you have inadvertently inserted blank lines into your document. Press [Backspace] to remove the blank lines.

3. Press **[Enter]** eight times. Notice the change in the status bar. The "At" section, which is the position from the top edge of the paper, is now 2.5"; the "Ln" section, the position from the top margin of the page, now reads "Ln 9."

   TROUBLE? If the "Ln" section displays 9 but the "At" section does not display 2.5", ask your instructor or technical support person to change the default font to Times New Roman 12 point. If the default font or its size cannot be changed, continue with the tutorial, keeping in mind that your screen, and eventually your printed document, will look different from the figures shown in this tutorial.

Denise has moved the insertion point so that she has 2.5 inches of blank space at the top of her document, and now she is ready to type the date. In the following steps, you will make an intentional error by entering an incorrect date. This is so you can practice correcting errors in text as you type.

To type the date:

❶ Type **February 22, 1985**. Notice the change in the "Col" section of the status bar. The "Col" indicator in the status bar changes as you move the insertion point to the right. See Figure 1-17.

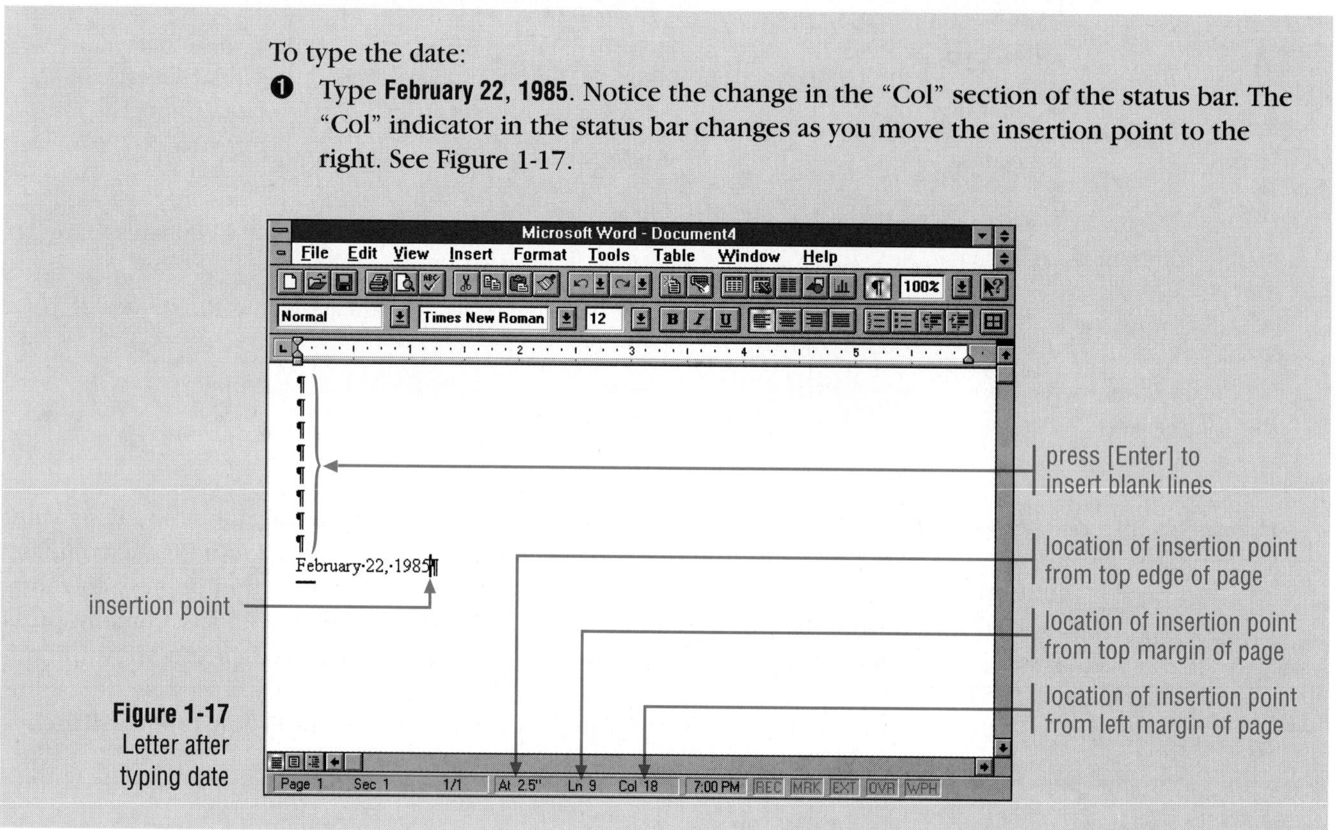

Figure 1-17 Letter after typing date

Denise notices that she typed 1985 instead of 1995. Because she discovers this typing error shortly after making it, she can press [Backspace] up to and including the error and then type the correct text. Pressing [Backspace] deletes characters or spaces to the left of the insertion point. There are other ways to correct errors, but for now let's use this method to correct your typing errors.

To correct an error using [Backspace]:

❶ Make sure the insertion point is after the "5" in 1985.

❷ Press **[Backspace]** twice to delete the "5" and then the "8."

❸ Type **95**. The date is now correct.

Now Denise is ready to type the inside address. She needs to move the insertion point to the left margin and to insert three blank lines before the inside address.

To insert blank lines then type the inside address:

1. Press **[Enter]** one time to move the insertion point to the left margin, then press **[Enter]** three more times to insert three blank lines after the date.
2. Type **Mr. Mike Gonzales** (the first line of the inside address).
3. Press **[Enter]**.
4. Continue to enter the remaining three lines of the inside address, as shown in Figure 1-18. Press **[Enter]** at the end of each short line in the inside address to move the insertion point to the left margin of the next line. Make sure you press **[Enter]** at the end of the last line of the inside address as well.

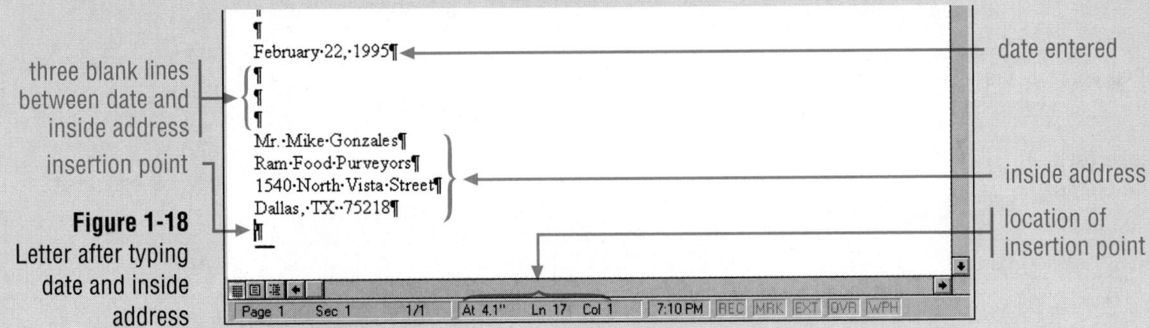

Figure 1-18
Letter after typing date and inside address

You have now typed the inside address of the letter. Next add a blank line after the inside address, then type the salutation.

5. Press **[Enter]** to insert a blank line after the inside address.
6. Type **Dear Mr. Gonzales:** then press **[Enter]** twice to leave a blank line between the salutation and beginning of the body of the letter.

Now you are ready to begin typing the body of the letter. As you type the letter, however, you do not have to press [Enter] at the end of the line as you did when you typed the date, inside address, and salutation. As you are entering text, if a word does not fit completely on the line, Word automatically moves it to the beginning of the next line for you. This feature is known as **word wrap**.

To type the body of the letter:

1. Type the first paragraph of the body of the letter, as shown in Figure 1-19. Remember—do not press [Enter] at the end of each full line. Let Word do the work for you. Notice that some lines inserted at the top of the letter are now no longer in view.

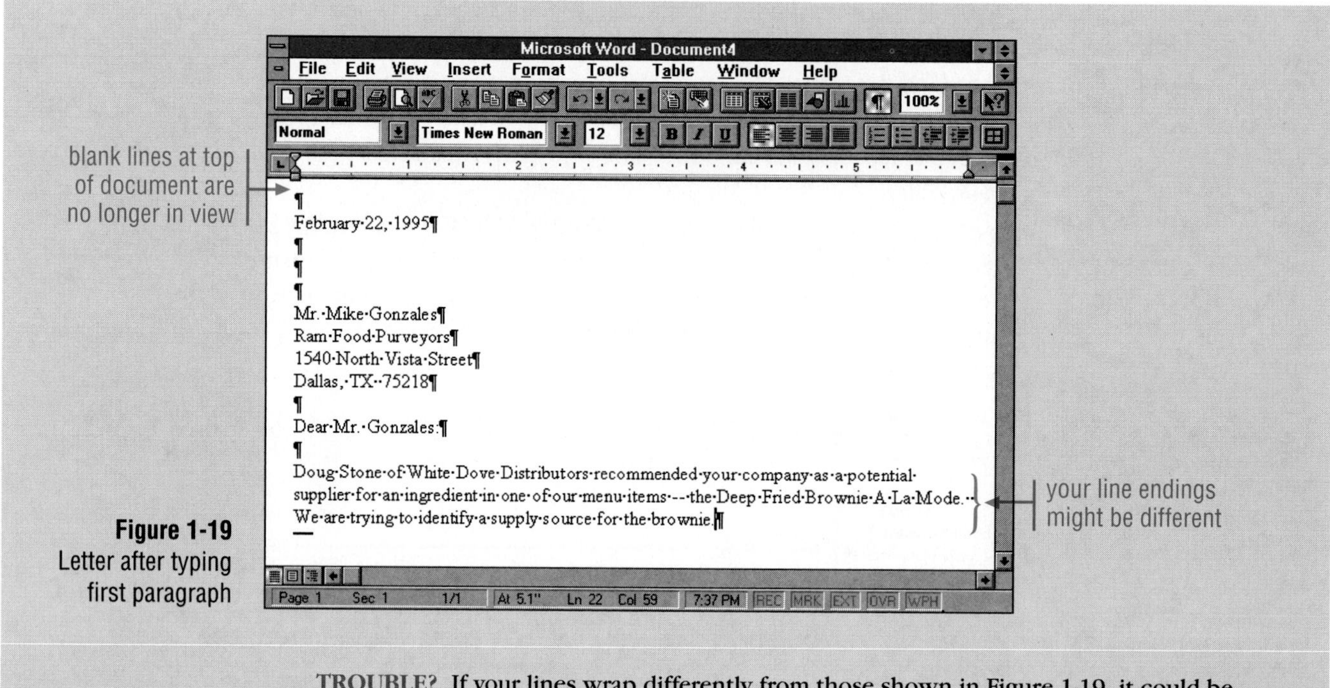

Figure 1-19 Letter after typing first paragraph

TROUBLE? If your lines wrap differently from those shown in Figure 1-19, it could be because you have a printer selected that is different from the one used to prepare this tutorial. Don't worry; just continue with the tutorial.

2. Press **[Enter]** to end the first paragraph, then press **[Enter]** again to insert a blank line between the first and second paragraphs.
3. Finish typing the rest of the letter, as shown in Figure 1-20, *including the three deliberate typographical errors in the last paragraph*. Press **[Enter]** twice at the end of each paragraph to insert a blank line between paragraphs.

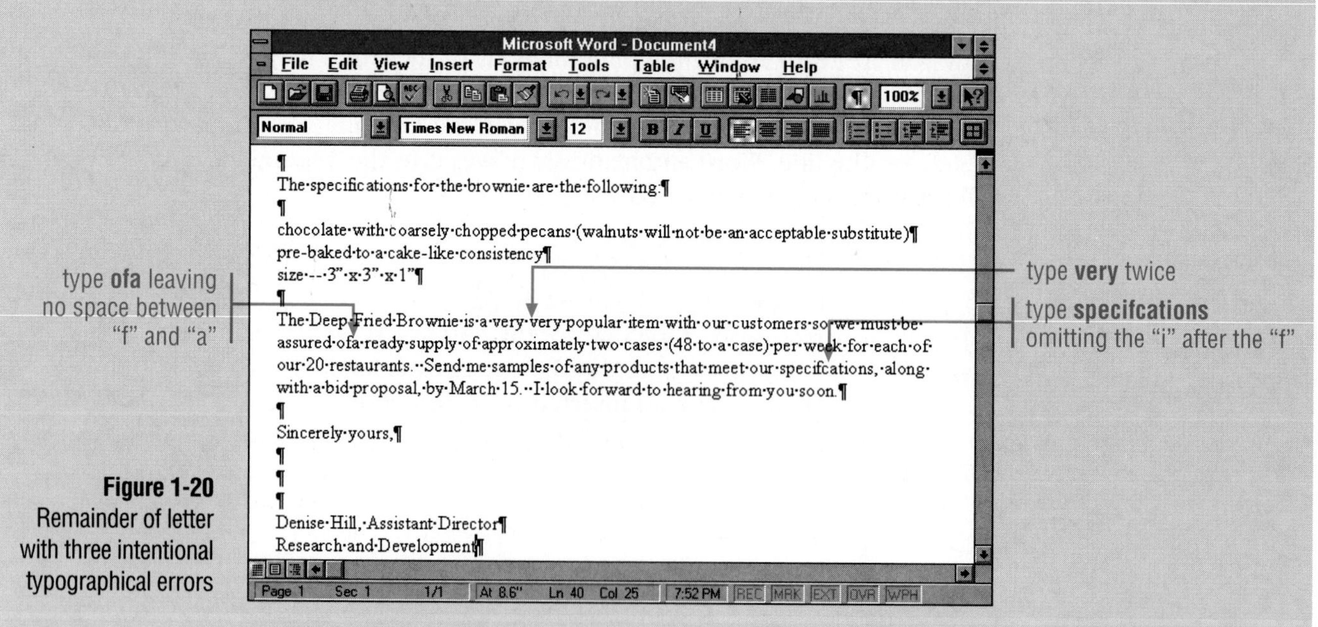

Figure 1-20 Remainder of letter with three intentional typographical errors

Denise has finished entering the text of her letter, and now she is ready to save her work.

Saving a Document

While you were creating Denise's document, it was not stored permanently to disk. A default feature of Word, AutoSave, automatically saves changes made to a document every specified number of minutes to a temporary file in case of a power failure. The changes are not saved to the permanent file, however, until you save the document. It is a good idea to save your work to disk at least every 15 minutes or when you finish something you wouldn't want to do again. When you save a document, it is preserved permanently on the disk in its own file with its own filename.

Naming Files

Word's filenames can be any legal filename; that is, they can contain from one to eight characters and no spaces. The extension "DOC" is added automatically to Word document files. Each filename must be unique, should be descriptive of the file's content, and should follow a naming scheme.

Before you save your work, you need to understand the file naming scheme used in this book, which was designed to help you and your instructor recognize the origin and content of documents. You will create many files, but some files have already been created for you and are stored on your Student Disk. As shown in Figure 1-21, you will be working with four categories of files. Those files provided for you on the Student Disk are for use in the Tutorial Cases, Tutorial Assignments, and Case Problems. The filenames of any files used in Tutorial Cases begin with C; Tutorial Assignments begin with T; and Case Problems begin with P. However, all files that you are instructed to save throughout these tutorials will have a filename that begins with S (for "saved").

File Category	Description
Tutorial **C**ases	The files you use to work through each tutorial
Tutorial Assignments	The files that contain the documents you need to complete the Tutorial Assignments at the end of each tutorial
Case **P**roblems	The files that contain the documents you need to complete the Case Problems at the end of each tutorial
Saved Document	Any document that you save

Figure 1-21
Types of tutorial files

In the file naming convention used in these tutorials, the second character of the filename identifies the number of the tutorial to which the file relates. The last six characters of the filenames represent a description of the document's content—a word or an abbreviation that helps to identify the document. Thus, the filename S1RAM would represent a file you saved in Tutorial 1 that has something to do with Ram Food Purveyors.

Saving a Document for the First Time

The first time you save a document after it has been created, you must tell Word the filename that you want to give your document and where you want the document saved.

Let's save the work you have completed so far and name the document S1RAM.

To save the document for the first time:

❶ Make sure your Student Disk is in drive A.

❷ Click the **Save button** on the Standard toolbar (or click **File** then click **Save** or **Save As...**). The Save As dialog box appears with the default filename doc4.doc highlighted in the File Name text box.

❸ In the File Name text box, type **s1ram**. *Do not press [Enter].* Because the default filename doc4.doc was highlighted, typing s1ram automatically replaces the selected text. Word automatically adds the extension "DOC" to the filename when you complete the dialog box. You can type the filename using uppercase or lowercase letters.

You want to save this document to your Student Disk, not the hard drive, so you must change the destination, or target drive, information.

❹ Click the **Drives list box down arrow**. A list of available target drives appears.

❺ Click the letter of the drive in which you put your Student Disk. This tutorial assumes that your Student Disk is in drive A. Notice that the Directories section of the dialog box also changes to reflect the change in the target drive. See Figure 1-22.

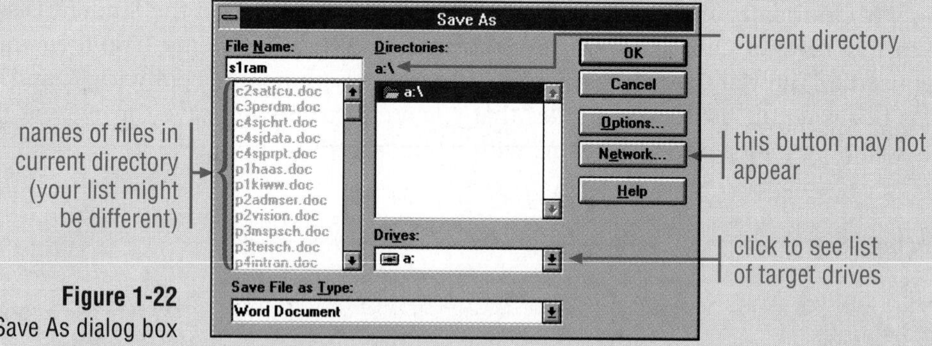

Figure 1-22
Save As dialog box

❻ Click **OK** or press **[Enter]** to save the document. Notice that the title bar has changed to reflect the new filename, S1RAM.DOC.

Now that Denise has created her letter and saved it, she decides to take a break before she begins editing her letter to Ram Food Purveyors. First, she needs to exit Word.

Exiting Word

You can exit Word by double-clicking the Word window Control menu box, or by choosing Exit from the File menu.

To exit Word:

1. Double-click the **Word window Control menu box** (or click **File** then click **Exit**). Be sure not to double-click the document window Control menu box. The message, "Do you want to save changes to Document3?" appears because Document3 is still open.
2. Click **No**. You do not need to save Document3.
3. Double-click the **Microsoft Office group window Control menu box** to close it. You return to the Program Manager.
4. At the Program Manager, either exit Windows or start another application.

If you want to take a break and resume the tutorial at a later time, you can do so now. When you want to resume the tutorial, start Word and place your Student Disk in the disk drive. Remember to complete the screen check procedure described earlier in this tutorial. Then continue with the tutorial.

■ ■ ■

Editing a Document

Editing a document involves changing its content by inserting, deleting, or moving text. The purpose of editing is to refine a document so that its meaning is clear and it is free of errors. The most efficient way to edit a document is first to make changes in content and then to check for spelling and typographical errors.

Opening an Existing Document

To resume work on the letter, you must first open the file that contains that document. You can either click the Open button on the Standard toolbar or choose the Open command from the File menu to display the Open dialog box, in which you specify the file you want to open.

You can also open a document that you have worked on recently from the File menu. The four most recently closed documents are listed at the bottom of the File menu. See Figure 1-23. (Your list might include other filenames.) Just click the name of the document on which you want to work, and it will open.

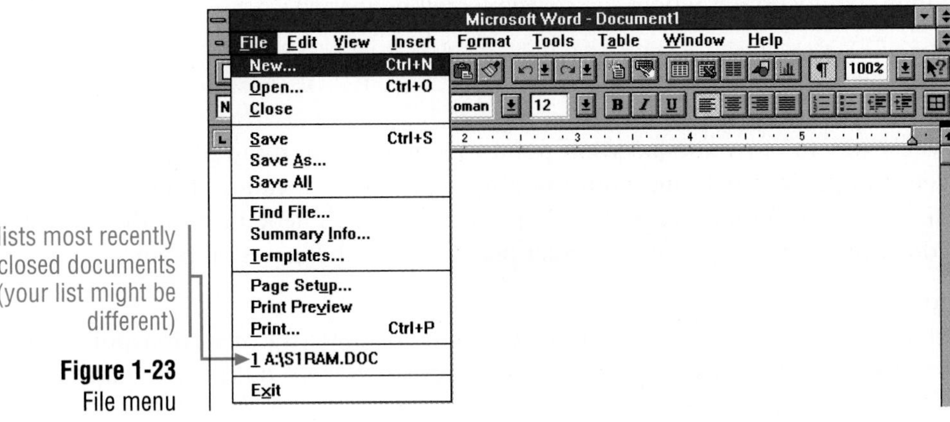

Figure 1-23
File menu

Let's open the file S1RAM, which you saved on your Student Disk.

To open the S1RAM document:

1. If necessary, start Word and conduct the screen check of your Word screen as described in the "Screen Check" section earlier in this tutorial.
2. Click the **Open button** on the Standard toolbar (or click **File** then click **Open...**). Word displays the Open dialog box.
3. Click the **Drives list box down arrow**. The list of available drives appears.
4. Click the letter of the drive containing your Student Disk. Notice that the Directories section of the dialog box changes to reflect the selected drive. Scroll through the list of files until s1ram.doc appears.
5. Click **s1ram.doc**. The name of the selected file now appears in the File Name text box. See Figure 1-24.

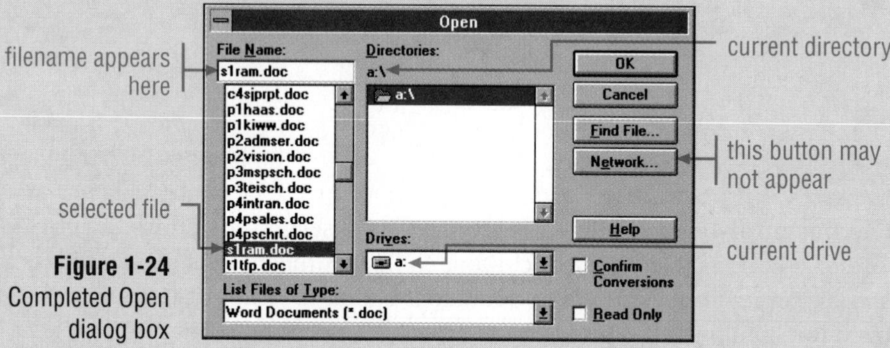

Figure 1-24
Completed Open dialog box

TROUBLE? If you can't find a file named S1RAM.DOC, make sure the Drives section indicates the location of your Student Disk. If the Drives section indicates the correct drive name, perhaps you accidentally saved the file to the hard drive. If you are working on the same computer as you were when you saved the document, check drive C. If you still cannot locate your file, check with your instructor or technical support person.

6. Click **OK** or press **[Enter]**. The document S1RAM.DOC opens with the insertion point at the top of the document.

After reading through her letter, Denise decides to make a few changes to its content. Before she can make these changes, however, she must move the insertion point to the location in the document where the revisions will be made.

Moving the Insertion Point

The fastest way to move the insertion point to a new location in the window you are currently viewing is to move the mouse pointer to the new location, then click the mouse button. The mouse pointer takes the shape of an I-beam I when it is in the workspace of the Word window to aid you in the exact placement of the insertion point.

Keyboard Techniques

Skilled keyboarders might find it more efficient to move the insertion point with keyboard shortcuts rather than with the mouse, because they do not have to take their hands off the keyboard. The basic keyboard movement keys are the arrow keys: [→], [←], [↑], [↓]. To move the insertion point further with the keyboard, however, you need to use the keyboard movement techniques listed in Figure 1-25. To perform a movement that involves two keys, hold down the first key listed while pressing the second key listed. For instance, hold down [Ctrl] while pressing [End] to move the insertion point to the end of the document.

To move the insertion point:	Press:
Left or right one character at a time	[←] or [→]
Up or down one line at a time	[↑] or [↓]
Left or right one word at a time	[Ctrl][←] or [Ctrl][→]
Down one paragraph at a time	[Ctrl][↑] or [Ctrl][↓]
To the previous screen	[PgUp]
To the next screen	[PgDn]
To the top of the screen	[Ctrl][PgUp]
To the bottom of the screen	[Ctrl][PgDn]
To the beginning of the previous page	[Alt][Ctrl][PgUp]
To the beginning of the next page	[Alt][Ctrl][PgDn]
To the beginning of the current line	[Home]
To the end of the current line	[End]
To the top of the document	[Ctrl][Home]
To the bottom of the document	[Ctrl][End]

Figure 1-25
Keyboard movement techniques

Let's practice moving the insertion point using the keyboard. Look at the status bar to determine the location of the insertion point before you begin. Because you just opened the document, the insertion point should be at the top of the document.

To change the location of the insertion point using keyboard techniques:

1. Press **[Ctrl][End]** to move to the end of the document. Notice that the status bar reflects the change in the location of the insertion point.

   TROUBLE? If the insertion point didn't move to the end of the document, perhaps you released [Ctrl] before you pressed [End]. Try again; this time continue to hold down [Ctrl] while you press [End].

2. Press **[Ctrl][Home]**. The insertion point moves to the top of the document.
3. Press **[Ctrl][PgDn]**. Notice that you see the same text on the screen, but the insertion point moves to the last line on the screen.
4. Press [↓] until the insertion point is in the first paragraph of the body of the letter.

5. Press **[Ctrl][→]** once. Word moves the insertion point forward one word. Practice moving forward a word at a time a few more times.
6. Press **[End]**. The insertion point moves to the end of the current line.
7. Press **[Home]**. The insertion point moves to the beginning of the current line.
8. Press **[Ctrl][↓]** once. The insertion point moves to the next paragraph. To Word, a paragraph is any string of characters that ends with a paragraph mark, including a paragraph mark on a line by itself.
9. Press **[Ctrl][Home]**. The insertion point moves to the beginning of the document.

Mouse Techniques

Now let's practice moving the insertion point with the mouse by using the point-and-click method. The insertion point is at the top of the document, but Denise wants to move it in front of the word Street in the inside address.

To move the insertion point using the point-and-click method:

1. Move the pointer so that the I-beam is in front of the "S" in Street. The insertion point is still at the top of the document. See Figure 1-26.

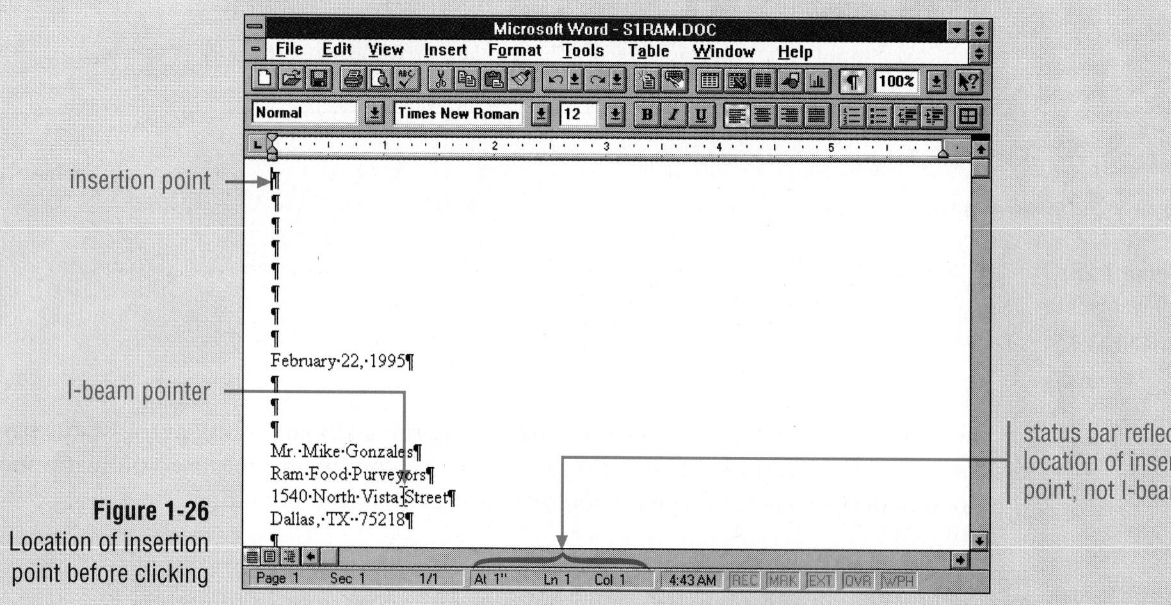

Figure 1-26
Location of insertion point before clicking

2. Click the mouse button. Move the mouse pointer out of the way so that you can see the insertion point in its new location. Notice the change in the status bar.

The point-and-click method of moving the insertion point with the mouse is useful when the part of the document you need to move to is visible on the screen. If you can't see the place in your document to which you want to move, you must use the scroll bars first to move the new location into view, then click the I-beam at the point where the revision needs to be made.

Word's vertical and horizontal scroll bars contain the same elements as Windows' scroll bars—scroll arrows and a scroll box. Let's practice using the scroll bars. Take note of the status bar to determine the current location of the insertion point.

To scroll through a document:

1. Click the **down arrow** at the bottom of the vertical scroll bar several times. Notice that the location of the insertion point does not change. You can use the down arrow and the up arrow on the vertical scroll bar to scroll through your document line by line.
2. Click once below the scroll box in the vertical scroll bar. When you click below or above the scroll box, you scroll one window of text at a time.
3. Drag the scroll box to the bottom of the vertical scroll bar to move quickly through the document. Although you can see the end of your document on the screen, you cannot see the insertion point.
4. Move the I-beam anywhere in the last line of text you can see on the screen, then click. Now the location of the insertion point changes.
5. Drag the scroll box in the horizontal scroll bar all the way to the right. You lose sight of your document. Drag the scroll box back to the left edge of the horizontal scroll bar. Your document comes back into view.

You can use the scroll bars to bring different parts of your document into view. However, until you click the mouse pointer, the insertion point does not move to a new location.

Inserting New Text

Now that Denise knows how to move within her document and change the location of the insertion point quickly, she can modify her document. She sees several changes she wants to make. First, she decides to insert the letter "n" and the word "alternate" before the word "supply" in the last sentence of the first paragraph.

To insert new text into previously created text, move the insertion point and type in the new text. Word's default typing preference mode is **Insert mode**; that is, as new characters are inserted into previously typed text, Word moves the existing text to the right and adjusts the line endings to accommodate the changes.

To insert the new text in the first paragraph:

1. Place the insertion point in the first paragraph of the body of the letter, immediately after the "a" in "identify a..."
2. Type **n** and press **[Spacebar]**, then type **alternate**. As you type the new text, the existing text moves to the right. See Figure 1-27.

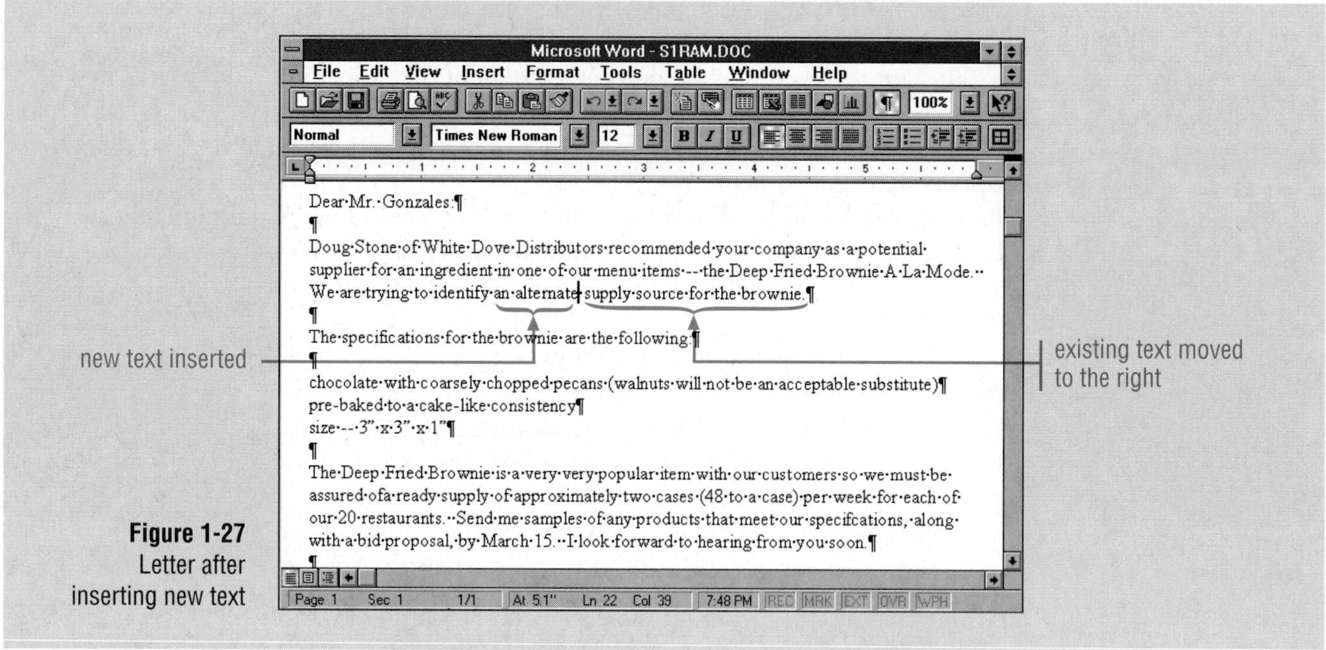

Figure 1-27 Letter after inserting new text

Deleting Text

Thus far, you have been correcting your errors by backspacing over them. Backspacing deletes the character or space to the left of the insertion point. To delete a space or character to the *right* of the insertion point, you press [Del]. Denise notices that she capitalized the words "A La" in A La Mode, but they should be lowercase. Let's delete the capital A and capital L and replace them with lowercase letters.

To use [Del] to delete the text:

1. Place the insertion point directly in front of the "A" in A La.
2. Press **[Del]** three times to remove the "A," the space, and the "L." Notice that the text closes up after the characters are deleted.
3. Type **a** then press **[Spacebar]** and type **l**. The correction is inserted, and the existing text moves to the right. See Figure 1-28.

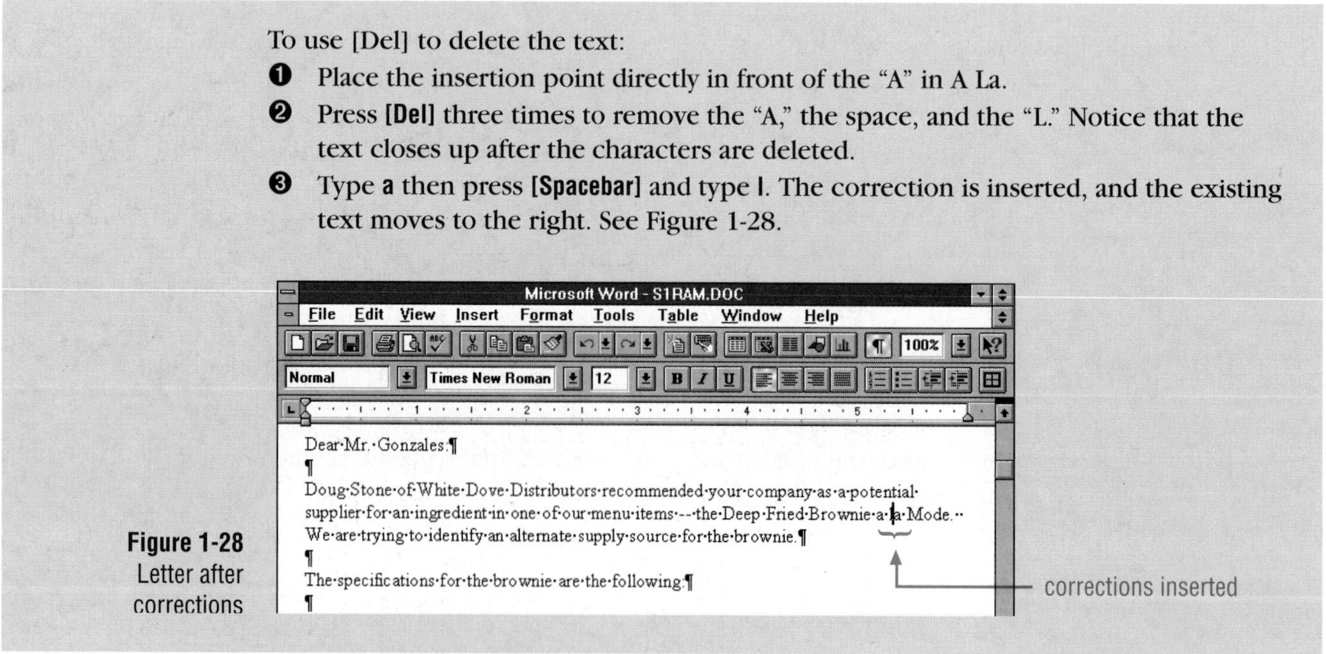

Figure 1-28 Letter after corrections

Deleting text one character at a time is inefficient if you have several characters to delete. Figure 1-29 describes other keyboard deletion techniques you can use.

To delete:	Press:
The character to the right of the insertion point	[Del]
The character to the left of the insertion point	[Backspace]
Text from the insertion point to the end of the word	[Ctrl][Del]
The word to the left of the insertion point	[Ctrl][Backspace]

Figure 1-29
Keyboard deletion techniques

Denise wants to delete the word "The" in the sentence beginning "The specifications..." and change it to "Our."

To delete the word "The":

1. Place the insertion point in front of "The" at the beginning of the second paragraph.
2. Press **[Ctrl][Del]**. Notice that the word "The" and the space after it are deleted.

Using Undo

Sometimes Word makes it so easy to delete text that you might delete something unintentionally. In such a case, you could use another feature of Word, the Undo command. If you accidentally delete text, you can click the Undo button on the Standard toolbar or choose Undo from the Edit menu. The Standard toolbar also contains a Redo button, which redoes the previously undone action. The text you deleted reappears in its original location. The word or words that follow Undo on the Edit menu change to reflect the type of action that Word can undo at that point (for instance, "Undo Typing"). Note that some actions cannot be undone at any time. In that case, "Can't Undo" appears dimmed in the Edit menu to indicate that the command is not currently available for use.

Denise has just deleted the word "The" at the beginning of the second paragraph. Let's practice using the Undo feature to reinsert the deleted word.

To undo the text deletion:

1. Click the **Undo button** on the Standard toolbar (or click **Edit** then click **Undo Delete Word**). The deleted word is recovered.

Now try reversing the undo action to delete the word "The" again.

2. Click the **Redo button** on the Standard toolbar (or click **Edit** then click **Redo Delete Word**). Your previous undone action is reversed. "The" is deleted again.

Now you can insert the word "Our" in place of "The."

3. Type **Our** then press **[Spacebar]**. The sentence is corrected. See Figure 1-30.

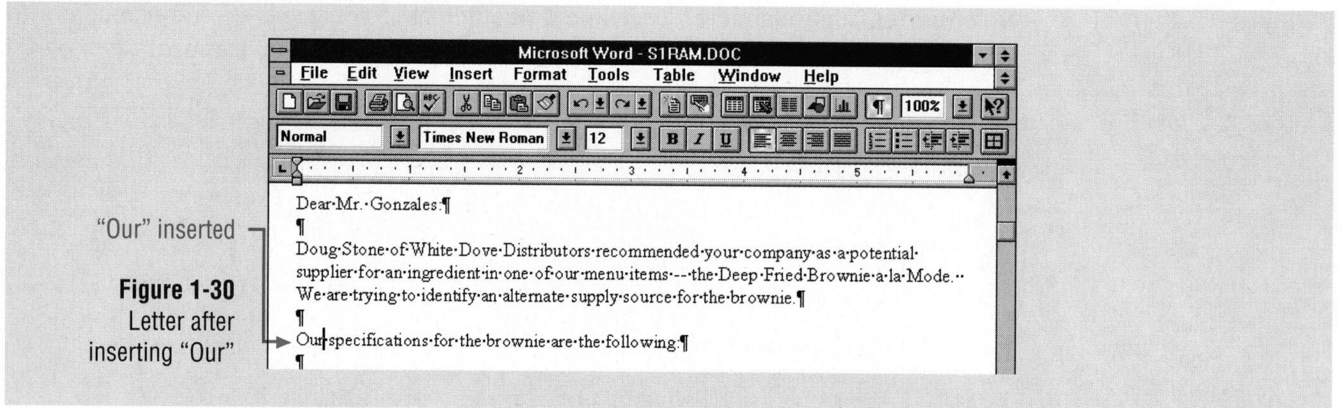

Figure 1-30 Letter after inserting "Our"

You can also undo more than just your last action. Clicking the down arrow next to the Undo button displays a list of all actions that can be reversed. You then select the action to be undone, and that action is undone as well as all subsequent actions. The Redo button has a similar list of all actions that can be redone.

Using Overtype Mode

As you learned earlier, Word's default typing preference is Insert mode. You can deactivate Insert mode by pressing [Ins] or by double-clicking the dimmed OVR indicator in the status bar. The Insert key acts as a **toggle switch;** in other words, you can activate and deactivate Insert mode by pressing the same key.

When you deactivate Insert mode, you overwrite existing text as you type new text. This mode of typing is called **Overtype mode.** When you activate Overtype mode, the abbreviation OVR changes from dimmed to bolded in the status bar.

Let's use Overtype mode to correct an error in Denise's letter. She notices that the address of Ram Food Purveyors is incorrect—it should be 1540 North Vista Avenue instead of Street. She wants to type Avenue over Street.

To type the word Avenue over the word Street:

1. Place the insertion point in front of the "S" in Street in the inside address.
2. Press **[Ins]**. In the status bar, OVR appears darker to remind you that you have changed to Overtype mode. See Figure 1-31.

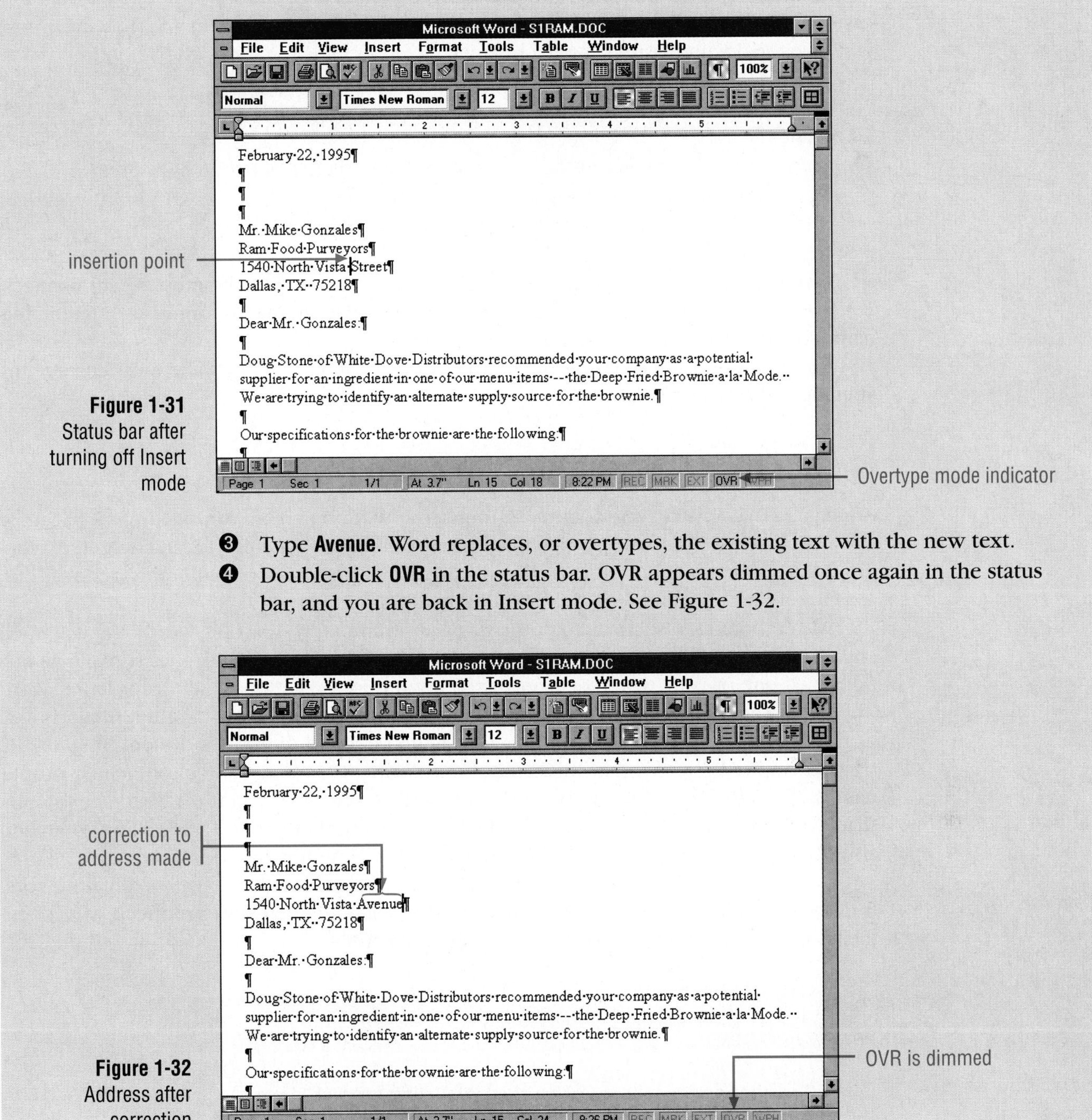

Figure 1-31 Status bar after turning off Insert mode

❸ Type **Avenue**. Word replaces, or overtypes, the existing text with the new text.

❹ Double-click **OVR** in the status bar. OVR appears dimmed once again in the status bar, and you are back in Insert mode. See Figure 1-32.

Figure 1-32 Address after correction

Updating a File

You have now made several changes to Denise's letter, but these changes are not automatically saved. You must instruct Word to update your file to reflect any changes made since you last saved your document. Once a Word document is saved and given a name, all you have to do to save again is click the Save button on the Standard toolbar or choose Save from the File menu. The Save As dialog box will not appear.

As mentioned earlier, the AutoSave feature saves changes to a temporary file just in case of a power failure. The changes are not saved to the permanent file, however, until you save the document in the usual manner.

To update the file:

1. Click the **Save button** on the Standard toolbar (or click **File** then click **Save**). Notice that the Save As dialog box does not appear.

If you wanted to save both the original file and the file with the most recent changes, you would choose the Save As command from the File menu, then give a different filename to the most recent version of your document.

Denise has finished revising the content of her document. Now she must correct any spelling and typographical errors.

Checking Spelling

After you have edited your document to get the wording right, you need to check it for misspelled words and typographical errors. Proofing a document for spelling and typographical errors can be tedious. Word's Spelling command considerably reduces the amount of time you spend on this part of the editing process.

Word contains a standard dictionary of approximately 130,000 words. As you spell check a document, Word compares each word in your document with the words in its dictionary. If one of your words doesn't match a word in its dictionary letter for letter, Word highlights the misspelled word in your document and opens the Spelling dialog box. Correctly spelled words would still be highlighted if Word did not find them in its dictionary. Examples of words that might not be in Word's standard dictionary include proper names, specialized vocabulary, foreign words, and acronyms. If you use a word consistently that Word doesn't recognize, you can add it to a custom dictionary. The Spelling command also points out instances of repeated or doubled words within your document.

A word of caution: don't rely solely on the Spelling command to catch all your errors. It does not catch grammatical and syntax errors. You should always proofread your documents to make the final decisions about their correctness.

REFERENCE WINDOW

Checking the Spelling of a Document

- Click the Spelling button on the Standard toolbar (or click Tools then click Spelling...).
- Change the spelling or ignore Word's suggestion for each flagged word.
- Click OK or press [Enter] when the spell check is finished.

Recall that you made some intentional typing mistakes in the last paragraph of Denise's letter. Let's use the Spelling command to locate and correct these errors. If you made other mistakes, Word will stop at additional places in your document.

To check the spelling of your document:

1. Press **[Ctrl][Home]** to move the insertion point to the top of the document. Word checks your document from the location of the insertion point to the end of the document.
2. Click the **Spelling button** on the Standard toolbar (or click **Tools** then click **Spelling...**). The Spelling dialog box appears. See Figure 1-33. The word "Gonzales" is not found in Word's dictionary, which is typical for most proper nouns. Notice that the word "Gonzales" is highlighted in the text and also appears in the Not in Dictionary text box of the dialog box. Word has no suggested correct spellings.

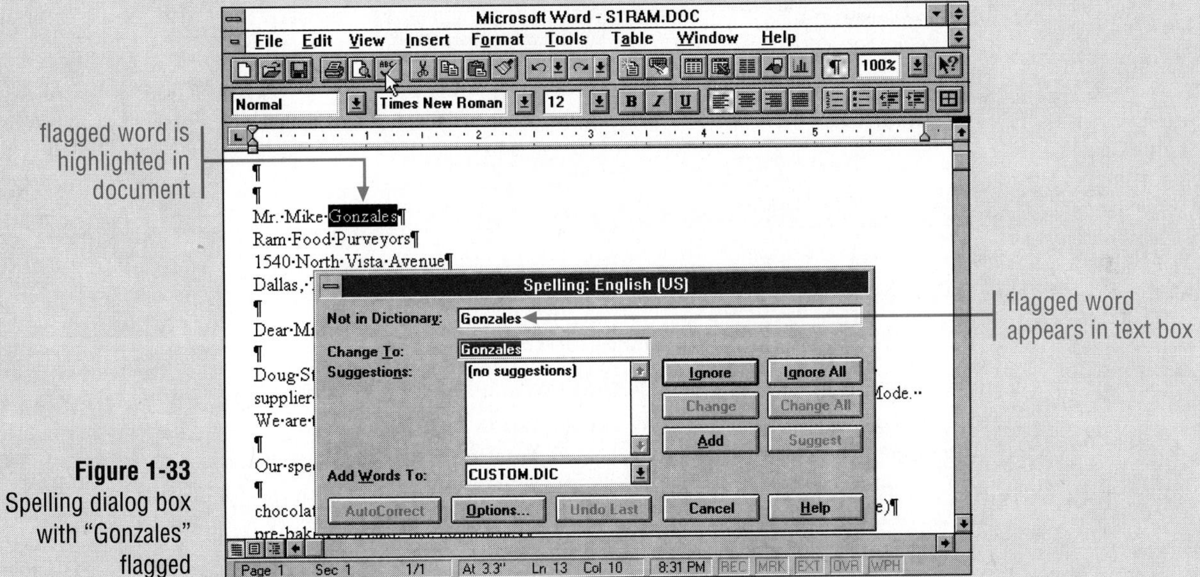

Figure 1-33 Spelling dialog box with "Gonzales" flagged

Denise knows that this is the correct spelling, so she wants to tell Word to ignore this word as well as all other instances of "Gonzales" in her letter.

3. Click **Ignore All** in the Spelling dialog box. Word will not stop at the next instance of "Gonzales" in the salutation.

Word continues to check the spelling in the document and next flags the occurrence of a repeated word "very." The repeated word is highlighted in the document and flagged in the Spelling dialog box. Notice that the text box in the Spelling dialog box changes to Repeated Word instead of Not in Dictionary, and that the Change button is now a Delete button. See Figure 1-34.

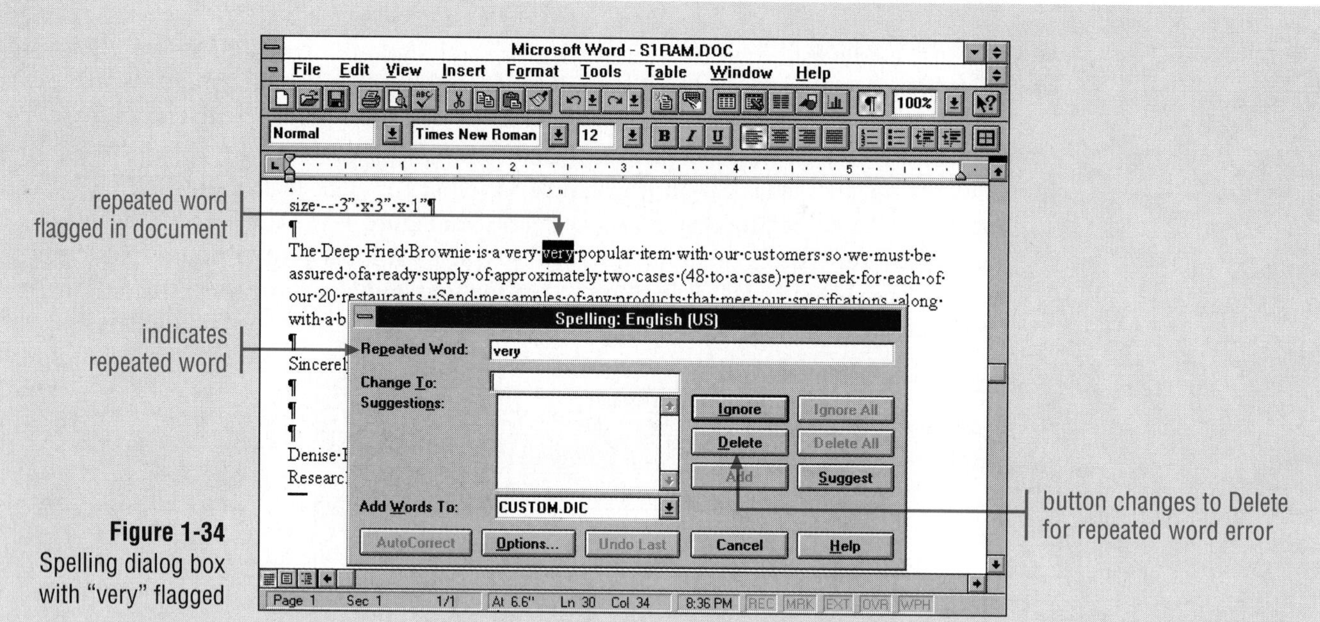

Figure 1-34
Spelling dialog box with "very" flagged

Denise decides to delete the second occurrence of the word "very."

❹ Click **Delete** in the Spelling dialog box.

Word edits your document by deleting the second instance of "very," then stops at another typographical error, "ofa." As shown in Figure 1-35, Word's suggestions for correcting "ofa" are not appropriate, so you must edit this word manually.

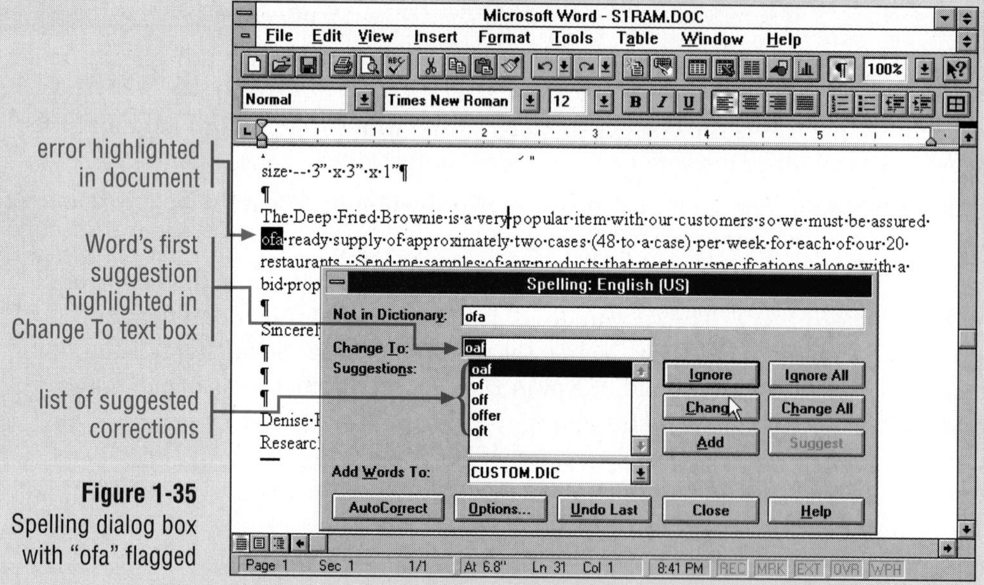

Figure 1-35
Spelling dialog box with "ofa" flagged

❺ Click after the highlighted word "oaf" in the Change To text box to remove the highlighting.

❻ Press **[Backspace]** twice, then type **f** and press **[Spacebar]**, then type **a**. The Change To text box should now contain the correct text, "of a."

❼ Click **Change** in the Spelling dialog box to instruct Word to insert the correct text in the document.

Word moves to the next misspelled word, "specifcations." Notice that the Change To text box contains the correct spelling. If you accept the suggested spelling, Word edits your text for you by replacing the misspelled word in your document with the correct spelling.

❽ Click **Change** to accept Word's suggested spelling.

Word finds no more spelling errors (unless you made additional errors), and a message box appears. You're finished checking the document for spelling errors, so let's exit Spelling and save the corrections you've made.

To exit Spelling and save changes:

❶ Click **OK** or press **[Enter]**.

❷ Click the **Save button** on the Standard toolbar (or click **File** then click **Save**) to save the changes you have made.

Denise proofreads her letter one last time, looking for any errors that the spell check would not catch. The content of her letter is correct and free from errors, and she has saved all of the changes she has made so far. Now she's ready to format her document.

If you want to take a break and resume the tutorial at a later time, you can do so now. Follow the procedure for exiting Word. When you want to resume the tutorial, start Word and place your Student Disk in the disk drive. Remember to complete the screen check procedure described earlier in this tutorial. Then open the file S1RAM.DOC and continue with the tutorial.

■ ■ ■

Formatting a Document

Formatting is the process of controlling how your printed document looks. The purpose of formatting is to improve the readability and attractiveness of your document so that the reader can concentrate on your message. To implement this phase of the productivity strategy efficiently, you should format your document only after you have created and edited the text.

Select, Then Do

When you want to format, you must first indicate to Word the portion of your document you want formatted. You give Word this information by selecting the text you want to change. To **select** text means to highlight it. You can select one character, the whole document, or any amount of text in between. Once you have selected the text you want to format, you then issue the commands to change the highlighted text. Simply stated, the process is "select, then do."

You can select text with either the mouse or the keyboard. Because the mouse is the most efficient way to select text, this book focuses on mouse techniques. The **selection bar** is the area located in the left margin of the document screen. It is one way you select a line or a paragraph of text. The I-beam pointer changes to ↗ whenever it passes into the selection bar.

The mouse technique most frequently used to select small amounts of text is the click-and-drag technique: you click and hold the I-beam in front of the first character to be selected, then drag the pointer across all the text you want selected. The selected text is highlighted. Figure 1-36 summarizes the various techniques for selecting text.

To select:	Then:
A word	Double-click in the word
A sentence	Press [Ctrl] and click within the sentence
A line	Click in the selection bar next to the line
Multiple lines	Click and drag in the selection bar next to lines
A paragraph	Double-click in the selection bar next to the paragraph
Multiple paragraphs	Click and drag in the selection bar next to the paragraphs
Entire document	Triple-click in the selection bar or press [Ctrl] and click
Non-standard block of text	Click at beginning of block, then press [Shift] and click at end of block

Figure 1-36
Selection techniques

Selected text is extremely sensitive to change, so be careful. Word immediately carries out whatever command you issue after you have selected text. If you select text and then press [Enter], for instance, Word replaces your highlighted text with a paragraph mark. If you want your replaced text back, just click the Undo button on the Standard toolbar or select Undo from the Edit menu.

Once you become more familiar with Word and working with selected text, you will see that selecting and replacing text can be a very useful editing tool. For example, earlier you deleted the word "The" and typed the word "Our" to replace it. You could also select the word "The" then simply type "Our" to both delete the selected text and insert the new text in one step.

It is best to deselect text as soon as you can. To deselect highlighted text, you click anywhere off the selected text in the workspace or press any of the arrow keys.

Let's apply the principle of "select, then do" by practicing with the first sentence of Denise's letter.

To select the first sentence in the letter:

1. Place the insertion point anywhere within the first sentence of the first paragraph of the body of the letter.

❷ Press and hold **[Ctrl]** and click within the first sentence. The entire first sentence plus the period and the spaces following are selected. The selected text appears highlighted. See Figure 1-37.

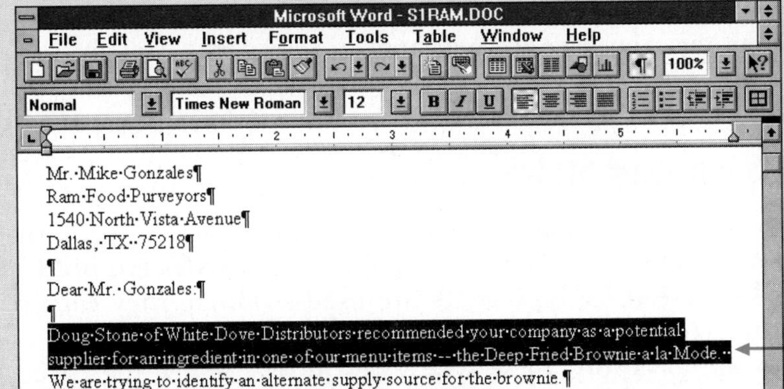

Figure 1-37 Letter with first sentence highlighted

selected area includes two spaces at the end of sentence

TROUBLE? If the entire first sentence is not selected, make sure the insertion point is visible within the first sentence, then press [Ctrl] while you click the left mouse button.

Now let's practice the "do" part of the principle: issuing a command to Word. Let's intentionally make an error, then undo it. If you type something rather than issue a formatting command after you select text, Word will replace your highlighted text with your typing. The principle here is "typing replaces selection." Let's try it.

❸ Press **[Enter]**. Your selection disappears and is replaced with a paragraph mark. See Figure 1-38.

illustrates "typing replaces selection"

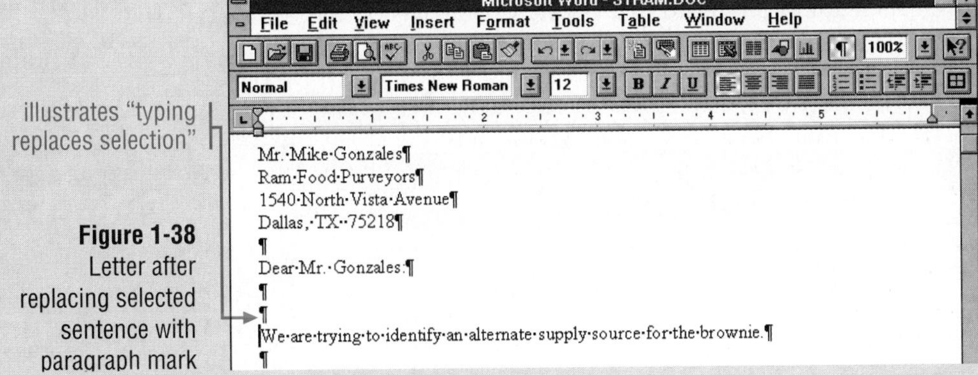

Figure 1-38 Letter after replacing selected sentence with paragraph mark

Don't worry that your sentence disappeared. Word carried out your command. You can recover your selected text by reversing the last command.

❹ Click the **Undo button** on the Standard toolbar (or click **Edit** then click **Undo Typing**). The text returns to its original location and is still highlighted.

To reduce the risk of error, it is always a good idea to deselect highlighted text as soon as possible after you are finished working with it.

To deselect the first sentence:

❶ Click in the workspace outside the selected area or press one of the arrow keys. The highlighting is removed from the first sentence.

Now that you have learned how to select text, you are ready to format Denise's document.

Applying Type Styles

One common formatting technique is to add emphasis to words by changing the style of the printed type. The three most popular type styles are **bold**, *italic*, and underline. Because these three type styles are used so often, they each have a button on the Formatting toolbar.

To add, or **apply**, these type styles to text, follow the "select, then do" principle. Select the text you want to change, then click the appropriate type style button on the Formatting toolbar. The type style is applied only to the selected text.

Denise wants to emphasize several words in her letter so that Mr. Gonzales will pay particular attention to them. She wants to italicize "not" in the first specification.

To italicize the word "not":

❶ Double-click **not** in the first specification ("walnuts will not be...") to select it. When you double-click a word, you select the word and the space after it.

Now let's issue the command to italicize the word you've selected.

❷ Click the **Italic button** on the Formatting toolbar. Notice that the Italic button appears lighter to indicate that the italic type style is in effect, or activated, for the highlighted text. See Figure 1-39.

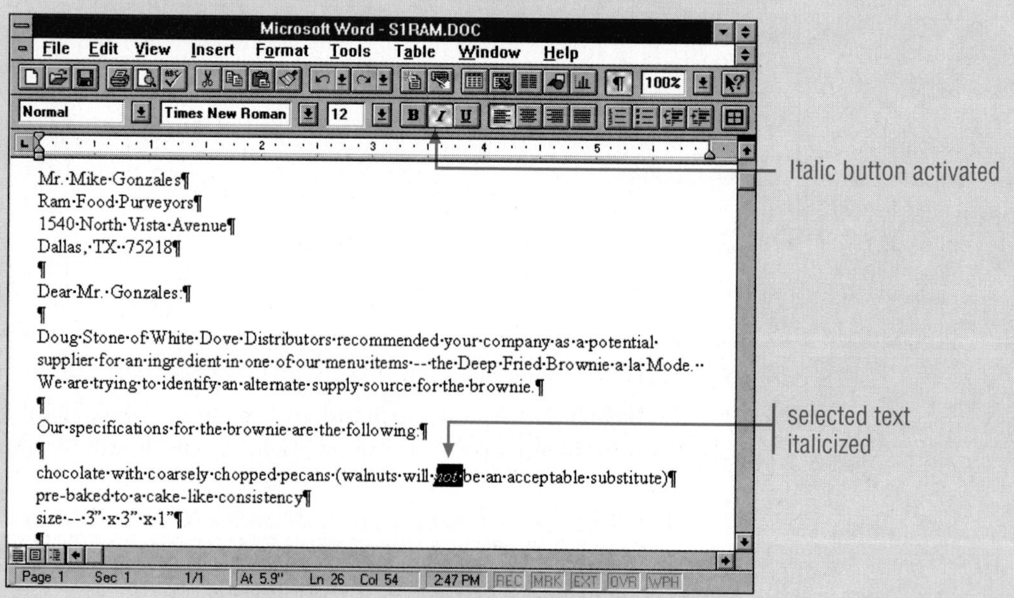

Figure 1-39 Letter with "not" italicized

You are essentially "pressing" the Italic button to activate that type style. By selecting the text first, though, you instruct Word to start and end the italic type style with the selected text.

❸ Click anywhere to deselect the highlighted text so that you can see the change in the type style of "not."

Next Denise wants to emphasize the date by which she needs the bid proposal from Mr. Gonzales. She decides to bold "March 15."

To bold the text "March 15":

❶ Click and hold the I-beam in front of the "M" in March, drag across and through March 15, then release the mouse button.

TROUBLE? If you have difficulty highlighting March 15, deselect the text by clicking in the workspace or pressing one of the arrow keys. Then start over. The insertion point serves as an anchor for whatever you want to select. As long as you do not release the mouse button, you can reduce or expand the amount of text you have highlighted. Once you have selected the text, you are ready to give a formatting command.

❷ Click the **Bold button** B on the Formatting toolbar. The Bold button appears lighter to indicate it has been applied to the selected text.

❸ Deselect the text to see the effect of the bold type style. See Figure 1-40.

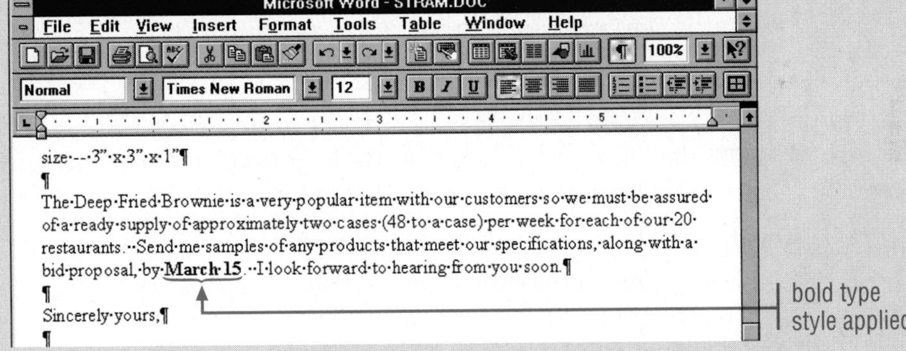

Figure 1-40 Letter with "March 15" bolded

You can apply more than one type style to selected text. Denise wants the word "not," which she italicized in the first specification, to really stand out, so she decides to bold it, too. Let's do that now.

To apply more than one type style to the word "not":

❶ Double-click **not** in the first specification. Notice that the Italic button *I* becomes lighter because the word "not" has been italicized. The appearance of the button on the Formatting toolbar changes to reflect the format applied to the selected text.

❷ Click the **Bold button** B on the Formatting toolbar. Notice that the Bold button also becomes lighter. Both type styles have now been applied to the word.

❸ Deselect the text to see the effect of adding the bold type style to the italicized text.

4. Click the **Save button** on the Standard toolbar (or click **File** then click **Save**) to save the changes you have made so far.

Denise wants to emphasize "the Deep Fried Brownie a la Mode" in the first paragraph, so she decides to underline it. Although she could use the click-and-drag method to select the text, she decides to try a selection technique that gives her more control over what she wants to select.

Let's use the shift-click technique to highlight "the Deep Fried Brownie a la Mode" in the first paragraph before you underline it.

To underline the text:

1. Place the insertion point in front of the "t" in the word "the" in the first sentence of the first paragraph.
2. Move the I-beam after the "e" in Mode. Just move the I-beam to the end of the block—do not drag the mouse pointer over the text. See Figure 1-41.

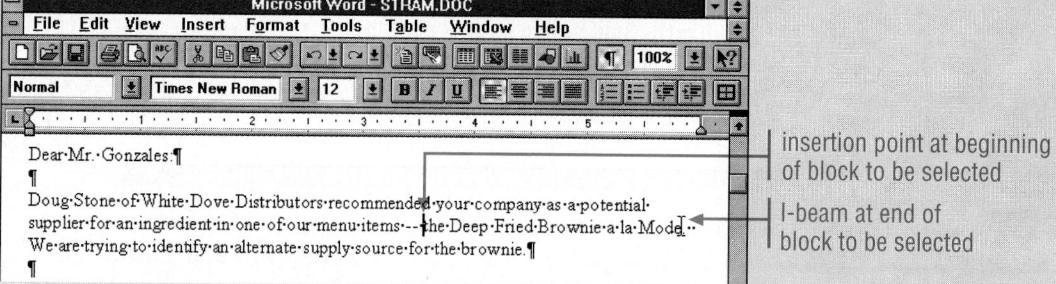

Figure 1-41 Preparing to use the shift-click selection technique

3. With the I-beam after the "e" in Mode, press **[Shift]** then click. Just the block of text, "the Deep Fried Brownie a la Mode," is highlighted.

Now that you have selected the text, you are ready to underline it.

4. Click the **Underline button** on the Formatting toolbar to underline the selected text. The Underline button is activated. See Figure 1-42.

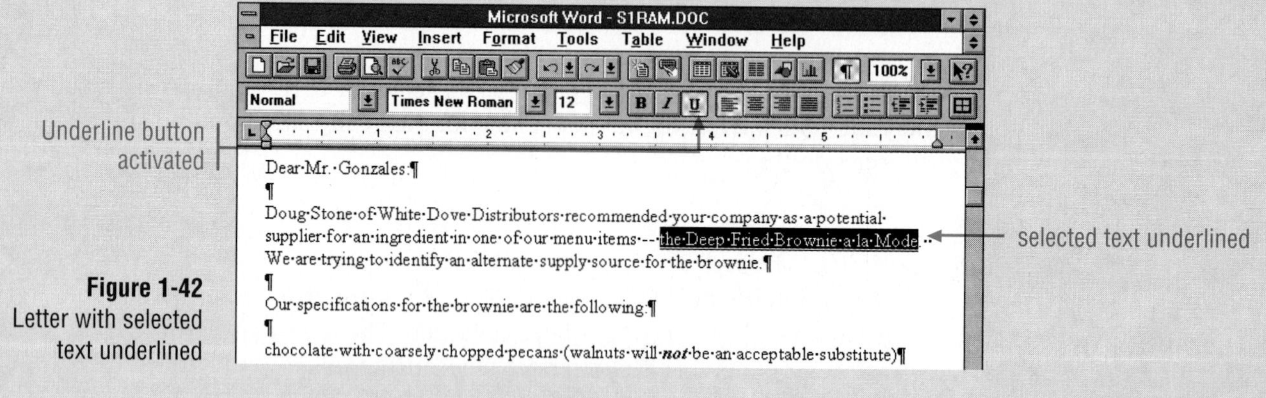

Figure 1-42 Letter with selected text underlined

5. Deselect the text to see the effect of the underlining.

Now you have seen how the shift-click technique gives you more control over the block of text you need to select.

Removing Type Styles

Denise changes her mind about the underlining and wants to remove it. She knows that to remove a type style format, such as bold, italic, or underline, all she has to do is select the formatted text she wants to change, then click the button of the type style she wants to remove. Let's try it.

To remove the underlining:

1. Use the shift-click method again to select "the Deep Fried Brownie a la Mode." Notice that the Underline button U becomes lighter to indicate that it is activated for the selected text.
2. Click U and notice that the button is deactivated.
3. Deselect the text to see that the underlining is removed.

The type style buttons are toggle switches; you turn the type styles on and off with the same button.

Adding Bullets

Another way to format documents is to add special characters—often heavy dots—to call attention to a particular passage or list of items. These characters are called **bullets**. The Bullets button on the Formatting toolbar makes it easy for you to add or remove these special characters because it also acts like a toggle switch. To add a bullet to selected text, simply click the Bullets button; to remove a bullet from selected text, click the Bullets button again to deactivate the feature.

Denise decides to emphasize the three specifications for the brownie by placing a bullet in front of each of them. She could select each specification individually and then click the Bullets button, but the more efficient procedure would be to select all three specifications at once, then format the entire selection with the bullets. She decides to use the selection bar to highlight all three specifications.

To apply bullets to the list of specifications:

1. Move the I-beam into the selection bar next to the first specification, "chocolate..." The pointer changes to ↗ when you move it into the selection bar.
2. Press and drag the pointer down until the last specification, "size ...," is highlighted.
3. Click the **Bullets button** on the Formatting toolbar. A special character, the rounded bullet, appears in front of each item. Notice that the button appears lighter to indicate that it is activated.
4. Deselect the text to view the bullets. See Figure 1-43.

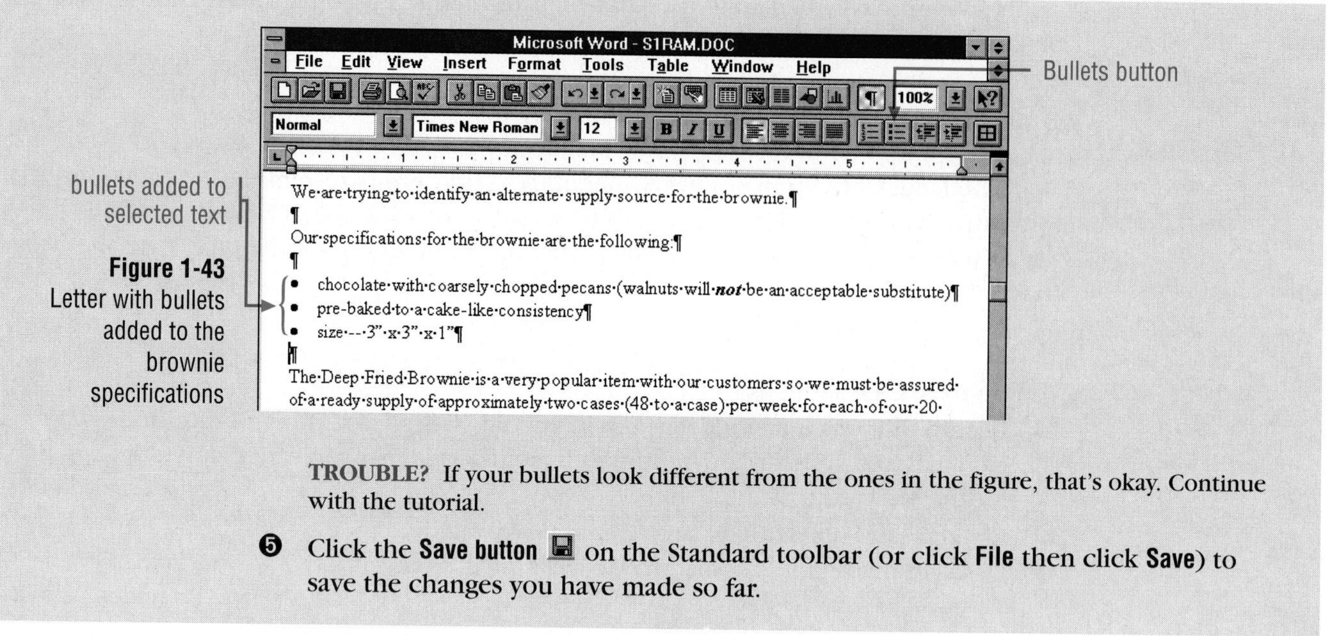

Figure 1-43
Letter with bullets added to the brownie specifications

TROUBLE? If your bullets look different from the ones in the figure, that's okay. Continue with the tutorial.

5. Click the **Save button** on the Standard toolbar (or click **File** then click **Save**) to save the changes you have made so far.

Denise is now finished with three of the four phases of the productivity strategy. She began by entering the text, keeping in mind her plan for organizing her letter as she typed. Then she edited her letter by making changes in content and correcting any errors she found during proofreading, including spell checking her document. Next she used the various techniques for selecting text with the mouse to format her document so that it is more readable and attractive. Now she is ready to print her document.

Previewing and Printing a Document

During the first three phases of the production strategy, you typically use only Word's normal editing view. Now it is time to see a printed version of your document.

It is not necessary to actually print a hard copy of your document to see how it will look when printed. Rather, you can preview your printed document on screen. You can use the Print Preview button on the Standard toolbar to see a miniaturized view of your document as it would look printed. You can also choose Print Preview from the File menu. Then you can either edit the document while in print preview or return to your document to make adjustments. If the document needs no modifications, you can print it directly from the Preview window. Previewing your document before actually printing it saves time and resources.

To preview then print the document:

1. Make sure your printer is on and contains paper.
2. Click the **Print Preview button** on the Standard toolbar (or click **File** then click **Print Preview**). The Preview window opens and displays a reduced version of your document. See Figure 1-44.

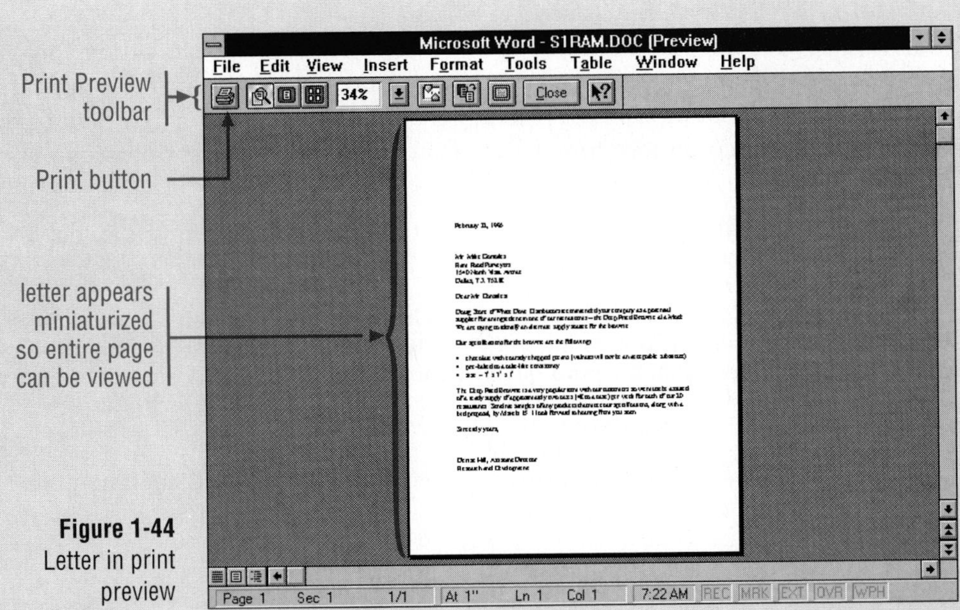

Figure 1-44 Letter in print preview

The letter looks evenly balanced on the page, both vertically and horizontally, so Denise decides to print the letter. However, she wants to check the print settings first. To do so, she needs to choose the Print command from the File menu instead of clicking the Print button on the toolbar. The Print button sends the document directly to the printer; the Print command displays the Print dialog box in which you can modify the print settings. Both the Print button and the Print command are also available from the document window.

❸ Click **File** then click **Print...**. The Print dialog box appears. See Figure 1-45. Notice that the Print dialog box provides options for printing all the pages in your document, the current page only, or selected pages that you specify. You can also choose to print multiple copies of your document.

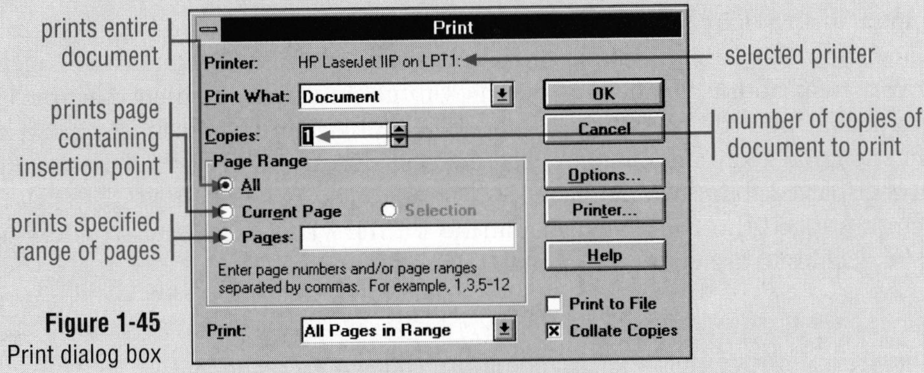

Figure 1-45 Print dialog box

Always check the Printer section of the dialog box to make sure that it shows the correct printer.

TROUBLE? If the correct printer is not selected, click Cancel in the Print dialog box. Click File, click Print..., then click Printer.... Select the correct printer from the list of available printers. If you change a document's printer after formatting a document, the way your document displays and prints might be different from the way you intended.

4. Click **OK** or press **[Enter]**. A message appears briefly in the status bar letting you know that your document is being sent to the printer. A printer icon also appears briefly in the time slot of the status bar along with the number of pages sent to the printer. To cancel a print job from within Word, double-click the printer icon in the status bar.

   Once your letter prints, it should look similar to Figure 1-1 without the Sweet T's letterhead.

   TROUBLE? If your document hasn't printed yet, check the status of your document in Windows Program Manager by pressing [Alt][Tab] until the Print Manager title bar appears. Remove your document from the print queue before returning to your document, then send the document to print again. If it still doesn't print, check with your instructor or technical support person.

5. Click the **Close button** on the Print Preview toolbar to return to the document.

Getting Help

Although the tutorials in this book will help you learn a great deal about Word's operations, you might want to explore a topic not taught yet or refresh your memory about a procedure already covered. In any case, you need to be able to find your own answers to word processing questions that might arise in the future.

Word's on-line Help system gives you quick access to information about Word's features, commands, and procedures. You can get help by using context-sensitive Help as you work, by looking up a topic in Word Help Contents, or by using the Help Search feature.

Using Context-Sensitive Help

Context-sensitive Help allows you to find out information about menu commands, buttons, toolbars, rulers, or other screen elements as you are working with them in your document. You click the Help button on the Standard toolbar or press [Shift][F1] to change the pointer to the Help pointer. Then you click the screen item you want to know about and the related Help topic appears automatically. Most dialog and message boxes also have a Help button, which you can click to get information about that specific feature's options. Once you have initiated context-sensitive Help, you can also use it to find out what function a key combination performs—just press the key combination and information is displayed about that command.

Denise noticed the Full Screen command on the View menu and wonders what it does. She decides to use context-sensitive Help to find out.

To use context-sensitive Help to learn about the Full Screen command:

1. Click the **Help button** on the Standard toolbar. The mouse pointer changes to the Help pointer.
2. Click **View** then click **Full Screen**. The Word Help window appears and displays the topic, "Full Screen command (View menu)."
3. Read the information in the topic window, using the scroll bar to view the entire topic if necessary.

Denise is ready to exit Word Help.

❹ Double-click the **Word Help window Control menu box** (or click **File** then click **Exit** in the Word Help window).

Using the Help Contents Window

If you want general information about Word's features, you should open the Word Help Contents window, which serves as a table of contents for all topics in on-line Help. You can even have Word demonstrate some of its features for you. To access the Help Contents window, you press [F1] or choose Contents from the Help menu. From this window you can move to topics of interest by clicking the appropriate **hot topic,** a solid underlined word or phrase.

Denise is interested in finding out more about Outline view. She decides to look it up using the Help Contents window.

To use the Help Contents window to find information about Outline view:

❶ Press **[F1]** (or click **Help** then click **Contents**). The Word Help Contents window appears in front of the document and becomes the active window. See Figure 1-46.

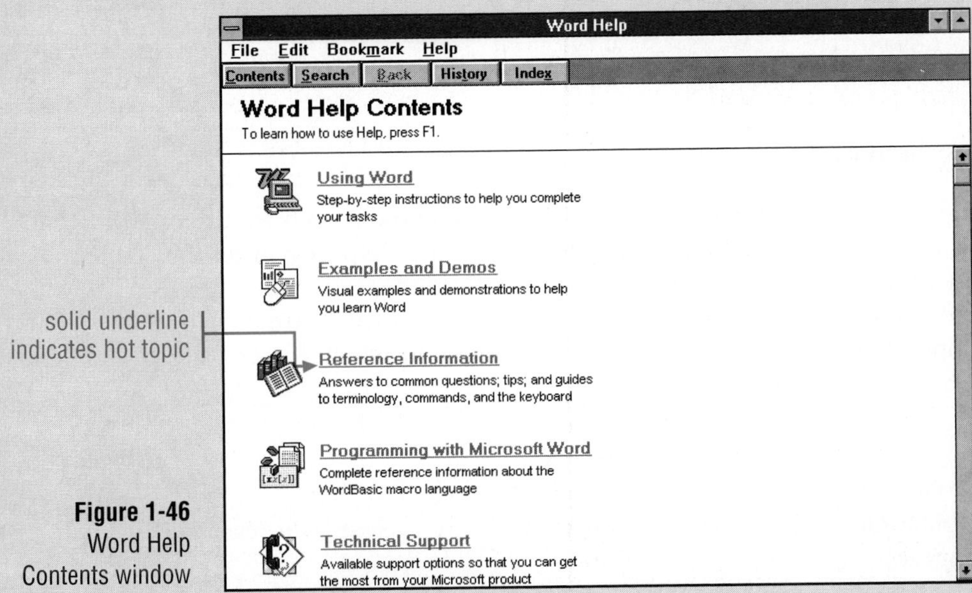

Figure 1-46 Word Help Contents window

❷ Click the **Reference Information** hot topic, then click **Definitions** in the General Reference Information section. Notice that the pointer changes to a hand when placed over a topic. An alphabetical listing of terms opens. The dotted underlined words are known as *hot words*. To see a definition of a hot word, simply click it.

Because you're looking for information on Outline view, you need to move to the topics that begin with the letter "O."

❸ Click the **O button** then click the **outline view** hot word. A definition of Outline view appears in a separate window. See Figure 1-47.

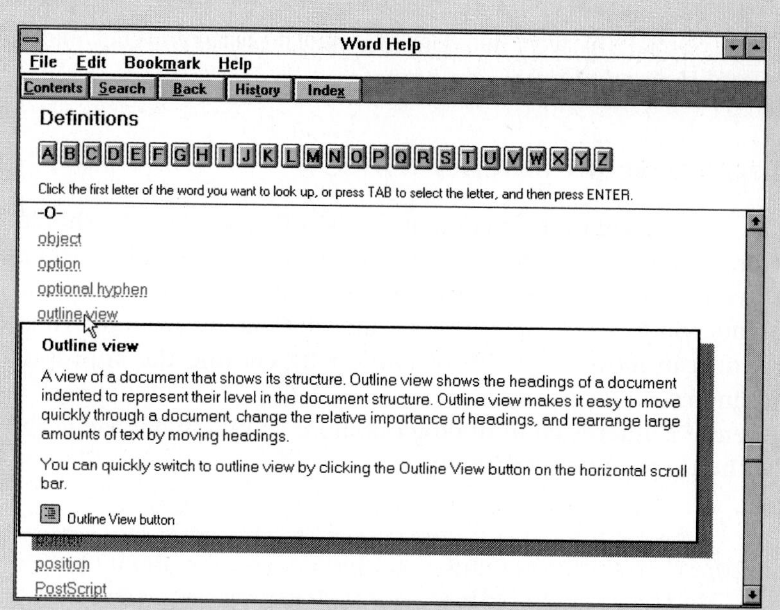

Figure 1-47 Definition of outline view

4. Read the information then press **[Esc]** to dismiss the definition window.

Denise now has a better understanding of outline view and is ready to exit Help.

5. Close the Word Help Contents window.

Using Search

You can let Word do the leg work for you by using the Search feature of Word Help. You access the Search dialog box by double-clicking the Help button on the Standard toolbar or choosing the Search for Help on command from the Help menu.

Denise decides to use the Search feature to find information about printing envelopes, because she needs a printed envelope in which to send her completed letter to Ram Food Purveyors.

To search in Word Help for information on printing envelopes:

1. Double-click the **Help button** on the Standard toolbar. The Search dialog box appears.
2. Type **e** in the "search for" text box. The list of topics shown changes to those topics starting with "e."
3. Type **nv** after the "e" in the "search for" text box. The list of topics shown changes to those starting with "env" and the topic "envelopes" is now highlighted.
4. Click **Show Topics** or press **[Enter]**. Several related topics appear in the lower half of the window. See Figure 1-48.

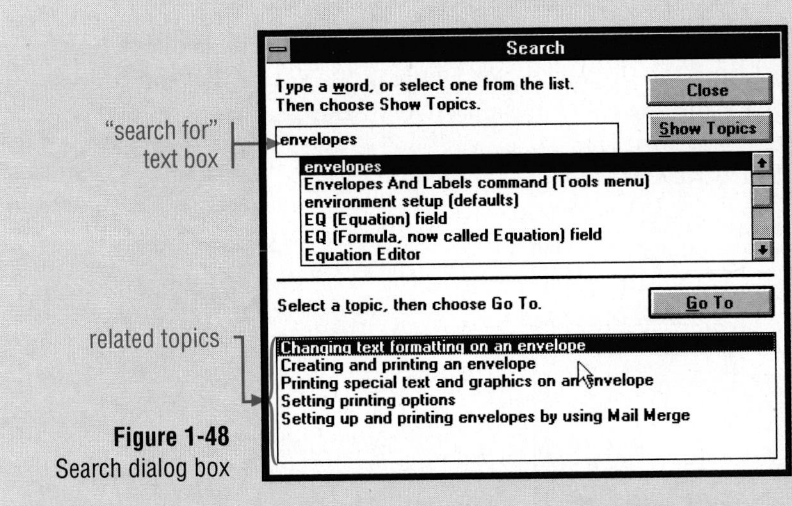

Figure 1-48
Search dialog box

5. Click **Creating and printing an envelope**, then click **Go To** or press **[Enter]**. The How To window for Creating and Printing Envelopes appears.
6. Maximize the How To window. How To windows have their own button bars, including an On Top button, which keeps the window visible so you can return to your document and still see the procedures for completing the task.
7. Read the information about creating envelopes, double-click the **How To window Control menu box**, then double-click the **Help Contents window Control menu box** (or click **File** then click **Exit** in the Help Contents window) to close the window and return to the document.

Now that Denise has read the information about creating and printing envelopes, she decides to print the envelope for her letter to Mr. Gonzales.

Printing an Envelope

Envelopes have always been difficult to address on computers and, until recently, almost impossible to print on ordinary printers. It was generally easier just to type the address on an envelope using a typewriter rather than spend time figuring out how to do it on a computer. Word now makes it extremely easy to address the envelope, but you must still have a printer capable of printing envelopes. *Before you attempt this section of the tutorial, check with your instructor or technical support person to determine whether your printer can print envelopes.*

Denise inserts an envelope into the envelope feeder of her printer and is now ready to print her envelope.

To print an envelope:

1. Insert an envelope into the envelope feeder on your printer. Check with your instructor or technical support person to make sure your printer can print envelopes before continuing. If your printer doesn't have an envelope feeder or you don't have an envelope, try printing the address on a regular sheet of paper.

2. Click **Tools** then click **Envelopes and Labels...**. The Envelopes and Labels dialog box appears with the Envelopes tab displayed. See Figure 1-49. Notice that the address for Mr. Gonzales appears automatically in the Delivery Address box.

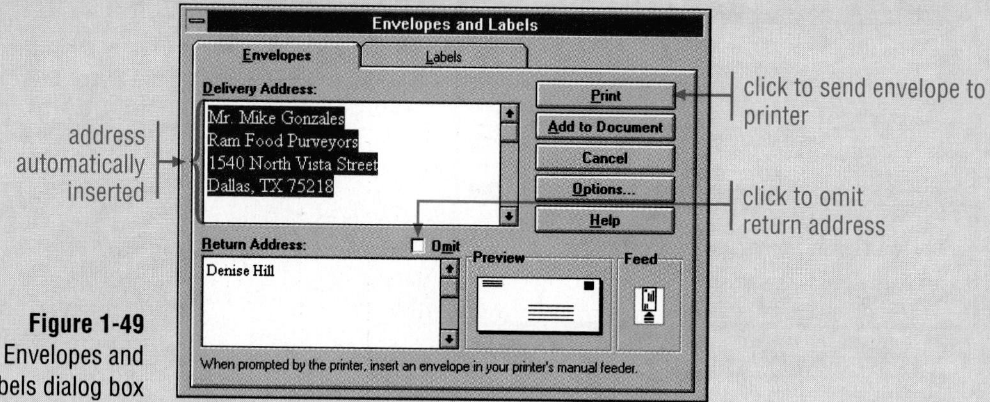

Figure 1-49 Envelopes and Labels dialog box

The information in your Return Address box will vary, depending on who installed Word on your computer. Generally in a business situation, the Omit check box would be selected because a company's return address is already printed on the envelope. However, you will enter your name and address in the Return Address box so that you can distinguish your printed envelope from those of other students.

3. If the Omit check box is selected, click the box to clear it.
4. Select any text that appears in the Return Address box, then type your name and address.

Ask your instructor or technical support person about your printer's ability to print envelopes before completing the next step. If your printer cannot print envelopes, click Cancel in the dialog box instead of completing the next step.

5. Click **Print**. Because you have inserted your name and address in the Return Address box, Word wants to know if you want to change the default so that your name and address will automatically appear as the return address.
6. Click **No**. A printing message appears briefly in the status bar.
7. Save the changes you have made.

TROUBLE? If your envelope didn't print, your printer might not be able to print envelopes. Check with your instructor or technical support person to determine what to do next.

Your envelope should look like the envelope in Figure 1-1 except that your name and address will appear where the Sweet T's, Inc. preprinted address appears.

Now that Denise has printed both her letter and her envelope, she decides to close her document and exit Word.

To close the document and exit Word:

1. Double-click the **document window Control menu box** (or click **File** then click **Close**). Notice the difference in the menu bar of the Word window—just the File and Help menus are available on the menu bar. Also, the status bar is blank. See Figure 1-50. When you have no other documents open, Word displays this window, known as the Nil menu screen.

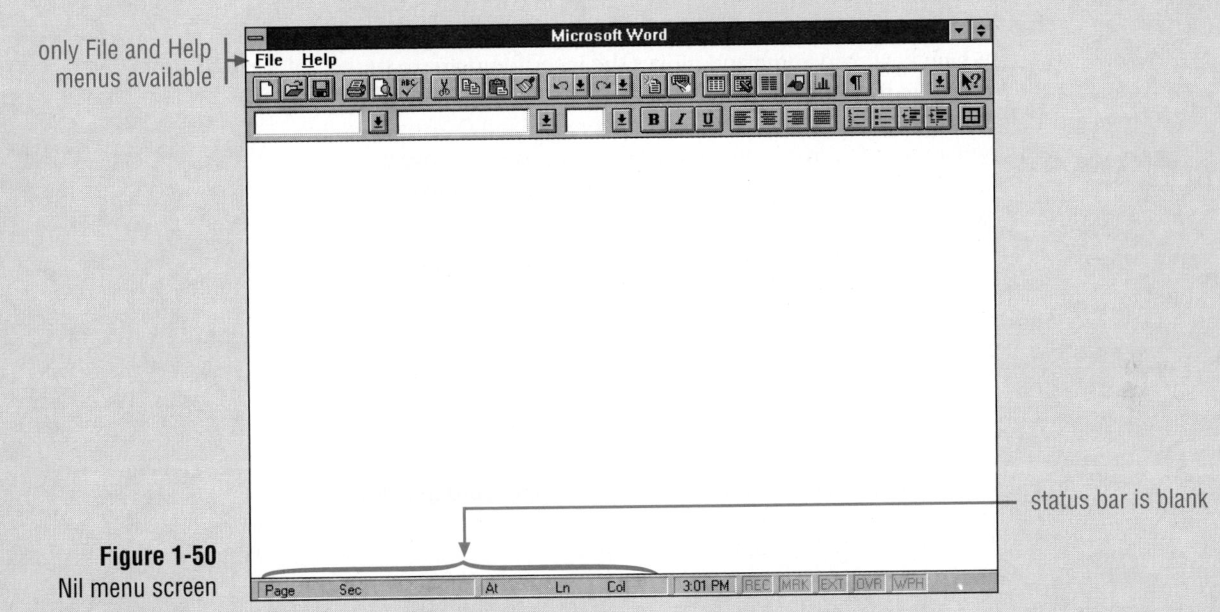

Figure 1-50
Nil menu screen

You could create a new document or open an existing document if you wanted to continue to work in Word, but in this case you will exit Word.

2. Double-click the **Word window Control menu box** (or click **File** then click **Exit**). You return to the Program Manager. The Microsoft Office group window is still open.

   TROUBLE? If you are asked to save changes to any documents other than S1RAM.DOC, click No.

3. Double-click the **Microsoft Office group window Control menu box** to close this window.
4. Exit Windows.

■ ■ ■

Denise has completed all phases of her productivity strategy—creating, editing, formatting, and printing—and is now is ready to mail her letter.

Questions

1. List and briefly describe the four phases of the productivity strategy.
2. Describe the differences between the Word window and the document window.
3. What are the six questions you should answer at the beginning of each new Word session to determine whether your Word screen is arranged properly?
4. How do you display the shortcut Toolbar menu?

5. What is the difference between an open document and an active document?
6. Describe two methods for switching between open documents.
7. What are default settings for a Word document?
8. In the status bar, what do the following indicate about the location of the insertion point?
   a. At 7.2"
   b. Ln 20
   c. Col 29
9. Which key do you press to insert a blank line in your document?
10. What is the difference between using [Backspace] and [Del] to correct errors?
11. Which keyboard command moves the insertion point to the top of the document?
12. Describe the difference between the insertion point and the I-beam.
13. What is the difference between Insert mode and Overtype mode?
14. What types of errors will the Spelling command discover?
15. Explain the principle of "select, then do." Give examples.
16. Where is the selection bar located?
17. What is the purpose of the print preview feature?
18. What is the difference between a dotted underscored word and a solid underscored word in a Word Help topic window?

Use Word Help to answer Questions 19 through 22:

E 19. How do you open a file in Word that was created by another application?

E 20. What is the purpose of the Summary Info dialog box?

E 21. How would you check the spelling of just one word in a document?

E 22. How do you modify the format of a bullet?

Tutorial Assignments

Start Word, if necessary, and make sure your Student Disk is in the disk drive. Conduct a screen check, then open T1TFP.DOC and complete the following:

1. Change the date to October 5, 1995.
2. Use the selection bar to select the inside address, then insert your name and address.
3. Change the salutation appropriately.
4. Move the insertion point into the last paragraph and change the date, March 15, to October 31. Bold and italicize the date.
5. Remove the applied type styles from "not" in the last brownie specification.
6. Spell check and proofread for additional errors.
7. Save the letter as S1TFP.DOC to your Student Disk.
8. Preview the letter.
9. Print the letter and an envelope, if your printer has the capability to print envelopes.
10. Save the changes, if necessary.

E 11. Apply bullets to the brownie specifications, but change the shape of the bullet to ⇒. Save the document as S1TFP2.DOC.

12. Print the document.

E 13. Use Word Help to look up how to remove bullets. Then print the Help Topic on "Adding or removing bullets or numbers in a list."

Case Problems

1. A Confirmation Letter to Haas Petroleum

Lillian May coordinates off-campus credit offerings for Western Hills Community College in Colorado Springs, Colorado. She has worked for several years with Fred Maxwell, Human Resources director at Haas Petroleum, to schedule academic classes for Haas employees at their site. She needs to write a letter confirming next semester's schedule. To save time, she uses the document she wrote last year, making a couple of changes.

Open P1HAAS.DOC from your Student Disk and complete the following:

1. Change the date to today's date.
2. Save the document as S1HAAS.DOC.
3. Insert the course description shown in Figure 1-51 one blank line below the course description for GOVT 2301.

> CSCI 1301. Introduction to Computer Information Systems. (3-0) Tuesday, 5-8 p.m.
>
> This course is designed to teach you computer concepts by providing a general knowledge of mainframes and microcomputers, their functions, and applications.

Figure 1-51

4. Delete the entire course description for PSYC 1301.
5. Edit the wording of the letter to make it appropriate for next semester.
6. Bold the course abbreviation and number for each course description.
7. Italicize each course name.
8. Remove the underlining from days and times in GOVT 2301 and ENGL 1302.
9. Spell check the document and proofread for all errors.
10. Save the changes.
11. Preview the letter.
12. Print the letter.
13. Print an envelope, if your printer supports printing envelopes. Include your name and address in the return address. Save the changes.
14. Close the document.

2. A Response to a High School Student

As program manager for KIWW, a radio station in your home town, you often receive requests from local high school students interested in radio and television. Marcus Vincente wrote to you asking for sources of information about radio or television for a research paper he has to write.

Open P1KIWW.DOC from your Student Disk and complete the following to respond to his request:

1. Insert seven blank lines at the top of the document.
2. Save the document as S1KIWW.DOC.
3. Type today's date then insert three blank lines after the date.
4. Insert the names of the three books shown in Figure 1-52 and insert a blank line after the sentence "Check with your school librarian for the following books."

> Handbook of American Popular Culture
> Les Brown's Encyclopedia of Television
> The Encyclopedia of Television Series, Pilots, and Specials, 1937-1973

Figure 1-52

5. Move to the end of the document, type your name, press [Enter], then type Program Manager.
6. Spell check the document and proofread for all errors.
7. Save your changes.
8. Format your document to improve its readability and appearance by italicizing the names of books and adding rounded bullets to the list of books.
9. Save your changes.
10. Preview then print your document.
11. **E** Remove the bullets from the list of books, then print the letter again. Save the document as S1KIWW2.DOC.
12. Close the document.

3. Inquiring About a Sweet Tooth Cafe Franchise

You are interested in opening a Sweet Tooth Cafe franchise in your area. Write a letter to Jocelyn Titus, president of Sweet T's, requesting information about franchising and convincing her of the need for a Sweet Tooth Cafe in your town. Her address is Oklahoma Bank Building, One Main Street, Oklahoma City, OK 73112.

1. Plan your letter then type it.
2. Save the document as S1SWEET1.DOC.
3. Correct all errors, including spelling.
4. Save your changes.
5. Format your document to improve its readability and appearance.
6. Save your changes.
7. Preview then print your document.
8. Close the document.

T U T O R I A L 2

Using Page, Paragraph, and Font Formatting Commands

Creating a Cover Memo and Agenda

OBJECTIVES

In this tutorial you will:

- Rename a file
- Move text within a document
- Change page formatting options such as document margins
- Change paragraph formatting options such as indentation, tabs, line spacing, alignment, borders, and rules
- Insert leader characters
- Number paragraphs
- Change font formatting options such as font type, point size, type style, and between-character spacing
- Insert special symbols
- Preview and print multiple pages

CASE

Seattle Area Teachers Federal Credit Union

Marcus Jenkins recently was hired by the Seattle Area Teachers Federal Credit Union as an administrative assistant to the president of the credit union, Michael Brown. The credit union provides financial services for its approximately 10,000 members, all of whom are employees or former employees of school districts within greater metropolitan Seattle.

Michael is responsible for the daily operations of the credit union and its staff. However, overall policy decisions are made by the Board of Directors, who are elected from the credit union's membership. Part of Marcus's new job is to develop the agenda for the monthly meetings of the board, along with a cover memo announcing the meeting and outlining the agenda for the board members. Because this is his first attempt at completing these documents, Marcus asks Michael to review them and make corrections. Michael suggests that Marcus submit his draft free of any formatting so that Michael can concentrate on the wording.

In this tutorial you will edit, format, and print the cover memo and agenda for Marcus. Marcus decides to use the productivity strategy to complete his assignment. He will first create a draft of the cover memo and agenda, then edit the document to include any additions or corrections Michael wants to make. Marcus will next format the cover memo and agenda and finally print his document.

Before creating the first draft of his cover memo and agenda, Marcus reviews the files from several previous meetings to see how his predecessor had created these documents. He notes that the content of the various cover memos and the order of the items on the agendas remain essentially the same from meeting to meeting. He also notices that occasionally more information is included in the memo than just the announcement of the meeting, and that the agenda items are sometimes rearranged. Marcus then creates a draft cover memo and agenda, which he submits to Michael, using basically the same wording as previous cover memos and the same order of agenda items, changing only the dates. As Michael requested, Marcus submits an unformatted document for his review.

Michael returns the draft of the cover memo and agenda with his edits. He attaches notes with additional information he wants inserted in the memo and some suggestions for reordering and formatting the agenda (shown in Figure 2-1). Marcus looks over his comments and is ready to begin editing the document.

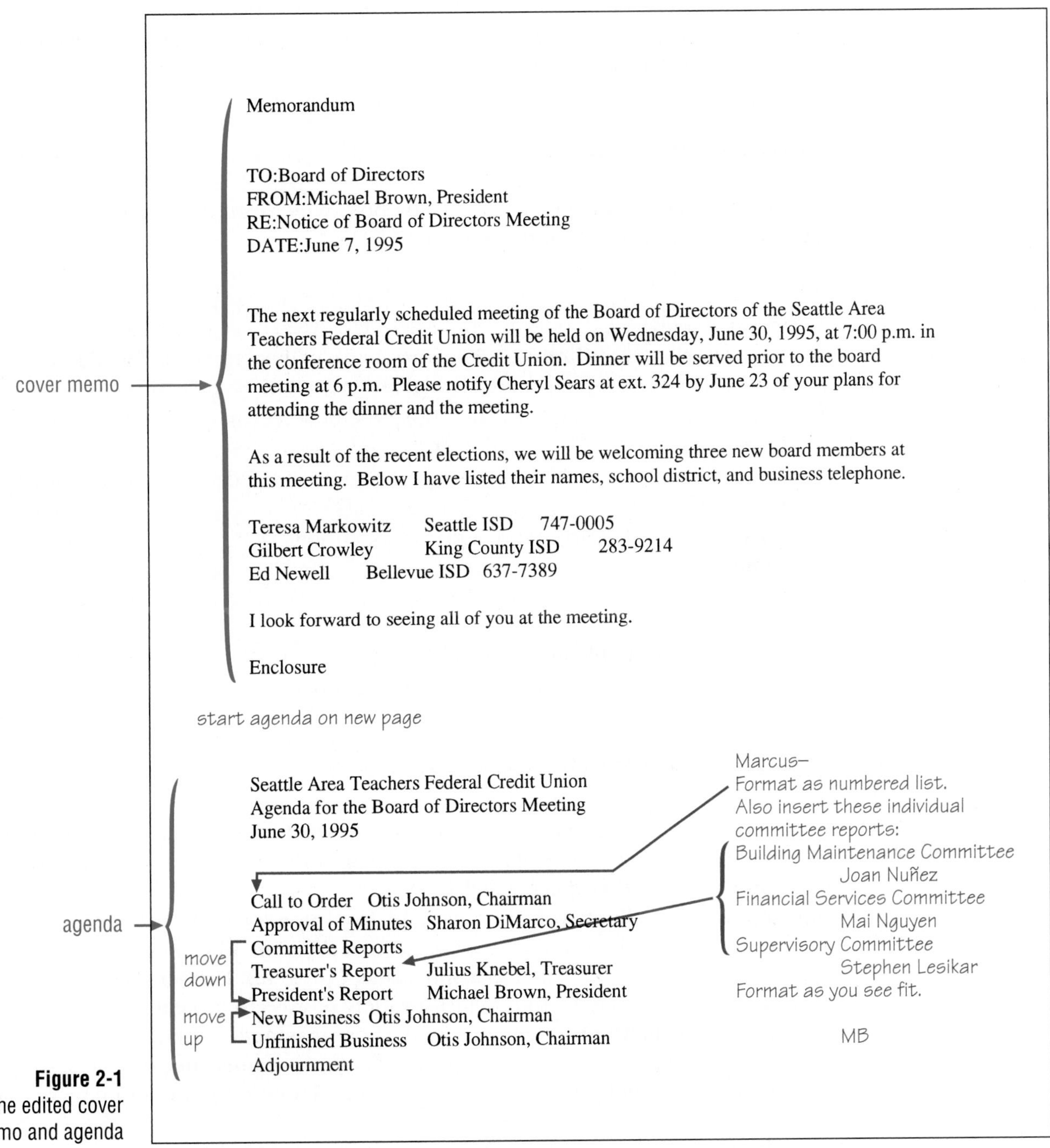
Memorandum

TO:Board of Directors
FROM:Michael Brown, President
RE:Notice of Board of Directors Meeting
DATE:June 7, 1995

The next regularly scheduled meeting of the Board of Directors of the Seattle Area Teachers Federal Credit Union will be held on Wednesday, June 30, 1995, at 7:00 p.m. in the conference room of the Credit Union. Dinner will be served prior to the board meeting at 6 p.m. Please notify Cheryl Sears at ext. 324 by June 23 of your plans for attending the dinner and the meeting.

As a result of the recent elections, we will be welcoming three new board members at this meeting. Below I have listed their names, school district, and business telephone.

Teresa Markowitz Seattle ISD 747-0005
Gilbert Crowley King County ISD 283-9214
Ed Newell Bellevue ISD 637-7389

I look forward to seeing all of you at the meeting.

Enclosure

Seattle Area Teachers Federal Credit Union
Agenda for the Board of Directors Meeting
June 30, 1995

Call to Order Otis Johnson, Chairman
Approval of Minutes Sharon DiMarco, Secretary
Committee Reports
Treasurer's Report Julius Knebel, Treasurer
President's Report Michael Brown, President
New Business Otis Johnson, Chairman
Unfinished Business Otis Johnson, Chairman
Adjournment

Figure 2-1
The edited cover memo and agenda

Let's begin by opening Marcus's unformatted document.

To open the document containing the cover memo and agenda:

1. Start Word, if necessary, and conduct the screen check as described in Tutorial 1.
2. Insert your Student Disk in the disk drive, then open the file C2SATFCU.DOC from your Student Disk. If you do not remember how to open an existing file, refer to Tutorial 1. After C2SATFCU.DOC is open, scroll through the document to become familiar with it.

Before Marcus begins making changes to the document, he decides to save the file with a new name. He wants to keep the original version intact in case he needs it later. To do so, he must rename the file.

Renaming a File

You rename a file using the Save As dialog box, which you used in Tutorial 1 to name a document when saving it for the first time.

To rename the file:

1. Click **File** then click **Save As...**. The Save As dialog box appears. The file's current name, "c2satfcu.doc," appears highlighted in the File Name text box.
2. Type **s2satfcu** in the File Name text box. The new filename replaces the previous filename.
3. Make sure the Drives list box displays the name of the drive containing your Student Disk.
4. Click **OK** or press **[Enter]**. Word adds the extension "DOC" automatically to the filename.

Marcus saved the file he will work in as S2SATFCU.DOC, and he still has the original version of the file. Now he can begin editing the document.

Moving Text Within a Document

In the process of editing a document, you might want to rearrange the content by changing the location of an entire block of text. One of the advantages of word processing is that you can move text quickly and easily from its original location to another without retyping it. Word allows you to move text from one location in a Word document to another location in the *same document,* or to a *different Word document,* or to a *different application program,* such as a spreadsheet program. Furthermore, for each type of move you want to make, Word provides a variety of ways to make it.

The easiest method for moving text short distances within the same document involves the feature known as **drag-and-drop**, so named because you simply *drag* selected text to its new spot in your document and then *drop* it in place by releasing the mouse button.

Michael suggested a change in the order of the agenda items, and Marcus decides to use the drag-and-drop feature to relocate the Committee Reports agenda item after the President's Report agenda item and before the New Business agenda item.

To move the agenda items using drag-and-drop:

1. Click in the selection bar next to Committee Reports to select that line (Ln 37), including the paragraph mark at the end of the line.

   TROUBLE? If you don't remember how to use the selection bar or the other techniques for selecting text, refer to Tutorial 1.

❷ Move the mouse pointer over the selected text. Notice that the shape of the pointer changes to ↖.

❸ Press and continue to hold down the mouse button. The drag-and-drop pointer appears. Use the dashed insertion point of the pointer to help guide you as you drag the selected text to its new location.

❹ Drag the selected text to its new location so that the dashed insertion point is in front of the "N" in New Business. See Figure 2-2.

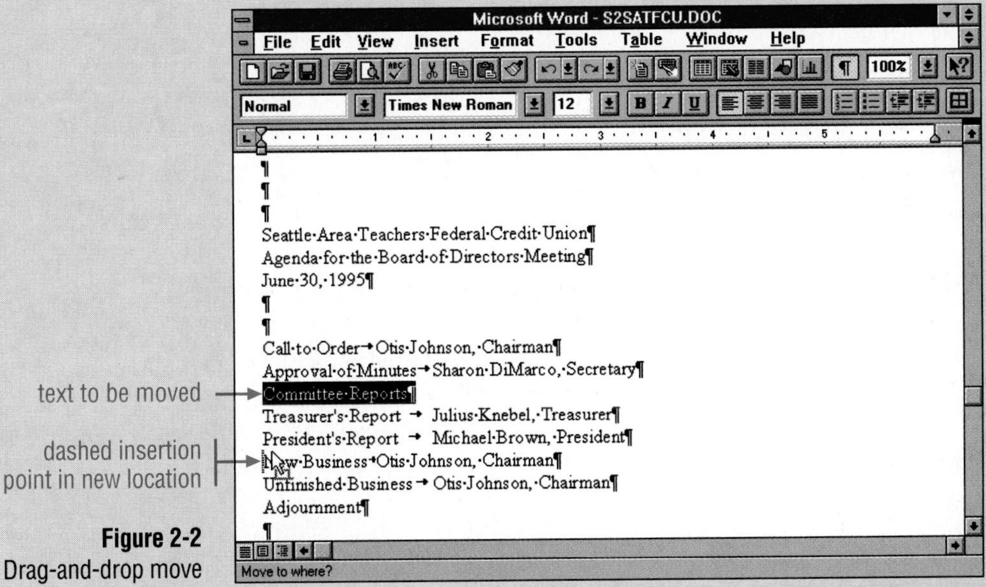

Figure 2-2
Drag-and-drop move

❺ Release the mouse button. The selected text is moved to its new location and is still highlighted.

❻ Deselect the highlighted text.

TROUBLE? If the move did not work, click the Undo button on the Standard toolbar (or click Edit then click Undo Move). Repeat the steps above, making sure that you do not release the mouse button until the dashed insertion point is in front of the "N" in New Business.

Moving Text with the Move Command ([F2])

The keyboard equivalent for the drag-and-drop feature is the Move command ([F2]). Marcus also needs to move the Unfinished Business agenda item before New Business, but this time he decides to use the Move command.

To move the agenda item using the Move command:

❶ Click in the selection bar next to Unfinished Business to select that line, including the paragraph mark.

❷ Press **[F2]**. Notice that the status bar displays the message "Move to where?"

❸ Place the insertion point in front of the "N" in New Business. Notice that the insertion point changes to a dashed vertical line.

❹ Press **[Enter]**. Unfinished Business is moved above New Business. See Figure 2-3.

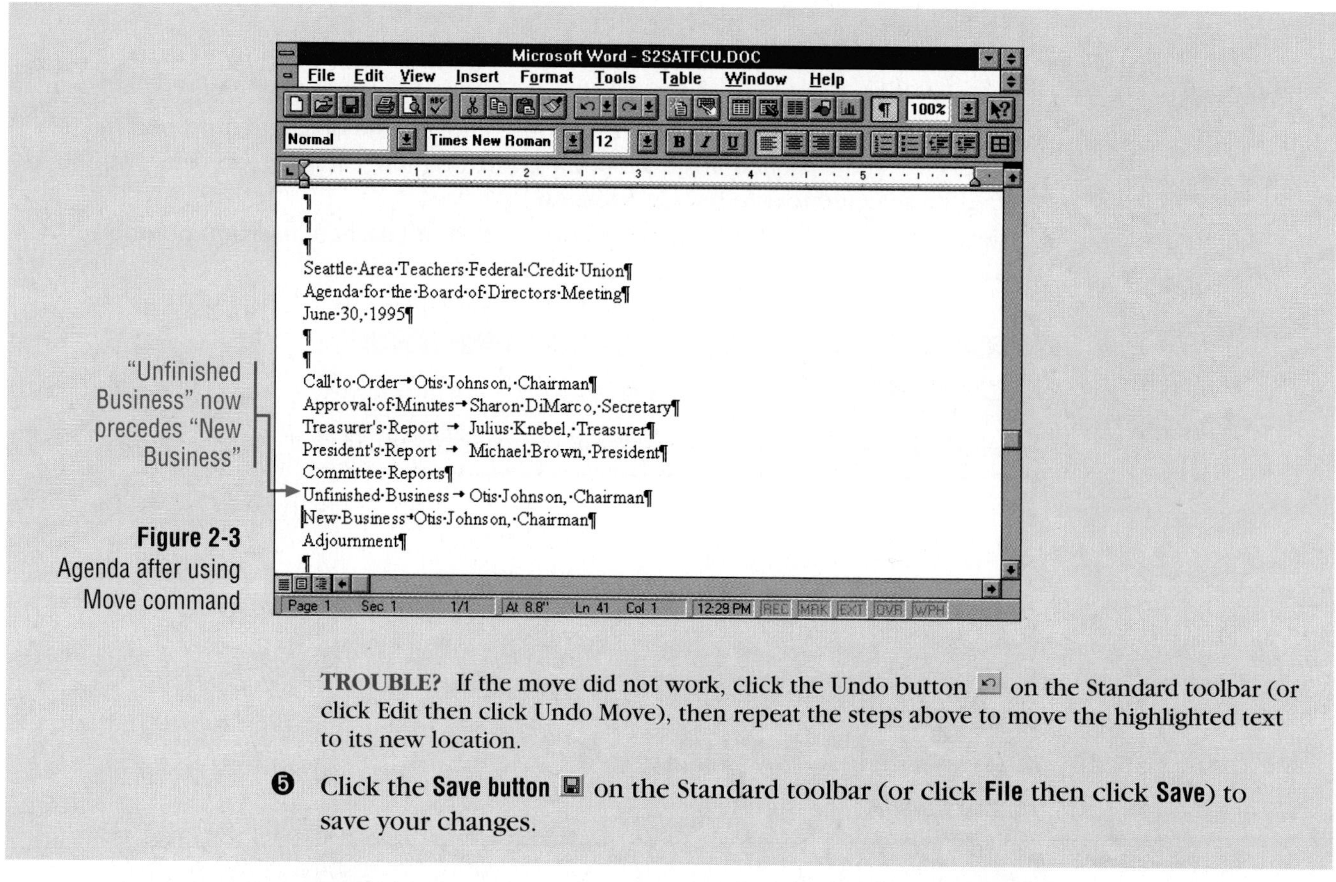

Figure 2-3
Agenda after using Move command

TROUBLE? If the move did not work, click the Undo button on the Standard toolbar (or click Edit then click Undo Move), then repeat the steps above to move the highlighted text to its new location.

5. Click the **Save button** on the Standard toolbar (or click **File** then click **Save**) to save your changes.

Marcus is ready to move to the next phase of the productivity strategy: formatting the document.

Applying Direct Formatting Options

Word divides its formatting options into three groups: document-level or page setup commands, paragraph-level commands, and character-level or font commands. To work efficiently, start with decisions that affect the entire document (page setup decisions), then move to decisions about paragraph formatting options, and finally make decisions about font formatting options. By starting with those options that affect your entire document and moving to more specific formatting choices, you eliminate retracing your steps. You can apply individual formatting options directly to specific elements of your document by selecting the element and then choosing the appropriate formatting command, or you can apply several formatting options at once through the use of Word's styles. In this tutorial you will use direct formatting; in Tutorial 3 you will learn about using styles to apply formatting to a document.

Both the cover memo and the agenda require a great deal of formatting, so Marcus decides to begin by making the changes that affect the overall appearance of the document.

Page Setup Options

Word's page setup features govern the size of your document's text area—in other words, how many lines of text will fit on a page. Setting margins is a page formatting decision that affects the size of the available text area. Two other factors affecting your document's text area are paper size (8.5 x 11 or 8.5 x 14) and page orientation (tall or wide). The default page orientation is tall, or **portrait**, but you can change it to wide, or **landscape**. You can make changes to the margins, paper size, or page orientation by choosing Page Setup from the File menu.

Changing Margins

Word uses a default width of 1.25 inches for the left and right margins, and a default width of 1 inch for the top and bottom margins. Any changes to the margins affect the entire document, not just the current page. The area that remains after allowing for the margin settings is called the **available text area** (Figure 2-4).

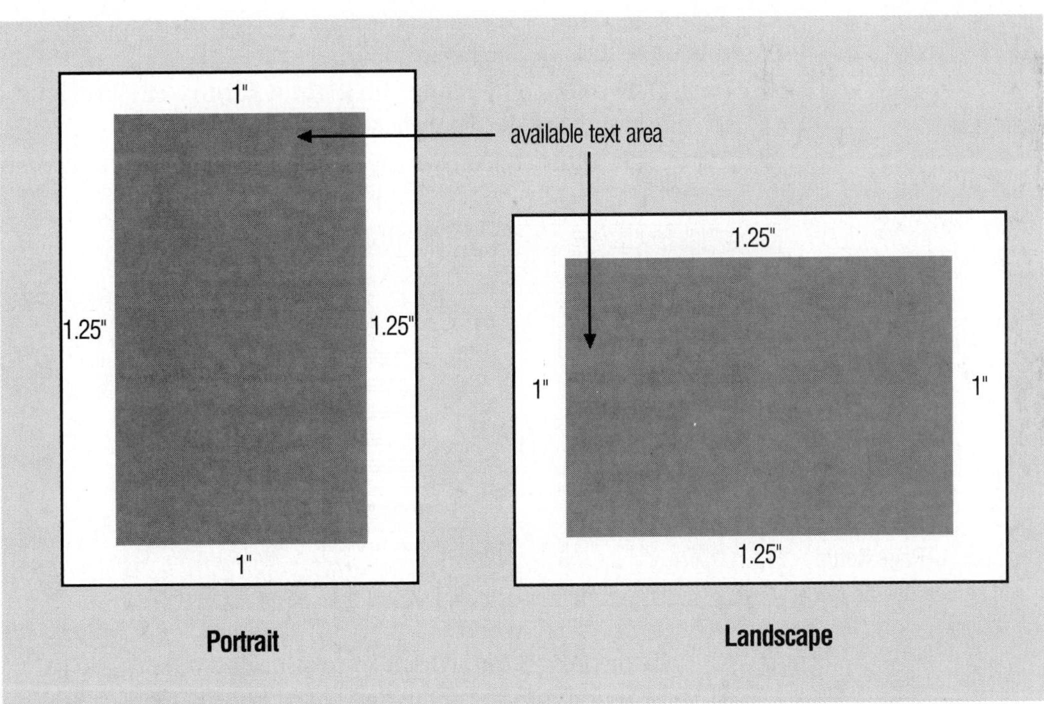

Figure 2-4
Available text area

The ruler, displayed below the Formatting toolbar on the Word screen, shows the length of the typing line, given the width of the current left and right margins. For instance, the default left and right margin settings of 1.25 inches provide a typing line of 6 inches (8.5 - 1.25 - 1.25 = 6). The numbers on the ruler scale indicate distances in inches from the left margin *not* from the left edge of the paper; therefore, the scale starts with 0. The tick marks on the ruler scale indicate increments of ⅛ inch.

To create a more balanced frame of white space around the text, making the document more attractive to the reader, Marcus wants to increase the top margin to 1.5 inches and the left and right margins to 1.75 inches.

To change the top, left, and right margins:

1. Press **[Ctrl][Home]** to move to the beginning of the document.
2. Click **File** then click **Page Setup...**. The Page Setup dialog box appears. From this dialog box, you can also change paper size and orientation, and paper source. The Preview section allows you to preview any changes you make to the page setup.

   TROUBLE? If you do not see the Page Setup dialog box with the Margins tab displayed, as shown in Figure 2-5, click the Margins tab at the top of the dialog box.

Marcus wants to increase the top margin to 1.5 inches.

3. Click the **Top text box up arrow** until it reads 1.5". Notice that the Preview section changes as you change the value for the top margin.

Next, Marcus wants to change the left and right margin settings to 1.75 inches. This setting is not available in the list of settings, so he needs to type 1.75 in the Left and Right text boxes.

4. Press **[Tab]** twice to highlight the Left text box.
5. Type **1.75**. Note that you do not have to type the quotation mark to indicate inches; this is the assumed measurement.
6. Press **[Tab]** once to highlight the Right text box. The Preview section now changes to reflect the new left margin setting.
7. Type **1.75**. Figure 2-5 shows the completed Page Setup dialog box.

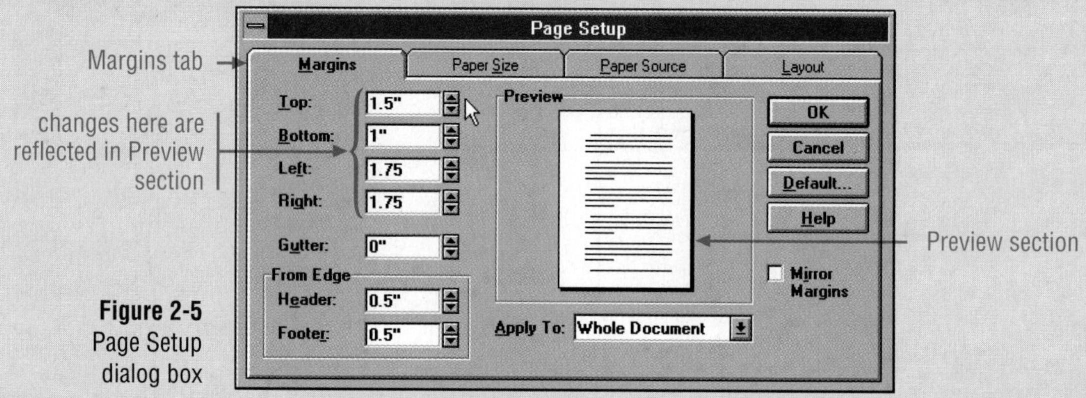

Figure 2-5 Page Setup dialog box

8. Click **OK** or press **[Enter]** to return to your document. The ruler changes to reflect the new length of the typing line based on the new left and right margin settings (8.5 - 1.75 - 1.75 = 5). Also, notice the changes in the status bar, which now indicates that the first line begins 1.5 inches from the top of the page and that the document has two pages (as indicated by 1/2, meaning page 1 of 2). The increased top margin forced the text of the document onto a second page.
9. Click the **Save button** on the Standard toolbar (or click **File** then click **Save**) to save your changes.

Now that Marcus has made changes to the document's margins, he needs to adjust where the pages end within his document.

Soft Page Breaks

When you enter enough text to fill up a page, Word automatically starts a new page for you. To indicate the start of a new page, a row of dots appears across the page. This row of dots is called a **soft page break** because as you insert and delete text, the position of the soft page break can change. The status bar also changes to indicate the increase or decrease in the number of pages in the document.

Because his document has increased to two pages, Marcus must see where the second page starts. Michael wants the agenda to appear on a page by itself.

To view the soft page break in the document:

❶ Drag the vertical scroll box to the bottom of the scroll bar to move quickly to the end of your document. Notice the row of dots across the page. See Figure 2-6. This is Word's indication that you have filled one page of text and started another.

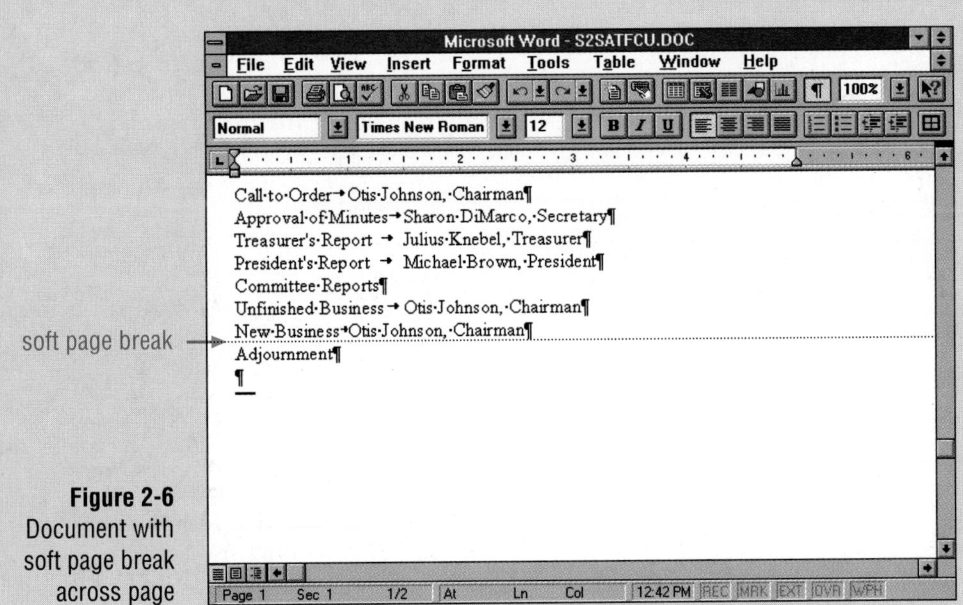

Figure 2-6 Document with soft page break across page

TROUBLE? Depending on the type of monitor or printer that you're using, the soft page break might occur in a different location. Just continue with the tutorial.

❷ Place the insertion point in the line of text directly *below* the soft page break. Notice the status bar. After the soft page break, the insertion point is located on page 2 of your document.

❸ Press [↑] to move the insertion point up one line of text, directly *above* the soft page break. The status bar now shows that the insertion point is on page 1.

Because the soft page break does not fall at the beginning of the agenda, Marcus must force the agenda to appear on a page by itself. He will do so by inserting a hard page break.

Inserting Hard Page Breaks

At times you might want to force a page to end at a particular spot in your document. To start a new page, you must insert a **hard page break**, also called a **manual page break**.

You can insert a hard page break by pressing [Ctrl][Enter] or by choosing Break from the Insert menu.

A hard page break is indicated by a row of dots across the page, like those used for a soft page break, but the words "Page Break" appear in the center of the row of dots. To delete a hard page break, select the page break then press [Del].

Let's insert a hard page break so that the agenda appears on a page by itself.

To insert the hard page break:

1. Place the insertion point in front of the "S" in Seattle in the first line of the agenda heading (Ln 32).

   TROUBLE? If the first line of the agenda title in your document does not fall at the same point, perhaps you accidentally pressed [Enter] and inserted extra blank lines. Or, perhaps you have not changed the point size from 10 to 12. Ask your instructor or technical support person to do this for you. The line variation might also be due to the selection of a printer different from the one used in this book. Continue with the tutorial, keeping in mind this difference between your screen and the figures in this tutorial; use any line number indications as a point of reference.

2. Press **[Ctrl][Enter]**. The status bar indicates that the insertion point is on page 2. See Figure 2-7.

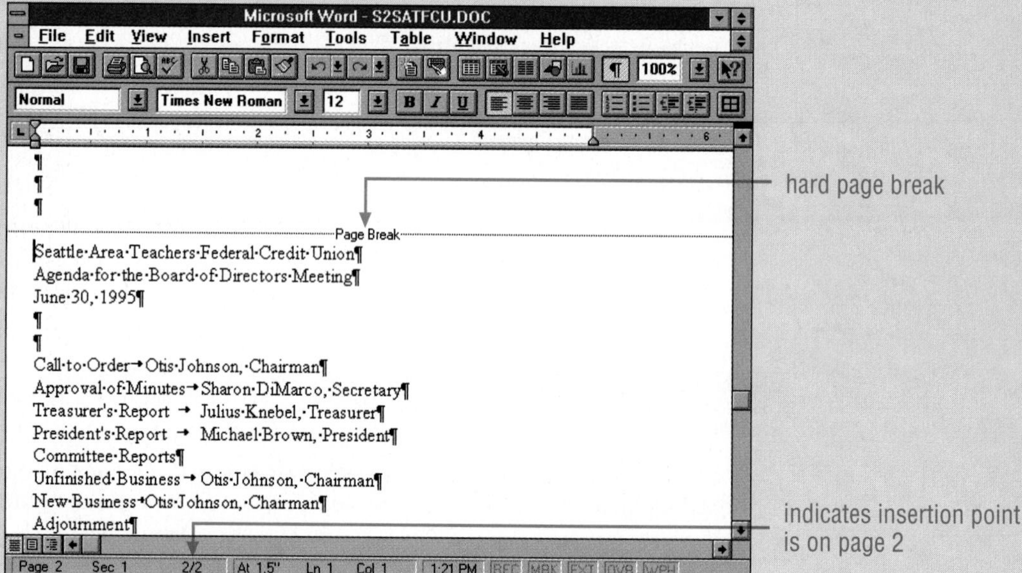

Figure 2-7 Screen after inserting hard page break

   TROUBLE? If you do not see a hard page break across your page, perhaps you did not hold down [Ctrl] while you pressed [Enter]. Click the Undo button on the Standard toolbar (or click Edit then click Undo Page Break), then repeat Step 2.

3. Press [↑] to move the insertion point to the hard page break. Notice that the status bar changes to indicate that the insertion point is on page 1, Ln 32. Even though you have not filled page 1 completely with text, inserting a hard page break forced one page to end and another to begin.

4. Click the **Save button** on the Standard toolbar (or click **File** then click **Save**) to save your changes.

Marcus has completed making the document-level formatting decisions.

If you want to take a break and resume the tutorial at a later time, you can close the current document then exit Word by double-clicking the Control menu box in the upper-left corner of the screen. When you want to resume the tutorial, start Word, place your Student Disk in the disk drive, then complete the screen check procedure described in Tutorial 1. Open the file S2SATFCU.DOC then continue with the tutorial.

■ ■ ■

Now Marcus moves to the next group of formatting decisions: paragraph formatting options.

Paragraph Formatting

Paragraph formatting includes a wide variety of features such as paragraph indentations, tabs, numbered paragraphs, line spacing, paragraph alignment, paragraph borders, and rules. Some of the most often used paragraph formatting features are available on the Formatting toolbar; others are available only through the Paragraph command and the Borders and Shading command on the Format menu.

Remember that Word defines a paragraph as any amount of text that ends with a paragraph mark (¶). Word stores the paragraph formatting options that have been applied to a paragraph in the paragraph mark at the end of that paragraph. If you accidentally delete a paragraph mark, immediately click the Undo button or choose Undo from the Edit menu to restore the paragraph mark and any paragraph formatting changes that you might have made.

To make paragraph formatting changes, you first select the paragraph or paragraphs to be changed and then choose the paragraph formatting options you want to apply to the selection. To select a *single* paragraph, all you need to do is position the insertion point anywhere in that paragraph. Once you have selected a paragraph, you can make the necessary paragraph formatting changes. To make changes to *multiple* paragraphs, you can select the paragraphs and then apply paragraph formatting options. As you can see, the principle of "select, then do" pertains to formatting, too.

Marcus will begin formatting the paragraphs in his document by changing paragraph indentations.

Changing Paragraph Indentations

You might want to call attention to certain paragraphs within your document by indenting them from the left or right margin, or both, thus changing the length of your typing line. As you learned previously, changing margins is one way to change the length of the typing line; however, changing margins is a document-level option that affects the entire document, rather than just a paragraph. Word provides four ways to indent paragraph text from the margins without adjusting the entire document's margins—first-line indents, left indents, right indents, and hanging indents—as shown in Figure 2-8. The text in Figure 2-8 describes the different types of indents.

This is an example of a paragraph in which the first line is indented from the left margin. You can create this type of indent by moving only the *first-line indent marker* on the ruler.

This is an example of a paragraph in which all lines are indented from the left margin. You can create this type of indent by moving the *rectangle* below the left indent marker.

This is an example of a hanging indent, that is, a paragraph in which all lines except the first line are indented from the left margin. You can create this type of indent by moving only the *left indent marker* on the ruler.

This is an example of a paragraph in which all lines are indented from the right margin. You can create this type of indent by moving the *right indent marker* on the ruler.

Figure 2-8
Samples of Word's indents

As usual, Word gives you a variety of ways to apply these features. You can create all these indents using the ruler or the Paragraph command on the Format menu. You can also use the Formatting toolbar to create left indents and hanging indents.

The ruler allows you to change paragraph indents quickly through the use of the indent markers (Figure 2-9). By default the indent markers are even with the left and right margins. The top triangle at the left end of the ruler, called the **first-line indent marker**, controls the amount of indentation from the left margin for the *first line* of a selected paragraph. The bottom triangle at the left end of the ruler, called the **left indent marker**, controls the amount of indentation from the left margin for *all* lines in the selected paragraph *except* the first line. The **rectangle** below the left indent marker controls the amount of indentation from the left margin for *all* lines in the selected paragraph, including the first line. The triangle at the right end of the ruler, called the **right indent marker**, controls the amount of indentation from the *right* margin for all lines in the selected paragraph. Any changes to the indentation level affect only the paragraph with the insertion point or any selected paragraphs. If you indent a paragraph and do not like the indentation you have chosen, you can click the Undo button and start again.

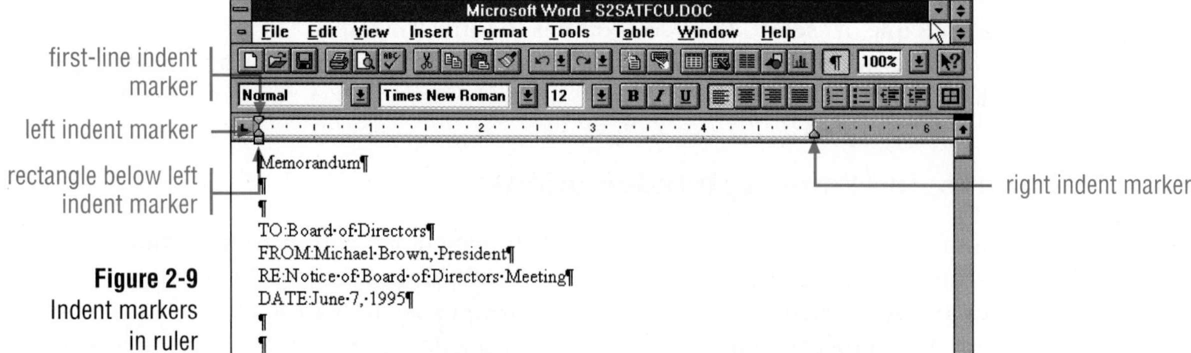

Figure 2-9
Indent markers in ruler

You change the indent level for a paragraph by following the "select, then do" principle: select the appropriate paragraph or paragraphs to be changed and then drag the appropriate indent marker to a new position on the ruler.

REFERENCE WINDOW

Indenting a Paragraph

- Select the paragraph or paragraphs to be indented.
- Point to the indent marker you want to change and drag it to its new location on the ruler scale.

To indent:	*Do the following:*
Only the first line	Drag the first-line indent marker
All lines but the first line	Drag the left indent marker
All lines	Drag the rectangle under the left indent marker
All lines from the right margin	Drag the right indent marker

or

- Select the paragraph or paragraphs to be indented.
- Click Format then click Paragraph.... If necessary, click the Indents and Spacing tab in the Paragraph dialog box.
- From the Indentation section of the Paragraph dialog box, do one or more of the following:
  - In the Left text box, select or type the distance that you want to indent the paragraph from the left margin.
  - In the Right text box, select or type the distance that you want to indent the paragraph from the right margin.
  - In the Special section, select First Line, then select or type the negative or positive distance that you want to indent the first line of the paragraph from the *left indent*.
  - In the Special section, select Hanging, then select or type the negative or positive distance that you want to hang text after the first line.
- Click OK or press [Enter].

Marcus wants to try indenting the first line of each paragraph of the body of the memo by 0.5 inch, to see if this improves the appearance of the memo. He'll do so by changing the first-line indent marker. Because he's not sure if this is the format he wants, Marcus decides to indent just the first paragraph to see the results.

To indent the first line of the first paragraph:

1. Place the insertion point anywhere in the first paragraph of the body of the memo, which begins "The next regularly..."
2. Point to the first-line indent marker (top triangle), then click and drag it to the right 0.5 inch. The first line of the first paragraph is indented, but the remaining lines of the paragraph do not change. See Figure 2-10. Also notice that the other paragraphs in the memo were not affected by the change.

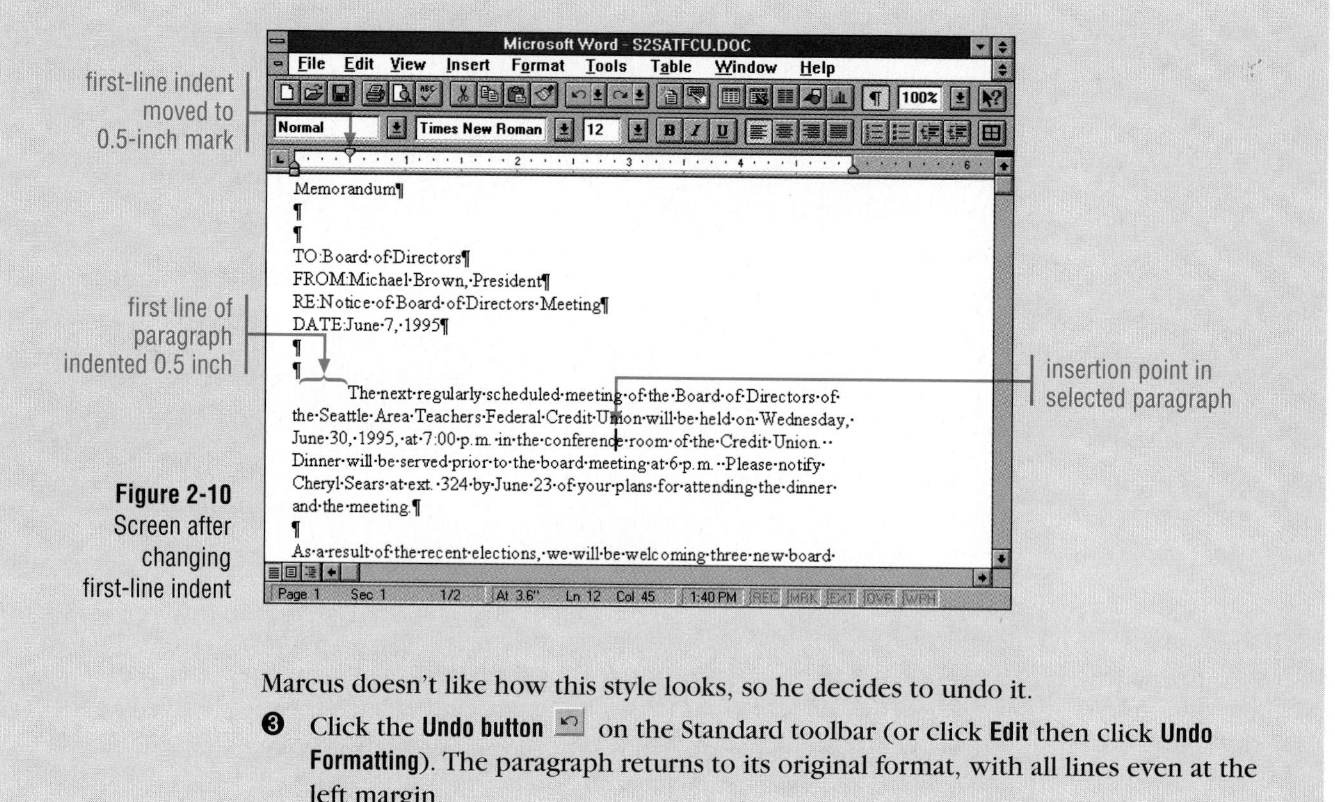

Figure 2-10 Screen after changing first-line indent

Marcus doesn't like how this style looks, so he decides to undo it.

❸ Click the **Undo button** on the Standard toolbar (or click **Edit** then click **Undo Formatting**). The paragraph returns to its original format, with all lines even at the left margin.

Next Marcus decides to indent *all* lines of the paragraph 1 inch from the left margin. He could drag the rectangle to move both the first-line indent and the left indent to the 1-inch mark on the ruler, or he could use the Increase Indent button on the Formatting toolbar. Whenever you click the Increase Indent button, both the first-line and left indent markers move to the next tab stop to the right on the ruler. (You learn about tab stops in the next section.) You can just as easily "unindent" selected paragraphs by clicking the Decrease Indent button on the Formatting toolbar. Each time you click the Decrease Indent button, the first-line and left indent markers move to the previous tab stop to the left.

Marcus decides to use the Increase Indent button on the Formatting toolbar to indent all of the paragraphs of the body of the memo and the enclosure notation to the 1-inch mark on the ruler.

To indent the paragraphs using the Increase Indent button:

❶ Use the selection bar to select all the paragraphs in the body of the memo, from the first paragraph in the body of the memo ("The next regularly...") through Enclosure.

Next, let's make an intentional error and move the indentation too far to the right.

❷ Click the **Increase Indent button** on the Formatting toolbar three times. The selected paragraphs move to the right. Notice that the first-line and left indent markers have moved to the 1.5-inch mark on the ruler—half an inch too far to the right of where Marcus wants them.

3. Click the **Decrease Indent button** on the Formatting toolbar. All selected paragraphs move to the left 0.5 inch. Notice that the first-line and left indent markers have moved to the 1-inch mark on the ruler.
4. Deselect the highlighted text and then scroll through the document. The body of the memo is indented to the 1-inch mark, but the rest of the document remains at the left margin. See Figure 2-11.

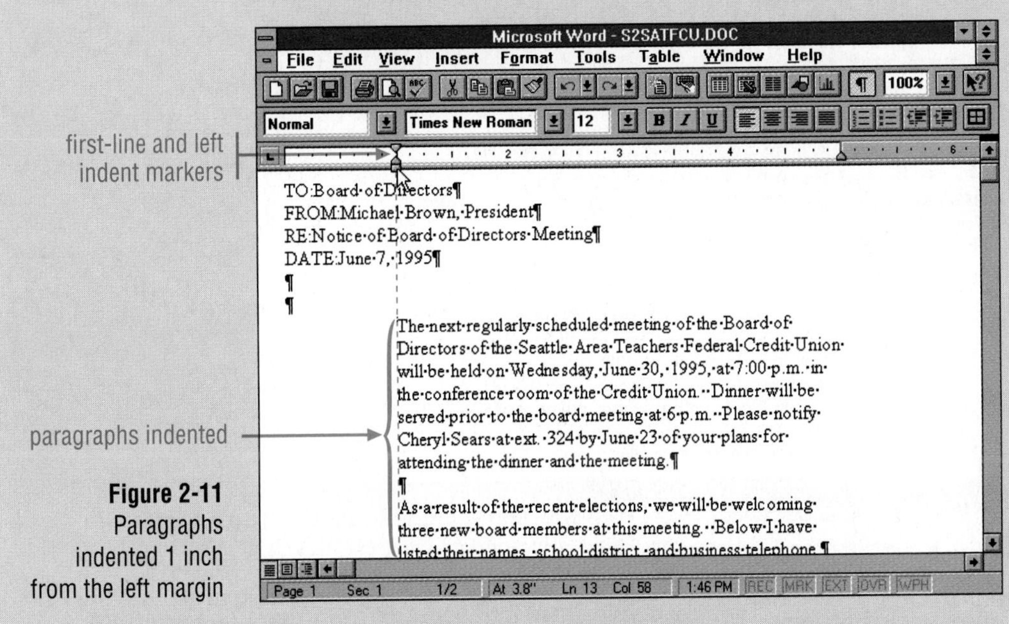

Figure 2-11 Paragraphs indented 1 inch from the left margin

5. Save the changes you have made.

Next, to improve the appearance of the memo, Marcus wants to align the information vertically after the memo headings (TO:, FROM:, RE:, and DATE:) at the 1-inch mark on the ruler. This will match the indentation of the paragraphs in the body of the memo. To make this paragraph formatting change, Marcus will use Word's default tab settings.

Using Default Tabs

A **tab stop** is a predefined stopping point along your document's typing line. Each time you press [Tab], the insertion point moves to the next tab stop. If the Show/Hide ¶ option is activated, a tab character (→) appears on the screen at the point where you pressed [Tab]. Word's default tabs are set every 0.5 inch. To delete a tab character, you place the insertion to the left of the → then press [Del], or place the insertion point to the right of the → then press [Backspace].

Tabs are useful for aligning text or numerical data vertically in columns. Marcus will insert tabs to align the information after the memo headings.

To align the information after the memo headings by inserting tabs:

1. Place the insertion point after the colon in the first memo heading (TO:).
2. Press **[Tab]** twice. Notice that two tab characters appear and that the text aligns vertically under the 1-inch mark on the ruler. See Figure 2-12.

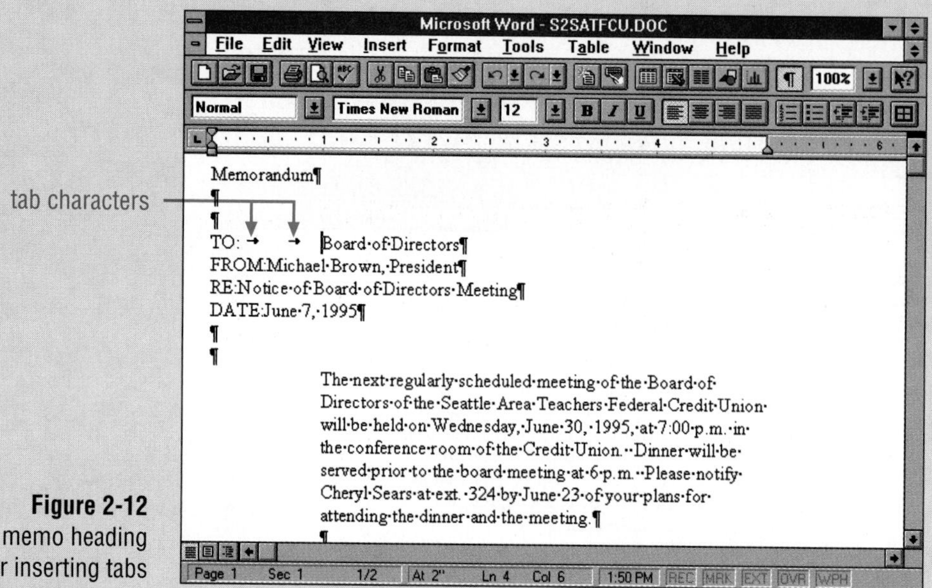

Figure 2-12
First memo heading after inserting tabs

TROUBLE? If you don't see the tab characters on your screen, you need to activate the Show/Hide ¶ option by clicking the Show/Hide ¶ button ¶ on the Standard toolbar.

3. Place the insertion point after the colon in the second memo heading (FROM:), then press **[Tab]** twice. The text aligns vertically at the 1.5-inch mark instead of at the 1-inch mark.

Marcus wants all the information to align at the 1-inch mark, so he must delete one of the tabs.

4. Press **[Backspace]** once. The second tab character is deleted, and the text aligns vertically at the 1-inch mark.
5. Place the insertion point after the colon in the third memo heading (RE:), then press **[Tab]** twice.
6. Place the insertion point after the colon in the fourth memo heading (DATE:), then press **[Tab]** twice.

Because you inserted tabs between the headings and the information that follows them, the information aligns vertically.

Marcus now wants to format the information in the memo about the three new board members so that the three columns of information are more balanced on the page. To do so, he needs to set custom tab stops.

Setting Custom Tab Stops

Sometimes you might want to set tab stops at locations other than those of the default settings. In other words, you might want to customize the tab stops. Word allows you to set custom tabs using different alignment tab styles, namely, left, right, centered, or decimal (Figure 2-13). The default tab style, which you just used, is **left-aligned**, meaning that text at that tab stop is positioned even at the left and extends to the right from the tab stop. The **centered** tab aligns text evenly on either side of the tab stop, while the **right-aligned** tab creates text that is positioned even at the right and extends to the left from the tab stop. With **decimal-aligned** tabs, a number aligns at the decimal point, but text aligns to the right. You can use the tab alignment selector on the left side of the ruler or the Tabs command on the Format menu to set custom tabs.

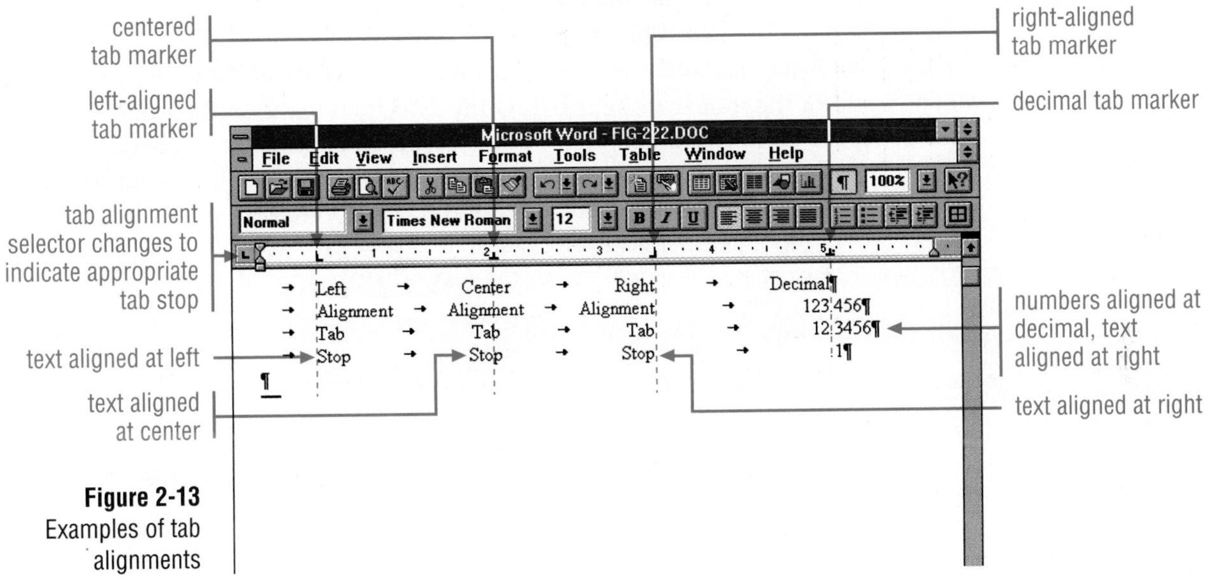

Figure 2-13
Examples of tab alignments

REFERENCE WINDOW

Setting Custom Tab Stops

- Select the paragraph or paragraphs for which you want to set custom tab stops.
- Click the tab alignment selector on the ruler until the appropriate icon for the tab alignment appears.
- Click at the point in the ruler where you want to set the custom tab stop.

or

- Click Format then click Tabs.... The Tabs dialog box appears.
- Type the position where you want to set the custom tab stop in the Tab Stop Position text box.
- Click the appropriate tab alignment option in the Alignment section.
- Click Set.
- Repeat the above steps for each additional tab stop to be set.
- Click OK or press [Enter].

Originally, Marcus entered the information about the board members by inserting a tab between each column of information, that is, between the board member's name and the school district, and between the school district and the telephone number. Now he wants to set a centered tab stop for the column containing the school districts, and a right-aligned tab stop for the column containing the telephone numbers.

To set the centered and right-aligned tab stops using the ruler:

❶ Select the three lines of information in the memo about the new board members ("Teresa Markowitz..." through "...637-7389").

❷ Click the **tab alignment selector** on the ruler until the **centered tab button** appears.

❸ Move the tip of the mouse pointer below the 2.75-inch mark on the ruler, then click to set the centered tab at that point. A centered tab marker is inserted into the ruler. See Figure 2-14. Notice that the text *after* the first tab character in each of the selected lines shifts to the location of the centered tab stop.

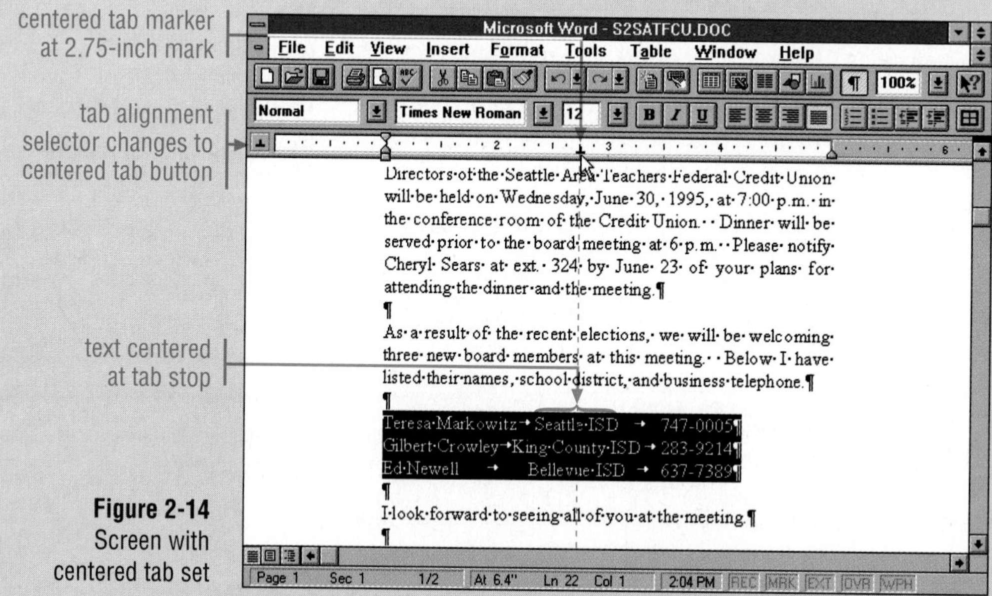

Figure 2-14 Screen with centered tab set

Now Marcus wants to set a right-aligned tab stop for the last column of information.

❹ Click the **tab alignment selector** on the ruler until the **right-aligned tab button** appears.

Marcus decides to set the tab at the 4.75-inch mark on the ruler, but he wants to make sure he gets the tab exactly in place.

❺ Press and hold **[Alt]**, move the mouse pointer to the 4.75-inch mark (approximately) on the ruler, then press and hold down the mouse button. As you do, the ruler indicates the exact distances from the left and right indents.

❻ When the ruler indicates that you are exactly 3.75" from the left indent, release [Alt] and the mouse button. A right-aligned tab marker is inserted into the ruler. The text after the second tab character in each of the selected lines moves to the new tab stop, and the default tabs between the centered tab marker and the right-aligned tab marker on the ruler are cleared. See Figure 2-15.

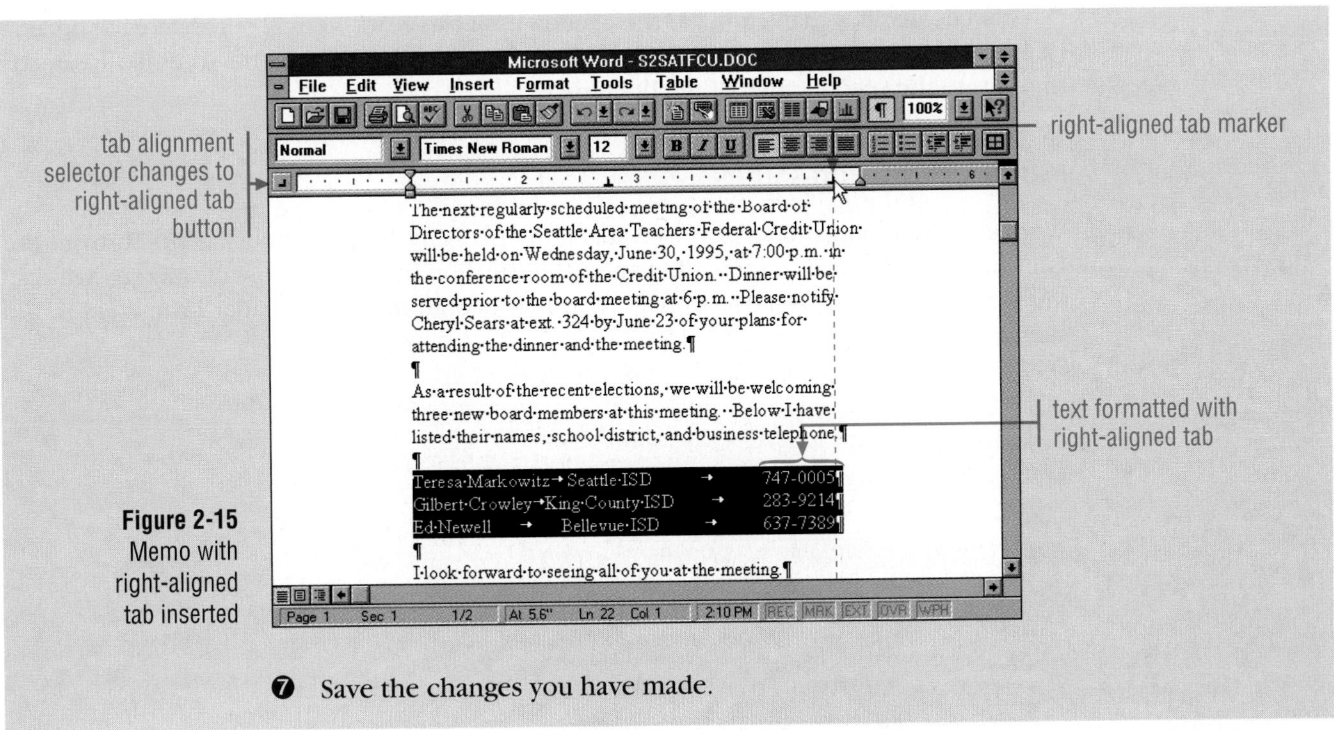

Figure 2-15 Memo with right-aligned tab inserted

❼ Save the changes you have made.

Marcus notices that the second column containing the names of the school districts is too close to the first column. He decides to move the second column to the right so that it looks evenly centered between the first and third columns.

Moving Tab Stops

You can adjust the location of a custom tab stop simply by dragging its marker to a new location on the ruler. Marcus will drag the right-aligned and centered tab markers to improve the format of the three columns.

To move the right-aligned and centered tab stops using the ruler:

❶ Select the information in the memo about the three new board members, if it is not already selected.

❷ Point to the right-aligned tab marker (at the 4.75-inch mark) in the ruler, then click and drag it to the 5-inch mark, on top of the right indent marker. The selected text adjusts to the new setting.

❸ Point to the centered tab marker (at the 2.75-inch mark) in the ruler, then click and drag it to the 3.25-inch mark. If necessary, continue to adjust the centered tab marker on the ruler until the items look evenly centered between the board members' names and their telephone numbers.

❹ Deselect the highlighted text.

❺ Save the changes you have made.

You can clear a custom tab stop just as easily as you can change its location. Simply point to the custom tab stop you want to remove, drag it down below the ruler, then release the mouse button.

Marcus decides that, to make the agenda easier to read, he will separate each agenda item from its presenter with a series of dots, called leader characters. To do so he needs to move to the second page of the document.

Moving Between Pages

Word's Go To command, which is available by pressing [F5] or choosing Go To from the Edit menu, allows you to move to a specified location in your document. Marcus will use the Go To command to move to page 2 so that he can insert the leader characters in the agenda items.

To move to page 2:

❶ Press **[F5]**. The Go To dialog box appears. See Figure 2-16.

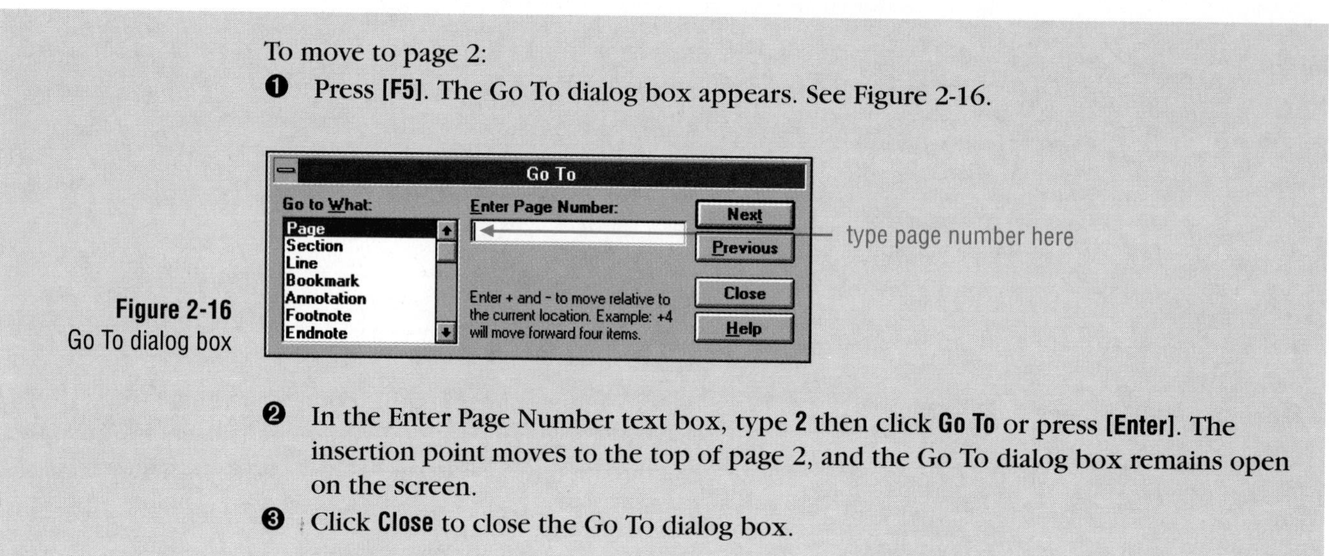

Figure 2-16
Go To dialog box

❷ In the Enter Page Number text box, type **2** then click **Go To** or press **[Enter]**. The insertion point moves to the top of page 2, and the Go To dialog box remains open on the screen.

❸ Click **Close** to close the Go To dialog box.

When formatting the rest of the document, you can use the Go To command to move between the two pages.

Now Marcus can insert the leader characters.

Inserting Leader Characters

Leader characters are repeated characters that help guide the reader's eye from one column of text formatted with tabs to another. Word provides you with three choices of leader characters: dots, dashed lines, or solid lines. The leader character you choose is inserted into the space preceding the designated tab stop.

REFERENCE WINDOW

Inserting Leader Characters

- Select the paragraph or paragraphs for which you want to set custom tab stops, or select the paragraph or paragraphs containing the existing tab stops.
- Click Format then click Tabs.... The Tabs dialog box appears.
- In the Tab Stop Position text box, type the position where you want to set the custom tab stop (if necessary).
- Select the appropriate type of tab alignment option from the Alignment section (if necessary).
- Select the appropriate type of leader character from the Leader section.
- Click Set then click OK or press [Enter].

Marcus originally entered the agenda items with a tab between the agenda item and the presenter's name. Now he will insert leader characters between the two columns. In addition, he will right-align the names of the presenters at the right indent (the 5-inch mark).

To insert leader characters in the agenda items:

1. Select all the agenda items, beginning with Call to Order and ending with Adjournment.
2. Click **Format** then click **Tabs...**. The Tabs dialog box appears.
3. Type **5** in the Tab Stop Position text box to set the location of the custom tab stop at the same position as the right indent.
4. Click the **Right radio button** in the Alignment section to right-align text typed at this tab.
5. Click the **2 radio button** (dot leaders) in the Leader section.
6. Click **Set**. A tab is set at the position you have indicated in the Tab Stop Position text box with the options you have chosen in the Tabs dialog box. Dot leaders will be inserted in the blank space leading up to the right-aligned tab set at the 5-inch mark. See Figure 2-17.

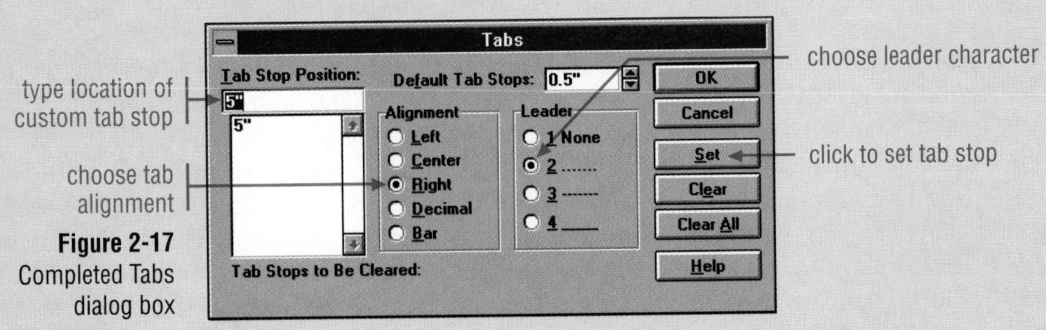

Figure 2-17 Completed Tabs dialog box

7. Click **OK** or press **[Enter]**. A right-aligned tab marker appears in the ruler at the 5-inch mark (on top of the right indent). Dot leaders appear in the tab space leading

up to the names of the presenters, and the names of the presenters are right-aligned at the 5-inch mark. All default tabs to the left of the right-aligned tab stop at the 5-inch mark are cleared (for the selected paragraphs).

8. Deselect the highlighted text. See Figure 2-18.

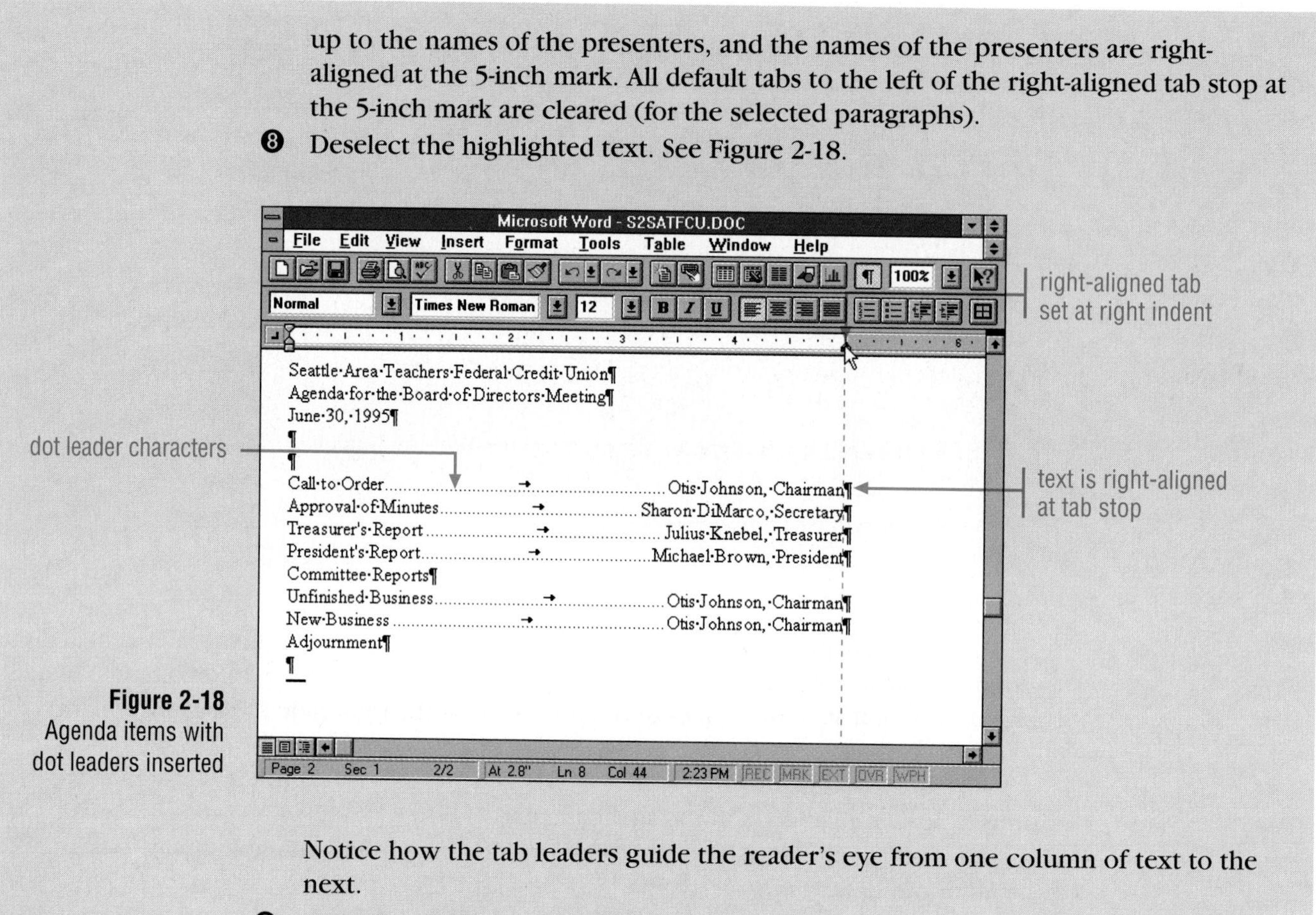

Figure 2-18
Agenda items with dot leaders inserted

Notice how the tab leaders guide the reader's eye from one column of text to the next.

9. Save the changes you have made.

Marcus reviews the changes Michael requested (Figure 2-1) and notes that Michael wants to add three new agenda items (under Committee Reports), and he wants the list of agenda items to be numbered. However, the new items Marcus needs to insert under Committee Reports should not be numbered—only the main item (Committee Reports) should be numbered. To format the list in this way, Marcus will use Word's New Line command when entering the new agenda items.

Using the New Line Command

As you learned in Tutorial 1, Word treats any block of text that ends with a paragraph mark (¶), including a paragraph mark on a line by itself, as a paragraph. Because of the way Word formats paragraphs, treating a series of short lines as a single paragraph rather than several paragraphs is sometimes desirable. If you want to start a new *line*, but you do not want to start a new *paragraph*, use the **New Line command**, [Shift][Enter]. Word will insert a new line mark (↵) on the screen to indicate the use of the New Line command.

To format the agenda items in the numbered list as Michael requested, Marcus needs the line Committee Reports and the three new committee agenda items to be treated as *one paragraph* rather than as four short paragraphs. Therefore, when he types the new agenda items, Marcus must end all but the last item (Supervisory Committee) with a new line mark (↵).

To enter the new agenda items with new line marks:

1. Place the insertion point after the "s" in the agenda item Committee Reports and before the paragraph mark.
2. Press **[Shift][Enter]**. A new line mark (↵) is inserted after Committee Reports and Unfinished Business is forced to the next line.

   TROUBLE? If you inserted a paragraph mark instead of a new line mark, you did not hold down [Shift] while you pressed [Enter]. Press [Backspace] to delete the paragraph mark, then repeat Step 2.

Now let's enter the three new individual committee report items Michael wants inserted. You will separate the committee name from the presenter's name with a tab. When you do, the dot leaders will automatically be inserted because the Committee Reports paragraph mark stores the leader characters as part of its format.

3. Type **Building Maintenance Committee** then press **[Tab]**. Pressing [Tab] inserts a tab character (→) and moves the insertion point to the next tab stop. The dot leaders are also inserted.
4. Type **Joan Nunez** then press **[Shift][Enter]**.
5. Type **Financial Services Committee** then press **[Tab]**.
6. Type **Mai Nguyen** then press **[Shift][Enter]**.
7. Type **Supervisory Committee** then press **[Tab]**.
8. Type **Stephen Lesikar**. *Do not press [Enter]* because there is a paragraph mark already following Stephen Lesikar, signifying the end of the paragraph. The paragraph consists of the text "Committee Reports" through "Stephen Lesikar," even though the text appears on different lines. See Figure 2-19.

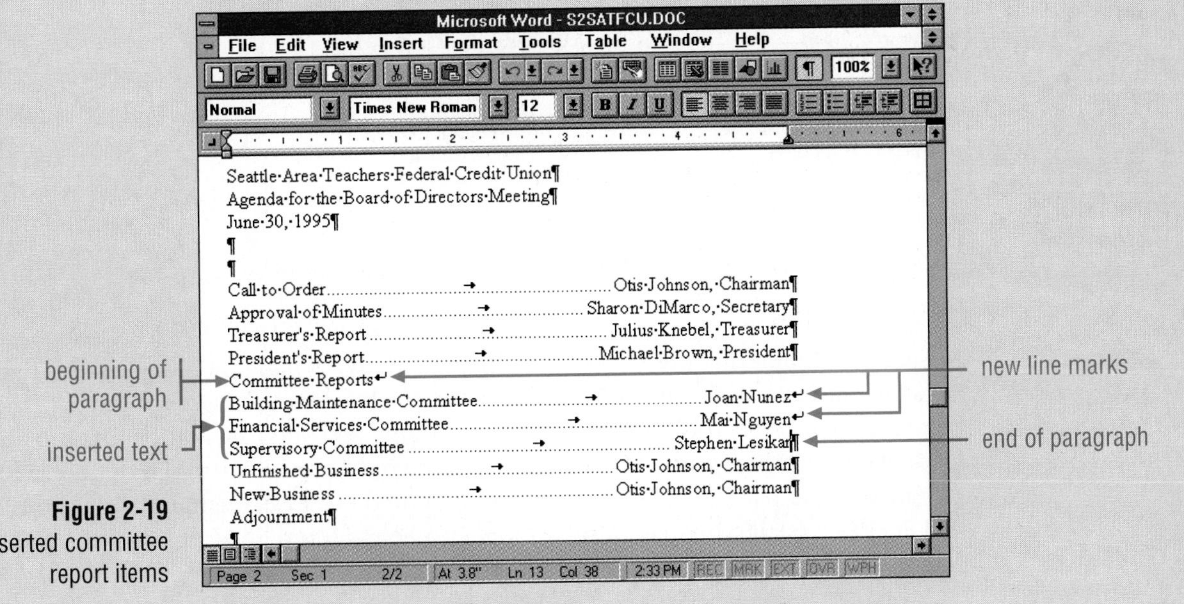

Figure 2-19 Inserted committee report items

Now Marcus can number the agenda items, as Michael requested, so that the order of presentation in the meeting is clear.

Numbering Paragraphs

Adding numbers to a group of paragraphs is another paragraph formatting option that might make your document easier to understand. To create a numbered list of paragraphs, you select the paragraphs you want to number and then click the Numbering button on the Formatting toolbar. Although you can use the Numbering button to apply or remove this option to selected paragraphs, you must choose Bullets and Numbering from the Format menu to reformat the numbers.

Marcus will use the Numbering button to number the agenda items.

To add numbers to the list of agenda items:

1. Select all the agenda items, from Call to Order through Adjournment.
2. Click the **Numbering button** on the Formatting toolbar. Each paragraph in the selected text is numbered consecutively.
3. Click within the numbered list to deselect the highlighted text. Notice the indent markers in the ruler for the numbered paragraphs. See Figure 2-20.

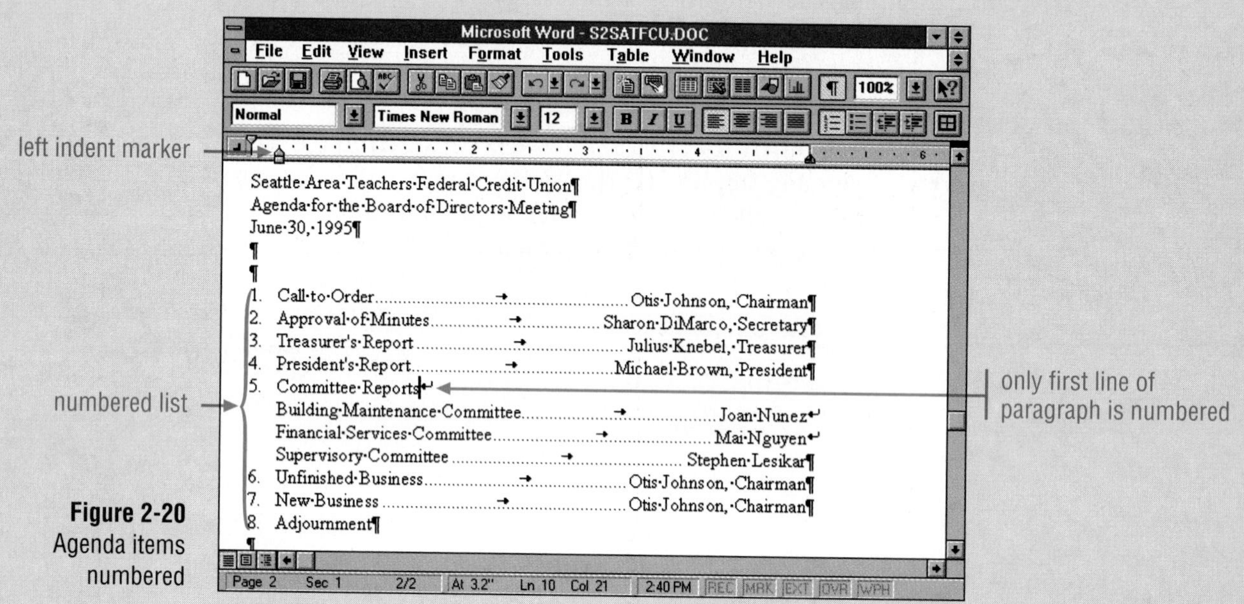

Figure 2-20 Agenda items numbered

Using the Numbering button formats the paragraphs as hanging indents, with the first-line indent marker at the left margin and the left indent marker at the 0.25-inch mark. For example, look at agenda item 5, Committee Reports. Notice that the individual committee report items were not numbered because Word did not consider them separate paragraphs, but they were indented because a hanging indent causes all lines of a paragraph except the first line to be indented.

Marcus wants the agenda items to start at the 0.5-inch mark instead of the 0.25-inch mark. Because of the change to the left indent, the agenda items moved to the point of the indent at the 0.25-inch mark instead of to the first default tab stop at the 0.5-inch mark. Marcus must adjust the amount of the hanging indent for the numbered agenda items.

To adjust the hanging indent for the numbered list:

1. Select all the agenda items again.
2. Click **Format** then click **Bullets and Numbering...**. The Bullets and Numbering dialog box appears. Notice that the Numbered tab is selected.

Marcus needs to modify the numbering options.

3. Click **Modify...**. The Modify Numbered List dialog box appears.
4. In the Number Position section, click the **Distance from Indent to Text up arrow** until it reads 0.5". See Figure 2-21. The Preview section changes to reflect the change in the value for the hanging indent.

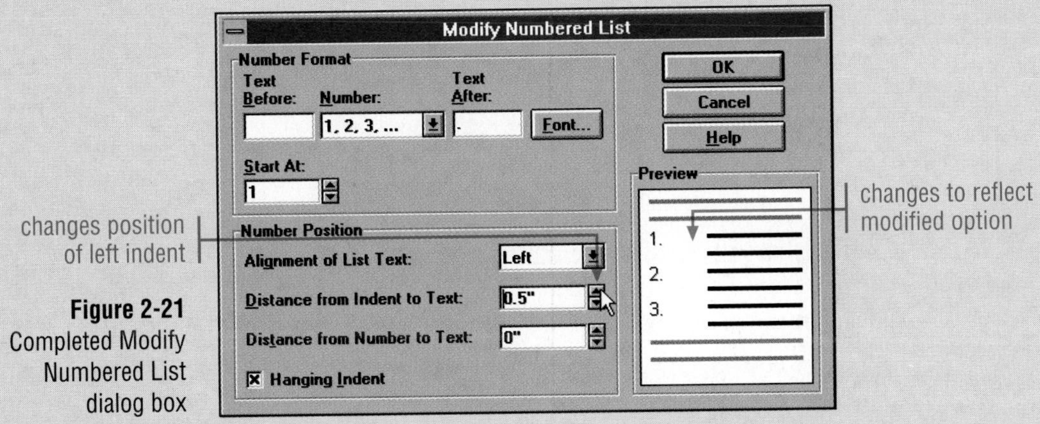

Figure 2-21 Completed Modify Numbered List dialog box

5. Click **OK** or press **[Enter]**. The amount of the left indent is changed, and the agenda items start at the 0.5-inch mark on the ruler.
6. Deselect the highlighted text.
7. Save the changes you have made.

Viewing the numbered list, Marcus decides that it would look better if he added more space between the lines of text in the list. This will help to distinguish the items from each other.

Adjusting Line Spacing

The default line spacing in Word documents is single spacing. Sometimes, however, you might want to use 1.5 spacing or double spacing. Because these options do not appear on the Formatting toolbar, the quickest way to apply line spacing options is through shortcut key combinations. The shortcut key combination for single spacing is [Ctrl][1]; for 1.5 spacing, [Ctrl][5]; and for double spacing, [Ctrl][2]. Other line spacing options are available when you choose Paragraph from the Format menu. Changes in line spacing affect only the selected paragraph or paragraphs.

Marcus wants to double space the agenda items to make them stand out more. He'll use the Paragraph command on the Format menu to do so.

To double space the agenda items using the Paragraph command:

1. Select all the agenda items from Call to Order through Adjournment.
2. Click **Format** then click **Paragraph...** to display the Paragraph dialog box.
3. Click the **Line Spacing list box down arrow**. The list of line spacing options appears. See Figure 2-22.

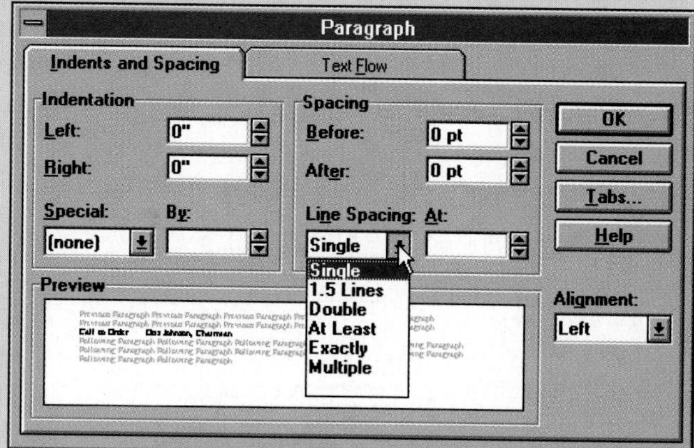

Figure 2-22 Line spacing options on Indents and Spacing tab

4. Click **Double** in the list of line spacing options. Notice that the Preview section changes to reflect the new line spacing setting.
5. Click **OK** or press **[Enter]**. The agenda items are now double-spaced.
6. Deselect the highlighted text.

Marcus also decides to double space the memo headings on the first page, to make them stand out more. This time, he'll use the shortcut key combination.

To double space the memo headings using the shortcut key combination:

1. Place the insertion point at the top of page 1.
2. Select the four lines of the memo headings (TO:, FROM:, RE:, DATE:).
3. Press **[Ctrl][2]**. Notice that only the selected area is affected by the paragraph format change to double spacing.
4. Deselect the highlighted text.
5. Save the changes you have made.

Next, Marcus wants to change how text aligns in some of the paragraphs in his document.

Aligning Paragraphs

Paragraph alignment involves specifying how you want the text within a paragraph to align horizontally in relation to its left and right *indents*. Remember, initially the left and right indents are located at the same point as the left and right *margins*. With **left alignment**, the paragraph text is set even with the left indent and ragged at the right; with **centered alignment**, the paragraph text is positioned evenly between the left and right indents; with **right alignment**, the lines of text within a paragraph are set even at the right indent and ragged at the left; and with **justified alignment**, the paragraph text at both the left and right indents is even. Left alignment is the default alignment setting.

Buttons for each of these alignment options appear on the Formatting toolbar. Alternatively, you can apply the different alignment options by using shortcut key combinations: [Ctrl][l] for left alignment, [Ctrl][e] for centered alignment, [Ctrl][r] for right alignment, or [Ctrl][j] for justified alignment. You can also choose the Paragraph command from the Format menu and then select the appropriate alignment option from the Paragraph dialog box.

Marcus wants to apply centered alignment to the memo title Memorandum and to the three-line agenda title, because titles are often centered on the page so that they stand out. He also wants to justify the text in the body of the memo, for a more formal appearance.

To apply centered alignment to the memo title:

1. Place the insertion point anywhere within the paragraph, Memorandum. Remember that because of the way Word defines a paragraph, you merely position the insertion point anywhere within the paragraph to select it and Word will apply any paragraph formatting changes to the entire paragraph.
2. Click the **Center button** on the Formatting toolbar. The text is centered between the left and right indents, and the Center button appears lighter to indicate that it is activated for the selected text. See Figure 2-23.

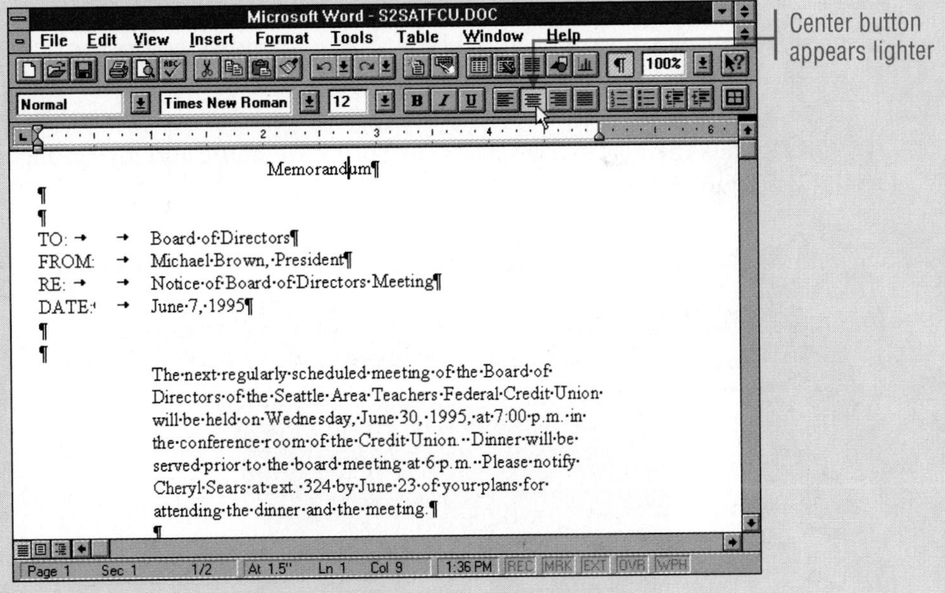

Figure 2-23 "Memorandum" centered

Now Marcus needs to center the three lines of the agenda title. Because each line of the agenda title is a separate paragraph, he must first select all three paragraphs.

To apply centered alignment to the paragraphs of the agenda title:

1. Move to page 2.
2. Use the selection bar to select the three lines of the agenda title.

3. Press **[Ctrl][e]**, the shortcut key combination for centered alignment. Notice that the Center button on the Formatting toolbar appears lighter, and the three paragraphs that you selected are centered.
4. Deselect the highlighted text. See Figure 2-24.

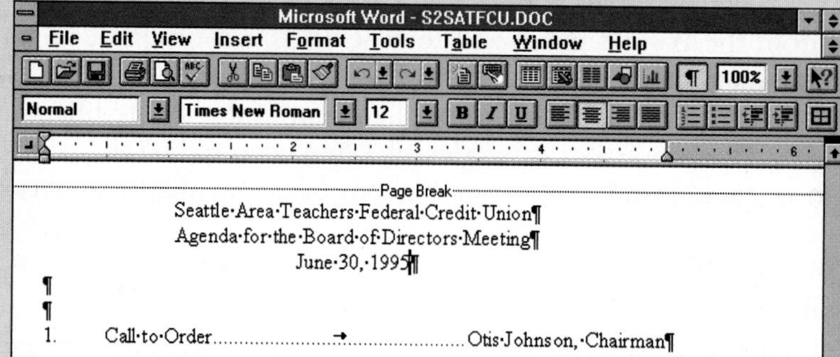

Figure 2-24 Agenda title lines centered

Next Marcus decides to justify all paragraphs in the body of the memo to give the memo a more formal appearance. He decides to use the shortcut editing and formatting menu to do so.

To justify all paragraphs in the body of the memo using the shortcut menu:

1. Move to page 1, then use the selection bar to select all the paragraphs in the body of the memo from "The next regularly scheduled..." through "...at the meeting."
2. Click the **right mouse button**. The shortcut editing and formatting menu appears. See Figure 2-25.

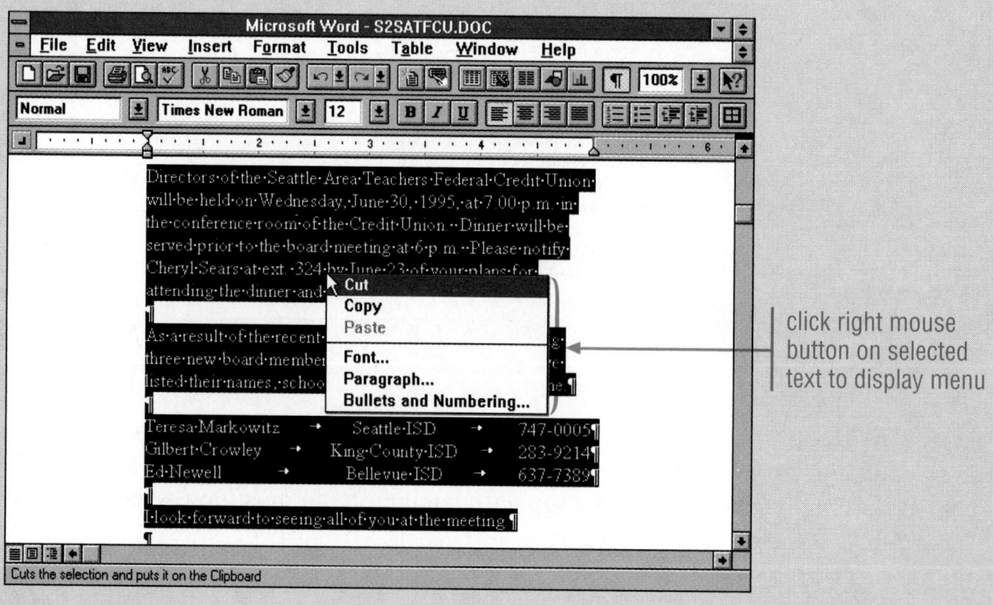

Microsoft Word - S2SATFCU.DOC
File Edit View Insert Format Tools Table Window Help
Normal
Times New Roman
12
100%
Directors·of·the·Seattle·Area·Teachers·Federal·Credit·Union·
will·be·held·on·Wednesday,·June·30,·1995,·at·7:00·p.m.·in·
the·conference·room·of·the·Credit·Union.··Dinner·will·be·
served·prior·to·the·board·meeting·at·6·p.m.··Please·notify·
Cut
Copy
Paste
Font...
Paragraph...
Bullets and Numbering...
Teresa·Markowitz Seattle·ISD 747-0005¶
Gilbert·Crowley King·County·ISD 283-9214¶
Ed·Newell Bellevue·ISD 637-7389¶
I·look·forward·to·seeing·all·of·you·at·the·meeting.¶
Cuts the selection and puts it on the Clipboard
click right mouse button on selected text to display menu

Figure 2-25 Shortcut editing and formatting menu

3. Click **Paragraph...**. The Paragraph dialog box appears.

4. Click the **Indents and Spacing tab**, if necessary. Notice that the Alignment section on the right side of the dialog box currently shows "Left" as the alignment.
5. Click the **Alignment list box down arrow**. The list of alignment options appears.
6. Click **Justified**. The Preview section changes to reflect the new alignment option.
7. Click **OK** or press **[Enter]**.
8. Deselect the highlighted text.
9. Scroll through the memo to see the effect of justifying the body of the memo. Notice that only those lines that take up a full line of typing are affected by justification.
10. Save the changes you have made.

Marcus is pleased with how the agenda looks, but he wants to emphasize its three-line title by putting a border around it. He also wants to separate the memo headings from the memo text by inserting a rule from the left margin to the right margin.

Creating Paragraph Borders and Rules

Applying borders and rules to paragraphs is another paragraph formatting technique. A **border** is a box that you use to frame text or graphics. A **rule** is a horizontal or vertical line that you use to enhance the appearance of your document. You can add borders and rules using either the Borders and Shading command on the Format menu or the Borders toolbar.

Marcus decides to put a shadow border, also called a drop shadow, around the three-line title of the agenda. Remember that each line of the title is actually a paragraph.

To create a border around the agenda title lines:

1. Move to page 2.
2. Select the three lines of the agenda title from "Seattle Area..." through "...1995."
3. Click **Format** then click **Borders and Shading...**. The Paragraph Borders and Shading dialog box appears.
4. Click the **Borders tab**, if necessary. The Border section allows you to preview changes you make.
5. Click the **Shadow icon** in the Presets section. Notice the change in the Border section.

Next Marcus needs to decide on the thickness of the line style. The choices are given in point sizes, with 1 point equal to 1/72".

6. In the Line section, under Style, click **3/4 pt** (if it's not already selected). Figure 2-26 shows the completed Paragraph Borders and Shading dialog box.

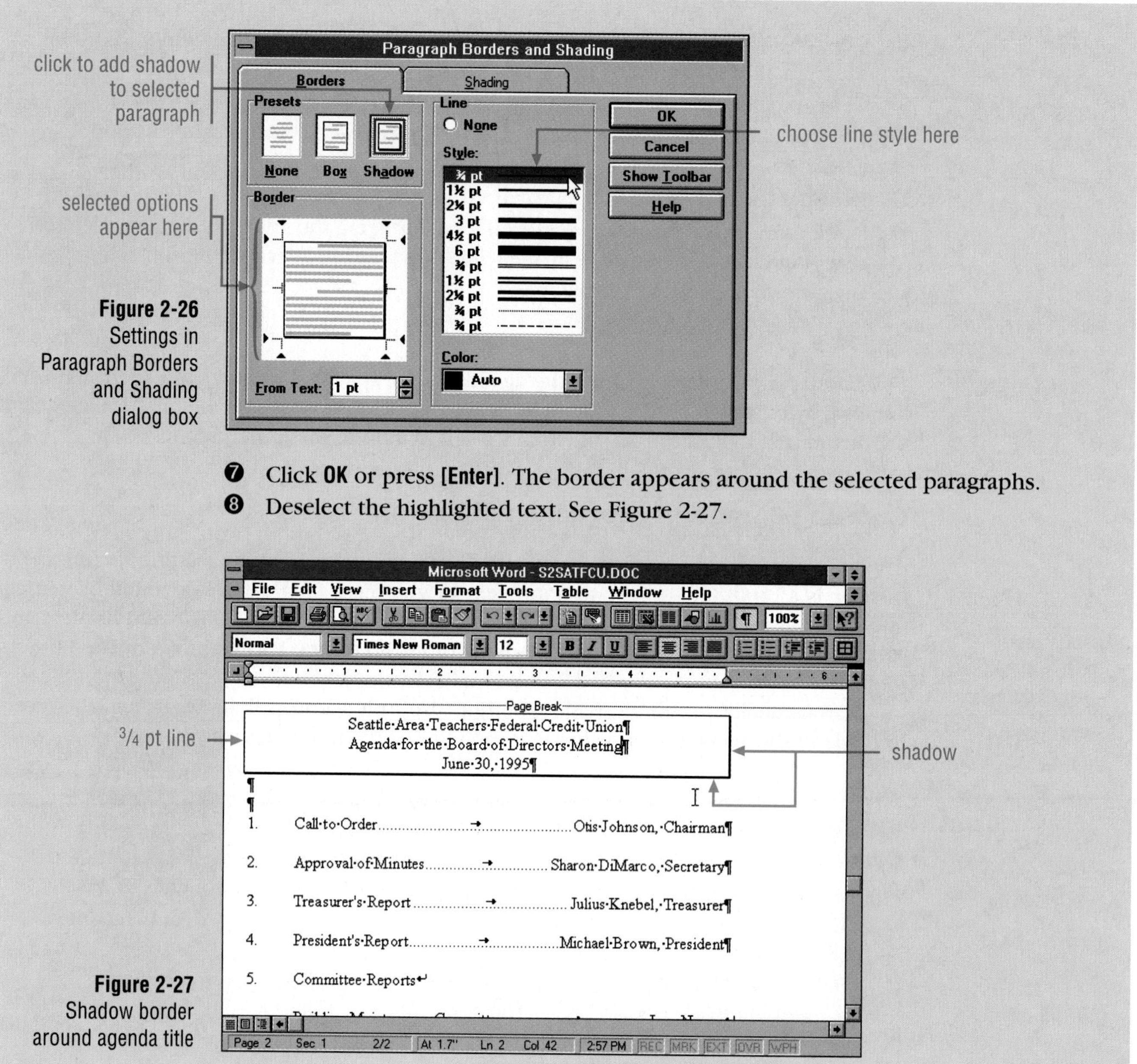

Figure 2-26 Settings in Paragraph Borders and Shading dialog box

❼ Click **OK** or press **[Enter]**. The border appears around the selected paragraphs.
❽ Deselect the highlighted text. See Figure 2-27.

Figure 2-27 Shadow border around agenda title

Marcus follows basically the same procedure to add a rule between the date line in the memo headings and the body of the memo, except this time he'll use the Borders toolbar.

To insert a rule below the memo headings:

❶ Move to page 1.
❷ Place the insertion point in front of the first paragraph mark below the date of the memo. Even though this line has no text on it, Word considers it a paragraph.
❸ Click the **Borders button** on the Formatting toolbar. The Borders toolbar appears. See Figure 2-28.

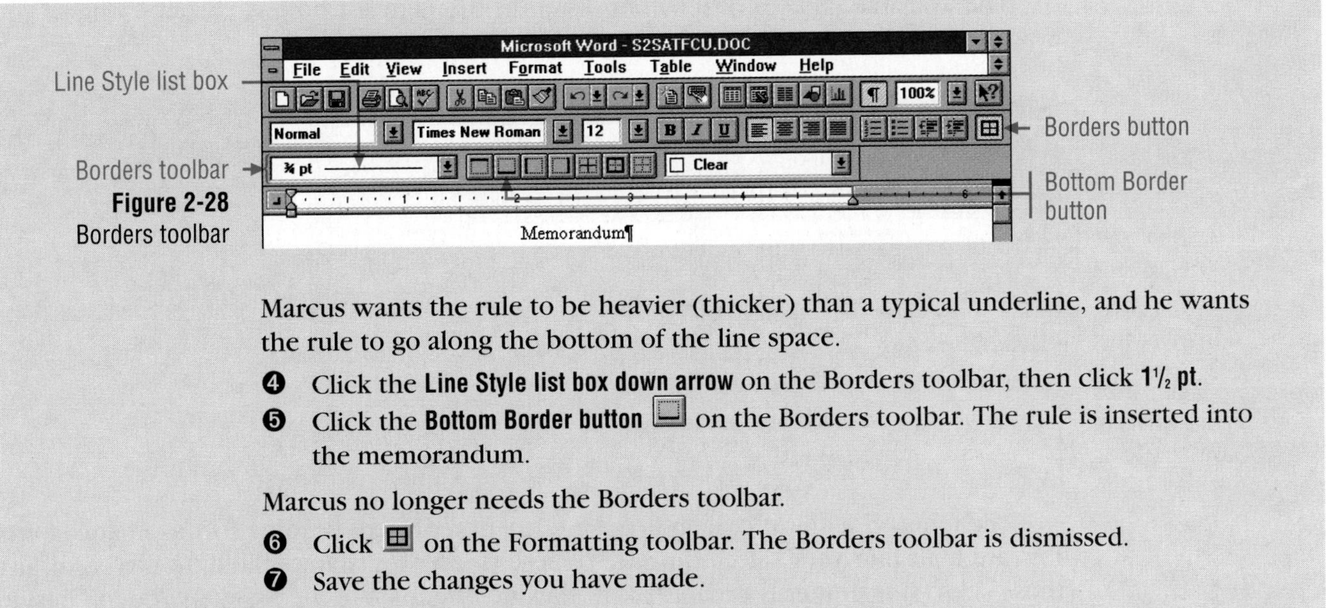

Figure 2-28
Borders toolbar

Marcus wants the rule to be heavier (thicker) than a typical underline, and he wants the rule to go along the bottom of the line space.

4. Click the **Line Style list box down arrow** on the Borders toolbar, then click **1½ pt.**
5. Click the **Bottom Border button** on the Borders toolbar. The rule is inserted into the memorandum.

Marcus no longer needs the Borders toolbar.

6. Click on the Formatting toolbar. The Borders toolbar is dismissed.
7. Save the changes you have made.

To remove a border or rule, select the paragraph or paragraphs to be changed. Choose Borders and Shading from the Format menu, then click the None radio button in the Line section of the Paragraph Borders and Shading dialog box. You can also click the No Border button on the Borders toolbar to remove a border or rule from a selected paragraph.

Marcus has now completed the paragraph formatting phase for his document.

If you want to take a break and resume the tutorial at a later time, you can close the current document then exit Word by double-clicking the Control menu box in the upper-left corner of the screen. When you want to resume the tutorial, start Word, place your Student Disk in the disk drive, then complete the screen check procedure described in Tutorial 1. Open the file S2SATFCU.DOC, press [Shift][F5], Word's Go Back command, to return to your last point in the document, then continue with the tutorial.

■ ■ ■

Next, Marcus begins the final stage of formatting: font-level formatting.

Font Formatting

A **font** is the general shape of the characters in your document. A **character** is any letter, number, punctuation mark, or symbol that you enter in your document. Font formatting involves choices about how the individual characters in your document appear on the screen and in print. These different choices are known as **character attributes**. Font formatting changes are made through the Formatting toolbar or the Font command on the Format menu. You can change the font type, the size of the characters, the style of the characters, the space between characters, the vertical position of characters, and even the color of the characters. In Tutorial 1 you learned how to change the type style of characters using the Bold, Italic, and Underline buttons on the Formatting toolbar. In this tutorial you will also use the Formatting toolbar and the Font command to make font-level formatting changes.

The available choices of fonts are listed in the Font list box. A partial listing of the available fonts is shown in Figure 2-29.

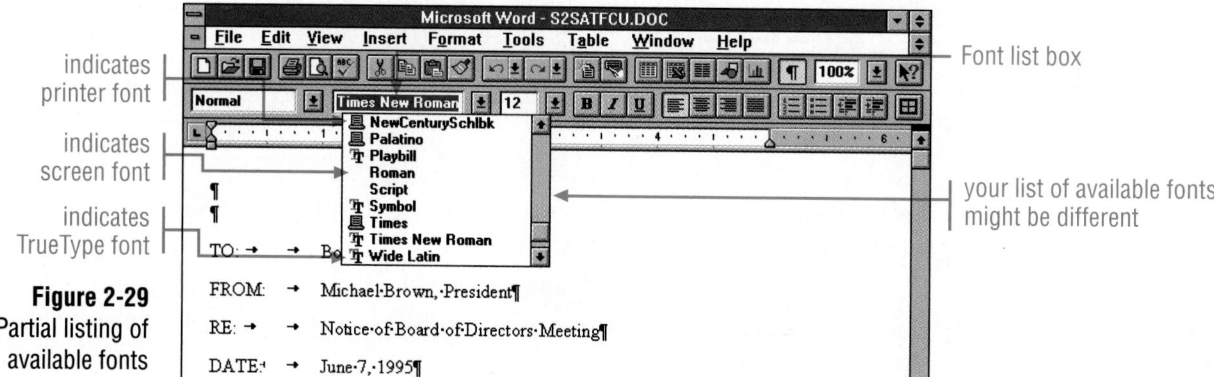

Figure 2-29 Partial listing of available fonts

The fonts with a printer icon in front of them represent **printer fonts**—that is, fonts that are built into your selected printer. These printer fonts are limited, however, to just those sizes your printer is capable of producing. The fonts in the list with no icon beside them are **screen fonts** only; if you choose a screen font, the way your document appears on your screen might be different from the way it looks when it is printed. The fonts in the list with double "Ts" in front of them are TrueType fonts, a special type of font that is available only in Windows 3.1. **TrueType fonts** work with every printer, including dot matrix printers, and any size can be specified. Word provides you with several TrueType fonts. Figure 2-30 illustrates each TrueType font available in Word. Although all these different fonts are available to you, you should limit to two or three the number of different fonts you use in any one document.

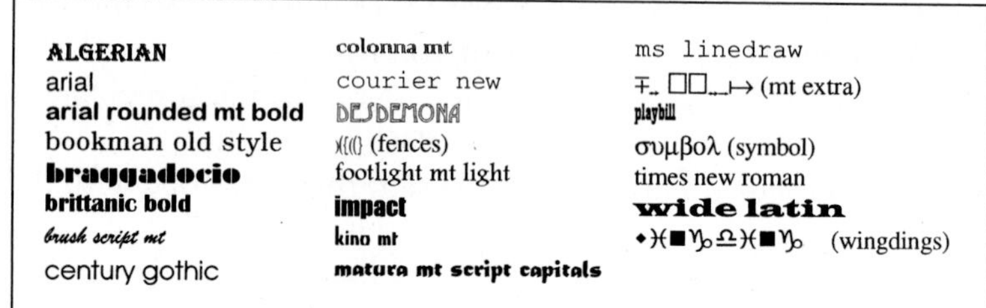

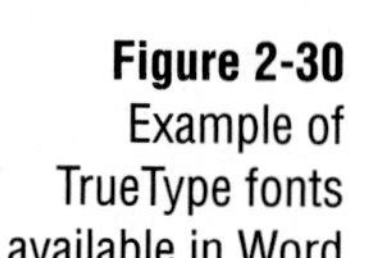
Figure 2-30 Example of TrueType fonts available in Word

The size of a font is measured in **points**; there are 72 points in an inch. The larger the point size of a font, the larger the font will be displayed and printed. The Font Size list box shows the sizes available for the font you have selected. Available point sizes vary depending on the font selected. The basic TrueType fonts are available, however, in sizes ranging from 4 points to 127 points. Figure 2-31 illustrates various font sizes.

This is Arial 12 point

This is Arial 24 point

This is Arial 36 point

Figure 2-31 Various font sizes

Another character attribute that you can change is type style. You have already used the bold, italic, and underline type styles, but Word provides other effects in the Font dialog box, such as strikethrough, all caps, small caps, and color (if you print on a color printer). The Character Spacing tab also provides you with the option to decrease or increase the space between characters and create superscript or subscript characters.

Marcus wants to change several character attributes of the memo title, Memorandum.

Changing Several Character Attributes at Once

Marcus wants to make the title Memorandum stand out from the rest of the memo text. He decides to change the font type of the memo title to the TrueType font Arial, make its size 14 point, make its font style bold and all caps, and expand the amount of space between each character. He decides to use the Font dialog box to change all these character attributes at once.

To change the character attributes at one time:

1. Select the memo heading **Memorandum**. Because you are now changing font formats, you must select all the characters you want to change; you cannot simply click the insertion point in the paragraph.
2. Click **Format** then click **Font...**. The Font dialog box appears.

   The Font list box displays the available font types in alphabetical order.
3. Scroll up the list of fonts, then click **Arial**. Notice that the Preview section changes to reflect the new font choice.

   TROUBLE? If you cannot locate Arial at the top of your font list, then perhaps your system is using a previous version of Windows. Ask your instructor or technical support person which font to use instead of Arial.
4. Click **Bold** in the Font Style list box. The Preview section changes to reflect the new type style choice.
5. Click **14** in the Size list box. The Preview section changes to reflect the new point size.
6. Click the **All Caps check box** in the Effects section. Figure 2-32 shows the completed settings on the Font tab of the Font dialog box.

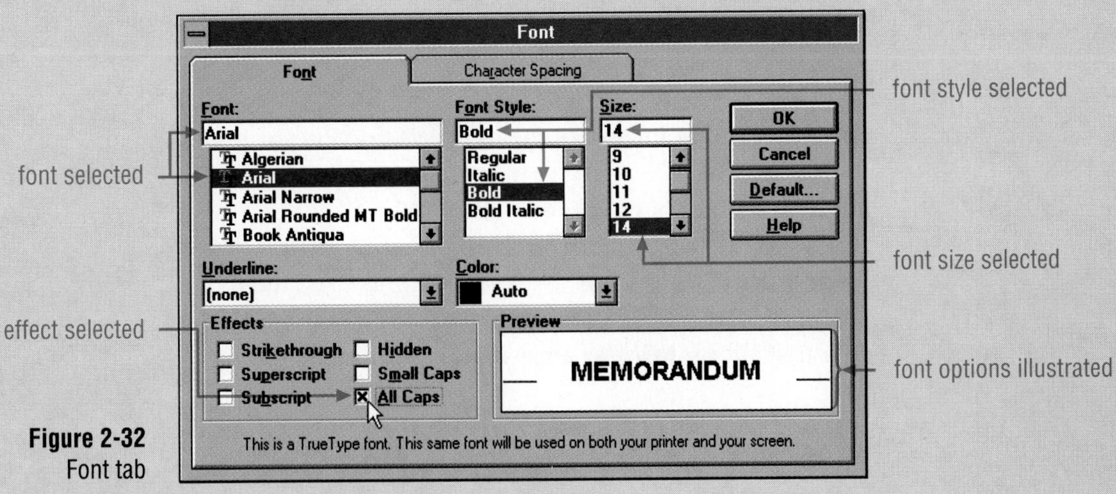

Figure 2-32
Font tab

Next, Marcus wants to increase the spacing between characters, so he needs to move to the Character Spacing tab of the Font dialog box.

7. Click the **Character Spacing tab**, then click the **Spacing list box down arrow** to display the available spacing options.
8. Click **Expanded**. An additional 1 point of space will be inserted between each character of the selected text. See Figure 2-33.

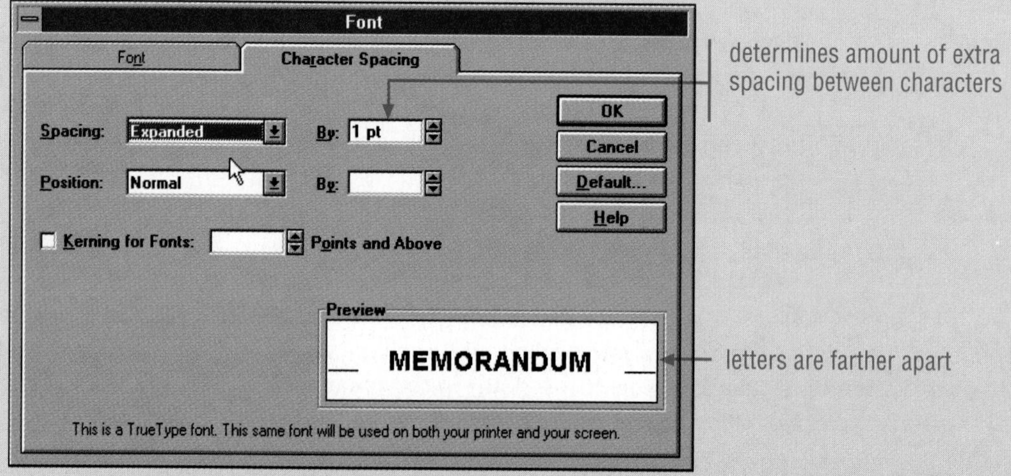

Figure 2-33 Character Spacing tab

9. Click **OK** or press **[Enter]**. All the character attribute changes you made are applied to the title Memorandum.
10. Deselect the highlighted text, then save the changes you have made.

Next, Marcus wants to change the agenda's title to make it stand out more from the list of agenda items.

Changing Font and Point Size Using the Formatting Toolbar

Marcus decides to change the font and enlarge the type size of the agenda's title lines. He decides to change the font to Arial and the point size to 14 using the Formatting toolbar. He also wants to bold the title lines.

To change the font and point size of the agenda's title lines using the Formatting toolbar:

1. Move to page 2.
2. Select the three lines of the agenda title.
3. Click the **Font list box down arrow** on the Formatting toolbar to open the font list. At the top of the list, Word keeps track of the fonts used most recently in a document.
4. Click the **Arial**. The selected text changes to reflect the new font choice.
5. Click the **Font Size list box down arrow** on the Formatting toolbar to open the Font Size list.
6. Click **14**. The selected text changes to reflect the new point size choice.
7. Click the **Bold button** B. The selected text changes to reflect the new type style choice.

❽ Deselect the highlighted text. See Figure 2-34.

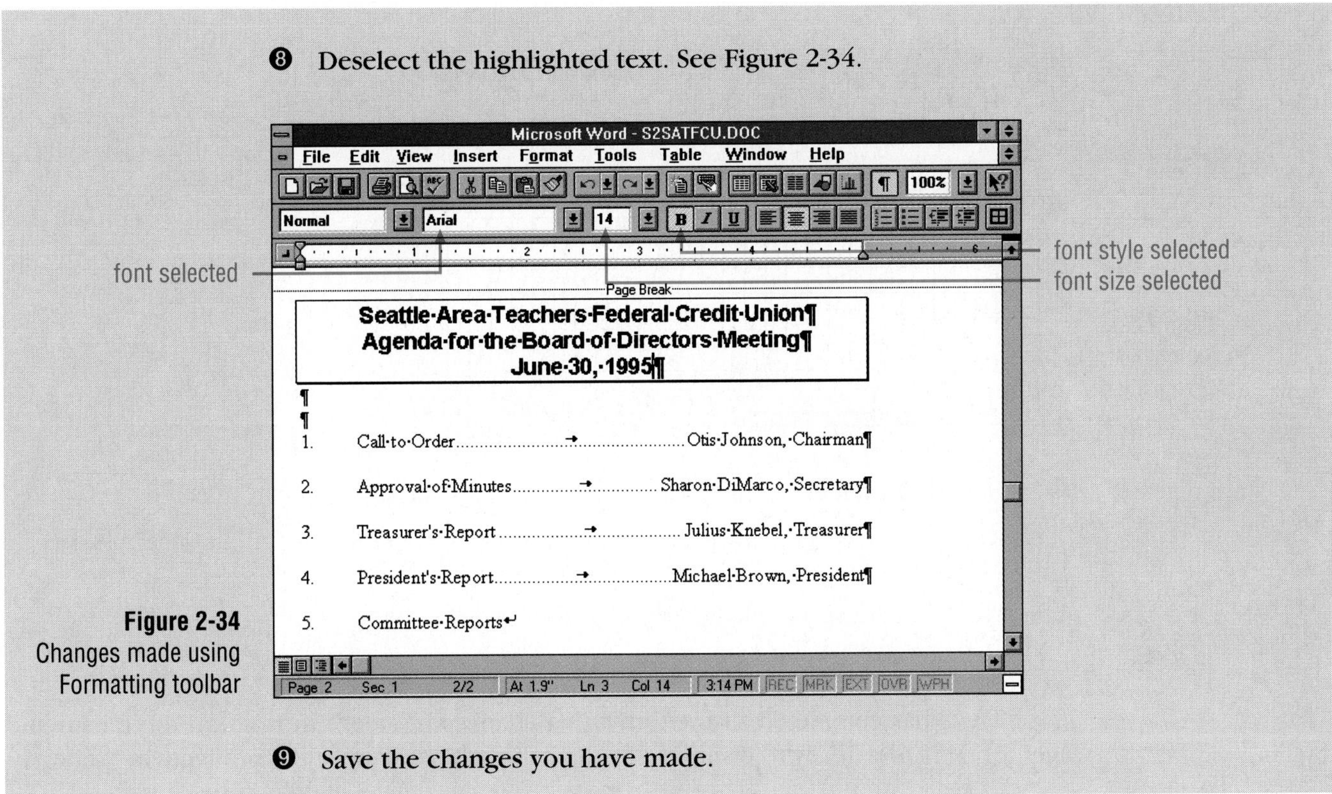

Figure 2-34
Changes made using Formatting toolbar

❾ Save the changes you have made.

Marcus decides to insert the tilde (~) above the second "n" in Nuñez, the last name of one of the presenters on the agenda.

Inserting Special Symbols

Word provides an easy way to insert special symbols called **character sets** in your documents. The character sets available depend on the selected printer; you choose them using the Symbol command on the Insert menu. Each character set has a variety of available characters or symbols. Once you have selected a character, it is placed in your document at the insertion point. To delete an inserted symbol, you must first select it and then press [Del].

The (normal text) character set contains the symbol with the tilde above the letter "n," which is the symbol Marcus wants to insert in this document.

To insert the tilde above the "n" in Nunez:

❶ Move the insertion point to page 2, if necessary.

❷ Select the second "n" in Nunez, the last name of the presenter for the Building Maintenance Committee report. Only the "n" should be highlighted.

❸ Click **Insert** then click **Symbol...**. The Symbol dialog box appears and the Symbols tab is selected.

❹ Click the **Font list box down arrow** to display the available character sets. Scroll up, then click **(normal text)** at the top of the list. The (normal text) character set is displayed.

❺ Click the **ñ symbol** to select it. (You will find it in the last row.) The symbol "ñ" now appears much bigger. See Figure 2-35.

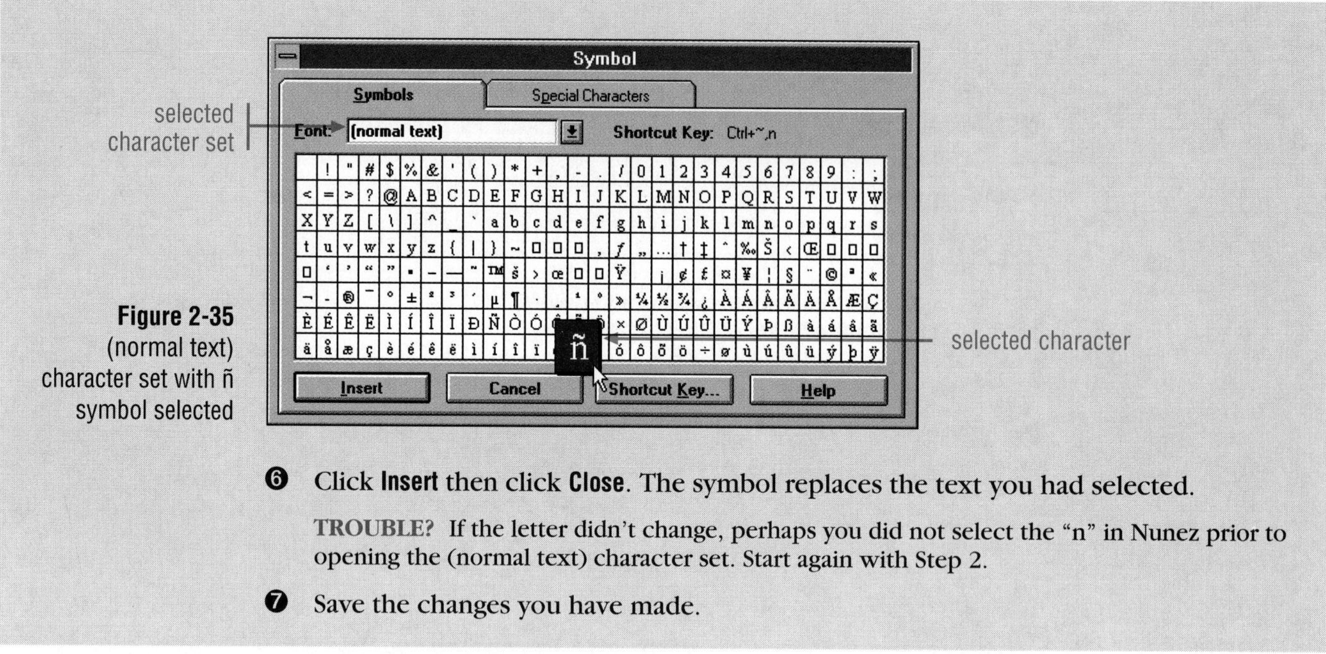

Figure 2-35 (normal text) character set with ñ symbol selected

6. Click **Insert** then click **Close**. The symbol replaces the text you had selected.

   TROUBLE? If the letter didn't change, perhaps you did not select the "n" in Nunez prior to opening the (normal text) character set. Start again with Step 2.

7. Save the changes you have made.

Marcus has completed all the formatting changes he needs to make to the memo and agenda. He is now ready to print his document—the final stage of the productivity strategy.

Previewing and Printing Multiple Pages

Now you are ready to print a copy of Marcus's memo and agenda. Before you do, you'll first spell check the document and correct any errors. Then, you'll view the document in print preview to see how it will look when printed. One of the options in print preview, Multiple Pages, allows you to view several pages of your document side by side.

To spell check the document:

1. Press **[Ctrl][Home]** to move to the beginning of the document.
2. Click the **Spelling button** on the Standard toolbar (or click **Tools** then click **Spelling...**). Follow the procedures described in Tutorial 1 for performing a spell check.
3. Save your changes if necessary.

Now you can preview and print the document.

To preview both pages at the same time, then print the document:

1. Click the **Print Preview button** on the Standard toolbar (or click **File** then click **Print Preview**).

   TROUBLE? If two pages are already displayed in print preview, skip to Step 4.

2. Click the **Multiple Pages button** on the Print Preview toolbar.

3. Drag the mouse pointer across two of the page icons to indicate that you want to view two pages side by side, then release the mouse button. Both pages of your document appear in the Preview window. See Figure 2-36.

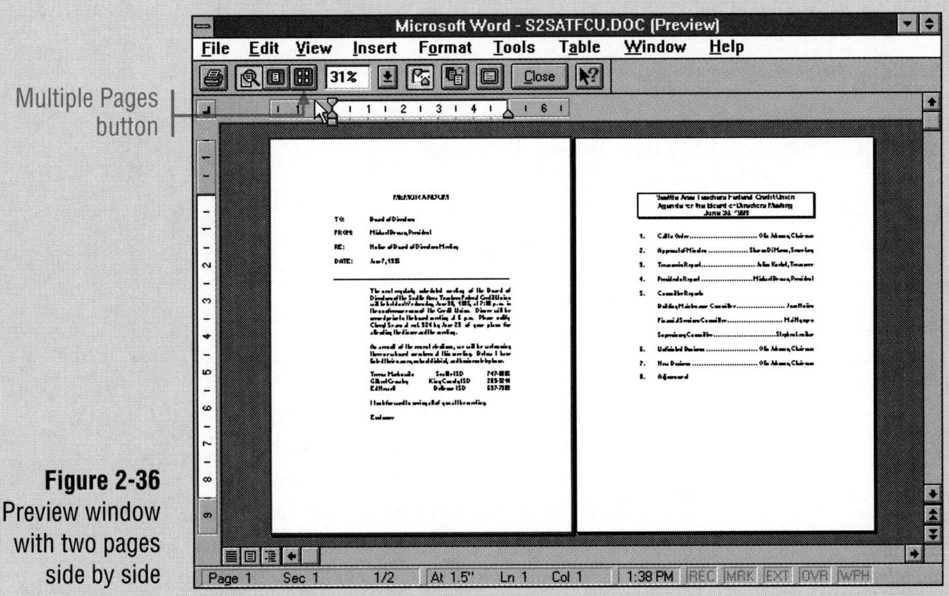

Figure 2-36 Preview window with two pages side by side

4. Click the **Print button** on the Print Preview toolbar if you are satisfied with the appearance of your document. Otherwise, click **Close**, return to your document to make changes, then repeat Steps 1 through 4. Your final document should look like Figure 2-37.
5. Click the **Close button** on the Print Preview toolbar to return to your document.
6. Close the document and exit Word.

MEMORANDUM

TO: Board of Directors

FROM: Michael Brown, President

RE: Notice of Board of Directors Meeting

DATE: June 7, 1995

The next regularly scheduled meeting of the Board of Directors of the Seattle Area Teachers Federal Credit Union will be held on Wednesday, June 30, 1995, at 7:00 p.m. in the conference room of the Credit Union. Dinner will be served prior to the board meeting at 6 p.m. Please notify Cheryl Sears at ext. 324 by June 23 of your plans for attending the dinner and the meeting.

As a result of the recent elections, we will be welcoming three new board members at this meeting. Below I have listed their names, school district, and business telephone.

Teresa Markowitz	Seattle ISD	747-0005
Gilbert Crowley	King County ISD	283-9214
Ed Newell	Bellevue ISD	637-7389

I look forward to seeing all of you at the meeting.

Enclosure

Figure 2-37 Marcus's final document (page 1 of 2)

Seattle Area Teachers Federal Credit Union
Agenda for the Board of Directors Meeting
June 30, 1995

1. Call to Order .... Otis Johnson, Chairman
2. Approval of Minutes............................. Sharon DiMarco, Secretary
3. Treasurer's Report.................................... Julius Knebel, Treasurer
4. President's Report...................................Michael Brown, President
5. Committee Reports

   Building Maintenance Committee ....Joan Nuñez

   Financial Services Committee ....Mai Nguyen

   Supervisory Committee .... Stephen Lesikar
6. Unfinished Business................................... Otis Johnson, Chairman
7. New Business... Otis Johnson, Chairman
8. Adjournment

Figure 2-37 Marcus's final document (page 2 of 2)

■ ■ ■

Marcus is pleased with his final document. He gives it to Michael for distribution to the board members.

Questions

1. Explain the purpose of Word's drag-and-drop feature. What is another way to accomplish the same purpose?
2. Explain the uses of a new line mark.
3. What command do you choose to rename an existing file?
4. Explain the differences among page setup, paragraph formatting, and font formatting.
5. What would the length of your typing line be if you changed your left and right margins both to 1 inch?
6. Explain the difference between a soft page break and a hard page break.
7. What different methods can you use to move quickly between pages in a document?
8. What is the difference between portrait page orientation and landscape page orientation? What command do you choose to change page orientation?
9. What are Word's four types of indent formats? How do you create them using the indent markers on the ruler?
10. Describe the effect of the following paragraph alignment options:
    a. Left
    b. Centered
    c. Right
    d. Justified
11. What are the shortcut keyboard combinations for the following line spacing options?
    a. Single spacing
    b. 1.5 spacing
    c. Double spacing
12. Explain the difference between an indent and a tab.
13. What are the four types of tab alignments? How do you set tabs using the ruler?
14. What is the difference between paragraph alignment and tab alignment?
15. What are the three types of leader characters? How do you set leader characters?
16. What is the difference between a border and a rule? How do you create a border around a paragraph?
17. Describe the different types of character attributes.
18. If you wanted to print a word so that it appeared 1.5 inches high, what point size would you apply to the selected word?
19. What are the advantages of using TrueType fonts rather than printer fonts?
20. What is a character set?

Use Word Help to find the answers to the following questions:

E 21. What is the keyboard equivalent command to indent all lines of a paragraph to the next tab stop?

E 22. How do you remove the numbers from a numbered list of items?

E 23. How do you change the number format of a numbered list of items?

E 24. What is the keyboard equivalent command to remove all font formatting from selected text?

E 25. What is the procedure for inserting a vertical bar between tabbed columns of information?

Tutorial Assignments

Start Word, if necessary, and conduct a screen check. Open T2SATMIN.DOC from your Student Disk, then complete the following:

1. On the line after the Attendance section heading, type the names given below of the members in attendance. Press [Tab] once after the name in the first column, then type the name in the second column.

Joan Nuñez	Michael Brown
Gilbert Crowley	Sharon DiMarco
Otis Johnson	Julius Knebel
Stephen Lesikar	Teresa Markowitz
Ed Newell	Mai Nguyen

2. Insert new line marks so that the Committee Reports section (from Committee Reports through the Supervisory Committee) is all one paragraph.
3. Move the President's report after the Treasurer's report.
4. Change the top margin to 1.5 inches and the side margins to 1 inch.
5. Center the three-line heading.
6. Indent the names of the members in attendance 1 inch from the left margin.
7. Insert a left-aligned tab so that the second column of the members in attendance starts at the 3.5-inch mark on the ruler.
8. Number the paragraphs of the body of the minutes.
9. Right-align the closing lines (Respectfully submitted through Board of Directors).
10. Change the three-line heading to 14 point, Century Gothic, bold.
11. Bold each of the section headings (Attendance, Treasurer's Report, etc.) and italicize the headings for each of the committee reports.
12. Save the document as S2SATMIN.DOC.
13. Spell check, preview, then print the document.
14. **E** Number the paragraphs of the body of the minutes using roman numeral format.
15. Change the amount of the hanging indent for the numbered list to 0.5 inch.
16. Save the document as S2MIN2.DOC.
17. Preview then print the document.
18. Close the document.

Case Problems

1. The Cost of Administrative Services at Tyler Fasteners

Marjorie Rominofski is the administrative services manager for Tyler Fasteners, which manufactures a variety of fasteners for the construction industry. One of her responsibilities each month is to write a memo to the department heads in the plant. In this memo she informs the department heads about the cost of administrative services charged to each department's budget. You will format Marjorie's memo.

Open P2ADMSER.DOC from your Student Disk, then complete the following:

1. Insert the title Memorandum at the top of the document, then press [Enter] twice.
2. Align the information after the memo headings (TO:, FROM:, and so on) at the 1-inch mark.
3. Change the top margin to 2 inches and the left and right margins to 1.75 inches.
4. Double space the memo headings.
5. Move the sentence beginning "These amounts . . ." and the two spaces after it to the beginning of the last paragraph ("If you have . . .").
6. Center the title Memorandum.
7. Insert a 1½ point, double line border around Memorandum.

8. Indent the three expenditure lines (Photocopies, and so on) to the 1-inch mark.
9. Align the decimal for the amounts in the expenditure lines at the 4-inch mark.
10. Change Memorandum to 18-point Bookman Old Style, bold, and all caps.
11. Save the document as S2ADMSER.DOC.
12. Spell check, preview, then print the document.
13. Change the left and right margins to 1.25 inches and move the tab for the expenditures from the 4-inch mark to the 4.5-inch mark.

E 14. Remove the border from the title Memorandum.

E 15. Change the font to Arial for all the text except the title.

16. Save the document as S2TYLER.DOC.
17. Preview then print the document.
18. Dismiss the Borders toolbar, if necessary, and close the document.

2. Total Quality Management at English Engineering, Inc.

Janetta Coleman is the manager of the Human Resources Development Department for English Engineering, Inc., an aeronautical engineering systems firm in Huntsville, Alabama. As part of the team of contractors responsible for the life-support system on board the space shuttle, English is participating in the total quality management program mandated by the federal government of all space shuttle contractors. At a recent retreat, Janetta's staff developed its vision statement. Janetta created and edited a simple flyer that will serve as a reminder to her staff of their vision for the direction of the department. Now she needs to format and print it.

Open P2VISION.DOC from your Student Disk, then complete the following:

1. Scroll through the document. The flyer consists of three parts—the heading Vision on Ln 5, the vision statement on Ln 18 through 20, and the department identification on Ln 33 through 35.
2. Center the heading Vision and the vision statement.
3. Right-align and double space the department identification.
4. Place a $1\frac{1}{2}$ point double rule approximately 1 inch above and below the vision statement.
5. Add the following character attributes to Vision:
   a. Century Gothic font
   b. 36 point
   c. bold
   d. italic
   e. all caps
   f. expanded spacing
6. Add the following character attributes to the vision statement:
   a. Century Gothic font
   b. 24 point
   c. bold
   d. italic
7. Add the following character attributes to the department identification:
   a. Century Gothic font
   b. 18 point
   c. bold
8. Save the document as S2VISION.DOC.
9. Preview then print the document.

E 10. Insert the Wingdings character set symbol A (you will find it on the seventh row) at the beginning of the line, Human Resources Development Department.

11. Increase the amount of space between each character in the heading Vision to 3 point.
12. Save the document as S2HRD2.DOC.
13. Preview then print the document.
14. Dismiss the Borders toolbar then close the document.

3. Safety Measures at University General Hospital

Raul Fernandez is the director of the Environmental and Physical Safety Department of University General Hospital. He has decided to prepare a memo motivating employees to be aware of the potential safety hazards in their work environment and informing them whom to call for information or help.

Complete the following:

1. Create the document as shown in Figure 2-38. Type the memo headings, body of the memo, and telephone information without making any formatting decisions. When typing the memo headings (TO:, FROM:, and so on), insert one tab between the heading and the information that follows. When typing the personnel information, insert a tab between the title (for example, Director) and the name (Raul Fernandez).

Memorandum

TO: Hospital Staff
FROM: Raul Fernandez
RE: Safe and healthful work environments
DATE: September 2, 1995

Whether you work in a laboratory, hospital ward, or an office, it is important for you to be aware of the hazards and safety procedures for your work area. Attend safety meetings, learn about fire extinguishers, evacuation plans, personal protective equipment, and techniques for handling and storing potentially harmful materials.

The Environmental and Physical Safety Department maintains programs in chemical safety, radiation safety, biosafety, asbestos control, hazardous waste management, fire safety, hazard communication, and general safety. On the next page is a list of the individuals responsible for these programs. Please keep this sheet readily available, and contact the appropriate person whenever you have a question or concern about safety issues. Thank you!

Whom to Call

749-4271

Director Raul Fernandez
Manager, Fire and Physical Safety Bob Lane
Manager, Hazardous Materials Janet Hunter
Manager, Radiation Safety Le Chiu
Office Manager Ann Schuler

Figure 2-38

2. Save the document as S2SAFETY.DOC.
3. Double space the memo headings and the personnel information.
4. Center the title Memorandum.
5. Justify the body of the memo.
6. Indent the body of the memo to the 1-inch mark.
7. Align the colons in the memo headings by inserting a right-aligned tab stop at the 0.75-inch mark, then inserting a tab in front of each heading.
8. Insert a hard page break before Whom to Call.
9. Insert a $\frac{3}{4}$ point single rule below Whom to Call.
10. Center the telephone number.
11. Indent the personnel information from both margins 1 inch.
12. Set a right-aligned, dot leader tab for the personnel information at the 5-inch mark.
13. Bold the title Memorandum.
14. Change the font for all the text on page 2 to Arial Rounded MT Bold.
15. Change the telephone number to 24 point.
16. Save the document.
17. Spell check, preview, then print the document.

E

18. Insert the Wingdings special character set symbol for the telephone above the telephone number.
19. Center the telephone.
20. Change the telephone special character to 36 point.
21. Save the document as S2UGH2.DOC.
22. Preview then print the document.
23. Dismiss the Borders toolbar and close the document.

TUTORIAL 3

Creating a Multiple-Page Document with Tables

Developing a Travel Expense Policy Report

OBJECTIVES

In this tutorial you will:

- Create a table
- Use AutoCorrect
- Use the Clipboard for cutting, copying, and pasting text
- Find and replace text
- Select cells, rows, columns, text, or an entire table
- Modify a table structure
- Sort information in a table
- Perform mathematical calculations in a table
- Insert a caption
- Insert headers and footers
- Use and apply styles
- Format a table automatically with borders, rules, and shading

CASE **Powell International Petroleum Services, Inc.** Barbara Svoboda is a recent business school graduate with a specialty in human resources management. For the last two years, she has been working for Powell International Petroleum Services, Inc. (PIPSI) at its corporate headquarters in Baton Rouge, Louisiana. PIPSI specializes in retrofitting older refineries and pipelines with the latest production technologies. Most recently, PIPSI has started numerous projects in the Commonwealth of Independent States; as a result, employee travel expenses have increased.

PIPSI's executive management has asked Barbara's manager, Nancy McDermott, to develop a new travel expense policy that will control domestic and foreign travel expenses. Nancy has almost finished the policy statement but has been called out of town. She gives Barbara the disk containing the report and tells her to finish the report, then edit and format it before submitting it to management.

Barbara decides to use the productivity strategy to complete her task. She will finish creating the travel expense policy, then edit the document for any changes or corrections she needs to make. Next, she will format the policy statement following the format used for other policy statements in the company's policy manual. Barbara will then print the completed travel expense policy.

To start Word and open the document that Nancy created:

1. Start Word, if necessary, and conduct the screen check as described in Tutorial 1.
2. Insert your Student Disk in the disk drive, then open the file C3PERDM.DOC from your Student Disk. After C3PERDM.DOC is open, scroll through the document to become familiar with it. Compare your document to Figure 3-1 on the following page. Notice that the document is two pages long and divided into four major sections—Standard Per Diem Allowance, Domestic Travel, Foreign Travel, and Exceptions. Eventually, the Domestic Travel and Foreign Travel sections will contain basically the same information arranged in the same order.
3. Click **File** then click **Save As...** and save the document as S3PERDM.DOC to your Student Disk.
4. Click **OK** or press **[Enter]**. The title bar changes to reflect the new document name.

Barbara begins by looking over the printed copy of the unfinished travel expense policy that Nancy left (Figure 3-1). She decides to begin her work in the document by adding the following: explanations for the components of the per diem allowance (Insert A), a table of information about the domestic travel per diem (Insert B), and a table of information about foreign travel per diem (Insert C). Depending on the printer selected, your document might break between pages one and two at a point different from that shown in Figure 3-1.

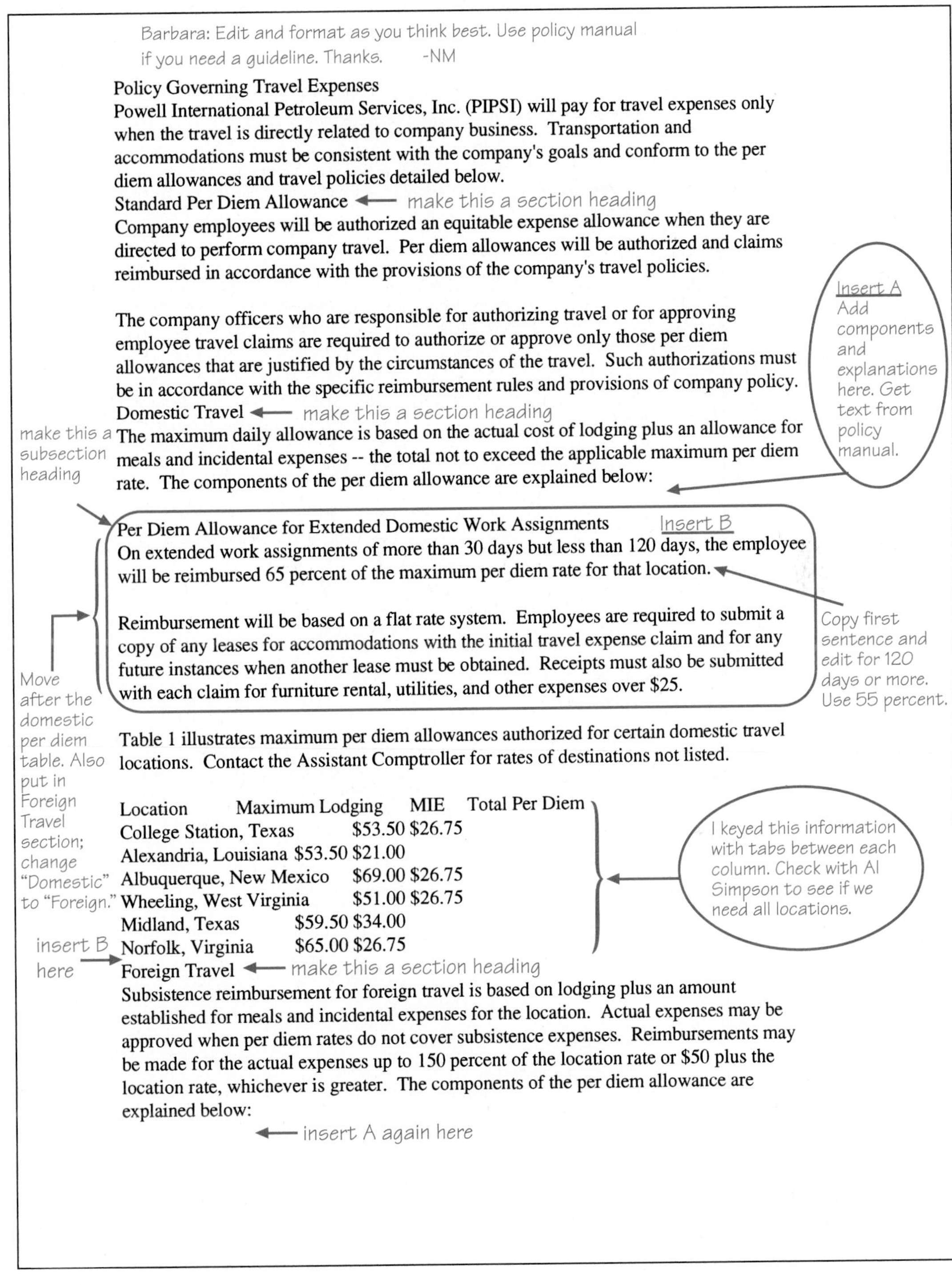

Barbara: Edit and format as you think best. Use policy manual if you need a guideline. Thanks. -NM

Policy Governing Travel Expenses
Powell International Petroleum Services, Inc. (PIPSI) will pay for travel expenses only when the travel is directly related to company business. Transportation and accommodations must be consistent with the company's goals and conform to the per diem allowances and travel policies detailed below.

Standard Per Diem Allowance

Company employees will be authorized an equitable expense allowance when they are directed to perform company travel. Per diem allowances will be authorized and claims reimbursed in accordance with the provisions of the company's travel policies.

The company officers who are responsible for authorizing travel or for approving employee travel claims are required to authorize or approve only those per diem allowances that are justified by the circumstances of the travel. Such authorizations must be in accordance with the specific reimbursement rules and provisions of company policy.

Domestic Travel

The maximum daily allowance is based on the actual cost of lodging plus an allowance for meals and incidental expenses -- the total not to exceed the applicable maximum per diem rate. The components of the per diem allowance are explained below:

Per Diem Allowance for Extended Domestic Work Assignments

On extended work assignments of more than 30 days but less than 120 days, the employee will be reimbursed 65 percent of the maximum per diem rate for that location.

Copy first sentence and edit for 120 days or more. Use 55 percent.

Reimbursement will be based on a flat rate system. Employees are required to submit a copy of any leases for accommodations with the initial travel expense claim and for any future instances when another lease must be obtained. Receipts must also be submitted with each claim for furniture rental, utilities, and other expenses over $25.

Table 1 illustrates maximum per diem allowances authorized for certain domestic travel locations. Contact the Assistant Comptroller for rates of destinations not listed.

Location	Maximum Lodging	MIE	Total Per Diem
College Station, Texas	$53.50	$26.75	
Alexandria, Louisiana	$53.50	$21.00	
Albuquerque, New Mexico	$69.00	$26.75	
Wheeling, West Virginia	$51.00	$26.75	
Midland, Texas	$59.50	$34.00	
Norfolk, Virginia	$65.00	$26.75	

I keyed this information with tabs between each column. Check with Al Simpson to see if we need all locations.

insert B here

Foreign Travel

Subsistence reimbursement for foreign travel is based on lodging plus an amount established for meals and incidental expenses for the location. Actual expenses may be approved when per diem rates do not cover subsistence expenses. Reimbursements may be made for the actual expenses up to 150 percent of the location rate or $50 plus the location rate, whichever is greater. The components of the per diem allowance are explained below:

← insert A again here

Figure 3-1
Nancy's edited document (page 1 of 2)

Table 2 illustrates maximum per diem allowances authorized for certain foreign travel locations. Contact the Assistant Comptroller for rates of destinations not listed.

← insert C here

← insert B here

Exceptions ← make this a section heading

Any exceptions to the standard per diem allowance must be in writing to the Assistant Comptroller's office.

Here's the information for the Foreign Travel Per Diem table. Check with Al to see if there are other locations.

Location	Maximum Lodging	MIE	Maximum Per Diem	
Usinsk, Komi	$23	$8	$31	
Baku, Azerbaijan	$35	$12	$47	
Lisitschansk, Ukraine	$40	$12	$52	Insert C

Figure 3-1
Nancy's edited document (page 2 of 2)

Creating a Table

Tables are an important means of communicating information in business documents, because they allow the reader to analyze complex data quickly. A **table** is simply information organized horizontally in rows and vertically in columns. The intersection of a row and column is called a **cell**.

In Tutorial 2 you learned to align text vertically by using tabs. That procedure works well for information in two or three columns, with each item in the table containing only one row of information. But if the information is more complex, or if you want a more professional-looking table, using tabs to create tables becomes awkward and tedious.

Word's table feature relieves the tedium of setting up data in columns and rows. It also enables you to lay out other types of information, such as text and graphics, side by side in a more readable format. The elements of a Word table are illustrated in Figure 3-2. Like text typed in a paragraph, text entered in a cell wraps automatically within that cell.

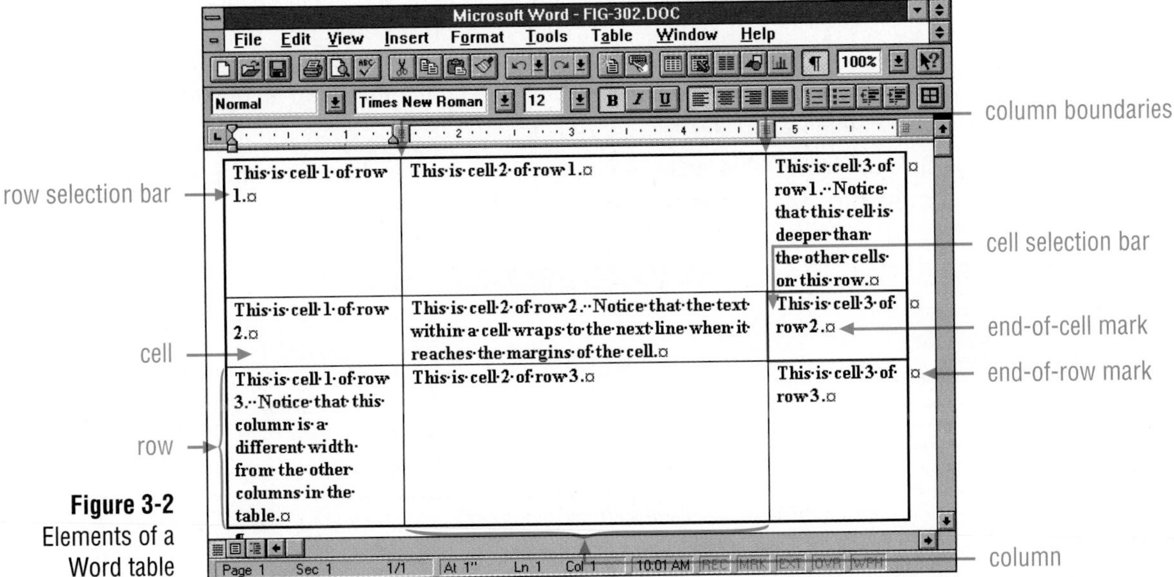

Figure 3-2 Elements of a Word table

Word's table feature allows you to create a blank table, then insert information in it, or to convert existing text to a table. Whichever method you choose, Word makes it easy for you to create the **structure**—the number of rows and columns—of a table.

To see the outline of the table structure in your document, the Gridlines option on the Table menu must be activated, which it is by default. To check whether the Gridlines option is activated, open the Table menu and look for a checkmark in front of the Gridlines option. The gridlines that are used to display the blank table structure do not print, however. If you want a border around any part of a table, you must specifically format the table or individual cells with borders.

Creating a Table Using the Table Button

In addition to arranging data in rows and columns, Word's table feature allows you to create side-by-side text paragraphs, such as when you need to define words or include explanations of catalog items. One method to create a blank table structure is to use the Insert Table button on the Standard toolbar to specify the number of rows and columns you need in your table. Word then inserts a blank table structure with the specified number of rows and columns at the insertion point.

As she noted on page 1 of her draft, Nancy wants Barbara to insert explanations of the two components of the per diem allowance: "Maximum lodging expense allowance" and "Meals and incidental expense allowance." Barbara will use the table feature to create side-by-side text paragraphs, with the per diem component name on the left side and the explanation of the component on the right side. Barbara needs to create a table that has two rows and two columns. She decides to use the Insert Table button to specify the table structure.

To create a blank table structure using the Insert Table button:

1. Scroll through the document until you see the Domestic Travel heading.
2. Place the insertion point in front of the heading, Per Diem Allowance for Extended Domestic Work Assignments (Page 1, Ln 20).

   TROUBLE? Your choice of printer might affect the location of the insertion point shown in your status bar. Use the line reference given in the tutorial as a guide, but continue to refer to the figures.

3. Click the **Insert Table button** on the Standard toolbar. The Insert Table button grid, a miniature table, appears. See Figure 3-3.

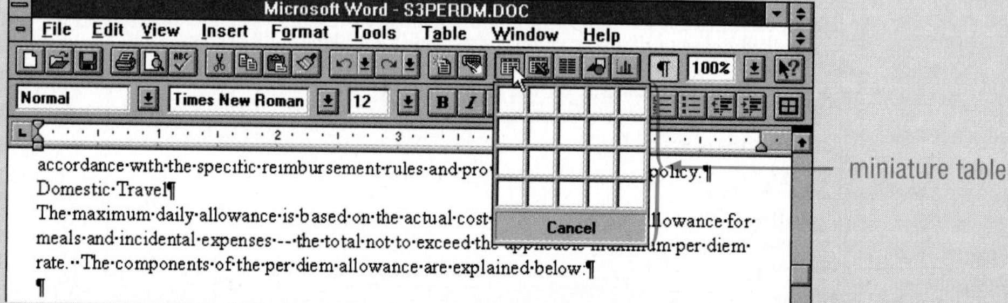

Figure 3-3 Insert Table button grid

4. Place the pointer in the upper-left cell of the miniature table, then click and drag it across the grid so that two rows and two columns are highlighted. As you highlight cells, Word indicates the size of the table at the bottom of the grid (rows x columns).
5. Release the mouse button. An empty 2 x 2 table grid structure appears in the document, and the insertion point is in cell 1 of row 1. See Figure 3-4.

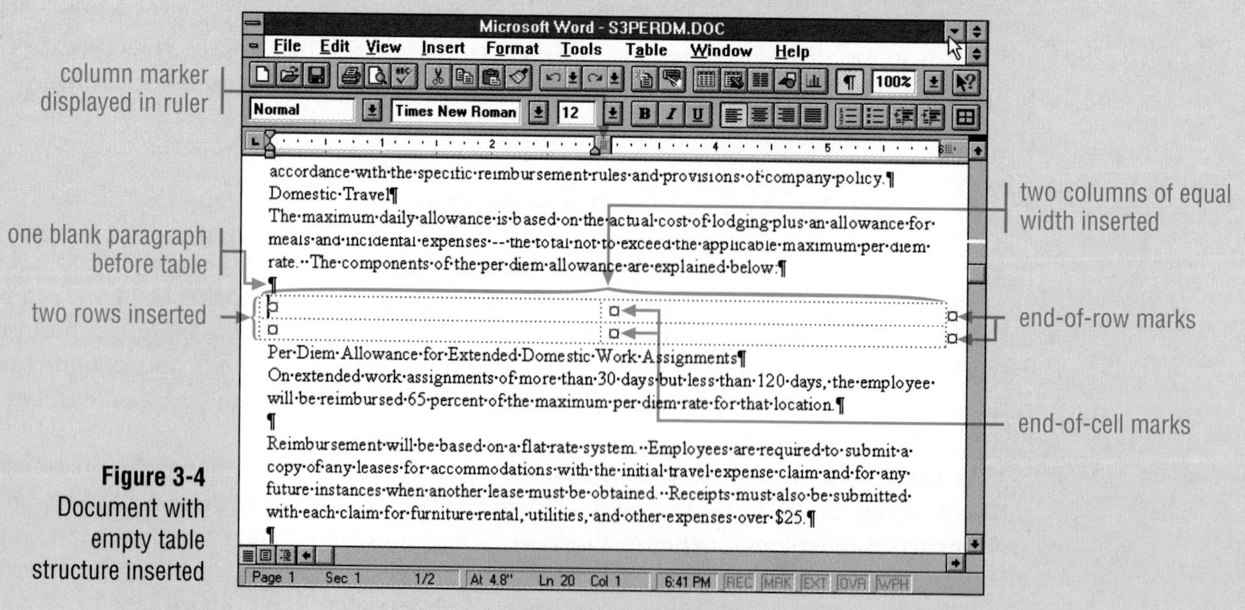

Figure 3-4 Document with empty table structure inserted

Notice that, by default, Word automatically creates two columns of equal width between the margins of the document. Each cell contains an end-of-cell mark, and each row contains an end-of-row mark. Also notice the change in the ruler: each column is indicated by column markers on the ruler, the indent markers for the active cell are displayed, and between column spacing has been inserted.

TROUBLE? If you are not satisfied with the table you created, immediately click the Undo button on the Standard toolbar (or click Edit then click Undo Insert Table), then repeat Steps 2 through 5.

TROUBLE? If you do not see the end-of-cell and end-of-row marks, you need to click the Show/Hide ¶ button on the Standard toolbar.

6 Click the **Save button** on the Standard toolbar (or click **File** then click **Save**) to save your changes.

Now that Barbara has created the structure for her table, she is ready to enter text in it.

Entering Text in a Table and Using AutoCorrect

You enter text in tables just as you do in the rest of your document—simply start typing. If the text in a cell takes up more than one line, Word automatically wraps the text to the next line and increases the height of the cell. To move to a new cell, either click in that cell to move the insertion point or press [Tab]. Press [Shift][Tab] to move the insertion point to the previous cell. If a cell that you are moving to contains text or data, using [Tab] or [Shift][Tab] will highlight the contents of the cell. Figure 3-5 lists other keyboard techniques for moving within a table.

To move the insertion point:	Press:
One cell to the right or to the first cell in the next row	[Tab]
One cell to the left	[Shift][Tab]
The first cell in the current row	[Alt][Home]
The last cell in the current row	[Alt][End]
The top cell in the current column	[Alt][PgUp]
The bottom cell in the current column	[Alt][PgDn]

Figure 3-5
Keyboard techniques for moving within a table

When entering text in a table, you can correct errors just as you correct errors when typing text in the main document. In addition, the Spelling command will find spelling errors in the text of a table.

Word's AutoCorrect feature corrects some of the more common typing mistakes you might make when entering text anywhere in a document, including a table. For instance, if you mistakenly type *teh* for *the* or *adn* for *and*, AutoCorrect automatically corrects the error after you press the Spacebar. Figure 3-6 shows the AutoCorrect dialog box, which you display by choosing the AutoCorrect command from the Tools menu.

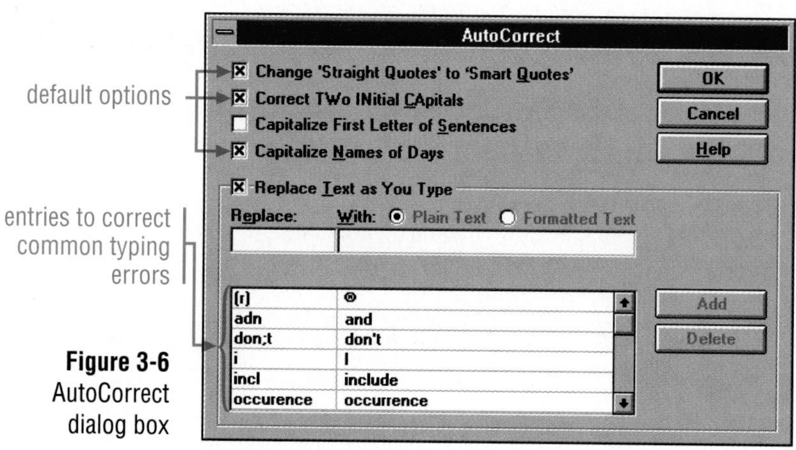

Figure 3-6
AutoCorrect dialog box

Word provides AutoCorrect entries for many common typing errors, and you can also add your own entries for the typing errors you make most often. In addition, the dialog box provides default options that automatically change straight quotes to smart (curly) quotes; correct words typed with two initial capital letters; and capitalize the days of the week as you type.

Now that Barbara has created the table structure, she is ready to insert the components of the per diem allowance ("Maximum lodging expense allowance" and "Meals and incidental expense allowance") and their explanations in the table, as specified in Figure 3-1, Insert A. When she does, she'll make some intentional typing errors to see how AutoCorrect fixes them.

To enter the text in the table:

1. Place the insertion point in the first cell in row 1, if it is not already there.
2. Type **Maximum lodging expense allowance**. The end-of-cell mark moves to the right as you type within the cell.
3. Press **[Tab]**. The insertion point moves to cell 2 in row 1.

   TROUBLE? If you accidentally press [Enter] instead of [Tab], you will create a new paragraph within a cell rather than move the insertion point to another cell. Simply delete the paragraph mark or click the Undo button (or click Edit then click Undo Typing). Then press [Tab] to move to the next cell.

To see how AutoCorrect works, you'll make a typing error.

4. Type **Teh** then press **[Spacebar]**. Notice how Word automatically corrects your typing mistake.

   TROUBLE? If the error is not corrected after you press [Spacebar], the AutoCorrect feature has been deactivated. Correct the error then type the remaining text for the explanation as shown in Figure 3-7, then skip to Step 7.

5. Type **per diem rates authorized under this category**. When you reach the end of the first line in the cell, Word automatically wraps the insertion point to the next line, which increases the height of the cells across the entire row. By increasing the height of the cells, you can keep the explanation of the component next to the name of the per diem component.

The AutoCorrect feature also expands abbreviations you might substitute for text when typing. In the next step, you'll see how this works.

6. Press **[Spacebar]**, type **incl** then press **[Spacebar]**. Notice how Word automatically expands the abbreviation "incl" to the complete word "include." Type the remaining explanation of the first term as shown in Figure 3-7.

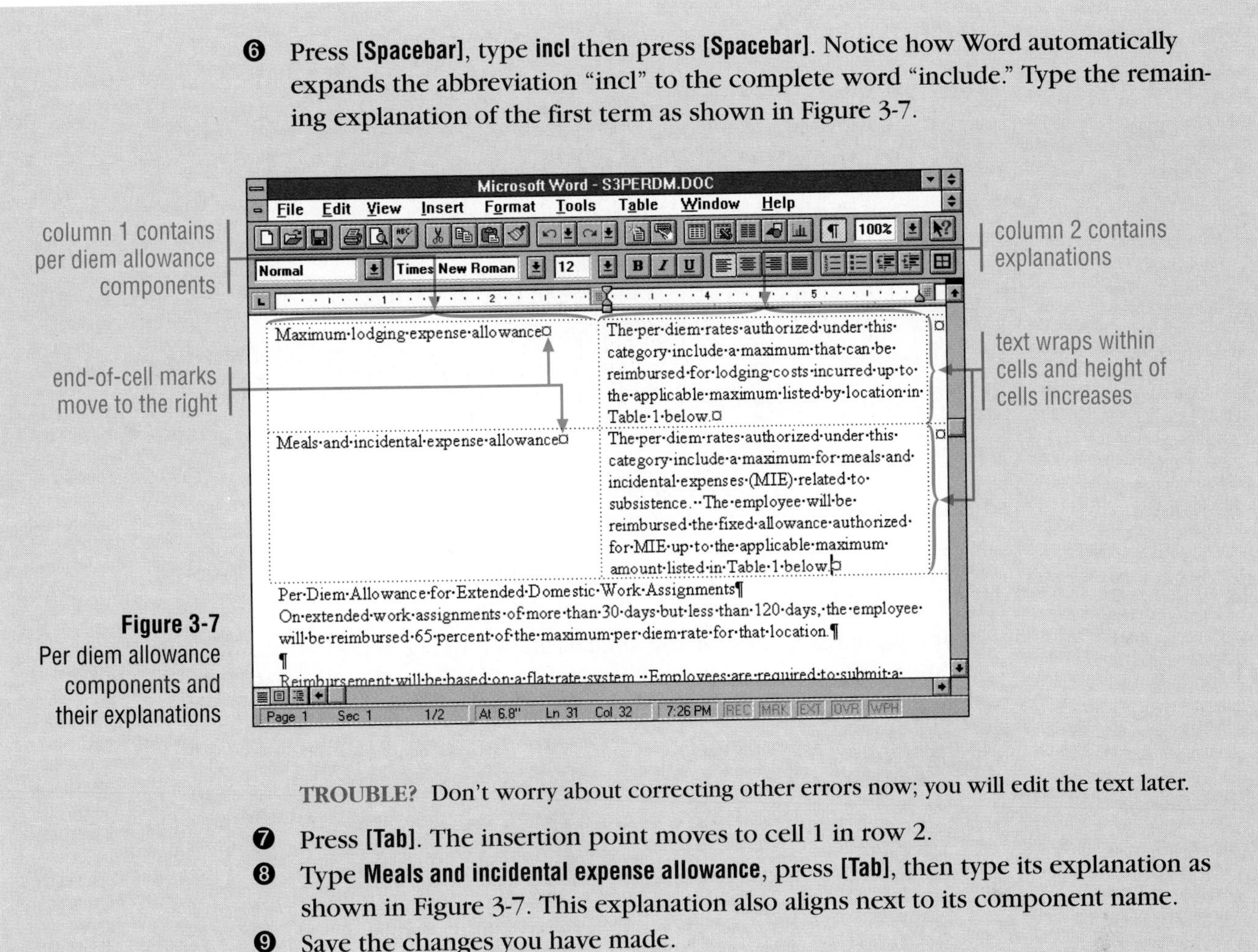
column 1 contains per diem allowance components
end-of-cell marks move to the right
column 2 contains explanations
text wraps within cells and height of cells increases

Figure 3-7
Per diem allowance components and their explanations

TROUBLE? Don't worry about correcting other errors now; you will edit the text later.

7. Press **[Tab]**. The insertion point moves to cell 1 in row 2.
8. Type **Meals and incidental expense allowance**, press **[Tab]**, then type its explanation as shown in Figure 3-7. This explanation also aligns next to its component name.
9. Save the changes you have made.

Barbara next decides to create a table for the foreign travel per diem data that Nancy wants her to insert at the end of the Foreign Travel section (Figure 3-1, Insert C). Barbara thinks she needs a table structure that is four rows by four columns; she knows that if this is not the right size, she can easily change the table structure. She decides to use the Insert Table command to create this table.

Creating a Table Using the Insert Table Command

The Insert Table command on the Table menu displays the Insert Table dialog box. In this dialog box, you can specify additional features for your table that are not available with the Insert Table button, such as the exact width for each column or a predefined format for the table with the Table AutoFormat option. You can also have Word take you step by step through the creation of a table with the Table Wizard option.

Barbara will use the Insert Table command to create the table containing the foreign travel per diem data.

To insert the table using the Insert Table command:

1. Scroll to the end of the document until you see the Exceptions heading, then place the insertion point in front of the "E" in Exceptions (Pg 2, Ln 17).
2. Click **Table** then click **Insert Table...**. The Insert Table dialog box appears.
3. Click the **Number of Columns up arrow** until it reaches 4.
4. Click the **Number of Rows up arrow** until it reaches 4. See Figure 3-8. Barbara decides to create evenly spaced columns so she leaves the Column Width setting at Auto.

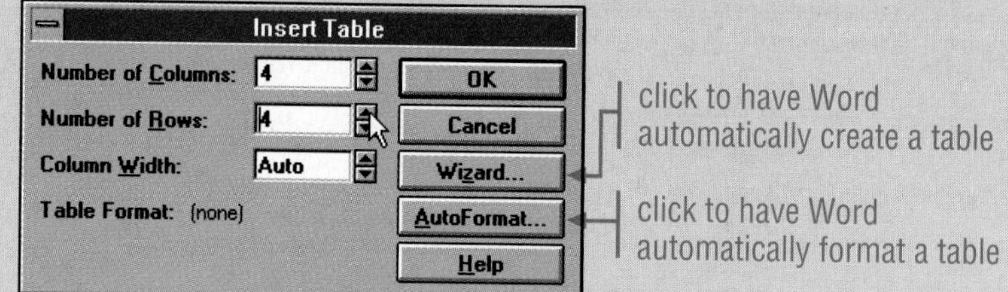

Figure 3-8 Insert Table dialog box

5. Click **OK** or press **[Enter]**. A blank 4 x 4 table appears on the screen, and the insertion point is placed in cell 1 of row 1. Notice that the columns are of equal width.
6. Type the information for the table as shown in Figure 3-9. Remember to press [Tab] to move to the next cell; to move to a previous cell, press [Shift][Tab]. Leave the cells below the last column heading, Total Per Diem, blank for now.

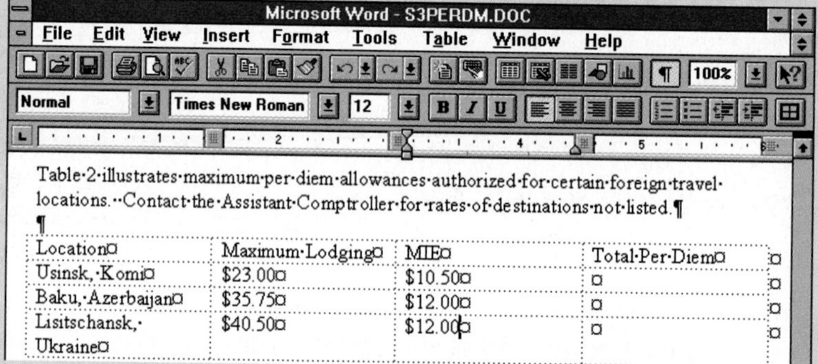

Figure 3-9 Completed Foreign Travel Per Diem table

7. Save the changes you have made.

Word provides several ways to insert an empty table structure in a document. Moreover, Word can convert existing text to a table so that you can lay out the information more easily.

Converting Existing Text to a Table

You can convert existing text that is consistently separated by paragraph marks, tabs, or commas to a table. Word uses these three types of characters to separate the selected text into cells.

REFERENCE WINDOW

Converting Text to a Table

- Select the text to be converted to a table.
- Click the Insert Table button on the Standard toolbar (or click Table then click Convert Text to Table...). If the selected text contains a variety of possible separator characters, such as paragraph marks, tabs, or commas, then the Convert Text to Table dialog box appears.
- Choose the appropriate option to convert the text to a table according to either the paragraph marks, tabs, or commas in the text.
- Click OK or press [Enter].

Barbara needs to convert to a table the data about the domestic travel per diem rates that Nancy originally typed. This text will be easy to convert because Nancy separated each piece of data with a tab and put a paragraph mark at the end of each line.

To convert the text to a table:

1. Scroll through the document until you see the data for the domestic per diem rates (Pg 1, Ln 45). Notice that each piece of information in a row is separated by a tab character and that each row ends with a paragraph mark.
2. Use the selection bar to select the rows from "Location..." through "Norfolk, Virginia..."
3. Click the **Insert Table button** on the Standard toolbar (or click **Table** then click **Insert Table...**). Because the text was originally separated by tabs, Word creates a table with four columns of equal width, replacing the tabs with column boundaries. Eventually Barbara will calculate the total per diem amounts to complete the last column of the table.
4. Deselect the table. Notice that the table splits across the page break between pages 1 and 2. See Figure 3-10. By default, Word inserts the page break *within* a row if the entire row won't fit at the bottom of the page. Word does not move the entire row to the next page.

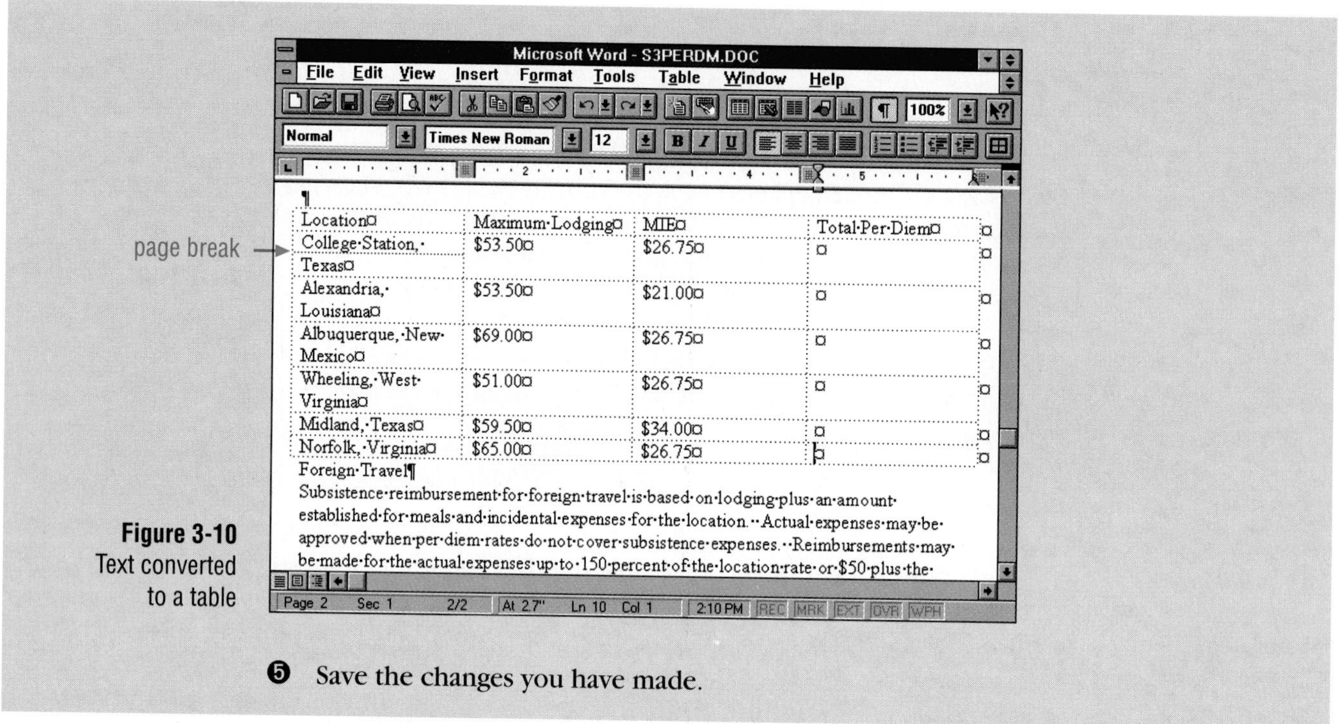

Figure 3-10 Text converted to a table

5. Save the changes you have made.

If you want to take a break and resume the tutorial at a later time, you can close the current document, then exit Word by double-clicking the Control menu box in the upper-left corner of the screen. When you want to resume the tutorial, start Word, place your Student Disk in the disk drive, then complete the screen check procedure described in Tutorial 1. Open the document S3PERDM.DOC, make sure the Gridlines option is activated on the Table menu, press [Shift][F5] to return to your last point in the document, then continue with the tutorial.

■ ■ ■

Barbara has several tasks to complete during the editing phase of the productivity strategy, some of which will be done more easily with the use of the Clipboard.

Using the Clipboard

The **Clipboard**, a standard feature in Windows applications, provides a temporary storage area for information that you need to copy or move from one location to another. To **copy** information means that the original text stays in its current location and a duplicate is created in a new location; to **move** information means that the original text is removed from its current location and placed in a new location. You would use the Clipboard when you need to copy or move information more than once or when you need to copy or move information between Word documents or between Word and other applications, such as spreadsheets. Clipboard operations using the Cut, Copy, and Paste commands from Word's Edit menu operate as they do in Windows. Word also provides Cut, Copy, and Paste buttons on the Standard toolbar.

Once you place information on the Clipboard by cutting or copying, you can paste the contents of the Clipboard as many times as you need. The contents of the Clipboard are overwritten, however, with any new text that you subsequently cut or copy.

Copying and Pasting Text

The Copy command is helpful when you need to use similarly worded text throughout a document. By using the Copy command, you eliminate possible keyboarding errors and you save time.

Barbara needs to add a second sentence to the end of the first paragraph after the heading, Per Diem Allowance for Extended Domestic Work Assignments, concerning work assignments of 120 days or more. The wording of the new sentence is similar to the first sentence with only a few corrections, so Barbara decides to copy the first sentence and paste it at the end of the paragraph; then she will edit the pasted sentence appropriately.

To copy and paste the sentence about per diem allowances:

1. Place the insertion point in the first sentence of the first paragraph below the heading, Per Diem Allowance for Extended Domestic Work Assignments (Pg 1, Ln 34).
2. Press **[Ctrl]** and click to select the entire sentence, including the period. Note that the ending paragraph mark is *not* selected. See Figure 3-11.

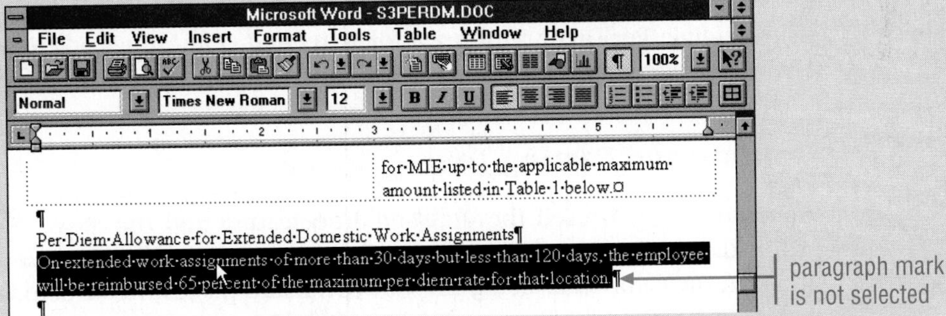

Figure 3-11 Selected sentence to be copied

3. Click the **Copy button** on the Standard toolbar (or click **Edit** then click **Copy**). The selected text is copied to the Clipboard and remains highlighted.

   TROUBLE? If the selected text disappeared, you chose Cut instead of Copy. Click the Undo button on the Standard toolbar (or click Edit then click Undo Cut). Then repeat Steps 2 and 3.

4. Place the insertion point after the period at the end of the selected sentence. The text is deselected.
5. Click the **Paste button** on the Standard toolbar (or click **Edit** then click **Paste**). The copied selection appears at the insertion point, with one space between the two sentences. Adding spaces to pasted text is part of Word's Smart Cut and Paste feature.

Barbara wants two spaces between sentences, and she needs to edit the pasted sentence.

6. Place the insertion point between the two sentences, press **[Spacebar]**, then edit the pasted sentence to read "On extended work assignments of *120 days or more*, the employee will be reimbursed 55 percent of the maximum per diem rate for that location." See Figure 3-12. Do not type the quotation marks or use italics.

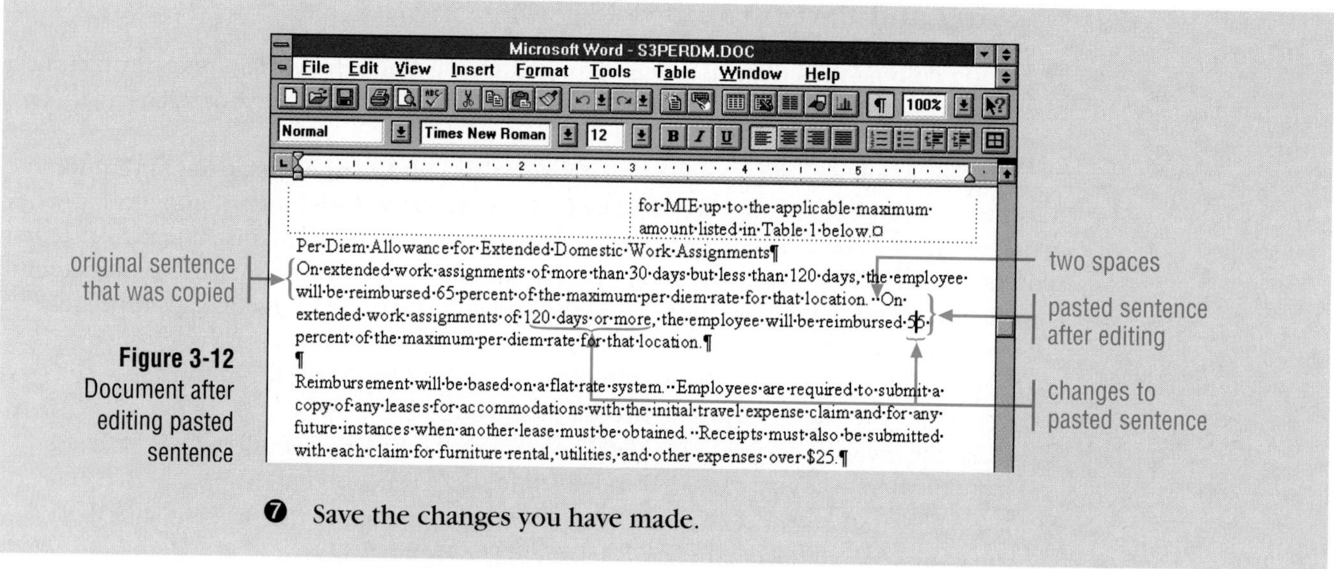

Figure 3-12 Document after editing pasted sentence

7. Save the changes you have made.

Barbara checks Nancy's draft of the policy statement and sees that she needs to move the heading, Per Diem Allowance for Extended Domestic Work Assignments, and the two following paragraphs just before the Foreign Travel section.

Cutting and Pasting Text

In Tutorial 2 you used the drag-and-drop feature and the Move command to move text short distances within a document. These commands, however, do not place the selected text on the Clipboard. Using the Cut command places the selected text on the Clipboard so that you can paste the text as many times as you need.

Barbara will use the Cut and Paste buttons to move the heading about extended domestic work assignments and the two following paragraphs.

To cut and paste the heading and the two following paragraphs:

1. Use the selection bar to select from the heading, Per Diem Allowance for Extended Domestic Work Assignments (Pg 1, Ln 33) through "...expenses over $25." Do not include the blank paragraph after the second paragraph. See Figure 3-13.

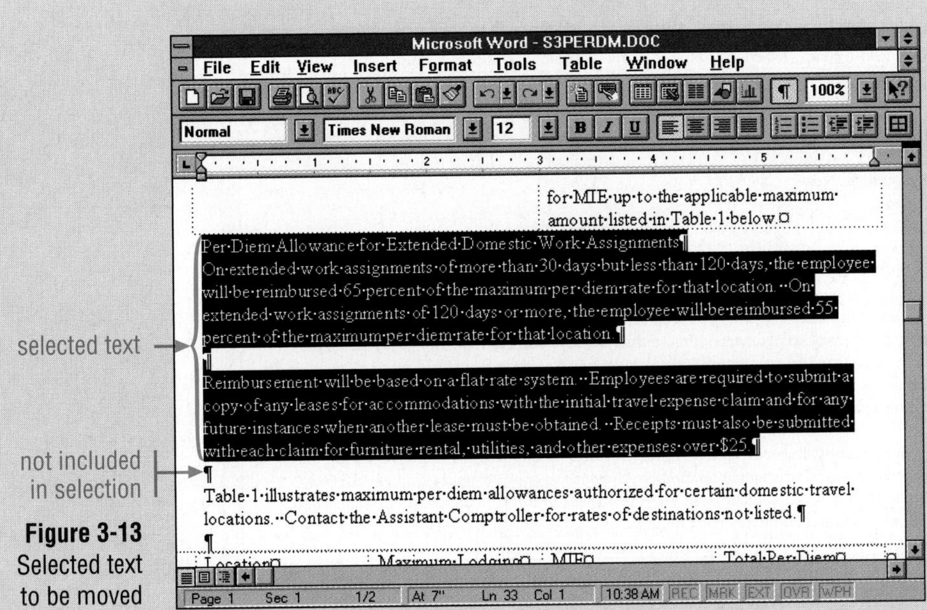

Figure 3-13 Selected text to be moved

2. Click the **Cut button** on the Standard toolbar (or click **Edit** then click **Cut**). The selected text disappears. The Clipboard now contains the cut text instead of the previously copied text.

Barbara wants to move the text to the end of the Domestic Travel section.

3. Place the insertion point directly before the "F" in the Foreign Travel heading (Pg 2, Ln 2).
4. Click the **Paste button** on the Standard toolbar (or click **Edit** then click **Paste**). The cut text appears at the insertion point.

   TROUBLE? If you moved the text to the wrong location, click the Undo button on the Standard toolbar (or click Edit then click Undo Paste). The pasted text is removed from the document, but it still remains on the Clipboard. Place the insertion point in the correct location, then paste again.

5. Scroll through the document to see that the cut text has been pasted to the correct location. See Figure 3-14.

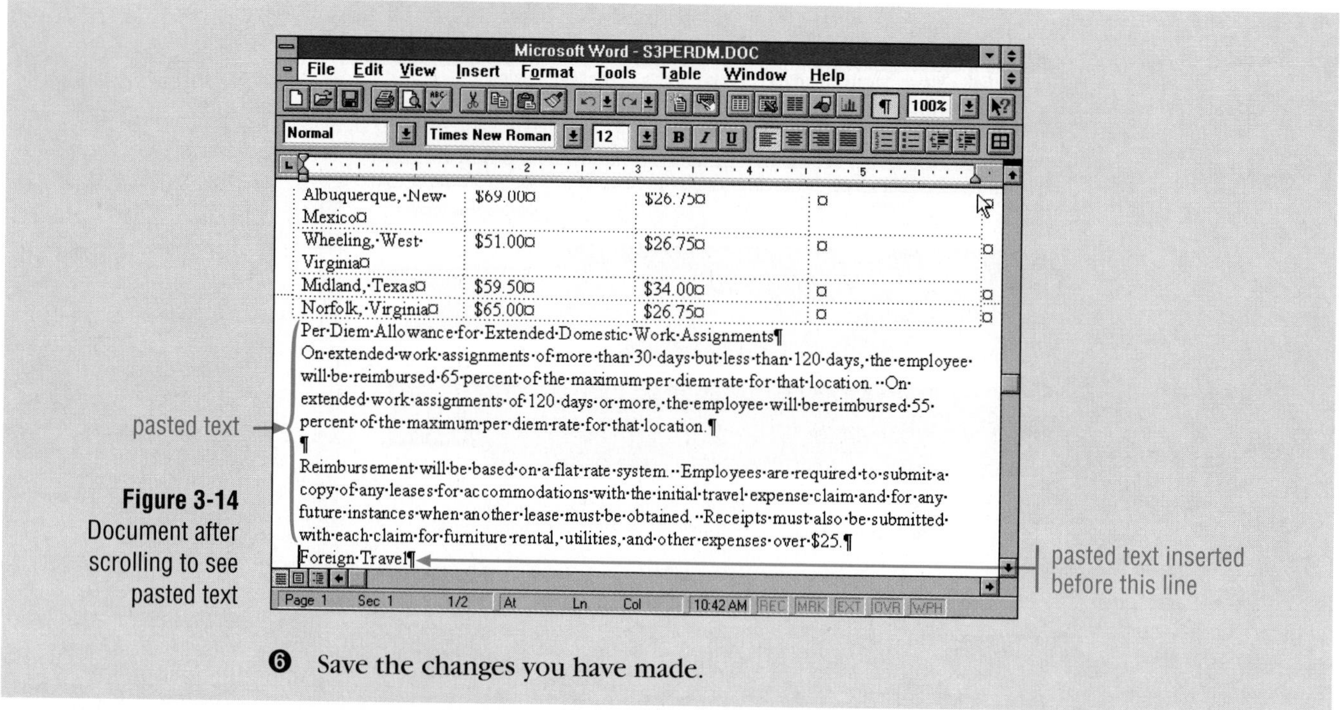

Figure 3-14 Document after scrolling to see pasted text

❻ Save the changes you have made.

Next, Barbara needs to put the same information at the end of the Foreign Travel section just before the Exceptions heading. Rather than retype it, she can paste that information again from the Clipboard, then edit the title appropriately.

To paste the heading and the two following paragraphs again:

❶ Place the insertion point in front of the "E" in the Exceptions heading at the end of the document (Pg 2, Ln 28).

❷ Click the **Paste button** on the Standard toolbar (or click **Edit** then click **Paste**). The previously pasted text is pasted again in the new location.

❸ Scroll through the document to verify that the text has been pasted at the proper location.

❹ Select the word **Domestic** in the second occurrence of the pasted text and change it to **Foreign**.

❺ Save the changes you have made.

Barbara now sees some editorial changes she wants to make to Nancy's draft. She wants to replace references to "the company" or "company" with the acronym of the company's name—PIPSI—to make the travel expense policy sound less formal.

Finding and Replacing Text

In editing long documents, you often need to change every occurrence of a word or string of characters within the document. Word makes this process easy with the Replace command on the Edit menu. This command allows you to find specified text or formatting, then replace it with different text or formatting. Word can also find and replace special

You are already familiar with using the selection bar to the left of your document to select text. Each element of a table—cell, row, column—also has its own selection bar. The selection bar for an individual cell is located at the left edge of the cell. The pointer changes to ↗ when it moves into the cell selection bar, and it changes to ⬇ when it moves into the column selection bar. Figure 3-17 describes different selection techniques for various elements of a table.

To:	Do this:	Or:	Or:
Select a cell	Click in the cell selection bar	Drag across the contents of a cell, including the end-of-cell mark	Press [Tab] to select the contents of the next cell
Select a row	Click in the row selection bar next to the row to be selected	Place the insertion point in the row to be selected, click Table, then click Select Row	Double-click in the cell selection bar of any cell in the row to be selected
Select a column	Click in the column selection bar above the column to be selected	Place the insertion point in the column to be selected, click Table, then click Select Column	
Select a table	Place the insertion point anywhere within the table to be selected, click Table, then click Select Table	Press [Alt][5] (on the numeric keypad) with Num Lock turned off	

Figure 3-17
Table selection techniques

Barbara needs to add the components of the standard per diem and their explanations to the Foreign Travel section. She decides to copy that information from the Domestic Travel section and paste it. First she needs to select the table before copying it.

To select the table:

1. Place the insertion point anywhere within the table created for the explanations of the per diem allowance components in the Domestic Travel section (beginning on Pg 1, Ln 20).
2. Click **Table** then click **Select Table**. The entire table is selected.

   TROUBLE? If the Select Table command is dimmed, you did not have the insertion point within the table before you chose Select Table from the Table menu. Repeat Steps 1 and 2.

Now Barbara is ready to copy the selected table, then paste it after the first paragraph of the Foreign Travel section.

To copy and paste the selected table:

1. Click the **Copy button** on the Standard toolbar (or click **Edit** then click **Copy**). The selected table is copied to the Clipboard.
2. Deselect the table.
3. Place the insertion point in the blank line between the first and second paragraphs in the Foreign Travel section (Pg 2, Ln 19), then press **[Enter]** once. This inserts a blank line above the table.
4. Click the **Paste button** on the Standard toolbar (or click **Edit** then click **Paste**). The copied table is pasted in its new location.
5. Scroll through the document to verify that the table has been pasted correctly.

Barbara notices that she must change the pasted text to read Table 2 instead of Table 1.

6. Change the two instances of Table 1 to Table 2 in the pasted table. See Figure 3-18.

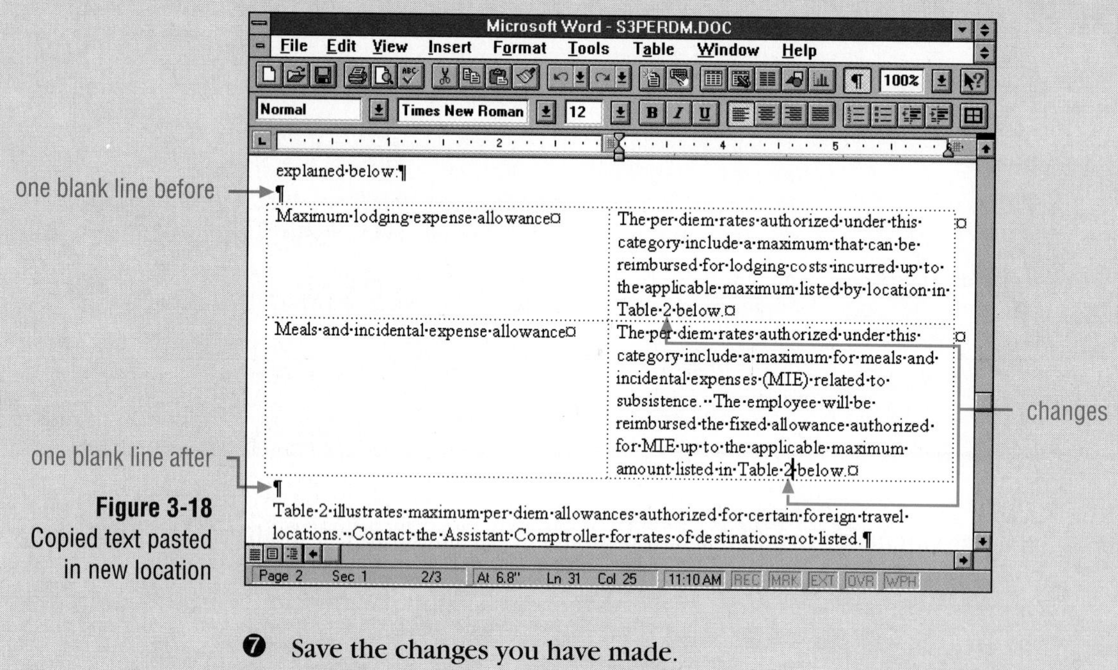

Figure 3-18 Copied text pasted in new location

7. Save the changes you have made.

Next, based on the information from Al Simpson, Barbara needs to add the other location to Table 2.

Modifying a Table Structure

When you originally create the structure for a table, you often do not know how many rows or columns you will actually need. However, you can easily modify or change a table's structure after creating it. Figure 3-19 describes the various ways to insert or delete rows or columns in a table.

To:	Within a table:	At the end of a table:
Insert a row	Select the entire row below the one you want to add, click Table, then click Insert Rows	Place the insertion point in the last cell of the last row, then press [Tab]
Insert a column	Select the entire column to the left of the one you want to add, click Table, then click Insert Columns	Select the end-of-row markers, click Table, then click Insert Columns
Delete a row	Select the entire row or rows you want to delete, click Table, then click Delete Rows	
Delete a column	Select the entire column or columns you want to delete, click Table, then click Delete Columns	

Figure 3-19
Techniques for inserting and deleting rows and columns

Barbara decides to insert the new location at the bottom of Table 2. To do so she must insert a row.

To insert a blank row at the bottom of Table 2 and add the information about the new location:

1. Place the insertion point in the last cell of the last row in Table 2 (Pg 2, Ln 40). This cell is currently empty.
2. Press **[Tab]**. A blank row is added to the bottom of the table with the same characteristics as the row above it.

   TROUBLE? If a blank row is not added to the bottom of the table, perhaps you did not have the insertion point in the last cell of the last row. Repeat Steps 1 and 2.

3. Type **Radusny, Western Siberia** then press **[Tab]**; type **$23.00** then press **[Tab]**; type **$10.50**. See Figure 3-20.

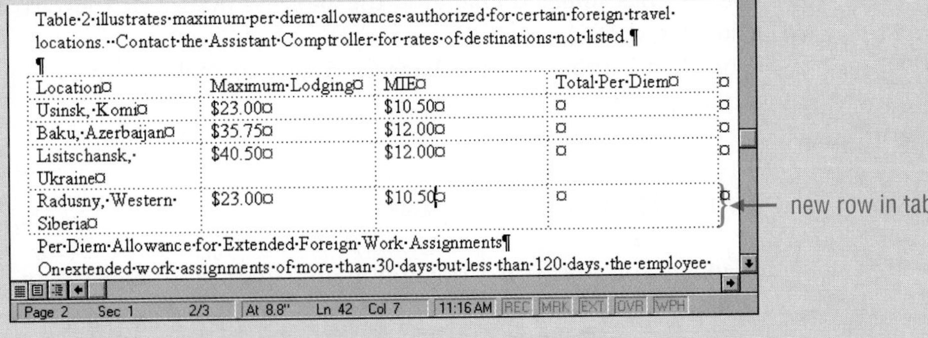
Table·2·illustrates·maximum·per·diem·allowances·authorized·for·certain·foreign·travel· locations.··Contact·the·Assistant·Comptroller·for·rates·of·destinations·not·listed.¶

¶

Location¤	Maximum·Lodging¤	MIE¤	Total·Per·Diem¤
Usinsk,·Komi¤	$23.00¤	$10.50¤	¤
Baku,·Azerbaijan¤	$35.75¤	$12.00¤	¤
Lisitschansk,·Ukraine¤	$40.50¤	$12.00¤	¤
Radusny,·Western·Siberia¤	$23.00¤	$10.50¤	¤

Per·Diem·Allowance·for·Extended·Foreign·Work·Assignments¶

On·extended·work·assignments·of·more·than·30·days·but·less·than·120·days,·the·employee·

Page 2 Sec 1 2/3 At 8.8" Ln 42 Col 7 11:16 AM REC MRK EXT OVR WPH

Figure 3-20
Table 2 after inserting row at bottom

4. Save the changes you have made.

Barbara now needs to delete the row containing information about Wheeling, West Virginia, from Table 1 per instructions from Al Simpson.

With Word, you can delete either the *contents* of the cells in a selected row or the *entire row* from a table. To delete the contents of the cells in a selected row, just press the

Delete key. However, to delete the selected row entirely from the table structure, including the contents of the cells, you must choose the Delete Rows command from the Table menu.

According to Al Simpson, Barbara needs to remove the information about Wheeling, West Virginia, from Table 1 because PIPSI has completed work at the location and no longer sends employees there. Barbara decides to use the Shortcut Table menu, which contains the most often used commands for working with tables, to delete the row.

To delete the row for Wheeling, West Virginia, using the Shortcut Table menu:

1. Place the insertion point in the Wheeling, West Virginia, row of Table 1 (Pg 1, Ln 44).
2. Click **Table** then click **Select Row** (or double-click in the cell selection bar of any cell in the row).

To display the Shortcut Table menu, you simply place the insertion point within a table, then click the right mouse button.

3. With the mouse pointer over the selected text, click the **right mouse button**. The Shortcut Table menu appears. See Figure 3-21.

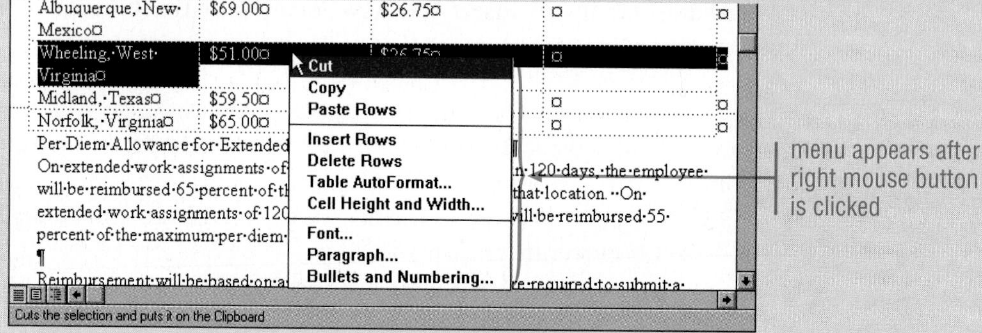

Figure 3-21 Shortcut Table menu

4. Click **Delete Rows**. The selected row is deleted from the table structure.
5. Save the changes you have made.

Barbara has finished changing the table structure of the tables in her document by inserting and deleting rows.

The next editing change Barbara needs to make is to arrange the travel locations alphabetically in Tables 1 and 2.

Sorting Rows in a Table

Word allows you to sort information in alphabetical, numerical, or date order quickly and easily. The most common use for sorting is to rearrange rows in a table, but you can use the sorting feature to sort any list of information. You can sort a table by up to three columns within a table. Word recognizes whether or not your table contains a header row, that is, whether the first row of the table contains column headings.

Barbara decides to arrange the locations in Table 1 in alphabetical order.

To sort the information in Table 1:

1. Place the insertion point anywhere within Table 1, if necessary.

❷ Click **Table** then click **Sort...**. The entire table is selected, and the Sort dialog box appears. See Figure 3-22.

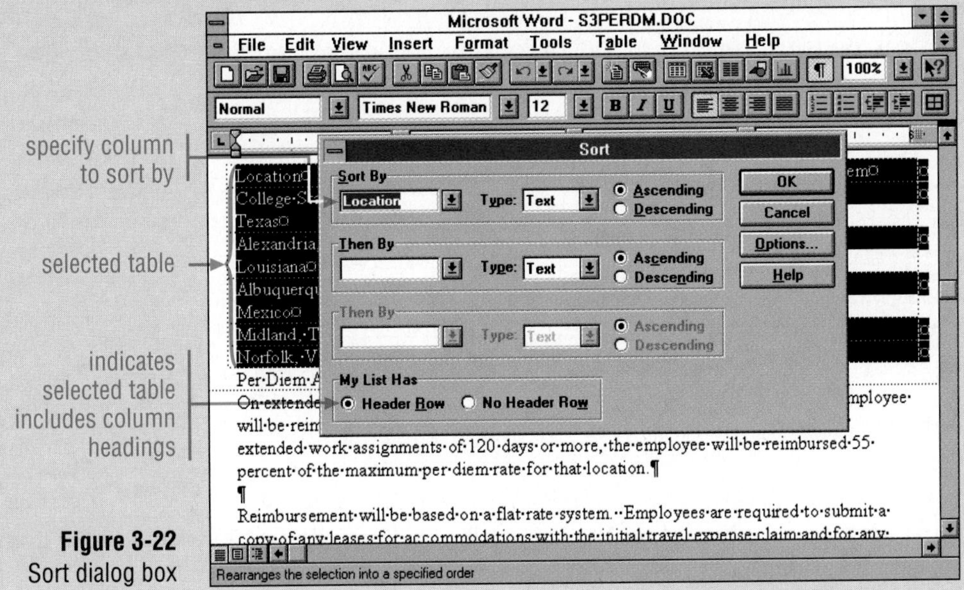

Figure 3-22
Sort dialog box

Barbara can sort by any column in the table, but she wants to sort by the Location column in *ascending* alphabetical order—that is, from A to Z—rather than in *descending* alphabetical order (from Z to A), so she doesn't need to change any of the settings in the dialog box. "Location" appears in the Sort By list box automatically because it is the first column heading in the table. Also, Word recognizes that the first row of the table contains the column headings; therefore, the Header Row option is selected in the My List Has section. This means that the contents of the first row will not be sorted. If you wanted to include the first row in the sort, you would click the No Header Row button.

❸ Click **OK** or press **[Enter]** then deselect the highlighted rows. Rows 2 through 6 of Table 1 are arranged alphabetically by the first word in the Location column. See Figure 3-23.

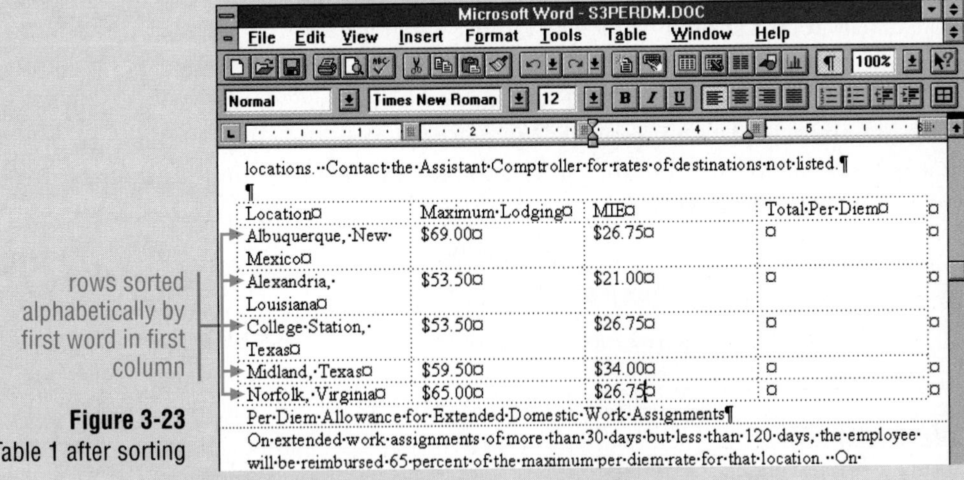

Figure 3-23
Table 1 after sorting

TROUBLE? If the sort was unsuccessful, immediately click the Undo button on the Standard toolbar (or click Edit then click Undo Sort). Then repeat Steps 1 through 3.

Now Barbara needs to sort the locations in Table 2.

4. Repeat Steps 1 through 3 to sort by location in Table 2. Deselect the table. See Figure 3-24.

rows sorted alphabetically by first word in first column

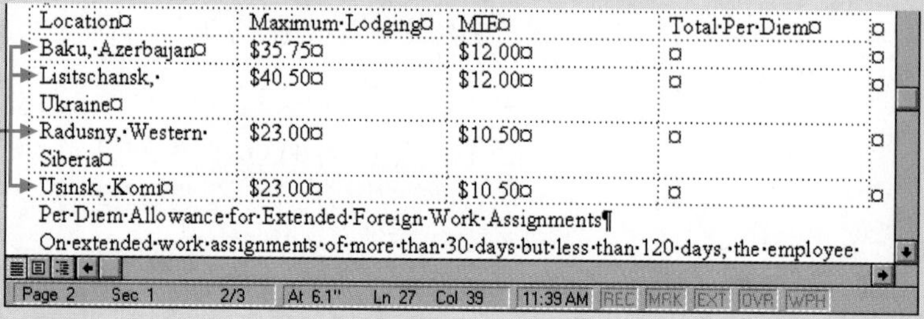

Location	Maximum Lodging	MIE	Total Per Diem
Baku, Azerbaijan	$35.75	$12.00	
Lisitschansk, Ukraine	$40.50	$12.00	
Radusny, Western Siberia	$23.00	$10.50	
Usinsk, Komi	$23.00	$10.50	

Per Diem Allowance for Extended Foreign Work Assignments¶
On extended work assignments of more than 30 days but less than 120 days, the employee

Page 2 Sec 1 2/3 At 6.1" Ln 27 Col 39 11:39 AM REC MRK EXT OVR WPH

Figure 3-24
Table 2 after sorting

5. Save the changes you have made.

Next, Barbara needs to calculate the total per diem allowed for each of the domestic and foreign locations.

Performing Mathematical Calculations in Tables

A popular use of tables is to display data, perhaps showing the results of a mathematical calculation like a sum of numbers. Word's Table Formula command allows you to perform simple calculations, such as adding, subtracting, multiplying, dividing, and calculating percentages, averages, and minimum and maximum values. For involved calculations, you would use a spreadsheet application like Microsoft Excel, then link or embed the spreadsheet in your Word document.

Barbara needs to calculate the total per diem values for the domestic and foreign locations. Because these are simple calculations, she decides to use Word's Table Formula command.

To calculate the total per diem values in Table 1 and Table 2:

1. Place the insertion point in the last cell of the second row in Table 1(Pg 1, Ln 38).
2. Click **Table** then click **Formula...**. The Formula dialog box appears. Word analyzes the table, then displays a formula based on the data in the table, in this case one that will sum all numbers in the cells to the left of the insertion point. This is the correct formula. See Figure 3-25.

indicates that numbers to the left of the insertion point will be summed

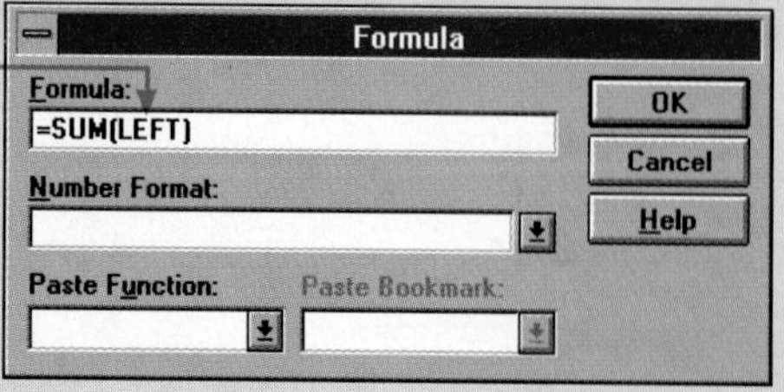

Formula
Formula: =SUM(LEFT)
Number Format:
Paste Function: Paste Bookmark:
OK
Cancel
Help

Figure 3-25
Formula dialog box

3. Click **OK** or press **[Enter]**. The sum of the two numbers ($95.75) appears, properly formatted as currency.

Barbara needs to repeat this procedure for each total needed in this table, as well as those in Table 2. She decides to use Word's Repeat command [F4], which repeats the last change made to a document.

4. Place the insertion point in the next empty cell below, then press **[F4]**. The sum for that set of numbers appears.
5. Repeat Step 4 for each of the remaining rows in Table 1, scroll to Table 2 (Pg 2, Ln 36), then repeat Step 4 for each row in it also. Pressing [F4] will not repeat the scrolling; it will still repeat the last command, which sums the row of numbers.
6. Save the changes you have made.

If a value used in a calculation subsequently changes, the new result will not be automatically updated. You must delete the current answer, then choose the Table Formula command again.

Next, Barbara wants to insert captions identifying the tables because the document refers to them as Table 1 and Table 2.

Inserting a Caption

A **caption** is a number or title that identifies tables or figures in a document. The Insert Caption command allows you to add automatically numbered captions easily to tables and figures.

Barbara decides to insert table captions containing both a number and a title so that employees reading the travel expense policy can better identify the tables' contents.

To insert captions for Table 1 and Table 2:

1. Select all the rows in Table 1, click **Insert**, then click **Caption...**. The Caption dialog box appears with the text Table 1 inserted in the Caption text box. Word analyzes the selected text and inserts an appropriate label, in this instance Table. You can, however, change the caption label if you want.
2. Type . (a period), press **[Spacebar]** twice, then type **Domestic Travel Per Diem**.

Barbara wants the captions to appear below the tables, so she needs to change the Position setting.

3. If necessary, click the **Position list box down arrow**, then click **Below Selected Item**. See Figure 3-26.

caption for table

determines placement of caption

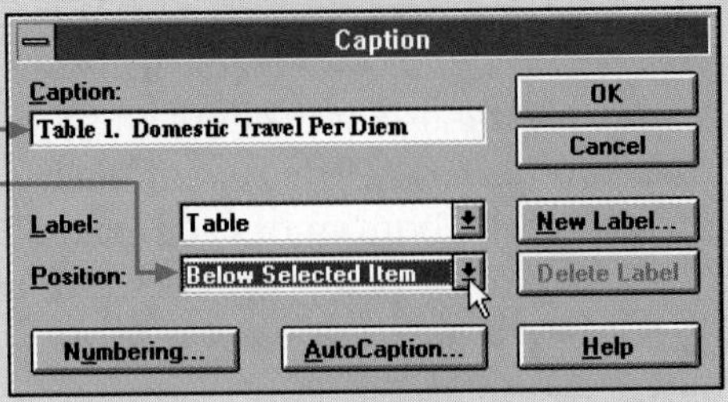

Figure 3-26
Completed Caption dialog box

4. Click **OK**. The specified caption is inserted below Table 1. See Figure 3-27. Notice that Word applied a predefined set of formats, also called a style, to the caption, which you can change if you want. You will learn more about styles later in this tutorial.

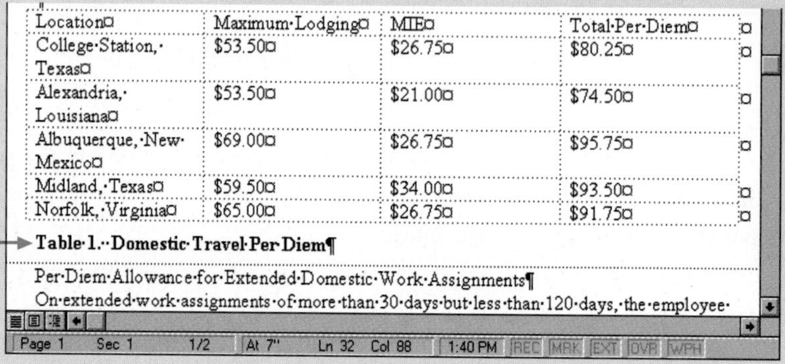

Location	Maximum Lodging	MIE	Total Per Diem
College Station, Texas	$53.50	$26.75	$80.25
Alexandria, Louisiana	$53.50	$21.00	$74.50
Albuquerque, New Mexico	$69.00	$26.75	$95.75
Midland, Texas	$59.50	$34.00	$93.50
Norfolk, Virginia	$65.00	$26.75	$91.75

caption → **Table 1. Domestic Travel Per Diem¶**

Per Diem Allowance for Extended Domestic Work Assignments¶
On extended work assignments of more than 30 days but less than 120 days, the employee

Page 1 Sec 1 1/2 At 7" Ln 32 Col 88 1:40 PM REC MRK EXT OVR WPH

Figure 3-27 Caption below Table 1

5. Select all the rows in Table 2, then repeat Steps 1 through 4 to insert the following caption: **Table 2. Foreign Travel Per Diem**.
6. Save the changes you have made.

If you delete a table with a numbered caption, Word will automatically renumber the captions for the remaining tables.

If you want to take a break and resume the tutorial at a later time, you can close the current document, then exit Word by double-clicking the Control menu box in the upper-left corner of the screen. When you want to resume the tutorial, start Word, place your Student Disk in the disk drive, then complete the screen check procedure described in Tutorial 1. Open the document S3PERDM.DOC, make sure the Gridlines option is activated on the Table menu, press [Shift][F5] to return to your last point in the document, then continue with the tutorial.

■ ■ ■

To follow the format used in the company policy manual, Barbara needs to insert page numbers at the top of her document on all pages but the first, and insert the title of the document and the revision date at the bottom of all pages.

Using Headers and Footers

As you learned in Tutorial 2, you should format a document starting with the page-level decisions, then proceed to the paragraph- and font-level decisions. One of Word's more popular page-level formatting features is the use of headers and footers.

A **header** is information that is repeated at the top of each page of a document. A **footer** is information that is repeated at the bottom of each page. In addition to including text in a header or footer, you can also insert page numbers, the date, and the time. You can format the contents of a header or footer just as you format text in the document, including inserting borders, rules, or graphics.

When you insert headers or footers in a document, Word changes to page layout view and the insertion point moves to the point in the document where the header will print. To speed the process of inserting headers or footers, Word provides you with a Header and Footer toolbar.

Inserting a Header

Barbara wants to insert the page number at the top right margin of all pages of her document except the first. It is a standard practice to omit the page number from the first page of a document.

To insert a header containing the page number:

❶ Press **[Ctrl][Home]** to move the insertion point to page 1, click **View**, then click **Header and Footer**. The Header and Footer toolbar appears, the insertion point is placed in the Header text area at the top of page 1 surrounded by a dashed line, the main text of the document becomes dimmed, and the screen changes to page layout view. See Figure 3-28.

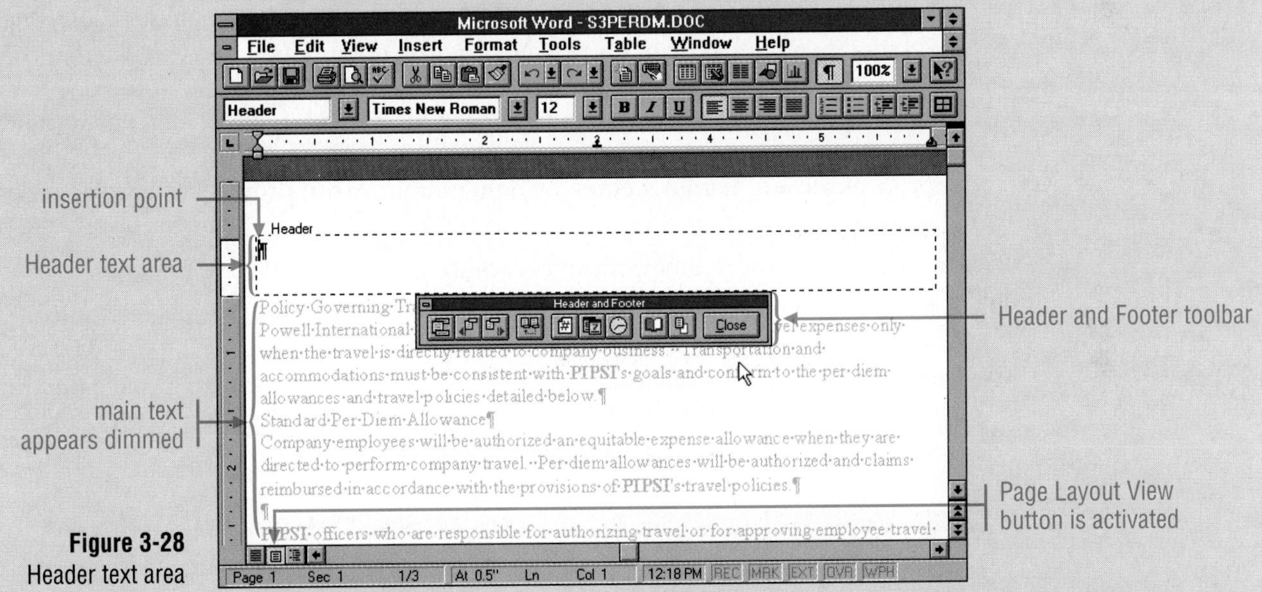

Figure 3-28
Header text area

TROUBLE? If the Header and Footer toolbar obscures the Header text area, drag the toolbar out of the way.

TROUBLE? Depending on the type of monitor you're using, the main text of the document might not appear on the screen; just continue with the tutorial.

Barbara does not want the header to appear on the first page.

❷ Click the **Page Setup button** on the Header and Footer toolbar (or click **File** then click **Page Setup...**). The Layout tab of the Page Setup dialog box appears.

❸ Click the **Different First Page check box** in the Headers and Footers section. See Figure 3-29.

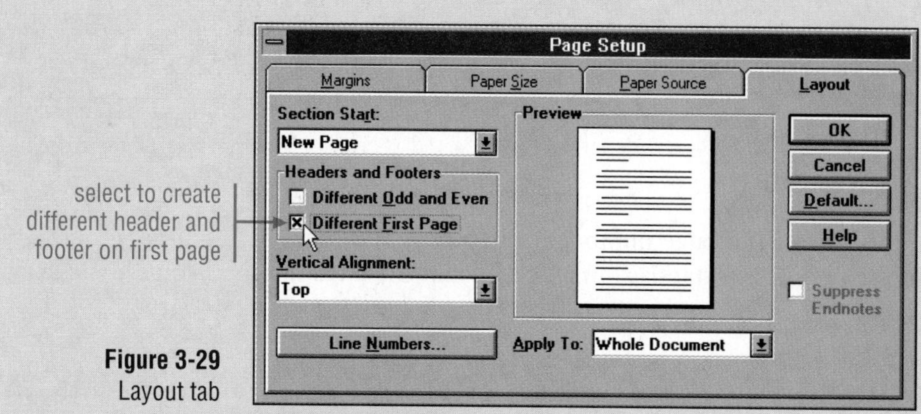

Figure 3-29 Layout tab

4. Click **OK** or press **[Enter]**. You return to the document, but now the Header text area is labeled First Page Header. Any text typed here would print only on the first page.

Barbara does not want any text to appear in the header on the first page of the document so she can move to the Header text area on page 2.

5. Click the **Show Next button** on the Header and Footer toolbar. Notice that the insertion point moves to page 2. Now the Header text area is labeled "Header"; any text typed here would print on this and all subsequent pages. Notice also that the ruler in effect for the header is different from the ruler for the rest of the document: it contains a centered tab at the 3-inch mark and a right-aligned tab at the 6-inch mark, even with the right margin. Because header and footer text typically appears at the left margin, center, or right margin, Word provides formats for these text areas.

Barbara wants the page number of the document to appear at the right margin.

6. Press **[Tab]** twice to move the insertion point to the right-aligned tab stop at the right margin of the Header text area.
7. Click the **Page Numbers button** on the Header and Footer toolbar. A page number appears at the right-aligned tab. Word also automatically places the correct page number on all subsequent pages of the document. See Figure 3-30.

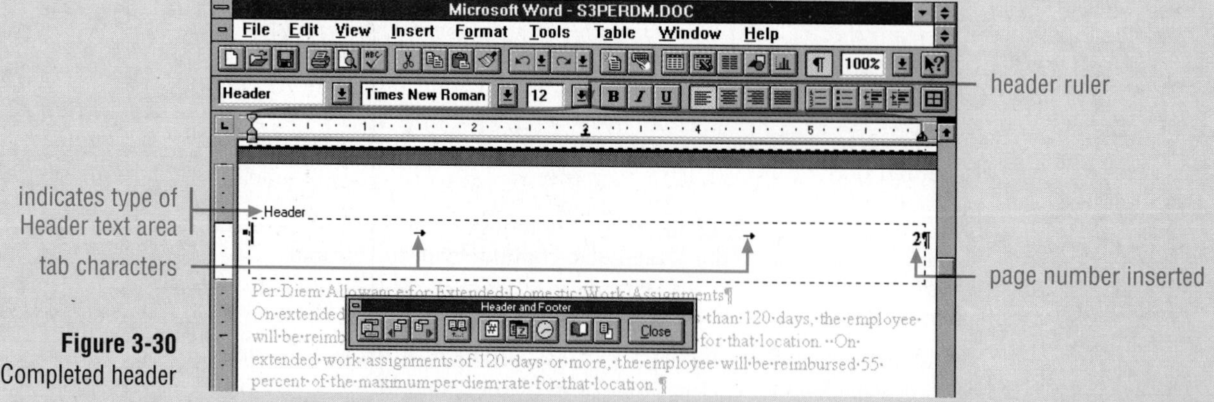

Figure 3-30 Completed header

8. Click the **Close button** on the Header and Footer toolbar. You return to the document. Normal view does not display headers and footers; you need to switch to print preview (or page layout view) to see the header you just inserted.

9. Click the **Print Preview button** on the Standard toolbar (or click **File** then click **Print Preview**). Notice that the header does not appear on page 1 but that it does appear on pages 2 and 3.

   TROUBLE? If you cannot see all three pages at one time in print preview, click the Multiple Pages button on the Print Preview toolbar, then drag across the grid to select three pages.

10. Click the **Close button** on the Print Preview toolbar. You return to the document in normal view.

Next Barbara wants to add a footer containing the text, Policy Governing Travel Expenses, and the current date.

Inserting a Footer

Even though Barbara wants the same footer information to appear on all pages, including the first, she must insert it twice—in both the First Page Footer text area and the Footer text area—because the Different First Page check box is selected in the Page Setup dialog box. This setting affects both headers and footers. She also wants the footer text to appear in 10-point bold type.

To insert the footer:

1. Click **View** then click **Header and Footer**. The insertion point appears in the First Page Header text area of the document.

Barbara needs to switch to the First Page Footer text area.

2. Click the **Switch Between Header and Footer button** on the Header and Footer toolbar. The insertion point is placed in the First Page Footer text area.

Barbara wants the text "Policy Governing Travel Expenses" to appear at the left margin of the footer and the date to appear at the right.

3. Type **Policy Governing Travel Expenses** then press **[Tab]** twice.
4. Click the **Date button** on the Header and Footer toolbar. The current date appears. The date will be updated automatically each time the document is printed.

   TROUBLE? If you chose the wrong button from the Header and Footer toolbar, you must select the incorrect text, then press [Del] before inserting the correct text.

Barbara wants to format the footer text in 10-point bold type.

5. Click in the selection bar to select the entire footer, then use the Formatting toolbar to change the font format to 10 point and bold. Deselect the text. See Figure 3-31. Note that the date shown on your screen will be different from the one shown in the figure.

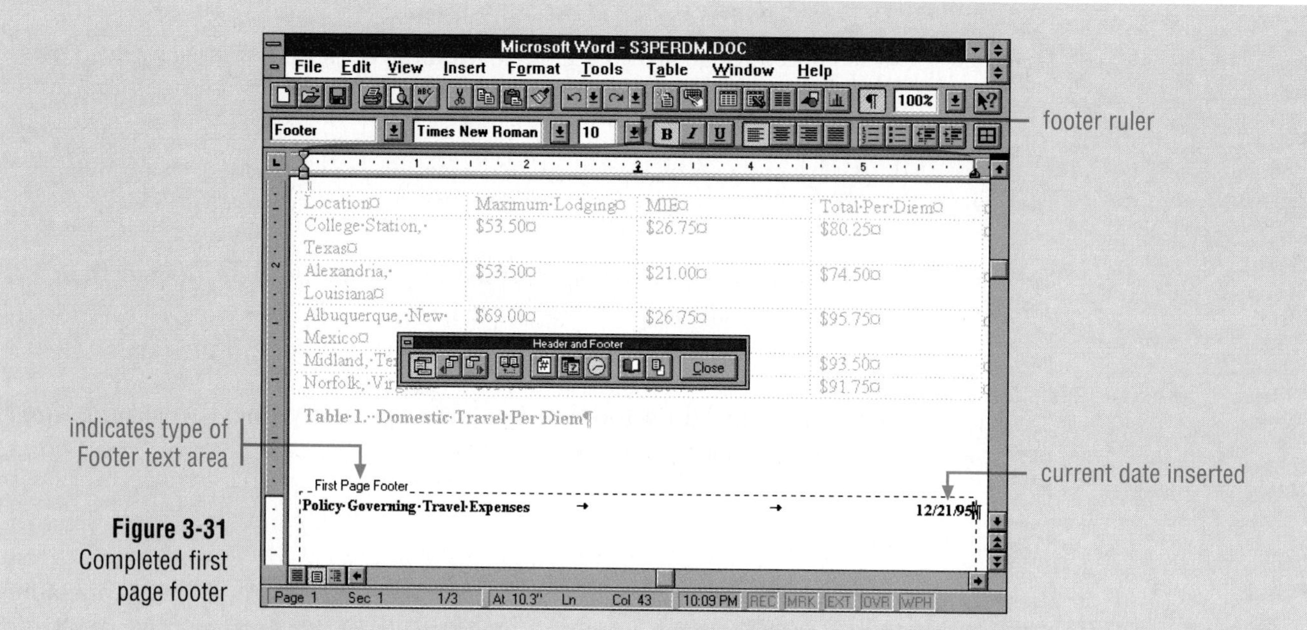

Figure 3-31 Completed first page footer

Barbara decides to use the Copy and Paste buttons to copy the footer information from the First Page Footer text area to the Footer text area. Copying and pasting the footer eliminates the need to type and format the text again, and ensures that the same text appears in the footer on all pages.

6. Click in the selection bar to select the entire footer, then click the **Copy button** on the Standard toolbar (or click **Edit** then click **Copy**).
7. Click the **Show Next button** on the Header and Footer toolbar to move the insertion point to the Footer text area.
8. Click the **Paste button** on the Standard toolbar (or click **Edit** then click **Paste**) to paste the copied text in the Footer text area. You need to insert the footer on page 2 only, and it will appear on all remaining pages.
9. Click the **Close button** on the Header and Footer toolbar to return to your document.

Barbara wants to view the document in print preview to make sure she entered the footer information correctly.

To view the footer information in print preview:

1. Click the **Print Preview button** on the Standard toolbar (or click **File** then click **Print Preview**). Notice that the footer appears on all pages of the document.

   TROUBLE? If you cannot see all three pages at one time in print preview, click the Multiple Pages button on the Print Preview toolbar, then drag across the grid to select three pages.

2. Click the **Close button** on the Print Preview toolbar to return to the document in normal view.
3. Save the changes you have made.

Barbara wants the different parts of her document to be attractively formatted with a variety of paragraph and font formats. She doesn't, however, want to take the time to select each of the different parts and then directly apply formats one at a time. She decides to use Word's Style feature to speed up the formatting process.

Using Styles

In Tutorial 2 you used direct formatting to change the appearance of text within your document. Another method for changing the formatting of a document is to use Word's style feature. A **character style** is a collection of font formatting options that you save and reuse. A **paragraph style** is a collection of font and paragraph formatting options that you save and reuse. A paragraph style can include any and all of the following formatting options: tab settings, font, point size, type style, line spacing, borders, and indents. Rather than apply each formatting option individually, you apply a style that contains all the formatting options you want. A **style sheet** is a listing, which you can print, that describes the formatting characteristics of each style used in a document.

Each Word document comes with a set of standard paragraph styles: Normal (the default paragraph style for a Word document), Heading 1, Heading 2, and Heading 3. Word also contains a default character style called Default Paragraph Font. The current style is shown in the Style list box on the Formatting toolbar, and all styles available in a document are listed in the Style list, which you display by clicking the down arrow next to the Style list box. You can also use the Format Style command to view the paragraph and font attributes of each style in use. When certain other features, such as headers, footers, and captions, are used in a document, their styles are automatically added to the list.

You can define your own styles for use in documents, or you can use the predefined styles in Word's templates. A **document template** is a pattern, or model, on which a document is built. All documents based on a template take on the features defined for that template. In addition to its styles, a template's features can include boilerplate, or standard, text and specialized menu bars, toolbars, or keyboard shortcuts. These defined features help to automate the production of a document.

The NORMAL template is Word's default template, but Word contains many templates for other types of typical business communications. Figure 3-32 lists the names of the predefined templates available in Word. The file extension for a Word template is "DOT."

BROCHURE1	DIRECTR1	FAXCOVR1	FAXCOVR2
INVOICE	LETTER1	LETTER2	LETTER3
MANUAL1	MANUSCR1	MANUSCR3	MEMO1
MEMO2	MEMO3	NORMAL	PRESENT1
PRESREL1	PRESREL2	PRESREL3	PURCHORD
REPORT1	REPORT2	REPORT3	RESUME1
RESUME2A	RESUME4	THESIS1	WEEKTIME

Figure 3-32
Word's templates

To use the styles in one of the predefined templates, you can choose a template other than NORMAL when you first create a document, or you can *attach* a template to a document you've already created using the NORMAL template.

REFERENCE WINDOW

Attaching a Template to the Current Document

- Click File then click Templates.... The Templates and Add-ins dialog box appears.
- Click the Automatically Update Document Styles check box.
- Click Attach.... The Attach Template dialog box appears with all of Word's predefined templates listed.
- Click the template to be attached, then click OK or press [Enter] to close the Attach Template dialog box.
- Click OK or press [Enter] to close the Templates and Add-ins dialog box.

If you want to preview the predefined styles of a template before attaching it to the current document, you can use Word's Style Gallery feature. You can preview the styles of any template or document by using this feature.

Barbara's document contains several levels of headings, and she wants to differentiate among them with different paragraph styles. She decides to use the predefined styles of the MANUAL1 template. It has been a while since she used this template, so she decides to review its styles using Word's Style Gallery feature.

To use the Style Gallery to preview the MANUAL1 template styles:

1. Click the **Style list box down arrow**. The list of styles assigned to the NORMAL template appears. The paragraph styles are bolded, and the character styles are shown in lighter type. Press **[Esc]** to close the list without selecting any styles.
2. Click **Format** then click **Style Gallery...**. The Style Gallery dialog box appears with the current document displayed in the Preview section.

Barbara wants to review each style assigned to the MANUAL1 template.

3. Click **Manual1** then click the **Style Samples radio button**. Each style defined for this template is displayed with the specific paragraph and font formatting characteristics applied to sample text. See Figure 3-33.

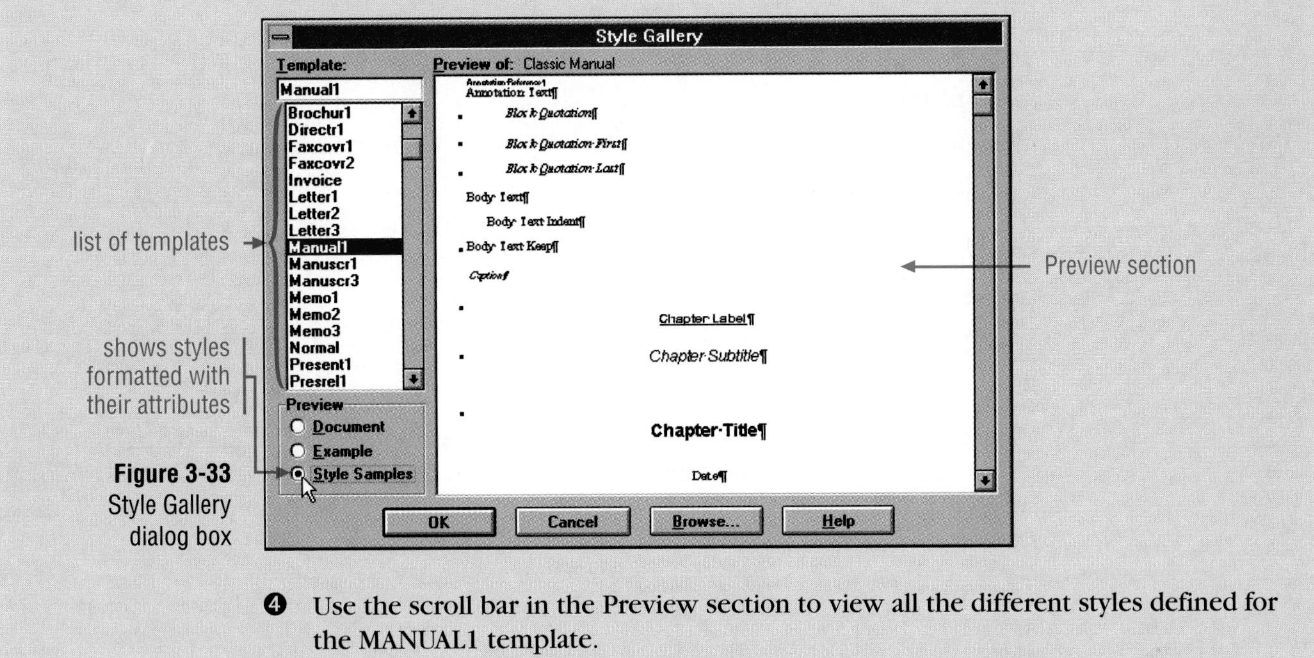

Figure 3-33 Style Gallery dialog box

❹ Use the scroll bar in the Preview section to view all the different styles defined for the MANUAL1 template.

❺ Click **Cancel** to return to the document.

Barbara wants to attach the MANUAL1 template to her current document so she can use the styles provided in the template. Note that any existing style in Barbara's document having the same name as a style in the new template she attaches will be overwritten by the new style.

To attach the MANUAL1 template to the document:

❶ Click **File** then click **Templates...**. The Templates and Add-ins dialog box appears with "normal" in the Document Template text box.

❷ Click **Attach...**. The Attach Template dialog box appears. Only the template files are listed in the File Name list box. See Figure 3-34.

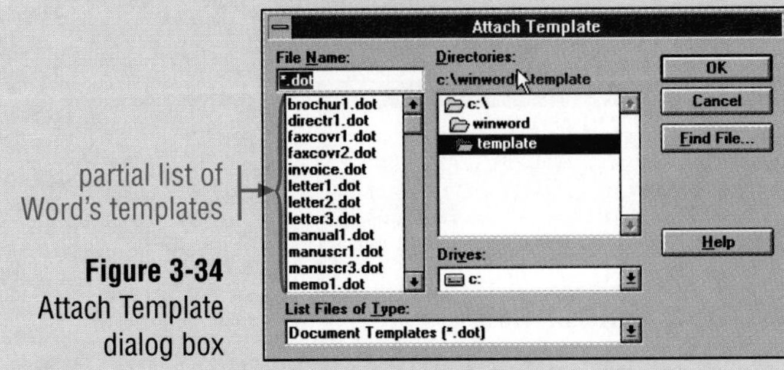

Figure 3-34 Attach Template dialog box

❸ Click **manual1.dot**, then click **OK** or press **[Enter]**. You return to the Templates and Add-ins dialog box; the name and file location of the new template now appear in the Document Template text box.

❹ Click the **Automatically Update Document Styles check box** to update your document with the new styles.

5. Click **OK** or press **[Enter]** to return to the document. Notice that the font size in your document has changed to 10 point, which is the default font size for the MANUAL1 template.

Barbara must change the font size for the entire document to 12 point.

6. Click **Edit**, click **Select All**, then change the font size to 12 point.
7. Click the **Style list box down arrow**. Scroll through the list to see that all the styles of the MANUAL1 template have been copied to the document.
8. Press **[Esc]** to close the list without making any choices.
9. Save the changes you have made.

Barbara's document contains several levels of headings, and she decides to differentiate among them by using different paragraph styles. She attached the MANUAL1 template to her document so she could use its predefined styles. Now she needs to apply those styles.

Applying Styles

Once you determine which styles you want to use—either Word's default styles or styles that you define—you must apply them to the text in your document to format it. The easiest way to apply a style to selected text is to use the Style list box.

Barbara is ready to apply paragraph styles to her document.

To apply paragraph styles to selected text using the Style list box:

1. Click anywhere within the document title, **Policy Governing Travel Expenses**.
2. Click the **Style list box down arrow** on the Formatting toolbar to open the Style list. Scroll through the list, then click **Title**. The combination of paragraph and font formatting attributes assigned to the Title style is applied to the selected paragraph. See Figure 3-35. Note that a small black box appears in the margin indicating that the text was formatted with one of Word's predefined styles. This box does not appear for text formatted with user-defined styles.

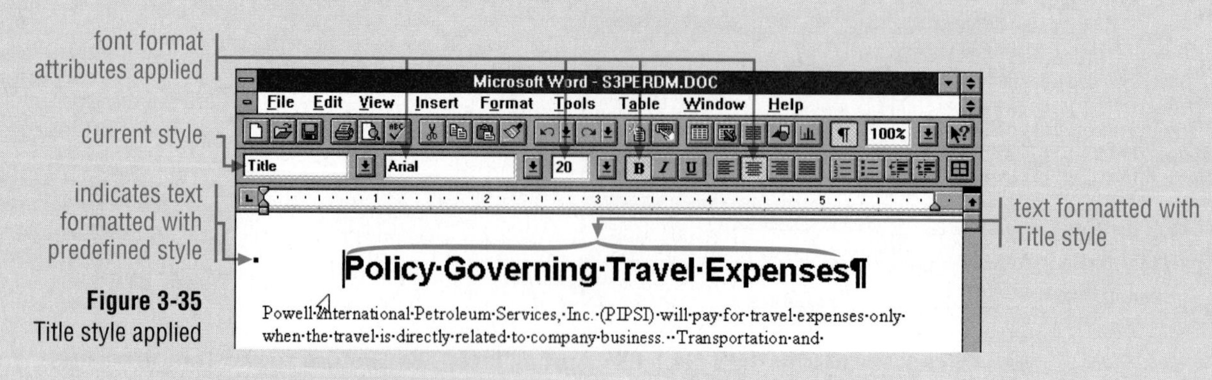

Figure 3-35
Title style applied

While she can see from the Formatting toolbar that the font format has changed, Barbara wants to review the exact attributes assigned to the Title style.

Using Reveal Formats

The Reveal Formats feature allows you to display information about the formatting that has been applied to paragraphs or characters either directly (as you learned in Tutorial 2) or through the use of styles. To use the Reveal Formats feature, click the Help button on the Standard toolbar, then click the Help pointer on the character or paragraph you want information about. Word displays an information box describing the formatting applied to the selected text. To dismiss the information box, press [Esc] or click the Help button.

To check the formats applied to the title:

1. Click the **Help button** on the Standard toolbar, then click anywhere in the title, **Policy Governing Travel Expenses**. The Reveal Formats box appears. See Figure 3-36. The description indicates that the font used in the Title style has the following font formatting: Arial, 20 pt, bold; and the following paragraph formatting: a blank line equal to 18 pt inserted above the paragraph and a blank line equal to 8 pt inserted below the paragraph. Notice that no direct formatting has been applied to this text.

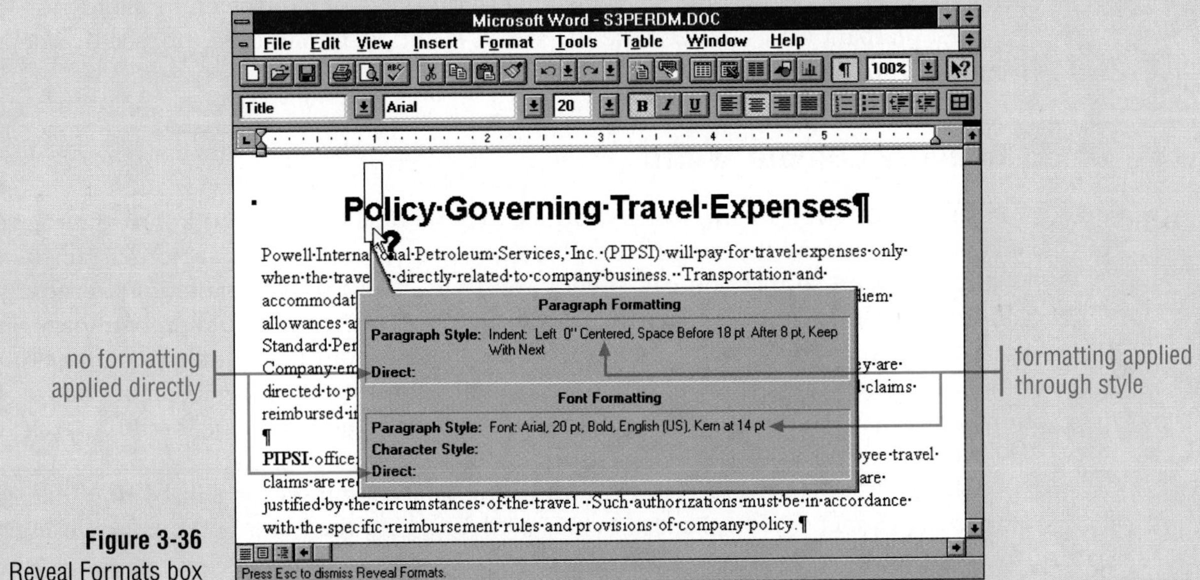

Figure 3-36
Reveal Formats box

2. Press **[Esc]** or click to close the Reveal Formats box.

Barbara continues to apply styles to the rest of the document.

3. Click anywhere within the **Standard Per Diem Allowance** heading (Pg 1, Ln 6) to select it.
4. Click the **Style list box down arrow** on the Formatting toolbar, then click **Heading 1**. The formatting attributes for the Heading 1 style are applied to the selected text. Use the Reveal Formats feature to determine the attributes applied to the selected heading.
5. Click anywhere in the **Domestic Travel** heading (Pg 1, Ln 15), click the **Style list box down arrow**, then click **Heading 1**. The formatting attributes of the Heading 1 style are applied to the selected paragraph.

6. Click anywhere in the heading, **Per Diem Allowance for Extended Domestic Work Assignments** (Pg 2, Ln 8), click the **Style list box down arrow**, then click **Heading 2**. The Heading 2 style is applied to the selected text.
7. Repeat Steps 5 and 6 for those similar headings in the Foreign Travel section.
8. Click anywhere in the **Exceptions** heading, click the **Style list box down arrow**, then click **Heading 1**.
9. Save the changes you have made.

Barbara is now ready to format the tables in her document.

Formatting Tables

Word provides a variety of features to enhance the appearance of tables in documents. You can change the width of columns, the height of rows, or the alignment of text within cells; and you can place borders around cells, parts of a table, or the entire table.

First, Barbara wants to decrease the width of the first column in the side-by-side text paragraphs so that this table takes up fewer lines.

Changing Column Width

You sometimes need to adjust the width of the columns in a table to improve its appearance. If you need the column to be a precise measurement, use the Table Cell Height and Width command so that you can specify the exact width of the column. Otherwise you can drag either the right column marker on the ruler or the right column boundary (gridline) of the column you want to change to the desired position. All other columns to the right are resized proportionately, but the overall width of the table does not change. For more information about other options for adjusting the width of a column, see the *Microsoft Word User's Guide*.

Barbara wants to decrease the width of the first column in the side-by-side text paragraphs to 1.5 inches. She decides to do so by dragging the column boundary, using the ruler as a guide.

To change the width of the first column by dragging the column boundary:

1. Place the insertion point anywhere in the table containing the side-by-side text paragraphs in the Domestic Travel section (beginning Pg 1, Ln 20). Make sure that you do not have any cells selected.
2. Move the mouse pointer over the boundary between columns 1 and 2. The mouse pointer changes to ⇹.
3. Click and drag the pointer to the 1.5" mark on the ruler, then release the mouse button. Notice that as the first column decreases in width, the second column increases, but the overall width of the table does not change.

Barbara wants to make two other formatting changes to the table: she wants to increase the space between the two rows and bold the text in the first column.

To finish making formatting changes to the table:

1. Place the insertion point in row 1 of the table, click the **right mouse button** to display the Table Shortcut menu, then click **Paragraph...**. The Paragraph dialog box appears.
2. Increase the Spacing After box to **12 pt**, then click **OK** or press **[Enter]**.
3. Select the first column of text, then click the **Bold button** on the Formatting toolbar. Deselect the selected cells. See Figure 3-37.

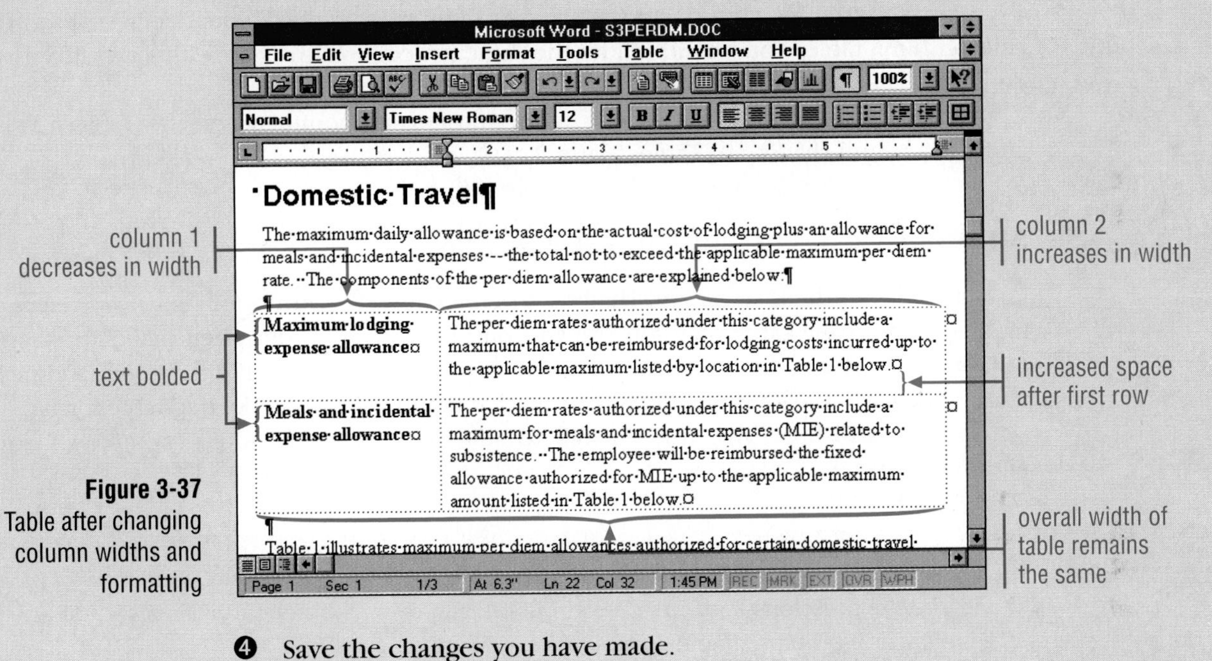

Figure 3-37 Table after changing column widths and formatting

4. Save the changes you have made.

Next Barbara needs to make the same formatting changes to the same table in the Foreign Travel section of the document. This time she'll use the column marker instead of the column boundary to change the column width.

To format the table in the Foreign Travel section:

1. Place the insertion point in the table containing side-by-side text paragraphs in the Foreign Travel section of the document (beginning Pg 2, Ln 21).
2. Move the mouse pointer over the column marker in the ruler between columns 1 and 2. The mouse pointer changes to ↔.

❸ Click and drag the column marker to the 1.5" mark on the ruler, then release the mouse button.

❹ Place the insertion point in row 1 of the table, click the **right mouse button** to display the Table Shortcut menu, then click **Paragraph...**. The Paragraph dialog box appears.

❺ Increase the Spacing After box to **12 pt**, then click **OK** or press **[Enter]**.

❻ Select the first column of text, then click the **Bold button** on the Formatting toolbar. Deselect the selected cells.

❼ Save the changes you have made.

Word also allows you to change the width of selected individual cells or groups of cells within a table. You would follow the same procedures to change their widths as you do for changing entire columns.

Next, Barbara decides to use the Table AutoFormat command on the Table menu to add borders and shading to Tables 1 and 2.

Automatically Formatting Tables

You can add borders, rules, and shading to tables just as you do for text: first select the table or part of the table that you want to outline with a border, then make appropriate option choices from the Borders toolbar. However, the Table AutoFormat command makes it much easier to create professionally formatted tables using a predefined table format.

Barbara will use Table AutoFormat to add borders and shading to Tables 1 and 2 automatically.

To add borders and shading to the tables using the Table AutoFormat command:

❶ Place the insertion point in Table 1, click **Table**, then click **Table AutoFormat...**. The Table AutoFormat dialog box appears.

Barbara is not sure which format she wants to use so she decides to explore her options.

❷ Click several different table format options in the Formats list to view the various formats available.

Barbara decides that the Classic 2 format is the one that suits her data the best.

❸ Click **Classic 2**. See Figure 3-38. Barbara wants Word to adjust the width of the column so that each column is only as wide as the longest item in the column, so she leaves the AutoFit option in the Formats to Apply section activated.

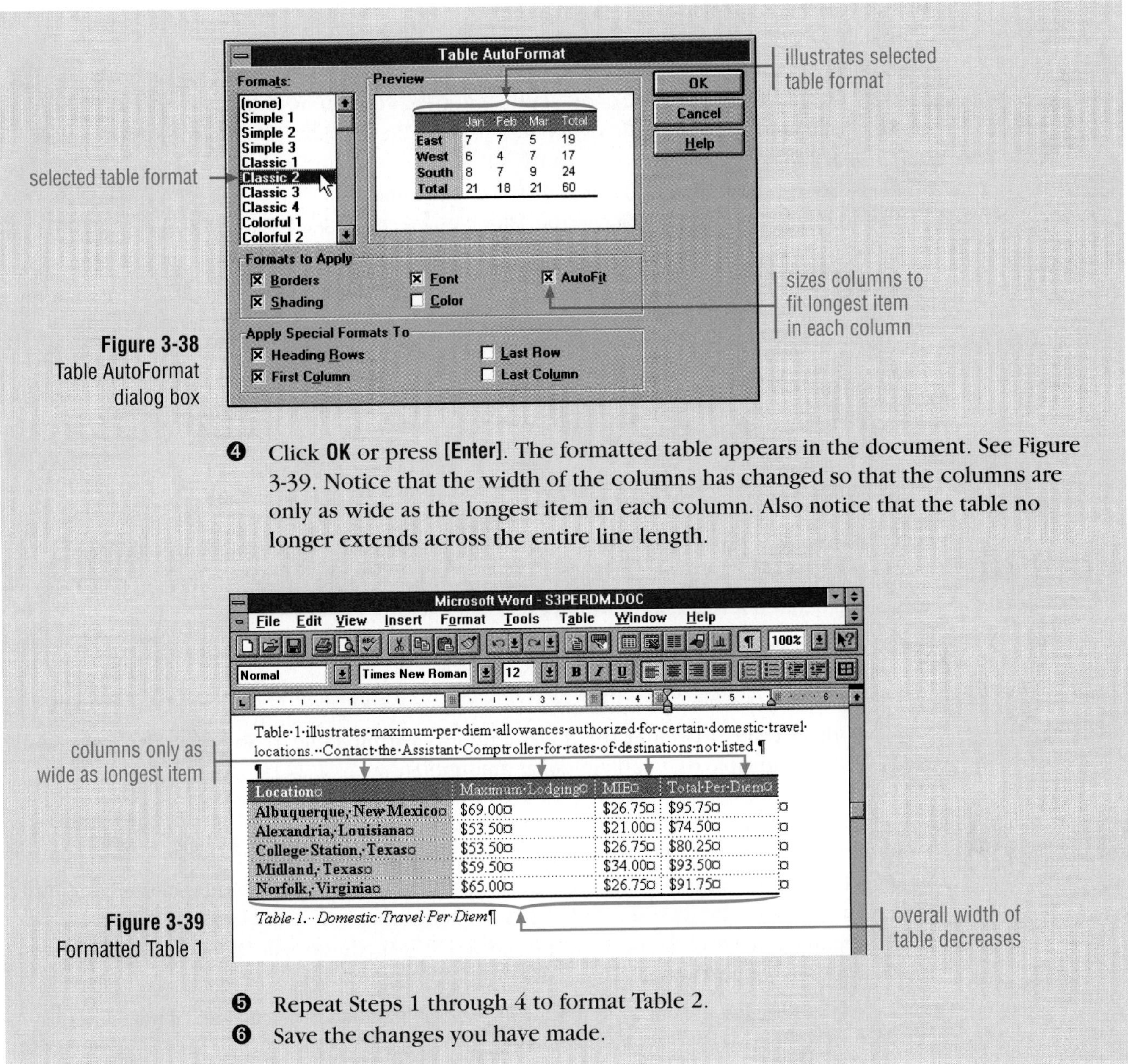

Figure 3-38 Table AutoFormat dialog box

4. Click **OK** or press **[Enter]**. The formatted table appears in the document. See Figure 3-39. Notice that the width of the columns has changed so that the columns are only as wide as the longest item in each column. Also notice that the table no longer extends across the entire line length.

Figure 3-39 Formatted Table 1

5. Repeat Steps 1 through 4 to format Table 2.
6. Save the changes you have made.

Keep in mind that the gridlines you use to see the table structure on the screen are not the same as the borders that you apply using the Borders toolbar or the Table AutoFormat command; gridlines do not print.

Next Barbara decides to center the table across the page, center the dollar amounts within the cells, and center the caption below the table.

Centering a Table

If a table does not take up the entire width of a line, you might want to center it between the left and right margins. If you use the Center button on the Formatting toolbar to center a selected table, the *text* within the cells is centered between each cell boundary; the table is not centered across the page. To center a table, you must use the Table Cell Height and Width command.

Barbara begins by centering Table 1.

To center Table 1 across the page, then center the column headings:

1. Place the insertion point anywhere within Table 1, click **Table**, then click **Cell Height and Width....** The Cell Height and Width dialog box appears.
2. Click the **Row tab**, if necessary. The Row tab appears.
3. Click the **Center radio button** in the Alignment section. See Figure 3-40.

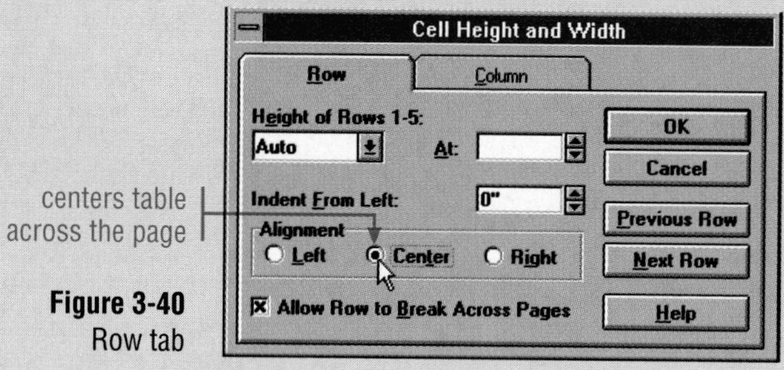

Figure 3-40
Row tab

4. Click **OK** or press **[Enter]**. Table 1 is adjusted so that it is centered across the page.

Next Barbara wants to center the column headings for Table 1. She must first select the row containing the column headings.

5. Select the first row, then click the **Center button** on the Formatting toolbar.

Barbara wants to center the dollar amounts within Table 1. She must first select only the cells in the table that contain dollar amounts.

To center the text in the cells containing dollar amounts in Table 1:

1. Click in the cell selection bar of the first dollar amount, $69.00 (Maximum Lodging amount for Albuquerque, New Mexico). The entire cell is selected.
2. Press the mouse button, drag through $91.75 (Maximum Per Diem amount for Norfolk, Virginia), then release the mouse button.

   TROUBLE? Just the dollar amounts within the table should be highlighted. If not, click the Undo button (or click Edit then click Undo), then start again.

3. Click the **Center button** on the Formatting toolbar. Just the highlighted dollar amounts are centered. Deselect the text.
4. Save the changes you have made.

Next Barbara wants the caption centered across the page below Table 1.

To center the caption for Table 1:

1. Click anywhere within the caption for Table 1.
2. Click the **Center button** on the Formatting toolbar. See Figure 3-41.

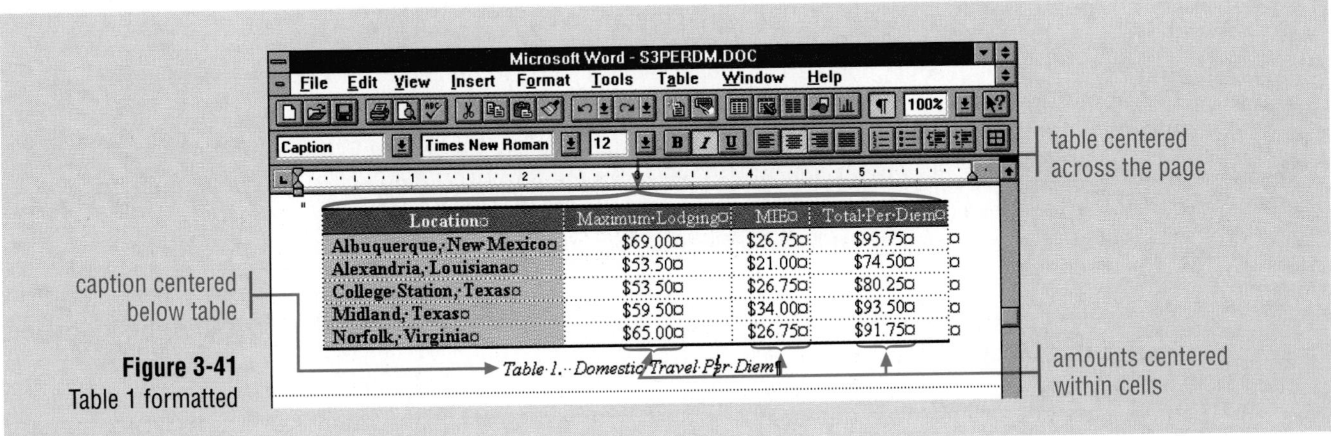

Location	Maximum Lodging	MIE	Total Per Diem
Albuquerque, New Mexico	$69.00	$26.75	$95.75
Alexandria, Louisiana	$53.50	$21.00	$74.50
College Station, Texas	$53.50	$26.75	$80.25
Midland, Texas	$59.50	$34.00	$93.50
Norfolk, Virginia	$65.00	$26.75	$91.75

Figure 3-41
Table 1 formatted

Barbara has applied formatting changes to Table 1. She now needs to make the same format changes to Table 2 (Pg 2, Ln 31). Use what you have learned in the preceding steps to help you make the changes to this table.

To apply format changes to Table 2:

1. Center the table across the page, then center the column headings.
2. Center the dollar amounts.
3. Center the caption under Table 2. See Figure 3-42.

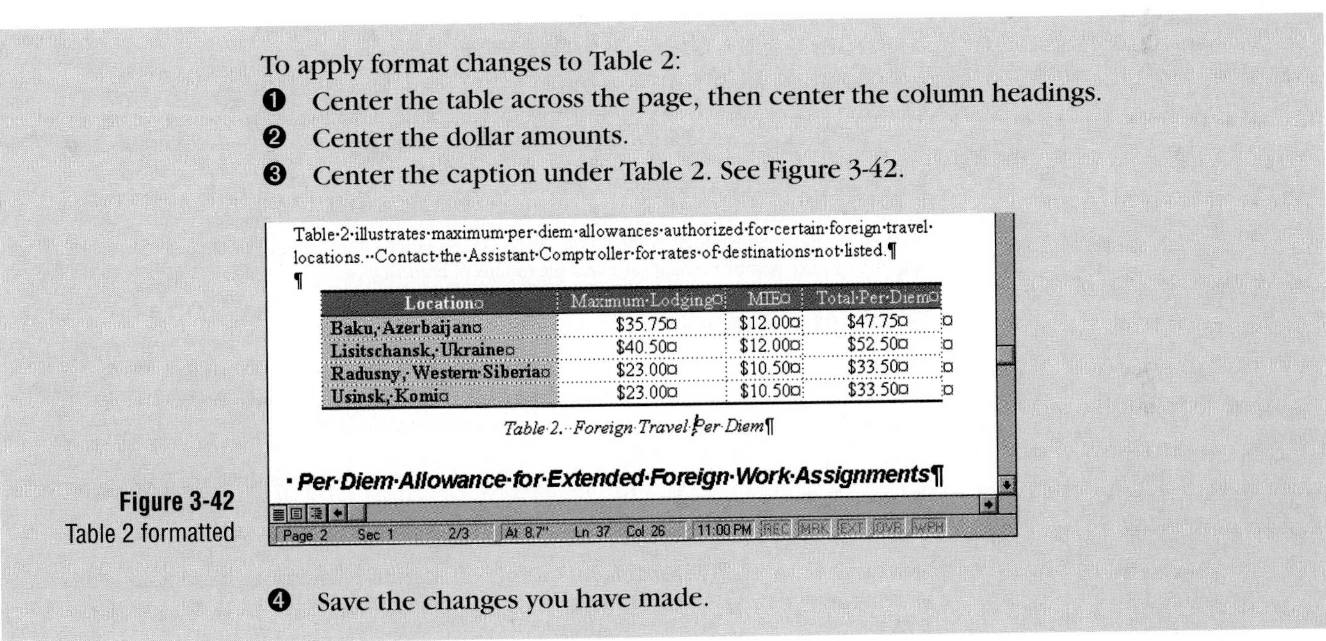
Table 2 illustrates maximum per diem allowances authorized for certain foreign travel locations. Contact the Assistant Comptroller for rates of destinations not listed.

Location	Maximum Lodging	MIE	Total Per Diem
Baku, Azerbaijan	$35.75	$12.00	$47.75
Lisitschansk, Ukraine	$40.50	$12.00	$52.50
Radusny, Western Siberia	$23.00	$10.50	$33.50
Usinsk, Komi	$23.00	$10.50	$33.50

Table 2. Foreign Travel Per Diem

Per Diem Allowance for Extended Foreign Work Assignments

Figure 3-42
Table 2 formatted

4. Save the changes you have made.

Barbara has finished formatting her document and now is ready to spell check, preview, then print it.

To spell check, preview, then print the document:

1. Click the **Spelling button** on the Standard toolbar (or click **Tools** then click **Spelling...**). Complete the spell check following the procedures you learned in Tutorial 1, then save your changes as necessary.
2. Click the **Print Preview button** on the Standard toolbar (or click **File** then click **Print Preview**).

3. If necessary, click the **Multiple Pages button** on the Print Preview toolbar, then select three pages to display all pages of the document.
4. Click the **Print button** on the Print Preview toolbar to print the document.
5. Click the **Close button** on the Print Preview toolbar. You return to the document.
6. Close the document then exit Word.

Barbara's completed document appears in Figure 3-43 on this page and the following two pages.

Policy Governing Travel Expenses

Powell International Petroleum Services, Inc. (PIPSI) will pay for travel expenses only when the travel is directly related to company business. Transportation and accommodations must be consistent with **PIPSI**'s goals and conform to the per diem allowances and travel policies detailed below.

Standard Per Diem Allowance

Company employees will be authorized an equitable expense allowance when they are directed to perform company travel. Per diem allowances will be authorized and claims reimbursed in accordance with the provisions of **PIPSI**'s travel policies.

PIPSI officers who are responsible for authorizing travel or for approving employee travel claims are required to authorize or approve only those per diem allowances that are justified by the circumstances of the travel. Such authorizations must be in accordance with the specific reimbursement rules and provisions of company policy.

Domestic Travel

The maximum daily allowance is based on the actual cost of lodging plus an allowance for meals and incidental expenses -- the total not to exceed the applicable maximum per diem rate. The components of the per diem allowance are explained below:

Maximum lodging expense allowance The per diem rates authorized under this category include a maximum that can be reimbursed for lodging costs incurred up to the applicable maximum listed by location in Table 1 below.

Meals and incidental expense allowance The per diem rates authorized under this category include a maximum for meals and incidental expenses (MIE) related to subsistence. The employee will be reimbursed the fixed allowance authorized for MIE up to the applicable maximum amount listed in Table 1 below.

Table 1 illustrates maximum per diem allowances authorized for certain domestic travel locations. Contact the Assistant Comptroller for rates of destinations not listed.

Location	Maximum Lodging	MIE	Total Per Diem
Albuquerque, New Mexico	$69.00	$26.75	$95.75
Alexandria, Louisiana	$53.50	$21.00	$74.50
College Station, Texas	$53.50	$26.75	$80.25
Midland, Texas	$59.50	$34.00	$93.50
Norfolk, Virginia	$65.00	$26.75	$91.75

Table 1. Domestic Travel Per Diem

Policy Governing Travel Expenses **12/21/95**

Figure 3-43 Completed document (page 1 of 3)

2

Per Diem Allowance for Extended Domestic Work Assignments

On extended work assignments of more than 30 days but less than 120 days, the employee will be reimbursed 65 percent of the maximum per diem rate for that location. On extended work assignments of 120 days or more, the employee will be reimbursed 55 percent of the maximum per diem rate for that location.

Reimbursement will be based on a flat rate system. Employees are required to submit a copy of any leases for accommodations with the initial travel expense claim and for any future instances when another lease must be obtained. Receipts must also be submitted with each claim for furniture rental, utilities, and other expenses over $25.

Foreign Travel

Subsistence reimbursement for foreign travel is based on lodging plus an amount established for meals and incidental expenses for the location. Actual expenses may be approved when per diem rates do not cover subsistence expenses. Reimbursements may be made for the actual expenses up to 150 percent of the location rate or $50 plus the location rate, whichever is greater. The components of the per diem allowance are explained below:

Maximum lodging expense allowance The per diem rates authorized under this category include a maximum that can be reimbursed for lodging costs incurred up to the applicable maximum listed by location in Table 2 below.

Meals and incidental expense allowance The per diem rates authorized under this category include a maximum for meals and incidental expenses (MIE) related to subsistence. The employee will be reimbursed the fixed allowance authorized for MIE up to the applicable maximum amount listed in Table 2 below.

Table 2 illustrates maximum per diem allowances authorized for certain foreign travel locations. Contact the Assistant Comptroller for rates of destinations not listed.

Location	Maximum Lodging	MIE	Total Per Diem
Baku, Azerbaijan	$35.75	$12.00	$47.75
Lisitschansk, Ukraine	$40.50	$12.00	$52.50
Radusny, Western Siberia	$23.00	$10.50	$33.50
Usinsk, Komi	$23.00	$10.50	$33.50

Table 2. Foreign Travel Per Diem

Per Diem Allowance for Extended Foreign Work Assignments

On extended work assignments of more than 30 days but less than 120 days, the employee will be reimbursed 65 percent of the maximum per diem rate for that location. On

Policy Governing Travel Expenses 12/21/95

Figure 3-43
Completed document (page 2 of 3)

3

extended work assignments of 120 days or more, the employee will be reimbursed 55 percent of the maximum per diem rate for that location.

Reimbursement will be based on a flat rate system. Employees are required to submit a copy of any leases for accommodations with the initial travel expense claim and for any future instances when another lease must be obtained. Receipts must also be submitted with each claim for furniture rental, utilities, and other expenses over $25.

Exceptions

Any exceptions to the standard per diem allowance must be submitted in writing to the Assistant Comptroller's office.

Policy Governing Travel Expenses **12/21/95**

Figure 3-43
Completed document
(page 3 of 3)

■ ■ ■

Barbara faxes Nancy a copy of the finished travel expense policy. Nancy is pleased with the document's appearance and gives Barbara her approval to submit it to management.

Questions

1. Describe three methods for creating tables.
2. Describe the elements of a table.
3. Explain the purpose of the AutoCorrect feature.
4. Explain the difference between the Cut and Paste procedure and the Copy and Paste procedure.
5. Explain the purpose of the Replace command on the Edit menu.
6. Explain the process for inserting a row:
   a. Between existing rows of a table
   b. At the bottom of a table
7. Explain the procedure for inserting a column:
   a. Between existing columns of a table
   b. At the end of a table
8. Explain the procedure for sorting information within a table.
9. What is the function key that repeats the last change to a document?
10. Explain the procedure for adding a caption to a table.
11. Explain the difference between a header and a footer.
12. Briefly define each of the following terms:
    a. template
    b. paragraph style
    c. character style
    d. style sheet
13. Describe the procedure for attaching a template other than the NORMAL template to the current document.
14. Describe the procedure for using the Style Gallery to preview a template's styles.
15. Describe the different methods for changing column widths.
16. Describe the procedure for using the Table AutoFormat command to apply formatting to a table.

Use Word Help to answer Questions 17 through 23.

E 17. What is a Table Wizard?

E 18. How do you copy and paste or cut and paste from one Word document to another Word document?

E 19. How do you print the style sheet for a document?

E 20. What is the purpose of the Find command on the Edit menu?

E 21. What is the procedure to merge cells within a table?

E 22. How do you change the numbering format used in a caption?

E 23. How do you print a range of pages within a document?

Tutorial Assignments

Start Word, if necessary, and conduct a screen check. Open the file T3PIPSI1.DOC from your Student Disk, then complete the following:

1. Save the document as S3PIPSI1.DOC.
2. Move the entire Domestic Travel section after the Foreign Travel section.
3. Change all occurrences of "company" to PIPSI (not bolded).

4. Change the header so that:
   a. The page number is centered rather than at the right margin.
   b. It is Arial 12 point bold.
   c. It does not print on the first page.
5. Apply the Heading 1 style to the heading Standard Per Diem Allowance.
6. Apply the Heading 2 style to the headings Domestic Travel and Foreign Travel.
7. Apply the Heading 3 style to the Per Diem Allowance for Extended Work Assignments headings in both sections.

E

8. Replace all instances of three consecutive paragraph marks with one paragraph mark.
9. Save your changes.
10. Preview, print, then close the document.

Open the file T3PIPSI2.DOC from your Student Disk, then complete the following:

11. Save the document as S3PIPSI2.DOC.
12. Decrease the width of the column containing the component names (Maximum lodging expense allowance and Meals and incidental expense allowance) to 1.25 inches without decreasing the overall width of the table.
13. Bold and center the component names, then change the font to Arial.
14. Insert a 12 point blank line after row 1 of the side-by-side text table, which explains the per diem components.
15. Insert a row at the top of the Foreign Travel Per Diem table to contain column headings: Location (in cell 1), Maximum Lodging (in cell 2), MIE (in cell 3), and Total Per Diem (in cell 4).
16. Insert the two rows of information shown in Figure 3-44 at the bottom of the Foreign Travel Per Diem table without changing the overall width of the table.

Volgograd, Russia	$40.25	$12.50
Tbilisi, Georgia	$35.75	$12.50

Figure 3-44

17. Calculate the total per diem amounts in the Foreign Travel Per Diem table.
18. Add a caption above the Foreign Travel Per Diem table that reads: Table 1. Foreign Travel Per Diem. Center the caption across the page.
19. Sort the rows in the table in descending order based on the total per diem amounts in the last column, then alphabetically by the Location column.
20. Insert a footer to appear on all pages with your name at the left margin, the current date at the right margin, and a $1\frac{1}{2}$ point single rule across the top of the line space.
21. Use the Style Gallery to view the styles in the MANUSCR1 template, then attach the template to the document.
22. Apply the Part Title style to the heading Policy Governing Travel Expenses.
23. Apply the Heading 1 style to the headings Standard Per Diem Allowance and Exceptions.
24. Apply the Heading 2 style to the heading Foreign Travel.
25. Apply the Heading 3 style to the heading Per Diem Allowance for Extended Foreign Work Assignments.
26. Apply the Body Text style to all the text paragraphs in the document, but not to the tables.
27. Format the Foreign Travel Per Diem table using the predefined Columns 5 table format. Deselect the shading option in the Formats section, and select the Last Column option in the Special Formats to Apply section.
28. Save your changes.
29. Preview then print the document.

E

30. Insert a tab at the beginning of each text paragraph. (*Hint:* Each paragraph is preceded by one paragraph mark. Tab characters and paragraph marks are special characters.)

31. Save the document as S3PIPSI3.DOC.
32. Preview then print the document.
33. Close all documents.

Case Problems

1. Hiring Practices at Teisch Manufacturing, Inc.

Jerome Ellis is the assistant director of Personnel Services for Teisch Manufacturing, Inc., of St. Louis, Missouri. His manager, Felicia Santana, has asked him to write a memo covering the company's hiring practices during the past year. Jerome is to report on how many males and females were hired so that Felicia can determine whether Teisch has complied with Equal Employment Opportunity Commission (EEOC) guidelines.

Open the file P3TEISCH.DOC then complete the following:

1. Save the document as S3TEISCH.DOC.
2. Insert a memo heading at the top of the document, including the title Memorandum and heading information: TO: Executive Committee; FROM: Jerome Ellis; RE: New Hire Mix; DATE: February 26, 1995.
3. Insert a hard page break at the end of the document.
4. Create a table on page 2 for the data shown in Figure 3-45.

Position	Female	Male	Total
Equipment Operator	17	10	
Plant Supervisor	1	4	
Administrative Assistant	2	4	
Salesperson	11	10	
Total			

Figure 3-45

5. Add a caption below the table that reads: Table 1. Gender Mix Among 1994 New Hires.
6. Save your changes.
7. Replace all instances of "the corporation" in the body of the memo with "Teisch."
8. Insert a first-page footer that includes the page number centered. Insert a header for subsequent pages that includes the text "Executive Committee" at the left margin, the page number at the center, and the memo date at the right margin. Add bolding to Executive Committee.
9. Apply the Document Label paragraph style to the title Memorandum.
10. Apply the Message Header First paragraph style to the memo heading TO:; apply the Message Header paragraph style to the memo headings FROM: and RE:; apply the Message Header Last paragraph style to the memo heading DATE; apply the Message Header Label character style to just the memo headings.
11. Apply the Body Text style to the body of the memo.
12. Format the table using the Columns 3 predefined table format. Select the Last Row option in the Apply Special Formats section.
13. Center the table across the page, and center the caption below the table.
14. Center the numbers of new hires within the cells.
15. Save your changes.
16. Preview then print the document.
17. Delete the caption below the table.
18. Insert one row at the top of the table.
19. **E** Merge the cells in the inserted row.
20. Type "Gender Mix for 1994 New Hires" in the cell.

21. Apply the Heading 2 style to the cell, then center the text across the cell.
22. Save the document as S3MIX.DOC.
23. E Preview then print just page 2 of the document.
24. Close the document.

2. AMICI Training Schedule

Cecilia Vance is the coordinator of staff development programs for AMICI Exploration and Production's headquarters in Houston. She asked Murry Kyle, the manager of the Information Support Services division, to provide her with a schedule of dates in June and July when the staff of the Help Desk Department could offer several training classes requested by the Headquarters' employees. Cecilia received the file today from Murry and wants to send out a flyer for distribution to all personnel.

Open P3MSPSCH.DOC then complete the following:

1. Save the document as S3MSPSCH.DOC.
2. Select all of the lines of text in the file, then convert them to a table.
3. Insert a row at the top of the table.
4. Type the following column headings in the cells of the new row: Course Name, Dates, Prerequisite.
5. Sort the table alphabetically by course name. Specify that the table contains a header row.
6. Insert the following three-line title above the table: Microsoft Products, Training Schedule, Summer Session.
7. Type the text shown in Figure 3-46 below the table.

Figure 3-46

> Class size is limited to ten students. Please call Cecilia Vance at 4-4091 or send an e-mail message to reserve your place. Observe the suggested prerequisites.

8. Change the top margin to 2.0".
9. Format the three-line title with the following attributes:
   a. Center alignment
   b. Matura MT Script Capitals (If this font is not available, choose another script font.)
   c. 24 point
10. Insert a 12 point blank line below the last line in the title and above the last paragraph ("Class size is ...").
11. Format the table using the Grid 8 predefined table format.
12. Center the table across the page and the column headings within their cells.
13. Save the document.
14. Preview then print the document.
15. E Use Word Help to learn about moving columns in a table, then move the Prerequisite column between the Course Name and the Dates columns.
16. E Use Word Help to learn about changing the row height in tables, then select all rows in the table. Change the row height to Exactly 24 point.
17. Save the document as S3MOVCOL.DOC.
18. Preview, print, then close the document.

3. Creating Your Own Résumé

Complete the following:

1. Create a new document.
2. Type your name, address, and telephone number on separate lines.
3. Press [Enter] twice.
4. Create a five-row by two-column table. (Note: If your résumé extends beyond one page, you will need to adjust the table structure and formatting accordingly.)

5. Decrease the width of column 1 to 1.5 inches, but do not change the overall size of the table.
6. Type the following section headings in the cells in the first column: Career Objective (in row 1), Education (in row 2), Employment (in row 3), Extracurricular Activities and Honors (in row 4), and References (in row 5).
7. In cell 2 of row 1 (next to Career Objective), type your career objective. Use the Paragraph command to insert a 12 point blank line at the bottom of the cell.
8. In cell 2 of row 2 (next to Education), list your college, its location, degree earned or expected to be earned, major, and date of graduation. Press [Enter] twice then list all the courses you have completed in your major. Use the Paragraph command to insert a 12 point blank line after the last line in the cell.
9. In cell 2 of row 3 (next to Employment), list the position title, company, location, and dates of employment for each position you have held. Start with your most recent position. On the next line, give a brief description of your duties. Skip a line between each job. Use the Paragraph command to insert a blank line after the last entry in the cell.
10. In cell 2 of row 4 (next to Extracurricular Activities and Honors), list any organizations you participate in and any awards you have received. Use the Paragraph command to insert a blank line after the last entry in the cell.
11. In cell 2 of row 5 (next to References), type "Available upon request."
12. Center your name, address, and telephone number. Change the font to 14 point Arial, then bold your name, address, and telephone number.
13. Change the section headings in column 1 of the table to bold and all capitals.
14. Insert bullets in front of each course in your major.
15. Bold each title of the positions you have held.
16. Spell check the document.
17. Save the document as S3RESUME.DOC.
18. Preview, print, then close the document.

T U T O R I A L 4

Creating Reports

Writing a Report with a Table of Contents

OBJECTIVES

In this tutorial you will:

- Use Word's Thesaurus
- Check grammar
- Assign bookmarks
- Insert section breaks
- Align a page vertically
- Insert headers and footers in a multi-section document
- Define, apply, and redefine styles
- Transfer data between documents
- Create a preface page with a table of contents and a table of figures
- Create a customized document template

CASE

Connolly/Bayle and Associates Jessica Pangiana is a research assistant with Connolly/Bayle and Associates of San Francisco, a marketing research and analysis firm specializing in investigating economic development opportunities for municipalities. One of the firm's current clients, the Research Division of the Greater San Juan Economic Development Foundation, has contracted with Connolly/Bayle to develop a demographic and industrial profile of the greater San Juan area. The foundation will use the information to apply for grants from the federal and state governments for job training programs and to attract new businesses to the San Juan area.

Henry Santiago is Jessica's manager. He has asked her to create a preliminary report of the demographic and industrial staffing patterns in the San Juan area based on the data she has gathered. He will then use the information in this preliminary report to create a more extensive final report, which will go to the client.

Jessica will follow the productivity strategy to complete her task. In her report document, she has already created a title page, a page for the table of contents, and a third page with the body of her report—unedited and unformatted (Figure 4-1). She separated the three pages with hard page breaks. The body of the report contains three major sections: Methodology, Summary of Major Findings, and Conclusion. Both the Methodology and Summary of Major Findings sections are divided into smaller sections to help the reader digest the information. Jessica has printed the first draft of her report and indicated the changes to be made.

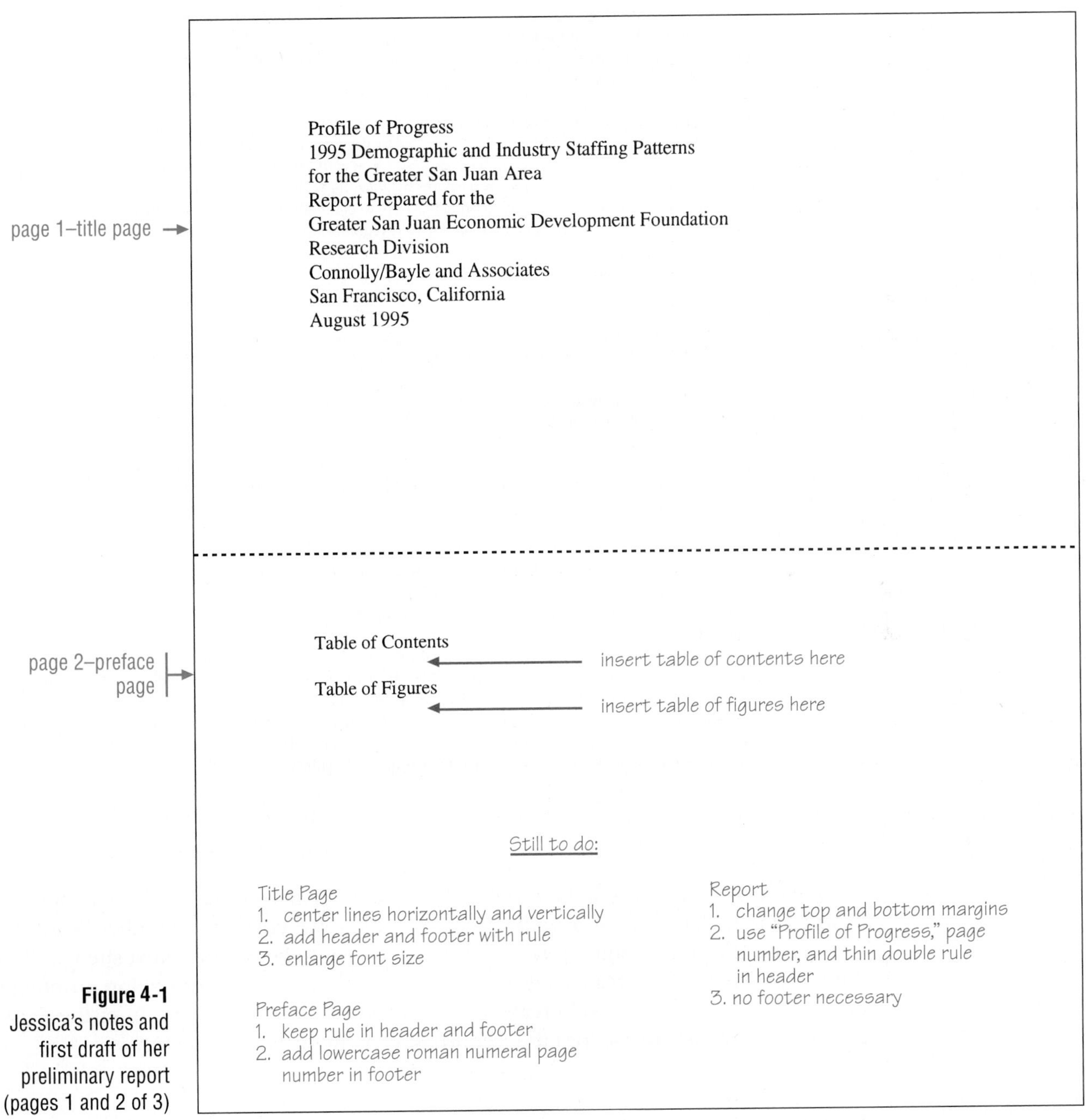

Figure 4-1
Jessica's notes and first draft of her preliminary report (pages 1 and 2 of 3)

page 3–report →

Introduction
The Profile of Progress is a compilation of industrial data designed to give the reader an overview of the population, job base, and job growth trends of the Greater San Juan area. The region, which encompasses San Juan, Bellville, Santa Maria, and Williston, continues to lead the way in California's recovery from the economic slump during the early '90s. The following report discusses both the data collection methodology and a summary of the findings.
Methodology
The Sample
The sample for this study was selected from the first quarter 1995 Employment and Wages report submitted to the California Department of Labor by the region's employers. The universe was stratified by standard industrial classification codes. Procedures involved all certainty cases.
Collection Procedures
The majority of the data was colected by mail. Each selected establishment received a structured schedule for there specific industry. The survey from included the following: instructions, occupational titles and definitions, business identification, and a standard industrial classification code. Survey procedures included three follow-up mailings to non-respondents. The telephone was used extensively to clarify data and to canvas critical non-respondents. The demographic statistics for the region was extracted from the 1990 census data.
Summary of Major Findings
Population
The 1995 Profile of Progress presents a growth statistic that continues to display the dynamic growth of the San Juan region. In 1990, the total population of the San Juan region was 192,457. This represents an increase of 48 percent over the 1980 figures and an increase of 150 percent increase over the 1970 figures. Greater numbers of jobs in the defense and computer industries accounted primarily for the population increases. Figure 1 depicts this dramatic growth.

insert chart 1 →

Diversifying San Juan
Diversification, induced in part by natural forces, along with the ingenuity of area business leaders is largely responsible for the continued growth in the San Juan area. Figure 2 shows the makeup of the employing community.

insert chart 2 →

Job Openings
According to our survey of the region's employers, on average, the occupational groups requiring the most education will also see the fastest job growth opportunities. Figure 3 lists the projected job openings during the next five years, including those due to replacement needs and those due to employment increases.

insert chart 3 →

Conclusion
Current population growth trends indicate that the Greater San Juan area will provide a steady job force for the next five to ten years. The diversity of the area's industries will continue to provide 4,000 to 5,000 new jobs over the next five years if current trends continue. These jobs will be largely in the professions, administrative support, and service industries. The San Juan region is a vital area that has grown rapidly over the past two decades and will continue to grow well into the twenty-first century.

Figure 4-1
Jessica's notes and first draft of her preliminary report (page 3 of 3)

Jessica will edit the report, proofreading the document using Word's Thesaurus and Grammar tools. She will also transfer charts, which she created in another Word document using Microsoft Graph, from the chart document to her report. Next she will format the report. Then she'll create a table of contents and a table of figures before printing the document. Finally Jessica will create a customized document template from the existing document that she can use for other reports she might develop in the future.

To start Word and open the document that Jessica created:

1. Start Word then conduct the screen check as described in Tutorial 1.

❷ Insert your Student Disk in the disk drive, then open the file C4SJPRPT.DOC from your Student Disk. Scroll through the document to become familiar with it. Compare your document to Figure 4-1. Notice that the document contains three pages.

❸ Click **File** then click **Save As...**, and save the document to your Student Disk as S4SJPRPT.DOC.

❹ Click **OK** or press **[Enter]**. The title bar changes to reflect the new document name.

Now Jessica is ready to start the editing phase of the productivity strategy. She begins by looking up an alternative meaning for a word she has used in her report.

Using Word's Thesaurus

You have used one of Word's proofreading tools, the Spelling command, to spell check a document for errors. Another proofreading tool that facilitates the editing process is the Thesaurus. Word's **Thesaurus** command provides synonyms and some antonyms for a selected word. Once you have looked up an alternative meaning for a word, you can immediately replace the selected word in the document with its synonym.

Jessica notices that she used the term "economic slump" in the first paragraph of the report text to describe the conditions of the local economy. She thinks that "slump" might be too negative, so she decides to use the Thesaurus command to find a synonym with a more positive meaning.

To look up a synonym for "slump" using the Thesaurus command:

❶ Move to page 3 then select the word "slump" (Pg 3, Ln 5).

❷ Click **Tools** then click **Thesaurus...**. The Thesaurus dialog box appears with the word "slump" inserted in the Looked Up list box and three alternative choices in the Meanings list box. See Figure 4-2.

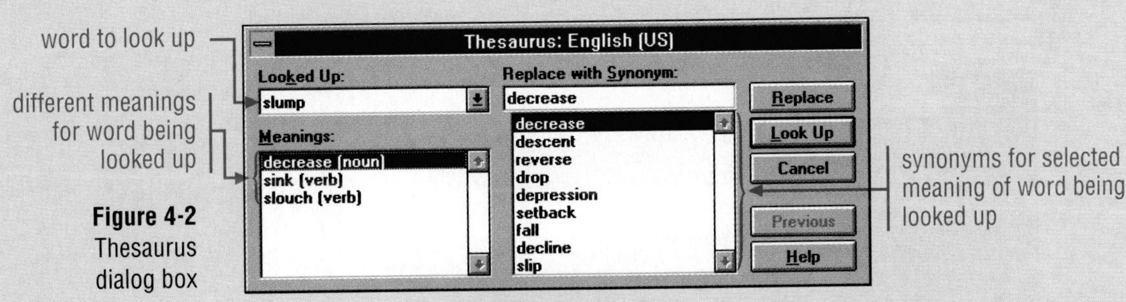

Figure 4-2 Thesaurus dialog box

The highlighted choice "decrease (noun)" in the Meanings list box is the appropriate meaning given the context of the word "slump" in her report, but Jessica doesn't like the choice of synonyms provided by Word. She decides to look up additional meanings for one of the listed synonyms, "depression."

❸ Click **depression** in the Replace with Synonym list box, then click **Look Up** or press **[Enter]**. The choices in the Meanings list box change to reflect options for the word "depression"; an option for antonyms also appears. The most appropriate meaning given the context in Jessica's report is "recession (noun)," not the highlighted choice "hollow (noun)."

4. Click **recession (noun)** in the Meanings list box, then click **Look Up** or press **[Enter]**. Two meanings for recession appear in the Meanings list box, as well as an entry for Related Words.

"Economic slump (noun)" is the appropriate meaning, given the context. Jessica decides that "slowdown" is the synonym that seems most positive.

5. Click **slowdown** in the Replace with Synonym list box, then click **Replace**. The selected word, "slowdown," replaces the original word, "slump," in the document.
6. Save the changes you have made.

Next, Jessica will check her report for grammatical errors.

Checking Grammar

Another proofreading tool available in Word is the Grammar command. The **Grammar** command checks your document for proper grammar usage and style, in addition to checking for spelling errors.

Jessica added the Methodology section after she had checked the other sections for spelling and grammar errors, so she needs to check the grammar in just that part of her document.

To check the grammar in the Methodology section:

1. Scroll through the document, then select the Methodology section of your document (Pg 3, Ln 8). See Figure 4-3.

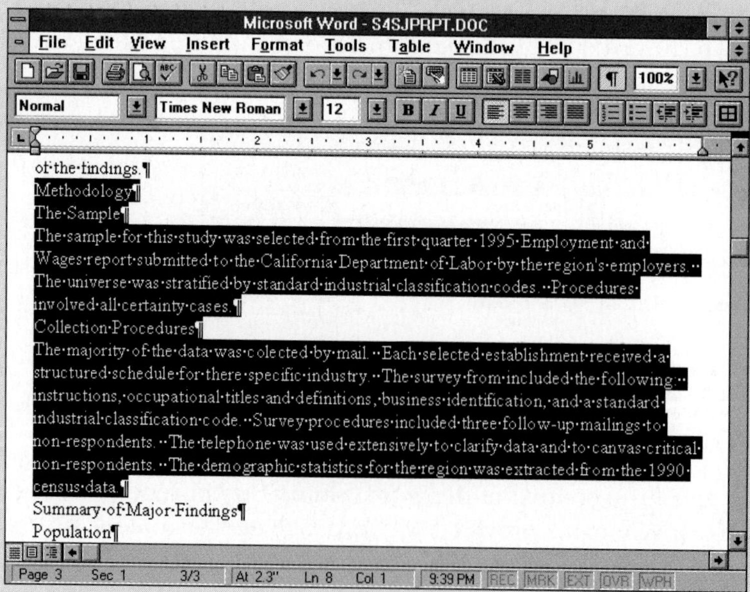

Figure 4-3 Document after selecting Methodology section

TROUBLE? Don't worry if your line endings differ from those shown here; continue with the tutorial.

❷ Click **Tools** then click **Grammar...**. Word stops and highlights the sentence containing the first instance of a grammar usage or style problem. The Grammar dialog box also appears. See Figure 4-4. The sentence containing the flagged error appears in the Sentence box of the dialog box with the "problem" word or words printed in red. Word's suggestions to solve the problem appear in the Suggestions box.

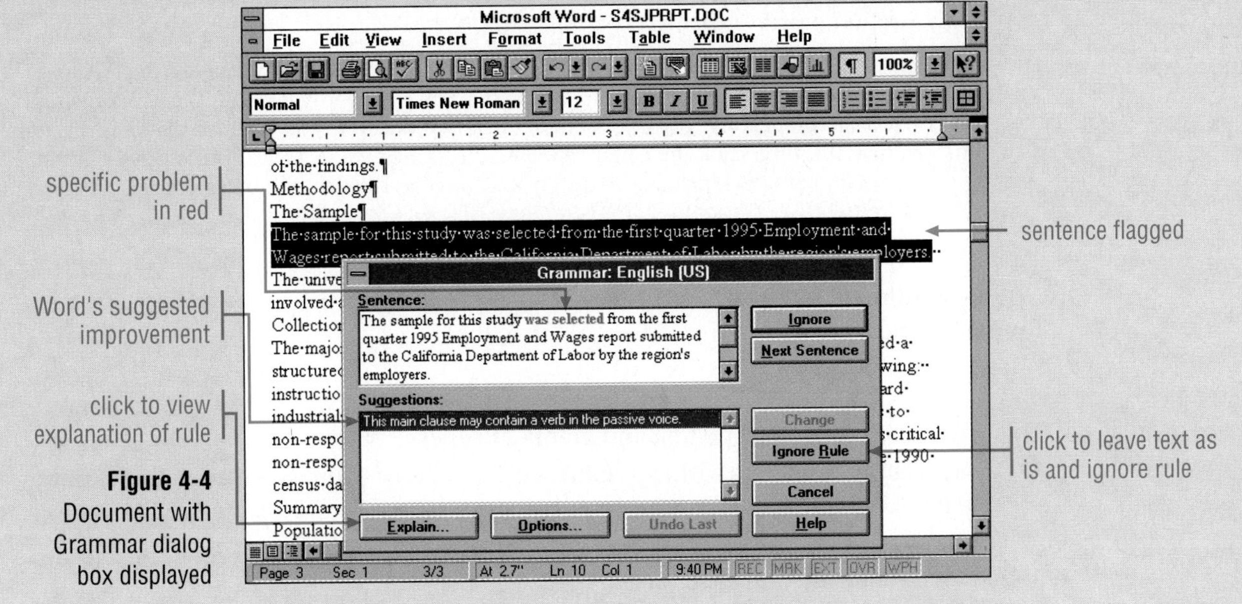

Figure 4-4 Document with Grammar dialog box displayed

Jessica needs further explanation of the problem and Word's suggested improvement.

To view the rule for the flagged grammatical error:

❶ Click **Explain...**. An explanation of the grammar rule that applies to this sentence is displayed. See Figure 4-5.

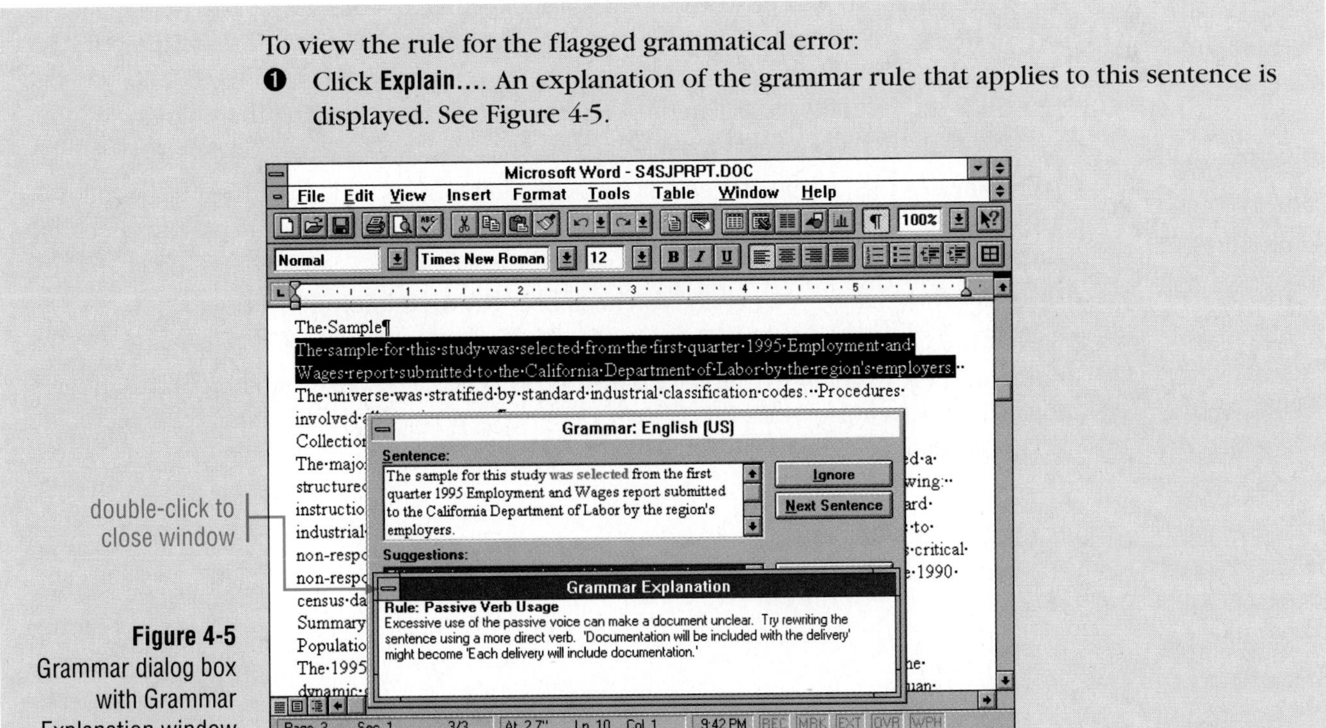

Figure 4-5 Grammar dialog box with Grammar Explanation window

❷ After reading the explanation, double-click the **Control menu box** of the Grammar Explanation window to close it.

Although active voice is often preferable to passive voice, Jessica thinks that it is acceptable for a report of this nature, and she decides to ignore the rule for the flagged error.

❸ Click **Ignore Rule**. Word continues the grammar check process and stops at an incorrectly spelled word, "colected."

TROUBLE? If Word did not find the misspelled word "colected," someone has deactivated the Spelling feature for the Thesaurus command. Click Cancel to close the Grammar dialog box. To activate the feature, click Tools then click Options.... In the Options dialog box, click the Grammar tab, then click the Check Spelling check box. Click OK or press [Enter], then repeat the grammar check procedure described above in this and the preceding set of steps.

As mentioned before, Word also checks for spelling errors at the same time it checks for grammatical errors.

To correct the remaining spelling and grammatical errors:

❶ Click **Change** to accept Word's spelling of "collected." Word next stops at the potential misuse of "there." Read the problem sentence and Word's suggested change.

TROUBLE? If Word stops at errors other than those discussed in this section, click Ignore Rule and continue with the tutorial.

❷ Click **Change** to accept Word's suggestion. Word next stops at the potential misuse of the word "from." Read the problem sentence and Word's suggested change.

❸ Click **Change** to accept Word's suggestion. Word next stops at the potential misuse of the word "canvas." Read the problem sentence and Word's suggested change.

❹ Click **Change** to accept Word's suggestion. Word next stops at the potential misuse of the word "statistics." This time Word offers two solutions to this subject/verb agreement problem.

❺ Click the **second suggestion** in the Suggestions box (for changing the word "was" to "were"), then click **Change**.

Word finishes the grammar check of the selected block of text, and displays the following message: "Word finished checking the selection. Do you want to continue checking the remainder of the document?"

❻ Click **No** because you needed to check only the Methodology section.

Next Word calculates the readability of the selected text and displays statistics about its content in the Readability Statistics dialog box. This dialog box contains data about various counts, averages, and criteria that measure how easy your document or selected text is to read. See Figure 4-6.

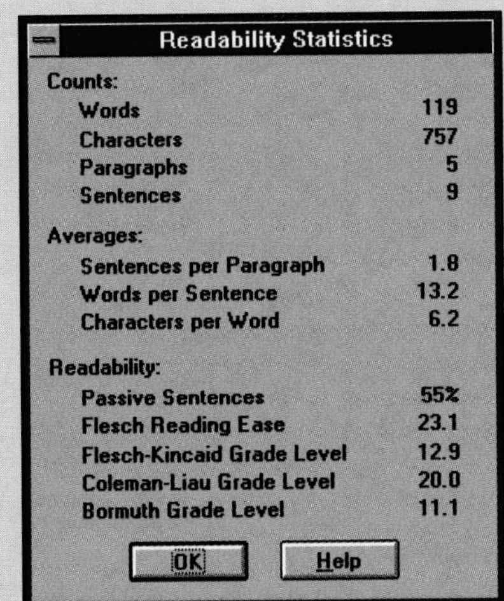

Figure 4-6
Readability Statistics dialog box

Jessica isn't sure how to interpret the statistics so she decides to use Word Help.

❼ Click **Help** in the Readability Statistics dialog box. Read the information in the Help topic, then close the Word Help window.

❽ After looking over the readability statistics for the selected text, click **OK**, then deselect the text.

❾ Save the changes you have made.

Jessica has one more editing change to make before she moves on to the formatting phase of her task. To help her move quickly to the locations in her report where she needs to insert the three charts, she decides to mark those locations with bookmarks.

Assigning Bookmarks

You can assign a **bookmark** to mark the location of the insertion point, selected text or graphics, or other items that you need to move to quickly. You simply select the location, text, or graphics that you want to mark, then choose the Bookmark command from the Edit menu. You then give the bookmark a name. A bookmark name must begin with a letter, cannot contain more than 40 characters, and cannot contain spaces.

Jessica wants to mark the locations for the charts she must transfer to the report document (Figure 4-1).

To assign bookmarks to the three chart locations:

❶ Place the insertion point in the Population section after the sentence "Figure 1 depicts..." (Pg 3, Ln 29), then press **[Enter]**. This will be the location of Figure 1, which will show one of the charts.

❷ Click **Edit** then click **Bookmark...**. The Bookmark dialog box appears.

❸ Type **figure1** in the Bookmark Name text box. See Figure 4-7.

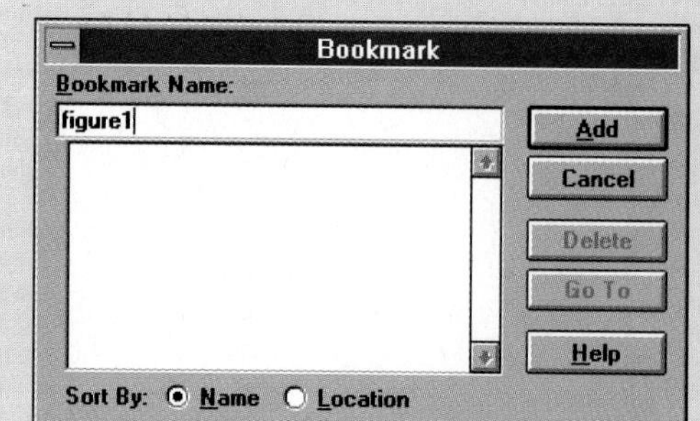

Figure 4-7 Bookmark dialog box

4. Click **Add** or press **[Enter]**. You return to the document.

Jessica wants to be able to view the bookmark locations in her document.

5. Click **Tools**, click **Options...**, then click the **View tab** (if necessary).
6. Click the **Bookmarks check box** in the Show section to select the option, then click **OK** or press **[Enter]**. The figure1 bookmark is now visible as a large I-beam. If you had marked text instead of a location, then the marked text would appear enclosed in square brackets.

   TROUBLE? If the Bookmarks check box is already selected, do not clear it.

7. Save the changes you have made.
8. Place the insertion point in the Diversifying San Juan section after the sentence "Figure 2 shows..." (Pg 3, Ln 34), press **[Enter]**, then repeat Steps 2 through 4, naming the bookmark **figure2**. The figure2 bookmark is now visible.
9. Place the insertion point in the Job Openings section after the sentence "Figure 3 lists..." (Pg 3, Ln 40), press **[Enter]**, then repeat Steps 2 through 4, naming the bookmark **figure3**. See Figure 4-8. Note that you might need to scroll the window to see all three bookmarks at one time.

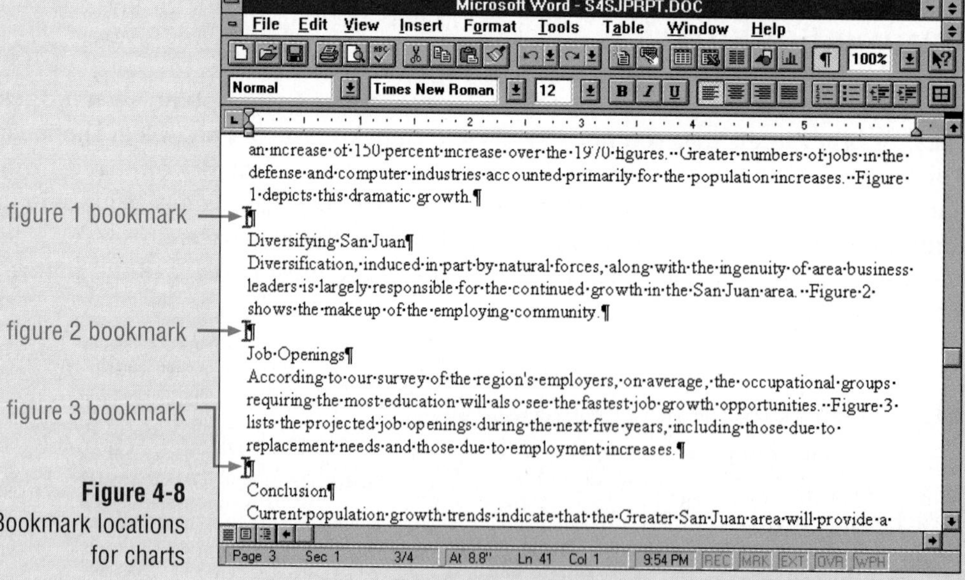

Figure 4-8 Bookmark locations for charts

10. Save the changes you have made.

Jessica has finished the editing phase of the productivity strategy. Now she is ready to format the document.

Formatting Sections in a Document

Jessica's report poses some interesting formatting challenges. In consulting her notes (Figure 4-1), Jessica sees that she needs to align the title page vertically, change the top and bottom margins for the report pages, and create headers and footers for the title page and the table of contents that are different from the headers and footers for the report. Each of these formatting changes—adjusting vertical alignment, changing margins, and inserting different headers and footers—are page-level, or document-level, decisions. As such, they cannot be confined to specific pages as Jessica needs. In addition to these changes, she must make paragraph and font formatting changes to the title page, table of contents page, and the report.

Word's solution to situations like Jessica's is to divide a document into mini-documents called sections, each with its own page-level formatting options. A **section** is a portion of a document in which you can change page setup options, such as page orientation, margins, headers and footers, and vertical alignment. To create a section, you insert a **section break**, a division between sections in a document. When you insert a section break, a double dotted line appears across the page with the words "End of Section," and the status bar changes to reflect an increase in the number of sections in the document. You can either insert a section break using the Break command on the Insert menu, then make the necessary page-level changes, or you can use the Page Setup command on the File menu to insert section breaks as well as apply page-level formatting changes.

When Jessica created her document, she inserted a *page break* between the title page and table of contents page, and between the table of contents page and the text of the preliminary report. She wants to format the title page differently from the table of contents page and from the rest of the document, so she needs to delete the page breaks and insert *section breaks* in their place. Then Jessica can make her page-level changes to each section of the document.

Jessica's first step in making her formatting changes is to insert a section break between pages 1 and 2.

To insert a section break between pages 1 and 2:

1. Place the insertion point at the top of page 2, directly before the "T" in Table of Contents, then press **[Backspace]** to remove the page break. The title page and table of contents page are combined temporarily. Notice that the status bar indicates that the insertion point is on page 1 of section 1. Until you insert a section break, your entire document is considered one section.
2. Click **Insert** then click **Break...**. The Break dialog box appears. See Figure 4-9.

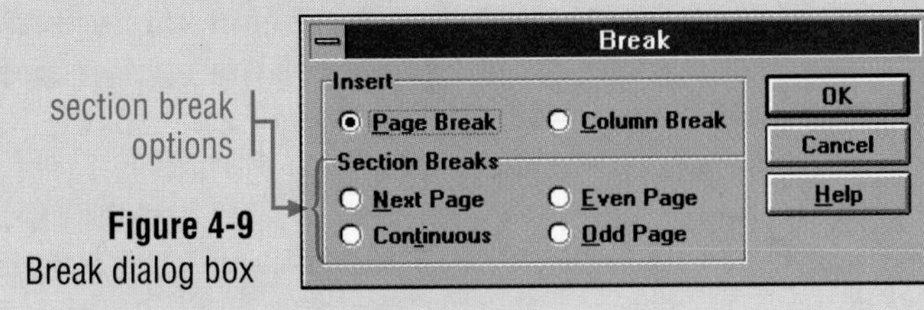

Figure 4-9
Break dialog box

Jessica wants to insert a section break, and she wants the text after the break to start on a new page.

❸ Click the **Next Page radio button** in the Section Breaks section, then click **OK** or press **[Enter]**. A double dotted line and the words "End of Section" are inserted across the page to indicate that a section break has been inserted. Notice that the status bar now indicates that the document has two sections and that the insertion point is on page 2 of section 2. See Figure 4-10.

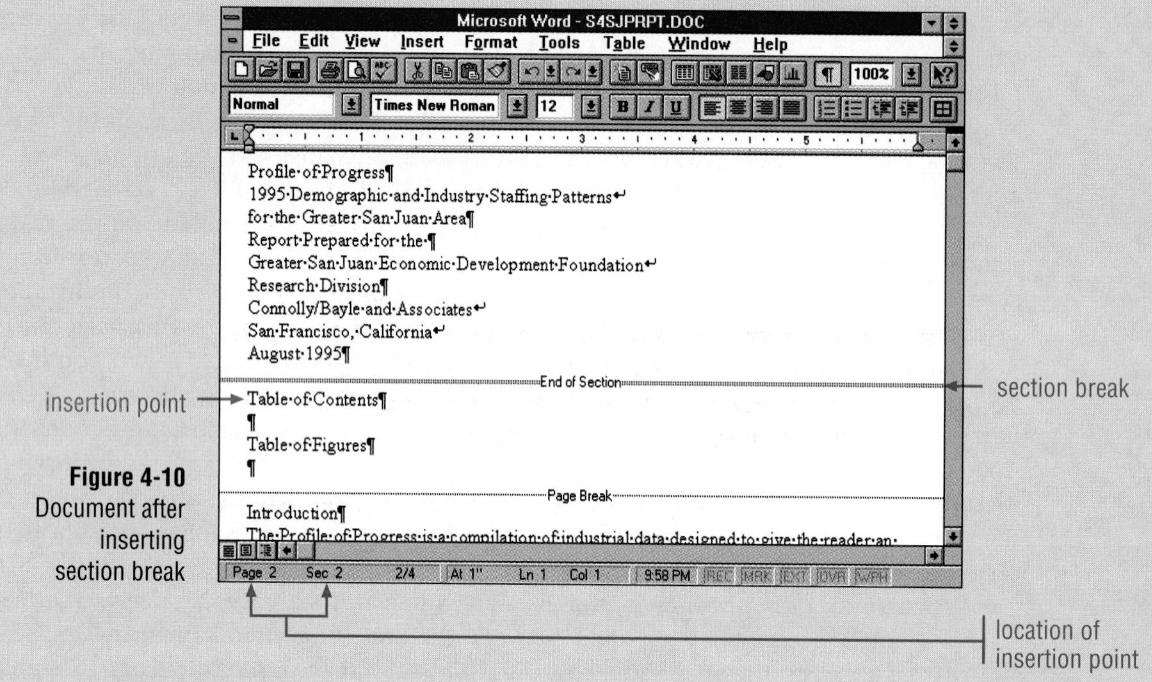

Figure 4-10 Document after inserting section break

❹ Save the changes you have made.

Jessica wants to insert another section break between pages 2 and 3, and she wants the text after the break to start on a new page. She wants 0.75" top and bottom margins for just the text portion of the report.

To insert a section break between pages 2 and 3 then format the sections:

❶ Place the insertion point at the top of page 3, directly before the "I" in Introduction, then press **[Backspace]** to remove the page break.

❷ Click **File** then click **Page Setup...**. The Page Setup dialog box appears, with the Margins tab displayed.

❸ Change the top and bottom margins to 0.75", click the **Apply To list box down arrow**, then click **This Point Forward**. This option inserts a section break before the insertion point and applies the changes you just made to the margins from the section break to the end of the document. See Figure 4-11.

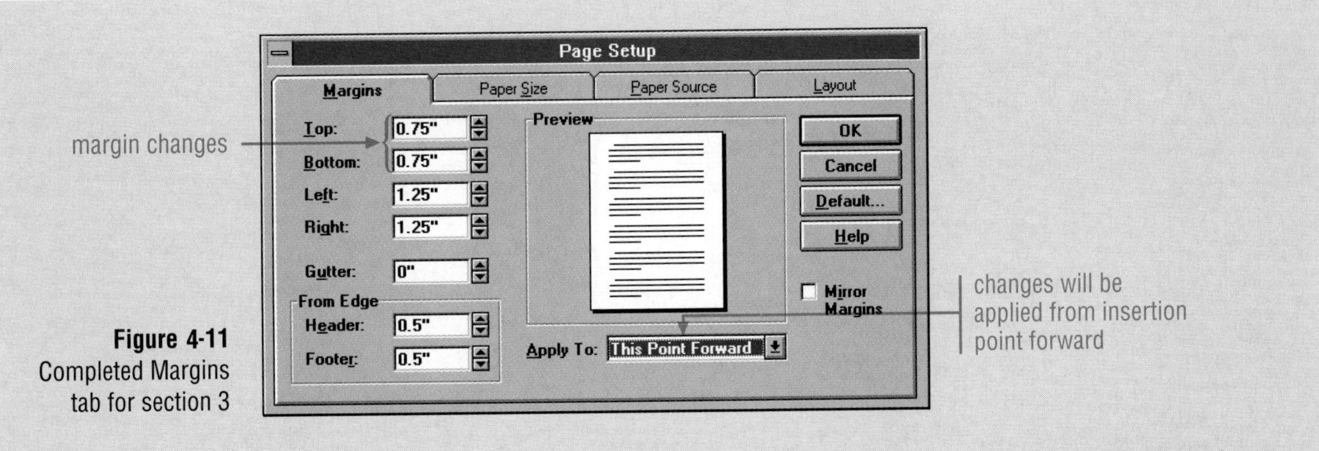

Figure 4-11
Completed Margins tab for section 3

4. Click **OK** or press **[Enter]**. You return to your document. Notice that a section break is inserted between pages 2 and 3, and the status bar indicates that the insertion point is in section 3 of the document.
5. Save the changes you have made.

Now that each part of the document—the title page, the table of contents page, and the body of the report—is in its own section, Jessica can format each section individually.

To start, Jessica can align the title page vertically without affecting the rest of the document. When you align text vertically on a page, you align it between the top and bottom margins.

Before changing the vertical alignment option, Jessica must first move the insertion point into the section to be affected by the change. You can use the Go To command [F5] to move quickly between sections.

To change the vertical alignment of the title page:

1. Press **[F5]**. The Go To dialog box appears.
2. Click **Section** in the Go To What list box, press **[Tab]** to move to the Enter Section Number text box, type **1**, then click **Go To** or press **[Enter]**. The insertion point moves to section 1.
3. Click **Close** in the Go To dialog box.

Now that Jessica has moved the insertion point into section 1, she can change the appropriate page-level options.

4. Click **File** then click **Page Setup...**. The Page Setup dialog box appears.
5. Click the **Layout tab**, click the **Vertical Alignment list box down arrow**, then click **Justified**. See Figure 4-12.

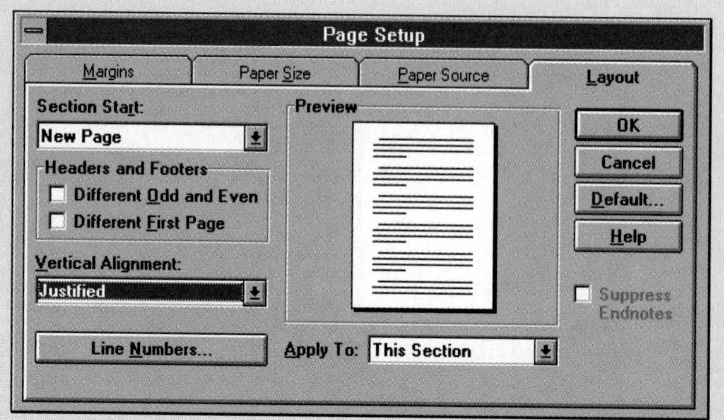

Figure 4-12
Completed Layout tab for section 1

Notice that the Apply To list box indicates that the selected option applies only to the current section. The default Top alignment option in the Vertical Alignment list box places the contents of a page at the top margin; the Center option centers paragraphs between the top and bottom margins; and the Justified option increases the space between paragraphs on a page so that the first line is even with the top margin and the last line is even with the bottom margin.

6. Click **OK** or press **[Enter]**.

Looking at the document in normal view, Jessica cannot tell if the title page is justified. She decides to switch to print preview.

7. Click the **Print Preview button** on the Standard toolbar (or click **File** then click **Print Preview**). Notice that the title page is justified between the top and bottom margins. The change in the vertical alignment of a page is a document-level option, but it affects only the section in which it is applied.

   TROUBLE? If you do not see all three pages side by side in print preview, click the Multiple Pages button on the Print Preview toolbar, then drag across the grid to display three pages.

8. Click the **Close button** on the Print Preview toolbar.
9. Save the changes you have made.

Inserting Headers and Footers in a Multi-Section Document

Jessica indicated that she wanted to have headers and footers in all sections of her document, but, as she noted in Figure 4-1, she wants the title page and table of contents page to have both a header and a footer, and the rest of the document to have a slightly different header from the title page and no footer. Unlike other page-level formatting options applied to a section, changes to headers or footers in a section are connected to one another; that is, the header or footer in the first section becomes the default for the entire document. In addition, changes to the headers or footers in any section are reflected in all sections.

Jessica begins by inserting a header and footer in section 1.

To insert a header and footer in section 1:

1. Place the insertion point in section 1, click **View**, then click **Header and Footer**. The Header text area, now labeled Header -Section 1, appears along with the Header and Footer toolbar.

Jessica wants the header and footer on the title page to be a ¾ point double rule across the page.

2. Click the **Borders button** on the Formatting toolbar, click the **Line Style list box down arrow**, then click the **¾ pt double rule**.

Jessica wants the rule to appear at the bottom of the line space in the header.

3. Click the **Bottom Border button** on the Borders toolbar. The double rule appears across the line space.

Next Jessica wants to place the same type of rule at the top of the line space in the footer for section 1.

4. Click the **Switch Between Header and Footer button** on the Header and Footer toolbar. The insertion point moves into the Footer text area, which is labeled Footer -Section 1.

The ¾ pt double rule is already selected on the Borders toolbar, so Jessica must only specify its placement.

5. Click the **Top Border button** on the Borders toolbar to place the double rule at the top of the line space in the footer.
6. Click the **Close button** on the Header and Footer toolbar.

Jessica wants to see how the changes to the title page appear.

7. Click the **Print Preview button** on the Standard toolbar (or click **File** then click **Print Preview**). See Figure 4-13.

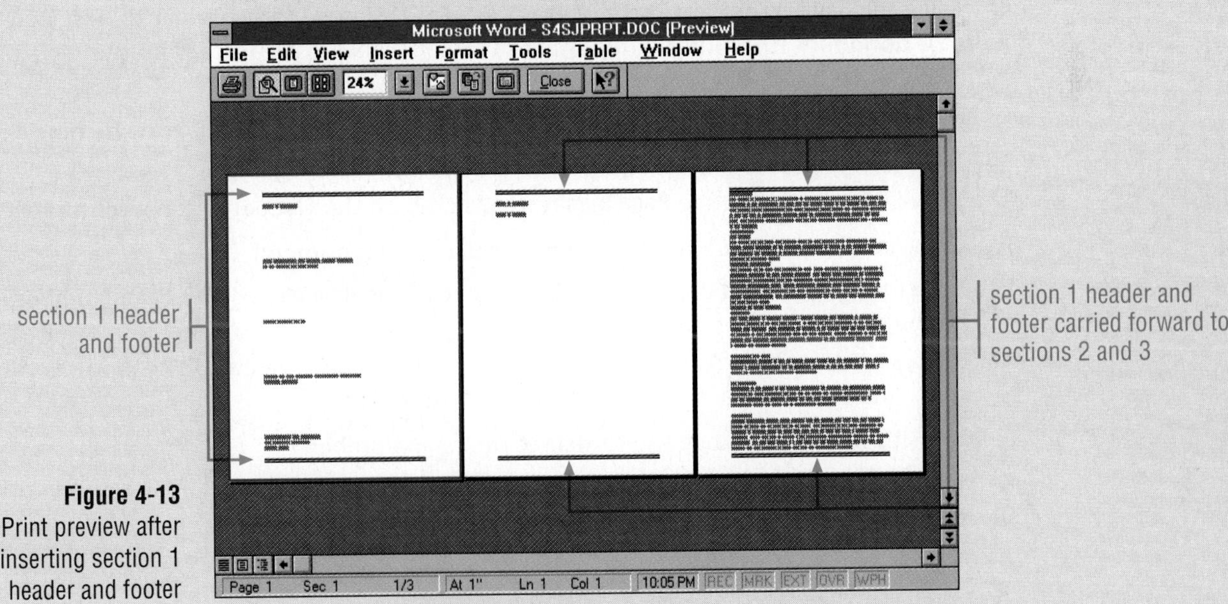

Figure 4-13
Print preview after inserting section 1 header and footer

Notice that the header and the footer appear on all pages of the document, even the pages in sections 2 and 3. Header and footer changes carry forward through the next sections of a document unless they are changed.

TROUBLE? If you do not see all three pages side by side in print preview, click the Multiple Pages button on the Print Preview toolbar, then drag across the grid to display three pages.

8. Click the **Close button** on the Print Preview toolbar to return to your document.
9. Save the changes you have made.

Jessica wants the same type of rule in both the header and footer of section 2, which is the table of contents page, but she also wants the page number to appear at the center bottom of this page as a lowercase roman numeral. She must, therefore, change the format of the page number. Furthermore, she doesn't want a page number to appear in section 1.

To change the page number format:

1. Place the insertion point in section 2, click **View**, then click **Header and Footer**. Notice that the label "Same as Previous" appears at the right of the Header text area and that the Same as Previous button on the Header and Footer toolbar is highlighted. This indicates that, unless you specify otherwise, the header for this section will be the same as the header of the previous section (in this case, section 1).

Jessica wants the double rule to appear in the section 2 header, so she can now move to the footer.

2. Click the **Switch Between Header and Footer button** on the Header and Footer toolbar. The Footer -Section 2 text area appears with Same as Previous displayed on the right.

Jessica does *not* want the section 2 footer connected to the section 1 footer because she does not want a page number to appear in section 1.

3. Click the **Same as Previous button** on the Header and Footer toolbar to deselect that option for this footer. The Same as Previous label disappears from the Footer -Section 2 text area.

Next Jessica wants to insert a page number at the center of the footer, and she needs to change the number format to lowercase roman numerals.

4. Press **[Tab]** then click the **Page Numbers button** on the Header and Footer toolbar.

Jessica wants the page number to be a lowercase roman numeral.

5. Select the page number, click **Insert**, then click **Page Numbers...**. The Page Numbers dialog box appears.
6. Make sure the Show Number on First Page check box is selected. This option will place the page number on the first page *of the section*.

Now Jessica needs to change the format of the page number.

7. Click **Format...**. The Page Number Format dialog box appears.
8. Click the **Number Format list box down arrow**, then click **i, ii, iii, ...**. See Figure 4-14.

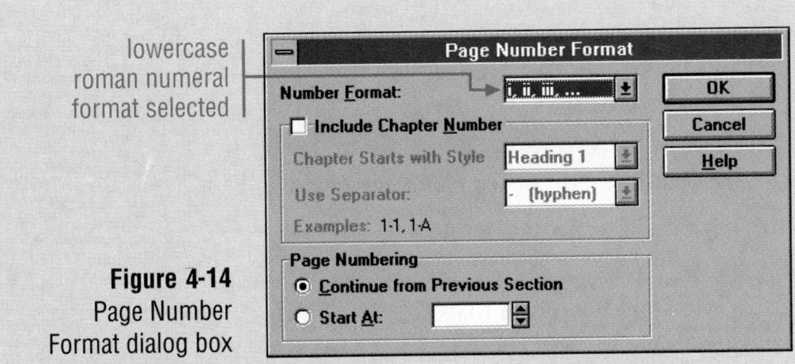

Figure 4-14
Page Number Format dialog box

9. Click **OK** or press **[Enter]**. You return to the Page Numbers dialog box. Click **OK** or press **[Enter]**. The page number format is changed to a lowercase roman numeral.
10. Close the Header and Footer toolbar, then save the changes you have made.

Jessica now needs to format the header and footer for section 3 of her document. Recall from Figure 4-1 that she wants to keep the ¾ point double rule in the section 3 header and add the name of the report and the page number. She wants to eliminate the footer altogether in section 3, because she'll include the page number in the header in this section.

To create different headers and footers in section 3 of the document:

1. Place the insertion point in section 3, click **View**, then click **Header and Footer**. The Header -Section 3 text area opens. Notice that the Same as Previous label appears on the right and that the Same as Previous button on the Header and Footer toolbar is highlighted, indicating that the header in this section is connected to the previous section. Also notice that the double rule doesn't appear completely because the header is too close to the text of the report.

Jessica doesn't want the header in the previous section of the document to be the same as the header in this section.

2. Click on the Header and Footer toolbar to deselect it. The double rule remains at the bottom of the line space, but the changes you are about to make to this header will not be reflected in the section 2 header.
3. Type **Profile of Progress**, then press **[Tab]** twice. Type **Page**, press **[Spacebar]**, then click the **Page Numbers button** on the Header and Footer toolbar. Select **Profile of Progress** then change its font formatting to **14 pt**, **Bold**, and **Italic**. Select **Page 3** then change its font formatting to **Bold**. Deselect the text.

Next Jessica wants to insert a blank line after the header so that it is not so close to the body of the report.

4. Click the **right mouse button** on the header text to open the shortcut editing and formatting menu, click **Paragraph...** (or click **Format** then click **Paragraph...**), then increase the Spacing After option to **12 pt**. Click **OK** or press **[Enter]**. The additional space inserted below the double rule in the header makes the double rule completely visible now.
5. Click the **Switch Between Header and Footer button** on the Header and Footer toolbar. Notice that the Footer text area is labeled Footer -Section 3, that the Same as Previous label appears on the right, and that the button is again highlighted.

Jessica wants to delete the footer in section 3 completely.

6. Click [icon] on the Header and Footer toolbar to deselect the button, then click the **No Border button** [icon] on the Borders toolbar.
7. Drag across the page number in the footer to select the number, then press **[Del]**.
8. Click the **Close button** on the Header and Footer toolbar to return to your document.

Jessica wants to see how the headers and footers look.

9. Click the **Print Preview button** [icon] on the Standard toolbar (or click **File** then click **Print Preview**). Notice that the footer has been eliminated from section 3.
10. Click the **Close button** on the Print Preview toolbar, then save the changes you have made.

If you want to take a break and resume the tutorial at a later time, you can close the current document then exit Word by double-clicking the Control menu box in the upper-left corner of the screen. When you want to resume the tutorial, start Word, place your Student Disk in the disk drive, then complete the screen check procedure described in Tutorial 1. Open the document S4SJPRPT.DOC, then continue with the tutorial.

■ ■ ■

Jessica has finished inserting headers and footers into the different sections of her document. Now she is ready to add paragraph-level and font-level formatting, which will also enhance her report's appearance.

Defining Styles

In Tutorial 3, you learned to apply Word's predefined styles. If you do not want to use any of the styles in Word's predefined templates, you can define your own. Word provides two ways to define a new style. You can define a style by **example**—that is, by basing it on an existing paragraph that already contains the formatting options you want. You can also use the Style command on the Format menu to define a style by specifying each formatting option. Unless you indicate otherwise, user-defined styles are automatically added to the NORMAL template and, therefore, are available globally to all documents.

Jessica used the Style Gallery to preview the styles in Word's existing templates, but she did not find a template that contained the styles to fit her needs exactly. She decides to define her own styles, then save them in a customized document template, which she can use again if she needs to format a similar report.

Defining a New Style by Example

Jessica wants to apply a variety of paragraph and font formats to each line of text on the title page to improve its appearance. She wants some lines to be Arial, bold, 24 point, with centered alignment, a 72 point line space before, and a 36 point line space after. She wants other lines to be Arial, bold, 18 point, with centered alignment, and a 36 point line space before and after. Rather than apply each formatting option individually to each line, Jessica decides to define two new styles to contain the set of formats she wants to use, then apply the appropriate style to each line on the title page.

One way to define a new paragraph style is by example—that is, by using a paragraph that already has all the formats you want.

REFERENCE WINDOW

Defining a New Style by Example

- Select the example paragraph.
- Click the Style list box on the Formatting toolbar to highlight the name of the current style.
- Type a name for the new style.
- Press [Enter].

Jessica wants to define a new style for those lines on the title page that will be Arial, bold, 24 point, with centered alignment, a 72 point line space before, and a 36 point line space after the paragraph. She must first create an example paragraph with these formats, then define the style by example. Because she will be accumulating these styles eventually in a customized document template and doesn't want these new styles to be available globally, Jessica must also prevent Word from automatically saving them to the NORMAL template, thus altering the NORMAL template.

To define a new style by example:

1. Click **Tools** then click **Options...**. The Options dialog box appears.
2. Click the **Save tab**.

Jessica wants to make sure that the styles she creates and modifies will not affect the NORMAL template.

3. Click the **Prompt to Save Normal.dot check box**, then click **OK** or press **[Enter]**. When you select this setting, Word will display a message box asking you to confirm any changes to the NORMAL template when you exit Word. This will allow you to avoid changing the NORMAL template inadvertently.

   TROUBLE? If the check box is already activated, skip to Step 4 below.

4. Move to page 1 then select the first line, **Profile of Progress**. Notice that the Normal style is in effect for the selected text.
5. Change the font formatting of the selected text to **Arial**, **24 pt**, **Bold**; then change its paragraph formatting options to a **72 pt** line space before, a **36 pt** line space after, and **Centered** alignment.

Now that you have created your "example," you will use it as the basis for your new style. The text should still be selected.

6. Click the style named **Normal** in the Style list box on the Formatting toolbar. This highlights the Normal style.

   TROUBLE? Do not click the Style list box arrow and choose Normal from the list of styles. Simply select (highlight) the word Normal in the Style list box on the Formatting toolbar.

Next Jessica names the new style by typing a name to replace the highlighted word, Normal. A style name can be up to 253 characters in length and can contain spaces.

Style names are case sensitive so "*T*itle 1" and "*t*itle 1" can be the names given to two different styles. Make sure that names of new styles are unique and are not used by Word in its own predefined styles. Jessica wants to name this style "Title 1."

7. Type **Title**, press **[Spacebar]**, then type **1**. "Title 1" replaces "Normal" in the Style list box.
8. Press **[Enter]** then deselect the text.

Jessica next wants to see if the new style has been added to the Style list.

9. Click the **Style list box down arrow** to display the Style list. The style name Title 1 is added to the Style list. The style in effect for the current location of the insertion point is highlighted. See Figure 4-15.

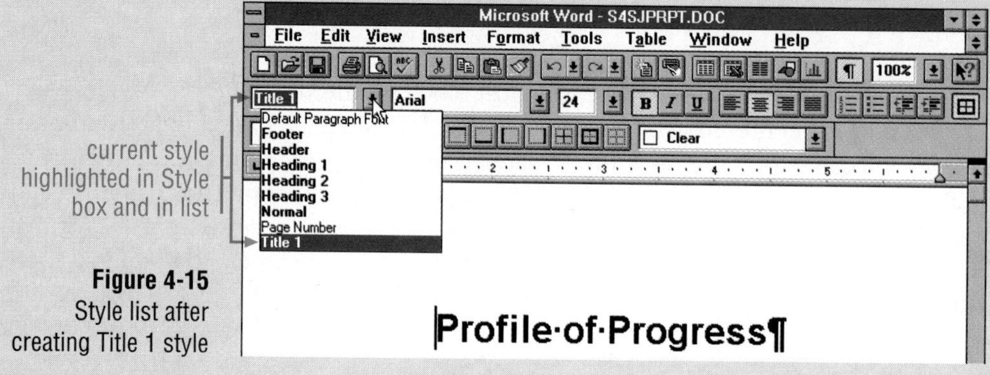

Figure 4-15 Style list after creating Title 1 style

10. Press **[Esc]** to close the Style list.

Jessica will apply this newly defined style to other parts of the title page later, but now she needs to define another style for use on her title page.

Defining a New Style Using the Style Command

The second method for defining a new style is to use the Style command on the Format menu. Essentially you build the style from scratch by specifying all the formatting options you want the style to contain.

REFERENCE WINDOW

Defining a New Style Using the Style Command

- Click Format then click Style.... The Style dialog box appears.
- Click New.... The New Style dialog box appears.
- Type the name of the new style in the Name text box.
- Click Format to specify the formatting options you want assigned to the style.
- Click OK to close the New Style dialog box and save your changes.
- Click Apply to apply the new style to the current paragraph or click Close to close the Style dialog box without applying the style.

Jessica wants to name her second new style "Title 2" and to define it with the following attributes: Arial, bold, 18 point, centered alignment, and a 36 point line space before and after the paragraph. She decides to define this new style by using the Style command on the Format menu.

To define the new title style using the Style command:

❶ Select the paragraph "1995 Demographic and Industry Staffing Patterns for the Greater San Juan Area," click **Format**, then click **Style....** The Style dialog box appears with Normal highlighted and checked in the Styles list box. See Figure 4-16. The Styles list includes only those styles that have been used in the current document. The two Preview sections show the current paragraph and character styles. The Description section describes the formatting characteristics of the style applied to the selected paragraph.

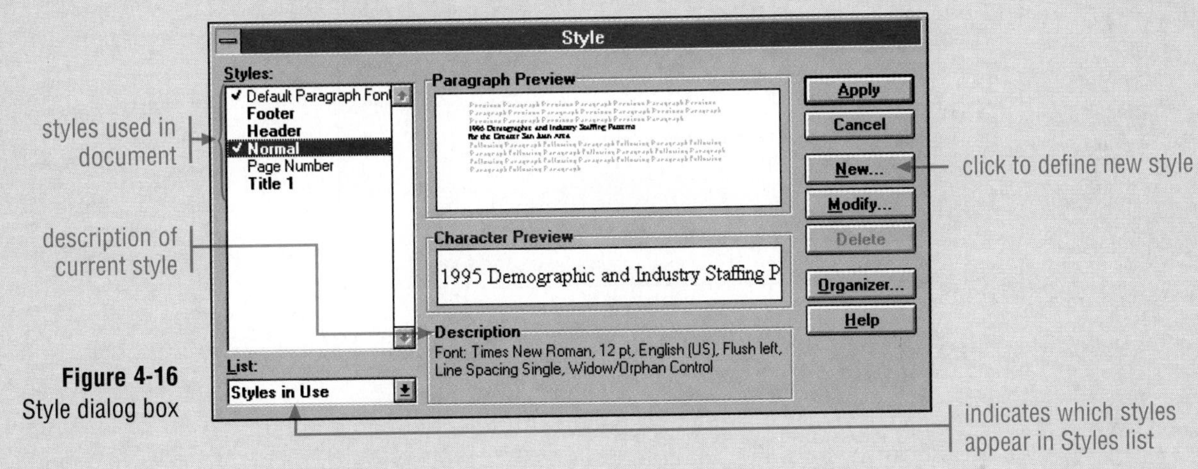

Figure 4-16
Style dialog box

TROUBLE? If your Styles list includes more styles than shown in Figure 4-16, click the List box down arrow then click Styles in Use.

Jessica needs to define a new style.

❷ Click **New....** The New Style dialog box appears, with the suggested style name "Style1" highlighted in the Name text box.

Now Jessica needs to replace the style name supplied by Word with "Title 2."

❸ Type **Title 2** in the Name text box to name the new style. You can specify whether the new style is a paragraph style or a character style, which style the new style is based on, and even which style is in effect after you create a new paragraph with the new style then press [Enter]. Unless otherwise specified, new styles are based on the style applied to the paragraph currently selected.

"Normal +" appears in the Description section, signifying that the new style is based on the Normal style but could also contain additional features specifically defined for the new style. The name of the base style Normal also appears in the Based On list box.

Next Jessica specifies the formatting characteristics of the new style.

❹ Click **Format** then click **Font....** The Font dialog box appears.

❺ Change the font formatting options to **Arial**, **Bold**, **18 pt**.

6. Click **OK** or press **[Enter]**. The selected font options are previewed and added to the description in the New Style dialog box.

Now Jessica is ready to add the paragraph formatting options to the Title 2 style definition.

7. Click **Format** then click **Paragraph...**. The Paragraph dialog box appears.
8. Increase the Spacing Before and Spacing After options to **36 pt**, then click **Centered** in the Alignment list box. Click **OK** or press **[Enter]**. You return to the New Style dialog box. Notice that the Description section has been updated to reflect the formatting characteristics of the new style. See Figure 4-17.

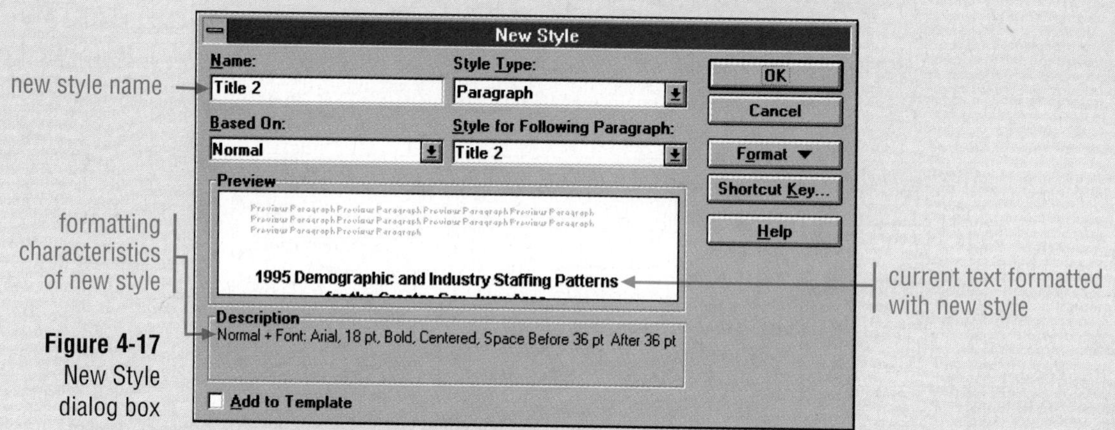

Figure 4-17 New Style dialog box

9. Click **OK** or press **[Enter]**. You return to the Style dialog box. Title 2 has been added to the Styles list.

Jessica can now apply the new style to the selected paragraph or close the Style dialog box. Because she is not going to define any more styles for the title page, she decides to apply the style from the Style dialog box.

10. Click **Apply** in the Style dialog box or press **[Enter]**. The new style is applied to the currently selected paragraph.

Jessica is now ready to apply the styles she has defined to the rest of the text on the title page.

Applying Styles

Word provides several methods to apply styles. As you learned in Tutorial 3, the easiest way to apply a style to selected text is to use the Style list box.

Jessica has created two new styles for her title page, and now she is ready to apply those styles to the appropriate paragraphs.

To apply styles on the title page and the table of contents page:

1. Select the paragraph **Report Prepared for the**. The currently assigned style is Normal.
2. Click the **Style list box down arrow** on the Formatting toolbar, then click **Title 2**. All the formatting attributes you defined for the Title 2 style are applied to the selected text.

3. Select the paragraph **Greater San Juan Economic Development Foundation Research Division**, then apply the Title 1 style to it.
4. Select the paragraph **Connolly/Bayle and Associates, San Francisco, California, August 1995**, then apply the Title 2 style to it.

Jessica decides to use the Repeat command ([F4]) to apply the Title 2 style to the titles on the table of contents page.

5. Place the insertion point in the title Table of Contents on page 2, then press **[F4]**. Word repeats the steps to apply the Title 2 style to the selected paragraph.
6. Place the insertion point in the title Table of Figures on page 2, then press **[F4]**. The Title 2 style is applied to the selected text.

Jessica wants to see how the title page and the table of contents page will appear when printed with the new styles applied.

7. Click the **Print Preview button** on the Standard toolbar (or click **File** then click **Print Preview**). Notice the changes to the first two pages of the document. See Figure 4-18.

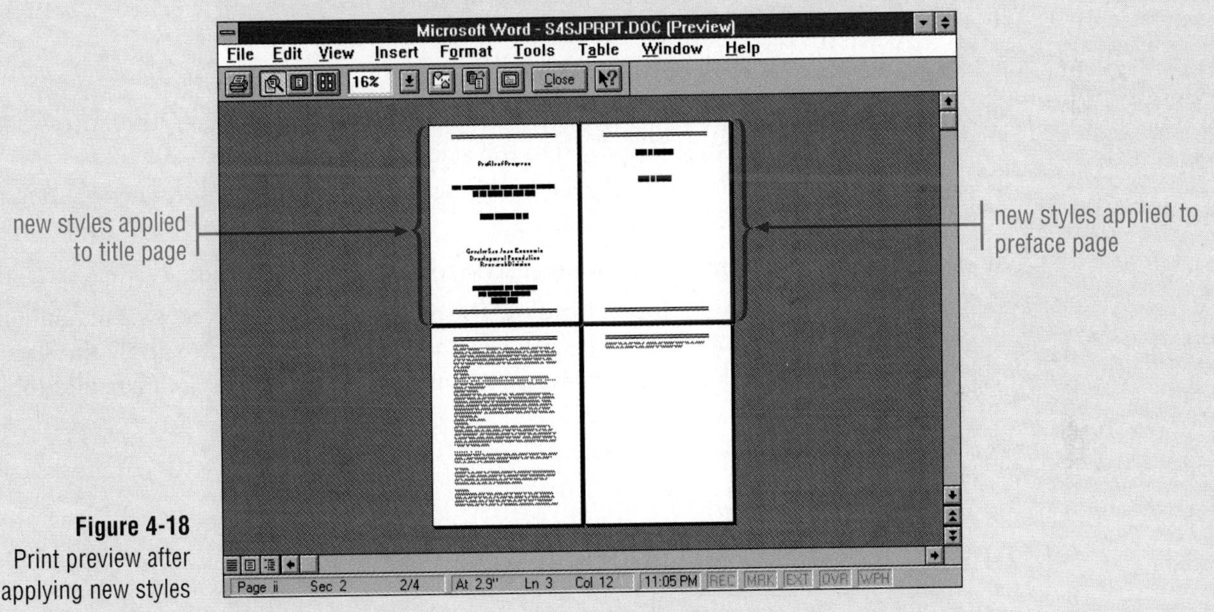

Figure 4-18
Print preview after applying new styles

TROUBLE? If you do not see all four pages in print preview, click the Multiple Pages button on the Print Preview toolbar, then select four pages.

8. Click the **Close button** on the Print Preview toolbar.
9. Save the changes you have made.

Jessica has defined and applied styles to the title page and to the table of contents page. Now she wants to apply the predefined styles Heading 1, Heading 2, and Heading 3 to the headings in her report. Rather than using the Formatting toolbar to apply these styles, she uses the Style command on the Format menu.

To apply the heading styles using the Style command:

1. Place the insertion point at the beginning of the heading Introduction on page 3.
2. Click **Format** then click **Style...**. The Style dialog box appears. Notice that only the styles specifically applied to text in the current document appear in the list of styles; the predefined styles Heading 1, Heading 2, and Heading 3 are not available as they are in the Style list box on the Formatting toolbar.

Jessica wants to apply the Heading 1 style to Introduction.

3. Click the **List box down arrow**, then click **All Styles**. All of the user-defined and predefined styles are listed in the Styles list box.
4. Scroll through the list of styles, then click **Heading 1**.
5. Click **Apply** or press **[Enter]**. The Heading 1 style is applied to the heading Introduction.

Next Jessica wants to apply the Heading 2 style to the headings Methodology, Summary of Major Findings, and Conclusion.

6. Place the insertion point in the heading Methodology, then repeat Steps 2, 4, and 5 except click **Heading 2** in the Styles list.

Jessica uses the Repeat command to apply the Heading 2 style to the other headings.

7. Place the insertion point in the heading Summary of Major Findings, then press **[F4]**. The Heading 2 style is applied to the selected heading.
8. Place the insertion point in the heading Conclusion, then press **[F4]**. The Heading 2 style is applied to the selected heading.

Next Jessica wants to apply the Heading 3 style to the remaining headings.

9. Place the insertion point in the heading The Sample, then repeat Steps 2, 4, and 5 except click **Heading 3** in the Styles list. Use the Repeat command to apply the style to the headings: Collection Procedures, Population, Diversifying San Juan, and Job Openings.
10. Save the changes you have made.

Applying Styles Using Shortcut Keys

Jessica has applied styles to all elements of her document except to the main text paragraphs of the report. She decides to use one of Word's predefined styles, Body Text Indent, for the main text paragraphs. Because she has so many paragraphs to format with the Body Text Indent style, she decides to define a shortcut key for that style to reduce the amount of time she'll spend formatting the text.

To assign a shortcut key for applying the Body Text Indent style:

1. Place the insertion point in the first text paragraph on page 3, click **Format**, then click **Style...**. The Style dialog box appears. Because you are going to apply the style after assigning the shortcut key, you need to place the insertion point in a paragraph to which you want to apply the style before choosing the Style command.
2. Scroll through the Styles list, then click **Body Text Indent**. The Description section identifies the characteristics of the selected style.
3. Click **Modify...**. The Modify Style dialog box appears. See Figure 4-19.

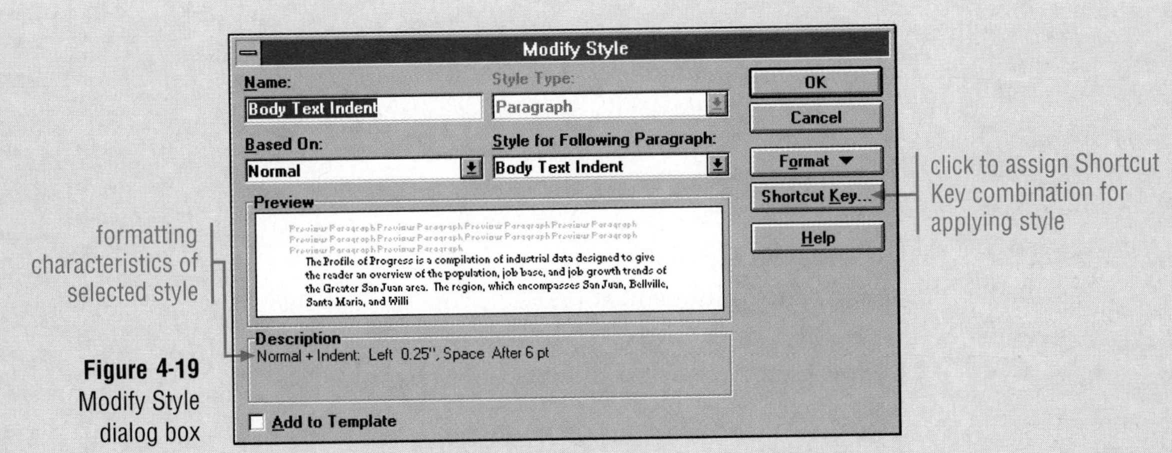

Figure 4-19 Modify Style dialog box

❹ Click **Shortcut Key...**. The Customize dialog box appears with the Keyboard tab displayed.

Word already has some shortcut keys assigned to options so Jessica must be certain to use a unique combination of keys. She decides to try [Alt][b] as the shortcut key combination.

❺ Press and hold **[Alt]** and press **[b]**. Release both keys. Notice that "Alt+B" appears in the Press New Shortcut Key text box, and a message appears indicating that this key combination is currently unassigned as a shortcut key combination for any other style.

❻ Click **Assign** or press **[Enter]**. The assigned shortcut key appears in the Current Keys list box. See Figure 4-20.

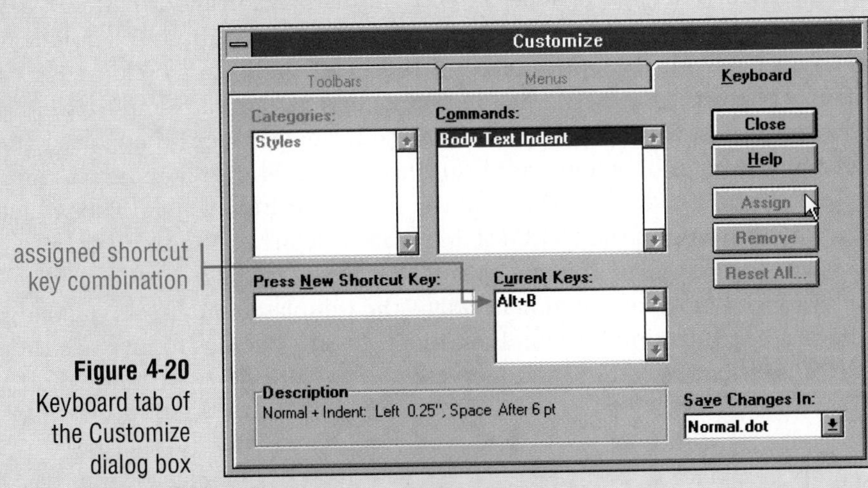

Figure 4-20 Keyboard tab of the Customize dialog box

❼ Click **Close** or press **[Enter]**. You return to the Modify Style dialog box.

❽ Click **OK**. You return to the Style dialog box.

❾ Click **Apply** or press **[Enter]**. The attributes of the Body Text Indent style are applied to the selected paragraph.

❿ Save the changes you have made.

Next Jessica needs to apply this style to the remaining text paragraphs in her document.

To apply the Body Text Indent style using the shortcut key:

1. Place the insertion point in the second text paragraph ("The sample for…").
2. Press **[Alt][b]**. The attributes of the Body Text Indent style are applied to the selected paragraph.
3. Continue applying the Body Text Indent style to the remaining text paragraphs using the assigned shortcut key combination.
4. Save the changes you have made.

Jessica decides to view the document in page layout view so that she can see how it will print.

5. Click the **Page Layout View button** in the status bar (or click **View** then click **Page Layout**).
6. Scroll through the document in page layout view.
7. Click the **Normal View button** in the status bar (or click **View** then click **Normal**) to return to normal view.

Jessica has applied styles to all elements of her document, but as she looked at the document in page layout view, she decided that she could further improve its appearance by modifying some of the styles.

Modifying Styles

You can redefine, or modify, any style, either Word's predefined styles or those that you have defined. Word automatically updates any paragraphs previously formatted with the style, thus saving you time and assuring consistent formatting throughout the document.

Jessica isn't satisfied with the appearance of the headings in her document. Rather than making manual changes to each heading in the document, she can simply redefine the formatting characteristics of the styles applied to these headings. Word then automatically updates each heading in the document based on these styles. She decides to redefine the Heading 1, Heading 2, and Heading 3 styles, and the Body Text Indent style. These changes would automatically be stored in the NORMAL template if Jessica had not first chosen the Save option to have Word confirm changes to the NORMAL template. In this way, Jessica can modify the styles for her report document only—the template will remain unchanged.

To make the heading Introduction stand out more, Jessica decides to increase the font size, change it to all uppercase letters, and increase the amount of space before and after the heading.

To modify the Heading 1 style using the Style command:

1. Move to the top of page 3, then place the insertion point in the heading Introduction. "Heading 1" appears in the Style list box on the Formatting toolbar.
2. Click **Format** then click **Style…**. The Style dialog box appears.
3. Click **Modify…**. The Modify Style dialog box appears. Notice that the current definition of the Heading 1 style appears in the Description section.
4. Click **Format**, click **Font…**, then make the following changes: **24 pt, All Caps**.
5. Click **OK** or press **[Enter]**. You return to the Modify Style dialog box.

Next Jessica needs to change the paragraph formats for the Heading 1 style.

6. Click **Format**, click **Paragraph...**, then make the following changes: **Spacing Before 48 pt** and **Spacing After 24 pt**.
7. Click **OK** or press **[Enter]**. You return to the Modify Style dialog box. Notice the change in the Description section.
8. Click **OK** or press **[Enter]**. You return to the Style dialog box.
9. Click **Close**. Notice that the newly defined Heading 1 style is applied to Introduction. This is the only instance of a Heading 1 style in the report.
10. Save the changes you have made.

You can also redefine a style by example using the Style list box on the Formatting toolbar.

REFERENCE WINDOW

Redefining a Style by Example

- Select a paragraph formatted with the style you want to redefine.
- Make the necessary formatting changes.
- Click the Style list box on the Formatting toolbar to select the style name in effect.
- Press [Enter]. The Reapply Style dialog box appears.
- Click the "Redefine the style using the selection as an example?" radio button, then click OK or press [Enter].

To keep the remaining headings proportional in size to the Introduction heading, Jessica also needs to redefine the predefined styles, Heading 2 and Heading 3. She used each of these styles throughout her document.

To redefine the Heading 2 style by example:

1. Select the heading **Methodology**. The entire heading must be highlighted. The Style list box on the Formatting toolbar changes to reflect the style applied to Methodology, which is Heading 2.

Jessica wants to change several formatting options.

2. Click the **right mouse button** on the selected text (or click **Format**), click **Font...**, then make the following changes: **18 pt**, **All Caps**.
3. Click **OK** or press **[Enter]**.
4. Click the **right mouse button** on the selected text (or click **Format**), click **Paragraph...**, then make the following changes: **Spacing Before 24 pt** and **Spacing After 6 pt**.
5. Click **OK** or press **[Enter]**.

Jessica wants to add a rule to the Heading 2 style definition.

6. Click the **3/4 pt single rule** in the Line Style list box on the Borders toolbar, if necessary, then click the **Top Border button**.

TROUBLE? If the Borders toolbar is not displayed, click the Borders button on the Formatting toolbar, then complete Step 6.

Now that Jessica has an example of the way she wants the Heading 2 style to appear, she is ready to redefine the style.

❼ Click the **Style list box** on the Formatting toolbar to select Heading 2, then press **[Enter]**. The Reapply Style dialog box appears for Heading 2. See Figure 4-21.

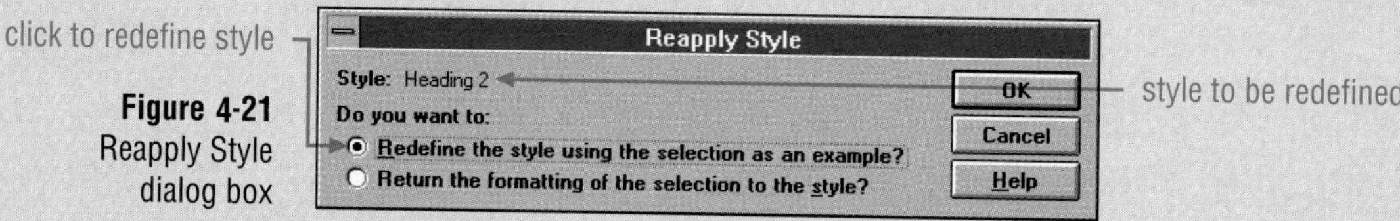

Figure 4-21 Reapply Style dialog box

❽ Make sure the radio button for the option "Redefine the style using the selection as an example?" is selected, then click **OK** or press **[Enter]**.

❾ Scroll through the document to see that the new formatting characteristics for the Heading 2 style were also applied automatically to the headings Summary of Major Findings and Conclusion.

Next Jessica wants to change the formatting characteristics for the Heading 3 style and for the Body Text Indent style.

To redefine the Heading 3 and Body Text Indent styles by example:

❶ Select the heading **The Sample**. The entire heading must be highlighted. Use the Formatting toolbar to make the following font formatting changes: **Arial**, **14 pt**.

❷ Click the right mouse button on the selected text (or click **Format**), click **Paragraph...**, then make the following changes: **Spacing After 12 pt**. (Spacing Before is already set to 12 pt.)

❸ Click **OK** or press **[Enter]**.

❹ Click the **Style list box** on the Formatting toolbar to select Heading 3, then press **[Enter]**. The Reapply Style dialog box appears.

❺ Make sure the radio button for the option "Redefine the style using the selection as an example?" is selected, then click **OK** or press **[Enter]**. Scroll through the document to see that all headings formatted with the Heading 3 style were automatically updated.

Now Jessica modifies the Body Text Indent style.

❻ Place the insertion point anywhere within a main text paragraph, then drag the indent markers on the ruler to the 1-inch mark.

❼ Click the **Justify button** on the Formatting toolbar.

❽ Repeat Steps 4 and 5 to complete modifying the Body Text Indent style by example.

9. Save the changes you have made.
10. Hide the Borders toolbar. See Figure 4-22.

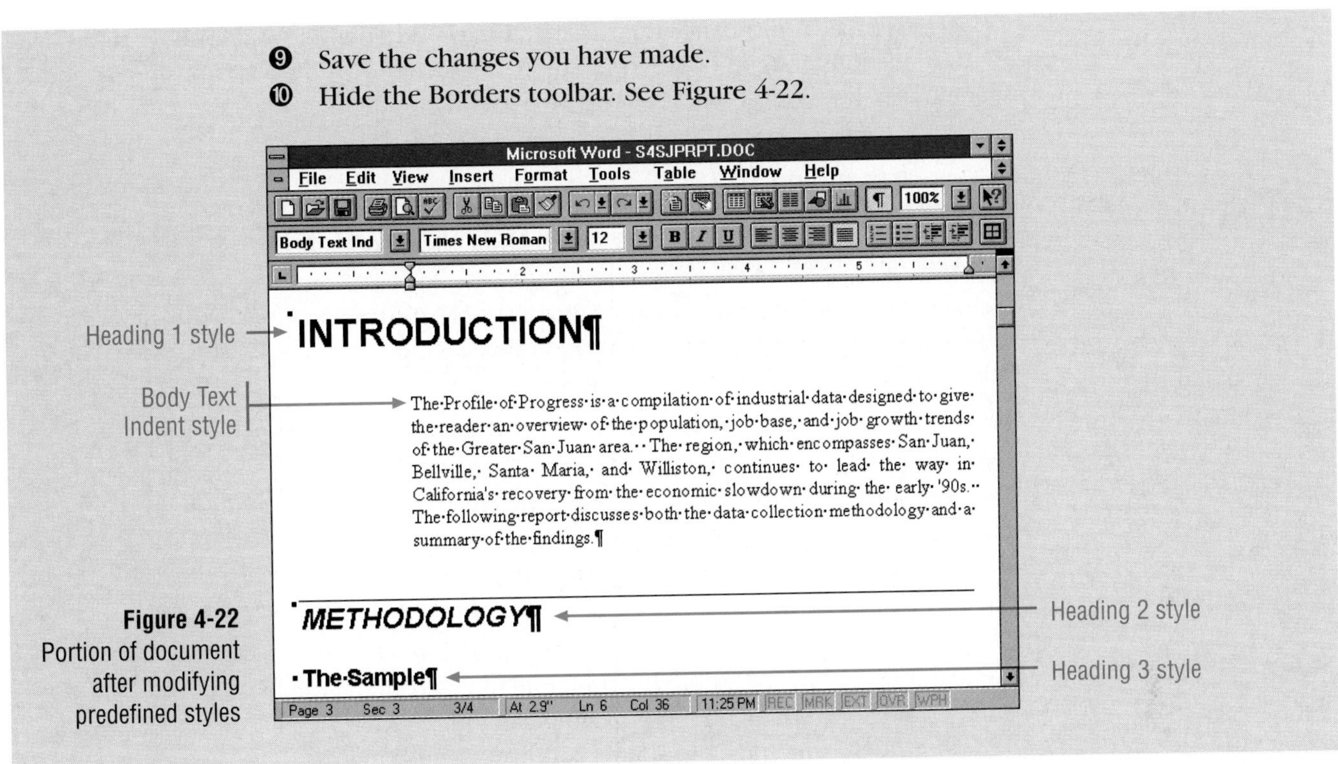

Figure 4-22 Portion of document after modifying predefined styles

Now that she has finished editing and formatting the text of her report, Jessica is ready to transfer the charts she created previously in another document.

Transferring Data Between Documents

One of the hallmarks of the Windows environment is the ease with which you can move or copy information. In previous tutorials, you learned ways to move or copy text *within* a document either by using the Clipboard or by using the drag-and-drop feature. The options for moving or copying information from one Word document to *another* Word document are basically the same as moving and copying text within a document. You can use either the Clipboard or the drag-and-drop feature.

Using the Clipboard to Transfer Data Between Documents

One way to transfer data between documents is by using the Clipboard. You can cut or copy selected text from one document, then paste the contents of the Clipboard in another document. Because the text is on the Clipboard, you can paste the cut or copied text as many times as you need to as many different documents as you need, including documents in other Windows applications.

Jessica thinks that the use of charts will enable the readers of the report to understand more easily the numeric data that she has gathered in her research. A **chart** is a visual display of numerical data in graph form. Jessica used Microsoft Graph to create the charts she needs to insert into the preliminary report and saved them in the file C4SJCHRT.DOC. Microsoft Graph is an **applet**, a small application designed to work with Windows programs such as Microsoft Word or Excel. To learn more about the use of Microsoft Graph, consult the *Microsoft Word User's Guide*.

Now Jessica needs to transfer the three charts she created in C4SJCHRT.DOC to their appropriate locations in S4SJPRPT.DOC. She marked the locations previously with bookmarks. She'll use the Go To command to move to the bookmarks.

To transfer the first chart using the Clipboard:

1. Press **[F5]** to display the Go To dialog box, then click **Bookmark** in the Go to What list box.
2. Click **figure1** in the Enter Bookmark Name list box, if necessary, then click **Go To** or press **[Enter]**. The insertion point moves to the selected bookmark. Close the Go To dialog box.

Now Jessica must open the document that contains the three charts she created.

3. Open the file C4SJCHRT.DOC from your Student Disk. S4SJPRPT.DOC remains open, but it is not visible. Scroll through the chart document to view the three charts Jessica created: a 3-D column chart of population growth data for the area, a 3-D pie chart showing the different types of businesses in the area, and a 2-D stacked column chart showing projected job openings in the area. Each chart is on a separate page.

Jessica will follow the "select, then do" principle to copy the first chart to the Clipboard. To select a chart, you move the mouse pointer over the chart, then click. *Selection handles*, resembling small boxes, appear around the chart to indicate that it is selected. A selected chart is just as susceptible to change as selected text, *so be careful*.

4. Move the mouse pointer over the 3-D Population column chart.
5. Click the chart. Selection handles appear around the chart to indicate that it is selected. See Figure 4-23.

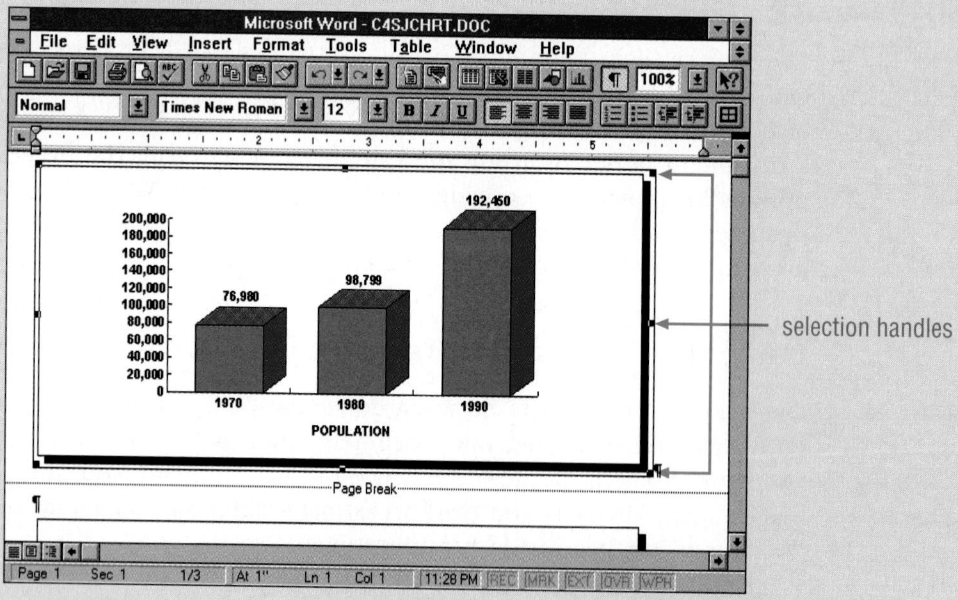

Figure 4-23 Selected Population chart

TROUBLE? If you accidentally delete a chart, click the Undo button on the Standard toolbar (or click Edit then click Undo Delete).

Now that the chart is selected, Jessica can copy it to the Clipboard.

❻ Click the **Copy button** on the Standard toolbar (or click **Edit** then click **Copy**).

Next Jessica will paste the copied chart from the Clipboard to its appropriate location in S4SJPRPT.DOC, but first she must make it the active document.

❼ Click **Window** then click **S4SJPRPT.DOC** to make it the active document. Notice that the insertion point is in the same location (figure1 bookmark) as it was before you switched. C4SJCHRT.DOC is still open, just not visible.

❽ Click the **Paste button** on the Standard toolbar (or click **Edit** then click **Paste**). The Population chart is pasted from the Clipboard to the report document. Notice that the bookmark has increased in size to match the size of the chart. See Figure 4-24. Press [↓] to see the entire chart.

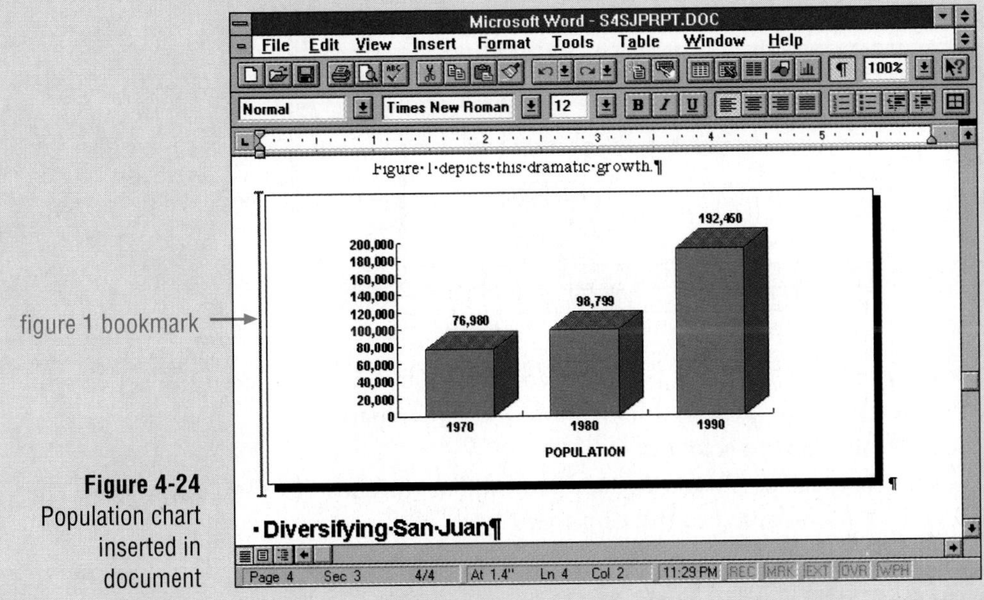

Figure 4-24
Population chart inserted in document

❾ Save the changes you have made.

Jessica next wants to transfer the pie chart from the chart document to the report document, but she decides to view both documents at once rather than switching between the two.

To arrange open documents on the screen:

❶ Go to the location of the figure2 bookmark in the report document, then close the Go To dialog box.

Rather than switch to the chart document, Jessica now arranges the screen so that both the chart document and the report document are visible at the same time.

❷ Click **Window**. Notice that C4SJCHRT.DOC and S4SJPRPT.DOC are the only two documents open.

TROUBLE? If other documents are listed, select them, then close them.

❸ Click **Arrange All**. Each document appears in its own document window, and S4SJPRPT.DOC is the active document. Notice also that the active document has its own document Control menu box and sizing buttons. See Figure 4-25.

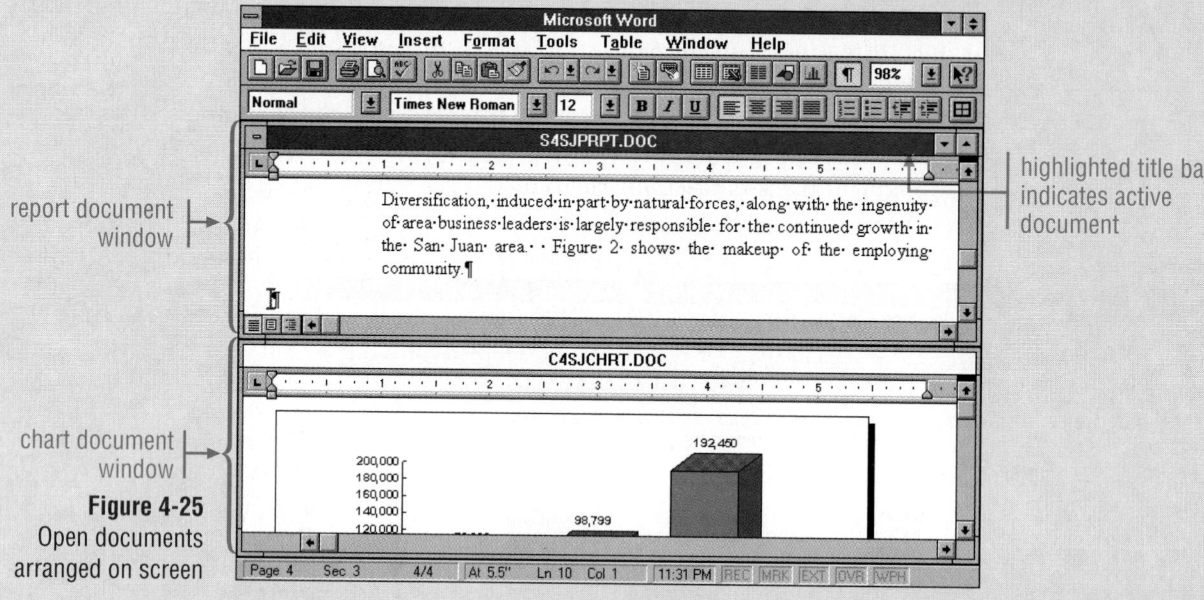

Figure 4-25
Open documents arranged on screen

❹ Click in the C4SJCHRT.DOC window (or press **[Ctrl][F6]**) to make it the active window, then move to page 2, the location of the pie chart.

❺ Click the pie chart to select it.

❻ Click the **Copy button** on the Standard toolbar (or click **Edit** then click **Copy**). The selected chart is copied to the Clipboard.

Next Jessica must paste the copied chart from the Clipboard to the report document.

❼ Click in the S4SJPRPT.DOC window (or press **[Ctrl][F6]**) to make it the active document. The insertion point is located at the figure2 bookmark.

❽ Click the **Paste button** on the Standard toolbar (or click **Edit** then click **Paste**). The pie chart is copied to its new location in the report document.

❾ Save the changes you have made.

Jessica has one more chart to copy to the report document. She decides to use the drag-and-drop feature to transfer the stacked column chart.

Using Drag-and-Drop Between Documents

In Tutorial 2 you learned to use drag-and-drop to move text within a document. With Word, you can also use drag-and-drop to *copy* text within a document simply by holding down the Control key as you drag the selected text. If you have the screen arranged so that two documents are visible at once, you can even use drag-and-drop to transfer data *between* documents.

To copy the third chart between the two documents using drag-and-drop:

1. Go to the location of the figure3 bookmark in the report document, then close the Go To dialog box. The insertion point moves to the location of the figure3 bookmark.
2. Click in the C4SJCHRT.DOC window (or press **[Ctrl][F6]**) to make it the active window, then move to page 3.
3. Scroll until part of the stacked column chart is visible, then select the chart.
4. Move the mouse pointer over the selected chart. Notice that the pointer changes to [pointer icon] just as it does when it is over selected text.
5. Press and hold **[Ctrl]** and hold down the **left mouse button**. The pointer changes to [copy pointer icon] to indicate that you are *copying* rather than *moving* the chart. See Figure 4-26. Do not release [Ctrl] until the copy is complete.

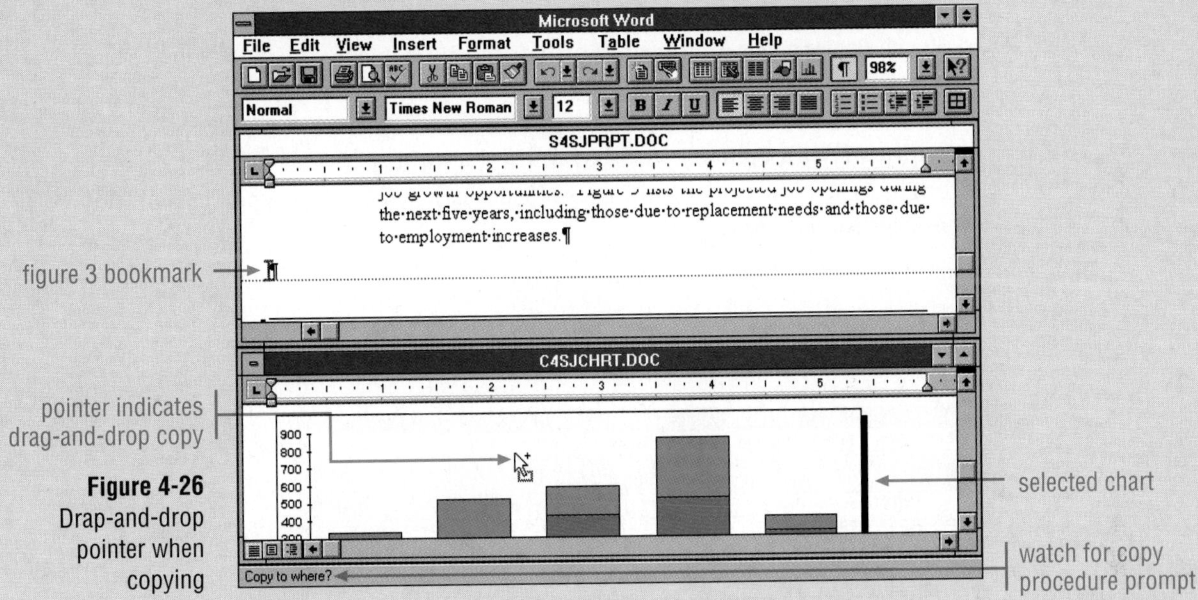

Figure 4-26 Drap-and-drop pointer when copying

6. Drag the selected chart from the chart document over the title bar of C4SJCHRT.DOC until the dashed insertion point of the pointer is after the figure3 bookmark, then release [Ctrl] and the mouse button. The stacked column chart is copied from the chart document to the report and is still selected.
7. Deselect the chart. Remember that when using the drag-and-drop procedure, the selected data is *not* placed on the Clipboard.

   TROUBLE? If you notice that the selected chart was moved instead of copied, you released [Ctrl] too soon. Click the Undo button [Undo icon] on the Standard toolbar (or click Edit then click Undo Move), then repeat Steps 3 through 7.

Jessica no longer needs to see both documents at the same time.

8. Click anywhere in the C4SJCHRT.DOC (or press **[Ctrl][F6]**), then close it without saving changes.

S4SJPRPT.DOC is still open but needs to be maximized.

9. Click the **Maximize button** for the S4SJPRPT.DOC window.
10. Save the changes you have made.

Now that Jessica has transferred the charts to the report document, she needs to format them by centering them and adding captions.

Adding Captions to Charts

Jessica formatted the charts when she created them in Microsoft Graph, but she thinks she can improve their appearance by centering them horizontally and adding an identifying caption.

To center the first chart and add a caption:

1. Go to the figure1 bookmark, then click the chart to select it. If you use the Go To dialog box to move to the bookmarks in the steps, make sure you close the dialog box before continuing.
2. Click the **Center button** on the Formatting toolbar. The chart is centered across the page.
3. With the chart still selected, click **Insert** then click **Caption...**. The Caption dialog box appears with Figure 1 inserted in the Caption text box.
4. After Figure 1, type : (a colon), press **[Spacebar]** twice, then type **Population Growth in the Greater San Juan Area**.

The Position list box indicates that the caption is to be inserted below the selected chart.

5. Click **OK** or press **[Enter]**. The caption is centered below the chart. See Figure 4-27.

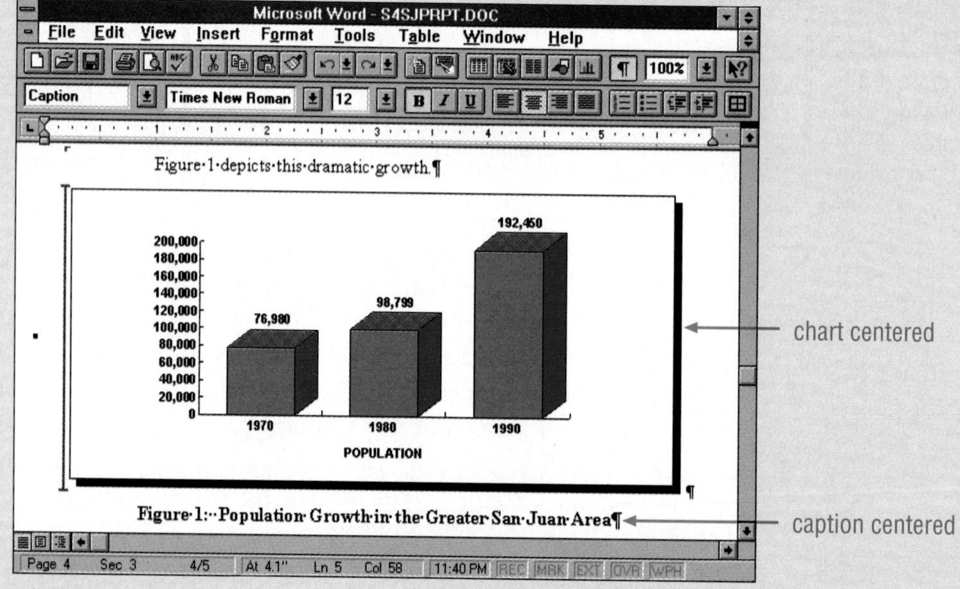

Figure 4-27
Formatted Population chart

6. Go to the figure2 bookmark, then select the pie chart. Repeat Steps 2 through 5, except insert the caption **Figure 2: Industrial Mix in the Greater San Juan Area**.
7. Go to the figure3 bookmark, then select the stacked column chart. Repeat Steps 2 through 5, except insert the caption **Figure 3: Projected Job Openings**.
8. Save the changes you have made.

Jessica wants to see how the pages split now that she has finished formatting her charts.

❾ Click the **Print Preview button** on the Standard toolbar (or click **File** then click **Print Preview**). Notice the location of the charts on pages 4 and 5. See Figure 4-28.

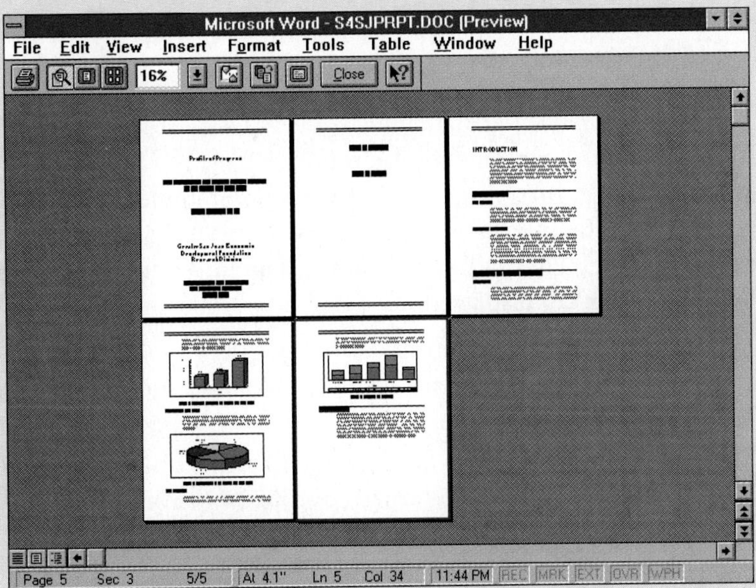

Figure 4-28
Formatted text and charts in print preview

TROUBLE? If you do not see all five pages, click the Multiple Pages button on the Print Preview toolbar, then select six pages.

❿ Click the **Close button** on the Print Preview toolbar.

Jessica no longer needs to see the bookmarks for the charts because she has inserted all three charts in her document. She can now deactivate the bookmarks.

To deactivate the bookmarks:

❶ Click **Tools**, click **Options...**, then click the **Bookmarks check box** on the View tab to deselect this option.

❷ Click **OK** or press **[Enter]**.

Jessica has finished formatting her report, and now she is ready to insert the table of contents.

Creating the Preface Page

In business reports, particularly long business reports, it's customary to include one or more preface pages immediately following the title page. The **preface pages** typically provide a list of the main topics so that a reader can go quickly to that topic without having to read the whole report. This list of main topics is called a **table of contents**. Word allows you to create a table of contents quickly, as well as a table of figures or a table of tables, if you have consistently applied styles to the various levels of topic headings or captions within a document.

Creating a Table of Contents

Jessica wants to insert a table of contents on the preface page between the title page and the text of the report.

To insert the table of contents for the report:

1. Move to page 2, then place the insertion point immediately before the blank paragraph below the title Table of Contents.
2. Click **Insert** then click **Index and Tables...**. The Index and Tables dialog box appears with the Index tab displayed.
3. Click the **Table of Contents tab**.

Word provides a variety of formats for the Table of Contents page, but Jessica prefers the Formal style.

4. Click **Formal** in the Formats box. Notice that the sample text in the Preview section changes to reflect the new formats. See Figure 4-29.

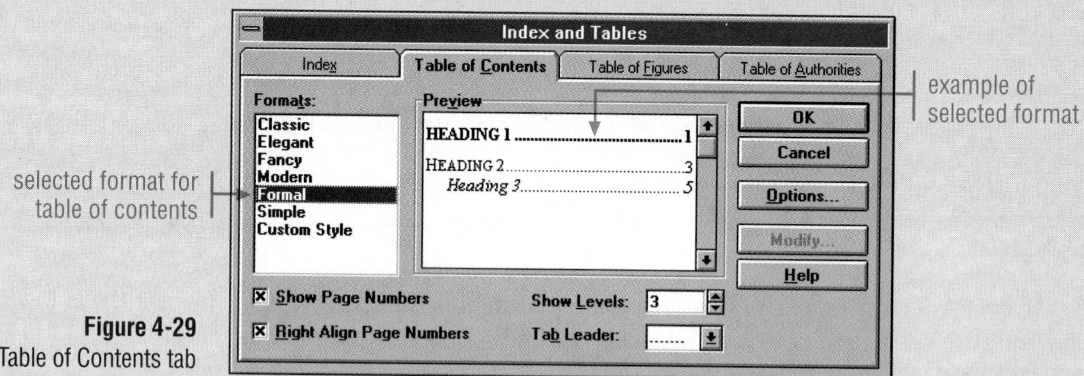

Figure 4-29
Table of Contents tab

Word will look for any text labeled with Heading 1, Heading 2, or Heading 3 styles, then display the text along with its corresponding page number in the Table of Contents.

5. Click **OK** or press **[Enter]**. The Table of Contents based on text labeled with Heading 1, 2, or 3 styles appears at the insertion point. Recall that the title page used the styles Title 1 and Title 2, therefore, the text labeled with those styles was not included in the Table of Contents.
6. Save the changes you have made.

Creating a Table of Figures

Next Jessica wants to insert a table of figures, which will list the names of the charts and their locations within the report. She will put the table of figures on the same page as the table of contents.

To insert a table of figures:

1. Place the insertion point before the blank paragraph below the title Table of Figures on page 2.
2. Click **Insert** then click **Index and Tables....**
3. Click the **Table of Figures tab**.

Jessica wants the table of figures to appear in a format similar to the table of contents.

4. Click **Formal** in the Formats list box. See Figure 4-30.

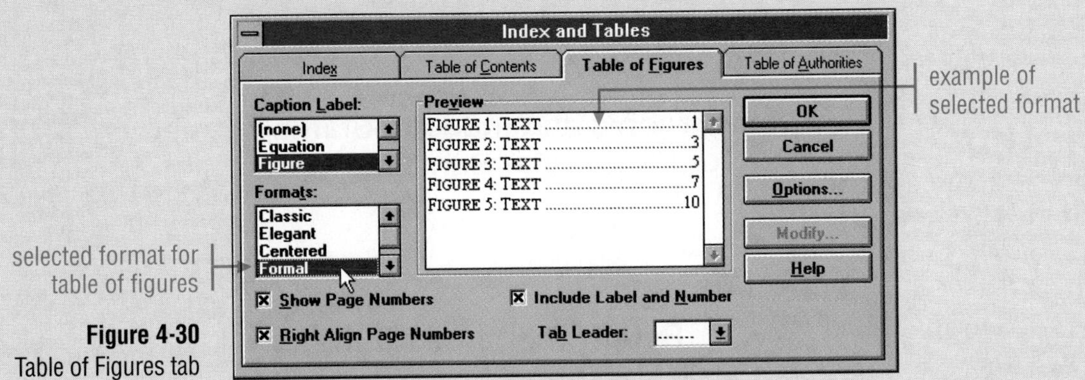

Figure 4-30
Table of Figures tab

5. Click **OK** or press **[Enter]**. Word builds a table of figures based on the captions inserted below each chart.
6. Save the changes you have made.
7. Hide the Borders toolbar, if necessary.

Printing the Report

With her report complete, Jessica is anxious to print the document, but she decides to spell check it one more time because she has inserted text since she conducted the grammar check. After spell checking, she'll preview then print her document.

To spell check, preview, then print the document:

1. Click the **Spelling button** on the Standard toolbar (or click **Tools** then click **Spelling...**) to spell check the document. If additional spelling errors are found, correct them, then save the changes.
2. Click the **Print Preview button** on the Standard toolbar (or click **File** then click **Print Preview**). Jessica is satisfied with the appearance of her report.
3. Click the **Print button** on the Print Preview toolbar. The printed document should be similar to Figure 4-31 on the following pages.
4. Click the **Close button** on the Print Preview toolbar.

Profile of Progress

1995 Demographic and Industry Staffing Patterns for the Greater San Juan Area

Report Prepared for the

Greater San Juan Economic Development Foundation Research Division

Connolly/Bayle and Associates
San Francisco, California
August 1995

Figure 4-31
Jessica's completed report (page 1 of 5)

Table of Contents

Table of Figures

Figure 4-31
Jessica's completed report (page 2 of 5)

Profile of Progress **Page 3**

INTRODUCTION

The Profile of Progress is a compilation of industrial data designed to give the reader an overview of the population, job base, and job growth trends of the Greater San Juan area. The region, which encompasses San Juan, Bellville, Santa Maria, and Williston, continues to lead the way in California's recovery from the economic slowdown during the early '90s. The following report discusses both the data collection methodology and a summary of the findings.

METHODOLOGY

The Sample

The sample for this study was selected from the first quarter 1995 Employment and Wages report submitted to the California Department of Labor by the region's employers. The universe was stratified by standard industrial classification codes. Procedures involved all certainty cases.

Collection Procedures

The majority of the data was collected by mail. Each selected establishment received a structured schedule for their specific industry. The survey form included the following: instructions, occupational titles and definitions, business identification, and a standard industrial classification code. Survey procedures included three follow-up mailings to non-respondents. The telephone was used extensively to clarify data and to canvass critical non-respondents. The demographic statistics for the region were extracted from the 1990 census data.

SUMMARY OF MAJOR FINDINGS

Population

The 1995 Profile of Progress presents a growth statistic that continues to display the dynamic growth of the San Juan region. In 1990, the total population of the San Juan region was 192,457. This represents an increase of 48 percent over the 1980 figures and an increase of 150 percent

Figure 4-31
Jessica's completed report (page 3 of 5)

Profile of Progress **Page 4**

increase over the 1970 figures. Greater numbers of jobs in the defense and computer industries accounted primarily for the population increases. Figure 1 depicts this dramatic growth.

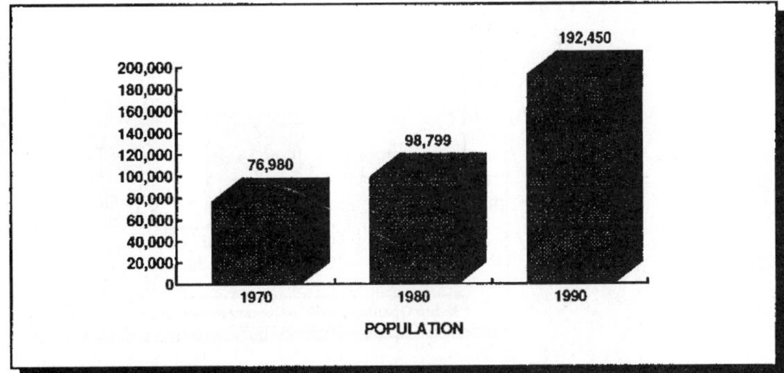

Figure 1: Population Growth in the Greater San Juan Area

Diversifying San Juan

Diversification, induced in part by natural forces, along with the ingenuity of area business leaders is largely responsible for the continued growth in the San Juan area. Figure 2 shows the makeup of the employing community.

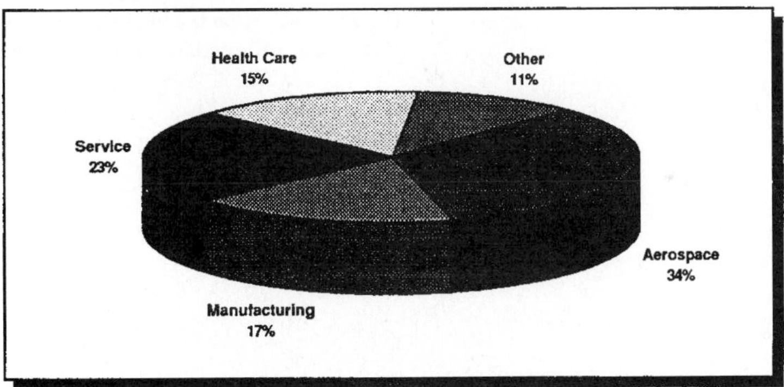

Figure 2: Industrial Mix in the Greater San Juan Area

Job Openings

According to our survey of the region's employers, on average, the occupational groups requiring the most education will also see the fastest

Figure 4-31
Jessica's completed report (page 4 of 5)

job growth opportunities. Figure 3 lists the projected job openings during the next five years, including those due to replacement needs and those due to employment increases.

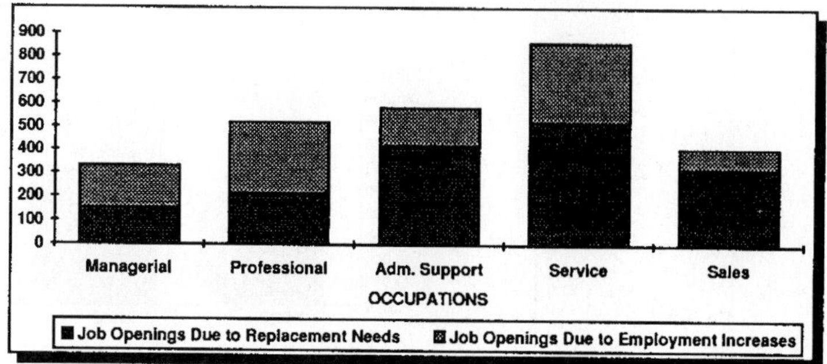

Figure 3: Projected Job Openings

CONCLUSION

Current population growth trends indicate that the Greater San Juan area will provide a steady job force for the next five to ten years. The diversity of the area's industries will continue to provide 4,000 to 5,000 new jobs over the next five years if current trends continue. These jobs will be largely in the professions, administrative support, and service industries. The San Juan region is a vital area that has grown rapidly over the past two decades and will continue to grow well into the twenty-first century.

Figure 4-31
Jessica's completed report (page 5 of 5)

Jessica has printed her document, but before she quits Word she wants to create a customized document template that will contain all the formatting and styles she has worked so hard to define in this report.

Creating a Customized Document Template

While Word's predefined document templates are indeed powerful, they might not exactly fit your needs, so you can create your own customized document templates. Once created, you use the user-defined document templates in the same way you use the predefined templates. Word provides you with several ways to create a customized document template, but the easiest way is to create a template from an existing document.

Jessica divided the original report document into three sections, each with its own specific formats such as headers and footers, margins, and vertical alignment. Although the formats and the styles she defined will be the same for future reports she might create, the text is likely to be different. Thus, her customized report template needs only to contain the styles and the section breaks. She must first prepare her document to be saved as a document template.

To prepare the document as a template:

❶ Make sure you have saved your most recent changes to S4SJPRPT.DOC.

Jessica wants to preserve the formatting in each of the three sections that she has created so she cannot delete any of the section breaks. She does not need any of the text in the document, however.

❷ Move to page 1, then select all the text on page 1 up to, but not including, the section break between pages 1 and 2. By not deleting the section break, the page-level changes made specifically for this section will be preserved.

❸ Press **[Del]**. Word deletes the text, but the styles applied to the text are still available.

Next Jessica moves to the page containing the table of contents. She does not want to delete the section break between pages 2 and 3.

❹ Move to page 2. Select the table of contents that you inserted, but *do not include* the title "Table of Contents" or the blank paragraph below the inserted table of contents.

❺ Press **[Del]**.

❻ Select the table of figures that you inserted, but *do not include* the title "Table of Figures" or the blank paragraph below the inserted table of figures.

❼ Press **[Del]**. The section break between pages 2 and 3 should not be deleted.

Finally, Jessica needs to delete all of the text in the report itself.

❽ Place the insertion point at the top of page 3, then press **[Ctrl][Shift][End]** to select all text and charts from the insertion point to the end of the document.

❾ Press **[Del]**.

Now Jessica is ready to save her prepared document as a customized document template.

To save the document as a template.

❶ Click **File** then click **Save As...**. The Save As dialog box appears.

❷ Click the **Save File as Type list box down arrow**, then click **Document Template**.

Ordinarily you would save your document templates to the Template subdirectory of the Winword directory along with Word's predefined document templates, but you will need to save this template to your Student Disk.

❸ Type **a:\s4report** in the File Name text box. Word will automatically add the template extension "DOT" to the filename. See Figure 4-32.

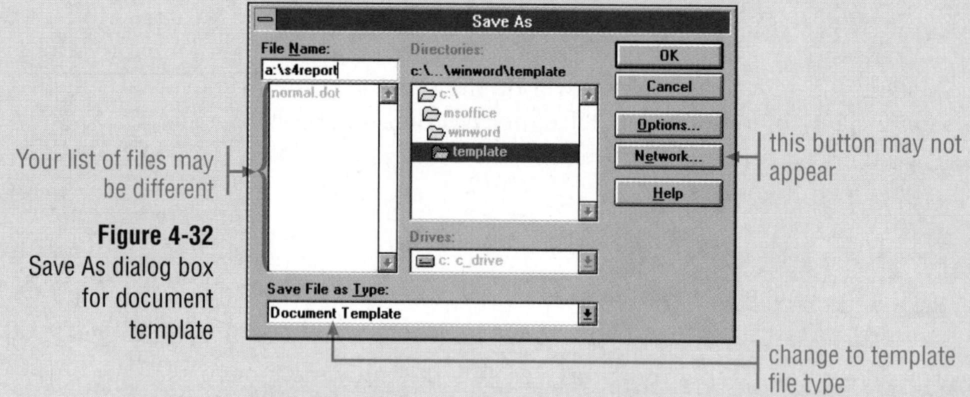

Figure 4-32 Save As dialog box for document template

❹ Click **OK** or press **[Enter]**. Notice the change in the title bar.

For future reference, Jessica wants to print the style sheet, which is a list of the formats defined for each style, for her customized document template.

❺ Click **File** then click **Print...**.

❻ Click the **Print What list box down arrow**, then click **Styles**.

❼ Click **OK** or press **[Enter]**. The style sheet is printed.

❽ Close the document and exit Word. A message box appears asking if you want to save the changes you made to NORMAL.DOT. Recall that, at the beginning of this tutorial, you selected the option that displays this dialog box as a precaution. See Figure 4-33.

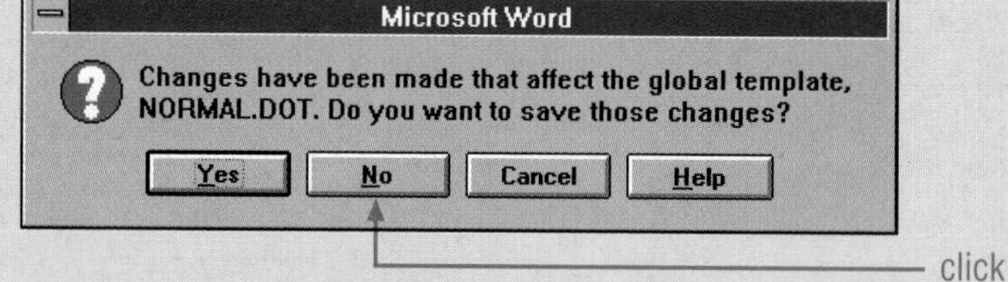

Figure 4-33 Microsoft Word message box

Jessica does *not* want these changes to affect the NORMAL template.

❾ Click **No**. The following message appears: "You placed a large amount of text in the Clipboard. Do you want this text to be available to other applications after Word quits?"

❿ Click **No**.

■ ■ ■

Jessica submits the preliminary report to Henry. He is pleased with the report and is anxious to incorporate it into the final report.

Questions

1. What is the purpose of the Thesaurus feature?
2. What is the purpose of the Grammar feature?
3. What is the purpose of the Bookmark feature?
4. Under what circumstances would you want to insert a section break into a document?
5. What are two methods for inserting section breaks in a document?
6. What is the command sequence to go to section 3 in a document?
7. Describe the procedure for justifying a page vertically.
8. What is the significance of the Same as Previous indication in a header or footer?
9. How do you change page number formats within sections of a document?
10. Describe two procedures for defining a new style.
11. Describe three procedures for applying a new style.
12. Describe two procedures for redefining a style.
13. Describe the procedure for transferring information from one Word document to another Word document using the Clipboard.
14. Describe the procedure for transferring information from one Word document to another Word document using drag-and-drop.
15. Describe the procedure for arranging open documents on the screen so that they are all visible at the same time.
16. How do you know if a chart within a Word document is selected?
17. Describe the procedure for creating a document template from an existing document.
18. What is the procedure for inserting a table of contents in a document?

19. In the Print dialog box, how would you specify that you want to print only pages 3 through 5 in section 2 of a document?

Tutorial Assignments

Start Word, if necessary, and conduct a screen check. Open T4PROFIL.DOC from your Student Disk, then complete the following:

1. Save the document as S4PROFIL.DOC.
2. Use the Thesaurus to substitute an appropriate synonym for the word "variety" in the first paragraph on page 2.
3. Proofread the document for grammar and spelling errors, then save your changes.
4. Insert three bookmarks in the document to mark the appropriate locations of the three referenced charts. Make sure you place the bookmarks on the blank line following the figure references. Use the Tools Options command to display the bookmark symbol in your document, if necessary. Name the bookmarks Chart1, Chart2, and Chart3.
5. Substitute a Next Page section break for the page break between pages 1 and 2.
6. Insert a header into section 2 only. The header is to display on all pages except the first page of section 2. Section 1 should not contain a header at all.
7. Center the title page vertically.
8. Click Tools, click Options..., then click the Save tab, and make sure the Prompt to Save Normal.dot option is selected.
9. On the title page, apply the Heading 1 style to the following paragraphs: Profile of Progress and Greater San Juan Economic Development Foundation. Apply the Heading 2 style to the remaining headings on the title page. Save the changes.
10. Define a new style named "Main Text" for the main text paragraphs in section 2 of the document with the following paragraph formatting options: First Line Indentation set to 0.5" and Line Spacing set to double. Apply the style to the four text paragraphs in the Executive Summary.

11. In the Executive Summary, apply the Title style to the title Executive Summary; apply the Heading 3 style to the headings Population, Diversifying San Juan, and Job Openings.
12. Modify the Heading 3 style so that the Spacing After option is increased to 12 pt. Save the changes.
13. As header text for page 2, and all subsequent pages of section 2, insert the header "Executive Summary" at the left margin and the word "Page" plus the page number code at the right margin. Bold the entire header. Increase the Spacing After option for the header to 12 pt. Save the changes.
14. Open T4ESCHRT.DOC from your Student Disk, then copy the chart on page 1 to the Chart1 bookmark in S4PROFIL.DOC.
15. Copy the chart on page 2 of T4ESCHRT.DOC to the Chart2 bookmark in S4PROFIL.DOC.
16. Copy the chart on page 3 of T4ESCHRT.DOC to the Chart3 bookmark in S4PROFIL.DOC.
17. Close T4ESCHRT.DOC without saving any changes, center Figure 1 across the page, then insert the following caption above it: Figure 1: Population Growth in the Greater San Juan Area.
18. Center Figure 2 across the page, then insert the following caption above it: Figure 2: Industrial Mix in the Greater San Juan Area.
19. Center Figure 3 across the page, then insert the following caption above it: Figure 3: Job Openings. Save the changes.
20. Check the spelling in the document. Preview the document, making adjustments if necessary. (If the heading "Diversifying San Juan" appears as the last line on page 2, insert a hard page break before the heading to force it to the top of page 3.) Print the document.

21. Use Word Help to determine how to specify in the Header text area that page numbers are to start at page 1 of section 2. Make the change in your document, then save the changes as S4EXSUM.DOC. Preview the document then print just section 2.
22. Close the document. Do *not* save any changes to NORMAL.DOT.

Case Problems

1. Reporting on Printers at Buffington Engineering

Clinton Williams works as a hardware specialist in the Internal Information Technology Consulting Group of Buffington Engineering, a large consulting firm specializing in traffic engineering, urban planning, and engineering design of roadways, drainage, and structures. Buffington needs to upgrade the printers used by its staff, and Clinton's supervisor, Lyn Follmar, has assigned him to investigate the alternatives. After his initial investigation, Clinton wrote a memo to Lyn explaining his findings. He is now ready to insert a chart illustrating the data he gathered on printer sales.

Open P4PSALES.DOC from your Student Disk, then complete the following:

1. Save the document as S4BUFENG.DOC.
2. Check grammar usage and spelling in the document.
3. Attach the MEMO2 template to the document.
4. Apply the Title style to the heading Memorandum; apply the Message Header style to the paragraphs beginning "TO:..." through "...1995"; apply the Body Text Indent style to the memo text.
5. Open P4PSCHRT.DOC from your Student Disk, then copy the chart and place it a double space below the memo text in S4BUFENG.DOC.
6. Center the chart across the page.
7. Insert the following caption below the chart: Figure 1: Printer Sales.
8. Save the changes to the document.

9. Preview the document, then print it.

E 10. Use Word Help to find out how to select vertical blocks of text. Select just the memo headings TO:, FROM:, RE:, and DATE:, then bold the vertical block of selected text. Save the document as S4VERT.DOC.

11. Print then close the document.

2. Informational Handout on Inter-Tran Translation Services

Minh Vuong owns a language translation business, Inter-Tran, in Washington, D.C. She has prepared the basic text of a two-page informational handout about the services her company provides. She brings the document to you and asks you to help her improve the appearance of the handout.

Open P4INTRAN.DOC from your Student Disk, then complete the following:

1. Review the document then save it as S4INTRAN.DOC.
2. Insert a Next Page section break between pages 1 and 2.
3. Center page 1 vertically.
4. Change the top margin of section 2 to 2" and the left and right margins to 1.75".
5. Insert appropriate headers and footers in sections 1 and 2.
6. Save the changes.
7. Click Tools, click Options..., then click the Save tab, and make sure the Prompt to Save Normal.dot option is selected.
8. Define attractive styles for the various elements of the handout, including at least two different styles for page 1 and two additional styles for page 2, one for the headings and one for the main text.
9. Apply the styles to the document. Save the changes.
10. Preview the document then print it.
11. Create a document template from S4INTRAN.DOC. Save it to your Student Disk as S4STYLES.DOT.
12. Print a style sheet for the styles used in your document.
13. Close the document. Do *not* save any changes to NORMAL.DOT.

3. Report on Career Opportunities

Write a double-spaced, two- to three-page report on the career opportunities in your major. Base your report on at least two sources, one of which should be the *Occupational Outlook Quarterly*. Consult your school's career counselor or reference librarian for other possible sources. Include in your report a discussion of potential job titles, salary expectations, academic preparation, and job mobility.

Complete the following:

1. Type your report, including a title page. Use different levels of headings to break your report into subtopics. Save the document as S4CAREER.DOC.
2. Edit the report. Check for correct grammar and spelling, but also proofread the report very carefully on your own.
3. Format the report. Center the title page vertically. Insert appropriate headers and footers. Use the standard heading styles in Word or redefine them to fit your preferences. Save the changes.
4. Insert a Table of Contents.
5. Preview the report then print it. Also print the style sheet for the report.
6. Close the document. Do *not* save any changes to NORMAL.DOT.

Index

D

H

I

J

K

M

R

S

U

V

W

TASK REFERENCE

Microsoft Word 6.0 for Windows

Italicized page numbers indicate the first discussion of each task.

TASK	MOUSE	MENU	KEYBOARD
Apply or define a style, *W 134*	Click Style box arrow, click style	Click Format, click Style..., choose style options, click Apply	[Alt][O], [S], choose style options, [Alt][A] or [Enter]
Arrange open documents, *W 179*		Click Window, click Arrange All	[Alt][W], [A]
Attach a template, *W 131*		Click File, click Templates..., choose template, click OK	[Alt][F], [T], choose template, [Enter]
AutoCorrect entries, change, *W 107*		Click Tools, click AutoCorrect..., make changes, click OK	[Alt][T], [A], make changes, [Enter]
Between character spacing, change, *W 90*		Click Format, click Font..., click Character Spacing tab, change spacing options, click OK	[Alt][O], [F], [Alt][R], change spacing options, [Enter]
Bold selected text, *W 43*	B	Click Format, click Font..., click Font tab, click Bold, click OK	[Alt][O], [F], [Alt][N], click Bold, [Enter]
Bookmark, assign, *W 157*		Click Edit, click Bookmark..., enter bookmark information, click Add	[Alt][E], [B], enter bookmark information, [Alt][A] or [Enter]
Border or shading, add to selected paragraphs and tables, *W 85*	⊞, choose border and shading options in Borders toolbar	Click Format, click Borders and Shading..., click appropriate tab, choose border and shading options, click OK	[Alt][O], [B], [B] or [S], choose border and shading options, [Enter]
Bulleted list, create, *W 45*	☰	Click Format, click Bullets and Numbering..., click Bulleted tab, click list format, click OK	[Alt][O], [N], [Alt][B], choose list format, [Enter]
Calculations, perform in tables, *W 124*		Click Table, click Formula..., enter calculation, click OK	[Alt][A], [O], enter calculation, [Enter]
Caption, insert, *W 125*		Click Insert, click Caption..., specify caption and format, click OK	[Alt][I], [I], specify caption and format, [Enter]
Center a selected table, *W 139*		Click Table, click Cell Height and Width..., click Row tab, click Center, click OK	[Alt][A], [W], [Alt][R], [Alt][T], [Enter]
Center selected text, *W 82*	☰	Click Format, click Paragraph..., click Indents and Spacing tab, click Alignment arrow, click Centered, click OK	[Ctrl][E], or [Alt][O], [P], [Alt][I], [Alt][G], choose Centered, [Enter]
Close a document, *W 19*	Double-click document Control menu box	Click File, click Close	[Alt][F], [C]
Column width, change, *W 136*	Drag boundary between columns using ↔	Click Table, click Cell Height and Width..., click Column tab, change column width options, click OK	[Alt][A], [W], [Alt][C], change column width options, [Enter]

TASK REFERENCE

Microsoft Word 6.0 for Windows

Italicized page numbers indicate the first discussion of each task.

TASK	MOUSE	MENU	KEYBOARD
Continuous section break, insert, *W 159*		Click Insert, click Break..., click Continuous, click OK	[Alt][I], [B], [Alt][T], [Enter]
Convert existing text to a table, *W 110*		Click Table, click Convert Text to Table..., choose table options, click OK	[Alt][A], [V], choose table options, [Enter]
Copy selected text or graphics to Clipboard, *W 113*		Click Edit, click Copy	[Ctrl][C], or [Alt][E], [C]
Copy selected text without using the Clipboard, *W 61*			[Shift][F2], place insertion point in location, [Enter]
Cut selected text or graphics to Clipboard, *W 114*		Click Edit, click Cut	[Ctrl][X], or [Alt][E], [T]
Decimal tab, insert, *W 73*		Click Format, click Tabs..., click Decimal, click OK	[Alt][O], [T], [Alt][D], [Enter]
Double-space text, *W 81*		Click Format, click Paragraph..., click Indents and Spacing tab, click Line Spacing arrow, click Double, click OK	[Ctrl][2], or [Alt][O], [P], [Alt][I], [Alt][N], choose Double, [Enter]
Exit Word, *W 26*	Double-click Word Control menu box	Click File, click Exit	[Alt][F4], or [Alt][F], [X]
Font, change, *W 88*	Click Font list box arrow, click font	Click Format, click Font..., click Font tab, click font, click OK	[Alt][O], [F], [Alt][N], choose font, [Enter]
Formats, display, *W 135*	Click , then click text		
Formatting toolbar, activate/deactivate, *W 14*		Click View, click Toolbars..., click Formatting, click OK	[Alt][V], [T], click Formatting, [Enter]
Go to a position in a document, *W 76*		Click Edit, click Go To...	[F5], or [Alt][E], [G], or [Ctrl][G]
Grammar, check, *W 155*		Click Tools, click Grammar...	[Alt][T], [G]
Hard page break, insert, *W 65*		Click Insert, click Break..., click Page Break, click OK	[Ctrl][Enter], or [Alt][I], [B], [Alt][P], [Enter]
Headers and footers, insert, *W 127*		Click View, click Header and Footer, enter headers and footers, click Close	[Alt][V], [H], enter headers and footers, click Close
Help, access, *W 48*		Click Help, click Contents	[F1], or [Alt][H], [C]
Indent selected paragraph to next tab stop, *W 70*			[Ctrl][M]
Italicize text, *W 42*	*I*	Click Format, click Font..., click Font tab, click Italic, click OK	[Ctrl][I], or [Alt][O], [F], [Alt][N], click Italic, [Enter]
Justify text, *W 83*		Click Format, click Paragraph..., click Indents and Spacing tab, click Alignment arrow, click Justified, click OK	[Ctrl][J], or [Alt][O], [P], [Alt][I], [Alt][G], choose Justified, [Enter]
Left-align text, *W 82*		Click Format, click Paragraph..., click Indents and Spacing tab, click Alignment arrow, click Left, click OK	[Ctrl][L], or [Alt][O], [P], [Alt][I], [Alt][G], click Left, [Enter]

TASK REFERENCE

Microsoft Word 6.0 for Windows

Italicized page numbers indicate the first discussion of each task.

TASK	MOUSE	MENU	KEYBOARD
Left-aligned tab, insert, *W 73*		Click Format, click Tabs..., click Left, click OK	[Alt][O], [T], [Alt][L], [Enter]
Margins, change, *W 63*		Click File, click Page Setup..., click Margins tab, change margin settings, click OK	[Alt][F], [U], [Alt][M], change margin settings, [Enter]
Move selected text without using the Clipboard, *W 61*			[F2], place insertion point in location, [Enter]
Move to previous location in a document, *W 87*			[Shift][F5]
New line mark, insert, *W 78*			[Shift][Enter]
Next Page section break, insert, *W 159*		Click Insert, click Break..., click Next Page, click OK	[Alt][I], [B], [Alt][N], [Enter]
Normal view, change to, *W 12*		Click View, click Normal	[Alt][V], [N]
Numbered list, create, *W 80*		Click Format, click Bullets and Numbering..., click Numbered tab, click list format, click OK	[Alt][O], [N], [Alt][N], choose list format, [Enter]
Open a new document, *W 17*		Click File, click New..., click a template, click OK	[Ctrl][O], or [Alt][F], [N], click a template, [Enter]
Open an existing document, *W 27*		Click File, click Open..., click document name, click OK	[Ctrl][F12], or [Alt][F], [O], click document name, [Enter]
Outline view, change to, *W 12*		Click View, click Outline	[Alt][V], [O]
Overtype mode, activate/ deactivate, *W 34*	Double-click OVR in the status bar	Click Tools, click Options..., click the Edit tab, click Overtype Mode, click OK	[Insert] or [Alt][T], [O], click the Edit tab, click Overtype Mode, [Enter]
Page layout view, change to, *W 12*		Click View, click Page Layout	[Alt][V], [P]
Paste text or graphics from the Clipboard, *W 113*		Click Edit, click Paste	[Ctrl][V], or [Alt][E], [P]
Point size, change, *W 89*	Click Font Size box arrow, click size	Click Format, click Font..., click Font tab, click size, click OK	[Alt][O], [F], [Alt][N], choose size, [Enter]
Print a document, *W 46*		Click File, click Print..., specify print options, click OK	[Ctrl][P], or [Alt][F], [P], specify print options, [Enter]
Print an envelope, *W 51*		Click Tools, click Envelopes and Labels..., click Envelopes tab, click Print	[Alt][T], [E], [Alt][E], [Alt][P]
Print Preview a document, *W 46*		Click File, click Print Preview	[Alt][F], [V]
Redo a previous undone action, *W 33*		Click Edit, click Redo	[Ctrl][Y], or [Alt][E], [R]
Rename a file, *W 60*		Click File, click Save As..., type filename, click OK	[Alt][F], [A], type filename, [Enter]

TASK REFERENCE

Microsoft Word 6.0 for Windows

Italicized page numbers indicate the first discussion of each task.

TASK	MOUSE	MENU	KEYBOARD
Repeat last action, *W 125*			[F4]
Replace text or formatting, *W 116*		Click Edit, click Replace..., specify replace options, click Replace or Replace All	[Ctrl][H] or [Alt][E], [E], specify replace options, [Alt][R] or [Alt][A]
Right-align text, *W 83*		Click Format, click Paragraph..., click Indents and Spacing tab, click Alignment arrow, click Right, click OK	[Ctrl][R], or [Alt][O], [P], [Alt][I], [Alt][G], click Right, [Enter]
Right-aligned tab, insert, *W 73*		Click Format, click Tabs..., click Right, click OK	[Alt][O], [T], [Alt][R], [Enter]
Save a document for the first time, *W 25*	, enter filename, click OK	Click File, click Save or Save As..., enter filename, click OK	[Ctrl][S] or [Alt][F], [S] or [A], enter filename, [Enter]
Save a document, *W 35*		Click File, click Save	[Ctrl][S], or [Shift][F12], or [Alt][F], [S]
Single space text, *W 81*		Click Format, click Paragraph..., click Indents and Spacing tab, click Line Spacing arrow, click Single, click OK	[Ctrl][1], or [Alt][O], [P], [Alt][I], [Alt][N], click Single, [Enter]
Sort rows in a table, *W 122*		Click Table, click Sort..., specify sort options, click OK	[Alt][A], [T], specify sort options, [Enter]
Spacing before or after a selected paragraph, change, *W 137*		Click Format, click Paragraph..., click Indents and Spacing tab, change Spacing Before or After options, click OK	[Alt][O], [P], [Alt][I], change Spacing Before or After options, [Enter]
Spelling, check, *W 36*		Click Tools, click Spelling...	[Alt][T], [S], or [F7]
Standard toolbar, activate/deactivate, *W 14*		Click View, click Toolbars..., click Standard, click OK	[Alt][V], [T], click Standard, [Enter]
Style Gallery, access, *W 132*		Click Format, click Style Gallery...	[Alt][O], [G]
Switch between open documents, *W 18*		Click Window, click document name	[Ctrl][F6], or [Alt][W], click document name
Symbol, insert, *W 91*		Click Insert, click Symbol..., click Symbols tab, click symbol, click Insert, click Close	[Alt][I], [S], [Alt][S], click symbol, [Alt][I], [Enter]
Table, create, *W 105*		Click Table, click Insert Table..., choose table options, click OK	[Alt][A], [I], choose table options, [Enter]
Table, format, *W 138*		Click Table, click Table AutoFormat..., choose format options, click OK	[Alt][A], [F], choose format options, [Enter]
Table of contents, insert, *W 184*		Click Insert, click Index and Tables..., click Table of Contents tab, choose table of contents options, click OK	[Alt][I], [X], [Alt][C], choose table of contents options, [Enter]

TASK REFERENCE

Microsoft Word 6.0 for Windows

Italicized page numbers indicate the first discussion of each task.

TASK	MOUSE	MENU	KEYBOARD
Table of figures, insert, *W 185*		Click Insert, click Index and Tables..., click Table of Figures tab, choose table of figures options, click OK	[Ctrl][N], or [Alt][I], [X], [Alt][F], choose table of figures options, [Enter]
Thesaurus, access, *W 153*		Click Tools, click Thesaurus...	[Shift][F7], or [Alt][T], [T]
ToolTips, activate/deactivate, *W 14*		Click View, click Toolbars..., click Show ToolTips, click OK	[Alt][V], [T], [Alt][S], [Enter]
Underline text, *W 44*	U	Click Format, click Font..., click Font tab, click Underline arrow, click underline option, click OK	[Ctrl][U], or [Alt][O], [F], [Alt][N], [Alt][U], click underline option, [Enter]
Undo last action, *W 33*		Click Edit, click Undo	[Ctrl][Z], or [Alt][E], [U]
Unindent text to previous tab stop, *W 71*			[Ctrl][Shift][M]
Vertical alignment, change, *W 161*		Click File, click Page Setup..., click Layout tab, click Vertical Alignment option, click OK	[Alt][F], [U], [Alt][L], [Alt][V], choose alignment option, [Enter]

Introductory Microsoft Excel® 5.0 for Windows™ Tutorials

1 Using Worksheets to Make Business Decisions

2 Planning, Building, Testing, and Documenting Worksheets

3 Formatting and Printing

4 Functions, Formulas, and Absolute References

5 Charts and Graphing

Read This Before You Begin

To the Student

To use this book, you must have a Student Disk. Your instructor will either provide you with one or ask you to make your own by following the instructions in the section "Making Your Excel Student Disk" in Tutorial 1. See your instructor or technical support person for further information. If you are going to work through this book using your own computer, you need a computer system running Microsoft Windows 3.1, Microsoft Excel 5.0 for Windows, and a Student Disk. *You will not be able to complete the tutorials and exercises in this book using your own computer until you have a Student Disk.*

Any references to "this book" or to a tutorial (such as "Tutorial 1") refer to the Microsoft Excel 5.0 tutorials of *this* Microsoft Office Professional book.

To the Instructor

Making the Student Disk To complete the tutorials in this book, your students must have a copy of the Student Disk. To relieve you of having to make multiple Student Disks from a single master copy, we provide you with the CTI WinApps Setup Disk, which contains an automatic Student Disk generating program. Once you install the Setup Disk on a network or standalone workstation, students can easily make their own Student Disks by double-clicking the "Make Excel 5.0 Office Student Disk" icon in the CTI WinApps icon group. Double-clicking this icon transfers all the data files students will need to complete the tutorials, Tutorial Assignments, and Case Problems to a high-density disk in drive A or B. If some of your students will use their own computers to complete the tutorials and exercises in this book, they must first get the Student Disk. The section called "Making Your Excel Student Disk" in Tutorial 1 provides complete instructions on how to make the Student Disk.

Installing the CTI WinApps Setup Disk To install the CTI WinApps icon group from the Setup Disk, follow the instructions inside the disk envelope that was bundled with your book. By adopting this book, you are granted a license to install this software on any computer or computer network used by you or your students.

README File A README.TXT file located on the Setup Disk provides additional technical notes, troubleshooting advice, and tips for using the CTI WinApps software in your school's computer lab. You can view the README.TXT file using any word processor you choose.

Microsoft Excel Installation

Make sure the Microsoft Excel software has been installed on your computer using the complete setup option, rather than the laptop or typical installation. Make sure the video driver is set to 16-color to avoid VRAM problems when using ChartWizard.

System Requirements

The minimum software and hardware requirements for your computer system are as follows:

- Microsoft Windows Version 3.1 or later on a local hard drive or a network drive.
- A 286 or higher processor with a minimum of 4 MB RAM.
- A mouse supported by Windows 3.1.
- A printer supported by Windows 3.1.
- A VGA 64 × 480 16-color display is recommended; an 800 × 600 or 1024 × 768 SVGA, VGA monochrome, or EGA display is acceptable.
- At least 9 MB free hard disk space for a laptop (minimum) installation. A custom installation requires 20 MB free hard disk space.
- Student workstations with at least 1 high-density disk drive.
- If you want to install the CTI WinApps Setup Disk on a network drive, your network must support Microsoft Windows.

TUTORIAL 1

Using Worksheets to Make Business Decisions

Evaluating Sites for a World-Class Golf Course

OBJECTIVES

In this tutorial you will:

- Make an Excel Student Disk
- Launch and exit Excel
- Discover how Excel is used in business
- Identify the major components of the Excel window
- Open, save, print, and close a worksheet
- Correct mistakes and use the Undo button
- Use an Excel decision-support worksheet
- Scroll a worksheet
- Split a worksheet window
- Create, save, and print a chart
- Learn how Excel uses values, text, formulas, and functions

CASE

InWood Design Group In Japan, golf is big business. Spurred by the Japanese passion for the sport, golf is enjoying unprecedented popularity. But in that small mountainous country of 12 million golfers, there are fewer than 2,000 courses, the average fee for 18 holes on a public course is between $200 and $300, and golf club memberships are bought and sold like stock shares. The market potential is phenomenal, but building a golf course in Japan is expensive because of inflated property values, difficult terrain, and strict environmental regulations.

InWood Design Group is planning to build a world-class golf course, and one of the four sites under consideration for the course is in Chiba Prefecture, Japan. The other possible sites are Kauai, Hawaii; Edmonton, Canada; and Scottsdale, Arizona. Mike Mazzuchi and Pamela Kopenski are members of the InWood Design Group site selection team. The team is responsible for collecting information on the sites, evaluating that information, and recommending the best site for the new golf course.

The team identified five factors that are likely to determine the success of a golf course: climate, competition, market size, topography, and transportation. The team collected information on these factors for each of the four potential golf course sites. The next step is to analyze the information and make a site recommendation to management.

Using Microsoft Excel 5.0 for Windows, Mike created a worksheet that the team can use to evaluate the four sites. He will bring the worksheet to the next meeting to help the team evaluate the sites and reach a decision.

In this tutorial you will learn how to use Excel as you work along with the InWood team to select the best site for the golf course.

Using the Tutorials Effectively

The tutorials will help you learn about Microsoft Excel 5.0. They are designed to be used at your computer. Begin by reading the text that explains the concepts. Then when you come to the numbered steps, follow the steps on your computer. Read each step carefully and completely before you try it.

As you work, compare your screen with the figures to verify your results. Don't worry if your screen display differs slightly from the figures. The important parts of the screen display are labeled in each figure. Just make sure you have these parts on your screen.

Don't worry about making mistakes; that's part of the learning process. **TROUBLE?** paragraphs identify common problems and explain how to get back on track. You should complete the steps in the **TROUBLE?** paragraph *only* if you are having the problem described.

After you read the conceptual information and complete the steps, you can do the exercises found at the end of each tutorial in the sections entitled "Questions," "Tutorial Assignments," and "Case Problems." The exercises are carefully structured to help you review what you learned in the tutorials and apply your knowledge to new situations.

When you are doing the exercises, refer back to the Reference Window boxes. These boxes, which are found throughout the tutorials, provide you with short summaries of frequently used procedures. You can also use the Task Reference at the end of the tutorials; it summarizes how to accomplish tasks using the mouse, the menus, and the keyboard.

Before you begin the tutorials, you should know how to use the menus, dialog boxes, Help facility, Program Manager, and File Manager in Microsoft Windows. Course Technology, Inc. publishes two excellent texts for learning Windows: *A Guide to Microsoft Windows 3.1* and *An Introduction to Microsoft Windows 3.1*.

Making Your Excel Student Disk

Before you can work along with the InWood design team, you need to make a Student Disk that contains all the practice files you need for the tutorials, the Tutorial Assignments, and the Case Problems. If your instructor or technical support person provides you with your Student Disk, you may skip this section and go to the section entitled "Launching Excel." If your instructor asks you to make your own Student Disk, you need to follow the steps in this section.

To make your Student Disk you need:

- A blank, formatted, high-density 3.5-inch disk
- A computer with Microsoft Windows 3.1, Microsoft Excel 5.0, and the CTI WinApps group icon installed on it

If you are using your own computer, the CTI WinApps group icon will not be installed on it. Before you proceed, you must go to your school's computer lab and use a computer with the CTI WinApps group icon installed on it to make your Student Disk. Once you have made your own Student Disk, you can use it to complete all the tutorials and exercises in this book on any computer you choose.

To make your Excel Office Student Disk:

1. Launch Windows and make sure the Program Manager window is open.

   TROUBLE? The exact steps you follow to launch Microsoft Windows 3.1 might vary depending on how your computer is set up. On many computer systems, type WIN then press [Enter] to launch Windows. If you don't know how to launch Windows, ask your technical support person.

2. Label your formatted disk "Excel 5.0 Office Student Disk" and place it in drive A.

   TROUBLE? If your computer has more than one disk drive, drive A is usually on top. If your Student Disk does not fit into drive A, then place it in drive B and substitute "drive B" anywhere you see "drive A" in the tutorial steps.

3. Look for an icon labeled "CTI WinApps" like the one in Figure 1-1 or a window labeled "CTI WinApps" like the one in Figure 1-2.

   TROUBLE? If you cannot find anything labeled "CTI WinApps," the CTI software might not be installed on the computer you are using. See your technical support person for assistance.

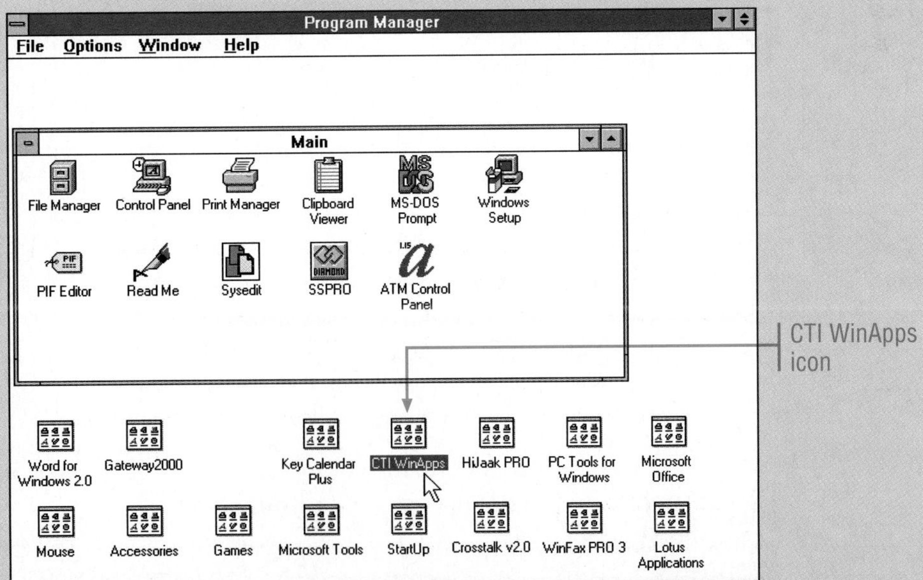

Figure 1-1 The CTI WinApps icon

TROUBLE? If you are running Office Manager, your screen will also include the Office Manager toolbar. This book assumes Office Manager is not running.

CTI WinApps group window

Make Excel 5.0 Office Student Disk icon

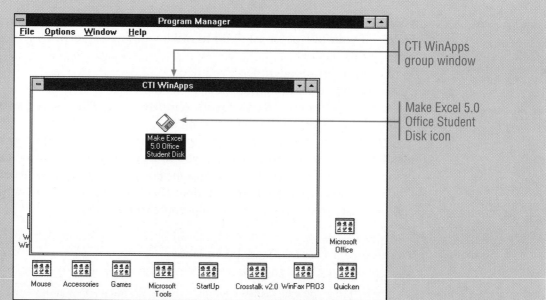

Figure 1-2 Making your Excel Office Student Disk

❹ If you see an icon labeled "CTI WinApps," double-click the **CTI WinApps icon** to open the CTI WinApps group window. If the CTI WinApps window is already open, go to Step 5.

❺ Double-click the **Make Excel 5.0 Office Student Disk icon**. The Make Excel 5.0 Office Student Disk window opens. See Figure 1-3.

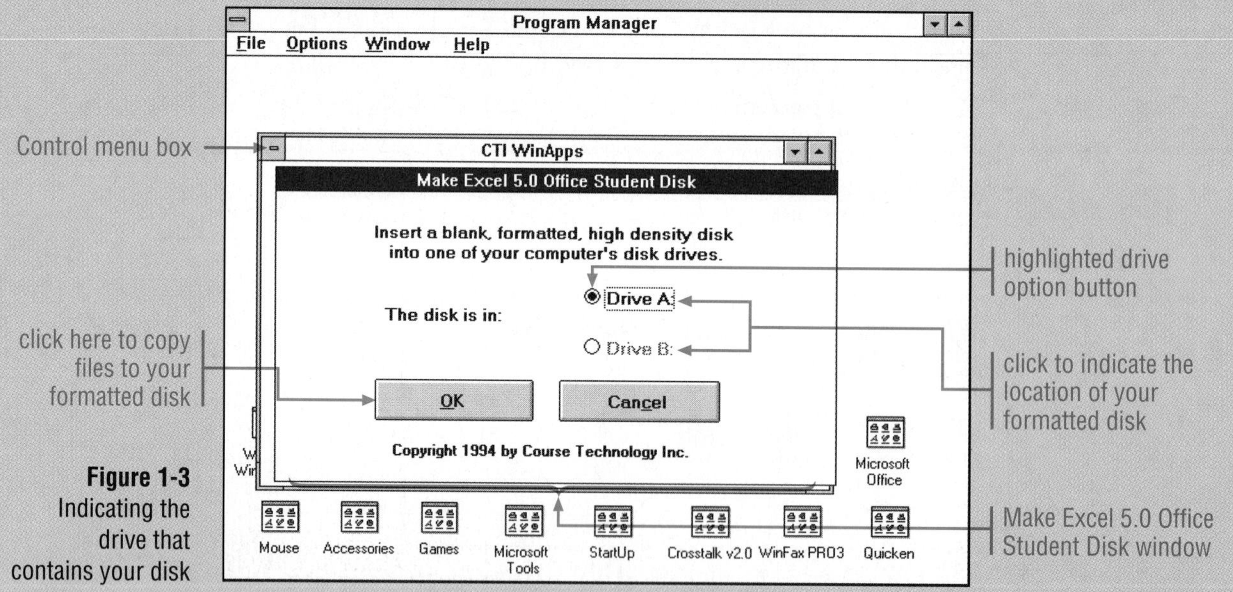

Figure 1-3 Indicating the drive that contains your disk

❻ Make sure the drive that contains your disk corresponds to the drive option button that is highlighted in the dialog box on your screen.

❼ Click the **OK button** to copy the practice files to your formatted data disk.

❽ When the copying is complete, a message indicates the number of files copied to your disk. Click the **OK button**.

❾ To close the CTI WinApps window, double-click the **Control menu box** on the CTI WinApps window.

Launching Excel

Mike arrives at the meeting a few minutes early so he can open his laptop computer and connect it to the large screen monitor in the company conference room. In a few moments Windows is up and running, Mike launches Excel, and the meeting is ready to begin.

Let's launch Excel to follow along with Mike as he works with the design team to make a decision about the golf course site.

To launch Excel:

❶ Look for an icon or window titled "Microsoft Office." See Figure 1-4.

TROUBLE? If you don't see anything called "Microsoft Office," click Window on the menu bar and, if you find "Microsoft Excel 5.0" in the list, click it. If you still can't find anything called "Microsoft Excel 5.0," ask your technical support person for help on how to launch Excel. If you are using your own computer, make sure the Excel software has been installed.

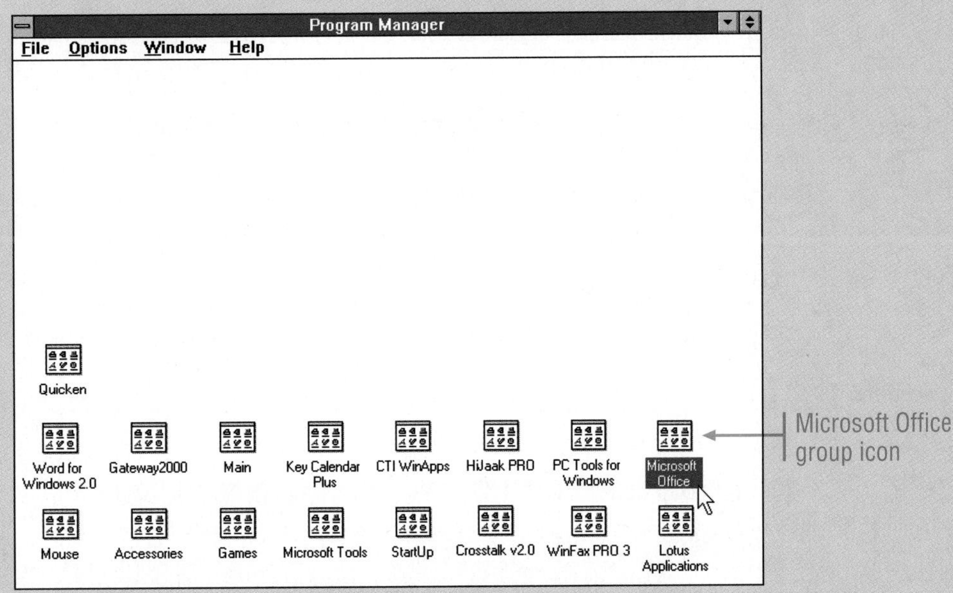

Figure 1-4
Launching Excel

❷ If you see the Microsoft Office group icon, double-click the **Microsoft Office group icon** to open the group window. If you see the Microsoft Office *group window* instead of the *group icon*, go to Step 3.

❸ Double-click the **Microsoft Excel program-item icon**. After a short pause, the Excel copyright information appears in a box and remains on the screen until Excel is ready for use. Excel is ready when your screen looks similar to Figure 1-5. Don't worry if your screen doesn't look *exactly* the same as Figure 1-5. You are ready to continue when you see the Excel menu bar.

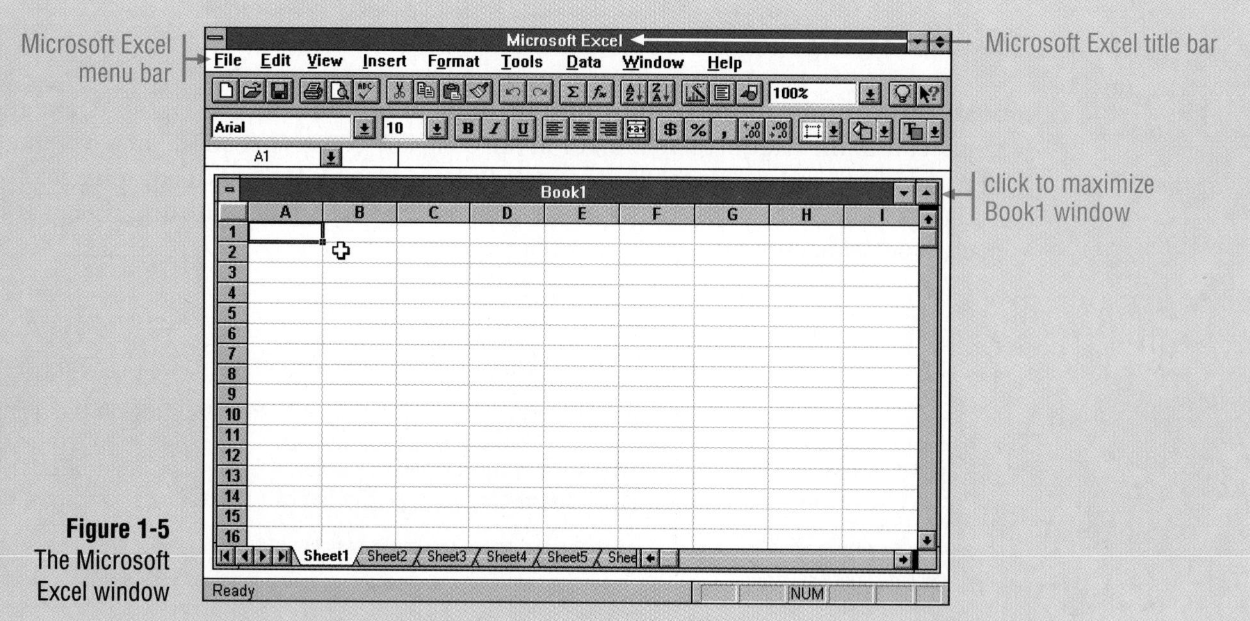

Figure 1-5 The Microsoft Excel window

4. Click the **application window Maximize button** if your Microsoft Excel application window is not maximized.
5. Click the **document window Maximize button** to maximize the Book1 window. Figure 1-6 shows the maximized Microsoft Excel and Book1 windows.

   TROUBLE? Your screen might display a little more or a little less of the grid shown in Figure 1-6 if you are using a display type that is different from the one used to produce the figures in the tutorials. This should not be a problem as you continue with the tutorial.

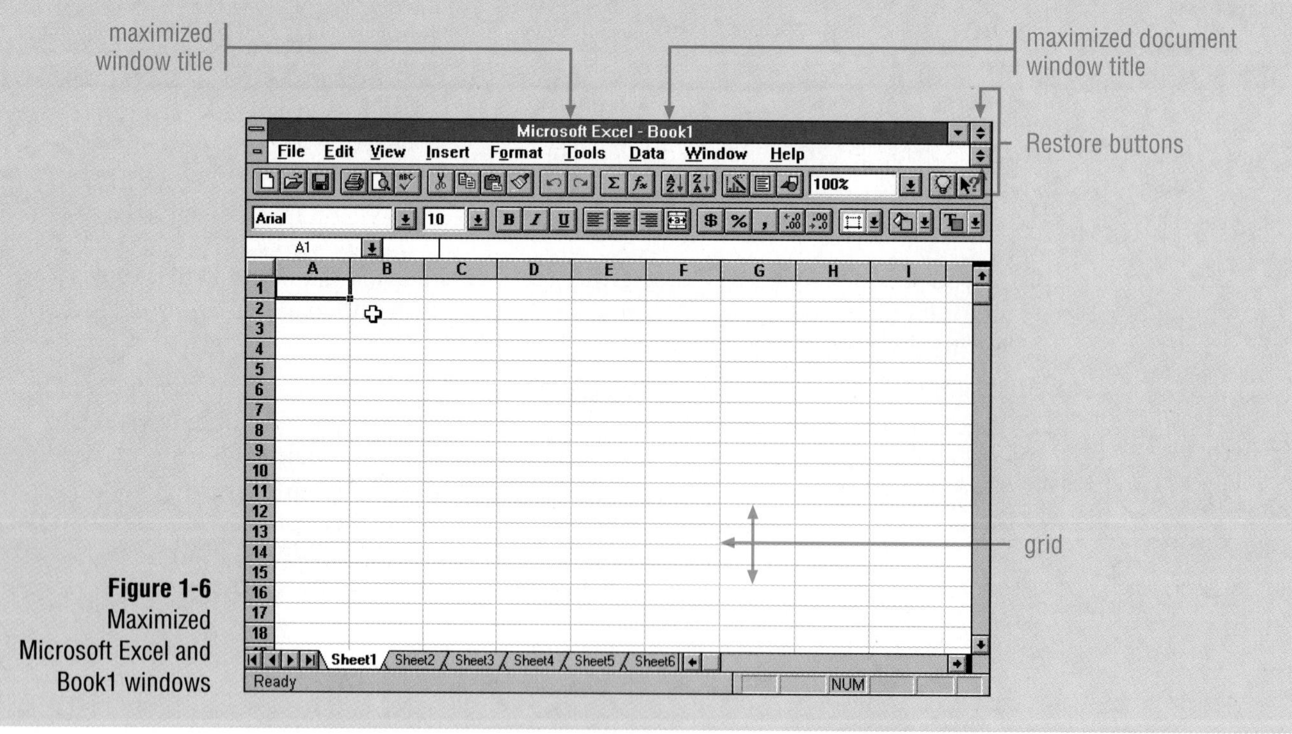

Figure 1-6 Maximized Microsoft Excel and Book1 windows

What Is Excel?

Excel is a computerized spreadsheet. A **spreadsheet** is an important business tool that helps you analyze and evaluate information. Spreadsheets are often used for cash flow analysis, budgeting, decision making, cost estimating, inventory management, and financial reporting. For example, an accountant might use a spreadsheet for a budget like the one in Figure 1-7.

Cash Budget Forecast

	January Estimated	*January Actual*
Cash in Bank (Start of Month)	$1,400.00	$1,400.00
Cash in Register (Start of Month)	100.00	100.00
Total Cash	$1,500.00	$1,500.00
Expected Cash Sales	$1,200.00	$1,420.00
Expected Collections	400.00	380.00
Other Money Expected	100.00	52.00
Total Income	$1,700.00	$1,852.00
Total Cash and Income	$3,200.00	$3,352.00
All Expenses (for Month)	$1,200.00	$1,192.00
Cash Balance at End of Month	$2,000.00	$2,160.00

Figure 1-7 A budget spreadsheet

To produce the spreadsheet in Figure 1-7, you could manually calculate the totals and then type your results, or you could use a computer and spreadsheet program to perform the calculations and print the results. Spreadsheet programs are also referred to as spreadsheet applications, electronic spreadsheets, computerized spreadsheets, or just spreadsheets.

In Excel 5.0, the document you create is called a **workbook.** You'll notice that the document currently on your screen is titled Book1, which is short for Workbook #1. Each workbook is made up of individual worksheets, or **sheets**, just as a spiral notebook is made up of sheets of paper. You'll learn more about using multiple sheets in later tutorials. For now, just keep in mind that the terms "worksheet" and "sheet" are often used interchangeably.

The Excel Window

Excel operates like most other Windows programs. If you have used other Windows programs, many of the Excel window controls will be familiar. Figure 1-8 shows the main components of the Excel window. Let's take a look at these components so you are familiar with their location.

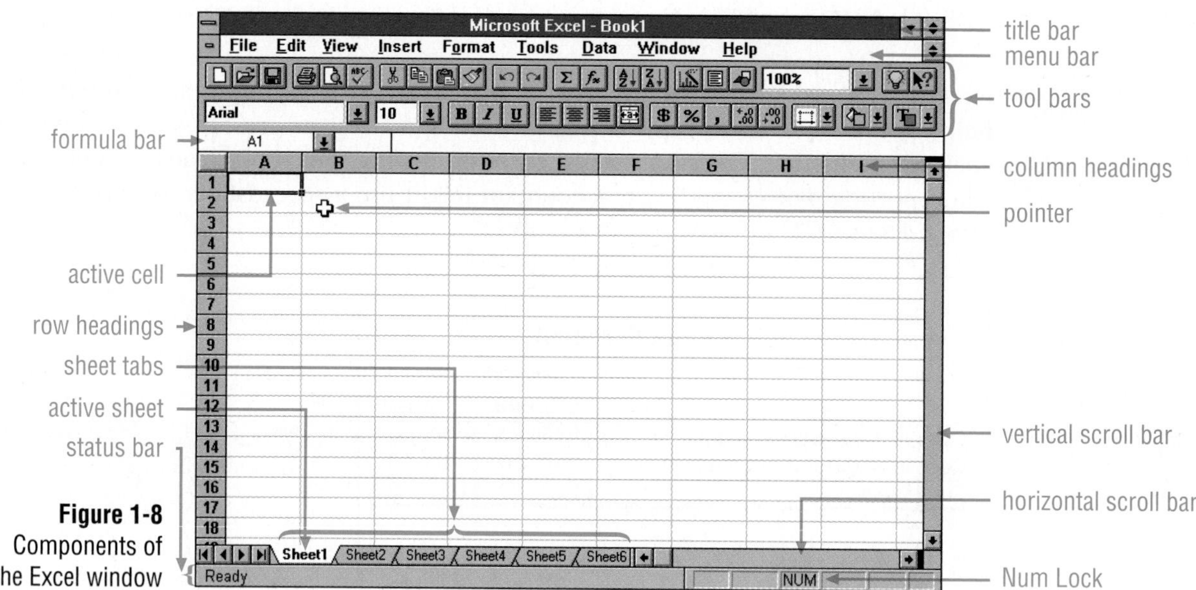

Figure 1-8
Components of the Excel window

The Title Bar

The **title bar** at the top of a window identifies the window. On your screen and in Figure 1-8 the title bar displays "Microsoft Excel - Book1." The title of the application window is "Microsoft Excel." Because the document window is maximized, the title of the document window, "Book1," is also displayed on the title bar.

The Menu Bar

The **menu bar** is located directly below the title bar. Each word in the menu bar is the title of a menu you can open to display a list of commands and options. The menu bar provides easy access to all the features of the Excel spreadsheet program.

The Toolbars

The two rows of square buttons (or tools) and drop-down list boxes, located below the menu bar, make up the **toolbars**. These buttons and boxes provide shortcuts for accessing the most commonly used features of Excel.

The Formula Bar

The **formula bar**, located immediately below the toolbars, displays the data you enter or edit.

The Worksheet Window

The document window, usually referred to as the **worksheet window**, contains the sheet you are creating, editing, or using. The worksheet window includes a series of vertical columns indicated by lettered **column headings** and a series of horizontal rows indicated by numbered **row headings**.

A **cell** is the rectangular area at the intersection of a column and row. Each cell is identified by a **cell reference**, which is its column and row location. For example, the cell reference B6 indicates the cell at the intersection of column B and row 6. The column letter is always specified first in the cell reference. B6 is a correct cell reference, but 6B is not.

In Figure 1-8 the active cell is A1. The **active cell**, indicated by a black border, is the cell you have selected to work with. You can change the active cell when you want to work in a different location on the worksheet.

The Pointer

The **pointer** is the indicator that moves on your screen as you move your mouse. The pointer changes shape to indicate the type of task you can perform at a particular location. When you click a mouse button, something happens at the location of the pointer. In Figure 1-8 the pointer, which is located in cell B2, looks like a white plus sign. Let's see what other shapes the pointer can assume.

To explore pointer shapes:

1. Move the pointer slowly down the row numbers on the far left of the workbook window. Then move it slowly, from left to right, across the formula bar. Notice how the pointer changes shape as you move it over different parts of the window. Do *not* click the mouse button yet. You will have a chance to do so later in the tutorial. You can also use the pointer to display the name of each button in the tool bar. This is helpful when you can't remember the function of a button.
2. Move the pointer to the Cut button. After a short pause, the name of the button—"Cut"—appears just below the pointer. The message "Cuts selection and places it onto Clipboard" appears in the status bar.

Scroll Bars and Sheet Tabs

The **vertical scroll bar** (on the far right side of the workbook window) and the **horizontal scroll bar** (in the lower-right corner of the workbook window) allow you to move quickly around the worksheet. The **sheet tabs** allow you to move quickly between sheets by simply clicking on the sheet tab. Again, you'll learn how to use the sheet tabs in later tutorials.

The Status Bar

The **status bar** is located at the bottom of the Excel window. The left side of the status bar provides a brief description of the current command or task in progress. The right side of the status bar shows the status of important keys such as Caps Lock and Num Lock. In Figure 1-8 the status bar shows that the Num Lock mode is in effect, which means you can use your numeric keypad to enter numbers.

Opening a Workbook

When you want to use a workbook you have previously created, you must first open it. When you **open a workbook**, a copy of the workbook file is transferred into the random access memory (RAM) of your computer and displayed on your screen. Figure 1-9 shows that when you open a workbook called "GOLF.XLS," Excel copies the file from the hard drive or disk into RAM. When the workbook is open, GOLF.XLS is both in RAM and on the disk.

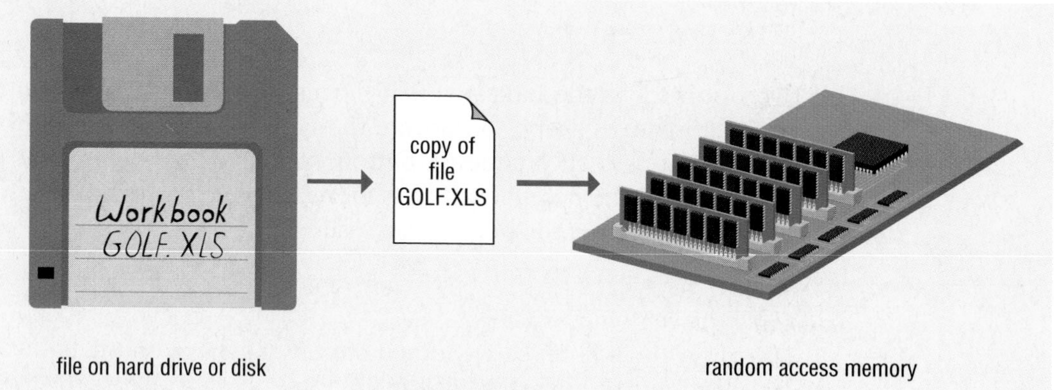

Figure 1-9 Opening a workbook

After you open a workbook, you can view, edit, print, or save it again on your disk.

REFERENCE WINDOW

Opening a Workbook

- Click the Open button on the Excel toolbar.

  or

  Click File, then click Open....
- Make sure the Drives box displays the icon for the drive that contains the workbook you want to open.
- Make sure the Directories box shows an open file folder for the directory that contains the workbook you want to open.
- Double-click the filename that contains the workbook you want to open.

Mike created a worksheet to help the site selection team evaluate the four potential locations for the golf course. The workbook, GOLF.XLS, is stored on your Student Disk. Let's open this file to display Mike's worksheet.

To open the GOLF.XLS workbook:

1. Make sure your Excel Student Disk is in drive A.

   TROUBLE? If you don't have a Student Disk, then you need to get one. Your instructor will either give you one or ask you to make your own by following the steps described earlier in this tutorial in "Making Your Excel Student Disk." See your instructor or technical support person for information.

TROUBLE? If your Student Disk won't fit in drive A, then try drive B. If drive B is the correct drive, then substitute "drive B" for "drive A" throughout these tutorials.

2. Click the **Open button** to display the Open dialog box. Figure 1-10 shows the location of the Open button and the correct dialog box settings for opening the GOLF.XLS workbook.

TROUBLE? If the a: drive icon is not displayed in the Drives box, click the down arrow button on the Drives box; then from the list of drives, click the a: drive icon.

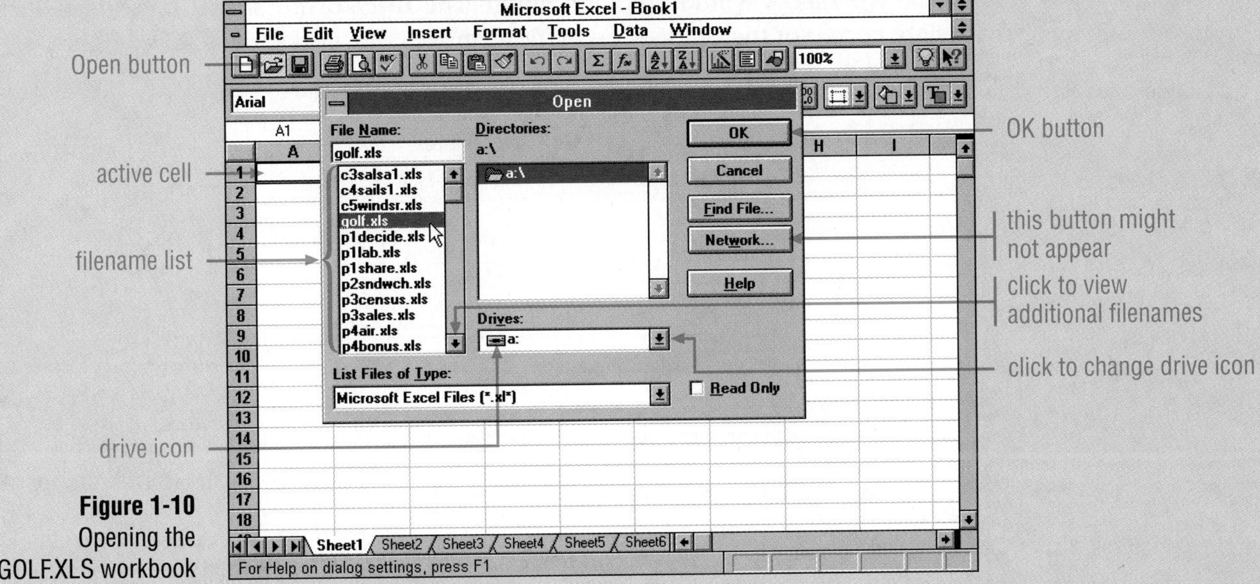

Figure 1-10 Opening the GOLF.XLS workbook

3. Double-click the filename **GOLF.XLS** in the File Name list. The GOLF.XLS workbook appears. See Figure 1-11.

TROUBLE? If you do not see GOLF.XLS in the File Name list, use the scroll bar to view additional filenames.

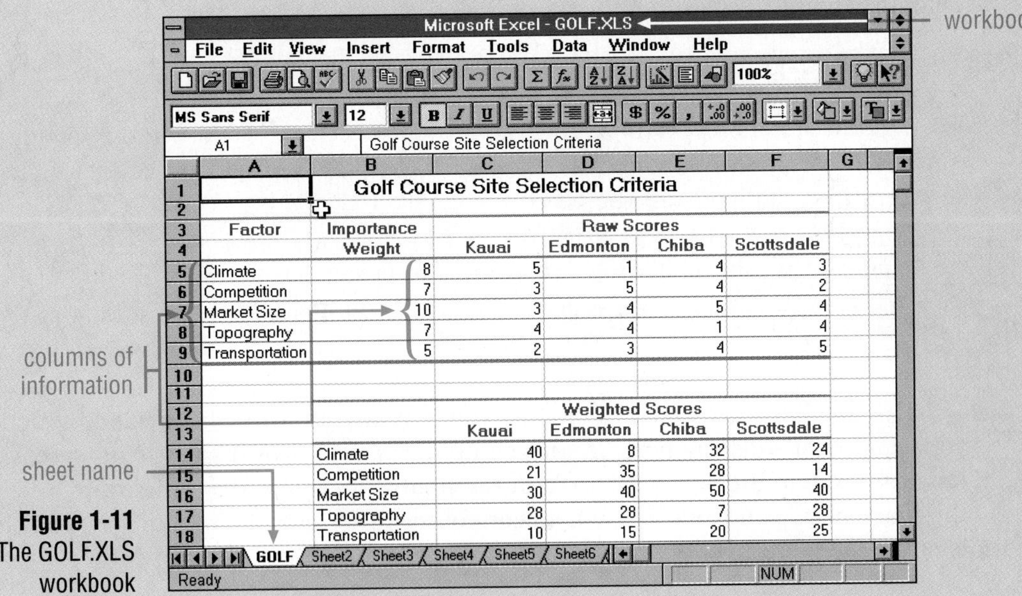

Factor	Importance Weight	Kauai	Edmonton	Chiba	Scottsdale
Climate	8	5	1	4	3
Competition	7	3	5	4	2
Market Size	10	3	4	5	4
Topography	7	4	4	1	4
Transportation	5	2	3	4	5

Weighted Scores	Kauai	Edmonton	Chiba	Scottsdale
Climate	40	8	32	24
Competition	21	35	28	14
Market Size	30	40	50	40
Topography	28	28	7	28
Transportation	10	15	20	25

Figure 1-11 The GOLF.XLS workbook

Mike's worksheet contains columns of information and a chart. To see the chart you must scroll the worksheet.

Scrolling the Worksheet

The worksheet window has a horizontal scroll bar and a vertical scroll bar, as shown in Figure 1-12. The **vertical scroll bar**, located at the right edge of the worksheet window, moves the worksheet window up and down. The **horizontal scroll bar**, located at the lower-right corner of the worksheet window, moves the worksheet left and right.

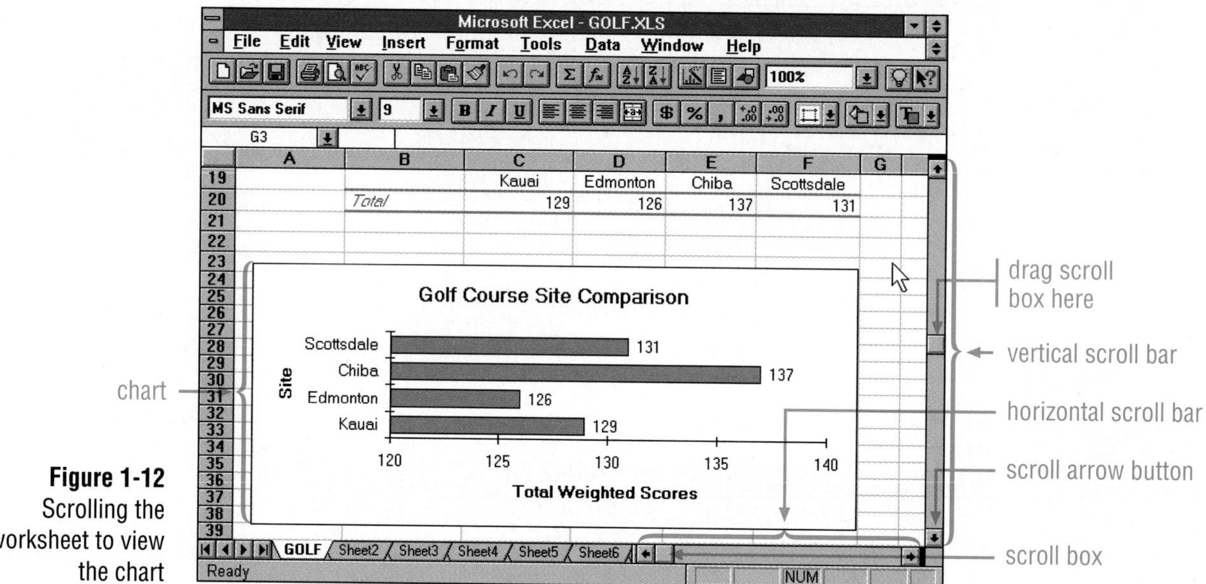

Figure 1-12 Scrolling the worksheet to view the chart

You click the scroll arrow buttons on the scroll bar to move the window one row or column at a time. You drag the **scroll box** to move the window more than one row or column at a time. Let's scroll the worksheet to view the chart.

To scroll the worksheet to view the chart:

1. Drag the scroll box on the vertical scroll bar about half way down the screen. Release the mouse button. The worksheet window displays the section of the worksheet that contains the chart. See Figure 1-12.

   TROUBLE? If you drag the scroll box too far, or if the chart is not positioned like the one in Figure 1-12, use the scroll arrow buttons or scroll box until your screen matches Figure 1-12.

2. After you view the chart, scroll the worksheet until you can see rows 3 through 20.

The number of rows and columns you see in your worksheet window depends on your computer's display type. If your computer has an EGA display, your screen displays fewer rows than the screens shown in the figures, but now that you know how to scroll the worksheet, you can scroll whenever you need to view an area of the worksheet that is not in the worksheet window.

Using a Decision-Support Worksheet

Mike explains the general layout of the decision-support worksheet to the rest of the team (Figure 1-13). Cells A5 through A9 contain the five factors on which the team is basing its decision: climate, competition, market size, topography, and transportation. The team assigned an *importance weight* to each factor to show its relative importance to the success of the golf course. The team assigned importance weights using a scale from 1 to 10; Mike entered the weights in cells B5 through B9. Market size, with an importance weight of 10, is the most important factor. The least important factor is transportation.

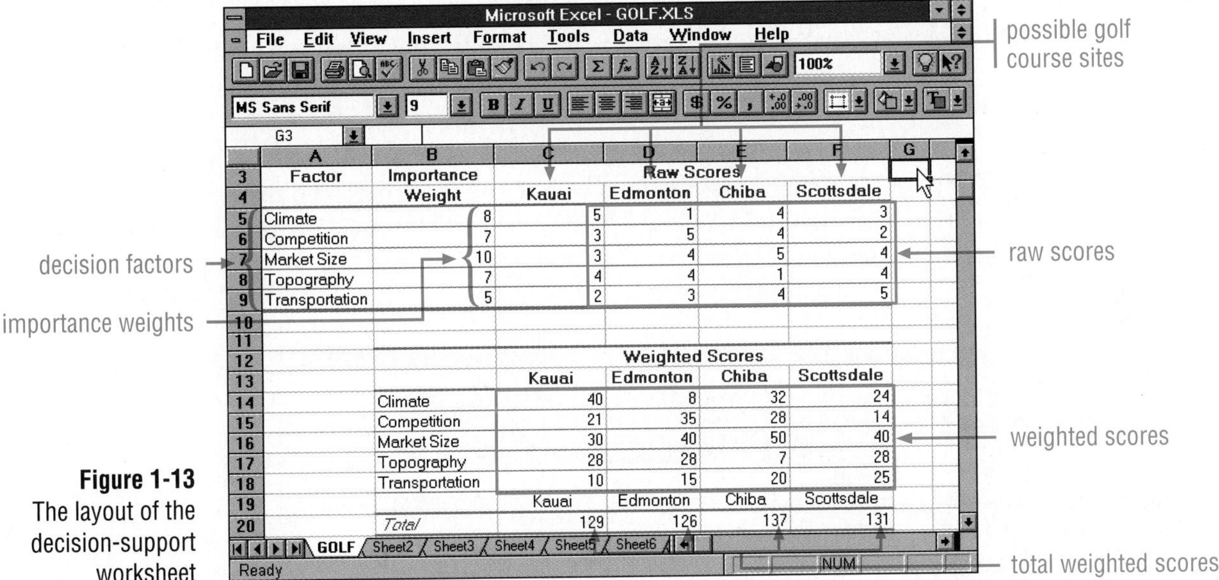

Figure 1-13
The layout of the decision-support worksheet

The four sites under consideration are listed in cells C4 through F4. The team used a scale of 1 to 5 to assign a *raw score* to each location for climate, competition, market size, topography, and transportation. Larger raw scores indicate the site is very strong in that factor. Smaller raw scores indicate the site is weak in that factor. For example, the raw score for Kauai's climate is 5. The other locations have scores of 1, 4, and 3 so it appears that Kauai, with warm, sunny days for 12 months of the year, has the best climate for the golf course. Edmonton, on the other hand, has cold weather and only received a climate raw score of 1.

The raw scores do not take into account the importance of each factor. Climate is important, but the team considers market size to be the most important factor. Therefore, the raw scores are not used for the final decision. Instead, the raw scores are multiplied by the importance weight to produce *weighted scores*. Which site has the highest weighted score for any factor? If you look at the scores in cells C14 through F18, you will see that Chiba's score of 50 for market size is the highest weighted score for any factor.

Cells C20 through F20 contain the total weighted scores for each location. With the current weighting and raw scores, it appears that Chiba is the most promising site, with a total score of 137.

As the team examines the worksheet, Pamela asks if the raw scores take into account the recent news that a competing design group has announced plans to build a $325 million golf resort just 10 miles away from InWood's Chiba site. Mike admits that he assigned the values before the announcement, so they do not reflect the increased competition in the Chiba market. Pamela suggests that they revise Chiba's raw score for competition to reflect this market change.

Changing Values and Observing Results

When you change a value in a worksheet, Excel recalculates the worksheet to display updated results. This feature makes Excel an extremely useful decision-making tool because it allows you to factor in changing conditions quickly and easily.

Another development group has announced plans to construct a new golf course in the Chiba area, so the team decides to lower the competition raw score for the Chiba site from 4 to 2.

To change the competition raw score for Chiba from 4 to 2:

1. Click cell **E6**. A black border appears around cell E6 indicating it is the active cell. The formula bar shows E6 is the active cell and shows that the current value of cell E6 is 4.
2. Type **2**. Notice that 2 appears in the cell and in the formula bar, along with three new buttons. These buttons—the Cancel box, the Enter box, and the Function Wizard button—provide shortcuts for entering data and formulas. You will learn how to use some of these in later tutorials. For now, you can simply ignore them. See Figure 1-14.

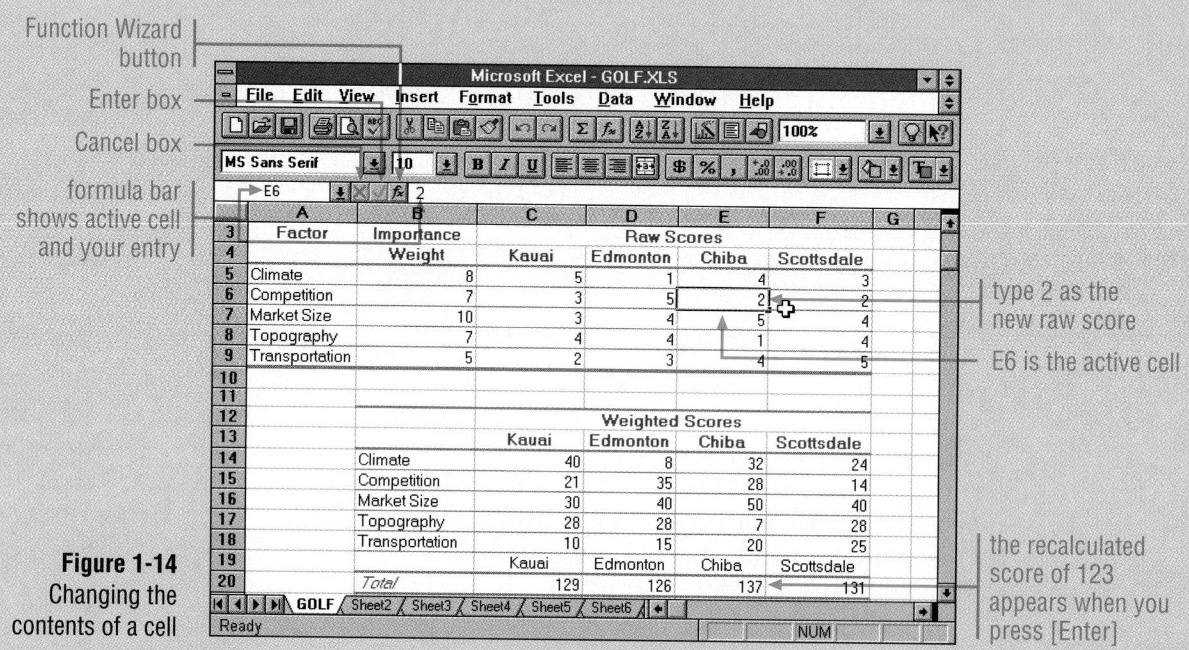

Factor	Importance Weight	Kauai	Edmonton	Chiba	Scottsdale
		Raw Scores			
Climate	8	5	1	4	3
Competition	7	3	5	2	2
Market Size	10	3	4	5	4
Topography	7	4	4	1	4
Transportation	5	2	3	4	5

Weighted Scores	Kauai	Edmonton	Chiba	Scottsdale
Climate	40	8	32	24
Competition	21	35	28	14
Market Size	30	40	50	40
Topography	28	28	7	28
Transportation	10	15	20	25
Total	129	126	137	131

Figure 1-14 Changing the contents of a cell

3. Press **[Enter]**. The worksheet recalculates the total weighted score for Chiba and displays it in cell E20. Cell E7 is now the active cell.

The team takes another look at the total weighted scores in row 20. Scottsdale just became the top ranking site, with a total weighted score of 131.

As the team continues to discuss the worksheet, several members express their concern over the importance weight used for transportation. On the current worksheet, transportation has an importance weight of 5. Pamela thinks they had agreed to use an importance weight of 2 at their last meeting. She asks Mike to change the importance weight for transportation.

To change the importance weight for transportation:

1. Click cell **B9** to make it the active cell.
2. Type **2** and press **[Enter]**. Cell B9 now contains the value 2 instead of 5. Cell B10 becomes the active cell.

With the change in the transportation importance weight, it appears that Kauai has pulled ahead as the most favorable site, with a total weighted score of 123.

Pamela, who has never used a spreadsheet program, asks Mike about mistakes. Mike explains that the most common mistake to make on a worksheet is a typing error. Typing mistakes are easy to correct, so Mike asks the group if he can take just a minute to demonstrate.

Correcting Mistakes

It is easy to correct a mistake as you are typing information in a cell, before you press the Enter key. If you need to correct a mistake as you are typing information in a cell, press the Backspace key to back up and delete one or more characters. When you are typing information in a cell, don't use the cursor arrow keys to edit because they move the cell pointer to another cell. Mike demonstrates how to correct a typing mistake by starting to type the word "Faktors" instead of "Factors."

To correct a mistake as you are typing:

1. Click cell **B12** to make it the active cell.
2. Type **Fak** to make an intentional error, *but don't press [Enter].*
3. Press **[Backspace]** to delete the "k."
4. Type **ctors** and press **[Enter]**.

Now the word "Factors" is in cell B12, but Mike really wants the word "Factor" in the cell. He explains that after you press the Enter key, you use a different method to change the contents of a cell. The F2 key puts Excel into **Edit mode**, which lets you use the Backspace key, Left Arrow key, Right Arrow key, and the mouse to make changes to the text displayed in the formula bar.

REFERENCE WINDOW

Correcting Mistakes Using Edit Mode

- Click the cell you want to edit to make it the active cell.
- Press [F2] to begin Edit mode and display the contents of the cell in the formula bar.
- Use [Backspace], [Delete], [→], [←], or the mouse to edit the cell contents in the formula bar.
- Press [Enter] when the edit is complete.

Mike uses Edit mode to demonstrate how to change "Factors" to "Factor" in cell B12.

To change the word "Factors" to "Factor" in cell B12:

1. Click cell **B12** if it is not already the active cell.
2. Press **[F2]** to begin Edit mode. Note that "Edit" appears in the status bar, reminding you that Excel is currently in Edit mode.
3. Press **[Backspace]** to delete the "s."
4. Press **[Enter]** to complete the edit.

Mike points out that sometimes you might inadvertently enter the wrong value in a cell. To cancel that type of error, you can use the Undo button.

The Undo Button

Excel's **Undo button** lets you cancel the last change—and only the last change—you made to the worksheet. You can use Undo not only to correct typing mistakes, but to correct almost anything you did to the worksheet that you wish you hadn't. For example, Undo cancels formatting changes, deletions, and cell entries. If you make a mistake, use Undo to put things back the way they were. But keep in mind that Excel can't reverse an entire series of actions. It can only reverse the most recent change you made to the worksheet.

Mike changes the font size (in other words, the size of the characters) for the label in cell B12. Then he uses the Undo button to cancel the font size change.

To change the font size and then cancel this change using the Undo feature:

1. Click cell **B12** if it is not already the active cell.
2. Click the **Font Size drop-down list-box arrow**. A list of font sizes appears. See Figure 1-15.

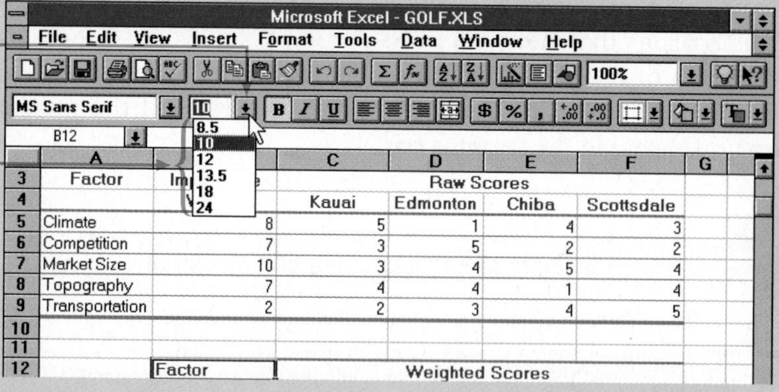

click here to open the font size drop-down list

font sizes

Figure 1-15
A font size mistake

3. Click **24** in the drop-down list. The size of the characters in cell B12 increases.
4. To undo the font size change, click the **Undo button**.

   TROUBLE? Make sure that you do not click the similar-looking Repeat button.

Now that you know how to correct typing mistakes and use the Undo button to cancel your last entry or command, you can apply these skills as you need them.

Mike says that the team must continue working on the golf course site selection. The team wants to see the chart and the scores at the same time. Mike says he can do that by splitting the worksheet window.

Splitting the Worksheet Window

The worksheet window displays only a section of the entire worksheet. Although you can scroll to any section of the worksheet, you might want to view two different parts of the worksheet at the same time. To do this, you can split the window into two or more separate window panes using the split bar, shown in Figure 1-16.

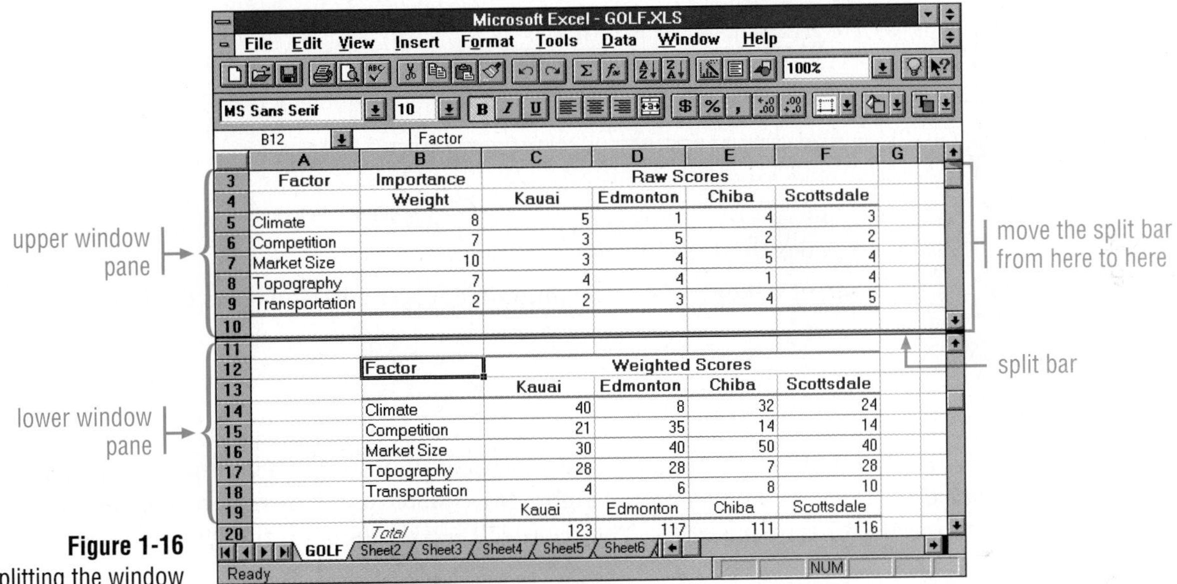

Figure 1-16
Splitting the window

A **window pane** is a subdivision of the worksheet window that can be scrolled separately to display a section of the worksheet. This is handy when you want to change some worksheet values and immediately see how these changes affect such things as totals or, as in this case, a chart.

Mike decides to split the worksheet window into two window panes. When he does this the top pane will display rows 3 through 9 of the worksheet. Then Mike needs to scroll the lower pane to display the chart.

To split the screen into two horizontal windows:

❶ Move ↖ over the horizontal split bar until it changes to ÷. Drag the split bar just below the bottom of row 10, then release the mouse button. Figure 1-16 shows the screen split into two horizontal windows.

Now you need to display the chart by using the scroll bar on the lower window pane.

❷ Drag the scroll box on the lower window pane about half way down the vertical scroll bar, then release the left mouse button. The lower window pane displays the chart. See Figure 1-17. Don't worry if your worksheet displays fewer rows than in the figure. Just make sure you can see row 9 in the upper window pane and the four bars of the chart in the lower window pane.

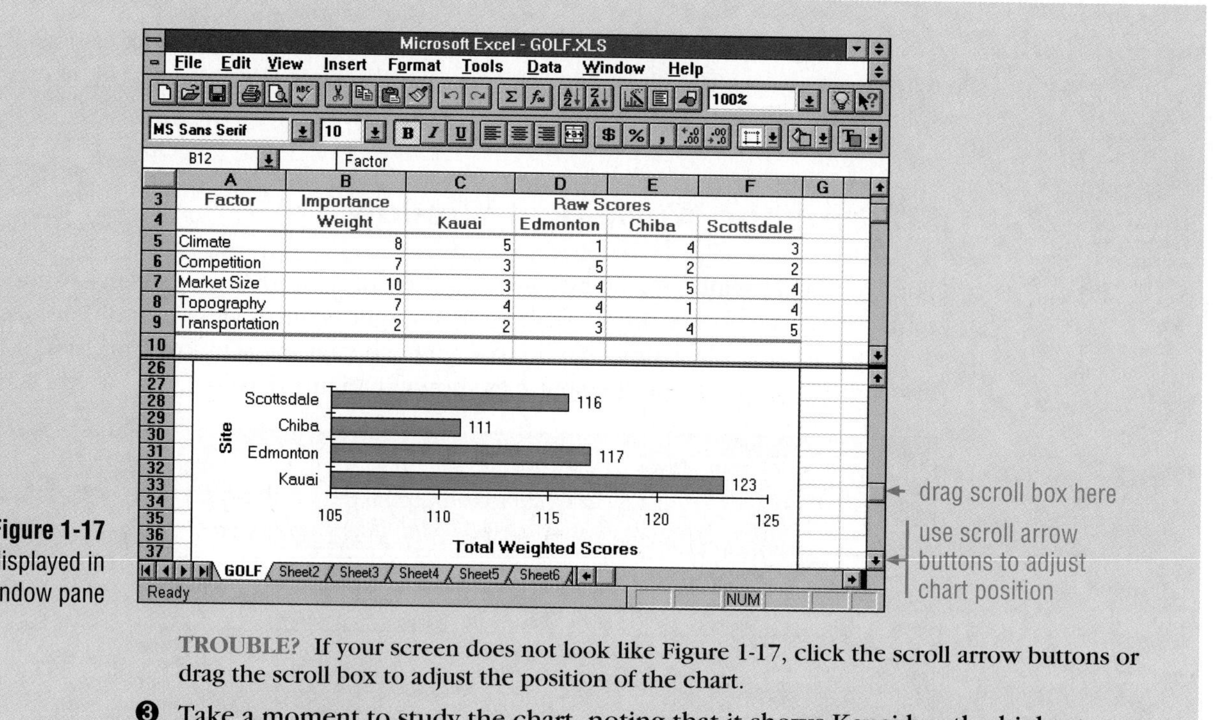

Figure 1-17
Chart displayed in lower window pane

TROUBLE? If your screen does not look like Figure 1-17, click the scroll arrow buttons or drag the scroll box to adjust the position of the chart.

3. Take a moment to study the chart, noting that it shows Kauai has the highest weighted score.

Pamela reviews her notes from the previous meetings and finds that the team had a long discussion about the importance of transportation, but eventually agreed to use 5 (instead of 2) as the importance weight. Now Mike needs to restore the original importance weight for transportation. The team will see its effect on the chart immediately.

To see the chart change when you change the importance weight in the worksheet:

1. Click cell **B9** to make it the active cell.
2. Type **5** and, as you press **[Enter]**, watch the chart change to reflect the new scores for all four sites.

Scottsdale once again ranks highest with a weighted score total of 131. Kauai ranks second with a total score of 129. Edmonton ranks third with a total score of 126. Chiba ranks last with a total score of 123.

Mike asks if everyone is satisfied with the current weightings and scores. The team agrees that the current worksheet is a reasonable representation of the factors that need to be considered for each site. Mike decides to remove the split screen so everyone can see all the scores and results on the worksheet.

Removing the Split Window

There are two ways to remove a split from your worksheet window. You can drag the split bar back to the top of the scroll bar, or you can use the Remove Split command on the Window menu. You can use whichever method you prefer. If you are using a mouse, it is probably easier to use the split bar.

Mike drags the split bar to remove the split window.

To remove the split window:

❶ Move the pointer over the split bar until it changes to ÷.

❷ Drag the split bar to the top of the scroll bar, then release the mouse button.

❸ If necessary, scroll the worksheet so you can see rows 3 through 20.

Making and Documenting the Decision

Pamela asks if the team is ready to recommend a final site. Mike wants to recommend Scottsdale as the primary site and Kauai as an alternative location. Pamela asks for a vote, and the team unanimously agrees with Mike's recommendation.

Mike suggests they save the modified worksheet under a different name. This will help document the decision process because it will preserve the original sheet showing Chiba with the highest score and it will save the current sheet, which shows Scottsdale with the highest score.

Saving the Workbook

When you save a workbook, it is copied from RAM onto your disk. Any charts that appear in the workbook are also saved.

Excel has more than one save command on the File menu. The two you'll use most often are the Save and Save As commands. The Save command copies the workbook onto a disk using the current filename. If an old version of the file exists, the new version will replace the old one. The Save As command asks for a filename before copying the workbook onto a disk. When you enter a new filename, the current file is saved under that new name. The previous version of the file remains on the disk under its original name. The flowchart in Figure 1-18 helps you decide whether to use the Save or the Save As command.

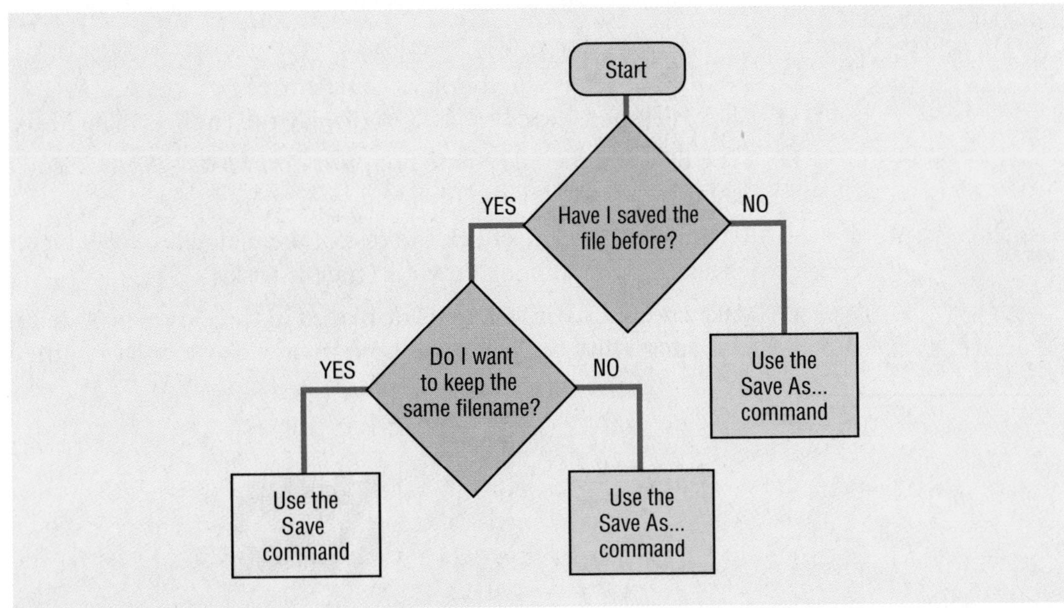

Figure 1-18
Deciding whether to use Save or Save As

When you type a filename, you can use either uppercase or lowercase letters. You do not need to type the .XLS extension. Excel automatically adds the extension when it saves the file.

REFERENCE WINDOW

Saving a Workbook with a New Filename

- Click File, then Save As....
- Type the filename for the modified workbook.
- Make sure the Drives box displays the drive in which you want to save your workbook.
- Make sure the Directories box shows an open file folder for the directory in which you want to store your workbook.
- Click the OK button.

As a general rule, use the Save As command the first time you save a file or whenever you have modified a file and want to save both the old and new versions. Use the Save command when you have modified a file and want to save only the current version.

It is a good idea to use the Save As command to save and name your file soon after you start a new workbook. Then, as you continue to work, periodically use the Save command to save the workbook. That way, if the power goes out or the computer stops working, you're less likely to lose your work. Because you use the Save command frequently, the toolbar has a Save button, which provides you with a single mouse-click shortcut for saving your workbook.

Mike's workbook is named GOLF.XLS. On the screen, Mike and the team are viewing a version of GOLF.XLS that they have modified during this work session. The original version of this workbook—the one that shows Chiba with the highest score—is still on Mike's disk. Mike decides to save the modified workbook as GOLF2.XLS on the disk in drive A. Then he will have two versions of the workbook on the disk—the original version named GOLF.XLS and the revised version named GOLF2.XLS.

To save the modified workbook as GOLF2.XLS:

❶ Click **File**, then click **Save As...** to display the Save As dialog box.

❷ Type **GOLF2** in the File Name box, *but don't press [Enter]*. You can use lowercase or uppercase to type the filename.

Before you proceed, check the rest of the dialog box specifications to ensure that you save the workbook on your Student Disk.

❸ Make sure the a: drive icon is displayed in the Drives box. If it is not, click the **down arrow button** on the Drives box, then click the **a: icon** in the list. See Figure 1-19.

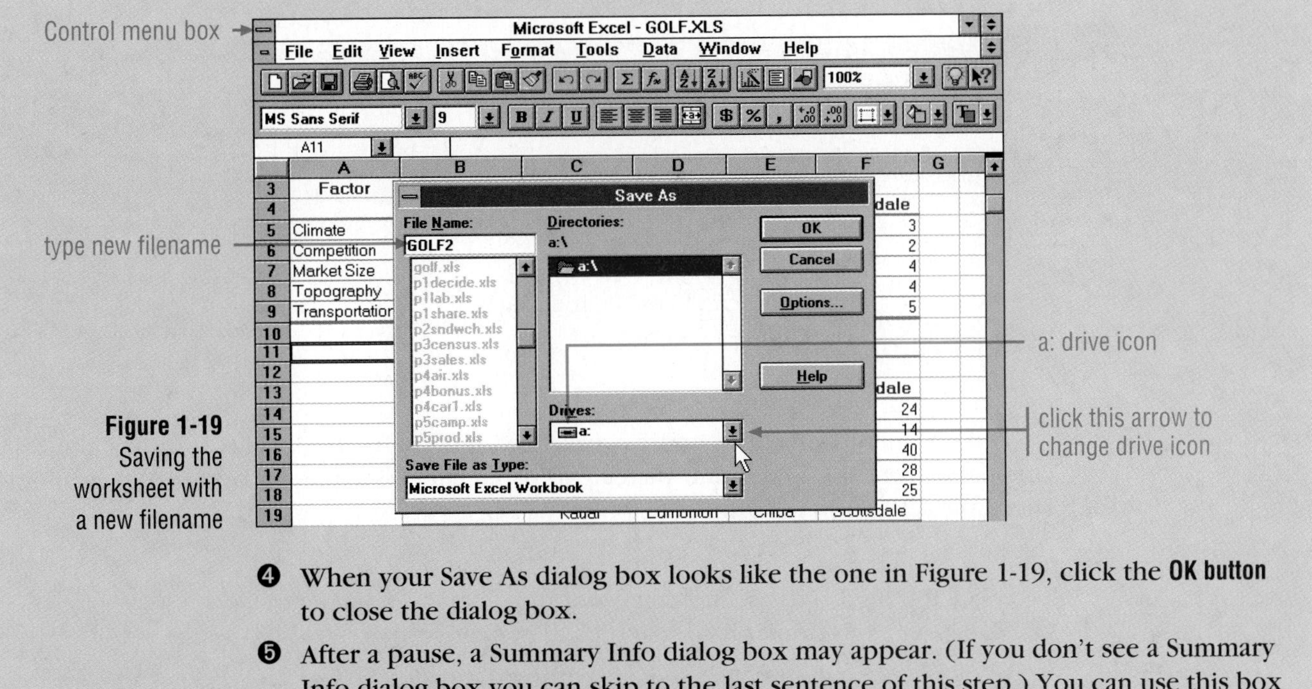

Figure 1-19
Saving the worksheet with a new filename

4. When your Save As dialog box looks like the one in Figure 1-19, click the **OK button** to close the dialog box.
5. After a pause, a Summary Info dialog box may appear. (If you don't see a Summary Info dialog box you can skip to the last sentence of this step.) You can use this box to record more information about the workbook—for example, you could enter your name in the Author box. When you are finished, click the **OK button** to return to the worksheet. The new workbook title, GOLF2.XLS, is displayed in the title bar.

If you want to take a break and resume the tutorial at a later time, you can exit Excel by double-clicking the Control menu box in the upper-left corner of the screen (shown in Figure 1-19). When you resume the tutorial, launch Excel, maximize the Microsoft Excel and Book1 windows, and place your Student Disk in the disk drive. Open the file GOLF2.XLS, then continue with the tutorial.

■ ■ ■

Printing the Worksheet and Chart

Pamela wants to have complete documentation for the team's written recommendation to management, so she asks Mike to print the worksheet and chart.

You can initiate the Print command using the File menu or the Print button. If you initiate printing with the Print command on the File menu, a dialog box lets you specify which pages of the worksheet you want to print, the number of copies you want to print, and the print quality. If you use the Print button, you will not have these options; Excel prints one copy of the entire worksheet at the default resolution, which is usually the highest resolution your printer can produce.

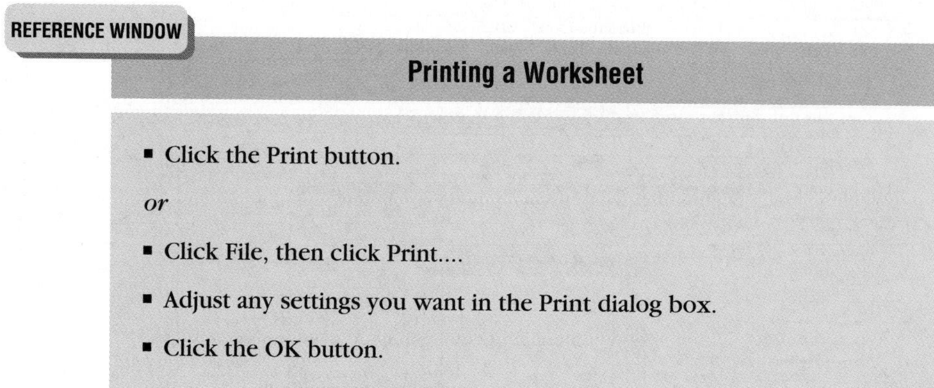

REFERENCE WINDOW

Printing a Worksheet

- Click the Print button.

or

- Click File, then click Print....
- Adjust any settings you want in the Print dialog box.
- Click the OK button.

Mike wants to print the entire worksheet and chart. He decides to select the Print command from the File menu instead of using the Print button because he wants to check the settings in the Print dialog box.

To check the print settings and then print the worksheet and chart:

1. Make sure your printer is turned on and contains paper.
2. Click **File**, then click **Print...** to display the Print dialog box.
3. Make sure your Print dialog box settings for Print What, Copies, and Page Range are the same as those in Figure 1-20.

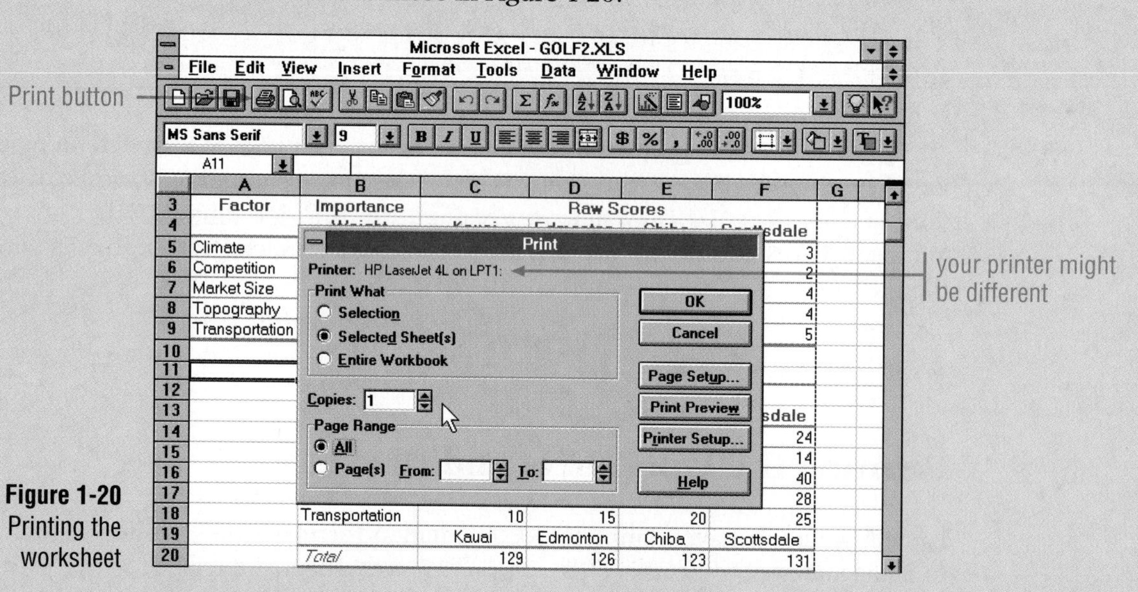

Figure 1-20 Printing the worksheet

4. Click the **OK button** to print the worksheet and chart. See Figure 1-21.

TROUBLE? If the worksheet and chart do not print, see your technical support person for assistance.

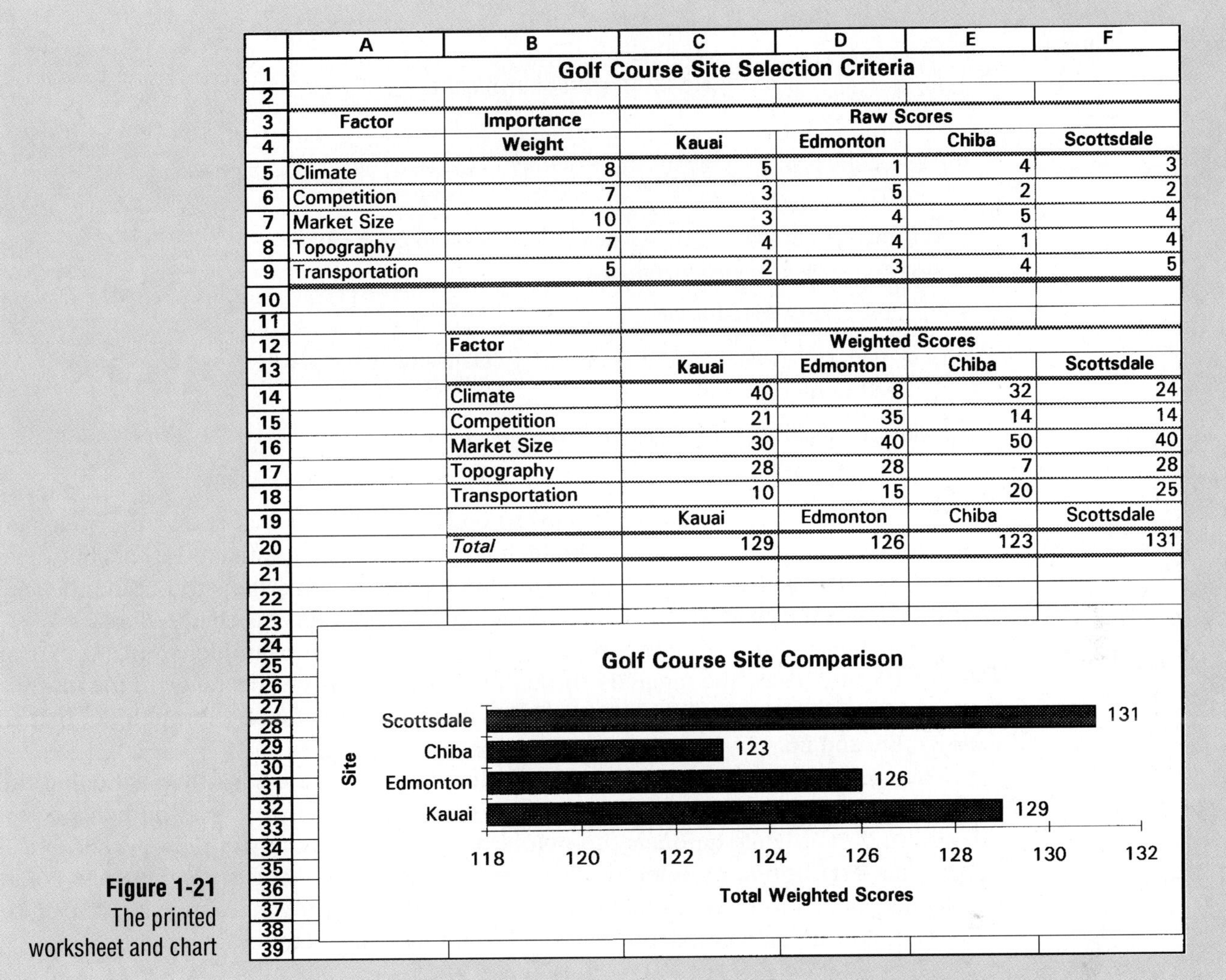

	A	B	C	D	E	F
1	Golf Course Site Selection Criteria					
2						
3	Factor	Importance	Raw Scores			
4		Weight	Kauai	Edmonton	Chiba	Scottsdale
5	Climate	8	5	1	4	3
6	Competition	7	3	5	2	2
7	Market Size	10	3	4	5	4
8	Topography	7	4	4	1	4
9	Transportation	5	2	3	4	5
10						
11						
12		Factor	Weighted Scores			
13			Kauai	Edmonton	Chiba	Scottsdale
14		Climate	40	8	32	24
15		Competition	21	35	14	14
16		Market Size	30	40	50	40
17		Topography	28	28	7	28
18		Transportation	10	15	20	25
19			Kauai	Edmonton	Chiba	Scottsdale
20		*Total*	129	126	123	131

Figure 1-21
The printed worksheet and chart

Pamela asks Mike if they can create a chart that illustrates the weighted scores for every factor for each site. Mike says he can easily do that with the Excel ChartWizard.

Creating a Chart with the ChartWizard

The **ChartWizard** guides you through five steps to create a chart. You can select from a variety of chart types, including bar charts, column charts, line charts, and pie charts. Tutorial 5 describes the chart types in detail. After you create a chart using the ChartWizard, you can change it, move it to a new location, or save it.

REFERENCE WINDOW

Creating a Chart with ChartWizard

- Position the pointer in the upper-left corner of the area you want to chart.
- Drag the pointer to highlight all the cells you want to chart. Make sure to include row and column titles.
- Click the ChartWizard button.
- Drag the pointer to outline the area in the worksheet where you want the chart to appear.
- Follow the ChartWizard instructions to complete the chart.

Mike is ready to use the ChartWizard to create a bar chart that shows the weighted scores for each of the four sites. First he highlights the cells that contain the data he wants to chart. Then he activates the ChartWizard and follows the five steps to outline the area where he wants the chart to appear and to specify how he wants his chart to look.

A rectangular block of cells is referred to as a **range**. For example, you can refer to cells B4, B5, and B6 as "the range B4 through B6." Excel displays this range in the formula bar as B4:B6. The colon in the notation B4:B6 indicates the range B4 through B6, that is, cells B4, B5, and B6.

When Mike highlights the range of cells for the chart, he begins by positioning the pointer on the cell that will be the upper-left corner of the range. Next, he holds down the mouse button while he drags the pointer to the cell in the lower-right corner of the range. This **highlights**, or **selects**, all the cells in the range; that is, they change color, usually becoming black. The cell in the upper-left corner of the range is the active cell, so it does not appear highlighted, but it is included in the range. Let's see how this works.

To highlight the data in the range B13:F18 for the chart:

1. Position the pointer on cell B13, the upper-left corner of the range you want to highlight.
2. Hold down the mouse button while you drag the pointer to cell F18.
3. Release the mouse button. The range of cells from B13 to F18 is highlighted, except for cell B13. Cell B13 does not appear to be highlighted because it is the active cell, but it is still included in the highlighted range. See Figure 1-22.

   TROUBLE? If your highlight does not correspond to Figure 1-22, repeat Steps 1–3.

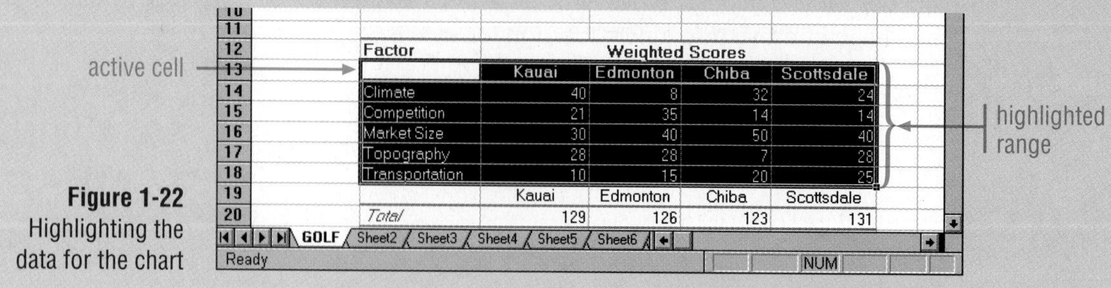

Figure 1-22 Highlighting the data for the chart

Next, Mike clicks the ChartWizard button and specifies the location of the chart. He wants to position the new chart between rows 45 and 64 on the worksheet, so he outlines the location for the new chart by dragging the pointer from cell A45 to cell F64.

To activate the ChartWizard and specify the location for the chart:

❶ Click the **ChartWizard button** . The prompt "Drag in document to create a chart" appears in the status bar and the pointer changes to .

❷ Use the vertical scroll bar to scroll the worksheet so you can view rows 45 through 64. (Note that the pointer becomes when positioned over the scroll bar.)

❸ Drag from cell A45 to cell F64 to outline the location of the chart. See Figure 1-23.

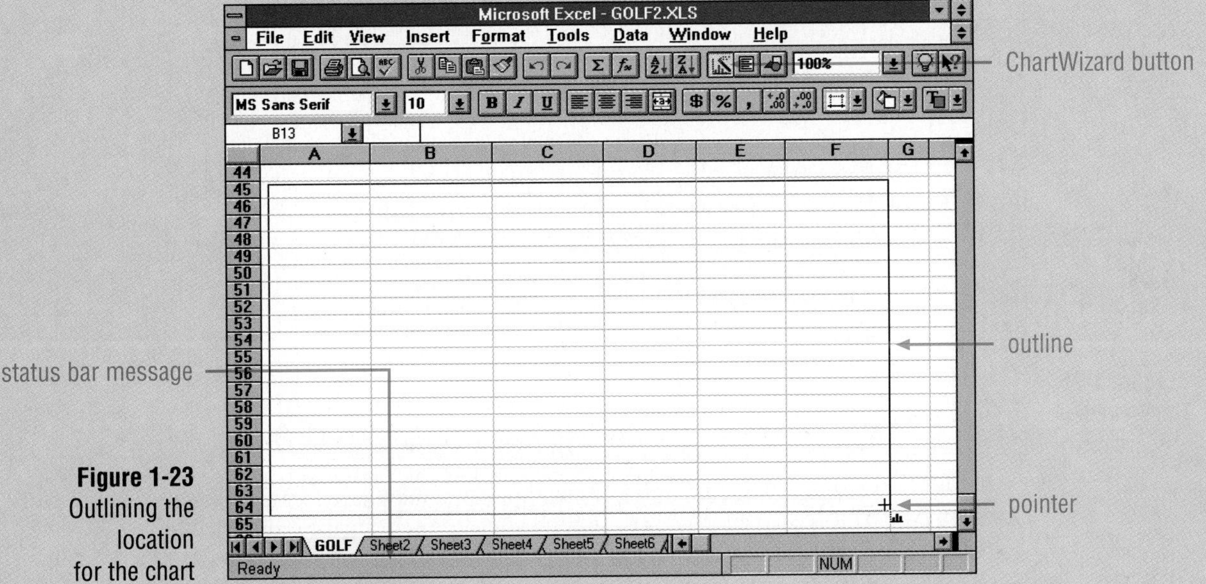

Figure 1-23
Outlining the location for the chart

❹ Release the mouse button.

❺ When the ChartWizard - Step 1 of 5 dialog box appears, make sure the Range box shows =$B$13:$F$18. See Figure 1-24. Don't be concerned about the dollar signs ($) in the cell references; you will learn about the dollar signs in Tutorial 4.

TROUBLE? If the Range box does not display $B$13:$F$18, you have highlighted the wrong cells to use for the chart. Drag the pointer from B13 to F18 and then release the mouse button.

ChartWizard - Step 1 of 5
If the selected cells do not contain the data you wish to chart, select a new range now.
Include the cells containing row and column labels if you want those labels to appear on the chart.
Range: =$B$13:$F$18
Help | Cancel | < Back | Next > | Finish

Range box
Next button

Figure 1-24
The ChartWizard - Step 1 of 5 dialog box

❻ Click the **Next > button** to display the ChartWizard - Step 2 of 5 dialog box.

❼ Double-click the chart type labeled **Bar**. The ChartWizard - Step 3 of 5 dialog box appears.

8. Double-click the box for format **6** to select a horizontal chart with gridlines. The ChartWizard - Step 4 of 5 dialog box appears, showing you a preview of your chart. Don't worry if the titles are not formatted correctly.
9. You will not make any additional changes to your chart at this point, so click the **Next > button** to display the ChartWizard - Step 5 of 5 dialog box.
10. Click the **Chart Title box**, then type **Weighted Scores** and click the **Finish button**. The chart appears in the worksheet. See Figure 1-25.

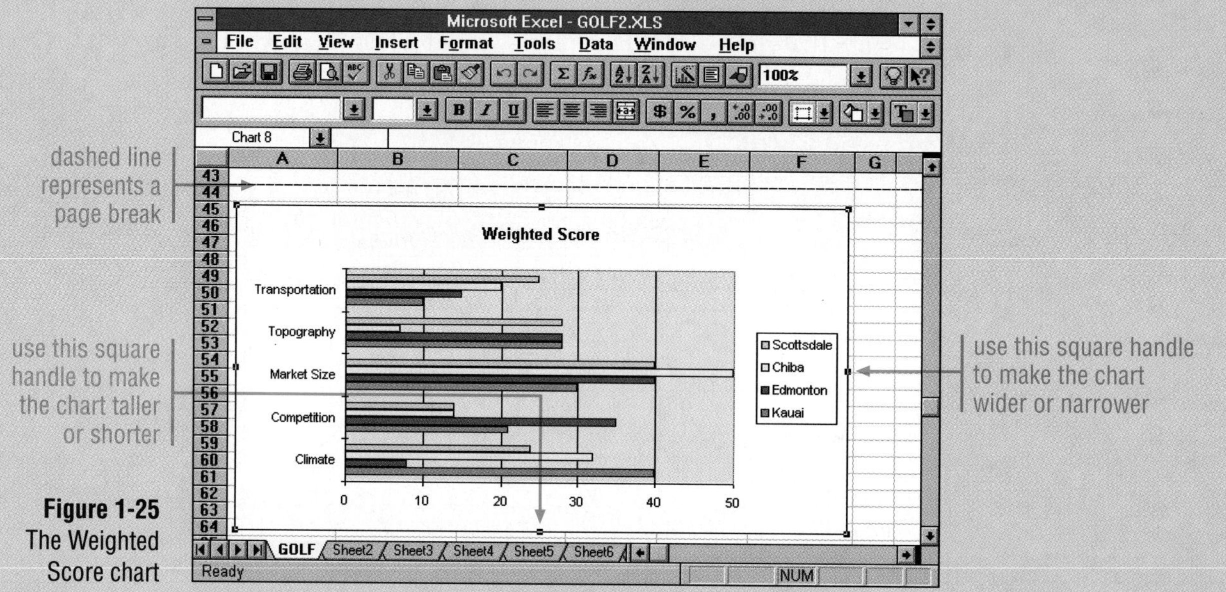

Figure 1-25 The Weighted Score chart

TROUBLE? You may see an extra toolbar appear somewhere in the worksheet, along with the chart. This is the Chart Toolbar, which you can use to make quick changes to the chart. Because you will not be making any changes to the chart, you can close the Chart Toolbar by double-clicking the Control menu box.

The entire team is impressed with the Weighted Scores chart. Pamela asks Mike to print it.

Printing a Specific Page

The Weighted Scores chart is on page 2 of the worksheet. On your screen and on Figure 1-25, the dashed line between row 43 and row 44 represents a page break. To print the Weighted Scores chart, Mike must print page 2 of the worksheet. The Print dialog box setting for "Page(s) From:__ To:__" lets you specify which page you want to start *from* and which page you want to print *to*. To print only page 2, Mike prints from page 2 to page 2.

To print page 2 of the worksheet containing the Weighted Scores chart:

1. Click **File**, then click **Print...** to display the Print dialog box. Figure 1-26 shows the Print dialog box settings you will have when you complete Steps 2 through 4.

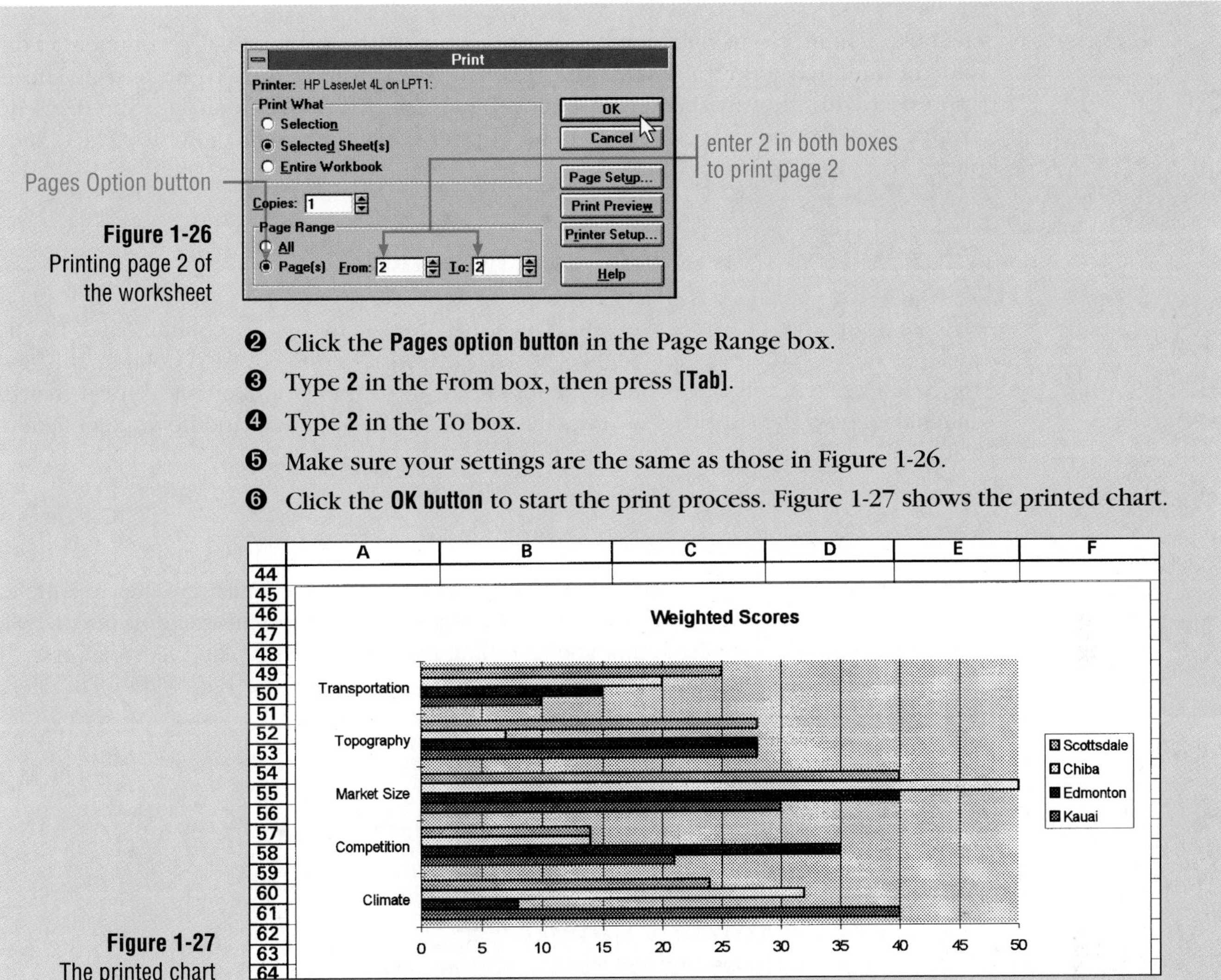

Figure 1-26
Printing page 2 of the worksheet

❷ Click the **Pages option button** in the Page Range box.

❸ Type **2** in the From box, then press **[Tab]**.

❹ Type **2** in the To box.

❺ Make sure your settings are the same as those in Figure 1-26.

❻ Click the **OK button** to start the print process. Figure 1-27 shows the printed chart.

Figure 1-27
The printed chart

Pamela suggests they save the worksheet and the Weighted Scores chart. They decide to save the workbook under the current name, GOLF2.XLS. This replaces the old version of GOLF2.XLS with the new version, which includes the Weighted Scores chart.

To save the workbook with the same filename:

❶ Click the **Save button** to replace the old version of the workbook with the new version.

If you want to take a break and resume the tutorial at a later time, you can exit Excel by double-clicking the Control menu box in the upper-left corner of the screen. When you resume the tutorial, launch Excel, maximize the Microsoft Excel and Book1 windows, and place your Student Disk in the disk drive. Open the file GOLF2.XLS, then continue with the tutorial.

■ ■ ■

Mike volunteers to put together the report with the team's final recommendation, and the meeting adjourns. After the meeting Pamela mentions to Mike that she is impressed with the way the spreadsheet program helped the team analyze the data and make a decision, but she admits that she doesn't really understand how it works. Mike offers to explain the basic concepts.

Values, Text, Formulas, and Functions

Mike explains that an Excel worksheet is a grid consisting of 256 columns and 16,384 rows. As noted earlier, the rectangular areas at the intersections of each column and row are called cells. A cell can contain a value, text, or a formula. Mike tells Pamela that to understand how the spreadsheet program works, she must understand how Excel manipulates values, text, formulas, and functions.

Values

Values are numbers, dates, and times that Excel can use for calculations. For example, 378, 11/29/94, and 4:40:31 are examples of values. As you type information into a cell, Excel determines if the characters you're typing can be used as a value. For example, if you type 456 Excel recognizes it as a value and displays it on the right side of the cell. Mike shows Pamela that cells B5 through B9 contain values.

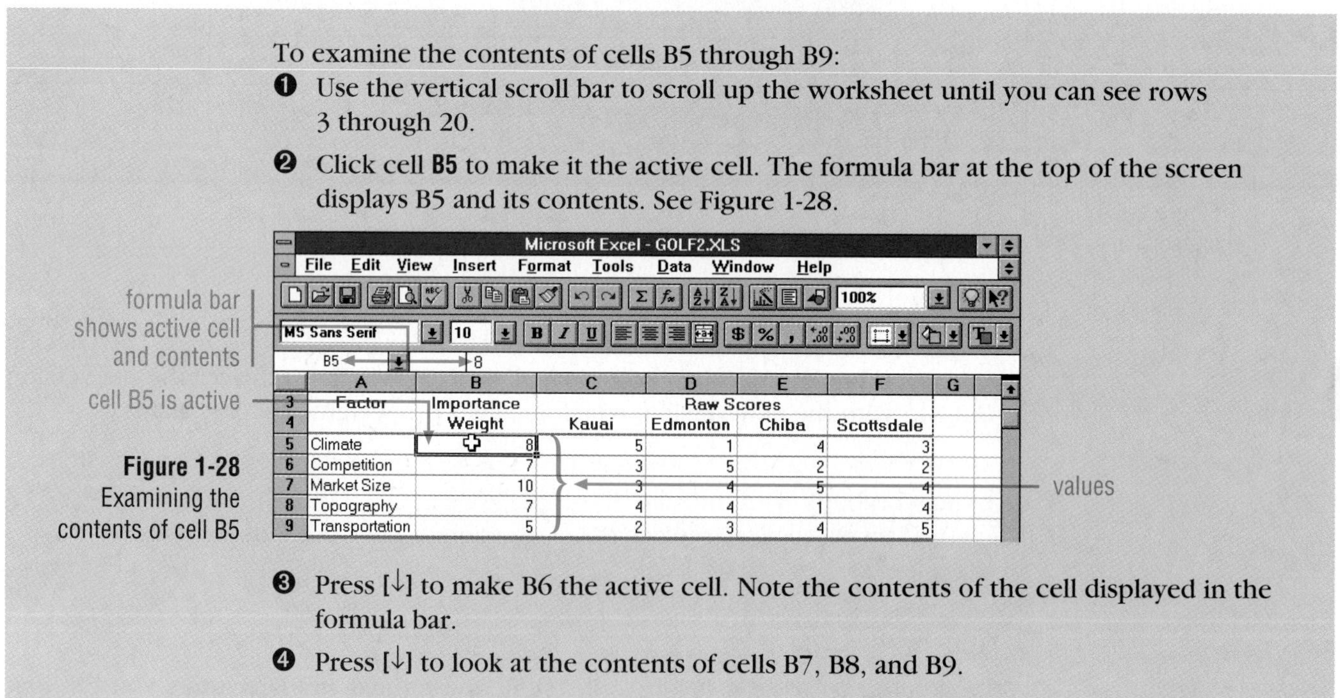

To examine the contents of cells B5 through B9:

1. Use the vertical scroll bar to scroll up the worksheet until you can see rows 3 through 20.
2. Click cell **B5** to make it the active cell. The formula bar at the top of the screen displays B5 and its contents. See Figure 1-28.

Figure 1-28 Examining the contents of cell B5

3. Press [↓] to make B6 the active cell. Note the contents of the cell displayed in the formula bar.
4. Press [↓] to look at the contents of cells B7, B8, and B9.

Text

Text is any set of characters that Excel does not interpret as a value. Text is often used to label the columns and rows in the worksheet. Examples of text are Total Sales, Acme Co., and Eastern Division.

Text entries cannot be used for calculations. Some data commonly referred to as "numbers" are treated as text by Excel. For example, a telephone number such as 227-1240 or a social security number such as 372-70-9654 is treated as text and cannot be used for calculations. Mike shows Pamela that cells A5 through A9 contain text.

To examine the contents of cells A5 through A9:

❶ Click cell **A5** to make it the active cell. The formula bar displays the cell reference A5 and the cell contents, "Climate." See Figure 1-29.

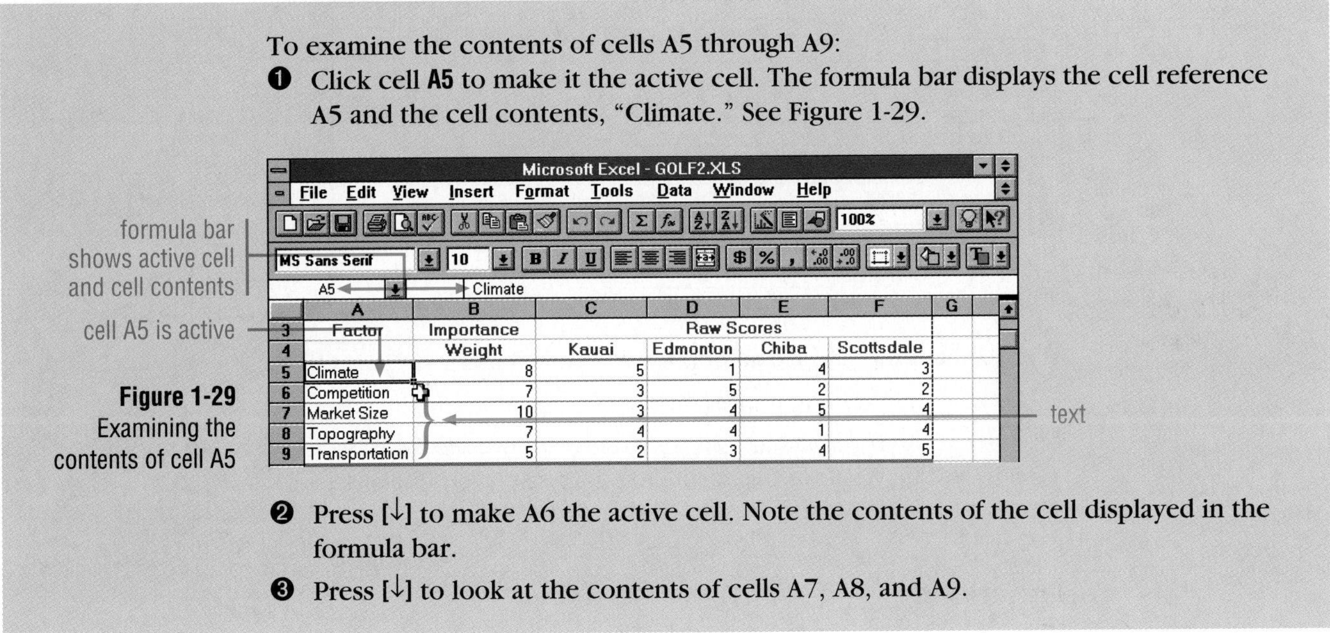

Figure 1-29 Examining the contents of cell A5

❷ Press [↓] to make A6 the active cell. Note the contents of the cell displayed in the formula bar.

❸ Press [↓] to look at the contents of cells A7, A8, and A9.

Formulas

Formulas specify the calculations you want Excel to perform. Formulas always begin with an equal sign (=). Most formulas contain **mathematical operators** such as +, –, *, / that specify how Excel should manipulate the numbers in the calculation. When you type a formula, use the asterisk (*) for multiplication and the slash (/) for division.

Formulas can contain numbers or cell references. Some examples of formulas are =20+10, =G9/2, and =C5*B5. The formula =C5*B5 instructs Excel to multiply the contents of cell C5 by the contents of cell B5.

The *result* of the formula is displayed in the cell in which you have entered the formula. To view the formula in a cell, you must first make that cell active, then look at the formula bar. Mike shows Pamela how to view formulas and their results.

To view the formula in cell C14:

❶ Click cell **C14** to make it the active cell. The formula bar shows =C5*B5 as the formula for cell C14. This formula multiplies the contents of cell C5 by the contents of cell B5. See Figure 1-30.

formula displayed in formula bar

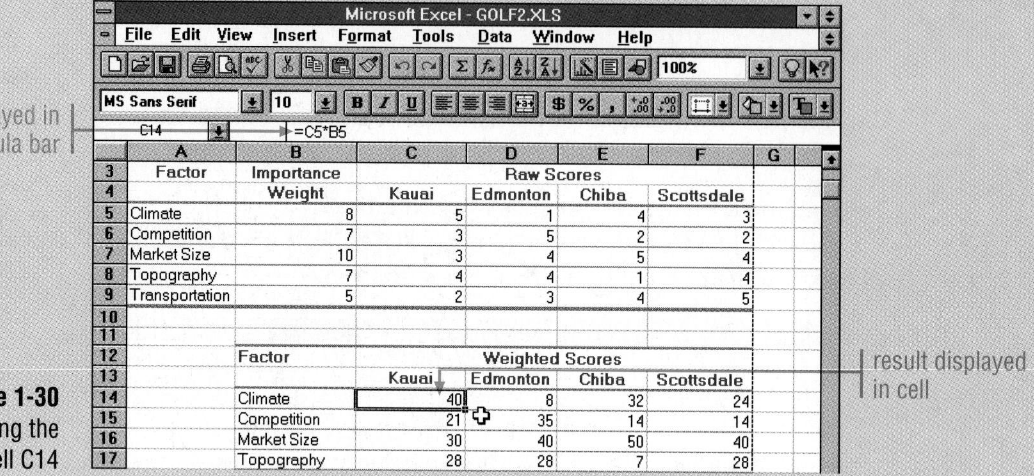

	A	B	C	D	E	F
3	Factor	Importance		Raw Scores		
4		Weight	Kauai	Edmonton	Chiba	Scottsdale
5	Climate	8	5	1	4	3
6	Competition	7	3	5	2	2
7	Market Size	10	3	4	5	4
8	Topography	7	4	4	1	4
9	Transportation	5	2	3	4	5
10						
11						
12		Factor		Weighted Scores		
13			Kauai	Edmonton	Chiba	Scottsdale
14		Climate	40	8	32	24
15		Competition	21	35	14	14
16		Market Size	30	40	50	40
17		Topography	28	28	7	28

result displayed in cell

Figure 1-30
Viewing the formula in cell C14

❷ Look at cell C5. The number in this cell is 5.

❸ Look at cell B5. The number in this cell is 8.

❹ Look at the formula bar. Multiplying the contents of C5 by B5 means to multiply 5 by 8. The result of this formula, 40, is displayed in cell C14.

Functions

A **function** is a special prewritten formula that provides a shortcut for commonly used calculations. For example, you can use the SUM function to create the formula =SUM(D14:D18) instead of typing the longer formula =D14+D15+D16+D17+D18. The SUM function in this example sums the range D14:D18. (Recall that D14:D18 refers to the rectangular block of cells beginning at D14 and ending at D18.) Other functions include AVERAGE, which calculates the average value; MIN, which finds the smallest value; and MAX, which finds the largest value.

To view the function in the formula in cell C20:

❶ Click cell **C20** to make it the active cell. See Figure 1-31.

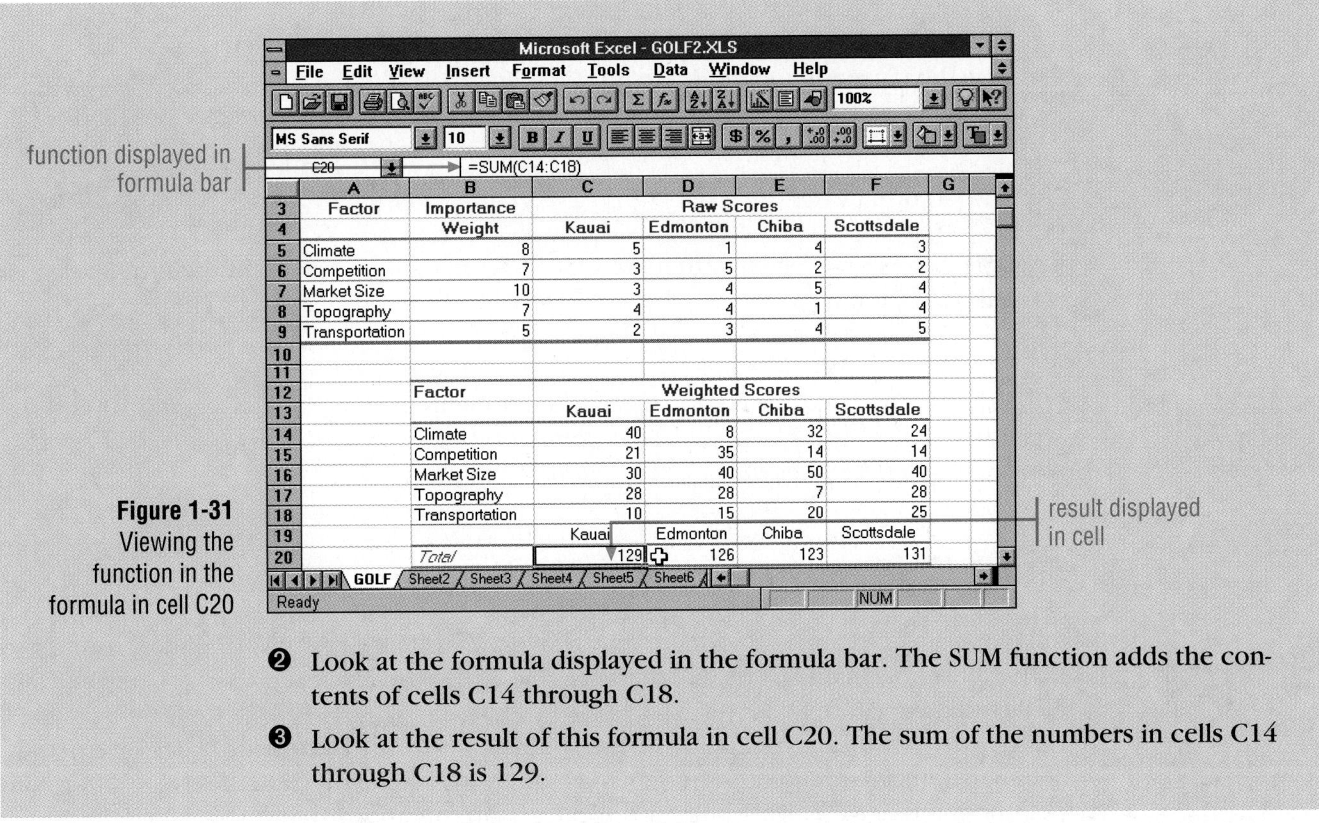

	A	B	C	D	E	F
3	Factor	Importance		Raw Scores		
4		Weight	Kauai	Edmonton	Chiba	Scottsdale
5	Climate	8	5	1	4	3
6	Competition	7	3	5	2	2
7	Market Size	10	3	4	5	4
8	Topography	7	4	4	1	4
9	Transportation	5	2	3	4	5
10						
11						
12		Factor		Weighted Scores		
13			Kauai	Edmonton	Chiba	Scottsdale
14		Climate	40	8	32	24
15		Competition	21	35	14	14
16		Market Size	30	40	50	40
17		Topography	28	28	7	28
18		Transportation	10	15	20	25
19			Kauai	Edmonton	Chiba	Scottsdale
20		Total	129	126	123	131

Figure 1-31 Viewing the function in the formula in cell C20

❷ Look at the formula displayed in the formula bar. The SUM function adds the contents of cells C14 through C18.

❸ Look at the result of this formula in cell C20. The sum of the numbers in cells C14 through C18 is 129.

Remember that the formula bar shows the *contents* of the cell, the formula =SUM(C14:C18). The worksheet cell shows the *result* of the formula. *To determine the actual contents of a cell, you must make that cell the active cell and view the contents in the formula bar.*

Automatic Recalculation

Mike explains that any time a value in a worksheet cell is changed, Excel automatically recalculates all the formulas. Changing a number in only one cell might result in many changes throughout the worksheet. Mike demonstrates by changing the importance weight for climate from 8 to 2.

To change the importance weight for climate:

1. Note the current importance weight for climate (8), the weighted scores for climate in each location (Kauai 40, Edmonton 8, Chiba 32, and Scottsdale 24), and the total weighted scores for each location (Kauai 129, Edmonton 126, Chiba 123, and Scottsdale 131).
2. Click cell **B5** to make it the active cell.
3. Type **2** and press **[Enter]**. Watch the worksheet update the results of the formulas in cells C14 through F14 and cells C20 through F20.

Note the updated results for the climate weighted scores (10, 2, 8, and 6) and the weighted totals (99, 120, 99, and 113). *Remember, when a value is changed in a worksheet, every cell that depends on that value is recalculated.*

Excel Help

Mike explains to Pamela that there are many spreadsheet programs to choose from, but he prefers Excel because it is one of the easiest to use. He especially likes the on-line Help facility that Excel provides.

Located on the far right side of the toolbar, the **Help button** provides information about any object you point to in the Excel window. When you click the Help button, the pointer changes to ?. This pointer indicates that you are in Help mode. In Help mode, you can move the Help pointer to a screen object to view a one-line description of the object in the status bar, or you can click the object to open the Microsoft Excel Help window and view a more complete explanation of the object and its function. The Help button is especially handy if you want to find out the function of menu options.

REFERENCE WINDOW

Using the Help Button

- Click the Help button to begin Help mode and display the Help pointer ?.
- Position ? on the screen object or menu item you want to know more about.
- If the Help message in the status bar is not sufficient, click the mouse button to open the Microsoft Excel Help window.
- When you are finished viewing the Microsoft Excel Help window, double-click the Control menu box for the window.
- If the Help pointer is still displayed and you want to exit Help mode, click the Help button again.

Mike shows Pamela how to use the Help button to learn the function of the Cells command on the Format menu.

To use the Help button to learn the function of the Cells command on the Format menu:

1. Click the **Help button** . The pointer changes to .
2. Click the word **Format** in the menu bar. The Format menu opens. In the status bar at the bottom of the screen, Excel displays the message "Changes cell font, border, alignment, and other formats."
3. To get detailed information on the Cells command, click **Cells...**. The Microsoft Excel Help window appears. See Figure 1-32. Note that the pointer changes shape to when you place it over the list of Help topics.

   TROUBLE? If your Microsoft Excel Help window is not the same size as the one in Figure 1-32, drag the borders to make it the same size.

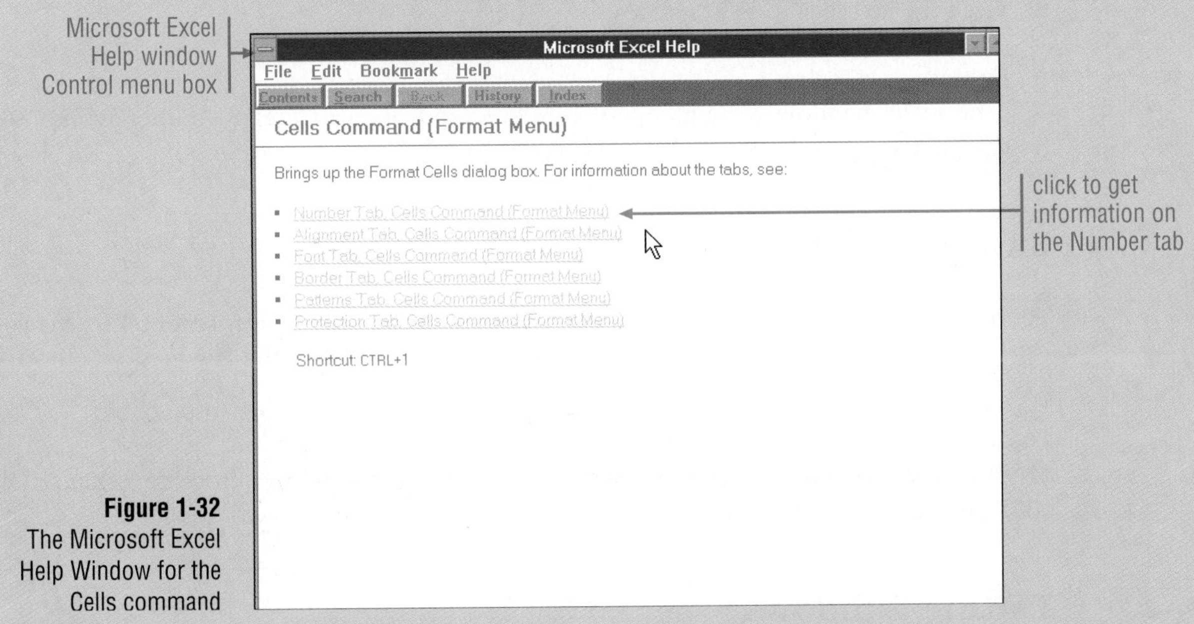

Figure 1-32
The Microsoft Excel Help Window for the Cells command

4. To get information on the first topic, click **Number Tab, Cells Command (Format Menu)**. Another Help window appears.
5. Read through the information in the Help window.
6. Double-click the **Microsoft Excel Help window Control menu box** to close the window and return to the worksheet.

Mike explains that when you close the Microsoft Excel Help window, you automatically exit Help mode and your pointer returns to the arrow or white plus shape.

Mike tells Pamela that the Help menu on the menu bar also gives you access to on-line Help. The Help menu works like the Help menu provided in most Windows programs. In addition, you can click the TipWizard button to display the TipWizard box. (The TipWizard button is the button with the lightbulb on it, next to the Help button.) This TipWizard box tells you about quicker, more efficient ways of performing actions you've just performed. Mike doesn't have time to show Pamela how to use these features, but he assures her that she can easily explore the options on her own.

Closing the Worksheet

Mike closes the worksheet window. He does not want to save the changes that he made while demonstrating the worksheet to Pamela, so he does not use the Save command or the Save As command. When he tries to close the worksheet window, a message asks if he wants to save the changes he has made. Mike responds by clicking the No button.

To close the GOLF2.XLS workbook without saving changes:

1. Click **File**, then click **Close**. A dialog box displays the message "Save changes in 'GOLF2.XLS?'"
2. Click the **No button** to exit without saving changes.

The Excel window remains open so Mike could open or create another workbook. He does not want to do this, so his next step is to exit Excel.

Exiting Excel

There are several ways to exit Excel. You can double-click the Control menu box, or you can use the Exit command on the File menu. Mike generally uses the File menu method.

To exit Excel using the File menu:

1. Click **File**, then click **Exit** to exit Excel and return to the Windows Program Manager.

Exiting Windows

Before Mike turns off his computer, he exits Windows. Mike knows that it is a good idea to exit Windows before he turns off his computer so all files are properly closed.

To exit Windows:

1. Click **File** on the Program Manager menu bar to display the File menu.
2. Click **Exit Windows...**. A dialog box displays the message "This will end your Windows session."
3. Click the **OK button** to exit Windows and return to the DOS prompt.

The InWood site selection team has completed its work. Mike's decision-support worksheet helped the team analyze the data and recommend Scottsdale as the best site for InWood's next golf course. Although the Japanese market was a strong factor in favor of locating the course in Japan's Chiba Prefecture, the mountainous terrain and competition from nearby courses reduced the desirability of this location.

■ ■ ■

Questions

1. List three uses of spreadsheets in business.
2. In your own words describe what a spreadsheet program does.
3. Identify each of the numbered components of the Excel window shown in Figure 1-33.

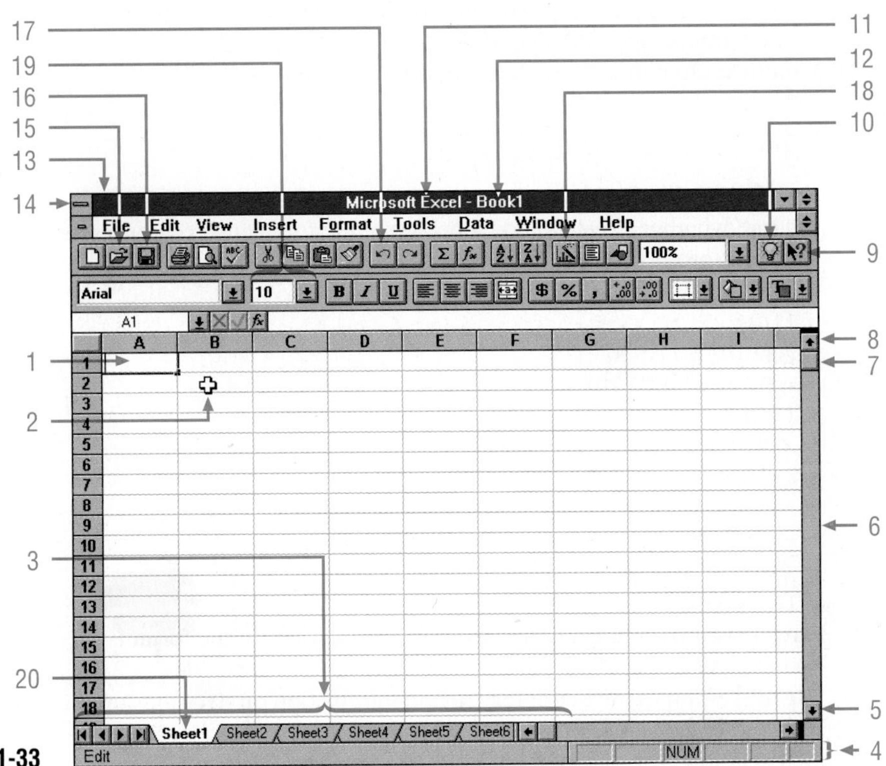

Figure 1-33

4. Identify each of the following buttons.
   a.
   b.
   c.
   d.
   e.
5. Draw four shapes the pointer can assume in the Excel window and describe the task you are performing when each pointer shape appears.
6. A(n) ________________ is the rectangular area at the intersection of a column and row.
7. When you ________________ a workbook, the computer copies it from your disk into RAM.
8. The cell with a black border around it is called the ________________.
9. To view more than one window pane, use the ________________ bar.
10. Use the ________________ command the first time you want to save a file.
11. The ________________ command is useful if you enter a number by mistake and want to restore the original value.
12. Any set of characters that Excel does not use for calculations is called ________________.
13. The ________________________ guides you through five steps to create a chart.

14. If you want to save the new version of a file in place of the old version, use the ________________ command.
15. Numbers, dates, and times that Excel uses for calculations are called ________________.
16. How can you tell exactly what a cell contains?
17. The colon in the notation B4:B6 indicates a(n) ________________.
18. A(n) ________________ is a special prewritten formula that provides a shortcut for commonly used calculations.
19. A(n) ________________ specifies the calculations you want Excel to make.
20. In the formula =B5*125, B5 is a(n) ________________.
21. Identify each of the following mathematical operators:
    a. *
    b. -
    c. +
    d. /
22. Indicate whether Excel would treat each of the following cell entries as a value, text, or a formula:
    a. Profit
    b. 11/09/95
    c. February 10, 1996
    d. =AVERAGE(B5:B20)
    e. 11:01:25
    f. =B9*225
    g. =A6*D8
    h. 227-1240
    i. =SUM(C1:C10)
    j. 372-80-2367
    k. 123 N. First St.
23. How do you write the function that is the equivalent of the formula =A1+A2+A3+A4?

E 24. Use the resources in your library to find information on decision-support systems. Write a one- or two-page paper that describes what a decision-support system is and how one might be used in a business. Also include your ideas on the relationship between spreadsheets and decision-support systems.

Tutorial Assignments

The other company that had planned a golf course in Chiba, Japan has run into financial difficulties. There are rumors that the project may be canceled. A copy of the final InWood Design team workbook is stored on your Student Disk in the file T1GOLF2.XLS. Do the Tutorial Assignments below to modify this worksheet to show the effect that the cancellation of the other project would have on your site selection. Print your results for Tutorial Assignment 14. Write your answers to Tutorial Assignments 15 through 17.

1. Launch Windows and Excel. Make sure your Student Disk is in the disk drive.
2. Open the file T1GOLF2.XLS.
3. Use the Save As command to save the workbook as S1GOLF2.XLS so you do not modify the original workbook for this set of Tutorial Assignments.
4. Click the TipWizard button to display the TipWizard box. As you complete the following Tutorial Assignments notice that the information in the TipWizard box changes.
5. In the S1GOLF2.XLS worksheet change the competition raw score for Chiba from 2 to 3.
6. Use the vertical scroll bar to view the effect on the chart showing Weighted Scores.

7. Enter the text "Scores if the Competing Project in Chiba, Japan is Canceled" in cell B2.

The importance weight assigned to each factor is a critical component in the site selection worksheet. Create a bar chart that shows the importance weights assigned to each factor.

8. Highlight cells A4 through B9.
9. Activate the ChartWizard.
10. Locate the chart in cells A66 through F85.
11. Use the ChartWizard - Steps 1 through 4 to select a bar chart using format 6.
12. For the ChartWizard - Step 5 of 5, enter "Importance Weights" as the chart title and indicate that you do not want to use a legend for the chart.
13. Save the worksheet and chart as S1GOLF2.XLS.
14. Print the entire worksheet, including the charts.

E 15. Use the Help button to learn the function of the four buttons shown in Figure 1-34.

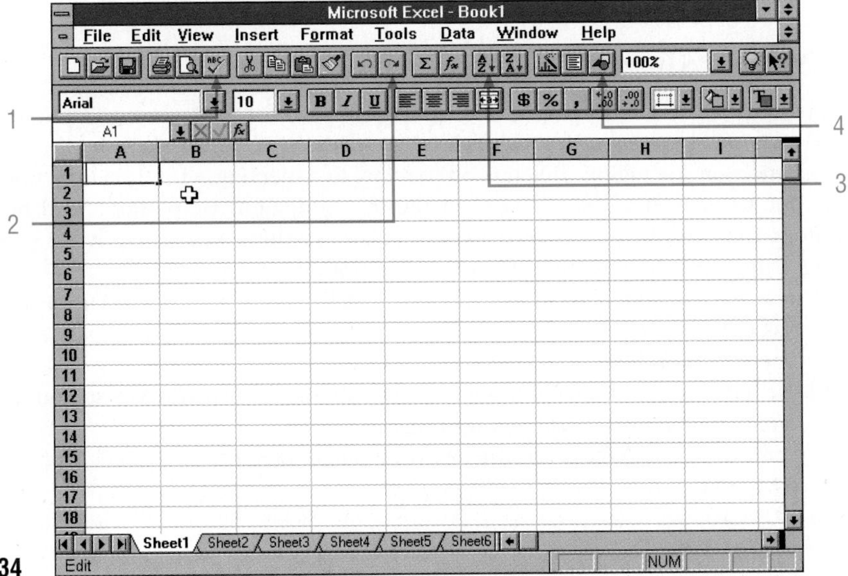

Figure 1-34

E 16. Use the Help button to learn more about the Print command on the File menu. How can you print a chart without printing the entire worksheet?

E 17. Use the scroll arrows to scroll through the tips in the TipWizard box. What new information did you learn? Click the TipWizard button in the toolbar to close the TipWizard box.

18. Exit Excel.

Case Problems

1. Selecting a Hospital Laboratory Computer System for Bridgeport Medical Center

David Choi is on the Laboratory Computer Selection Committee for the Bridgeport Medical Center. After an extensive search, the committee identified three vendors with products that appear to meet its needs. The Selection Committee prepared an Excel worksheet to help evaluate the strengths and weaknesses of the three potential vendors. The raw scores for two of the vendors, LabStar and Health Systems, have already been entered. Now the raw scores must be entered for the third vendor, MedTech. Which vendor's system is best for the Bridgeport Medical Center? Complete the following steps to find out:

1. If necessary, launch Windows and Excel. Make sure your Student Disk is in the disk drive.
2. Open the workbook P1LAB.XLS.
3. Use the Save As command to save the workbook as S1LAB.XLS so you don't modify the original workbook for this case.
4. Enter the following raw scores for MedTech:
   Cost = 6, Compatibility = 5, Vendor Reliability = 5, Size of Installed Base = 4, User Satisfaction = 5, Critical Functionality = 9, Additional Functionality = 8
5. Use the ChartWizard to create a column chart showing the total weighted scores for the three vendors. *Hint:* The chart will include cells C24 to E25. Position the chart below the worksheet in cells A28 to E46. Use a column chart with format 2. Enter "Total Weighted Scores" as the chart title.
6. Use the Save command to save the modified worksheet and chart.
7. Print the worksheet and chart.

2. Market Share Analysis at Aldon Industries

Helen Shalala is the Assistant to the Regional Director for Aldon Industries, a manufacturer of corporate voice mail systems. Helen prepared an analysis of the market share of the top vendors with installations in the region. Helen is on her way to a meeting with the marketing staff where she will use her worksheet to plan a new marketing campaign. Help Helen and her team evaluate the options and plan the best advertising campaign for Aldon Industries. Write your responses to questions 4 through 10, then create the chart and print it.

1. If necessary, launch Windows and Excel. Make sure your Student Disk is in the disk drive.
2. Open the workbook P1SHARE.XLS.
3. Use the Save As command to save the workbook as S1SHARE.XLS so you don't modify the original workbook for this case.
4. Examine the worksheet. Do the following ranges contain text, values, or formulas?
   a. B13:F13
   b. C3:C10
   c. A3:A10
   d. G3:G10
5. What is Aldon Industries' overall share of the market?
6. Examine the worksheet to determine in which state Aldon Industries currently has the highest market share.
7. Aldon Industries currently runs localized marketing campaigns in each state.
   a. In which state does Aldon Industries appear to have the most successful marketing campaign?
   b. In which state does Aldon Industries appear to have the least successful marketing campaign?
8. Which company is the overall market leader?
9. What is Aldon Industries' overall ranking in total market share (1st, 2nd, 3rd, etc.)?
10. Which companies rank ahead of Aldon Industries in total market share?
11. Michigan is the state in which Aldon Industries has its lowest market share. Use the ChartWizard to create a column chart showing the number of installations in Michigan for each company. *Hint:* The chart will include the range A2 through B10. Place the chart in cells A15 through F50. Select format 2 for the column chart. Enter "Installations in Michigan" as the chart title.
12. Save the worksheet and chart on your Student Disk.
13. Print the worksheet and chart.

3. Completing Your Own Decision Analysis

Think of a decision that you are trying to make. It might be choosing a new car, selecting a major, deciding where to go for vacation, or accepting a job offer. Use the workbook P1DECIDE.XLS to evaluate up to three options on the basis of up to five factors. Write your responses to questions 10 through 13 and print the worksheet and chart.

1. If necessary, launch Windows and Excel. Make sure your Student Disk is in the disk drive.
2. Open the workbook P1DECIDE.XLS.
3. Use the Save As command to save the workbook as S1DECIDE.XLS.
4. Click cell A1 and type the worksheet title.
5. Type the titles for up to three choices in cells C4, D4, and E4.
6. Type the titles for up to five factors in cells A6 to A10.
7. Type the importance weights for each of the five factors in cells B6 to B10.
8. Type the raw scores for each of your choices in columns C, D, and E.
9. Use the ChartWizard to create a column chart showing the total weighted scores for each choice.
10. Write a paragraph explaining your choice of factors and assignment of importance weights.
11. On the basis of the current importance weights and raw scores, which option appears most desirable?
12. How confident are you that the worksheet shows the most desirable choice?
13. Write a paragraph explaining your reaction to the results of the worksheet.
14. Save the worksheet and chart on your Student Disk.
15. Print the worksheet and chart.

T U T O R I A L 2

Planning, Building, Testing, and Documenting Worksheets

Creating a Standardized Income and Expense Template for Branch Offices

OBJECTIVES

In this tutorial you will:

- Plan, build, test, and document a worksheet
- Enter labels, values, and formulas
- Change column width
- Create a series with AutoFill
- Use the fill handle to copy data and formulas
- Learn about relative and absolute references
- Use the SUM function and the AutoSum button
- Insert a row
- Format cells with the AutoFormat command
- Add a text note to a worksheet
- Check the spelling of a worksheet
- Lock and unlock cells
- Create an Excel template

CASE

SGL Business Training and Consulting

SGL Business Training and Consulting, headquartered in Springfield, Massachusetts, provides consulting services and management training for small businesses. SGL has 12 regional branch offices throughout the United States. The managers of these branch offices prepare a quarterly report called an "Income and Expense Summary" and send it to Otis Nunley, a staff accountant who works at SGL headquarters.

Each quarter Otis must compile the income and expense information from the 12 reports. This task has not been easy because the branch managers do not use the same categories for income and expenses. For example, some of the managers have money they can use for advertising, and so they list advertising as an expense; other managers do not have money for advertising, and therefore advertising is not an expense on their reports.

Otis knows that he can simplify the task of consolidating the branch office information if he can convince the branch managers to use a standardized form for their reports. He gets approval from management to create an Excel template as the standardized form that branch managers will use to report income and expenses.

A **template** is a preformatted worksheet that contains labels and formulas, but does not contain any values. Otis will send the template to the branch managers. Each manager will fill in the template with income and expense information, then send it back to Otis. With all the information in a standard format, Otis will be able to consolidate it easily into a company-wide report.

Otis studies the branch managers' reports and then plans how to create a standardized worksheet template for reporting income and expenses. In this tutorial, you will work with Otis as he plans, builds, tests, and documents the worksheet template for the SGL branch managers.

Developing Effective Worksheets

An effective worksheet is well planned, carefully built, thoroughly tested, and comprehensively documented. When you develop a worksheet, therefore, you should do each of the following activities:

- *Plan* the worksheet by identifying the overall goal of the project; listing the requirements for input, output, and calculations; and sketching the layout of the worksheet.
- *Build* the worksheet by entering labels, values, and formulas, then format the worksheet so it has a professional appearance.
- *Test* the worksheet to make sure that it provides correct results.
- *Document* the worksheet by recording the information others will need to understand, use, and revise the worksheet.

Although planning is generally the first activity of the worksheet development process, the four development activities are not necessarily sequential. After you begin to enter labels, values, and formulas for the worksheet, you might need to return to the planning activity and revise your original plan. You are also likely to return to the building activity to change some values or formulas after you have tested the worksheet. And, it is important to note that documentation activities can and should take place throughout the process of worksheet development. For example, you might jot down some documentation notes as you are planning the worksheet, or you might enter documentation on the worksheet itself as you are building it.

Planning the Worksheet

To create a plan for the SGL worksheet template, Otis first studies the content and format of the reports from the branch managers. He notices that although there are 12 branches, there are only three different report formats.

The reports from four of the branch managers look similar to the sample report in Figure 2-1. On these reports the labels for each quarter are arranged on the left side of the report. The column titles, arranged across the top of the report, are Income, Expenses, and Profit. The profit for each quarter is calculated by subtracting the expenses from the income. Annual totals are displayed at the bottom of the report.

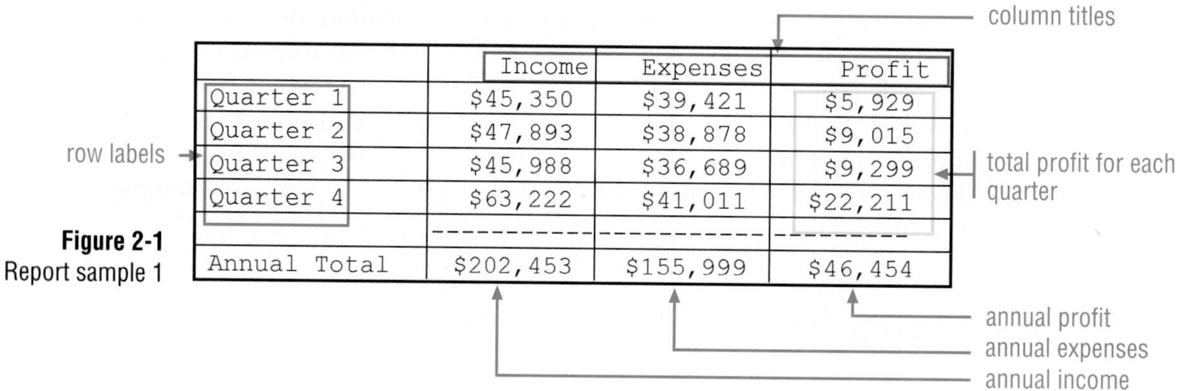

	Income	Expenses	Profit
Quarter 1	$45,350	$39,421	$5,929
Quarter 2	$47,893	$38,878	$9,015
Quarter 3	$45,988	$36,689	$9,299
Quarter 4	$63,222	$41,011	$22,211
	----------	----------	----------
Annual Total	$202,453	$155,999	$46,454

Figure 2-1
Report sample 1

The reports from five of the branch managers look similar to the sample report in Figure 2-2. The format of report sample 2 is very different from that of report sample 1. On report sample 2 the quarters are listed across the top as Q1, Q2, Q3, and Q4, rather than down the side. The income and expense categories are referred to as *revenue* and *expenses* and are listed down the left side of the report. This report has one revenue category and six expense categories. For each revenue or expense category, the sum of the amounts for each quarter produces the year-to-date totals shown on the right side of the report. The profit, shown at the bottom of the worksheet, is calculated by subtracting the total expenses from the total revenue.

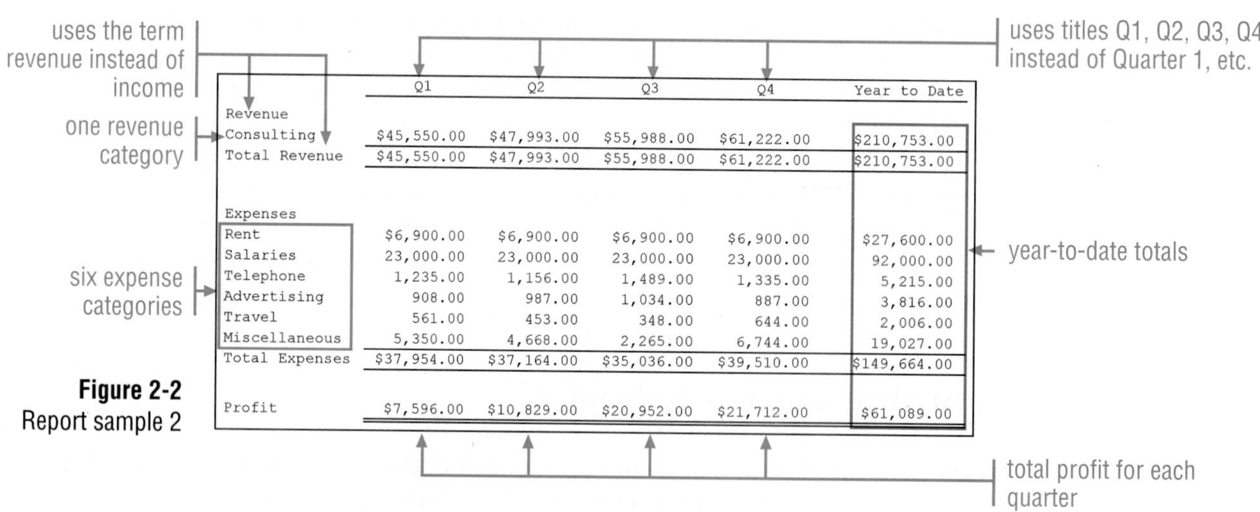

	Q1	Q2	Q3	Q4	Year to Date
Revenue					
Consulting	$45,550.00	$47,993.00	$55,988.00	$61,222.00	$210,753.00
Total Revenue	$45,550.00	$47,993.00	$55,988.00	$61,222.00	$210,753.00
Expenses					
Rent	$6,900.00	$6,900.00	$6,900.00	$6,900.00	$27,600.00
Salaries	23,000.00	23,000.00	23,000.00	23,000.00	92,000.00
Telephone	1,235.00	1,156.00	1,489.00	1,335.00	5,215.00
Advertising	908.00	987.00	1,034.00	887.00	3,816.00
Travel	561.00	453.00	348.00	644.00	2,006.00
Miscellaneous	5,350.00	4,668.00	2,265.00	6,744.00	19,027.00
Total Expenses	$37,954.00	$37,164.00	$35,036.00	$39,510.00	$149,664.00
Profit	$7,596.00	$10,829.00	$20,952.00	$21,712.00	$61,089.00

Figure 2-2
Report sample 2

The reports from the remaining branch managers look similar to the sample report in Figure 2-3. Notice the two income categories and eight expense categories. The titles for each quarter are listed across the top of the report. For each income or expense category, the sum of the amounts for each quarter produces the year-to-date totals shown on the right side of the report. The total profit for each quarter is shown in the last row of the report.

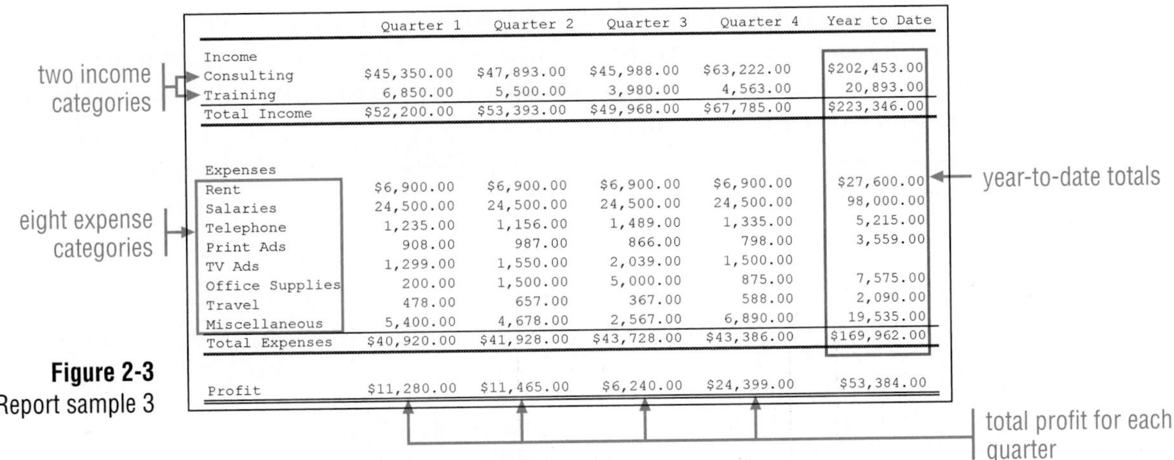

	Quarter 1	Quarter 2	Quarter 3	Quarter 4	Year to Date
Income					
Consulting	$45,350.00	$47,893.00	$45,988.00	$63,222.00	$202,453.00
Training	6,850.00	5,500.00	3,980.00	4,563.00	20,893.00
Total Income	$52,200.00	$53,393.00	$49,968.00	$67,785.00	$223,346.00
Expenses					
Rent	$6,900.00	$6,900.00	$6,900.00	$6,900.00	$27,600.00
Salaries	24,500.00	24,500.00	24,500.00	24,500.00	98,000.00
Telephone	1,235.00	1,156.00	1,489.00	1,335.00	5,215.00
Print Ads	908.00	987.00	866.00	798.00	3,559.00
TV Ads	1,299.00	1,550.00	2,039.00	1,500.00	
Office Supplies	200.00	1,500.00	5,000.00	875.00	7,575.00
Travel	478.00	657.00	367.00	588.00	2,090.00
Miscellaneous	5,400.00	4,678.00	2,567.00	6,890.00	19,535.00
Total Expenses	$40,920.00	$41,928.00	$43,728.00	$43,386.00	$169,962.00
Profit	$11,280.00	$11,465.00	$6,240.00	$24,399.00	$53,384.00

Figure 2-3
Report sample 3

After he studies the reports, Otis writes out a worksheet plan that:

- lists the goal(s) for the worksheet development project
- identifies the results, or *output*, that the worksheet must produce
- lists the information, or *input*, that is required to construct the worksheet
- specifies the calculations that use the input to produce the required output

The worksheet plan will guide Otis as he builds and tests the worksheet. Figure 2-4 shows the worksheet plan that Otis created.

Worksheet Plan for Loan Management Worksheet

My Goal:
To develop an Excel template that all branch managers can use to submit income and expense reports.

What results do I want to see?
Income categories for consulting and training.
Expense categories for rent, salaries, telephone, advertising, office supplies, travel, and miscellaneous.
Income and expenses for each quarter.
Total income for each quarter.
Total expenses for each quarter.
Total profit for each quarter.

What information do I need?
The amount for each income and expense category.

What calculations will I perform?
Total income = consulting income + training income
Total expenses = rent+salaries+telephone+advertising+office supplies+travel+miscellaneous
Profit = total income – total expenses

Figure 2-4
Otis's worksheet plan

After he completes the worksheet plan, Otis draws a sketch of the worksheet template, showing the worksheet titles, row labels, column titles, and formulas (Figure 2-5). He decides to list the income and expense categories down the left side of the worksheet and list the quarters across the top.

Income and Expense Summary				
	Quarter 1	Quarter 2	Quarter 3	Quarter 4
Income				
Consulting	$9,999,999.99	$9,999,999.99	$9,999,999.99	$9,999,999.99
Training	:	:	:	:
Total Income	${total income formula}	${total income formula}	${total income formula}	${total income formula}
Expenses				
Rent	$9,999,999.99	$9,999,999.99	$9,999,999.99	$9,999,999.99
Salaries	:	:	:	:
Telephone	:	:	:	:
Advertising	:	:	:	:
Office Supplies	:	:	:	:
Travel	:	:	:	:
Miscellaneous	:	:	:	:
Total Expenses	${total expenses formula}	${total expenses formula}	${total expenses formula}	${total expenses formula}
Profit	${profit formula}	${profit formula}	${profit formula}	${profit formula}

Figure 2-5
Otis's sketch of his planned worksheet

The dollar signs indicate that Otis will format these cells for currency. The number 9,999,999.99 indicates the largest number these cells can hold and specifies how wide these columns must be on the final version of the worksheet.

Otis indicates which cells will contain formulas by using "curly brackets," {}. The formulas are described in the calculation section of the worksheet plan in Figure 2-4. For example, the {total income formula} shown on the sketch is described in the worksheet plan as:

total income = consulting income + training income

Look in the calculation section of the worksheet plan in Figure 2-4 to find the descriptions for the rest of the formulas on Otis's worksheet sketch.

Now that Otis has completed the worksheet plan and the worksheet sketch, he is ready to start building the worksheet. Let's launch Excel now and work with Otis as he builds the worksheet.

To launch Excel and maximize the worksheet:

1. Launch Windows and Excel following your usual procedure.
2. Make sure your Student Disk is in the disk drive.
3. Make sure the Microsoft Excel and Book1 windows are maximized.

Building the Worksheet

As you learned in Tutorial 1, a worksheet generally contains values, labels that describe the values, and formulas that perform calculations. When you build a worksheet, you usually enter the labels first. What you enter next depends on how you intend to use the worksheet. If you intend to use the worksheet as a template, you will enter formulas, then enter values. If you are not creating a template, you would generally enter the values before you enter the formulas.

In addition to entering labels, formulas, and perhaps, values, when you build a worksheet you should format it so the information is displayed in a way that is clear and understandable.

Otis intends to create a template to send to the branch managers, so he will enter the labels, enter the formulas, then format the worksheet. The branch managers will enter the values later.

Entering Labels

When you build a worksheet, the first step is to enter the labels you defined in the planning stage. When you type a label in a cell, Excel aligns the label at the left side of the cell. Labels that are too long to fit in a cell spill over into the cell or cells to the right, if those cells are empty. If the cell to the right is not empty, Excel displays only as much of the label as fits in the cell. Otis begins by entering the worksheet title.

To enter the worksheet title:

1. Click cell **A1** to make it the active cell.
2. Type **Income and Expense Summary** and press **[Enter]**. The title appears in cell A1 and spills over into cells B1 and C1. Cell A2 is now the active cell.

Otis continues working in column A to enter the labels for the income and expense categories he defined on his worksheet sketch in Figure 2-5.

To enter the labels for the income categories:

1. Click cell **A3** to make it the active cell.

   TROUBLE? If you make a mistake while typing, remember that you can use the Backspace key to correct errors.
2. Type **Income** and press **[Enter]** to complete the entry and move to cell A4.
3. In cell A4 type **Consulting** and press **[Enter]**.
4. In cell A5 type **Training** and press **[Enter]**.
5. In cell A6 type **Total Income** and press **[Enter]**.

Next, Otis enters the labels for the expense categories.

To enter the labels for the expense categories:

❶ Click cell **A8** to make it the active cell.

❷ Type **Expenses** and press **[Enter]** to complete the entry and move to cell A9.

❸ Refer to Figure 2-6 and type the labels for cells A9 through A16: **Rent**, **Salaries**, **Telephone**, **Advertising**, **Office Supplies**, **Travel**, **Miscellaneous**, and **Total Expenses**.

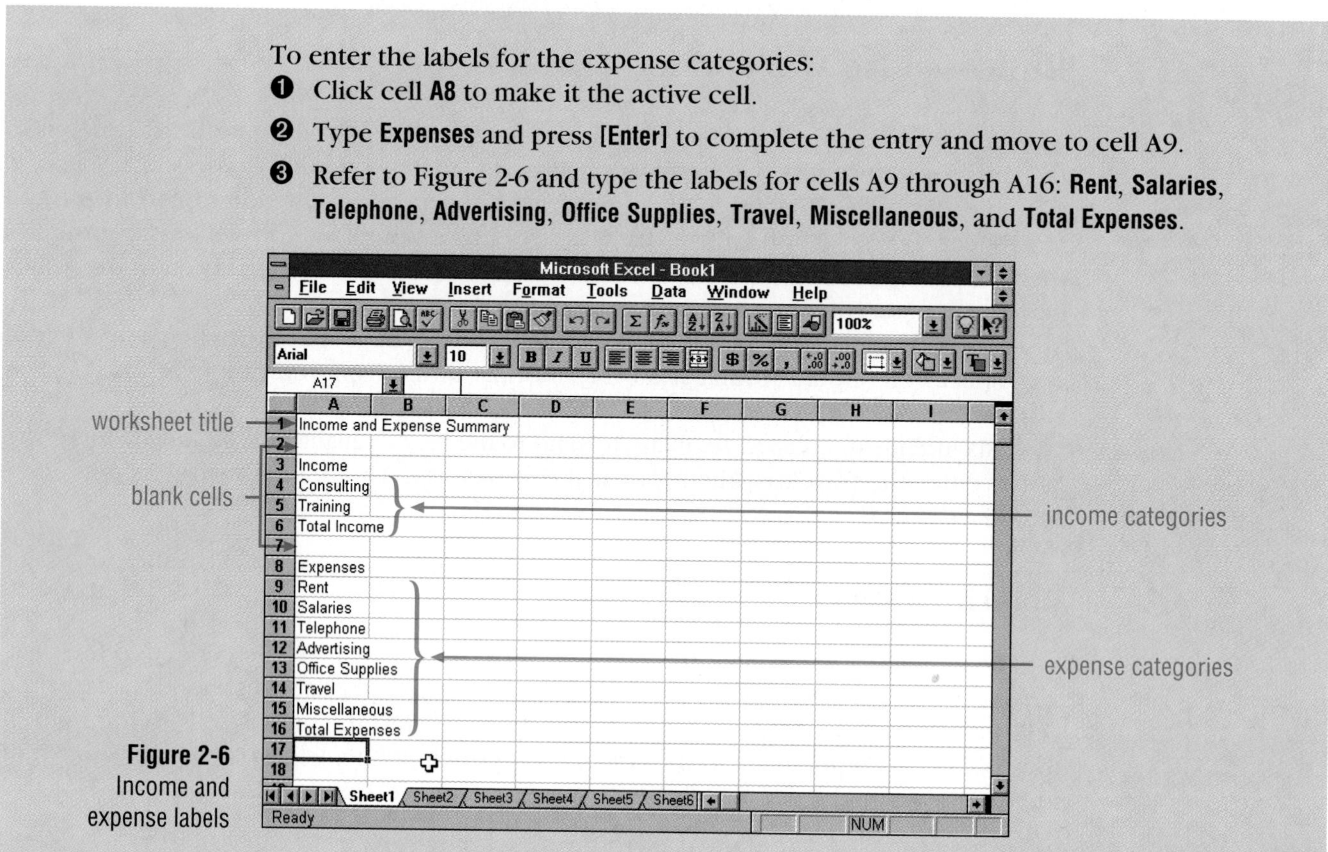

Figure 2-6
Income and expense labels

Otis wants to leave a blank row after the "Total Expenses" label and put the label "Profit" in cell A18.

To enter the label "Profit" in cell A18:

❶ Press [↓] until the active cell is A18.

❷ Type **Profit** and press **[Enter]**.

Otis notices that the text in some of the cells spills over into column B, so he decides to increase the width of column A.

Changing Column Width

The number of letters or numbers that Excel displays in a cell depends on the size and style of the lettering, or font, you are using and the width of the column. If you do not change the width of the columns on your worksheet, Excel automatically uses a column width that displays about eight and a half digits. To display the exact column width in the formula bar, simply press and hold the mouse button while the pointer is over the dividing line.

As shown in Figure 2-7, Excel provides several methods for changing column width. For example, you can click a column heading or drag the pointer to highlight a series of column headings and then use the Format menu. You can also use the dividing line between column headings. When you move the pointer over the dividing line between two column headings, the pointer changes to ✛. You can use the pointer to drag the dividing line to a new location. You can also double-click the dividing line to make the column as wide as the longest text label or number in the column.

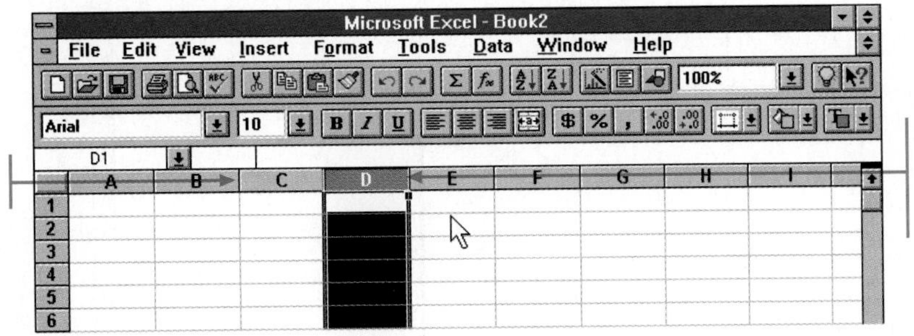

Figure 2-7
Changing column width

REFERENCE WINDOW

Changing Column Width

- Click the column heading(s) for which you want to change the width. Click Format, click Column, then click Width.... Use the Column Width dialog box to enter the new column width. Click AutoFit to make the column(s) as wide as the longest text label or number in the column(s).

or

- Drag the column heading dividing line to the right to increase column width or to the left to decrease column width.

or

- Double-click the column heading dividing line to make the column as wide as the longest text label or number in the column.

Otis wants to change the width of column A so that all the labels fit within the boundary of column A. He decides to double-click the column heading dividing line.

To change the width of column A:

❶ Position the pointer on the box that contains the column heading for column A.

❷ Move the pointer slowly to the right until it is positioned over the dividing line between column A and column B. Notice how the pointer changes to ✛.

❸ Double-click the dividing line. Column A automatically adjusts to the appropriate width and the worksheet title fits completely in cell A1. See Figure 2-8.

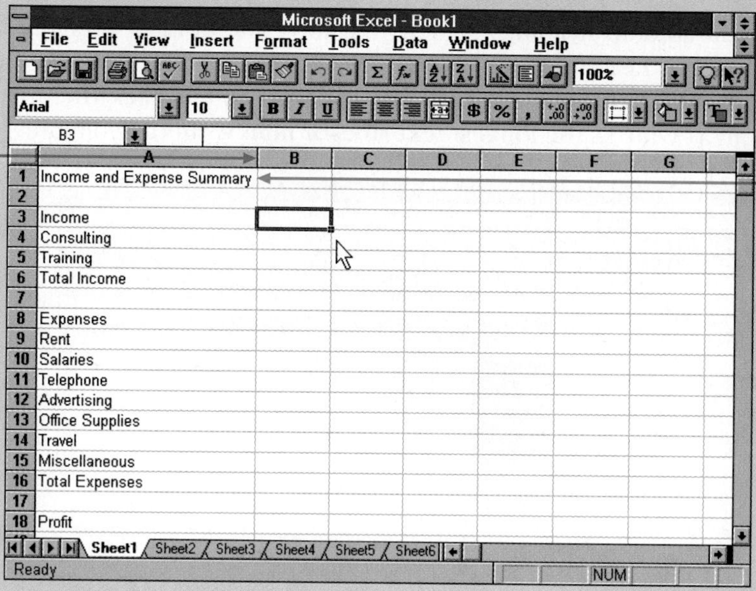

Figure 2-8
Changing the width of column A

Next, Otis begins to enter the column titles for each quarter. He starts by entering the label "Quarter 1" in cell B2.

To enter the label "Quarter 1" in cell B2:

❶ Click cell **B2** to make it the active cell.

❷ Type **Quarter 1** and press **[Enter]**.

Otis is not a fast typist. He wonders if there is any way to avoid typing the name of the next three quarters across the top of the worksheet. Then he remembers a feature called AutoFill.

Creating a Series with AutoFill

AutoFill is an Excel feature that automatically fills areas of the worksheet with a series of values or text. To use this feature you type one or two initial values or text entries, then AutoFill does the rest. AutoFill evaluates the initial entry or entries, determines the most likely sequence to follow, and completes the remaining entries in the range of cells you specify.

AutoFill recognizes series of numbers, dates, times, and certain labels. Figure 2-9 shows a selection of series that AutoFill recognizes and completes.

Initial Entry	Completed With
Monday	Tuesday, Wednesday, etc.
Mon	Tue, Wed, etc.
January	February, March, etc.
Jan	Feb, Mar, etc.
Quarter 1	Quarter 2, Quarter 3, etc.
Qtr1	Qtr2, Qtr3, etc.
11:00 AM	12:00 PM, 1:00 PM, etc.
Product 1	Product 2, Product 3, etc.
1992, 1993	1994, 1995, etc.
1, 2, 3, 4	5, 6, 7, etc.
1, 3, 5	7, 9, 11, etc.

Figure 2-9
Series completed by AutoFill

If you use a repeating series such as months or days of the week, you can begin anywhere in the series. If there are cells that need to be filled after the series ends, AutoFill repeats the series again from the beginning. For example, if you enter "October," AutoFill completes the series by entering "November" and "December," then it continues the series with "January," "February," and so on.

When you use AutoFill, you drag the fill handle to outline your initial entry and the cells you want to fill. The **fill handle**, shown in Figure 2-10, is the small black square in the lower-right corner of the active cell's border.

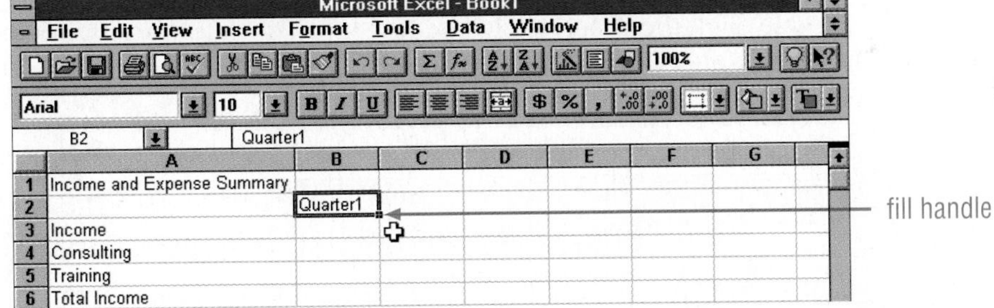

Figure 2-10
The fill handle

Otis uses AutoFill to enter the labels for the remaining quarters.

To fill in the labels for the rest of the quarters using AutoFill:

1. Click cell **B2** to make it the active cell. Look closely at the black border that appears around the cell. Notice the fill handle, the small black square in the lower-right corner of the border.
2. Move the pointer over the fill handle until the pointer changes to +.
3. Click and drag the pointer across the worksheet to outline cells B2 through E2. See Figure 2-11.

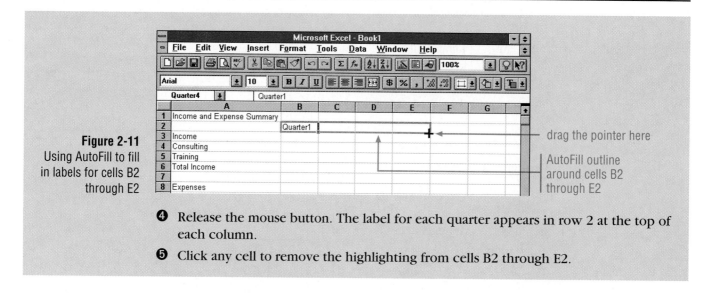

Figure 2-11
Using AutoFill to fill in labels for cells B2 through E2

drag the pointer here

AutoFill outline around cells B2 through E2

❹ Release the mouse button. The label for each quarter appears in row 2 at the top of each column.

❺ Click any cell to remove the highlighting from cells B2 through E2.

Renaming the Sheet

In the lower-left corner of the worksheet window, Otis notices that the sheet is currently named "Sheet1"—the name Excel uses automatically when it opens a new workbook. But now that the worksheet is taking shape, Otis decides to give it a more specific name: "Income and Expense." This way, if, in the future he uses other sheets in the workbook he'll be able to find the Income and Expense Summary quickly and easily.

To rename Sheet1:

❶ Double-click the **Sheet1 tab** in the lower-left corner of the worksheet to open the Rename Sheet dialog box. See Figure 2-12.

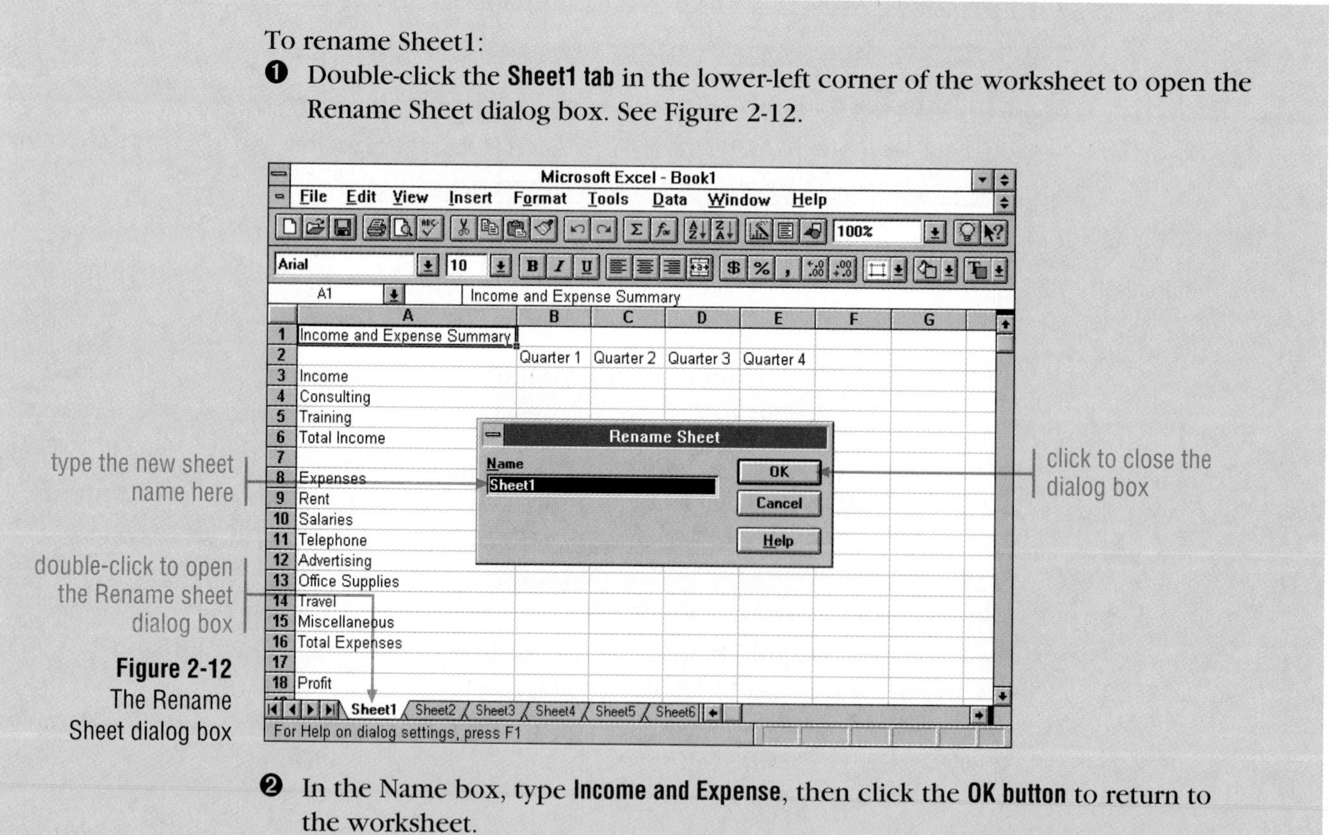

Figure 2-12
The Rename Sheet dialog box

❷ In the Name box, type **Income and Expense**, then click the **OK button** to return to the worksheet.

Saving the New Workbook

Otis decides to save the workbook so he won't lose his work if the power goes out. Since this is the first time he has saved since renaming this sheet, Otis uses the Save As command to save the workbook and name it S2INC.XLS.

Excel filenames can contain up to eight characters. These characters can be letters, numbers, or any symbols except for spaces, commas, or the following: []"/\:,*?. Excel automatically adds the .XLS extension to the filename.

It is not always easy to create a descriptive filename using only eight characters, but it is possible to design a file naming scheme that provides meaningful abbreviations. For example, the files on your Student Disk are named and categorized using the first letter of the filename, as shown in Figure 2-13.

Figure 2-13
Categories of files

First Character of Filename	File Category	Description of File Category
C	Tutorial **C**ase	The files you use to work through each tutorial
T	**T**utorial Assignments	The files that contain the worksheets you need to complete the Tutorial Assignments at the end of each tutorial
P	Case **P**roblems	The files that contain the worksheets you need to complete the Case Problems at the end of each tutorial
S	**S**aved Workbook	Any workbook that you save

The second character in the filenames on your Student Disk indicates the tutorial in which the file is created or used. For example, a filename that begins with C1 is a workbook you open in Tutorial 1; a filename that begins with S2 is a workbook you save in Tutorial 2. The remaining three to six characters of the filename are related to the content of the workbook. For example, in the next set of steps you will save your workbook as S2INC.XLS. The "S" signifies a file that you saved; the "2" means that you used the file in Tutorial 2; and "INC" refers to "income," to remind you that the file contains an income and expense summary worksheet. Let's save the file now.

To save the workbook as S2INC.XLS:

1. Click **File**, then click **Save As...** to display the Save As dialog box.
2. Type **S2INC** but don't press **[Enter]** because you need to check some additional settings. When you type the filename S2INC, you can use either uppercase or lowercase.

3. Make sure the Drives box displays the icon for the drive that contains your Student Disk. If the correct drive icon is not shown, click the **Drives box down arrow button** to display a list of drives, then click the correct drive. Your Save As dialog box should look like the dialog box in Figure 2-14.

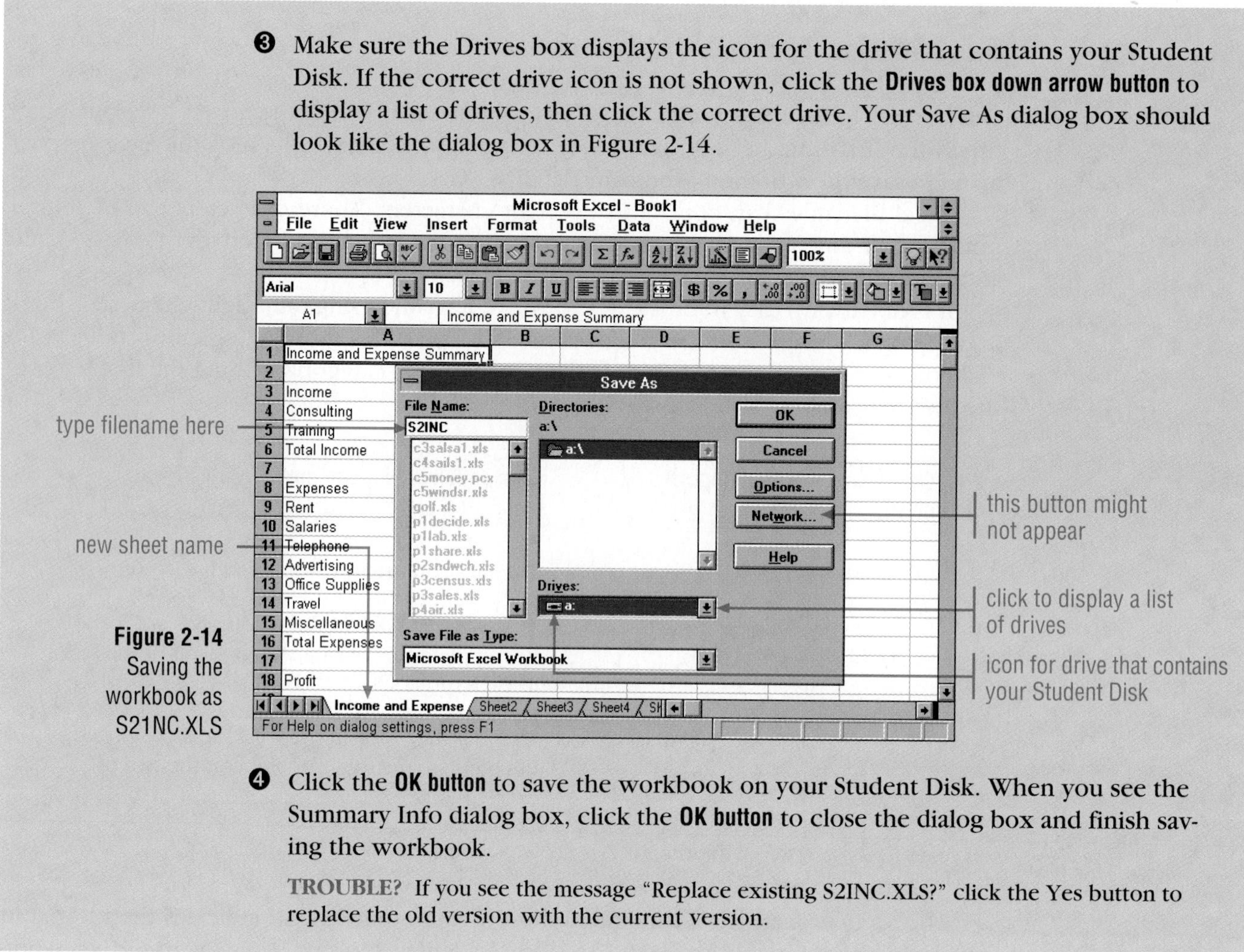

Figure 2-14 Saving the workbook as S21NC.XLS

4. Click the **OK button** to save the workbook on your Student Disk. When you see the Summary Info dialog box, click the **OK button** to close the dialog box and finish saving the workbook.

   TROUBLE? If you see the message "Replace existing S2INC.XLS?" click the Yes button to replace the old version with the current version.

Now that Otis has entered the labels for the worksheet template, his next step is to enter the formulas.

Entering Formulas

You will recall from Tutorial 1 that formulas tell Excel what to calculate. When you enter a formula in a cell, begin the formula by typing an equal sign (=). The equal sign tells Excel that the numbers or symbols that follow it constitute a formula, not just data. Formulas can contain cell references such as A1 and G14, operators such as * and +, and numbers such as 30 or 247. Figure 2-15 shows some examples of the numbers, operators, and references you can include in a formula.

Example	Description	Example	Description
30	a number	<	less than sign
+	addition operator	>=	greater than or equal to sign
-	subtraction operator	<=	less than or equal to sign
/	division operator	<>	not equal to sign
*	multiplication operator	A1	reference to cell
%	percentage operator	(A1:A5)	reference to a range of cells
^	exponentiation operator	(A:A)	reference to entire column A
&	connects two text labels	(1:1)	reference to entire row 1
=	equal sign	(1:3)	reference to entire rows 1-3
>	greater than sign		

Figure 2-15 Examples of numbers, operators, and references used in formulas

Figure 2-16 shows that Excel displays the results of a formula in the cell in which you typed the formula. To view the formula itself, you must look at the formula bar.

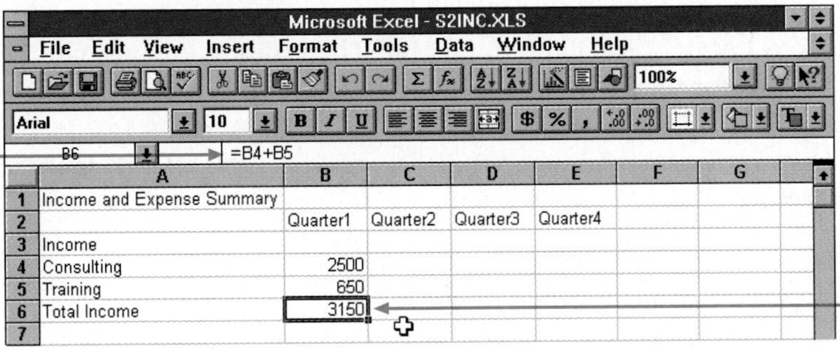

formula bar shows the formula that is in cell B6

cell displays result of formula

Figure 2-16 Viewing a formula and its result

When Excel calculates the results of a formula that contains more than one operator, it follows the standard order of operations shown in Figure 2-17.

Order	Operator	Description
1.	( )	parentheses
2.	^	exponentiation
3.	* /	multiplication or division
4.	+ -	addition or subtraction
5.	= <> > < >= <=	comparison

Figure 2-17 Order of operations

In accordance with the order of operations, Excel performs calculations by first doing any operations contained in parentheses, then any exponentiation, then any multiplication or division, and so on. For example, the result of the formula 3+4*5 is 23 because Excel completes the multiplication before the addition. The result of the formula (3+4)*5 is 35 because Excel calculates the operation in the parentheses first.

REFERENCE WINDOW

Entering a Formula

- Click the cell where you want the result to appear.
- Type = and then type the rest of the formula.
- For formulas that include cell references, such as B2 or D78, you can type the cell reference or you can use the mouse or arrow keys to select each cell.
- When the formula is complete, press [Enter].

Otis decides to enter the formula to calculate total income:

total income = consulting income + training income

The worksheet does not contain any values yet because Otis is building a template that will be filled in by the branch managers. Otis knows that when the consulting income is entered, it will be in cell B4. The training income will be in cell B5. Therefore, the formula for total income must add the contents of cells B4 and B5. Otis enters this formula as =B4+B5.

Otis wants the total income displayed in cell B6, so this is the cell in which he enters the formula.

To enter the formula for total income:

1. Click cell **B6** because this is where you want the total income displayed.
2. Type **=B4+B5** and press **[Enter]**. (You can use either uppercase or lowercase.) The result 0 appears in cell B6.

The result of the formula =B4+B5 is zero because cells B4 and B5 do not contain values.

Otis wants to enter the total income formulas for Quarters 2, 3, and 4. He could type the formula =C4+C5 in cell C6, then type the formula =D4+D5 in cell D6, and finally type the formula =E4+E5 in cell E6; but he can use a shortcut to copy the formula he entered for Quarter 1.

Using the Fill Handle to Copy a Formula

Earlier in this tutorial you used the fill handle in the lower-right corner of the active cell to fill the series that began with Quarter 1. You can also use the fill handle to copy the contents of a cell to other cells. Using the fill handle, you can copy formulas, values, and labels from one cell or from a group of cells.

REFERENCE WINDOW

Copying Cell Contents with the Fill Handle

- Click the cell that contains the label, value, or formula you want to copy. If you want to copy the contents of more than one cell, highlight the cells you want to copy.
- Drag the fill handle to outline the cells where you want the copy or copies to appear.
- Release the mouse button.

Otis wants to copy the formula from cell B6 to cells C6, D6, and E6.

To copy the formula from cell B6 to cells C6, D6, and E6:

1. Click cell **B6** to make it the active cell.
2. Position the pointer over the fill handle (in the lower-right corner of cell B6) until the pointer changes to +.
3. Drag the pointer across the worksheet to outline cells B6 through E6.
4. Release the mouse button. Zeros now appear in cells B6 through E6.
5. Click any cell to remove the highlighting.

Otis thinks he might have made a mistake. The formula in B6 is =B4+B5. Because he copied this formula to cells C6, D6, and E6, Otis is concerned that Quarters 2, 3, and 4 will show the same total income as Quarter 1 when the branch managers enter their data. Otis decides to look at the formulas in cells C6, D6, and E6.

To examine the formulas in cells C6, D6, and E6:

1. Click cell **C6**. The formula =C4+C5 appears in the formula bar.
   It appears that when the formula from cell B6 was copied to cell C6, the cell references changed. The formula =B4+B5 became =C4+C5 when Excel copied it to column C.
2. Click cell **D6**. The formula =D4+D5 appears in the formula bar. When Excel copied the formula to column D, the cell references changed from B to D.
3. Click cell **E6**. The formula =E4+E5 appears in the formula bar.

When Otis copied the formula from cell B6, Excel automatically changed the cell references in the formulas to reflect the new position of the formulas in the worksheet.

Relative and Absolute References

Otis just learned how Excel uses relative references. A **relative reference** tells Excel which cell to use based on its location *relative* to the cell containing the formula. When you copy or move a formula that contains a relative reference, Excel changes the cell references so they refer to cells located in the same position relative to the cell that contains the new copy of the formula. Figure 2-18 shows how this works.

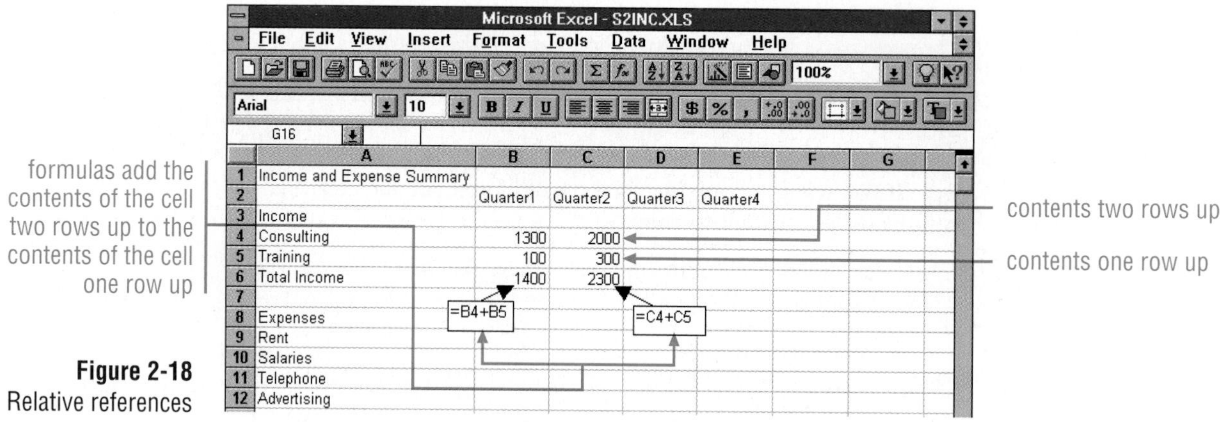

formulas add the contents of the cell two rows up to the contents of the cell one row up

contents two rows up

contents one row up

	A	B	C	D	E	F	G
1	Income and Expense Summary						
2		Quarter1	Quarter2	Quarter3	Quarter4		
3	Income						
4	Consulting	1300	2000				
5	Training	100	300				
6	Total Income	1400	2300				
7							
8	Expenses	=B4+B5		=C4+C5			
9	Rent						
10	Salaries						
11	Telephone						
12	Advertising						

Figure 2-18
Relative references

Otis's original formula =B4+B5 contains relative references. Excel interpreted this formula to mean add the value from the cell two rows up (B4) to the cell one row up (B5) and display the result in the current cell (B6).

When Otis copied this formula to cell C6, Excel created the new formula to perform the same calculation, but starting at cell C6 instead of B6. The new formula means to add the value from the cell two rows up (C4) to the cell one row up (C5) and display the result in the current cell (C6).

All references in formulas are relative references unless you specify otherwise. Most of the time, you will want to use relative references because you can then copy and move formulas easily to different cells on the worksheet.

From time to time, you might need to create a formula that refers to a cell in a fixed location on the worksheet. A reference that always points to the same cell is an **absolute reference**. Absolute references contain a dollar sign before the column letter, the row number, or both. Examples of absolute references include $A$4, $C$27, $A17, and D$32. You will learn more about absolute references in Tutorial 4.

Otis continues to enter the other formulas he planned to put in the worksheet template, starting with the formula to calculate total expenses.

The SUM Function

The **SUM function** provides you with a shortcut for entering formulas that total the values in rows or columns. You can use the SUM function to replace a lengthy formula such as =B9+B10+B11+B12+B13+B14+B15 with the more compact formula =SUM(B9:B15).

REFERENCE WINDOW

Entering the SUM Function

- Type = to begin the function.
- Type SUM in either uppercase or lowercase, followed by (—an opening parenthesis. Do not put a space between SUM and the parenthesis.
- Type the range of cells you want to sum, separating the first and last cells in the range with a colon, as in B9:B15, or drag the pointer to outline the cells you want to sum.

Otis wants to enter a formula in cell B16 to calculate the total expenses by summing the expenses such as rent, salaries, and so forth. He uses the SUM function to do this.

To calculate the total expenses using the SUM function:

1. Click cell **B16** because this is where you want to display the result of the formula.
2. Type **=SUM(** to begin the formula. Don't forget to include the open parenthesis.
3. Type **B9:B15)** and press **[Enter]**. Don't forget to include the closing parenthesis. The result, 0, appears in cell B16.

Normally, when typing a formula, you don't need to type the final parenthesis. Excel will automatically add it for you when you press [Enter]. You entered it yourself this time just for practice.

Now Otis can copy the formula in B16 to cells C16, D16, and E16.

To copy the formula from cell B16 to cells C16, D16, and E16:

1. Make sure that cell B16 is the active cell.
2. Drag the fill handle (in the lower-right corner of cell B16) to outline cells B16 through E16, then release the mouse button. Zeros appear in cells B16 through E16.
3. Click any cell to remove the highlighting.

Otis reviews his worksheet plan and sketch to see what he should do next. He sees that he needs to enter the profit formula and considers how to do this.

Using the Mouse to Select Cell References

Excel provides several ways for you to enter cell references in a formula. One way is to type the cell references directly, as Otis did when he created the formula =B4+B5. Recall that he typed the equal sign, then typed B4, a plus sign, and finally B5. Another way to put a cell reference in a formula is to select the cell using the mouse or arrow keys. To use this method to enter the formula =B4+B5, Otis would type the equal sign, then click cell B4, type the plus sign, then click cell B5. Using the mouse to select cell references is often the preferred method because it minimizes typing errors.

Otis wants to calculate the profit for the first quarter:

profit = total income - total expenses

Otis looks at the worksheet to locate the cell references for the profit formula. Cell B6 contains the total income and cell B16 contains the total expenses, so Otis knows that the formula should be =B6-B16. Let's see how Otis creates the formula to calculate profit by selecting the cell references with the mouse.

To create the formula to calculate profit by selecting cell references:

1. Click cell **B18** because this is where you want the result of the formula displayed.
2. Type = to begin the formula.

3. Click cell **B6**. Notice that a dashed box appears around cell B6. Also notice that B6 is added to the formula in the formula bar and in cell B18. See Figure 2-19.

   TROUBLE? If you happen to click the wrong cell simply click again on the correct cell, B6.

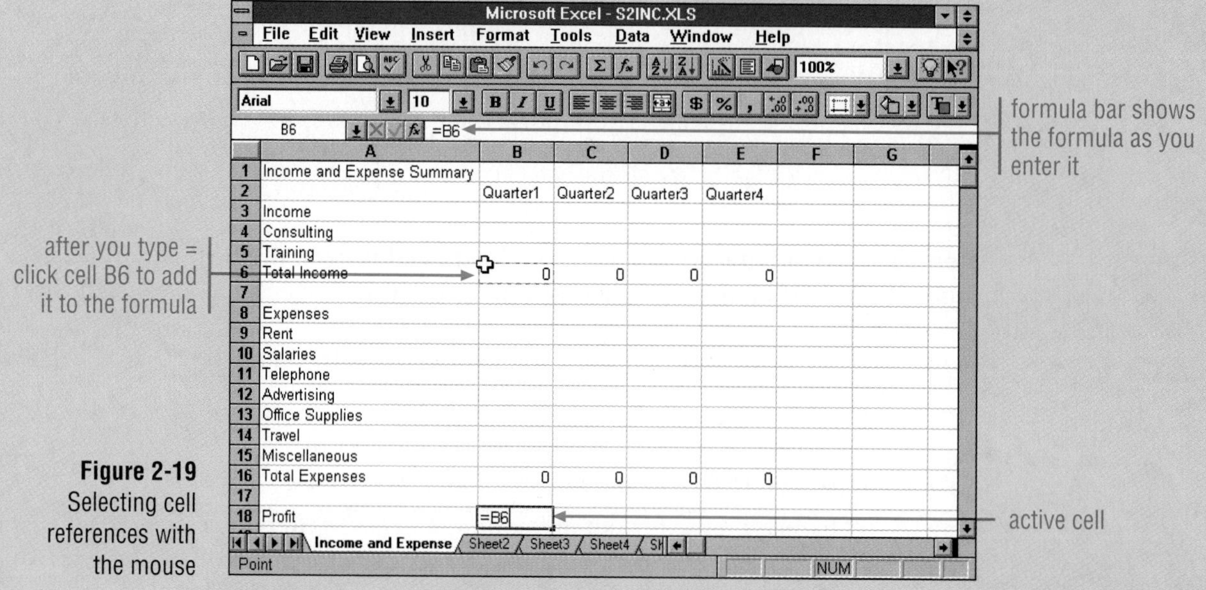

Figure 2-19 Selecting cell references with the mouse

4. Type – (a minus sign). Notice that the dashed box disappears from cell B6. The formula bar and cell B18 now display =B6-.
5. Click cell **B16**. A dashed box appears around cell B16, and the formula bar displays the entire formula =B6-B16.
6. Press **[Enter]** to complete the formula. The result 0 appears in cell B18.

Now Otis copies the formula in B18 to cells C18, D18, and E18.

To copy the formula from B18 to cells C18, D18, and E18:

1. Make cell B18 the active cell because it contains the formula you want to copy.
2. Drag the fill handle to outline cells B18 through E18. Release the mouse button. Zeros appear in cells B18 through E18.
3. Click any cell to remove the highlighting.

Now that all the formulas are entered, Otis decides to save the workbook.

4. Click the **Save button** .

If you want to take a break and resume the tutorial at a later time, you can exit Excel by double-clicking the Control menu box in the upper-left corner of the screen. When you resume the tutorial, launch Excel, maximize the Microsoft Excel and Book1 windows, and place your Student Disk in the disk drive. Open the file S2INC.XLS, then continue with the tutorial.

■ ■ ■

Otis has entered labels and formulas and functions for each quarter. Before he proceeds, he decides to test the worksheet by entering test values.

Testing the Worksheet

Test values are numbers that generate a known result. You enter the test values in your worksheet to determine if your formulas are accurate. After you enter the test values, you compare the results on your worksheet with the known results. If the results on your worksheet don't match the known results, you have probably made an error.

Test values can be numbers from a real sample or simple numbers that make it easy to determine if the worksheet is calculating correctly. As an example of test values from a real sample, Otis could use numbers from an income and expense report that he knows has been calculated correctly. As an example of simple numbers, Otis could enter the value 1 in all the cells. Then it would be easy to do the calculations "in his head" to verify that the formulas are accurate.

Otis decides to use the number 100 as a test value because he can easily check the accuracy of the formulas he entered in the worksheet.

To enter the test value 100 in cells B4 and B5:

1. Click cell **B4** to make it the active cell.
2. Type **100** and press **[Enter]** to move to cell B5.
3. Type **100** and press **[Enter]**. The value 200 appears in cell B6 and in cell B18.

Otis knows that 100 plus 100 equals 200. Since this is the result displayed in cell B6 for total income, it appears that the formula in this cell is correct. Otis decides to copy the test values from cells B4 and B5 to columns C, D, and E.

To copy the test values to cells C4 through E5:

1. Drag the pointer to highlight cells B4 and B5, then release the mouse button.
2. Drag the fill handle to outline cells B4 through E5. See Figure 2-20.

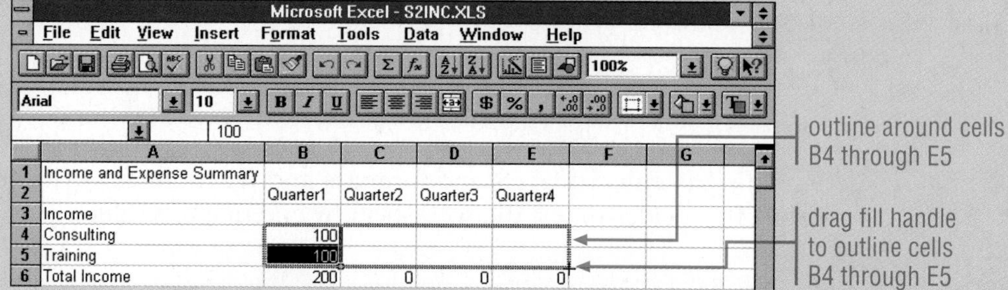

Figure 2-20 Copying test values

3. Release the mouse button. The test value 100 appears in cells B4 through E5.
4. Click any cell to remove the highlighting.

Otis notices that the formulas in cells B6, C6, D6, and E6 display 200 as the result of the formula that calculates total income. In addition, the formulas that calculate profit in cells B18, C18, D18, and E18 also display the value 200. This makes sense. The formula for profit is *total income - total expenses*. On the worksheet the total income is 200 and the total expenses are 0.

Otis decides to enter the test value 100 for each of the expense categories. He types the test value in cell B9, then copies it to cells B10 through B15. Then he copies the test values from column B to columns C, D, and E.

To enter a test value in cell B9, then copy it to cells B10 through B15:

1. Click cell **B9** to make it the active cell.
2. Type **100** and press **[Enter]**.
3. Press [↑] to make cell B9 the active cell again.
4. Drag the fill handle to outline cells B9 through B15, then release the mouse button. Do not remove the highlighting from the fill area. As a result the test value 100 appears in cells B9 through B15.
5. Drag the fill handle again to outline cells B9 through E15, then release the mouse button. The test value 100 appears in cells B9 through E15.
6. Click any cell to remove the highlighting. See Figure 2-21.

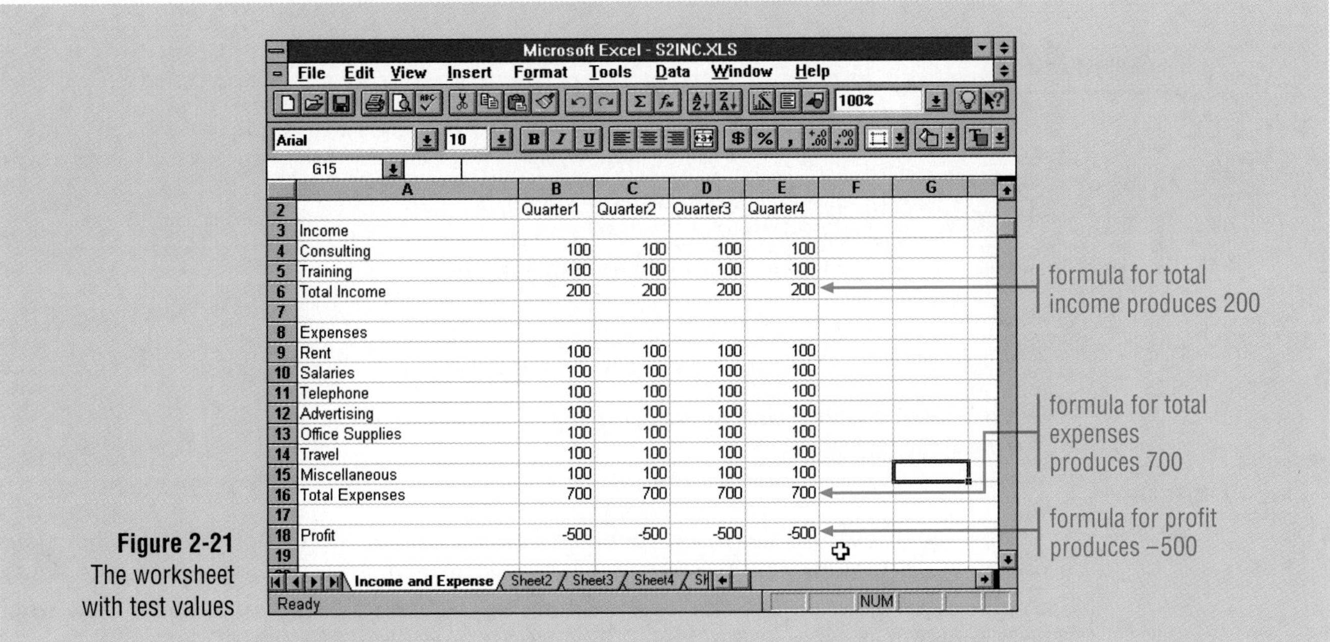

	A	B	C	D	E	F	G
2		Quarter1	Quarter2	Quarter3	Quarter4		
3	Income						
4	Consulting	100	100	100	100		
5	Training	100	100	100	100		
6	Total Income	200	200	200	200		
7							
8	Expenses						
9	Rent	100	100	100	100		
10	Salaries	100	100	100	100		
11	Telephone	100	100	100	100		
12	Advertising	100	100	100	100		
13	Office Supplies	100	100	100	100		
14	Travel	100	100	100	100		
15	Miscellaneous	100	100	100	100		
16	Total Expenses	700	700	700	700		
17							
18	Profit	-500	-500	-500	-500		
19							

Figure 2-21
The worksheet with test values

Otis takes a moment to make sure that the formulas have produced the results he expected. The formulas for total expenses in cells B16, C16, D16, and E16 display 700. This looks correct because there are seven expense categories, each containing the test value 100.

The formulas for profit in cells B18, C18, D18, and E18 display -500. This also looks correct. Total income is 200, total expenses are 700, and 200 minus 700 equals -500.

Now Otis compares this worksheet to his worksheet sketch (Figure 2-5). He notices that on the worksheet sketch he left row 1 blank for the branch managers to type in their branch office names. He forgot to leave row 1 blank when he entered the labels on the worksheet, and now there isn't any space for the branch office name. Does Otis need to start over? No, Otis can use the Insert command to insert a blank row.

Inserting a Row or Column

You can insert a row or column in a worksheet to make room for new data or to make the worksheet easier to read. When you insert rows or columns, Excel repositions the other rows and columns in the worksheet and automatically adjusts the cell references in formulas to reflect the new location of values used in calculations. Using the **Insert command** you can insert an entire row or multiple rows. You can insert an entire column or multiple columns.

REFERENCE WINDOW

Inserting a Row or Column

Use these instructions to insert a column by substituting "column" for "row."

- Click any cell in the row where you want to insert the new row.

  or

  Highlight a range of rows where you want to insert new rows.
- Click Insert and then click Rows. Excel inserts one row for every row in the highlighted range.

Otis decides to use the Insert menu to insert a row at the top of the worksheet. He cannot type a branch name in the new row because this template will be used by 12 branch offices. Instead, Otis decides to enter "SGL Branch Office Name" in the new row. The branch managers can then type the names of their branches when they use the worksheet. Let's see how Otis inserts a row for the branch office name.

To insert a row at the top of the worksheet:

1. Click cell **A1** because you want one new row to be inserted at the location of the current row.
2. Click **Insert** and then click **Rows**. Excel inserts a blank row at the top of the worksheet. All other rows shift down one row.
3. Make sure cell A1 is still active, then type **SGL Branch Office Name** and press **[Enter]**.

Adding a row changed the location of the data in the worksheet. For example, the consulting income that was originally in cell B4 is now in cell B5. Otis hopes that Excel adjusted the formulas to compensate for the new row.

Otis originally entered the formula =B4+B5 in cell B6 to calculate total income. Now the value for consulting income is in cell B5, and the value for training income is in cell B6. Let's take a look at the formula for total income, which is now located in cell B7.

To examine the contents of cell B7:

1. Click cell **B7**. The formula =B5+B6 appears in the formula bar.

Excel adjusted the formula to compensate for the new location of the data. Otis checks a few more formulas, just to be sure that they also have been adjusted.

To check the formulas in B17 and B19:

1. Click cell **B17**. The formula =SUM(B10:B16) appears in the formula bar. The original formula was =SUM(B9:B15). Excel adjusted this formula to compensate for the new location of the data.
2. Click cell **B19**. The formula =B7-B17 appears in the formula bar. This formula used to be =B6-B16.

After he examines the formulas in his worksheet, Otis concludes that Excel automatically adjusted all the formulas when he inserted the new row.

Now, Otis wants to use Excel's AutoFormat feature to improve the appearance of the worksheet by emphasizing the titles and displaying dollar signs in the cells that contain currency data.

Using AutoFormat

AutoFormat is a command that lets you change the appearance of your worksheet by selecting from a collection of predesigned worksheet formats. Each of the worksheet formats in the AutoFormat collection gives your worksheet a more professional appearance by using attractive fonts, borders, colors, and shading. AutoFormat also manipulates column widths, row heights, and the alignment of text in cells.

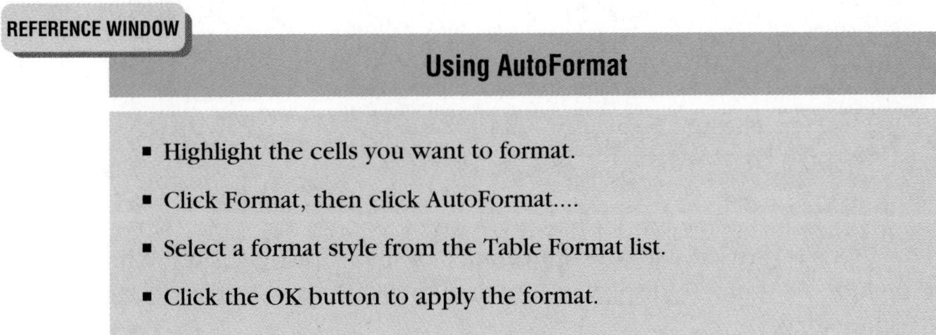

REFERENCE WINDOW

Using AutoFormat

- Highlight the cells you want to format.
- Click Format, then click AutoFormat....
- Select a format style from the Table Format list.
- Click the OK button to apply the format.

Otis decides to use AutoFormat's Financial 3 format to improve the appearance of the worksheet.

To apply AutoFormat's Financial 3 format:

1. Highlight cells A1 through E19, then release the mouse button.
2. Click **Format**, then click **AutoFormat...**. The AutoFormat dialog box appears. See Figure 2-22.

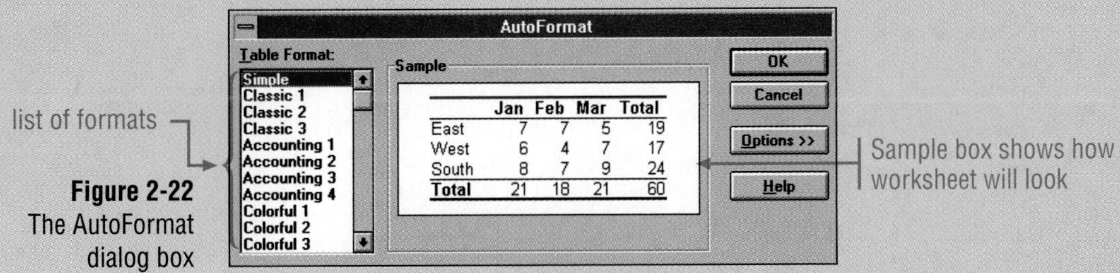

Figure 2-22 The AutoFormat dialog box

3. The Table Format box lists the formats available. The format called "Simple" is highlighted and the Sample box shows how the Simple format will look when applied to a worksheet.
4. Click each of the formats from Simple down to Accounting 4. Notice the different font styles and colors of each format shown in the Sample box.
5. Make sure that Accounting 3 is highlighted, then click the **OK button** to apply this format.

❻ Click any cell to remove the highlighting. The newly formatted worksheet is shown in Figure 2-23.

Microsoft Excel - S2INC.XLS

File Edit View Insert Format Tools Data Window Help

Arial 10 | G17 | 100%

	A	B	C	D	E	F	G
1	SGL Branch Office Name						
2	Income and Expense Summary						
3		Quarter1	Quarter2	Quarter3	Quarter4		
4	Income						
5	Consulting	$ 100.00	$ 100.00	$ 100.00	$ 100.00		
6	Training	100.00	100.00	100.00	100.00		
7	Total Income	$ 200.00	$ 200.00	$ 200.00	$ 200.00		
8							
9	Expenses						
10	Rent	$ 100.00	$ 100.00	$ 100.00	$ 100.00		
11	Salaries	100.00	100.00	100.00	100.00		
12	Telephone	100.00	100.00	100.00	100.00		
13	Advertising	100.00	100.00	100.00	100.00		
14	Office Supplies	100.00	100.00	100.00	100.00		
15	Travel	100.00	100.00	100.00	100.00		
16	Miscellaneous	100.00	100.00	100.00	100.00		
17	Total Expenses	$ 700.00	$ 700.00	$ 700.00	$ 700.00		

Income and Expense / Sheet2 / Sheet3 / Sheet4 / Sh

Ready NUM

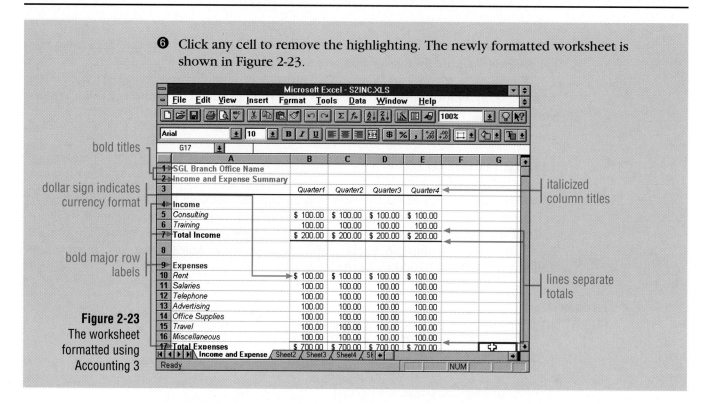

bold titles

dollar sign indicates currency format

bold major row labels

italicized column titles

lines separate totals

Figure 2-23 The worksheet formatted using Accounting 3

Otis is pleased with the appearance of his worksheet, but he realizes that he forgot to include a column to display year-to-date totals. He revises his worksheet plan, as shown in Figure 2-24.

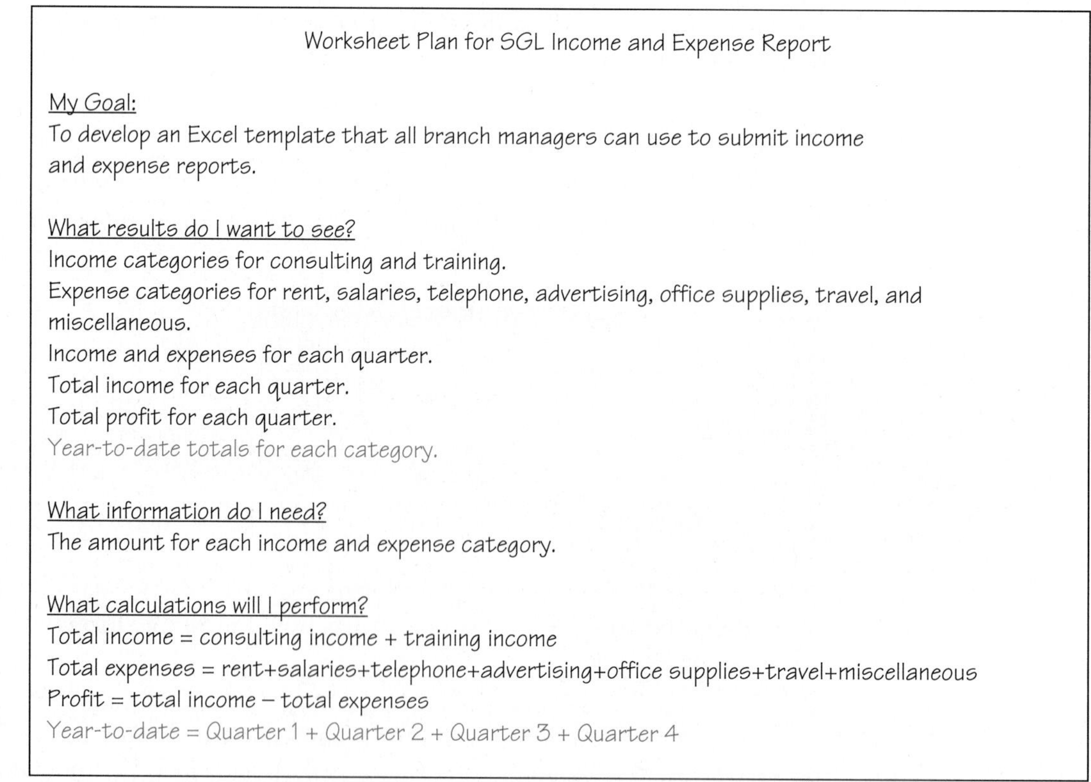
Worksheet Plan for SGL Income and Expense Report

My Goal:
To develop an Excel template that all branch managers can use to submit income and expense reports.

What results do I want to see?
Income categories for consulting and training.
Expense categories for rent, salaries, telephone, advertising, office supplies, travel, and miscellaneous.
Income and expenses for each quarter.
Total income for each quarter.
Total profit for each quarter.
Year-to-date totals for each category.

What information do I need?
The amount for each income and expense category.

What calculations will I perform?
Total income = consulting income + training income
Total expenses = rent+salaries+telephone+advertising+office supplies+travel+miscellaneous
Profit = total income – total expenses
Year-to-date = Quarter 1 + Quarter 2 + Quarter 3 + Quarter 4

Figure 2-24 Otis's revised worksheet plan

Otis also revises his worksheet sketch (Figure 2-25) to show the column titles, formulas, and formats for the Year to Date column.

Income and Expenses Summary					
	Quarter 1	Quarter 2	Quarter 3	Quarter 4	Year to Date
Income					
Consulting	$9,999,999.99	$9,999,999.99	$9,999,999.99	$9,999,999.99	${year-to-date formula}
Training	:	:	:	:	:
Total Income	${total income formula}	${total income formula}	${total income formula}	${total income formula}	${year-to-date formula}
Expenses					
Rent	$9,999,999.99	$9,999,999.99	$9,999,999.99	$9,999,999.99	${year-to-date formula}
Salaries	:	:	:	:	:
Telephone	:	:	:	:	:
Advertising	:	:	:	:	:
Office Supplies	:	:	:	:	:
Travel	:	:	:	:	:
Miscellaneous	:	:	:	:	:
Total Expenses	${total expenses formula}	${total expenses formula}	${total expenses formula}	${total expenses formula}	${year-to-date formula}
Profit	${profit formula}	${profit formula}	${profit formula}	${profit formula}	${year-to-date formula}

Figure 2-25
Otis's revised worksheet sketch

Otis begins by entering the title for the Year to Date column in cell F3.

To enter the title for column F:

1. Click cell **F3** to make it the active cell.
2. Type **Year to Date** and press **[Enter]**.

Next, Otis needs to enter a formula in cell F5 to calculate the year-to-date consulting income. He could type the formula =SUM(B5:E5), but he decides to use the AutoSum button to eliminate some extra typing.

The AutoSum Button

The **AutoSum button**, the Σ button on the toolbar, automatically creates formulas that contain the SUM function. To do this, Excel looks at the cells adjacent to the active cell, guesses which cells you want to sum, and displays a formula that contains a "best guess" about the range you want to sum. You can press the Enter key to accept the formula or you can drag the mouse over a different range of cells to change the range in the formula. Let's use the AutoSum button to enter the formula for year-to-date consulting income in cell F5.

To enter the formula in cell F5 using the AutoSum button:

1. Click cell **F5** because this is where you want to put the formula.
2. Click the **AutoSum button** Σ. See Figure 2-26. Excel determines that you probably want to sum the contents of the range B5 through E5, which is exactly what you want to do.

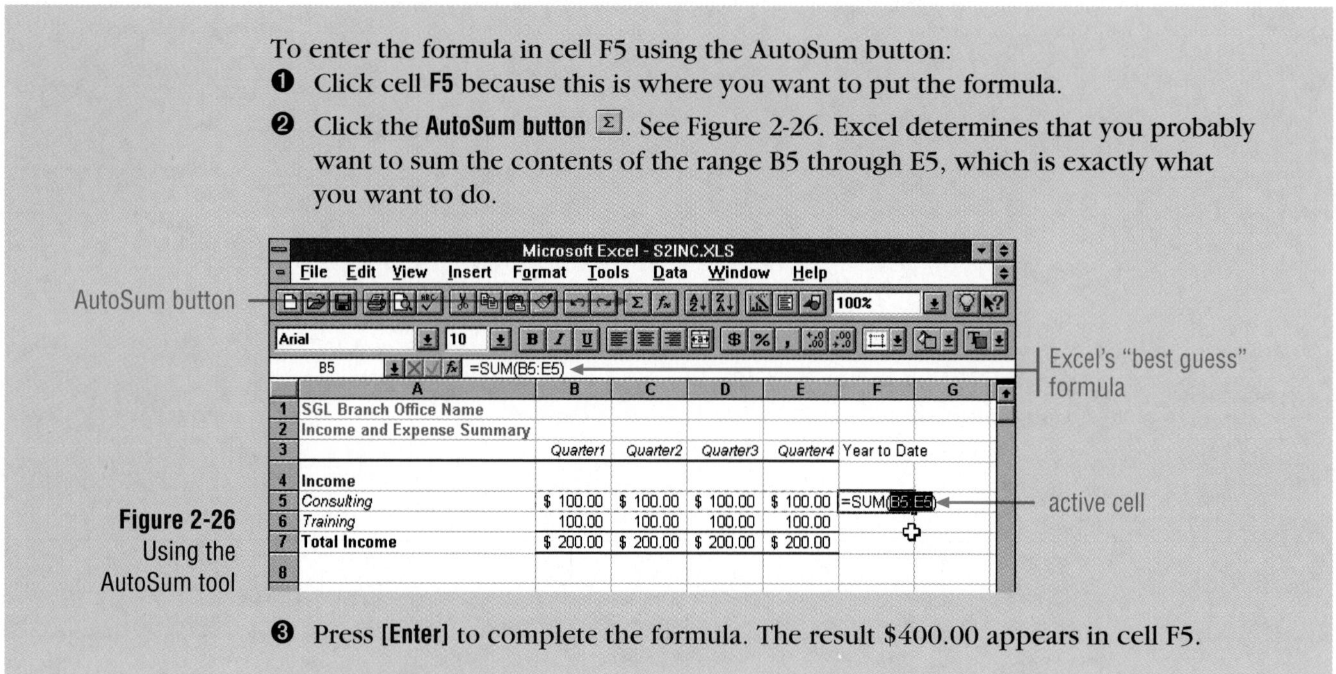

Figure 2-26 Using the AutoSum tool

3. Press **[Enter]** to complete the formula. The result $400.00 appears in cell F5.

Note that AutoSum assumed that you wanted to use the same format in cell F5 as you used in the cells containing the values for the sum. Therefore, cell F5 is formatted for currency with two decimal places.

Otis would like to use the same formula to calculate the year-to-date totals for all income and expense categories as well as the totals. He decides to use the fill handle to copy the formula from cell F5 to cells F6 through F19.

To copy the formula from cell F5 to cells F6 through F19:

1. Scroll the worksheet so you can see rows 5 through 19.
2. Click cell **F5** because this cell contains the formula you want to copy.
3. Drag the fill handle to outline cells F5 through F19, then release the mouse button.
4. Click any cell to remove the highlighting and view the results of the copy. See Figure 2-27.

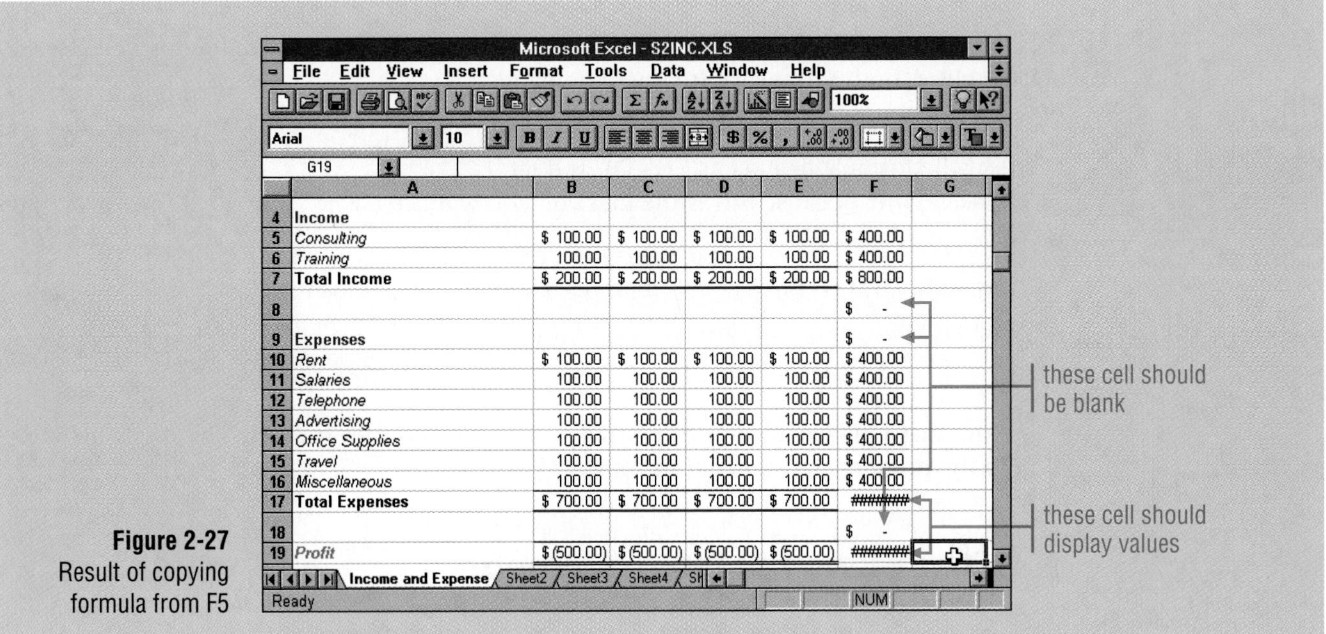

Figure 2-27 Result of copying formula from F5

Otis copied the formula from cell F5 to the range F6 through F19, but there are a few problems, as shown in Figure 2-26. Cells F8, F9, and F18 should be blank. Instead they contain a dollar sign and a hyphen. This is a result of the SUM function now located in those cells. Another problem is that number signs (###) appear in cells F17 and F19 instead of a value for the year-to-date total expenses and year-to-date profit.

Otis decides to clear the formulas from the cells in column F that should be blank.

Clearing Cells

If you want to erase the contents or the formats of a cell, you use either the Delete key or the Clear dialog box. Erasing the *contents* of a cell is known as *clearing a cell.* Keep in mind that clearing a cell is different from deleting the entire cell. When you *delete* a cell, the entire cell is removed from the worksheet and adjacent cells move to fill in the space left by the deleted cell.

When clearing a cell you have three choices. You can clear only the cell contents (i.e., the values or text entered in the cell), you can clear the formats in a cell, or you can clear both the cell contents and the formats. To do this, you can use the Delete key or the Clear dialog box on the Edit menu.

REFERENCE WINDOW

Clearing Cells

- Click the cell you want to clear or highlight a range of cells you want to clear.
- To delete the cell contents only, press [Del].
- To delete the formatting but not the contents, click Edit, click Clear, then click Formats.

Otis decides to clear the formula from cell F18 first. Then he highlights cells F8 and F9 and clears both formulas with one command.

To clear the formula from cells F18, F8, and F9:

1. Click cell **F18** because this is the first cell you want to clear.
2. Press **[Del]**.
3. Highlight cells F8 through F9, then release the mouse button.
4. Press **[Del]**.

Now that Otis has cleared the unwanted formulas from the cells, he turns his attention to the number signs in cells F17 and F19.

Number Sign (###) Replacement

If a value is too long to fit within the boundaries of a cell, Excel displays a series of number signs (###) in the cell. Excel displays the number signs as a signal that the number of digits in the value exceeds the width of the cell. It would be misleading to display only some of the digits of the value. For example, suppose you enter the value 5129 in a cell that is wide enough to display only two digits. Should Excel display the first two digits or the last two digits? You can see that either choice would be misleading, so Excel displays the number signs (###) instead. The values, formats, and formulas have *not* been erased from the cell. To display the value, you just need to increase the column width.

For example, on your worksheet cell F19 displays a maximum of eight entire digits. Because Excel formatted this cell for currency as a result of the AutoSum operation, Excel must have space in the column to display the dollar sign, the comma to indicate thousands, the decimal, two numbers after the decimal, and the parentheses for negative numbers. The value in this cell, ($2,000.00), requires a cell width of 11 digits.

Otis needs to make cells F17 and F19 wider. He also wants to have a double underline in cell F19, a thick single underline in cell F7, and single underlines in cells F3 and F17 so column F will look like the other columns in the worksheet. Rather than applying these formats separately, Otis decides to use AutoFormat again to reapply the Accounting 3 format to the entire worksheet. Reapplying the format will also widen column F because AutoFormat determines column width based on the numbers that are in the cells at the time you apply the format.

To reapply the Accounting 3 format to the entire worksheet:

1. Scroll the worksheet to display row 1.
2. Highlight cells A1 through F19, then release the mouse button.

   TROUBLE? If you don't see row 19 on the screen when you are highlighting the worksheet, move the pointer down past the bottom of the window and the worksheet will scroll.
3. Click **Format**, then click **AutoFormat...**. The AutoFormat dialog box appears.
4. Click the **Accounting 3** format, then click the **OK button** to apply the format.
5. Click any cell to remove the highlighting.

The entire worksheet is reformatted. Column F contains the same format as columns A through E. Otis wants to be sure that the width of column F was increased enough to display the value for year-to-date total expenses in cell F17 and year-to-date profit in cell F19.

To verify that cells F17 and F19 display values rather than number signs:

1. If necessary, scroll the worksheet until rows 17 and 19 are visible. Cell F17 displays $2,800.00 instead of number signs.
2. Cell F19 displays $(2,000.00) instead of number signs.

Otis still isn't satisfied with the format. He's not certain that the columns are wide enough. For example, what if a branch manager reports consulting income of $1 million for the first quarter? Will that value fit in cell B5? Let's try it.

To enter $1 million in cell B5:

1. Click cell **B5** to make it the active cell.
2. Type **1000000** and press **[Enter]**. Number signs appear in cells B5, B7, B19, F5, F7, and F19, as shown in Figure 2-28.

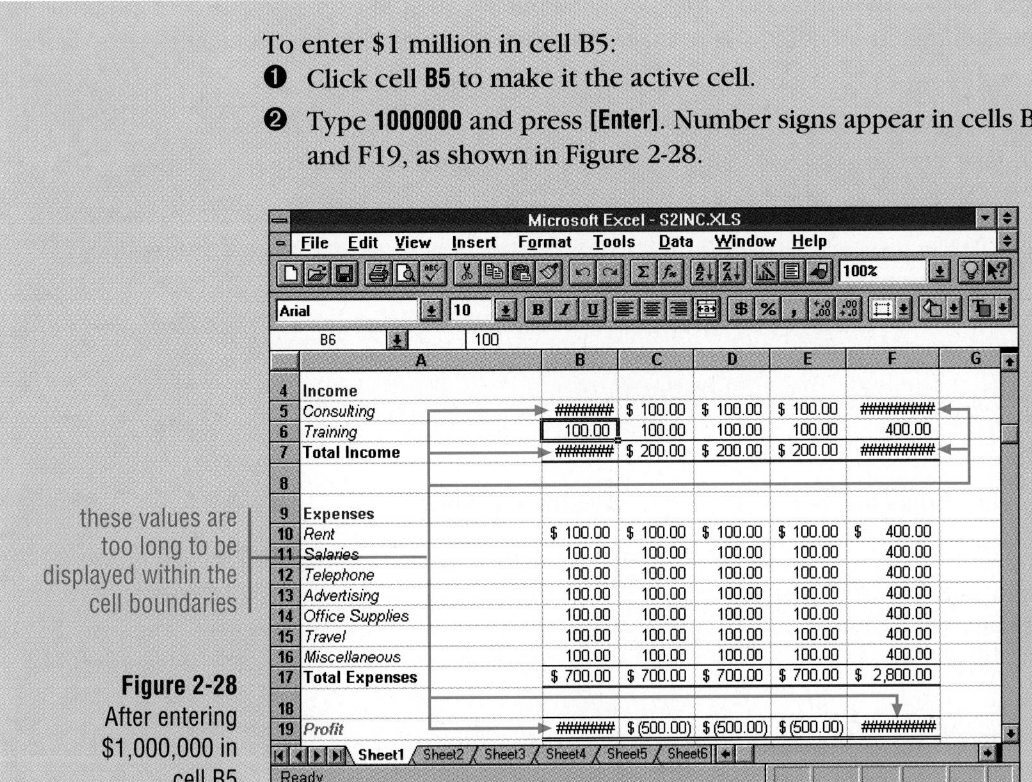

Figure 2-28
After entering $1,000,000 in cell B5

Otis realizes that columns B through F need to display at least 13 digits. Because Otis used small test values, AutoFormat did not make the cells as wide as they will need to be when the branch managers enter their data. Otis decides to change the column width using the Column Width command.

To change the width of columns B through F using the Column Width command:

1. Click the **column heading box** at the top of column B. This highlights column B.
2. Drag the pointer to column F, then release the mouse button. Columns B through F are highlighted.
3. Click **Format**.
4. Click **Column**, then click **Width...** to display the Column Width dialog box. The insertion point is flashing in the Column Width box.
5. Type **13** in the Column Width box, then click the **OK button**.
6. Click any cell to remove the highlighting and view the new column widths.

Otis thinks column A is too wide because the longest income or expense category label, "Total Expenses," is only 14 characters. He decides to allow the titles "SGL Branch Office Name" and "Income and Expense Summary" to spill over into adjacent columns. He adjusts the width of column A to make it just wide enough for the "Total Expenses" label.

To adjust the width of column A:

1. Make sure you can see cell A17, which contains the "Total Expenses" label.
2. Position the pointer on the column heading box at the top of column A.
3. Move the pointer slowly to the right until it is positioned over the dividing line between column A and column B and changes to ✛.
4. Drag the dividing line to the left, just to the right of the last "s" in the label "Total Expenses."
5. Release the mouse button. Column A adjusts to the new width.

Otis thinks this is a good time to save the workbook.

To save the workbook:

1. Click the **Save button** to save the workbook on your Student Disk.

If you want to take a break and resume the tutorial at a later time, you can exit Excel by double-clicking the Control menu box in the upper-left corner of the screen. When you resume the tutorial, launch Excel, maximize the Microsoft Excel and Book1 windows, and place your Student Disk in the disk drive. Open the file S2INC.XLS, then continue with the tutorial.

■ ■ ■

Otis next wants to test his worksheet using realistic data.

Testing the Worksheet with Realistic Data

Before you trust a worksheet and its results, you should test it to make sure you have entered the correct formulas and have specified appropriate formats. You want the worksheet to produce accurate results, and you want the results to be displayed clearly.

Earlier Otis used the test value 100 because it enabled him to make the worksheet calculations in his head and verify that the formulas were correct. So far, the formulas appear to be correct, but Otis is still not satisfied.

Otis knows that this is an extremely important worksheet. Branch managers will enter values into the worksheet, and they will assume the worksheet calculates the correct results. Otis's reputation, the reputations of the branch managers, and the success of the corporation could depend on the worksheet's providing correct results. Otis is determined to test the worksheet thoroughly before he distributes it to any branch offices.

Otis wants to test the worksheet using realistic data, so he decides to enter last year's values from the Littleton, North Carolina branch office report, which is shown in Figure 2-29.

Littleton, North Carolina
Income and Expense Data

	Quarter 1	Quarter 2	Quarter 3	Quarter 4	Year to Date
Income					
Consulting	$102,000	$150,000	$90,000	$110,000	$452,000
Training	$20,000	$22,000	$12,000	$15,000	$69,000
Total Income	$122,000	$172,000	$102,000	$125,000	$521,000
Expenses					
Rent	$6,800	$6,800	$6,800	$6,800	$27,200
Salaries	$80,900	$80,900	$80,900	$80,900	$323,600
Telephone	$1,125	$1,252	$1,056	$1,325	$4,758
Advertising	$700	$800	$1,200	$800	$3,500
Office Supplies	$215	$225	$102	$198	$740
Travel	$465	$1,650	$525	$1,466	$4,106
Miscellaneous	$1,488	$256	$555	$780	$3,079
Total Expenses	$91,693	$91,883	$91,138	$92,269	$366,983
Profit	$30,307	$80,117	$10,862	$32,731	$154,017

enter these test values

Figure 2-29
Littleton, North Carolina branch office data

To enter the Littleton test values:

1. Enter the test values shown in the blue-boxed area of Figure 2-29. Do not enter values in any cells that contain formulas. Because you have already formatted your worksheet, you should enter the test values without dollar signs or decimal places. Excel will automatically add the dollar signs and decimal places where appropriate.

   TROUBLE? If you enter a number in a cell that contains a formula and you notice it right away, click Edit, then click Undo Entry. If you don't notice the problem until after you have made other entries, retype the formula in the appropriate cell.

Next, Otis compares the results displayed on his worksheet with the results for the North Carolina branch values shown in the yellow-boxed area of Figure 2-29. The values produced by the formulas in his worksheet match the Littleton results. Now, Otis is more confident that the worksheet will provide the correct results.

Clearing Test Values from the Worksheet

The current worksheet contains test values that must not be included in the final worksheet template, so Otis needs to clear the test values from the worksheet.

To clear the test values from the worksheet:

1. Highlight cells B5 through E6, then release the mouse button. ***Do not drag to column F.*** Column F contains formulas and you don't want to clear them.

   TROUBLE? If you highlight column F, drag the pointer from B5 to E6 again.

2. Press **[Del]**.
3. Highlight cells B10 through E16, then release the mouse button. ***Do not drag to column F.***
4. Press **[Del]**.
5. Click any cell to remove the highlighting.

Otis knows that it is important to document his worksheet so the branch managers will know how it is set up.

Documenting the Worksheet

The purpose of documenting a worksheet is to provide the information necessary to use and modify the worksheet. The documentation for your worksheet can take many forms; if you work for a company that does not have documentation standards or requirements, you must decide what type of documentation is most effective for your worksheets.

Your worksheet plan and worksheet sketch provide one type of worksheet documentation. As you know, the worksheet plan and sketch give you a "blueprint" to follow as you build and test the worksheet. This can be useful information for someone who needs to modify your worksheet because it states your goals, specifies the required input, describes the output, and indicates the calculations you used to produce the output.

Excel also provides a way to print all the formulas you entered in the worksheet. This is a very useful form of documentation, which you will learn about in Tutorial 3.

The worksheet plan, the worksheet sketch, and the formula printout are not, however, part of the worksheet and might not be readily available to the person using the worksheet.

You can include documentation as part of your worksheet. This documentation might be as simple as a header with your name and the date you created the worksheet. More complete documentation might include the information from your worksheet plan typed on a page of the worksheet. You can also include documentation by adding a text note to your worksheet.

Adding a Text Note

A **text note** is text that is attached to a cell. The note does not appear on the worksheet unless you double-click the cell to which it is attached. Cells that contain text notes display a small square in the upper-right corner. On a color monitor this square is red. You can attach text notes to a cell even if it contains data.

Text notes are suitable for documentation that not every user needs to see. Because some users might not know that cells with squares in the upper-right corner contain notes, you cannot be certain that everyone will read your text notes. A text note, then, is appropriate for documentation that an experienced Excel user might want to see.

REFERENCE WINDOW

Adding a Text Note

- Click the cell to which you want to attach a text note.
- Click Insert, then click Note....
- Type the text of your note in the Text Note box. The insertion point will automatically move down when you reach the end of a line. If you need to type a short line and then move down, press [Enter].
- When you finish typing the note, click the OK button.

At SGL, management recommends that anyone who creates a worksheet should attach a text note to cell A1 with the following information:

- who created the worksheet
- the date the worksheet was created or revised
- a brief description of the worksheet

Otis adds a text note to his worksheet to provide the required documentation.

To add a text note to cell A1:

1. Click cell **A1** because this is the cell to which you want to attach the text note.
2. Click **Insert**, then click **Note...** to display the Cell Note dialog box.
3. Click in the **Text Note box** to make sure the insertion point is active, then type **Income and Expense Summary**.
4. Press **[Enter]** to move the insertion point to the next line.
5. Type **Created by Otis Nunley** and press **[Enter]**.
6. Type today's date and press **[Enter]**.
7. Type the rest of the note you see in Figure 2-30 without pressing [Enter]. Because the rest of the note is a paragraph, you do not need to press [Enter]; the words automatically wrap to the next line.

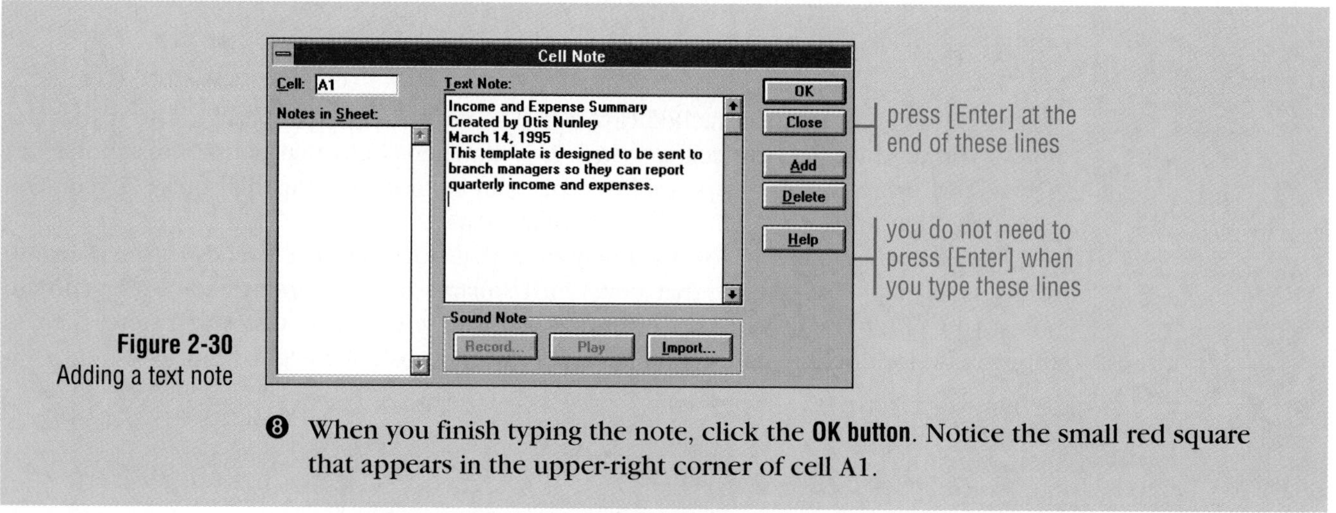

Figure 2-30
Adding a text note

8. When you finish typing the note, click the **OK button**. Notice the small red square that appears in the upper-right corner of cell A1.

Now that the worksheet is almost done, Otis wants to make sure that he hasn't misspelled any words.

Checking the Spelling of the Worksheet

Excel's **Spelling command** helps you find misspelled words in your worksheets. When you choose this command, Excel compares the words in your worksheet to the words in its dictionary. When it finds a word in your worksheet that is not in its dictionary, it shows you the word and provides options for correcting it or leaving it as is.

REFERENCE WINDOW

Using the Spelling Button

- Click cell A1 so you begin spell checking from the top of the worksheet.
- Click the Spelling button.
- Excel shows you any word that is in your worksheet, but not in its dictionary. Your options are:
  - If the word is correct and you do not want to change this one occurrence, click the Ignore button.
  - If the word is correct and you want Excel to ignore all future occurrences of the word, click the Ignore All button.
  - If you want Excel to suggest a correct spelling, click the Suggest button.
  - If you want to change the word to one of the suggestions listed in the Suggestions box, click the correct word, then click the Change button.
- If Excel does not provide an acceptable alternative, you can edit the word in the Change To box, then click the Change button.

Otis is ready to check the spelling of his worksheet.

To check the spelling of the entire worksheet:

1. Click cell **A1** so Excel begins spell checking at the first cell in the worksheet.
2. Click the **Spelling button** to check the spelling of the entire worksheet. Excel finds the word SGL. See Figure 2-31. SGL is the name of the company Otis works for. This word is not misspelled, but it is not in Excel's dictionary.

   TROUBLE? Don't worry if your list of suggested alternatives is different, simply continue with Step 3.

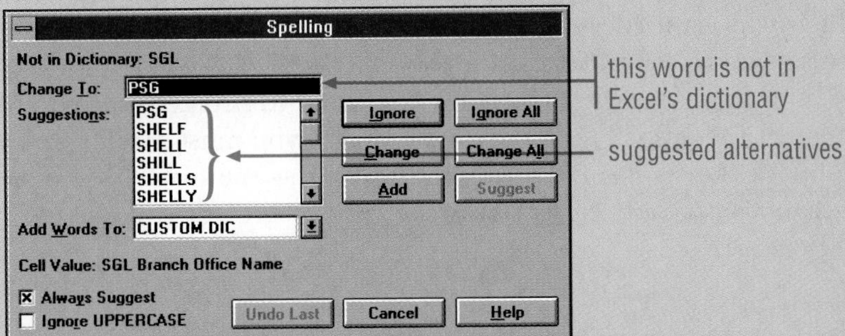

Figure 2-31
Checking the spelling in the worksheet

3. Click the **Ignore All button** because you do not want to change SGL here or anywhere else it appears on the worksheet.
4. When Excel finds the word "Otis" (in the text note) click the **Ignore All button** because you do not want to change this word here or anywhere else. Do the same for the word "Nunley."
5. If Excel finds any other misspelled words in your worksheet, use the Spelling dialog box buttons to make the appropriate changes.
6. When you see the message "Finished spell checking entire sheet" click the **OK button**.

Otis looks at the completed worksheet and thinks about the way it will be used. Branch managers will receive his template—a version of the worksheet with the titles and formulas, but with no values. At the start of each year, the branch managers will open a copy of the template and save it under a name that indicates the branch office name.

At the end of each quarter, the branch managers will retrieve the worksheet, enter the values for that quarter, then save and print the worksheet. The branch managers will send a printed copy to Otis, along with a disk containing a copy of the worksheet.

Otis foresees one problem with the template. What if a branch manager types a value over a cell containing a formula? The formula would be erased, the cell would not recalculate to reflect changes, and the worksheet would be unreliable. Otis needs some way to protect the worksheet.

Protecting Cells in the Worksheet

Excel lets you protect cells from changes while still allowing users to enter or change values in unprotected cells. Cells that are protected so that their contents cannot be changed are referred to as **locked cells**.

There are two commands you use to protect or unprotect cells: the Cell Protection command and the Protect Document command. The **Cell Protection command** lets you specify the protection status for any cell in the worksheet. In the worksheet you are currently building, the protection status of all cells is locked. How, then, can you change the contents of the cells in the worksheet when you build it? Here's where the Protect Document command comes into play. The protection status does not go into effect until you use the **Protect Document command** to put the worksheet into protected mode.

When you want to protect some cells in the worksheet, you first *unlock* the cells in which you want users to make entries. Then you use the Protection command on the Tools menu to activate the protection on those cells you left locked.

When you use the Protection command to protect the worksheet, Excel allows you to enter a password. If you use a password, you must make sure to remember it in order to unlock the worksheet in the future. Unless the material you are working on is confidential, it's probably easier not to use a password at all. You'll use one in this tutorial just for practice.

REFERENCE WINDOW

Protecting Cells

- Select the cells you want to *un*lock.
- Click Format, then click Cells....
- In the Format Cells dialog box, click the Protection tab.
- Remove the × from the Locked option box.
- Use the Tools, Protection, Protect Sheet... command to activate protection for the entire worksheet. All cells that were not set to unlocked will be protected.
- Save the modified worksheet.

Otis starts by unlocking the range of cells into which the managers *can* enter data. Then, he activates document protection for the rest of the worksheet.

To unlock the cells for data entry:

1. Highlight cells B5 through E6, then release the mouse button.
2. Click **Format**, then click **Cells...**. The Format Cells dialog box appears.
3. Click the **Protection tab**. Notice that the Locked box contains an ×. See Figure 2-32.

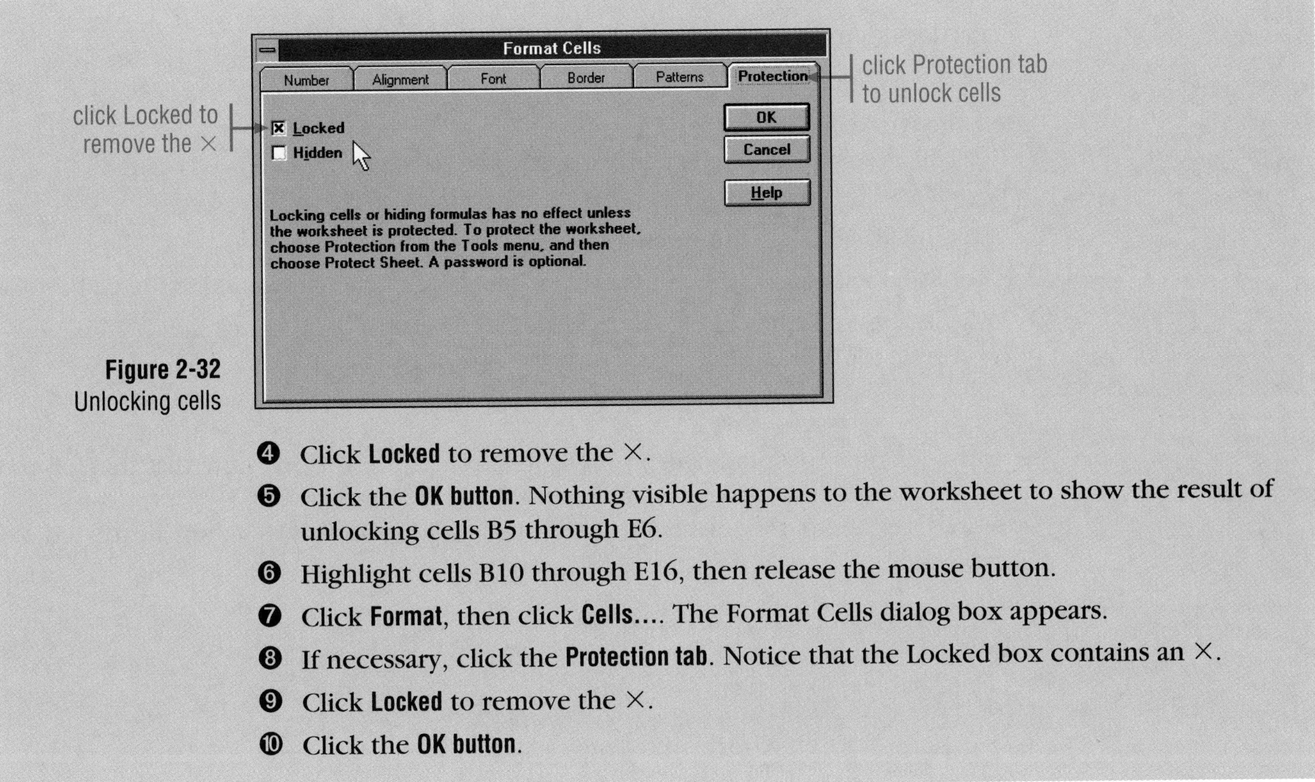

Figure 2-32
Unlocking cells

4. Click **Locked** to remove the ×.
5. Click the **OK button**. Nothing visible happens to the worksheet to show the result of unlocking cells B5 through E6.
6. Highlight cells B10 through E16, then release the mouse button.
7. Click **Format**, then click **Cells...**. The Format Cells dialog box appears.
8. If necessary, click the **Protection tab**. Notice that the Locked box contains an ×.
9. Click **Locked** to remove the ×.
10. Click the **OK button**.

In addition to entering data in the cells, the branch managers need to type the appropriate branch office name in row 1. Otis unlocks cell A1 to allow the managers to enter the branch office name.

To unlock cell A1:

1. Click **A1** to make it the active cell.
2. Click **Format**, then click **Cells...**. The Format Cells dialog box appears.
3. If necessary, click the **Protection tab**, then click **Locked** to remove the ×.
4. Click the **OK button**.

Now that Otis has unlocked the cells for data entry, he turns protection on for the entire worksheet. This protects every cell that he didn't unlock.

To turn protection on:

1. Click **Tools**, click **Protection**, then click **Protect Sheet...**. The Protect Sheet dialog box appears.
2. Type **bluesky** as the password. The letters appear as x's or *'s in the text box.
3. Click the **OK button**. You will be prompted to enter the password again to make sure that you remember it and that you entered it correctly the first time.
4. Type **bluesky** again, then click the **OK button**. Nothing visible happens to show that you protected the worksheet.

Otis decides to test the worksheet protection.

To test the worksheet protection:

1. Click **A8**, then type **5**. A dialog box displays the message, "Locked cells cannot be changed."
2. Click the **OK button** to continue.
3. Click **B10**, then type **3**. The number 3 appears in the formula bar and in the cell.
4. Press **[Enter]**. You can make an entry in cell B10 because you unlocked it before protecting the worksheet.

Otis tests the remaining cells in his worksheet. He is satisfied now that the cell protection will prevent the managers from overwriting the formulas.

Now Otis needs to delete the entry he made in cell B10 when he tested the cell protection.

To clear cell B10:

1. Click **B10**, then press **[Del]**.

Now the worksheet is complete and Otis is ready to save it as a template.

Saving the Worksheet as an Excel Template

Excel templates are stored with an .XLT extension rather than the .XLS extension used for workbooks.

Figure 2-33 shows that when you open a template, Excel copies it from the disk to RAM and displays the template on your screen (1). You fill in the template with values, as you would with any worksheet (2). When you save this workbook, Excel prompts you for a new filename so you do not overwrite the template. Excel then saves the completed workbook under the new filename (3).

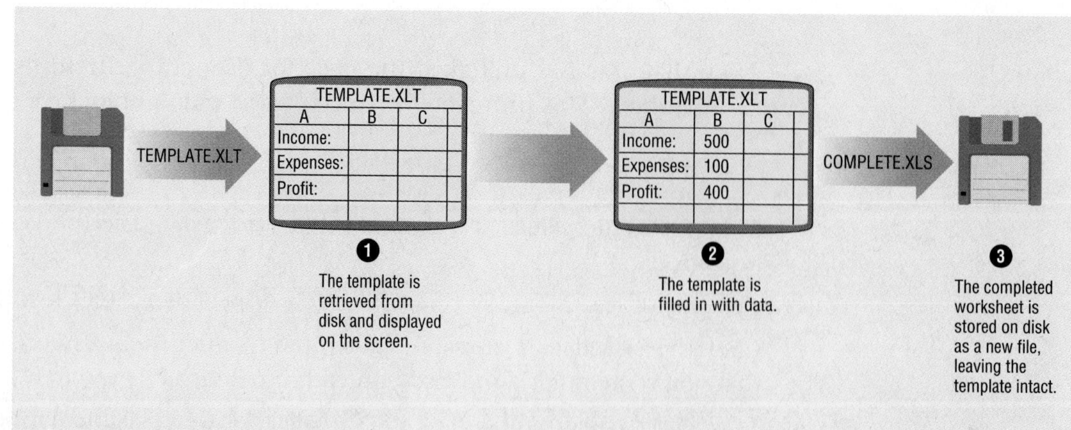

Figure 2-33
How a template works

Otis uses the Save As command to save the Income and Expense Summary worksheet as a template.

To save the worksheet as a template:

❶ Click **File**, then click **Save As...** to display the Save As dialog box.

❷ Click the **Save File as Type box down arrow button** to display a list of file types.

❸ Click **Template**. S2INC.XLT appears in the File Name box.

❹ Make sure the Drives box displays the icon for the disk drive that contains your Student Disk. See Figure 2-34.

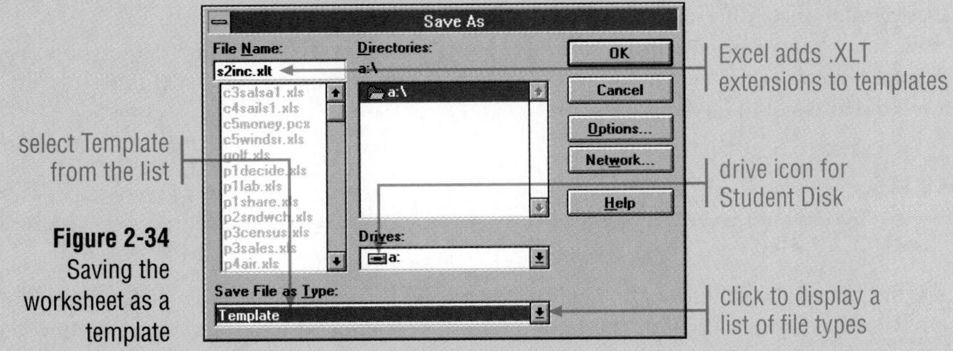

Figure 2-34 Saving the worksheet as a template

❺ Click the **OK button** to save the template. If you see the Summary Info dialog box, press **[Enter]** to close the dialog box and finish saving the template.

❻ Click **File**, then click **Close** to close the worksheet. Exit Excel if you are not going to proceed to the Tutorial Assignments.

Otis has finished his template and is ready to send it to the branch managers. He exits Excel and Windows before turning off his computer.

■ ■ ■

Questions

1. What command do you use to name a worksheet and save it?
2. The small black square in the lower-right corner of the active cell is called the __________________.
3. What are the four activities required to create an effective worksheet?
4. Why would you use 1 as a test value?
5. Using the correct order of operations, calculate the results of the following formulas:
   a. 2+3*6
   b. (4/2)*5
   c. 2^2+5
   d. 10+10/2
6. Describe the methods you can use to enter cell references in a formula.
7. All references in formulas are __________________ unless you specify otherwise.
8. When you copy a formula, what happens to the relative references?
9. To clear the contents of a cell (but not the formatting) click the cell and then click __________________.
10. Why does Excel display number signs (###) in a cell?
11. To protect a worksheet, you must first unlock those cells that the user will be allowed to change and then activate __________________.

12. ________________ references contain a dollar sign before the column letter, row number, or both.
13. What is the difference between clearing a cell and deleting a cell?
14. Explain the function of the following toolbar buttons:
    a. [Σ]
    b. [✓]...
    c. [■]
    d. [open]
15. How is a template different from a worksheet?
16. Which button will automatically complete a series such as Jan, Feb, Mar?
17. What are your options when you're using the Spelling command and Excel finds a word that is not in its dictionary?

Tutorial Assignments

You are the Branch Manager for the Duluth, Minnesota branch of SGL. Otis Nunley from the home office has just sent you a copy of the new quarterly income and expense summary template. Otis has asked you to test the template by filling in the information for the first two quarters of this year and sending a printed copy of the worksheet back to him. Open the template T2INC.XLT and do the following:

1. Enter your name in cell A1 in place of the branch office name.
2. Enter the values for Quarter 1 and Quarter 2 as shown in Figure 2-35.
3. Compare your results with those in Figure 2-35 to verify that the formulas are correct.
4. Save the workbook as S2DLTH.XLS.
5. Print the worksheet.

Figure 2-35

Duluth Branch Office					
Income and Expense Summary					
	Quarter 1	*Quarter 2*	*Quarter 3*	*Quarter 4*	***Year to Date***
Income					
Consulting	$27,930.00	$33,550.00			$61,480.00
Training	11,560.00	13,520.00			25,080.00
Total Income	$39,490.00	$47,070.00	$0.00	$0.00	$86,560.00
Expenses					
Rent	$2,300.00	$2,300.00			$4,600.00
Salaries	7,200.00	7,200.00			14,400.00
Telephone	547.00	615.00			1,162.00
Advertising	1,215.00	692.00			1,907.00
Office Supplies	315.00	297.00			612.00
Travel	1,257.00	1,408.00			2,665.00
Miscellaneous	928.00	802.00			1,730.00
Total Expenses	$13,762.00	$13,314.00	$0.00	$0.00	$27,076.00
Profit	$25,728.00	$33,756.00	$0.00	$0.00	$59,484.00

Otis shows the Quarterly Income and Expense Summary template to his boss, Joan LeValle. She suggests several additions to the template. Joan mentions that some of the branch offices have started long-term education programs for their employees, so she wants you to add a separate expense category for education.

6. Open the workbook S2INC.XLT, which you saved as a template at the end of this tutorial.
7. Deactivate document protection by clicking Tools, clicking Protection, then selecting Unprotect Sheet.... Type "bluesky" as the password, then click the OK button.

8. Insert a row where row 14 is currently located.
9. Enter the row label "Education" in cell A14.
10. Use the fill handle to copy the formula from cell F13 to cell F14.
11. Use the Protection command to reactivate document protection, using bluesky as the password.
12. Save the workbook as the template S2INC2.XLT and then close the workbook.
13. Open the template S2INC2.XLT and test it by entering 1 as the test value for each of the income and expense categories for each quarter. Make any revisions necessary to formulas, formats, or cell protection so it works according to Otis's plan.
14. Save the workbook with the test values as S2TEST.XLS, then print it.

Case Problems

1. Tracking Ticket Sales for the Brookstone Dance Group

Robin Yeh is the ticket sales coordinator for the Brookstone Dance Group, a community dance company. Brookstone sells five types of tickets: season tickets, reserved seating, general admission, student tickets, and senior citizen tickets.

Robin needs a way to track the sales of each of the five ticket types. She has done the initial planning for an Excel worksheet that will track ticket sales and has asked you to create the worksheet.

Study Robin's worksheet plan in Figure 2-36 and her worksheet sketch in Figure 2-37, then build, test, and document a template into which Robin can enter ticket sales data.

Worksheet Plan for Brookstone Dance Group

Goal:
To create a worksheet to track monthly ticket sales.

What results do I want to see?
Total ticket sales for each month.
Total annual sales for each of the five ticket types.
Total annual sales for all ticket types.

What information do I need?
The monthly sales for each type of ticket

What calculations will I perform?
Total ticket sales = season tickets + reserved seating + general admission + student tickets + senior citizen tickets

Season ticket annual sales = sum of each month's sales of season tickets
Reserved seating annual sales = sum of each month's sales of reserved seating
General admission annual sales = sum of each month's sales of general admission
Student ticket annual sales = sum of each month's sales of student tickets
Senior citizen ticket annual sales = sum of each month's sales of senior citizen tickets

Figure 2-36

Brookstone Dance Group Ticket Sales

	April	May	June	July	YTD
Season tickets	:	:	:	:	{season ticket annual sales formula}
Reserved seating	:	:	:	:	{reserved seating annual sales formula}
General admission	:	:	:	:	{general admission annual sales formula}
Student tickets	:	:	:	:	{student ticket annual sales formula}
Senior citizen tickets	:	:	:	:	{senior citizen ticket annual sales formula}
Total ticket sales	{total ticket sales formula}	{total ticket sales formula}	{total ticket sales formula}	{total ticket sales formula}	{total ticket sales formula}

Figure 2-37

1. Launch Excel and make sure you have a blank worksheet on your screen. If the Excel window is open and you do not have a blank worksheet, click the New Workbook button.
2. Enter the labels for the first column as shown in Figure 2-37.
3. Use AutoFill to automatically fill in the month names.
4. Enter YTD in the cell to the right of the cell containing the label July.
5. Create the formulas to calculate total ticket sales and year-to-date sales for each ticket type.
6. Use the AutoFormat Classic 3 style as the format for the worksheet. Adjust column widths as necessary.
7. Add a text note to cell A1 that includes your name, the date, and a short description of the template.
8. Rename Sheet1 "Ticket Sales."
9. Test the template using 1000 as the test value, then make any changes necessary for the template to work correctly.
10. Clear the test values from the cells.
11. Unprotect the cells in which Robin will enter data; then, protect the document using bluesky as the password.
12. Save the workbook as a template named S2TCKTS.XLT.
13. Print the template and close it.
14. Open the template S2TCKTS.XLT and enter some realistic data for April, May, and June. You can make up this data, keeping in mind that Brookstone typically has total ticket sales of about 500 per month.
15. Print the worksheet with the realistic test data, then close the workbook without saving it.

2. Tracking Customer Activity at Brownie's Sandwich Shop

Sherri McWilliams is the assistant manager at Brownie's Sandwich Shop. She is responsible for scheduling waitresses and cooks. To plan an effective schedule, Sherri wants to know the busiest days of the week and the busiest hours of the day. She started to create a worksheet to help track the customer activity in the shop, and she has asked if you could help her complete the worksheet. Open the workbook P2SNDWCH.XLS and do the following:

1. Save the workbook as S2SNDWCH.XLS so you will not modify the original file if you want to do this case again.
2. Use AutoFill to complete the column titles for the days of the week.
3. Use AutoFill to complete the labels showing open hours from 11:00AM to 10:00PM.
4. Use the AutoSum button to create a formula to calculate the total number of customers in cell B15.

5. Copy the formula in cell B15 to cells C15 through H15.
6. Enter the column title "Hourly" in cell I1, and the title "Average" in cell I2. Sherri plans to use column I to display the average number of customers for each one-hour time period.
7. Enter the formula =AVERAGE(B3:H3) in cell I3, then copy it to cells I4 through I15. **E**
8. Enter "Sandwich Shop Activity" in cell A1 as the worksheet title.
9. Add a text note to cell A1 that includes your name, the date, and a brief description of the worksheet.
10. Rename Sheet1 "Customer Activity."
11. Save the workbook as S2SNDWCH.XLS.
12. Print the worksheet.
13. On your printout, circle the busiest day of the week and the hour of the day with the highest average customer traffic.

3. Activity Reports for Magazines Unlimited

Norm McGruder was just hired as a fulfillment driver for Magazines Unlimited. He is responsible for stocking magazines in supermarkets and bookstores in his territory. Each week Norm goes to each store in his territory, removes the outdated magazines, and delivers the current issues.

Plan, build, test, and document a template that Norm can use to keep track of the number of magazines he removes and replaces from the Safeway supermarket during one week. Although Norm typically handles 100 to 150 different magazine titles at the Safeway store, for this Case Problem, create the template for only 12 of them: *Entertainment Weekly*, *Auto News*, *Fortune*, *Harpers*, *Time*, *The Atlantic*, *Newsweek*, *Ebony*, *PC Week*, *The New Republic*, *Forbes*, and *Vogue*.

Your worksheet should contain:

- a column that lists the magazine names
- a column that contains the number of magazines delivered
- a column that contains the number of magazines removed
- a column that contains a formula to calculate the number of magazines sold by subtracting the number of magazines removed from the number of magazines delivered
- a cell that displays the total number of magazines delivered
- a cell that displays the total number of magazines removed
- a cell that shows the total number of magazines sold during the week

To complete this Case Problem, do the following:

1. Create a worksheet plan similar to the one in Figure 2-4 at the beginning of the tutorial. Include a description of the worksheet goal, list the results you want to see, list the input information needed, and describe the calculations that must be performed.
2. Draw a worksheet sketch showing the layout for the template.
3. Build the worksheet by entering the title, the row labels, the column titles, and the formulas.
4. Format the worksheet using your choice of format from the AutoFormat list.
5. Test the worksheet using 1 as the test value. Make any changes necessary for the worksheet to function according to your plan.
6. Add a text note to cell A1 to document the worksheet.
7. Rename Sheet1 with an appropriate name.
8. Clear the test values from the worksheet.
9. Unprotect the cells in which you will enter the number of magazines delivered and removed; then, protect the entire document using bluesky as the password.
10. Save the workbook as a template called S2MAG.XLT.
11. Print the template, then enter some realistic test data and print it again.
12. Submit your worksheet plan, your worksheet sketch, the printout of the template, and the printout with the realistic test data.

TUTORIAL 3

Formatting and Printing

Producing a Projected Sales Impact Report

OBJECTIVES

In this tutorial you will:

- Change the font style, font size, and font
- Align cell contents
- Center text across columns
- Use the number, currency, and percentage formats
- Use borders, color, and patterns for emphasis
- Activate the Drawing toolbar
- Add comments to a worksheet
- Preview printouts
- Print in portrait and landscape orientations
- Center printouts on a page
- Remove cell gridlines from printouts
- Display formulas
- Use a module to print formulas

CASE

Pronto Authentic Recipe Salsa Company

Anne Castelar is the owner of the Pronto Authentic Recipe Salsa Company, a successful business located in the heart of Tex-Mex country. She is working on a plan to add a new product, Salsa de Chile Guero Medium, to Pronto's line of gourmet salsas.

Anne wants to take out a bank loan to purchase additional food processing equipment to handle the increase in production required for the new salsa. She has an appointment with her bank loan officer at 2:00 this afternoon. In preparation for the meeting, Anne is creating a worksheet to show the projected sales of the new salsa and the expected effect on profitability.

Although the numbers and formulas are in place on the worksheet, Anne has not had time to format the worksheet for the best impact. She was planning to do that now, but an unexpected problem with today's produce shipment requires her to leave the office for a few hours. Anne asks her office manager, Maria Stevens, to complete the worksheet. Anne shows Maria a printout of the unformatted worksheet and explains that she wants the finished worksheet to look very professional—like the examples you see in business magazines. She also asks Maria to make sure that the worksheet emphasizes the profits expected from sales of the new salsa.

After Anne leaves, Maria develops the worksheet plan in Figure 3-1 and the worksheet format plan in Figure 3-2.

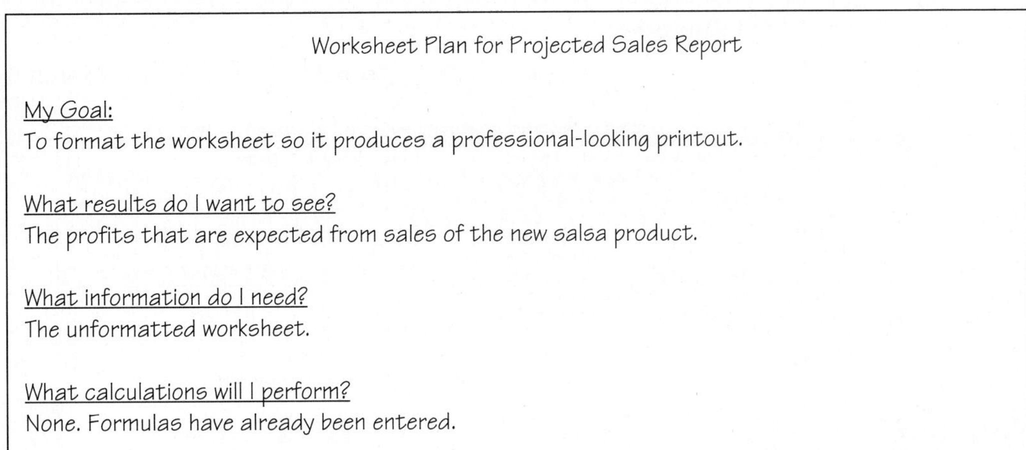

Worksheet Plan for Projected Sales Report

My Goal:
To format the worksheet so it produces a professional-looking printout.

What results do I want to see?
The profits that are expected from sales of the new salsa product.

What information do I need?
The unformatted worksheet.

What calculations will I perform?
None. Formulas have already been entered.

Figure 3-1
Maria's worksheet plan

adjust column widths as necessary

change title font; boldface, center, and enlarge titles for emphasis; also put a border around this title

boldface and center all column titles

display labels in italics

separate column titles from data with a line

format as currency with two decimal places

separate data from totals with a line

add text box and comment

display numbers with commas

display as a percent

display as currency with no decimal places

	A	B	C	D	E	F	G	H	I
1	Pronto Authentic Recipe Salsa Company								
2	Projected Sales Impact of New Product								
3									
4			Wholesale		Units	Total	Profit	Share of	
5	Product	Cost	Price	Profit	Sold	Sales	from Sales	Sales (Units)	
6	Salsa Verde	1.05	1.89	0.84	62100	117369	52164	0.180373	
7	Salsa Fresc	0.95	1.77	0.82	75400	133458	61828	0.21379	
8	Salsa Mexic	0.95	1.77	0.82	75500	133635	61910	0.214073	
9	Salsa Picar	1.21	2.09	0.88	54600	114114	48048	0.166141	
10	Salsa de Ch	0.78	1.65	0.87	75000	123750	65250	0.225622	
11				Total	342600	622326	289200		

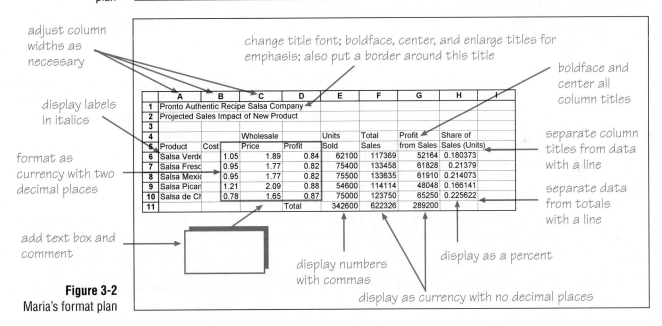

Figure 3-2
Maria's format plan

Now Maria is ready to launch Excel and open the worksheet. To begin, you need to launch Excel and maximize the application and document windows to organize your desktop.

To launch Excel and organize your desktop:

❶ Launch Excel following your usual procedure.

❷ Make sure your Student Disk is in the disk drive.

❸ Make sure the Microsoft Excel and Book1 windows are maximized.

Anne stored the workbook as C3SALSA1.XLS. Now Maria needs to open this file.

To open the C3SALSA1.XLS workbook:

1. Click the **Open button** to display the Open dialog box.
2. Double-click **C3SALSA1.XLS** in the File Name box to display the workbook shown in Figure 3-3.

   TROUBLE? Make sure the Drives list box displays the drive your Student Disk is in.

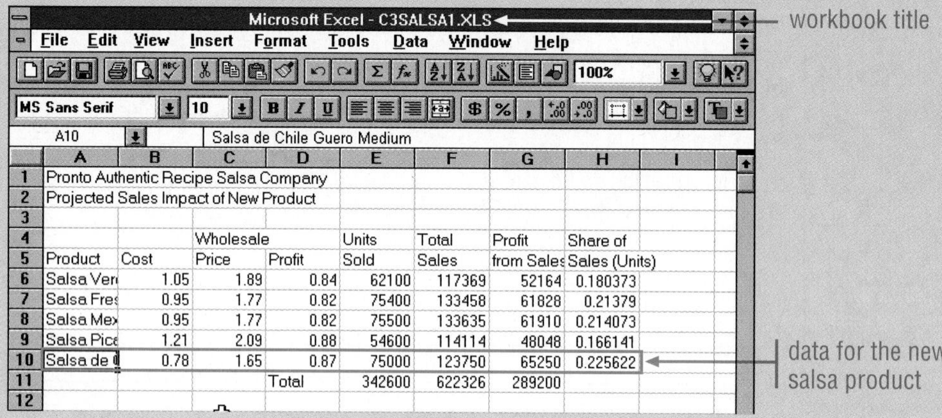

	A	B	C	D	E	F	G	H
1	Pronto Authentic Recipe Salsa Company							
2	Projected Sales Impact of New Product							
3								
4			Wholesale		Units	Total	Profit	Share of
5	Product	Cost	Price	Profit	Sold	Sales	from Sales	Sales (Units)
6	Salsa Ver	1.05	1.89	0.84	62100	117369	52164	0.180373
7	Salsa Fres	0.95	1.77	0.82	75400	133458	61828	0.21379
8	Salsa Mex	0.95	1.77	0.82	75500	133635	61910	0.214073
9	Salsa Pica	1.21	2.09	0.88	54600	114114	48048	0.166141
10	Salsa de C	0.78	1.65	0.87	75000	123750	65250	0.225622
11				Total	342600	622326	289200	
12								

Figure 3-3 The C3SALSA1.XLS workbook

Before you begin to make changes to the workbook, let's save it using the filename S3SALSA1.XLS so you can work on a copy of the workbook. The original workbook, C3SALSA1.XLS, will be left in its original state in case you want to do this tutorial again.

To save the workbook as S3SALSA1.XLS:

1. Click **File**, then click **Save As...** to display the Save As dialog box.
2. Type **S3SALSA1** using either uppercase or lowercase.
3. Click the **OK button** to save the workbook under the new filename. When the save is complete, you should see the new filename, S3SALSA1.XLS, displayed in the title bar.

   TROUBLE? If you see the message "Replace existing C3SALSA1.XLS?" click the Cancel button and go back to Step 1. If you see the message "Replace existing S3SALSA1.XLS?" click the OK button to replace the old version of S3SALSA1.XLS with your new version.

Maria studies the worksheet and notices that the salsa names do not fit in column A. It would be easy to make column A wider, but Maria knows that if she widens this column some of the worksheet will scroll off the screen. It will be easier to do the other formatting tasks if she can see the entire worksheet, so she decides to make other formatting changes first.

Formatting Worksheet Data

Formatting is the process of changing the appearance of the data in the cells of the worksheet. Formatting can make your worksheets easier to understand and draw attention to important points.

Formatting changes only the appearance of the data; it does not change the text or numbers stored in the cells. For example, if you format the number .123653 using a percentage format that displays only one decimal place, the number will appear on the worksheet as 12.4%; however, the original number .123653 remains stored in the cell.

When you enter data in cells, Excel applies an automatic format, referred to as the General format. The **General format** aligns numbers at the right side of the cell and displays them without trailing zeros to the right of the decimal point. You can change the General format by using AutoFormat, the Format menu, the Shortcut menu, or toolbar buttons.

In Tutorial 2 you used AutoFormat to apply a predefined format to your entire workbook. AutoFormat is easy to use, but the predefined formats might not be suitable for every worksheet. If you decide to customize the format of a workbook, you can use Excel's extensive array of formatting options. When you select your own formats, you can format an individual cell or a range of cells.

There are multiple ways to access Excel's formatting options. The Format menu provides access to all the formatting commands (Figure 3-4).

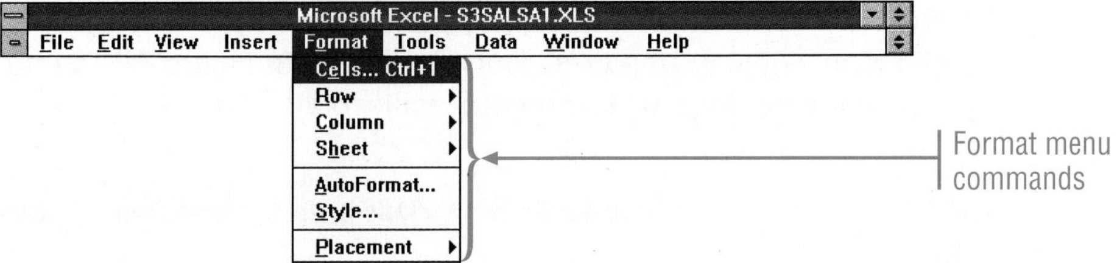

Figure 3-4
The Format menu

The Shortcut menu provides quick access to the Format dialog box (Figure 3-5). To display the Shortcut menu, make sure the pointer is on one of the cells in the range you have highlighted to format, then click the *right* mouse button.

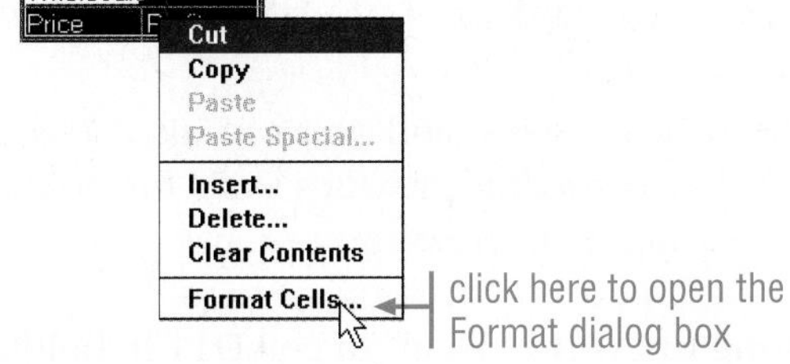

Figure 3-5
The Shortcut menu

The formatting toolbar contains formatting buttons, including the style buttons, font style box, font size box, and alignment buttons (Figure 3-6).

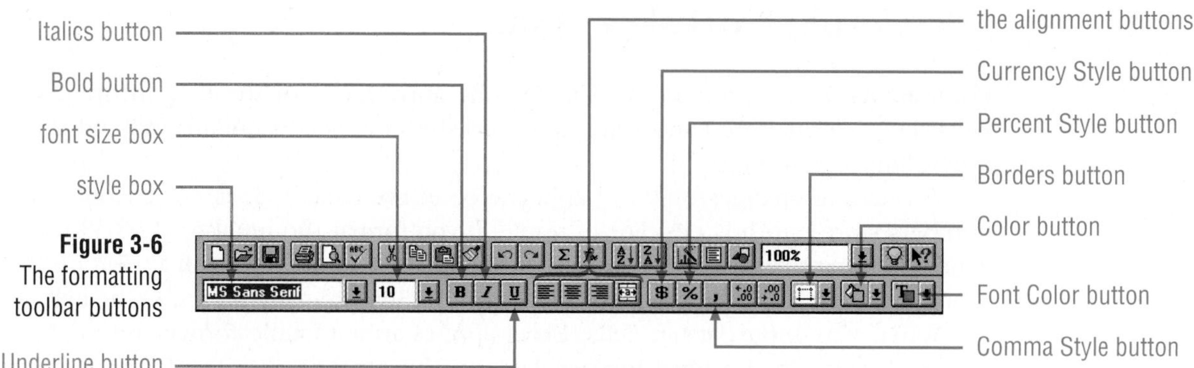

Figure 3-6
The formatting toolbar buttons

Most experienced Excel users develop a preference for which menu or buttons they use to access Excel's formatting options; however, most beginners find it easy to remember that all the formatting options are available from the Format menu.

Maria decides to use the Bold button to change the font style to boldface for some of the titles on the worksheet.

Changing the Font, Font Style, and Font Size

A **font** is a set of letters, numbers, punctuation marks, and symbols with a specific size and design. Some examples of fonts are shown in Figure 3-7. A font can have one or more of the following **font styles**: regular, italic, bold, and bold italic.

Figure 3-7
A selection of fonts

Font	Regular Style	Italic Style	Bold Style	Bold Italic Style
Times	AaBbCc	*AaBbCc*	**AaBbCc**	***AaBbCc***
Courier	AaBbCc	*AaBbCc*	**AaBbCc**	***AaBbCc***
Garamond	AaBbCc	*AaBbCc*	**AaBbCc**	***AaBbCc***
Helvetica Condensed	AaBbCc	*AaBbCc*	**AaBbCc**	***AaBbCc***

Most fonts are available in many sizes, and you can also select font effects, such as strikeout, underline, and color. The toolbar provides tools for boldface, italics, underline, changing font style, and increasing or decreasing font size. To access other font effects, you can open the Cells... dialog box from the Format menu.

Maria begins by formatting the word "Total" in cell D11 in boldface letters.

To change the font style for cell D11 to boldface:

1. Click cell **D11**.
2. Click the **Bold button** [B] to set the font style to boldface. See Figure 3-6 for the location of the Bold tool.

Maria also wants to display the worksheet titles and the column titles in boldface letters. To do this she first highlights the range she wants to format, then she clicks the Bold button to apply the format.

To display the worksheet titles and column titles in boldface:

1. Highlight cells A1 through H5.
2. Click the **Bold button** [B] to apply the bold font style.
3. Click any cell to remove the highlighting.

Next, Maria decides to display the names of the salsa products in italics.

To italicize the row labels:

1. Highlight cells A6 through A10.
2. Click the **Italics button** [I] to apply the italic font style. See Figure 3-6 for the location of the Italics tool.
3. Click any cell to remove the highlighting and view the formatting you have done so far. For now, don't worry that the labels aren't fully displayed. You'll widen the column later. See Figure 3-8.

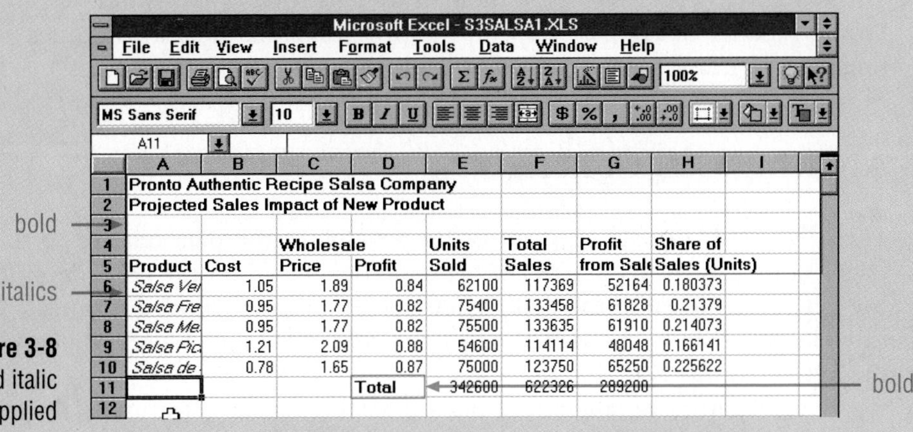

Figure 3-8 Bold and italic formats applied

Maria wants to increase the size of the worksheet titles for emphasis. She also wants to use a different font for the titles of this worksheet. Maria decides to use the Font dialog box (instead of the toolbar) so she can preview her changes. Remember, even though the worksheet titles appear to be in columns A through E, they are just spilling over from column A. To format the titles, Maria needs to highlight only cells A1 and A2—the cells in which the titles are entered.

To change the font and font size of the worksheet titles:

1. Highlight cells A1 through A2.
2. Click **Format**, then click **Cells...** to display the Format Cells dialog box.
3. Click the **Font tab**.
4. Use the Font box scroll bar to find the Times New Roman font. Click the **Times New Roman** font to select it.
5. Make sure the Font Style box is set to "Bold."
6. Click **14** in the Size box. A sample of the font Maria has chosen appears in the Preview box. See Figure 3-9.

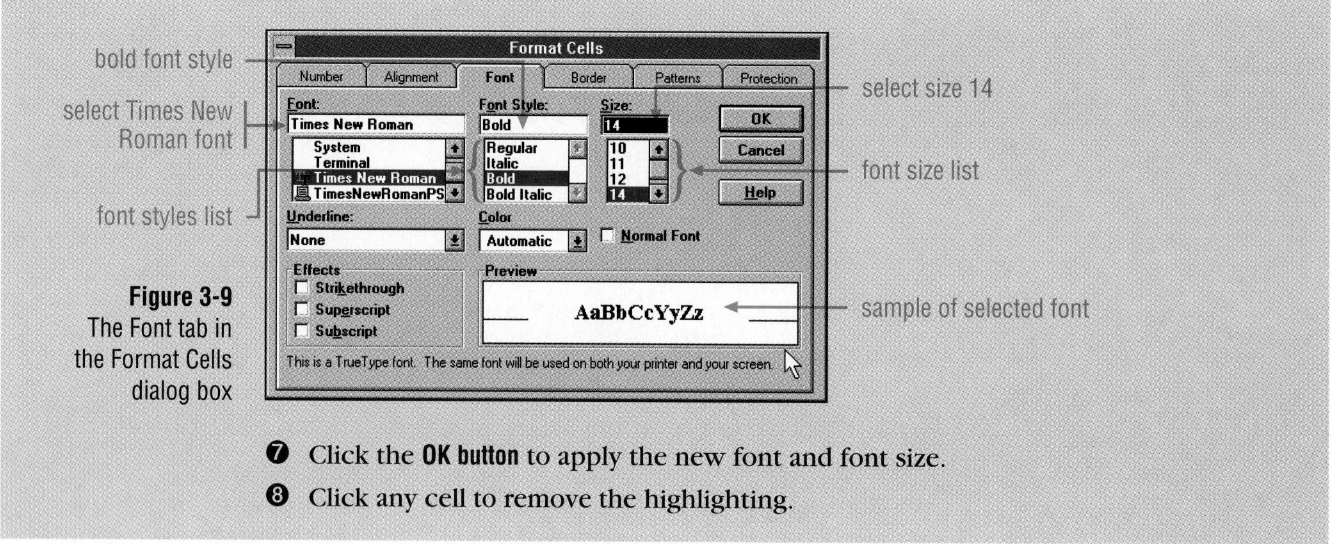

Figure 3-9 The Font tab in the Format Cells dialog box

7. Click the **OK button** to apply the new font and font size.
8. Click any cell to remove the highlighting.

Maria likes the Times New Roman font because it looks like the font used on the Pronto salsa jar labels. Pleased with her progress so far, Maria continues with her formatting plan. Her next step is to adjust the alignment of the column titles.

Aligning Cell Contents

The **alignment** of data in a cell is the position of the data relative to the right and left edges of the cell. The contents of cells can be aligned on the left side or the right side of the cell, or centered in the cell. When you enter numbers and formulas, Excel automatically aligns them on the right side of the cell. Excel automatically aligns text entries on the left side of the cell.

Excel's automatic alignment does not always create the most readable worksheet. Figure 3-10 shows a worksheet with the column titles left-aligned and the numbers in the columns right-aligned.

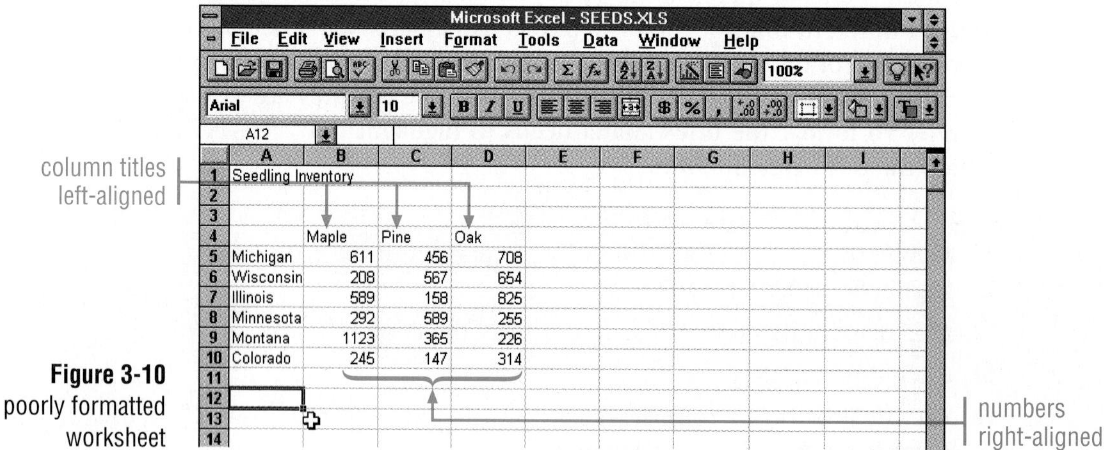

Figure 3-10 A poorly formatted worksheet

Notice how difficult it is to sort out which numbers go with each column title. The readability of the worksheet in Figure 3-10 would be improved by centering the column titles or aligning them on the right. As a general rule, you should center column titles, format columns of numbers so the decimal places are in line, and leave columns of text aligned on the left.

The Excel toolbar provides four alignment tools, as shown in Figure 3-11. You can access additional alignment options by selecting Alignment from the Format menu.

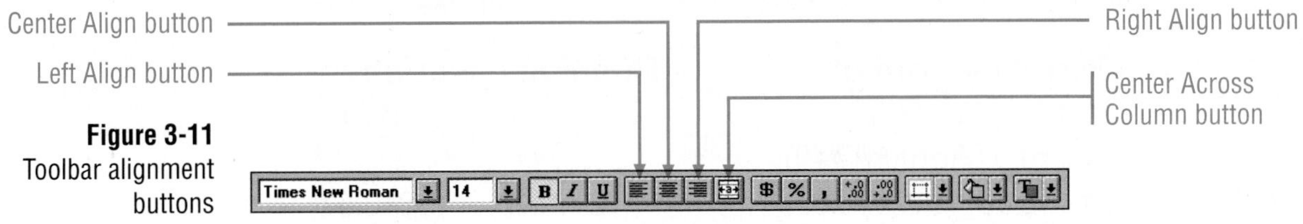

Figure 3-11 Toolbar alignment buttons

Maria decides to center the column titles.

To center the column titles:

1. Highlight cells A4 through H5.
2. Click the **Center button** on the toolbar to center the cell contents.
3. Click any cell to remove the highlighting and view the centered titles. See Figure 3-12.

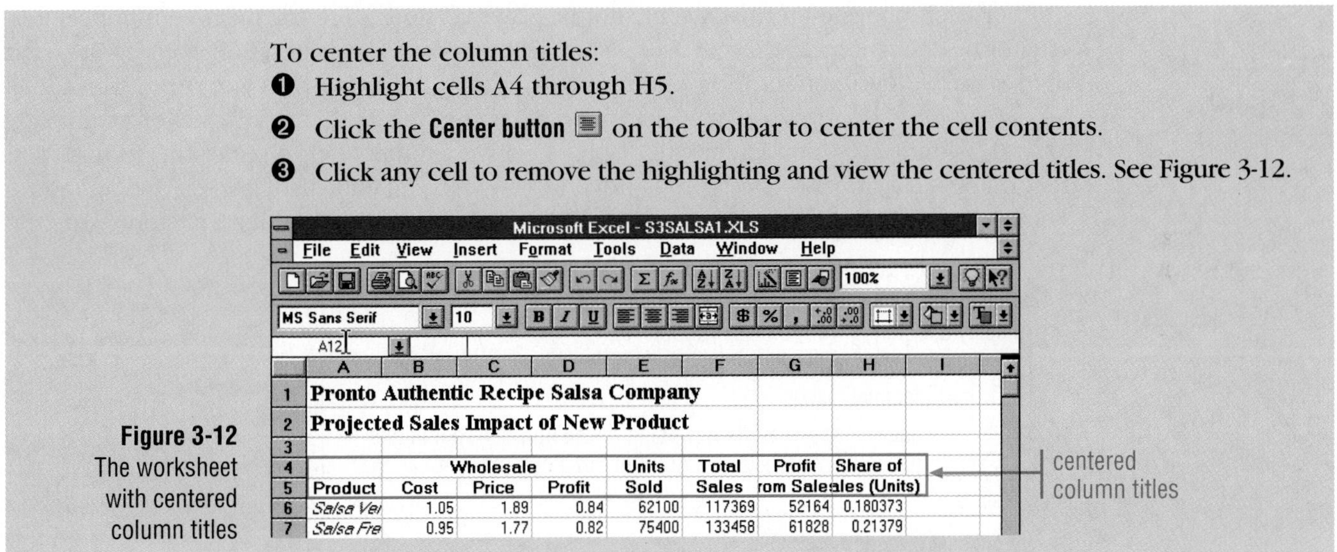

Figure 3-12 The worksheet with centered column titles

Maria notices that eventually she will need to change the width of columns G and H to display the entire column title, but for now she decides to center the main worksheet titles.

Centering Text Across Columns

Sometimes you might want to center the contents of a cell across more than one column. This is particularly useful for centering the titles at the top of a worksheet.

Maria uses the Center Across Columns button to center the worksheet titles in cells A1 and A2 across columns A through H.

To center the worksheet titles across columns A through H:

1. Highlight cells A1 through H2.
2. Click the **Center Across Columns button** to center the titles across columns A through H.
3. Click any cell to remove the highlighting.

Maria looks at her plan and sees that she needs to display the cost, price, profit, and total sales figures as currency.

Currency Formats

Excel provides four currency formats, as shown in Figure 3-13.

Currency Format	Positive	Negative
$#,##0_);($#,##0)	$214	($214)
$#,##0_);[Red]($#,##0)	$214	($214)
$#,##0.00_);($#,##0.00)	$213.52	($213.52)
$#,##0.00_);[Red]($#,##0.00)	$213.52	($213.52)

Figure 3-13
Examples of Excel's currency formats

For each currency format Excel supplies two versions, one for positive numbers and one for negative numbers. Excel uses a special set of symbols, or notation, to describe each of the currency formats. For example, in Figure 3-13 the first currency format is $#,##0_);($#,##0). How do you decipher what this means? The first set of symbols—$#,##0_)—indicates how Excel will display positive amounts if you select this format. The second set of symbols—($#,##0)—indicates how Excel will display negative amounts. The meaning of the $#,0_ symbols in the currency notation is explained in Figure 3-14.

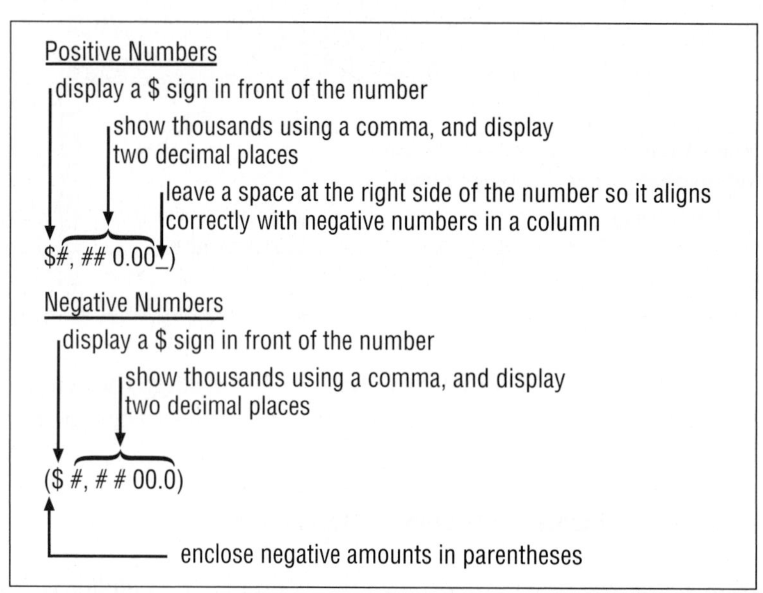

Figure 3-14
Notation for currency formats

Maria wants to format the amounts in columns B, C, and D as currency with two decimal places.

To format columns B, C, and D as currency with two decimal places:

1. Highlight cells B6 through D10.
2. Click **Format**, then click **Cells...** to display the Format Cells dialog box.
3. Click the **Number tab**.
4. Click **Currency** in the Category box.
5. Click the third option down, **$#,##0.00_);($#,##0.00)** in the Format Codes box. A sample of this format appears at the bottom of the dialog box. See Figure 3-15.

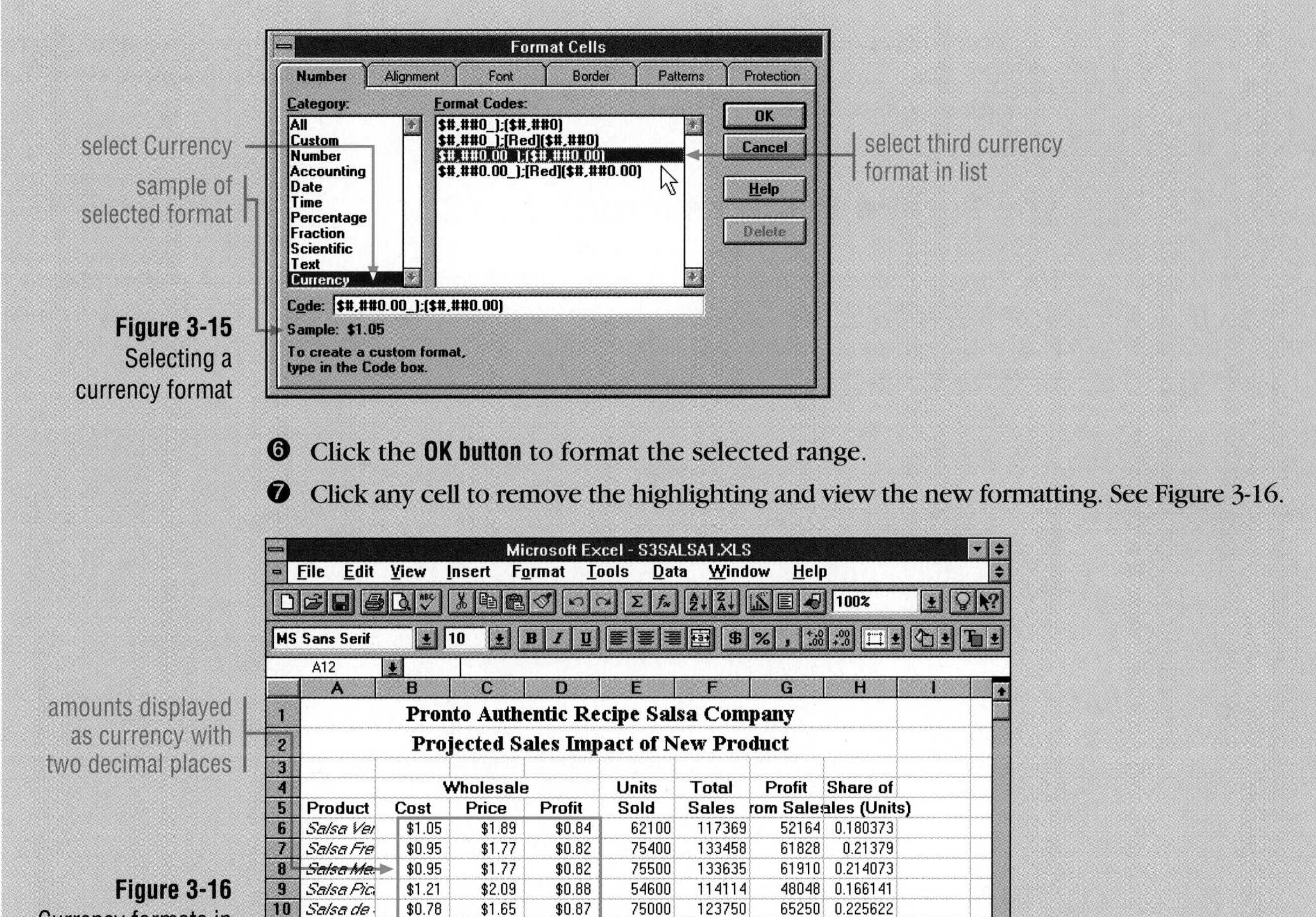

Figure 3-15
Selecting a currency format

❻ Click the **OK button** to format the selected range.

❼ Click any cell to remove the highlighting and view the new formatting. See Figure 3-16.

	A	B	C	D	E	F	G	H
1		Pronto Authentic Recipe Salsa Company						
2		Projected Sales Impact of New Product						
3								
4			Wholesale		Units	Total	Profit	Share of
5	Product	Cost	Price	Profit	Sold	Sales	rom Sale	ales (Units)
6	Salsa Ver	$1.05	$1.89	$0.84	62100	117369	52164	0.180373
7	Salsa Fre	$0.95	$1.77	$0.82	75400	133458	61828	0.21379
8	Salsa Me	$0.95	$1.77	$0.82	75500	133635	61910	0.214073
9	Salsa Pic	$1.21	$2.09	$0.88	54600	114114	48048	0.166141
10	Salsa de	$0.78	$1.65	$0.87	75000	123750	65250	0.225622
11				Total	342600	622326	289200	
12								

Figure 3-16
Currency formats in columns B, C, and D

When you have large dollar amounts in your worksheet, you might want to use a currency format that does not display any decimal places. To do this you can use the first or second currency format listed in the Cell Format dialog box. These formats round the amount to the nearest dollar; $15,612.56 becomes $15,613; $16,507.49 becomes $16,507; and so on.

Maria decides to format the Total Sales column as currency rounded to the nearest dollar.

To format cells F6 through F11 as currency rounded to the nearest dollar:

❶ Highlight cells F6 through F11.

❷ Click **Format**, then click **Cells...** to display the Format Cells dialog box.

❸ If necessary, click the **Number tab**.

❹ Click **Currency** in the Category box.

❺ Click the first option, **$#,##0_);($#,##0)**, in the Format Codes box and notice the sample format.

❻ Click the **OK button** to apply the format.

❼ Click any cell to remove the highlighting.

After formatting the Total Sales figures in column F, Maria realizes she should have used the same format for the numbers in column G. To save time, she'll simply copy the formatting from column F to column G.

The Format Painter Button

The Format Painter button allows you to copy formats quickly from one cell or range to another. You simply click a cell containing the formats you want to copy, click the Format Painter button, and then drag through the range to which you want to apply the formats.

Maria decides to use the Format Painter button now.

To copy the format from cell F6:

1. Click cell **F6** because it contains the format you want to copy.
2. Click the **Format Painter button**. The pointer turns into .
3. Highlight cells G6 through G11. When you release the mouse button, the cells appear in the proper format.

Now all the cells that contain cost, price, profit, and total sales data are formatted as currency. Next, Maria wants to apply formats to the numbers in columns E and H so they are easier to read.

Number Formats

You can select number formats to specify:

- the number of decimal places displayed
- whether to display a comma to delimit thousands, millions, and billions
- whether to display negative numbers with a minus sign, parentheses, or red numerals

Figure 3-17 shows Excel's number formats and examples of each. To access the Excel number formats, you would use the Number tab in the Format Cells dialog box.

Figure 3-17
Examples of Excel's number formats

Number Format	Positive	Negative
0	1556	-1556
0.00	1556.33	-1556.33
#,##0	1,556	-1,556
#,##0.00	1,556.33	-1,556.33
#,##0_);(#,##0)	1,556	(1,556)
#,##0_);[Red](#,##0)	1,556	(1,556)
#,##0.00_);(#,##0.00)	1,556.33	(1,556.33)
#,##0.00_);[Red](#,##0.00)	1,556.33	(1,556.33)

Maria wants to include a comma in the number format for column E, and she does not want to display any decimal places.

To format the contents in column E with a comma:

❶ Highlight cells E6 through E11.

❷ Click **Format**, then click **Cells...** to display the Format Cells dialog box.

❸ If necessary, click the **Number tab**.

❹ Click **Number** in the Category box.

❺ Click the fourth option, **#,##0**, in the Format Codes box.

❻ Click the **OK button** to apply the format.

❼ Click any cell to remove the highlighting and view the format results. See Figure 3-18.

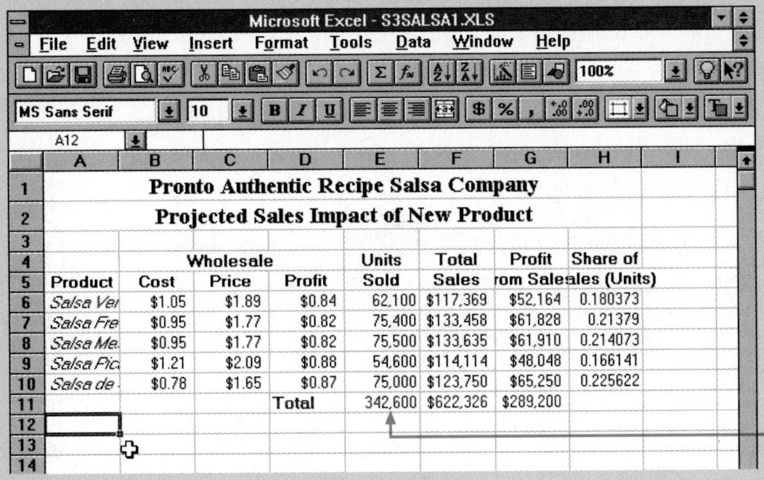

	A	B	C	D	E	F	G	H
1		**Pronto Authentic Recipe Salsa Company**						
2		**Projected Sales Impact of New Product**						
3								
4			Wholesale		Units	Total	Profit	Share of
5	Product	Cost	Price	Profit	Sold	Sales	rom Sale	ales (Units)
6	*Salsa Ver*	$1.05	$1.89	$0.84	62,100	$117,369	$52,164	0.180373
7	*Salsa Fre*	$0.95	$1.77	$0.82	75,400	$133,458	$61,828	0.21379
8	*Salsa Me*	$0.95	$1.77	$0.82	75,500	$133,635	$61,910	0.214073
9	*Salsa Pic*	$1.21	$2.09	$0.88	54,600	$114,114	$48,048	0.166141
10	*Salsa de*	$0.78	$1.65	$0.87	75,000	$123,750	$65,250	0.225622
11				Total	342,600	$622,326	$289,200	

Figure 3-18
Comma format

Maria thinks the numbers in column H are difficult to interpret and decides that it is not necessary to display so many decimal places. What are her options for displaying percentages?

Percentage Formats

Excel provides two percentage formats: the 0% format and the 0.00% format. If you have the number 0.18037 in a cell, the 0% format would display this number as 18%, without any decimal places. The 0.00% format would display the number as 18.04%, with two decimal places.

Maria's format plan specifies a percentage format with no decimal places for the values in column H. She could use the Number tab to choose this format. But it's faster to use the Percent Style button. (Note that if Maria wanted to use the 0.00% style, she would have to select it using the Number tab in the Format Cells dialog box.)

To format the values in column H as a percentage with no decimal places:

❶ Highlight cells H6 through H10.

❷ Click the **Percent Style button** [%].

❸ Click any cell to remove the highlighting and view the percentage format.

Maria checks her plan once again and confirms that she selected formats for all the cells on the worksheet. She delayed making any change to the width of column A because she knew that it would cause some of the columns to scroll off the screen and force her to scroll around the worksheet to format all the labels and values. Now that she has finished formatting the labels and values, she can change all the columns to the appropriate width to best display the information in them.

To do this, Maria could double-click the right column heading border for each column she wants to widen. But since she needs to widen several columns, it's easier to use the Format menu.

To change the width of the columns using the Format menu:

1. Highlight cells A4 through H11.
2. Click **Format**, click **Column**, then click **AutoFit Selection**.
3. Click any cell to remove the highlighting and view the results of the change in column width. See Figure 3-19.

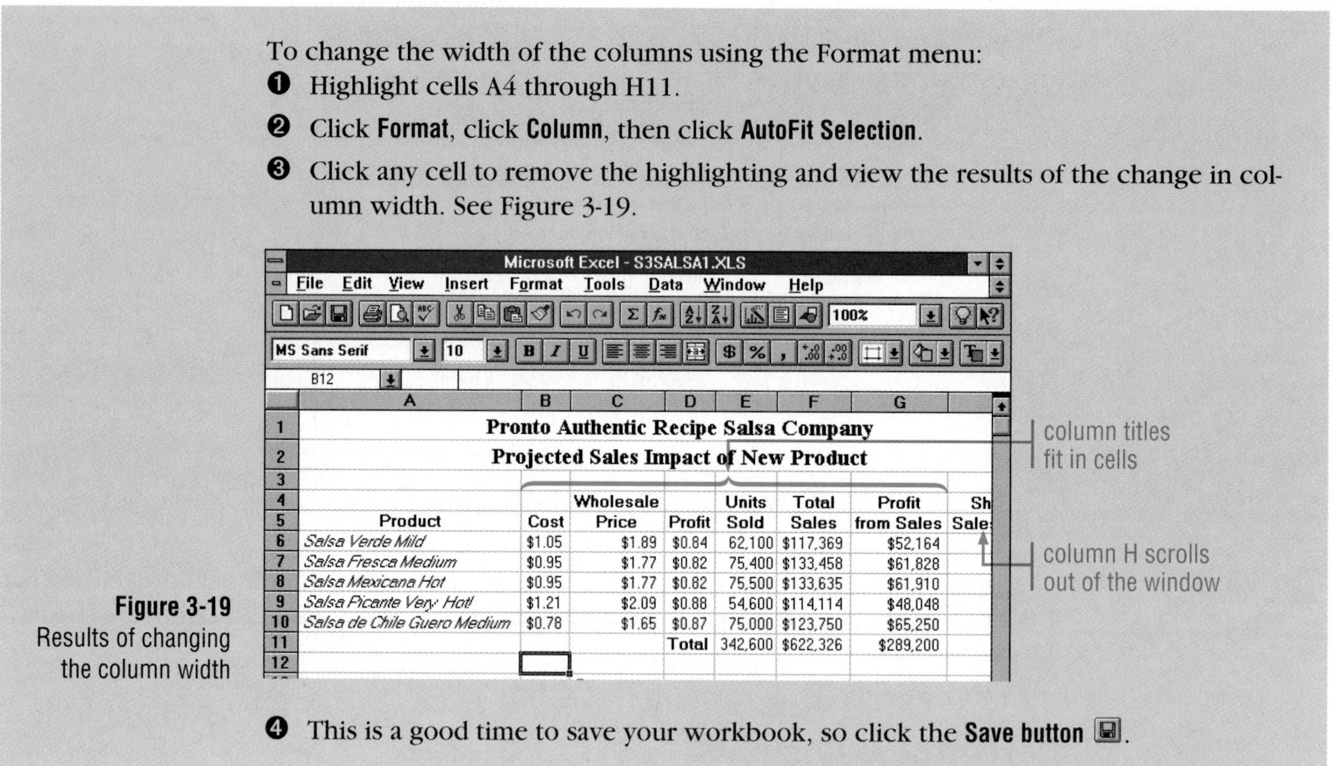

	A	B	C	D	E	F	G
4			Wholesale		Units	Total	Profit
5	Product	Cost	Price	Profit	Sold	Sales	from Sales
6	*Salsa Verde Mild*	$1.05	$1.89	$0.84	62,100	$117,369	$52,164
7	*Salsa Fresca Medium*	$0.95	$1.77	$0.82	75,400	$133,458	$61,828
8	*Salsa Mexicana Hot*	$0.95	$1.77	$0.82	75,500	$133,635	$61,910
9	*Salsa Picante Very Hot!*	$1.21	$2.09	$0.88	54,600	$114,114	$48,048
10	*Salsa de Chile Guero Medium*	$0.78	$1.65	$0.87	75,000	$123,750	$65,250
11				Total	342,600	$622,326	$289,200

Figure 3-19 Results of changing the column width

4. This is a good time to save your workbook, so click the **Save button**.

As Maria expected, the worksheet is now too wide to fit on the screen. She might need to scroll from side to side to complete some additional formatting tasks. Remember from the previous tutorials that when you want to see a part of the worksheet that is not displayed, you can use the scroll bars. If you are highlighting a range, but some of the range is not displayed, you can drag the pointer to the edge of the screen and the worksheet will scroll. You'll see how this works when you add some borders in the next set of steps.

Adding and Removing Borders

A well-constructed worksheet is clearly divided into **zones** that visually group related information. Figure 3-20 shows the zones on Maria's worksheet. Lines, called **borders**, can help to distinguish between different zones of the worksheet and add visual interest.

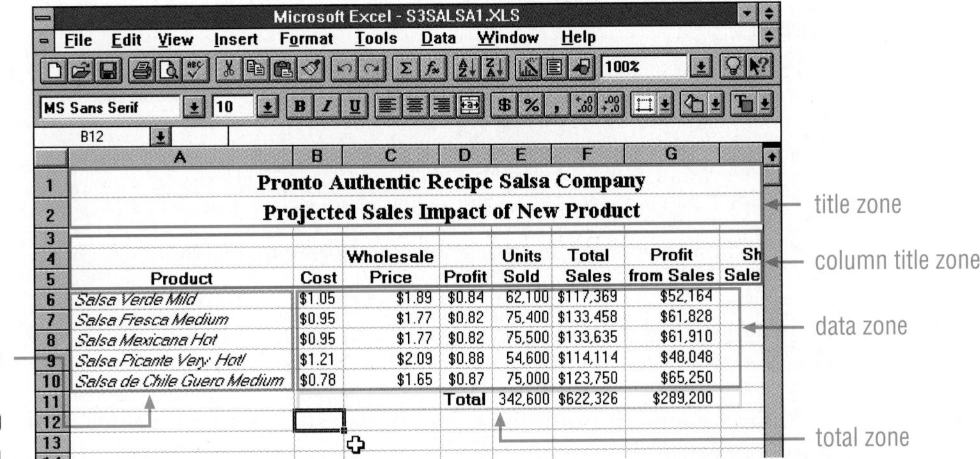

data label zone

Figure 3-20
Zones of information

You can create lines and borders using either the Borders button or the Border tab in the Format Cells dialog box. You can put a border around a single cell or a group of cells using the Outline option. To create a horizontal line, you create a border at the top or bottom of a cell. To create a vertical line, you create a border on the right or left of a cell.

The border tab allows you to choose from numerous border styles, including different line thicknesses, double lines, dashed lines, and different line colors. With the Border Styles button, your choice of border styles is limited.

REFERENCE WINDOW

Adding a Border

- Select the cell to which you want to add the border.
- Click Format, click Cells..., then click Border.
- Click the Outline, Top, Bottom, Left, and/or Right border box to indicate where you want to put the border.
- Select the border style and color.
- Click the OK button.

or

- Select the cell to which you want to add the border.
- Click the Borders drop-down arrow, then click the type of border you want.

If you want to remove a border from a cell or group of cells, you can use the Border dialog box. To remove all borders from a selected range of cells, make sure the Outline, Top, Bottom, Left, and Right border boxes are blank. Excel shades in a border box to show that some cells in the selected range contain a border but others do not. If a border box is gray and you want to remove the border, click the box to remove the gray shading.

REFERENCE WINDOW

Removing a Border

- Select the cell or cells that contain the border you want to remove.
- Click Format, click Cells..., then click Border.
- Look for the border box that contains a border or shading, then click this box until it is empty.
- Click the OK button.

Maria wants to put a thick line under all the column titles. To do this, she'll use the Borders button.

To put a line under the column titles:

1. Highlight cells A5 through H5.

   TROUBLE? If cell H5 is not displayed on your screen, drag the pointer from cell A5 to G5 then, without releasing the mouse button, continue moving the pointer to the right. The worksheet window will scroll so you can include cell H5 in the highlighted range. If the worksheet scrolls too fast and you highlight I, J, K, L, and M, move the mouse to the left—without releasing the mouse button—until H5 is the right-most cell in the highlighted range. If you released the mouse button too soon, use the scroll bars to scroll column A back on the screen, then go back to Step 1.

2. Click the **Borders button drop-down arrow**. The Borders palette appears.
3. Click the thick underline button in the second row. See Figure 3-21.

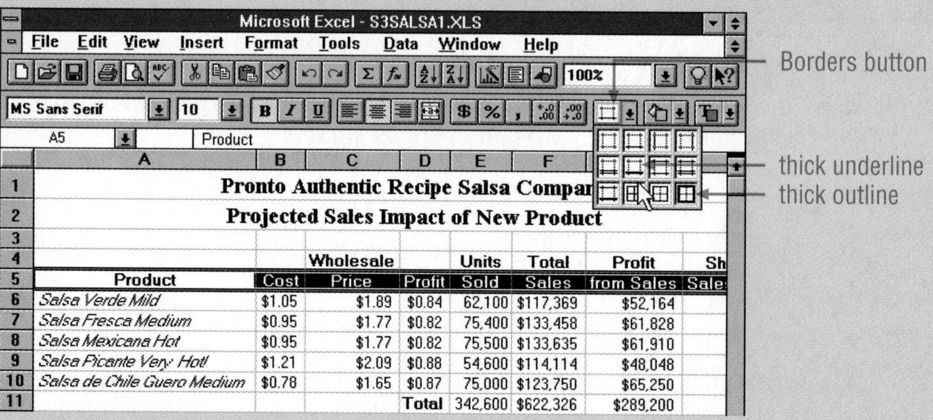

Figure 3-21
The new border

4. Click any cell to remove the highlighting and view the border.

Maria also wants to use a line to separate the data from the totals in row 11. This time she will use the Border tab in the Format Cells dialog box. First Maria highlights cells A11 through H11, then she selects a thick top border from the Border tab. Why would she use a top border here, when she used a bottom border for the column titles? It is good practice not to attach borders to the cells in the data zone because when you copy cells, the cell formats are also copied. Maria knows from experience that if she attaches borders to the wrong cells, she can end up with borders in every cell, or she can end up erasing borders she wanted when she copies cell contents down a column.

To add a line separating the data and the totals:

1. Highlight cells A11 through H11.
2. Click **Format**, click **Cells...**, then click the **Border tab**.
3. Click **Top** to select a top border.
4. Click the thickest line in the Style box.
5. Click the **OK button** to apply the border.
6. Click any cell to remove the highlighting and view the border.

Maria consults her format sketch and sees that she planned to put a border around the title zone to add a professional touch. Let's add this border now.

To place an outline border around the title zone:

1. Highlight cells A1 through H2.
2. Click the **Borders button drop-down arrow**.
3. Click the thick outline button. See Figure 3-21.
4. Click any cell to remove the highlighting and view the border. See Figure 3-22.

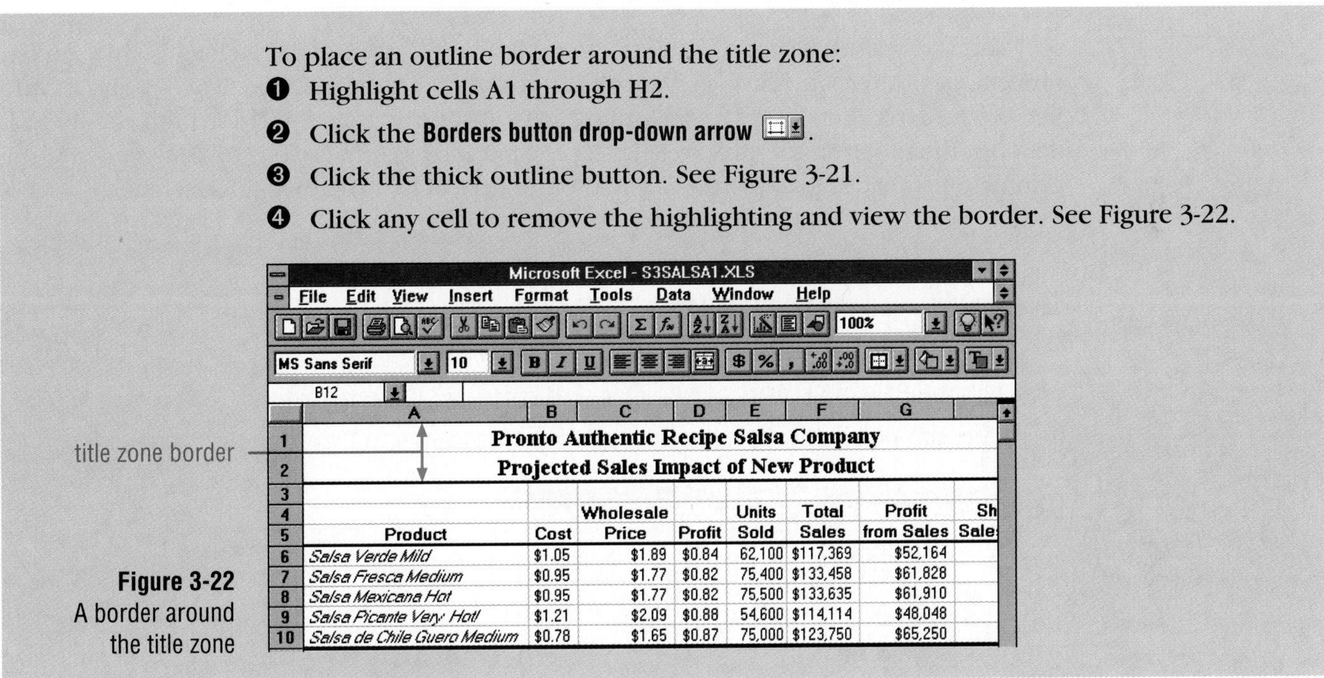

Figure 3-22
A border around the title zone

In addition to a border around the title zone, Maria wants to add color and a shaded pattern in the title zone.

Using Patterns and Color for Emphasis

Patterns and colors can provide visual interest, emphasize zones of the worksheet, or indicate data-entry areas. The use of patterns or colors should be based on the way you intend to use the worksheet. If you print the worksheet on a color printer and distribute it in hardcopy format, or if you are going to use a color projection device to display a screen image of your worksheet, you might want to take advantage of Excel's color formatting options. On the other hand, a printout you produce on a printer without color capability might look better if you use patterns, because it is difficult to predict how the colors you see on your screen will be translated into shades of gray on your printout.

REFERENCE WINDOW

Applying Patterns and Color

- Highlight the cells you want to fill with a pattern or color.
- Click Format, click Cells..., then click the Patterns tab.
- Select a pattern from the Pattern box. If you want the pattern to appear in a color, select a color from the Pattern box, too.
- If you want to select a background color, select it from the Cell Shading box. You can also select colors by clicking the Color button on the toolbar and then clicking the desired color.

Maria wants her worksheet to look good when it is printed in black and white on the office laser printer, but she also wants it to look good on the screen when she shows it to her boss. Maria decides to use a yellow background with a light dot pattern, since it matches the color on the Pronto Salsa labels and looks fairly good on the screen and the printer. She decides to apply this format to the title zone using the Patterns tab.

To apply a pattern and color to the title zone:

1. Highlight cells A1 through H2.
2. Click **Format**, click **Cells...**, then click the **Patterns tab**.
3. Click the **Pattern box down arrow button** to display the patterns palette.
4. Select the polka-dot pattern in the top row, as shown in Figure 3-23.

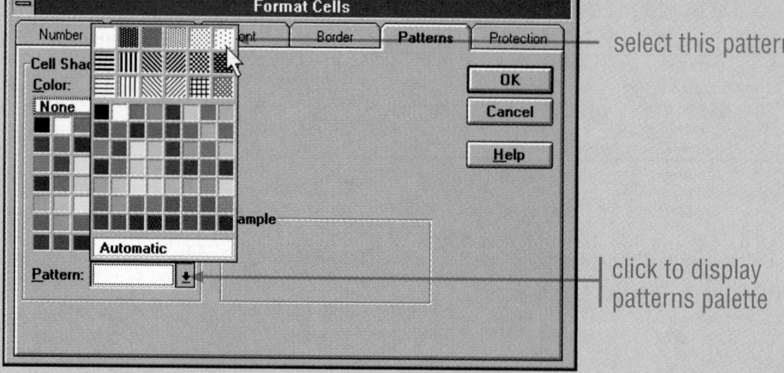

Figure 3-23 Selecting a pattern from the patterns palette

5. Click the yellow square in the top row of the Cell Shading box. A sample of the color and pattern you selected appears in the Sample box.

   TROUBLE? If you are using a monochrome monitor, skip Step 5.
6. Click the **OK button** to apply the pattern and the color.
7. Click any cell to remove the highlighting and view the pattern and color in the title zone. See Figure 3-24.

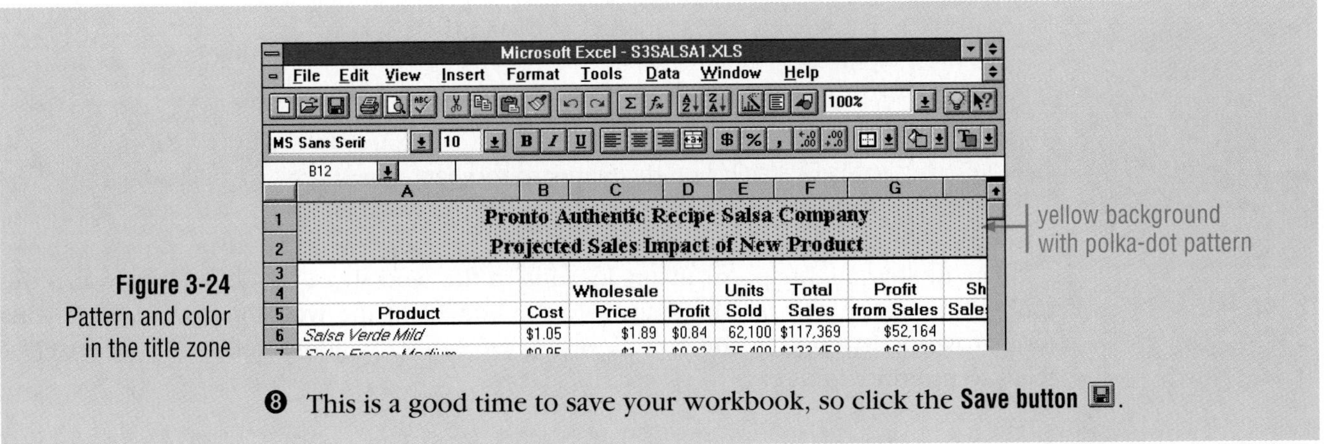

Figure 3-24 Pattern and color in the title zone

❽ This is a good time to save your workbook, so click the **Save button** .

If you want to take a break and resume the tutorial at a later time, you can exit Excel by double-clicking the Control menu box in the upper-left corner of the screen. When you resume the tutorial, launch Excel, maximize the Microsoft Excel and Book1 windows, and place your Student Disk in the disk drive. Open the file S3SALSA1.XLS, then continue with the tutorial.

■ ■ ■

Maria's next formatting task is to add a comment to the worksheet to emphasize the high profits expected from the new salsa product. She wants to put the comment in a box. To do this, she must use the Drawing toolbar.

Activating a Toolbar

Excel contains more than one toolbar. The two toolbars you have been using are called the Standard toolbar and the Formatting toolbar. (The Standard toolbar is the one on top.) Excel also has a number of other toolbars, including a Chart toolbar, a Drawing toolbar, and a Formatting toolbar. To activate a toolbar, it's usually easiest to use the toolbar shortcut menu, but to active the Drawing toolbar you can simply click the Drawing button on the Standard toolbar. When you are finished using a toolbar, you can easily remove it from the worksheet.

REFERENCE WINDOW

Activating and Removing Toolbars

- To activate a toolbar, click on any toolbar with the right mouse button to display the toolbar shortcut menu. Then click the name of the toolbar you want to use.
- To remove a toolbar, click on any toolbar with the right mouse button to display the toolbar shortcut menu. Then click the name of the toolbar you want to remove.

Maria needs the Drawing toolbar to accomplish her next formatting task.

To add the Drawing toolbar:

❶ Click the **Drawing button** on the Standard toolbar.

The toolbar might appear in any location in the worksheet window. Maria wants the toolbar out of the way, so she drags it to the bottom of the worksheet window. If your toolbar is not attached to the bottom of the worksheet window, follow the next set of steps to position it there.

To attach the Drawing toolbar to the bottom of the worksheet window:

❶ Position the pointer on the title bar of the Drawing toolbar.

❷ Drag the toolbar to the bottom of the screen. The outline of the toolbar changes to a long, narrow rectangle, as shown in Figure 3-25.

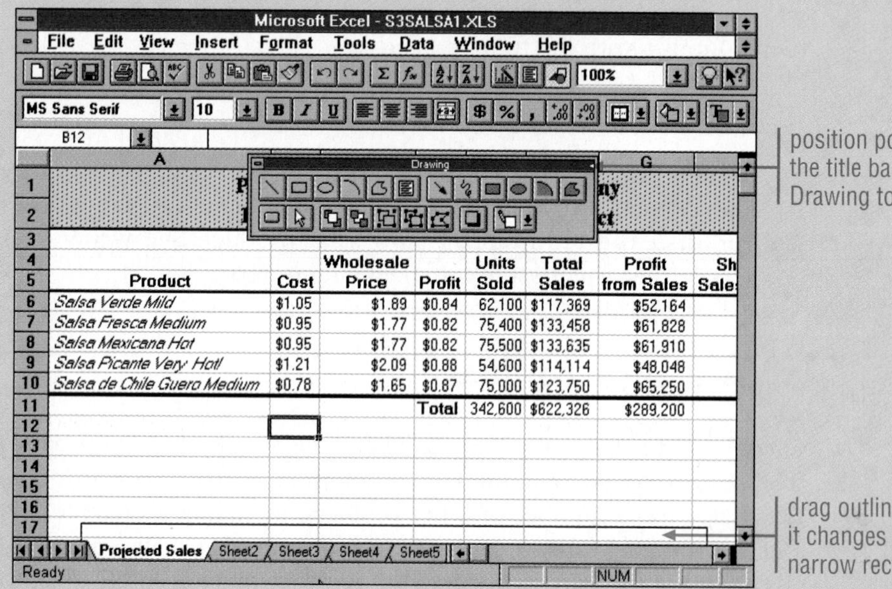
Microsoft Excel - S3SALSA1.XLS
position pointer on the title bar of the Drawing toolbar
drag outline here until it changes to a long, narrow rectangle

Figure 3-25 Positioning the Drawing toolbar

❸ Release the mouse button to attach the Drawing toolbar to the bottom of the worksheet window. See Figure 3-26.

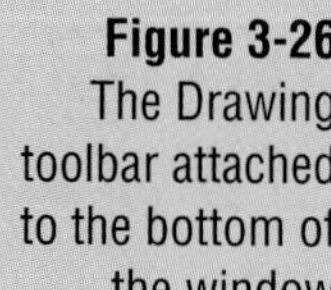

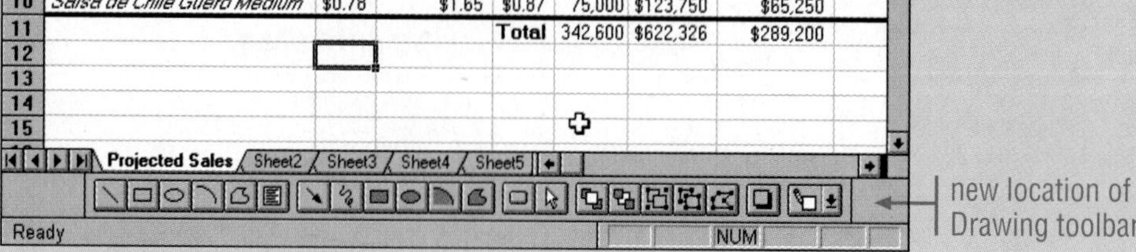
new location of Drawing toolbar

Figure 3-26 The Drawing toolbar attached to the bottom of the window

Now that the Drawing toolbar is where she wants it, Maria is ready to proceed with her plan to add a comment to the worksheet.

Adding Comments to the Worksheet

Excel's text box feature enables you to display a comment on a worksheet. Unlike the text note you attached to a cell in Tutorial 2, a **comment** is like an electronic "post-it" note that you paste on the worksheet inside a rectangular text box. You do not need to double-click a cell to display a comment as you do to display a text note.

To add a comment to your worksheet, you create a text box using the Text Box tool. Then you simply enter the text in the box. (Note that there are two Text Box tools, one on the Drawing toolbar and one on the Standard toolbar. You can use whichever one is more convenient.)

REFERENCE WINDOW

Adding a Text Box and Comment

- Click the Text Box button either in the Drawing toolbar or in the Standard toolbar.
- Position + where you want the text box to appear on the worksheet.
- Drag + to outline the size and shape of the text box you want.
- Type the text of the comment you want to display in the text box.
- Click any cell outside the text box when the comment is complete.

A text box is one example of an Excel object. Excel objects include shapes, arrows, and text boxes. If you need to move, modify, or delete an object, you must select it first. To select an object, you move the pointer over the object until the pointer changes to ↖, then click. When the object is selected, small square handles appear. You use the handles to adjust the size of an object, change the location of an object, or delete an object.

Maria wants to draw attention to the low price and high profit margin of the new salsa product. To do this, she plans to add a text box that contains a comment about expected profits. Refer to Maria's format plan in Figure 3-2 to see where she wants to locate the text box.

To add a comment in a text box:

1. Click the **Text Box button** on the Drawing toolbar. The pointer changes to +.
2. Position the pointer in cell A13 to mark the upper-left corner of the text box.
3. Drag + to cell C17, then release the mouse button to mark the lower-right corner of the text box. See Figure 3-27.

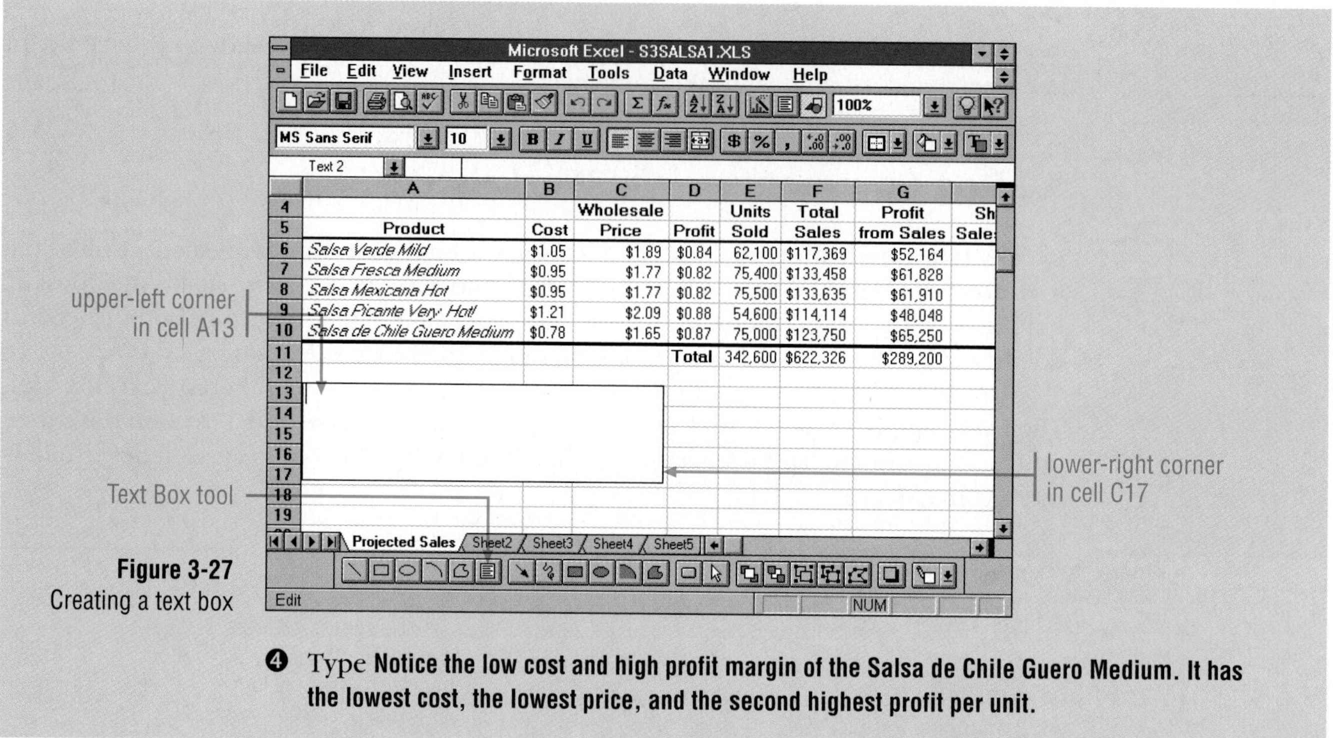

Figure 3-27
Creating a text box

4. Type **Notice the low cost and high profit margin of the Salsa de Chile Guero Medium. It has the lowest cost, the lowest price, and the second highest profit per unit.**

Maria wants to use a different font style to emphasize the name of the new salsa product in the text box.

To italicize the name of the new salsa product:

1. Position I in the text box just before the word "Salsa."

   TROUBLE? If the size of your text box is slightly different from the one in the figure, the lines of text might break between different words. Don't worry if the text in your text box is not arranged exactly like the text in the figure.

2. Drag I to the end of the word "Medium," then release the mouse button. See Figure 3-28.

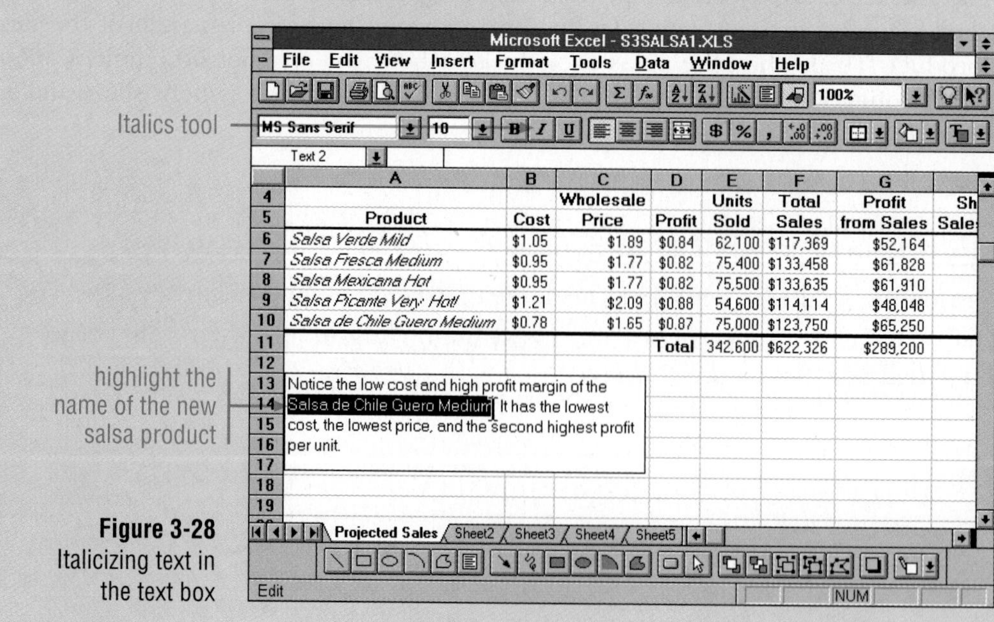

Figure 3-28
Italicizing text in the text box

❸ Click the **Italics button** $\boxed{I}$.

❹ Click any cell to remove the highlighting. Now the new product name is italicized.

Maria decides to change the size of the text box so there is no empty space at the bottom of it.

To change the size of the text box:

❶ Click anywhere within the borders of the **text box** to select it and display the thick border with handles.

❷ Position the pointer on the center handle at the bottom of the box. The pointer changes to ↕. See Figure 3-29.

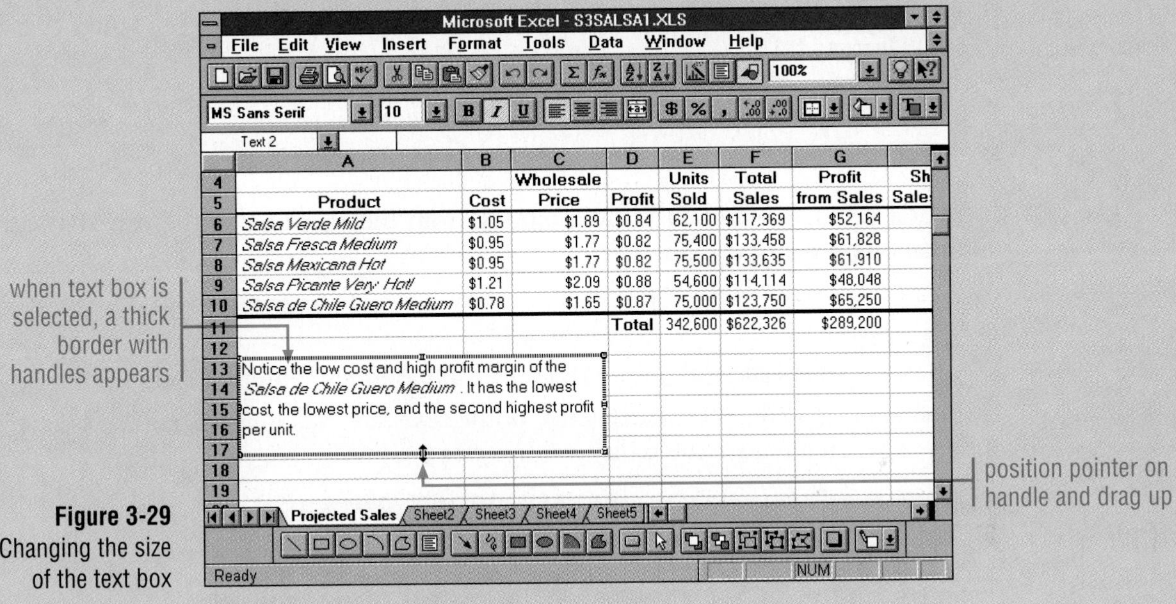

Figure 3-29 Changing the size of the text box

❸ Click and drag + up to shorten the box, then release the mouse button.

Maria wants to make a few more modifications to the text box. First she wants to add a 3-D drop shadow.

To add a drop shadow:

❶ Make sure the text box is still selected, as indicated by the thick border and handles.

❷ Click the **Drop Shadow button** ▢ in the Drawing toolbar.

Now Maria wants to make the text border thicker.

To modify the border of the text box:

❶ Make sure the text box is still selected.

❷ Click **Format**, click **Object...** to display the Format Object dialog box, then click the **Patterns tab**.

❸ Click the **Weight box down arrow button** to display the border thicknesses.

❹ Click the third border weight in the list, as shown in Figure 3-30. Notice that the Shadow box contains an ×. That's because you already added a shadow using the Drop Shadow button.

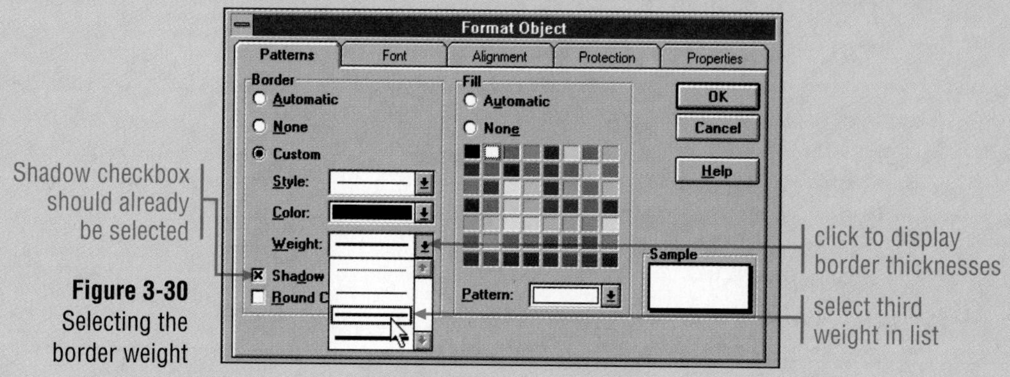

Figure 3-30 Selecting the border weight

❺ Click the **OK button**, then click any cell to deselect the text box.

Maria decides to add an arrow pointing from the text box to the row that contains information on the new salsa.

To add an arrow:

❶ Click the **Arrow button** on the Drawing toolbar. The pointer changes to +.

❷ Position the pointer on the top edge of the text box in cell B12. Drag the pointer to cell B10, then release the mouse button. See Figure 3-31.

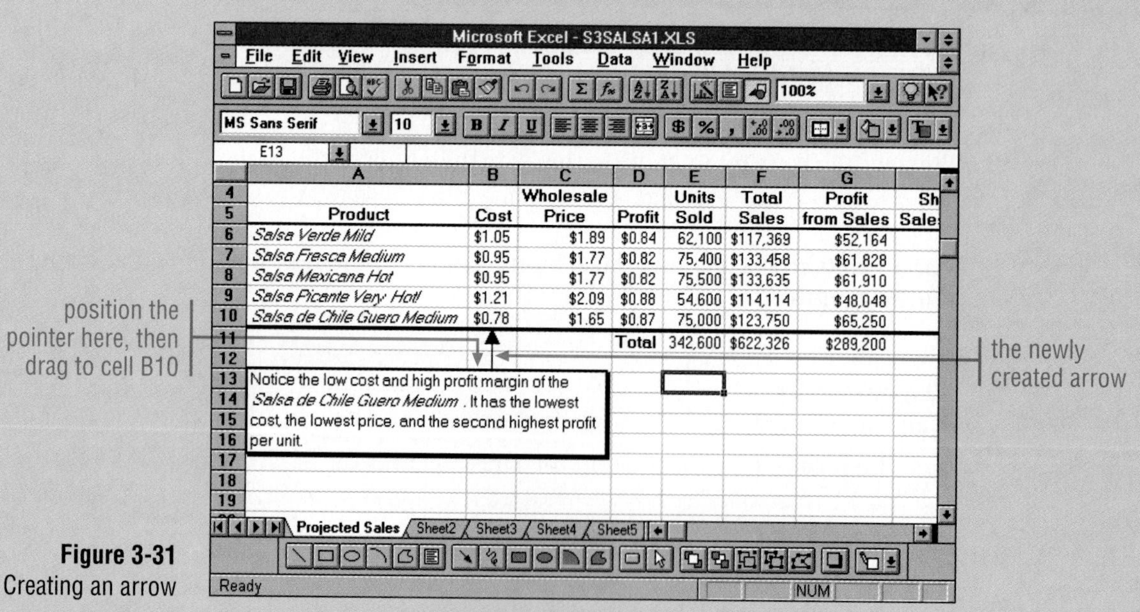

Figure 3-31 Creating an arrow

❸ Click any cell to deselect the arrow.

Like a text box, an arrow is an Excel object. To modify the arrow object, you must select it. When you select an arrow object, two small square handles appear on it. You can reposition either end of the arrow by dragging one of the handles to a new position.

Maria wants the arrow to point to cell D10 instead of B10. Let's see how you can reposition the arrow.

To reposition the arrow:

❶ Move the pointer over the arrow object. The pointer changes to ↖.

❷ Click the mouse button to select the arrow. Handles appear at each end of the arrow.

❸ Move the pointer to the top handle on the arrowhead until the pointer changes to +.

❹ Drag + to cell D10, then release the mouse button.

❺ Click any cell to deselect the arrow object. See Figure 3-32.

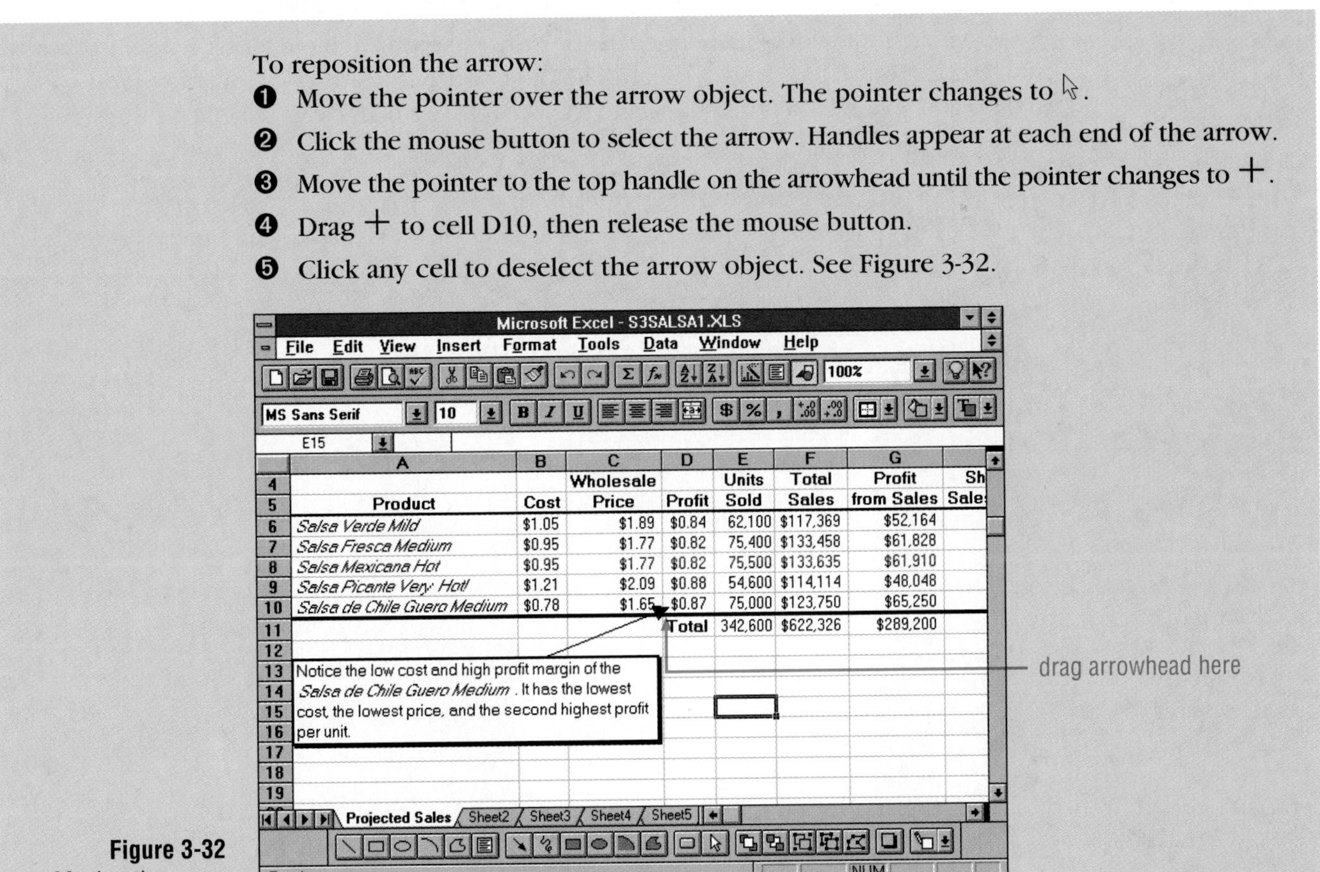

	A	B	C	D	E	F	G	
4			Wholesale		Units	Total	Profit	Sh
5	Product	Cost	Price	Profit	Sold	Sales	from Sales	Sale
6	*Salsa Verde Mild*	$1.05	$1.89	$0.84	62,100	$117,369	$52,164	
7	*Salsa Fresca Medium*	$0.95	$1.77	$0.82	75,400	$133,458	$61,828	
8	*Salsa Mexicana Hot*	$0.95	$1.77	$0.82	75,500	$133,635	$61,910	
9	*Salsa Picante Very Hot!*	$1.21	$2.09	$0.88	54,600	$114,114	$48,048	
10	*Salsa de Chile Guero Medium*	$0.78	$1.65	$0.87	75,000	$123,750	$65,250	
11				Total	342,600	$622,326	$289,200	

Figure 3-32
Moving the arrow

Now that the text box is finished, you can remove the Drawing toolbar from the worksheet.

To remove the Drawing toolbar:

❶ Click the **Drawing button** on the Standard toolbar.

❷ This is a good time to save your workbook, so click the **Save button**.

If you want to take a break and resume the tutorial at a later time, you can exit Excel by double-clicking the Control menu box in the upper-left corner of the screen. When you resume the tutorial, launch Excel, maximize the Microsoft Excel and Book1 windows, and place your Student Disk in the disk drive. Open the file S3SALSA1.XLS, then continue with the tutorial.

■ ■ ■

The text box and arrow effectively call attention to the profits expected from the new salsa product. Now Maria is ready to print the worksheet.

Print Preview

Before you print a worksheet, you can see how the worksheet will look when it is printed by using Excel's print preview feature. When you request a print preview, you can see the margins, page breaks, headers, and footers that are not always visible on the screen.

To preview the worksheet before you print it:

1. Click the **Print Preview button**. After a moment Excel displays the first page of the worksheet in the Print Preview window. See Figure 3-33.

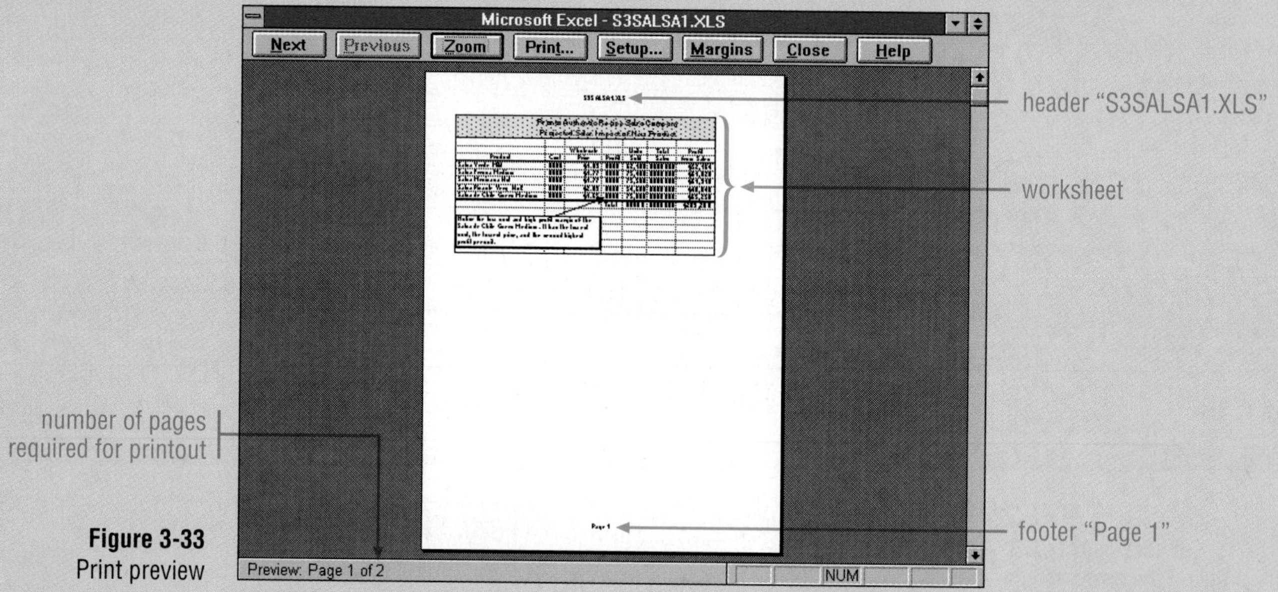

Figure 3-33
Print preview

2. Click the **Next button** to view the second page of the worksheet. Only one column is displayed on this page.
3. Click the **Previous button** to display the first page again.

When Excel displays a full page on the print preview screen, it is usually difficult to see the text of the worksheet because it is so small. If you want to read the text, you can use the Zoom button.

To display an enlarged section of the print preview:

1. Click the **Zoom button** to display an enlarged section of the print preview.
2. Click the **Zoom button** again to return to the full page view.

The print preview screen contains several other buttons. The Print button lets you access the Print dialog box directly from the preview screen. The Setup button lets you change the way the page is set up by adjusting the margins, creating headers and footers, adding page numbers, changing the paper size, or centering the worksheet on the page. The Margins button allows you to adjust the margins and immediately view the result of that change. The Close button returns you to the worksheet window.

By looking at the print preview, Maria sees that the worksheet is too wide to fit on a single page. She decides to print the worksheet sideways so it will fit on a single sheet of paper.

Portrait and Landscape Orientations

Excel provides two print orientations, portrait and landscape. The **portrait** orientation prints the worksheet with the paper positioned so it is taller than it is wide. The **landscape** orientation prints the worksheet with the paper positioned so it is wider than it is tall. Because many worksheets are wider than they are tall, landscape orientation is used frequently.

You can specify the print orientation using the Page Setup command on the File menu or by using the Setup button on the print preview screen. Let's use the landscape orientation for Maria's worksheet.

To change the print orientation to landscape:

❶ Click the **Setup... button** to display the Page Setup dialog box. If necessary, click the **Page tab**.

❷ Click **Landscape** in the Orientation box. The sample diagram—the sheet of paper with the large "A" on it—shows that the page will be oriented so it is wider than it is tall. See Figure 3-34.

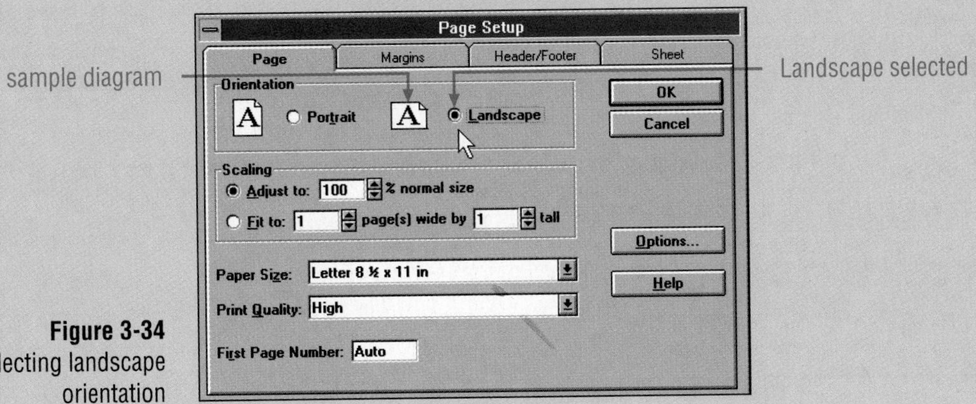

Figure 3-34
Selecting landscape orientation

While the Page Setup dialog box is open, let's use the Header/Footer tab to document the worksheet.

Headers and Footers

A **header** is text that is printed in the top margin of every page of a worksheet. A **footer** is text that is printed in the bottom margin of every page of a worksheet. Headers and footers are not displayed as part of the worksheet window. To see them, you must look at a print preview or a worksheet printout.

You can use a header or footer to provide basic documentation about your worksheet. A worksheet header could contain the name of the person who created the worksheet, the date the worksheet was created, and the filename of the worksheet. Excel automatically attaches a centered header containing the worksheet filename and a centered footer containing the page number, unless you specify otherwise. Refer back to Figure 3-33 to see the headers and footers displayed in the print preview.

Excel uses formatting codes in headers and footers. **Formatting codes** produce dates, times, and filenames that you might want to include in a header or footer. You can type these codes, or you can click a formatting code button to insert the code. Figure 3-35 shows the formatting codes and the tools you can use to insert them.

Tool	Tool Name	Formatting Code	Action
A	Font tool	none	set font size
#	Page Number tool	&[Page]	print page number
	Total Pages tool	&[Pages]	print total number of pages
	Date tool	&[Date]	print date
	Time tool	&[Time]	print time
	Filename tool	&[File]	print filename
	Tabname tool	&[Tab]	print tabname

Figure 3-35
The header and footer formatting

Maria wants to change the header and footer that Excel added automatically.

To change the worksheet header:

1. Make sure the Page Setup dialog box is still open, then click the **Header/Footer tab**.
2. Click the **Custom Header... button** to display the Header dialog box.
3. Drag the pointer over &[File] in the Center Section box to highlight it. See Figure 3-36.

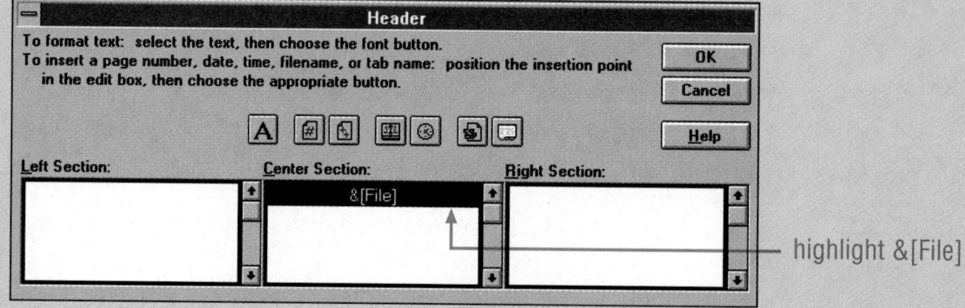

Figure 3-36
Deleting a header

4. Press **[Del]** to delete &[File].
5. Click the **Right Section box** to move the insertion point there. You should be able to see the insertion point blinking on the far right border of the box.

6. Type **Pronto Salsa Company** and then press **[Spacebar]** so the company name doesn't run into the next item in the header.
7. Click the **Date button** to add &[Date] to the header, then press **[Spacebar]**.
8. Click the **Filename button** to add &[File] to the header. See Figure 3-37.

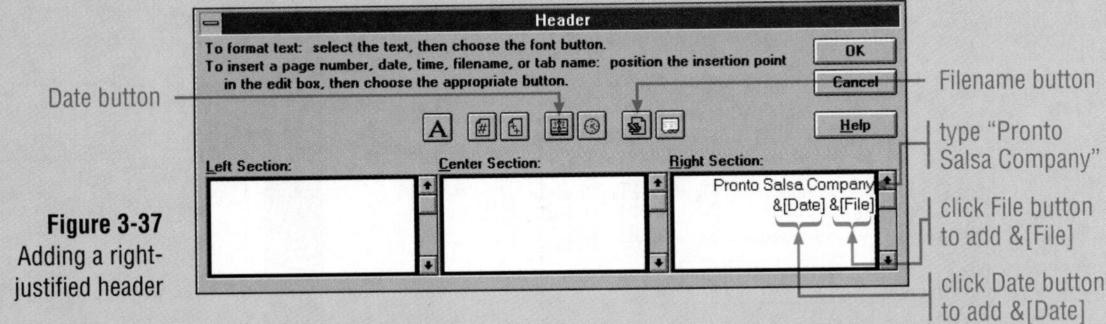

Figure 3-37 Adding a right-justified header

TROUBLE? Don't worry if &[Date] and &[File] are in different lines from "Pronto Salsa Company."

9. Click the **OK button** to complete the header and return to the Page Setup dialog box.

Centering the Printout and Removing Cell Gridlines and Row/Column Headings

Maria thinks that worksheet printouts look more professional without gridlines and row/column headings. In her opinion, the row/column headings—the letters A, B, C, and so forth that identify the columns—are useful when you design and create the worksheet but are distracting on the printout. Maria also likes her worksheets to be centered on the printed page. Let's make those changes now.

To center the printout and remove the row/column headings and gridlines:

1. Make sure the Page Setup dialog box is still open.
2. Click the **Margins tab**.
3. If the Horizontally box does not contain an ×, click the **Horizontally box** to place an × in it.
4. If the Vertically box does not contain an ×, click the **Vertically box** to place an × in it.
5. Click the **Sheet tab**.
6. If the Gridlines box contains an ×, click the **Gridlines box** to remove the × from it.
7. Make sure the Row & Column Headings box is empty.

8. Click the **OK button** to complete the Page Setup changes and display a print preview that shows the effect of the changes you made. See Figure 3-38.

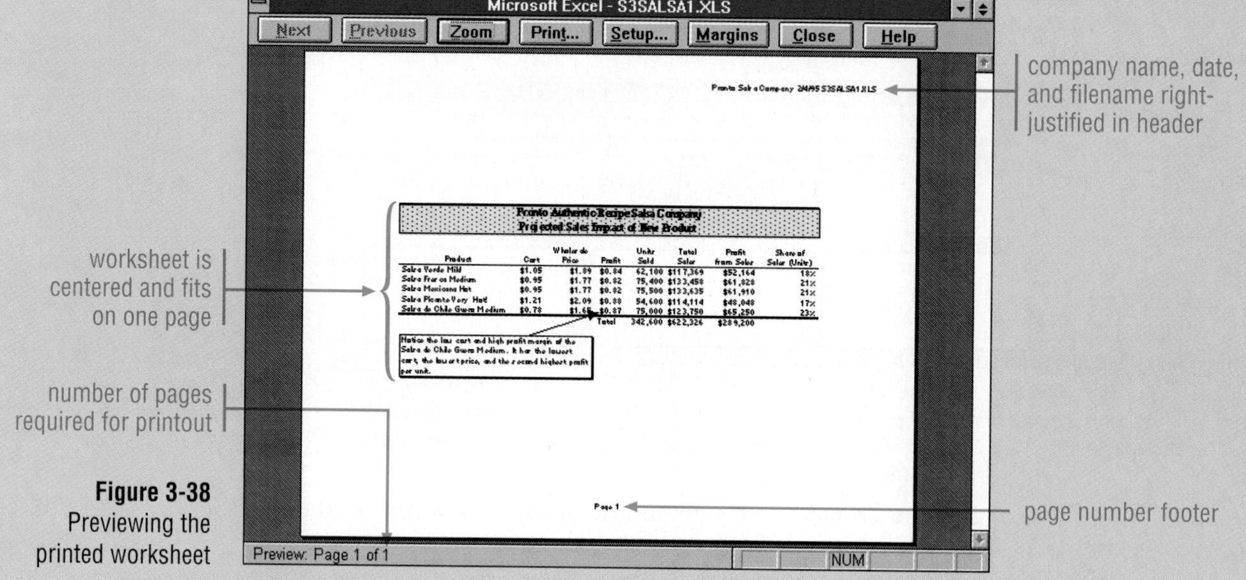

Figure 3-38
Previewing the printed worksheet

9. If your screen doesn't match the figure, make any necessary adjustments using the Page Setup dialog box. When you're ready, click the **Close button** to close the print preview window.

The worksheet is ready to print, but Maria always saves her work before printing.

To save and print the worksheet:

1. Click the **Save button** .
2. Click the **Print button** .

TROUBLE? If you see a message that indicates you have a printer problem, click the Cancel button to cancel the printout. Check your printer to make sure it is turned on and is on-line; also make sure it has paper. Then go back and try Step 2 again. If you do not have a printer available, click the Cancel button.

Figure 3-39 shows Maria's printout. Maria is pleased with her work.

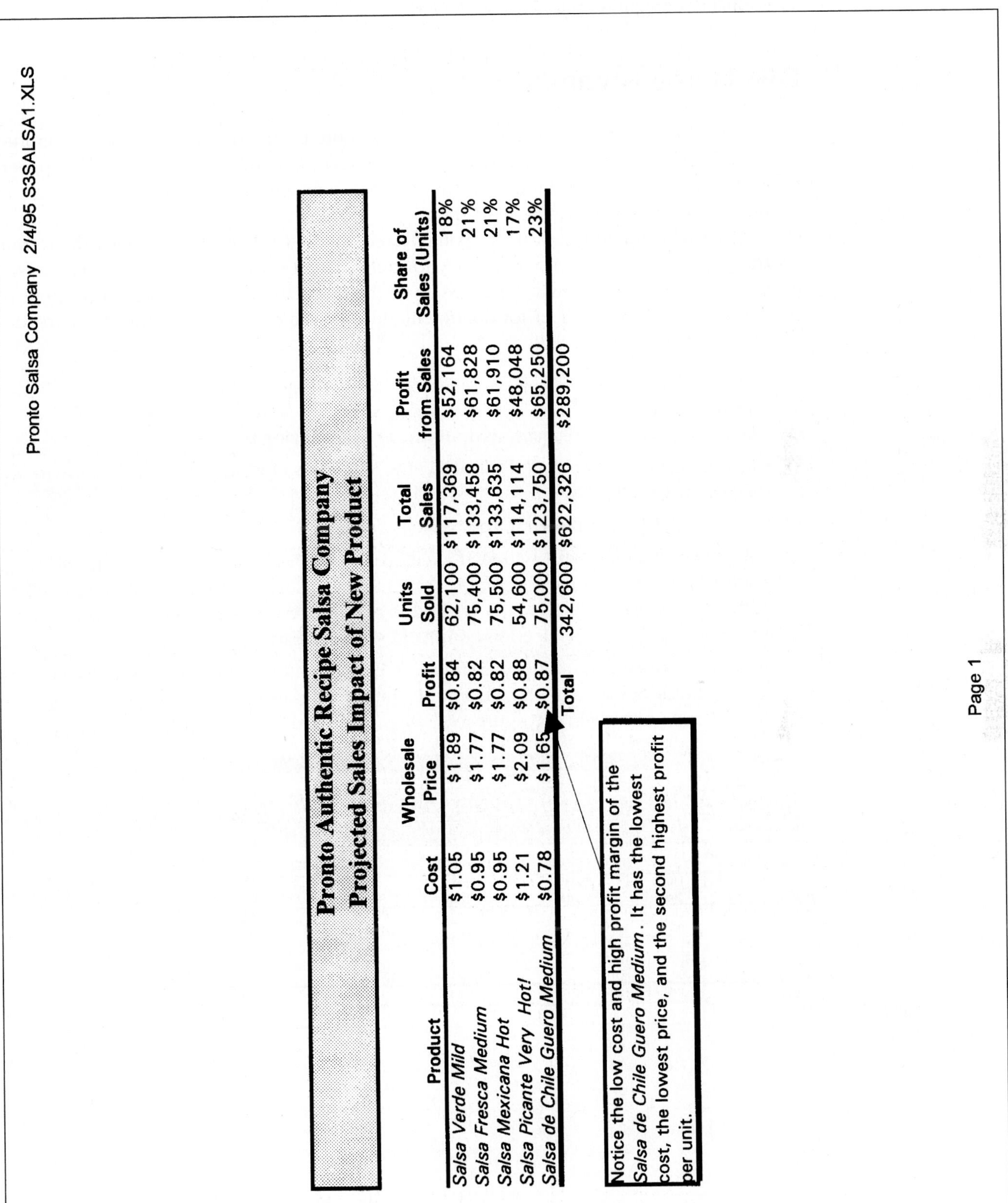

Pronto Salsa Company 2/4/95 S3SALSA1.XLS

Pronto Authentic Recipe Salsa Company
Projected Sales Impact of New Product

Product	Cost	Wholesale Price	Profit	Units Sold	Total Sales	Profit from Sales	Share of Sales (Units)
Salsa Verde Mild	$1.05	$1.89	$0.84	62,100	$117,369	$52,164	18%
Salsa Fresca Medium	$0.95	$1.77	$0.82	75,400	$133,458	$61,828	21%
Salsa Mexicana Hot	$0.95	$1.77	$0.82	75,500	$133,635	$61,910	21%
Salsa Picante Very Hot!	$1.21	$2.09	$0.88	54,600	$114,114	$48,048	17%
Salsa de Chile Guero Medium	$0.78	$1.65	$0.87	75,000	$123,750	$65,250	23%
			Total	342,600	$622,326	$289,200	

Notice the low cost and high profit margin of the *Salsa de Chile Guero Medium*. It has the lowest cost, the lowest price, and the second highest profit per unit.

Page 1

Figure 3-39
Maria's printed worksheet

Since she has a few minutes before her boss returns, Maria decides to produce some additional documentation for the worksheet.

Displaying Formulas

In Tutorial 2 you learned that you can add a text note to incorporate documentation into your worksheet, and you learned that the worksheet plan and sketch are valuable paper-based worksheet documentation. In this tutorial, you will learn how to document the formulas you used to create the worksheet.

You can document the formulas you entered on a worksheet by displaying the formulas and printing them. When you display formulas, Excel shows the formulas you entered in each cell instead of showing the results of the calculations. Maria wants a printout of the formulas in her worksheet for documentation. To see how she does this, let's first display the formulas she entered.

To display formulas:

1. Click **Tools**, then click **Options**, to open the Options dialog box.
2. Click the **View tab**, then click **Formulas** in the Windows Option box to place an × in the Formulas box.
3. Click the **OK button** to return to the worksheet.

The worksheet columns have widened excessively, but Maria isn't concerned about worksheet format right now. She simply wants to make sure the formulas are displayed properly in the worksheet. (If Maria wanted to readjust the column width, she would have to repeat the AutoFit Selection command she used earlier.)

4. Scroll the worksheet to look at columns D, E, F, G, and H—the columns that contain formulas. See Figure 3-40. (Don't be concerned if the columns on your screen are wider than those in the figure.)

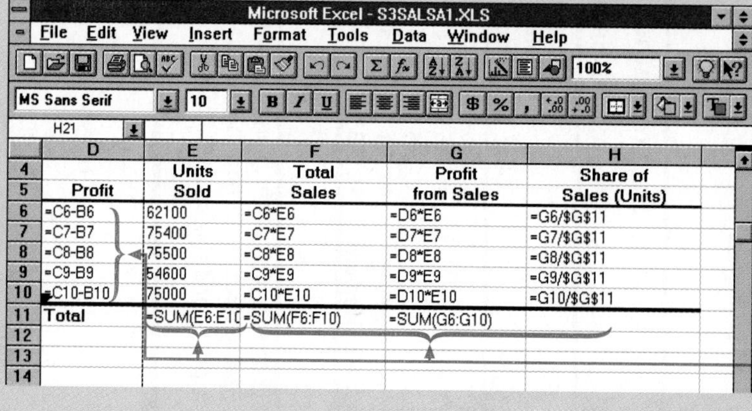

Figure 3-40
Displaying formulas

Maria could manually make the settings to print the worksheet with the formulas displayed, but to do so would be time consuming because she would have to change the column widths and make the appropriate settings in the Page Setup dialog box to show the gridlines and the row/column headings, center the worksheet on the page, and fit the printout on a single page. To avoid doing all this work every time she wants to print formulas, Maria created a Visual Basic module to automate this printing task.

Before you look at Maria's module, let's turn off the formulas display.

To turn off the formulas display:

1. Click **Tools**, then click **Options**, to open the Options dialog box.
2. Click the **View tab** if necessary, then click **Formulas** to remove the ×.
3. Click the **OK button** to return to the worksheet. The formulas are no longer displayed.
4. Scroll the worksheet so you can see column A.

A Visual Basic Module to Print Formulas

A Visual Basic **module**, also called a macro, automatically performs a sequence of tasks or commands such as menu selections, dialog box selections, or keystrokes. You create modules to automate the Excel tasks that you perform frequently and that require a series of steps. To create a module you can record the series of steps as you perform them, or you can enter a series of commands (in the Visual Basic programming language) that tell Excel how to do the task.

In this section of the tutorial, you will have the opportunity to use a prewritten module that prints formulas. You will learn how to run the module, and you will look at the commands that constitute the module. As you will discover, the print formulas module is very useful for documenting the worksheets you complete as course assignments.

Opening a Module

Your Student Disk contains a copy of Maria's module, which displays and prints worksheet formulas automatically. Maria created her print formulas module to do the following:

- Make a copy of the worksheet in a separate sheet
- Display formulas
- Adjust column width for best fit
- Turn on cell gridlines and row/column headings
- Fit the printout on a single page in landscape orientation
- Print the worksheet
- Erase the copy of the worksheet and return to the original worksheet

The module that prints worksheet formulas is stored in a workbook called PRINT1.XLM. The .XLM extension tells you that this workbook contains only a Visual Basic module. Let's open the workbook and look at the commands.

To open the PRINT1.XLM module:

1. Click the **Open button** to display the Open dialog box.
2. Double-click **PRINT1.XLM** to open the workbook. The print module appears, along with the Visual Basic toolbar. See Figure 3-41.

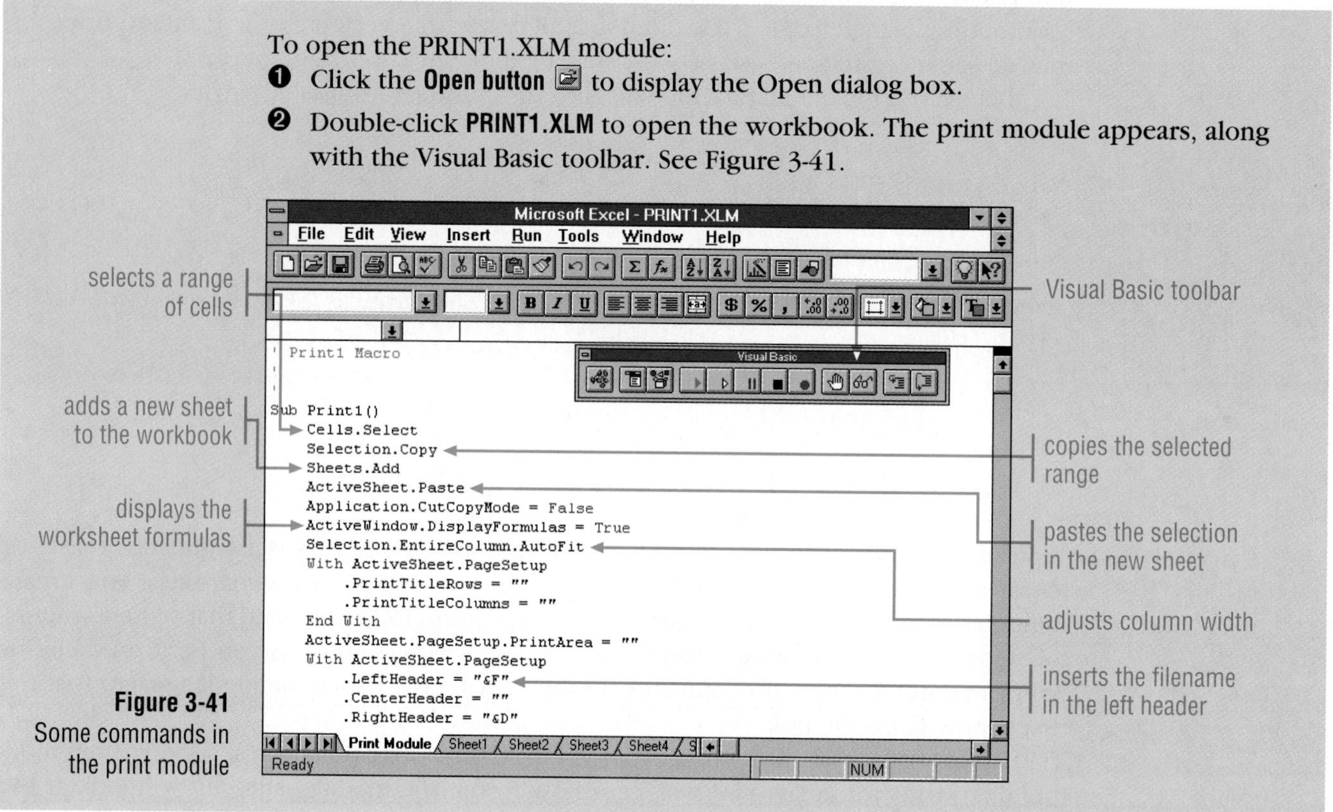

Figure 3-41
Some commands in the print module

Maria created this module by performing the steps for the formula printout while Excel recorded what she did. When Maria completed the steps, Excel translated her actions into the commands you see on the screen. Each row of the module displays one command. The Visual Basic toolbar allows you to run the module or make adjustments to it simply by clicking the proper toolbar button.

While the commands may seem difficult to understand at first, you can probably decipher a few just by taking a close look. For example, Sheets.Add tells Excel to add a new sheet to the workbook. Then, as you might expect, the next command, ActiveSheet.Paste tells Excel to paste something into the active sheet. Other commands are explained in Figure 3-41.

Running a Module

To use a module, you first insert a copy of the module in the workbook you're working on. Then you use the Macro command on the Tools menu to run the module. When you're finished, you should save the workbook, along with the newly added module sheet, so you can use the module whenever you open that workbook.

Maria begins by copying the module to the S3SALSA1.XLS workbook.

To copy the module:

1. Click **Edit**, then click **Move or Copy Sheet...** to open the Move or Copy dialog box.
2. Click the **To Book down arrow button** and select **S3SALSA1.XLS**. Then click the **Create a Copy checkbox** to insert an ×.
3. In the Before Sheet box, click **Sheet2**. This tells Excel to place the module sheet, before Sheet2, directly after the Projected Sales sheet.
4. Check that the dialog box on your screen matches Figure 3-42. Then click the **OK button** to make the copy.

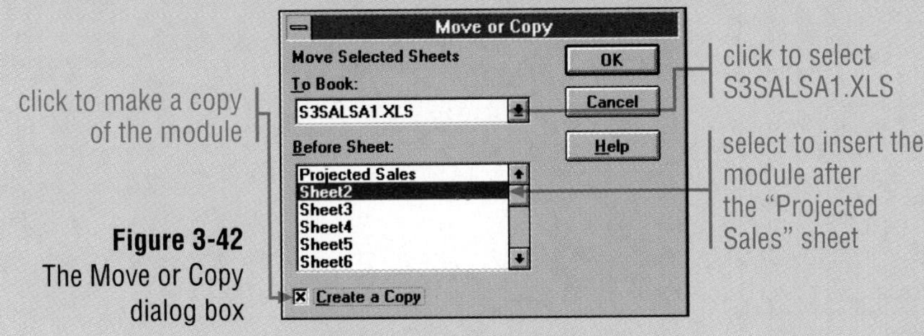

Figure 3-42
The Move or Copy dialog box

Excel adds a module sheet to Maria's workbook. The module appears in the sheet exactly as it appeared in the PRINT1.XLM workbook.

Now, you're ready to run the macro and print the formulas.

To run the module:

1. Click the **Projected Sales tab** to display the Projected Sales sheet.
2. Click **Tools**, then click **Macro...** to display the Macro dialog box.
3. Click **Print1** to display Print1 in the Macro Name/Reference box.
4. Click the **Run button**.
5. After a moment, you'll see the message "Selected sheets will be permanently deleted. Continue?" Click the **OK button** because you do not want to save the copy of the worksheet that the module created. As a result, you will return to your Projected Sales worksheet. Excel prints the worksheet formulas. Notice that the formatting is slightly different on the printed worksheet due to the AutoFit command in the module.

Normally you would save the workbook with the new module sheet. But since you will be improving on the print module in the Tutorial Assignments, you don't want to save this version of the module.

6. Use the File menu to close the workbook. When you see the message "Save changes in 'S3SALSA1.XLS'?" click the **No button**.
7. Close the PRINT1.XLM workbook.

   TROUBLE? If you accidentally made some changes to the module, you will see the message "Save changes in 'PRINT1.XLM'?" Click the No button to save the module in its original form.

8. Exit Excel if you are not going to do the Tutorial Assignments right away.

Now Maria has a printout of the formulas in her worksheet (Figure 3-43), in addition to the printout showing the results of the formula calculations.

S3SALSA1.XLS 2/4/95

Pronto Authentic Recipe Salsa Company
Projected Sales Impact of New Product

Product	Cost	Wholesale Price	Profit	Units Sold	Total Sales	Profit from Sales	Share of Sales (Units)
Salsa Verde Mild	1.05	1.89	=C6-B6	62100	=C6*E6	=D6*E6	=G6/$G$11
Salsa Fresca Medium	0.95	1.77	=C7-B7	75400	=C7*E7	=D7*E7	=G7/$G$11
Salsa Mexicana Hot	0.95	1.77	=C8-B8	75500	=C8*E8	=D8*E8	=G8/$G$11
Salsa Picante Very Hot!	1.21	2.09	=C9-B9	54600	=C9*E9	=D9*E9	=G9/$G$11
Salsa de Chile Guero Medium	0.78	1.65	=C10-B1	75000	=C10*E10	=D10*E10	=G10/$G$11
			Total	=SUM(E6:E10)	=SUM(F6:F10)	=SUM(G6:G10)	

Notice the low cost and high profit margin of the *Salsa de Chile Guero Medium*. It has the lowest cost, the lowest price, and the second highest profit per unit.

Page 1

Figure 3-43

Tips for Using the Print Formulas Module

The print formulas module you used in this tutorial helped Maria print the formulas for her worksheet. In the Tutorial Assignments you will modify this module to create your own customized print formulas module called S3MYMOD.XLM. Your customized module will automatically print your name in the header of the formulas printout. You can use your customized module to print out the formulas for any worksheet you create.

Many of the Tutorial Assignments and Case Problems require you to produce a printout of your worksheet formulas, in addition to a printout of the results of the formula calculations. When you are completing worksheets for the Tutorial Assignments and Case Problems, you should follow these general steps:

1. Create the worksheet and format it as required.
2. When you are ready to print the worksheet, use the Print Preview command to see how the worksheet fits on the printed page. Make adjustments to the column widths on the worksheet if necessary.
3. Use the Page Setup dialog box to center the printout on the page and turn off the cell gridlines and row/column headings. Add your name to the header, and include the date and filename.
4. Print the worksheet.
5. Save the workbook at this point to save your print specifications.
6. Open your customized workbook, S3MYMOD.XLM
7. Use the Move or Copy Sheet command on the Edit menu to move a copy of the module worksheet to the workbook containing the sheet you want to print. Make sure you click the Create a Copy box.
8. Display the sheet containing the formulas you want to print.
9. Use the Macro… command on the Tools menu to open the Macro dialog box and select the print module. Then click the Run button.
10. When the module asks if you want to continue, click the OK button.
11. When you are sure the module is working properly, save the workbook with the new module worksheet.
12. If you are not going to print any other worksheets during your computing session, use the Window menu to activate the module workbook, then close it.

As Maria looks over the printed worksheet and formula printout, Anne returns and asks to see the formatted worksheet. Anne examines the printouts and briefly checks the accuracy of the formulas shown on the formulas printout. She praises Maria for her excellent work before rushing off to her appointment with the loan officer.

■ ■ ■

Questions

1. If the number .128912 is in a cell, what will Excel display if you:
   a. format the number using the 0% percentage format
   b. format the number using the $#,##0_) currency format
   c. format the number using the $#,##0.00_) currency format
2. Define the following terms using your own words:
   a. column titles
   b. font style
   c. Visual Basic module
   d. formatting
   e. formatting codes
   f. font effects
   g. headers
   h. footers
   i. column headings
3. Explain the advantages and disadvantages of using the AutoFormat command to apply a predefined format to your worksheet.
4. List three ways you can access formatting commands, options, and tools.
5. Explain why Excel might display 3,045.39 in a cell, but when you look at the contents of the cell in the formula bar, it displays 3045.38672.
6. List the formatting buttons that are available on the formatting toolbar.
7. Explain the options Excel provides for aligning data.
8. What is the general rule you should follow for aligning column headings, numbers, and text labels?
9. List four ways you can change column widths.
10. What is a potential problem with the way Excel automatically aligns data?
11. Why is it useful to include a comma to separate thousands, millions, and billions?
12. List the Excel formatting features you can use to draw attention to data or to provide visual interest.
13. List the toolbars that you can activate in Excel. Which of these toolbars have you used in Tutorials 1 through 3?
14. **E** Use the *Excel On-line Help*, the *Microsoft Excel User's Guide*, the *Microsoft-Windows 3.1 User's Guide*, or other similar documentation to learn more about objects. Write a short paragraph describing what you learned and how you might use objects when you design your own worksheets.
15. Explain how you should position borders so they are not disrupted when you copy cell contents.
16. Make a list of things you should look for when you do a print preview to ensure that your printed worksheets look professional.

Tutorial Assignments

Launch Windows and Excel, if necessary. Insert your Student Disk in the disk drive. Make sure the Excel and Book1 windows are maximized. Complete the following steps to customize the print formulas module so it automatically places your name in the header.

1. Open the module workbook PRINT1.XLM.
2. Move I to the line that reads .RightHeader = "&D".
3. Position I after the first quotation mark and click.

4. Type your own name, and make sure there is a space between your name and the &D formatting code.
5. Scroll back up to the fourth line of the module. Replace "Print1" with "MyMod" in the fourth line. The modified line should now read: Sub MyMod ( ).
6. Edit the first line so that it reads: ' MyMod Macro. Then click at the very beginning of the line to insert the insertion pointer before the apostrophe.
7. Save the revised module as S3MYMOD.XLM.
8. Test the module. Open the S3SALSA1.XLS workbook, then use the Window menu to activate the S3MYMOD.XLM workbook again.
9. Use the Move or Copy Sheet command on the Edit menu to insert a copy of the module in the S3SALSA1.XLS workbook. Then select the sheet containing the formulas you want to print.
10. Use the Macro... command on the Tools menu to open the Macro dialog box and select MYMOD. Your name, the date, and the filename S3SALSA1.XLS should appear in the header of the printed worksheet.

Next, revise the S3SALSA1.XLS workbook by doing the following:

11. Make the text box higher and narrower so it fits in columns A and B.
12. Move the tail-end of the arrow that goes from the top of the text box to cell D10, so that it comes from the right side of the text box.
13. Center the percentages displayed in column H.
14. Make the contents of cells A10 through H10 bold to emphasize the new product. Make any necessary column width adjustments.
15. Add shading to cells A10 through H10 using the same dot pattern and color you used for the titles.
16. Put your name in the header so it appears on the printout of the worksheet. Make sure the header also prints the date and worksheet filename.
17. Make sure the Page Setup menu settings are for landscape orientation, centered horizontally and vertically, no row/column headings, and no cell gridlines.
18. Preview the printout to make sure it fits on one page.
19. Print the worksheet.
20. Save your workbook.

Case Problems

1. Fresh Air Sales Incentive Program

Carl Stambaugh is the assistant sales manager at Fresh Air Inc., a manufacturer of outdoor and expedition clothing. Fresh Air sales representatives contact retail chains and individual retail outlets to sell the Fresh Air line of outdoor clothing products.

This year, to spur sales Carl has decided to run a sales incentive program for the sales representatives. Each sales representative has been assigned a sales goal 15% higher than his or her total sales for last year. All sales representatives who reach this new goal will be awarded an all-expense paid trip for two to Cozumel, Mexico.

Carl has been tracking the results of the sales incentive program with an Excel worksheet. He has asked you to format the worksheet so it will look professional. He also wants a printout before he presents the worksheet at the next sales meeting. Complete the following steps to format and print the worksheet:

1. Launch Windows and Excel as usual.
2. Open the workbook P3SALES.XLS, maximize the worksheet window, then save the workbook as S3SALES.XLS.

3. Make the formatting changes shown in Figure 3-44.

P3SALES.XLS ← delete this header

add header containing your name, date, filename

format using 0% format

center title across columns, enlarge font using Increase Font Size tool

right justify this label

center all headings

add bottom border

	A	B	C	D	E	F	G	H	I	J
1	Fresh Air Sales Representative Incentive Program									
2										
3										
4		Goal % Increase	0.15							
5										
6			1994	1st Qtr	2nd Qtr	3rd Qtr	4th Qtr	1994	1994	% Goal
7	Territory	Name	Sales	Actual	Actual	Actual	Actual	Actual	Goal	Reached
8	Western	Delman, Amy	142789	47899	41567	81266	96782	267514	164207.4	1.629128
9	Western	Trout, Patricia	152402	35008.2	68909	66328	91344	261589.2	175262.3	1.492558
10	Western	Valentino, Elizabeth	163284	33567	70929.7	63213	99345	267054.7	187776.6	1.422194
11	Southern	Schuda, Jay	156782	56893	62332	89547	45877	254649	180299.3	1.412368
12	Central	Oliver, Deby	182018	66897	56874	66345	93234	283350	209320.7	1.353664
13	Western	Chu, Johnathon	166324	41889	75892	87445	51678	256904	191272.6	1.34313
14	Western	Shalala, Donna	161300	36221.5	71563	62341	76432	246557.5	185495	1.329187
15	Western	Leatherman, Courtney	136589	34327	37899	64333	67894	204453	157077.4	1.301607
16	Southern	Epstein, Lee	159778	33258	65700	65789	44661	209408	183744.7	1.139668
17	Western	Cook, Pamela	157896	42339	45233	58566	45328	191466	181580.4	1.054442
18	Southern	Rose, Ann C.	155840	33258	61788	46777	42215	184038	179216	1.026906
19	Western	Vagelos, Paul	155329	43667	39086	68733	31566	183052	178628.4	1.024765
20	Central	Richstone, Ellen	176900	43658	65223	59087	38900	206868	203435	1.016875
21	Central	Azevedo, Tricia	179385	53278	47895	53334	43445	197952	206292.8	0.959568
22	Eastern	Gyorog, Mike	211408	55789	65996	69023	42215	233023	243119.2	0.958472
23	Southern	Dufallo, Basil	166805	46899	48912	45687	38999	180497	191825.8	0.940942
24	Central	Johnson, Carole	145823	34122	34557	39700	46789	155168	167696.5	0.925291
25	Central	Crawford, Lori	226050	56821	72100	66872	44122	239915	259957.5	0.922901
26	Eastern	Haag, Candee	156877	31566	43677	48043.5	41566	164852.5	180408.6	0.913773
27	Central	Lewis, Kathryn	156998	39800	46772	45687	29876	162135	180547.7	0.898018
28	Southern	Kim, Choong Soon	207630	51233	66721	61788	29878	209620	238774.5	0.877899
29	Southern	Baer, Joachim	206850	56821	55781	51223	38900	202725	237877.5	0.852224
30	Western	Massalska, Angela	172894	35998	41566	44366	38071.1	160001.1	198828.1	0.804721
31	Eastern	Sako, Mari	176504	36221.5	45987	46033.8	33546	161788.3	202979.6	0.797067
32	Central	McChesney, Darlene	189600	37889	56894	45687	32172.2	172642.2	218040	0.791791
33	Southern	Free, Valerie	195365	47822	48900	48043.5	33123	177888.5	224669.8	0.791778
34	Western	Widnall, Sheila	172369	31567	45987	44024.1	33156	154734.1	198224.4	0.780601
35	Eastern	Dupre, William	195887	43223	38900	45789	46877	174789	225270.1	0.775909
36	Western	Lahiri, Nayanjot	238605	61233	72344	41277	32172.2	207026.2	274395.8	0.75448
37	Eastern	Horiuchi, Kotaro	208695	44105	61788	45687	26273.3	177853.3	239999.3	0.741058
38	Eastern	Luck,Steven P.	214689	56821	32678	45789	46877	182165	246892.4	0.737832
39	Southern	Hess, Lisa	212550	32778	65996	42334	37650	178758	244432.5	0.731318
40	Southern	Wertheim, Andrea	193250	42666	35874	34788	47888	161216	222237.5	0.725422
41	Eastern	Catoe, Chris	189560	38766	34566	41555	41233	156120	217994	0.716166
42	Eastern	Bolitho, Jason	215600	42177	56894	49800	20374.4	169245.4	247940	0.682606
43	Eastern	Jansson, Maija	227588	33794.9	55223	46512	29876	165405.9	261726.2	0.631981

format this column using 0.00% format

format regions in bold italics

adjust column widths to best fit

Figure 3-44

4. Use the Page Setup dialog box to scale the worksheet to fit on one page printed in landscape mode.
5. Center the worksheet horizontally and vertically.
6. Add a header, shown in Figure 3-44, and delete the formatting code &[File] from the Center Section of the header.
7. Save the workbook.
8. Preview the worksheet and make any page setup adjustments necessary to obtain the printed results you want.
9. Print the worksheet.
10. Use S3MYMOD.XLM, which you created in the Tutorial Assignments, to print the formulas for your worksheet.

2. Age Group Changes in the U.S. Population

Rick Stephanopolous is preparing a report on changes in the U.S. population. Part of the report focuses on age group changes in the population from 1970 through 1980. Rick has created a worksheet that contains information from the U.S. Census reports, and he is ready to format the worksheet. Complete the following steps to format the worksheet:

1. Launch Windows and Excel as usual.
2. Open the workbook P3CENSUS.XLS, maximize the worksheet window, then save the workbook as S3CENSUS.XLS.
3. Make the formatting changes shown in Figure 3-45, adjusting column widths as necessary.

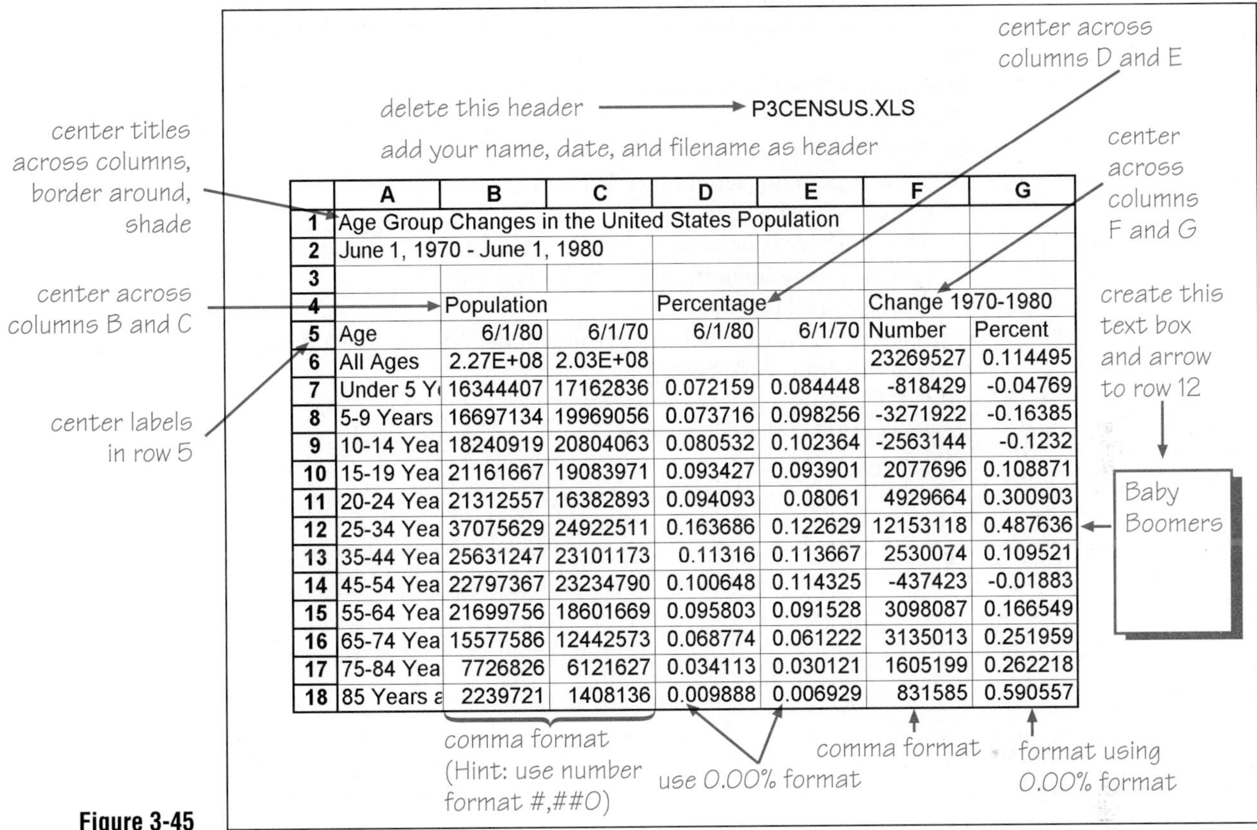

	A	B	C	D	E	F	G
1	Age Group Changes in the United States Population						
2	June 1, 1970 - June 1, 1980						
3							
4		Population		Percentage		Change 1970-1980	
5	Age	6/1/80	6/1/70	6/1/80	6/1/70	Number	Percent
6	All Ages	2.27E+08	2.03E+08			23269527	0.114495
7	Under 5 Y	16344407	17162836	0.072159	0.084448	-818429	-0.04769
8	5-9 Years	16697134	19969056	0.073716	0.098256	-3271922	-0.16385
9	10-14 Yea	18240919	20804063	0.080532	0.102364	-2563144	-0.1232
10	15-19 Yea	21161667	19083971	0.093427	0.093901	2077696	0.108871
11	20-24 Yea	21312557	16382893	0.094093	0.08061	4929664	0.300903
12	25-34 Yea	37075629	24922511	0.163686	0.122629	12153118	0.487636
13	35-44 Yea	25631247	23101173	0.11316	0.113667	2530074	0.109521
14	45-54 Yea	22797367	23234790	0.100648	0.114325	-437423	-0.01883
15	55-64 Yea	21699756	18601669	0.095803	0.091528	3098087	0.166549
16	65-74 Yea	15577586	12442573	0.068774	0.061222	3135013	0.251959
17	75-84 Yea	7726826	6121627	0.034113	0.030121	1605199	0.262218
18	85 Years a	2239721	1408136	0.009888	0.006929	831585	0.590557

Figure 3-45

4. Use the Page Setup dialog box to modify the header so the Right Section consists of your name, a space, the current date, and the name of the file. Delete the contents of the Center Section of the header.
5. Save the workbook again.
6. Preview and print the worksheet.
7. Use S3MYMOD.XLM, which you created in the Tutorial Assignments, to print the formulas for your worksheet.

3. Creating and Formatting Your Own Worksheet

Design a worksheet for a problem with which you are familiar. The problem might be a business problem from one of your other business courses, or it could be a numeric problem from a biology, education, or sociology course. Follow the steps below to plan your worksheet, prepare your planning documents, and complete the worksheet.

1. Decide what problem you would like to solve.
2. Refer to Maria's worksheet plan in Figure 3-1 and Otis's worksheet plan in Figure 2-4. Write a similar document for the problem you would like to solve. Write a statement of your goal, list the results you want to see, list the information you need for the worksheet cells, and describe the formulas you will need for the worksheet calculations.

3. Sketch a plan for your worksheet showing the worksheet title(s), the data labels, column headings, and totals. Indicate the formats you will use for titles, headings, labels, data, and totals.
4. Build the worksheet by entering the titles and labels first, then entering the data and formulas.
5. Test the formulas using simple test data such as 1s or 10s.
6. After you are sure the formulas are correct, format the worksheet according to your plan.
7. Save the workbook periodically as you work.
8. When the worksheet is formatted, use Excel's print preview feature to determine the Page Setup settings you need to make.
9. Make the Page Setup settings needed to:
    a. center the worksheet
    b. print a header containing your name, the date, and the filename
    c. turn off row/column headings and cell gridlines
10. Print your worksheet.
11. Use S3MYMOD.XLM, which you created in the Tutorial Assignments, to print the formulas for your worksheet.
12. Submit the following to your instructor:
    a. your planning sheet
    b. your planning sketch
    c. a printout of the regular worksheet
    d. a printout of the worksheet formulas

TUTORIAL 4

Functions, Formulas, and Absolute References

Managing Loan Payments

OBJECTIVES

In this tutorial you will:

- Use the MAX function to find the largest number in a range of cells
- Use the MIN function to find the smallest number in a range of cells
- Use the AVERAGE function to calculate the average of a column of numbers
- Calculate monthly loan payments using the PMT function
- Create a formula using the IF function
- Use the TODAY function to display today's date
- Learn when to use absolute references in formulas

CASE

Superior Sails Charter Company The Superior Sails Charter Company is based in Sault Ste. Marie, Michigan, on the shores of Lake Superior and close to the North Channel, one of the most pristine boating areas in the Northern Hemisphere. The company owns a large fleet of boats purchased with bank loans. Shabir Ahmad works part time for the charter company to help pay for his college education. As of this month, the company finally has a computer. James LaSalle, the company owner, has asked Shabir to create some Excel worksheets so he will have better information with which to manage the business.

James asks Shabir to create a worksheet that contains the following information about each Superior Sails boat loan:

- original amount of the loan
- payments left to repay the loan
- interest rate of the loan
- payment amount per month

James also wants to see the total monthly amount that Superior Sails needs to pay for all of the loans, and he encourages Shabir to include any other information that might be useful for managing the boat loans.

Shabir thinks about the project, then develops the worksheet plan shown in Figure 4-1 and the sketch shown in Figure 4-2.

Worksheet Plan for Loan Management Worksheet

My Goal:
To develop a worksheet to help management keep track of loan payments for boats in the Superior Sails fleet.

What results do I want to see?
Total payments due this month.
The amounts of the largest and smallest loans.
The average loan amount.

What information do I need?
A list of all boats in the Superior Sails fleet.
The amount, interest rate, and number of monthly payments for each loan.
The loan status (paid or due) for each boat.

What calculations will I perform?
largest loan = MAX (all loans)
smallest loans = MIN (all loans)
average loans = AVERAGE (all loans)
monthly payment amount = PMT (interest rate, number of payments, loan amount)
payments due this month = IF (loan is not paid, display the loan payment)
total payments due = SUM (all payments for loans not paid off)
percent of total payment = loan payment/total payments due

Figure 4-1
Shabir's worksheet plan

Superior Sails Charter Company - Loan Management Worksheet

Boat Type and Length	Loan Amount	Annual Interest Rate	Number of Monthly Payments	Monthly Payment Amount	Current Loan Status	Payments Due this Month	Percent of Total Payment
O'Day 34	$37,700	11.00%	60	${monthly payment amount formula}	xxxx	${payments due this month formula}	{percent of total payment formula}%
:	:	:	:		:		
:	:	:	:		:		:
:	:	:	:	:	:	:	:
:	:	:	:	:	:	:	:
:	:	:	:	:	:	:	:
:	:	:	:	:	:	:	:
:	:	:	:	:	:	:	:
Largest loan:	${largest loan formula}		Total Payments Due			${total payments due formula}	
Smallest loan:	${smallest loan formula}						
Average loan:	${average loan formula}						

Figure 4-2
Shabir's worksheet sketch

He decides that the worksheet should show the largest loan, the smallest loan, and the average amount of the loans, in addition to the information James specified. Shabir also decides to add a column that shows what percent each loan payment is of the total payment. This information might be useful if James decides to sell or replace any of his boats.

James approves Shabir's plan, then shows him where to find the information on the boat loans. Shabir begins to develop the worksheet according to his plan.

In this tutorial you will work with Shabir to create a worksheet to help James manage his boat loans. You will use several Excel functions to simplify the formulas you enter, and you will learn when to use absolute references in formulas. Let's get started by launching Excel and organizing the desktop.

To launch Excel and organize the desktop:

1. Launch Windows and Excel following your usual procedure.
2. Make sure your Student Disk is in the disk drive.
3. Make sure the Microsoft Excel and Book1 windows are maximized.

Shabir already entered the labels for the worksheet and the loan data provided by James. Let's open Shabir's worksheet and look at what he has done so far.

To open the C4SAILS1.XLS workbook:

1. Click the **Open button** to display the Open dialog box.
2. Double-click **C4SAILS1.XLS** in the File Name box to display the workbook shown in Figure 4-3.

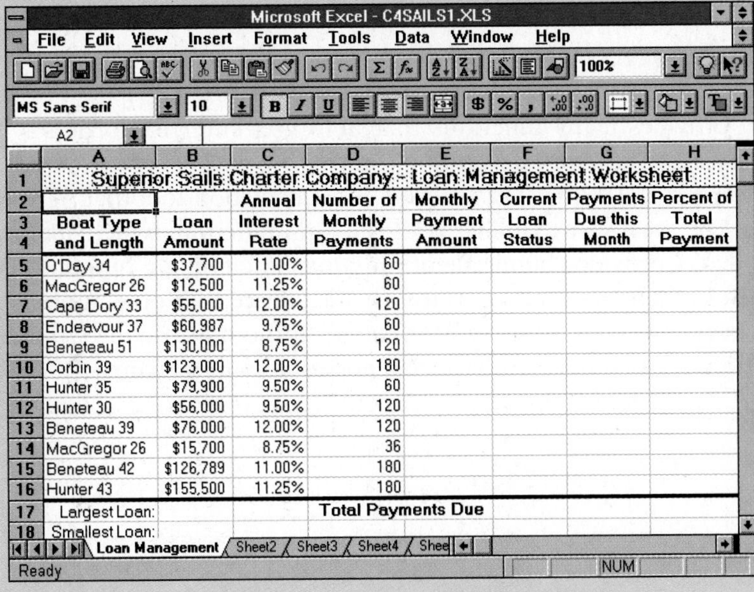

	A	B	C	D	E	F	G	H
1	Superior Sails Charter Company - Loan Management Worksheet							
2			Annual	Number of	Monthly	Current	Payments	Percent of
3	Boat Type	Loan	Interest	Monthly	Payment	Loan	Due this	Total
4	and Length	Amount	Rate	Payments	Amount	Status	Month	Payment
5	O'Day 34	$37,700	11.00%	60				
6	MacGregor 26	$12,500	11.25%	60				
7	Cape Dory 33	$55,000	12.00%	120				
8	Endeavour 37	$60,987	9.75%	60				
9	Beneteau 51	$130,000	8.75%	120				
10	Corbin 39	$123,000	12.00%	180				
11	Hunter 35	$79,900	9.50%	60				
12	Hunter 30	$56,000	9.50%	120				
13	Beneteau 39	$76,000	12.00%	120				
14	MacGregor 26	$15,700	8.75%	36				
15	Beneteau 42	$126,789	11.00%	180				
16	Hunter 43	$155,500	11.25%	180				
17	Largest Loan:			Total Payments Due				
18	Smallest Loan:							

Figure 4-3 The C4SAILS1.XLS workbook

Shabir listed the boats in column A and the loan amounts in column B; for example, the Beneteau 51-foot sailboat was purchased with a $130,000 loan. Shabir entered the annual interest rate for each loan in column C and formatted this column to display percents. Column D contains the number of monthly payments required to pay off the loan. The loans are payable in 3 years (36 months), 5 years (60 months), 10 years (120 months), or 15 years (180 months). Although columns E through H do not contain data yet, Shabir typed the titles for these columns and selected appropriate formats.

Now that you have had an opportunity to study what Shabir has done so far, let's save the workbook under a different name, so your changes will not alter the original file.

To save the workbook under a different filename:

1. Click **File**, then click **Save As...** to display the Save As dialog box.
2. Type **S4SAILS1** in either uppercase or lowercase.
3. Click the **OK button** to save the workbook under the new filename on your Student Disk. Notice that the new workbook filename, S4SAILS1.XLS, appears in the title bar.

TROUBLE? If you see the message "Replace existing C4SAILS1.XLS?" click the Cancel button and make sure you entered S4SAILS1 as the filename. If you see the message "Replace existing S4SAILS1.XLS?" click the OK button to replace the old version of S4SAILS1.XLS with your current version.

Shabir plans to use several Excel functions to simplify the formulas for the loan management worksheet. He researches the functions in the *Microsoft Excel On-line Help* and the *Microsoft Excel Users Guide*. The next section includes information summarized from this reference manual.

Excel Functions

Excel provides many functions that help you enter formulas for calculations and other specialized tasks, even if you don't know the mathematical details of the calculation. As you learned in Tutorial 1, a function is a calculation tool that performs a predefined operation. You are already familiar with the SUM function, which adds the values in a range of cells. Excel provides hundreds of functions, including a function to calculate the average of a list of numbers, a function to find the square root of a number, a function to calculate loan payments, and a function to calculate the number of days between two dates. The functions are organized into the categories shown in Figure 4-4.

Function Category	Examples of Functions in this Category
Financial	Calculate loan payments, depreciation, interest rate, internal rate of return
Date & Time	Display today's date and/or time; calculate the number of days between two dates
Math & Trig	Round off numbers; calculate sums, logs, and least common multiple; generate random numbers
Statistical	Calculate average, standard deviation, and frequencies; find minimum, maximum; count how many numbers are in a list
Lookup & Reference	Look for a value in a range of cells; find the row or column location of a reference
Database	Perform crosstabs, averages, counts, and standard deviation for an Excel database
Text	Convert numbers to text; compare two text entries; find the length of a text entry
Logical	Perform conditional calculations
Engineering	Convert binary to hexadecimal and binary to decimal; calculate Bessel function

Figure 4-4
Excel function categories

Each function has a **syntax**, which tells you the order in which you must type the parts of the function, and where to put commas, parentheses, and other punctuation. The general syntax of an Excel function is:

NAME*(argument1, argument2,...)*

The syntax of most functions requires you to type the function name followed by one or more arguments in parentheses. Function arguments specify the values that Excel must use in the calculation, or the cell references that Excel must include in the calculation. For example, in the function SUM(A1:A20) the function name is SUM and the argument is A1:A20.

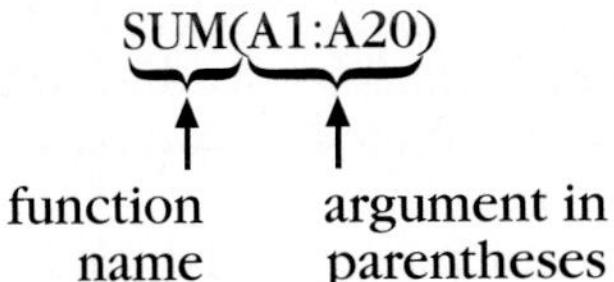

You can use a function in a simple formula such as =SUM(A1:A20), or a more complex formula such as =SUM(A1:A20)*26. As with all formulas, you enter the formula that contains a function in the cell where you want to display the results. The easiest way to enter functions in a cell is to use the Function Wizard, which asks you for the arguments and then enters the function for you.

REFERENCE WINDOW

Using the Function Wizard

- Click the cell where you want to display the results of the function. Then click the Function Wizard button to open the Function Wizard - Step 1 of 2 dialog box.
- Click the type of function you want in the Function Category box. (This will narrow the possibilities in the Function Name box.)
- Click the function you want in the Function Name box.
- Click the Next button to move on to the Step 2 of 2 box.
- Enter values for each argument in the function either by typing in the appropriate cell addresses or by using the mouse to click the appropriate cells.
- Press [Enter] (or click the Finish button) to close the dialog box and display the results of the function in the cell.

If you prefer, you can type the function directly in the cell. Although the function name is always shown in uppercase, you can type it in either uppercase or lowercase. Also, even though the arguments are enclosed in parentheses, you do not have to type the closing parenthesis if the function is at the end of the formula. Excel automatically adds the closing parenthesis when you press the Enter key to complete the formula.

REFERENCE WINDOW

Typing Functions Directly in a Cell

- Click the cell where you want to display the result of the formula.
- Type = to begin the formula.
- Type the function name in either uppercase or lowercase.
- Type (, an opening parenthesis.
- Enter the appropriate arguments using the keyboard or mouse.
- When the arguments are complete, press [Enter]. Excel enters the closing parenthesis and displays the results of the function in the cell.

Shabir consults his plan and decides that he wants to enter a formula to find the largest loan amount. To do this, he uses the MAX function.

The MAX Function

MAX is a statistical function that finds the largest number. The syntax of the MAX function is:

MAX(*number1,number2,...*)

In the MAX function, *number* can be a constant number such as 345, a cell reference such as B6, or a range of cells such as B5:B16. You can use the MAX function to simply display the largest number or to use the largest number in a calculation.

REFERENCE WINDOW

Using MAX to Display the Largest Number in a Range of Cells

- Click the cell where you want to display the result of the function.
- Click the Function Wizard button, then select the statistical function MAX.

  or

  Type =MAX(to begin the formula.
- Drag the pointer to outline the range of cells in which you want to find the largest number.
- Press [Enter] to complete the function.

Shabir wants to find the largest loan amount in the range of cells from B5 through B16. He wants to display the largest amount in cell B17 next to the label "Largest Loan:."

To use the MAX function to find the largest loan amount:

1. Click cell **B17** to move to the cell where you want to type the formula that uses the MAX function.
2. Type **=MAX(** to begin the formula.
3. Drag the pointer to outline cells B5 through B16, then release the mouse button. See Figure 4-5.

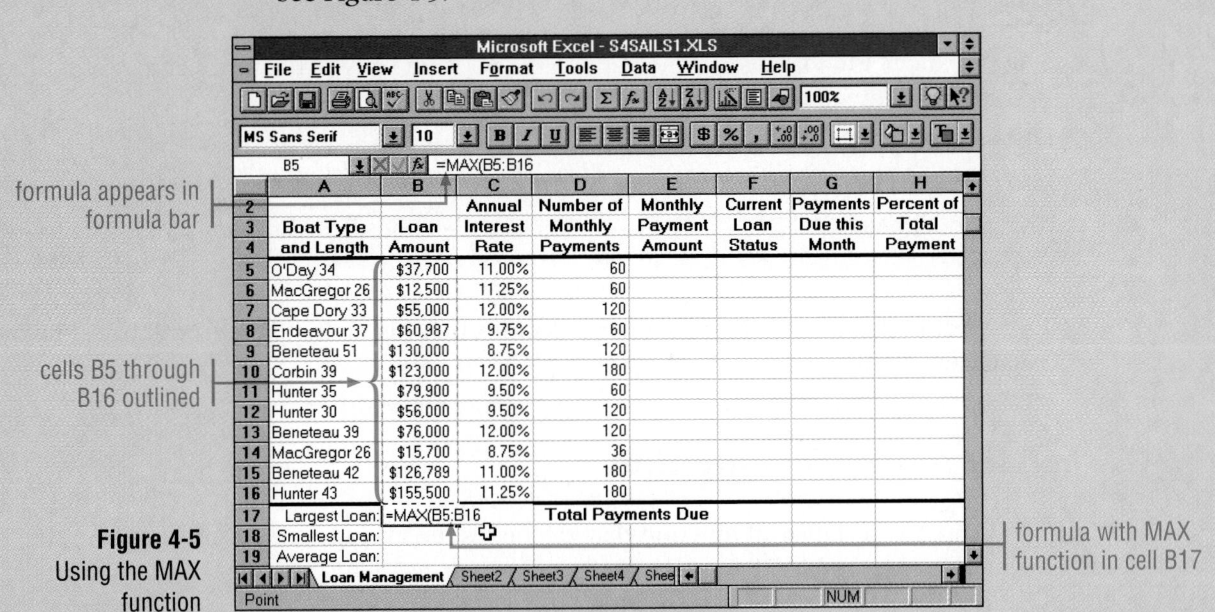

Figure 4-5 Using the MAX function

4. Press **[Enter]**. Excel adds the closing parenthesis to complete the formula. Cell B17 displays $155,500 as the largest loan amount.

Next, Shabir wants to find the smallest loan amount.

The MIN Function

MIN is a statistical function that finds the smallest number. The syntax of the MIN function is:

MIN(*number1,number2,...*)

You can use the MIN function to simply display the smallest number or to use the smallest number in a calculation.

REFERENCE WINDOW

Using MIN to Display the Smallest Number in a Range of Cells

- Click the cell where you want to display the result of the formula.
- Click the Function Wizard button, then select the statistical function MIN.

  or

  Type =MIN(to begin the function.
- Drag the pointer to outline the range of cells in which you want to find the smallest number.
- Press [Enter] to complete the function.

Shabir wants to find the smallest loan amount and display it in cell B18.

To use the MIN function to find the smallest loan amount:

1. Click cell **B18** to move to the cell where you want to type the formula that uses the MIN function.
2. Type **=MIN(** to begin the formula.
3. Drag the pointer to outline cells B5 through B16. Release the mouse button.
4. Press **[Enter]**. Cell B18 displays $12,500 as the smallest loan amount.

Shabir consults his plan again and decides that his next step is to calculate the average loan amount.

The AVERAGE Function

AVERAGE is a statistical function that calculates the average, or the arithmetic mean. The syntax for the AVERAGE function is:

AVERAGE(*number1,number2,...*)

Most of the time when you use the AVERAGE function *number* will be a range of cells. To calculate the average of a range of cells, Excel sums the values in the range, then divides by the number of *non-blank* cells in the range. Figure 4-6 shows the results of using the AVERAGE function on three ranges.

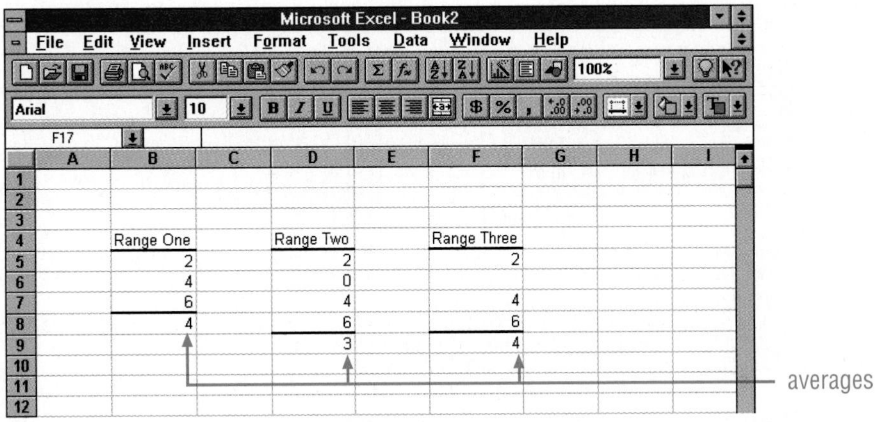

Range One	Range Two	Range Three
2	2	2
4	0	
6	4	4
4	6	6
	3	4

averages

Figure 4-6
How the AVERAGE function handles zeros and blank cells

The first range has no blank cells or cells that contain zeros, so the sum of the numbers, 12, is divided by 3 to find the average. In the second range, the cells with zeros are counted, so the sum, 12, is divided by 4 to find the average. In the third range, the blank cells are not counted, so the sum, 12, is divided by 3 to find the average.

REFERENCE WINDOW

Using AVERAGE to Calculate the Average of the Numbers in a Range of Cells

- Click the cell where you want to display the result of the formula.
- Click the Function Wizard button, then select the statistical function AVERAGE.

  or

  Type =AVERAGE(to begin the function.
- Drag the pointer to outline the range of cells you want to average.
- Press [Enter] to complete the function.

Shabir wants to calculate the average of the boat loans listed in cells B5 through B16, and he wants to display the average in cell B19. Shabir is not certain about the syntax of the AVERAGE function. He decides to use the Function Wizard button because the Function Wizard dialog box shows the syntax for the AVERAGE function. This way Shabir can be sure he uses the correct syntax.

To enter the AVERAGE function into cell B19 using the Function Wizard button:

1. Click cell **B19** to move to the cell where you want to enter the AVERAGE function.
2. Click the **Function Wizard button** to display the Function Wizard - Step 1 of 2 dialog box. See Figure 4-7.

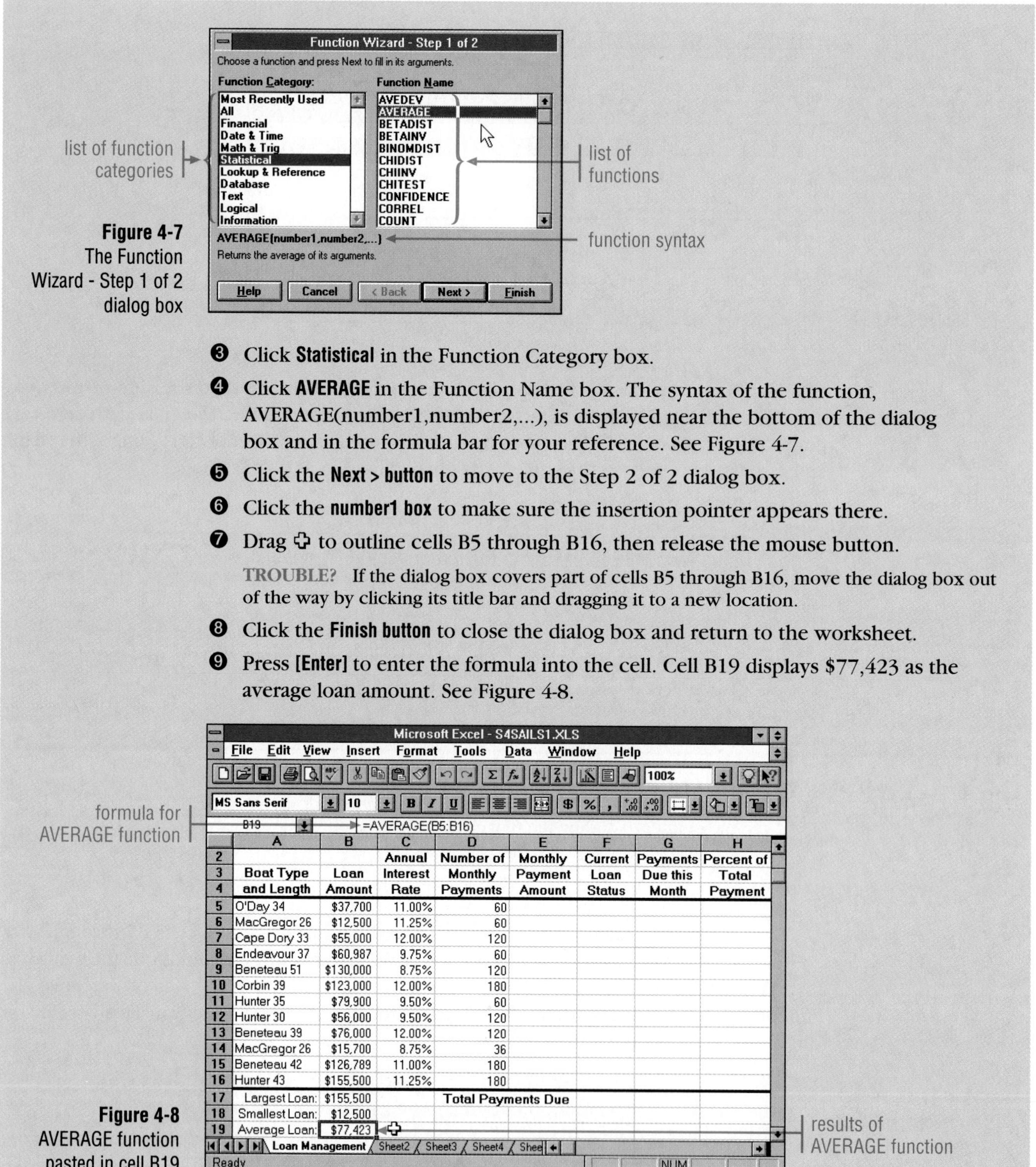

Figure 4-7 The Function Wizard - Step 1 of 2 dialog box

❸ Click **Statistical** in the Function Category box.

❹ Click **AVERAGE** in the Function Name box. The syntax of the function, AVERAGE(number1,number2,...), is displayed near the bottom of the dialog box and in the formula bar for your reference. See Figure 4-7.

❺ Click the **Next > button** to move to the Step 2 of 2 dialog box.

❻ Click the **number1 box** to make sure the insertion pointer appears there.

❼ Drag ✥ to outline cells B5 through B16, then release the mouse button.

TROUBLE? If the dialog box covers part of cells B5 through B16, move the dialog box out of the way by clicking its title bar and dragging it to a new location.

❽ Click the **Finish button** to close the dialog box and return to the worksheet.

❾ Press **[Enter]** to enter the formula into the cell. Cell B19 displays $77,423 as the average loan amount. See Figure 4-8.

	A	B	C	D	E	F	G	H
2			Annual	Number of	Monthly	Current	Payments	Percent of
3	Boat Type	Loan	Interest	Monthly	Payment	Loan	Due this	Total
4	and Length	Amount	Rate	Payments	Amount	Status	Month	Payment
5	O'Day 34	$37,700	11.00%	60				
6	MacGregor 26	$12,500	11.25%	60				
7	Cape Dory 33	$55,000	12.00%	120				
8	Endeavour 37	$60,987	9.75%	60				
9	Beneteau 51	$130,000	8.75%	120				
10	Corbin 39	$123,000	12.00%	180				
11	Hunter 35	$79,900	9.50%	60				
12	Hunter 30	$56,000	9.50%	120				
13	Beneteau 39	$76,000	12.00%	120				
14	MacGregor 26	$15,700	8.75%	36				
15	Beneteau 42	$126,789	11.00%	180				
16	Hunter 43	$155,500	11.25%	180				
17	Largest Loan:	$155,500		Total Payments Due				
18	Smallest Loan:	$12,500						
19	Average Loan:	$77,423						

Figure 4-8 AVERAGE function pasted in cell B19

Next, Shabir consults his plan and decides to create a formula to calculate the monthly payment for each loan.

Calculating Loan Payments with the PMT Function

PMT is a financial function that calculates the periodic payment amount for money borrowed. For example, if you want to borrow $5,000 at 11% interest, you can use the PMT function to find out that your monthly payment would be $108.71 for five years.

The syntax of the PMT function is:

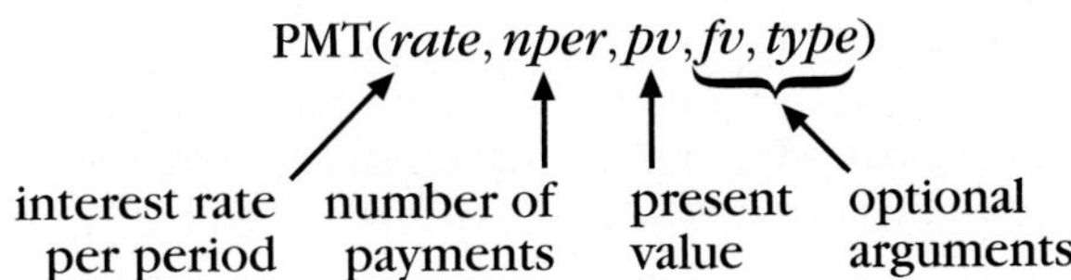

The last two arguments, *fv* and *type*, are optional; Shabir will not include them in the loan management worksheet. You can refer to the *Microsoft Excel On-line Help* if you want information about these two optional arguments.

The *rate* argument is the interest rate per period. Usually interest rates are expressed as annual rates. For example, a 10% interest rate means that if you borrow $1,000 for a year, you must pay back the $1,000 plus $100 interest—that's 10% of 1,000—at the end of the year.

The *nper* argument is the total number of payments required to pay back the loan.

The *pv* argument is the present value; in the case of a loan, this value is the total amount borrowed.

When you enter the arguments for the PMT function, you must be consistent about the units you use for *rate* and *nper*. For example, if you use the number of monthly payments for *nper*, then you must express the interest rate as the percentage per month. Usually, the loan payment period is monthly, but the interest is expressed as an annual rate. If you are repaying the loan in monthly installments, you need to divide the annual interest rate by 12 when you enter the rate as an argument for the PMT function.

To illustrate the PMT function, let's say that you wanted to know the monthly payment for a $5,000 loan at 11% annual interest that you must pay back in 36 months. You would use the PMT function in the formula:

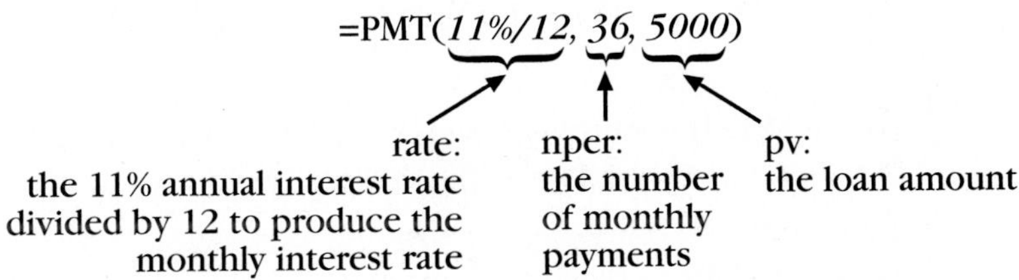

As another example, suppose you wanted to know the monthly payment for a $95,000 30-year loan at 9% (.09) interest. You would use the PMT function in the formula:

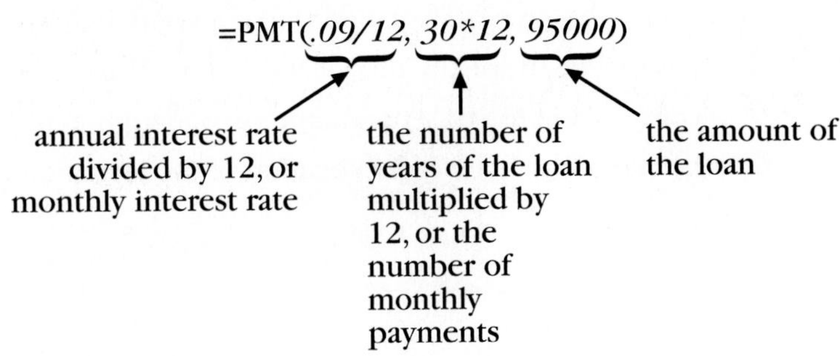

Excel displays the PMT function result as a negative number because you must pay it. Think of this as money that you subtract from your checkbook. If you prefer to display the payment amount as a positive number, place a minus sign in front of the PMT function.

REFERENCE WINDOW

Using PMT to Calculate a Monthly Payment

These directions assume you are typing the function in the cell. Keep in mind that you can also use the Function Wizard button and then enter the arguments in the Step 2 of 2 dialog box.

- Click the cell where you want to display the monthly payment amount.
- Type =PMT(if you want the result displayed as a negative number.

  or

  Type =-PMT(if you want the result displayed as a positive number.
- Type the annual interest rate, type %, then type /12 to divide it by 12 months.
- Type a comma to separate the interest rate from the next argument.
- Type the number of monthly payments that are required to pay back the loan, then type a comma to separate the number of payments from the next argument.
- Type the amount of the loan, then press [Enter].

Instead of typing the arguments, you can click the cells that contain the values you want to use for the arguments.

Shabir wants to display the monthly payment for the O'Day 34 loan in cell E5. The annual interest rate is in cell C5, but it must be divided by 12 to obtain the monthly interest rate. The number of periods is in cell D5, and the loan amount is in cell B5. Let's enter the =PMT(C5/12,D5,B5) formula for the O'Day 34 loan.

To calculate the monthly payment for the O'Day 34 loan:

1. Click cell **E5** to move to the cell where you want to enter the formula for the monthly payment.
2. Type **=PMT(** to begin the formula.
3. Click cell **C5** to specify the location of the annual interest rate.
4. Type **/12** to convert the annual interest rate to the monthly interest rate.
5. Type , (a comma) to separate the first argument from the second.
6. Click cell **D5** to specify the location of the number of payments.
7. Type , (a comma) to separate the second argument from the third.
8. Click cell **B5** to specify the location of the loan amount. See Figure 4-9.

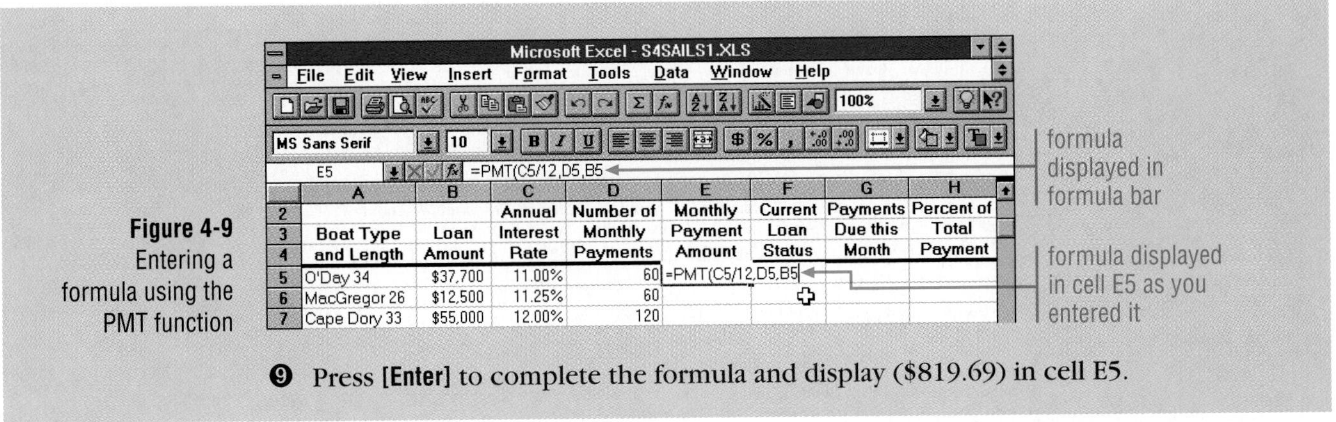

Figure 4-9 Entering a formula using the PMT function

❾ Press **[Enter]** to complete the formula and display ($819.69) in cell E5.

As expected, the PMT function displays the payment as a negative number, in parentheses. (If you are using a color monitor, the number may also appear in red.) Shabir decides to change the formula to display the payment as a positive number. He uses the F2 function key to change the contents of cell E5 to =-PMT(C5/12,D5,B5).

To display the payment as a positive number:

❶ Make sure cell E5 is the active cell.

❷ Press **[F2]** to edit the formula in cell E5.

❸ Press **[Home]** to position the insertion point at the beginning of the formula.

❹ Press [→] to move the insertion point between the equal sign and the "P" in PMT.

❺ Type **–** (a minus sign). The formula is now =-PMT(C5/12,D5,B5).

❻ Press **[Enter]** to complete the edit. Cell E5 displays the positive value $819.69. On a color monitor, the value appears in black.

Shabir tests this formula by comparing the result to a table of loan payment amounts. He finds that the amount in cell E5 on his worksheet is correct. Now that he is confident he has used the PMT function correctly, he can copy the formula in cell E5 to calculate the payments for the rest of the loans.

To copy the PMT formula to cells E6 through E16:

❶ Make sure cell E5 is the active cell.

❷ Position the pointer over the fill handle in the lower-right corner of cell E5 until it changes to +.

❸ Drag the pointer to cell E16, then release the mouse button.

❹ Click any cell to remove the highlighting and view the payment amounts displayed in cells E5 through E16. See Figure 4-10.

TROUBLE? If your formula did not copy to all the cells, repeat Steps 1 through 4.

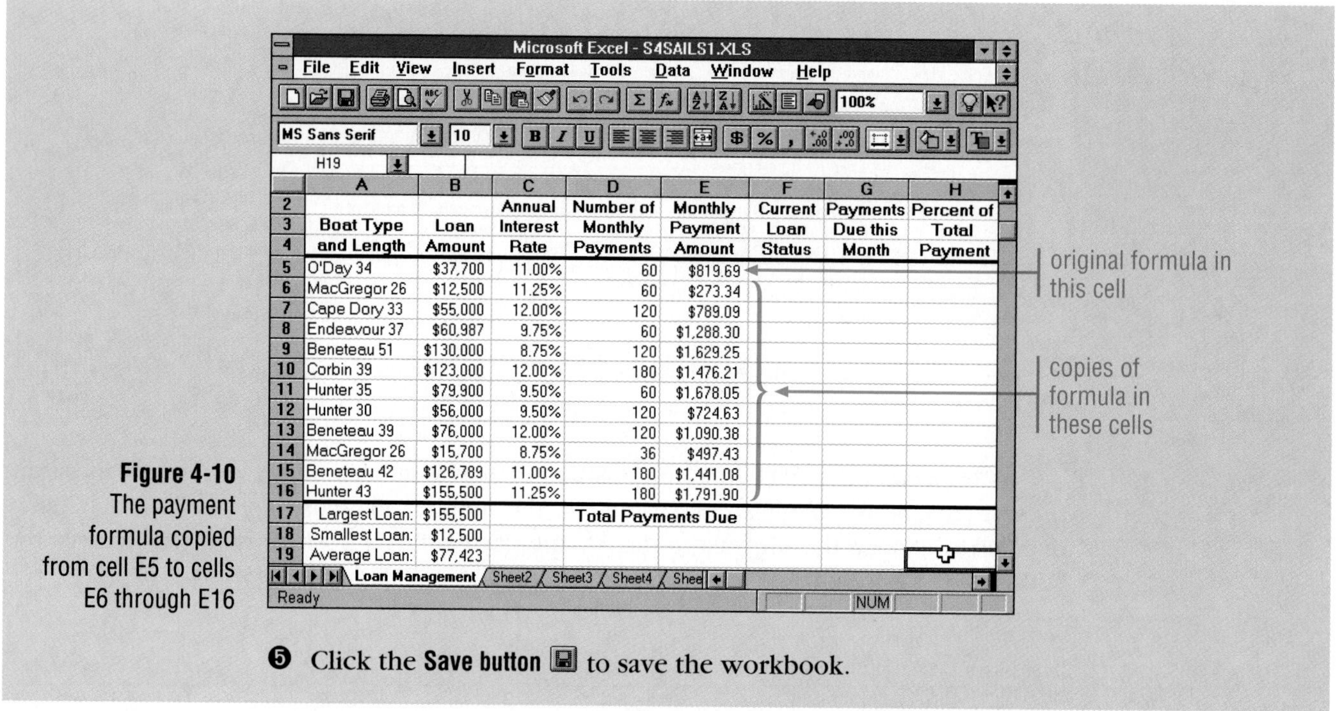

	A	B	C	D	E	F	G	H
2			Annual	Number of	Monthly	Current	Payments	Percent of
3	Boat Type	Loan	Interest	Monthly	Payment	Loan	Due this	Total
4	and Length	Amount	Rate	Payments	Amount	Status	Month	Payment
5	O'Day 34	$37,700	11.00%	60	$819.69			
6	MacGregor 26	$12,500	11.25%	60	$273.34			
7	Cape Dory 33	$55,000	12.00%	120	$789.09			
8	Endeavour 37	$60,987	9.75%	60	$1,288.30			
9	Beneteau 51	$130,000	8.75%	120	$1,629.25			
10	Corbin 39	$123,000	12.00%	180	$1,476.21			
11	Hunter 35	$79,900	9.50%	60	$1,678.05			
12	Hunter 30	$56,000	9.50%	120	$724.63			
13	Beneteau 39	$76,000	12.00%	120	$1,090.38			
14	MacGregor 26	$15,700	8.75%	36	$497.43			
15	Beneteau 42	$126,789	11.00%	180	$1,441.08			
16	Hunter 43	$155,500	11.25%	180	$1,791.90			
17	Largest Loan:	$155,500		Total Payments Due				
18	Smallest Loan:	$12,500						
19	Average Loan:	$77,423						

Figure 4-10 The payment formula copied from cell E5 to cells E6 through E16

❺ Click the **Save button** to save the workbook.

Shabir considers his plan again. James wants a listing of all the boat loans, but he wants a sum of only those payments that he must make this month. He doesn't need to make payments on boat loans that he has already paid off; therefore, Shabir realizes that there is no need to sum the values in column E.

If you want to take a break and resume the tutorial at a later time, you can exit Excel by double-clicking the Control menu box in the upper-left corner of the screen. When you resume the tutorial, launch Excel, maximize the Microsoft Excel and Book1 windows, and place your Student Disk in the disk drive. Open the file S4SAILS1.XLS, then continue with the tutorial.

■ ■ ■

Shabir looks at the loan paperwork and finds that the O'Day 34, the Endeavour 37, and the Beneteau 51 loans have been paid in full. Shabir's plan is to type the word "Paid" in column F if a boat loan has been paid off.

To enter the current loan status:

❶ Click cell **F5** because this is where you want to enter "Paid" for the O'Day 34.

❷ Type **Paid** and press **[Enter]**.

❸ Click cell **F8** because this is where you want to enter the status of the Endeavour 37.

❹ Type **Paid** and press **[Enter]**.

❺ If necessary, click cell **F9** because this is where you want to enter the status of the Beneteau 51.

❻ Type **Paid** and press **[Enter]**.

Next, Shabir wants to display the payment amounts for the loans that are not paid. To do this he uses the IF function in column G, which shows the payments due this month.

The IF Function

There are times when the value you store or display in a cell depends on certain conditions. The **IF function** provides you with a way to specify the if-then-else logic required to calculate or display information based on one or more conditions.

An example of an if-then-else condition in Shabir's worksheet is: *if* the loan status is paid, *then* place a zero in the payment due column, otherwise (*else*) display the monthly payment amount in the payment due column (Figure 4-11).

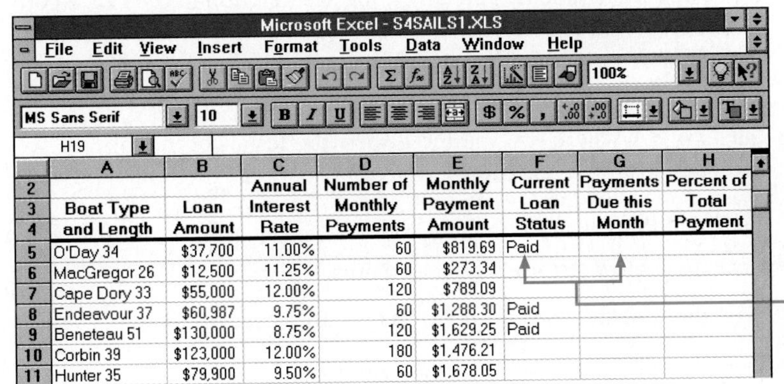

Microsoft Excel - S4SAILS1.XLS

	A	B	C	D	E	F	G	H
2–4	Boat Type and Length	Loan Amount	Annual Interest Rate	Number of Monthly Payments	Monthly Payment Amount	Current Loan Status	Payments Due this Month	Percent of Total Payment
5	O'Day 34	$37,700	11.00%	60	$819.69	Paid		
6	MacGregor 26	$12,500	11.25%	60	$273.34			
7	Cape Dory 33	$55,000	12.00%	120	$789.09			
8	Endeavour 37	$60,987	9.75%	60	$1,288.30	Paid		
9	Beneteau 51	$130,000	8.75%	120	$1,629.25	Paid		
10	Corbin 39	$123,000	12.00%	180	$1,476.21			
11	Hunter 35	$79,900	9.50%	60	$1,678.05			

if cell F5 contains Paid, put zero in cell G5, else display the monthly payment amount in cell G5

Figure 4-11
The conditions for displaying payments due this month

The syntax of the IF function is:

IF (*logical test*, *value if true*, *value if false*)

- *logical test*: Excel evaluates this expression to determine if it is true or false
- *value if true*: if the logical test is true, Excel uses this expression and displays the result
- *value if false*: if the logical test is false, Excel uses this expression and displays the result

The *logical test* is any value or expression that Excel evaluates as true or false. For example, Excel evaluates the expression 2=2 as true when you use it for a logical test. Excel evaluates the expression 2=1 as false. Most expressions you use for logical tests will contain numbers or cell references separated by one of the comparison operators shown in Figure 4-12.

Type of Comparison	Comparison Operator Symbol
less than	<
greater than	>
less than or equal to	<=
greater than or equal to	>=
equal to	=
not equal to	<>

Figure 4-12
Comparison operators

Some examples of expressions are 2>3, B5=C3, and B8<=0. An expression can also include text. Note that you must put quotation marks around any text that you use in the IF function.

The *value if true* argument specifies what to display in the cell if the expression for the logical test is true.

The *value if false* argument specifies what to display in the cell if the expression for the logical test is false.

REFERENCE WINDOW

Using the IF Function to Specify the Conditions

- These directions assume you are typing the function in the cell. Keep in mind that you can also use the Function Wizard button to select the logical function IF, then enter the arguments in the Step 2 of 2 dialog box.
- Click the cell where you want to display the results of the formula that contains the IF function.
- Type =IF(to begin the formula.
- Type the *logical test*, then type a comma.
- Type the specifications for *value if true*, then type a comma.
- Type the specifications for *value if false*.
- Press [Enter] to complete the formula.

Suppose you want Excel to display a warning message if the loan amount in cell B5 is greater than $150,000. You can use the formula:

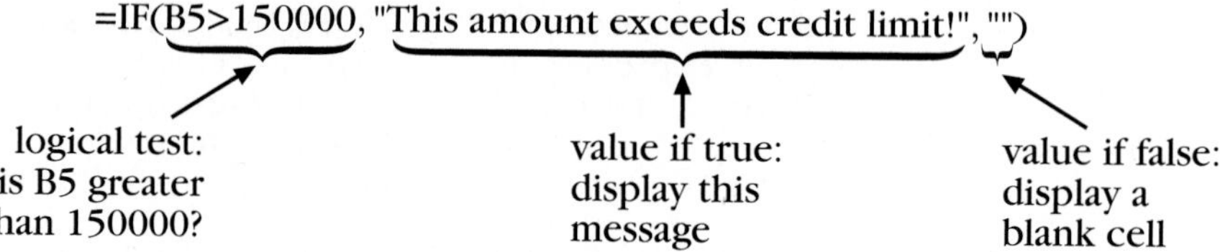

Notice the quotation marks around the text that contain the credit limit message and the quotation marks without any text, which will leave the cell blank. When you use text as an argument for the IF function, you *must* enclose it in quotation marks.

As another example, suppose you want to add a $100 bonus to the salary of any salesperson who sells more than $10,000 of merchandise. Look at Figure 4-13. The amount of merchandise sold by Sergio Armanti is in cell B9. Sergio's base salary is in cell C9.

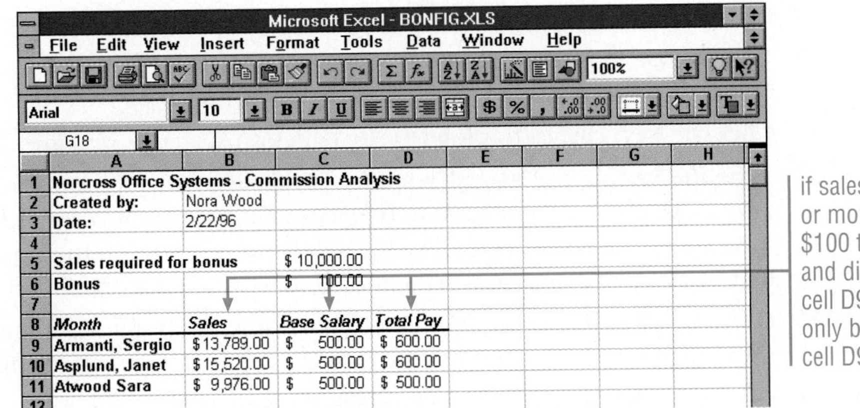

	A	B	C	D
1	Norcross Office Systems - Commission Analysis			
2	Created by:	Nora Wood		
3	Date:	2/22/96		
4				
5	Sales required for bonus		$ 10,000.00	
6	Bonus		$ 100.00	
7				
8	*Month*	*Sales*	*Base Salary*	*Total Pay*
9	Armanti, Sergio	$13,789.00	$ 500.00	$ 600.00
10	Asplund, Janet	$15,520.00	$ 500.00	$ 600.00
11	Atwood Sara	$ 9,976.00	$ 500.00	$ 500.00
12				

Microsoft Excel - BONFIG.XLS
File Edit View Insert Format Tools Data Window Help
Arial
10
100%
G18
if sales are $10,000 or more, then add $100 to base salary and display result in cell D9, else display only base salary in cell D9

Figure 4-13 Conditions for awarding a bonus to Sergio Armanti

To calculate Sergio's total pay, including the bonus if he earned it, you would enter the formula =IF(B9>=10000,C9+100,C9) in cell D9. In this case if the amount sold in cell B9 is at least $10,000, Excel would add $100 to the base salary and display it in cell D9. If the amount sold in cell B9 is less than $10,000, Excel will display the base salary in cell D9.

Unlike the previous example that displayed text, the arguments for the IF function that calculates Sergio's bonus are all numeric, so you would not use quotation marks.

Now let's consider the formula Shabir needs to use. In cell G5 he wants to display the amount of the payment that is due. The conditions for this situation are: if the current loan status is "Paid," then put a zero in the payments due column, otherwise, put the monthly payment amount in the payments due column. Shabir's formula will be:

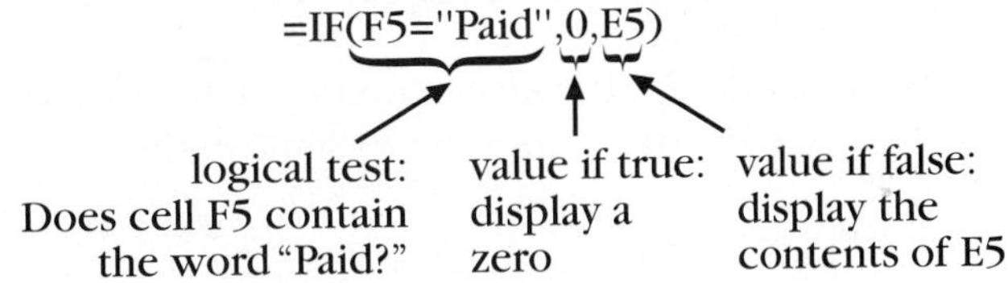

=IF(F5="Paid",0,E5)
logical test: Does cell F5 contain the word "Paid?"
value if true: display a zero
value if false: display the contents of E5

If this formula works, Shabir expects to see a zero in cell G5 because the O'Day 34 loan is paid off. Let's see if the formula produces the results he expects. This time Shabir will use the Function Wizard button in the formula bar (instead of the Function Wizard button in the tool bar) to enter the formula.

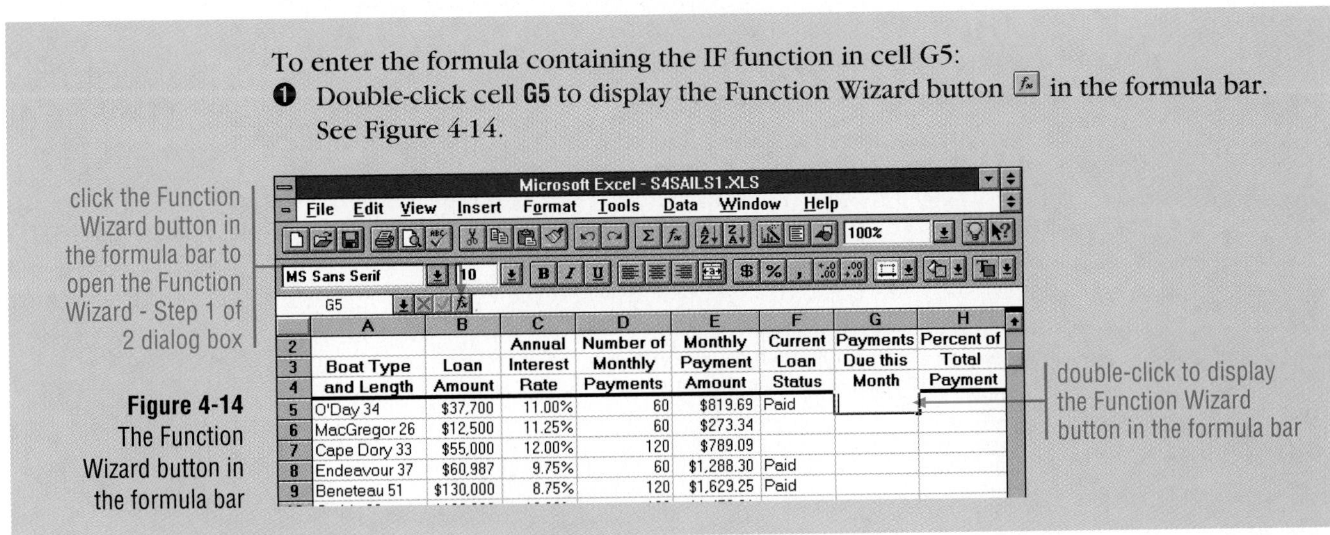

To enter the formula containing the IF function in cell G5:

1. Double-click cell **G5** to display the Function Wizard button in the formula bar. See Figure 4-14.

	A	B	C	D	E	F	G	H
2			Annual	Number of	Monthly	Current	Payments	Percent of
3	Boat Type	Loan	Interest	Monthly	Payment	Loan	Due this	Total
4	and Length	Amount	Rate	Payments	Amount	Status	Month	Payment
5	O'Day 34	$37,700	11.00%	60	$819.69	Paid		
6	MacGregor 26	$12,500	11.25%	60	$273.34			
7	Cape Dory 33	$55,000	12.00%	120	$789.09			
8	Endeavour 37	$60,987	9.75%	60	$1,288.30	Paid		
9	Beneteau 51	$130,000	8.75%	120	$1,629.25	Paid		

Microsoft Excel - S4SAILS1.XLS
File Edit View Insert Format Tools Data Window Help
MS Sans Serif
10
100%
G5
click the Function Wizard button in the formula bar to open the Function Wizard - Step 1 of 2 dialog box
double-click to display the Function Wizard button in the formula bar

Figure 4-14 The Function Wizard button in the formula bar

2. Click the **Function Wizard button** to open the Function Wizard - Step 1 of 2 dialog box.
3. Click **Logical** in the Function Category box, then click **IF** in the Function Name box. Notice the function syntax displayed in the formula bar.
4. Click the **Next > button** to move to the Function Wizard - Step 2 of 2 dialog box.
5. Type **F5="Paid"** in the logical_test box. Make sure you type the quotation marks. (Notice that you do not have to type commas to separate arguments when using the Function Wizard dialog box.) Excel displays "True" in the box next to the logical_test box because cell F5 *does* contain the entry "Paid."
6. Click the **value_if_true box** and type **0**. Make sure you type the number zero, and not the capital letter "O." The box next to the value_if_true box displays "0."
7. Click the **value_if_false box** and type **E5**. The box next to the value_if_false box displays "819.6893498," which is the value in cell E5 displayed without formatting. See Figure 4-15.

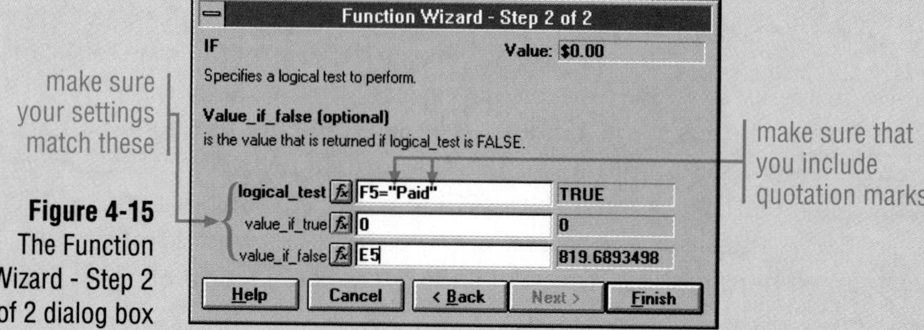

Figure 4-15 The Function Wizard - Step 2 of 2 dialog box

8. Click the **Finish button** to complete the formula and return to the worksheet. Then press **[Enter]** to enter the formula in the cell. Watch as $0.00 displays in cell G5.

   TROUBLE? If you see the error message #NAME? in cell G5, look carefully at the formula displayed in the formula bar to see if you included the quotation marks around "Paid." Use the F2 key to edit the formula.

The formula produced the expected results, so Shabir decides to copy the formula to cells G6 through G16.

To copy the If formula to cells G6 through G16:

1. Make sure that G5 is the active cell because it contains the formula you want to copy.
2. Move the pointer over the fill handle until it turns into +.
3. Drag the pointer to cell G16, then release the mouse button.
4. Click any cell to remove the highlighting and view the results displayed in cells G5 through G16. See Figure 4-16.

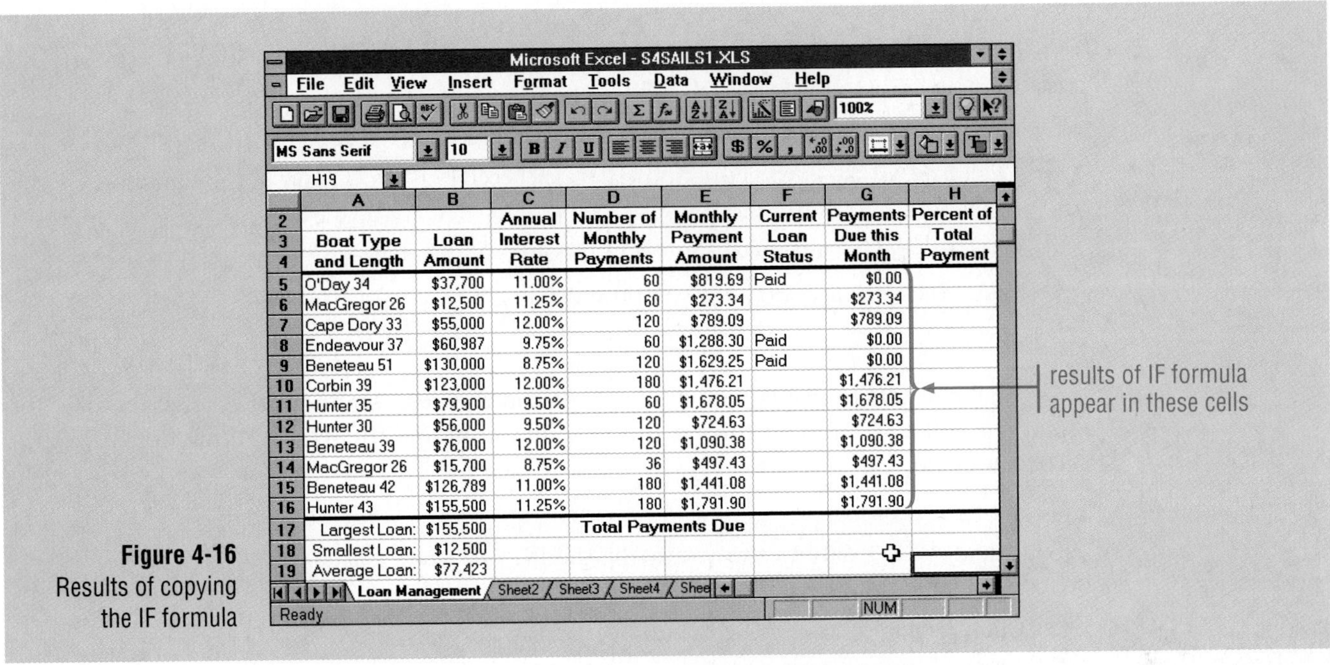

Figure 4-16
Results of copying the IF formula

Shabir carefully checks the results of the IF formulas in cells G5 through G16. He sees that the formulas produced zeros in cells G5, G8, and G9 because the loans for those boats are paid. In the other cells the IF formulas have correctly placed the same value as that displayed in column E. Shabir is satisfied that the formulas in column G are correct.

James wants a total of the payments due, so Shabir needs to sum the payments in column G. He plans to display the sum in cell G17.

To sum the payments due this month:

1. Click cell **G17** to move to the cell where you want to display the sum.
2. Click the **AutoSum button** Σ.
3. Make sure cells G5 through G16 are outlined.
4. Press **[Enter]**. The amount $9,762.10 is displayed in cell G17.

Now Shabir looks at the label for the total payments. He wants the label to indicate the month and year for which the payment is calculated. He can use Excel's TODAY function to display the date.

Displaying and Formatting the Date with the TODAY Function

The **TODAY function** reads the computer system clock and displays the current date in the cell that contains the TODAY function. The syntax of the TODAY function is:

TODAY( )

The empty parentheses indicate that no arguments are required for this function. You enter the function by typing only "TODAY( )." As an alternative to typing the TODAY function, you can use the Function Wizard dialog box. Shabir wants the date displayed in cell F17.

To enter the TODAY function in cell F17:

1. Click cell **F17** to move to the cell where you want to enter the function.
2. Click the **Function Wizard button** to open the Function Wizard - Step 1 of 2 dialog box.
3. Click **Date & Time** in the Function Category box, then click **Today** in the Function Name box.
4. Click the **Next > button** to move on to the Step 2 of 2 dialog box.
5. Press **[Enter]** to display the date in the cell.

Shabir wants to display only the month and the year, so he must change the date format for cell F17. He can format the cell that contains the TODAY function using the Format menu.

To format today's date to show only the month and year:

1. Make sure cell F17 is the active cell.
2. Click **Format**, then click **Cells...** to display the Format Cells dialog box.
3. Click the **Number tab**.
4. Click **Date** in the Category box.
5. Click **mmm-yy** in the Format Codes box to select the month-year format for the date.
6. Click the **OK button** to display the new date format.

The date doesn't look quite right. Shabir thinks it should be bold and aligned on the left side of the cell.

To bold the date and align it on the left side of the cell:

1. Make sure cell F17 is the active cell.
2. Click the **Bold button** on the toolbar.
3. Click the **Align Left button** on the toolbar. See Figure 4-17.

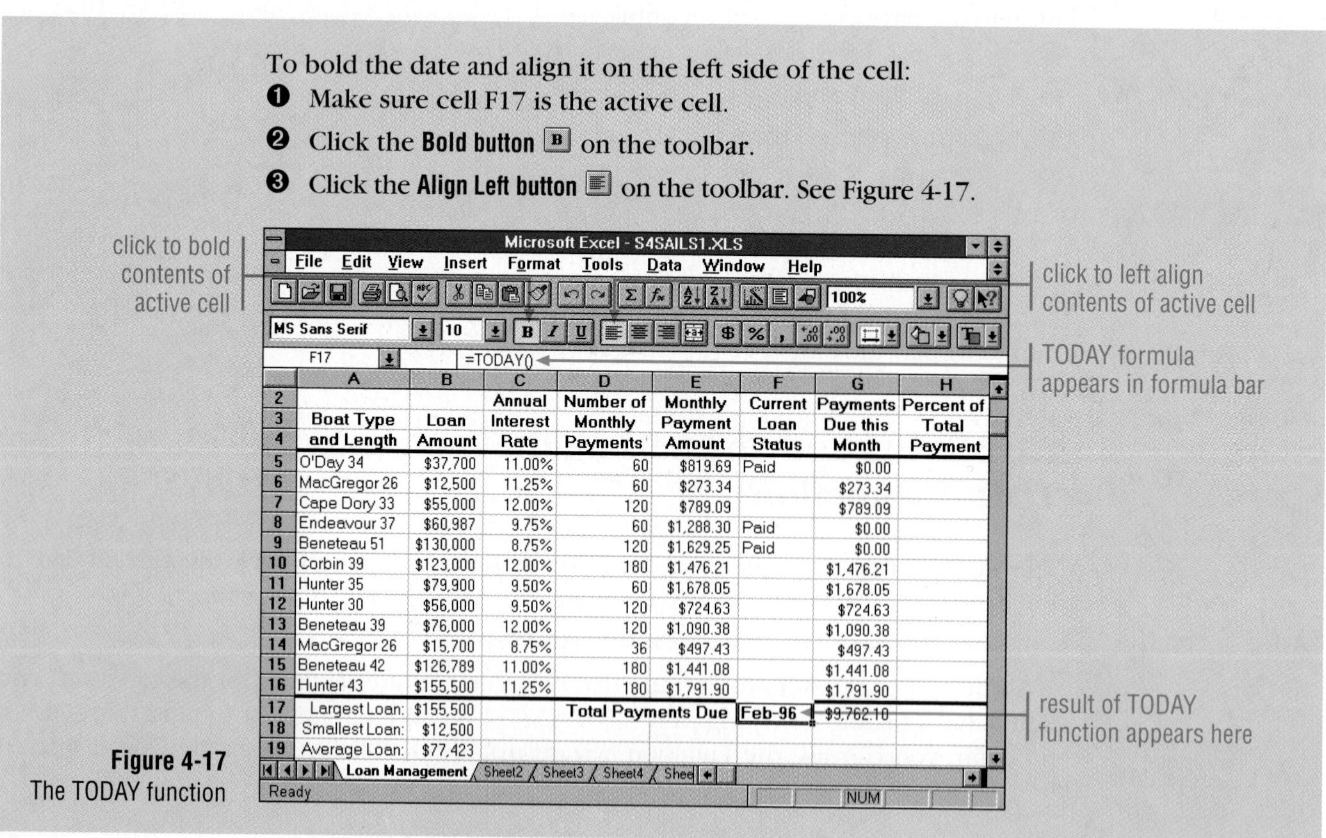

	A	B	C	D	E	F	G	H
2			Annual	Number of	Monthly	Current	Payments	Percent of
3	Boat Type	Loan	Interest	Monthly	Payment	Loan	Due this	Total
4	and Length	Amount	Rate	Payments	Amount	Status	Month	Payment
5	O'Day 34	$37,700	11.00%	60	$819.69	Paid	$0.00	
6	MacGregor 26	$12,500	11.25%	60	$273.34		$273.34	
7	Cape Dory 33	$55,000	12.00%	120	$789.09		$789.09	
8	Endeavour 37	$60,987	9.75%	60	$1,288.30	Paid	$0.00	
9	Beneteau 51	$130,000	8.75%	120	$1,629.25	Paid	$0.00	
10	Corbin 39	$123,000	12.00%	180	$1,476.21		$1,476.21	
11	Hunter 35	$79,900	9.50%	60	$1,678.05		$1,678.05	
12	Hunter 30	$56,000	9.50%	120	$724.63		$724.63	
13	Beneteau 39	$76,000	12.00%	120	$1,090.38		$1,090.38	
14	MacGregor 26	$15,700	8.75%	36	$497.43		$497.43	
15	Beneteau 42	$126,789	11.00%	180	$1,441.08		$1,441.08	
16	Hunter 43	$155,500	11.25%	180	$1,791.90		$1,791.90	
17	Largest Loan:	$155,500		Total Payments Due		Feb-96	$9,762.10	
18	Smallest Loan:	$12,500						
19	Average Loan:	$77,423						

Figure 4-17
The TODAY function

Now Shabir consults his worksheet sketch and sees that he has only one column left to complete the worksheet. He wants column H to display the percent of the total payment that each individual loan payment represents. For example, if the total of all the loan payments is $10,000 and the O'Day payment is $1,000, the O'Day payment is 10% of the total payment. To do this calculation Shabir needs to divide each payment by the total payment, as shown in the equation:

percent of total payment = payment due this month / total payments due

Shabir decides to enter the formula =G5/G17 in cell H5.

To enter the formula to calculate the percent of total payment in cell H5:

1. Click cell **H5** to move to the cell where you want to enter the formula.
2. Type **=G5/G17** and press **[Enter]** to complete the formula and display 0.00% in cell H5.

Cell H5 seems to display the correct result. James is paying $0 for the O'Day loan, which is 0% of the $9,762.10 total. Next, Shabir decides to copy the formula to cells H6 through H16.

To copy the percent formula to cells H6 through H16:

1. Make H5 the active cell. Then move the pointer over the fill handle in cell H5 until it changes to +.
2. Drag the pointer to cell H16. Release the mouse button.
3. Click any blank cell to remove the highlighting and view the message #DIV/0! displayed in cells H6 through H16.

Shabir knows something is wrong. Cells H6 through H16 display #DIV/0!, a message that means Excel was instructed to divide by zero, which is not possible. Shabir examines the formulas he copied into cells H6 through H16.

To examine the formulas in cells H6 through H16:

1. Click cell **H6** and look at the formula displayed in the formula bar. The first relative reference changed from G5 in the original formula to G6 in the copied formula. That's correct because the loan amount for row 6 is in cell G6. The second reference changed from G17 in the original formula to G18, which is not correct. This formula should be =G6/G17 because the total of the payments is in cell G17.
2. Look at the formulas in cells H7 through H16 and see how the relative references changed in each.

For a moment, Shabir is puzzled about the results, but then he remembers about relative and absolute references. Shabir realizes he should have used an absolute reference instead of a relative reference for cell G17 in the percent of total payment formula.

Absolute References

Sometimes when you copy a formula, you don't want Excel to automatically change all the cell references to reflect their new position in the worksheet. If you want a cell reference to point to the same location in the worksheet even when you copy it, you must use an absolute reference. An **absolute reference** is the row and column location of a cell that must not change if it is copied to other cells.

The reference to cell $G$17 is an absolute reference, whereas the reference to cell G17 is a relative reference. If you copy a formula that contains the absolute reference $G$17, the reference to $G$17 will not change. On the other hand, if you copy a formula containing the relative reference G17, the reference to G17 could change to G18, G19, G20 and so forth as it is copied to other cells.

To include an absolute reference in a formula, you can type the dollar sign when you type the cell reference, or you can use the F4 key to change the cell reference type. You can always edit a formula that contains the wrong cell reference type.

REFERENCE WINDOW

Editing Cell Reference Types

- Click the cell that contains the formula you want to edit.
- Press [F2] to begin editing in the formula bar.
- Use the arrow keys to move the insertion point to the cell reference you want to change.
- Press [F4] until the reference is correct.
- Press [Enter] to complete the edit.

Shabir used the wrong cell reference type when he entered the formula in cell H5. He should have used an absolute reference, instead of a relative reference, to indicate the location of the total payments. Now he must change the reference G17 to $G$17.

To change the formula in cell H5 from =G5/G17 to =G5/$G$17:

1. Click cell **H5** to move to the cell that contains the formula you want to edit.
2. Double-click the mouse button to edit the formula in the cell.
3. Make sure the insertion point is just to the right of the reference G17. See Figure 4-18.

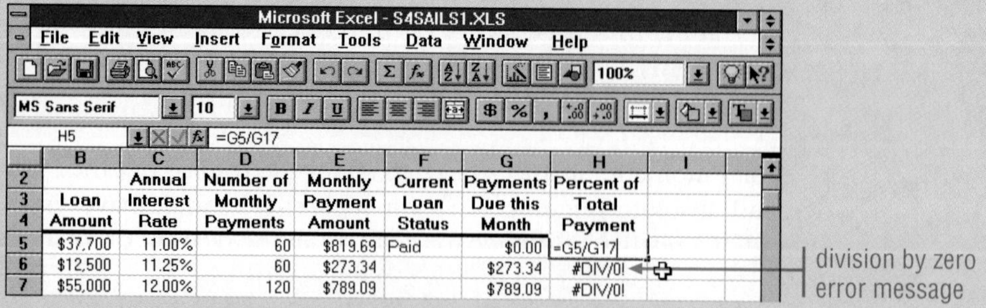

Figure 4-18 Error messages produced by copying the formula from cell H5

Microsoft Excel - S4SAILS1.XLS

File Edit View Insert Format Tools Data Window Help

H5 =G5/G17

	B	C	D	E	F	G	H
2		Annual	Number of	Monthly	Current	Payments	Percent of
3	Loan	Interest	Monthly	Payment	Loan	Due this	Total
4	Amount	Rate	Payments	Amount	Status	Month	Payment
5	$37,700	11.00%	60	$819.69	Paid	$0.00	=G5/G17
6	$12,500	11.25%	60	$273.34		$273.34	#DIV/0!
7	$55,000	12.00%	120	$789.09		$789.09	#DIV/0!

division by zero error message

4. Press **[F4]** to change the reference to $G$17.
5. Press **[Enter]** to update the formula in cell H5.

Cell H5 still displays 0.00% as the result of the formula, which is correct, but the problem in Shabir's original formula did not surface until he copied it to cells H6 through H16. He copies the revised formula and checks to see if it produces the correct results.

To copy the revised formula from cell H5 to cells H6 through H16:

1. Make sure cell H5 is the active cell, because it contains the revised formula that you want to copy.
2. Move the pointer to the fill handle until it changes to +.
3. Drag the pointer to cell H16, then release the mouse button.
4. Click any cell to remove the highlighting and view the results of the formula. See Figure 4-19.

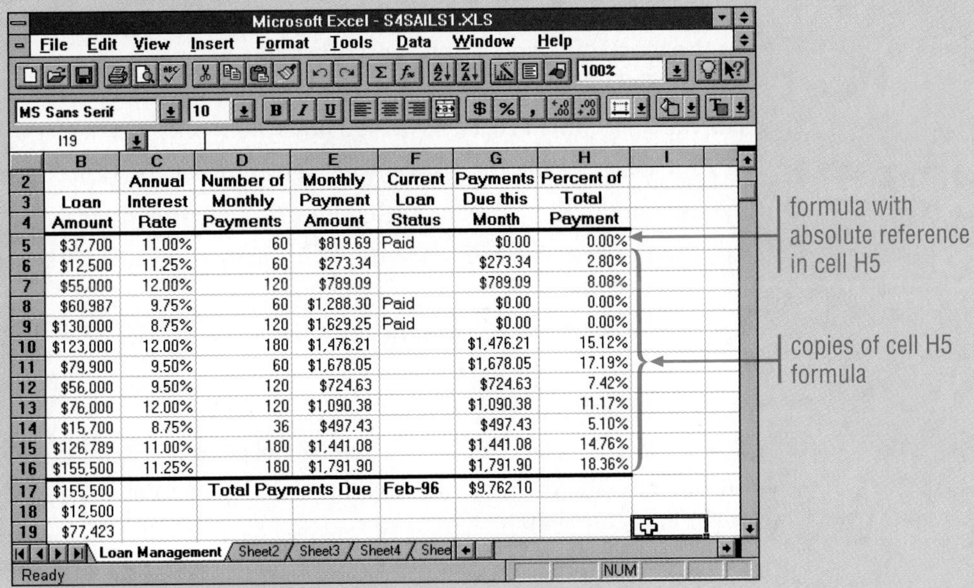

	B	C	D	E	F	G	H
2		Annual	Number of	Monthly	Current	Payments	Percent of
3	Loan	Interest	Monthly	Payment	Loan	Due this	Total
4	Amount	Rate	Payments	Amount	Status	Month	Payment
5	$37,700	11.00%	60	$819.69	Paid	$0.00	0.00%
6	$12,500	11.25%	60	$273.34		$273.34	2.80%
7	$55,000	12.00%	120	$789.09		$789.09	8.08%
8	$60,987	9.75%	60	$1,288.30	Paid	$0.00	0.00%
9	$130,000	8.75%	120	$1,629.25	Paid	$0.00	0.00%
10	$123,000	12.00%	180	$1,476.21		$1,476.21	15.12%
11	$79,900	9.50%	60	$1,678.05		$1,678.05	17.19%
12	$56,000	9.50%	120	$724.63		$724.63	7.42%
13	$76,000	12.00%	120	$1,090.38		$1,090.38	11.17%
14	$15,700	8.75%	36	$497.43		$497.43	5.10%
15	$126,789	11.00%	180	$1,441.08		$1,441.08	14.76%
16	$155,500	11.25%	180	$1,791.90		$1,791.90	18.36%
17	$155,500		Total Payments Due		Feb-96	$9,762.10	
18	$12,500						
19	$77,423						

Figure 4-19 The results of copying the formula with an absolute reference

The revised formula works correctly and Shabir is pleased.

Shabir is just about to close the worksheet when James stops in the office. Shabir shows him the worksheet. James thinks the worksheet looks great, but notices that the MacGregor 26 loan in row 6 should be marked "Paid" because he just made the last payment a month ago. Shabir says it is easy to make the change and explains that the worksheet will recalculate the amount for the total payments due this month.

To change the loan status of the MacGregor 26:

1. Click cell **F6** to make it the active cell.
2. Type **Paid** and watch cell G17 as you press **[Enter]**.

As a result of changing the loan status, the amount in cell G6 changes to $0.00, the total payments due in cell G17 changes to $9,488.76, and Excel recalculates the percentages in column H. James is impressed. Now Shabir can save the workbook and then print the worksheet.

He wants to print the worksheet in landscape orientation, center it from left to right on the page, center it from top to bottom on the page, omit the row/column headings, and omit the cell gridlines.

To save the workbook and print the worksheet:

1. Click the **Save button**.
2. Click the **Print Preview button** to see how the worksheet will look when you print it.
3. Click the **Setup... button** to display the Page Setup dialog box. Then click the **Page tab**.
4. If landscape orientation is not selected, click the **Landscape button**.
5. Click the **Margins tab**. Then click the **Horizontally** and **Vertically boxes** to center the worksheet on the page.
6. Click the **Sheet tab**. Make sure the Gridlines box and the Row and Column Headings box are empty.
7. Click the **OK button** to return to the print preview.
8. Click the **Print... button**, then click the **OK button** on the Print dialog box to send the worksheet to the printer. The final printout for the loan management worksheet is shown in Figure 4-20.

Shabir Ahmad 2/7/96 S4SAILS1.XLS

Superior Sails Charter Company - Loan Management Worksheet							
Boat Type and Length	Loan Amount	Annual Interest Rate	Number of Monthly Payments	Monthly Payment Amount	Current Loan Status	Payments Due this Month	Percent of Total Payment
O'Day 34	$37,700	11.00%	60	$819.69	Paid	$0.00	0.00%
MacGregor 26	$12,500	11.25%	60	$273.34	Paid	$0.00	0.00%
Cape Dory 33	$55,000	12.00%	120	$789.09		$789.09	8.32%
Endeavour 37	$60,987	9.75%	60	$1,288.30	Paid	$0.00	0.00%
Beneteau 51	$130,000	8.75%	120	$1,629.25	Paid	$0.00	0.00%
Corbin 39	$123,000	12.00%	180	$1,476.21		$1,476.21	15.56%
Hunter 35	$79,900	9.50%	60	$1,678.05		$1,678.05	17.68%
Hunter 30	$56,000	9.50%	120	$724.63		$724.63	7.64%
Beneteau 39	$76,000	12.00%	120	$1,090.38		$1,090.38	11.49%
MacGregor 26	$15,700	8.75%	36	$497.43		$497.43	5.24%
Beneteau 42	$126,789	11.00%	180	$1,441.08		$1,441.08	15.19%
Hunter 43	$155,500	11.25%	180	$1,791.90		$1,791.90	18.88%
Largest Loan:	$155,500			Total Payments Due	Feb-96	$9,488.76	
Smallest Loan:	$12,500						
Average Loan:	$77,423						

Page 1

Figure 4-20
Printout of loan management worksheet

❾ Save your file once again, so it includes the page setup format you specified.

If you want to take a break and resume the tutorial at a later time, you can exit Excel by double-clicking the Control menu box in the upper-left corner of the screen. When you resume the tutorial, launch Excel, maximize the Microsoft Excel and Book1 windows, and place your Student Disk in the disk drive. Open the file S4SAILS1.XLS, then continue with the tutorial.

■ ■ ■

Next, James wonders how much less his monthly payment would be if he refinanced some of the loans, so that instead of paying 12% interest he would pay 11%. Shabir shows him that this sort of what-if analysis is easy to do.

To change the interest rates and look at the effect on the total payment:

1. Click cell **C7**, which contains one of the 12% interest rates.
2. Type **11%** and press **[Enter]**. The total loan payment in cell G17 changes from $9,488.76 to $9,457.29.
3. Click cell **C10**, which contains another of the 12% interest rates.
4. Type **11%** and press **[Enter]**. The total loan payment in cell G17 changes to $9,379.10.
5. Click cell **C13**, which contains another of the 12% interest rates.
6. Type **11%** and press **[Enter]**. The total loan payment in cell G17 changes to $9,335.62.

James sees that he could save about $150 each month by refinancing the three loans that are at 12% interest. Now he wonders "what if" he bought a West Wight Potter 19 foot for $9,000 at 11% interest.

To add another boat to the list, Shabir must insert a row at the current location of row 17. Then he must copy the formulas to calculate the monthly payment amount, the payments due this month, and the percent of total payment to the new row.

To insert a row for the new boat and copy the necessary formulas:

1. Click cell **A17** because you want to insert a new row at this location.
2. Click **Insert**, click **Rows** to insert a blank row.
3. Highlight cells A16 through H17, then release the mouse button.
4. Click **Edit**, click **Fill**, then click **Down** to duplicate the formulas and data from row 16 to row 17. Click any cell to remove the highlighting and view the results. See Figure 4-21.

formulas and data from row 16 copied to row 17

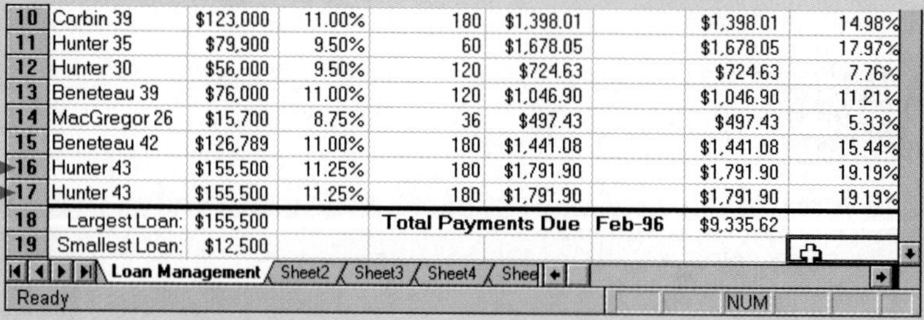

10	Corbin 39	$123,000	11.00%	180	$1,398.01		$1,398.01	14.98%
11	Hunter 35	$79,900	9.50%	60	$1,678.05		$1,678.05	17.97%
12	Hunter 30	$56,000	9.50%	120	$724.63		$724.63	7.76%
13	Beneteau 39	$76,000	11.00%	120	$1,046.90		$1,046.90	11.21%
14	MacGregor 26	$15,700	8.75%	36	$497.43		$497.43	5.33%
15	Beneteau 42	$126,789	11.00%	180	$1,441.08		$1,441.08	15.44%
16	Hunter 43	$155,500	11.25%	180	$1,791.90		$1,791.90	19.19%
17	Hunter 43	$155,500	11.25%	180	$1,791.90		$1,791.90	19.19%
18	Largest Loan:	$155,500		Total Payments Due		Feb-96	$9,335.62	
19	Smallest Loan:	$12,500						

Loan Management / Sheet2 / Sheet3 / Sheet4 / Shee

Ready NUM

Figure 4-21
Duplicating a row

The Fill Down command copied the data, as well as the formulas, to row 17. That does not present a problem because Shabir can easily type over the copied data with the data for the West Wight Potter 19. Now Shabir fills in row 17 with the information for the West Wight Potter.

To change the data in row 17:

❶ Click cell **A17**, type **W W Potter 19** and press [→].

❷ Type **9000** as the loan amount and press [→].

❸ Type **11%** as the interest and press [→].

❹ Type **60** as the number of payments and press **[Enter]**. The monthly payment for this loan, $195.68, is displayed in cell E17.

Shabir and James look at the total payments due in cell G18, and they notice that something is wrong. The amount in this cell did not change to reflect the addition of the West Wight Potter. They look at the formulas in cells G18, B18, B19, and B20 to find out what happened.

To view the contents of cells G18, B18, B19, and B20:

❶ Click cell **G18** to make it the active cell. The formula for this cell appears in the formula bar as =SUM(G5:G16). The formula was not updated to include cell G17.

❷ Click cell **B18** and look at the formula that appears in the formula bar. The formula =MAX(B5:B16) was not updated to include B17.

❸ Click cell **B19** and look at the formula that appears in the formula bar. The formula =MIN(B5:B16) was not updated.

❹ Click cell **B20** and look at the formula that appears in the formula bar. The formula =AVERAGE(B5:B16) was not updated after row 17 was inserted.

It is obvious that these formulas need to be updated to include row 17. Shabir explains to James that if you add a row in the location of any of the current rows in a formula, the formula will update. *However, if you add a row that is not included in a formula, you must manually update the formulas to include the new row.*

The original range in these formulas was B5:B16. Shabir could have inserted a row in the current location of row 10, for example, and the range in the total payment formula would have "stretched" to include cells G5 through G17. But, Shabir inserted row 17, which was not within the original range, so he needs to manually update the formulas in cells G18, B18, B19, and B20.

To update the formulas in cells G18, B18, B19, and B20:

❶ Double-click cell **G18**, which contains the formula you want to change.

❷ Place I at the end of the formula and click. Then press **[Backspace]** twice to delete the 6.

❸ Type **7** and press **[Enter]**.

❹ Repeat Steps 2 through 4 so that the formulas in cells B18, B19, and B20 contain the argument (B5:B17). See Figure 4-22.

14	MacGregor 26	$15,700	8.75%	36	$497.43		$497.43	5.22%
15	Beneteau 42	$126,789	11.00%	180	$1,441.08		$1,441.08	15.12%
16	Hunter 43	$155,500	11.25%	180	$1,791.90		$1,791.90	18.80%
17	WW Potter 19	$9,000	11.00%	60	$195.68		$195.68	2.05%
18	Largest Loan:	$155,500		**Total Payments Due**		**Feb-96**	$9,531.30	
19	Smallest Loan:	$9,000						
20	Average Loan:	$72,160						

Loan Management / Sheet2 / Sheet3 / Sheet4 / Shee

Ready NUM

updated formulas reflect correct values

Figure 4-22
Manually updated formulas

Now Shabir and James can see that the total loan payment would be $9,531.30 with the loan payment for a new West Wight Potter 19. The amount of the largest loan, shown in cell B18, did not change. The smallest loan, shown in cell B19, is now $9,000. The amount shown in cell B20 for the average loan changed from $77,423 to $72,160.

James now understands how important it is to check each formula to make sure it works. Shabir agrees and explains that there are many ways to test a worksheet to verify the accuracy of the results. For example, he can use test data or compare results with known values, such as those in loan payment tables.

James does not want a printout of the what-if analysis, so Shabir closes the workbook without saving it. Because he does not save the current version of the workbook, the version he has on disk will reflect the worksheet before he changed the interest rates from 12% to 11% and added the West Wight Potter.

To close the workbook without saving the what-if analysis:

1. Double-click the **document window Control menu box.**
2. Click the **No button** when you see the message "Save changes in S4SAILS1.XLS?"
3. Exit Excel if you are not proceeding directly to the Tutorial Assignments.

To complete his loan management worksheet, Shabir used many Excel functions to simplify the formulas he entered. He was able to troubleshoot the problem he encountered when he copied the percent of total payment formula and ended up with a column of #DIV/0! error messages because he remembered that absolute references don't change when copied to other cells. Shabir is pleased that James was impressed by the capabilities of the worksheet to do what-if analyses.

■ ■ ■

Questions

1. List the Excel functions you used in this tutorial.
   a. Briefly explain what each function does.
   b. Write out the syntax for each function.
   c. Write a sample function in which you use cell references or constant numbers for the arguments.

E 2. Use the Function Wizard, or the Excel On-line Help to find one function for each category listed in Figure 4-4.
   a. Indicate the category to which this function belongs.
   b. List the function name.
   c. Write a short description of what this function does.

3. Write the definition of a function, then refer to Tutorial 1 and write out the definition of a formula. Explain the relationship between functions and formulas.
4. Explain the difference between the way the AVERAGE function handles zeros and the way it handles blank cells that are included in the range of cells to be averaged.
5. In the tutorial, Shabir thought that the MAX and MIN functions would be especially useful for large lists that changed frequently. Explain the advantage of using the MAX and MIN functions on such lists.
6. What are the advantages of using the Function Wizard dialog box instead of typing a function directly into a cell?
7. Write the formula you would use to calculate the monthly payment for a $150,000 30-year home loan at 8.75% annual interest.
8. Write the formula you would use to calculate the monthly payment for a $10,000 loan at 8% annual interest that you must pay back in 48 months.
9. Write the formula you would use to display the value $100 if cell A9 contains the word "Bonus," but display $0 if cell A9 is empty.
10. Write the formula you would use to display the message "Over budget" whenever the amount in cell B5 is greater than or equal to $800,000, but display the message "Budget OK" if the amount in cell B5 is less than $800,000.
11. Explain the difference between absolute and relative references.
12. What is the significance of the empty parentheses in the TODAY function?
13. Explain the meaning of the message #DIV/0!.
14. Which function key can you use to change the cell reference type from relative to absolute?

Tutorial Assignments

Launch Windows and Excel, if necessary, then complete the Tutorial Assignments and print the results for Tutorial Assignments 10 and 17.

1. Open the file T4SAILS1.XLS, then save it as S4SAILSR.XLS on your Student Disk. Shabir did not have the paperwork for the CSY Gulfstar 42 loan, so it was not included in the worksheet. The CSY Gulfstar 42 was purchased with a $183,000 loan at 9.75% (.0975) interest for 20 years.
2. Insert a blank row between the Hunter 30 and the Beneteau 39 at row 13. *Hint:* Because you are adding the row in the middle of the range specified for the function arguments, you will not need to adjust the SUM, MAX, MIN, and AVERAGE formulas.
3. Enter the name of the boat, CSY Gulfstar 42, in column A.
4. Enter the loan amount in cell B13, the interest rate in cell C13, and the number of monthly payments in cell D13.
5. In cell E13 use the PMT function to calculate the monthly payment.
6. In cell G13 use the IF function to display $0.00 if the loan is not paid, or display the loan payment if the loan is paid.
7. Copy the formula from cell H12 to cell H13 to calculate the percent of total payment.
8. Edit the header and replace Shabir's name with yours.
9. Save the revised workbook.
10. Print the worksheet in landscape orientation; center it from top to bottom and from left to right. Do not print cell borders or row/column headings.
11. Use a felt marker or pen to indicate on your printout which cells display different results after the addition of the CSY Gulfstar 42.
12. Return to the worksheet on your screen and enter the label "Largest Payment:" in cell A21; then in cell B21 enter the formula to find the largest loan payment in column G.

13. Enter the label "Smallest Payment:" in cell A22; then in cell B22 enter the formula to find the smallest loan payment in column G.
14. Enter the label "Average Interest Rate:" in cell A23; then in cell B23 enter the formula to calculate the average of the interest rates shown in column C.
15. Format the text in cells A21 through A23 to align on the right side of the cell, and adjust the column width, if necessary.
16. Save the revised workbook.
17. Use your customized print formulas module, S3MYMOD.XLM, to print the formulas for your worksheet.

Case Problems

1. Compiling Data on the U.S. Airline Industry

The editor of *Aviation Week and Space Technology* has asked Muriel Guzzetti to research the current status of the U.S. airline industry. Muriel collects information on the revenue-miles and passenger-miles for each of the major U.S. airlines. She wants to calculate the following summary information to use in the article:

- total revenue-miles for the U.S. airline industry
- total passenger-miles for the U.S. airline industry
- each airline's share of the total revenue-miles
- each airline's share of the total passenger-miles
- the average revenue-miles for U.S. airlines
- the average passenger-miles for U.S. airlines

Complete the following steps:

1. Open the workbook P4AIR.XLS, then save it as S4AIR.XLS on your Student Disk.
2. Use the SUM function to calculate the industry total revenue-miles in cell B14.
3. Use the SUM function to calculate the industry total passenger-miles in cell D14.
4. In cell C7, enter the formula to calculate American Airlines' share of the total industry revenue-miles using the following equation:

$$\textit{American's share of total industry revenue-miles} = \frac{\textit{American's revenue-miles}}{\textit{industry total revenue-miles}}$$

   Hint: You are going to use this formula for the rest of the airlines, so consider which cell reference should be absolute.
5. Copy the formula from cell C7 to calculate each airline's share of the total industry revenue-miles.
6. In cell E7 enter the formula to calculate American Airlines' share of the total industry passenger-miles, then copy this formula for the other airlines.
7. In cell B15 use the AVERAGE function to calculate the average revenue-miles for the U.S. airline industry.
8. In cell D15 use the AVERAGE function to calculate the average passenger-miles for the U.S. airline industry.
9. Use the TODAY function to display the date in cell B3.
10. Enter your name in cell B2.
11. Format the worksheet so it is easier to read:
    a. Bold the titles and column headings.
    b. Center the title across the entire worksheet and center the column titles over each column.
    c. Add a border at the bottom of cells A6 through E6, and add a border at the top of cells A14 through E14.
    d. Format column B and column D to display numbers with commas; for example, the revenue-miles for American Airlines will display as 26,851 instead of 26851.
    e. Format columns C and E for percents that display two decimal places.

12. Save your workbook.
13. Make two printouts:
    a. Print the worksheet in portrait orientation, centered on the page, without cell gridlines or row/column headings.
    b. Print the formulas in landscape orientation, centered on the page, and include cell gridlines and row/column headings.

2. Commission Analysis at Norcross Office Systems

Maija Jansson is the sales manager for Norcross Office Systems, an office supply store. Maija is thinking of changing the commission structure to motivate the sales representatives to increase sales. Currently, sales representatives earn a monthly base salary of $500.00. In addition to the base salary, sales representatives earn a 6% (.06) commission on their total sales when their monthly sales volume is $6,000.00 or more.

To look at some options for changing the commission structure, Maija collected past payroll information for one of the employees, Jim Marley. Jim's monthly sales are typical of those of most of the Norcross sales representatives. Maija wants to design a worksheet that will help her look at how much money Jim would have earned in the past 12 months if the commission structure was different. Maija completed some of the worksheet and has asked you to help her finish it.

To complete the worksheet:

1. Open the workbook P4BONUS.XLS, then save it as S4BONUS.XLS on your Student Disk.
2. Enter your name in cell B2, then use the TODAY function to display the date in cell B3.
3. Enter the names of the months January through December in column A. *Hint:* Use the fill handle to automatically fill cells A9 through A20 with the names of the months.
4. In cell C9, enter a formula that uses the IF function to calculate Jim's bonus for January.
   For the *logical test* argument, enter the expression to check if Jim's sales are greater than or equal to the sales required for a commission in cell C5.
   For the *value if true* argument, multiply Jim's sales by the commission percent in cell C6.
   For the *value if false* argument, enter a zero.
5. Copy the formula from cell C9 to cells C10 through C20.
6. If your formulas produced zeros for every month, something is wrong. Examine the formula in cell C9 and determine which references need to be absolute. Edit the formula, then copy it again. Your formulas are correct if cell C18 shows that Jim earned a $433.56 commission.
7. In cell E9, enter a formula to calculate Jim's total pay for January. Calculate Jim's total pay by adding his commission to his base salary.
8. Copy the formula from cell E9 to cells E10 through E20.
9. In cell E21, use the SUM function to calculate Jim's total pay for the year.
10. Save the workbook.

E

11. Write out your answers to the following questions:
    a. How much did Jim earn in the last 12 months under the current commission structure?
    b. How much would Jim have earned last year if the commission was 8%?
    c. How much would Jim have earned in the last 12 months if the commission rate was 7%, but he had to make at least $6,500 in sales each month before he could earn a commission?

12. Print two versions of your worksheet:
    a. Print the worksheet showing what Jim would have earned if he had to sell $6,500 each month to earn a commission, and the commission was 7%. Center the worksheet on the page, but do not print cell gridlines or row/column headings.
    b. Display the formulas for the worksheet and adjust the column widths so there is no extra space. Print the formulas for the worksheet in portrait orientation. Print the entire worksheet on one page; include cell gridlines and row/column headings.

3. Calculating Car Loans at First Federal Bank

Paul Vagelos is a loan officer in the Consumer Loan Department of the First Federal Bank. Paul evaluates customer applications for car loans, and he wants to create a worksheet that will calculate the monthly payments, total payments, and total interest paid on a loan. Paul has finished most of the worksheet but needs to complete a few more sections. To complete the worksheet:

1. Open the workbook P4CAR1.XLS, then save it as S4CAR1.XLS on your Student Disk.
2. Enter a formula in cell B10 that uses the PMT function to calculate the monthly payment for the loan amount in cell B5, at the annual interest rate in cell B6, for the term in cell A10. Display the monthly payment as a positive amount.
3. Edit the formula in cell B10 so you use absolute references for any cell references that should not change when you copy the formula.
4. Copy the formula from cell B10 to cells B11 through B14.
5. Enter the formula in cell D10 to calculate the total interest using the following equation:

   total interest = total payments - loan amount
6. Edit the formula in cell D10 so you use absolute references for any cell references that should not change when you copy the formula.
7. Copy the formula from cell D10 to cells D11 through D14.
8. Type your name in cell B2, and enter the TODAY function in cell B3.
9. Make any formatting changes you think are appropriate to have a professional-looking worksheet.
10. Preview the printed worksheet. Make any page setup settings necessary to produce a professional-looking printout, then print the worksheet.
11. Save the workbook with formatting changes.
12. Use your customized print formulas module, S3MYMOD.XLM, to print the formulas for your worksheet.

T U T O R I A L 5

O B J E C T I V E S

In this tutorial you will:

- Plan and construct charts
- Create a pie chart, line chart, column chart, and 3-D column chart
- Identify the elements of the Excel chart
- Learn which type of chart will represent your data most effectively
- Select non-adjacent ranges
- Move a chart and change its size
- Add gridlines to a chart
- Change the format of chart lines
- Identify the differences between label text, attached text, and unattached text
- Add, edit, and format chart text
- Add pictures to a column chart
- Add color and borders to a chart
- Work with multiple sheets

Charts and Graphing

Charting Sales Information

CASE

Cast Iron Concepts Carl O'Brien is the assistant marketing director at Cast Iron Concepts, a distributor of traditional cast iron stoves. Carl is working on a new product catalog and his main concern is how much space to allocate for each product. In previous catalogs the Box Windsor stove was allocated one full page. The Star Windsor and the West Windsor stoves were each allocated a half page.

Carl has collected sales information about the three stove models, and he has discovered that Box Windsor stove sales have steadily decreased since 1991. Although the Box Windsor stove was the best-selling model during the 1980s, sales of Star Windsor stoves and West Windsor stoves have increased steadily and overtaken the Box Windsor sales. Carl believes that the space allocated to the Box Windsor stove should be reduced to a half page while the Star Windsor stove and the West Windsor stove should each have a full page.

Carl needs to convince the marketing director to change the space allocation in the new catalog, so he is preparing a presentation for the next department meeting. At the presentation Carl plans to show four charts that graphically illustrate the sales pattern of the Box Windsor, Star Windsor, and West Windsor stoves. Carl has stored the sales figures in a workbook named C5WINDSR.XLS. He will generate the charts from the data in the worksheet. Let's launch Windows, launch Excel, and then open Carl's worksheet.

To launch Excel, organize the desktop, and open the C5WINDSR.XLS workbook:

1. Launch Excel following your usual procedure.
2. Make sure your Student Disk is in the disk drive.
3. Make sure the Microsoft Excel and Book1 windows are maximized.
4. Click the **Open button** to display the Open dialog box.
5. Double-click **C5WINDSR.XLS** in the File Name box to display the workbook.

Let's save the workbook using the filename S5WINDSR.XLS so the changes you make will be made to a copy of the file, not the original.

To save the workbook as S5WINDSR.XLS:

1. Click **File**, then click **Save As...** to display the Save As dialog box.
2. Type **S5WINDSR** using either uppercase or lowercase.
3. Click the **OK button** to save the workbook under the new filename. When the save is complete, the new filename, S5WINDSR.XLS, appears in the title bar. See Figure 5-1.

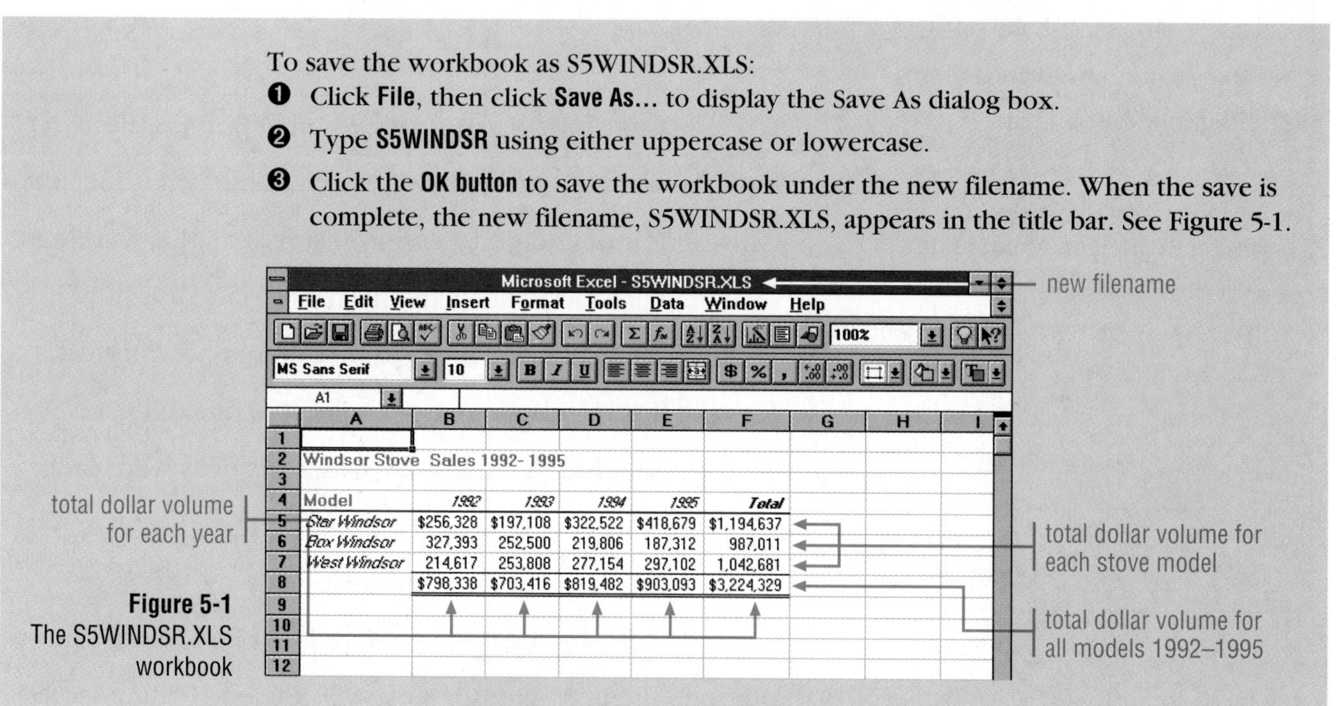

Figure 5-1
The S5WINDSR.XLS workbook

The worksheet shows the sales generated by each of the three Windsor stove models for the period 1992 through 1995. The total dollar volume during the four-year period for each model is displayed in column F. The total dollar volume for each year is displayed in row 8. Carl wants to make several charts that will help him convince the marketing director to change the catalog space allocated to each Windsor stove model. In this tutorial you will work with Carl as he plans and creates four charts for his presentation.

Excel Charts

As you learned in Tutorial 1, it is easy to graphically represent your worksheet data. You might think of these graphical representations as "graphs"; however, in Excel they are referred to as **charts**. Figure 5-2 shows the 15 **chart types** you can use to represent worksheet data. Of the 15 chart types, nine chart types produce two-dimensional (2-D) charts and six chart types produce three-dimensional (3-D) charts.

Icon	Chart Type	Purpose
Area	Area chart	Shows the magnitude of change over a period of time
Bar	Bar chart	Shows comparisons between the data represented by each bar
Column	Column chart	Shows comparisons between the data represented by each column
Line	Line chart	Shows trends or changes over time
Pie	Pie chart	Shows the proportion of parts to a whole
Radar	Radar chart	Shows changes in data relative to a center point
XY (Scatter)	XY chart	Shows the pattern or relationship between sets of (x,y) data points
Combination	Combination chart	Shows how one set of data corresponds to another set by superimposing one chart type over another
3-D Area	3-D Area chart	Shows the magnitude of each data series as a solid, three-dimensional shape
3-D Bar	3-D Bar chart	Similar to a 2-D Bar chart, but bars appear three-dimensional
3-D Column	3-D Column chart	Shows three-dimensional columns and some formats show data on x-, y-, and z- axes
3-D Line	3-D Line chart	Shows each chart line as a ribbon within a three-dimensional space
3-D Pie	3-D Pie chart	Shows the proportion of parts to a whole, with emphasis on the data values in the front wedges
3-D Surface	3-D Surface chart	Shows the interrelationship between large amounts of data
Doughnut	Doughnut chart	Shows the proportion of parts to whole

Figure 5-2
Excel chart types

Each chart type has several predefined **chart formats** that specify such format characteristics as gridlines, chart labels, axes, and so on. For example, the Area chart type has five predefined formats, as shown in Figure 5-3. You can find more information on chart types and formats in the *Microsoft Excel User's Guide*, in the Excel Help facility, and in the ChartWizard.

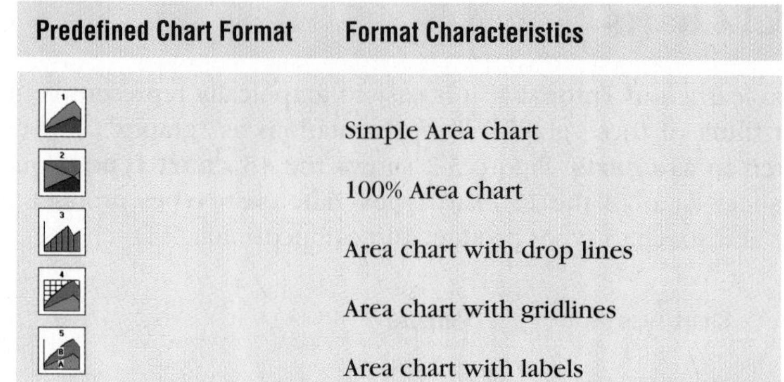

Predefined Chart Format	Format Characteristics
1	Simple Area chart
2	100% Area chart
3	Area chart with drop lines
4	Area chart with gridlines
5	Area chart with labels

Figure 5-3
Predefined formats for the Area chart type

Figure 5-4 shows the elements of a typical Excel chart. It is particularly important to understand the Excel chart terminology so you can successfully construct and edit charts.

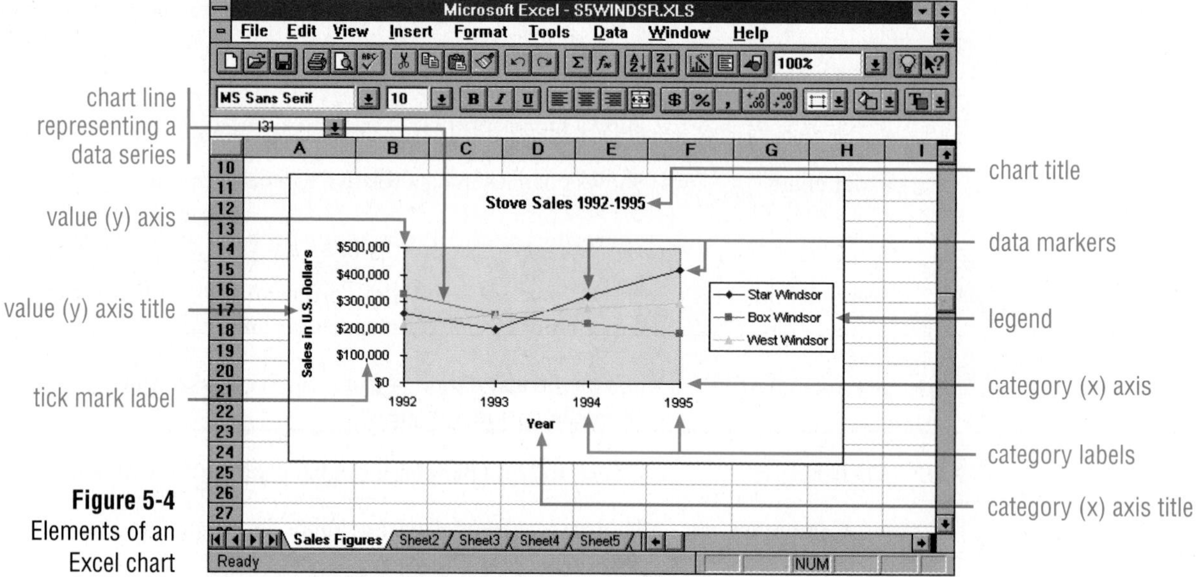

Figure 5-4
Elements of an Excel chart

The **chart title** identifies the chart. The horizontal axis of the chart is referred to as the **category axis** or the **x-axis**. The vertical axis is referred to as the **value axis** or the **y-axis**. Each axis on a chart can have a title that identifies the scale or categories of the chart data; in Figure 5-4 the x-axis title is "Year" and the y-axis title is "Sales in U.S. Dollars."

A **tick mark label** shows the scale for the y-axis. Excel automatically generates this scale based on the values selected for the chart. The **category names** or **category labels** correspond to the labels you use for the worksheet data and are usually displayed on the x-axis.

A **data point** is a single value in a cell in the worksheet. A **data marker** is a bar, area, wedge, or symbol that marks a single data point on a chart. For example, the 1995 sales of the Star Windsor stove in cell E5 of the worksheet on your screen is a data point. The small square on the chart line in Figure 5-4 that shows the 1995 sales of the Star Windsor stove is a data marker.

A **data series** is a group of related data points, such as the Star Windsor sales shown in cells B5 through E5 on your worksheet. On a chart such as the one in Figure 5-4, a data series is shown as a set of data markers connected by a chart line.

When you have more than one data series, your chart will contain more than one set of data markers. For example, Figure 5-4 has three chart lines, each representing a data series. When you show more than one data series on a chart, it is a good idea to use a **legend** to identify which data markers represent each data series. Figure 5-4 also shows the chart toolbar, which contains buttons for changing the chart type and some chart characteristics. You will use the menus instead of the chart toolbar in this tutorial, but don't be concerned if the chart toolbar appears in your Excel window.

Carl wants to show that the West Windsor and Star Windsor stove models generate a higher proportion of the total Windsor stove sales than the Box Windsor model. Because pie charts are an effective way to show the relationship of parts to the whole, Carl decides to use a pie chart to show the sales for each model as a percentage of total Windsor stove sales.

Carl knows that pie charts and 3-D pie charts illustrate the same relationships, but he decides to create a 3-D pie chart because he thinks it looks more professional. Since Carl will be creating a number of charts, he decides to put each chart on a separate sheet. This will allow him to switch quickly from one chart to the other, without having to scroll up and down through numerous charts. In the next set of steps, Carl renames Sheet2 "Pie Chart."

To rename Sheet2:

❶ Double-click the **Sheet2 tab** to open the Rename Sheet dialog box.

❷ Type **Pie Chart** in the Name box, then click the **OK button**. See Figure 5-5.

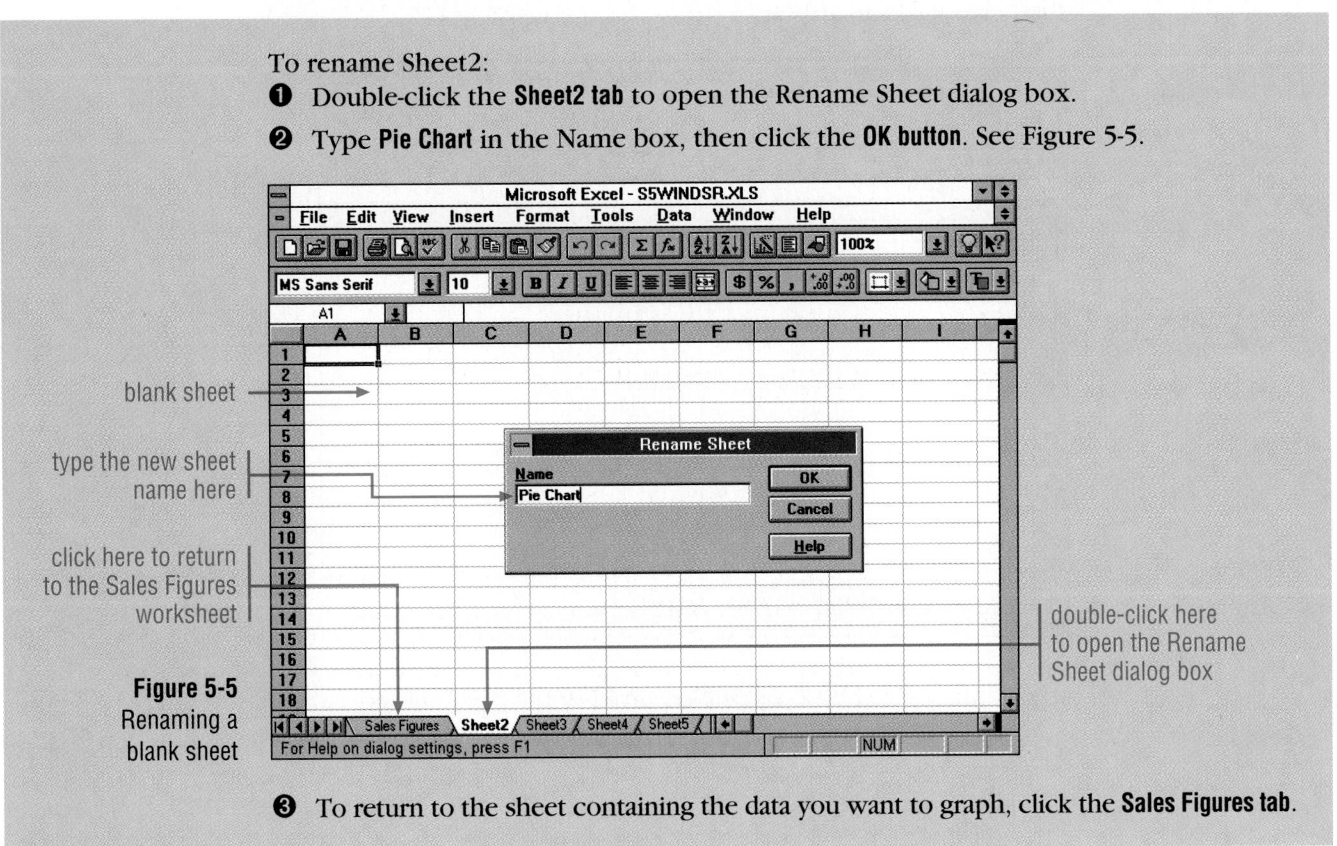

Figure 5-5
Renaming a blank sheet

❸ To return to the sheet containing the data you want to graph, click the **Sales Figures tab**.

Now Carl is ready to create a pie chart on the Pie Chart sheet.

Creating a 3-D Pie Chart

A **pie chart** represents one data series by displaying each data point as a wedge. The size of the wedge represents the proportion of the data point in the total circle, or "pie." When you create a pie chart, you generally specify two ranges. Excel uses the first range for the category labels and the second range for the data series. Excel automatically calculates the percentage for each wedge, draws the wedge to reflect the percentage, and gives you the option of displaying the percentage as a label on the completed chart.

A 3-D pie chart shows a three-dimensional view of a pie chart. The 3-D representation adds visual interest and emphasizes the data points in the front wedges, or in any wedges that are pulled out, or "exploded," from the circle. Each wedge on an Excel 3-D pie chart can be colored or patterned, displayed with category labels, or labeled with its percentage relative to the whole pie.

Carl wants to create a 3-D pie chart to show the percentage of sales generated by each of the three Windsor stove models during 1995. He draws a sketch showing the way he wants the pie chart to look (Figure 5-6). The pie chart will have three wedges, one for each of the stove models. Carl wants each wedge labeled with the stove model and its percentage of the total sales. Because Carl doesn't know the percentages until Excel calculates them and displays them on the chart, he puts "__%" on his sketch where he wants the percentages to appear.

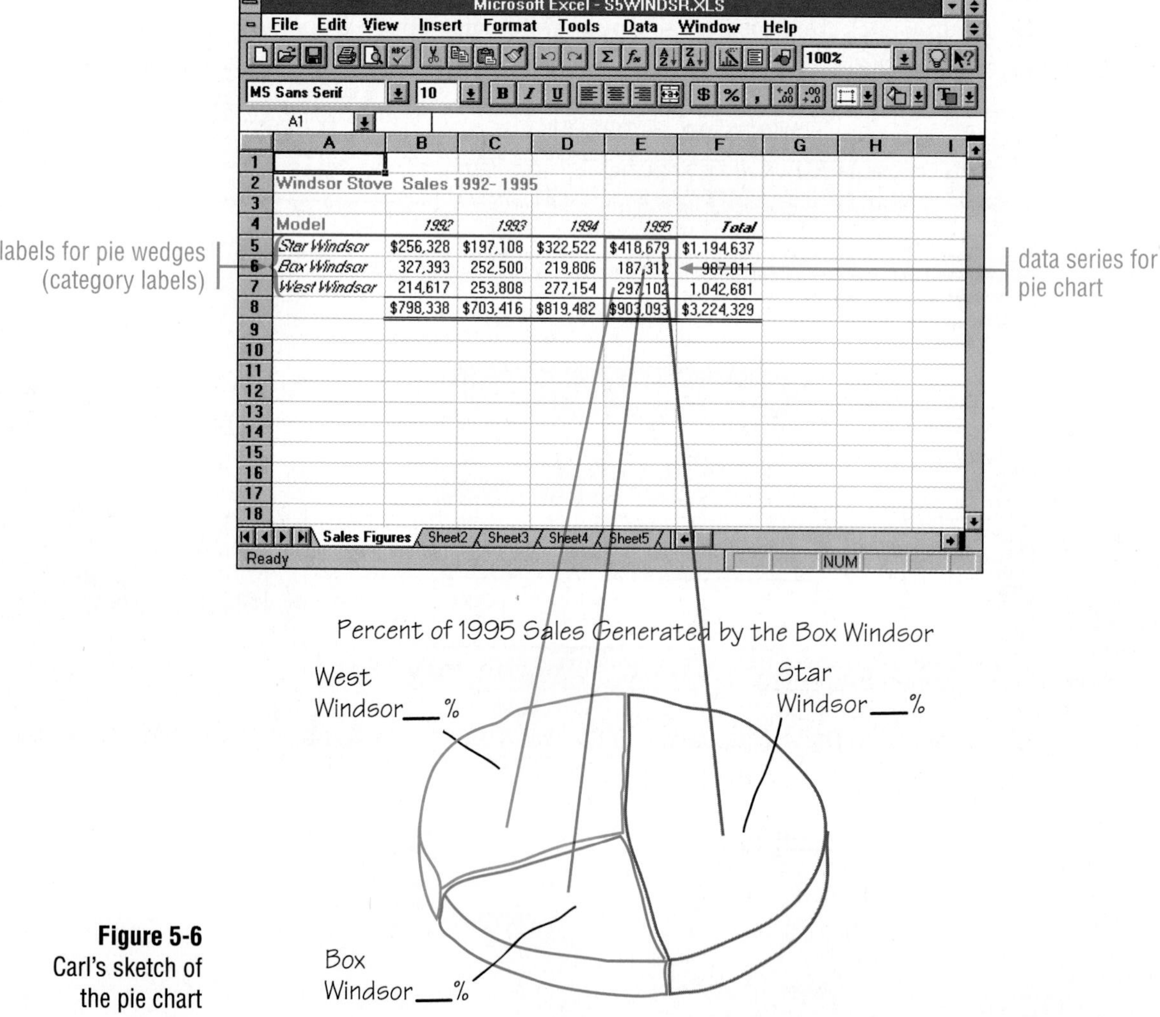

Figure 5-6 Carl's sketch of the pie chart

Carl's sketch shows roughly what he wants the chart to look like. It is difficult to envision exactly how a chart will appear until you know how the data series looks when it is plotted; therefore, it is not necessary to try to incorporate every detail on the chart sketch. As you construct the chart, you can take advantage of Excel's editing capabilities to try different formatting options until your chart looks just the way you want.

Carl refers back to his worksheet and notes in his sketch that the data labels for the pie wedges are in cells A5 through A7 and the data points representing the pie wedges are in cells E5 through E7. Carl must select these two ranges to tell the ChartWizard what he wants to chart, but he realizes that these ranges are not next to each other on the worksheet. He knows how to highlight a series of cells that are adjacent, but now he needs to select two separate ranges at the same time.

Selecting Non-adjacent Ranges

A **non-adjacent range** refers to a group of individual cells or ranges that are not next to each other. Selecting non-adjacent ranges is particularly useful when you construct charts because the cells that contain the data series and the data labels are often not next to each other on the worksheet. When you select non-adjacent ranges, the selected cells in each range are highlighted. You can then apply formats to the cells, clear the cells, or use them to construct a chart.

REFERENCE WINDOW

Selecting Non-adjacent Ranges

- Click the first cell or highlight the first range you want to select.
- Press and hold [Ctrl] while you click additional cells or highlight additional ranges.
- When you have selected all the cells you want to include, release [Ctrl].

To begin constructing the pie chart, Carl first selects the range A5:A7, which contains the data labels. Then he holds down the Control key while highlighting the range E5:E7, which contains the data points.

To select range A5:A7 and range E5:E7 in the Sales Figures sheet:

1. Make sure the Sales Figures sheet is active. Highlight cells A5 through A7, then release the mouse button.
2. Press and hold **[Ctrl]** while you highlight cells E5 through E7. Release **[Ctrl]**. Now two ranges are highlighted: A5:A7 and E5:E7.

   TROUBLE? If you don't highlight the cells you want on your first try, click any cell to remove the highlighting, then go back to Step 1 and try again.

Now that Carl has selected the cells he wants to use for the pie chart, he uses the ChartWizard button to specify the chart type, chart format, and chart titles.

To create the pie chart using the ChartWizard:

1. Click the **ChartWizard button**. The prompt "Drag in document to create chart" appears in the status bar. This prompt is asking you to specify where you want the chart to appear in the worksheet.
2. Click the **Pie Chart tab** to select the sheet where you want the chart to appear.
3. Move the pointer to cell A1 to set the upper-left corner where the chart will appear.
4. Hold down the mouse button and drag the pointer to cell F13 to outline the area where you want the chart to appear. Release the mouse button to display the ChartWizard - Step 1 of 5 dialog box. Now the dialog box appears over the Sales Figures sheet so you can correct the range address if necessary. See Figure 5-7.

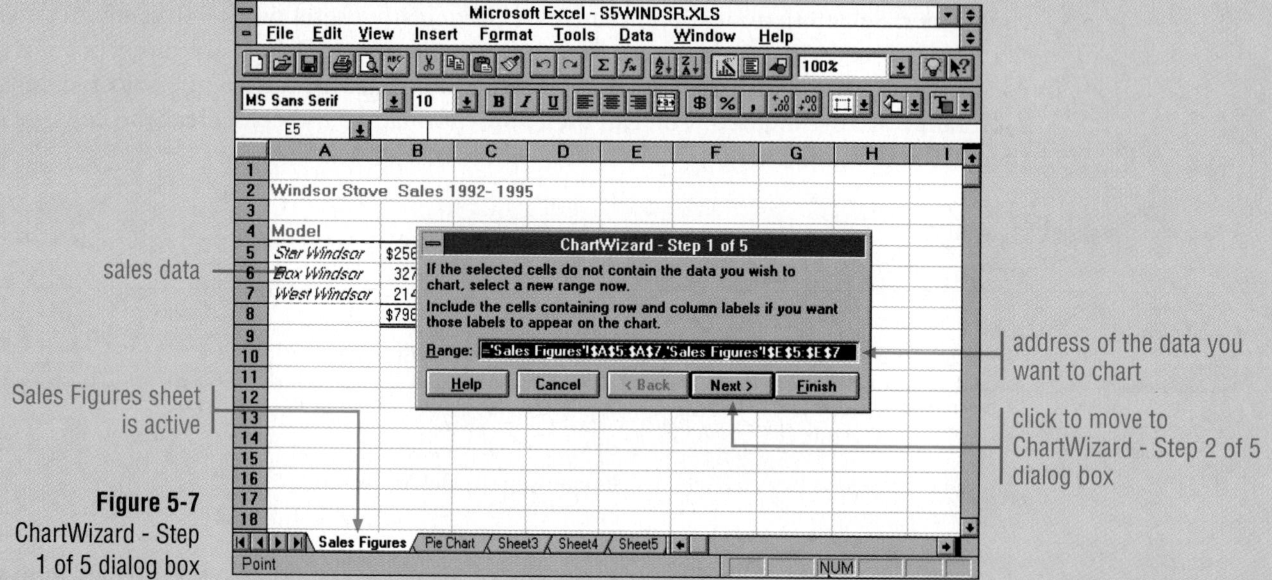

Figure 5-7
ChartWizard - Step 1 of 5 dialog box

Make sure the range is ='Sales Figures'!$A$5:$A$7,'Sales Figures'!$E$5:$E$7. These cell references are the absolute references of the ranges you selected in the previous set of steps. Note that the cell references also include the name of the sheet where the cells are located. The exclamation mark (!) indicates an absolute sheet reference.

TROUBLE? If the range displayed on your screen is not correct, type the necessary corrections in the Range box.

5. Click the **Next > button** to display the ChartWizard - Step 2 of 5 dialog box.
6. Double-click the **3-D Pie** chart type to display the ChartWizard - Step 3 of 5 dialog box.

7. Double-click chart format **7** so your chart will display labels and percentages for each wedge. ChartWizard - Step 4 of 5 shows you a sample of the chart. See Figure 5-8.

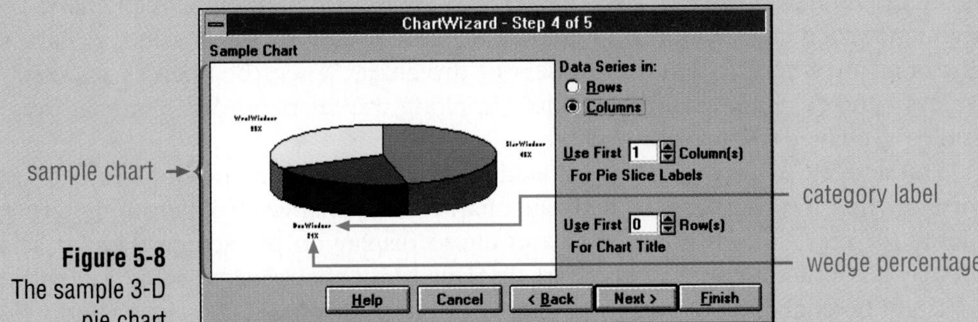

Figure 5-8
The sample 3-D pie chart

This looks right, so next you'll add a title to the chart.

8. Click the **Next > button** to display the ChartWizard - Step 5 of 5 dialog box.
9. Click the **Chart Title box**, then type **Percent of 1995 Sales Generated by the Box Windsor**. After a pause, Excel displays the new title in the Sample Chart box.
10. Click the **Finish button** to complete the chart. The new chart, along with the chart toolbar, appears in the Pie Chart sheet. Use the scroll bars, if necessary, to view the entire chart on the worksheet. See Figure 5-9.

    TROUBLE? If you have a monochrome monitor, the chart will be displayed in shades of gray instead of colors.

    TROUBLE? If the chart toolbar does not appear, click View, click Toolbars. . ., click the Chart check box to select it, then click OK.

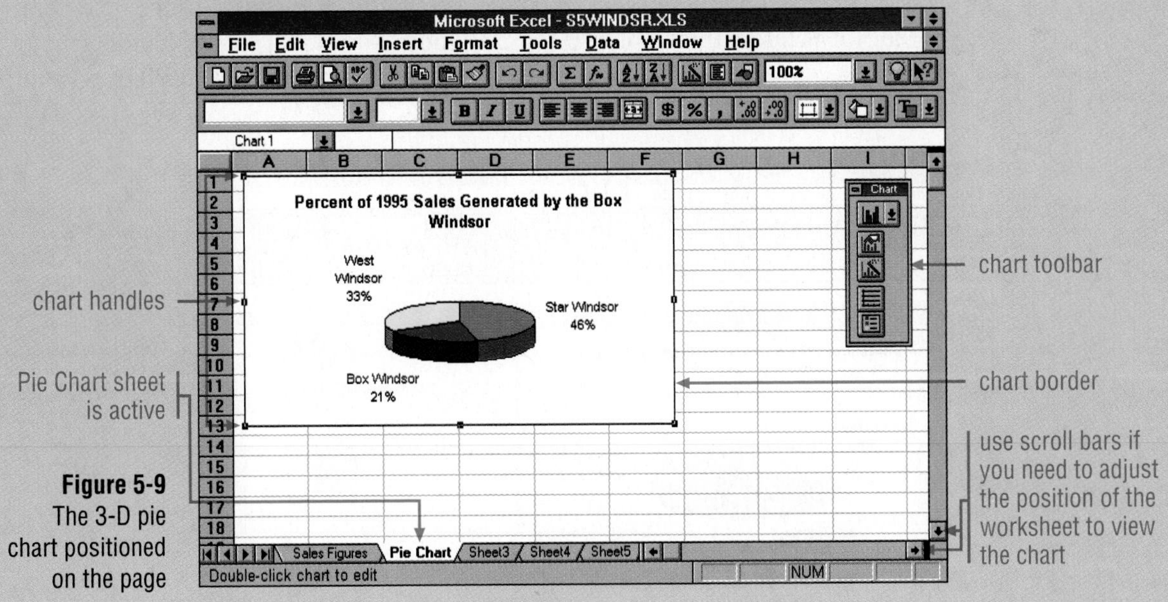

Figure 5-9
The 3-D pie chart positioned on the page

If your chart looks somewhat different from Figure 5-9, you might need to change the chart size, as explained later in this tutorial. For now, don't worry about the chart toolbar. You'll learn how to use it later in this tutorial.

Selecting and Activating the Chart

The chart you have created is called an embedded object or an embedded chart. To modify an embedded chart, you need to either select it or activate it. To select a chart, simply click once anywhere within the borders of the chart. When the chart is selected, Excel displays handles, eight small black squares, along the chart border. You can drag these handles to change the size of the chart.

You activate a chart by double-clicking anywhere within the borders of the chart. Usually, when the chart is activated, the chart border changes from a thin line to a thick colored (or gray) line. If the chart is too big to display on the screen without scrolling, you may see the entire activated chart displayed in a special chart window, with a title bar. Don't be concerned if you see one of your charts displayed in a chart window; it simply means you made your chart too big to fit in the worksheet window. Treat such a chart window just as you would an activated chart with a thick border.

Activating a chart gives you access to the chart commands on the menu bar. Also, when the chart is activated, you can double-click on any part of the chart to open a Format dialog box. Let's experiment with some of these techniques now.

To practice selecting and activating the chart:

1. Make sure the Pie Chart sheet is active. Click anywhere outside the chart border to make sure the chart is *not* selected. The chart toolbar disappears, along with the square handles around the chart border.
2. Click once anywhere within the chart border to select the chart. The chart toolbar appears, along with the square handles on the chart border.
3. To activate the chart, double-click anywhere within the chart border. The chart border turns into a thick colored (or gray) line. Additional square handles might appear along the edge of the chart. The horizontal and vertical scroll bars disappear from the worksheet window. See Figure 5-10.

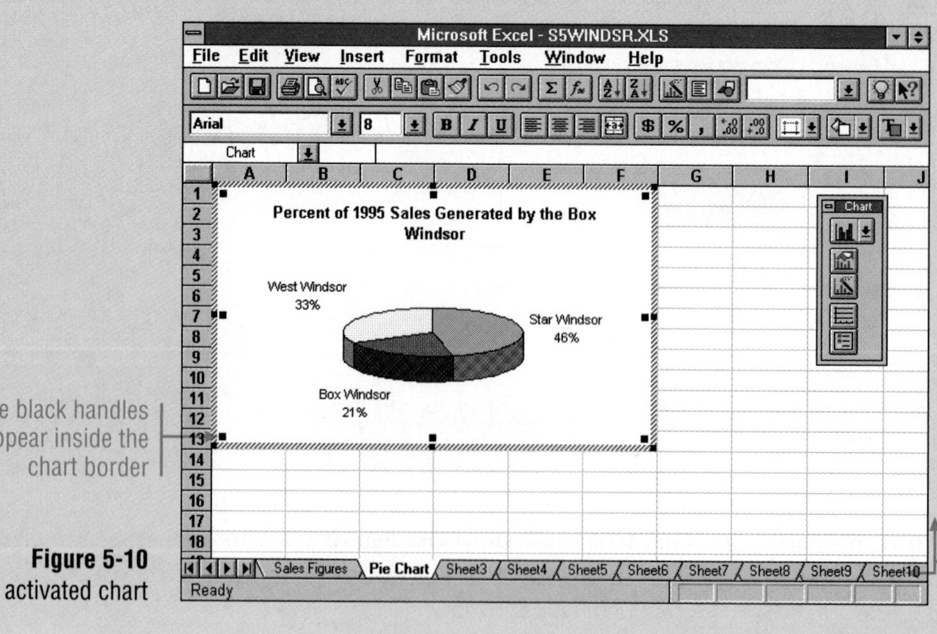

Figure 5-10
The activated chart

TROUBLE? If you don't see the large black handles as shown in Figure 5-10, try clicking the white area in the lower-right corner of the chart. If you see the chart displayed in a window with a menu bar, don't be concerned. Proceed with the following steps as if the chart were displayed within a thick border

Now that the chart is activated, you have access to the chart commands on the menu bar.

4. Click **Format**. The Format menu displays the chart formatting options. Click **Format** again to close the Format menu.
5. To open the Format Chart Area dialog box, double-click anywhere on the white space in the chart border. The Format Chart Area dialog box appears. See Figure 5-11.

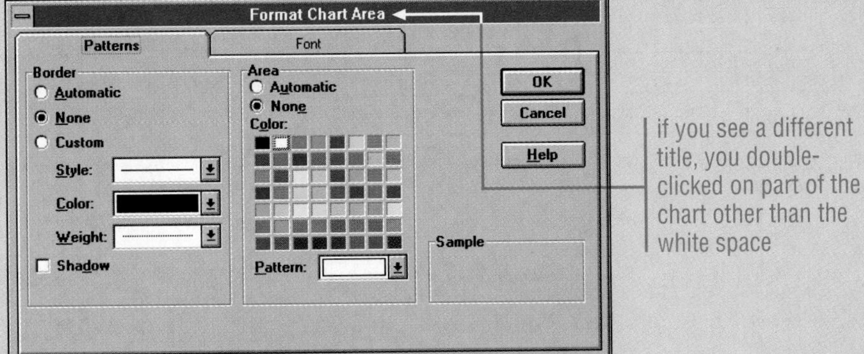

Figure 5-11
The Format Chart Area dialog box

TROUBLE? If you see a dialog box with a slightly different title, don't worry—it simply means that you double-clicked on a part of the chart other than the white space. As a result, Excel displays the dialog box appropriate for that part of the chart.

6. Click the **Cancel button** to close the dialog box and return to the Pie Chart sheet.
7. Double-click anywhere outside the chart border to deactivate the chart. The chart border turns into a thin line without handles, and the chart toolbar disappears.

Now that you're familiar with selecting and activating a chart, you can help Carl modify the pie chart.

Moving and Changing the Size of a Chart

When you use the ChartWizard to create a chart, you drag the pointer to outline the area of the worksheet where you want the chart to appear. If the area you outlined is not large enough, Excel positions the chart elements as best as it can, but the text on the chart might break in odd places. For example, in Figure 5-9 the word "Windsor" appears on a separate line. You can increase the size of the chart to eliminate this problem.

To change the size of a chart, you first click the chart to select it. You can move the chart to another position on the worksheet by clicking anywhere inside the chart border and dragging the chart to the new location. Let's practice moving the chart and changing its size.

To move and change the size of the chart:

1. Select the chart by clicking anywhere within the chart border. The black handles appear on the chart border.

❷ Position the pointer anywhere within the chart border, then hold down the mouse button and drag the chart two rows down. Release the mouse button to view the chart in its new position.

❸ Position the pointer over one of the handles on the right-hand chart border. Hold down the mouse button and drag the border one column to the right. Release the mouse button to view the new chart size.

❹ Adjust the size and position of your chart so it looks like Figure 5-12.

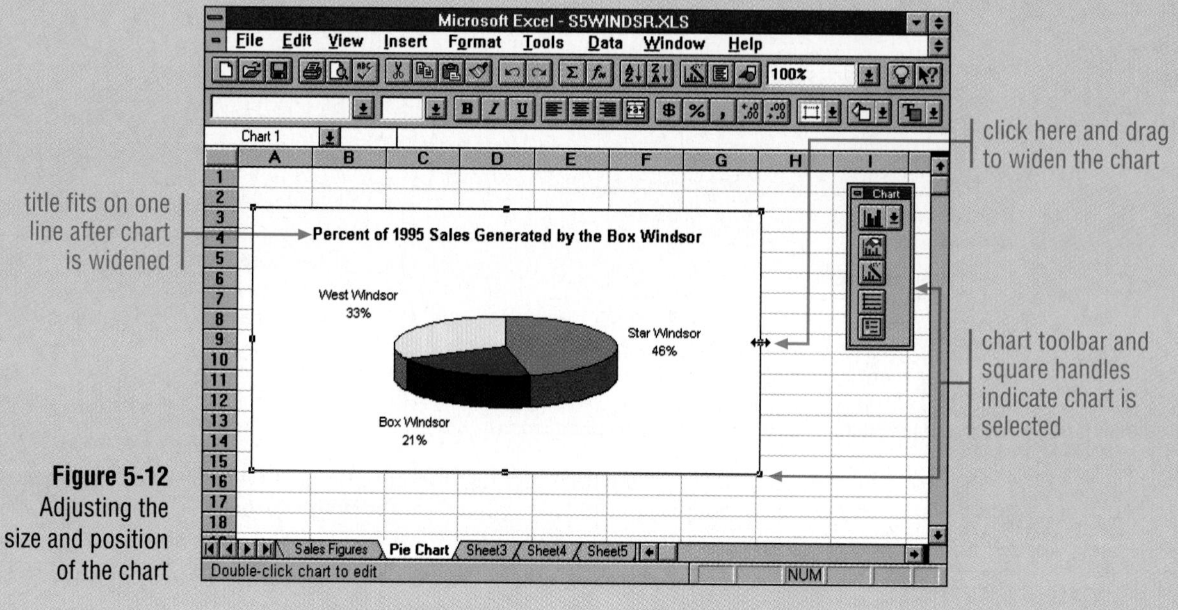

Figure 5-12 Adjusting the size and position of the chart

Carl decides to draw attention to the Box Windsor data by pulling out the wedge that represents its sales.

Pulling Out a Wedge of a Pie Chart

When the chart is activated, you can manipulate each part of the chart as you would any other Excel object. When you click a wedge of the pie chart, small black handles appear, showing you that the wedge is selected. You can then drag the wedge out of the circle or pull it back into the circle. Carl wants to pull out the wedge that represents sales for the Box Windsor stove.

To pull out the wedge that represents the Box Windsor stove sales:

❶ Double-click within the border of the chart to activate it. The border changes to a thick colored (or gray) line.

❷ Click the white space just inside the chart border to make sure the large black handles appear around the inside edge of the activated chart, as in Figure 5-10. These handles indicate that the entire chart border is selected.

❸ Click anywhere on the pie to select it. One square handle appears on each wedge of the pie.

4. Now that the entire pie is selected, you can select one part of it, the Box Windsor Wedge. Position over the wedge that represents Box Windsor sales, then click to select the wedge. Handles now appear on this wedge only. See Figure 5-13.

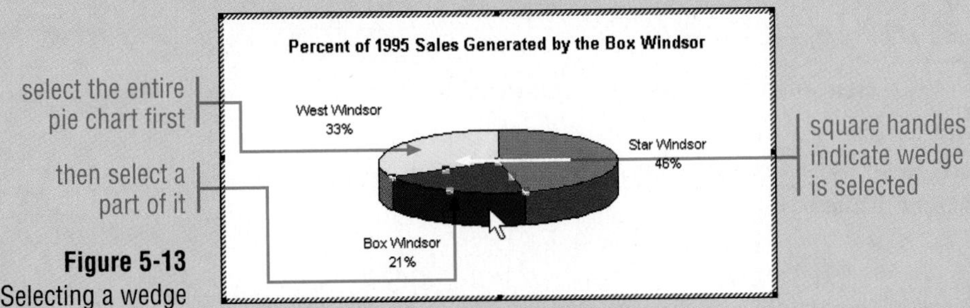

Figure 5-13
Selecting a wedge

TROUBLE? If the Box Windsor wedge is not selected, make sure the chart is activated and start again with Step 2. If you see the Format Chart Area dialog box, you accidentally double-clicked the activated chart. Click the Cancel button and start again with Step 2.

5. Hold down the mouse button to drag the wedge away from the center of the pie chart. Notice that the wedge will only slide directly in or out. It will not move to the side.

6. Move the wedge to the position shown in Figure 5-14.

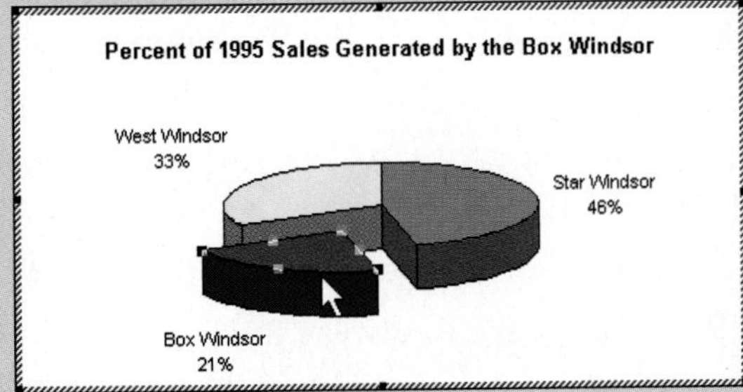

Figure 5-14
Moving a wedge

7. Release the mouse button to leave the wedge in its new position.

The chart on Carl's screen shows that the Box Windsor stove sales generated the smallest percentage of the total Windsor stove sales in 1995. Carl studies the chart on his screen and decides to add patterns to two of the chart wedges for more visual interest.

Changing Chart Patterns

Excel provides a variety of patterns that you can apply to data markers. Patterns add visual interest to a chart, and they can be useful when you use a printer without color capability. Although your charts appear in color on a color monitor, if your printer does not have color capability Excel translates colors to shades of gray for the printout. Some colors, particularly some of the darker colors, are difficult to distinguish from each other when they are translated to gray shades and then printed. You can make your charts more readable by selecting a different pattern for each data marker.

To apply a pattern to a data marker, such as a wedge in a pie chart, activate the chart, select the data marker to which you want to apply a pattern, then select the pattern you want from the Patterns dialog box.

REFERENCE WINDOW

Selecting a Pattern for a Data Marker

Make sure the chart is activated.

- Select the wedge, or column data marker, to which you want to apply a pattern.
- Click Format, then click Selected Data Point... to display the Format Data Point dialog box.

  or

  Double-click the wedge or column marker to which you want to apply a pattern to display the Format Data Point dialog box.
- Click the Patterns tab, then click the Patterns box down arrow button to display a list of patterns.
- Click the pattern you want to apply, then click the OK button to close the dialog box.

Carl wants to apply a dot pattern to the Box Windsor wedge, a horizontal stripe pattern to the Star Windsor wedge, and a grid pattern to the West Windsor wedge.

To apply patterns to the wedges:

1. Make sure the chart is activated.
2. If necesary, select the Box Windsor wedge to display the small black handles.
3. Double-click the Box Windsor wedge to display the Format Data Point dialog box.

   TROUBLE? If you see a dialog box with a different title, then you didn't select the wedge before double-clicking. Close the dialog box and start again with Step 2.
4. Click the **Pattern box down arrow button** to display the patterns.
5. Click the sparse dot pattern to select it. See Figure 5-15.

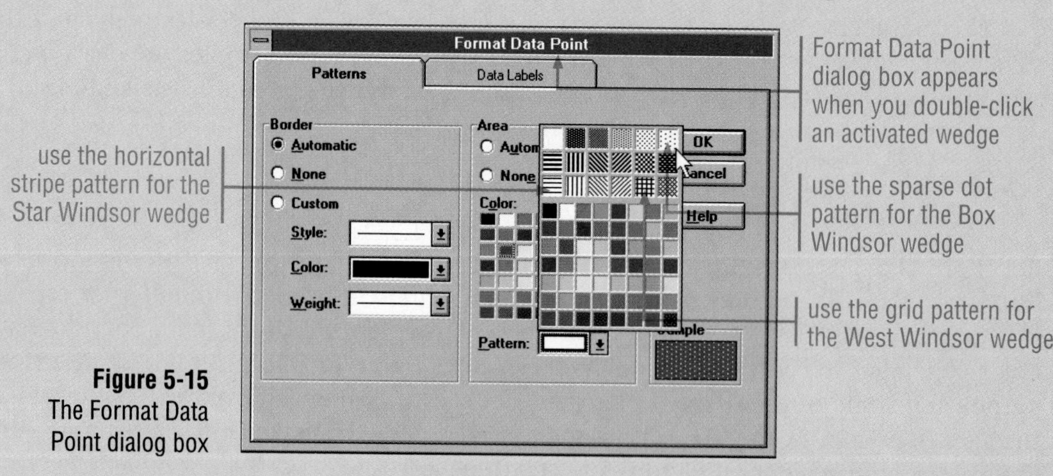
Format Data Point
Patterns
Data Labels
Border
Automatic
None
Custom
Style:
Color:
Weight:
Area
None
Color:
Pattern:
OK
Help
Format Data Point dialog box appears when you double-click an activated wedge
use the horizontal stripe pattern for the Star Windsor wedge
use the sparse dot pattern for the Box Windsor wedge
use the grid pattern for the West Windsor wedge

Figure 5-15
The Format Data Point dialog box

6. Click the **OK button** to close the dialog box and view the pattern.

7. Repeat Steps 2 through 6 to select a horizontal stripe pattern for the Star Windsor wedge, and again to select a grid pattern for the West Windsor wedge. After you select patterns for the Star Windsor and West Windsor wedges, your chart should look like Figure 5-16.

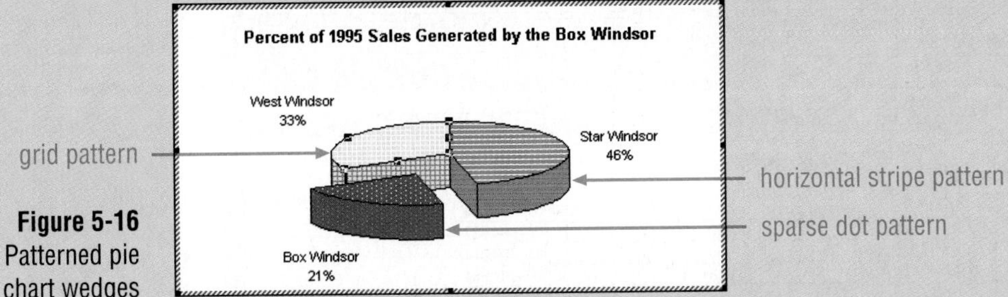

Figure 5-16 Patterned pie chart wedges

8. To deactivate and deselect the chart, double-click anywhere outside the chart border.
9. To return to the Sales Figures sheet, click the **Sales Figures tab**.

This chart is complete, so Carl saves the workbook with the new Pie Chart sheet.

10. Click the **Save button**.

If you want to take a break and resume the tutorial at a later time, you can exit Excel by double-clicking the Control menu box in the upper-left corner of the screen. When you resume the tutorial, launch Excel, maximize the Microsoft Excel and Book1 windows, and place your Student Disk in the disk drive. Open the file S5WINDSR.XLS, then continue with the tutorial.

■ ■ ■

Carl wants to show the change in sales volume for each model during the period 1992 through 1995. He decides to create a line chart to illustrate this change. He begins by renaming a blank sheet, just as he did with the pie chart.

To rename Sheet3:

1. Double-click the **Sheet3 tab** to open the Rename Sheet dialog box.
2. Type **Line Chart** in the Name box, then click the **OK button**.
3. To return to the sheet containing the data you want to graph, click the **Sales Figures tab**.

Creating a Line Chart

A **line chart** represents a data series by connecting each data point with a line. When you use a line chart to plot more than one data series, each data series is represented by one line on the chart. The primary use of a line chart is to show trends or changes over time. Generally, the category labels for the x-axis reflect the time periods for the data, such as days, months, or years. If you are charting more than one data series, make sure you use a legend to indicate which data series is represented by each line.

As with the pie chart, Carl begins by making a sketch of the line chart he wants to create. (Figure 5-17). He uses the years 1992, 1993, 1994, and 1995 for the category labels on the x-axis. The category labels are in row 4 of the worksheet.

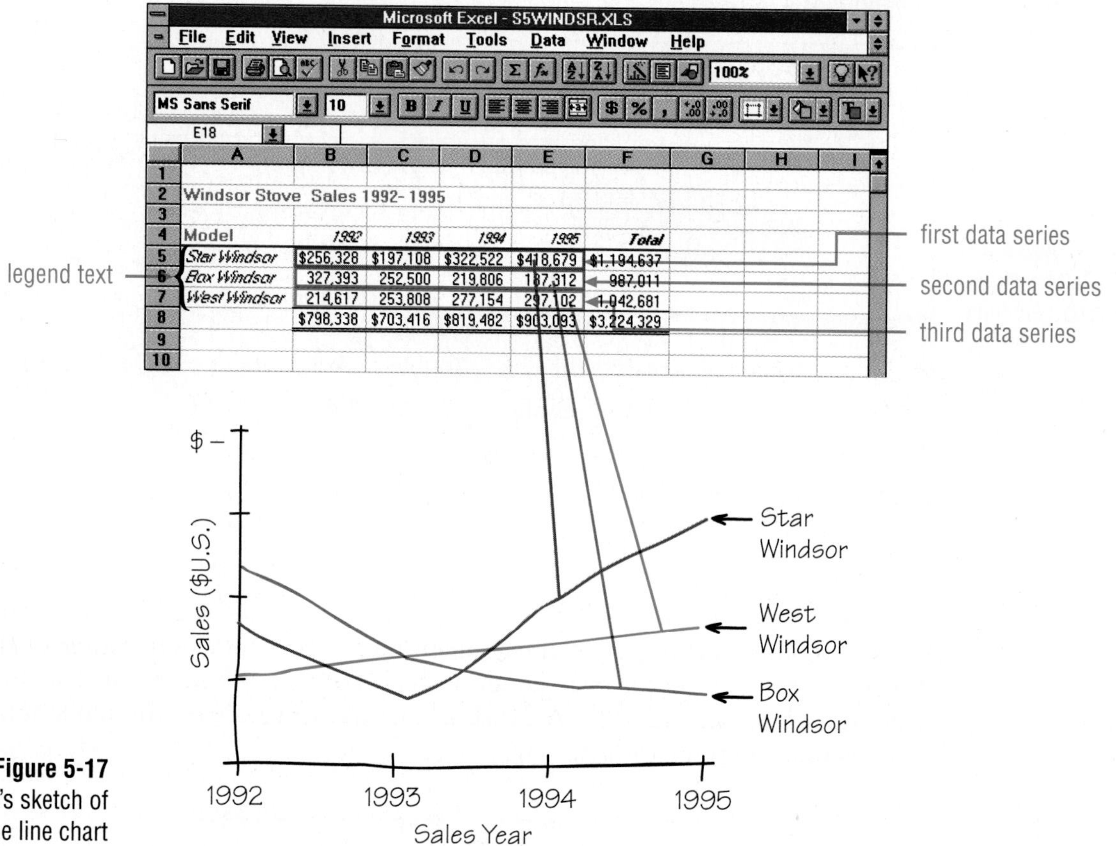

Figure 5-17 Carl's sketch of the line chart

The first chart line will show the Star Windsor sales for the four-year period. The values for this chart line are in row 5. The second chart line will show the Box Windsor sales for the four-year period. The values for the second chart line are in row 6. The third chart line will show the West Windsor sales for the four-year period. The values for the third chart line are in row 7.

Carl does not include any of the total sales figures from column F or row 8 in the chart. Carl knows that it would be confusing to show yearly sales and total sales on the same chart.

To highlight the chart range:

1. Click the **Sales Figures tab** to make sure the Sales Figures sheet is active.
2. Highlight cells A4 through E7, then release the mouse button. Make sure you have not highlighted any cells in column F or in row 8.

Now that he has highlighted the chart range, Carl uses the ChartWizard to create the line chart on the Line Chart sheet.

To create the line chart using the ChartWizard:

1. Click the **ChartWizard button** .
2. Click the **Line Chart tab** to display the Line Chart sheet.
3. Drag the pointer to outline cells A1 through G14. Release the mouse button to display the ChartWizard - Step 1 of 5 dialog box.
4. Make sure the Range box displays ='Sales Figures'!$A$4:$E$7, then click the **Next > button** to display the Chart Wizard - Step 2 of 5 dialog box.

   TROUBLE? If the range shown on your screen is not ='Sales Figures'!$A$4:$E$7, drag the pointer to highlight the correct range on the Sales Figures sheet.
5. Double-click the **Line** chart type to select the line chart and display the ChartWizard - Step 3 of 5 dialog box.
6. Double-click chart format **1** to select the chart format with lines that connect data markers.
7. When you see ChartWizard - Step 4 of 5, compare Carl's sketch in Figure 5-13 to the sample chart shown on your screen and in Figure 5-18. Even though the sample chart is too blurry to allow you to read all the text, it's clear that the chart is not turning out according to Carl's sketch.

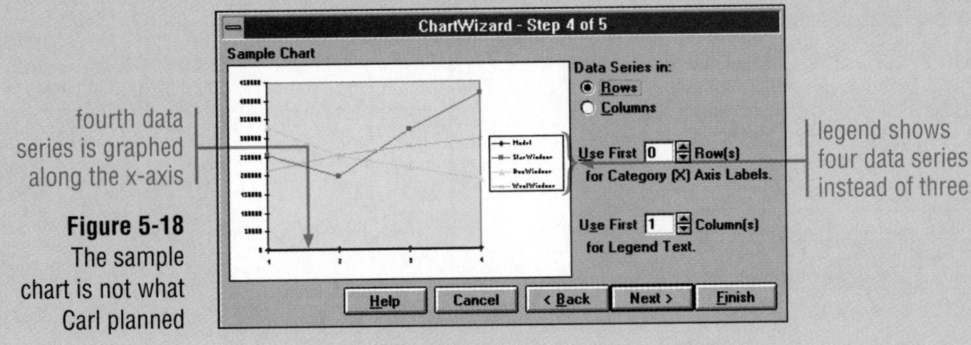

Figure 5-18 The sample chart is not what Carl planned

What's wrong with the sample chart? The legend for the sample chart on your screen shows four colored lines representing four data series: Model, Star Windsor, Box Windsor, and West Windsor. Carl's plan was to plot only three data series: the Box Windsor sales, the Star Windsor Sales, and the West Windsor sales.

The ChartWizard, however, plotted the range A4:F4 as an additional data series. The cells in this range contain the label "Model" and the values 1992, 1993, 1994, and 1995. These values are represented by the dark blue chart line that appears on the x-axis. Carl wants to use these values as labels instead of data, so he needs to revise the ChartWizard settings. Let's look at the options in the ChartWizard - Step 4 of 5 dialog box to find out how to do this.

The first dialog box option, "Data Series in:," lets you specify whether the data series are in rows or columns. Looking at Carl's sketch, you see that the data series are in rows. For example, the first line on the chart should plot the Star Windsor sales in row 5: $256,328; $197,108; $322,522; and $418,679. The Rows option button is selected in the dialog box. This is correct, so Carl does not need to change this setting.

The second dialog box option, "Use first __ Row(s) for Category (X) Axis Labels," lets you specify whether you want to use any rows as category labels for the x-axis. The first row that Carl highlighted for the chart contains the values 1992, 1993, 1994, and 1995. Carl wants to use these values as the category labels, so he needs to change the setting to 1. Before doing that, let's look at the last option in the dialog box.

The third dialog box option, "Use First __ columns for Legend Text" lets you specify whether you want to use any columns for the legend text. The first column that Carl highlighted for the chart was column A, which contains the name of each stove model. Carl wants to use the labels in this column as legend text so the chart clearly shows which line represents the sales data for each stove. Excel automatically selects the first column for the legend text. Carl does not need to change the setting for this option.

Carl needs to change the setting for the Category (X) Axis Labels, so that the values in the first row become the x-axis labels instead of the first data series. Let's do that now.

To use the first row for x-axis labels:

1. Click the **up arrow button** for the Category (X) Axis Labels option to select 1 as the new setting. See Figure 5-19.

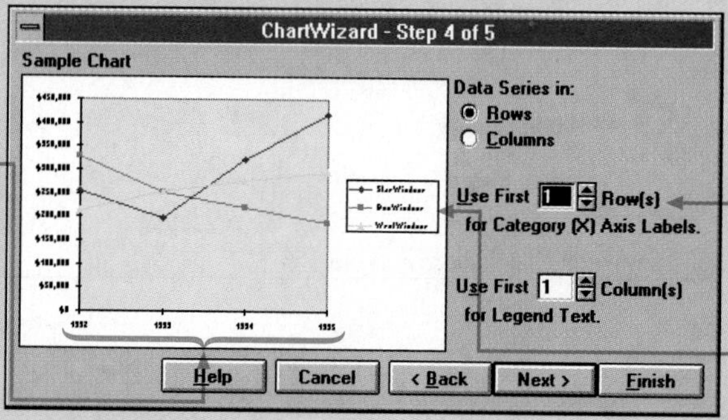

Figure 5-19 The revised sample chart

Carl likes the layout of the revised chart. The x-axis is labeled with the years, the legend box contains the labels for each stove model, and the chart displays one colored line for each stove model. Let's complete the chart by adding the chart title and the x-axis title.

To add the chart title and x-axis title:

1. Click the **Next > button** to display the ChartWizard - Step 5 of 5 dialog box.
2. Click the **Chart Title box**, then type **Sales by Model 1992–1995** as the chart title, but don't press [Enter]. You also need to type the x-axis title.

   TROUBLE? If you inadvertently pressed [Enter] and the ChartWizard disappeared, don't worry about it for now; just continue with Step 5.
3. Press **[Tab]** to move the pointer to the Category (X) box.
4. Type **Sales Year** and press **[Enter]** to complete the chart and display it on the Line Chart sheet. See Figure 5-20.

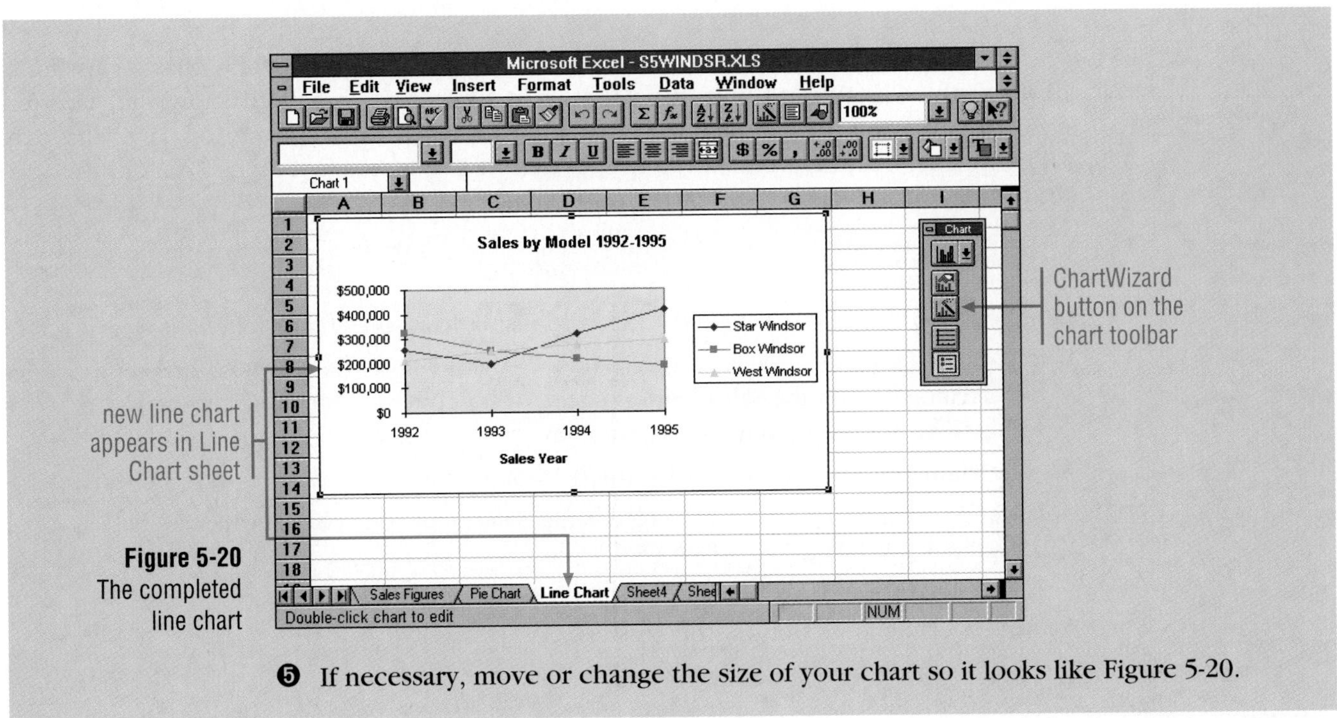

Figure 5-20
The completed line chart

❺ If necessary, move or change the size of your chart so it looks like Figure 5-20.

Carl is concerned because the chart shows that the sales of the Star Windsor declined between 1992 and 1993. He thinks he could make a stronger point if he includes only the years 1993 through 1995 in the chart. But can he revise the chart without starting over?

Revising the Chart Data Series

After you create a chart, you might discover that you specified the wrong data range, or you might decide that your chart should display different data series. Whatever your reason, you do not need to start over if you want to revise the chart's data series.

REFERENCE WINDOW

Revising the Chart Data Series Using the ChartWizard

- Click the chart to select it.
- Click the ChartWizard button to display the ChartWizard - Step 1 of 2 dialog box.
- Drag the pointer to outline the range of cells you want to include in the revised chart, then click the Next > button.
- Make any revisions necessary on the ChartWizard - Step 2 of 2 dialog box, then click the OK button.

Carl will use the ChartWizard to revise the data series for his line chart. This time, he'll use the ChartWizard button on the Chart toolbar. He wants to show the sales for each stove during the period 1993 through 1995, instead of the period 1992 through 1995. He examines his worksheet and sees that he needs to select range A4:A7 as the text for the legend and range C4:E7 as the data series.

To revise the line chart:

1. If the line chart is not selected, click it to display the small black handles.
2. Click the **ChartWizard button** on the chart toolbar to display the ChartWizard - Step 1 of 2 dialog box on the Sales Figures sheet. See Figure 5-20 for the location of the ChartWizard button on the Chart toolbar.
3. Highlight cells A4 through A7 for the first range, then release the mouse button.

   TROUBLE? If the ChartWizard dialog box hides the range you need to highlight, drag the title of the dialog box to a new location.
4. Press and hold **[Ctrl]** while you highlight cells C4 through E7.
5. Release the mouse button, then release [Ctrl].
6. Make sure the Range box displays ='Sales Figures'!$A$4:$A$7,'Sales Figures'!$C$4:$E$7, then click the **Next > button** to display the ChartWizard - Step 2 of 2 dialog box.
7. Look at the sample chart to verify that it now shows three years on the x-axis. (You probably can't actually read the labels, but you should be able to tell if they're displayed at all.) Don't worry if the dates are split onto two lines.
8. Click the **OK button** to close the ChartWizard dialog box and return to the Line Chart sheet. See Figure 5-21.

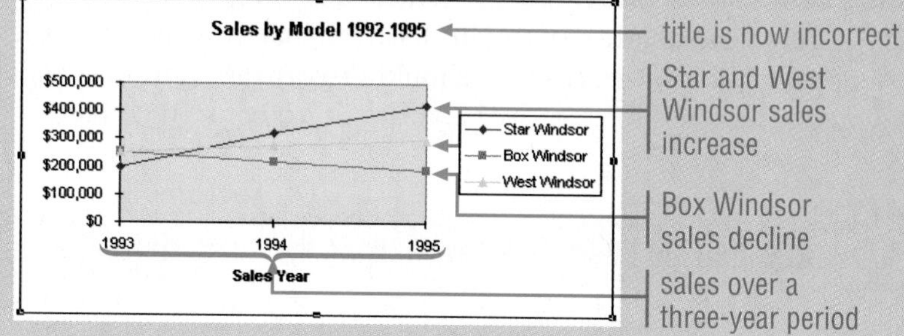

Figure 5-21 The revised line chart

The revised chart clearly shows that sales of the Box Windsor have decreased, while sales of the Star Windsor and West Windsor have increased. Carl notices that he now needs to change the text of the chart title to reflect the revisions.

Adding and Editing Chart Text

Excel classifies the text on your charts into three categories: label text, attached text, or unattached text. **Label text** includes the category names, the tick mark labels, the x-axis labels, and the legend text. Label text is often derived from the cells on the worksheet and is usually specified using the ChartWizard or the Edit Series command on the Chart menu.

Attached text includes the chart title, the x-axis title, and the y-axis title. Attached text appears in a predefined position. You can edit attached text and move it by clicking and dragging. To add attached text, you use the Titles command on the Insert menu. To edit attached text, you click the text, then type the changes.

Unattached text includes text boxes or comments that you type on the chart. You can position unattached text anywhere on the chart. To add unattached text to a chart, you use the Text Box tool.

As noted earlier, Carl needs to change the chart title to reflect the revised data series. To do this he must activate the chart, select the chart title, then change "1992" to "1993."

To revise the chart title:

1. Double-click the chart to activate it.
2. Click the chart title to select it and display the gray border and small black handles. See Figure 5-22.

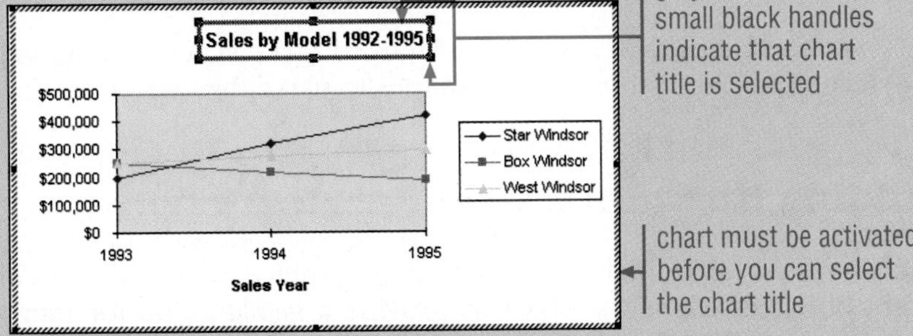

Figure 5-22 Revising the chart title

3. Position the I-bar pointer in the chart title text box just to the right of "1992," then click to display the flashing insertion point.
4. Press **[Backspace]** to delete the 2, then type **3** to change 1992 to 1993.
5. Click anywhere on the chart to complete the change.

Carl checks his original sketch and notices that he forgot to include a y-axis title. He uses the Titles... command to add this title.

To add a y-axis title:

1. Make sure the chart is still activated.
2. Click **Insert**, then click **Titles...** to display the Titles dialog box.
3. Click the **Value (Y) Axis option button** to indicate that you want to add a title for the y-axis.
4. Click the **OK button** to close the Titles dialog box. Eight black handles and a gray border appear, surrounding the letter "Y" on the y-axis.
5. Type **Sales ($U.S.)**. Notice that the letters appear in the formula bar as you type.
6. Press **[Enter]** to add the y-axis title to the chart.

   TROUBLE? If you need to revise the y-axis title after you press [Enter], make sure the title is selected, then type your revisions in the formula bar.

Now that the titles accurately describe the chart data, Carl sees that all he has left to do is format the chart labels.

Using Boldface for the Legend and Axis Labels

You can change the format of any chart text by using the Standard toolbar buttons or the Format menu. Each text item on a chart is an object; as with any object, you must click the object to select it before you can change it.

Carl looks at the chart and decides that it will look better if he bolds the legend text and the category labels along the x-axis.

To bold the legend text and the category labels:

1. Make sure the chart is still activated, then click the chart legend to select it and display the square black handles.
2. Click the **Bold button** [B] to change the font in the chart legend to bold.
3. Click the **x-axis**, the bottom horizontal line of the chart. Two square handles appear on the x-axis.
4. Click [B] to change the x-axis text to bold.

Carl examines the chart and decides to make several additional enhancements. First, he decides to display horizontal gridlines to make the chart easier to read.

Adding Horizontal Gridlines to a Chart

You can add horizontal gridlines to most types of 2-D and 3-D charts. Gridlines stretch from one axis across the chart to provide a visual guide for more easily estimating the value or category of each data marker. You can specify gridlines when you select the format for your chart using the ChartWizard, or you can add gridlines later by activating the chart and using the Gridlines... command from the Insert menu.

To add horizontal gridlines to the chart:

1. Make sure the chart is still activated, then click the **Horizontal Gridlines button** on the Chart toolbar. Horizontal gridlines appear on the chart. See Figure 5-23.

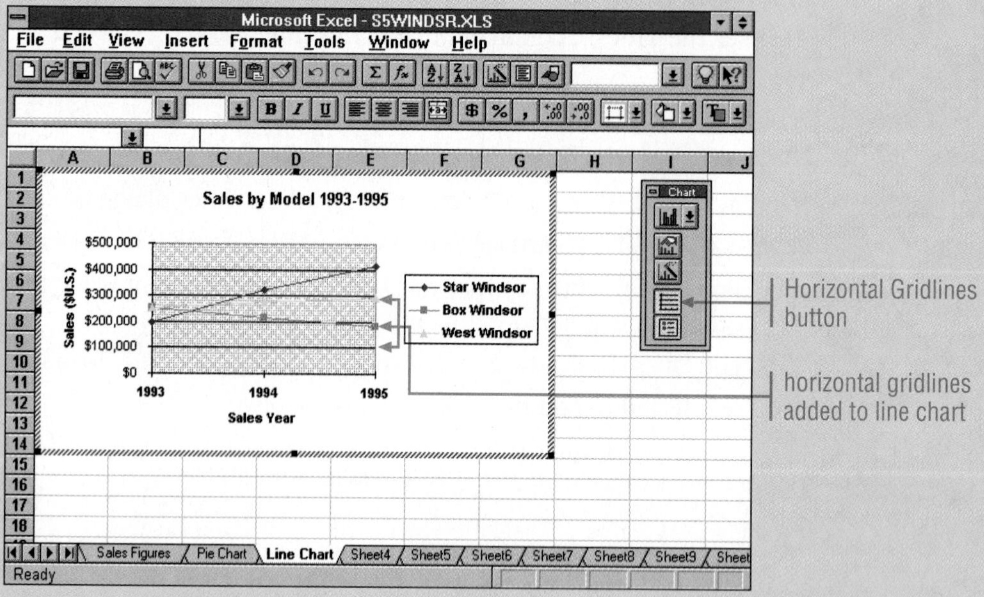

Microsoft Excel - S5WINDSR.XLS

File Edit View Insert Format Tools Window Help

Sales by Model 1993-1995

$500,000
$400,000
$300,000
$200,000
$100,000
$0

Sales ($U.S.)

1993 1994 1995

Sales Year

Star Windsor
Box Windsor
West Windsor

Chart

Sales Figures / Pie Chart / Line Chart / Sheet4 / Sheet5 / Sheet6 / Sheet7 / Sheet8 / Sheet9 / Sheet

Ready

Horizontal Gridlines button

horizontal gridlines added to line chart

Figure 5-23
Adding horizontal gridlines

Next Carl wants to improve the appearance of the lines that represent data on the chart.

Formatting Chart Lines

You can change the format or appearance of the lines and data markers on a chart. In this case, Carl wants to make each chart line thicker. Excel provides a variety of line colors, line styles such as dashed lines and dotted lines, and line weights or thicknesses. Excel also provides a variety of data marker colors and styles, such as triangles, squares, and circles. As with any changes you make to a chart, the chart must be activated before you can change the appearance of the chart lines.

Each chart line is an object, so when you want to format a chart line, you must first select the chart line to display the handles. Once you select a chart line, you can apply formats using the Data Series dialog box.

To format the chart lines:

1. Make sure the chart is still activated, then click the blue line that represents the sales trend for the Star Windsor stove. When the line is selected, handles appear. Also, the formula bar displays the address of the cells containing each data point represented on the line.

   TROUBLE? If you are using a monochrome monitor, refer to Figure 5-24 for the location of the blue line.

2. Click **Format**, click **Selected Data Series...**, then click the **Patterns tab** in the Format Data Series dialog box.
3. Click the **Weight box down arrow button** to display the available line weights. Click the thickest line weight to select it.
4. Click the **OK button** to make the changes.
5. Repeat Steps 1 through 5, but select the pink line that represents Box Windsor sales.
6. Repeat Steps 1 through 5, but select the yellow line that represents West Windsor sales.
7. Click any empty area of the chart to deselect the line representing West Windsor sales. Your chart should look like Figure 5-24.

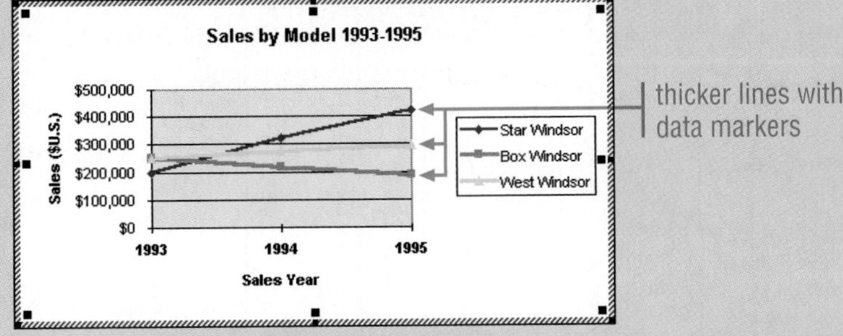

Figure 5-24 The completed line chart

8. Click the **Save button** to save the workbook.

Carl is pleased with the line chart because it supports his argument for allocating less catalog space to the Box Windsor stove. Carl wants to drive his point home by creating a column chart that compares the total dollar sales for each model.

If you want to take a break and resume the tutorial at a later time, you can exit Excel by double-clicking the Control menu box in the upper-left corner of the screen. When you resume the tutorial, launch Excel, maximize the Microsoft Excel and Book1 windows, and place your Student Disk in the disk drive. Open the file S5WINDSR.XLS, then continue with the tutorial.

■ ■ ■

Creating a Column Chart

As you saw in Figure 5-2, Excel's **column chart** type uses vertical bars to represent data. You might want to call this a "bar chart," but Excel has another chart type called a bar chart that uses horizontal bars to represent data. Both the column chart and the bar chart are excellent choices if you want to show comparisons. It is easy to construct either of these chart types with the ChartWizard.

Carl decides that he wants to make a column chart to compare the total sales of each stove model for the entire four-year period. Figure 5-25 shows Carl's sketch of this chart. He examines his worksheet and notes that the data labels are located in column A. The data series for the column chart is located in column F.

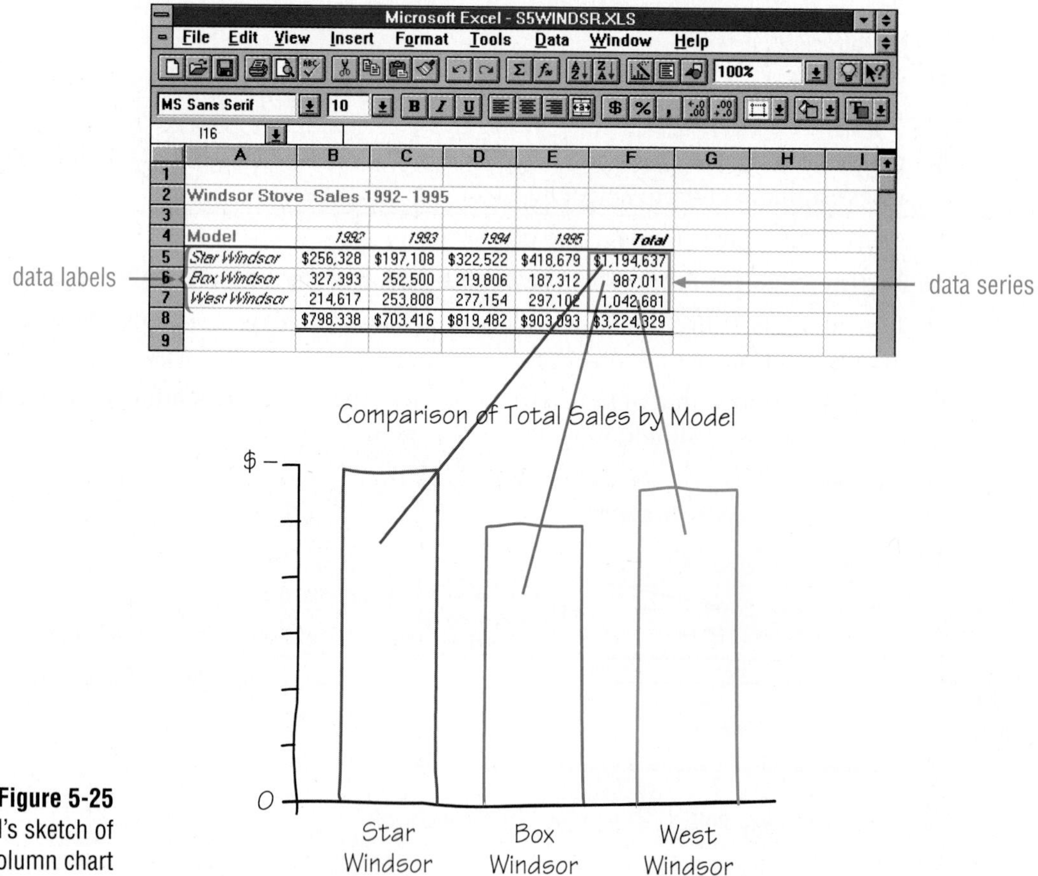

Figure 5-25
Carl's sketch of the column chart

To create the column chart, Carl renames a blank sheet. Then he selects the nonadjacent ranges that contain the data labels and the data series.

To rename Sheet4 and then select the non-adjacent ranges for the column chart:

1. Double-click the **Sheet4 tab** to open the Rename Sheet dialog box.
2. Type **Column Chart** in the Name box, then click the **OK button**.
3. To return to the sheet containing the data you want to graph, click the **Sales Figures tab**.
4. Highlight cells A5 through A7, which contain the labels for the chart.
5. Press and hold **[Ctrl]** while you highlight cells F5 through F7, which contain the data for the chart.
6. Release [Ctrl], then release the mouse button.

Next, Carl uses the ChartWizard to create a column chart in the Column Chart sheet.

To create the column chart:

1. Click the **ChartWizard tool**.
2. Click the **Column Chart tab** to activate the sheet where you want to create the chart.
3. Drag the pointer from cell A1 to cell G18 to outline the area where the chart should appear. Release the mouse button and the ChartWizard - Step 1 of 5 dialog box appears.
4. Make sure the range is ='Sales Figures'!$A$5:$A$7,'Sales Figures'!$F$5:$F$7, then click the **Next > button** to display the ChartWizard - Step 2 of 5 dialog box.
5. Double-click the **Column** chart type to display the chart formats.
6. Double-click chart format **2**. ChartWizard - Step 4 of 5 displays the sample chart.

Carl compares the sample chart to his sketch to make sure that the ChartWizard option buttons are set correctly. The chart appears to be what Carl expected, so he continues to the next step.

7. Click the **Next > button** to continue.
8. Click the **Chart Title** box, then type **Comparison of Total Sales by Model**.
9. Click the **Finish button** to complete the chart and view it on the worksheet. See Figure 5-26. Change the size of your chart, if necessary, so it looks like the figure.

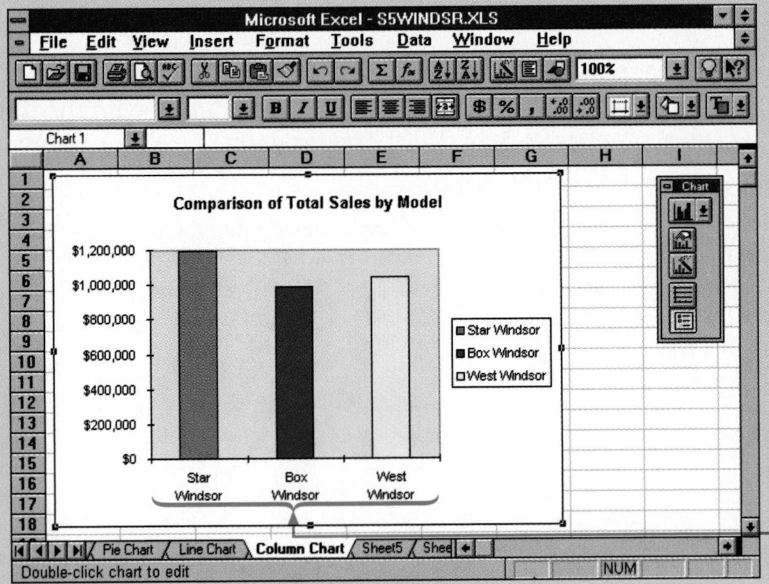

Figure 5-26
The column chart embedded in the worksheet

Carl has heard that it is possible to use pictures instead of colored bars for bar charts and column charts in Excel. Carl decides to try using a picture in this chart.

Using Pictures in a Column Chart

When the ChartWizard creates a column or bar chart, it uses a plain bar as the data marker. You can add visual impact to your charts by using pictures or graphical objects instead of a plain bar. You can stretch or shrink these pictures to show the chart values, or you can create a stack of pictures to show the chart values.

REFERENCE WINDOW

Creating a Picture Chart

- Create a bar or column chart using the ChartWizard.
- Switch to the Windows application that contains the picture you want to use.
- Copy the picture to the Clipboard.
- Return to Excel.
- Select the data marker you want to replace with the picture.
- Click Edit, then click Paste.

Carl remembers that last month, one of the graphic artists in the marketing department created a picture of a stack of money to use in an advertisement. Carl thinks it would be clever to use the picture as the data marker in his column chart. Carl checks with the artist and learns that the filename for the picture is C5MONEY.PCX. His plan is to use the Windows Paintbrush application to open the picture, copy it to the Clipboard, then paste the picture into the columns of the Excel chart.

To copy the picture to the Clipboard:

1. Press and hold **[Alt]** while you press **[Tab]** until a box with the title "Program Manager" appears. Release [Alt]. The Program Manager window appears.
2. Locate the Accessories window.

   TROUBLE? If you can't find the Accessories window, look for the Accessories group icon and double-click it. If you cannot see the Accessories window or group icon, click Window, then click Accessories.

3. Locate the Paintbrush icon in the Accessories window. Double-click the **Paintbrush icon** to start the Paintbrush application.
4. On the Paintbrush menu bar, click **File**, then click **Open...** to display the Open dialog box. Make sure the Drives box displays the icon for the drive that contains your Student Disk.
5. Click the **List Files of Type down arrow button**, then click **PCX files (*.PCX)**.
6. Double-click **C5MONEY.PCX** to open the file that contains the picture Carl wants to use on the chart. See Figure 5-27.

Figure 5-27
Copying the picture to the Clipboard

7. Click the **Pick button** on the right column of the toolbar. Move the pointer to the drawing area; it changes to +.
8. Position + in the upper-left corner of the picture. Drag the pointer to outline the picture. Release the mouse button.
9. On the Paintbrush menu bar, click **Edit**, then click **Copy** to copy the picture to the Clipboard.
10. Click **File**, then click **Exit** to exit Paintbrush. Minimize the Program Manager window to return to Excel.

    TROUBLE? If you see the message "Do you want to save current changes?" click the No button. If you do not return to Excel, press [Alt][Tab] until you see the Excel box.

Now that the picture is on the Clipboard, Carl needs to select one of the columns of the chart, and use the Paste command to replace the plain bars with the picture.

To copy the picture to the column chart:

1. Make sure the entire chart is visible on the screen, then double-click the column chart to activate it.
2. Click any column in the chart. As a result, all three columns display handles.
3. Click **Edit**, then click **Paste** to paste the contents of the Clipboard into the columns. The picture of money appears in each column. See Figure 5-28. Notice that each picture is "stretched" to reflect the different values.

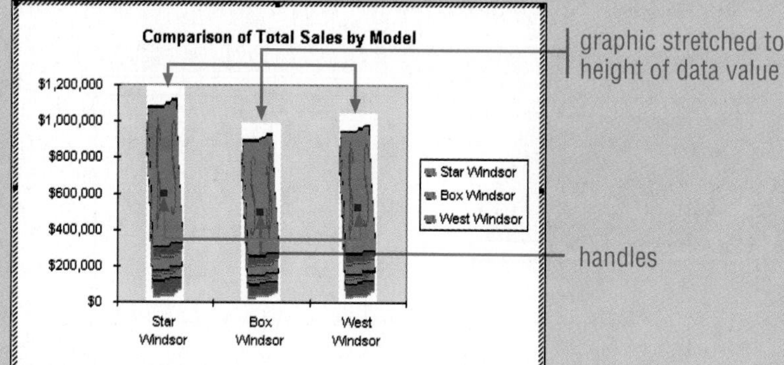

Figure 5-28 The picture chart with stretched graphics

When you paste a picture into a bar or column chart, Excel automatically stretches the picture to show the different values of each bar. Carl doesn't like the way the picture looks when it is stretched. He knows that Excel also provides a way to stack the pictures instead of stretching them, so he decides to try it.

Stretching and Stacking Pictures

The picture or graphical object you use as the data marker on a column chart can be either stretched or stacked to represent the height of the bar. Some pictures stretch well, whereas other pictures become very distorted and detract from, rather than add to, the impact of the chart. You should use your artistic judgment to decide whether to stretch or stack the pictures you use for data markers on your charts.

Carl thinks the money is too distorted when it is stretched, so he tries stacking it instead.

To stack the data marker picture:

1. If the handles have disappeared from the columns, click any column in the chart to select all columns.
2. Click **Format**, click **Selected Data Series...**, then click the **Patterns tab** in the Format Data Series dialog box.

3. Click **Stack**.
4. Click the **OK button** to apply the format. See Figure 5-29.

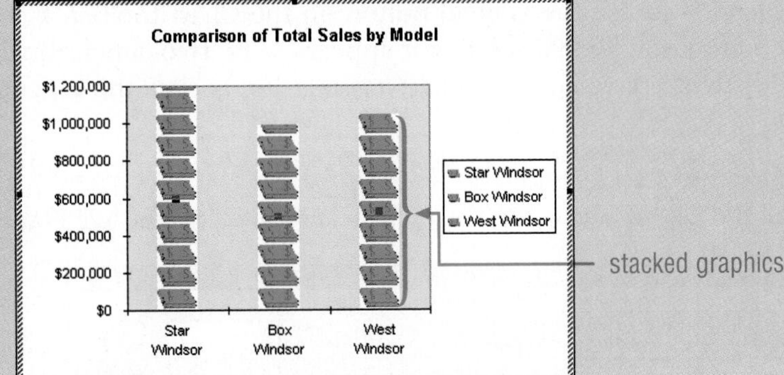

Figure 5-29
The picture chart with stacked graphics

Carl looks at the chart and decides that the stacked graphics effectively show that the Box Windsor stove has produced the lowest dollar volume of the three stove models. He notices that the chart title needs a box around it for emphasis.

Displaying the Title in a Colored Box with a Shadow

As mentioned earlier, the title on a chart is an object that you can select and then format using the menu options and toolbar buttons. To add emphasis to the title, Carl decides to fill the title area with green and then add a thick border around the title. To complete the title format, he creates a shadow effect under the title box.

To display the title in a colored box with a shadow:

1. Click the title to select it and display the handles.
2. Click **Format**, click **Selected Chart Title...**, then click the **Patterns tab** in the Format Chart Title dialog box.
3. Click the **bright green box** in the top row of the Color palette.

   TROUBLE? If you have a monochrome system, select a light gray shade.
4. Click the **Weight box down arrow button** in the Border section to display a list of border weights.
5. Click the thickest line in the list.
6. Click **Shadow** to display a shadow under the title.
7. Click the **OK button** to apply the format.

The chart looks better now that the title is emphasized. Now Carl notices that because all the column markers are identical in color, the chart legend is not necessary. The x-axis labels are sufficient to differentiate between the columns. The easiest way to delete the chart legend is to use the Legend button on the Chart toolbar. If you look closely at the Legend button now, you'll see that it appears to be two-dimensional, indicating that a legend *is* displayed. To remove the chart legend, simply click the Legend button.

To remove the chart legend:

1. Click the **Legend button**. The chart legend disappears. See Figure 5-30.

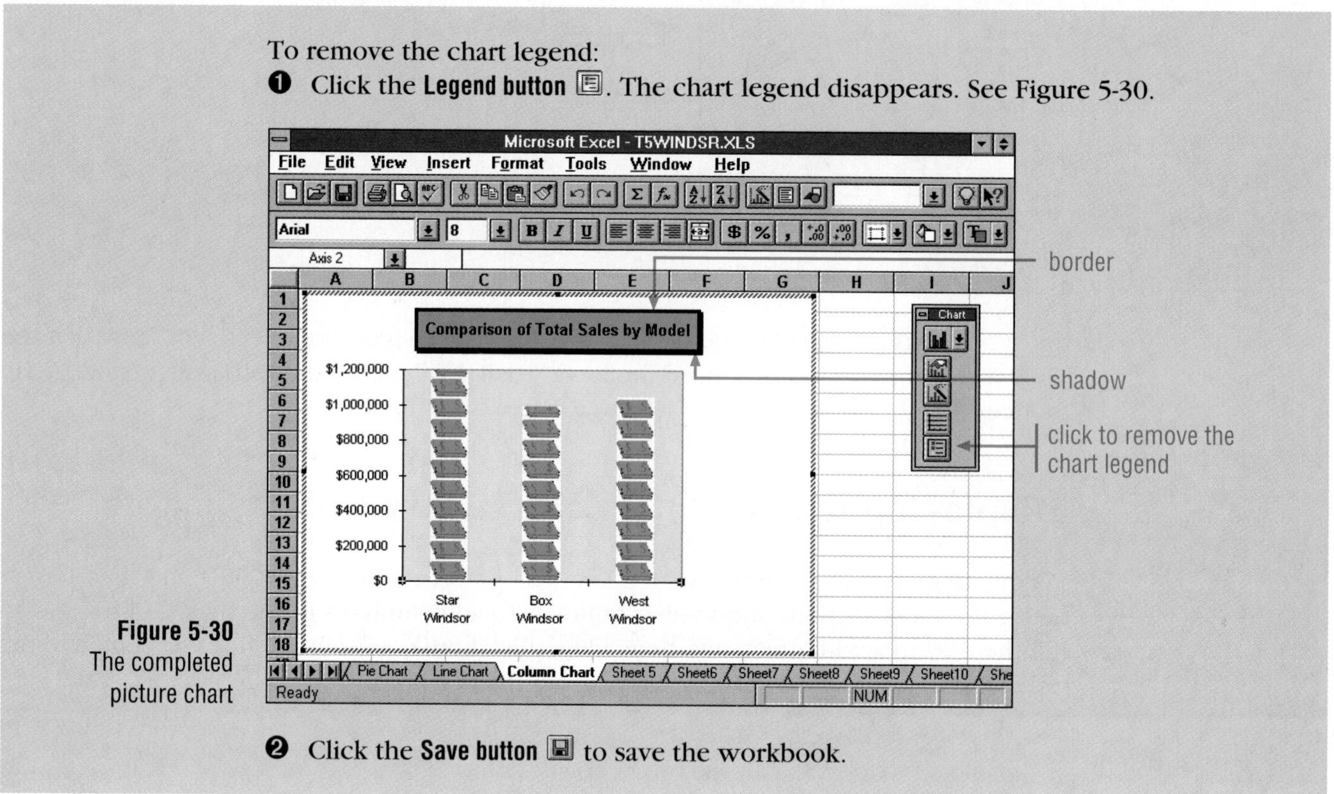

Figure 5-30 The completed picture chart

2. Click the **Save button** to save the workbook.

The picture chart is complete. Now Carl decides to create a 3-D chart to show the sales figures for each of the three stove models from 1992 to 1995.

If you want to take a break and resume the tutorial at a later time, you can exit Excel by double-clicking the Control menu box in the upper-left corner of the screen. When you resume the tutorial, launch Excel, maximize the Microsoft Excel and Book1 windows, and place your Student Disk in the disk drive. Open the file S5WINDSR.XLS, then continue with the tutorial.

■ ■ ■

Creating a 3-D Column Chart

A 3-D column chart displays three-dimensional vertical bars plotted on either two or three axes. Excel provides eight different formats for 3-D column charts, as shown in Figure 5-31.

Predefined Chart Format	Format Characteristics
1	Column chart displayed on x, y axes using three-dimensional columns, no gridlines
2	Stacked three-dimensional columns on x, y axes, no gridlines
3	Columns stacked and proportioned to show relationship to 100% of the data series
4	Column chart displayed on x, y, z axes with x-axis and y-axis gridlines
5	Column chart displayed on x, y, z axes using three-dimensional columns, no gridlines
6	Column chart displayed on x, y, z axes using three-dimensional columns and showing gridlines
7	Column chart displayed on x, y, z axes with gridlines, using three-dimensional columns
8	Three-dimensional columns displayed on two-dimensional, x, y axes with gridlines

Figure 5-31
Predefined formats for 3-D column charts

Formats 1, 2, 3, and 4 convey the same information as 2-D column charts but with the added visual appeal of three-dimensional columns. Like their 2-D counterparts, 3-D formats 1, 2, 3, and 4 use two axes: the horizontal x-axis and the vertical y-axis. Formats 5, 6, and 7 display the data on three axes: the x-axis in the front of the chart, the y-axis on the side of the chart, and a vertical axis called the z-axis.

The three-dimensional arrangement of data on a chart with three axes makes it easier to view the data in different ways. For example, suppose you wanted to compare the number of employees in a company that work in clerical and managerial positions. Suppose you also were interested in the number of males and females in clerical and managerial positions. Figure 5-32 shows a 2-D column chart and a 3-D column chart that were created using the same data range. Both charts were designed to compare the number of male, female, clerical, and managerial employees.

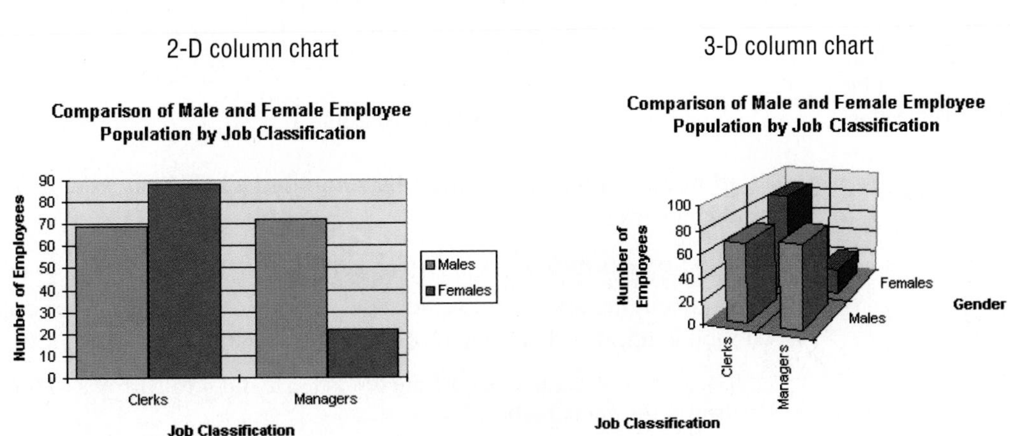

Figure 5-32
2-D and 3-D column charts

The 2-D chart in Figure 5-32 shows the comparison between the number of males and females by job classification. You can see clearly that there are more female clerical workers than males, and that there are fewer female managers. It is not as apparent in this chart that there are more men in clerical positions than in managerial positions. The 3-D column chart in Figure 5-32 shows comparisons based on both gender and job classification.

Carl wants to create a 3-D column chart to compare the sales data in two ways. He wants it to show the sales trends by model; for example, how the sales of the Star Windsor changed from 1992 to 1995. He also wants the chart to show sales by year; for example, the relative sales of each model in 1995. Carl thinks that a 3-D column chart will make it easier to examine the sales data by year or by model.

Carl's sketch of the 3-D column chart is shown in Figure 5-33, along with a note about the two relationships that he wants the chart to illustrate. It is not easy to draw a 3-D column chart by hand so Carl's sketch is not complete, but he tries to show what will appear on each of the three axes of the graph.

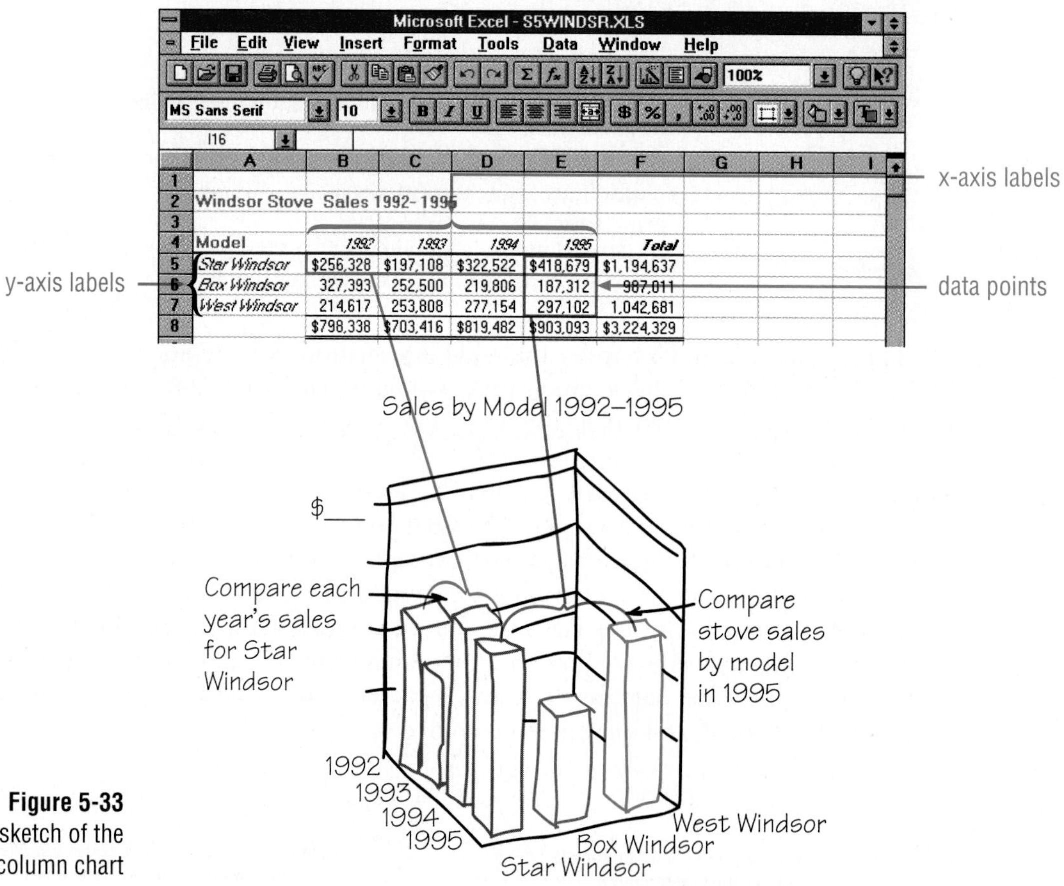

Figure 5-33
Carl's sketch of the 3-D column chart

Carl begins creating the chart by renaming a blank sheet and then selecting the range for the data series.

To rename a blank sheet and select the range for the 3-D column chart:

1. Double-click the **Sheet5 tab** to open the Rename Sheet dialog box.

   TROUBLE? If you can't see the Sheet5 tab, use the scroll arrows to the left of the sheet tabs to display the Sheet5 tab.

❷ Type **3-D Column Chart** in the Name box, then click the **OK button**.

❸ To return to the sheet containing the data you want to graph, click the **Sales Figures tab**. You might have to click the left sheet tab scroller (just to the left of the sheet tabs) to see it.

❹ Highlight cells A4 through E7, then release the mouse button.

Next, Carl uses the ChartWizard to position the chart on the 3-D Column Chart sheet, select the chart type, select the chart format, and enter the chart text.

To create the chart using the ChartWizard:

❶ Click the **ChartWizard icon** .

❷ Click the **3-D Column Chart tab** to activate the sheet where you want the chart to appear.

❸ Hold down the mouse button and drag the pointer from cell A1 to cell G15 to outline the range where you want the chart to appear. Release the mouse button and the ChartWizard - Step 1 of 5 dialog box appears.

❹ Make sure the range is ='Sales Figures'!$A$4:$E$7, then click the **Next > button** to display the ChartWizard - Step 2 of 5 dialog box.

❺ Double-click the **3-D Column chart type** to display the ChartWizard - Step 3 of 5 dialog box.

❻ Double-click chart format **6** to view the sample chart. See Figure 5-34.

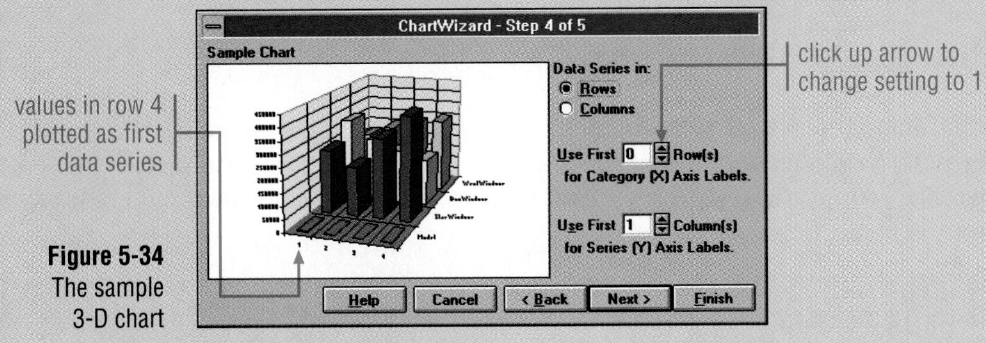

Figure 5-34
The sample 3-D chart

Compare the sample chart on your screen with Carl's sketch in Figure 5-33. The sample chart shows that Excel used the values in row 4 as the first data series. This is the same problem Carl encountered when he created the line chart. Carl must tell Excel to use the values in row 4 (the first row of the chart range) as x-axis labels, not as a data series.

To tell Excel to use the values in row 4 as x-axis labels:

❶ Click the **up arrow button** to change the Category (X) Axis Labels setting to 1.

Now the chart looks more like Carl's sketch. Let's add the title to complete the chart.

❷ Click the **Next > button** to continue to the next ChartWizard step.

❸ Click the **Chart Title box** to activate the flashing insertion point.

❹ Type **Sales by Model 1992–1995** and click the **Finish button** to complete the chart. See Figure 5-35.

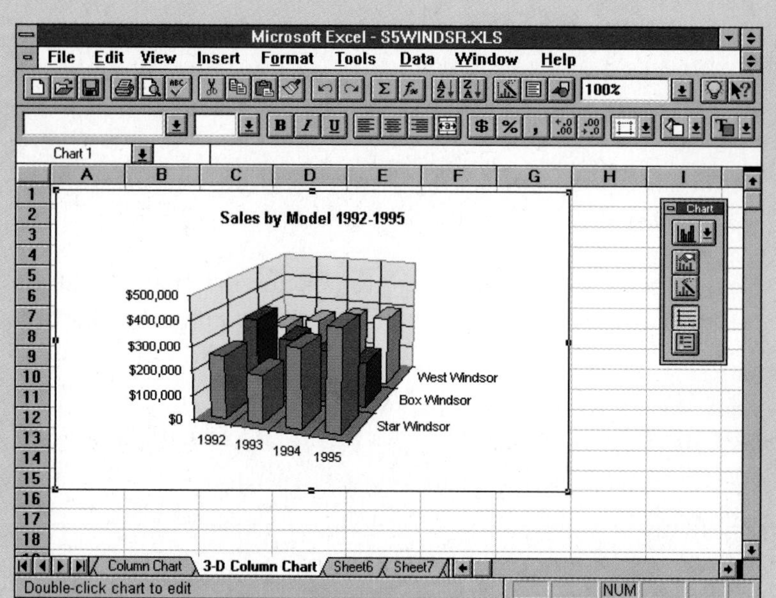

Figure 5-35 The 3-D column chart embedded in the worksheet

❺ If necessary, drag the handles to change the dimensions of the chart to display all the chart text.

Carl notices that some of the bars are hidden by other bars. He can fix this by rotating the chart.

Rotating a 3-D Column Chart

You can use the 3-D View dialog box on the Format menu to rotate a 3-D column chart by ten-degree increments in either a clockwise or counterclockwise direction. By rotating the chart you can display the clearest view of the columns or draw attention to the data from a certain viewpoint.

To rotate the chart:

❶ Double-click the 3-D column chart to activate the chart.

❷ Click **Format**, then click **3-D View...** to display the Format 3-D View dialog box. See Figure 5-36.

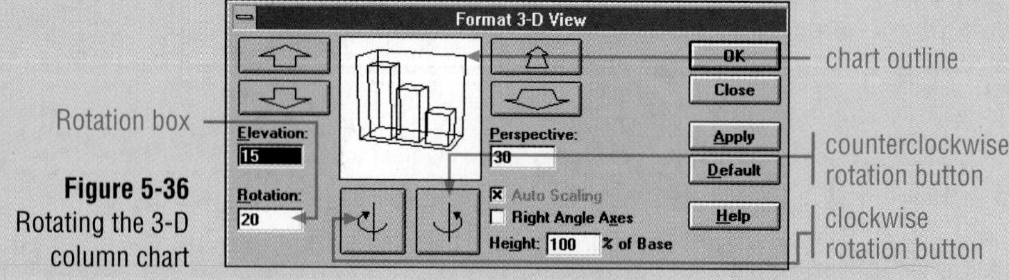

Figure 5-36 Rotating the 3-D column chart

❸ Click the **clockwise rotation button** until the Rotation box shows 140; as you do this, notice how the outline of the chart in the 3-D View dialog box rotates to show the new position.

4. Click the **OK button** to apply the changes. The chart is now rotated to make it easier to see all the columns.
5. Enlarge the chart by dragging the handle in the lower-right corner until you can see all the x- and y-axis labels displayed horizontally. You might need to drag the handle until part of the chart scrolls off the screen.

   TROUBLE? If you enlarge the chart so that it scrolls off the screen, you may see the chart displayed in a chart window the next time you activate it. This is Excel's way of allowing you to view the entire chart without scrolling. You can treat the chart in the chart window exactly as you would an activated chart with a thick border.

Applying a Border Around a Chart

You can customize the border that appears around a chart by using the options in the Patterns dialog box. A border helps to define a chart and to make it visually appealing. For good visual balance, the weight of the chart border should be equivalent to the weight of the chart elements—a chart with vividly colored columns and large, bold text elements should have a thicker border than a line chart with a lighter text font. Carl wants to put a thick, black border around the 3-D column chart.

To apply a black border around the chart:

1. Click any blank space in the upper-left corner of the chart window. Eight handles appear inside the chart border indicating that the chart border is selected.
2. Click **Format**, click **Selected Chart Area...**, then click the **Patterns tab** in the Format Chart Area dialog box.
3. Click the **Weight box down arrow button**, then click the thickest line.
4. Click the **OK button** to apply the changes.
5. Click anywhere outside the chart border to deactivate the chart.
6. If necessary, use the black handles on the chart border to adjust the size of the chart so it looks like Figure 5-37.

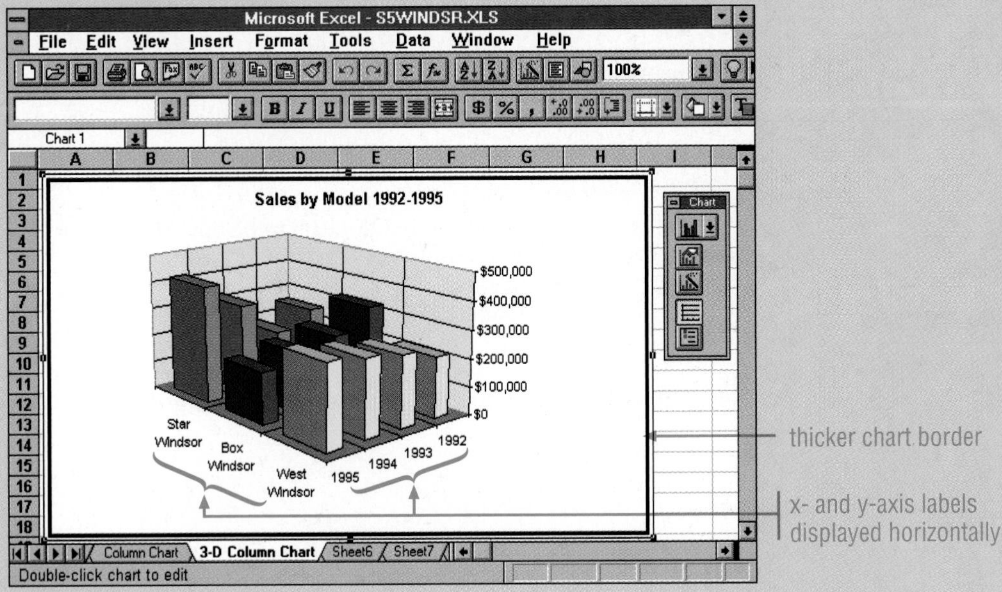

Figure 5-37 The completed 3-D column chart

The fourth chart is complete and Carl saves the workbook.

7. Click the **Save button** to save the workbook.

Previewing and Printing the Worksheet and Charts

Carl has four charts arranged vertically on four different sheets. What would the printed results look like? Carl uses the Print Preview button to find out.

To preview the 3-D Column chart before printing:

1. Make sure the 3-D Column chart sheet is still on your screen.
2. Click the **Print Preview button** to preview the chart. The chart appears in the Print Preview window.
3. If necessary, click the **Next button** to view the second page. (Don't worry if your chart doesn't fit on one page, you'll change the orientation to landscape in the next set of steps.)

Carl decides to use the scaling option in the Page Setup dialog box to enlarge the chart when it is printed. He also changes the orientation to landscape.

To adjust the Page Setup options:

1. Click the **Setup... button** at the top of the Print Preview dialog box, then click the **Page tab** to display the Page Setup dialog box.
2. Click **Landscape** to select landscape orientation.
3. In the Scaling box, change Adjust to: to **125%**.
4. Click the **Margins tab**.
5. Click the **Horizontally box** and click the **Vertically box** to put an × in each box.
6. Click the **sheet tab**.
7. If an × appears in the Print Gridlines box, remove it so the gridlines will not appear on the printout.
8. If an × appears in the Row & Column Headings box, remove it so the row and column headings will not appear on the printout.
9. Click the **OK button** to return to the print preview and view the result of the revised page setup settings.

   TROUBLE? If some of the chart text appears to be cut off, click the Zoom button to get a more accurate preview of the output.
10. Click the **Close button** to return to the worksheet.

Now Carl will adjust the settings for the remaining sheets in the workbook.

To adjust the Page Setup options for the remaining sheets:

1. Click the **Column Chart tab**. If necessary, use the scroll arrows on the sheet tab scroll bar to display the sheet tabs as you need them. See Figure 5-38.

use the scroll arrows to display the sheet tabs as you need them

Figure 5-38
The sheet tab scroll arrows

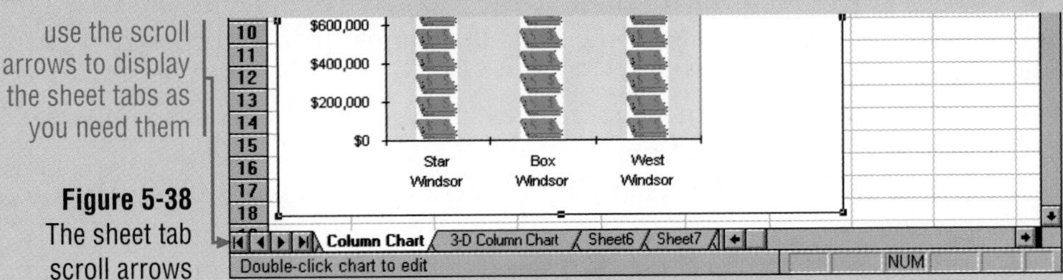

2. Click the **Print Preview button**, click the **Setup... button**, then click the **Page tab** to display the Page Setup dialog box.
3. Click **Landscape** to select landscape orientation. In the Scaling box, change Adjust to: to **125%**.
4. Click the **Margins tab**.
5. Click the **Horizontally box** and click the **Vertically box** to put an × in each box.
6. Click the **sheet tab**.
7. If an × appears in the Print Gridlines box, remove it so the gridlines will not appear on the printout.
8. If an × appears in the Row & Column Headings box, remove it so the row and column headings will not appear on the printout.
9. Click the **OK button** to return to the print preview and view the result of the revised page setup settings, then click the **Close button** to return to the worksheet.
10. Repeat Steps 2 through 9 for the Line Chart sheet, the Pie Chart sheet, and the Sales Figures sheet. Remember to use the scroll arrows on the sheet tab scroll bar to display the sheet tabs as you need them.

Carl likes the way his charts will print. He plans to print the charts on transparencies using a color printer. He will use an overhead projector to present the charts at the department meeting.

You do not need to print the charts from this tutorial now because you will have an opportunity to print them when you do the Tutorial Assignments. While Carl prints his charts, let's exit the print preview and save the workbook with the print specifications.

To exit the print preview and save the workbook:

1. Click the **Save button** .
2. Double-click the **document window Control menu box**.
3. Exit Excel if you are not proceeding directly to the Tutorial Assignments.

In this tutorial Carl created a 3-D pie chart, a line chart, a column chart, and a 3-D column chart. He modified the charts by formatting text, adding titles, adding gridlines, formatting chart lines, adding a border, and selecting chart colors. He adjusted the page setup options to position each chart to create an effective set of color transparencies for his presentation.

Tips for Creating Charts

Excel includes many additional chart types, chart formats, and chart options. You will have an opportunity to use some of these in the Tutorial Assignments and Case Problems at the end of this tutorial. Here are some hints that should help you construct charts that effectively represent your data.

- Use a line chart, a 3-D line chart, an area chart, or a 3-D area chart to show trends or change over a period of time.
- Use a column chart, a bar chart, a 3-D column chart, or a 3-D bar chart to show comparisons.
- Use a pie chart or a 3-D pie chart to show the relationship or proportion of parts to a whole.
- Before you begin to construct a chart using Excel, locate the cell ranges on the worksheet that contain the data series you want to chart and locate the cell range that contains the x-axis labels. Then draw a sketch showing the x-axis, the x-axis title, the x-axis category labels, the y-axis, the y-axis title, y-axis labels, and the data series.
- Design the chart so that viewers can understand the main point at first glance. Too much detail can make a chart difficult to interpret.
- Chart consistent categories of data. For example, if you want to chart monthly income, do not include the year-to-date income as one of the data points.
- Every chart should have a descriptive title, a title for the x-axis, a title for the y-axis, and category labels.

■ ■ ■

Questions

1. Identify each of the numbered elements in Figure 5-39.

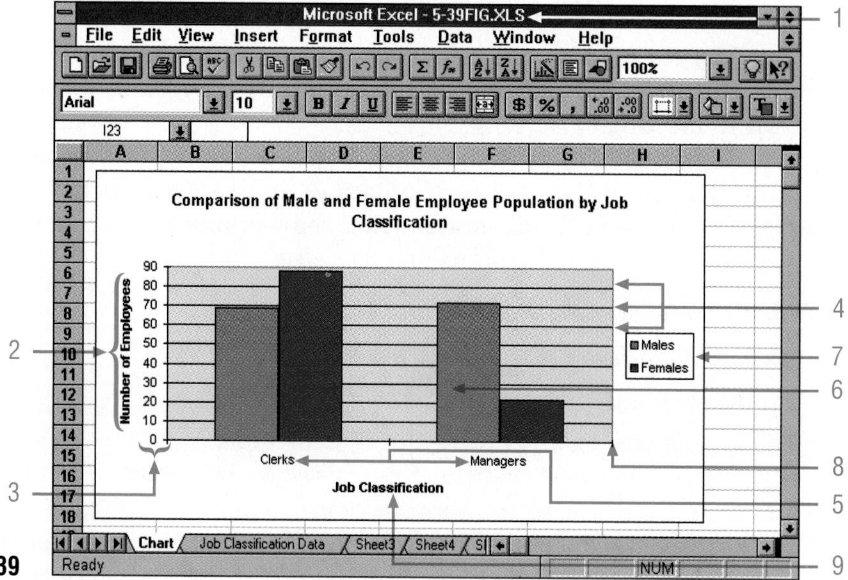

Figure 5-39

2. Write a one-sentence definition for each of the following terms:
   a. data point
   b. data marker
   c. data series
   d. non-adjacent range
3. Explain the difference between a chart type and a chart format.
4. List the chart types that are effective for showing change over time.
5. When do you need to activate a chart?
6. How many data series can you show using a pie chart?
7. List the chart types that are effective for showing comparisons.
8. Describe how Carl set up his workbook so each chart would be displayed on a separate sheet.
9. Suppose you wanted to use the data from Figure 5-1 to chart the sales trend for the Star Windsor stove.
   a. What range contains the category (x) axis labels?
   b. What range contains the data series?
   c. Would you include cell F5 in the data range? Why or why not?
   d. How many data series would you chart?
10. Describe the advantage of using a 3-D pie chart rather than a 2-D pie chart.
11. Explain how to rotate a 3-D chart.
12. Use your library resources to research the topic of graphing (called charting in Excel). Compile a one- to two-page list of tips for creating effective graphs (charts). Make sure you include a bibliography.
13. Look for examples of charts in magazines, books, or the textbooks you use for other courses. Select one chart and photocopy it.
    a. Label each of the chart components.
    b. Write a one-page evaluation of the effectiveness of the chart. Explain how the chart might be improved.

Tutorial Assignments

Carl wants to create a line chart that shows the change in total stove sales between 1992 and 1995. To do this:

1. Open the file T5WINDSR.XLS.
2. Save the file under the new name S5CHARTS.XLS.
3. Rename Sheet6 "Line Chart #2."
4. On the Sales Figures sheet highlight the non-adjacent ranges that contain the dates and the total sales.
5. Use the ChartWizard to create a chart positioned between rows 1 and 16 of the Line Chart #2 sheet.
6. Continue using the ChartWizard to select the Line chart type and format 2.
7. Use first row for the Category (X) Axis Labels at the prompt.
8. Enter "Total Stove Sales 1992–1995" as the chart title.
9. Activate the chart and make the chart line thicker.
10. Remove the chart legend.

Charts such as those Carl created in the tutorial are part of a series of related charts and, therefore, should have similar formats. To standardize the format of the charts that Carl created, do the following for each chart:

11. Put a box around the title of the chart.
12. Fill the title box with the bright green color and put a shadow under it.
13. Select yellow for the background color of the chart and put a thick border around the entire chart.
14. Bold all the text in the chart and adjust the chart size, as necessary, so that the chart text is formatted correctly.

After you have completed the format changes for each chart, do the following:

15. Revise the worksheet header so it includes your name, the filename, and the date.
16. Preview the new charts. Adjust the page setup options as necessary to print each chart centered on the page, enlarged to 125%, without gridlines.
17. Save the workbook, then select and print each chart. (You could choose the Entire Workbook option in the Print dialog box, and print the entire workbook at once, but you may have problems getting the charts to print properly.)

Case Problems

1. Charting Production Data at TekStar Electronics

Julia Backes is the Executive Assistant to the President of TekStar Electronics, a manufacturer of consumer electronics. Julia is compiling the yearly manufacturing reports. She has collected the production totals for each of TekStar's four manufacturing plants and has created a worksheet containing the production totals. Julia has asked you to help her create a 3-D pie chart and a column chart to accompany the report.

To help Julia create a 3-D pie chart showing the relative percentage of CD players produced at the four plants:

1. Open the file P5PROD.XLS.
2. Use the ChartWizard to create the 3-D pie chart on a separate sheet. Use chart format 7 to show the plant name and the percentage of CD players produced at that plant.
3. Enter "Total CD Player Production" as the chart title.
4. Adjust the size of the chart so that all the labels are displayed correctly.
5. Activate the chart and pull out the slice representing CD player production at the Madison plant.
6. Select patterns and colors for the chart that will give it visual impact when it is printed.
7. Save the workbook as S5PROD.XLS.

To help Julia create a column chart showing production totals for all four plants:

8. Use the ChartWizard to create the column chart. Use chart format 4 to show the production totals of VCRs, CD players, and TVs for each plant.
9. Enter "Total Production Quantities" as the chart title.
10. Adjust the size of the chart so that all labels are displayed correctly.
11. Put a shadowed box around the chart title.
12. Select patterns and colors to give the chart good visual impact.
13. Preview the worksheets. Adjust the size and position of the charts if necessary. Turn off row and column headings and cell gridlines.
14. Save the workbook as S5PROD.XLS.
15. Select and print each sheet in the workbook.

2. Showing Sales Trends at Bentley Twig Furniture

You are a marketing assistant at Bentley Twig Furniture, a small manufacturer of rustic furniture. Bentley's major products are rustic twig chairs, rockers, and tables. Your boss, Jack Armstrong, has asked you to create a line chart showing the sales of the three best-selling products during the period 1992 through 1995.

You have collected the necessary sales figures, entered them into a worksheet, and are ready to prepare the line chart.

1. Open the workbook P5TWIG.XLS.
2. Use the ChartWizard to prepare a line chart that shows the change in sales for the three best-selling items over the period 1992 through 1995. If you like, create the chart on the Sales Figures sheet, below the sales data. Use chart format 2.

3. Enter "Total Unit Sales 1992–1995" as the chart title.
4. Size the chart as necessary so that all the labels are displayed correctly.
5. Bold the x-axis and y-axis labels.
6. Change all the lines to a heavier line weight and assign each line a different data marker.
7. Add a shadow border around the entire chart.
8. Adjust the size and placement of the chart as needed.
9. Save the workbook with chart as S5TWIG.XLS.
10. Preview your work and make any changes necessary to position the printed worksheet and chart for the best visual impact.
11. Print the worksheet and chart.

3. Sales Comparisons at Trail Ridge Outfitters

You are working in the marketing department of Trail Ridge Outfitters, a manufacturer of camping equipment. Trail Ridge management is considering an expansion of its Canadian marketing efforts. You have been asked to prepare a chart showing the relative sales of major camping equipment items in the United States and Canada. You have prepared a simple worksheet containing the latest figures for Trail Ridge sales of camp stoves, sleeping bags, and tents in the U.S. and Canadian markets. You now want to prepare a 3-D column chart to illustrate the relative sales in each market.

1. Open the file P5CAMP.XLS.
2. Use the ChartWizard to create a 3-D column chart showing the relative sales in each market. Create the chart either on a separate sheet or on the Sales Figures sheet, below the sales data. Use 3-D column chart format 6.
3. Enter "U.S. and Canadian Unit Sales" as the chart title.
4. Adjust the size of the chart so the labels are displayed correctly.
5. Rotate the chart so that the Canadian figures are clearly visible.
6. Put a shadowed box around the chart title.
7. Change the x-, y-, and z-axis labels to boldface text.
8. Switch back to the worksheet and adjust the size of the chart so all titles are displayed correctly.
9. Preview the chart. If you created the chart on the Sales Figures sheet, you may need to adjust the size of the chart to fit the worksheet and chart on a single page.
10. Save the workbook as S5CAMP.XLS.
11. Print the worksheet and chart.

4. Duplicating a Printed Chart

Look through books, business magazines, or textbooks for your other courses to find an attractive chart. When you have selected a chart, photocopy it. Create a worksheet that contains the data displayed on the chart. You can estimate the data values that are plotted on the chart. Do your best to duplicate the chart you found. You might not be able to duplicate the chart fonts or colors exactly, but choose the closest available substitutes. When your chart is complete, save it, preview it, and print it. Submit the photocopy of the original chart as well as the printout of the chart you created.

Index

Special Characters

A

B

C

D

G

H

I

K

L

M

N

O

X

Y

Z

TASK REFERENCE

MICROSOFT EXCEL 5.0 FOR WINDOWS

*Italicized page numbers indicate the first discussion of each task. An * in the Mouse or Keyboard column indicates that instructions continue from the * in the Menu column.*

TASK	MOUSE	MENU	KEYBOARD
AutoFill a range of cells *EX 50*	Drag fill handle to highlight the cells to be filled.		
AutoFormat a range of cells *EX 65*	See Reference Window "Using AutoFormat."		
AutoSum button, activate *EX 68*	Click the cell where you want the sum to appear. Click Σ. Make sure the range address in the formula is the same as the range you want to sum.		Click the cell where you want the sum to appear. Press Alt =. Make sure the range address in the formula is the same as the range you want to sum.
Bold cell contents *EX 90*	Highlight the cell or range you want to format. Click B.	Highlight the cell or range you want to format. Click Format, click Cells..., click the Font tab, then click Bold in the Font Style list box.	Highlight the cell or range you want to format. Press Ctrl B.
Border, add *EX 98*	See Reference Window "Adding a Border."		
Border, remove *EX 98*	See Reference Window "Removing a Border."		
Cancel action			Press Esc.
Cell references, edit *EX 148*	See Reference Window "Editing Cell Reference Types."		
Center cell contents *EX 92*	Highlight the cell or range you want to format. Click ☰.	Highlight the cell or range you want to format. Click Format, click Cells.... *Click the Alignment tab, then click the Center option button in the Horizontal box.	Highlight the cell or range you want to format. Press Alt O, then press E.*
Center text across columns *EX 92*	Highlight a range—include the text you want to center and at least one cell in each of the columns across which you want to center the text. Click ⊞.	Highlight a range—include the text you want to center and at least one cell in each of the columns across which you want to center the text. Click Format, then click Cells.... *Click the Alignment tab, then click the Center across selection option button in the Horizontal box.	Highlight a range—include the text you want to center and at least one cell in each of the columns across which you want to center the text. Press Alt O, then press E.*

TASK REFERENCE

MICROSOFT EXCEL 5.0 FOR WINDOWS

Italicized page numbers indicate the first discussion of each task. An * in the Mouse or Keyboard column indicates that instructions continue from the * in the Menu column.

TASK	MOUSE	MENU	KEYBOARD
Center the printout *EX 113*		Click File, click Page Setup...., click the Margins tab, then click Horizontally and/or Vertically	Press Alt F, press U, press M, then press Alt Z and/or Alt V.
Chart, add or remove gridlines *EX 180*	Select the chart. Click ▤ on the Chart toolbar.		
Chart, adjust size *EX 169*	Select the chart and drag handles.		
Chart, applying a pattern to a data marker *EX 172*	See Reference Window "Selecting a Pattern for a Data Marker."		
Chart, activate *EX 168*	Double-click anywhere within the chart border.		
Chart border *EX 193*	See "Applying a Border Around a Chart" in Tutorial 5.		
Chart, delete		Select the chart. Click Edit, then click Cut.	Select the chart. Press Del.
Chart, creating picture chart *EX 184*	See Reference Window "Creating a Picture Chart."		
Chart, move *EX 169*	Select the chart and drag it to a new location.		
Chart, revising using the ChartWizard *EX 177*	See Reference Window "Revising the Chart Data Series Using the ChartWizard."		
Chart, rotating a 3-D chart *EX 192*	Activate a 3-D chart. Click the intersection of any two axes to select the corners of the chart. Drag any corner to adjust the elevation and rotation of the chart.	Activate a 3-D chart. Click Format, then click 3-D View.... *Type the values you want in the elevation and rotation boxes.	Activate a 3-D chart. Press Alt O, then press V.*
Chart, select *EX 168*	Click anywhere within the chart border.		
Chart title, add *EX 176*		Activate the chart. Click Insert, click Titles..., click the chart title box to display an ×, then click the OK button. *Highlight the word "Title" in the chart title, press Del, then type the desired title.	Activate the chart. Press Alt I, press T, press T, then press Enter.*
ChartWizard, activate *EX 25*	See Reference Window "Creating a Chart with ChartWizard."		

TASK REFERENCE

MICROSOFT EXCEL 5.0 FOR WINDOWS

*Italicized page numbers indicate the first discussion of each task. An * in the Mouse or Keyboard column indicates that instructions continue from the * in the Menu column.*

TASK	MOUSE	MENU	KEYBOARD
Clear cell contents *EX 69*	See Reference Window "Clearing Cells."		
Close the worksheet *EX 36*	Double-click the worksheet Control menu box ▭.	Click File, then click Close.	Press Alt F, then press C.
Column width, adjust *EX 48*	See Reference Window "Changing Column Width."		
Colors, applying to a range of cells *EX 101*	See Reference Window "Applying Patterns and Color."		
Copy cell contents using the Copy command	Highlight the cell or range you want to copy, then click ▭.	Highlight the cell or range you want to copy, click Edit, then click Copy.	Highlight the cell or range you want to copy, press Alt E, then press C.
Copy cell contents using the fill handle *EX 56*	See Reference Window "Copying Cell Contents with the Fill Handle."		
Delete a row or column		Click the heading(s) of the row(s) or column(s) you want to delete, click Edit, then click Delete....	Click the heading(s) of the row(s) or column(s) you want to delete, press Alt E, then press D.
Display formulas *EX 116*		Click Tools, then click Options.... *Click View tab, then click the Formulas box in the Windows Options box to display an ×.	Press Alt T, then press O.*
Enter a formula *EX 54*	See Reference Window "Entering a Formula."		
Exit Excel *EX 36*	Double-click the Excel Control menu box ▭.	Click File, then click Exit.	Press Alt F, then press X.
Font, select *EX 90*	Highlight the cell or range you want to format. Click the Font down arrow button in the toolbar, then click the desired font.	Highlight the cell or range you want to format. Click Format, then click Cells.... *Click the Font tab, then click the desired font in the Font box.	Highlight the cell or range you want to format. Press Alt O, then press E.*
Font, size *EX 90*	Highlight the cell or range you want to format. Click the Font Size down arrow button in the toolbar, then click the desired font size.	Highlight the cell or range you want to format. Click Format, then click Cells.... *Click the Font tab then click the desired font size in the Size box.	Highlight the cell or range you want to format. Press Alt O, then press O.*

TASK	MOUSE	MENU	KEYBOARD
Footer, edit *EX 111*	Click the Setup button in the Print Preview window.*	Click File, then click Page Setup.... *Click the Header/ Footer tab in the Page Setup dialog box. Click the Footer down arrow button to choose a preset footer, or click the Custom Footer button and edit the existing footer in the Footer dialog box.	Press Alt F, then press U.*
Format currency *EX 94*	Select the cell or range of cells you want to format. Click $.	Select the cell or range of cells you want to format. Click Format, then click Cells.... *Click the Number tab, click Currency in the Category box, then click the desired format code.	Select the cell or range of cells you want to format. Press Alt O, then press E.*
Format date *EX 145*		Select the cell or range of cells you want to format. Click Format, then click Cells.... *Click the Number tab, click Date in the Category box, then click the desired format code.	Select the cell or range of cells you want to format. Press Alt O, then press E.*
Format percentage *EX 97*	Select the cell or range of cells you want to format. Click %.	Select the cell or range of cells you want to format. Click Format, then click Cells.... *Click the Number tab, click Percentage in the Category box, then click the desired format code.	Select the cell or range of cells you want to format. Press Alt O, then press E.*
Format Painter button, activate *EX 96*	Select the cell or range of cells with the format you want to copy. Click [Format Painter], then select the cell or range of cells you want to format.		
Function, enter *EX 130*	See Reference Window "Typing Functions Directly in a Cell."		
Function, AVERAGE *EX 134*	See Reference Window "Using AVERAGE to Calculate the Average of the Numbers in a Range of Cells."		
Function, IF *EX 141*	See Reference Window "Using the IF Function to Specify the Conditions."		
Function, MAX *EX 132*	See Reference Window "Using MAX to Display the Largest Number in a Range of Cells."		

TASK REFERENCE

MICROSOFT EXCEL 5.0 FOR WINDOWS

Italicized page numbers indicate the first discussion of each task. An * in the Mouse or Keyboard column indicates that instructions continue from the * in the Menu column.

TASK	MOUSE	MENU	KEYBOARD
Function, MIN *EX 134*	See Reference Window "Using MIN to Display the Smallest Number in a Range of Cells."		
Function, PMT *EX 137*	See Reference Window "Using PMT to Calculate a Monthly Payment."		
Function, SUM *EX 58*	See Reference Window "Entering the SUM Function."		
Function Wizard, activate *EX 132*	See Reference Window "Using the Function Wizard."		
Gridlines, add or remove from printout *EX 113*	Click the Setup button in the Print Preview window.*	Click File, then click Page Setup. *Click the Sheet tab in the Page Setup dialog box. In the Print box, insert an × in the Gridlines box to add gridlines, delete the × to remove gridlines.	Press Alt F, then press U.*
Header, edit *EX 111*	Click the Setup button in the Print Preview window.*	Click File, then click Page Setup. *Click the Header/ Footer tab in the Page Setup dialog box. Click the Header down arrow button to select a preset header , or click the Custom Header button to edit the existing header in the Header dialog box.	Press Alt F, then press U.*
Help button, activate *EX 34*	See Reference Window "Using the Help Button."		
Highlight a range *EX 26*	Position pointer on the first cell of the range. Press and hold the mouse button and drag the mouse through the cells you want, then release the mouse button.		Select the first cell of the range. Press and hold down Shift and use the arrow keys to select the cells you want, then release Shift.
Insert a row or column *EX 63*	See Reference Window "Inserting a Row or Column."		
Italicize cell contents *EX 90*	Highlight the cell or range you want to format. Click *I*.	Highlight the cell or range you want to format. Click Format, click Cells..., click the Font tab, then click Italic in the Font Style list box.	Highlight the cell or range you want to format. Press Ctrl I.
Landscape (sideways) printing *EX 111*	Click the Setup button in the Print Preview window.*	Click File, then click Page Setup.... *Click the Page tab in the Page Setup dialog box, then click the Landscape option button in the Orientation box.	Press Alt F, then press U .*

TASK REFERENCE

MICROSOFT EXCEL 5.0 FOR WINDOWS

*Italicized page numbers indicate the first discussion of each task. An * in the Mouse or Keyboard column indicates that instructions continue from the * in the Menu column.*

TASK	MOUSE	MENU	KEYBOARD
Launch Excel *EX 7*	Double-click the MS Excel icon.		
Left-align cell contents *EX 146*	Highlight the cell or range you want to format. Click [left-align button].	Highlight the cell or range you want to format. Click Format, click Cells..., click the Alignment tab, then click the Left option button.	Highlight the cell or range you want to format. Press Alt O, press E, then press Alt L.
Module, run *EX 118*		Click Tools, then click Macro. *Select macro name, then click Run.	Press Alt T, then press M.*
Manual page break, add		Select the cell where you want to start a new page. Click Insert, then click Page Break.	Select the cell where you want to start a new page. Press Alt I, then press B.
Manual page break, remove		Select any cell directly below a horizontal page break or to the right of a vertical page break. Click Insert, then click Remove Page Break.	Select any cell directly below a horizontal page break or to the right of a vertical page break. Press Alt I, then press B.
Maximize a window *EX 8*	Click [maximize button] on the window.		
Minimize a window *EX 8*	Click [minimize button] on the window.		
Non-adjacent ranges, selecting *EX 165*	See Reference Window "Selecting Non-adjacent Ranges."		
Open a worksheet or workbook *EX 12*	See Reference Window "Opening a Worksheet."		
Paste the contents of the clipboard into a cell or range of cells	Click [paste button].	Click Edit, then click Paste.	Press Ctrl V.
Patterns, applying to a range of cells *EX 101*	See Reference Window "Applying Patterns and Color."		
Portrait (normal) printing *EX 111*	Click the Setup button in the Print Preview window.*	Click File, then click Page Setup. *Click the Page tab in the Page Setup dialog box,* then click the Portrait option button in the Orientation box.	Press Alt F, then press V.*
Print a worksheet *EX 23*	See Reference Window "Printing a Worksheet."		
Print Formulas module *EX 117*	See "Tips for Using the Print Formulas Module" in Tutorial 3.		

TASK REFERENCE

MICROSOFT EXCEL 5.0 FOR WINDOWS

*Italicized page numbers indicate the first discussion of each task. An * in the Mouse or Keyboard column indicates that instructions continue from the * in the Menu column.*

TASK	MOUSE	MENU	KEYBOARD
Print Preview *EX 110*	Click [Print Preview button].	Click File, then click Print Preview.	Press Alt F, then press V.
Protecting cells *EX 77*	See Reference Window "Protecting Cells."		
Remove split worksheet window *EX 20*	Double-click any part of the split bar.	Click Window, then click Remove Split.	Press Alt W, then press S.
Right-align cell contents *EX 92*	Highlight the cell or range you want to format. Click [Align Right button].	Highlight the cell or range you want to format. Click Format, click Cells.... *Click the Alignment tab, then click the Right option button in the Horizontal box.	Highlight the cell or range you want to format. Press Alt O, then press E.*
Save workbook as a template *EX 80*		Create a workbook, click File, then click Save As. *Type the name you want for the template, select the drive and directory in the File Name box. Click Template in the File Save As Type box.	Create a workbook, press Alt F, then press A.*
Save workbook with the same filename *EX 21*	Click [Save button].	Click File, then click Save.	Press Ctrl S.
Save workbook with a new filename *EX 21*	See Reference Window "Saving a Workbook with a New Filename."		
Select entire column	Click column heading.		
Select entire row	Click row heading.		
Select entire worksheet	Click the Select All button [Select All button].		
Select range *EX 26*	See Highlight a range.		
Sheet, activating	Click the sheet tab for the desired sheet.		
Sheet, move or copy		Click Edit, then click Move or Copy Sheet.... *Select the workbook you want to move or copy the sheet to in the To Book box. Indicate where you want the sheet to appear in the workbook in the Before box. Click Create a Copy if you want to Copy the sheet instead of removing it from its original location.	Press Alt E, then press M.*

TASK REFERENCE

MICROSOFT EXCEL 5.0 FOR WINDOWS

*Italicized page numbers indicate the first discussion of each task. An * in the Mouse or Keyboard column indicates that instructions continue from the * in the Menu column.*

TASK	MOUSE	MENU	KEYBOARD
Sheet tab, rename *EX 52*	Double-click the sheet tab.*	Select the sheet, click Format, click Sheet, then click Rename. *Type the new sheet name in the Rename Sheet dialog box.	Select the sheet, press Alt O, press H, then press R.*
Shortcut menu, activate *EX 89*	Select the cells or objects to which you want to apply the command, click the right mouse button, then select the command you want.		Select the cells or objects to which you want to apply the command, press Shift F10, then select the command you want.
Spelling button, activate *EX 76*	See Reference Window "Using the Spelling Button."		
Split the worksheet window *EX 19*	Drag the horizontal or vertical split box to the desired position.	For vertical pages, select a column, click Window, then click Split. For horizontal pages, select a row, click Window, then click Split.	For vertical pages, select a column, press Alt W, then press S. For horizontal pages, select a row, press Alt W, then press S.
Split window, move to	Click the window.		
Text box, add *EX 105*	See Reference Window "Adding a Text Box and Comment."		
Text note, add *EX 75*	See Reference Window "Adding a Text Note."		
Text note, read or edit	Double-click the cell containing the text note.		
Toolbar, add or remove *EX 103*	See Reference Window "Activating and Removing Toolbars."		
Underline cell contents *EX 90*	Highlight the cell or range you want to format. Click [U].	Highlight the cell or range you want to format. Click Format, click Cells..., then click the Font tab. Click the Underline down arrow button, then select the desired type of underline.	Highlight the cell or range you want to format. Press Ctrl U.
Undo the previous action *EX 18*	Click [Undo].	Click Edit, then click Undo.	Press Alt E, then press U.
Unprotecting worksheets *EX 79*		Click Tools, click Protection, then click Unprotect Sheet.... *If you previously entered a password, enter the password in the Unprotect Sheet dialog box.	Press Alt T, then press P.*

Introductory Microsoft Access® 2.0 for Windows™ Tutorials

1 Introduction to Database Concepts and Access

2 Creating Access Tables

3 Maintaining Database Tables

4 Querying Database Tables

5 Designing Forms

6 Creating Reports

Read This Before You Begin

To the Student

To use this book, you must have a Student Disk. Your instructor will either provide you with one or ask you to make your own by following the instructions in the section "Your Student Disk" in Tutorial 1. See your instructor or technical support person for further information. If you are going to work through this book using your own computer, you need a computer system running Microsoft Windows 3.1 and Microsoft Access 2.0, and a Student Disk. *You will not be able to complete the tutorials and exercises in this book using your own computer until you have a Student Disk.*

To the Instructor

Making the Student Disk To complete the tutorials in this book, your students must have a copy of the Student Disk. To relieve you of having to make multiple Student Disks from a single master copy, we provide you with the CTI WinApps Setup Disk, which contains an automatic Student Disk generating program. Once you install the Setup Disk on a network or standalone workstation, students can easily make their own Student Disks by double-clicking the "Make Access 2.0 Student Disk" icon in the CTI WinApps icon group. Double-clicking this icon transfers all the data files students will need to complete the tutorials, Tutorial Assignments, and Case Problems to a high-density disk in drive A or B. If some of your students will use their own computers to complete the tutorials and exercises in this book, they must first get the Student Disk. The section called "Your Student Disk" in Tutorial 1 provides complete instructions on how to make the Student Disk.

Installing the CTI WinApps Setup Disk To install the CTI WinApps icon group from the Setup Disk, follow the instructions inside the disk envelope that was bundled with your book. By adopting this book, you are granted a license to install this software on any computer or computer network used by you or your students.

README File A README.TXT file located on the Setup Disk provides additional technical notes, troubleshooting advice, and tips for using the CTI WinApps software in your school's computer lab. You can view the README.TXT file using any word processor you choose.

System Requirements

The minimum software and hardware requirements for your computer system are as follows:

- Microsoft Windows Version 3.1 or later on a local hard drive or a network drive.
- A 386 or higher processor with a minimum of 6 MB RAM (8 MB RAM or more is strongly recommended).
- A mouse supported by Windows 3.1.
- A printer supported by Windows 3.1.
- A VGA 640 × 480 16-color display is recommended; an 800 × 600 or 1024 × 768 SVGA, VGA monochrome, or EGA display is acceptable.
- 19 MB free hard disk space.
- Student workstations with at least 1 high-density 3.5-inch disk drive.
- If you wish to install the CTI WinApps Setup Disk on a network drive, your network must support Microsoft Windows.

TUTORIAL 1

Introduction to Database Concepts and Access

Planning a Special Magazine Issue

OBJECTIVES

In this tutorial you will:

- Learn terms used with databases
- Launch and exit Access
- Identify the components of Access windows
- Open and close an Access database
- Open and close Access objects
- View an Access table using a datasheet and a form
- Print an Access table
- Use the Access Help system

CASE

Vision Publishers Brian Murphy is the president of Vision Publishers, which produces five specialized monthly magazines from its Chicago headquarters. Brian founded the company in March 1970 when he began publishing *Business Perspective*, a magazine featuring articles, editorials, interviews, and investigative reports that are widely respected in the financial and business communities. Using the concept, format, style, and strong writing of *Business Perspective* as a model, Brian began *Total Sports* in 1975, *Media Scene* in 1978, *Science Outlook* in 1984, and *Travel Vista* in 1987. All five magazines are leaders in their fields and have experienced consistent annual increases in circulation and advertising revenue.

Brian decides to do something special to commemorate the upcoming 25th anniversary of *Business Perspective* and schedules a meeting with four key employees of the magazine. At the meeting are Judith Rossi, managing editor; Harold Larson, marketing director; Elena Sanchez, special projects editor; and Helen Chung, print production director. After reviewing alternatives, they agree that they will create a special 25th-anniversary issue of *Business Perspective*. The issue will include several articles reviewing the past 25 years of the magazine and of the business and financial worlds during those years. Most of the special issue, however, will consist of articles from previous issues, a top article from each year of the magazine's existence. They expect to sign up many advertisers for the issue and to use it as an incentive bonus gift for new and renewing subscribers.

Brian instructs Judith to select past articles, Elena to plan for the special issue, Harold to contact advertisers and plan the marketing campaign, and Helen to prepare the production schedule. Brian will decide on the concept for the new articles and will communicate assignments to the writers.

Judith begins her assignment by using the Vision Publishers database that contains all articles ever published in the five magazines. From this Access for Windows 2.0 database, Judith will scan the articles from *Business Perspective* and select the top articles.

Elena will also use Access for Windows 2.0 for her assignment. Once Judith and Brian determine which articles will be in the special issue, Elena will use Access for Windows 2.0 to store information about the selected business articles and their writers.

In this tutorial, you will follow along as Judith completes her task. You will also learn about databases and how to use the features of Access for Windows 2.0 to view and print your data.

Using the Tutorials Effectively

The tutorials will help you learn about Access for Windows 2.0. They are designed to be used at your computer. Begin by reading the text that explains the concepts. Then when you come to the numbered steps, follow the steps on your computer. Read each step carefully and completely before you try it.

As you work, compare your screen with the figures in the tutorials to verify your results. Don't worry if your screen display differs slightly from the figures. The important parts of the screen display are labeled in each figure. Just be sure you have these parts on your screen.

Don't worry about making mistakes; that's part of the learning process. TROUBLE? paragraphs identify common problems and explain how to get back on track. You complete the steps in a TROUBLE? paragraph *only* if you are having the problem described.

After you read the conceptual information and complete the steps, you can do the exercises found at the end of each tutorial in the sections entitled "Questions," "Tutorial Assignments," and "Case Problems." The exercises are carefully structured to help you review what you learned in the tutorials and apply your knowledge to new situations.

When you are doing the exercises, refer back to the Reference Window boxes. These boxes, which are found throughout the tutorials, provide you with short summaries of frequently used procedures. You can also use the Task Reference at the end of the tutorials; it summarizes how to accomplish tasks using the mouse, the menus, and the keyboard.

Before you begin the tutorials, you should know how to use the menus, dialog boxes, Help facility, Program Manager, and File Manager in Microsoft Windows. Course Technology, Inc. publishes two excellent texts for learning Windows: *A Guide to Microsoft Windows 3.1* and *An Introduction to Microsoft Windows 3.1*.

From this point on, the tutorials refer to Access for Windows 2.0 simply as Access.

Your Student Disk

To complete the tutorials and exercises in this book, you must have a Student Disk. The Student Disk contains all the practice files you need for the tutorials, the Tutorial Assignments, and the Case Problems. If your technical support person or instructor provides you with your Student Disk, you can skip this section and go to the section "Introduction to Database Concepts." If your instructor asks you to make your own Student Disk, follow the steps in this section.

To make your Student Disk, you need:

- a blank, formatted, high-density 3.5-inch disk
- a computer with Microsoft Windows 3.1, Microsoft Access 2.0, and the CTI WinApps icon group installed on it

If you are using your own computer, the CTI WinApps icon group will not be installed on it. Before you proceed, you must go to your school's computer lab and find a computer with the CTI WinApps icon group installed on it. Once you have made your own Student Disk, you can use it to complete all the tutorials and exercises in this book on any computer you choose.

To make your Access 2.0 Student Disk:

1. Launch Windows and make sure the Program Manager window is open.

   TROUBLE? The exact steps you follow to launch Microsoft Windows 3.1 might vary depending on how your computer is set up. On many computer systems, type WIN then press [Enter] to launch Windows. If you don't know how to launch Windows, ask your instructor or technical support person.

2. Label your formatted disk "Access 2.0 Student Disk" and place it in drive A.

   TROUBLE? If your computer has more than one disk drive, drive A is usually on top or on the left. If your Student Disk does not fit into drive A, then place it in drive B and substitute "drive B" anywhere you see "drive A" in the tutorial steps.

3. Look for an icon labeled "CTI WinApps" like the one in Figure 1-1, or a window labeled "CTI WinApps," like the one in Figure 1-2 on the following page.

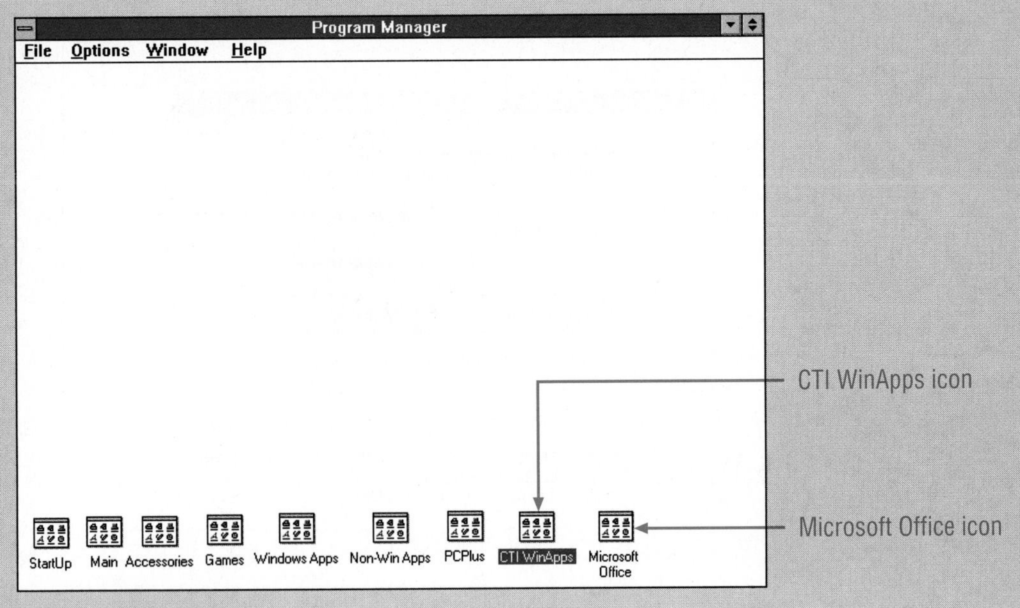

Figure 1-1
The CTI WinApps icon

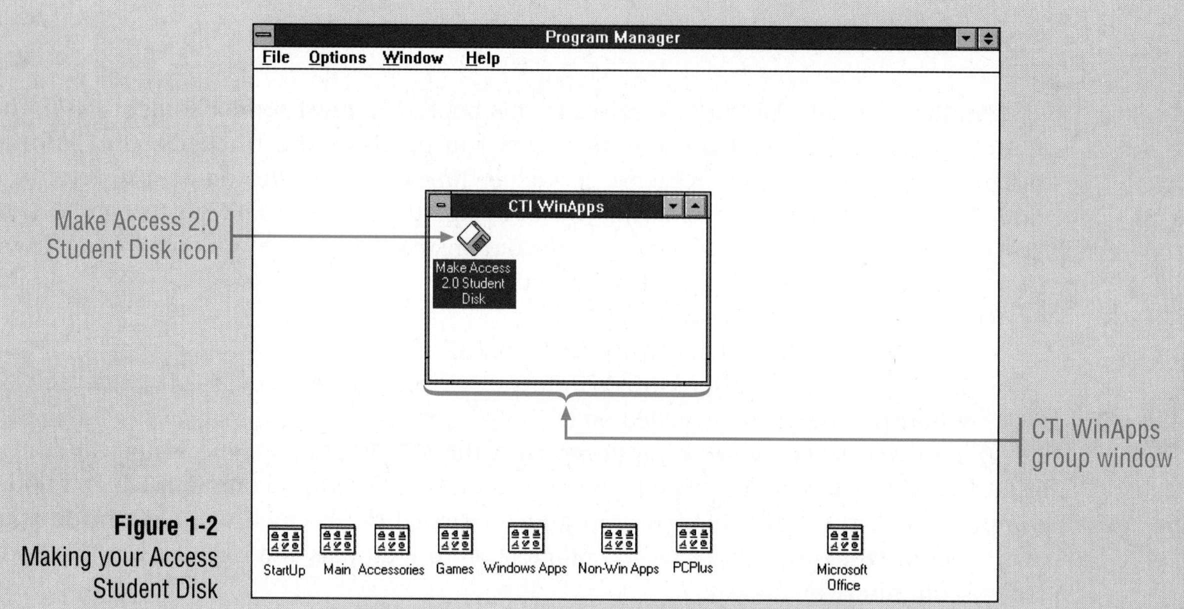

Figure 1-2
Making your Access Student Disk

TROUBLE? If you can't find anything labeled "CTI WinApps," the CTI software might not be installed on your computer. If you are in a computer lab, ask your instructor or technical support person for assistance. ***If you are using your own computer***, you will not be able to make your Student Disk. To make it, you need access to the CTI WinApps icon group, which is, most likely, installed on your school's lab computers. Ask your instructor or technical support person for further information on where to locate the CTI WinApps icon group. Once you create your Student Disk, you can use it to complete all the tutorials and exercises in this book on any computer you choose.

4. If you see an icon labeled "CTI WinApps," double-click it to open the CTI WinApps group window. If the CTI WinApps window is already open, go to Step 5.
5. Double-click the icon labeled "Make Access 2.0 Student Disk." The Make Access 2.0 Student Disk window opens. See Figure 1-3.

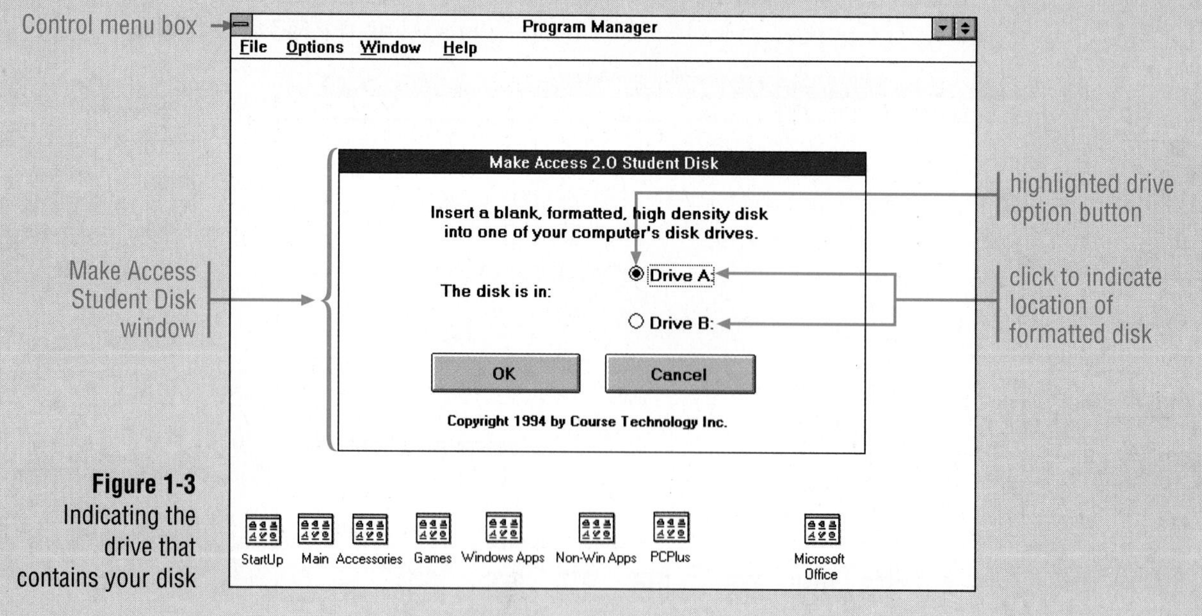

Figure 1-3
Indicating the drive that contains your disk

6. Make sure the drive that contains your formatted disk corresponds to the drive option button that is highlighted in the dialog box on your screen.
7. Click the **OK button** to copy the practice files to your formatted disk.
8. When the copying is complete, a message indicates the number of files copied to your disk. Click the **OK button**.
9. To close the CTI WinApps window, double-click the **Control menu box** on the CTI WinApps window.

Introduction to Database Concepts

Before you work along with Judith on her Vision Publishers assignment, you need to understand a few key terms and concepts associated with databases.

Organizing Data

Data is a valuable resource to companies. At Vision Publishers, for example, writers' names and payments and past magazine article titles and publication dates are data of great value. Organizing, creating, storing, maintaining, retrieving, and sorting such data are important activities that lead to the display and printing of information useful to a company.

When you plan to create and store new types of data either manually or on a computer, you follow a general three-step procedure:

- Identify the individual fields.
- Group fields for each entity.
- Store the field values for each record.

You first identify the individual fields. A **field** is a single characteristic of an entity. An **entity** is a person, place, object, event, or idea. Article title and article length are examples of two fields that Vision Publishers tracks for the entity magazine articles. The company also tracks the fields of writer name and writer address for the entity writers. A field is also called a **data element**, **data item**, or **attribute**.

You next group together all fields for a specific entity into a structure called a **table**. Among its many tables, Vision Publishers has a MAGAZINE ARTICLES table and a WRITERS table, as shown in Figure 1-4. The MAGAZINE ARTICLES table has fields named Article Title, Magazine Issue, Magazine Name, and Article Length. The WRITERS table has fields named Writer Name, Writer Address, and Phone Number. By identifying the fields for each entity and organizing them into tables, you have created the physical structure for your data.

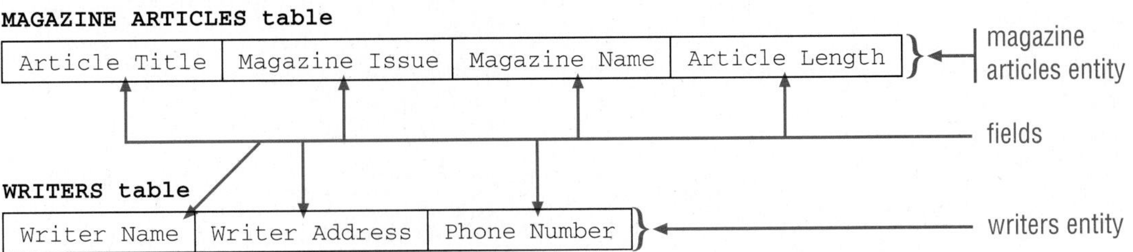

Figure 1-4 Fields organized in two tables

Your final step is to store specific values for the fields of each table. The specific value, or content, of a field is called the **field value**. In the MAGAZINE ARTICLES table, for example, the first set of field values for Article Title, Magazine Issue, Magazine Name, and Article Length are, respectively, Trans-Alaskan Oil Pipeline Opening, 1977 JUL, Business Perspective, and 803 (Figure 1-5). This set of field values is called a **record**. Each separate stored magazine article is a separate record. Nine records are shown in Figure 1-5; each row of field values is a record.

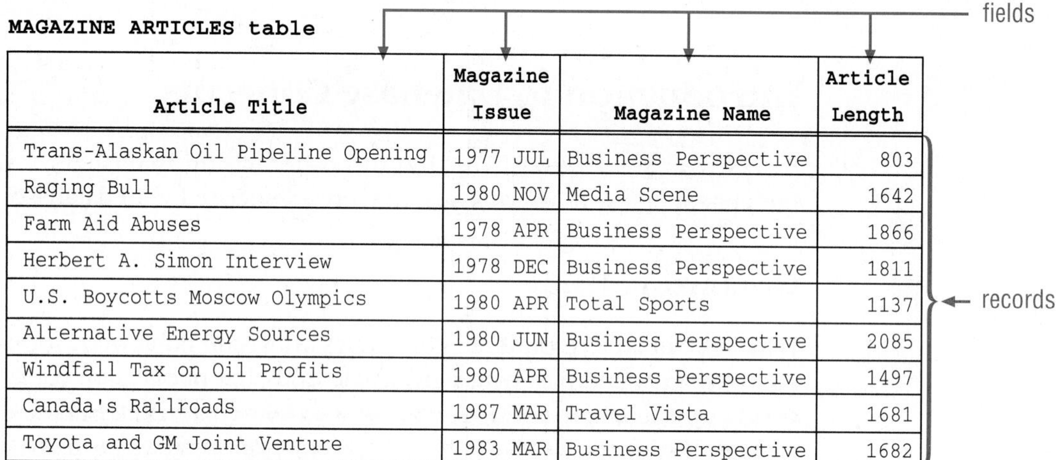

Article Title	Magazine Issue	Magazine Name	Article Length
Trans-Alaskan Oil Pipeline Opening	1977 JUL	Business Perspective	803
Raging Bull	1980 NOV	Media Scene	1642
Farm Aid Abuses	1978 APR	Business Perspective	1866
Herbert A. Simon Interview	1978 DEC	Business Perspective	1811
U.S. Boycotts Moscow Olympics	1980 APR	Total Sports	1137
Alternative Energy Sources	1980 JUN	Business Perspective	2085
Windfall Tax on Oil Profits	1980 APR	Business Perspective	1497
Canada's Railroads	1987 MAR	Travel Vista	1681
Toyota and GM Joint Venture	1983 MAR	Business Perspective	1682

Figure 1-5
Data organization for a table of magazine articles

Databases and Relationships

A collection of related tables is called a **database**, or a **relational database**. Two related tables at Vision Publishers, for example, are the WRITERS table and the MAGAZINE ARTICLES table. Sometimes you might want information about writers and the articles they wrote. To obtain this information you must have a way to connect records from the WRITERS table to records from the MAGAZINE ARTICLES table. You connect the records from the separate tables through a **common field** that appears in both tables. Each record in the MAGAZINE ARTICLES table has a field named Writer ID, which is also a field in the WRITERS table (Figure 1-6). For example, Leroy W. Johnson is the third writer in the WRITERS table and has a Writer ID field value of J525. This same Writer ID field value, J525, appears in the first and third records of the MAGAZINE ARTICLES table. Leroy W. Johnson is therefore the writer of these two articles. Tables are also often called **relations**, because records can be connected to form relationships between tables.

MAGAZINE ARTICLES table

Article Title	Magazine Issue	Magazine Name	Article Length	Writer ID
Trans-Alaskan Oil Pipeline Opening	1977 JUL	Business Perspective	803	J525
Raging Bull	1980 NOV	Media Scene	1642	S253
Farm Aid Abuses	1978 APR	Business Perspective	1866	J525
Herbert A. Simon Interview	1978 DEC	Business Perspective	1811	C200
U.S. Boycotts Moscow Olympics	1980 APR	Total Sports	1137	R543
Alternative Energy Sources	1980 JUN	Business Perspective	2085	S260
Windfall Tax on Oil Profits	1980 APR	Business Perspective	1497	K500
Canada's Railroads	1987 MAR	Travel Vista	1681	H655
Toyota and GM Joint Venture	1983 MAR	Business Perspective	1682	S260

WRITERS table

Writer ID	Writer Name	Phone Number	Last Contact Date	Freelance?
C200	Kelly Cox	(204)783-5415	11/14/82	Yes
H655	Maria L. Hernandez	(916)669-6518	4/9/94	No
J525	Leroy W. Johnson	(209)895-2046	1/29/91	Yes
K500	Chong Kim	(807)729-5364	5/19/94	No
R543	Adam Reynolds	(211)457-9811	10/30/88	No
S253	Myra Schneider	(819)534-6785	2/28/89	No
S260	Wilhelm Seeger	(306)423-0932	12/24/93	Yes

Figure 1-6
Database relationship between tables for magazine articles and writers

Each Writer ID value in the WRITERS table must be unique, so that we can distinguish one writer from another and identify the writer of specific articles in the MAGAZINE ARTICLES table. We call the Writer ID field the primary key of the WRITERS table. A **primary key** is a field, or a collection of fields, whose values uniquely identify each record in a table.

When we include a primary key from one table in a second table to form a relationship between the two tables, we call it a **foreign key** in the second table. For example, Writer ID is the primary key in the WRITERS table and is a foreign key in the MAGAZINE ARTICLES table. Although the primary key Writer ID has unique values in the WRITERS table, the same field as a foreign key in the MAGAZINE ARTICLES table does not have unique values. The Writer ID values J525 and S260, for example, each appear in two records in the MAGAZINE ARTICLES table. Each foreign key value, however, must match one of the field values for the primary key in the other table. Each Writer ID value in the MAGAZINE ARTICLES table, for instance, appears as a Writer ID value in the WRITERS table. The two tables are related, enabling us to tie together the facts about magazine articles with the facts about writers.

Relational Database Management Systems

To manage its databases, a company purchases a database management system. A **database management system (DBMS)** is a software package that lets us create databases and then manipulate data in the databases. Most of today's database management systems, including Access, are called relational database management systems. In a **relational database management system**, data is organized as a collection of tables. These tables are formally called relations, which is how the term relational databases originated.

A relationship between two tables in a relational DBMS is formed through a common field. A relational DBMS controls the physical databases on disk storage by carrying out data creation and manipulation requests. Specifically, a relational DBMS has the following functions (Figure 1-7 summarizes these functions):

- It allows you to create database structures containing fields, tables, and table relationships.
- It lets you easily add new records, change field values in existing records, and delete records.
- It contains a built-in query language, which lets you obtain immediate answers to the questions you ask about your data.
- It contains a built-in report generator, which lets you produce professional-looking, formatted, hardcopy reports from your data.
- It provides protection of databases through security, control, and recovery facilities.

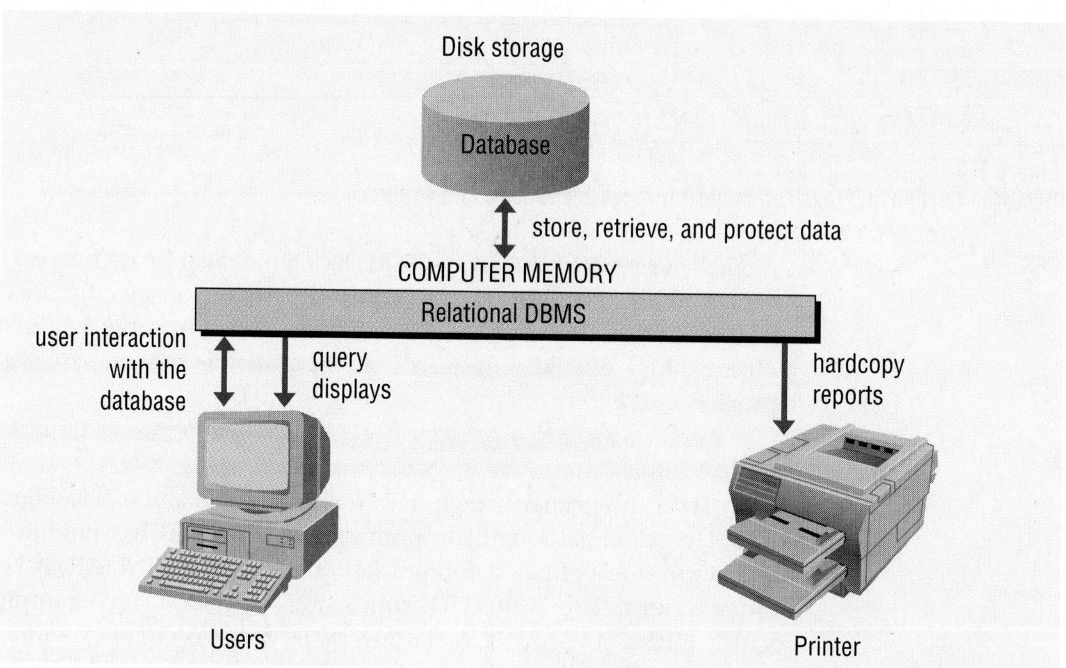

Figure 1-7
A relational database management system

A company like Vision Publishers additionally benefits from a relational DBMS because it allows several people working in different departments to share the same data. More than one person can enter data into a database, and more than one person can retrieve and analyze data that was entered by others. For example, Vision Publishers keeps only one copy of the WRITERS table, and all employees use it to satisfy their specific needs for writer information.

Finally, unlike other software tools, such as spreadsheets, a DBMS can handle massive amounts of data and can easily form relationships among multiple tables. Each Access database, for example, can be up to 1 gigabyte in size and can contain up to 32,768 tables.

Launching and Exiting Access

Access, marketed by Microsoft Corporation, is rapidly becoming one of the most popular relational DBMSs in the Windows environment. For the rest of this tutorial, you will learn to use Access as you work with Judith Rossi on her project.

You first need to learn how to launch Access, so let's launch Access from the Program Manager window.

To launch Access:

❶ Make sure you have created your copy of the Access Student Disk. The Microsoft Office group icon should be visible in the Program Manager window, as you saw in Figure 1-1.

TROUBLE? If you don't have a group icon labeled Microsoft Office, then look for a group icon labeled Microsoft Access and use it instead. If you do not have either of these group icons, ask your technical support person or instructor for help finding the proper icon. Perhaps Access has not been installed on the computer you are using. If you are using your own computer, make sure you have installed the Access software.

TROUBLE? If you don't have a Student Disk, then you need to get one. Your instructor will either give you one or ask you to make your own by following the steps earlier in this tutorial in the section called "Your Student Disk." See your instructor for information.

❷ Double-click the **Microsoft Office group icon** in the Program Manager window. The Microsoft Office group window opens. See Figure 1-8.

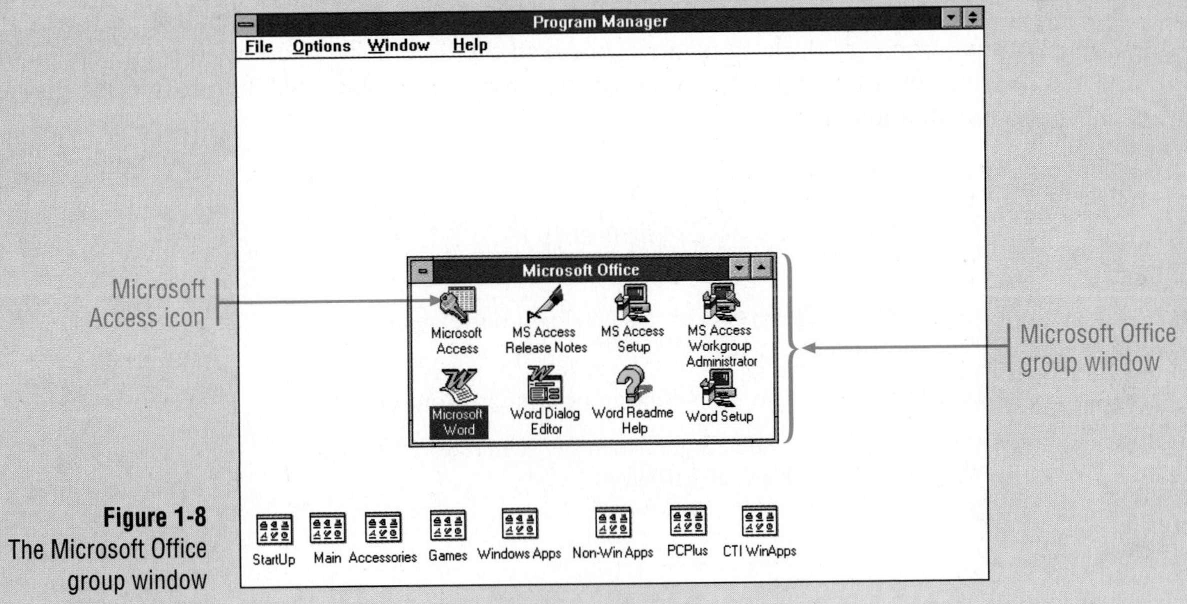

Figure 1-8 The Microsoft Office group window

❸ Double-click the **Microsoft Access icon** in the Microsoft Office group window. After a short pause, the Access copyright information appears in a message box and remains on the screen until Access is ready for use. See Figure 1-9.

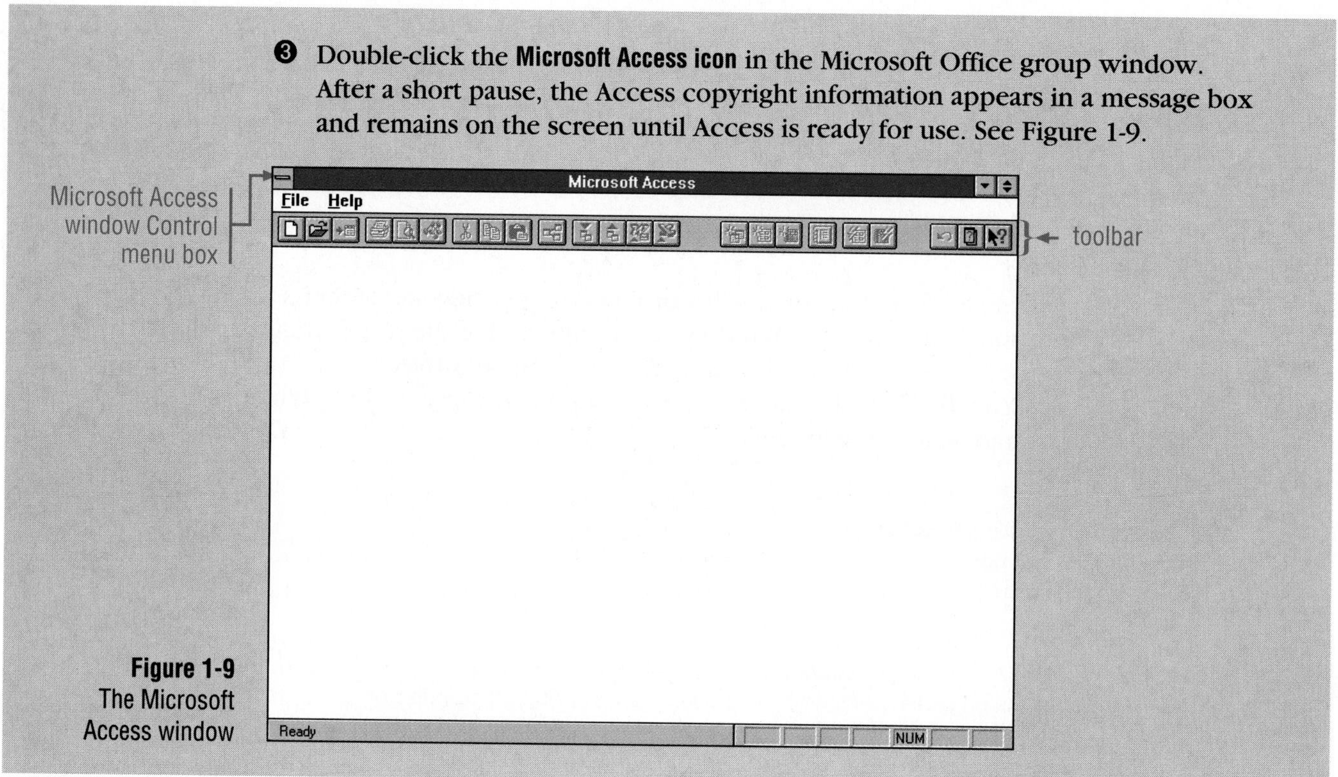

Figure 1-9
The Microsoft Access window

Access is now loaded into your computer's memory. Although Judith wants to work with an existing database, it's always a good idea to know how to exit a software package when you first start working with it. In case you need to end your working session with the package to do something else or if you want to start all over again, you should feel comfortable that you can exit the package at any time.

The Reference Window called "Exiting Access" lists the general steps for exiting Access. Don't try these steps now. Just read the Reference Window to get a general idea of what you are going to do. Specific steps for you to follow will be provided in the next section of numbered steps.

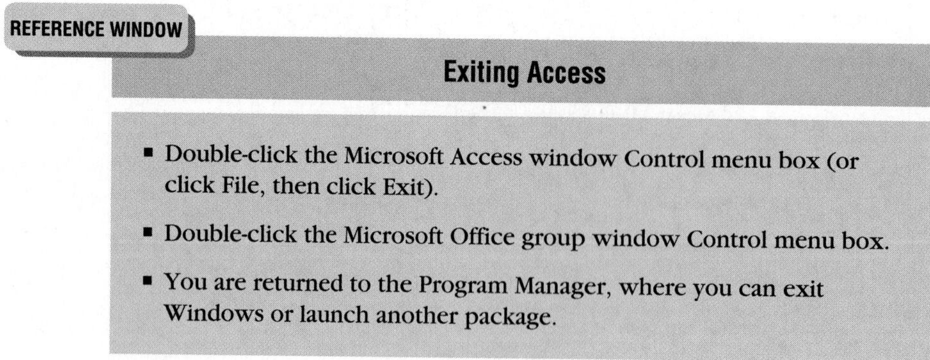

REFERENCE WINDOW

Exiting Access

- Double-click the Microsoft Access window Control menu box (or click File, then click Exit).
- Double-click the Microsoft Office group window Control menu box.
- You are returned to the Program Manager, where you can exit Windows or launch another package.

Practice exiting Access by completing the following set of steps. You can exit Access almost any time, no matter what you are doing, by following these steps. If you ever try to exit Access and find you cannot, your active window is likely to be an open dialog box. An open dialog box will prevent you from immediately exiting Access. Simply cancel the dialog box, and you will then be able to exit Access.

To exit Access:

1. Double-click the Microsoft Access window **Control menu box** (or click **File**, then click **Exit**).
2. Double-click the Microsoft Office group window **Control menu box** to close it. You are returned to the Program Manager.

After exiting Access, you should follow the steps to launch Access when you continue with the next section of the tutorial.

Opening a Database

To select the anniversary issue articles, Judith will work with an existing database, so her first step is to open that database. When you want to use a database that was previously created, you must first open it. When you open a database, a copy of the database file is transferred into the random access memory (RAM) of your computer and becomes available for your use. You can then view, print, modify, or save it on your disk.

REFERENCE WINDOW

Opening a Database

- Click the Open Database button on the toolbar in the Microsoft Access window. The Open Database dialog box appears.
- Change the drive and directory information, if necessary, to the disk location of the database.
- Scroll through the File Name list box until the database name appears and then click it. The name appears in the File Name text box.
- Click OK or press [Enter] to accept the changes in the Open Database dialog box.

You open a database by using the Open Database button on the toolbar. The **toolbar buttons** on the toolbar represent common operations you perform with your database. For example, the Help button is used to ask for help about Access tasks. When you switch to different windows in Access, both the toolbar and menu bar change to provide you with the appropriate common operations relevant to that window.

When you first view the toolbar, you will probably be unsure of the function associated with each toolbar button. Fortunately, when you stop the mouse pointer on a toolbar button, Access displays a ToolTip under the button and a description of the button in the status bar at the bottom of the screen. A **ToolTip** is a boxed caption showing the name of the indicated toolbar button.

Let's display the ToolTip for the Open Database button. If you exited Access earlier, launch Access before you follow the next step.

To display a ToolTip:

1. Move the mouse pointer to the toolbar and stop the pointer on the second button from the left. After a short pause, Access displays a ToolTip under the button and the button's description in the status bar. See Figure 1-10.

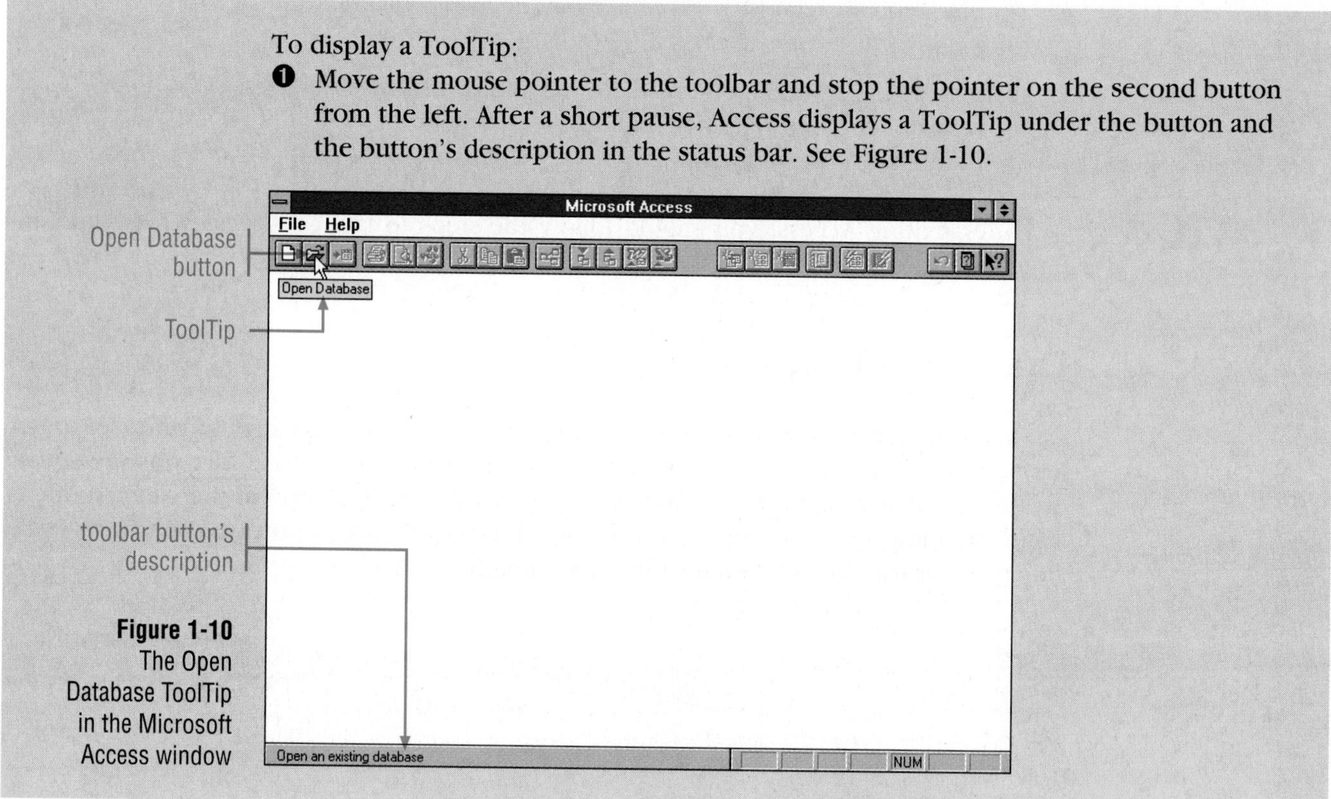

Figure 1-10 The Open Database ToolTip in the Microsoft Access window

Some toolbar buttons appear dimmed because they are not active now. They will become active later, after you have opened a database or taken some other action. You can spend a few moments stopping at each toolbar button to view its ToolTip and status bar description.

Let's now open the database for Vision Publishers.

To open an existing database:

1. Make sure your Access Student Disk is in the appropriate drive—either drive A or drive B.
2. Click the **Open Database button** in the Microsoft Access window. Access displays the Open Database dialog box. See Figure 1-11.

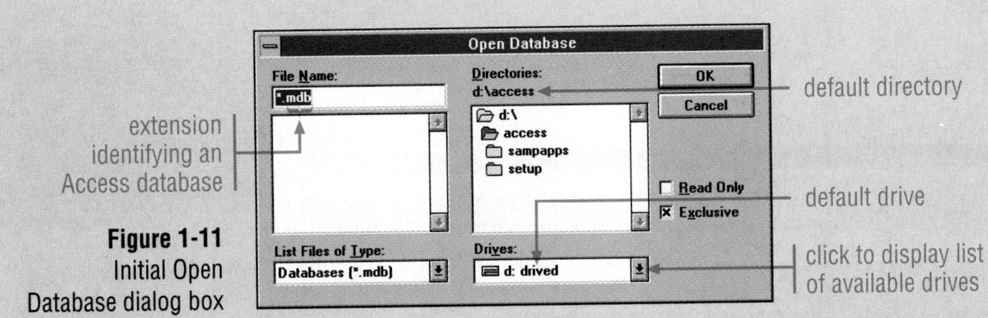

Figure 1-11
Initial Open Database dialog box

3. Click the **down arrow button** on the right side of the Drives box. A list of available drives drops down. Click the letter of the drive in which you put your Student Disk. Notice that the Directories section of the dialog box also changes as you change your selection in the drop-down Drives box.
4. Click **vision.mdb** in the File Name list box. The name of the selected file now appears in the File Name text box. See Figure 1-12.

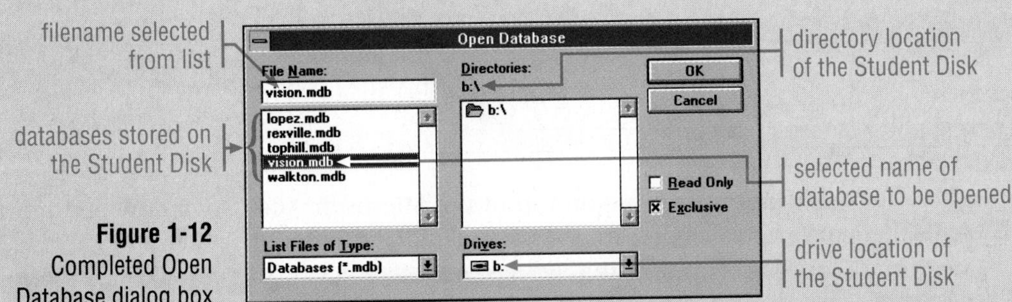

Figure 1-12
Completed Open Database dialog box

TROUBLE? If you can't find a file named vision.mdb, check that the Drives box indicates the location of your Student Disk. If the Drives box shows the correct drive, perhaps you are using the wrong disk in the drive. Check your disk to be sure it's your Student Disk. If it is the correct disk, check with your technical support person or instructor. If it is not the correct disk, place the correct Student Disk in the drive and resume your work from Step 3.

5. Click the **OK button** to let Access know you have completed the Open Database dialog box. Access opens the Vision.mdb database and displays the Database window.

After opening the Vision Publishers database, Judith checks the window on the screen to familiarize herself with her options. After making this check she will begin her assignment for Brian. Judith wants to review magazine article titles to select past articles for the special edition of *Business Perspective*.

The Database Window

After a database is opened, Access displays the Database window. Because you have experience with the Windows graphical user interface (GUI), you already recognize these components of the Database window: the Microsoft Access window Control menu box, the title bar, the Microsoft Access window sizing buttons, the menu bar, the toolbar, the toolbar buttons, the Database window Control menu box, the Database window sizing buttons, the status bar, and the Microsoft Access window. These are labeled in blue in Figure 1-13 on the following page. Components of the Database window that are new to you appear in red in Figure 1-13.

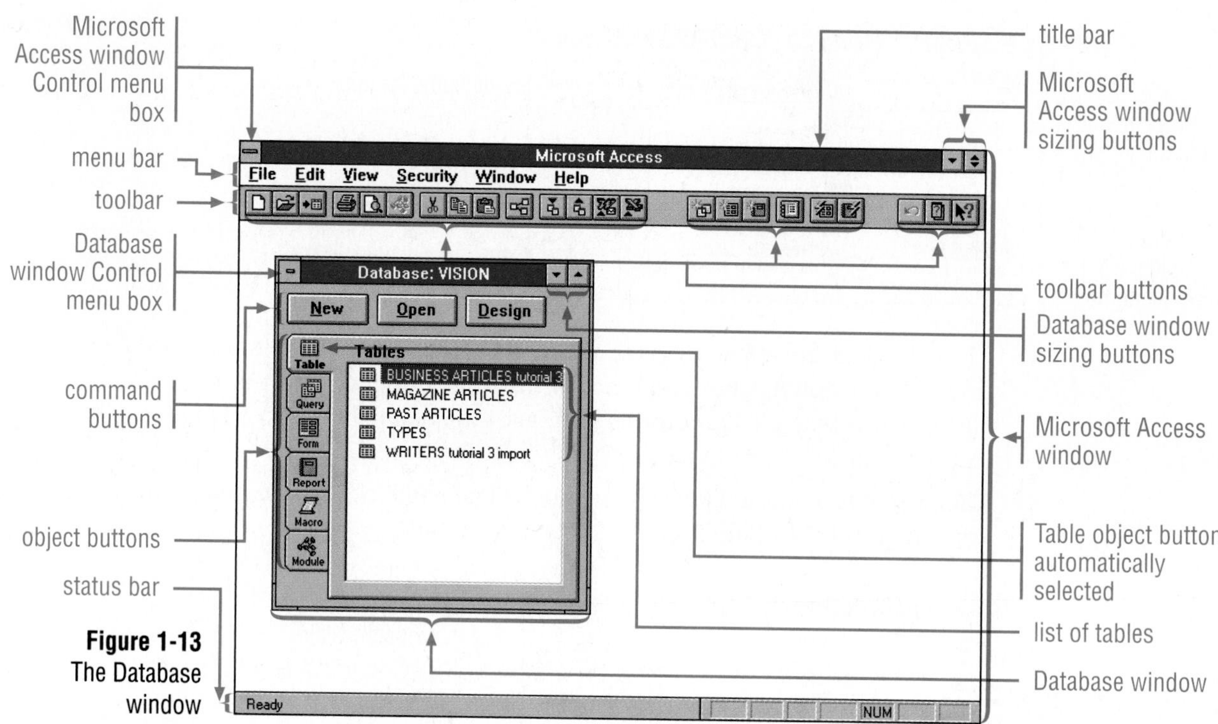

Figure 1-13 The Database window

- The Database window appears on top of the Microsoft Access window and represents the main control center for working with a database.
- The object buttons represent the six types of objects you can create for an Access database. Unlike most other DBMSs, Access stores each database in a single file. The database contains all the tables you define for it, along with all queries, forms, reports, macros, and modules; these collectively are the objects that make up the database. Each separate query and each separate report, for example, is a separate object so that, if Vision Publishers has three tables, five queries, and four reports in a database, Access treats them as 12 separate objects.

You already know what a table is, so let's consider the other five objects. You use the built-in Access query language to create a query (or question) about data from your tables. For example, if Judith needs to find records from the MAGAZINE ARTICLES table for a specific writer she can use a query for this purpose. You use a form to store, display, and view records from your tables. For example, Judith can create a form for others to use that displays one record at a time from the WRITERS table. You use a report to print data from tables in a customized format. For example, Brian might need a printed list that shows all writer information; a report can be used to generate this list. A **macro** is a saved list of operations to be performed on data. Access carries out the operations when you run the macro. Judith can use a macro, for example, to open a special form automatically whenever someone opens the company database. Finally, Access has a built-in programming language called Access Basic. A **module** is a set of one or more Access Basic programmed procedures. Vision Publishers uses a module, for example, to calculate payments to its writers for the articles they write.

- The three command buttons represent the major operations performed on tables. You can create a new table by clicking the New button. For an existing table, click the Open button to view table records or click the Design button to change the table structure.
- Notice that the Table object button is automatically selected when you first open a database, and a list of available tables for the database appears. When you click one of the other object buttons, that object button becomes the one that is selected; a list of available objects of that type then appears.

Viewing and Printing a Table

Now that you have opened a database and familiarized yourself with the components of the Database window, you are ready to view and print an existing Access table. If you are interested in looking up information from a small number of records in a table, you usually view them on the screen. However, if you need information from a large number of records or need to present the information to other people, you usually print a hardcopy of the table.

Datasheet View Window

Vision Publishers has a table named MAGAZINE ARTICLES that contains data about all the magazine articles published by the company. Judith opens this table to start her selection of top articles from *Business Perspective* magazine.

REFERENCE WINDOW

Opening the Datasheet View Window for a Table

- Scroll through the Tables list box until the table name appears and then click it.
- Click the Open command button.

Let's open the MAGAZINE ARTICLES table for Vision Publishers.

To open the Datasheet View window for the MAGAZINE ARTICLES table:

1. Click **MAGAZINE ARTICLES**, then click the **Open command button**. The Datasheet View window for the MAGAZINE ARTICLES table appears on top of the previous windows. See Figure 1-14 on the following page.

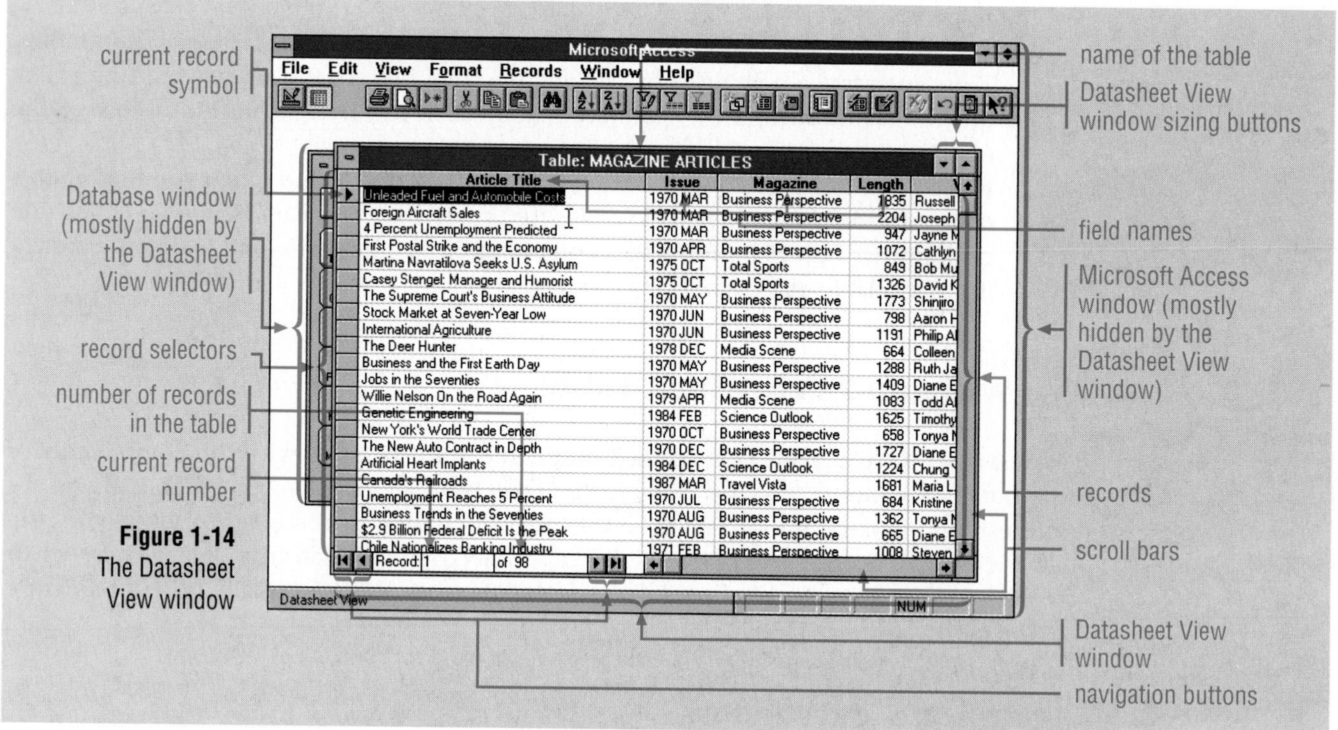

Figure 1-14
The Datasheet View window

The **Datasheet View window** shows a table's contents as a **datasheet** in rows and columns, similar to a spreadsheet. Each row is a separate record in the table, and each column contains the field values for one field from the table. Each column is headed by a field name. When you first open a datasheet, Access automatically selects the first field value in the first record for processing. Notice that this field is highlighted and that a darkened triangle symbol, called the current record symbol, appears in the record selector to the left of the first record. The **current record symbol** identifies the currently selected record. If you move your mouse pointer over any field value, it changes to I. If you then click the I on a field value in another row, that field value becomes the currently selected field. Although the entire field value is not highlighted, the insertion point stays where you clicked, the new record becomes the current record, and the current record number, between the navigation buttons at the bottom of the screen, changes. Practice clicking the I on different fields and records and notice the changes that occur in the datasheet.

Although the MAGAZINE ARTICLES table has only five fields, the Datasheet View window isn't large enough to display the entire writer name field. Similarly, you see only the first group of records from the table. One way to see different parts of a table is to use the vertical and horizontal scroll bars and arrows on the right and bottom of the datasheet. Practice clicking these scroll bars and arrows to become comfortable with their use.

Using the lower-left navigation buttons is another way to move vertically through the records. From left to right respectively, the **navigation buttons** advance the selected record to the first record, the previous record, the next record, and the last record in the table (Figure 1-15). The current record number appears between the two pairs of navigation buttons, as does the total number of records in the table. Practice clicking the four navigation buttons and notice the changes that occur in the datasheet, in the current record number, and in the placement of the current record symbol.

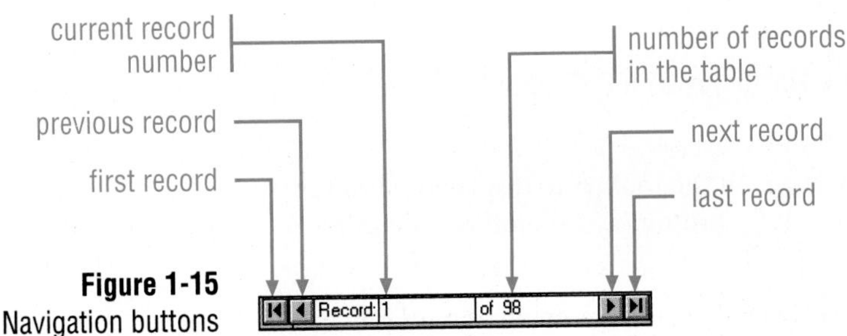

Figure 1-15
Navigation buttons

Judith decides to print the records from the first datasheet page of the table to study their contents more closely, but first she maximizes the Datasheet View window.

To maximize the Datasheet View window:

1. Click the **maximize button** for the Datasheet View window to expand the window. See Figure 1-16. Notice that a restore button replaces the minimize and maximize buttons and that the table title appears in the Access title bar.

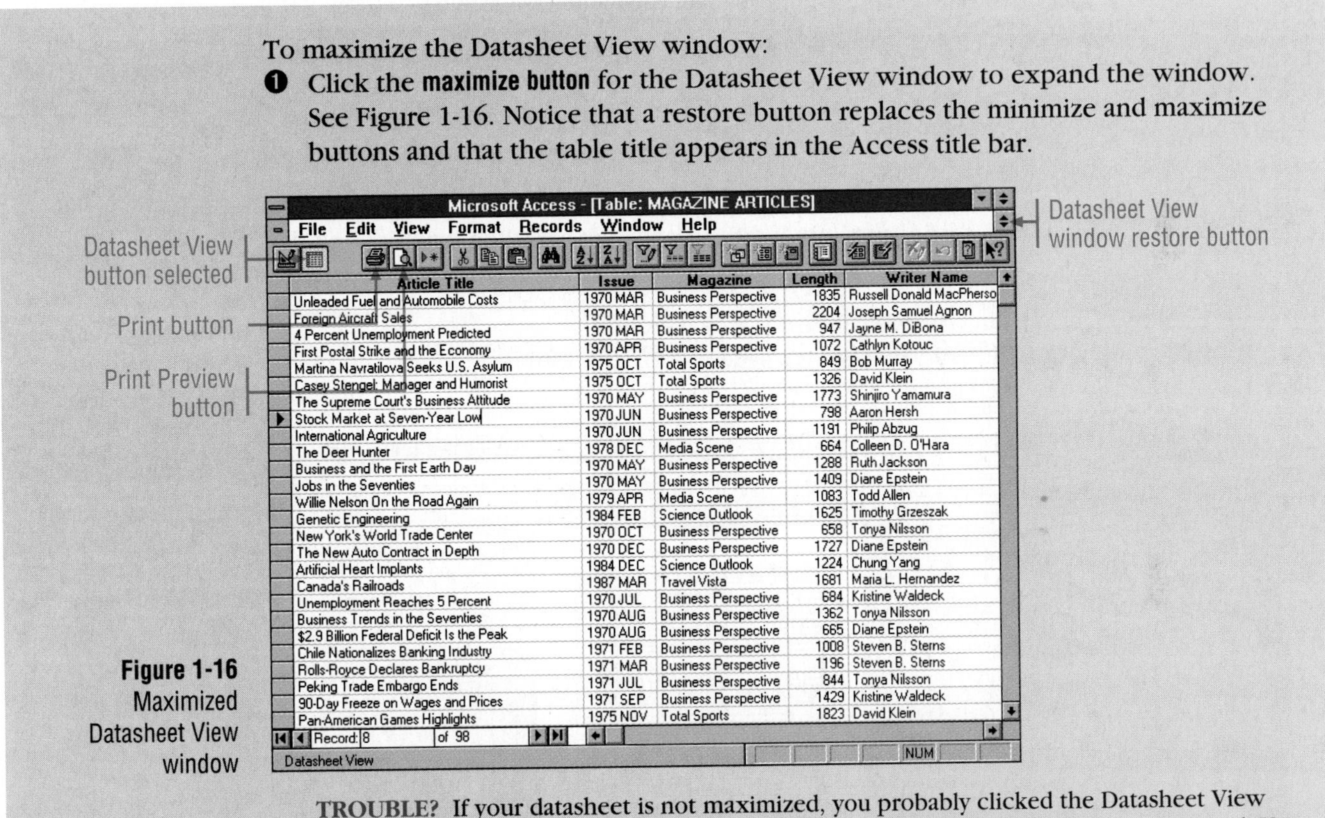

Article Title	Issue	Magazine	Length	Writer Name
Unleaded Fuel and Automobile Costs	1970 MAR	Business Perspective	1835	Russell Donald MacPherso
Foreign Aircraft Sales	1970 MAR	Business Perspective	2204	Joseph Samuel Agnon
4 Percent Unemployment Predicted	1970 MAR	Business Perspective	947	Jayne M. DiBona
First Postal Strike and the Economy	1970 APR	Business Perspective	1072	Cathlyn Kotouc
Martina Navratilova Seeks U.S. Asylum	1975 OCT	Total Sports	849	Bob Murray
Casey Stengel: Manager and Humorist	1975 OCT	Total Sports	1326	David Klein
The Supreme Court's Business Attitude	1970 MAY	Business Perspective	1773	Shinjiro Yamamura
Stock Market at Seven-Year Low	1970 JUN	Business Perspective	798	Aaron Hersh
International Agriculture	1970 JUN	Business Perspective	1191	Philip Abzug
The Deer Hunter	1978 DEC	Media Scene	664	Colleen D. O'Hara
Business and the First Earth Day	1970 MAY	Business Perspective	1288	Ruth Jackson
Jobs in the Seventies	1970 MAY	Business Perspective	1409	Diane Epstein
Willie Nelson On the Road Again	1979 APR	Media Scene	1083	Todd Allen
Genetic Engineering	1984 FEB	Science Outlook	1625	Timothy Grzeszak
New York's World Trade Center	1970 OCT	Business Perspective	658	Tonya Nilsson
The New Auto Contract in Depth	1970 DEC	Business Perspective	1727	Diane Epstein
Artificial Heart Implants	1984 DEC	Science Outlook	1224	Chung Yang
Canada's Railroads	1987 MAR	Travel Vista	1681	Maria L. Hernandez
Unemployment Reaches 5 Percent	1970 JUL	Business Perspective	684	Kristine Waldeck
Business Trends in the Seventies	1970 AUG	Business Perspective	1362	Tonya Nilsson
$2.9 Billion Federal Deficit Is the Peak	1970 AUG	Business Perspective	665	Diane Epstein
Chile Nationalizes Banking Industry	1971 FEB	Business Perspective	1008	Steven B. Sterns
Rolls-Royce Declares Bankruptcy	1971 MAR	Business Perspective	1196	Steven B. Sterns
Peking Trade Embargo Ends	1971 JUL	Business Perspective	844	Tonya Nilsson
90-Day Freeze on Wages and Prices	1971 SEP	Business Perspective	1429	Kristine Waldeck
Pan-American Games Highlights	1975 NOV	Total Sports	1823	David Klein

Figure 1-16
Maximized Datasheet View window

TROUBLE? If your datasheet is not maximized, you probably clicked the Datasheet View window minimize button or one of the Microsoft Access window sizing buttons instead. Use the appropriate sizing button to restore your screen to its previous condition, and then refer to Figure 1-14 for the location of the Datasheet View window maximize button.

You might have noticed that one toolbar button, the Datasheet View button is selected, as shown in Figure 1-16. You can click the Datasheet View button to switch to the Datasheet View window of your table whenever you see this button on the toolbar. To the right of the Datasheet View button are the Print and Print Preview buttons. You click the Print Preview button whenever you want to review the appearance of a datasheet on screen before you print a hardcopy of it. Use the **Print button** instead, if you want to print a hardcopy without reviewing it on screen.

REFERENCE WINDOW

Printing a Hardcopy of a Datasheet

- Click the Print Preview button on the toolbar to display the Print Preview window. Click the Print button on the toolbar. The Print dialog box appears.
- Select the Copies box if you want to change the number of copies you want to print.
- Click Pages in the Print Range section if your want to print only a portion of your datasheet. Specify the beginning page in the range in the From box and the ending page in the range in the To box.
- Click All in the Print Range section if you want to print all the pages in your datasheet.
- Click the OK button or press [Enter].

Let's print preview Judith's datasheet and then print its first page.

To print preview and print a datasheet:

❶ Click the **Print Preview button** on the toolbar. The Print Preview window appears. See Figure 1-17.

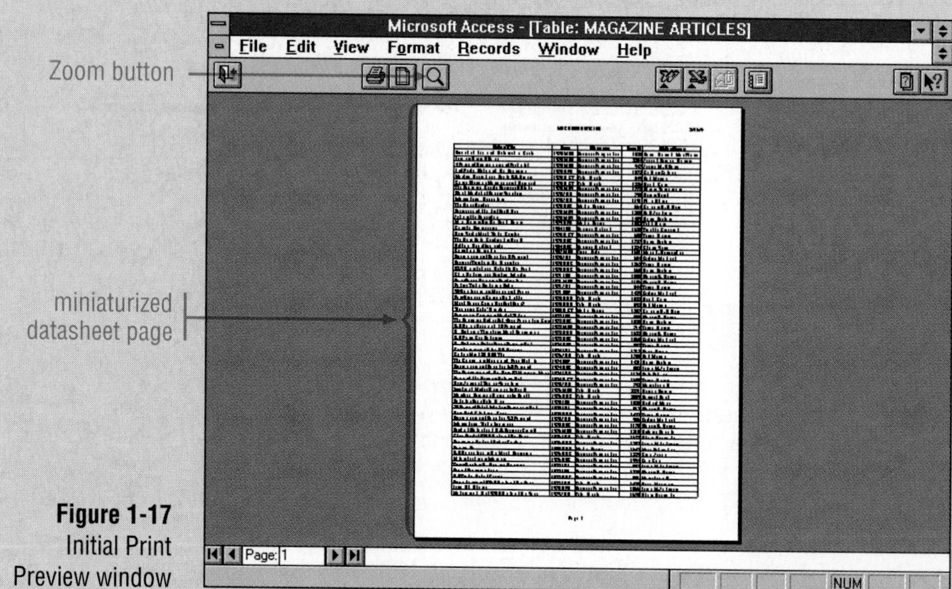

Figure 1-17 Initial Print Preview window

When you move the mouse pointer over the datasheet page, it changes to 🔍. You can click the 🔍 or click the toolbar Zoom button to see a close-up of the datasheet page. Judith decides to preview a close-up of the page.

❷ Click the **Zoom button**, or click the when it is positioned over the miniaturized page. A close-up of the page appears. See Figure 1-18. Depending on whether you clicked the or the, your screen might differ from the illustration.

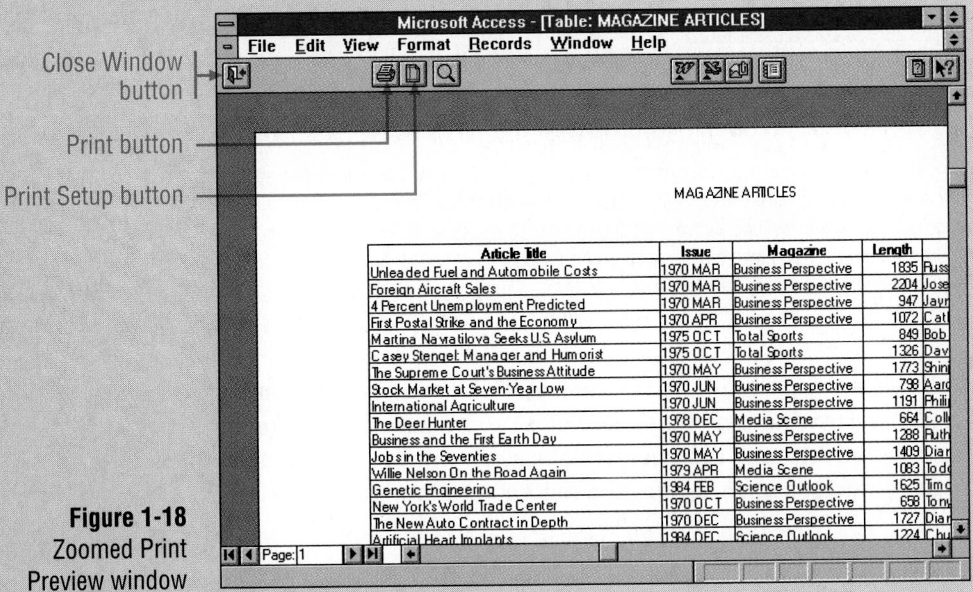

Figure 1-18 Zoomed Print Preview window

If you click the or the a second time, the page returns to its original miniaturized view. Practice clicking the, the, and the navigation buttons. When you are done practicing, you are ready to print the datasheet page.

❸ Make sure your printer is on-line and ready to print. Click the **Print button** on the toolbar. The Print dialog box appears. See Figure 1-19. Check the Printer section of the dialog box to make sure your printer is selected.

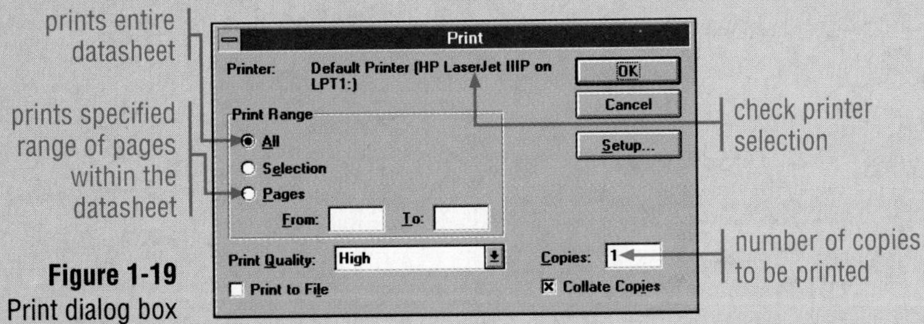

Figure 1-19 Print dialog box

TROUBLE? If the correct printer is not selected, click the Setup... button in the Print dialog box, select the correct printer from the Specified Printer list, and click the OK button.

❹ Because you want to print just the first datasheet page, click the **Pages option button**, type **1**, press **[Tab]**, type **1**, and click the **OK button**. A dialog box appears to inform you that your datasheet page is being sent to the printer. See Figure 1-20 on the following page.

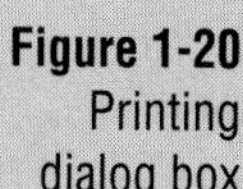

Figure 1-20 Printing dialog box

❺ After the dialog box disappears, click the **Close Window button** in the Print Preview window toolbar to return to the Datasheet View window.

TROUBLE? If your document hasn't printed yet, check the print status in the Windows Print Manager by pressing [Alt][Tab] until the Print Manager title bar appears, and then release. Remove your document from the print queue before returning to your datasheet and then print the first datasheet page again. If it still doesn't print, check with your technical support person or instructor.

Judith is ready to close the Datasheet View window. Whenever you finish your work with a particular window, you should close the window. This frees up memory, speeds up processing, and removes unnecessary clutter from your screen. Any object—a table using a datasheet, a query, a form, a report, a macro, or a module—is closed in a similar way.

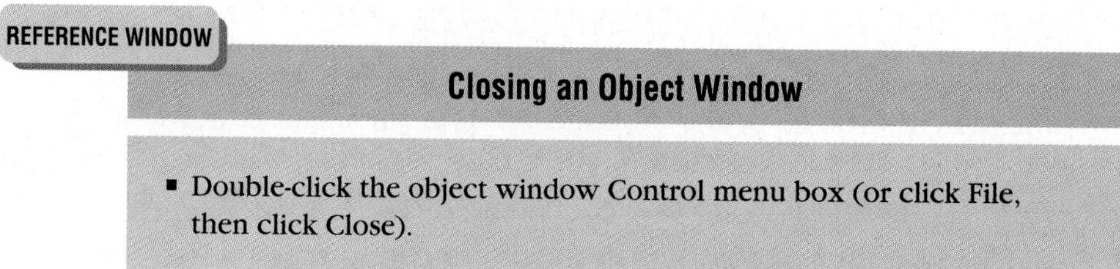

REFERENCE WINDOW

Closing an Object Window

- Double-click the object window Control menu box (or click File, then click Close).

Let's close the Datasheet View window you have been using.

To close the Datasheet View window (or other object window):

❶ Click **File** to open the File menu. See Figure 1-21.

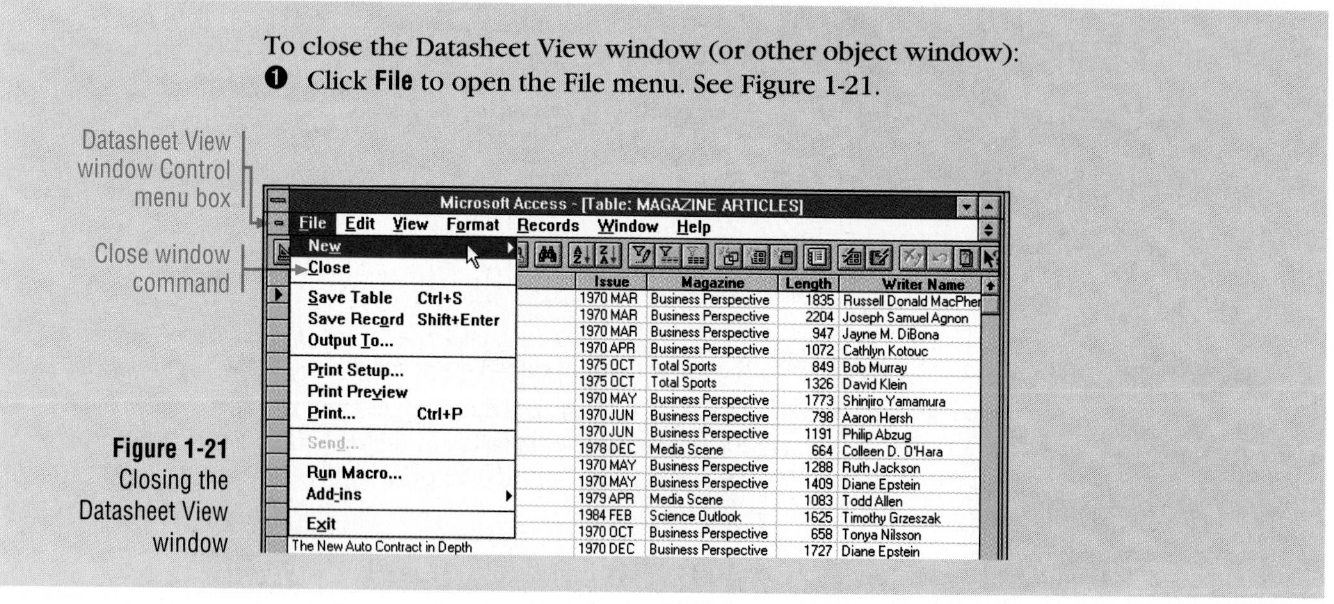

Figure 1-21 Closing the Datasheet View window

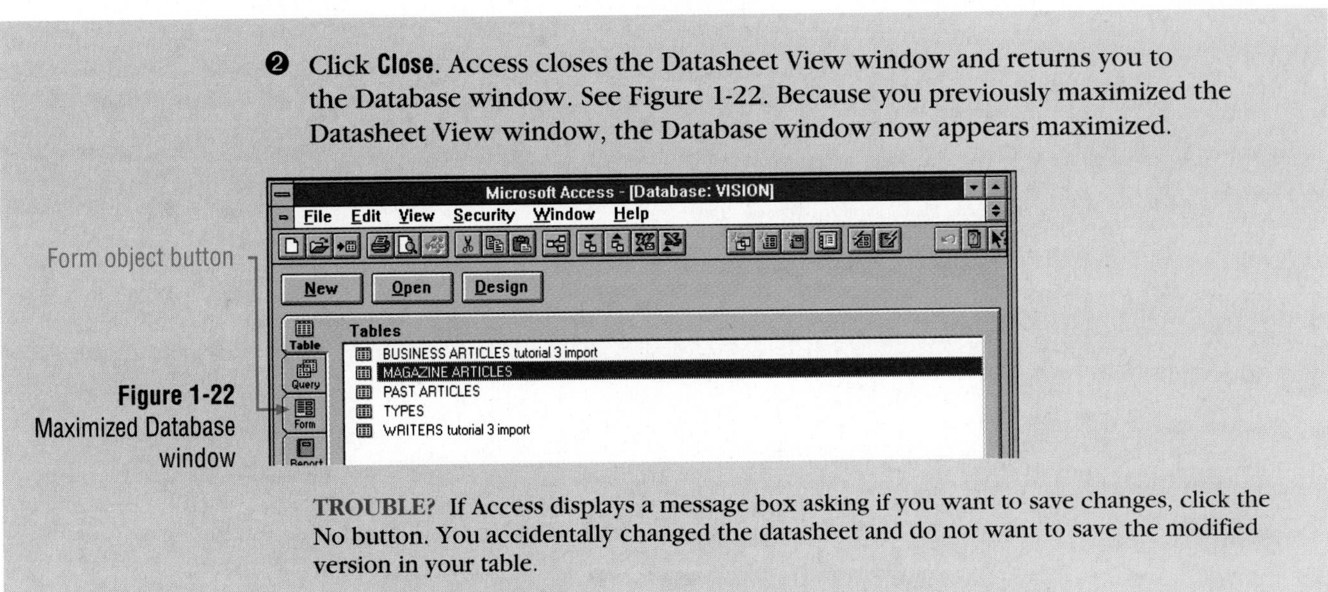

❷ Click **Close**. Access closes the Datasheet View window and returns you to the Database window. See Figure 1-22. Because you previously maximized the Datasheet View window, the Database window now appears maximized.

Figure 1-22
Maximized Database window

TROUBLE? If Access displays a message box asking if you want to save changes, click the No button. You accidentally changed the datasheet and do not want to save the modified version in your table.

If you want to take a break and resume the tutorial at a later time, you can exit Access by double-clicking the Microsoft Access window Control menu box in the upper-left corner of the screen. When you resume the tutorial, place your Student Disk in the appropriate drive and launch Access. Open the database vision.mdb, maximize the Database window, and then continue working on the next section of the tutorial.

■ ■ ■

Form View Window

Judith now opens an existing form to view the records from the MAGAZINE ARTICLES table. A form gives you a customized view of data from a database. You use a form, for example, to view one record from a table at a time, to view data in a more readable format, or to view related data from two or more tables. The way you open a form is similar to the way you opened a datasheet and the way you open all other database objects.

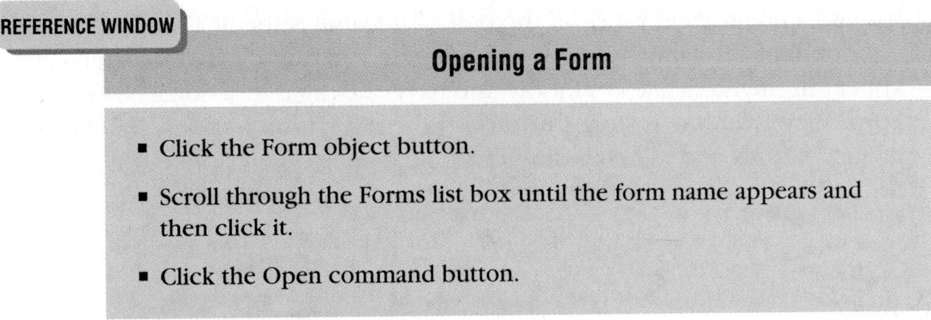
REFERENCE WINDOW

Opening a Form

- Click the Form object button.
- Scroll through the Forms list box until the form name appears and then click it.
- Click the Open command button.

Let's now open the form named Magazine Articles.

To open a form:

❶ Click the **Form object button**. A list of available forms appears in the Forms list box. See Figure 1-23.

Form object button

list of forms

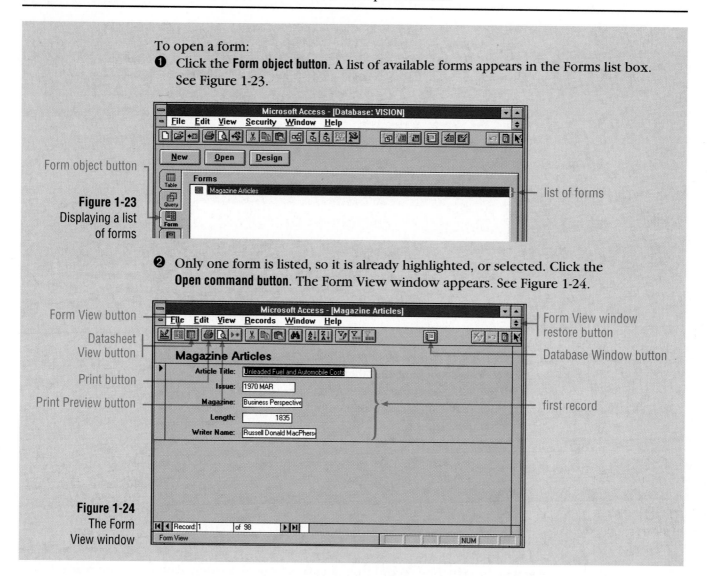

Figure 1-23
Displaying a list of forms

❷ Only one form is listed, so it is already highlighted, or selected. Click the **Open command button**. The Form View window appears. See Figure 1-24.

Form View button

Datasheet View button

Print button

Print Preview button

Form View window restore button

Database Window button

first record

Figure 1-24
The Form View window

The **Form View window** shows a table's contents in a customized format, usually one record at a time. The form, as shown in Figure 1-24, displays all five fields from the MAGAZINE ARTICLES table vertically, one record at a time. Each field has a label on the left and a boxed field value on the right. The label is the field name.

Some of the same window components you saw in the Datasheet View window also appear in the Form View window and have the same functions. Notice the location of the Form View window restore button and the navigation buttons. Practice clicking the navigation buttons and clicking different field values. Then notice the changes that occur in the form.

You should also practice clicking the Datasheet View and Form View toolbar buttons. Clicking the Datasheet View button switches you from the Form View window to the Datasheet View window. Clicking the Form View button switches you from the Datasheet View window to the Form View window.

Judith prints the first page of records from the Form View window but does not first use the Print Preview option. Access prints as many form records as can fit on a printed page. The steps you follow to print from the Form View window are similar to the steps you followed when you printed from the Datasheet View window.

To print a form page:

1. Before continuing, be sure you are in the Form View window with the first record appearing in a maximized window. Click the **Print button** on the toolbar. The Print dialog box appears.
2. Make sure your printer is on-line and ready to print. Check the Printer section of the dialog box to make sure the correct printer is selected. Click the **Pages option button**, type **1**, press **[Tab]**, type **1**, and then click the **OK button**. A dialog box informs you that your datasheet page is being sent to the printer. After the dialog box disappears, Access returns you to the Form View window.

Closing a Database

Judith is done working on both the form and the database, so she closes the database. She could close the Form View window, as she previously closed the Datasheet View window, and then close the database. However, whenever you close a database without closing the Form View window or any other open object window, Access automatically closes all open windows before closing the database.

REFERENCE WINDOW

Closing a Database

- Click the Database Window button in an open object window to make the Database window visible and make it the active window.
- Double-click the Database window Control menu box.

Let's close the Vision Publishers database that you have been using.

To close a database:

1. Click the **Database Window button** on the toolbar to activate the Database window on top of a smaller-sized Form View window. See Figure 1-25.

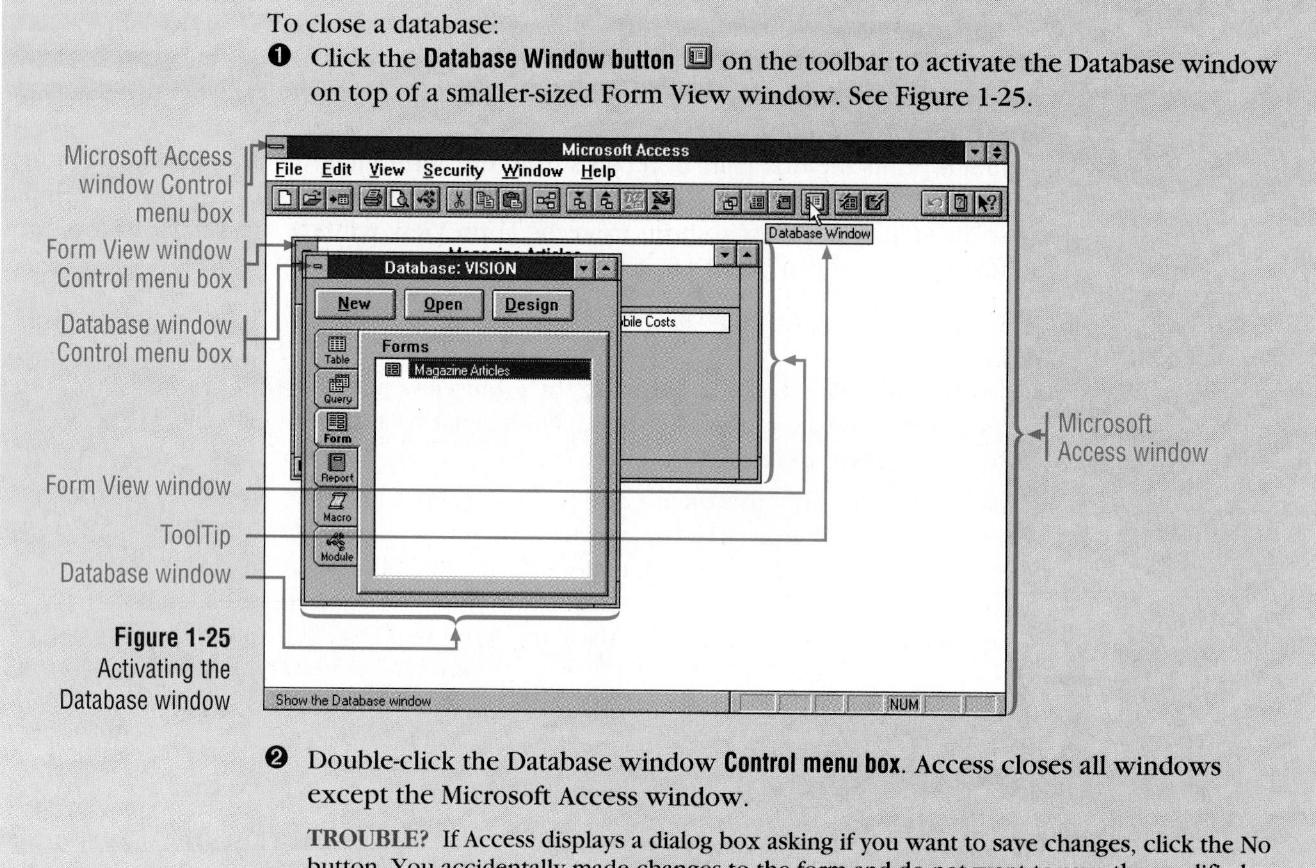

Figure 1-25
Activating the Database window

2. Double-click the Database window **Control menu box**. Access closes all windows except the Microsoft Access window.

   TROUBLE? If Access displays a dialog box asking if you want to save changes, click the No button. You accidentally made changes to the form and do not want to save the modified version in your table.

Getting Help

While you are using Access on your computer, there might be times when you are puzzled about how to complete a task. You might also need to clarify a definition or Access feature or investigate more advanced Access capabilities. You can use Access's Help system to give you on-line information about your specific questions. There are four ways you can get on-line help as you work: by using the Help Contents, the Search feature, the Glossary feature, or the context-sensitive Help system. Let's practice using the Access Help system.

Starting Help and Using the Help Contents

Judith has some questions about moving the toolbar and about shortcut menus and uses the Access Help system to find answers. One way to use the Access Help system is to click Help and then click Contents.

To start Help:

1. Click **Help** and then click **Contents**. The Microsoft Access Help window becomes the active window and displays the Microsoft Access Help Contents topic. See Figure 1-26.

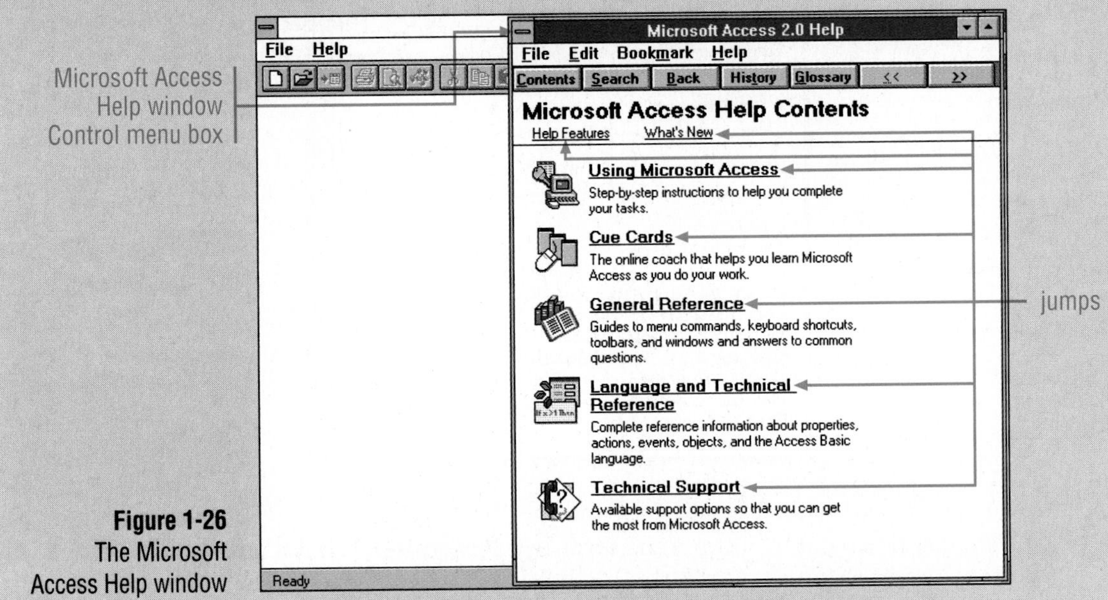

Figure 1-26 The Microsoft Access Help window

TROUBLE? If the size or position of your Microsoft Access Help window is different from what is shown in the illustration, don't worry. Continue with the tutorial.

The underlined words and topics in the Microsoft Access Help window serve as a top-level table of contents. You can get detailed information on each of these words or topics by clicking one of the words or topics. The mouse pointer changes to ☝ when you move it over any of the words or topics. Underlined words or topics are called jumps. A **jump** provides a link to other Help topics or to more information or a definition about the current word or topic.

Judith wants to find out how to use Help and decides that clicking Help on the Microsoft Access Help menu bar might tell her how to do this.

To get help on using Access Help:

1. Press **[F1]** while the Microsoft Access Help window is active (or click **Help** within the Microsoft Access Help window, then click **How to Use Help**). See Figure 1-27 on the following page. Judith wants more information about the scroll bar jump.

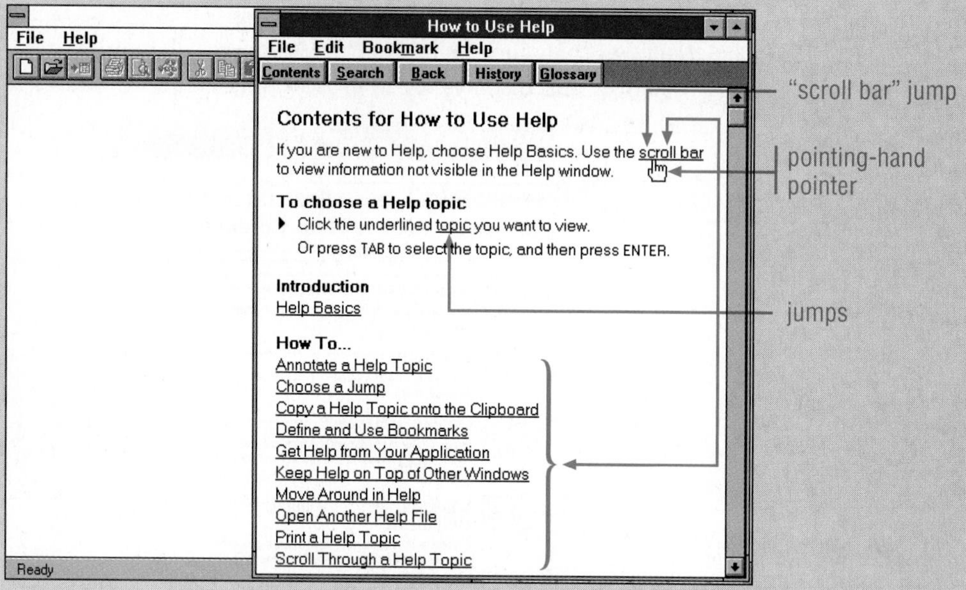

"scroll bar" jump

pointing-hand pointer

jumps

Figure 1-27
The How to Use Help window

❷ Click the words **scroll bar** when the mouse pointer changes to [hand pointer] over them. Access Help displays a description of the term. See Figure 1-28. The pointer changes back to [arrow pointer].

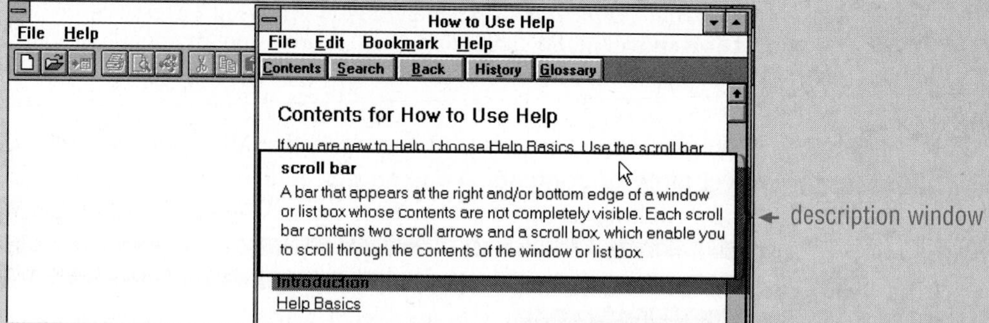

Figure 1-28
Description of "scroll bar"

TROUBLE? If you get the message "Help topic does not exist," you might not have the complete Access Help system installed on your system. Ask your technical support person or instructor for assistance.

❸ Click the words **scroll bar** again. The description window disappears.

❹ Read the material under the heading Contents for How to Use Help. Use the scroll bar to view the entire topic.

Judith sees the Search for a Help Topic jump as she scrolls through Contents for How to Use Help and decides to view that jump.

To view the Contents for How to Use Help jump:

1. Find and click the jump **Search for a Help Topic**.
2. Read the information under Search for a Help Topic, using the scroll bar to view the entire topic.

Using the Search feature of Help appears to be what Judith needs to use to get answers to her questions. Because the How to Use Help window is active, however, she must switch back to the Microsoft Access Help window before she can use the Search feature. If she does not switch back, she will be searching for Help topics rather than Access topics.

To return to the Microsoft Access Help window:

1. Click the **Back button** in the Help button bar two times. Notice that the title bar changes to Microsoft Access 2.0 Help.

Using Search

Having read about the Search feature in Access Help, Judith uses that feature to search for information about moving toolbars.

To use the search feature in Access Help:

1. Click the **Search button** on the Help button bar. The Search dialog box appears. See Figure 1-29.

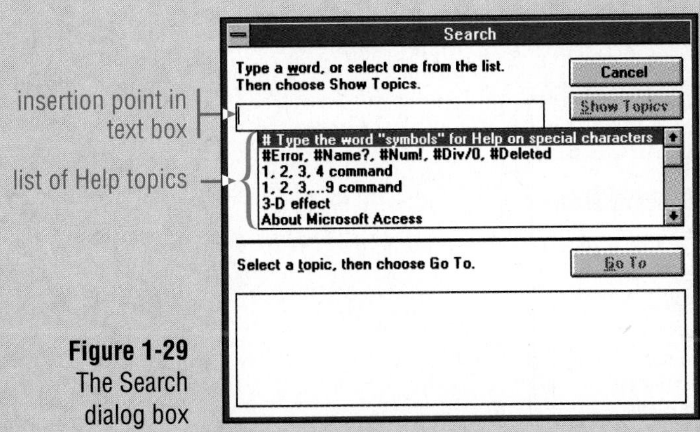

Figure 1-29 The Search dialog box

2. Type **m** in the text box. The list of topics shown changes to those topics starting with *m*.
3. Type **oving t** after the *m* in the text box. The list of topics shown changes to those starting with the letters "moving t" and the topic moving toolbars is visible in the list box.
4. Click **moving toolbars** in the list box and then click the **Show Topics button**. See Figure 1-30 on the following page.

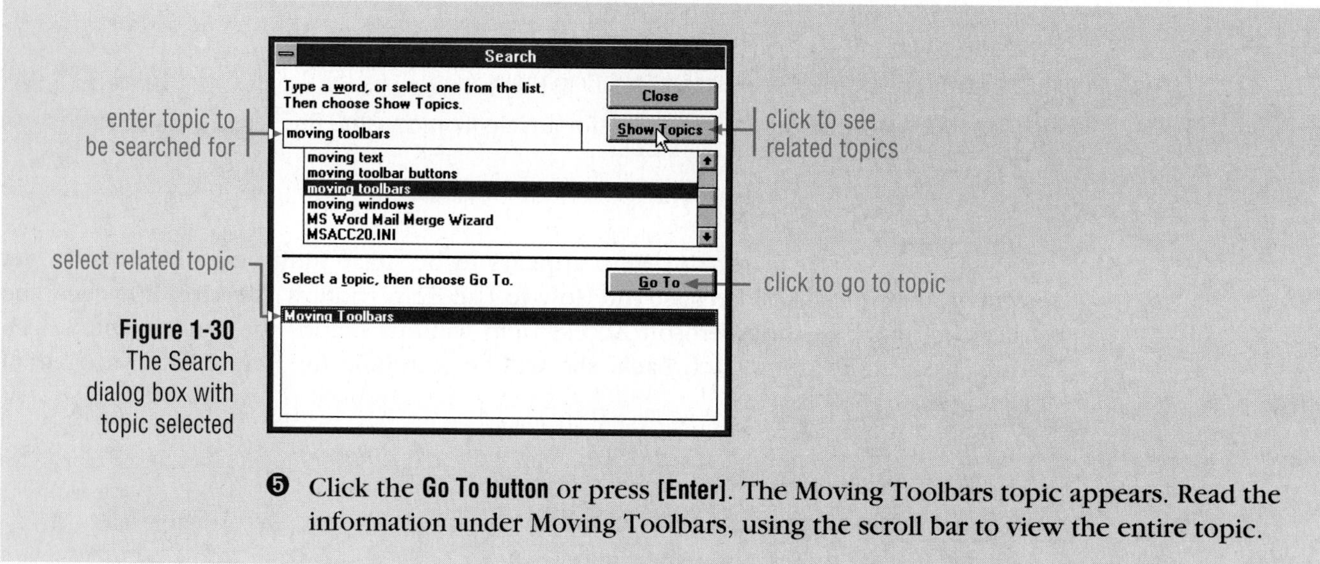

Figure 1-30 The Search dialog box with topic selected

❺ Click the **Go To button** or press **[Enter]**. The Moving Toolbars topic appears. Read the information under Moving Toolbars, using the scroll bar to view the entire topic.

Judith has the answers she needs to her questions about moving toolbars and next looks up the definition of the term Shortcut menu in the glossary.

Using the Glossary

The Glossary contains Access terms and their definitions. Judith uses the Glossary feature to read the definition of Shortcut menu.

To use the Glossary feature in Access Help:

❶ Click the **Glossary button** on the Help button bar. The Glossary topic appears. See Figure 1-31.

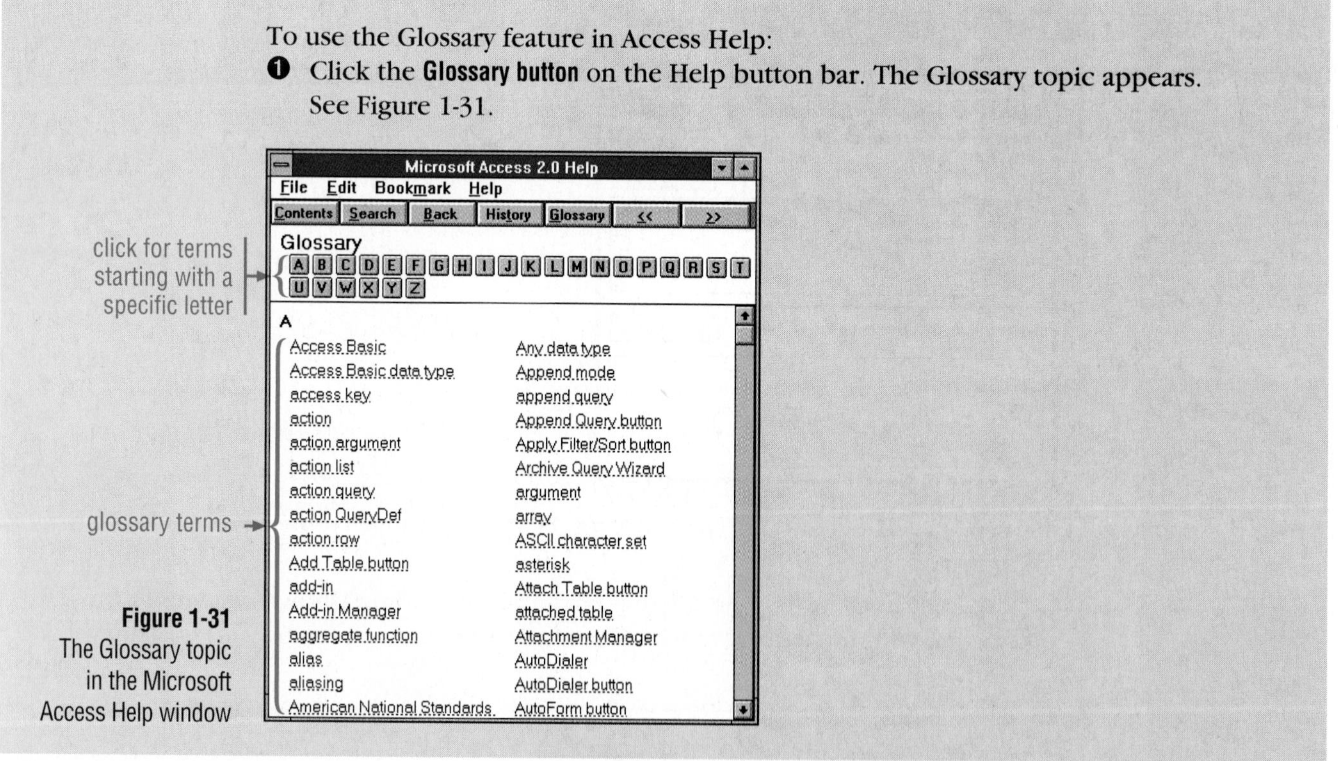

Figure 1-31 The Glossary topic in the Microsoft Access Help window

❷ Click the **S button**. Access displays the beginning of the list of terms beginning with the letter S.

❸ Scroll until the term Shortcut menu appears. Click the words **Shortcut menu**. Access displays the corresponding definition window. Read the definition.

❹ Click the words **shortcut menu** again. The definition window disappears.

Judith has the answers to her questions and is ready to exit Help.

To exit Help:

❶ Double-click the Microsoft Access Help **Control menu box**. The Help window closes.

Using Context-Sensitive Help

When you start Help by pressing [F1] instead of using the Help menu, the Microsoft Access Help window you see is **context sensitive**, which means that Access displays information that is relevant to the window or operation that is active when you start Help. If you want Help information about a particular component of an Access window, click the Help button on the toolbar instead of pressing [F1]. The mouse pointer changes to ?, which is the Help pointer. You then click the ? on the window component you want information about, and Help opens a window specific to that component.

Judith learns more about the Access toolbar by clicking the Help button.

To use context-sensitive Help on a specific window component:

❶ Click the **Help button** on the toolbar. The mouse pointer changes to ?. See Figure 1-32.

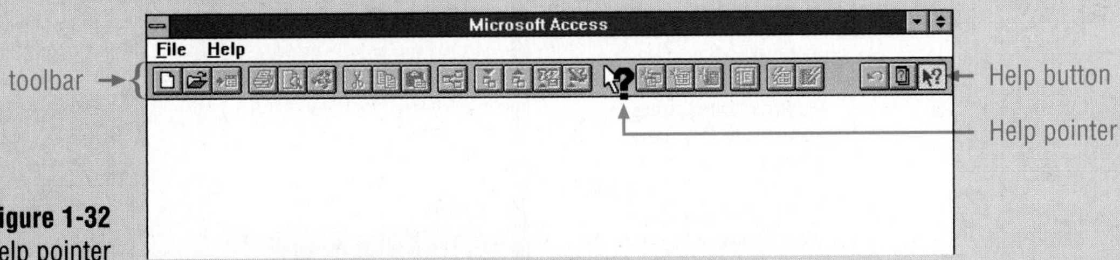

Figure 1-32
Help pointer

❷ Do not click any of the toolbar buttons. Instead, click anywhere else in the toolbar with the Help pointer. Help opens the Database Window Toolbar topic window. See Figure 1-33 on the following page.

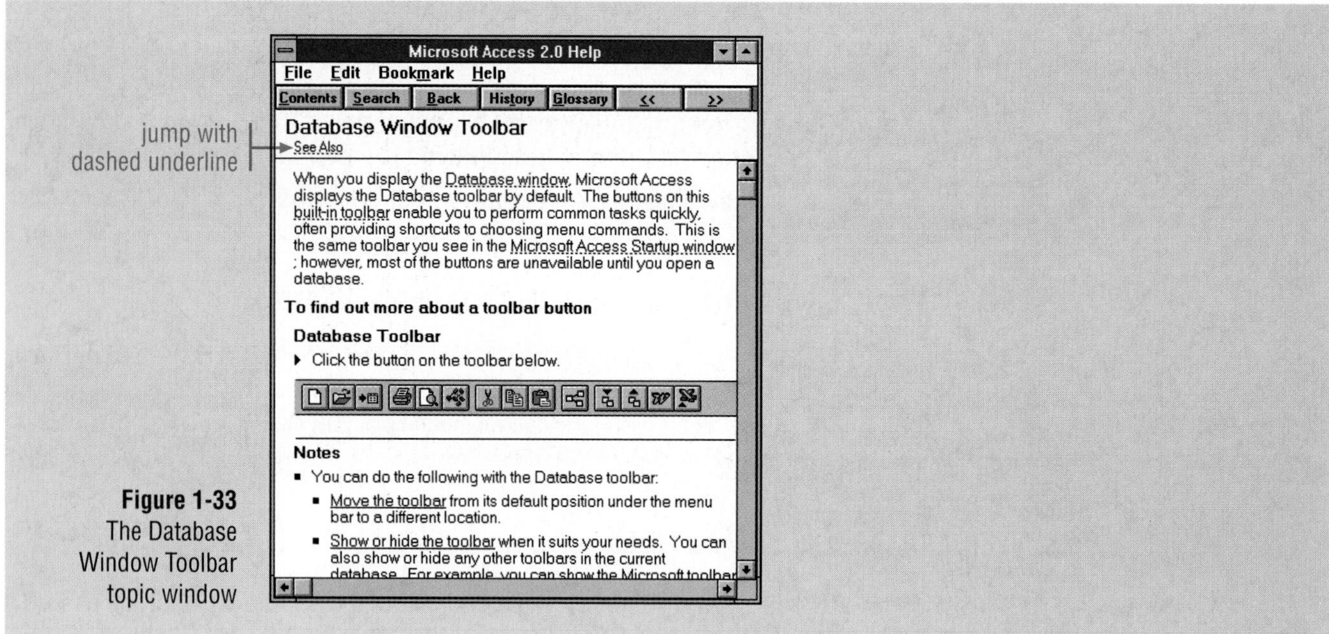

Figure 1-33 The Database Window Toolbar topic window

Judith notices the See Also jump, wonders what it means, and clicks it.

To view the See Also jump:

1. Click the words **See Also**. Access Help displays a window containing other topics that are related to the Database Window Toolbar topic. See Figure 1-34.

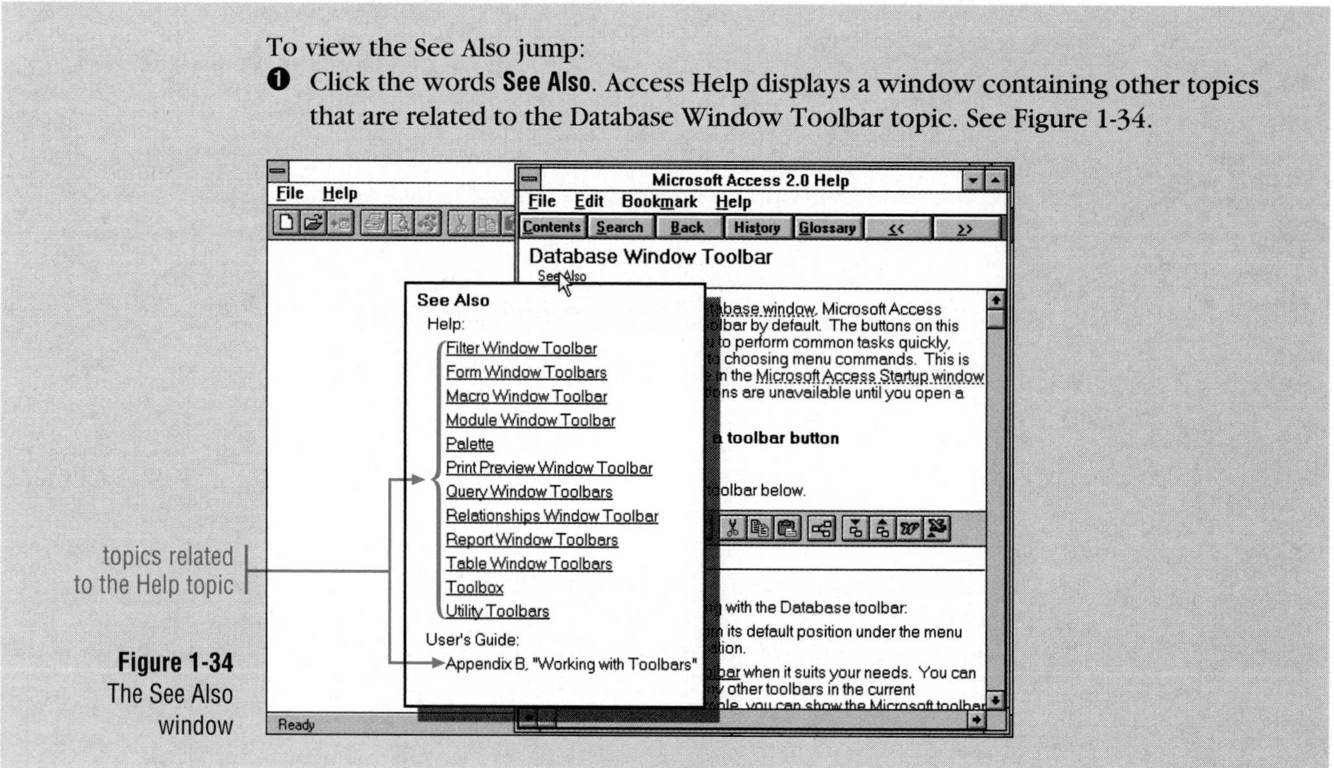

Figure 1-34 The See Also window

Her curiosity satisfied, Judith is done using Help and follows up by experimenting with Shortcut menus and moving the toolbar.

Shortcut Menus

As described in the Help glossary, a **Shortcut menu** contains a list of commands that relate to the object you click. To display a Shortcut menu window, you position the mouse pointer on a specific object or area and click the right mouse button. Using a Shortcut menu is often faster than using a menu or toolbar button.

Judith closes the Help window, opens the Vision database, and then displays a Shortcut menu.

To exit Help and open a database:

1. Click the words **See Also** to close the jump window.
2. Double-click the Microsoft Access Help **Control menu box** to close the Help window.
3. Open the vision.mdb database.

Judith now opens the Shortcut menu for the table objects.

To display a Shortcut menu:

1. Move the mouse pointer into the Database window and position it just below the last table listed.
2. Click the right mouse button. Access displays the Shortcut menu. See Figure 1-35.

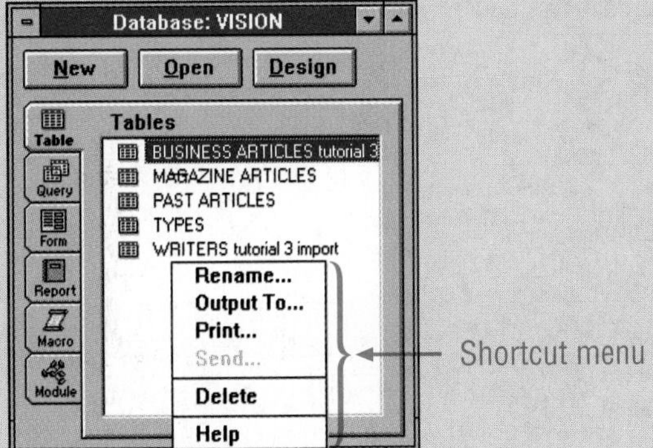

Figure 1-35
The Shortcut menu

If you select a Shortcut menu command, it applies to the highlighted table. Judith does not want to select a command, so she closes the Shortcut menu.

To close a Shortcut menu:

1. Click the right mouse button again to close the Shortcut menu.

   TROUBLE? If the Shortcut menu does not disappear, move the mouse pointer slightly outside the Shortcut menu and click the right mouse button again.

Judith experiments moving the toolbar to a different location on the screen.

Moving the Toolbar

The default location for the toolbar is just below the menu bar at the top of the screen. Most Windows software packages position the toolbar in the same location, so you do not usually want to move the toolbar to a different location on the screen. If you launch Access and find the toolbar in a location other than the default location, however, you should know how to move it back to its default location.

To move the toolbar to a different location:

1. Click anywhere in the toolbar's background but not on a toolbar button.
2. Click again in the toolbar's background and drag the toolbar to the bottom of the screen. As you drag the toolbar, the toolbar outline shows where the toolbar will be positioned if you release the mouse button. Release the mouse button when the toolbar is positioned as shown in Figure 1-36.

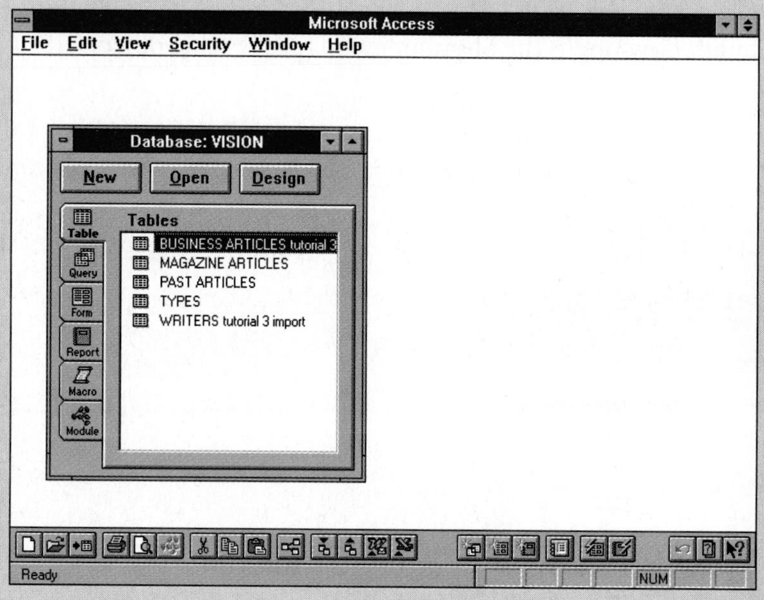

Figure 1-36 The toolbar at the bottom of the screen

Judith next moves the toolbar back to its default location. Although she could repeat the steps she previously used, Judith uses a command on the View menu instead.

To move the toolbar to its default location:

1. Click **View** and then click **Toolbars...** to display the Toolbars dialog box. See Figure 1-37.

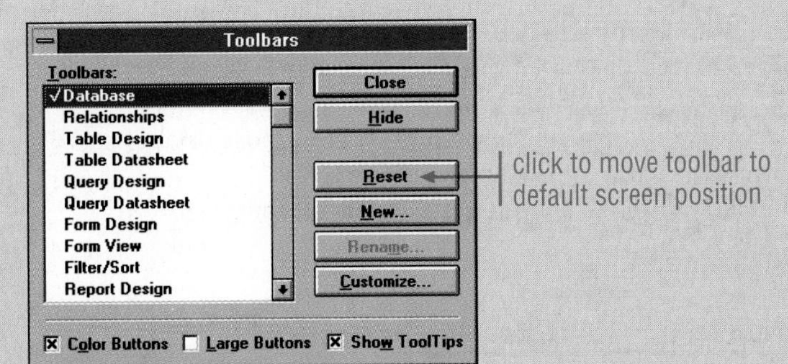

Figure 1-37 The Toolbars dialog box

❷ Be sure that Database is checked in the Toolbars list box and then click the **Reset button**. Access displays a dialog box that asks if you are sure you want to reset all changes to the toolbar.

❸ Click the **OK button** to close the dialog box. Access moves the toolbar back to its default location.

❹ Click the **Close button** in the Toolbars dialog box.

Judith is done experimenting with Access and exits Access.

To exit Access:

❶ Double-click the Microsoft Access window **Control menu box** to exit Access. Double-click the Microsoft Office group window **Control menu box** to close it. You are returned to the Program Manager.

■ ■ ■

Judith has completed her initial assignment. In the next tutorial she will meet with Brian to give him her business article selections.

Questions

1. What three steps should you generally follow when you plan to create and store a new type of data?
2. What are fields and entities, and how are they related?
3. How do you form a relationship between two tables?
4. What are the differences between a primary key and a foreign key?
5. Describe what a DBMS is designed to do.
6. What is a ToolTip?
7. What are the six different objects you can create for an Access database?
8. What do the columns and rows of a datasheet represent?

9. To which record do you advance when you use each of the four navigation buttons?
10. Which open object, the table or form object, allows you to switch between datasheet view and form view?
11. Where in Access do you find jumps, and what purpose do they serve?
12. Explain the steps for using context-sensitive Help.

Use the data in Figure 1-38 to answer Questions 13 through 18.

CHECKING ACCOUNTS table

Account Number	Name	Balance
2173	Theodore Lamont	842.27
4519	Beatrice Whalley	2071.92
8005	Benjamin Hoskins	1132.00

CHECKS table

Account Number	Check Number	Date	Amount
4519	1371	10/22/95	45.00
4519	1372	10/23/95	115.00
2173	1370	10/24/95	50.00
4519	1377	10/27/95	60.00
2173	1371	10/29/95	20.00

Figure 1-38

13. How many fields are in the CHECKING ACCOUNTS table?
14. Name the fields in the CHECKS table.
15. How many records are in the CHECKS table?
16. What is the primary key of the CHECKING ACCOUNTS table?
17. **E** What is the primary key of the CHECKS table?
18. **E** Which table has a foreign key, and what is the field name of the foreign key?

Use the Access Help feature to answer Questions 19 through 21.

19. **E** When you use the Close command on the File menu, do you need to save the changes to your data first?
20. **E** You can use the navigation buttons to move from one record to another. How can you move to a specific record number in datasheet view or form view?
21. **E** How can you print a Help topic?

Tutorial Assignments

Launch Access, open the Vision.mdb database on your Student Disk, and do the following:

1. Open the MAGAZINE ARTICLES table in the Datasheet View window.
2. Print preview the datasheet.
3. Print the last page of the datasheet.
4. Close the Datasheet View window.
5. Open the Magazine Articles form.
6. Print preview the form. What is the page number of the last page?
7. Print the last two pages of the form.
8. **E** Use Access Help with the following active windows: the Database window, the Datasheet View window, and the Print Preview window. Describe the differences you see in each situation in the initial Microsoft Access Help window.

TUTORIAL 2

Creating Access Tables

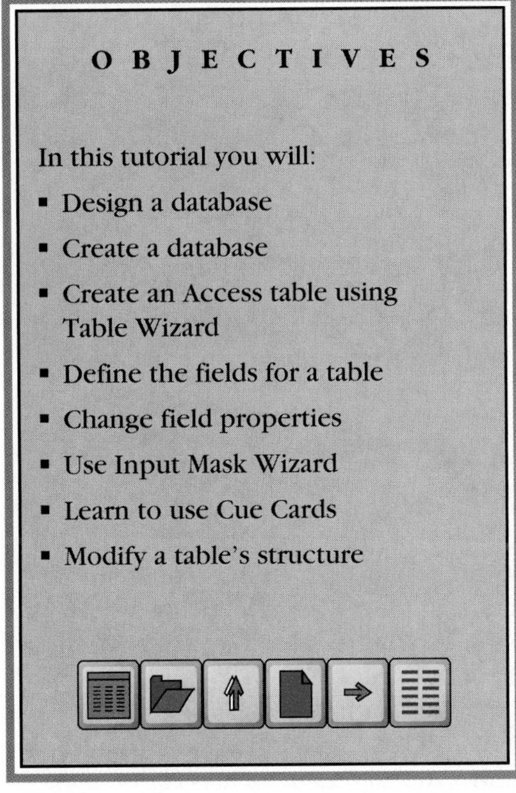

OBJECTIVES

In this tutorial you will:

- Design a database
- Create a database
- Create an Access table using Table Wizard
- Define the fields for a table
- Change field properties
- Use Input Mask Wizard
- Learn to use Cue Cards
- Modify a table's structure

Creating the WRITERS Table at Vision Publishers

CASE

Vision Publishers Brian Murphy, Judith Rossi, and Elena Sanchez meet to exchange ideas about the cover design and article layout for the 25th-anniversary issue of *Business Perspective*. Because Elena will coordinate all production phases of the special issue, she will be in contact with writers, editors, and marketing. First, she concentrates on creating a table of all the writers.

From Judith, Elena needs information about the articles from past issues, specifically, the article title, the issue of *Business Perspective* in which the article appeared, the length of the article, and the writer name. Because she will need to phone all the writers to tell them about their inclusion in the special issue, she also needs each writer's phone number.

Brian reminds Elena that only freelancers will need to be paid for reprints of their articles. In her database design, Elena will need to indicate if the writer is a freelancer and, if so, what the reprint payment amount is.

After scanning the articles, Elena remarks that the 25 articles were written by only 13 writers and Chong Kim wrote four of them. Brian points out that the writer of "Cola Advertising War" is a different Chong Kim, so Elena realizes that a writer name is not unique. She will need to identify the writer of each article with a unique writer ID. The data that Elena recorded during the meeting is shown in Figure 2-1.

Figure 2-1
Elena's data requirements

article title	writer phone number
issue of Business Perspective	is the writer a freelancer?
length of article	freelancer reprint payment amount
writer name	writer ID

Elena knows from her previous work with databases that, before she can create her database tables on the computer, she must first design the database.

Database Design Guidelines

A database management system can be a useful tool, but only if you first carefully design your database to represent your data requirements accurately. In database design, you determine the fields, tables, and relationships needed to satisfy your data and processing requirements. Some database designs can be complicated because the underlying data requirements are complex. Most data requirements and their resulting database designs are much simpler, however, and these are the ones we will consider in the tutorials.

When you design a database, you should follow these guidelines:

- Identify all fields needed to produce the required information. For example, Elena needs information for contacting writers and for planning a magazine layout, so she listed the fields that would satisfy those informational requirements (Figure 2-1).
- Identify the entities involved in the data requirements. Recall that an entity is a person, place, object, event, or idea for which you want to store and process data. Elena's data requirements, for example, involve two entities, articles and writers. Entities usually become the names for the tables in a database.
- Group fields that describe each entity. Recall that fields are characteristics, or attributes, of entities, so it's logical to group together the characteristics of an entity. An entity and the fields that describe that entity represent a table in your database. Elena has articles and writers as entities, and she groups the fields for them under each entity name, as shown in Figure 2-2. So far, Elena's database design has an ARTICLES table and a WRITERS table.

Figure 2-2
Elena's fields describing each entity

ARTICLES	WRITERS
article title	writer ID
issue of Business Perspective	writer name
length of article	writer phone number
	is the writer a freelancer?
	freelancer reprint payment amount

- Determine each table's primary key. Recall that a primary key uniquely identifies each record in a table. Although a primary key is not mandatory in Access, it's usually a good idea to have one for each table. Without a primary key, selecting the proper record can be a problem. For example, Elena has decided to include a writer ID to identify uniquely each writer because she needs to distinguish between the two writers named Chong Kim. At this point, however, Elena does not have a primary key for the ARTICLES table. No field in the table is guaranteed to have unique field values. Even a combination of these fields cannot be guaranteed to be unique. Elena delays a final decision on a primary key for the ARTICLES table until later in the database design process.
- Include a common field in related tables. You use the common field to link one table logically with another table. For example, in the ARTICLES table Elena includes writer ID, which is the primary key for the WRITERS table. When she views a record in the ARTICLES table, writer ID serves as a foreign key. She uses the foreign key value to find the one record in the WRITERS table having that field value as a primary key. This process allows Elena to know who wrote which article. She can also find all articles written by a writer; she uses the writer ID value for that writer and searches the ARTICLES table for all articles with that writer ID value.
- Avoid data redundancy. **Data redundancy** occurs when you store the same data in more than one place. With the exception of common fields to relate tables, you should avoid redundancy. Figure 2-3 shows a correct database design for an ARTICLES table and a WRITERS table with no redundancy. The Writer ID field serves as the common field to link the two tables.

ARTICLES table

Article Title	Issue of Business Perspective	Article Length	Writer ID
Trans-Alaskan Oil Pipeline Opening	1977 JUL	803	J525
Farm Aid Abuses	1978 APR	1866	J525
Herbert A. Simon Interview	1978 DEC	1811	C200
Alternative Energy Sources	1980 JUN	2085	S260
Windfall Tax on Oil Profits	1980 APR	1497	K500
Toyota and GM Joint Venture	1983 MAR	1682	S260

WRITERS table

Writer ID	Writer Name	Writer Phone Number	Freelancer?	Reprint Payment Amount
C200	Kelly Cox	(204)783-5415	Yes	$100
J525	Leroy W. Johnson	(209)895-2046	Yes	$125
K500	Chong Kim	(807)729-5364	No	$0
S260	Wilhelm Seeger	(306)423-0932	Yes	$250

Figure 2-3
Correct database design with no redundancy

Data redundancy wastes storage space. Data redundancy can also cause inconsistencies, if, for instance, you type a field value one way in one table and a different way in the same table or in a second table. Figure 2-4 on the following page shows two examples of incorrect database design. Both designs illustrate data redundancy and the resulting waste of storage space and problem of inconsistent field values.

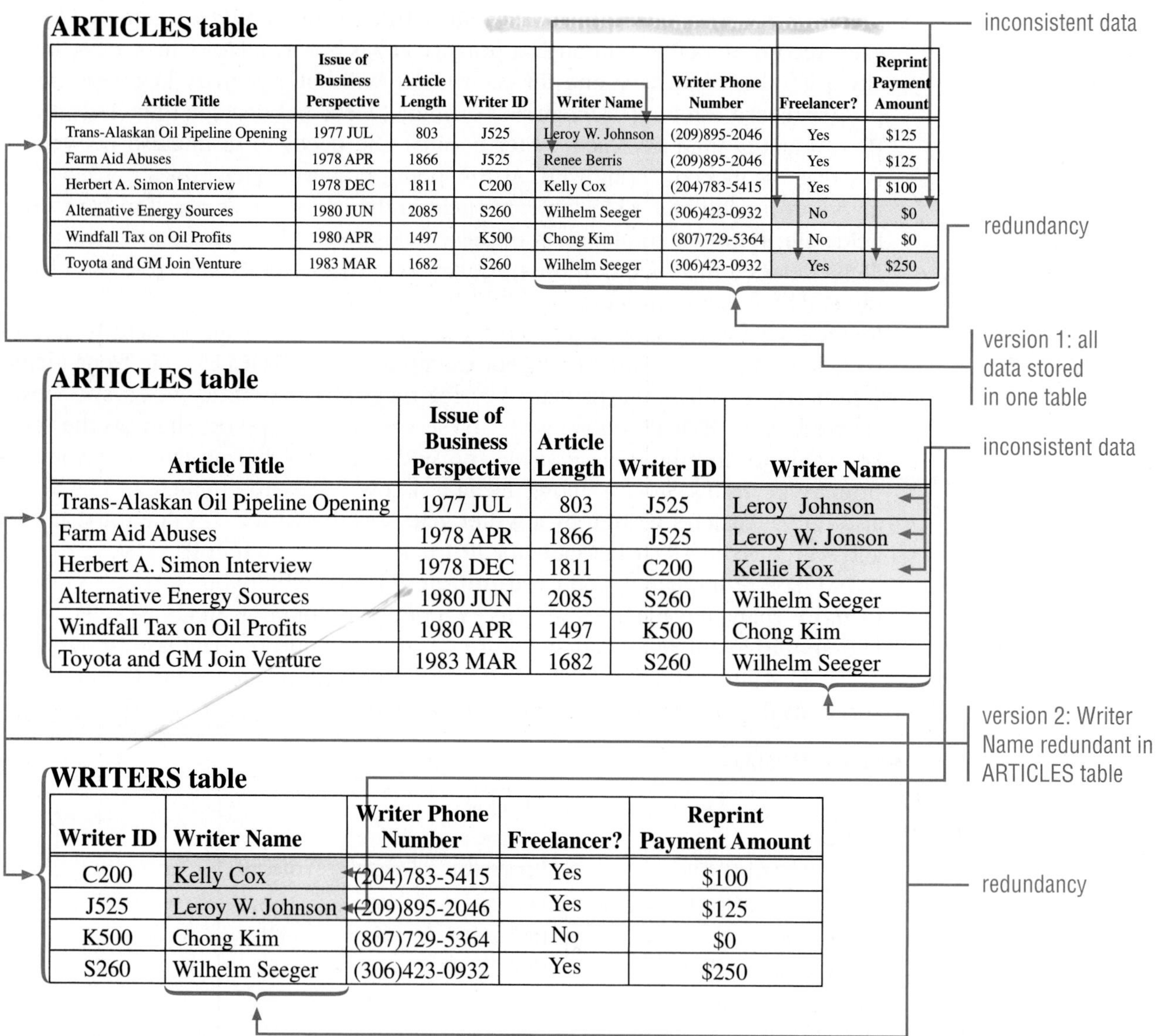

ARTICLES table

Article Title	Issue of Business Perspective	Article Length	Writer ID	Writer Name	Writer Phone Number	Freelancer?	Reprint Payment Amount
Trans-Alaskan Oil Pipeline Opening	1977 JUL	803	J525	Leroy W. Johnson	(209)895-2046	Yes	$125
Farm Aid Abuses	1978 APR	1866	J525	Renee Berris	(209)895-2046	Yes	$125
Herbert A. Simon Interview	1978 DEC	1811	C200	Kelly Cox	(204)783-5415	Yes	$100
Alternative Energy Sources	1980 JUN	2085	S260	Wilhelm Seeger	(306)423-0932	No	$0
Windfall Tax on Oil Profits	1980 APR	1497	K500	Chong Kim	(807)729-5364	No	$0
Toyota and GM Join Venture	1983 MAR	1682	S260	Wilhelm Seeger	(306)423-0932	Yes	$250

ARTICLES table

Article Title	Issue of Business Perspective	Article Length	Writer ID	Writer Name
Trans-Alaskan Oil Pipeline Opening	1977 JUL	803	J525	Leroy Johnson
Farm Aid Abuses	1978 APR	1866	J525	Leroy W. Jonson
Herbert A. Simon Interview	1978 DEC	1811	C200	Kellie Kox
Alternative Energy Sources	1980 JUN	2085	S260	Wilhelm Seeger
Windfall Tax on Oil Profits	1980 APR	1497	K500	Chong Kim
Toyota and GM Join Venture	1983 MAR	1682	S260	Wilhelm Seeger

WRITERS table

Writer ID	Writer Name	Writer Phone Number	Freelancer?	Reprint Payment Amount
C200	Kelly Cox	(204)783-5415	Yes	$100
J525	Leroy W. Johnson	(209)895-2046	Yes	$125
K500	Chong Kim	(807)729-5364	No	$0
S260	Wilhelm Seeger	(306)423-0932	Yes	$250

Figure 2-4
Incorrect database designs with redundancy

- Determine the properties of each field. You need to describe to the DBMS the **properties**, or characteristics, of each field, so that the DBMS knows how to store, display, and process the field. These properties include the field name, the field's maximum number of characters or digits, the field's description or explanation, and other field characteristics. For example, Elena notes that Length of Article is a field name, which has a maximum of four digits. You will learn more details about field properties later in this tutorial.

A diagram depicting the database design guidelines is shown in Figure 2-5.

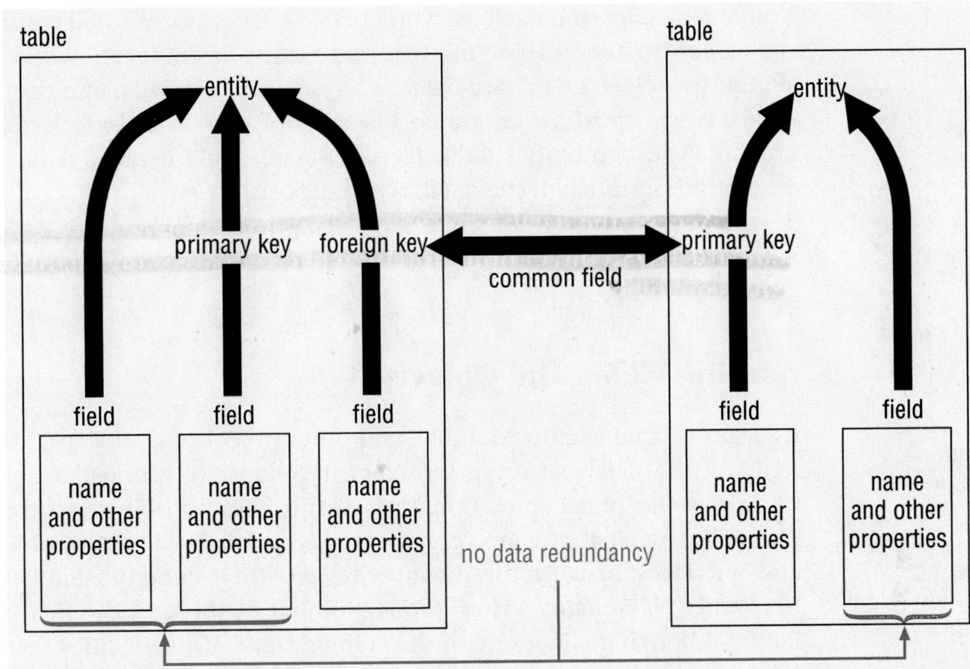

Figure 2-5 Database design guidelines

Keeping the database design guidelines in mind, Elena develops her initial database design, as shown in Figure 2-6.

ARTICLES table
Article Title
Issue of Business Perspective
Length of Article
Writer ID—foreign key

WRITERS table
Writer ID—primary key
Writer Name
Writer Phone Number
Is the Writer a Freelancer?
Freelancer Reprint Payment Amount

Figure 2-6 Elena's initial database design

Guidelines for Creating an Access Table

In addition to following the database design guidelines, you must follow rules imposed by Access when you create a database. These rules apply to naming a database, naming fields and objects, and defining the properties of fields and objects. Rather than discuss all the property definition rules, let's initially consider the naming rules and three field-property rules.

Naming Databases

You must name each database you create. Access stores the database as a file on disk with the name you choose. You use that same name in the future when you open the database. When you select a database name, choose a descriptive name that will remind you of the database's purpose or contents. Vision Publishers' database is named Vision because it contains the company's data. Elena chooses for her new database the name Issue25, which is descriptive of the database's purpose.

In Access, the database name contains up to eight characters and must conform to standard DOS conventions for filenames. Access automatically adds the filename extension .mdb.

Naming Fields and Objects

You must name each field, table, and other object in a database. Access then stores these items in the database using the names you supply. Choose a field or object name that describes the purpose or contents of the field or object, so that later you can easily remember what the name represents. Elena names her two tables BUSINESS ARTICLES and WRITERS, because these names suggest their contents. Similarly, she chooses Writer ID, Writer Name, and Writer Phone Number as three of the field names in the WRITERS table. Although it is not one of the naming rules, Elena decides that identifying her critical tables might be easier if she uses a convention of all uppercase letters for table names and an appropriate mix of uppercase and lowercase for field names and the names of other database objects.

One set of rules applies to the naming of fields and objects:

- They can be up to 64 characters long.
- They can contain letters, numbers, spaces, and special characters except a period, exclamation mark, and square brackets.
- They must not start with a space.

Assigning Field Descriptions

When you define a field, you can assign an optional description for the field. If you choose a descriptive field name, you probably do not need to supply a description. Because, for example, Elena selected the descriptive field names Writer Name and Writer Phone Number, she does not plan to enter a description for these fields. For the Writer ID field in the BUSINESS ARTICLES table, however, Elena plans to assign the description "foreign key."

The field description can be up to 255 characters long. If you enter a description, choose one that explains the purpose or usage of the field.

Assigning Field Data Types

You must assign a data type for each field. The **data type** determines what field values you can enter for that field and what other properties the field will have. For example, Elena's Length of Article field is a number, so she tells Access that the field has the number data type. Access will allow Elena to enter only numbers as values for the field and will enable her to perform calculations on the field values.

In Access, you assign one of the following eight data types to each field:

- The **text data type** allows field values containing letters, digits, spaces, and special characters. Text fields can be up to 255 characters long. You should assign the text data type to fields in which you will store names, addresses, and descriptions, and to fields containing digits that are not used in calculations. Elena, for example, assigns the text data type to the Writer ID field; the Writer Name field; and the Writer Phone Number field, which contains digits not used in calculations.
- The **memo data type**, like the text data type, allows field values containing letters, digits, spaces, and special characters. Memo fields, however, can be up to 64,000 characters long and are used for long comments or explanations. Elena does not plan to assign the memo data type to any of her fields.
- The **number data type** limits field values to digits, an optional leading sign (+ or –), and an optional decimal point. Use the number data type for fields that you will use in calculations, except calculations involving money. Elena assigns the number data type to the Length of Article field in the BUSINESS ARTICLES table.
- The **date/time data type** allows field values containing valid dates and times only. Usually you enter dates in mm/dd/yy format, where mm is a two-digit month, dd is a two-digit day of the month, and yy are the last two digits of the year. This data type also permits other date formats and a variety of time formats. When using this data type, you can perform calculations on dates and times and you can sort them. The number of days between two dates, for example, can be determined. Elena does not assign the date/time data type to any of her fields.
- The **currency data type** allows field values similar to those for the number data type. Unlike calculations with number data type decimal values, calculations performed using the currency data type match to the penny exactly. Elena assigns the currency data type to the Freelancer Reprint Payment Amount field in the WRITERS table.
- The **counter data type** consists of integers that are values automatically controlled by Access. Access enters a value of 1 for the field in the first record of a table and adds 1 for each successive record's field value. This guarantees a unique field value, so that such a field can serve as a table's primary key. Elena does not assign the counter data type to any of her fields.
- The **yes/no data type** limits field values to yes and no entries. Use this data type for fields that indicate the presence or absence of a condition, such as whether an order has been filled, or if an employee is eligible for the company dental plan. Elena assigns the yes/no data type to the Is the Writer a Freelancer? field in the WRITERS table.
- The **OLE object data type** allows field values that are created in other software packages as objects, such as photographs, video images, graphics, drawings, sound recordings, voice-mail messages, spreadsheets, and word processing documents. **OLE** is an acronym for object linking and embedding. You can either import the object or link to the object, but you cannot modify it in Access. Elena does not assign the OLE object data type to any of her fields.

Assigning Field Sizes

The **field size** property defines a field value's maximum storage size for text and number fields only. The other data types have no field size property, because their storage size is either a fixed, predetermined amount or is variable, as shown in Figure 2-7 on the following page. You should still document every field's maximum size, however, so that you allow enough room for it on entry screens and on reports and other outputs, without wasting space.

Data Type	Storage Size
Text	1 to 255 bytes 50 bytes default
Memo	64,000 maximum exact size depends on field value
Number	1 to 8 bytes 8 bytes default
Date/Time	8 bytes
Currency	8 bytes
Counter	4 bytes
Yes/no	1 bit
OLE object	1 gigabyte maximum exact size depends on object size

Figure 2-7
Data type storage sizes

A text field has a default field size of 50 characters. You set its field size by entering a number in the range 1 to 255. You select the field size for a number field from the five choices of byte, integer, long integer, double, and single, as shown in Figure 2-8. Double is the default field size for a number field.

Field Size	Storage Size (Bytes)	Number Type	Field Values Allowed
Byte	1	Integer	0 to 255
Integer	2	Integer	-32,768 to 32,767
Long Integer	4	Integer	-2,147,483,648 to 2,147,483,647
Double	8	Decimal	15 significant digits
Single	4	Decimal	7 significant digits

Figure 2-8
Number data type field size

Elena's Writer ID field is a text field that is always exactly four characters long, so she documents its field size as 4. Writer Name is also a text field, but each field value varies in size. After studying the different field values, she finds that a field size of 25 will accommodate the largest field value for the Writer Name field. In a similar fashion, Elena determines the field size for the other fields in her database.

Creating an Access Table

Before you create a database and its objects on the computer, you should spend time carefully documenting your data requirements. You must understand, and accurately represent, the structure of each table in the database.

Planning the Table Structure

Now that you have learned the guidelines for designing databases and creating Access tables, you are ready to work with Elena to create the Issue25 database. Elena first develops the structure of the WRITERS and BUSINESS ARTICLES tables. For each field, she documents the field name and its data type, input/display field size, and description (Figure 2-9).

	Data Type	Input/Display Field Size	Description
WRITERS table			
Writer ID	text	4	primary key
Writer Name	text	25	
Writer Phone Number	text	14	(999) 999-9999 format
Is the Writer a Freelancer?	yes/no	3	
Freelancer Reprint Payment Amount	currency	4	$250 maximum
BUSINESS ARTICLES table			
Article Title	text	44	
Issue of Business Perspective	text	8	
Length of Article	number	4	integer field size
Writer ID	text	4	foreign key

Figure 2-9
Elena's table structures for the WRITERS and BUSINESS ARTICLES tables

With the exception of some new information, the file structures for these two tables are consistent with the planning Elena has done so far. The five fields in the WRITERS table are Writer ID, Writer Name, Writer Phone Number, Is the Writer a Freelancer? and Freelancer Reprint Payment Amount. The four fields in the BUSINESS ARTICLES table are Article Title, Issue of Business Perspective, Length of Article, and Writer ID. Six of these nine fields are text fields, while Is the Writer a Freelancer? is a yes/no field, Freelancer Reprint Payment Amount is a currency field, and Length of Article is a number field.

Elena needs to choose field sizes only for text and number fields. However, she decides that documenting the maximum field sizes for all data types will help her plan how many positions each field requires for input and for screen and report display. For this purpose, she includes a column labeled Input/Display Field Size. Freelancers will receive $250 at most for their articles, so she plans a field size of four for the Freelancer Reprint Payment Amount currency field.

Finally, she adds descriptions for Length of Article to remind her of its field size, for Writer Phone Number to specify its format, and for Freelancer Reprint Payment Amount to document its format and size.

Creating a Database

Having completed the planning for her table structures, Elena creates the database named Issue25. When you create a database, you give it a unique eight-character name that conforms to standard DOS conventions for filenames. Access stores the database by that name as a file on disk with an .mdb extension. A new Access database uses 64KB of disk space. Most of this is used when you add your first fields, tables, and other objects. As your database grows in size and needs more disk storage, Access increases its size in 32KB increments.

REFERENCE WINDOW

Creating a Database

- Click the New Database button on the toolbar. The New Database dialog box appears.
- With the File Name text box highlighted, type the name of the database you want to create. Do not press [Enter] yet.
- Change the drive and directory information, if necessary.
- Click the OK button or press [Enter] to accept the changes in the New Database dialog box.

Let's create the Issue25 database. If you have not done so, launch Access before you follow the next set of steps.

To create a database:

1. Click the **New Database button** on the toolbar in the Microsoft Access window. Access displays the New Database dialog box. See Figure 2-10. The File Name text box highlights the default name, db1.mdb.

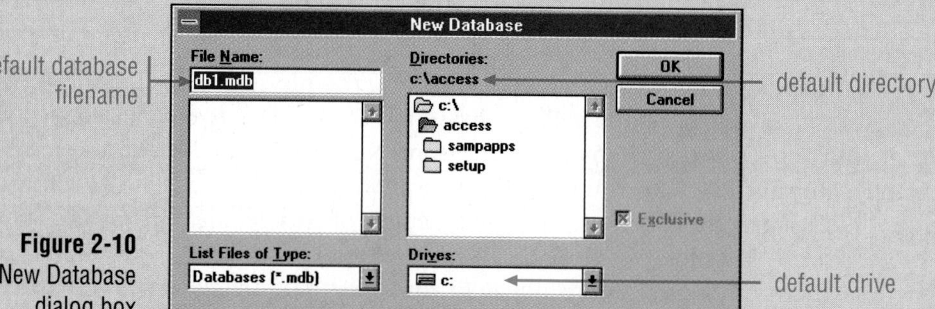

Figure 2-10 Initial New Database dialog box

2. Type **issue25** in the File Name text box. Click the **down arrow button** on the right side of the Drives box. A list of available drives drops down. Click the letter of the drive in which you put your Student Disk. See Figure 2-11. Your drive might be different.

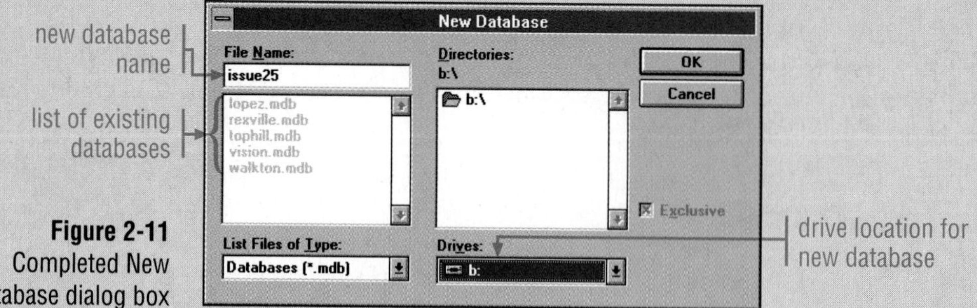

Figure 2-11 Completed New Database dialog box

TROUBLE? If the contents of the File Name text box do not show issue25, the text box might not have been highlighted when you began typing. If this is the case, highlight the contents of the text box and retype issue25.

❸ Click the **OK button** to let Access know you have completed the New Database dialog box. Access creates the Issue25 database, adding the extension .mdb, and opens the Database window. See Figure 2-12. Because this is a new database, no tables appear in the Tables list box.

Figure 2-12 The Database window for a new database

Creating the Table Structure with Table Wizard

Having created her new database, Elena's next step is to create the WRITERS table structure. Creating a table structure consists of creating a table and defining the fields for the table. Therefore, Elena will create the WRITERS table and define its fields: Writer ID, Writer Name, Writer Phone Number, Is the Writer a Freelancer? and Freelancer Reprint Payment Amount.

In Access, you can keyboard the fields for a table or use Table Wizard to automate the table creation process. A **Wizard** is an Access tool that helps you create objects such as tables and reports by asking you a series of questions and then creating the objects based on your answers. **Table Wizard** asks you questions about your table and then creates the table based on your answers. Whether you use Table Wizard or keyboard the table fields, you can change a table's design after it is created.

Elena uses Table Wizard to create the WRITERS table.

To activate Table Wizard:

❶ Click the **New command button** in the Database window. Access displays the New Table dialog box. See Figure 2-13.

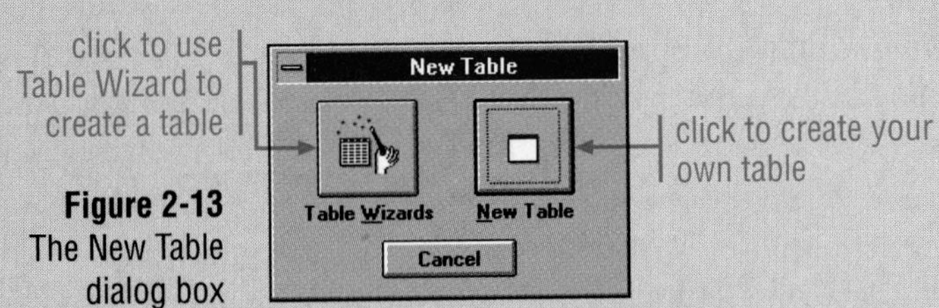

Figure 2-13 The New Table dialog box

❷ Click the **Table Wizards button**. The first Table Wizard dialog box appears. See Figure 2-14 on the following page.

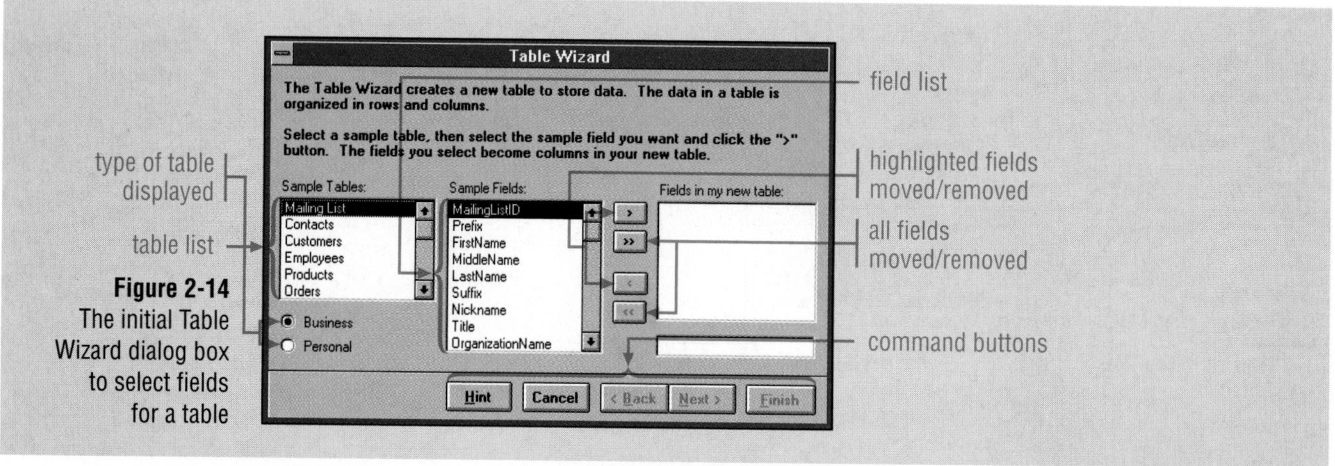

Figure 2-14
The initial Table Wizard dialog box to select fields for a table

In the first Table Wizard dialog box, you select the fields for your table from sample fields in dozens of sample tables. The sample tables include those for business and personal use; simply click the Business or Personal radio button to display the corresponding list of sample tables. Scroll through the Sample Tables list until you find an appropriate table and then select fields to add to your table from the Sample Fields list. If necessary, you can select fields from more than one table. Do not be concerned about selecting field names that exactly match the ones you need because you can change the names later. Instead, select fields that seem like they have the general properties you need for your fields. If a field's properties do not exactly match, you can change the properties later.

You select fields in the order you want them to appear in your table. If you want to select fields one at a time, highlight a field by clicking it, and then click the > button. If you want to select all the fields, click the >> button. The fields appear in the list box on the right as you select them. If you make a mistake, click the << button to remove all the fields from the list box on the right or highlight a field and click the < button to remove fields one at a time.

At the bottom of each Table Wizard dialog box is a set of command buttons. These command buttons allow you to move quickly to other Table Wizard dialog boxes, to cancel the table creation process, and to display hints. You can display a hint for a Table Wizard dialog box by clicking the Hint command button. After reading the hint, click OK to remove the hint and continue with your work.

Elena selects fields from the Mailing List sample table to create the WRITERS table.

To select fields for a new table:

1. If Mailing List is not highlighted in the Sample Tables list box, click it, so that it is highlighted. Click **MailingListID** in the Sample Fields list box and then click the **> button**. Access places MailingListID into the list box on the right as the first field in the new table.
2. In order, select LastName, HomePhone, MembershipStatus, and DuesAmount for the WRITERS table by clicking the field name in the Sample Fields list box, scrolling as needed, and then clicking the **> button**.

Elena has selected all the fields she needs for her table, so she continues through the remaining Table Wizard dialog boxes to finish creating the WRITERS table.

To finish creating a table using Table Wizard:

1. Click the **Next > button**. Access displays the second Table Wizard dialog box.
2. Type **WRITERS** in the text box and then click the **radio button** beside "Set the primary key myself." See Figure 2-15.

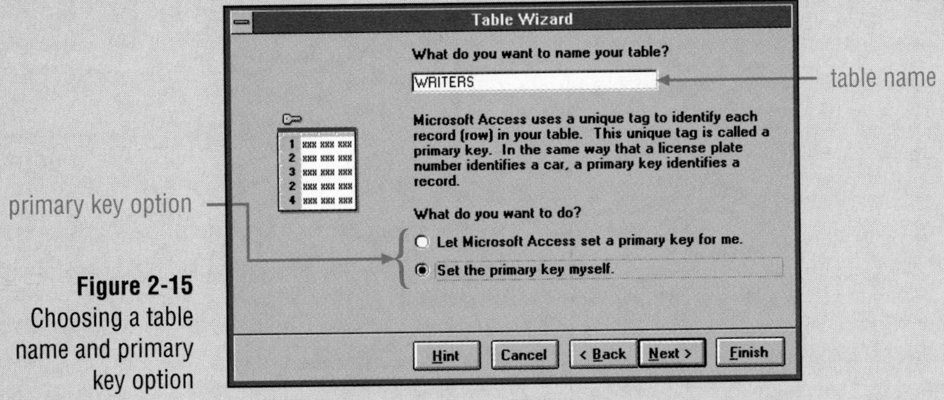

Figure 2-15 Choosing a table name and primary key option

3. Click the **Next > button**. Access displays the third Table Wizard dialog box.
4. Let MailingListID remain in the text box at the top of the dialog box and click the **bottom radio button**, so that the primary key will contain "Numbers and/or letters I enter when I add new records." You have now selected MailingListID as the primary key for the table. See Figure 2-16.

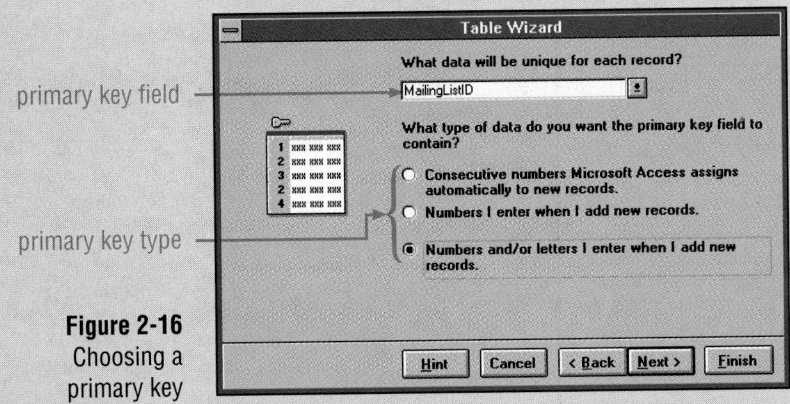

Figure 2-16 Choosing a primary key

5. Click the **Next > button**. Access displays the final Table Wizard dialog box.

Elena needs to change the field names and other field properties for the sample fields inserted into the WRITERS table by Table Wizard, so that they agree with her table design. To make these changes she must modify the table design. First, she must exit Table Wizard.

To exit Table Wizard:

1. Be sure that the "Modify the table design" radio button is on and that the Cue Cards box at the bottom is unchecked. See Figure 2-17 on the following page.

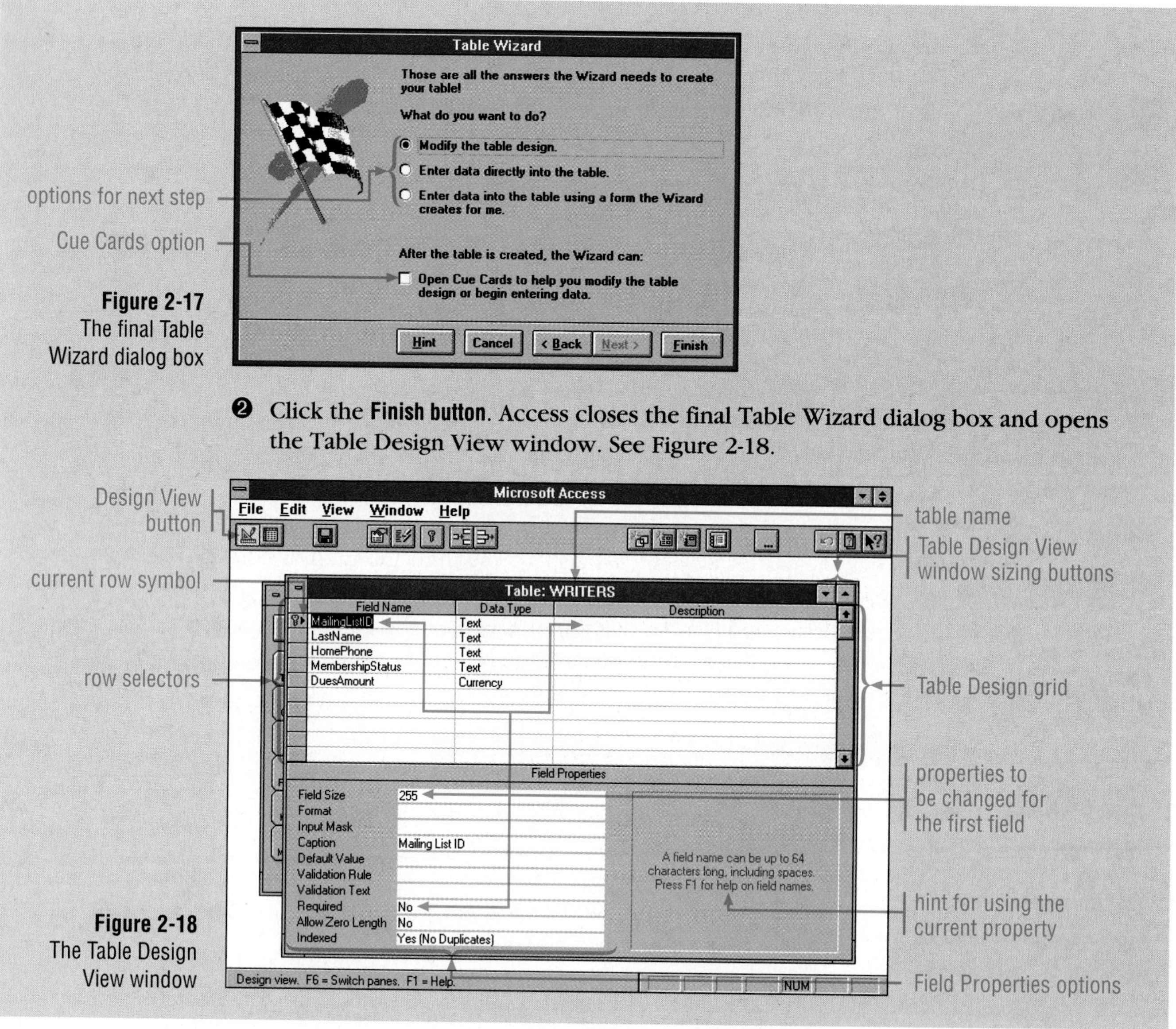

Figure 2-17 The final Table Wizard dialog box

❷ Click the **Finish button**. Access closes the final Table Wizard dialog box and opens the Table Design View window. See Figure 2-18.

Figure 2-18 The Table Design View window

Changing the Sample Field Properties

You use the Table Design View window to define or modify a table structure or the properties for the fields in a table. If you create a table without using Table Wizard, you enter the fields and their properties for your table directly in this window.

Initially, the Design View button on the toolbar is selected, the table name appears in the Table Design View window title bar, the first field name is highlighted, and the current row symbol is positioned in the first row selector of the Table Design grid. When you click a row selector, Access highlights the entire row and moves the current row symbol to that row. If you click a field name, data type, or description for a different field, Access moves the current row symbol to that row but does not highlight the entire row.

A hint for using the current property appears in the lower-right corner of the Table Design View window. As you press [Tab] or click a different property, the hint changes to define or explain the new property. If the hint does not answer your questions about the property, press [F1] for a full explanation.

The field name, data type, and description field properties appear in the top half of the Table Design View window. In the Field Properties sheet, which appears in the lower-left corner of the window, you view and change other properties for the current field. For example, in the property sheet you can change the size of a text field or the number of decimal places for a number field. The Field Properties displayed are appropriate for the data type of the currently selected field.

For the first field, Elena changes the field name to Writer ID, the Field Size property to 4, the Required property to Yes, and adds "primary key" as a description.

To change the first field's properties:

1. If MailingListID is not highlighted in the first row of the Field Name column, double-click it. Then type **Writer ID** to replace the highlighted MailingListID and press **[Tab]** twice to move the I to the Description box.
2. Type **primary key** as the Description for the first field.
3. Double-click **255** in the Field Size property box to highlight it and then type **4**.
4. Click **Mailing List ID** in the Caption property box, press **[F2]** to highlight it, and then press **[Del]** to delete it.
5. Click anywhere in the **Required property text box** and then click the **down arrow button** that appears in that box to display the Required list box. Click **Yes** in the Required list box to choose that as the property value.

Setting the **Required property** to Yes for a field means you must enter a value in the field for every record in the table. Every primary-key field should have the Required property set to Yes, so that each record has a unique value. Fields other than a primary key usually have the Required property set to No, which is the default value.

The Caption property allows you to use a **caption**, which is text that replaces the default field name in the datasheet column heading box and in the label on a form. Elena deletes all Caption property values because they do not represent the new field names she will use.

Elena next changes some of the properties for each of the remaining fields in the WRITERS table. If you make a mistake in typing a field name or description value, click that box, press [F2] to select the entire property value, and retype the value.

To change the properties of the remaining fields:

1. Double-click **LastName** in the second row's Field Name text box and type **Writer Name**. Double-click **50** in the Field Size property box to highlight it and then type **25**. Finally, click **Last Name** in the Caption property box, press **[F2]** to highlight it, and then press **[Del]** to delete it.
2. Double-click **HomePhone** in the third row's Field Name text box and type **Writer Phone Number**. Press **[Tab]** twice and type **(999) 999-9999 format** in the Description text box. Double-click **30** in the Field Size property box to highlight it and then type **14**. Finally, click **Home Phone** in the Caption property box, press **[F2]** to highlight it, and then press **[Del]** to delete it.
3. Double-click **MembershipStatus** in the fourth row's Field Name text box and type **Is the Writer a Freelancer?** Press **[Tab]** and then click the **down arrow button** in the Data Type text box to display the Data Type list box. See Figure 2-19 on the following page.

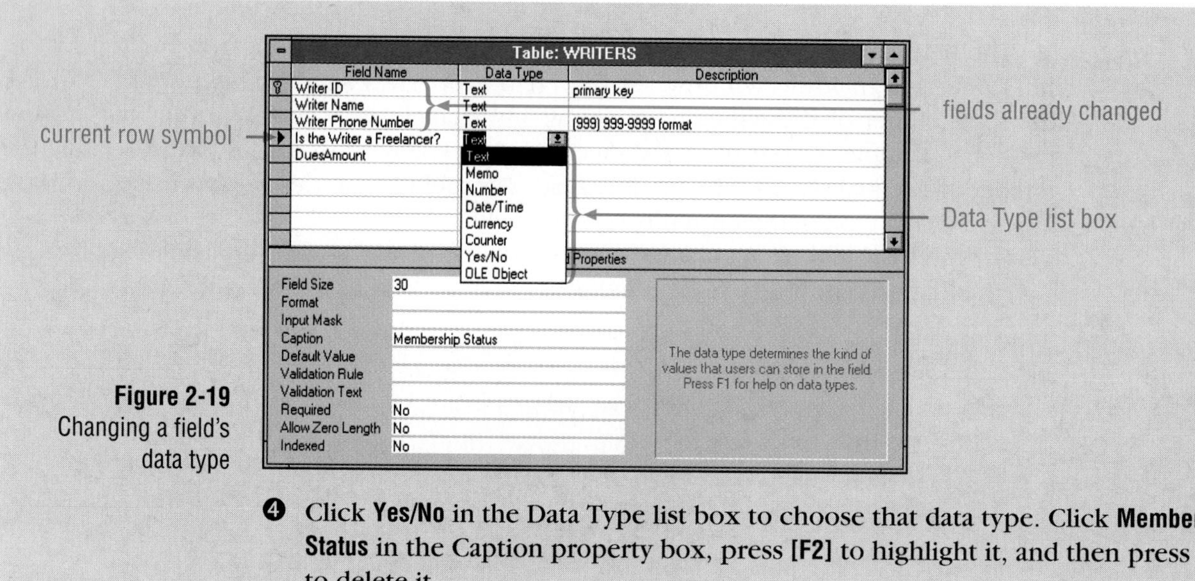

Figure 2-19 Changing a field's data type

❹ Click **Yes/No** in the Data Type list box to choose that data type. Click **Membership Status** in the Caption property box, press **[F2]** to highlight it, and then press **[Del]** to delete it.

❺ Double-click **DuesAmount** in the fifth row's Field Name text box, type **Freelancer Reprint Payment Amount**, press **[Tab]**, and then type **cu** in the Data Type box. "Currency" replaces the "cu" you typed in the Data Type box.

❻ Press **[Tab]**, and then type **$250 maximum** to enter the field's Description property. Click **Dues Amount** in the Caption property box, press **[F2]** to highlight it, and then press **[Del]** to delete it. See Figure 2-20.

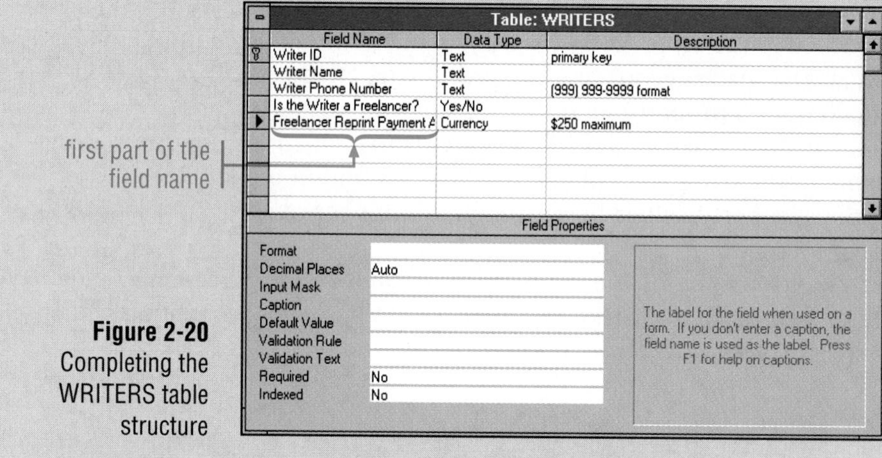

Figure 2-20 Completing the WRITERS table structure

Instead of selecting a field's data type by clicking one of the choices in the Data Type list box, you can type the entire data type in the field's Data Type box. Alternatively, type just the first character—or the first two characters for currency and counter—of the data type to select that data type.

Field names can be up to 64 characters long. However, the Field Name text box is not wide enough to show an entire long name. Freelancer Reprint Payment Amount is an example of a long field name.

Saving the Table Structure

Elena has finished defining and changing the WRITERS table structure, so she saves the table. When you first create a table, you save the table with its field definitions to add the table structure permanently to your database. If you use Table Wizard, Access saves your table before you switch to the Table Design View window. Elena saves the table, so that her field property changes are retained in the database.

To save a table:

1. Click the **Save button** on the toolbar. Access saves the WRITERS table on your Student Disk.

Switching to the Datasheet View Window

Once you have defined a table, you can view the table in either the Table Design View window or the Datasheet View window. Use the Table Design View window to view or change a table's fields, and use the Datasheet View window to view or change the field values and records stored in a table. Even though she has not yet entered field values and records in the WRITERS table, Elena displays the WRITERS table in the Datasheet View window. She wants to study the datasheet to determine if she needs to make further changes to the table structure.

To switch from the Table Design View window to the Datasheet View window:

1. Click the **Datasheet View button** on the toolbar. Access displays the Datasheet View window for the WRITERS table. See Figure 2-21.

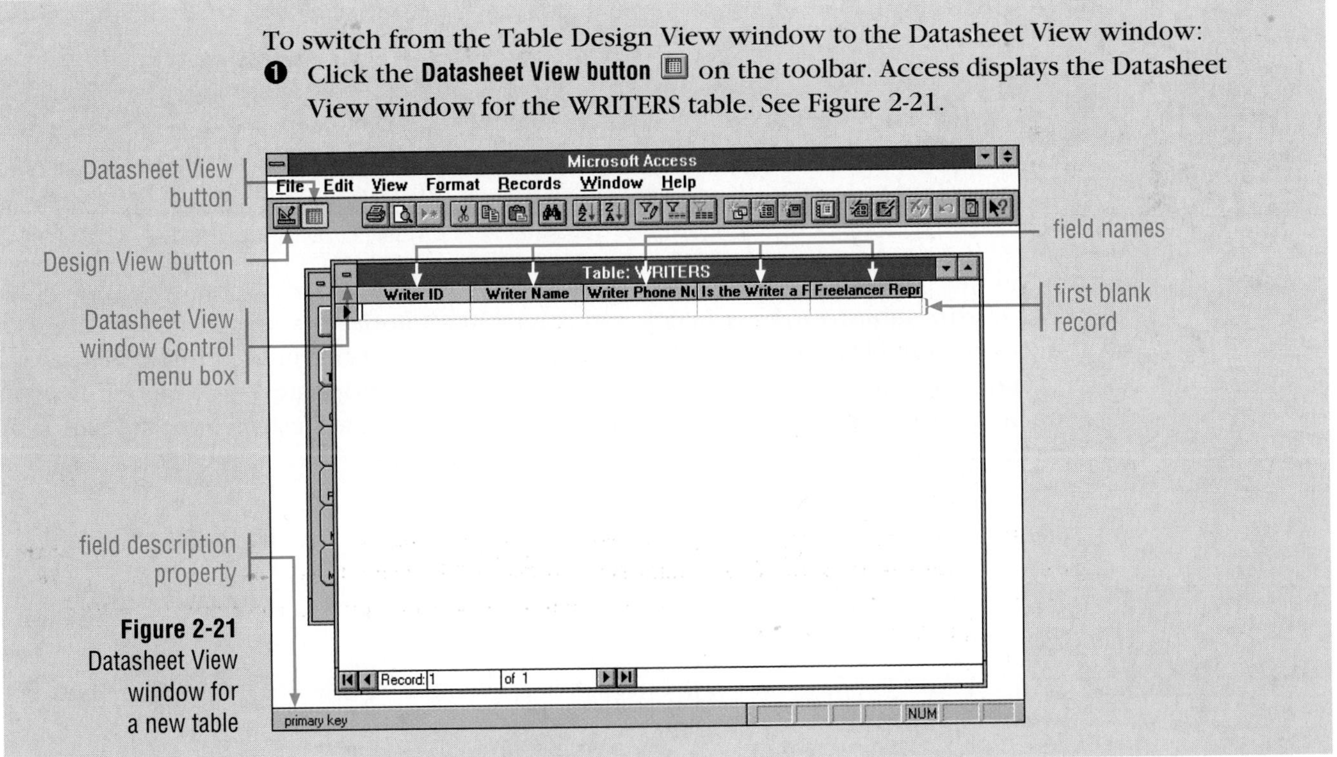

Figure 2-21 Datasheet View window for a new table

Elena notices that the description property for Writer ID appears in the status bar. Also, the first record has no field values. Thus, no records exist for the new WRITERS table. This is correct because Elena has not yet entered field values in the table.

Elena sees two problems in the Datasheet View window of the WRITERS table that she wants to correct. First, the field names Writer Phone Number, Is the Writer a Freelancer? and Freelancer Reprint Payment Amount are only partially displayed, and their field value boxes are wider than they need to be to accommodate the field values that will be entered. Second, the Writer Name field value box is too narrow to display the entire field value.

Printing a Datasheet

Before making any changes, Elena prints the datasheet for the WRITERS table, so that she can refer to it when she makes the field changes to correct the problems she discovered.

To print the datasheet:

1. Click the **Print button** on the toolbar to open the Print dialog box.
2. Check the Printer section of the Print dialog box to make sure your computer's printer is selected. Click the **OK button** to initiate printing. After the message box disappears, Access returns you to the Datasheet View window.

Elena switches back to the Table Design View window to make her field property changes.

To switch from the Datasheet View window to the Table Design View window:

1. Click the **Design View button** on the toolbar. Access again displays the Table Design View window for the WRITERS table.

If you want to take a break and resume the tutorial at a later time, you can exit Access by double-clicking the Microsoft Access window Control menu box. When you resume the tutorial, place your Student Disk in the appropriate drive, launch Access, open the Issue25 database on your Student Disk, and click the Design command button to open the Table Design View window for the WRITERS table.

■ ■ ■

Changing Field Properties

The first changes Elena makes are to shorten the field names for Writer Phone Number and Is the Writer a Freelancer? The field name for Freelancer Reprint Payment Amount is also too wide to fit in the datasheet column heading box. Rather than change the field name, however, Elena uses its Caption property to replace the default field name in the datasheet column heading box and in the label on a form. You use the Caption property to display a shorter version of a longer, more descriptive table field name.

Changing Field Names and Entering Captions

Let's change the names for the fields Writer Phone Number and Is the Writer a Freelancer?

To change a table field name in the Table Design View window:

1. Double-click **Number** in the Field Name box for Writer Phone Number to highlight it. Press **[Backspace]** twice to leave Writer Phone as the new field name.
2. Click anywhere in the Field Name box for Is the Writer a Freelancer? and then press **[F2]** to highlight the entire field name.
3. Type **Freelancer** to make it the new field name.

Suppose you make a change that you immediately realize is a mistake. You can click the **Undo button** on the toolbar to cancel your change. Not all changes can be undone; the Undo button is dimmed in those cases.

Let's make a field name change to Writer Name that we will immediately undo.

To undo a change:

1. Click anywhere in the Field Name box for Writer Name and then press **[F2]** to select the entire field name. Type **Amount**, which becomes the new field name.
2. Click the **Undo button**. Access restores the previous field name, Writer Name.

Having completed her field name changes, Elena enters a caption for Freelancer Reprint Payment Amount.

To enter a caption:

❶ Click anywhere in the Field Name box for Freelancer Reprint Payment Amount. The current row symbol moves to the Freelancer Reprint Payment Amount row, and the Field Properties options apply to this current field. Click the **Caption text box** and then type **Amount**. See Figure 2-22.

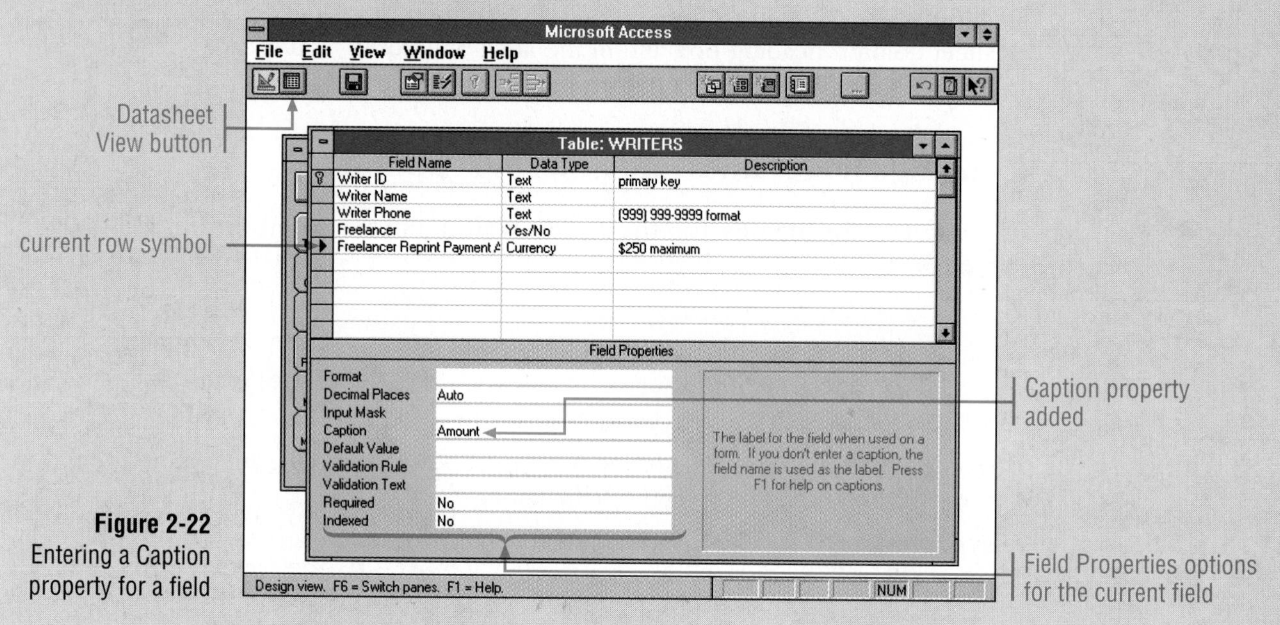

Figure 2-22
Entering a Caption property for a field

Elena switches to the Datasheet View window to review the effects of the changes she's made so far.

To switch to the Datasheet View window:

❶ Click the **Datasheet View button** on the toolbar. Access displays the "Save now?" dialog box. See Figure 2-23.

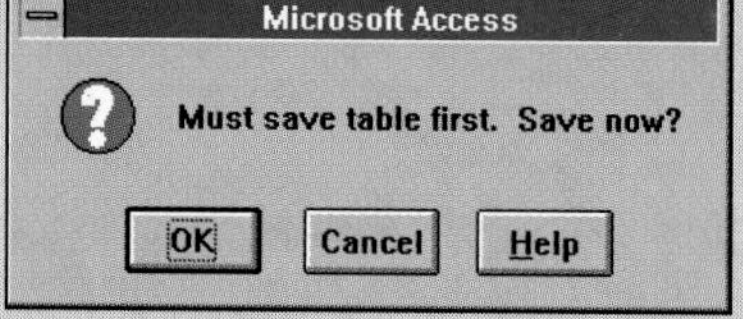

Figure 2-23
The "Save now?" dialog box

Access makes your table structure changes permanent only when you take action to save the changes or to close the Table Design View window. Switching to the Datasheet View window first involves closing the Table Design View window, so Access displays the dialog box to ask you about saving your table changes. If you want to keep the Table Design View window open and continue making table structure changes, click the **Cancel button**. If you would rather switch to the Datasheet View window, you need to save your changes first.

❷ Click the **OK button**. Access saves your table structure changes, closes the Table Design View window, and opens the Datasheet View window. See Figure 2-24.

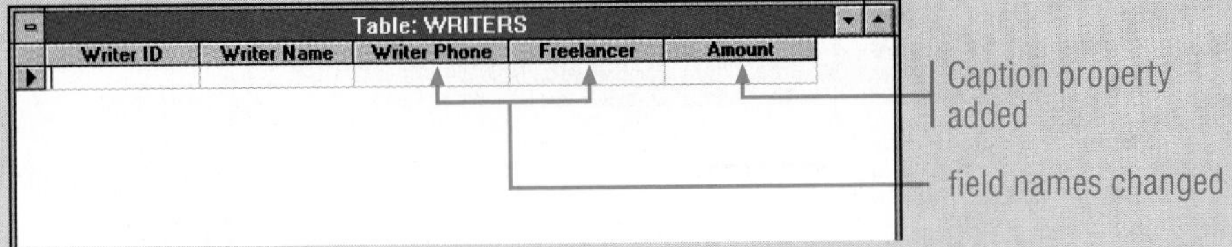

Figure 2-24 Reviewing file structure changes in the Datasheet View window

Elena reviews the changes she has made to the WRITERS table structure. The two new field names, Writer Phone and Freelancer, appear; and the Amount caption replaces the Freelancer Reprint Payment Amount field name. Elena is still bothered by the column widths in some of the fields in the datasheet, so she changes them.

Resizing Columns in a Datasheet

There are often several ways to accomplish a task in Access. For example, you can close a database by double-clicking the Database window Control menu box; by clicking File and then clicking Close Database; or by pressing and holding [Alt] and then pressing [F], then releasing both keys, and then pressing [C]. Elena has been choosing the simplest and fastest method to accomplish her tasks and has not spent time experimenting with alternative methods. However, Elena has never resized datasheet columns before, so she wants to practice three different techniques.

Let's first resize a datasheet column using the Format menu.

To resize datasheet columns using the Format menu:

❶ Click anywhere in the **Writer ID column**, click **Format**, and then click **Column Width...**. Access opens the Column Width dialog box. See Figure 2-25. Access has automatically selected the default, standard column width of 18.8 positions and has checked the Standard Width check box.

Figure 2-25 The Column Width dialog box

❷ Type **11** and then click the **OK button**. The Column Width dialog box disappears, and Access resizes the Writer ID column from 18.8 to 11 positions.

Changing a datasheet column width does not change the field size for the table field. The standard column width of 18.8 positions is approximately 1" wide on the screen. The actual number of characters you can place in a column depends on the typeface and font size you are using. Elena chooses not to change the typeface and font size.

Elena resizes the Writer Name field with a second resizing method, which uses the mouse pointer to drag the column's right edge. To resize this way, you must first position the mouse pointer in the field's **column selector**, which is the gray box that contains the field name at the top of the column. A column selector is also called a **field selector**.

To resize datasheet columns using the mouse pointer to drag the column's right edge:

1. Move the mouse pointer to the right edge of the Writer Name column selector until it changes to ✥. See Figure 2-26.

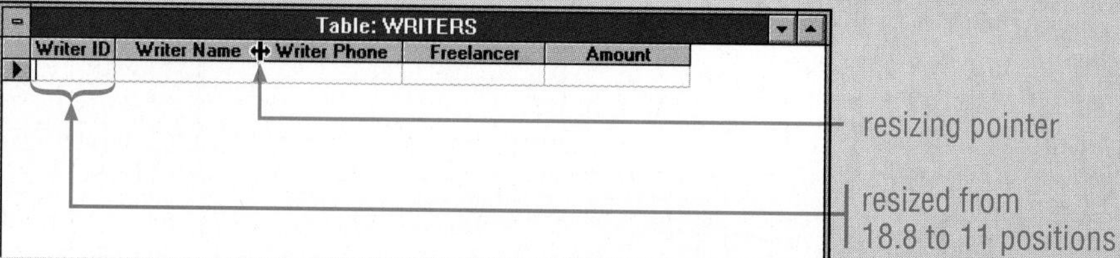

Figure 2-26 Resizing columns using the resizing pointer

2. Click-and-drag the pointer to the right until the column width is approximately twice its original size.

3. Release the mouse button to complete the resizing of the Writer Name field.

TROUBLE? Be sure that all five fields are still visible in the Datasheet View window. If not, you can repeat the previous steps to make the column narrower.

Elena tries a third technique—the best-fit column width method—to resize the Freelancer and Amount columns. When you use the **best-fit column width** method, Access automatically resizes the column to accommodate its largest value, including the field name at the top of the column. To use this method, you position the mouse pointer at the right edge of the column selector for the field and, when the mouse pointer changes to ✥, double-click the left mouse button. Access then automatically resizes the column. (A fourth method for resizing columns is to use the Best Fit button in the Column Width dialog box, but Elena does not experiment with this method.)

For both best-fit methods, you can resize two or more adjacent columns at the same time. Simply move the mouse pointer to the column selector of the leftmost of the fields. When the pointer changes to ⬇, click-and-drag it to the column selector of the rightmost field and then release the mouse button. You then double-click the ✥ at the right edge of the column selector for the rightmost field.

To resize datasheet columns using the best-fit column width method:

1. Move the mouse pointer to the Freelancer column selector. When it changes to ⬇, click the left mouse button, drag the pointer to the right to the Amount column selector, and then release the mouse button. Both columns are now highlighted.

2. Move the mouse pointer to the right edge of the Amount column selector. When it changes to ✥, double-click the left mouse button. Access automatically resizes both columns to their best fits. See Figure 2-27.

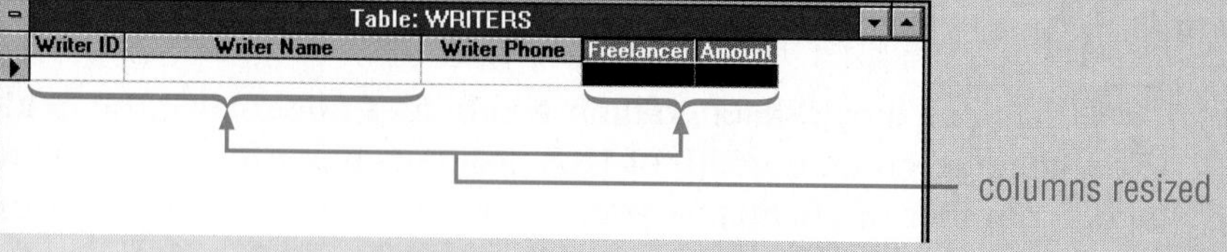

Figure 2-27 Four columns resized

For her final set of table structure changes, Elena assigns a default value to the Freelancer field, eliminates the decimal places in the Amount field, and adds an input mask to the Writer Phone field. These changes must be made in the Table Design View window, so Elena first switches from the Datasheet View window.

Assigning Default Values

With a few exceptions, Elena knows which writers are freelancers and which are staff writers. To be safe, Elena will assume that the exceptions are freelancers until she finds out for sure. She assigns the default value Yes to the Freelancer field, which means each writer will have the value Yes in the Freelancer field unless it is changed individually to No.

To assign a default value:

1. Click the **Design View button** on the toolbar to switch to the Table Design View window.
2. Click anywhere in the **Freelancer field row** to make it the current field, click the Field Properties **Default Value text box**, and then type **Yes**. See Figure 2-28.

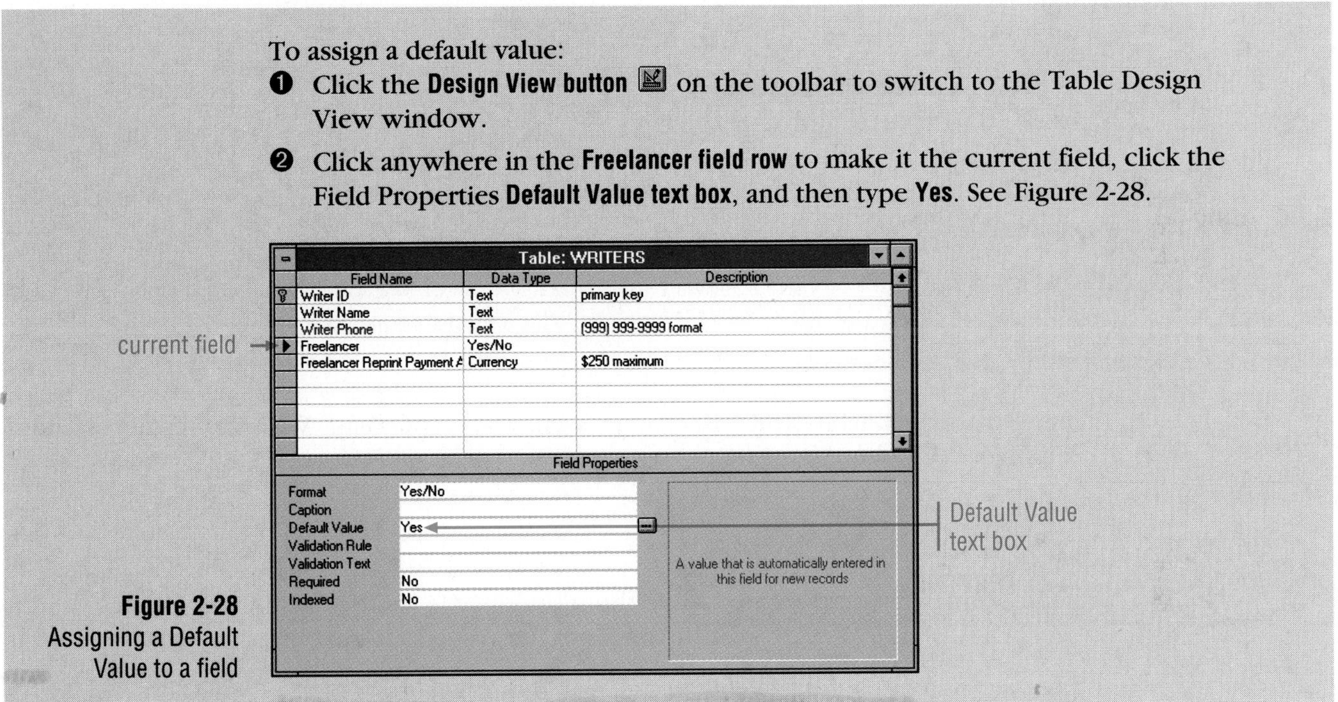

Figure 2-28
Assigning a Default Value to a field

Elena's next table structure change is to eliminate the decimal places in the Freelancer Reprint Payment Amount field.

Changing Decimal Places

Vision Publishers pays freelancers at most $250 for reprint rights to their articles. Some freelancers will be paid less, but in all cases, a whole dollar amount will be paid. Elena changes the Freelancer Reprint Payment Amount field to show only whole dollar amounts. To do this, she modifies the Decimal Places property for the field.

To change the number of decimal places displayed:

1. Click anywhere in the **Freelancer Reprint Payment Amount field row** to make it the current field and to display its Field Properties options.
2. Click the **Decimal Places text box**, and then click the **down arrow button** that appears in the box. Access displays the Decimal Places list box. See Figure 2-29.

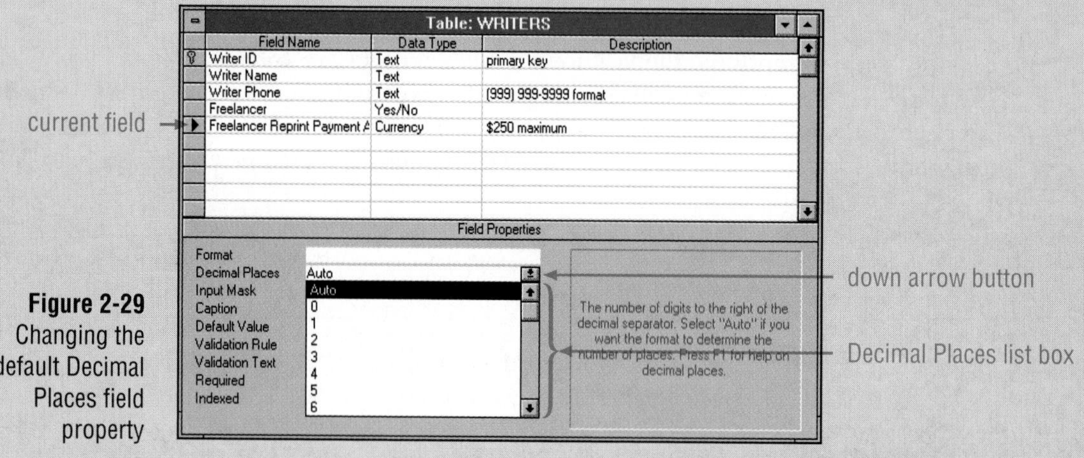

Figure 2-29 Changing the default Decimal Places field property

3. Click the **0** in the Decimal Places list box. The Decimal Places list box disappears, and 0 is now the value for the Decimal Places field property.

For the final table structure change, Elena uses Input Mask Wizard to create an input mask for the Writer Phone field.

Using Input Mask Wizard

One standard way to format a telephone number is with parentheses, a space, and a hyphen—as in (917) 729-5364. If you want these special formatting characters to appear whenever Writer Phone field values are entered, you need to create an input mask. An **input mask** is a predefined format you use to enter data in a field. An easy way to create an input mask is to use **Input Mask Wizard**, which is an Access tool that guides you in creating a predefined format for a field. To start Input Mask Wizard, click the text box for the Input Mask property and then click either the Build button that appears to the right of the text box or the Build button on the toolbar. You use the **Build button** to start a builder or wizard, which are Access tools to help you perform a task.

Let's use Input Mask Wizard to create an input mask for the Writer Phone field.

To start Input Mask Wizard:

1. Click anywhere in the **Writer Phone field row** to make it the current field and to display its Field Properties options.
2. Click the **Input Mask text box**. A Build button appears to the right of the Input Mask text box. See Figure 2-30.

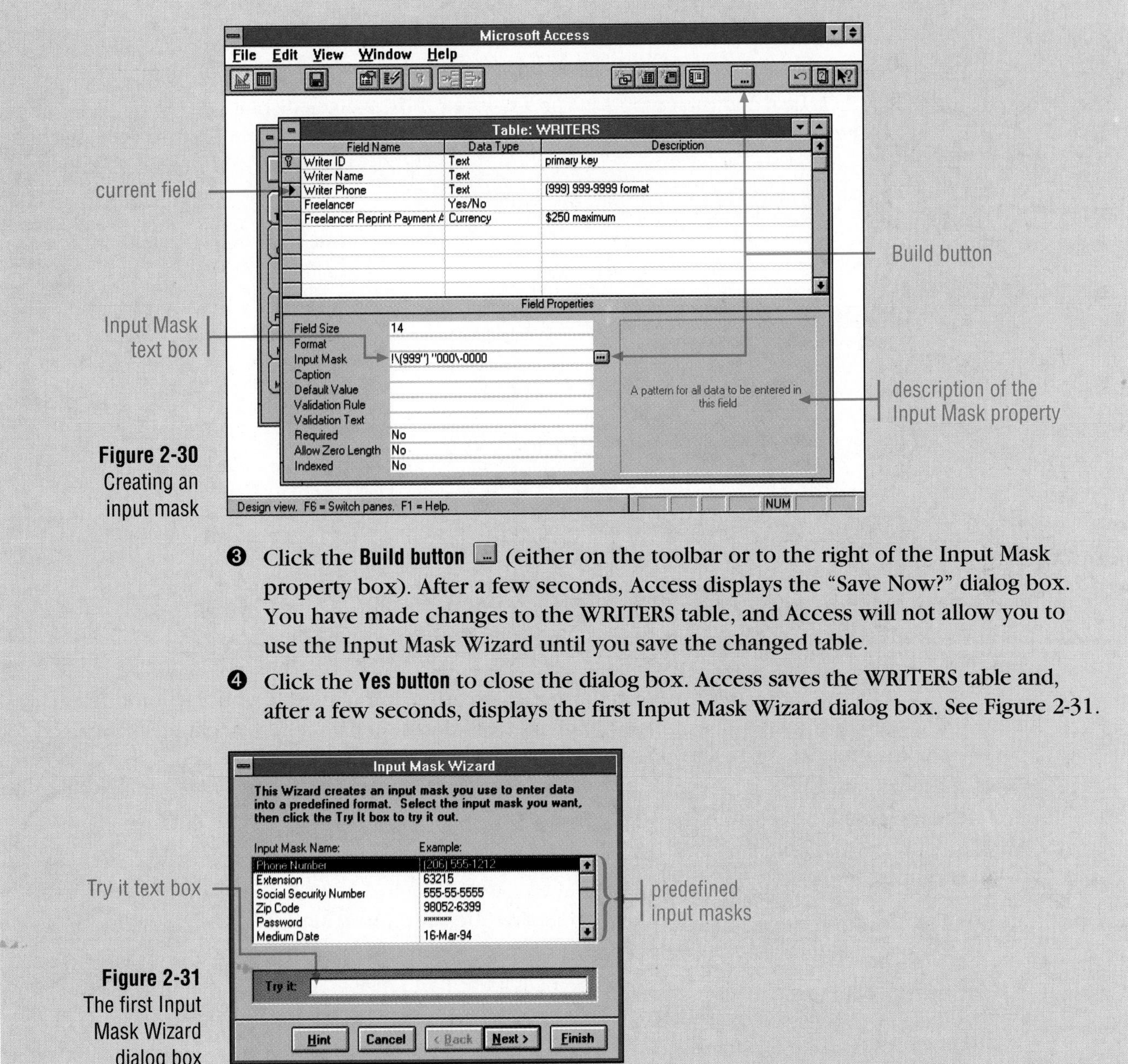

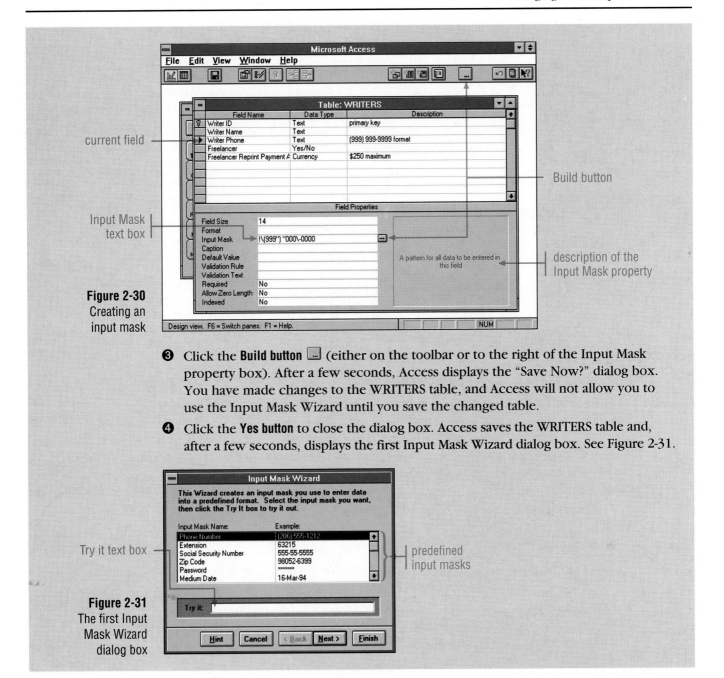

Figure 2-30 Creating an input mask

❸ Click the **Build button** (either on the toolbar or to the right of the Input Mask property box). After a few seconds, Access displays the "Save Now?" dialog box. You have made changes to the WRITERS table, and Access will not allow you to use the Input Mask Wizard until you save the changed table.

❹ Click the **Yes button** to close the dialog box. Access saves the WRITERS table and, after a few seconds, displays the first Input Mask Wizard dialog box. See Figure 2-31.

Figure 2-31 The first Input Mask Wizard dialog box

You scroll through the Input Mask Name list box, select the input mask you want, and then enter representative values to experiment with the input mask. Elena selects the Phone Number input mask for the Writer Phone field.

To select an input mask:

1. If necessary, click **Phone Number** in the Input Mask Name list box to highlight it.
2. Click **Try it** and then type **9** in the Try it text box. Access displays (9__) ___-____ in the Try it text box. The underscores are placeholder characters that are replaced as you type.
3. Type **876543210** to complete the sample entry.
4. Click the **Next > button**. Access displays the second Input Mask Wizard dialog box. See Figure 2-32.

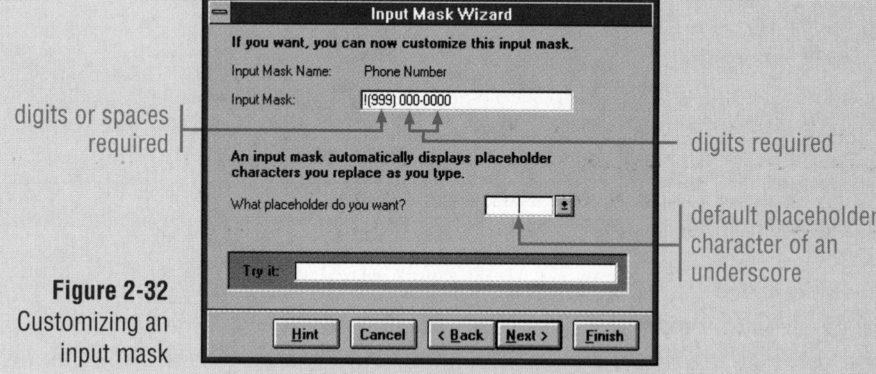

Figure 2-32
Customizing an input mask

When you have more experience creating input masks, you can modify, or customize, the input mask. You can change the default underscore placeholder character, for example, to a space or one of the following special characters: #, @, !, $, %, or *. For now, Elena accepts the predefined input mask and continues through the remaining Input Mask Wizard dialog boxes.

To finish an input mask:

1. Click the **Next > button**. Access displays the third Input Mask Wizard dialog box.
2. Click the **top radio button**, so that you store the data "With the symbols in the mask, like this: (206) 555-1212." Then click the **Next > button**. Access displays the final Input Mask Wizard dialog box.
3. Click the **Finish button**. Access ends Input Mask Wizard and displays the newly created input mask for Writer Phone.

Elena is done with her initial work on the WRITERS table structure, so she exits Access.

To exit Access after changing a table structure:

1. Double-click the Microsoft Access window **Control menu box**. A dialog box asks, "Save changes to Table 'WRITERS'?"
2. Click the **Yes button** to save your changes to the WRITERS table structure. Access saves the table structure changes, closes all windows, and then exits to Windows.

Selecting the Primary Key

As Elena thinks about her Issue25 database later that day, she can't remember if she made Writer ID the primary key of the WRITERS table. Although Access does not require that tables have a primary key, Elena knows that choosing a primary key has several advantages.

- Based on its definition, a primary key does serve to identify uniquely each record in a table. For example, Elena is using Writer ID to distinguish one writer from another when both have the same name.
- Access does not allow duplicate values in the primary key field. If Elena already has a record with N425 as the field value for Writer ID, Access prevents her from adding another record with this same field value in the Writer ID field. Preventing duplicate values ensures the uniqueness of the primary key field.
- Access enforces entity integrity on the primary key field. **Entity integrity** means that every record's primary key field must have a value. If you do not enter a value for a field, you have actually given the field what is known as a **null value**. You cannot give a null value to the primary key field; Access will not store the record for you unless you've entered a field value in the primary-key field.
- Access displays records in primary key sequence when you view a table in the Datasheet View window or the Form View window. If you enter records in no specific order, you are ensured that you will later be able to work with them in a more meaningful, primary key sequence.
- Access responds faster to your requests for specific records based on the primary key.

To verify that Writer ID is the primary key of the WRITERS table, Elena launches Access, opens the Issue25 database, and then opens the WRITERS table in the Table Design View window.

To open a table in the Table Design View window:

1. Launch Access.
2. Open the Issue25 database.
3. WRITERS should be highlighted in the Tables list box, so click the **Design button**. Access opens the Table Design View window for the WRITERS table. See Figure 2-33.

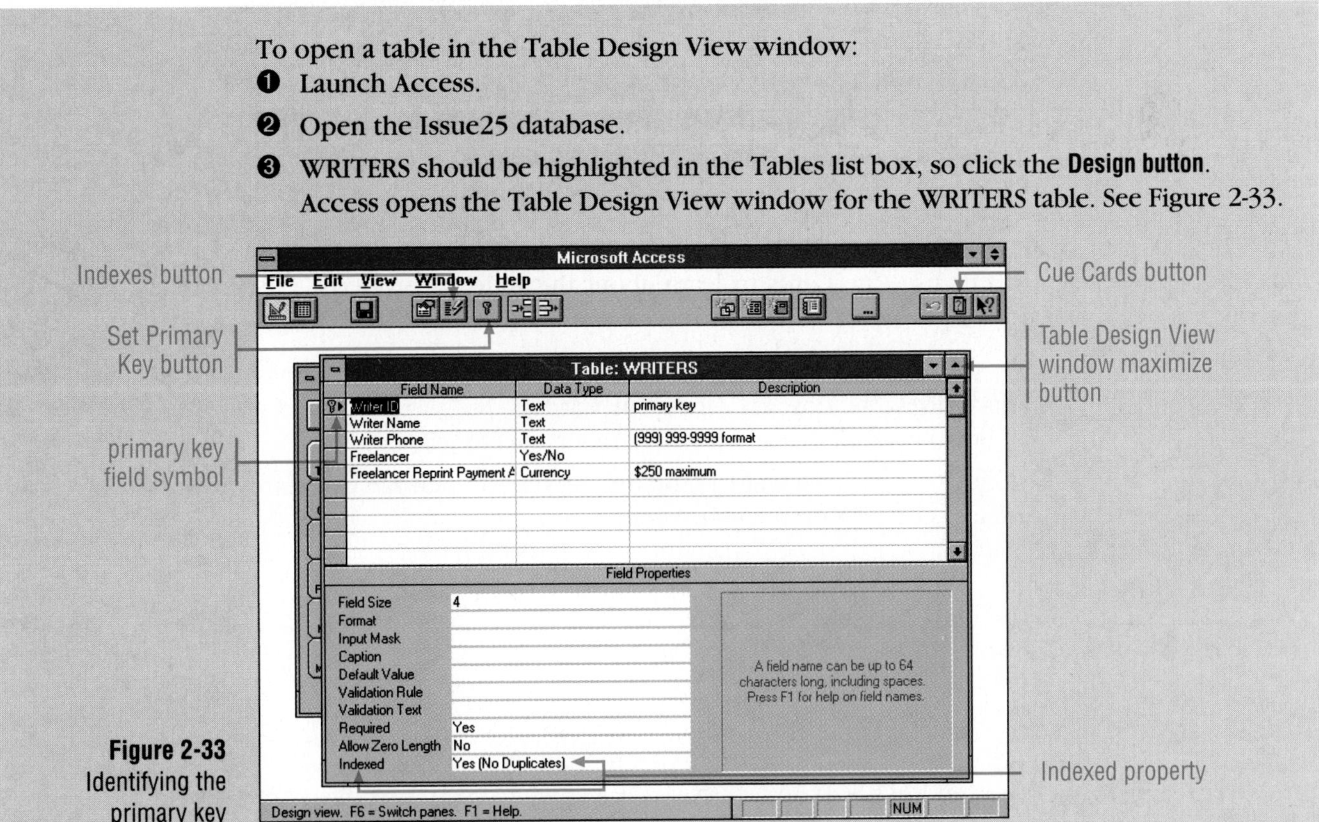

Figure 2-33 Identifying the primary key

Writer ID is highlighted and has the current row symbol in its row selector because Writer ID is the current field. Elena sees a key symbol to the left of the current row symbol. Access uses the key symbol as a **primary key field symbol** to identify the table's primary key. To change the primary key to another field, click the other field's row selector and then click the Set Primary Key button on the toolbar; Access will move the primary-key field symbol to that other field. If the primary key consists of two or more fields, hold down [Ctrl], click the row selector for each field, and then click the Set Primary Key button. Access will move the primary-key field symbol to all selected fields.

Elena sees the toolbar Indexes button to the left of the Set Primary Key button and the Indexed property as one of the Field Properties options. Elena uses Cue Cards to learn more about indexes.

Using Cue Cards and Creating Indexes

The Access Help system contains a Cue Cards feature. **Cue Cards** are interactive Access tutorials that remain visible to help you while you do the most common database tasks. They provide examples, guidance, and shortcuts to Access Help information.

REFERENCE WINDOW

Opening and Using Cue Cards

- Click the Cue Cards button on the toolbar. The Cue Cards window appears.
- Click the Cue Cards option you want to use.
- As each successive display appears, read the coaching information, and then click the option button of your choice. Continue until you have the information you need.
- When you finish using the Cue Cards, double-click the Cue Cards window Control menu box to close the Cue Cards window.

Let's use Cue Cards to learn about the Indexes property. First, maximize the Table Design View window so that the Cue Cards hide less of the window.

To maximize a window and open Cue Cards:

1. Click the Table Design View window **maximize button**.
2. Click the **Cue Cards button** on the toolbar to open the Cue Cards window. See Figure 2-34 on the following page.

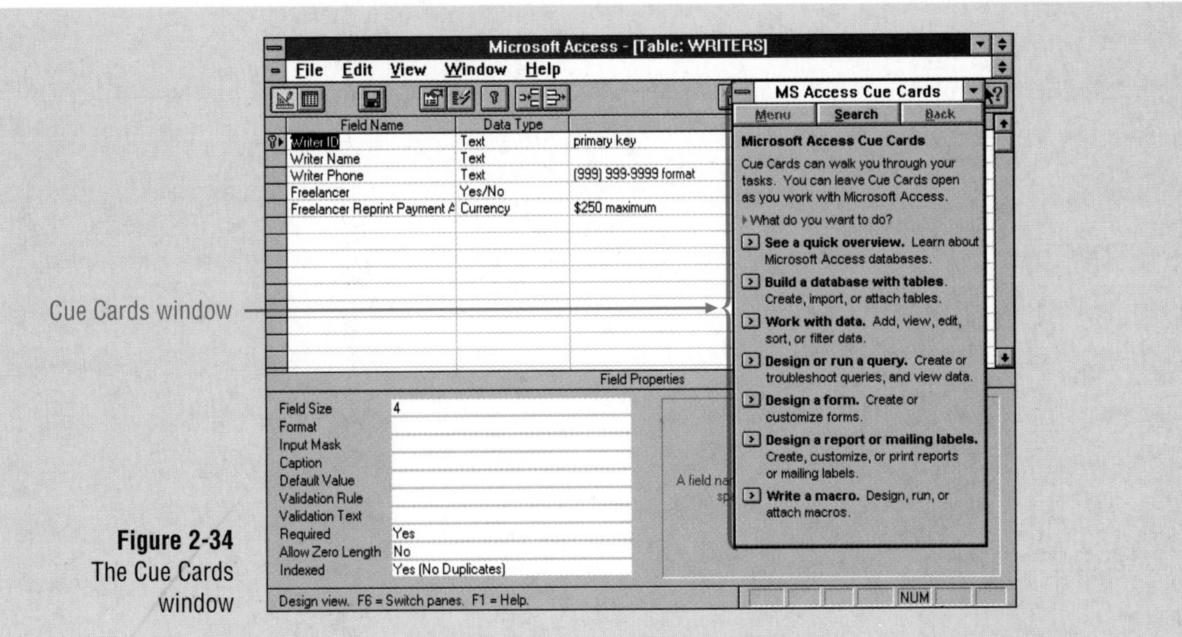

Figure 2-34 The Cue Cards window

The Cue Cards window appears as an active window. Although normally only one window at a time is active, the Table Design View window is now also an active window. You can perform tasks in either window. If you switch from the Table Design View window to another Access window and from the current Cue Cards window to another Cue Cards window, both new windows will become active windows.

Review the displayed Cue Cards options. If you have time, you might want to investigate the Cue Cards topic called "See a quick overview." If you do, be sure to complete the topic so that you return to the Cue Cards window shown in Figure 2-34 before continuing with the tutorial.

Elena wants guidance working with table indexes, so she first chooses the Cue Cards topic "Build a database with tables" and then makes the appropriate choices on subsequent Cue Cards windows.

To open a Cue Cards topic:

❶ Click the **Build a database with tables button** to open the Cue Cards Build a Database with Tables window. See Figure 2-35.

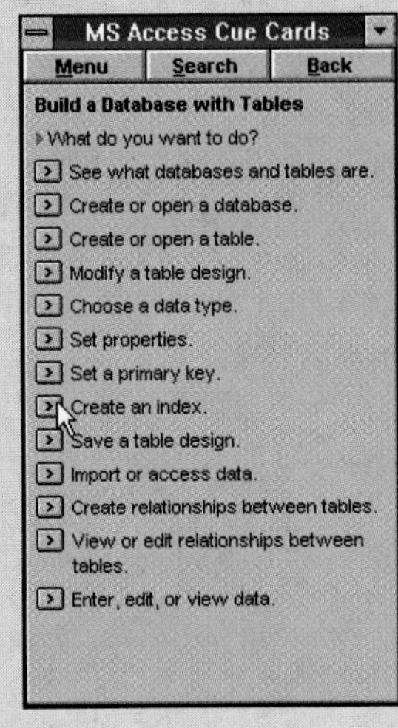

Figure 2-35 The Cue Cards Build a Database with Tables window

2. Click the **Create an index button** to see the next Cue Cards window.
3. Carefully read the contents of each Cue Cards window, then click the **Next button** in each Cue Cards window until you reach the last Cue Cards window in the sequence. See Figure 2-36.

Cue Cards Control menu box

MS Access Cue Cards
Menu | Search | Back
Build a Database with Tables
What do you want to do now?
Create and design a new table.
Modify a table design.
Save a table design.
Create relationships between tables.
Enter, edit, or view data.
I've finished working with databases and tables.

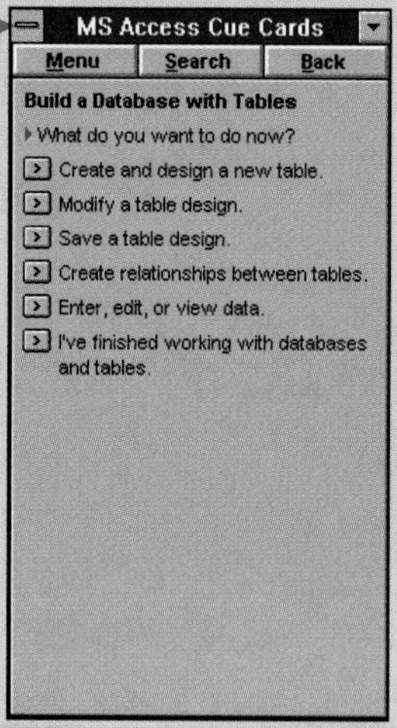

Figure 2-36
The last Cue Cards Build a Database with Tables window

4. Double-click the Cue Cards **Control menu box** to close the Cue Cards feature.

Elena has learned that Access automatically creates and maintains an index for the primary key field. An **index**, in this case, is a list of primary-key values and their corresponding record numbers. For a primary-key field, the index cannot have duplicate values. The index adds to the database disk storage requirements and takes time to maintain as you add and delete records. These are two disadvantages of having a primary key and its corresponding index for a table, but they are insignificant compared with the many advantages of an index. You cannot index fields that have the data types memo, yes/no, and OLE object, but this restriction should never be a problem.

You can also create indexes for other selected table fields. Do so to improve processing speed if you think you will often sort or find records based on data in those fields. However, each index requires extra disk space and additional processing time when records are added, changed, or deleted in the table.

Elena views the indexes that currently exist for the WRITERS table by using the Indexes button on the toolbar.

To display the indexes for a table:

1. Click the **Indexes button** on the toolbar. Access displays the Indexes window. See Figure 2-37.

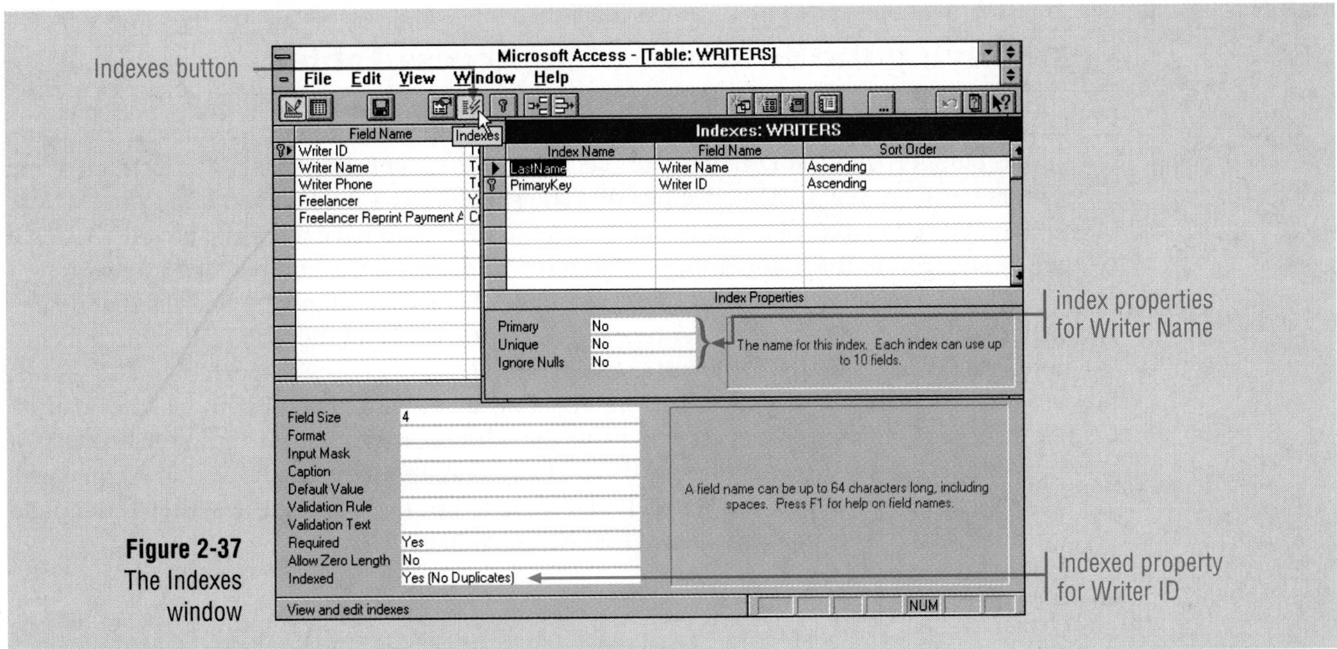

Figure 2-37 The Indexes window

Two indexes appear in the Indexes window: one for the primary-key field of Writer ID and a second one for the Writer Name field. How was the second index created? Recall that you used Table Wizard to create the WRITERS table. When you select Table Wizard fields, you also select all their predefined properties. One of the fields you selected was LastName, which had "Yes (Duplicates OK)" as the value for its Indexed property. When you changed LastName to Writer Name, the field retained this Indexed property value.

Elena doesn't think she needs an index for Writer Name, so she deletes the index. If she ever needs an index for this field in the future, she can add it back by using the Indexes window or the Indexed property for Writer Name.

To delete an index:

1. Position the mouse pointer in the first row of the Indexes window with the Index Name LastName and click the right mouse button. Access displays the Shortcut menu.
2. Using the left mouse button, click **Delete Row**. Access deletes the index for Writer Name from the Indexes window.
3. Click the **Indexes button** on the toolbar to close the Indexes window.

If you want to take a break and resume the tutorial at a later time, you can exit Access by double-clicking the Microsoft Access window Control menu box and then clicking Yes in the dialog box that asks if you want to save your table changes. When you resume the tutorial, place your Student Disk in the appropriate drive, launch Access, open the Issue25 database on your Student Disk, and open the Table Design View window for the WRITERS table.

■ ■ ■

Modifying the Structure of an Access Table

Elena learns that Vision Publishers has a writer contact list containing each writer's name, phone number, and last contact date. Because Vision Publishers has not contacted some writers for many years, Elena decides that she should add a field named Last Contact Date to her WRITERS table. She will contact those writers who have a reasonably current date before she tries to track down those who wrote articles for the company many years ago.

When Elena shows Brian the WRITERS table she is developing, he realizes that he can use this information to contact writers and asks for a list of all the WRITERS table information arranged alphabetically by writer last name.

After the meeting, Elena realizes she has a problem with giving Brian this information. She had been planning to enter names in the Writer Name field in the regular order of first, middle, and last name. She needs to change her strategy for the Writer Name field. Her solution is to change the WRITERS table structure by deleting the Writer Name field and adding two fields that she names Last Name and First Name.

Deleting a Field

After meeting with Brian, Elena makes her table structure modifications to the WRITERS table. She first deletes the Writer Name field.

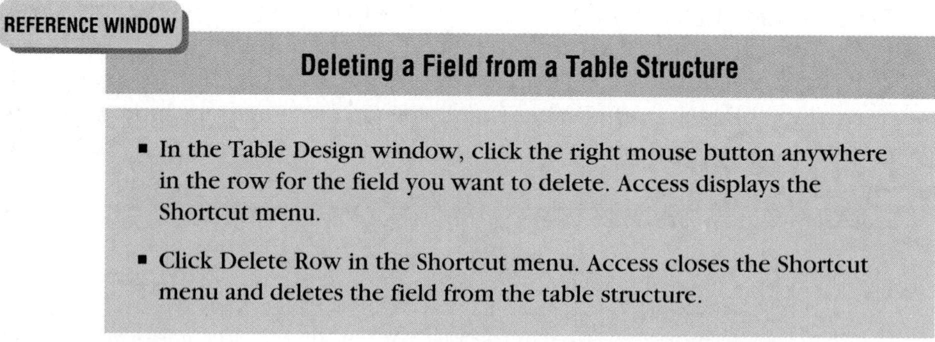

REFERENCE WINDOW

Deleting a Field from a Table Structure

- In the Table Design window, click the right mouse button anywhere in the row for the field you want to delete. Access displays the Shortcut menu.
- Click Delete Row in the Shortcut menu. Access closes the Shortcut menu and deletes the field from the table structure.

Let's delete the Writer Name field from the WRITERS table.

To delete a field from a table structure:

1. Move the mouse pointer to the row for the Writer Name field and click the right mouse button. Access displays the Shortcut menu. See Figure 2-38.

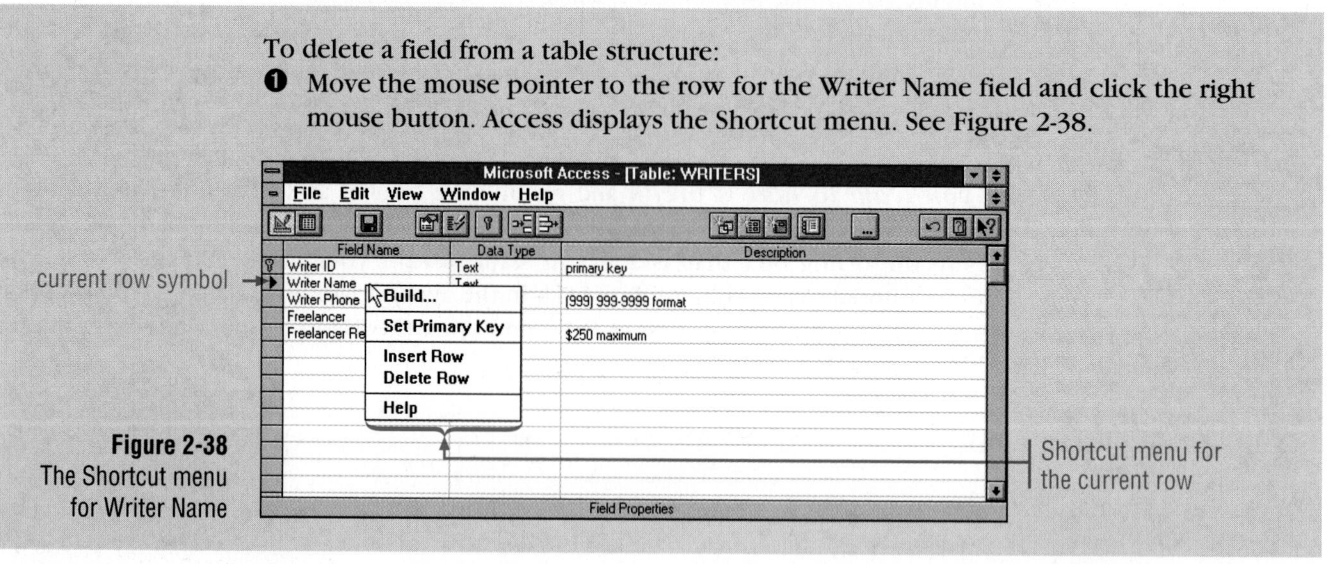

Figure 2-38 The Shortcut menu for Writer Name

❷ Click **Delete Row** in the Shortcut menu. Access deletes the Writer Name field from the WRITERS table structure. The row where Writer Name had been positioned is also deleted.

TROUBLE? If you deleted the wrong field, immediately click the Undo button. The field you deleted reappears. You should repeat the deletion steps from the beginning for the correct field.

Adding a Field

The order of fields in the Table Design window determines the order of the fields in the Datasheet View window. Therefore, Elena decides that the two new fields, Last Name and First Name, should be positioned right after the Writer ID row. Then she will position the third new field, Last Contact Date, between the Writer Phone and Freelancer rows.

REFERENCE WINDOW

Adding a Field to a Table Structure

- In the Table Design window, open the Shortcut menu by clicking the right mouse button anywhere in the row that will end up below the field you are adding. If the new field is to be added to the end of the table, click the Field Name column for the first blank row and skip the next step.
- Click Insert Row in the Shortcut menu. Access inserts a blank row.
- Define the new field by entering a field name, data type, and optional description in the new row.

Let's add the three fields to the WRITERS table.

To add a field to a table structure:

❶ Click the right mouse button anywhere in the **Writer Phone row**. Above this row you want to insert two blank rows in preparation for adding two fields. Access displays the Shortcut menu.

❷ Click **Insert Row** in the Shortcut menu. Access adds a blank row between the Writer ID and Writer Phone rows and closes the Shortcut menu.

❸ Because you need to add two rows, click the right mouse button anywhere in the **Writer Phone row** and then click **Insert Row** in the Shortcut menu to insert the second blank row. See Figure 2-39.

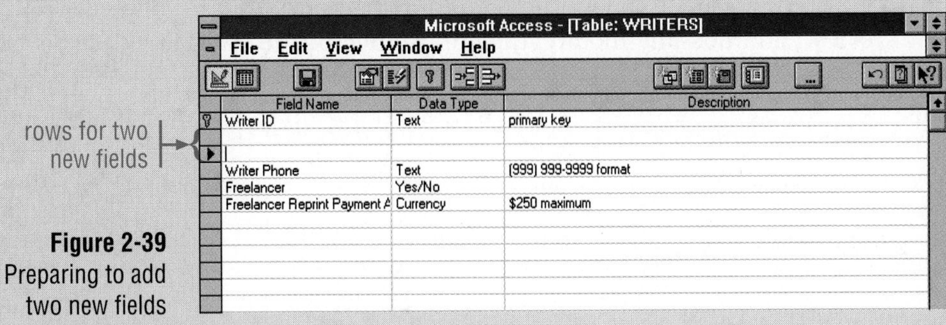

Figure 2-39
Preparing to add two new fields

4. Click the Field Name box for the first of the two new rows. To define the Last Name field, type **Last Name**, press **[Tab]**, and highlight the 50 in the Field Size box. Then type **15** and click the Field Name box for the second of the two new rows.
5. To define the First Name field, type **First Name**, press **[Tab]**, highlight the 50 in the Field Size box, and then type **15**. See Figure 2-40.

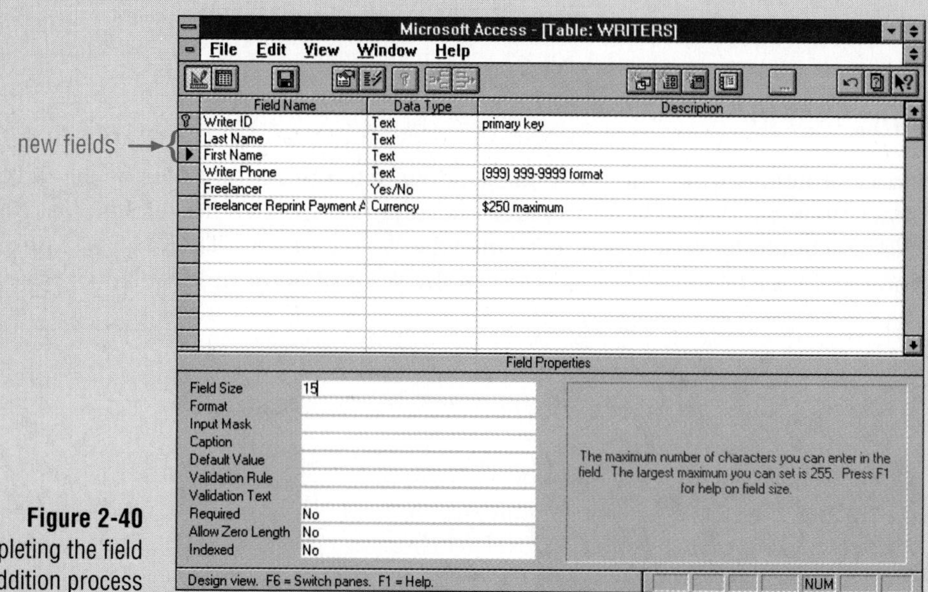

Figure 2-40
Completing the field addition process

6. After adding Last Name and First Name, Elena next adds Last Contact Date to the WRITERS table. Click the right mouse button anywhere in the Freelancer row and then click **Insert Row** in the Shortcut menu to insert a row between the Writer Phone and Freelancer rows. Access places the insertion point in the Field Name box of the new row.
7. Type **Last Contact Date**, press **[Tab]**, type **d**, and then press **[Tab]**. See Figure 2-41. Last Contact Date is a date/time field.

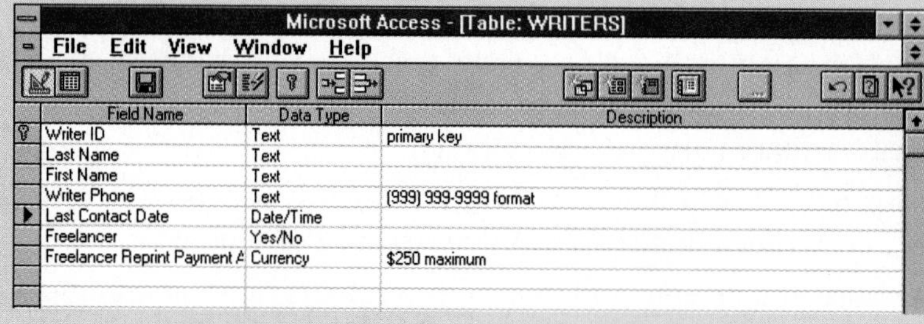

Figure 2-41
Last Contact Date field added

Elena has now defined the WRITERS table structure. Once again, however, she wants to review, and possibly modify, the appearance of the WRITERS datasheet before exiting Access.

To review and modify a datasheet:

❶ Click the **Datasheet View button** ▦. The "Save now?" dialog box appears.

❷ Click the **OK button**. Access displays the Datasheet View window. The Last Name and First Name fields appear to the right of the Writer ID field, and Last Contact Date is to the right of Writer Phone. The one change you should make is to widen the column for Last Contact Date so the whole field name will be visible.

❸ Resize the column for Last Contact Date so that the entire field name appears in the heading box. See Figure 2-42.

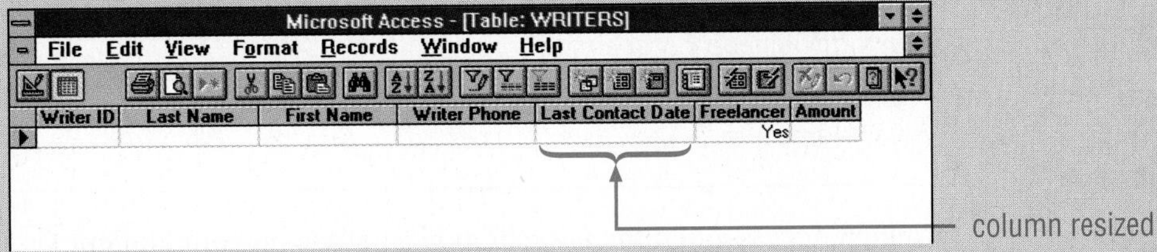

Figure 2-42 The final Datasheet View window for the WRITERS table

❹ Double-click the Microsoft Access window **Control menu box**, and then click the **Yes button** in the "Save layout changes to table 'WRITERS'" dialog box to save your table changes and exit Access.

■ ■ ■

Elena has defined the WRITERS table structure and refined the table's datasheet. In the next tutorial, Elena will add data to the WRITERS table.

Questions

1. What two types of keys represent a common field when you form a relationship between tables?
2. What is data redundancy?
3. Which Access names must conform to standard DOS conventions for filenames?
4. Which Access field property can be up to 255 characters long?
5. What are the eight Access data types?
6. Which data type could automatically serve as a table's primary key because Access itself fills in each field value to guarantee uniqueness?
7. Which data types have the Field Size property?
8. What is a caption?
9. Describe three different ways to select a field's data type.
10. When is it appropriate to use the Undo button?
11. Describe three different ways to resize a datasheet column.
12. What is an input mask?
13. Explain entity integrity.
14. What are Cue Cards?
15. When is it possible to have two active windows?

E 16. Using Cue Cards for information on the technique, explain how to move a field in the Table Design View window.

E 17. Using Cue Cards for information, document for your instructor the tips for choosing a data type.

E 18. Use the "Work with data" Cue Cards to describe a method for rearranging columns in a datasheet while the Datasheet View window is active.

Tutorial Assignments

Elena creates the BUSINESS ARTICLES table structure, as shown in Figure 2-43.

BUSINESS ARTICLES table	Data Type	Input/Display Field Size	Description
Article Title	text	44	
Issue of Business Perspective	text	8	yyyy mmm format
Length of Article	number	4	Integer field size
Writer Name	text	25	

Figure 2-43

Launch Access, open the Issue25.mdb database on your Student Disk, and do the following:

1. Create a new table without using Table Wizard. Use Figure 2-43 to define these properties, as appropriate, for each of the four fields in the table: field name, data type, description, and field size. For the number data type field, use the Description column in Figure 2-43 to set its Field Size property.
2. Save the table with the name BUSINESS ARTICLES. Do not select a primary key.
3. Switch to the Datasheet View window and resize columns so that the entire field name can be read in the column heading for every field.
4. Print the datasheet for the table.
5. In the Table Design View window, change the field name Length of Article to Article Length. For the field Issue of Business Perspective, add the Caption property Issue. Resize the columns, if necessary, for these two fields in the Datasheet View window.
6. Print the datasheet for the table.
7. Delete the field Writer Name from the table structure.
8. Add a four-character text field named Writer ID to the end of the table. For a description, enter "foreign key."
9. Change the data type of the field Issue of Business Perspective to date/time.
10. Add a three-character text field named Type between the Article Length and Writer ID fields. For this new field, enter the description "article type" and the Default Value BUS, which represents a business article.
11. Resize columns, as necessary, in the Datasheet View window.
12. Print the datasheet for the table.
13. **E** Switch the order of the Article Length and Type columns in the datasheet, using the "Work with data" Cue Cards for guidance. Do not switch their order in the table structure. Print the datasheet for the table.
14. **E** Using Cue Cards for guidance, move the field named Type in the Table Design View window so that it follows the field named Article Title. Print the datasheet for the table and then close the Issue25 database.

Case Problems

1. Walkton Daily Press Carriers

Grant Sherman, circulation manager of the Walkton Daily Press, wants a better way to keep track of the carriers who deliver the newspaper. Grant meets with Robin Witkop, one of the newspaper's computer experts, to discuss what can be done to improve his current tracking system.

Robin reviews Grant's informational needs and recommends that she design a database to keep track of carriers and their outstanding balances. Grant agrees and, after obtaining her manager's approval, Robin designs a database that has two tables: CARRIERS and BILLINGS. Robin first creates the CARRIERS table structure, as shown in Figure 2-44.

CARRIERS table

Field Name	Data Type	Input/Display Field Size	Description
Carrier ID	counter	3	primary key; unique carrier identification number
Carrier First Name	text	14	
Carrier Last Name	text	15	
Carrier Phone	number	8	Long Integer field size
Carrier Birthdate	date/time	8	

Figure 2-44

Launch Access and do the following:

1. Create a new database on your Student Disk with the name Press.
2. Create a new table without using Table Wizard. Use Figure 2-44 to define these properties, as appropriate, for each of the five fields in the table: field name, data type, and description. Define the Field Size property for only the text and number fields, using the Description column in Figure 2-44 to set the Field Size property for the number field.
3. Select Carrier ID as the table's primary key.
4. Save the table with the name CARRIERS.
5. Switch to the Datasheet View window and resize columns so that the entire field name can be read in the column heading for every field.
6. Print the datasheet for the table.
7. In the Table Design View window, change the field name Carrier Birthdate to Birthdate. Add the Caption property First Name for the field Carrier First Name. Add the Caption property Last Name for the field Carrier Last Name. Resize the columns, if necessary, for the fields in the Datasheet View window.
8. Print the datasheet for the table.
9. **E** Using Cue Cards for guidance, move the field named Carrier Last Name in the Table Design View window so that it follows the field named Carrier ID. Print the datasheet for the table and then close the Datasheet View window.

Robin next creates the BILLINGS table structure, as shown in Figure 2-45.

BILLINGS table

Field Name	Data Type	Input/Display Field Size	Description
Route ID	text	4	primary key
Carrier ID	number	3	Long Integer field size; carrier assigned to the route; foreign key
Balance Amount	currency	5	outstanding balance due from the carrier

Figure 2-45

Launch Access, if necessary, and do the following:

10. Open the database named Press.mdb on your Student Disk.
11. Create a new table without using Table Wizard. Use Figure 2-45 to define these properties, as appropriate, for each of the three fields in the table: field name, data type, and description. Define the Field Size property for only the text and number fields, using the Description column in Figure 2-45 to set the Field Size property for the number field.
12. Select Route ID as the primary key and then save the table with the name BILLINGS.
13. Switch to the Datasheet View window and resize columns so that the entire field name can be read in the column heading for every field.
14. Print the datasheet for the table.
15. In the Table Design View window, add the Caption property Balance for the field Balance Amount, and change the Decimal Places property for the field Balance Amount from Auto to 2. Resize the columns, if necessary, for the fields in the Datasheet View window.
16. Print the datasheet for the table and then close the Press database.

2. Lopez Used Cars

Maria and Hector Lopez own a chain of used-car lots throughout Texas. They have used a computer in their business for several years to handle their payroll and normal accounting functions. Their phenomenal expansion, both in the number of used-car locations and the number of used cars handled, forces them to develop a database to track their used-car inventory. They design a database that has two tables: USED CARS and LOCATIONS. They first create the USED CARS table structure, as shown in Figure 2-46.

USED CARS table

Field Name	Data Type	Input/Display Field Size	Description
Vehicle ID	text	5	primary key
Manufacturer	text	13	
Model	text	15	
Class Type	text	2	code for the type of sedan, van, truck, and so on; foreign key
Transmission Type	text	3	code for type of transmission; foreign key
Year	number	4	Integer field size
Cost	currency		
Selling Price	currency		
Location Code	text	2	lot location within the state; foreign key

Figure 2-46

Launch Access and do the following:

1. Create a new database on your Student Disk with the name Usedcars.
2. Create a new table without using Table Wizard. Use Figure 2-46 to define these properties, as appropriate, for each of the nine fields in the table: field name, data type, and description. Define the Field Size property for only the text and number fields, using the Description column in Figure 2-46 to set the Field Size property for the number field.

3. Select Vehicle ID as the table's primary key.
4. Save the table with the name USED CARS.
5. Switch to the Datasheet View window and resize columns so that the entire field name can be read in the column heading for every field. Maximize the Datasheet View window, and continue to resize columns until you can see all column headings on the screen at one time.
6. Print the datasheet for the table.
7. In the Table Design View window, change the field name Class Type to Class. Add the Caption property Transmission for the field Transmission Type and the Caption property Location for the field Location Code. Resize the columns, if necessary, for the fields in the Datasheet View window.
8. Print the datasheet for the table.

E 9. Using Cue Cards for guidance, move the field named Location Code in the Table Design View window so that it follows the field named Year. Print the datasheet for the table and then close the Datasheet View window.

Hector and Maria next create the LOCATIONS table structure, as shown in Figure 2-47.

LOCATIONS table

Field Name	Data Type	Input/Display Field Size	Description
Location Code	text	2	primary key
Location Name	text	15	
Manager Name	text	25	

Figure 2-47

Launch Access, if necessary, and do the following:

10. Open the database named Usedcars.mdb on your Student Disk.
11. Create a new table without using Table Wizard. Use Figure 2-47 to define these properties, as appropriate, for each of the three fields in the table: field name, data type, description, and field size.
12. Select Location Code as the primary key and then save the table with the name LOCATIONS.
13. Switch to the Datasheet View window and resize columns so that the entire field name can be read in the column heading for every field.
14. Print the datasheet for the table and then close the Usedcars database.

3. Tophill University Student Employment

Olivia Tyler is an administrative assistant in the Student Employment office of the Financial Aid department at Tophill University. She is responsible for tracking the companies that have announced part-time jobs for students. She keeps track of each available job and the person to contact at each company. Olivia had previously relied on student workers to do the paperwork, but reductions in the university budget have forced her department to reduce the number of part-time student workers. As a result, Olivia's backlog of work is increasing. After discussing the problem with her supervisor, Olivia meets with Lee Chang, a database analyst on the staff of the university computer center.

Lee questions Olivia in detail about her requirements and suggests that he could develop a database to reduce her workload. He designs a database that has two tables: JOBS and EMPLOYERS. He first creates the JOBS table structure, as shown in Figure 2-48 on the following page.

JOBS table

Field Name	Data Type	Input/Display Field Size	Description
Job Order	counter	5	primary key; unique number assigned to the job position
Employer ID	text	4	foreign key
Job Title	text	30	
Wage	currency	6	rate per hour
Hours	number	2	Integer field size; hours per week

Figure 2-48

Launch Access and do the following:

1. Create a new database on your Student Disk with the name Parttime.
2. Create a new table without using Table Wizard. Use Figure 2-48 to define these properties, as appropriate, for each of the five fields in the table: field name, data type, and description. Define the Field Size property for only the text and number fields, using the Description column in Figure 2-48 to set the Field Size property for the number field.
3. Select Job Order as the table's primary key.
4. Save the table with the name JOBS.
5. Switch to the Datasheet View window and resize columns so that the entire field name can be read in the column heading for every field.
6. Print the datasheet for the table.
7. In the Table Design View window, change the field name Hours to Hours/Week. Add the Caption property Job# for the field Job Order and the Caption property Wages for the field Wage. Resize the columns, if necessary, for the fields in the Datasheet View window.
8. Print the datasheet for the table.
9. **E** Using Cue Cards for guidance, move the field named Hours/Week in the Table Design View window so that it follows the field named Job Order. Print the datasheet for the table and then close the Datasheet View window.

Lee next creates the EMPLOYERS table structure, as shown in Figure 2-49.

EMPLOYERS table

Field Name	Data Type	Input/Display Field Size	Description
Employer ID	text	4	primary key
Employer Name	text	40	
Contact Name	text	25	
Contact Phone	text	8	999-9999 format

Figure 2-49

Launch Access, if necessary, and do the following:

10. Open the database named Parttime.mdb on your Student Disk.
11. Create a new table without using Table Wizard. Use Figure 2-49 to define these properties, as appropriate, for each of the four fields in the table: field name, data type, description, and field size.
12. Select Employer ID as the primary key and then save the table with the name EMPLOYERS.
13. Switch to the Datasheet View window and resize columns so that the entire field name can be read in the column heading for every field.
14. Print the datasheet for the table and then close the Parttime database.

4. Rexville Business Licenses

Chester Pearce works as a clerk in the town hall in Rexville, North Dakota. He has just been assigned responsibility for maintaining the licenses issued to businesses in the town. He learns that the town issues over 30 different types of licenses to over 1,500 businesses, and that most licenses must be renewed annually by March 1.

The clerk formerly responsible for the processing gives Chester the license information in two full boxes of file folders. Chester has been using a computer to help him with his other work, so he designs a database to keep track of the town's business licenses. When he completes his database design, he has two tables to create. One table, named LICENSES, contains data about the different types of business licenses the town issues. The second table, named BUSINESSES, contains data about all the businesses in town. Chester first creates the LICENSES table structure, as shown in Figure 2-50.

LICENSES table

Field Name	Data Type	Input/Display Field Size	Description
License Type	text	2	primary key
License Name	text	60	license description
Basic Cost	currency	4	cost of the license

Figure 2-50

Launch Access and do the following:

1. Create a new database on your Student Disk with the name Buslic.
2. Create a new table without using Table Wizard. Use Figure 2-50 to define these properties, as appropriate, for each of the three fields in the table: field name, data type, and description. Define the Field Size property for the text fields only.
3. Select License Type as the table's primary key.
4. Save the table with the name LICENSES.
5. Switch to the Datasheet View window and resize columns so that the entire field name can be read in the column heading for every field.
6. Print the datasheet for the table.
7. In the Table Design View window, change the field name License Name to License Description. Add the Caption property License Code for the field License Type. Change the Decimal Places property of the field Basic Cost from Auto to 0. Resize the columns, if necessary, for the fields in the Datasheet View window.
8. Print the datasheet for the table and then close the Datasheet View window.

Chester next creates the BUSINESSES table structure, as shown in Figure 2-51.

BUSINESSES table

Field Name	Data Type	Input/Display Field Size	Description
Business ID	counter	4	primary key; unique number assigned to a business
Business Name	text	35	official business name
Street Number	number	4	business street number; Integer field size
Street Name	text	25	
Proprietor	text	25	business owner name
Phone Number	text	8	999-9999 format

Figure 2-51

Launch Access, if necessary, and do the following:

9. Open the database named Buslic.mdb on your Student Disk.
10. Create a new table without using Table Wizard. Use Figure 2-51 to define these properties, as appropriate, for each of the six fields in the table: field name, data type, description, and field size. Define the Field Size property for only the text and number fields, using the Description column in Figure 2-51 to set the Field Size property for the number field.
11. Select Business ID as the primary key and then save the table with the name BUSINESSES.
12. Switch to the Datasheet View window and resize columns so that the entire field name can be read in the column heading for every field.
13. Print the datasheet for the table.
14. In the Table Design View window, add the Caption property Street# for the field Street Number. Resize the columns, if necessary, for the fields in the Datasheet View window.
15. Print the datasheet for the table.

E 16. Using Cue Cards for guidance, move the field named Phone Number in the Table Design View window so that it follows the field named Street Name. Print the datasheet for the table and then close the Buslic database.

TUTORIAL 3

OBJECTIVES

In this tutorial you will:

- Add and change data in a table
- Move the insertion and selection points
- Change table structure and datasheet properties
- Delete records from a table
- Import data
- Delete and rename a table
- Find field values in a table
- Replace data in a table
- Sort records in a datasheet
- Print table documentation
- Back up and compact a database

Maintaining Database Tables

Maintaining the WRITERS Table at Vision Publishers

CASE

Vision Publishers Special projects editor Elena Sanchez meets with the production staff of Vision Publishers to set the schedule for the special 25th-anniversary issue of *Business Perspective*. After the meeting, she plans the work she needs to do with the WRITERS table. Because Elena has already created the WRITERS table structure, she is ready to enter the writers' data.

Based on her prior experience working with databases, Elena decides to enter only three records into the WRITERS table. Then she will review the table structure and the datasheet. If she finds a difference between a field's values and its definition, she will change the table structure to correct the problem. For example, if Elena defined the field size for a text field as 25 characters and finds some field values as large as 30 characters, she can change the field size to 30. Elena might also need to change the table's datasheet. For example, if a field's column is too narrow to show the entire field value, she can resize the datasheet column to make it wider.

Elena plans to confirm her list of writers and articles for the special magazine issue with president Brian Murphy and managing editor Judith Rossi before entering the remaining records into the WRITERS table. Finally, Elena will examine the WRITERS table records and correct any errors she finds. Elena takes her written plan, as shown in Figure 3-1, to her computer and starts her work with the WRITERS table.

WRITERS table task list:
- Enter complete information for three writers
- Change the table structure, if necessary
- Change the table datasheet, if necessary
- Confirm the WRITERS table data
- Enter complete information for remaining writers
- Correct errors

Figure 3-1
Elena's task list for the WRITERS table

Updating a Database

Elena built the table structure for the WRITERS table by defining the table's fields and their properties. Before the Issue25 database can provide useful and accurate information, however, Elena must update the database. **Updating a database**, or **maintaining a database**, is the process of adding, changing, and deleting records in database tables to keep them current and accurate.

Recall that the first step in creating a database is carefully planning the contents of the table structures. Similarly, the first step in updating a database is planning the field and record modifications that are needed. For example, preparing a task list of modifications was Elena's first step in updating the WRITERS table. In this tutorial, you will learn how to update the tables in a database.

Adding Records

When you initially create a database, adding records to the tables is the first step in updating a database. You also add records whenever you encounter new occurrences of the entities represented by the tables. At Vision Publishers, for example, an editorial assistant adds one record to the MAGAZINE ARTICLES table for each article in a new issue of one of its five magazines.

Using the Datasheet to Enter Data

In Tutorial 1 you used the Datasheet View window to view a table's records. You can also use a table's datasheet to update a table by adding, changing, and deleting its records. As her first step in updating the Issue25 database, for example, Elena adds to the WRITERS table the three records shown in Figure 3-2. She uses the WRITERS table datasheet to enter these records.

Figure 3-2 The first three WRITERS table records

WRITERS table data

	Writer ID	Last Name	First Name	Writer Phone	Last Contact Date	Freelancer	Amount
Record 1:	N425	Nilsson	Tonya	(909) 702-4082	7/9/77	No	$0
Record 2:	S260	Seeger	Wilhelm	(706) 423-0932	12/24/93	Yes	$350
Record 3:	S365	Sterns	Steven B.	(710) 669-6518	12/13/84	No	$0

Let's add the same three records to the WRITERS table. If you have not done so, place your Student Disk in the appropriate drive, launch Access, open the Issue25 database on your Student Disk, maximize the Database window, click the WRITERS table, and then click the Open command button. The Datasheet View window appears, and the insertion point is at the beginning of the Writer ID field for the first record.

To add records in a table's datasheet:

1. Type **N425**, which is the first record's Writer ID field value, and press **[Tab]**. Each time you press **[Tab]**, the insertion point moves to the right to the next field in the record.
2. Continue to enter the field values for all three records shown in Figure 3-2. For the Writer Phone field values, type the digits only. Access automatically supplies the parentheses, spaces, and hyphens from the field's input mask. If the value for the Freelancer field is the default value Yes, simply press **[Tab]** to accept the displayed value and move to the next field. Press **[Tab]** to move from the Amount field in the first two rows to the start of the next record, but do not press **[Tab]** after typing the Amount field for the third record. See Figure 3-3.

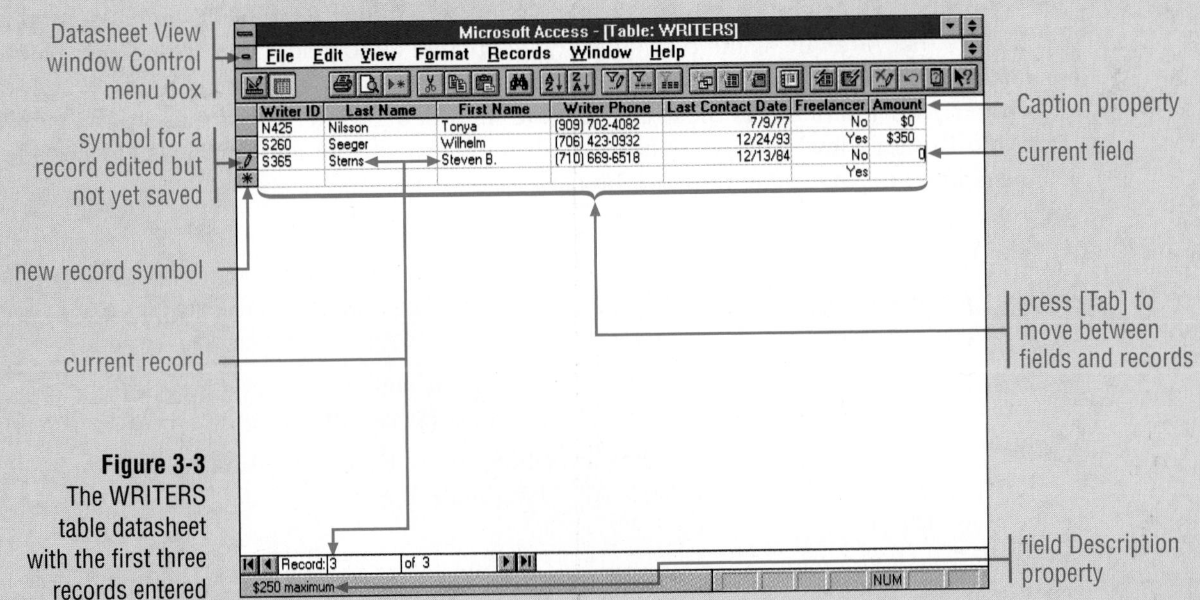

Figure 3-3 The WRITERS table datasheet with the first three records entered

TROUBLE? If you enter any field value incorrectly, double-click the field value to highlight it and retype the field value correctly to replace it.

Two new symbols appear in the record selectors for rows three and four. The pencil symbol in the third row indicates that you have made changes to the current record and have not yet saved the changes. The asterisk symbol in the fourth row shows you the next row available for entering a new record.

TROUBLE? If the pencil symbol and the asterisk symbol do not appear exactly as shown in Figure 3-3, the insertion point might be in the fourth row. If the current record symbol (a black, right-facing triangle) appears in the record selector for row four, then just observe these two new symbols the next time you make a change. If the pencil symbol and asterisk symbol appear in the fourth and fifth rows, then you should double-click the Datasheet View window Control menu box and click the OK button two times to close the datasheet and return to the Database window. Then click the WRITERS table and click the Open command button to redisplay the datasheet.

Elena has completed her first task, so she continues with the next two tasks on her list.

Changing a Field's Properties

Elena's next two tasks are to change the WRITERS table structure and the table datasheet if changes are needed. Because all field values and field names fit in their datasheet boxes, Elena does not need to change the datasheet. If a datasheet column were too narrow to display the entire field name and all the field values, however, Elena could resize the column for that field to widen it.

The value $350 in the Amount field for the second record catches Elena's eye, because the field's description in the status bar reads "$250 maximum." Elena realizes that $250 is a maximum for each reprinted article and not a maximum value for the field. She changes the field description in the Table Design View window to "$250 maximum per article." Elena also reassesses the field name Freelancer Reprint Payment Amount and decides that Amount would be a shorter, acceptable table field name. This table structure change makes the field name and the field caption the same, so Elena deletes the Caption property for the field. All these changes are field definition changes that are made in the Table Design View window. You can add fields to a table and modify field properties even after you have added data to the table.

To change properties for a field:

1. Click the **Design View button** to close the datasheet and open the Table Design View window.
2. To change the description for the field, click the right end of the Description box for Freelancer Reprint Payment Amount, press **[Spacebar]**, and then type **per article**.
3. To change the field's name, click anywhere in the Field Name box for Freelancer Reprint Payment Amount, press **[F2]** to highlight the entire field name, and then type **Amount**.
4. To delete the field's Caption property, double-click **Amount** in the Caption text box, click the right mouse button in the same text box to open the Shortcut menu, and then click **Cut** in the Shortcut menu.

Now that she has changed field properties, Elena meets with Judith to discuss the list of articles for the special issue.

Changing Records

During the meeting with Judith, Elena notices some differences between the preliminary and final lists of writers for the special issue. First, Tonya Nilsson, who is one of the three writers she just added to the WRITERS table, is a freelancer and will be paid $450 for her two reprint articles. Elena entered Nilsson as a staff writer, so she needs to change both the Freelancer and Amount fields for Nilsson. Elena also added Steven B. Sterns to the WRITERS table, and he does not appear in the final list. Thus, Elena needs to delete his record from the table.

Changing Field Values

Elena's next task is to change the two field values for Tonya Nilsson in the WRITERS table datasheet. The field values for Freelancer and for Amount are to be Yes and $450, respectively. The Table Design View window for the WRITERS table should still be displayed on the screen, so Elena first opens the WRITERS table datasheet.

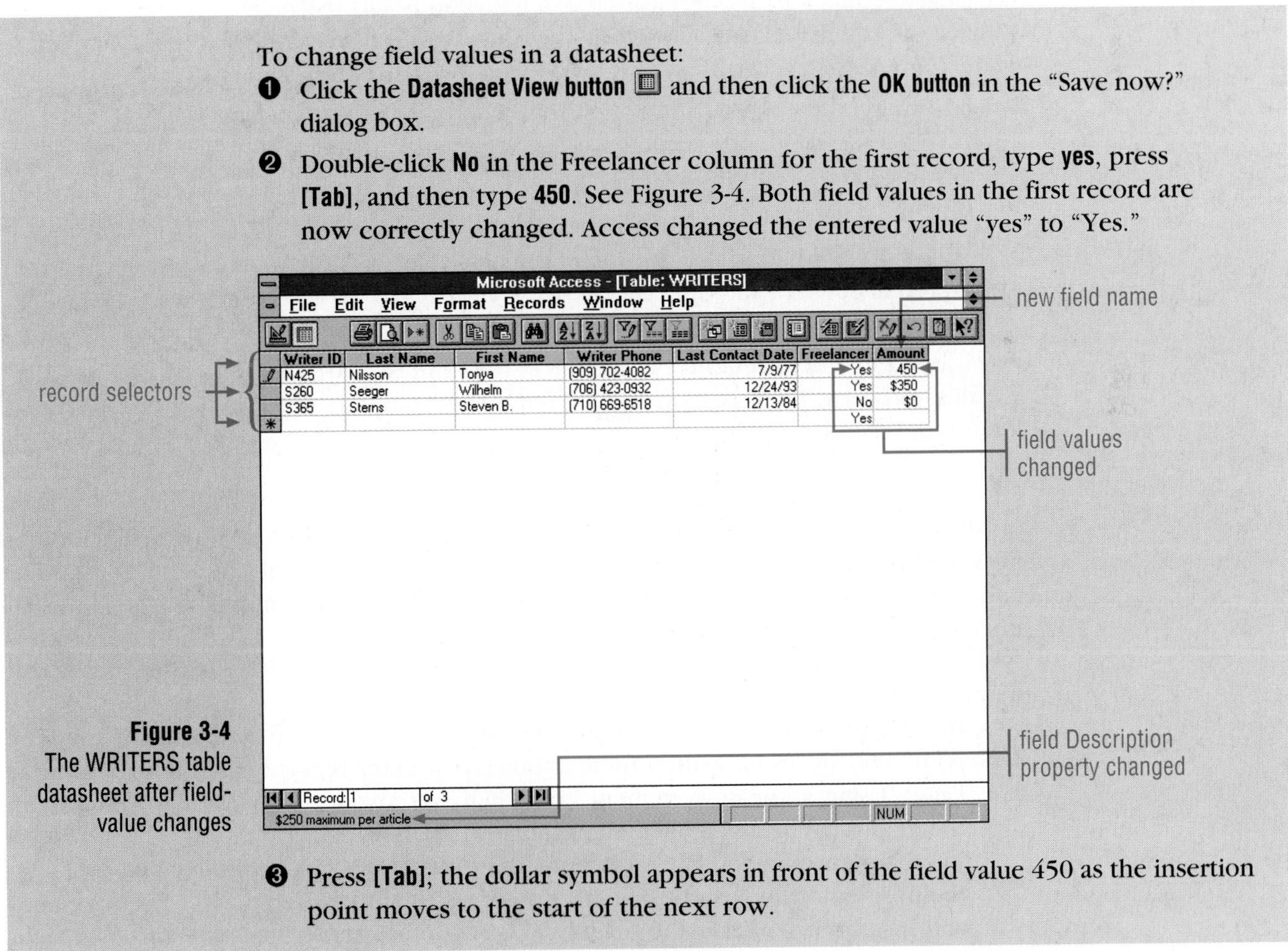

To change field values in a datasheet:

❶ Click the **Datasheet View button** and then click the **OK button** in the "Save now?" dialog box.

❷ Double-click **No** in the Freelancer column for the first record, type **yes**, press **[Tab]**, and then type **450**. See Figure 3-4. Both field values in the first record are now correctly changed. Access changed the entered value "yes" to "Yes."

Figure 3-4
The WRITERS table datasheet after field-value changes

❸ Press **[Tab]**; the dollar symbol appears in front of the field value 450 as the insertion point moves to the start of the next row.

Access saves the changes you make to the current record whenever you move to a different record. Thus, your data is kept current as you make changes, and you do not need to worry about losing your changes if a hardware or software problem occurs.

Using the Mouse and Keyboard

You use the mouse to move through the fields and records in a datasheet or to make changes to field values. The mouse techniques you use include those for movement, selection, and placement. To move to a specific record in the Datasheet View window, for example, you click combinations of the scroll bars and arrows on the right and at the bottom, the navigation buttons on the lower-left, and the record selectors on the left. Also, clicking a record selector when the pointer appears as ➡ selects an entire row, and clicking a field name box when the pointer appears as ⬇ selects an entire column. You can also select entire field values by clicking the ⇗ that appears when you position the mouse pointer near the left side of a field-value box. Finally, when the pointer changes to I, clicking a field-value box makes that row the current record and places the insertion point at that field-value position.

Let's practice these mouse techniques on the WRITERS datasheet that you are now viewing.

To change the location of the selection and insertion points using a mouse:

1. Click the **Last Record navigation button** ▶| to highlight the Writer ID field value in the third, or last, record. The third row becomes the current record.
2. Click the record selector for the first row when the pointer changes to ➡. Access highlights the entire first record.
3. Click the **Writer Phone field-name box** when the pointer changes to ⬇. Access highlights the entire fourth column.
4. Position the pointer on the left side of the field-value box for Wilhelm in the First Name column, and then click when it changes to ⇗. The entire field value is highlighted, and the second row becomes the current record.
5. Position the I between the 1 and the 3 in the third record's Last Contact Date field value and click. The insertion point appears there, and the third row becomes the current record.

Most Access keyboard techniques are also compatible with those used in a Windows environment, but Access has some keyboard techniques that might be new to you. For example, Access handles navigation and selection through a combination of the usual cursor-movement keystrokes and the [F2] key.

The **[F2] key** is a toggle that you use to switch between navigation mode and editing mode.

- In **navigation mode**, Access highlights, or selects, an entire field value. If you type while you are in navigation mode, your typed entry replaces the highlighted field value. Using a cursor-movement key when you are in navigation mode results in the field value being highlighted in the new location.
- In **editing mode**, you can replace or insert characters in a field-value box based on the position ofthe insertion point. You press [Ins] to switch between replacement and insertion, which is the default. When you are replacing characters, the right side of the status bar at the bottom of the screen displays the letters OVR, which is an abbreviation for "overtype," and one character is highlighted. The character you type replaces the highlighted character. When you are inserting characters, the right side of the status bar displays spaces, and the insertion point blinks between characters. The character you type is inserted between the characters.

The navigation-mode and editing-mode keyboard movement techniques are shown in Figure 3-5. They allow numerous selection and insertion-point movement possibilities. You can perform moves that involve two keys by holding down the first key and pressing the second key. You will find, however, that using the mouse is faster than using the keyboard. Use Figure 3-5 for reference or if you want to practice some of the keyboard movement techniques.

Press	To Move the Selection Point in Navigation Mode	To Move the Insertion Point in Editing Mode
[Left Arrow]	Left one field value at a time	Left one character at a time
[Right Arrow] or [Tab] or [Enter]	Right one field value at a time	Right one character at a time
[Home]	Left to the first field value in the record	Before the first character in the field value
[End]	Right to the last field value in the record	After the last character in the field value
[Up Arrow] or [Down Arrow]	Up or down one record at a time	Up or down one record at a time and switch to navigation mode
[Pg Up]	To previous screen	To previous screen and switch to navigation mode
[Pg Dn]	To next screen	To next screen and switch to navigation mode
[Ctrl] [Left Arrow] or [Ctrl] [Right Arrow]	Left or right one field value at a time	Left or right one word at a time
[Ctrl] [Up Arrow] or [Ctrl] [Down Arrow]	To first or last record	Before the first character or after the last character in the field
[Ctrl] [PgUp]	Left to first field value in the record	Before the first character in the field value
[Ctrl] [PgDn]	Right to the last field value in the record	After the last character in the field value
[Ctrl] [Home]	To the first field value in the first record	Before the first character in the field value
[Ctrl] [End]	To the last field value in the last record	After the last character in the field value

Figure 3-5
Navigation-and editing-mode keyboard movement techniques

When you are in editing mode, Access supports the usual Windows keyboard deletion techniques, as shown in Figure 3-6 on the following page. If you are in navigation mode, however, using any of the deletion keystrokes causes Access to delete the entire selection.

Press	To Delete
[Del]	The character to the right of the insertion point
[Backspace]	The character to the left of the insertion point
[Ctrl] [Del]	Text from the insertion point to the end of the word
[Ctrl] [Backspace]	Text from the insertion point to the beginning of the word

Figure 3-6
Keyboard deletion techniques in editing mode

Let's practice these deletion techniques in editing mode.

To use the keyboard deletion techniques in editing mode:

1. If you have moved the cursor, click between the 1 and the 3 in the third record's Last Contact Date field-value box to place the insertion point there and to switch to editing mode. Press **[Del]** to remove the 3 and then press **[Backspace]** to remove the 1.
2. Press **[Ctrl][Backspace]** to remove the 12/ and then press **[Ctrl][Del]** to remove the /84. The field value should now be null.
3. To restore the original field value, click the **Undo Current Field/Record button** on the toolbar. Access highlights the entire field value and switches from editing mode to navigation mode.

Changing Datasheet Properties

Elena has completed her initial changes to the WRITERS table. Before continuing with her next task, however, Elena changes the datasheet font to a larger size. Because you can create tables with dozens of fields, Access uses the default font MS Sans Serif and the default font size 8 for screen display. The small font size allows Access to display more data on the screen than it could with a larger font size. If your table has few fields, you can make the data easier to read by choosing a larger font size.

REFERENCE WINDOW

Changing a Datasheet's Font Properties

- Open the Format menu.
- Click Font... to open the Font dialog box.
- Select the font from the Font list box.
- Select the font style from the Font Style list box.
- Select the font size from the Size list box.
- Click the Underline check box if you want to select this special effect.
- A sample of the font characteristics appears in the Sample box as options are chosen. Click the OK button to accept the changes in the Font dialog box.

Let's change the font size for the WRITERS datasheet.

To change the datasheet font size:

1. Click **Format**, and then click **Font...** to display the Font dialog box. See Figure 3-7.

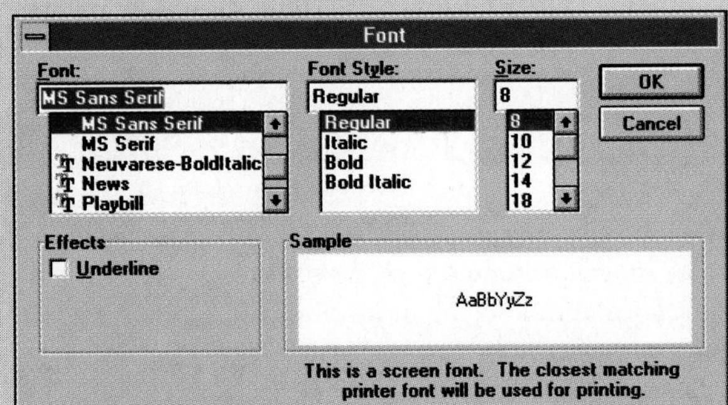

Figure 3-7 The Font dialog box

2. Click **10** in the Size list box. The Sample box changes to show the larger font size.
3. Click the **OK button** to accept the font size change. The Font dialog box disappears, and the datasheet displays the selected font size in place of the original default size.

Access automatically increases the row height to accommodate the larger font size. You can change the row height using the Format menu, but it is usually better to let Access make row height adjustments automatically.

Now that Elena has changed the datasheet font size, she notices that several of the field name boxes no longer display the field names in their entirety. She resizes the datasheet column widths for all the datasheet fields.

To resize datasheet column widths:

1. Use the Format menu, the mouse pointer, or the best-fit column width method to resize datasheet columns until each field-name box displays the entire field name. Fit the entire datasheet on the screen by narrowing some column widths, if necessary. See Figure 3-8.

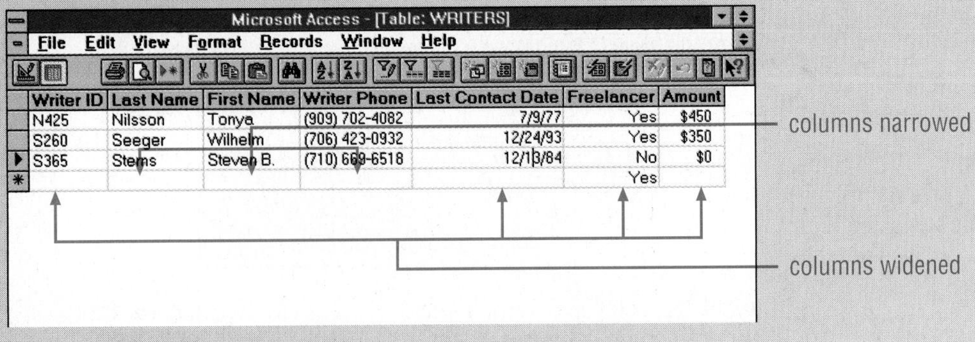

Figure 3-8 The datasheet after column width changes

Deleting Records

Elena needs to make one last update to the WRITERS table. Steven B. Sterns should not be included in the final list of writers for the special anniversary issue, so Elena deletes his record from the table.

REFERENCE WINDOW

Deleting Records from a Table

- Click the record selector of the record you want to delete. If you want to delete two or more consecutive records, click the record selector of the first record and hold the mouse button, while dragging the ➡ to the last record selector of the group, and then release.
- Click the right mouse button in the record selector to display the Shortcut menu.
- Click Cut in the Shortcut menu. The "Delete record" dialog box appears.
- Click the OK button to delete the record or records.

Let's delete the third record from the WRITERS datasheet and then close the datasheet.

To delete a datasheet record and close a datasheet:

❶ Click the record selector for the third record. Access highlights the entire third row.

❷ Click the right mouse button in the record selector for the third record. Access displays the Shortcut menu.

❸ Click **Cut** in the Shortcut menu. Access displays the "Delete record" dialog box. See Figure 3-9. The current record indicator is positioned in the third row's record selector, and all field values (except default values) in the third record have disappeared.

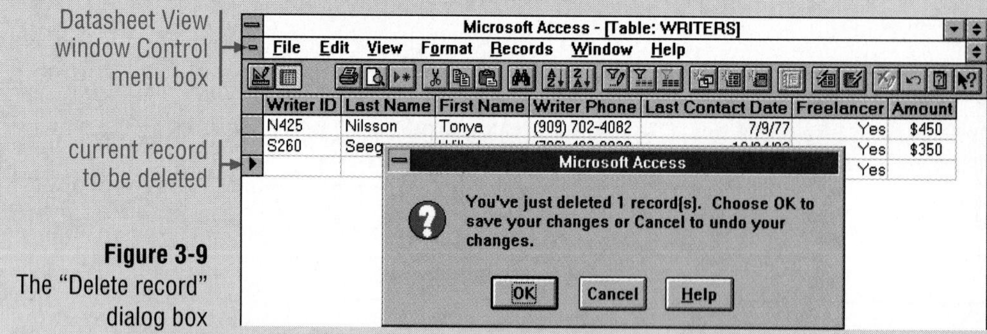

Figure 3-9
The "Delete record" dialog box

TROUBLE? If you selected the wrong record for deletion, click the Cancel button. Access ends the deletion process and redisplays the deleted record. Repeat Steps 1 and 2 for the third record.

❹ Click the **OK button**. Access deletes the third record from the WRITERS table.

❺ Double-click the Datasheet View window **Control menu box**. Access displays the message "Save layout changes to Table 'WRITERS'?"

❻ Click the **Yes button**. The dialog box disappears, and then the datasheet disappears. The Database window becomes the active window.

If you want to take a break and resume the tutorial at a later time, you can exit Access by double-clicking the Microsoft Access window Control menu box. When you resume the tutorial, place your Student Disk in the appropriate drive, launch Access, open the Issue25 database on your Student Disk, and maximize the Database window.

■ ■ ■

Importing Data

After Elena finishes deleting the table record, she asks Judith to help her add the remaining writers to the WRITERS table. While Judith and Brian were selecting the final articles for the special anniversary issue, Judith was also maintaining a database table containing data about the selected writers. If they use Access to transfer writers' data from Judith's database to Elena's database, Elena will save time and will be sure that the data is accurate.

Judith first verifies that she has all the fields Elena needs for the WRITERS table and finds that their table structures are compatible. Judith will show Elena how to import this special table from the Vision database to the Issue25 database.

Importing data involves copying data from a text file, spreadsheet, or database table into a new Access table. You can also import objects from another Access database into an open database. You can import data from Access tables; from spreadsheets, such as Excel and Lotus 1-2-3; from database management systems, such as Paradox, dBASE, and FoxPro; and from delimited text and fixed-width text files. Importing existing data, as shown in Figure 3-10, saves you time and eliminates potential data-entry errors.

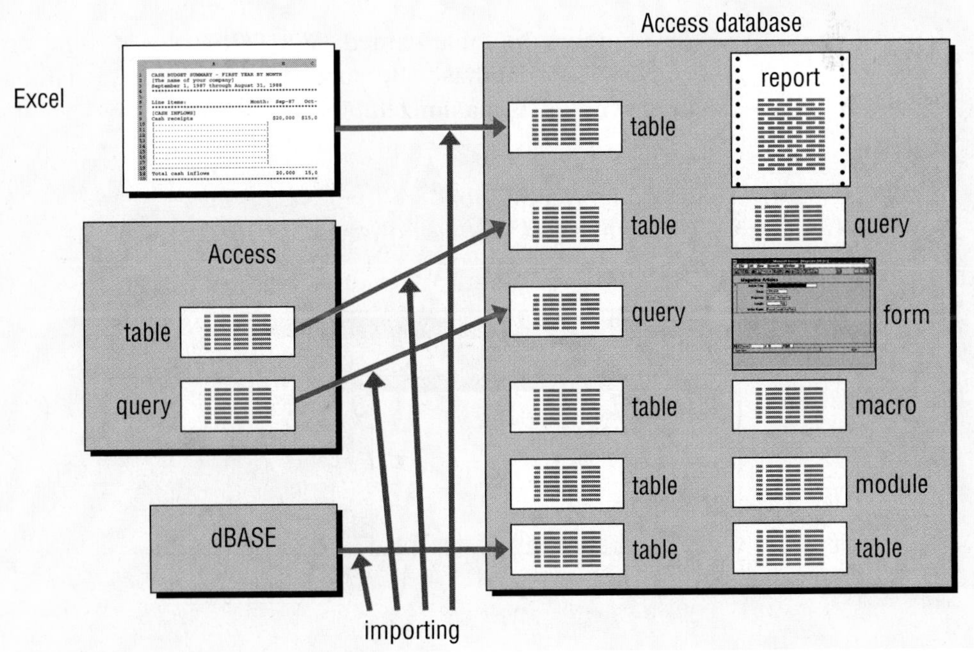

Figure 3-10
Importing data

REFERENCE WINDOW

Importing an Access Table

- Click the toolbar Import button (or click File, and then click Import...). The Import dialog box appears.
- Select Microsoft Access in the Data Source list box, and then click the OK button. The Import dialog box disappears, and the Select Microsoft Access Database dialog box appears.
- Select the drive and directory combination that has the database containing the table you want to import. From the File Name list box, select the database name.
- Click the OK button to accept your selections and close the dialog box. Access displays the Import Objects dialog box.
- Select Tables in the Object Type list box, select the desired table name from the Objects list box, click the Structure and Data option button, and then click the Import button to complete your selections. If you want to import only the table structure and not the table's records, click the Structure Only option button instead of the Structure and Data option button.
- Access imports the table and displays the "Successfully Imported" dialog box.
- Click the OK button in the dialog box, and then click Close in the Import Objects dialog box. Access adds the imported table name to the Tables list box in the Database window.

Let's import the table named "WRITERS tutorial 3 import" from the Vision database to your Issue25 database. Be sure that the Issue25 database is open and the active Database window is maximized.

To import an Access table:

1. Click the **Import button** on the toolbar. Access displays the Import dialog box. See Figure 3-11.

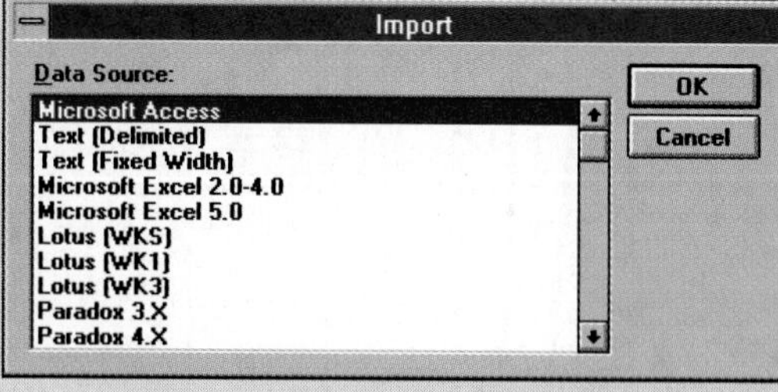

Figure 3-11 The Import dialog box

❷ If necessary, click **Microsoft Access** in the Data Source list box to highlight it; then click the **OK button**. The dialog box disappears, and Access displays the Select Microsoft Access Database dialog box.

❸ In the Drives drop-down list box, select the drive that contains your Student Disk. Next, scroll down the File Name list box and click **vision.mdb**. See Figure 3-12.

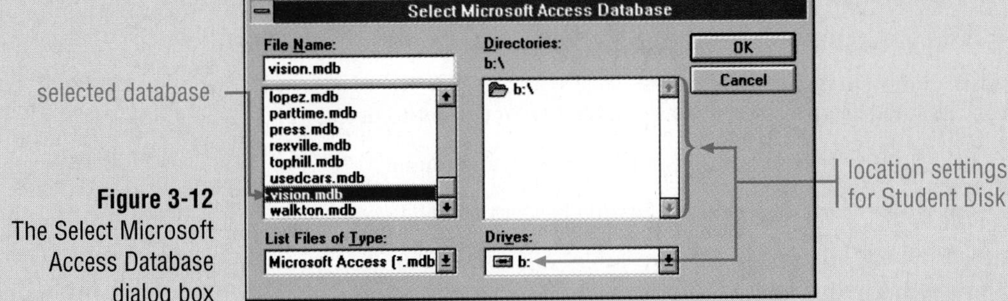

Figure 3-12
The Select Microsoft Access Database dialog box

❹ Click the **OK button**. The dialog box disappears, and Access displays the Import Objects dialog box. See Figure 3-13.

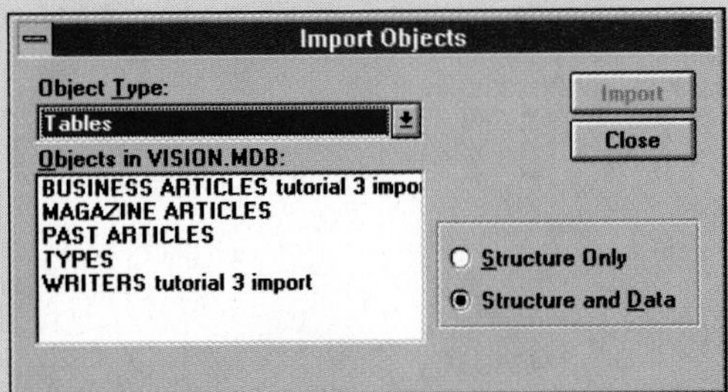

Figure 3-13
The Import Objects dialog box

❺ The Tables selection should be highlighted in the Object Type list box. If not, then click **Tables** in the drop-down list box. Next, click **WRITERS tutorial 3 import** in the Objects in VISION.MDB list box, click the **Structure and Data button**, and then click the **Import button**. Access imports the table, and displays the "Successfully Imported" dialog box on top of the Import Objects dialog box.

❻ Click the **OK button** in the "Successfully Imported" dialog box to close the dialog box, and then click the **Close button** in the Import Objects dialog box. The dialog box disappears.

❼ The Database window now displays the new table in the Tables list box. If you want, you can open this new table to view its 14 records, but do not update any of the records. When you are done viewing the records, close the table by double-clicking the Datasheet View window Control menu box.

Deleting a Table

Because the "WRITERS tutorial 3 import" table contains the records she needs, Elena no longer needs the WRITERS table. She deletes this table.

REFERENCE WINDOW

Deleting a Table

- In the Database window, click the table that you want to delete.
- Click the right mouse button to open the Shortcut menu.
- Click Delete. The "Delete Table" dialog box appears.
- Click the OK button. The "Delete Table" dialog box disappears, and Access deletes the table. When the active Database window appears, it does not list the table you just deleted.

Let's delete the WRITERS table.

To delete a table:

1. Click the **WRITERS** table and then click the **WRITERS** table again with the right mouse button. Access displays the Shortcut menu.
2. Click **Delete**. The "Delete Table" dialog box appears. See Figure 3-14.

Figure 3-14 The "Delete Table" dialog box

3. Click the **OK button**. The dialog box disappears, and the WRITERS table no longer appears in the Tables list box.

Renaming a Table

Elena renames the "WRITERS tutorial 3 import" table to WRITERS.

To rename a table:

1. Click **WRITERS tutorial 3 import** in the Tables list box and then click **WRITERS tutorial 3 import** again with the right mouse button. Access displays the Shortcut menu. See Figure 3-15.

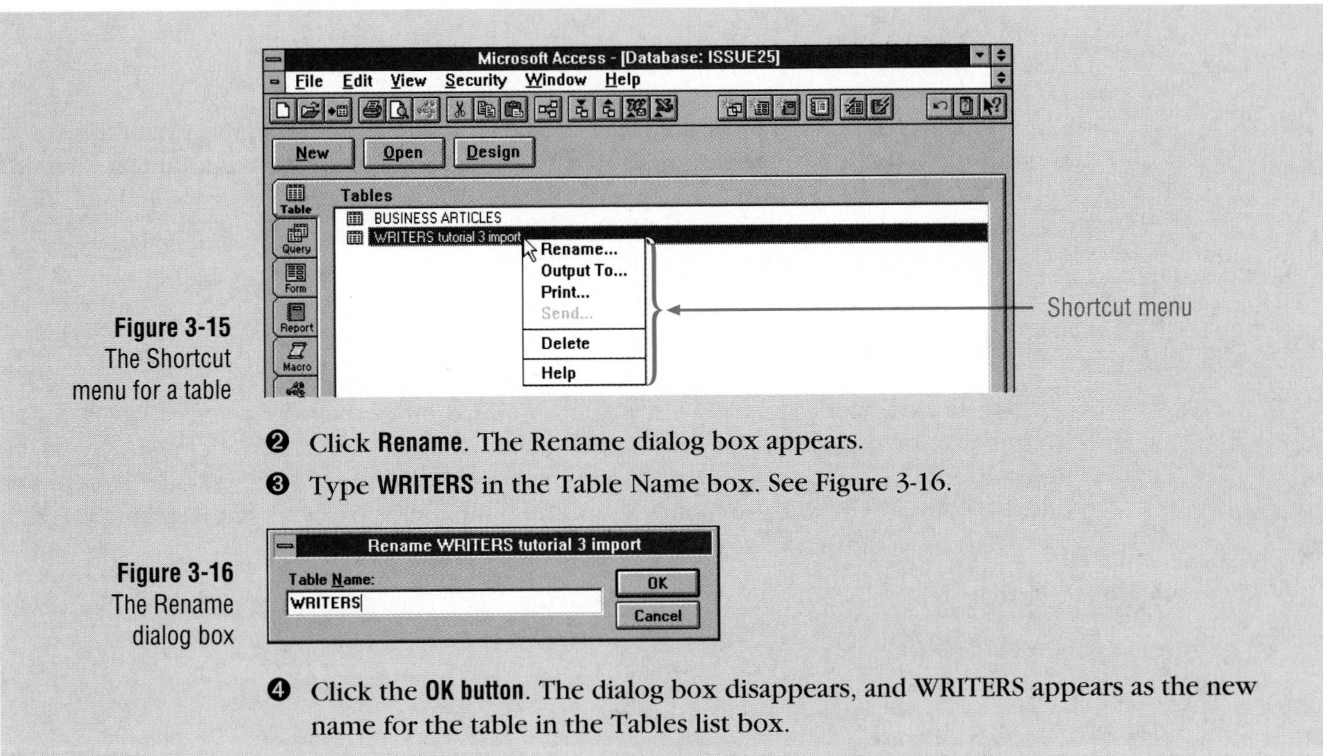

Figure 3-15 The Shortcut menu for a table

❷ Click **Rename**. The Rename dialog box appears.

❸ Type **WRITERS** in the Table Name box. See Figure 3-16.

Figure 3-16 The Rename dialog box

❹ Click the **OK button**. The dialog box disappears, and WRITERS appears as the new name for the table in the Tables list box.

Elena next reviews the imported records in the WRITERS table by opening the datasheet.

To open the WRITERS table datasheet:

❶ Double-click **WRITERS** in the Tables list box. The datasheet becomes the active window, and the records appear arranged in order by Writer ID, which is the primary key. See Figure 3-17.

Microsoft Access - [Table: WRITERS]

File Edit View Format Records Window Help

Writer ID	Last Name	First Name	Writer Phone	Last Contact Date	Freelancer	Amount
C200	Cox	Kelly	(210) 783-5415	11/14/82	Yes	$100
C500	Cohen	Julia Rice	(909) 338-1875	2/28/95	No	$0
E235	Epstein	Diane	(610) 349-9689	11/14/79	Yes	$30
H400	Hall	Valerie	(710) 918-7767	9/16/94	No	$0
J525	Johnson	Leroy W.	(210) 895-2046	1/29/91	Yes	$125
K500	Kim	Chong	(917) 729-5364	5/19/94	No	$0
K501	Kim	Chong	(710) 116-4683	8/27/88	Yes	$40
L130	Leavitt	Morris	(810) 270-2927	3/6/95	No	$0
M635	Martinez	Santos	(610) 502-8244	1/18/95	No	$0
N200	Ngo	Thuy	(706) 636-0046	3/6/95	No	$0
N425	Nilsson	Tonya	(909) 702-4082	7/9/77	Yes	$450
S260	Seeger	Wilhelm	(706) 423-0932	12/24/93	Yes	$350
W432	Waldeck	Kristine	(917) 361-8181	4/1/86	No	$0
Y556	Yamamura	Shinjiro	(905) 551-1293	9/26/72	No	$0
					Yes	$0

Figure 3-17 The WRITERS datasheet with newly imported records

To open a table's datasheet from the Database window, you click the table name and then click the Open command button. You can also open a datasheet by double-clicking the table name. Because the second method is faster, you will use it in future tutorials.

Finding and Replacing Data in a Datasheet

Even though records are physically stored on disk in the order in which you add them to a table, Access displays them in primary-key sequence in the datasheet. Finding a record in the WRITERS table based on a specific Writer ID value, therefore, is a simple process. Because of the small size of the WRITERS table, finding records based on a specific value for another field is also relatively simple.

Finding Data

Finding records based on a specific value for a field other than the primary key is not so simple when you are working with larger tables. You can spend considerable time trying to locate the records and can easily miss one or more of them in your visual search. For these situations, you can use the Find button on the toolbar to help your search.

REFERENCE WINDOW

Finding Data in a Table

- Click anywhere in the field column you want to search.
- Click the Find button on the toolbar.
- In the Find What box, type the field value you want to find.
- To find field values that entirely match a value, select Match Whole Field in the Where box.
- To find a match between a value and any part of a field's value, select Any Part of Field in the Where box.
- To find a match between a value and the start of a field's value, select Start of Field in the Where box.
- To search all fields for the search value, click the All Fields option button.
- To find matches with a certain pattern of lowercase and uppercase letters, click the Match Case option box.
- Click the Up option button if you want the search to go from the current record to earlier records in the table, rather than down, which is the default.
- Click the Find First button to have Access begin the search at the top of the table, or click the Find Next button to begin the search at the current record. If a match is found, Access scrolls the table and highlights the field value.
- Click the Find Next button to continue the search for the next match. Access displays the "End of records" dialog box if the search began at a record other than the first and it reaches the last record without finding a match. Click the Yes button to continue searching from the first record.
- Click the Close button to stop the search operation.

Let's search the WRITERS table for phone numbers that have a 909 area code.

To find data in a table:

1. Click the **Writer Phone box** for the fourth record.
2. Click the **Find button** on the toolbar. Access displays the Find dialog box. See Figure 3-18.

Figure 3-18
The Find dialog box

3. Type the search value **909** in the Find What text box. The left parenthesis, which is the first character of the Writer Phone field, is part of the input mask and not part of the field value. Therefore, searching for 909 at the start of the field is the same as searching for 909 area codes.
4. Click the **down arrow button** in the Where drop-down list box, and then click **Start of Field** to restrict the search to the first three digits of the Writer Phone field. To start the search, click the **Find Next button**. Access finds a match in the 11th record. Record 11 is displayed as the current record number at the bottom of the screen between the navigation buttons, and the field value is hidden behind the dialog box. See Figure 3-19.

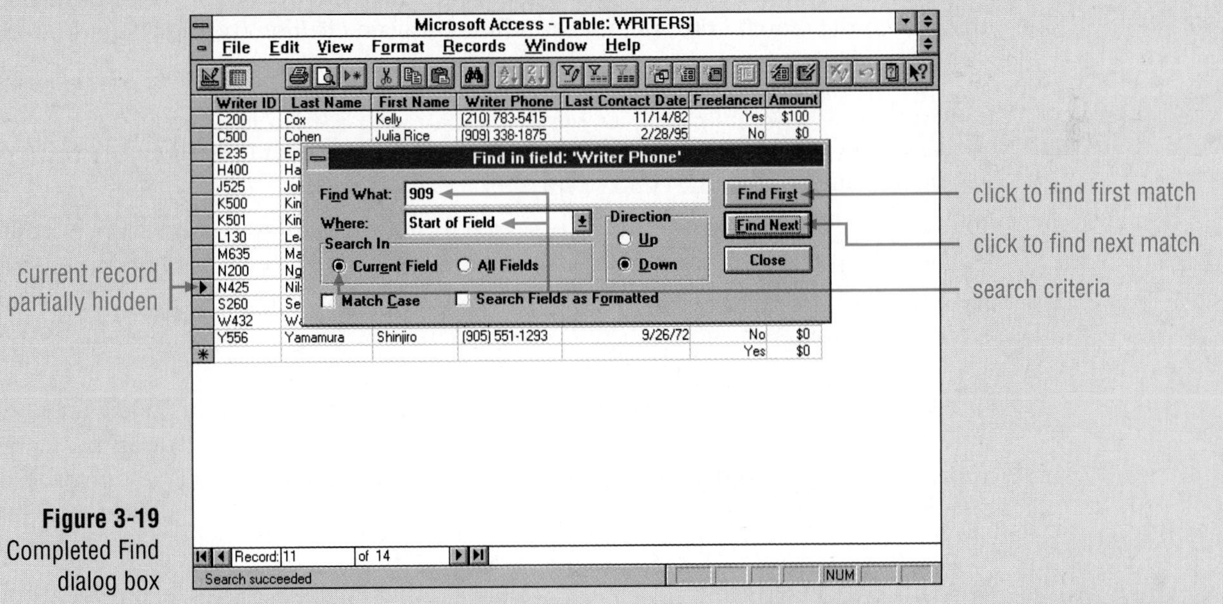

Figure 3-19
Completed Find dialog box

TROUBLE? If the second record becomes the current record instead of the 11th record, you did not click the Writer Phone box for the fourth record in Step 1. Click the Close button in the Find dialog box and repeat your work starting with Step 1.

The Find dialog box remains open and hides a portion of the datasheet. You can move the dialog box so that it covers less critical parts of the datasheet.

To move a dialog box:

1. Click the Find dialog box **title bar** and hold down the mouse button.
2. Drag the dialog box outline to the lower-right corner of the screen and release the mouse button. See Figure 3-20.

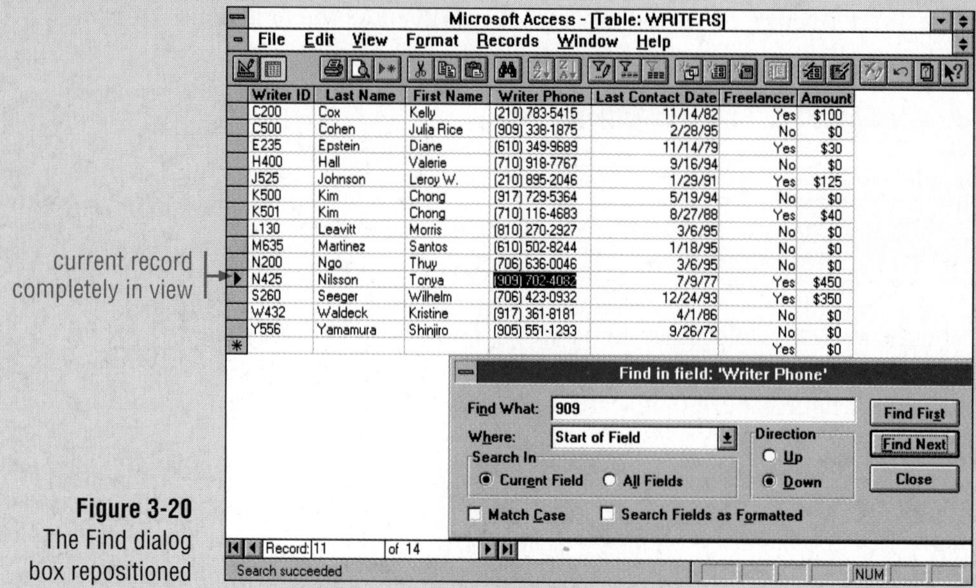

current record completely in view

Figure 3-20
The Find dialog box repositioned

You can now see the entire record found by the Find operation. To find other records that match the search criterion, you continue by again clicking the Find Next button.

To continue a Find operation:

1. Click the **Find Next button**. Access reaches the end of the table without finding a match and displays the "End of records" dialog box.
2. Click the **Yes button** to continue the search from the beginning of the table. Access finds a match in the second record and highlights the entire Writer Phone field value.
3. Click the **Close button** in the Find dialog box. The Find dialog box disappears.

You can use the standard DOS wildcard characters in the Find What text box. Use an asterisk (*) to represent any sequence of characters, and use a question mark (?) to represent any single character. You can also use the number symbol (#) to represent any single digit.

Replacing Data

While verifying the WRITERS data, Judith and Elena notice that the digits 909 appear only in the area code portion of the Writer Phone field. If they need to search for records having a 909 area code again that day, they will not need to restrict the search to the start of the field. They also notice that the two records with 909 area codes should have 905 area codes instead. Elena corrects these values by using the Replace option on the Edit menu. You use the Replace option to find a specific value in your records and replace that value with another value.

REFERENCE WINDOW

Replacing Data in a Table

- Click anywhere in the field column in which you want to replace data.
- Click Edit and then click Replace....
- In the Find What box, type the field value you want to find.
- Type the replacement value in the Replace With box.
- To search all fields for the search value, click the All Fields option button.
- To find field values that entirely match a value, click the Match Whole Field option box.
- To find matches with a certain pattern of lowercase and uppercase letters, click the Match Case option box.
- Click the Find Next button to begin the search at the current record. If a match is found, Access scrolls the table and highlights the field value.
- Click the Replace button to substitute the replacement value for the search value, or click the Find Next button to leave the highlighted value unchanged and to continue the search for the next match.
- Access displays the "End of records" dialog box if the replacement began at a record other than the first and it reaches the last record without finding its next match. Click the Yes button to continue searching from the first record.
- Click the Replace All button to perform the search and replace without stopping for confirmation of each replacement.
- Click the Close button to stop the replacement operation.

Let's search the WRITERS table and replace the 909 phone number area codes with 905.

To replace data in a table:

❶ Click the **Writer Phone box** for the fifth record.

❷ Click **Edit**, and then click **Replace....** Access displays the Replace dialog box. See Figure 3-21. Because you previously repositioned the Find dialog box, the Replace dialog box is similarly positioned. Your previous search value, 909, appears in the new Find What box.

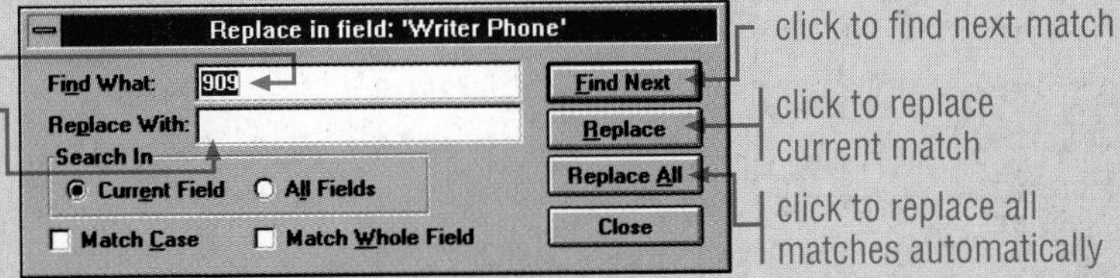

Figure 3-21 The Replace dialog box

❸ Press **[Tab]** and then type **905** in the Replace With text box.

❹ To start the replacement process, click the **Replace All button**. Access finds all 909 area codes in the table and replaces them with 905 area codes.

5. You might get one or more different "End of records" dialog boxes. For each one, click the **Yes button** or the **OK button**, as appropriate, to close the dialog box and continue the replace operation.
6. Access displays a dialog box that states: "You won't be able to undo this replace operation. Choose OK to continue or Cancel to undo the change(s) you just made." Access displays this message when more than one replacement occurs, because it cannot undo all the replacements it makes. When this message box appears, click the **OK button** to complete the replacement operation.
7. Click the **Close button** in the Replace dialog box.

   TROUBLE? If no replacement occurred, try repeating the preceding steps starting with Step 2. Be sure the Match Whole Field option is not checked in the Replace dialog box before Step 4.
8. Preview and print a copy of the datasheet, using the Print Preview button as you have done before.

   TROUBLE? If, in the printed copy, a field, such as Writer Phone, contains only parts of the field values, return to the Datasheet View window, resize the column, and reprint the datasheet. Also, if the printed copy takes up two pages, return to the Datasheet View window, resize columns to make them narrower, without hiding any of the field names or field values, and reprint the datasheet.

You can use the standard DOS wildcard characters in the Find What text box, but not in the Replace With text box.

Sorting Records in a Datasheet

Elena will be contacting the writers who are listed in the WRITERS datasheet. She feels she will be more successful reaching those writers having a recent contact date, so she wants to view the datasheet records arranged by the Last Contact Date field. Because the datasheet displays records in Writer ID, or primary-key, sequence, Elena needs to sort the records in the datasheet.

Sorting is the process of rearranging records in a specified order or sequence. Most companies sort their data before they display or print it because staff use the information in different ways according to their job responsibilities. For example, Brian might want to review writer information arranged by the Amount field because he is interested in knowing what the writers will be paid. On the other hand, Elena wants her information arranged by date of last contact because she will be calling the writers.

When you sort records in a datasheet, Access does not change the sequence of records in the underlying table. Only the records in the datasheet are rearranged according to your specifications.

To sort a table's records, you select the **sort key**, which is the field used to determine the order of the records in the datasheet. For example, Elena wants to sort the WRITERS data by last contact date, so the Last Contact Date field will be the sort key. Sort keys can be text, number, date/time, currency, counter, or yes/no fields, but not memo or OLE object fields.

You sort records in either ascending (increasing) or descending (decreasing) order. Sorting the WRITERS data in descending order by last contact date means that the record with the most recent date will be the first record in the datasheet. The record with the earliest, or oldest, date will be the last record in the datasheet. If the sort key is a number, currency, or counter field, ascending order means from lowest to highest numeric value; descending means the reverse. If the sort key is a text field, ascending order means alphabetical order beginning with A. Descending order begins with Z. For yes/no fields, ascending order means yes values appear first; descending order means no values appear first.

Sort keys can be unique or nonunique. Sort keys are **unique** if the value of the sort-key field for each record is different. The Writer ID field in the WRITERS table is an example of a unique sort key, because each writer has a different value in the ID field. Sort keys are **nonunique** if more than one record can have the same value for the sort key field. The Freelancer field in the WRITERS table is a nonunique sort key because more than one record has the same value (either yes or no).

When the sort key is nonunique, records with the same sort-key value are grouped together, but they are not in a specific order within the group. To arrange these grouped records in a specific order, you can specify a **secondary sort key**, which is a second sort-key field. The first sort-key field is called the **primary sort key**. Note that the primary sort key is not the same as the table's primary-key field. A table has at most one primary key, which must be unique, whereas any field in a table can serve as a primary sort key.

Quick Sorting a Single Field

The **Sort Ascending** and the **Sort Descending buttons** on the toolbar are called quick-sort buttons. **Quick sort buttons** allow you to sort records immediately, based on the selected field. You first select the column on which you want to base the sort and then click the appropriate quick sort button on the toolbar to rearrange the records in either ascending or descending order.

Elena uses the Sort Descending button to rearrange the records in descending order by the Last Contact Date field.

To quick sort records in a datasheet:

❶ Click anywhere in the **Last Contact Date column** to establish that field as the current field.

❷ Click the **Sort Descending button** on the toolbar. Access rearranges the records in descending order by last contact date. See Figure 3-22.

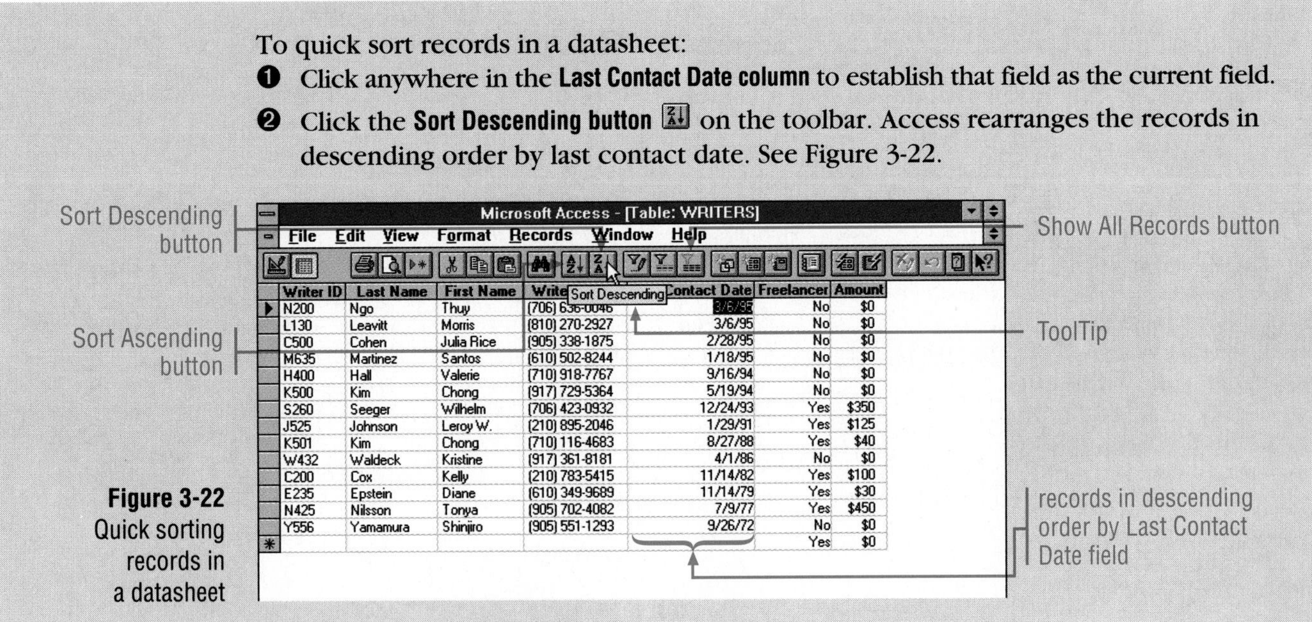

Writer ID	Last Name	First Name	Write	Contact Date	Freelancer	Amount
N200	Ngo	Thuy	(706) 636-0046	3/6/95	No	$0
L130	Leavitt	Morris	(810) 270-2927	3/6/95	No	$0
C500	Cohen	Julia Rice	(905) 338-1875	2/28/95	No	$0
M635	Martinez	Santos	(610) 502-8244	1/18/95	No	$0
H400	Hall	Valerie	(710) 918-7767	9/16/94	No	$0
K500	Kim	Chong	(917) 729-5364	5/19/94	No	$0
S260	Seeger	Wilhelm	(706) 423-0932	12/24/93	Yes	$350
J525	Johnson	Leroy W.	(210) 895-2046	1/29/91	Yes	$125
K501	Kim	Chong	(710) 116-4683	8/27/88	Yes	$40
W432	Waldeck	Kristine	(917) 361-8181	4/1/86	No	$0
C200	Cox	Kelly	(210) 783-5415	11/14/82	Yes	$100
E235	Epstein	Diane	(610) 349-9689	11/14/79	Yes	$30
N425	Nilsson	Tonya	(905) 702-4082	7/9/77	Yes	$450
Y556	Yamamura	Shinjiro	(905) 551-1293	9/26/72	No	$0
*					Yes	$0

Figure 3-22 Quick sorting records in a datasheet

You can restore the records to their original Writer ID order by clicking the Show All Records button on the toolbar.

To restore records to their original order:

1. Click the **Show All Records button** on the toolbar. Access rearranges the records in ascending Writer ID order.

Quick Sorting Multiple Fields

Access allows you to quick sort a datasheet using two or more sort keys. The sort-key fields must be in adjacent columns in the datasheet. You highlight the columns, and Access sorts first by the first column and then by each other highlighted column in order from left to right. Because you click either the Sort Ascending or the Sort Descending button to perform a quick sort, each of the multiple sort-key fields is in either ascending or descending sort order.

Elena selects the adjacent fields Freelancer and Amount and performs an ascending-order quick sort.

To use multiple sort keys to quick sort records in a datasheet:

1. Click the **Freelancer field selector**, which is the gray box containing the field name at the top of the column, and, while holding down the mouse button, drag the ⬇ to the right until both the Freelancer and Amount columns are highlighted. Then release the mouse button.
2. Click the **Sort Ascending button** on the toolbar. Access rearranges the records to place them in ascending order by Freelancer and, when the Freelancer field values are the same, in ascending order by Amount. See Figure 3-23.

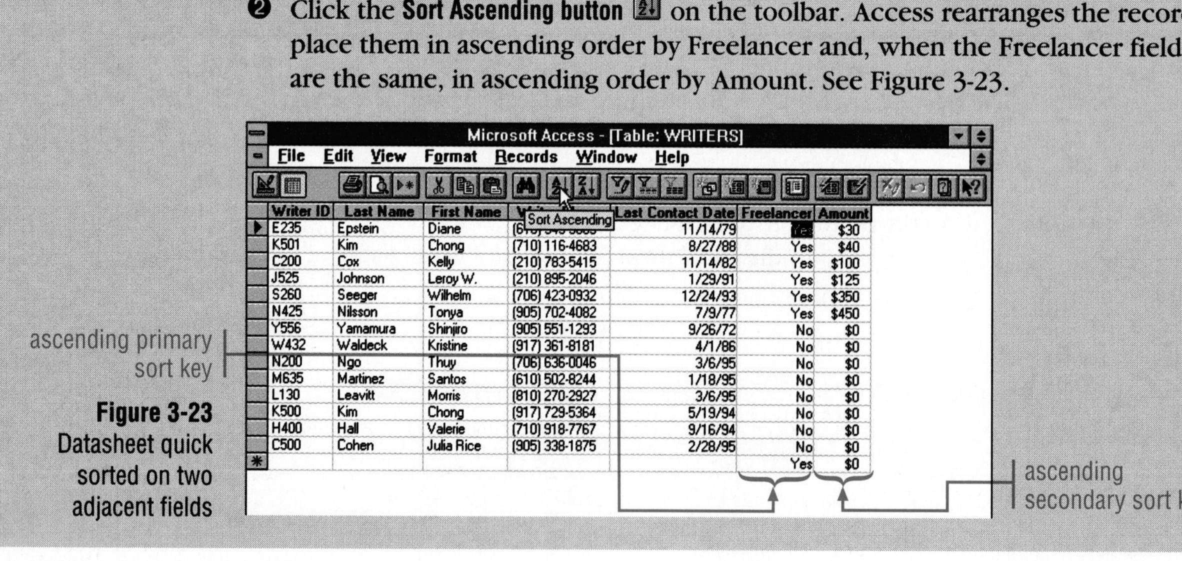

Writer ID	Last Name	First Name	W[illegible]	Last Contact Date	Freelancer	Amount
E235	Epstein	Diane	(61[illegible]	11/14/79	Yes	$30
K501	Kim	Chong	(710) 116-4683	8/27/88	Yes	$40
C200	Cox	Kelly	(210) 783-5415	11/14/82	Yes	$100
J525	Johnson	Leroy W.	(210) 895-2046	1/29/91	Yes	$125
S260	Seeger	Wilhelm	(706) 423-0932	12/24/93	Yes	$350
N425	Nilsson	Tonya	(905) 702-4082	7/9/77	Yes	$450
Y556	Yamamura	Shinjiro	(905) 551-1293	9/26/72	No	$0
W432	Waldeck	Kristine	(917) 361-8181	4/1/86	No	$0
N200	Ngo	Thuy	(706) 636-0046	3/6/95	No	$0
M635	Martinez	Santos	(610) 502-8244	1/18/95	No	$0
L130	Leavitt	Morris	(810) 270-2927	3/6/95	No	$0
K500	Kim	Chong	(917) 729-5364	5/19/94	No	$0
H400	Hall	Valerie	(710) 918-7767	9/16/94	No	$0
C500	Cohen	Julia Rice	(905) 338-1875	2/28/95	No	$0
*					Yes	$0

Figure 3-23
Datasheet quick sorted on two adjacent fields

Elena does a final review of the data in the WRITERS table and determines that she is finished with her updates. She next uses the Access Database Documentor for the WRITERS table.

Printing Table Documentation

Access has a **Database Documentor**, which you use to print the characteristics of a database or of selected database objects. For a table, Access prints the table fields and their properties.

Let's print the Access documentation for the WRITERS table.

To start the Database Documentor:

1. Double-click the Datasheet View window **Control menu box** to close the datasheet and activate the Database window.
2. Be sure the WRITERS table is highlighted in the Tables list box. Click **File** and then click **Print Definition...** to open the Print Table Definition dialog box. See Figure 3-24.

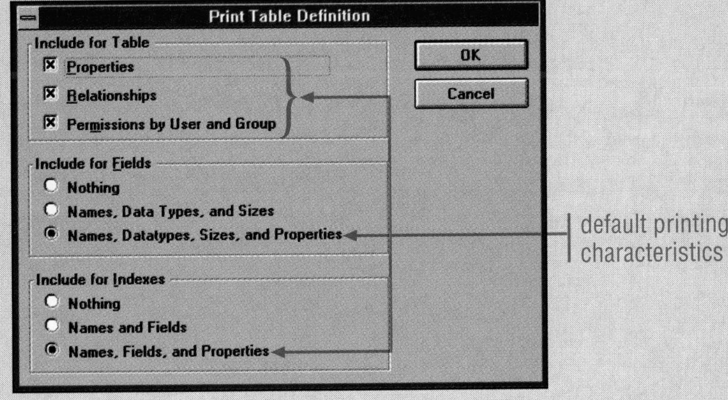

Figure 3-24 The Print Table Definition dialog box

The default characteristics for fields and indexes are fine. Because she has not yet defined any relationships or permissions for the WRITERS table, however, Elena turns off these check boxes.

To print table documentation:

1. Click the **Relationships check box** and the **Permissions by User and Group check box** so that these table characteristics do not print.

   TROUBLE? If your Print Table Definition dialog box looks different from Figure 3-24, just be sure that only the Properties box is checked and only the radio buttons shown are turned on.

2. Click the **OK button** to close the dialog box. After a short wait, Access opens the Print Preview window and displays the top of the first page of the documentation. See Figure 3-25 on the following page.

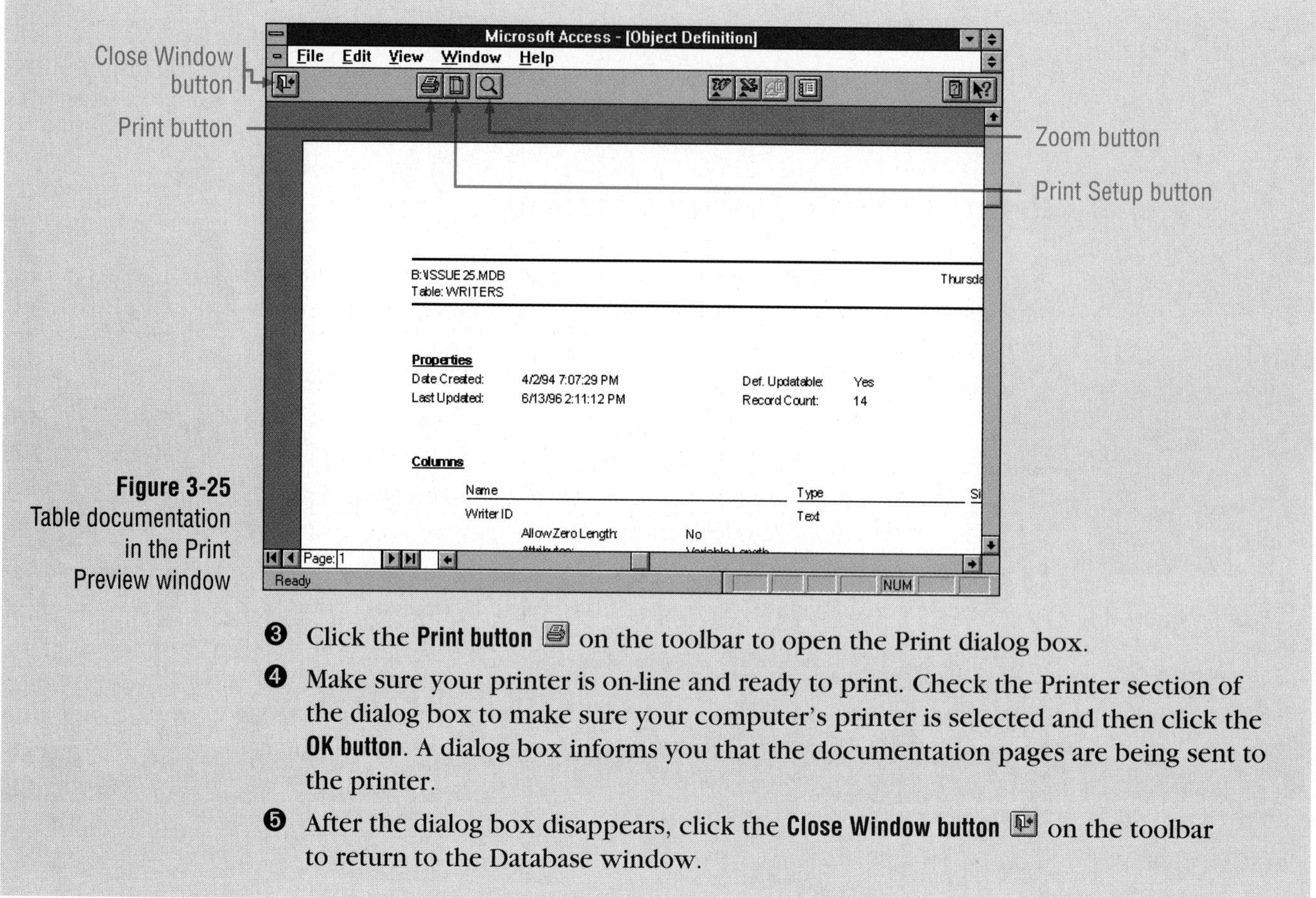

Figure 3-25 Table documentation in the Print Preview window

3. Click the **Print button** on the toolbar to open the Print dialog box.
4. Make sure your printer is on-line and ready to print. Check the Printer section of the dialog box to make sure your computer's printer is selected and then click the **OK button**. A dialog box informs you that the documentation pages are being sent to the printer.
5. After the dialog box disappears, click the **Close Window button** on the toolbar to return to the Database window.

Backing Up a Database

Elena is done with her work on the WRITERS table. Before exiting Access, however, Elena backs up the Issue25 database. **Backing up** is the process of making a duplicate copy of a database on a different disk. Elena does this to protect against loss of or damage to the original database. If problems occur, she can simply use the backup database.

In Access, a database and all its objects are contained in a single file, so backing up an Access database consists of copying the database file from one disk to another disk. Before backing up a database file, however, you must close the database in Access.

Access does not have its own backup command, so you use the Windows File Manager to back up an Access database from one disk to another disk. If you have both a drive A and drive B, you copy the Issue25 database from the drive containing your Student Disk to the other drive. If you have a drive A but not a drive B, however, you copy the Issue25 database from your Student Disk in drive A to the hard disk. Next, you place a different disk, which serves as the backup disk, in drive A and move the database to it from the hard disk.

Let's back up the Issue25 database from your Student Disk to your backup disk.

To back up a database:

1. Double-click the Database window **Control menu box** to close the Issue25 database.
2. Switch to the Windows Program Manager without exiting Access using **[Alt] [Tab]**, and launch File Manager.
3. Copy the issue25.mdb file from your Student Disk to a backup disk, using the procedure appropriate for your disk configuration.
4. Exit File Manager.
5. Be sure that your Student Disk is in the same drive you've been using for your Access work.
6. Switch back to Access. The Access window is the active window.

Compacting a Database

Elena deleted a record from the WRITERS table during her updating work. She knows that, when records are deleted in Access, the space occupied by the deleted records does not become available for other records. The same is true if an object, such as a form or report, is deleted. To make the space available, you must compact the database. When you **compact a database**, Access removes deleted records and objects and creates a smaller version of the database. Unlike backing up a database, which you do to protect your database against loss or damage, you compact a database to make it smaller, thereby making more space available on your disk. Before compacting a database, you must close it.

REFERENCE WINDOW

Compacting a Database

- Close any database you are using, so that the Microsoft Access window is active.
- Click File, and then click Compact Database... to open the Database to Compact From dialog box.
- In the Drives list box and in the Directories list box, select the drive and directory that contain the database you want to compact.
- In the File Name list box, select the database you want to compact.
- Click the OK button. Access closes the Database to Compact From dialog box and opens the Database to Compact Into dialog box.
- In the Drives list box and in the Directories list box, select the drive and directory for the location of the compacted form of the database.
- Type the name you want to assign to the compacted form of the database.
- Click the OK button. The Database to Compact Into dialog box disappears, and Access starts compacting the database.
- If you use the same name for both the original and compacted database, Access displays the message "Replace existing file?" Click Yes to continue compacting the database.
- After the database compacting is complete, Access returns you to the Microsoft Access window.

Elena compacts the Issue25 database before exiting Access. Because she has just made a backup copy, she uses Issue25 as the compacted database name. You can use the same name, or a different name, for your original and compacted databases. If you use the same name, you should back up the original database first in case a hardware or software malfunction occurs in the middle of the compacting process.

Let's compact the Issue25 database and then exit Access.

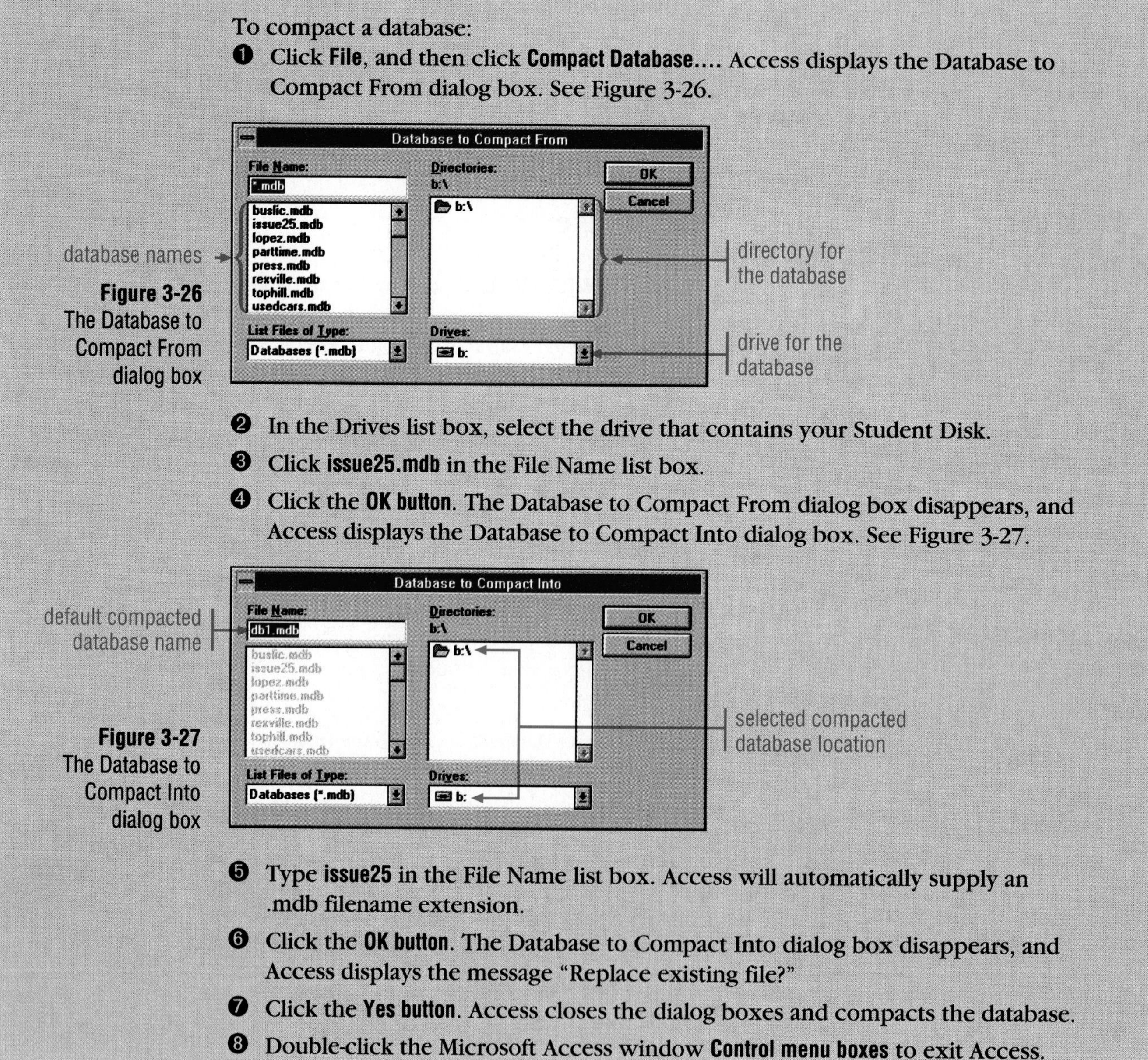

To compact a database:

1. Click **File**, and then click **Compact Database...**. Access displays the Database to Compact From dialog box. See Figure 3-26.

Figure 3-26 The Database to Compact From dialog box

2. In the Drives list box, select the drive that contains your Student Disk.
3. Click **issue25.mdb** in the File Name list box.
4. Click the **OK button**. The Database to Compact From dialog box disappears, and Access displays the Database to Compact Into dialog box. See Figure 3-27.

Figure 3-27 The Database to Compact Into dialog box

5. Type **issue25** in the File Name list box. Access will automatically supply an .mdb filename extension.
6. Click the **OK button**. The Database to Compact Into dialog box disappears, and Access displays the message "Replace existing file?"
7. Click the **Yes button**. Access closes the dialog boxes and compacts the database.
8. Double-click the Microsoft Access window **Control menu boxes** to exit Access.

■ ■ ■

Elena has finished updating the WRITERS table. In the next tutorial, she will use the Access query feature to answer questions about the data in the WRITERS table.

Questions

1. What operations are performed when you update a database?
2. What does a pencil symbol signify in a record selector? What does an asterisk symbol signify in a record selector?
3. **E** You can use the Format menu to hide columns in a datasheet. Use the Access Help system to learn a reason for hiding columns in a datasheet.
4. When you make changes to a field value, what mode are you in when an entire field is highlighted? What mode do you change to if you then press [F2]?
5. When you change a datasheet's font size, what other datasheet property is automatically changed?
6. **E** Use the Access Help system to document for your instructor the difference between exporting and importing.
7. In what sequence are records displayed in a datasheet?
8. When might you consider using a secondary sort key?
9. What is the Database Documentor?
10. How many different files do you copy when you back up one Access database?
11. **E** Use Cue Cards to document for your instructor how to save changes to a record without moving to another record.
12. **E** Use Cue Cards to find out which update operations you cannot undo.
13. What is the purpose of compacting a database?

Tutorial Assignments

Elena imports one of Judith's Vision database tables to replace her BUSINESS ARTICLES table in the Issue25 database. After importing the table, Elena adds, changes, and deletes data in the BUSINESS ARTICLES table.

Launch Access, open the Issue25 database on your Student Disk, maximize the Database window, and do the following:

1. Delete the BUSINESS ARTICLES table.
2. Import the "BUSINESS ARTICLES tutorial 3 import" table from the Vision database on your Student Disk.
3. Change the table name "BUSINESS ARTICLES tutorial 3 import" to BUSINESS ARTICLES.
4. Open the BUSINESS ARTICLES table. It should contain 23 records.
5. Print the BUSINESS ARTICLES datasheet.
6. Delete the third record, which is an article that appeared in a 1972 issue.
7. In the Type field, change the type of the 1988 article from LAW to POL.
8. Switch to the Table Design View window. Make the row for the Issue of Business Perspective field the current field, click in its Format property box, and start the Access Help system. Click Search..., type date/time, click the Show Topics button, click Format Property, and then click the Go To button. Next, click the Date/Time Data Types jump and read the explanation about the date/time format "yyyy mmm." Exit the Access Help system, switch back to the Datasheet View window, and observe the format of the field values in the Issue column.
9. Add the three new records shown in Figure 3-28 on the following page to the end of the BUSINESS ARTICLES table. Notice the format of the Issue field and enter the three new Issue field values in the exact same format.

BUSINESS ARTICLES table data

	Article Title	Type	Issue	Article Length	Writer ID
Record 1:	The Economy Under Sub-Zero Population Growth	BUS	1972 Dec	1020	E235
Record 2:	New York City Fiscal Crisis	POL	1975 Nov	1477	N425
Record 3:	Toyota and GM Joint Venture	INT	1983 Mar	1682	S260

Figure 3-28

10. Resize the datasheet columns so that all field names and field values appear on the screen.
11. Print the datasheet.
12. Back up the Issue25 database from your Student Disk to your backup disk.
13. Compact the Issue25 database using Issue25 as the File Name in the Database to Compact Into dialog box.

Case Problems

1. Walkton Daily Press Carriers

Robin Witkop has created a database to help Grant Sherman track newspaper carriers and their outstanding balances. Grant starts his maintenance of the CARRIERS table. He imports data to his database and then adds, changes, and deletes data to update the CARRIERS table.

Launch Access and do the following:

1. Open the Press database on your Student Disk and maximize the Database window.
2. Delete the CARRIERS table.
3. Import the "CARRIERS starting data" table from the Walkton database on your Student Disk.
4. Change the table name "CARRIERS starting data" to CARRIERS.
5. Open the CARRIERS table, which should contain 19 records.
6. Print the CARRIERS datasheet.
7. Delete the record that has a value of 10 in the Carrier ID field. This is the record for Joe Carrasco.
8. In the Last Name field of the record having a Carrier ID value of 11, change Thompson to Thomson.
9. Make the following changes to the record that has a Carrier ID value of 17, which is the record for Bradley Slachter: change the First Name field to Sean; change the Birthdate field value 3/4/79 to 3/14/79.
10. Add the two new records shown in Figure 3-29 to the end of the CARRIERS table. Because Access automatically controls fields that are assigned a counter data type, press [Tab] instead of typing a field value in the Carrier ID field.

CARRIERS table data

	Carrier ID	Last Name	First Name	Carrier Phone	Birthdate
Record 1:	20	Rivera	Nelia	281-3787	6/3/80
Record 2:	21	Hansen	Gunnar	949-6745	4/30/81

Figure 3-29

11. Resize the datasheet columns, if necessary, so that all field names and field values appear on the screen.
12. Print the datasheet.
13. Back up the Press database from your Student Disk to your backup disk.
14. Compact the Press database using Press as the File Name in the Database to Compact Into dialog box.

2. Lopez Used Cars

Maria and Hector Lopez have created a database to track their used-car inventory in the lots they own throughout Texas. They start their maintenance of the USED CARS table. They import data and then add, change, and delete data to update the USED CARS table.

Launch Access and do the following:

1. Open the Usedcars database on your Student Disk and maximize the Database window.
2. Delete the USED CARS table.
3. Import the "USED CARS starting data" table from the Lopez database on your Student Disk.
4. Change the table name "USED CARS starting data" to USED CARS.
5. Open the USED CARS table. It should contain 25 records.
6. Print the USED CARS datasheet.
7. Delete the record that has the value JT4AA in the Vehicle ID field. The record is for a Cadillac Fleetwood.
8. In the Cost field of the record having the Vehicle ID QQRT6, which is a Nissan 240SX, change $6700 to $6200. You might need to resize the column to see the entire field value.
9. Make the following changes to the record that has the Vehicle ID value AB7J8, which is an Acura Legend: change the Model field from Legend to Integra; change the Cost field value from $300 to $4300.
10. Add the two new records shown in Figure 3-30 to the end of the USED CARS table.

USED CARS table data

	Vehicle ID	Manufacturer	Model	Class	Transmision Type	Year	Location Code	Cost	Selling Price
Record 1:	MX8M4	Ford	Taurus Wagon	WM	L4	1992	P1	5225	6600
Record 2:	BY7BZ	Subaru	Justy	S2	M5	1991	H1	1900	2700

Figure 3-30

11. Resize the datasheet columns so that all field names and field values appear on the screen.
12. Print the datasheet. If some columns are too narrow to print all field names and values, or if more than one page is needed to print the datasheet, resize the datasheet columns and reprint the datasheet.
13. Back up the Usedcars database from your Student Disk to your backup disk.
14. Compact the Usedcars database using Usedcars as the File Name in the Database to Compact Into dialog box.

3. Tophill University Student Employment

Lee Chang has created a database to help Olivia Tyler track employers and their advertised part-time jobs for students. Olivia starts her maintenance of the JOBS table. She imports data to her database and then adds, changes, and deletes data to update the JOBS table.

Launch Access and do the following:

1. Open the Parttime database on your Student Disk and maximize the Database window.
2. Delete the JOBS table.
3. Import the "JOBS starting data" table from the Tophill database on your Student Disk.
4. Change the table name "JOBS starting data" to JOBS.
5. Open the JOBS table. It should contain 17 records.

6. Print the JOBS datasheet.
7. Resize the datasheet columns so that all field names and field values appear on the screen.
8. Delete the record that has a value of 16 in the Job# field. This record describes a position for a night stock clerk.
9. In the Job Title field of the record having a Job# value of 3, change Computer Analyst to Computer Lab Associate.
10. Make the following changes to the record that has a Job# value of 13, which is the record describing a position for an actuarial aide: change the Employer ID field to BJ93; change the Wage field value $8.40 to $9.25.
11. Add the two new records shown in Figure 3-31 to the end of the JOBS table. Because Access automatically controls fields that are assigned a counter data type, press [Tab] instead of typing a field value in the Job# field.

JOBS table data

	Job Order	Hours/Week	Employer ID	Job Title	Wage
Record 1:	18	21	ME86	Lab Technician	5.30
Record 2:	19	18	BJ92	Desktop Publishing Aide	5.80

Figure 3-31

12. Print the datasheet. If some columns are too narrow to print all field names and values, or if more than one page is needed to print the datasheet, resize the datasheet columns and reprint the datasheet.
13. Back up the Parttime database from your Student Disk to your backup disk.
14. Compact the Parttime database using Parttime as the File Name in the Database to Compact Into dialog box.

4. Rexville Business Licenses

Chester Pearce has created a database to help him track the licenses issued to businesses in the town of Rexville. Chester starts his maintenance of the BUSINESSES table. He imports data to his database and then adds, changes, and deletes data to update the BUSINESSES table.

Launch Access and do the following:

1. Open the Buslic database on your Student Disk and maximize the Database window.
2. Delete the BUSINESSES table.
3. Import the "BUSINESSES starting data" table from the Rexville database on your Student Disk.
4. Change the table name "BUSINESSES starting data" to BUSINESSES.
5. Open the BUSINESSES table. It should contain 12 records.
6. Print the BUSINESSES datasheet.
7. Change to the Table Design View window. Enter the Caption property value Bus ID for the Business ID field and the Caption property value Phone# for the Phone Number field.

8. Resize the datasheet columns so that all field names and field values appear on the screen.
9. Delete the record that has a value of 3 in the Business ID field. The content of the Business Name field for this record is Take a Chance.
10. In the Street Name field of the record having a Business ID value of 9, change West Emerald Street to East Emerald Street.
11. Make the following changes to the record that has a Business ID value of 8. The Business Name for this field reads Lakeview House. Change the Business Name field to Rexville Billiards; change the Street# field value 2425 to 4252.
12. Add the two new records shown in Figure 3-32 to the end of the BUSINESSES table. Because Access automatically controls fields that are assigned a counter data type, press [Tab] instead of typing a field value in the Business ID field.

BUSINESSES table data

	Business ID	Business Name	Street Number	Street Name	Phone Number	Proprietor
Record 1:	13	Kyle Manufacturing, Inc.	4818	West Paris Road	942-9239	Myron Kyle
Record 2:	14	Merlin Auto Body	2922	Riverview Drive	243-5525	Lester Tiahrt

Figure 3-32

13. Print the datasheet. If some columns are too narrow to print all field names and values, or if more than one page is needed to print the datasheet, resize the datasheet columns and reprint the datasheet.
14. Back up the Buslic database from your Student Disk to your backup disk.
15. Compact the Buslic database using Buslic as the File Name in the Database to Compact Into dialog box.

TUTORIAL 4

Querying Database Tables

Querying the Issue25 Database at Vision Publishers

OBJECTIVES

In this tutorial you will:

- Define record selection criteria
- Sort records in a query
- Print a dynaset selection
- Save and open a query
- Define multiple selection criteria
- Perform query calculations
- Add relationships between tables
- Query more than one table
- Create a parameter query

CASE

Vision Publishers At the next progress meeting on the special 25th-anniversary issue of *Business Perspective*, Brian Murphy, Elena Sanchez, Judith Rossi, and Harold Larson discuss the information each needs to obtain from the database. Brian asks for a list of the freelancers, their phone numbers, and the amounts owed to them. He also wants to know the total amount owed to freelancers, the dollar impact of giving all writers an extra $50, and the dollar impact of giving the extra money to freelancers versus staff writers.

Judith and Elena decide to develop writer contact lists based on specific area codes and the last dates the writers were contacted. Because Elena is starting the magazine layout process, she wants to see the article titles and lengths.

Harold plans to highlight the diversity of articles in his marketing campaign, so he needs a list of writers, article titles, and article types arranged by article type. Harold also wants to feature one or two writers in the marketing campaign, and the group decides that Valerie Hall and Wilhelm Seeger should be the featured writers. Elena agrees to get Harold the contact information for these two writers.

After further discussion, the group agrees on a list of questions (Figure 4-1) that they want Elena to answer. Elena will use Access's query capability to obtain the answers.

Answer these questions:

1. What are the names, phone numbers, and amounts owed for all writers?
2. What is the complete information on Valerie Hall?
3. What are the names, phone numbers, last contact dates, and amounts owed for all freelancers?
4. What is the contact information for writers with 706 area codes, for Valerie Hall and Wilhelm Seger, and for writers last contacted prior to 1994?
5. Who are the staff writers and who are the freelancers, arranged in order by last contact date?
6. Who are the freelancers last contacted prior to 1990?
7. What is the phone contact information for freelancers with 210 or 706 area codes?
8. What is the impact of giving all writers an extra $50? What would be the total cost and average cost per writer with and without the extra $50? What would be the total cost and average cost for freelancers versus staff writers with and without the extra $50?
9. What are the article titles, types, and lengths for each writer in order by article type?
10. What are the article titles and lengths and the writer names for a specific article type in order by article title?

Figure 4-1
Elena's questions about the Issue25 database

Using a Query

A **query** is a question you ask about the data stored in a database. Elena's list of questions about the Issue25 database are examples of queries. When you create a query, you tell Access which fields you need and what criteria Access should use to select records for you. Access shows you just the information you want, so you don't need to scan through an entire database for that information.

Access has a powerful query capability that can:

- display selected fields and records from a table
- sort records
- perform calculations
- generate data for forms, reports, and other queries
- access data from two or more tables

The specific type of Access query Elena will use to answer her questions is called a select query. A **select query** asks a question about the data stored in a database and returns an answer in a format that is the same as the format of a datasheet. When you create a select query, you phrase the question with definitions of the fields and records you want Access to select for you.

Access has a set of **Query Wizards** that ask you questions about your queries and then create queries based on your answers. You use Query Wizards for specialized, complex queries such as finding duplicate records in a table and copying table records to a new table. For common queries such as select queries, however, you do not use Query Wizards.

You use Access's Query Design window to create a select query. In the Query Design window you specify the data you want to see by constructing a query by example. Using **query by example (QBE)**, you give Access an example of the information you are requesting. Access then retrieves the information that precisely matches your example.

Access also allows you to create queries using Structured Query Language (SQL). **SQL**, which can be pronounced either "sequel" or "ess cue ell," is a powerful computer language used in querying, updating, and managing relational databases. When you create a QBE query, Access automatically constructs the equivalent SQL statement. Although you will not use SQL in this tutorial, you can view the SQL statement by switching from the Query Design window to the SQL View window.

Access has a set of Cue Cards you can use while working with queries. Although we will not use these Cue Cards in this tutorial, you might find they enhance your understanding of queries. At any time during this tutorial, therefore, select Design a Query from the Cue Card menu window to launch the appropriate Cue Cards.

Creating a Query

Before Elena creates her first query, she compares the tables in the Issue25 database against those in the Vision database. She finds some differences and determines that the tables containing data about articles and article types are more complete and accurate in the Vision database. She imports these tables from the Vision database to the Issue25 database to make her data accurate.

Let's import the same two tables, named PAST ARTICLES and TYPES, to the Issue25 database. Doing so will ensure that your tables are consistent with the remaining tutorials even if you have not accurately completed previous Tutorial Assignments. If you have not done so, place your Student Disk in the appropriate drive, launch Access, and open the Issue25 database on your Student Disk.

To import tables:

1. Import the PAST ARTICLES table from the Vision database on your Student Disk. Be sure that the Structure and Data option button in the Import Objects dialog box is selected.
2. Click the **OK button** to close the "Successfully Imported" dialog box. The Import Objects dialog box becomes the active window. Do not close this window because you can import the next table from the same database by continuing in this active window.
3. In the Import Objects dialog box, click **TYPES** in the Objects list box. Be sure that the Structure and Data option button is selected and click the **Import button**.
4. Click the **OK button** to close the "Successfully Imported" dialog box and then click the **Close button** to close the Import Objects dialog box. The two new tables now appear in the Database window.

Elena has very little experience working with queries, so she practices with the first few questions on her list. She will not save any queries until she completes her practice. Elena creates her first query using the WRITERS table. She must first open the Query Design window.

REFERENCE WINDOW

Opening the Query Design Window for a Single Table

- In the Tables list box of the Database window, click the table name that you will use for the query.
- Click the New Query button. The New Query dialog box appears.
- Click the New Query button to open the Query Design window.

Let's open the Query Design window for the WRITERS table.

To open the Query Design window:

❶ Click **WRITERS** in the Tables list box. See Figure 4-2.

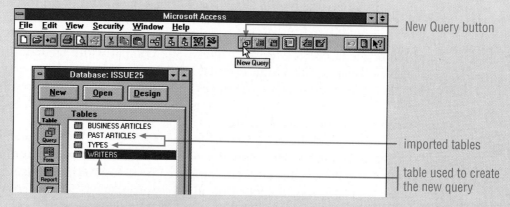

Figure 4-2 Database window showing imported tables PAST ARTICLES and TYPES

New Query button

imported tables

table used to create the new query

❷ Click the toolbar **New Query button** to open the New Query dialog box.

❸ Click the **New Query button** in the New Query dialog box. Access opens the Query Design window. See Figure 4-3.

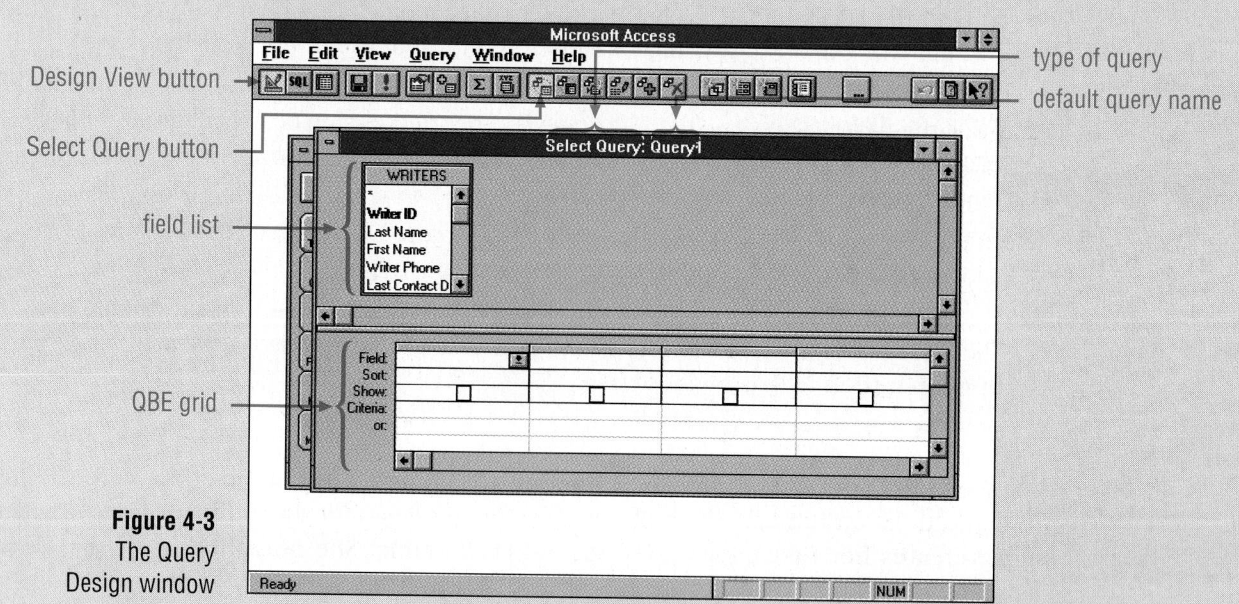

Figure 4-3 The Query Design window

The Query Design Window

The Query Design window contains the standard title bar, menu bar, toolbar, and status bar. On the toolbar, both the Design View and Select Query buttons are automatically selected to identify that you are in the Query Design window designing a select query. The title bar displays the query type, Select Query, and the default query name, Query1. You change the default query name to a more meaningful one when you save the query.

In addition to the standard window components, the Query Design window contains a field list and the QBE grid. The **field list**, in the upper-left part of the window, contains the fields for the table you are querying. The table name appears at the top of the list box. The fields are listed in the order in which they appear in the Table Design window. If your query needs fields from two or more tables, each table's field list appears in this upper portion of the Query Design window. You choose a field for your query by dragging its name from the field list to the QBE grid in the lower portion of the window.

In the **QBE grid**, you include the fields and record selection criteria for the information you want to see. Each column in the QBE grid contains specifications about a field you will use in the query.

If Elena's query uses all fields from the WRITERS table, she can choose one of three methods to transfer all the fields from the field list to the QBE grid. You use the three methods as follows:

- In the first method, you click and drag each field individually from the field list to the QBE grid. Use this method if you want the fields in your query to appear in an order that is different from that in the field list.
- In the second method, you double-click the asterisk in the field list. Access places WRITERS.* in the QBE grid. This signifies that the order of the fields will be the same in the query as it is in the field list. Use this method if the query does not need to be sorted or to have conditions for the records you want to select. The advantage of using this method is that you do not need to change the query if you add or delete fields from the underlying table structure. They will all automatically appear in the query.
- In the third method, you double-click the field list title bar to highlight all the fields. Click and drag one of the highlighted fields to the QBE grid. Access places each field in a separate column and arranges the fields in the order in which they appear in the field list. Use this method rather than the previous one if your query needs to be sorted or to have record selection criteria.

To help you understand the purpose and relationship of the field list and QBE grid better, let's create a simple query.

Adding All Fields Using the Asterisk Method

Elena's first query is to find the names, phone numbers, and amounts owed for all writers. She decides to use all the fields from the WRITERS table in her query.

To use the asterisk method to add all fields to the QBE grid:

❶ The insertion point should be in the QBE grid's first column Field box; if it is not, click that box. Double-click the **asterisk** in the WRITERS field list. Access places WRITERS.* in the QBE grid's first column Field box. See Figure 4-4.

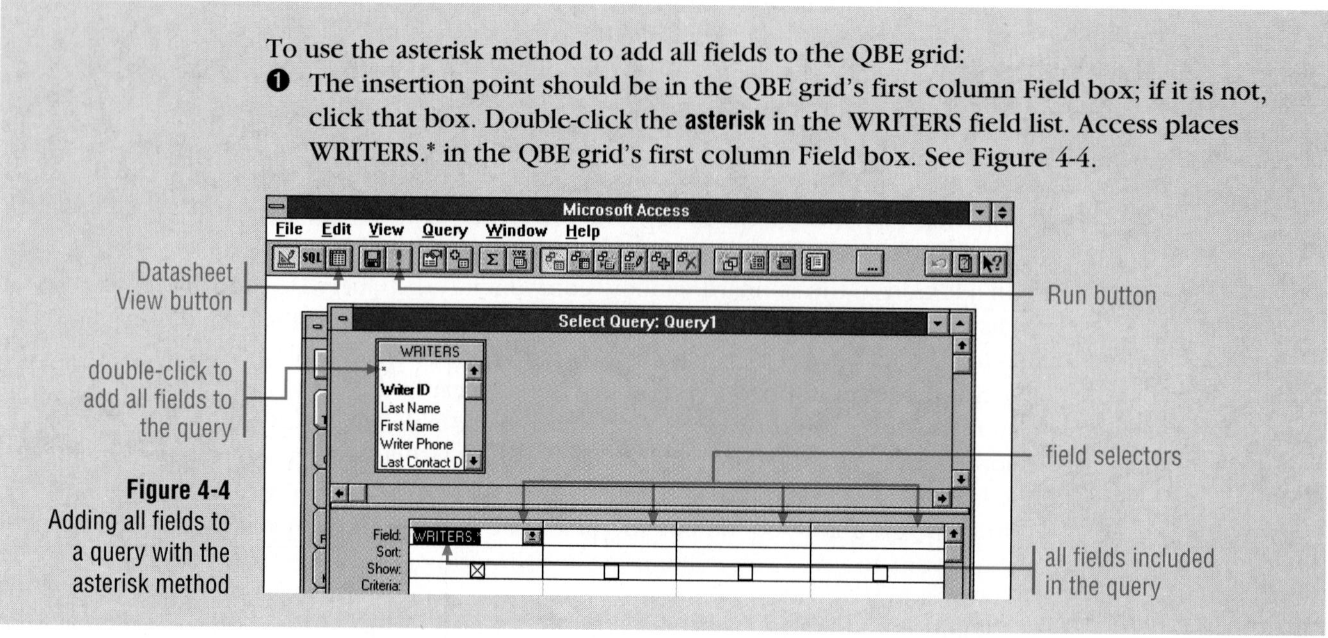

Figure 4-4 Adding all fields to a query with the asterisk method

While you are constructing a query, you can see the answer at any time by clicking the Run button or the Datasheet View button on the toolbar. In response, Access displays the **dynaset**, which is the set of fields and records that results from answering, or running, a query. Although a dynaset looks just like a table's datasheet and appears in the same Datasheet View window, the dynaset is temporary and its contents are based on the criteria you establish in the QBE grid. In contrast, the datasheet shows the permanent data in a table.

Elena views the dynaset for the query she just created.

To view a query's dynaset:

❶ Click the toolbar **Run button** [!]. Access displays the dynaset for the query. See Figure 4-5.

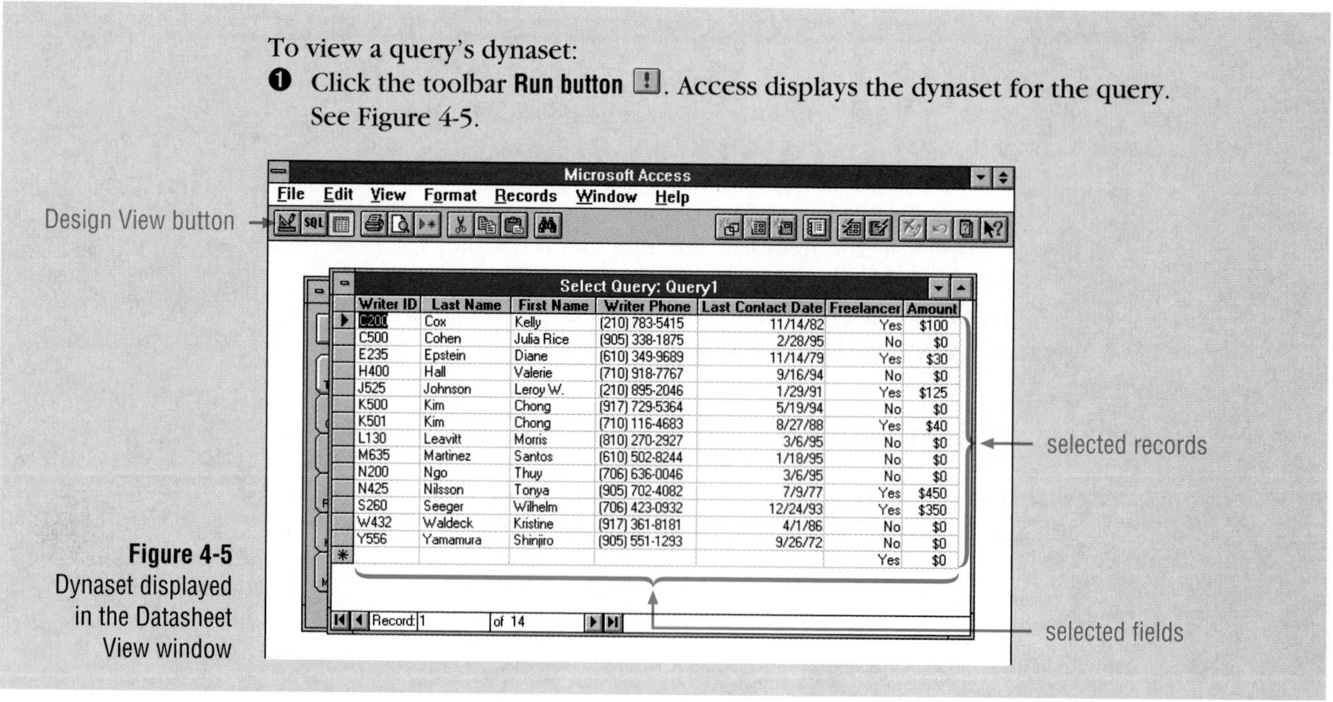

Writer ID	Last Name	First Name	Writer Phone	Last Contact Date	Freelancer	Amount
C200	Cox	Kelly	(210) 783-5415	11/14/82	Yes	$100
C500	Cohen	Julia Rice	(905) 338-1875	2/28/95	No	$0
E235	Epstein	Diane	(610) 349-9689	11/14/79	Yes	$30
H400	Hall	Valerie	(710) 918-7767	9/16/94	No	$0
J525	Johnson	Leroy W.	(210) 895-2046	1/29/91	Yes	$125
K500	Kim	Chong	(917) 729-5364	5/19/94	No	$0
K501	Kim	Chong	(710) 116-4683	8/27/88	Yes	$40
L130	Leavitt	Morris	(810) 270-2927	3/6/95	No	$0
M635	Martinez	Santos	(610) 502-8244	1/18/95	No	$0
N200	Ngo	Thuy	(706) 636-0046	3/6/95	No	$0
N425	Nilsson	Tonya	(905) 702-4082	7/9/77	Yes	$450
S260	Seeger	Wilhelm	(706) 423-0932	12/24/93	Yes	$350
W432	Waldeck	Kristine	(917) 361-8181	4/1/86	No	$0
Y556	Yamamura	Shinjiro	(905) 551-1293	9/26/72	No	$0
*					Yes	$0

Figure 4-5 Dynaset displayed in the Datasheet View window

Viewing the WRITERS table datasheet would have produced the same results as shown in the dynaset because all the fields and records appear in the same order in both. Elena realizes that she did not ask the right question, which was to list just the writer names, phone numbers, and amounts. To change the query, Elena switches back to the Query Design window by clicking the Design View button.

Deleting a Field

You will rarely create a query to list all the fields from a table. More often, you will want to include some fields and exclude other fields. You might also want to rearrange the order of the included fields. Therefore, you seldom use the asterisk method to add all fields to a query. Let's remove WRITERS.* from the QBE grid in preparation for creating the correct first query.

To delete a field from the QBE grid:

1. Click the toolbar **Design View button** to switch to the Query Design window.
2. The field selectors are the gray bars above the Field row in the QBE grid. Move the pointer to the field selector for the first column. When the pointer changes to ⬇, click to highlight or select the entire column.
3. Position the pointer again in the first column's field selector and click the right mouse button to display the Shortcut menu.
4. Click **Cut** in the Shortcut menu. The Shortcut menu disappears and the contents of the first QBE grid column are deleted.

Adding All Fields by Dragging

Elena uses another method to add all the fields to the QBE grid. She then deletes those fields she does not need.

To add all fields to the QBE grid by dragging:

1. Double-click the **title bar** of the WRITERS field list to highlight, or select, all the fields in the table. Notice that the asterisk in the first row of the field list is not highlighted.
2. Click and hold the mouse button anywhere in the highlighted area of the WRITERS field list.
3. Drag the pointer to the QBE grid's first column Field box. As you near the destination Field box, the pointer changes to . Release the mouse button in the Field box. Access adds each table field in a separate Field box, from left to right. See Figure 4-6 on the following page. You can use the QBE grid's horizontal scroll bars and arrows to see the fields that are off the screen.

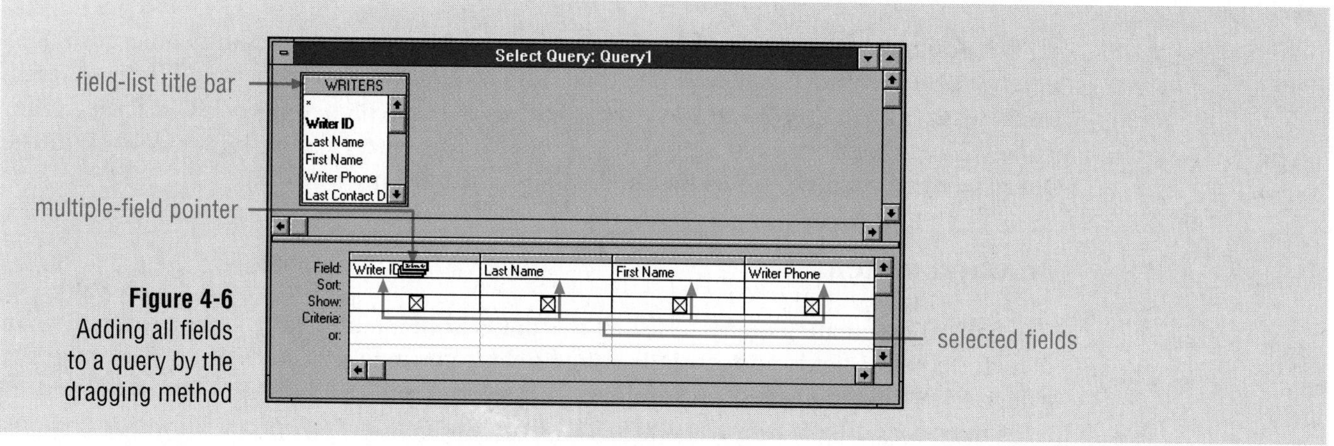

Figure 4-6 Adding all fields to a query by the dragging method

Moving a Field

Elena does not need the Writer ID, Last Contact Date, and Freelancer fields for her first query. She also thinks viewing the dynaset would be easier for everyone if the First Name field preceded the Last Name field. Elena deletes the three unneeded fields and then moves the First Name field.

To delete multiple fields from the QBE grid:

1. Move the pointer to the Writer ID field selector in the QBE grid. When the pointer changes to ⬇, click to select the entire column. Position the pointer again in the Writer ID field selector and click the right mouse button to display the Shortcut menu.
2. Click **Cut** in the Shortcut menu. The Shortcut menu disappears, and Access deletes the Writer ID column. The remaining fields shift one column to the left.
3. If necessary, click the horizontal scroll bar's **right arrow button** once so that the Last Contact Date and Freelancer fields are visible in the QBE grid.
4. Move the pointer to the Last Contact Date field selector. When the pointer changes to ⬇, click to select the entire column and, while holding the mouse button, drag the pointer to the right until the Freelancer field is also highlighted. Release the mouse button and click the right mouse button in either field selector to display the Shortcut menu.
5. Click **Cut** in the Shortcut menu. The Shortcut menu disappears, and Access deletes the Last Contact Date and Freelancer columns. Access moves the Freelancer Reprint Payment Amount field to the column next to the Writer Phone field.

Elena next moves the First Name field to the left of the Last Name field.

To move a field in the QBE grid:

1. If necessary, click the horizontal scroll bar's **left arrow button** once so that the Last Name field is visible in the QBE grid.
2. Click the **First Name field selector** to highlight the entire column. Click the **First Name field selector** again and drag the pointer, which appears as [pointer icon], to the left. When the pointer is anywhere in the Last Name column, release the mouse button. Access moves the First Name field to the left of the Last Name field. See Figure 4-7.

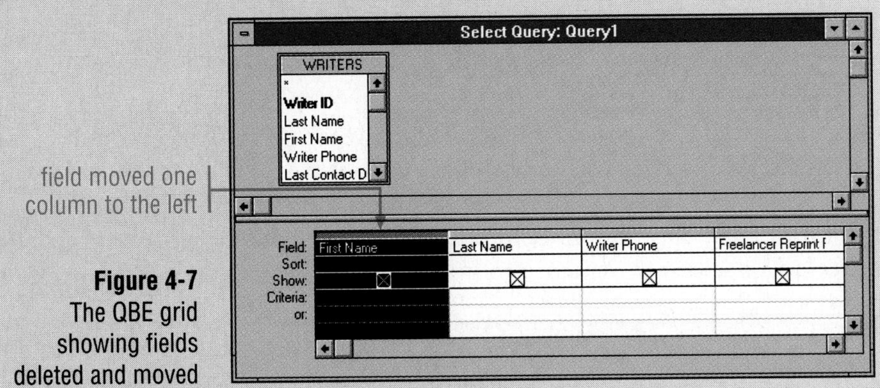

Figure 4-7 The QBE grid showing fields deleted and moved

TROUBLE? If the field does not move, you probably did not drag it far enough to the left. Repeat the move process to correct the problem.

Elena now views the dynaset for this query.

To view a dynaset for a query that uses a subset of the fields from a table:

1. Click the toolbar **Run button** [Run button icon]. Access displays the dynaset for the query. See Figure 4-8. The First Name field appears to the left of the Last Name field, and the three deleted fields do not appear in the dynaset.

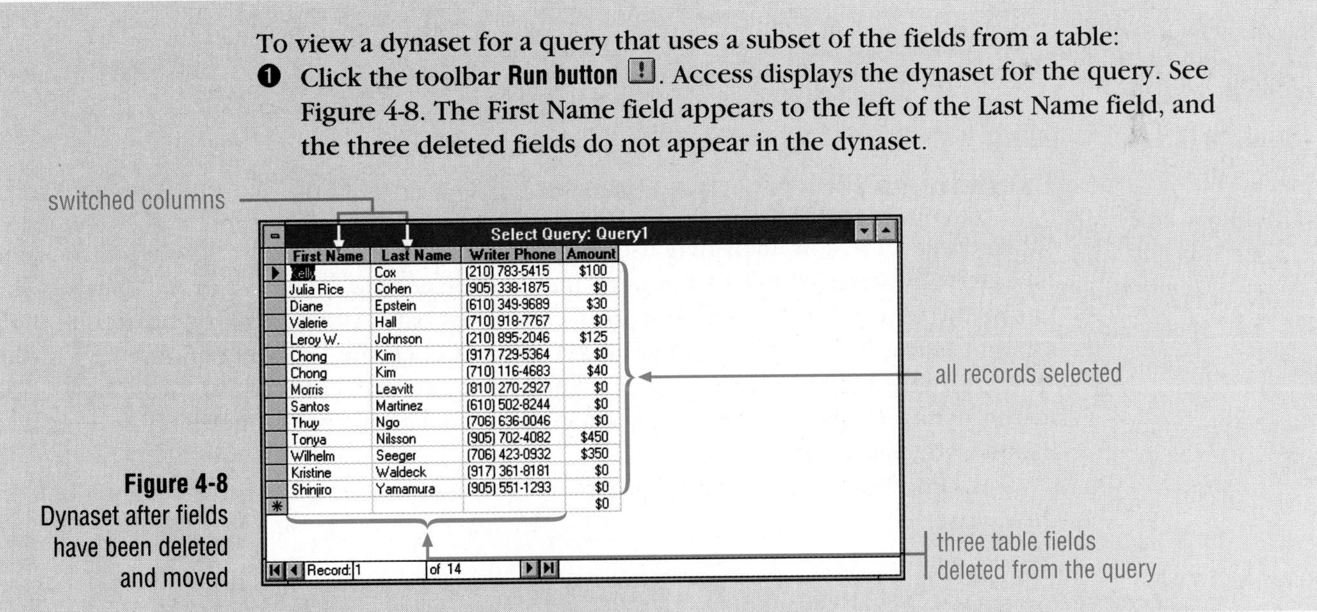

First Name	Last Name	Writer Phone	Amount
Kelly	Cox	(210) 783-5415	$100
Julia Rice	Cohen	(905) 338-1875	$0
Diane	Epstein	(610) 349-9689	$30
Valerie	Hall	(710) 918-7767	$0
Leroy W.	Johnson	(210) 895-2046	$125
Chong	Kim	(917) 729-5364	$0
Chong	Kim	(710) 116-4683	$40
Morris	Leavitt	(810) 270-2927	$0
Santos	Martinez	(610) 502-8244	$0
Thuy	Ngo	(706) 636-0046	$0
Tonya	Nilsson	(905) 702-4082	$450
Wilhelm	Seeger	(706) 423-0932	$350
Kristine	Waldeck	(917) 361-8181	$0
Shinjiro	Yamamura	(905) 551-1293	$0
			$0

Figure 4-8 Dynaset after fields have been deleted and moved

Deleting and moving fields in the query and resulting dynaset has no effect on the underlying WRITERS table. All fields remain in the table in the order you specified in the table structure design. With queries, you can view information any way you want without being restricted by the table structure.

Inserting a Field

Elena does not need to see the Freelancer field in this first query, but she realizes that others might want the field to appear in the dynaset. She adds the Freelancer field to the QBE grid between the Writer Phone and Freelancer Reprint Payment Amount fields.

To insert a field in the QBE grid:

1. Click the toolbar **Design View button** to switch to the Query Design window.
2. Scroll the WRITERS field list and click **Freelancer**. The Freelancer field becomes the only highlighted field in the WRITERS field list.
3. Drag Freelancer from the field list to the Freelancer Reprint Payment Amount column in the QBE grid, where the cursor changes to , and then release. See Figure 4-9. The Freelancer field is positioned between the Writer Phone and Freelancer Reprint Payment Amount columns. You might need to scroll to the right to see the Freelancer Reprint Payment Amount column.

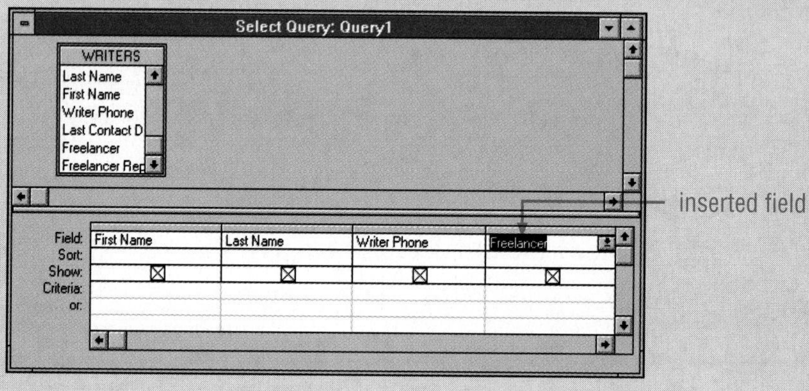

Figure 4-9 Inserting a field in the QBE grid

Excluding a Field from a Dynaset

When others at Vision Publishers use this query, they will simply run it. When Elena runs the query, however, she does not need the Freelancer field to appear in the dynaset. She knows the writers who are freelancers because they have values greater than zero in their Amount fields. Before she runs the query, she can click the Freelancer Show box in the QBE grid. This removes the × from the Show box and prevents the field from appearing in the dynaset. Clicking the Show box again puts the × back in the Show box and includes the field in the dynaset.

Let's use the Freelancer Show box to exclude and then include the Freelancer field in the dynaset.

To exclude and include a field in a dynaset:

1. Click the **Freelancer Show box** to remove the ×. Access will no longer show the Freelancer field in the dynaset.
2. Click the toolbar **Run button** to display the dynaset. The Freelancer field does not appear in the dynaset.
3. Click the toolbar **Design View button** to display the Query Design window.

❹ Click the **Freelancer Show box** to place the × back in the box. Access will now display the Freelancer field in the dynaset.

❺ Click the [!] to display the dynaset. The Freelancer field now appears in the dynaset.

❻ Click the [Design View] to return to the Query Design window.

Renaming Fields in a Query

Elena thinks that Phone Number would look better than Writer Phone as the dynaset column heading for this query. She could change the field name in the table structure. Instead, she renames the field in the Query Design window. You change a field name in the table structure when you want the change to be permanent and reflected throughout the database. Rename the field in the Query Design window when the name change is intended only for that query.

To rename a field in the Query Design window:

❶ Move the pointer to the beginning of the Field box in the QBE grid for Writer Phone. When the I appears on the left side of the W, click to position the insertion point there.

❷ Type **Phone Number:** to insert it before Writer Phone. See Figure 4-10. This name will now appear (without the colon) in the dynaset in place of the field name.

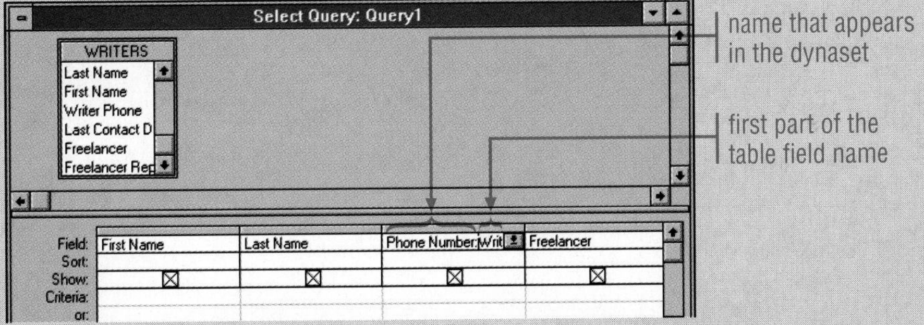

Figure 4-10 Renaming a field in a query

❸ Click the toolbar **Run button** [!]. Access displays the dynaset and shows Phone Number instead of Writer Phone.

TROUBLE? If you omit the colon, Access displays the Syntax error dialog box when you run the query. Click the OK button, insert the colon, and repeat step three.

❹ Click the toolbar **Design View button** [Design View] to switch back to the Query Design window.

After practicing with this query, Elena refers to her list of questions for her next task. She needs the Last Contact Date field for the next query, so she adds it to the QBE grid between the Phone Number and Freelancer fields.

To add a field to the QBE grid:

❶ Click **Last Contact Date** in the WRITERS field list.

❷ Drag Last Contact Date from the WRITERS field list to the Freelancer column in the QBE grid and then release the mouse button. The Last Contact Date field is now positioned between the Phone Number and the Freelancer columns.

Defining Record Selection Criteria

Elena's next few questions include showing the complete information on Valerie Hall, listing information on freelancers only, locating writers who have specific area codes, and finding which writers were last contacted prior to 1994. Unlike her first query, which selected some fields but all records from the WRITERS table, these questions ask Access to select specific records based on a condition.

A **condition** is a criterion, or rule, that determines which records are selected. For example, Elena wants records selected if they meet the condition that a writer is a freelancer. To define a condition for a field, you place in the QBE grid Criteria text box the condition for the field against which you want Access to match. To select only records for those writers who are freelancers, Elena can enter =Yes for the Freelancer field in the Criteria row of the QBE grid.

When you select records based on one condition, for a single field, you are using a **simple condition**. To form a simple condition, you enter a comparison operator and a value. A **comparison operator** asks Access to compare the relationship of two values and to select the record if the relationship is true. For example, the simple condition =Yes for the Freelancer field selects all records having Freelancer field values equal to Yes. The Access comparison operators are shown in Figure 4-11.

Operator	Meaning	Example
=	Equal to (optional, default operator)	="Hall"
<	Less than	<#1/1/94#
<=	Less than or equal to	<=100
>	Greater than	>"C400"
>=	Greater than or equal to	>=18.75
<>	Not equal to	<>"Hall"
Between...And	Between two values (inclusive)	Between 50 And 325
In ( )	In a list of values	In ("Hall", "Seeger")
Like	Matches a pattern that includes wildcards	Like "706*"

Figure 4-11
Access comparison operators

Simple conditions fit into the following categories. Do not be concerned about the details of the simple condition examples—they will be covered more thoroughly in the following sections.

- **Exact match**—selects records that have a value for the selected field exactly matching the simple condition value. To find information on freelancers, Elena will enter =Yes as the simple condition value.
- **Pattern match**—selects records that have a value for the selected field matching the pattern of the simple condition value. To find information on writers with 706 area codes, Elena will enter Like "706*" as the simple condition value.

- **List-of-values match**—selects records that have a value for the selected field matching one of two or more simple condition values. If Elena wants to obtain contact information for Valerie Hall and Wilhelm Seeger, she will enter In ("Hall","Seeger") as the simple condition value.
- **Non-matching value**—selects records that have a value for the selected field that does not match the simple condition value. To list contact information on writers having an area code other than 706, Elena will enter Not Like "706*" as the simple condition value.
- **Range-of-values match**—selects records that have a value for the selected field within a range specified in the simple condition. To find writers last contacted prior to 1994, Elena will enter <#1/1/94# as the simple condition value.

Using an Exact Match

Elena creates a query to select the complete information on Valerie Hall. She enters the simple condition ="Hall" in the Criteria text box for the Last Name field. When Elena runs the query, Access selects records that have the exact value Hall in the Last Name field. For text fields only, you need to use quotation marks around the condition value if the value contains spaces or punctuation. For text-field condition values without spaces or punctuation, the quotation marks are optional; Access inserts them automatically for you. Elena consistently uses the quotation marks for text-field condition values so that she will not accidentally omit them when they are required.

To select records that match a specific value:

1. Click the **Criteria text box** in the QBE grid for the Last Name field and then type **="Hall"**. See Figure 4-12. Access will select a record only if the Last Name field value matches Hall exactly. You can omit the equals symbol, because it is the default comparison operator automatically inserted by Access.

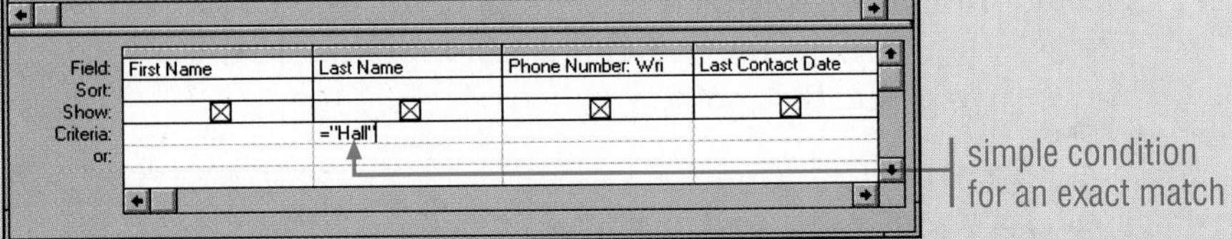

Figure 4-12
Record selection based on an exact match

2. Click the toolbar **Run button**. The dynaset appears, showing only the record for Valerie Hall.
3. Click the toolbar **Design View button** to switch back to the Query Design window.

Elena's third task is to create a query to show the names, phone numbers, last contact dates, and amounts owed for all freelancers. Before she continues her practice and enters the new condition in the QBE grid, she removes the previous condition.

To remove a previous condition from the QBE grid:

1. Click the **Criteria text box** for the Last Name field and press **[F2]** to highlight the entire condition.
2. Press **[Del]** and Access removes the previous condition.

Elena now enters the simple condition =Yes in the QBE grid for the Freelancer field. When she runs the query, Access selects records that have the value Yes for the Freelancer field.

To select records that match a specific value of a field with a yes/no data type:

1. If necessary, scroll to the right in the QBE grid to display the Freelancer column.
2. Click the **Criteria text box** in the QBE grid for the Freelancer field, and then type **=Yes** (note that you do not use quotation marks in a criterion for a yes/no data type).
3. Click the toolbar **Run button**. The dynaset appears and displays only records having the Freelancer field value Yes. See Figure 4-13.

Select Query: Query1

First Name	Last Name	Phone Number	Last Contact Date	Freelancer	Amount
Kelly	Cox	(210) 783-5415	11/14/82	Yes	$100
Leroy W.	Johnson	(210) 895-2046	1/29/91	Yes	$125
Chong	Kim	(710) 116-4683	8/27/88	Yes	$40
Diane	Epstein	(610) 349-9689	11/14/79	Yes	$30
Tonya	Nilsson	(905) 702-4082	7/9/77	Yes	$450
Wilhelm	Seeger	(706) 423-0932	12/24/93	Yes	$350
				Yes	$0

Figure 4-13 Dynaset showing records with Yes in the Freelancer field

4. Click the toolbar **Design View button** to switch back to the Query Design window.

Using a Pattern Match

The fourth question on Elena's list is to find the contact information for writers with 706 area codes. She can do this using the Like comparison operator. The **Like comparison operator** selects records by matching field values to a specific pattern that includes one or more wildcard characters—asterisk (*), question mark (?), and number symbol (#).

Elena enters the simple condition Like "706*" for the Phone Number field. Access will select records that have a Phone Number field value containing 706 in positions one through three. Any characters can appear in the last seven positions of the field value. Because the Phone Number field has an input mask, the displayed placeholder characters are not part of the field value.

To select records that match a specific pattern:

1. Click the **Criteria text box** for the Freelancer field, press **[F2]** to highlight the entire condition, and then press **[Del]** to remove the previous condition.
2. Click the **Criteria text box** in the QBE grid for the Phone Number field and then type **Like "706*"**. See Figure 4-14. Note that Access will automatically add Like and the quotation marks to the simple condition if you omit them.

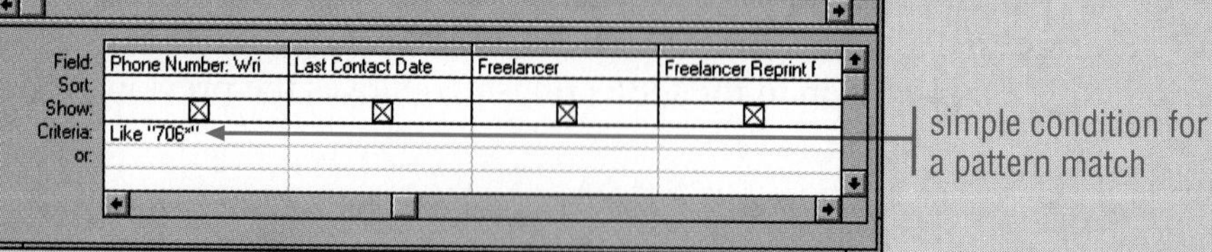

Figure 4-14 Record selection based on matching a specific pattern

3. Click the toolbar **Run button** [!]. The dynaset appears and displays the two records having the area code 706.
4. Click the toolbar **Design View button** to switch back to the Query Design window.

Using a List-of-Values Match

Elena's next task is to find the contact information for Valerie Hall and Wilhelm Seeger. She uses the In comparison operator to create the condition. The **In comparison operator** allows you to define a condition with two or more values. If a record's field value matches one value from the list of values, Access selects that record.

Elena wants records selected if the Last Name field value is equal to Hall or to Seeger. These are the values she will use with the In comparison operator. The simple condition she enters is: In ("hall","Seeger"). Because matching is not case-sensitive, Hall and HALL and other variations will also match. Notice that when you make a list of values, you place them inside parentheses.

To select records having a field value that matches a value in a list of values:

1. Click the **Criteria text box** for the Phone Number field, press **[F2]** to highlight the entire condition, and then press **[Del]** to remove the previous condition.
2. Scroll left in the QBE grid if necessary to display the Last Name column. Click the **Criteria text box** for the Last Name field and then type **In ("hall","Seeger")**. See Figure 4-15.

Figure 4-15 Record selection based on matching field values to a list of values

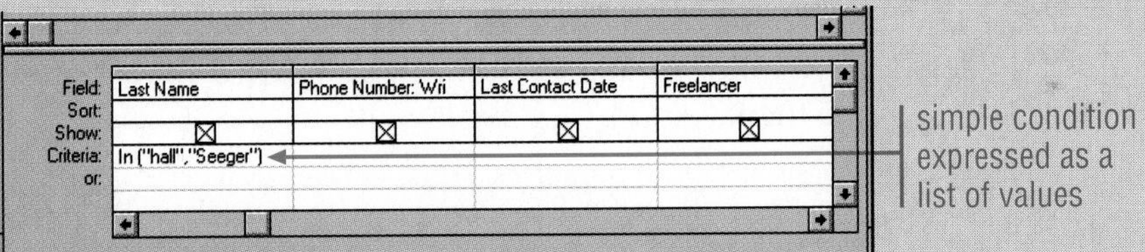

3. Click the toolbar **Run button** [!]. The dynaset appears and displays the two records having hall or Seeger in the Last Name field.
4. Click the toolbar **Design View button** to switch back to the Query Design window.

Using a Non-Matching Value

Elena now needs to find all writers who do not have 706 area codes. She uses a combination of the Like comparison operator and the Not logical operator. The **Not logical operator** allows you to find records that do not match a value. If Elena wants to find all records that do not have Hall in the Last Name field, for example, her condition is Not ="Hall".

Elena enters the simple condition Not Like "706*" in the Phone Number field to select writers who do not have 706 area codes.

To select records having a field value that does not match a specific pattern:

1. Click the **Criteria text box** for the Last Name field, press **[F2]** to highlight the entire condition, and then press **[Del]** to remove the previous condition.
2. Click the **Criteria text box** for the Phone Number field and then type **Not Like "706*"**. See Figure 4-16. Access will select a record only if the Phone Number field value does not have a 706 area code.

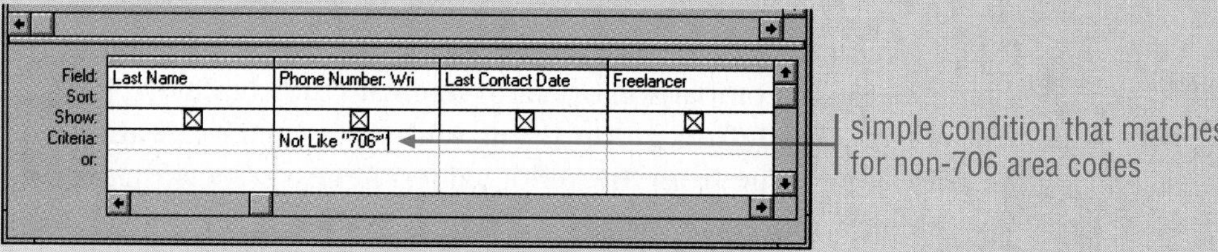

Figure 4-16 Record selection based on not matching a specific pattern

3. Click the toolbar **Datasheet View button**. The dynaset appears and displays only those records having a Phone Number field value that does not have a 706 area code.
4. Click the toolbar **Design View button** to switch back to the Query Design window.

Matching a Range of Values

Elena next finds all writers who were last contacted prior to 1994. She uses the less than (<) comparison operator with a date value of 1/1/94 and enters <#1/1/94# as the simple condition. Access will select records that have, in the Last Contact Date field, a date anywhere in the range of dates prior to January 1, 1994. You place date and time values inside number symbols (#). If you omit the number symbols, however, Access will automatically include them.

To select records having a field value in a range of values:

1. Click the **Criteria text box** for the Phone Number field, press **[F2]** to highlight the entire condition, and then press **[Del]** to remove the previous condition.
2. Click the **Criteria text box** for the Last Contact Date field and then type **<#1/1/94#**. See Figure 4-17. Access will select a record only if the Last Contact Date field value is in the range of dates prior to January 1, 1994.

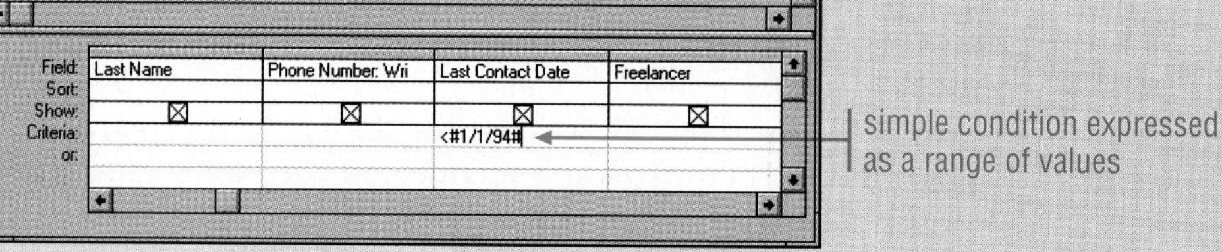

Figure 4-17 Record selection based on matching a value to a range of values

❸ Click the toolbar **Datasheet View button**. The dynaset appears and displays only those records having a Last Contact Date field value prior to 1994. See Figure 4-18.

Select Query: Query1

First Name	Last Name	Phone Number	Last Contact Date	Freelancer	Amount
Kelly	Cox	(210) 783-5415	11/14/82	Yes	$100
Leroy W.	Johnson	(210) 895-2046	1/29/91	Yes	$125
Chong	Kim	(710) 116-4683	8/27/88	Yes	$40
Kristine	Waldeck	(917) 361-8181	4/1/86	No	$0
Shinjiro	Yamamura	(905) 551-1293	9/26/72	No	$0
Diane	Epstein	(610) 349-9689	11/14/79	Yes	$30
Tonya	Nilsson	(905) 702-4082	7/9/77	Yes	$450
Wilhelm	Seeger	(706) 423-0932	12/24/93	Yes	$350
				Yes	$0

Figure 4-18 Selected records for writers last contacted prior to 1994

❹ Click the toolbar **Design View button** to switch back to the Query Design window.

As Elena finishes her query, Harold stops by to remind her of a meeting with the marketing staff. Elena quickly closes the Query Design window without saving the query.

To close the Query Design window without saving the query:

❶ Double-click the Query Design window **Control menu box**. The "Save changes to Query 'Query1'?" dialog box appears. See Figure 4-19.

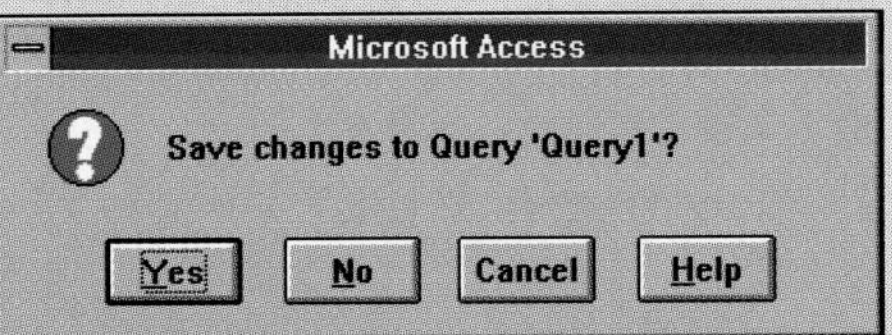

Figure 4-19 The "Save changes to Query 'Query1'?" dialog box

❷ Click the **No button**. Access closes the Query Design window without saving the query.

If you want to take a break and resume the tutorial at a later time, you can exit Access by double-clicking the Microsoft Access window Control menu box. When you resume the tutorial, place your Student Disk in the appropriate drive, launch Access, open the Issue25 database on your Student Disk, and click the WRITERS table.

■ ■ ■

Sorting Data

After the meeting, Elena resumes work on the Issue25 database queries. The next item on her list of questions asks for staff writers and freelancers in order by last contact date. Because the WRITERS table displays records in WRITER ID, or primary-key, sequence, Elena will need to sort records from the table to produce the requested information.

When you sort records from a table, Access does not change the sequence of records in the underlying table. Only the records in the dynaset are rearranged according to your specifications.

Sorting a Single Field

You sort records in an Access query by selecting one or more fields to be sort keys in the QBE grid. Elena chooses the Last Contact Date field to be the sort key for her next query. Because her last Access task was to return to the Database window, she first opens the Query Design window. Elena then adds all the fields from the WRITERS table to the QBE grid.

To start a new query for a single table:

1. Click the toolbar **New Query button** to open the New Query dialog box.
2. Click the **New Query button** in the New Query dialog box. Access opens the Query Design window.
3. Double-click the **title bar** of the WRITERS field list to highlight all the fields in the table.
4. Click and hold the mouse button anywhere in the highlighted area of the WRITERS field list.
5. Drag the pointer to the QBE grid's first column Field text box and release the mouse button when the pointer changes to . Access adds all the fields from the WRITERS table to separate boxes in the QBE grid.

Elena now selects the Last Contact Date field to be the sort key.

REFERENCE WINDOW

Selecting a Sort Key in the Query Window

- Click the Sort text box for the field designated as the sort key.
- Click the down arrow button on the right side of the Sort text box to display the Sort list.
- Click Ascending or Descending from the Sort list. The Sort list disappears, and Access displays the selected sort order in the Sort text box.

Elena decides a descending sort order for the Last Contact Date will be the best way to display the query results, and she now selects the sort key and its sort order. She does this by clicking the Sort text box for the last Contact Date column in the QBE grid. Access then displays a down arrow button on the right side of the text box. The text box has changed into a drop-down list box. Clicking the down arrow button displays the contents of the drop-down list box.

In most cases, you can use a quicker method to display the contents of the drop-down list box. If you click the text box near the right side, Access displays both the down arrow button and the contents of the drop-down list box.

To select a sort key and view a sorted dynaset:

1. If necessary, scroll right in the QBE grid to display the Last Contact Date column. Click the **Sort text box** in the QBE grid for the Last Contact Date field to position the insertion point there. A down arrow button appears on the right side of the Sort text box.
2. Click the **down arrow button** in the Sort text box. Access displays the Sort list. See Figure 4-20.

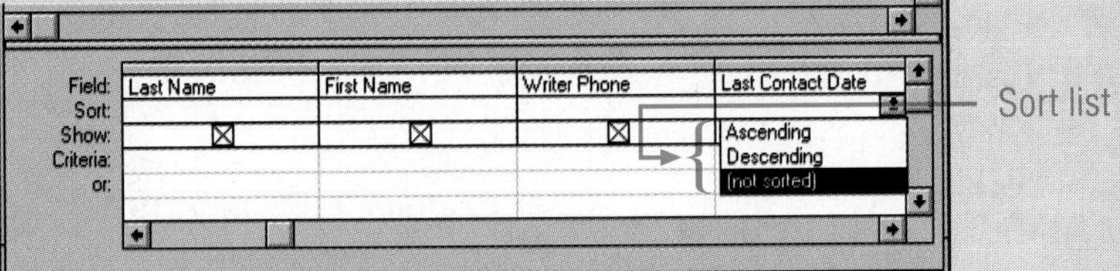

Figure 4-20 Specifying the sort order for the Last Contact Date field

3. Click **Descending** in the Sort list. The Sort list disappears, and Descending appears in the Sort text box as the selected sort order.
4. Click the toolbar **Run button** [!]. The dynaset appears and displays all the fields of the WRITERS table and all its records in descending order by last contact date. See Figure 4-21. Notice that Writer Phone appears in the column heading box instead of Phone Number. Recall that Writer Phone is the table field name that appears in a dynaset unless you rename the field in the Query window.

Select Query: Query1

Writer ID	Last Name	First Name	Writer Phone	Last Contact Date	Freelancer	Amount
N200	Ngo	Thuy	(706) 636-0046	3/6/95	No	$0
L130	Leavitt	Morris	(810) 270-2927	3/6/95	No	$0
C500	Cohen	Julia Rice	(905) 338-1875	2/28/95	No	$0
M635	Martinez	Santos	(610) 502-8244	1/18/95	No	$0
H400	Hall	Valerie	(710) 918-7767	9/16/94	No	$0
K500	Kim	Chong	(917) 729-5364	5/19/94	No	$0
S260	Seeger	Wilhelm	(706) 423-0932	12/24/93	Yes	$350
J525	Johnson	Leroy W.	(210) 895-2046	1/29/91	Yes	$125
K501	Kim	Chong	(710) 116-4683	8/27/88	Yes	$40
W432	Waldeck	Kristine	(917) 361-8181	4/1/86	No	$0
C200	Cox	Kelly	(210) 783-5415	11/14/82	Yes	$100
E235	Epstein	Diane	(610) 349-9689	11/14/79	Yes	$30
N425	Nilsson	Tonya	(905) 702-4082	7/9/77	Yes	$450
Y556	Yamamura	Shinjiro	(905) 551-1293	9/26/72	No	$0
*					Yes	$0

Record: 1 of 14

sort key

Figure 4-21 Records sorted in descending order based on last contact date

Elena studies the dynaset, rereads the question that the new query is supposed to answer, and realizes that her sort is incorrect. The question (Who are the staff writers and who are the freelancers, arranged in order by last contact date?) requires two sort keys. Elena needs to select Freelancer as the primary sort key and Last Contact Date as the secondary sort key.

Sorting Multiple Fields

Access allows you to select up to 10 different sort keys. When you have two or more sort keys, Access first uses the sort key that is leftmost in the QBE grid. Therefore, you must arrange the fields you want to sort from left to right in the QBE grid with the primary sort key being the leftmost sort-key field.

The Freelancer field appears to the right of the Last Contact Date field in the QBE grid. Because the Freelancer field is the primary sort key, Elena must move it to the left of the Last Contact Date field.

To move a field in the QBE grid:

1. If necessary, click the toolbar **Design View button** to switch back to the Query Design window.
2. Click the QBE grid horizontal scroll bar **right arrow button** until the Last Contact Date and Freelancer fields are visible.
3. Click the **Freelancer field selector** to highlight the entire column.
4. Click the **Freelancer field selector** again and drag the pointer, which appears as , to the left. When the pointer is anywhere in the Last Contact Date column, release the mouse button. Access moves the Freelancer field one column to the left.

Elena previously selected the Last Contact Date field to be a sort key and it is still in effect. She now chooses the appropriate sort order for the Freelancer field. Elena wants staff writers to appear first in the query, and they are identified in the Freelancer field by a value of No. Thus, Elena uses descending sort order for the Freelancer field so that all No values appear first. The Freelancer field will serve as the primary sort key because it is to the left of the Last Contact Date field, which will be the secondary sort key.

To select a sort key:

1. Click the **Sort text box** in the QBE grid for the Freelancer field to position the insertion point there. A down arrow button appears on the right side of the Sort text box.
2. Click the **down arrow button** in the Sort text box. Access displays the Sort list.
3. Click **Descending** in the Sort list. The Sort list disappears, and Descending appears in the Sort text box as the selected sort order. See Figure 4-22.

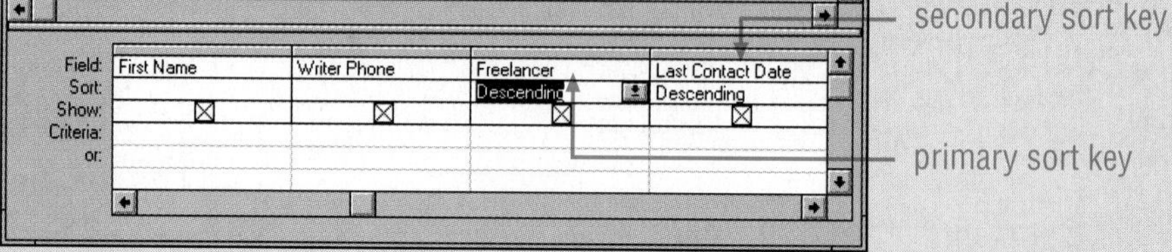

Figure 4-22 Sort orders specified for two fields

4. Click the toolbar **Run button** . The dynaset appears and displays all the fields of the WRITERS table and all its records, in descending order, based on the Freelancer field. Within the two groups of records that have the same Freelancer field value (No and Yes), the records are in descending order by last contact date. See Figure 4-23.

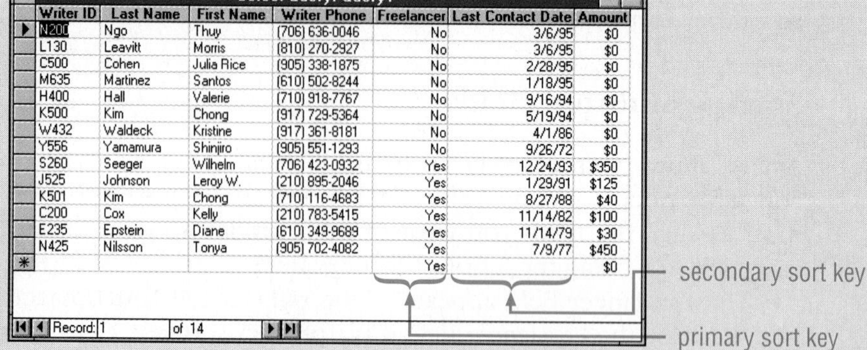

Select Query: Query1

Writer ID	Last Name	First Name	Writer Phone	Freelancer	Last Contact Date	Amount
N200	Ngo	Thuy	(706) 636-0046	No	3/6/95	$0
L130	Leavitt	Morris	(810) 270-2927	No	3/6/95	$0
C500	Cohen	Julia Rice	(905) 338-1875	No	2/28/95	$0
M635	Martinez	Santos	(610) 502-8244	No	1/18/95	$0
H400	Hall	Valerie	(710) 918-7767	No	9/16/94	$0
K500	Kim	Chong	(917) 729-5364	No	5/19/94	$0
W432	Waldeck	Kristine	(917) 361-8181	No	4/1/86	$0
Y556	Yamamura	Shinjiro	(905) 551-1293	No	9/26/72	$0
S260	Seeger	Wilhelm	(706) 423-0932	Yes	12/24/93	$350
J525	Johnson	Leroy W.	(210) 895-2046	Yes	1/29/91	$125
K501	Kim	Chong	(710) 116-4683	Yes	8/27/88	$40
C200	Cox	Kelly	(210) 783-5415	Yes	11/14/82	$100
E235	Epstein	Diane	(610) 349-9689	Yes	11/14/79	$30
N425	Nilsson	Tonya	(905) 702-4082	Yes	7/9/77	$450
*				Yes		$0

Record: 1 of 14

Figure 4-23 Dynaset sorted on two fields

Printing a Dynaset Selection

Next, Elena prints the dynaset. Rather than print the staff writers and freelancers together, however, she prints just the staff writers and then just the freelancers. Elena could change the query to select one group, run the query, print the dynaset, and then repeat the process for the other group. Instead, she selects one group in the dynaset, prints the dynaset selection, and then does the same for the other group. She uses this method because it is faster than changing the query.

To print a dynaset selection:

❶ Click the record selector for the first dynaset record and, while holding the mouse button, drag the pointer to the record selector of the last record that has a No value in the Freelancer field. Release the button. The group of records with Freelancer field values of No is highlighted. See Figure 4-24.

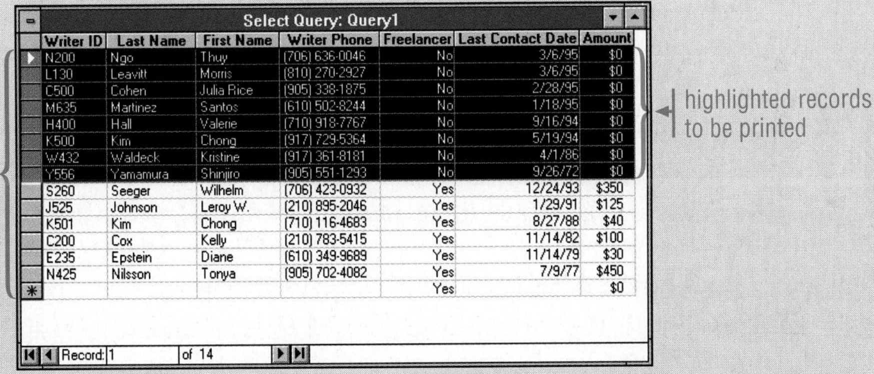

Select Query: Query1

Writer ID	Last Name	First Name	Writer Phone	Freelancer	Last Contact Date	Amount
N200	Ngo	Thuy	(706) 636-0046	No	3/6/95	$0
L130	Leavitt	Morris	(810) 270-2927	No	3/6/95	$0
C500	Cohen	Julia Rice	(905) 338-1875	No	2/28/95	$0
M635	Martinez	Santos	(610) 502-8244	No	1/18/95	$0
H400	Hall	Valerie	(710) 918-7767	No	9/16/94	$0
K500	Kim	Chong	(917) 729-5364	No	5/19/94	$0
W432	Waldeck	Kristine	(917) 361-8181	No	4/1/86	$0
Y556	Yamamura	Shinjiro	(905) 551-1293	No	9/26/72	$0
S260	Seeger	Wilhelm	(706) 423-0932	Yes	12/24/93	$350
J525	Johnson	Leroy W.	(210) 895-2046	Yes	1/29/91	$125
K501	Kim	Chong	(710) 116-4683	Yes	8/27/88	$40
C200	Cox	Kelly	(210) 783-5415	Yes	11/14/82	$100
E235	Epstein	Diane	(610) 349-9689	Yes	11/14/79	$30
N425	Nilsson	Tonya	(905) 702-4082	Yes	7/9/77	$450
*				Yes		$0

Record: 1 of 14

Figure 4-24 Dynaset records selected for printing

❷ Click the toolbar **Print button** to open the Print dialog box.

❸ Make sure your printer is on-line and ready to print.

❹ Check the Printer section of the Print dialog box to make sure that your computer's printer is selected.

❺ Click the **Selection radio button** to print just those records that are highlighted in the dynaset. See Figure 4-25.

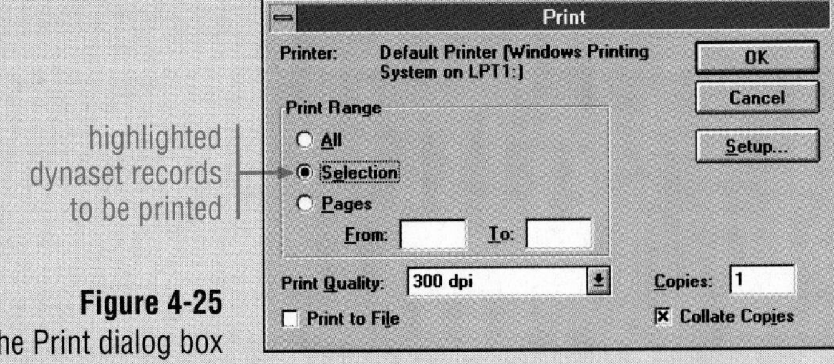

Figure 4-25 The Print dialog box

❻ Click the **OK button** to initiate printing. After the printing dialog box disappears, you are returned to the dynaset.

Saving a Query

Elena saves the query, so that she and others can open and run it again in the future.

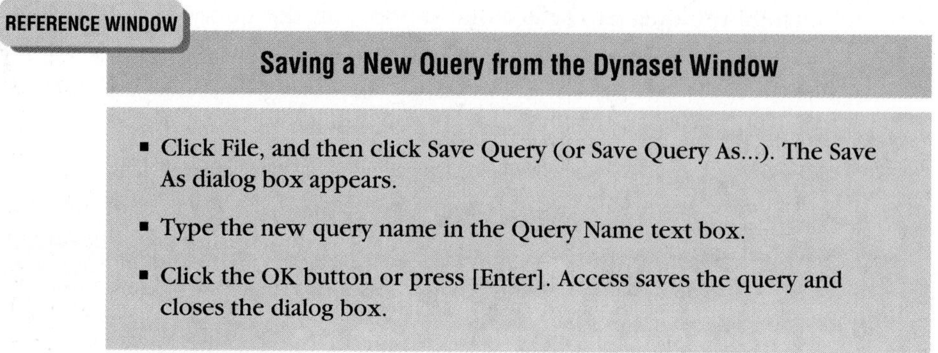

REFERENCE WINDOW

Saving a New Query from the Dynaset Window

- Click File, and then click Save Query (or Save Query As...). The Save As dialog box appears.
- Type the new query name in the Query Name text box.
- Click the OK button or press [Enter]. Access saves the query and closes the dialog box.

Elena saves the query using the name "WRITERS sorted by Freelancer, Last Contact Date."

To save a new query:

1. Click **File**, and then click **Save Query**. The Save As dialog box appears.

   TROUBLE? If the options in the File menu are Save and Save As..., then you are saving from the Query Design window. Click Save and continue with the next step.

2. Type **WRITERS sorted by Freelancer, Last Contact Date**.
3. Press **[Enter]**. The Save As dialog box disappears, and Access saves the query for later use.
4. Double-click the dynaset **Control menu box**. The dynaset disappears, and the Database window becomes the active window.
5. Click the **Query object button** and then click the **Database window maximize button**. Access displays the newly saved query in the Queries list box. See Figure 4-26.

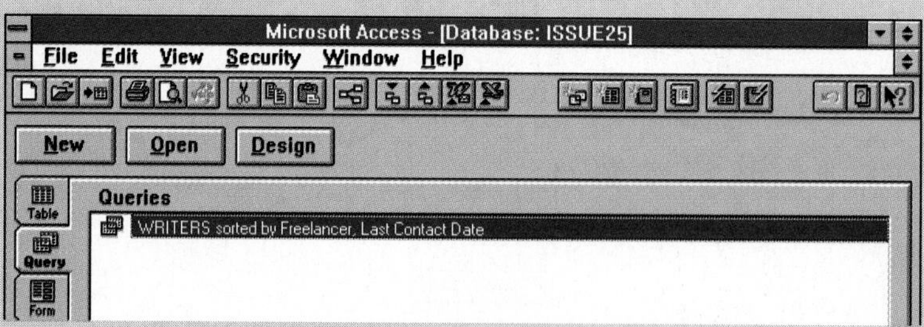

Figure 4-26
Query listed in the Database window

You can use a similar procedure to save a query from the Query Design window. In the Query Design window, the options on the File menu are Save and Save As.... If you try to close either the Query Design window or the dynaset without saving the query, Access displays a dialog box asking if you want to save the query. If you click Yes, Access displays the Save As dialog box.

If you want to take a break and resume the tutorial at a later time, you can exit Access by double-clicking the Microsoft Access window Control menu box. When you resume the tutorial, place your Student Disk in the appropriate drive, launch Access, open the Issue25 database on your Student Disk, maximize the Database window, and click the Query object button.

■ ■ ■

Opening a Query

Elena decides to use her saved query as a starting point for the next question on her list. She opens the saved query and then changes its design for the next query.

REFERENCE WINDOW

Opening a Saved Query

- Click the Query object button to display the Queries list box in the Database window.
- To view the query dynaset, either click the query name and then click the Open command button or double-click the left mouse button on the query name.
- Click the query name and then click the Design command button to open the Query Design window. You can change the query design in this window.

Let's open the Query Design window for the query saved with the name "WRITERS sorted by Freelancer, Last Contact Date."

To open a saved query to change its design:

1. If the Query object button is not selected, click it to display the Queries list box. The most recently saved query is highlighted in the Queries list box. In this case, there is only one saved query.
2. Click the **Design command button**. The Query Design window appears with the saved query on the screen.

Defining Multiple Selection Criteria

Elena's next task is to find all freelancers who were last contacted prior to 1990. This query involves two conditions.

Multiple conditions require you to use **logical operators** to combine two or more simple conditions. When you want a record selected only if two or more conditions are met, then you need to use the **And logical operator**. For an Access query, you use the And logical operator when you place two or more simple conditions in the same Criteria row of the QBE grid. If a record meets every one of the conditions in the Criteria row, then Access selects the record.

If you place multiple conditions in different Criteria rows, Access selects a record if at least one of the conditions is satisfied. If none of the conditions is satisfied, then Access does not select the record. This is known as the **Or logical operator**. The difference between the two logical operators is illustrated in Figure 4-27.

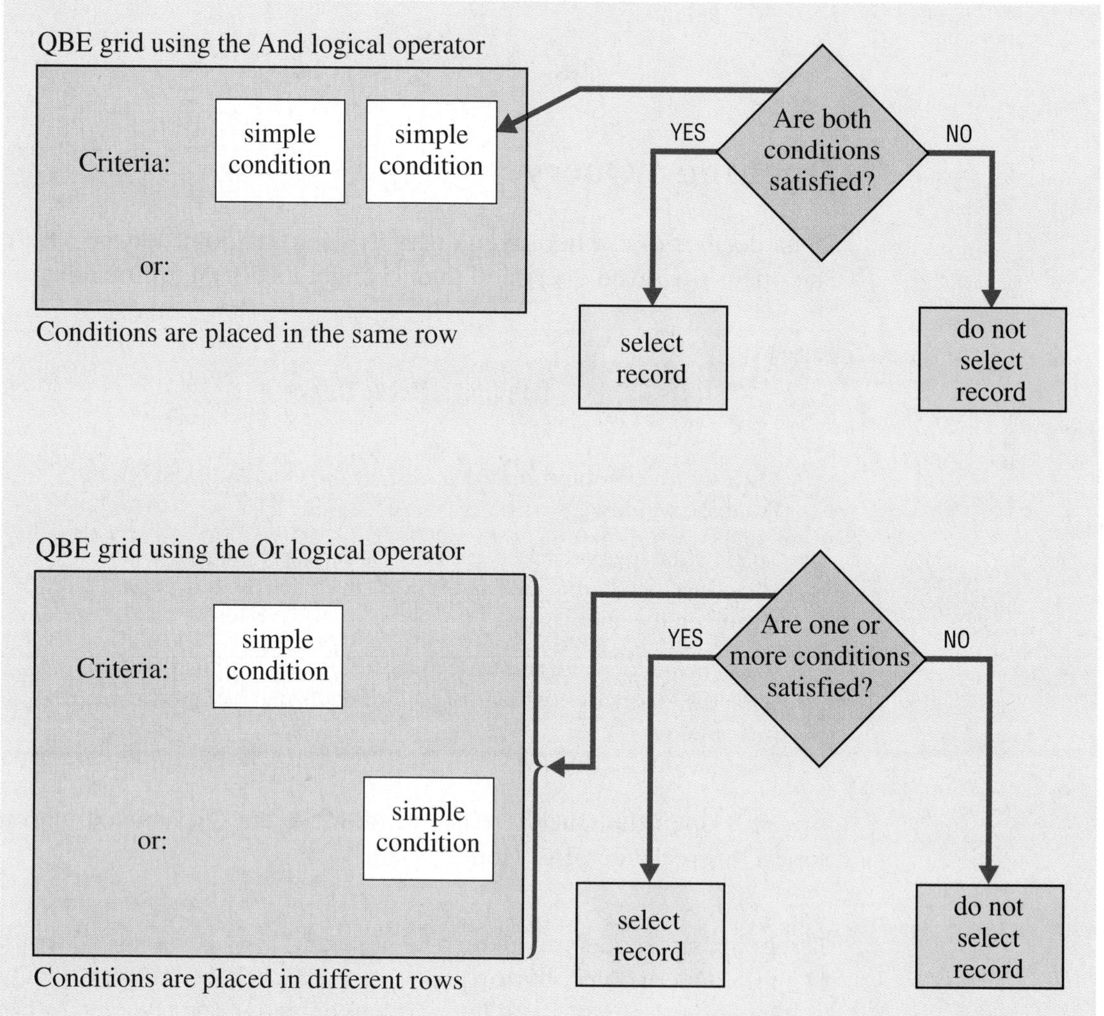

Figure 4-27 Logical operators And and Or for multiple selection criteria

The use of the word "and" in a question is usually a clue that you should use the And logical operator. The word "or" in a question usually means that you should use the Or logical operator.

The And Logical Operator

Elena will use the And logical operator and enter conditions for the Freelancer field and the Last Contact Date field in the same Criteria row. She will enter =Yes as the condition for the Freelancer field and <#1/1/90# as the condition for the Last Contact Date field. Because the conditions appear in the same Criteria row, Access selects records only if both conditions are met.

Elena's new query does not need sort keys, so Elena removes the sort keys for the Freelancer and Last Contact Date fields.

To remove sort keys from the QBE grid:

1. Click the **Sort text box** in the Freelancer column and then click the **down arrow button**. Access displays the Sort list.
2. Click **(not sorted)** in the Sort list. The Sort list disappears, and Access removes the sort order from the Sort text box.
3. If necessary, scroll to the right in the QBE grid until the Last Contact Date column appears. Click the **Sort text box** in the Last Contact Date column and then click the **down arrow button**. Access displays the Sort list.
4. Click **(not sorted)** in the Sort list. The Sort list disappears, and Access clears the sort order from the Sort text box.

Elena now enters the two conditions.

To select records using the And logical operator:

1. Click the **Freelancer Criteria text box** and then type **=Yes**.
2. Click the **Last Contact Date Criteria text box** and then type **<#1/1/90#**. See Figure 4-28. Access will select a record only if both conditions are met.

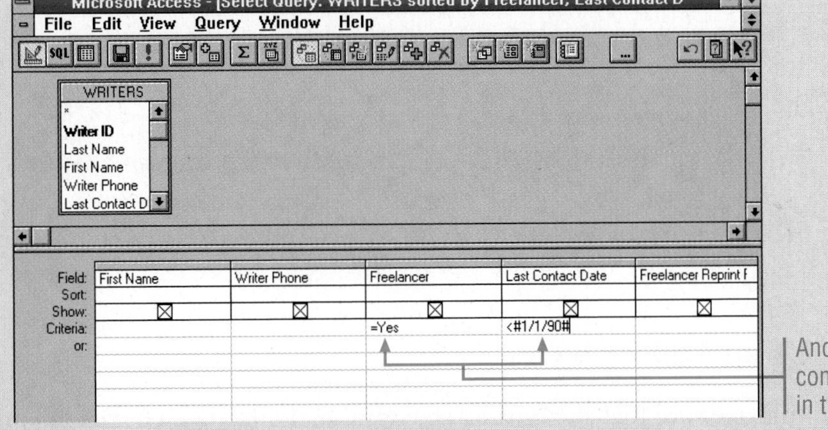

Figure 4-28 Criteria to find freelancers last contacted prior to 1990

3. Click the toolbar **Run button**. The dynaset appears and displays only records for freelancers last contacted prior to 1990.
4. Click the toolbar **Design View button** to switch back to the Query Design window.

The Or Logical Operator

Elena's next query asks for those writers who have 210 or 706 area codes. For this query, Elena uses the Or logical operator and enters conditions for the Writer Phone field in two different Criteria rows. She will enter Like "210*" in one row and Like "706*" in another row. Because the conditions appear in different Criteria rows, Access selects records if either condition is satisfied. The Or logical operator used in one field is similar to the In comparison operator.

To select records using the Or logical operator:

1. Move the pointer to the left side of the Criteria text box for the first column and click when the pointer changes to ➡. Access highlights the entire Criteria row.
2. Click the right mouse button in the first column's Criteria text box to display the Shortcut menu. Click **Cut** to remove the previous conditions from the QBE grid.

   TROUBLE? If the Shortcut menu does not appear, you clicked too far from the point where you originally clicked in Step 1. Repeat Step 1 and, without moving the mouse pointer, click the right mouse button once again.
3. Click the **Criteria text box** in the Writer Phone column and then type **Like "210*"**.
4. Click the **Criteria text box** below the one you just used and type **Like "706*"**. See Figure 4-29. Access will select a record if either condition is met.

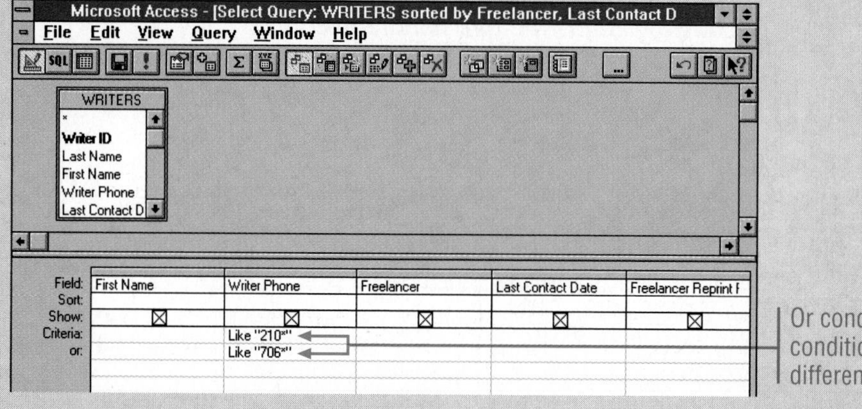

Figure 4-29 Criteria to find writers with 210 or 706 area codes

5. Click the toolbar **Run button** [!]. The dynaset appears and displays just those records for writers with 210 or 706 area codes.
6. Click the toolbar **Design View button** to switch back to the Query Design window.

Using And with Or

To make sure that she created the right query, Elena rechecks the question on her list and discovers she misread it. She really should be selecting records for freelancers who have 210 or 706 area codes. In other words, she really wants writers who are freelancers and have 210 area codes, or who are freelancers and have 706 area codes. To form this query, she needs to add the =Yes condition for the Freelancer field to both rows that already contain the Writer Phone conditions. Access will select a record if either And condition is met. Only freelancers will be selected, but only if their area codes are 210 or 706.

Elena adds the Freelancer conditions to the QBE grid to complete her new query.

To select records using the And logical operator with the Or logical operator:

1. Click the **Criteria text box** in the Freelancer column and then type **=Yes**.
2. Press [↓] and then type **=Yes**. See Figure 4-30. Access will select a record if either And condition is met.

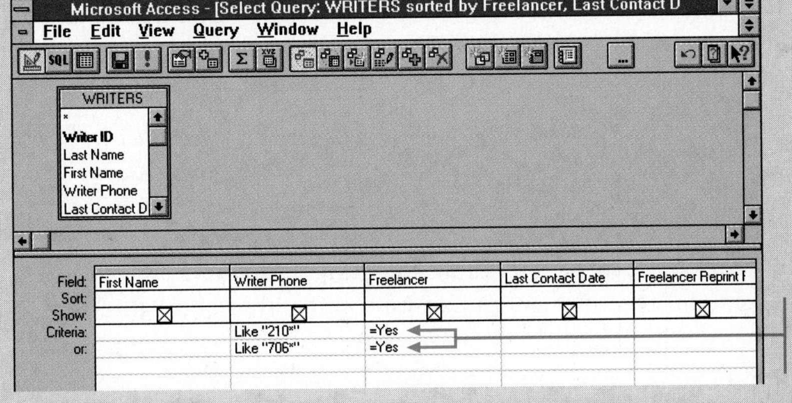

Figure 4-30
Criteria to find freelancers who have 210 or 706 area codes

3. Click the toolbar **Run button**. The dynaset appears and displays only records for freelancers with 210 or 706 area codes. See Figure 4-31.

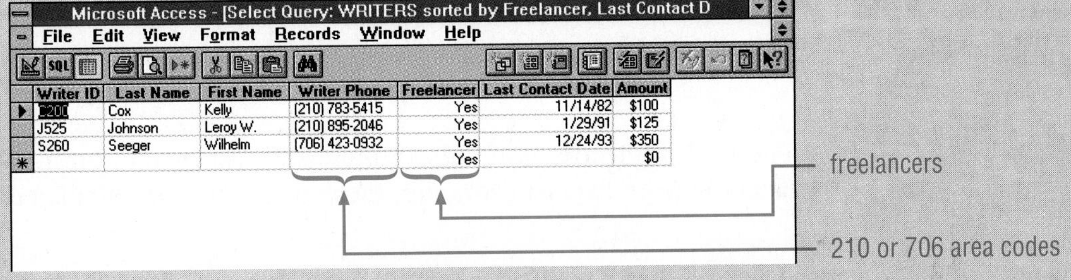

Writer ID	Last Name	First Name	Writer Phone	Freelancer	Last Contact Date	Amount
C200	Cox	Kelly	(210) 783-5415	Yes	11/14/82	$100
J525	Johnson	Leroy W.	(210) 895-2046	Yes	1/29/91	$125
S260	Seeger	Wilhelm	(706) 423-0932	Yes	12/24/93	$350
				Yes		$0

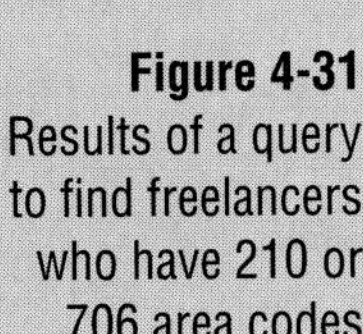

Figure 4-31
Results of a query to find freelancers who have 210 or 706 area codes

4. Click the toolbar **Design View button** to switch back to the Query Design window.

Performing Calculations

Elena's next task is to find the impact of giving all writers an extra $50. This query requires the addition of a calculated field in the QBE grid.

A **calculated field** is a new field that exists in a dynaset but does not exist in a database. The value of a calculated field is determined from fields that are in a database. You can define a calculated field in a query. When you run the query, Access determines the value for the calculated field. You perform your calculations using number, currency, or date/time fields from your database. Among the arithmetic operators you can use are those for addition (+), subtraction (–), multiplication (*), and division (/).

Using Calculated Fields

Elena creates a calculated field that adds 50 to the amount stored in the Freelancer Reprint Payment Amount field. Whenever a calculation includes a field name, you place brackets around the name to tell Access that the name is from your database. Elena's calculation, for example, will be expressed as [Freelancer Reprint Payment Amount]+50. Access supplies the default name Expr1 for your first calculated field, but you can change the name at any time. Elena uses Add50 as the name for the calculated field. Because the Field text box is too small to show the entire calculated field, Elena uses the Zoom box while she enters the calculated field. The **Zoom box** is a large text box for entering text or other values. You open the zoom box either by pressing [Shift][F2] or by using the Shortcut menu.

The new query will select all records in the WRITERS table, so Elena first removes the conditions in the two Criteria rows. At the same time, she decides to simplify the query by deleting three fields: Writer ID, Writer Phone, and Last Contact Date.

To remove conditions and delete fields from the QBE grid:

1. Move the pointer to the left side of the Criteria text box for the first column. The pointer changes to ➡. Click and, while holding the mouse button, drag the pointer down to the next row before releasing the mouse button. The two rows are highlighted. Click the right mouse button in either highlighted row to display the Shortcut menu and click **Cut** to remove the previous conditions from the QBE grid.
2. Scroll to make the Writer ID column visible. Move the pointer to the Writer ID field selector and then click it to highlight the entire column. Click the right mouse button in the Writer ID field selector to display the Shortcut menu and click **Cut** to delete the column.
3. In a similar manner, delete the Writer Phone and Last Contact Date columns in the QBE grid.

The QBE grid now contains four fields: Last Name, First Name, Freelancer, and Freelancer Reprint Payment Amount. Elena next adds the calculated field.

To add a calculated field to the QBE grid and run the query:

1. Click the right mouse button in the Field text box for the first unused column to open the Shortcut menu.
2. Click **Zoom...** to open the Zoom box.
3. Type **Add50:[Freelancer Reprint Payment Amount]+50**. See Figure 4-32.

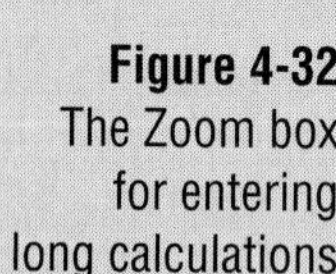

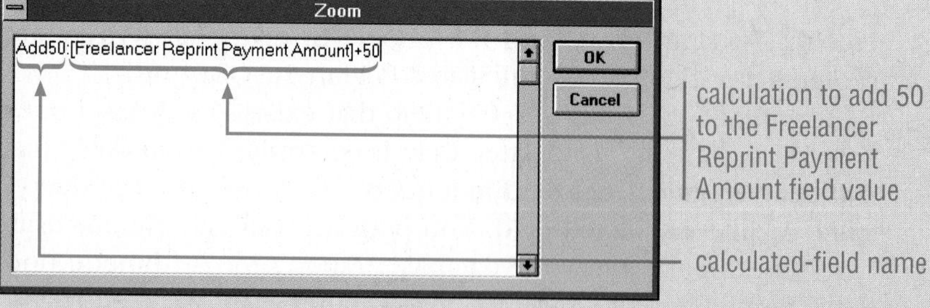

Figure 4-32 The Zoom box for entering long calculations

4. Click the **OK button**. The Zoom box disappears.

❺ Click the toolbar **Run button** [!]. The dynaset displays all records in the WRITERS table and includes the new calculated field. See Figure 4-33.

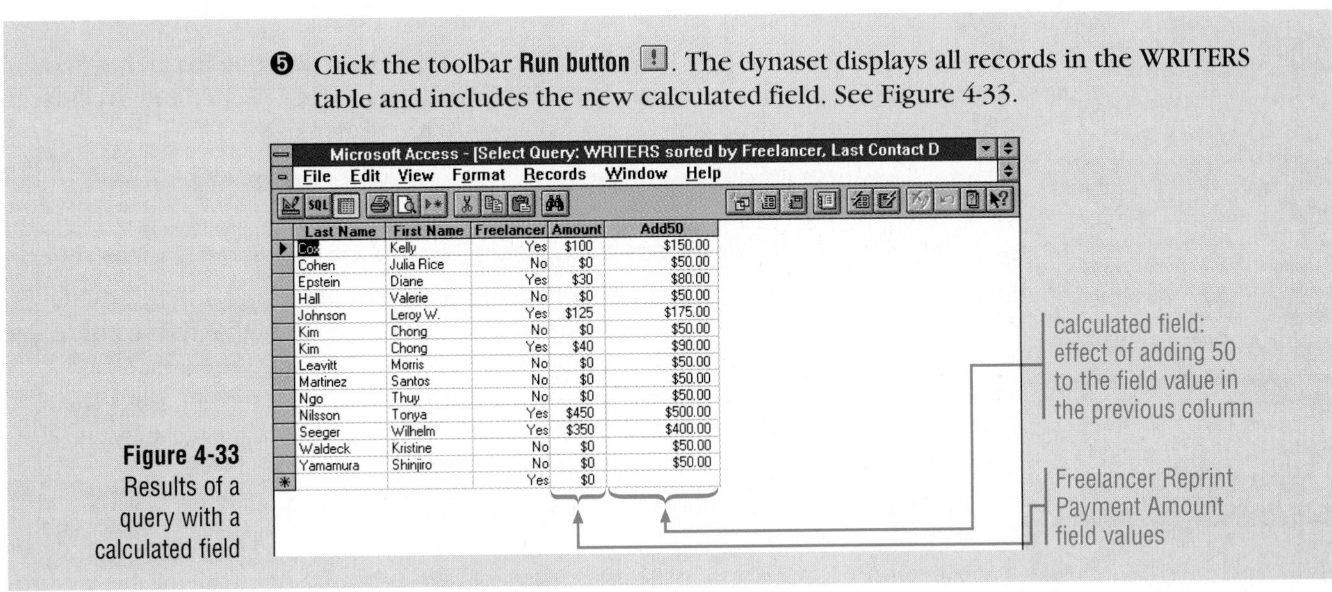

Figure 4-33 Results of a query with a calculated field

The calculated field values in the new Add50 column are $50 more than those in the Amount column, which is the Caption property name for the Freelancer Reprint Payment Amount field.

Using Record Calculations

Elena must now find both the total cost and the average cost per writer, with and without the extra $50. For this query, she uses aggregate functions. **Aggregate functions** perform arithmetic operations on the records in a database. The most frequently used aggregate functions are shown in Figure 4-34. Aggregate functions operate upon the records that meet a query's selection criteria. You specify an aggregate function for a specific field, and the appropriate operation applies to that field's values for the selected records.

Function	Meaning
Avg	Average of the field values for the selected records
Count	Number of records selected
Min	Lowest field value for the selected records
Max	Highest field value for the selected records
Sum	Total of the field values for the selected records

Figure 4-34 Frequently used aggregate functions

Elena uses the Sum and Avg aggregate functions for both the Freelancer Reprint Payment Amount field and for the calculated field she just created in her previous query. The Sum aggregate function gives the total of the field values, and the Avg aggregate function gives the average of the field values. Elena's query result will be a dynaset with one record displaying the four requested aggregate function values.

To use aggregate functions in the Query Design window, you click the toolbar Totals button. Access inserts a Total row between the Field and Sort rows in the QBE grid. You specify the aggregate functions you want to use in the Total row. When you run the query, one record appears in the dynaset with your selected aggregate function values. The individual table records themselves do not appear.

Elena does not need any fields other than the Freelancer Reprint Payment Amount field and the calculated field, so she deletes the Last Name, First Name, and Freelancer fields. She then restores the Query Design window to its smaller size.

To delete fields from the QBE grid:

1. Click the toolbar **Design View button** to switch back to the Query Design window.
2. If necessary, scroll to make the Last Name, First Name, and Freelancer fields visible. Move the pointer to the Last Name field selector. Then click to highlight the entire column, hold the mouse button, drag the pointer to the right until the First Name and Freelancer fields are also highlighted, and release the mouse button. Click the right mouse button in the field selector for one of these three fields to display the Shortcut menu, and click **Cut** to delete the three columns.

   TROUBLE? If the fields are not side by side, delete one column and then the others in separate steps.
3. Click the Query Design window **restore button**, which is on the right side of the menu bar.

Elena now has two fields left in the QBE grid: the Freelancer Reprint Payment Amount field and the Add50 calculated field. She needs two columns for each of these: one for a Sum aggregate function, and the other for an Avg aggregate function. The four columns will allow her to find the total cost and average cost per writer with and without the extra $50. She inserts a second copy of the Freelancer Reprint Payment Amount field in the QBE grid. She then renames the first Freelancer Reprint Payment Amount field AmountSum and the second AmountAvg. She likewise makes a second copy of the Add50 calculated field and renames the first one Add50Sum and the second Add50Avg.

First Elena adds the copy of the Freelancer Reprint Payment Amount field to the QBE grid and renames all three fields.

To add and rename fields in the QBE grid:

1. If necessary, scroll to the left to make both fields visible in the QBE grid. Click **Freelancer Reprint Payment Amount** in the WRITERS field list, drag it to the Add50 calculated field column in the QBE grid, and then release the mouse button. The three fields in the QBE grid, from left to right, are Freelancer Reprint Payment Amount, Freelancer Reprint Payment Amount, and Add50.
2. Click the beginning of the Field box for the first Freelancer Reprint Payment Amount field and type **AmountSum:**.
3. Click the beginning of the Field box for the second Freelancer Reprint Payment Amount field and type **AmountAvg:**.
4. Click just before the colon in the Field box for the Add50 calculated field and type **Sum**. The name of the calculated field is now Add50Sum.

Elena next selects aggregate functions for these three fields.

To select aggregate functions:

❶ Click the **Totals button** on the toolbar. The Total row appears in the QBE grid.

❷ Click the **Total text box** for the AmountSum field and then click the **down arrow button** that appears. Click **Sum** in the Total list box.

❸ Click the **Total text box** for the AmountAvg field and then click the **down arrow button** that appears. Click **Avg** in the Total list box.

❹ Click the **Total text box** for the Add50Sum field and then click the **down arrow button** that appears. See Figure 4-35.

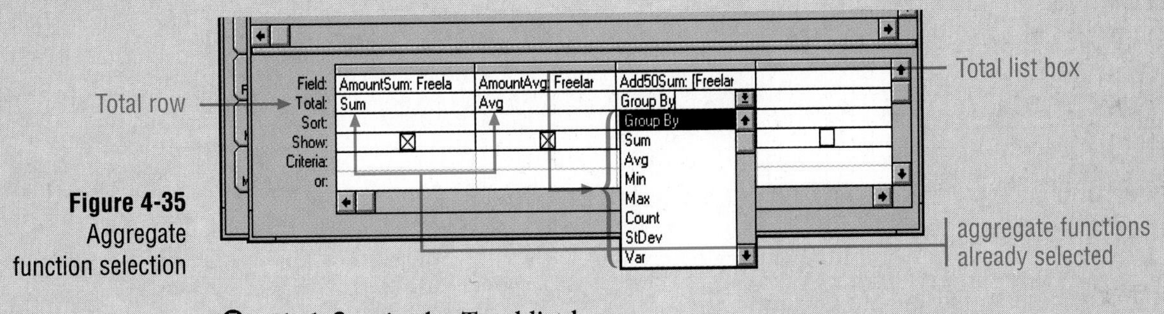

Figure 4-35 Aggregate function selection

❺ Click **Sum** in the Total list box.

Elena's last steps are to copy the calculated field, paste it to the fourth column, rename the new field Add50Avg, and change its Total text box to Avg.

To copy and paste a new calculated field with an aggregate function:

❶ Click the **Add50Sum field selector** to highlight the entire column.

❷ Click the right mouse button in the Add50Sum field selector to display the Shortcut menu and then click **Copy** to copy the column to the Clipboard.

❸ Click the **field selector** for the fourth column to highlight the entire column. Click the right mouse button in the fourth column's field selector to display the Shortcut menu and then click **Paste**. A copy of the third column appears in the fourth column.

❹ Highlight **Sum** in the Field text box for the fourth column and type **Avg**. The renamed field name is now Add50Avg.

❺ Click the **Total text box** for the Add50Avg column and then click the **down arrow button** that appears. Click **Avg** in the Total list box. See Figure 4-36.

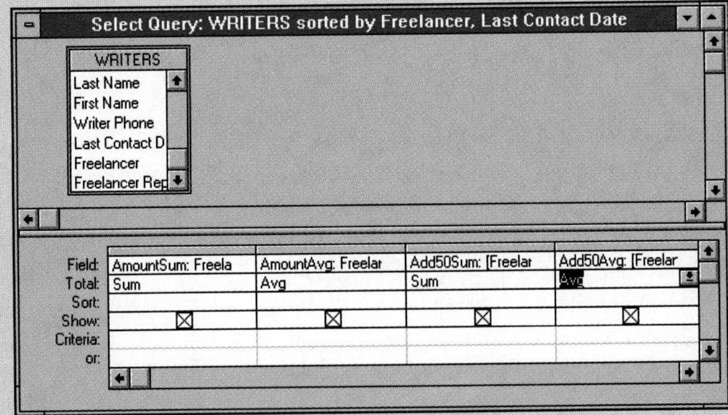

Figure 4-36 Calculating total cost and average cost per writer with and without an extra $50

As her final step, Elena views the query's dynaset.

To view a query dynaset:

1. Click the toolbar **Run button** [!]. The dynaset appears and displays one record containing the four aggregate function values. See Figure 4-37.

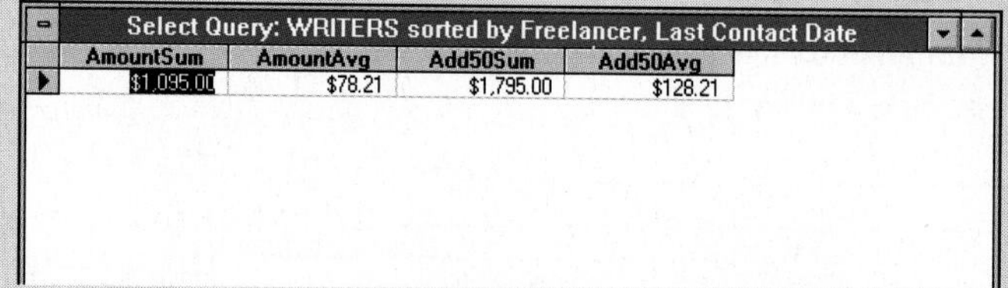

Select Query: WRITERS sorted by Freelancer, Last Contact Date

AmountSum	AmountAvg	Add50Sum	Add50Avg
$1,095.00	$78.21	$1,795.00	$128.21

Figure 4-37 Results of a query using aggregate functions

Using Record Group Calculations

Elena has one more query to create requiring the use of aggregate functions. Brian wants to know the total cost and average cost for freelancers versus staff writers with and without the extra $50. This query is exactly like her previous query, except Elena needs to add the Freelancer field and assign the Group By operator to it.

The **Group By operator** combines records with identical field values into a single record. The Group By operator used with the Freelancer field results in two records: one record for the Yes field values, and the other for the No field values. Subtotals for each of the two records are created if you use aggregate functions.

Elena adds the Freelancer field to the QBE grid in the first column, assigns it the Group By operator, and views the dynaset for the revised query.

To add a field with the Group By operator and view the dynaset:

1. Click the toolbar **Design View button** [icon] to switch back to the Query Design window.
2. Click **Freelancer** in the WRITERS field list and drag it to the first QBE grid column. The Total text box for the field shows the Group By operator by default. See Figure 4-38.

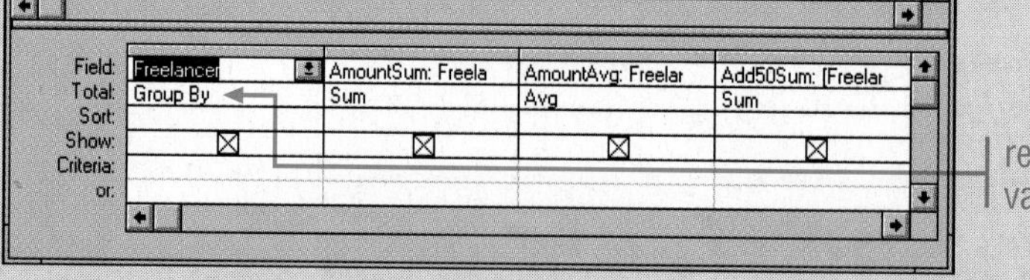

Figure 4-38 Query using aggregate functions on groups of records

3. Click the toolbar **Run button** [!]. The dynaset appears and displays two records, each containing the four aggregate function values. See Figure 4-39.

Select Query: WRITERS sorted by Freelancer, Last Contact Date

Freelancer	AmountSum	AmountAvg	Add50Sum	Add50Avg
Yes	$1,095.00	$182.50	$1,395.00	$232.50
No	$0.00	$0.00	$400.00	$50.00

Figure 4-39 Results of a query using aggregate functions on groups of records

Elena has some phone calls to make, so she closes the dynaset without saving her latest queries.

To close a dynaset without saving the query:

❶ Double-click the Datasheet View window **Control menu box**. The "Save changes to Query" dialog box appears.

❷ Click the **No button**. Access closes the dialog box and then closes the dynaset without saving the query.

If you want to take a break and resume the tutorial at a later time, you can exit Access by double-clicking the Microsoft Access window Control menu box. When you resume the tutorial, place your Student Disk in the appropriate drive, launch Access, open the Issue25 database on your Student Disk, and click the Query object button.

■ ■ ■

Establishing Table Relationships

One of the most powerful features of a database management system is its ability to establish relationships between tables. You use a common field to relate, or link, one table with another table. The process of linking tables is often called performing a **join**. When you link tables with a common field, you can extract data from them as if they were one larger table. For example, Elena links the WRITERS and PAST ARTICLES tables by using the Writer ID field in both tables as the common field. She can then use a query to extract all the article data for each writer, even though the fields are contained in two separate tables. The WRITERS and PAST ARTICLES tables have a type of relationship called a one-to-many relationship. The other two types of relationships are the one-to-one relationship and the many-to-many relationship.

Types of Relationships

A **one-to-one relationship** exists between two tables when each record in one table has exactly one matching record in the other table. For example, suppose Elena splits the WRITERS table into two tables, as shown in Figure 4-40. These two tables have a one-to-one relationship. Both the WRITERS CONTACT table and the WRITERS PAYMENT table have Writer ID as the primary key. Writer ID is also the common field between the two tables. Each record in the WRITERS CONTACT table matches one record in the WRITERS PAYMENT table through the common field. The reverse is also true that each record in the WRITERS PAYMENT table matches one record in the WRITERS CONTACT table through the common field. You can query the data from the two tables as if they were one table by linking, or joining, the two tables on the common field. Unless you set criteria to limit the dynaset to specific records, the resulting dynaset contains the same number of records each table has and fields from both tables—but only the fields you need.

WRITERS CONTACT table

Writer ID	Last Name	First Name	Writer Phone	Last Contact Date
C200	Cox	Kelly	(210)783-5415	11/14/82
C500	Cohen	Julia Rice	(905)338-1875	2/28/95
E235	Epstein	Diane	(610)349-9689	11/14/79
H400	Hall	Valerie	(710)918-7767	9/16/94
J525	Johnson	Leroy W.	(210)895-2046	1/29/91
K500	Kim	Chong	(917)729-5364	5/19/94

WRITERS PAYMENT table

Writer ID	Freelancer	Amount
C200	Yes	$100
C500	No	$0
E235	Yes	$30
H400	No	$0
J525	Yes	$125
K500	No	$0

query dynaset

Last Name	First Name	Amount
Cox	Kelly	$100
Cohen	Julia Rice	$0
Epstein	Diane	$30
Hall	Valerie	$0
Johnson	Leroy W.	$125
Kim	Chong	$0

common field and primary key

fields from WRITERS CONTACT table

fields from WRITERS PAYMENT table

Figure 4-40
One-to-one relationship

A **one-to-many relationship** exists between two tables when one record in the first table matches many records in the second table, but one record in the second table matches only one record in the first table. The relationship between the WRITERS CONTACT table and the PAST ARTICLES table, as shown in Figure 4-41 on the following page, is an example of a one-to-many relationship. Each record in the WRITERS CONTACT table matches many records in the PAST ARTICLES table. Valerie Hall's record in the WRITERS CONTACT table with a Writer ID of H400, for example, links to three records in the PAST ARTICLES table: "25% Tax Cut Bill Approved," "The BCCI Scandal Revealed," and "Computers in the Future." Many can also mean zero records or one record. There is no article listed for Leroy W. Johnson, for example. There is one article for Kelly Cox. Conversely, each record in the PAST ARTICLES table links to a single record in the WRITERS CONTACT table, with Writer ID used as the common field.

PAST ARTICLES table

Article Title	Type	Issue	Article Length	Writer ID
The Economy Under Sub-Zero Population Growth	BUS	1972 Dec	1020	E235
Milton Friedman Interview	ITV	1976 Dec	1994	C200
Chrysler Asks U.S. For $1 Billion	POL	1979 Aug	975	K500
25% Tax Cut Bill Approved	LAW	1981 Aug	2371	H400
AT&T Antitrust Settlement	BUS	1982 Feb	1600	K500
Building Trade Outlook	BUS	1984 Apr	1437	K500
Reagan's $1.09 Trillion Budget	POL	1988 Mar	1798	C500
The BCCI Scandal Revealed	EXP	1991 Jul	2461	H400
Computers in the Future	TEC	1994 Jan	2222	H400

common field as a foreign key

WRITERS CONTACT table

common field as a primary key

Writer ID	Last Name	First Name	Writer Phone	Last Contact Date
C200	Cox	Kelly	(210)783-5415	11/14/82
C500	Cohen	Julia Rice	(905)338-1875	2/28/95
E235	Epstein	Diane	(610)349-9689	11/14/79
H400	Hall	Valerie	(710)918-7767	9/16/94
J525	Johnson	Leroy W.	(210)895-2046	1/29/91
K500	Kim	Chong	(917)729-5364	5/19/94

query dynaset

Article Title	Issue	Last Name	First Name
The Economy Under Sub-Zero Population Growth	1972 Dec	Epstein	Diane
Milton Friedman Interwiew	1976 Dec	Cox	Kelly
Chrysler Asks U.S. For $1 Billion	1979 Aug	Kim	Chong
25% Tax Cut Bill Approved	1981 Aug	Hall	Valerie
AT&T Antitrust Settlement	1982 Feb	Kim	Chong
Building Trade Outlook	1984 Apr	Kim	Chong
Reagan's $1.09 Trillion Budget	1988 Mar	Cohen	Julia Rice
The BCCI Scandal Revealed	1991 Jul	Hall	Valerie
Computers in the Future	1994 Jan	Hall	Valerie

common field

fields from WRITERS CONTACT table

fields from PAST ARTICLES table

Figure 4-41
One-to-many relationship

For a one-to-many relationship, like a one-to-one relationship, you can query the data from the two tables as if they were one table by linking the two tables on the common field. The resulting dynaset can contain the same number of records as does the table that has the foreign key; this table is the table on the "many" side of the one-to-many relationship.

A **many-to-many relationship** exists between two tables when one record in the first table matches many records in the second table and one record in the second table matches many records in the first table. For example, suppose that an article was written by cowriters. The relationship between the WRITERS CONTACT and PAST ARTICLES tables would then be a many-to-many relationship, as shown in Figure 4-42. To handle this type of relationship, you first make sure that each table has a primary key. A counter field named Article ID needs to be added as a primary key to the PAST ARTICLES table, which did not have a primary key. Then you create a new table that has a primary key combining the primary keys of the other two tables. The WRITERS AND PAST ARTICLES table is created. Its primary key is Article ID *and* Writer ID. Each record in this new table represents one article and one of the article's writers. Even though an article ID and writer ID can appear more than once, each combination of article ID and writer ID is unique.

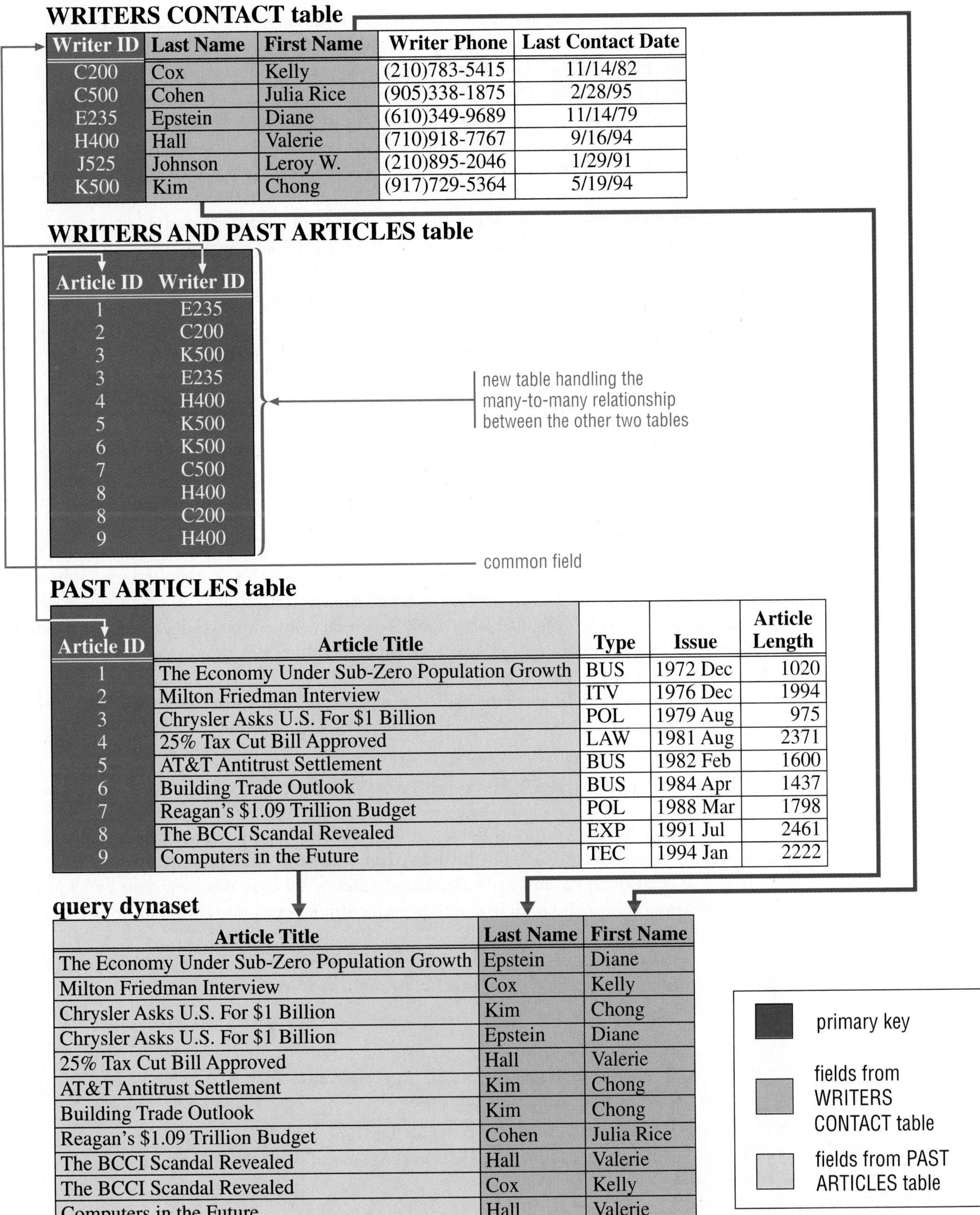

WRITERS CONTACT table

Writer ID	Last Name	First Name	Writer Phone	Last Contact Date
C200	Cox	Kelly	(210)783-5415	11/14/82
C500	Cohen	Julia Rice	(905)338-1875	2/28/95
E235	Epstein	Diane	(610)349-9689	11/14/79
H400	Hall	Valerie	(710)918-7767	9/16/94
J525	Johnson	Leroy W.	(210)895-2046	1/29/91
K500	Kim	Chong	(917)729-5364	5/19/94

WRITERS AND PAST ARTICLES table

Article ID	Writer ID
1	E235
2	C200
3	K500
3	E235
4	H400
5	K500
6	K500
7	C500
8	H400
8	C200
9	H400

PAST ARTICLES table

Article ID	Article Title	Type	Issue	Article Length
1	The Economy Under Sub-Zero Population Growth	BUS	1972 Dec	1020
2	Milton Friedman Interview	ITV	1976 Dec	1994
3	Chrysler Asks U.S. For $1 Billion	POL	1979 Aug	975
4	25% Tax Cut Bill Approved	LAW	1981 Aug	2371
5	AT&T Antitrust Settlement	BUS	1982 Feb	1600
6	Building Trade Outlook	BUS	1984 Apr	1437
7	Reagan's $1.09 Trillion Budget	POL	1988 Mar	1798
8	The BCCI Scandal Revealed	EXP	1991 Jul	2461
9	Computers in the Future	TEC	1994 Jan	2222

query dynaset

Article Title	Last Name	First Name
The Economy Under Sub-Zero Population Growth	Epstein	Diane
Milton Friedman Interview	Cox	Kelly
Chrysler Asks U.S. For $1 Billion	Kim	Chong
Chrysler Asks U.S. For $1 Billion	Epstein	Diane
25% Tax Cut Bill Approved	Hall	Valerie
AT&T Antitrust Settlement	Kim	Chong
Building Trade Outlook	Kim	Chong
Reagan's $1.09 Trillion Budget	Cohen	Julia Rice
The BCCI Scandal Revealed	Hall	Valerie
The BCCI Scandal Revealed	Cox	Kelly
Computers in the Future	Hall	Valerie

Figure 4-42
Many-to-many relationship

The many-to-many relationship between the WRITERS CONTACT and PAST ARTICLES tables has been changed into two one-to-many relationships. The WRITERS CONTACT table has a one-to-many relationship with the WRITERS AND PAST ARTICLES table, and the PAST ARTICLES table has a one-to-many relationship with the WRITERS AND PAST ARTICLES table.

For a many-to-many relationship, you can query the data from the tables as if they were one table by linking the tables on their common fields. For example, you link the WRITERS CONTACT and the WRITERS AND PAST ARTICLES tables on their common field, Writer ID, and you link the PAST ARTICLES and the WRITERS AND PAST ARTICLES tables on their common field, Article ID. The resulting dynaset can contain the same number of records as does the new table that you created—in this case, the WRITERS AND PAST ARTICLES table.

Access refers to the two tables that form a relationship as the primary table and the related table. The **primary table** is the one table in a one-to-many relationship, and the **related table** is the many table. In a one-to-one relationship, you can choose either table as the primary table and the other table as the related table.

When two tables are related, you can choose to enforce referential integrity rules. The **referential integrity** rules are:

- When you add a record to a related table, a matching record must already exist in the primary table.
- You cannot delete a record from a primary table if matching records exist in the related table, unless you choose to cascade deletes.

When you delete a record with a particular primary-key value from the primary table and choose to **cascade deletes**, Access automatically deletes from related tables all records having foreign-key values equal to that primary-key value. You can also choose to cascade updates. When you change a table's primary-key value and choose to **cascade updates**, Access automatically changes all related tables' foreign-key values that equal that primary-key value.

Let's see how to define relationships and choose referential integrity and cascade options in Access.

Adding a Relationship between Two Tables

When two tables have a common field, you can define the relationship between them in the Relationships window. The **Relationships window** illustrates the one-to-one and one-to-many relationships among a database's tables. In this window you can view or change existing relationships, define new relationships between tables, and rearrange the layout of the tables.

Elena defines the one-to-many relationship between the WRITERS and PAST ARTICLES tables. First, she opens the Relationships window.

To open the Relationships window:

1. Click the toolbar **Relationships button**. Access displays the Add Table dialog box on top of the Relationships window.
2. In the Add Table dialog box, double-click **WRITERS** and then double-click **PAST ARTICLES** in the Table/Query list box. Access adds both tables to the Relationships window.

❸ Click the **Close button** in the Add Table dialog box. Access closes the Add Table dialog box and reveals the entire Relationships window. See Figure 4-43.

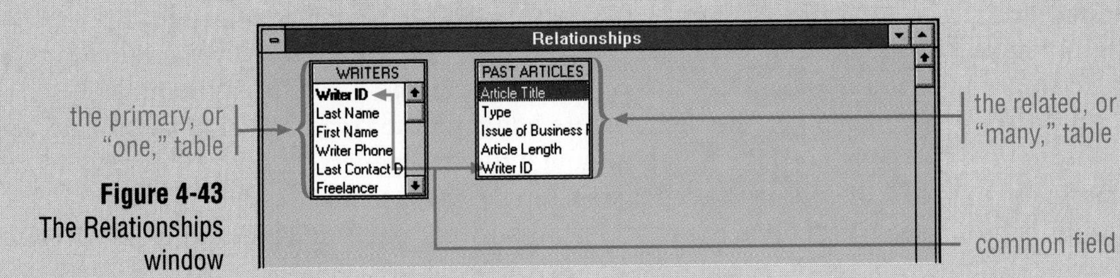

Figure 4-43
The Relationships window

To form a relationship between the two tables, you drag the common field from one table to the other table. Specifically, you click the primary-key field in the primary table and drag it to the foreign-key field in the related table. Access then displays the Relationships dialog box, in which you select the relationship options for the two tables.

Elena drags Writer ID from the WRITERS table to the PAST ARTICLES table and then selects the relationship options in the Relationships dialog box.

To define a relationship between two tables:

❶ Click **Writer ID** in the WRITERS table list and drag it to Writer ID in the PAST ARTICLES table list. When you release the mouse button, Access displays the Relationships dialog box.

❷ Click the **Enforce Referential Integrity check box** to turn this option on. Access turns on the Many radio button in the One To list.

❸ Click the **Cascade Update Related Fields check box** to turn this option on. See Figure 4-44. Do not turn on the Cascade Delete Related Records option.

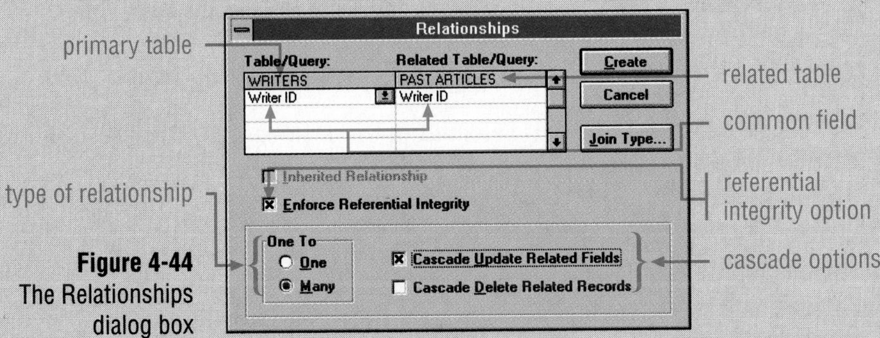

Figure 4-44
The Relationships dialog box

❹ Click the **Create button**. Access saves the defined relationship between the two tables, closes the Relationships dialog box, and reveals the entire Relationships window. See Figure 4-45.

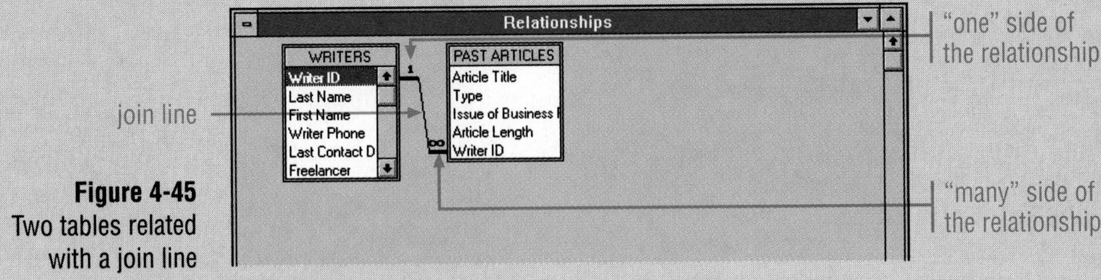

Figure 4-45
Two tables related with a join line

Notice the join line that connects the Writer ID fields common to the two tables. The **join line** shows you the common field between two tables. The common fields link (or join) the two tables, which have either a one-to-one or one-to-many relationship. The join line is bold at both ends; this signifies that you have chosen the option to enforce referential integrity. If you do not select this option, the join line is thin at both ends. The "one" side of the relationship has the digit 1 at its end, and the "many" side of the relationship has the infinity symbol (∞) at its end. Although the two tables are still separate tables, you have now defined the one-to-many relationship between them.

Now that she has defined the relationship between the WRITERS and PAST ARTICLES tables, Elena closes the Relationships window.

To close the Relationships window:

1. Double-click the Relationships window **Control menu box**. Access displays the "Save layout changes to 'Relationships'?" dialog box.
2. Click the **Yes button** to save the layout. Access closes the dialog box and the Relationships window and returns you to the Database window.

Elena can now build her next query, which requires data from both the WRITERS and PAST ARTICLES tables.

Querying More Than One Table

Elena's next query seeks the article titles, types, and lengths for each writer ordered by article type. This query involves fields from both the WRITERS and PAST ARTICLES tables and requires a sort.

Elena first opens the Query Design window and selects the two needed tables.

To start a query using two tables:

1. Be sure that the Query object button is selected in the Database window and then click the **New command button**. The New Query dialog box appears.
2. Click the **New Query button** in the dialog box. The Add Table dialog box appears on top of the Query Design window.
3. Double-click **WRITERS** and then double-click **PAST ARTICLES** in the Table/Query list box. Access displays the WRITERS and PAST ARTICLES field lists in the upper portion of the Query Design window.

❹ Click the **Close button**. The Add Table dialog box disappears. See Figure 4-46.

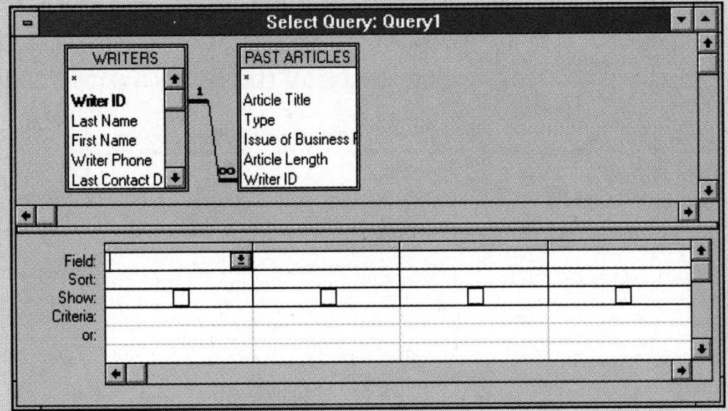

Figure 4-46
Two tables related with a join line in the Query Design window

Elena now defines the query. In the QBE grid she inserts the Article Title, Type, and Article Length fields from the PAST ARTICLES table. She inserts the Last Name and First Name fields from the WRITERS table. She then chooses ascending sort order for the Type field.

To define a query using two tables:

❶ Double-click **Article Title** in the PAST ARTICLES field list. Access places this field in the first column's Field text box.

❷ Double-click **Type** in the PAST ARTICLES field list. Access places this field in the second column's Field text box.

❸ Double-click **Article Length** in the PAST ARTICLES field list. Access places this field in the third column's Field text box.

❹ Double-click **Last Name** in the WRITERS field list. Access places this field in the fourth column's Field text box.

❺ Double-click **First Name** in the WRITERS field list. Access places this field in the fifth column's Field text box.

❻ Click the **Sort text box** for the Type field, and then click the **down arrow button** in the Sort text box. Access displays the Sort list.

❼ Click **Ascending** in the Sort list. The Sort list disappears, and Ascending appears in the Sort text box as the selected sort order.

Elena switches to the dynaset to verify her query.

To view a query dynaset:

❶ Click the toolbar **Run button** [!]. The dynaset appears and displays the fields from the two tables.

❷ Click the dynaset's **maximize button** to see all the fields and records. See Figure 4-47.

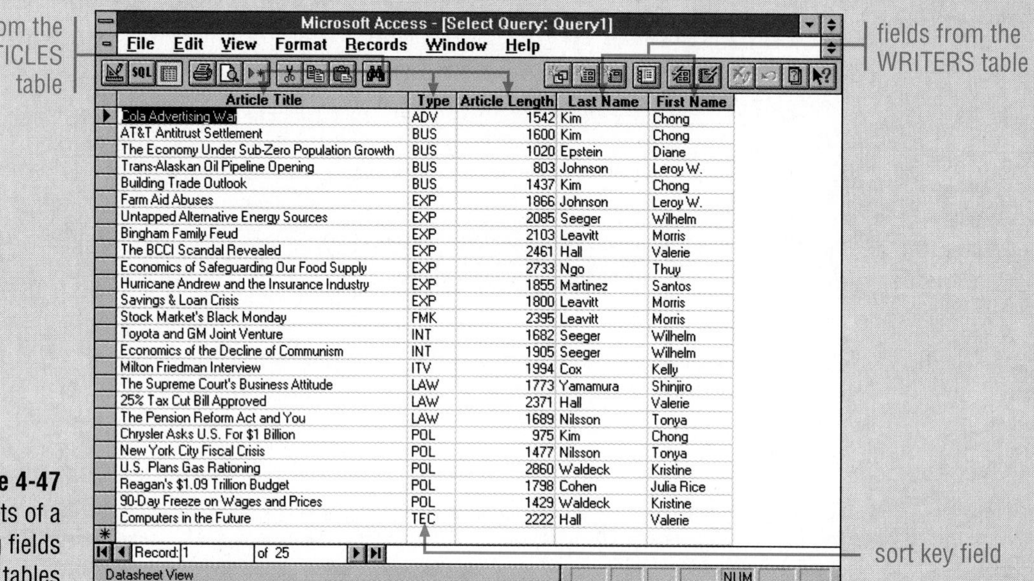

Article Title	Type	Article Length	Last Name	First Name
Cola Advertising War	ADV	1542	Kim	Chong
AT&T Antitrust Settlement	BUS	1600	Kim	Chong
The Economy Under Sub-Zero Population Growth	BUS	1020	Epstein	Diane
Trans-Alaskan Oil Pipeline Opening	BUS	803	Johnson	Leroy W.
Building Trade Outlook	BUS	1437	Kim	Chong
Farm Aid Abuses	EXP	1866	Johnson	Leroy W.
Untapped Alternative Energy Sources	EXP	2085	Seeger	Wilhelm
Bingham Family Feud	EXP	2103	Leavitt	Morris
The BCCI Scandal Revealed	EXP	2461	Hall	Valerie
Economics of Safeguarding Our Food Supply	EXP	2733	Ngo	Thuy
Hurricane Andrew and the Insurance Industry	EXP	1855	Martinez	Santos
Savings & Loan Crisis	EXP	1800	Leavitt	Morris
Stock Market's Black Monday	FMK	2395	Leavitt	Morris
Toyota and GM Joint Venture	INT	1682	Seeger	Wilhelm
Economics of the Decline of Communism	INT	1905	Seeger	Wilhelm
Milton Friedman Interview	ITV	1994	Cox	Kelly
The Supreme Court's Business Attitude	LAW	1773	Yamamura	Shinjiro
25% Tax Cut Bill Approved	LAW	2371	Hall	Valerie
The Pension Reform Act and You	LAW	1689	Nilsson	Tonya
Chrysler Asks U.S. For $1 Billion	POL	975	Kim	Chong
New York City Fiscal Crisis	POL	1477	Nilsson	Tonya
U.S. Plans Gas Rationing	POL	2860	Waldeck	Kristine
Reagan's $1.09 Trillion Budget	POL	1798	Cohen	Julia Rice
90-Day Freeze on Wages and Prices	POL	1429	Waldeck	Kristine
Computers in the Future	TEC	2222	Hall	Valerie

Figure 4-47 Results of a query using fields from two tables

TROUBLE? You should see 25 records in the dynaset. If you see none, then you probably did not import the PAST ARTICLES table correctly with the Data and Structure option. Save the query with the name Article Type Query. Delete the table and import it again. Then try running the query. If you see more than 25 records, then you created the relationship between the two tables incorrectly. Save the query with the name Article Type Query, repeat the steps for adding the relationship between the two tables, and then try running the query again.

Elena next saves this query and then closes the dynaset.

To save a new query:

❶ Click **File**, and then click **Save Query As...** The Save As dialog box appears.

❷ Type **Article Type Query**.

❸ Click the **OK button**. The Save As dialog box disappears, and Access saves the query for later use.

❹ Double-click the Datasheet View window **Control menu box**. The dynaset disappears, and the Database window becomes the active window and lists all saved queries alphabetically. See Figure 4-48.

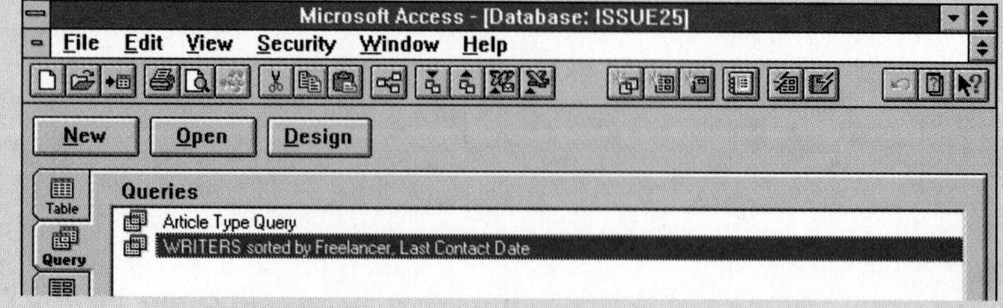

Figure 4-48 List of saved queries

Creating a Parameter Query

Elena's last query asks for the article titles and lengths and the writer names for a specific article type arranged by article title. She will use the PAST ARTICLES table for the Article Title, Article Length, and Type fields and the WRITERS table for the Last Name and First Name fields. Article Title will be the sort key and will have an ascending sort order. Because this query is similar to her last saved query, Elena will open the Article Type Query in the Query Design window and modify its design.

ADV for advertising, BUS for business, EXP for exposé, and POL for political are examples of specific article types. Elena can create a simple condition using an exact match for the Type field that she can change in the Query Design window every time she runs the query. Instead, Elena creates a parameter query.

For a **parameter query**, Access displays a dialog box and prompts you to enter your criteria, or parameters, when you run the query. Access then creates the dynaset just as if you had changed the criteria in the Query Design window.

REFERENCE WINDOW

Creating a Parameter Query

- Create a select query that includes all the fields that will appear in the dynaset. Also choose the sort keys and set the criteria that do not change when you run the query.
- Decide on the fields that will have prompts when you run the query. For each of them, type the prompt you want in the field's Criteria box and enclose the prompt in brackets.
- Highlight the prompt, but do not highlight the brackets. Click Edit and then click Copy to copy the prompt to the Clipboard.
- Click Query and then click Parameters... to open the Query Parameters dialog box.
- Press [Ctrl][V] to paste the contents of the Clipboard into the Parameter text box. Press [Tab] and select the field's data type.
- Click the OK button to close the Query Parameters dialog box.

Elena opens the query saved under the name Article Type Query in the Query Design window and changes its design.

To open a saved query and modify its design:

1. Be sure that the Database window is active and the Query object button is selected. Click **Article Type Query** in the Queries list box and then click the **Design command button** to open the Query Design window.
2. To remove the sort key for the Type field, click its Sort text box, click the **down arrow button**, and then click **(not sorted)**.
3. To add a sort key for the Article Title field, click its **Sort text box**, click the **down arrow button**, and then click **Ascending**.

Elena has completed the changes to the select query. She now changes the query to a parameter query.

To create a parameter query:

1. Click the **Criteria text box** for the Type field and type **[Enter an Article Type:]**. See Figure 4-49.

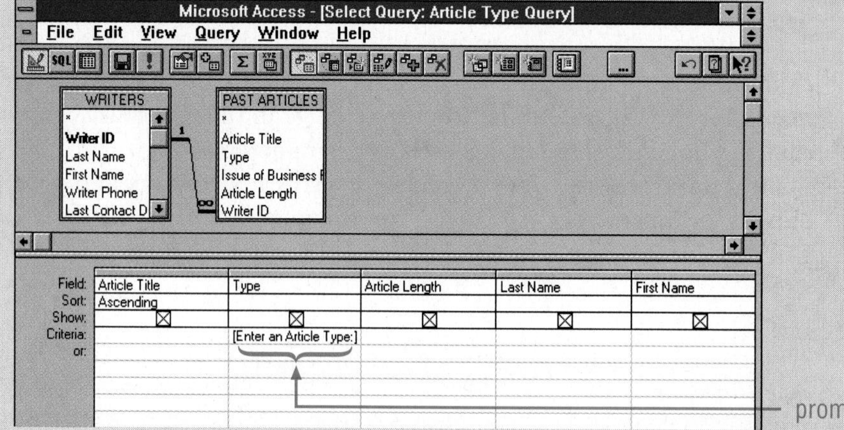

Figure 4-49 Entering a prompt for a parameter query

2. Highlight the prompt, including the colon, but do not highlight the brackets. The parameter query will not work unless "Enter an Article Type:" is exactly what you highlight. Click **Edit** and then click **Copy** to copy the prompt to the Clipboard.
3. Click **Query** and then click **Parameters...** to open the Query Parameters dialog box.
4. Press **[Ctrl][V]** to paste the prompt from the Clipboard into the Parameter text box and then press **[Tab]**. See Figure 4-50.

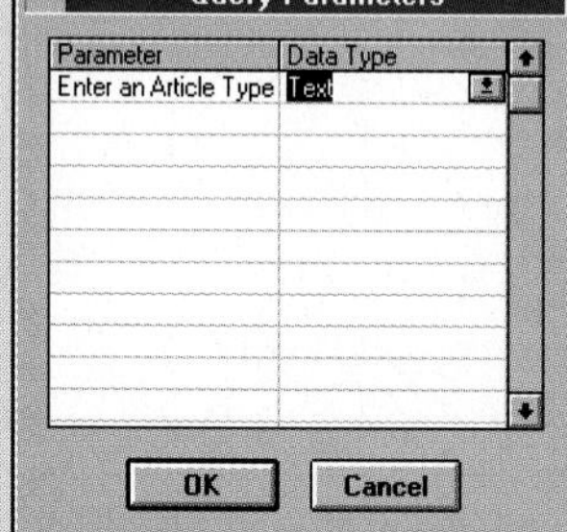

Figure 4-50 The Query Parameters dialog box

5. Your selection in the Data Type text box must be of the same data type as that of the Type field. Because the data type of the Type field is text, which is the default, click the **OK button** to close the Query Parameters dialog box.

Elena runs the parameter query, saves it with the name Article Type Parameter Query, and closes the dynaset. Elena wants to keep the saved version of the query named Article Type Query, as well as save the new parameter query. When she saves the parameter query, therefore, Elena uses the File menu's Save Query As... command instead of the Save Query command. If she were to use the Save Query command, Access would save the parameter query with the name Article Type Query after deleting the saved query.

To run and save a parameter query:

❶ Click the toolbar **Run button** [!]. The Enter Parameter Value dialog box appears with your prompt above the text box.

❷ To see all the articles that are exposés, type **EXP** in the text box. See Figure 4-51.

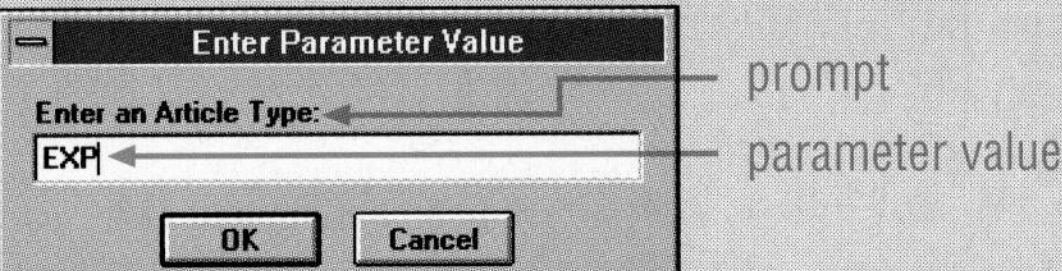

Figure 4-51
The Enter Parameter Value dialog box

❸ Press **[Enter]**. Access runs the parameter query and displays the dynaset. See Figure 4-52. Only records of type EXP appear, and the records are in ascending order by the Article Title field.

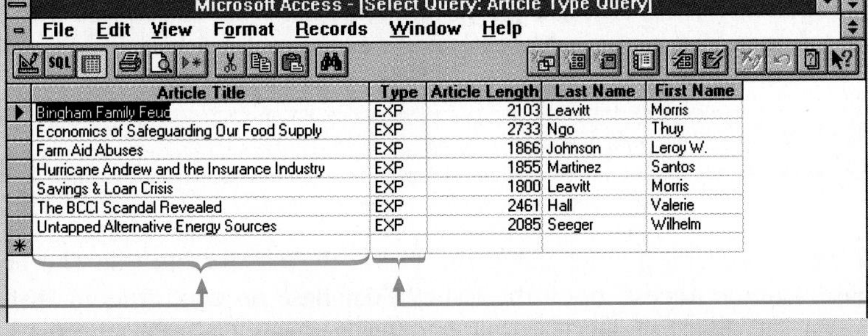

records in ascending sort order

parameter value entered

Figure 4-52
The dynaset for a parameter query

❹ To save the query, click **File** and then click **Save Query As...**. The Save As dialog box appears showing the query name Article Type Query, which is the name of the previously saved query. Place the insertion point just in front of the letter Q, type **Parameter**, press **[Spacebar]**, and then press **[Enter]** to name the new query.

❺ Double-click the Datasheet View window **Control menu box**. The dynaset disappears. The Database window becomes the active window and lists the newly saved query.

■ ■ ■

Elena exits Access and then schedules a meeting with her colleagues to review the results of her queries.

Questions

1. What is QBE?
2. What are three methods for adding all the fields from a table to the QBE grid?
3. What is a dynaset?
4. How do you exclude from a dynaset a field that appears in the QBE grid?
5. What are the two components of a simple condition?
6. What comparison operator is used to select records based on a specific pattern?
7. When do you use the In comparison operator?
8. How must you position the fields in the QBE grid when you have multiple sort keys?
9. When do you use logical operators?
10. What is a calculated field?

11. When do you use an aggregate function?
12. When do you use the Group By operator?
13. **E** Look for an example of a one-to-many relationship and an example of a many-to-many relationship in a newspaper, magazine, or everyday situation you encounter. For each one, name the entities and select the primary keys and common fields.
14. What are the two referential integrity rules?
15. What does a join line signify?
16. When do you use a parameter query?
17. **E** Use Cue Cards to document for your instructor four aggregate functions that do not appear in Figure 4-34.
18. **E** Suppose you create a calculated field in the Query Design window by typing NewField:[Writer ID]+50. Writer ID is a text field from the table you are using in your query and it appears in the QBE grid. When you run the query, the calculated field does not appear in the dynaset. Why did this occur?
19. **E** Suppose you want to print a dynaset selection, but the Selection option is dimmed out when the Print dialog box appears. What has caused this problem, and how do you correct it?

Tutorial Assignments

Elena creates several queries using the PAST ARTICLES table that she imported into the Issue25 database. Launch Access, open the Issue25 database on your Student Disk, maximize the Database window, click the PAST ARTICLES table, click the New Query button on the toolbar, and then click the New Query button in the New Query message box.

For each of the following questions, prepare an appropriate query in the Query Design window and print its entire dynaset. Whenever you use the Issue of Business Perspective field, rename it Issue. Whenever fields are listed in the question, display the fields in the order listed. Do not save any of the queries.

1. Which articles are of type BUS? Print all fields for this query.
2. What are the article titles and article lengths for all articles that have a length greater than 2103?
3. What are the article titles, article lengths, and writer IDs for all articles written by writers with writer IDs H400 or W432?
4. What are the article titles, article lengths, writer IDs, and issues for all articles published in *Business Perspective* in the 1980s?
5. What are the article lengths, article titles, writer IDs, and issues for all articles of type EXP that have a length less than 2100?
6. What are the article titles, writer IDs, and issues for all articles of type ITV or that were written by writer L130?
7. What are the article lengths, writer IDs, issues, types, and article titles for all articles that have a length less than 2000 and are of type BUS or LAW?
8. What are the article lengths, writer IDs, issues, types, and article titles for all articles that have a length less than 2000 and are of type BUS or LAW? Print in ascending order by length.
9. What are the article lengths, writer IDs, issues, types, and article titles for all articles in descending order by length?
10. What are the writer IDs, article titles, issues, types, and article lengths for all articles? Display the dynaset in ascending order with writer ID as the primary sort key and article length as the secondary sort key.
11. What are the article titles, writer IDs, issues, types, article lengths, and costs per article for all articles, based on a cost per article of three cents per word? Use the name CostPerArticle for the calculated field, assume that the Article Length field gives the number of words in the article, and use ascending sort order for the Article Length field.

12. What is the total cost, average cost, lowest cost, and highest cost for all articles? Assume that the Article Length field gives the number of words in an article and that the cost per article is three cents per word.
13. What is the total cost, average cost, lowest cost, and highest cost for all articles by type? Assume that the Article Length field gives the number of words in an article and that the cost per article is three cents per word.

E 14. Using the PAST ARTICLES and WRITERS tables, list the article titles, article types, issues, writer last names, and writer first names in ascending order by article length for all articles of type BUS, LAW, or POL. Do not print the Article Length field in the dynaset. Be sure that there is no Total row in the QBE grid.

15. Using the PAST ARTICLES and WRITERS tables, list the article titles, issues, writer last names, and writer first names in ascending order by article length for a selected article type. This query should be a parameter query.

Case Problems

1. Walkton Daily Press Carriers

Grant Sherman has created and updated his Press database and is now ready to query it. Launch Access and do the following:

1. Open the Press database on your Student Disk and maximize the Database window.
2. Delete the BILLINGS table.
3. Import the BILLINGS table from the Walkton database on your Student Disk.

Grant creates several queries using the CARRIERS table. For each of the following questions, prepare an appropriate query in the Query Design window and print its entire dynaset. Whenever you use one of the carrier name fields, rename it omitting the word "Carrier." Whenever fields are listed in the question, display the fields in the order listed.

4. What is all the carrier information on Ashley Shaub?
5. What is all the information on those carriers whose last names begin with the letter S?
6. What are the birthdates, phone numbers, first names, and last names of carriers born in 1981 or later?
7. What are the birthdates, phone numbers, last names, and first names of carriers whose phone numbers end with the digits 4 or 7?
8. What are the birthdates, carrier IDs, first names, and last names of those carriers born prior to 1980 who have a carrier ID either less than 5 or greater than 10?
9. What are the birthdates, carrier IDs, first names, last names, and phone numbers of all carriers in descending order by birthdate?

Close the dynaset to return to the Database window without saving your queries. Complete the following queries using the BILLINGS table.

E 10. What is the total, average, lowest, and highest balance amount for all carriers? Your four calculated fields should use the Balance Amount field as is. Note that Balance Amount is the table field name and Balance is the Caption property name.

E 11. What is the total, average, lowest, and highest balance amount, grouped by carrier?

12. Create a parameter query to display all the fields in the BILLINGS table based on a selected Carrier ID.

2. Lopez Used Cars

Maria and Hector Lopez have created and updated their Usedcars database and are now ready to query it. Launch Access and do the following:

1. Open the Usedcars database on your Student Disk and maximize the Database window.
2. Delete the LOCATIONS table.

3. Import the CLASSES, LOCATIONS, and TRANSMISSIONS tables from the Lopez database on your Student Disk.

Maria and Hector create several queries using the USED CARS table. For each of the following questions, prepare an appropriate query in the Query Design window and print its entire dynaset. Whenever fields are listed in the question, display the fields in the order listed. If a field has a Caption property, rename the field to match the name in the Query Design window.

4. What are the manufacturers, models, years, and selling prices for all cars?
5. What are the manufacturers, models, years, and selling prices for cars manufactured by Ford?
6. What are the manufacturers, models, years, costs, and selling prices for cars manufactured prior to 1989?
7. What are the manufacturers, models, years, costs, and selling prices for cars having a manufacturer that starts with the letter C or the letter N?
8. What are the manufacturers, models, classes, years, costs, and selling prices for cars manufactured prior to 1990 and having either an S2 or an S3 class?
9. What are the manufacturers, models, classes, years, costs, and selling prices for all cars in descending sequence by selling price?
10. Create a field that calculates the difference (profit) between the Selling Price and the Cost and name it Diff. What are the manufacturers, models, classes, years, costs, selling prices, and profits for all cars?

E 11. What is the total cost, total selling price, total profit, and average profit for all the cars?

E 12. What is the total cost, total selling price, total profit, and average profit grouped by year?

13. Create a parameter query to display all the fields from the USED CARS table based on a selected manufacturer.

Close the dynaset to return to the Database window without saving your query, and then complete the following problem.

E 14. Add a one-to-many relationship between the LOCATIONS and USED CARS tables using Location Code as the common field. Create a query to find the manufacturers, models, selling prices, location names, and manager names for all cars in descending sequence by manager name.

3. Tophill University Student Employment

Olivia Tyler has created and updated her Parttime database and is now ready to query it. Launch Access and do the following:

1. Open the Parttime database on your Student Disk and maximize the Database window.
2. Delete the EMPLOYERS table.
3. Import the EMPLOYERS table from the Tophill database on your Student Disk.

Olivia creates several queries using the JOBS table. For each of the following questions, prepare an appropriate query in the Query Design window and print its entire dynaset. Whenever fields are listed in the question, display the fields in the listed order. If a field has a Caption property, rename the field to match the name in the Query Design window.

4. What is all the job information on job order 7?
5. What is all the information on jobs having job titles that begin with Computer?
6. What are the job titles, hours per week, and wages of jobs paying wages greater than or equal to $7.05?
7. What are the job titles, hours per week, employer IDs, and wages of jobs requiring between 20 and 24 hours per week, inclusive?
8. What are the job titles, hours per week, employer IDs, and wages of jobs requiring between 20 and 24 hours per week, inclusive, and paying wages less than or equal to $6.75?

9. What are the job titles, hours per week, employer IDs, and wages of all jobs in order by ascending hours per week (the primary sort key) and by descending job title (the secondary sort key)?
10. Create a calculated field that is the product of hours per week and wage, and name it Weekly. What are the hours per week, wages, weekly wages, and job titles for all jobs?

E 11. What is the total, average, lowest, and highest weekly wage for all the jobs listed in the JOBS table?

E 12. What is the total, average, lowest, and highest weekly wage for all jobs grouped by employer ID?

13. Create a parameter query to display all the fields in the JOBS table based on a selected employer ID.

4. Rexville Business Licenses

Chester Pearce has created and updated his Buslic database and is now ready to query it. Launch Access and do the following:

1. Open the Buslic database on your Student Disk and maximize the Database window.
2. Delete the LICENSES table.
3. Import the LICENSES and ISSUED LICENSES tables from the Rexville database on your Student Disk.

Chester creates several queries using the BUSINESSES table. For each of the following questions, prepare an appropriate query in the Query Design window and print its entire dynaset. Whenever fields are listed in the question, display the fields in the listed order. If a field has a Caption property, rename the field to match the name in the Query Design window.

4. What is all the information for business ID 11?
5. What is all the information on those businesses that have the word "avenue" in the street-name field?
6. What are the business names, street numbers, street names, and proprietors for businesses having street numbers greater than 5100?
7. What are the business names, street numbers, street names, proprietors, and phone numbers for businesses having phone numbers starting 243 or 942?
8. What are the proprietors, business names, street numbers, street names, and phone numbers of all businesses in ascending sequence by business name?

Close the dynaset to return to the Database window without saving your query. Complete the following queries using the ISSUED LICENSES table.

E 9. What is the total amount, total count, and average amount for all issued licenses?

E 10. What is the total amount, total count, and average amount for all issued licenses grouped by license type?

11. Create a parameter query to display all the fields from the BUSINESSES table based on a selected business ID.

T U T O R I A L 5

Designing Forms

OBJECTIVES

In this tutorial you will:

- Create forms using Form Wizards
- Save and open a form
- View and maintain data using forms
- Find and sort data in a form
- Select and sort records with a filter
- Design and create a custom form
- Use Control Wizards

Creating Forms at Vision Publishers

CASE

Vision Publishers At the next Issue25 database meeting Brian Murphy, Judith Rossi, and Harold Larson are pleased when Elena Sanchez presents her query results. Everyone agrees that Elena should place the Issue25 database on the company network so that everyone can access and query the data.

Because some people seek information about a single writer, Elena creates a form to display one writer at a time on the screen. The form will be easier to read than a datasheet or dynaset and Elena can use the form to correct a writer's data.

Using a Form

A **form** is an object you use to maintain, view, and print records of data from a database. In Access, you can design your own form or use a Form Wizard to automate the form creation process. A **Form Wizard** is an Access tool that asks you a series of questions and then creates a form based on your answers. Whether you use a Form Wizard or design your own form, you can change a form's design after it is created.

Access has five different Form Wizards. Four of these Form Wizards are shown in Figure 5-1.

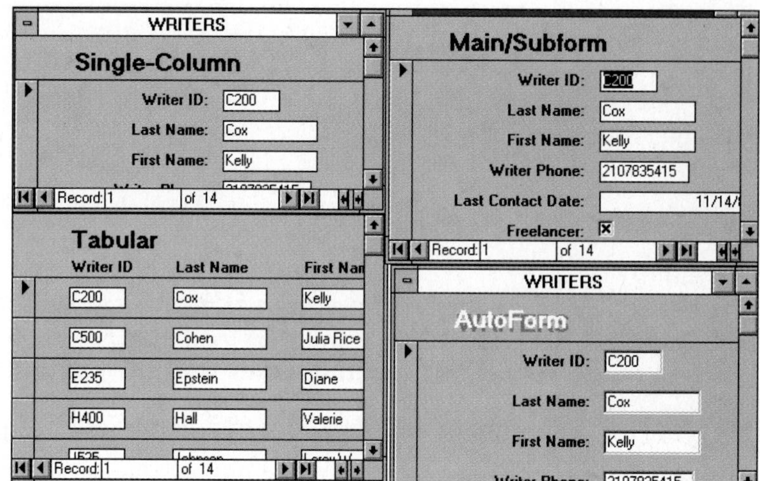

Figure 5-1
Four types of Form Wizards

- A **single-column form** displays the fields, one on a line, vertically on the form. Field values appear in boxes. Labels, which are the table field names, appear to the left of the field values.
- A **tabular form** displays multiple records and field values in a row-and-column format. Field values appear in boxes with the table field names as column headings.
- A **main/subform form** displays data from two or more related tables. One record from the primary table appears in single-column format in the main form at the top. Access displays one or more records in datasheet format from the related tables in the subforms at the bottom.
- An **AutoForm form** is a special single-column form that Access creates immediately without asking you further questions about the form's content and style. Access includes in the form all the fields from the underlying table or query.
- A **graph form** displays a graph of your designated data.

Each Form Wizard offers you a choice of five different form styles, as shown in Figure 5-2.

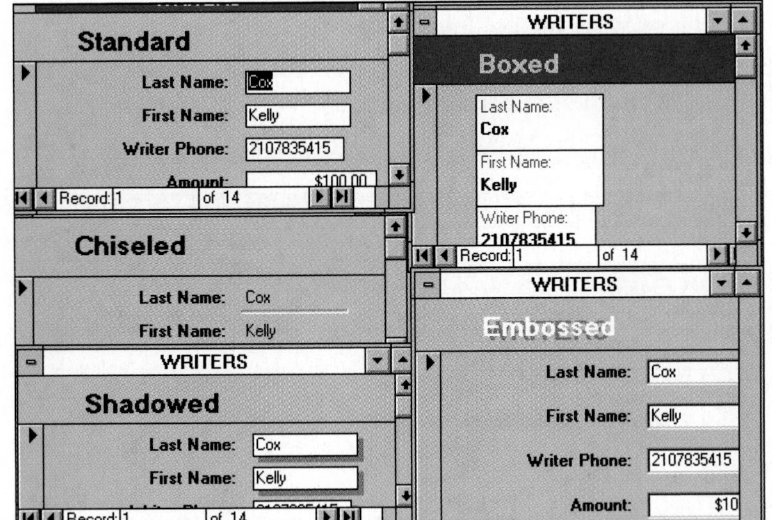

Figure 5-2
Form style options

- The **standard style** displays field values in white boxes on a light gray background.
- The **chiseled style** displays field values with sculpted underlines on a light gray background.
- The **shadowed style** is the same as the standard style with the addition of dark rectangles attached to the field-value boxes to give a shadowed, three-dimensional effect.
- The **boxed style** pairs field values and their labels inside white boxes on a light gray background with each label above its field value.
- The **embossed style** displays field values inside white boxes with a sunken, three-dimensional effect on a blue-green background.

Although you might find the last four styles to be more elegant, you should choose the standard style when you first begin working with forms. Some printers have problems printing colored forms, and changing a form's design by moving or resizing fields is easier when you use the standard style.

Access has a set of Cue Cards you can use while working with forms. Although we will not use these Cue Cards in this tutorial, you might find they enhance your understanding of forms. At any time during this tutorial, therefore, select Design a Form from the Cue Card menu window to launch the appropriate Cue Cards.

Creating Forms Using the AutoForm Wizard

The quickest way to create a form is to use the toolbar AutoForm button, which launches the AutoForm Wizard. When you click the **AutoForm button**, the AutoForm Wizard selects all the fields from the highlighted table or query in the Database window, creates a single-column form for these fields, and displays the form on the screen.

To create a form to display all the fields from the TYPES table, Elena uses the AutoForm button. If you have not done so, place your Student Disk in the appropriate drive, launch Access, and open the Issue25 database on your Student Disk.

To create a form using the AutoForm button:

❶ Click **TYPES** in the Tables list box. Access will place the fields from the TYPES table, which is now highlighted, into the form it creates when you click the toolbar AutoForm button.

❷ Locate on the toolbar. See Figure 5-3.

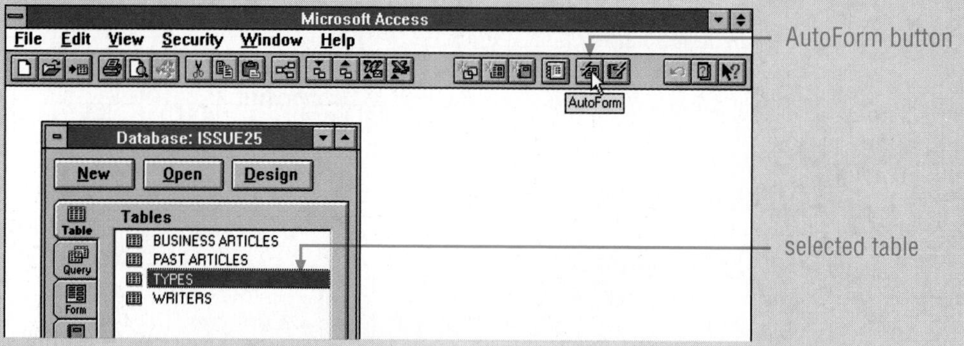

Figure 5-3
The toolbar AutoForm button

❸ Click . Access constructs and displays a form that contains the two fields from the TYPES table. See Figure 5-4.

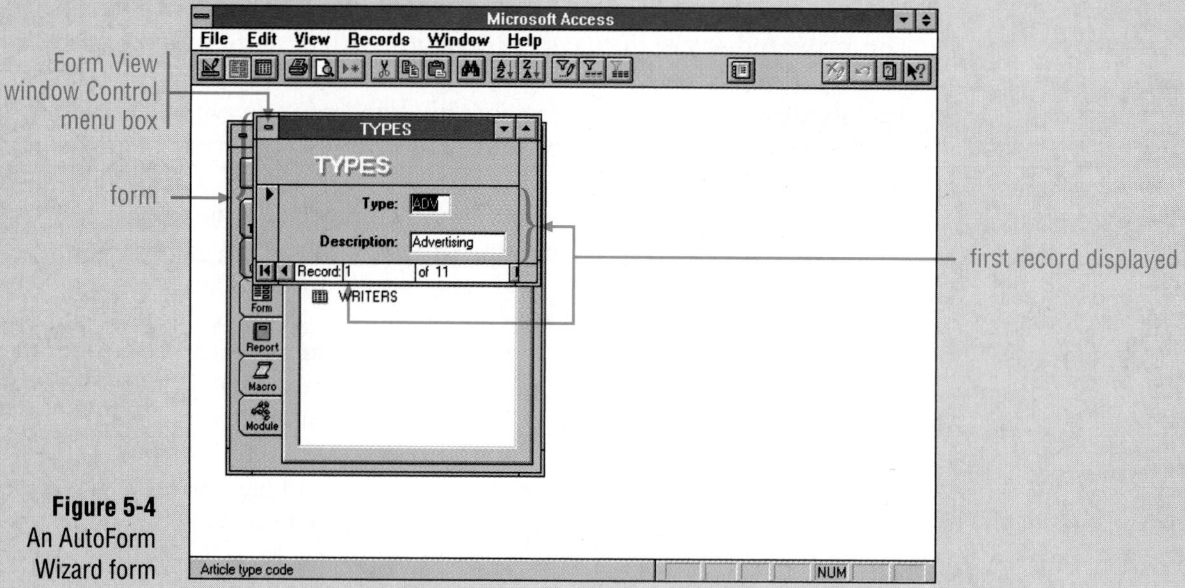

Figure 5-4
An AutoForm Wizard form

Access displays the first record from the TYPES table in the new form. If you want to view other records from the TYPES table, click the form navigation buttons or type a record number between the navigation buttons. You might need to resize the form to see all four navigation buttons.

Saving a Form

Elena saves the form so that she and others can use it for future work with data from the TYPES table. Elena saves the form, using the name TYPES form, and then closes the Form View window.

REFERENCE WINDOW

Saving a New Form

- Click File and then click Save Form As... Access opens the Save As dialog box.
- Type the new form name in the Form Name text box.
- Press [Enter] or click the OK button. Access saves the Form and closes the dialog box.

Let's save Elena's form.

To save and close a new form:

1. Click **File**, and then click **Save Form As...**. The Save As dialog box appears.
2. Type **TYPES form** in the Form Name text box.
3. Press **[Enter]**. The Save As dialog box disappears, and Access saves the form.
4. Double-click the Form View window **Control menu box**. The Form View window disappears, and the Database window becomes the active window.
5. Click the **Form object button**. Access lists the newly saved form. See Figure 5-5.

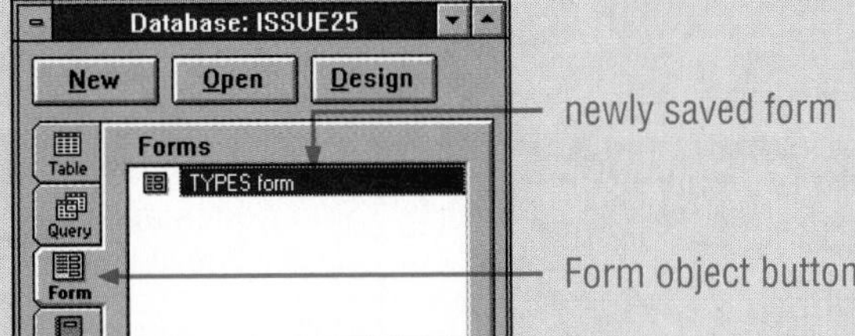

Figure 5-5
Listing a new form

Creating Forms Using Form Wizards

For her next form, Elena uses a Form Wizard to display data from the WRITERS table. She chooses to display all the fields from the table in a single-column form with the standard style.

Creating Single-Column Forms

Let's use a Form Wizard to create a single-column form type with the standard style.

To activate Form Wizards and select a form type:

1. Click the toolbar **New Form button**. The New Form dialog box appears.
2. Click the Select A Table/Query drop-down list box **down arrow button** to display the list of the Issue25 database tables and queries.

❸ Scroll through the Select A Table/Query drop-down list box and then click **WRITERS**. The drop-down list disappears and WRITERS appears highlighted in the box. See Figure 5-6.

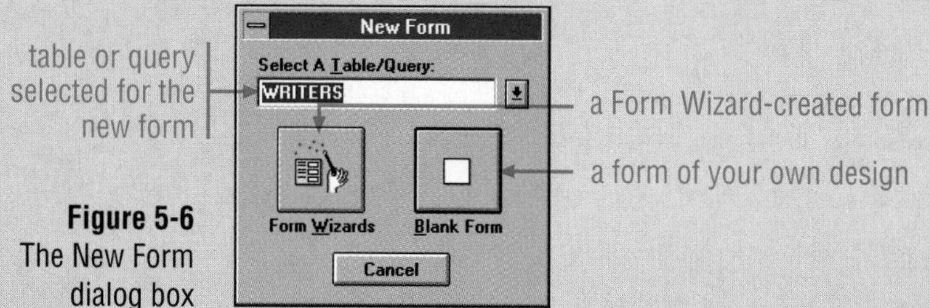

Figure 5-6
The New Form dialog box

❹ Click the **Form Wizards button**. The Form Wizards dialog box appears. This dialog box lists the five form types available through Form Wizards. See Figure 5-7.

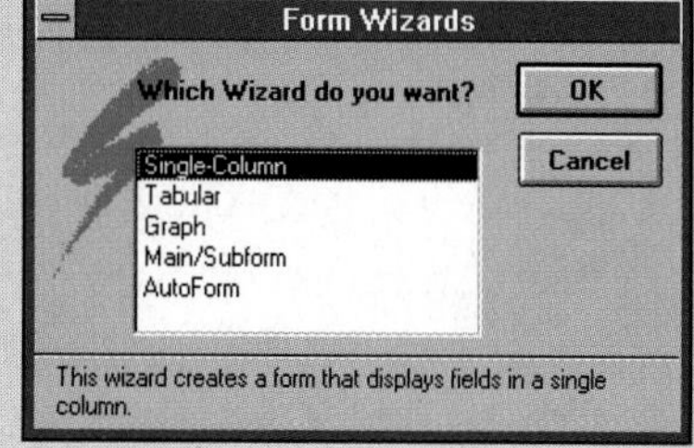

Figure 5-7
Choosing the form type

❺ If Single-Column is not highlighted, click it, and then click the **OK button**. The first Single-Column Form Wizard dialog box appears. See Figure 5-8.

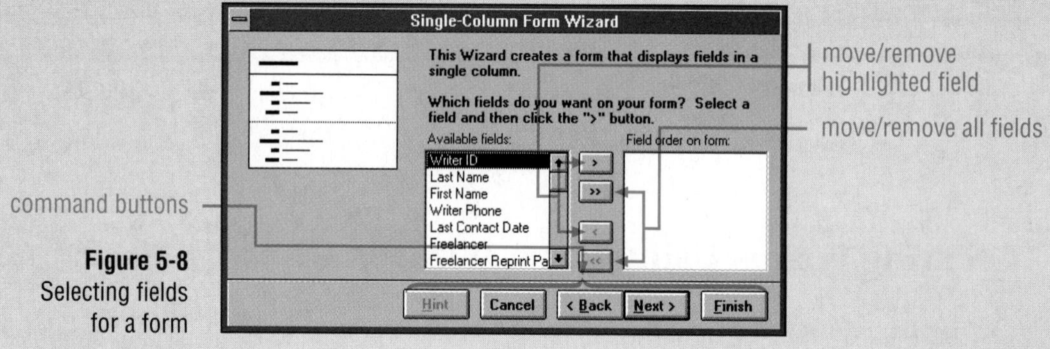

Figure 5-8
Selecting fields for a form

In this Single-Column Form Wizard dialog box, you select fields in the order you want them to appear on the form. If you want to select fields one at a time, highlight a field by clicking it, and then click the > button. If you want to select all fields, click the >> button. The selected fields move from the box on the left to the box on the right as you select them. If you make a mistake, click the << button to remove all fields from the box on the right or highlight a field and click the < button to remove fields one at a time.

Each Form Wizards dialog box displays command buttons on the bottom that allow you to move quickly to the other Form Wizards dialog boxes. You can go to the previous or next Form Wizards dialog box. You can also cancel the form creation process to return to the Database window; you can prematurely finish the form and accept the Form Wizards defaults for the remaining form options; and you can ask for hints about the Form Wizards options.

Elena wants her form to display all the fields from the WRITERS table in the order in which they appear in the table.

To finish creating a form using the Single-Column Form Wizards:

❶ Click the **>> button**. Access removes all the fields from the box on the left and places them in the same order in the box on the right.

❷ Click the **Next > button** to display the next Single-Column Form Wizard dialog box, in which you choose the form's style.

❸ Click the **Standard radio button** and then click the **Next > button**. Access displays the final Single-Column Form Wizard dialog box and shows the table name as the default for the title that will appear in the Form Header section. Elena wants to use the default form title. See Figure 5-9.

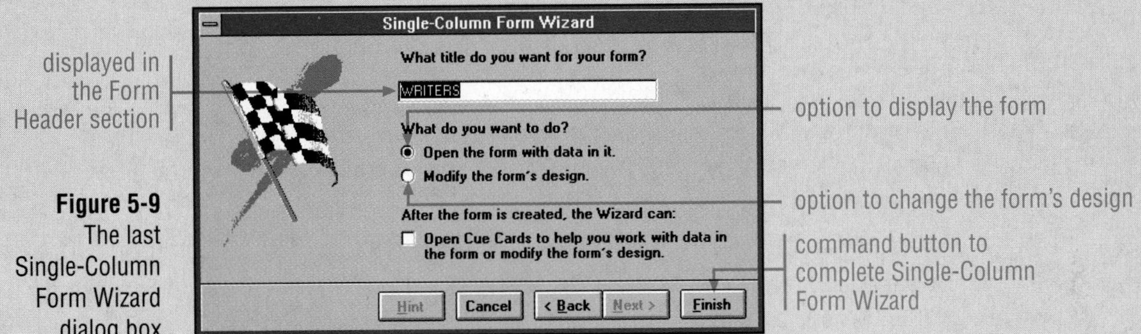

Figure 5-9 The last Single-Column Form Wizard dialog box

❹ Click the **Finish button**. The Form View window opens and displays the completed form. See Figure 5-10.

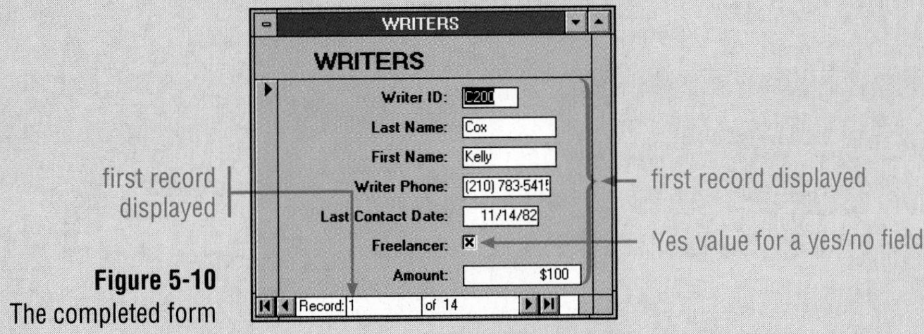

Figure 5-10 The completed form

Notice that Freelancer is a yes/no field and that Form Wizards automatically creates a check box for it. An empty check box indicates a value of No, and an × in the check box indicates a value of Yes.

Elena saves the form, using the name WRITERS form, and then closes the Form View window.

To save and close a new form:

❶ Click **File**, and then click **Save Form As...**. The Save As dialog box appears.

❷ Type **WRITERS form** in the Form Name text box.

❸ Press **[Enter]**. The Save As dialog box disappears, and Access saves the form.

❹ Double-click the Form View window **Control menu box**. The Form View window disappears, and the Database window becomes the active window.

Creating Main/Subform Forms

Elena next creates a form to show a specific writer and his or her articles. Elena will use this form to enter the writer and article data for the first two new articles written for the 25th-anniversary issue.

Because the main/subform form type allows you to work with data from two or more tables, Elena chooses this form type for her new form. The WRITERS table has a one-to-many relationship with the PAST ARTICLES table. Elena selects the WRITERS table for the main form because it is the primary table and the PAST ARTICLES table for the subform because it is the related table. Elena again uses a Form Wizard to create the form.

Because the Form object button is selected, Elena can create the new form by clicking either the toolbar New Form button or the New command button.

To activate Form Wizards and create a main/subform form type:

1. Click the **New command button**. The New Form dialog box appears.
2. Click the Select A Table/Query drop-down list box **down arrow button** to display the list of the Issue25 database tables and queries.
3. Scroll down the list and then click **WRITERS**. The drop-down list disappears and WRITERS appears highlighted in the box.
4. Click the **Form Wizards button**. The Form Wizards dialog box appears.
5. Click **Main/Subform** in the list box and then click the **OK button**. Access displays the first Main/Subform Wizard dialog box, in which you select the table or query for the subform. See Figure 5-11.

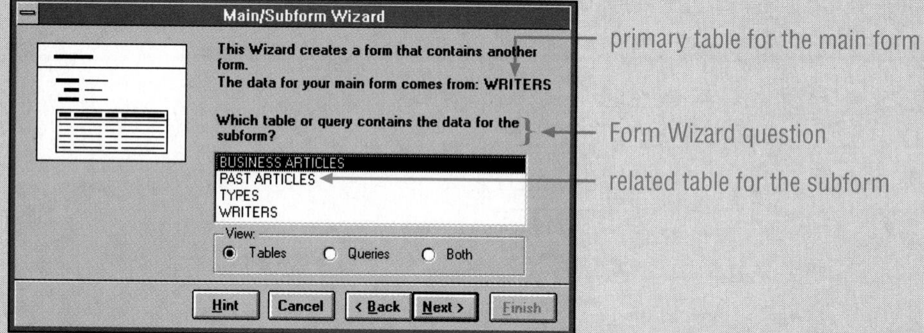

Figure 5-11 Selecting the subform table or query

6. Click **PAST ARTICLES** in the list box, and then click the **Next > button**. Access displays the next Main/Subform Wizard dialog box, in which you select the fields for the main form. Elena wants to display all the fields from the WRITERS table on the main form.
7. Click the **>> button** to select all fields and move them to the box on the right, and then click the **Next > button**. Access displays the next Main/Subform Wizard dialog box, in which you select the fields for the subform.

The Writer ID field will appear in the main form, so it is not needed in the subform. Otherwise, Elena wants to place all the fields from the PAST ARTICLES table on the subform.

To select the subform fields and a main/subform style:

1. Click the **>>button** to select all fields. If Writer ID is not highlighted in the box on the right, click it. Then click the **< button** to remove Writer ID from the box on the right. See Figure 5-12.

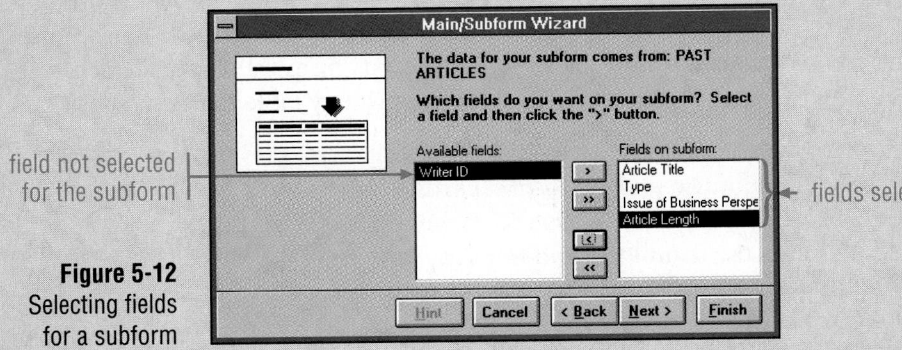

Figure 5-12 Selecting fields for a subform

2. Click the **Next > button**. Access displays the next Main/Subform Wizard dialog box, in which you select the form style.

3. Click the **Standard radio button** and then click the **Next > button**. Access displays the final Main/Subform Wizard window and shows the primary table name as the default form title.

Elena enters the form title WRITERS and PAST ARTICLES. This form title appears at the top of the form in the Form View window. The form itself is saved as two separate forms when you create a main/subform form type. You first save the subform and then you save the form/subform combination.

To title a form and save a subform:

1. Type **WRITERS and PAST ARTICLES**, and then click the **Finish button**. Access displays the "Save the subform" dialog box. You must save the subform before the Main/Subform Wizard can continue.

2. Click the **OK button**. The dialog box disappears, and the Save As dialog box appears.

3. Type **PAST ARTICLES subform** in the Form Name box and then press **[Enter]**. Access saves the subform and displays the completed main/subform window. See Figure 5-13.

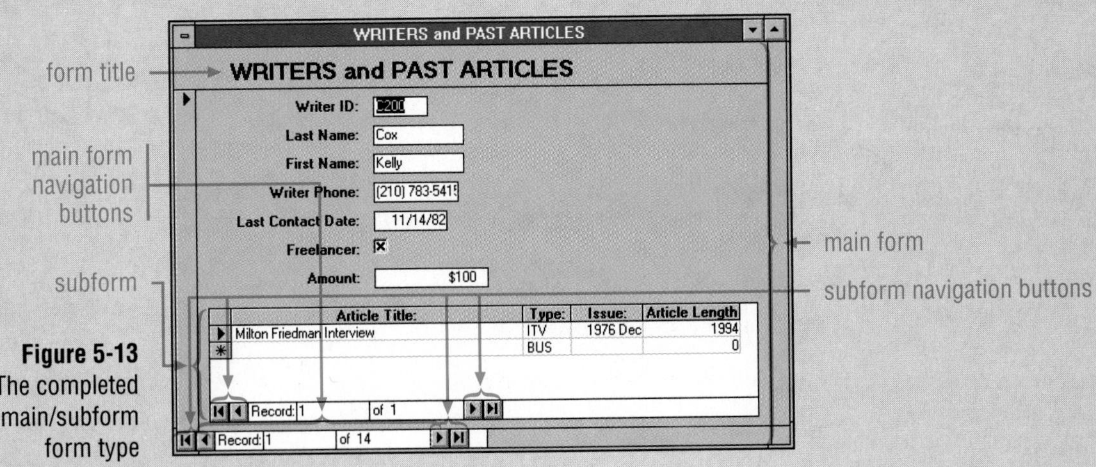

Figure 5-13 The completed main/subform form type

Access displays the fields from the first record in the WRITERS table in single-column format. The records in this main form appear in primary-key sequence. The writer Kelly Cox has one record in the PAST ARTICLES table that is shown at the bottom in datasheet format.

Elena wants to view the data for a writer who has more than one record in the PAST ARTICLES table. Two sets of navigation buttons appear at the bottom of the form. You use the top set of navigation buttons to select records from the related table in the subform and the bottom set to select records from the primary table in the main form.

To navigate to different main and subform records:

1. Click the main form **Next Record button** ▶ three times. Access displays the record for Valerie Hall in the main form and her three articles in the subform.
2. Click the subform ▶ once. Access changes the current record to the second article in the subform.

In addition to viewing data in a form and in a subform, you can also add, change, and delete field values and records. If a writer has four or more articles, Access adds a scroll bar on the right side of the subform.

Elena saves the main/subform combination using the name WRITERS and PAST ARTICLES form. This form name will appear in the Database window when you click the Form object button to display a list of the database's forms.

To save a new form/subform:

1. Click **File**, and then click **Save Form As...**. The Save As dialog box appears.
2. Type **WRITERS and PAST ARTICLES form**.
3. Press **[Enter]**. The Save As dialog box disappears, and Access saves the form.

Maintaining Table Data Using a Form

Elena needs to make two field value changes to one of Valerie Hall's articles. Then she will add two new articles to the database. The database modifications involve three articles and three writers, as shown in Figure 5-14.

Action	Table	Record and Fields
Change	PAST ARTICLES	Article Title: The BBCI Scandal Revealed (by Valerie Hall) Issue: from 1991 Jul to 1991 Aug Article Length: from 2461 to 2779
Add	PAST ARTICLES	Article Title: Advertising Over the Past 25 Years (by Thuy Ngo) Type: ADV Issue: 1994 Dec Article Length: 3285
Add	WRITERS	Writer ID: L350 Last Name: Lawton First Name: Pat Writer Phone: (705) 677-1991 Last Contact Date: 9/4/94 Freelancer: No Amount: $0
	PAST ARTICLES	Article Title: Law Over the Past 25 Years (by Pat Lawton) Type: LAW Issue: 1994 Dec Article Length: 2834

Figure 5-14
Maintenance changes to the Issue25 database

To maintain table data using a form, you must know how to move from field to field and from record to record. The mouse movement, selection, and placement techniques to do this are the standard Windows techniques that you used in Tutorial 3. If you are maintaining data in a subform, the keyboard techniques are also the same as those described in Tutorial 3. For other form types, you use the same keyboard deletion techniques that you use in editing mode and the same data entry and editing shortcut keys. The form navigation and editing mode keyboard movement techniques, however, differ slightly, as shown in Figure 5-15 on the following page.

Press	To Move the Selection Point in Navigation Mode	To Move the Insertion Point in Editing Mode
[Left Arrow]	To the previous field value	Left one character at a time
[Right Arrow] or [Tab] or [Enter]	To the next field value	Right one character at a time
[Home]	To the first field value in the record	Before the first character in the field value
[End]	To the last field value in the record	After the last character in the field value
[Up Arrow] or [Down Arrow]	To the previous or next field value	The insertion point does not move
[PgUp]	To the same field value in the previous record	To the same field value in the previous record and switch to navigation mode
[PgDn]	To the same field value in the next record	To the same field value in the next record and switch to navigation mode
[Ctrl][Left Arrow] or [Ctrl][Right Arrow]	To the previous or next field value	Left or right one word at a time
[Ctrl][Up Arrow] or [Ctrl][Down Arrow]	To the same field value in the first or last record	Before the first character or after the last character in the field value
[Ctrl][PgUp]	To the same field value in the previous record	Before the first character in the field value
[Ctrl][PgDn]	To the same field in the next record	After the last character in the field value
[Ctrl][Home]	To the first value in the first record	Before the first character in the field value
[Ctrl][End]	To the first subform field value for the last main form record	After the last character in the field value

Figure 5-15
Form navigation and editing mode keyboard movement techniques

Elena first makes the two changes to one of Valerie Hall's articles. Because the article she wants to change is already selected, Elena just moves to the field values in the subform and changes them.

To change table field values using a form:

1. Press **[Tab]** twice. The Issue field value 1991 Jul is highlighted.
2. Double-click Jul and then type **Aug** as the changed month value for the Issue field.
3. Press **[Tab]** to move to and highlight the Article Length field.
4. Type **2779** as the changed field value for the Article Length field.

Elena next adds records to the Issue25 database. She first adds one article for Thuy Ngo. There is already a record for Thuy Ngo in the WRITERS table, record number 10.

To add a record in a subform:

1. Click the record number that is displayed between the main form navigation buttons (4) and then press **[F2]** to highlight the number. Type **10** and then press **[Enter]**. Thuy Ngo's record appears, and the Article Title field is selected in the subform.
2. Press **[Down Arrow]** once to move to the Article Title field for the next available record in the subform.
3. Type **Advertising Over the Past 25 Years**, press **[Tab]**, type **ADV**, press **[Tab]**, type **1994 Dec**, press **[Tab]**, type **3285**, and then press **[Tab]**. See Figure 5-16. Access has added this record to the PAST ARTICLES table for Thuy Ngo.

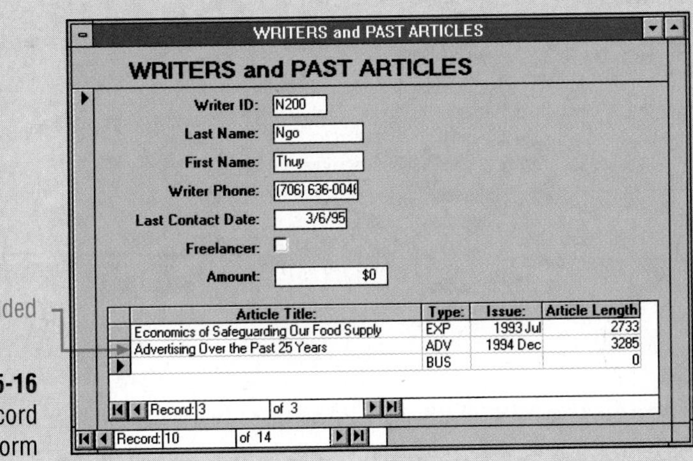

Figure 5-16 Adding a record in a subform

Elena's last change is to add one record to the WRITERS table and one record to the PAST ARTICLES table. To add a record to the WRITERS table, Elena navigates to the next available record in the table. You use the bottom set of navigation buttons to change which record Access displays in the main WRITERS form.

To add a new writer and a new article using a form:

1. Click the main form's **Last Record button**. Access displays the record for Shinjiro Yamamura in the main form and his one article in the subform.
2. Click the main form's **Next Record button**. Access moves to record 15 in the main form and to record 1 in the subform, clears all field values, and positions the insertion point in the subform's Article Title field.
3. Click the **field-value box** for the Writer ID field in the main form to position the insertion point there.
4. Type **L350**, press **[Tab]**, type **Lawton**, press **[Tab]**, type **Pat**, press **[Tab]**, type **7056771991**, press **[Tab]**, type **9/4/94**, and then press **[Tab]** to enter the first five field values. An ×, which indicates a value of Yes, appears in the Freelancer field value box.
5. Press **[Spacebar]** to change the Freelancer field value to No, and then press **[Tab]** to move to the Amount field.
6. Press **[Tab]**. Access saves the new record in the WRITERS table and positions the insertion point in the Article Title field in the subform.

7. Type **Law Over the Past 25 Years**, press **[Tab]**, type **LAW**, press **[Tab]**, type **1994 Dec**, press **[Tab]**, and then type **2834**. See Figure 5-17.

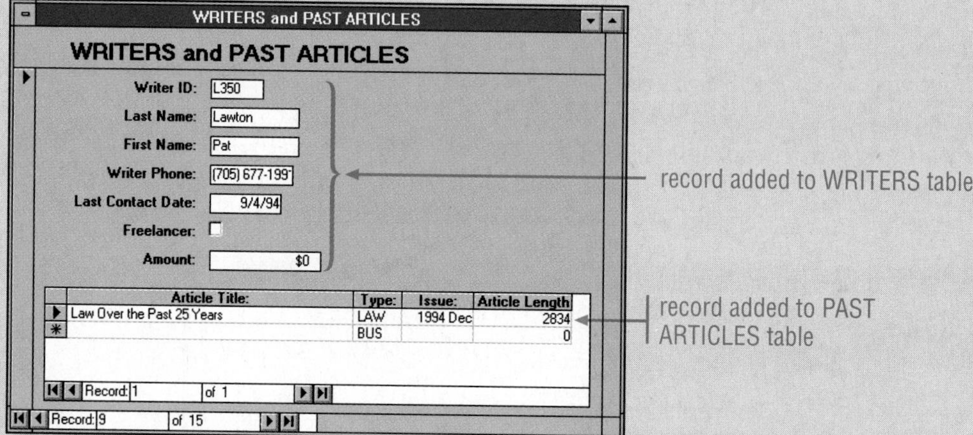

Figure 5-17 Adding records in a main form and a subform

8. Press **[Tab]**. Access saves the new record in the PAST ARTICLES table and positions the insertion point in the Article Title field for the next available record in the subform.

When you created the WRITERS and PAST ARTICLES form, you selected all fields from the WRITERS table for the main form. However, you did not select the Writer ID field for the subform. Because the Writer ID field is the common field between the two tables, Access uses the Writer ID field value from the main form when it saves the subform record in the PAST ARTICLES table.

Elena has completed her maintenance tasks, so she closes the Form View window and maximizes the Database window to see a list of the forms in the Issue25 database.

To close the Form View window and list the forms for a database:

1. Double-click the Form View window **Control menu box**. The Form View window disappears.
2. Click the Database window **maximize button**. Access displays a full list of the forms you created. See Figure 5-18.

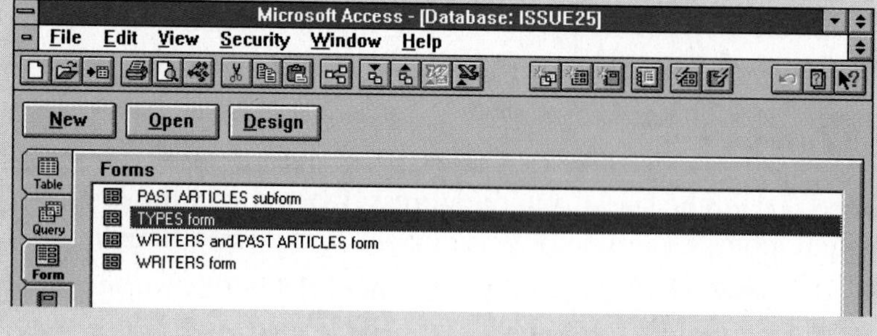

Figure 5-18 The Forms list in the Database window

If you want to take a break and resume the tutorial at a later time, you can exit Access by double-clicking the Microsoft Access window Control menu box. When you resume the tutorial, place your Student Disk in the appropriate drive, launch Access, open the Issue25 database on your Student Disk, maximize the Database window, and click the Form object button.

■ ■ ■

Finding and Sorting Records in a Form

Later that same day, Harold calls Elena to ask for the phone number of the freelance writer Chong Kim. Elena answers Harold's question by searching in the WRITERS and PAST ARTICLES form.

Using the Find Command

To find Chong Kim's phone number, Elena uses the toolbar Find button. Elena first opens the WRITERS and PAST ARTICLES form.

To open a form:

❶ If it is not already selected, click **WRITERS and PAST ARTICLES form** in the Database window's Forms list box.

❷ Click the **Open command button**. The Form View window that appears is maximized because you had maximized the Database window.

The left side of the toolbar in the Form View window has several buttons, as shown in Figure 5-19. You have already used some of these buttons. You will use the six buttons on the right side of Figure 5-19 in the next few steps of this tutorial.

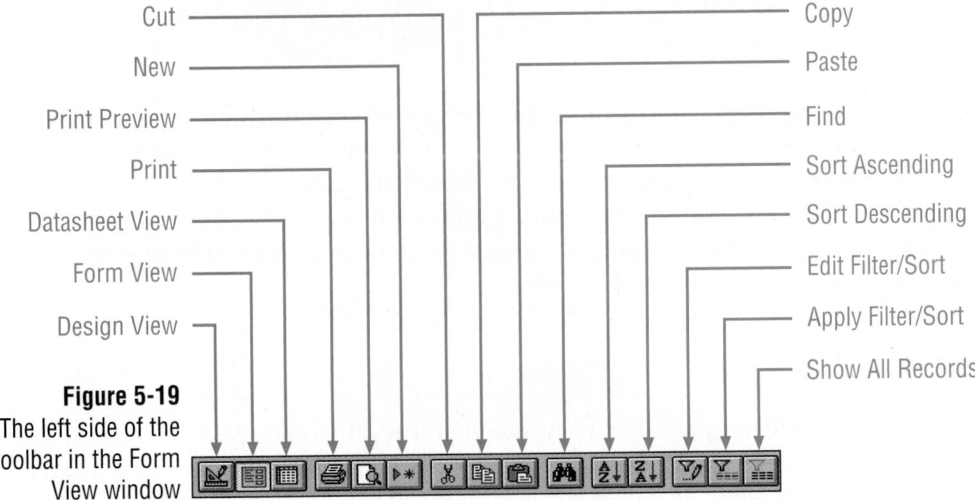

Figure 5-19
The left side of the toolbar in the Form View window

To find Chong Kim's record, Elena uses the Find button to search for a match on the Last Name field.

To find data in the Form View window:

❶ Click the main form's **field-value box** for the Last Name field to make it the search field for the Find command.

❷ Click the toolbar **Find button** . The Find dialog box appears.

❸ Click the title bar of the Find dialog box and drag the Find dialog box to the lower right to get a better view of the main form's field values and navigation buttons.

❹ Type **Kim** in the Find What text box, and then click the **Find First button** in the Find dialog box. Access finds the first Chong Kim and displays the sixth WRITERS table record. This Chong Kim is not a freelancer, so Elena searches for the next Chong Kim.

❺ Click the **Find Next button** in the Find dialog box. Access displays the next Chong Kim, whose record is the seventh WRITERS table record. His article is titled Cola Advertising War. This Chong Kim is a freelancer, so Elena has completed her search. She jots down the phone number.

❻ Click the **Close button**. The Find dialog box disappears.

Elena gives Chong Kim's phone number to Harold. Harold next asks Elena for the phone number and name of the writer with the oldest last contact date.

Quick Sorting in a Form

To find the writer with the oldest last contact date, Elena uses the toolbar Sort Ascending button to do a quick sort. She first selects the Last Contact Date field, so that the records will appear in the form in increasing order by this field.

To quick sort records in a form:

❶ Click the main form's **field-value box** for the Last Contact Date field to make it the selected field for the quick sort.

❷ Click the toolbar **Sort Ascending button** . Access displays the record for Shinjiro Yamamura, who has the earliest Last Contact Date field value, 9/26/72.

You can use the main form's Next Record navigation button to display the writer records, one at a time, in ascending order by last contact date. If you want Access to display the records in the default order by Writer ID, which is the primary key, click the toolbar's Show All Records button, and then use the navigation buttons.

Elena gives Shinjiro Yamamura's phone number to Harold. Harold next asks Elena for the phone numbers of all freelance writers.

Using a Filter

You use the Find command in a form when you want to see records that match a specific field value, and you use the quick sort buttons if you want Access to display all records in order by a single field. If you want Access to display selected records, display records sorted by two or more fields, or display selected records and sort them, you use a filter.

A **filter** is a set of criteria that describes the records you want to see in a form and their sequence. You enter record selection criteria in the Filter window in the same way you specify record selection criteria for a query. Elena wants to view only records for freelancers in her form, so she uses a filter to specify this criterion. Elena chooses a descending sort of the records based on the Last Contact Date field.

To open the Filter window and specify selection and sorting criteria:

1. Click the toolbar **Edit Filter/Sort button**. The Filter window appears.
2. Scroll the WRITERS field list to display the Freelancer field. Double-click **Freelancer** in the WRITERS field list. Access adds the Freelancer field to the second column of the Filter window grid. Because you selected the Last Contact Date field for the previous quick sort, it appears in the Filter window grid in the first column.
3. Click the **Criteria text box** in the Freelancer column and then type **Yes**.
4. Click the **Sort text box** in the Last Contact Date column, click the **down arrow button**, and click **Descending**. See Figure 5-20.

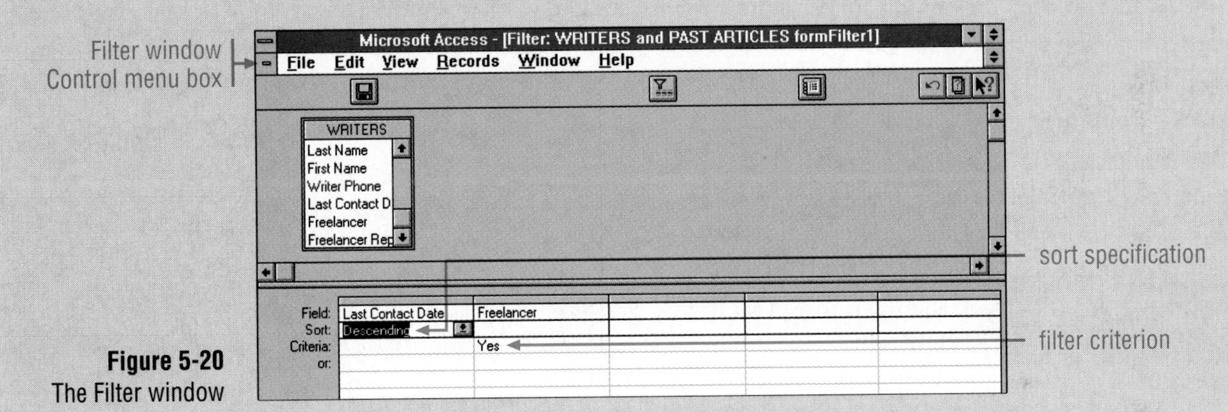

Figure 5-20
The Filter window

Elena has defined the filter; next she saves it as a query. By doing this, she can reuse the filter in the future by opening the saved query.

To save a filter as a query:

1. Click the toolbar **Save button**. The Save As Query dialog box appears.
2. Type **Freelancers and PAST ARTICLES** in the Query Name box and then press **[Enter]**. Access saves the filter as a query, and the Save As Query dialog box disappears.

Elena closes the Filter window and applies the filter. Applying the filter selects the records based on your selection criteria in the order specified by the sort criteria.

To close the Filter window and apply a filter:

1. Double-click the Filter window **Control menu box**. The Filter window disappears and Access displays the Form View window.

   TROUBLE? If you accidentally exit Access, launch Access, open the Issue25 database, maximize the Database window, click the Form object button, double-click the WRITERS and PAST ARTICLES form, click the Edit Filter/Sort button, click File, click Load From Query..., double-click Freelancers and PAST ARTICLES, and double-click the Filter window Control menu box. Then continue to Step 2.

2. Click the toolbar **Apply Filter/Sort button**. Access selects records based on the filter criteria and displays records in sort-key sequence. The record for Wilhelm Seeger is the first record to appear in the main form. His three articles appear in the subform.

3. Click the main form **Last Record button**. Access displays the record for Tonya Nilsson in the main form and her two articles in the subform.

The last record is record six. Because you view only the freelancer records when you apply the filter, you see only six of the 15 records in the table.

Elena gives Harold the phone numbers for all the freelancers. She then removes the filter. You remove a filter by clicking the Show All Records button on the toolbar.

To remove a filter:

1. Click the toolbar **Show All Records button**. Access displays the record from the WRITERS table with the lowest primary-key value. This is the record for Kelly Cox, who has a Writer ID of C200.

2. Click the main form **Last Record button**. Access displays the record from the WRITERS table with the highest primary key value. This is the record for Shinjiro Yamamura, who has a Writer ID of Y556.

When the filter is applied, Access displays one of the six records for freelancers from the WRITERS table. When you remove the filter, Access displays one of the 15 records stored in the WRITERS table.

Elena closes the Form View window and checks to be sure the filter was saved as a query.

To close the Form View window and view the query list:

1. Double-click the Form View window **Control menu box**. Access closes the Form View window and activates the Database window.

2. Click the **Query object button**. The Queries list box appears. See Figure 5-21.

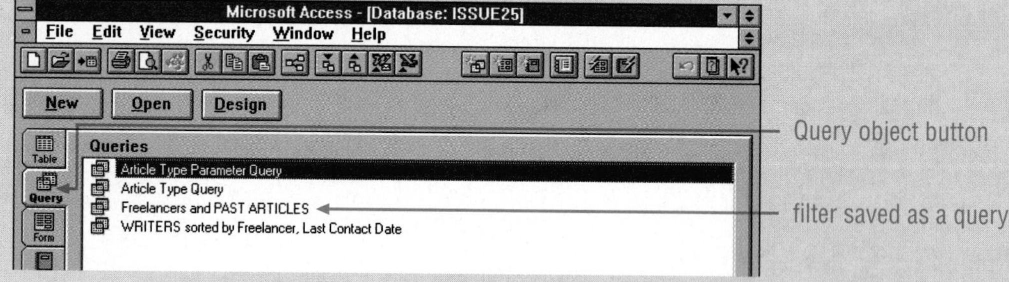

Figure 5-21 The Queries list box in the Database window

Elena wants to be sure she remembers how to apply a filter that she saved as a query. She opens the WRITERS and PAST ARTICLES form and applies the Freelancers and PAST ARTICLES query as a filter.

To apply a filter that was saved as a query:

1. Click the **Form object button** in the Database window and double-click **WRITERS and PAST ARTICLES form** in the Forms list box. The Form View window appears.
2. Click the toolbar **Edit Filter/Sort button**. Access displays the Filter window.
3. Click **File**, and then click **Load From Query...**. The Applicable Filter dialog box appears. See Figure 5-22.

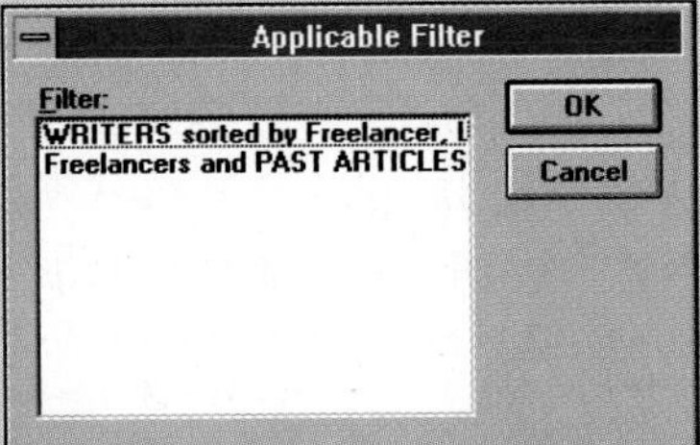

Figure 5-22 The Applicable Filter dialog box

4. Double-click **Freelancers and PAST ARTICLES**. The Applicable Filter dialog box disappears, and Access loads the saved query into the Filter grid.
5. Double-click the Filter window **Control menu box** to close the Filter window.
6. Click the toolbar **Apply Filter/Sort button**. Access applies the filter.
7. Click the main form **Last Record button**. Access displays the sixth freelancer record, which is for Tonya Nilsson.
8. Double-click the Form View window **Control menu box**. The Form View window disappears, and the Database window becomes the active window.

If you want to take a break and resume the tutorial at a later time, you can exit Access by double-clicking the Microsoft Access window Control menu box. When you resume the tutorial, place your Student Disk in the appropriate drive, launch Access, open the Issue25 database on your Student Disk, maximize the Database window, and click the Form object button.

■ ■ ■

Creating a Custom Form

Elena places the Issue25 database on the company network, and Harold, Judith, and Brian use it to answer their questions. The most popular query proves to be the Article Type Query, which lists the article title, type, and length, and the writer's first and last names. Harold tells Elena that he would like the option of viewing the same information in a form, and Elena designs a custom form based on the query.

If you modify a form created by a Form Wizard, or if you design and create a form without using a Form Wizard, you have developed a **custom form**. You might create a custom form, for example, to match a paper form, to display some fields side by side and others top to bottom, to highlight the form with color, or to add special buttons and list boxes.

Designing a Custom Form

Although Elena's custom form is relatively simple, she first designs the form's content and appearance on paper. Elena's finished design is shown in Figure 5-23.

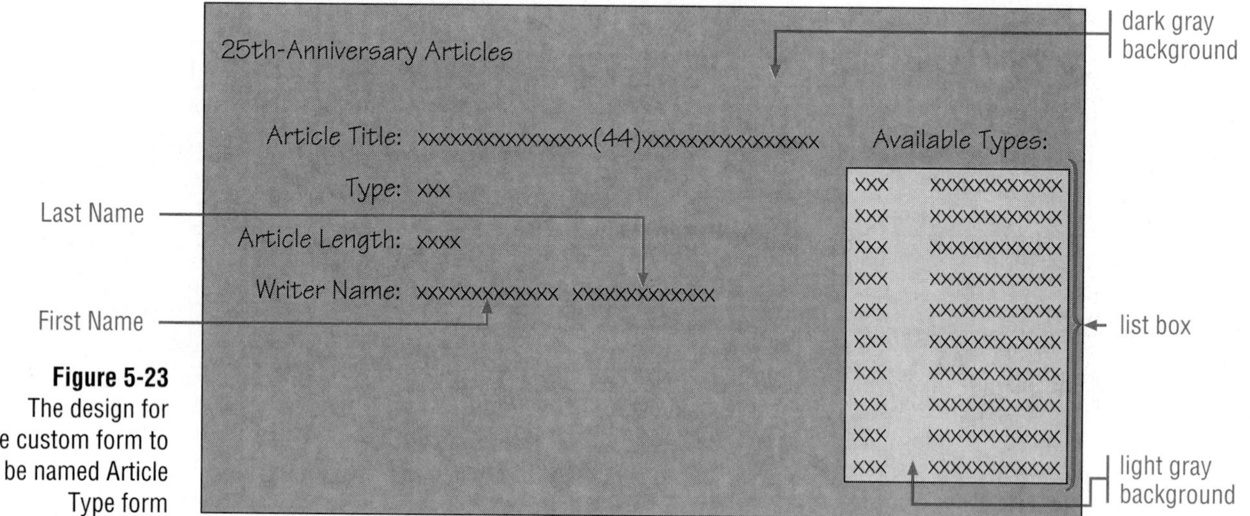

Figure 5-23
The design for the custom form to be named Article Type form

The title for the designed form is 25th-Anniversary Articles. The designed form displays all fields from the Article Type Query in single-column format, except for the writer's First Name and Last Name fields, which are side by side.

Each field value will appear in a text box and will be preceded by a label. Elena indicates the locations and lengths of each field value by a series of Xs. The three Xs that follow the Type field label indicate that the field value will be three characters wide.

Because many of her coworkers are unfamiliar with all the article type codes, a list box containing both the article types and their full descriptions will appear on the right. Elena plans to add background colors of light gray to the list box and dark gray to the rest of the form to make the form easier to read.

All the data Elena needs for her custom form is contained in the Article Type Query. Thus, unlike her previous Form Wizard forms that were based on tables, Elena will use a query to create the custom form and will use all the fields from the Article Type Query. This query obtains data from both the PAST ARTICLES and WRITERS tables and displays records in ascending order by Article Type. The form, which Elena plans to name Article Type form, will likewise display records in ascending Article Type.

The Form Design Window

You use the **Form Design window** to create and modify forms. To create the custom form, Elena creates a blank form based on the Article Type Query in the Form Design window.

To create a blank form in the Form Design window:

1. Click the toolbar **New Form button**. The New Form dialog box appears.
2. Click the Select A Table/Query drop-down list box **down arrow button**. Scroll if necessary, click **Article Type Query**, and then click the **Blank Form button**. The Form Design window appears. See Figure 5-24.

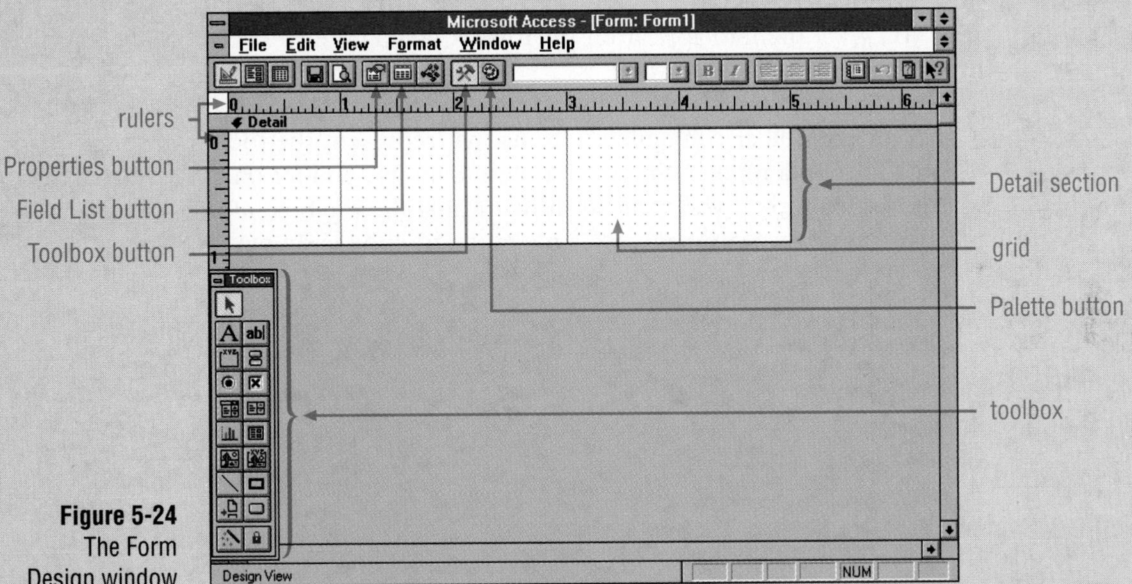

Figure 5-24 The Form Design window

TROUBLE? If the rulers, grid, or toolbox do not appear, click the View menu and then click Ruler, Grid, or Toolbox to display the missing component in the Form Design window. A check mark appears in front of these View menu commands when the components are displayed in the Form Design window. If the grid is still invisible, see your technical support person or instructor for assistance. If the Palette appears in the Form Design window, click the toolbar Palette button to close it until later in the tutorial. If the toolbar Properties button is selected, click it to close the property sheet.

The Form Design window contains four new components and four new toolbar buttons. The new components are the rulers, the Detail section, the grid, and the toolbox; the new toolbar buttons are the Properties button, the Field List button, the Toolbox button and the Palette button.

The **rulers** show the horizontal and vertical dimensions of the form and serve as a guide to the placement of controls on the form. A **control** is a graphical object, such as a text box, a list box, a rectangle, or a command button, that you place on a form or a report to display data, perform an action, or make the form or report easier to read and use. Access has three types of controls: bound controls, unbound controls, and calculated controls. A **bound control** is linked, or bound, to a field in the underlying table or query. You use a bound control to display or update a table field value. An **unbound control** is not linked to a field in the underlying table or query. You use an unbound control to display text, such as a form title or instructions, or to display graphics and pictures from other applications. If you use an unbound control to display text, the unbound control is called a **label**. You can have a label relate to a bound control—a field-name label and a field-value text box can be paired as a bound control, for example. A **calculated control** displays a value calculated from data from one or more fields.

When you want to create a bound control, click the toolbar **Field List button** to display a list of fields available from the underlying table or query. You click and drag fields from the field list box to the Form Design window, placing the bound controls where you want them to appear on the form. Clicking the Field List button a second time closes the field list box.

To place other controls on a form, you use the tool buttons on the toolbox. The **toolbox** is a specialized toolbar containing buttons that represent the tools you use to place controls on a form or a report. When you hold the mouse pointer on a tool, Access displays a ToolTip for that tool. If you want to show or hide the toolbox, click the toolbar **Toolbox button**. A summary of the tools available in the toolbox is shown in Figure 5-25.

Icon	Tool Name	Control Purpose on a Form or Report
	Select objects	Select, move, size, and edit controls
	Label	Display text, such as a title or instructions; an unbound control
	Text Box	Display a label attached to a text box that contains a bound control or a calculated control
	Option Group	Display a group frame containing toggle buttons, option buttons, or check boxes; can use Control Wizards to create
	Toggle Button	Signal if a situation is true (button is selected or pushed down) or false
	Option Button	Signal if a situation is true (black dot appears in the option button's center) or false; also called a radio button
	Check Box	Signal if a situation is true (× appears in the check box) or false
	Combo Box	Display a drop-down list box, so that you can either type a value or select a value from the list; can use Control Wizards to create
	List Box	Display a list of values from which you can choose one value; can use Control Wizards to create
	Graph	Display a graph that can be editd with Microsoft Graph; uses Graph Wizard
	Subform/Subreport	Display both a main form or report from a primary table and a subform or subreport form a related table
	Object Frame	Display a picture, graph, or other OLE object that is stored in an Access database table
	Bound Object Frame	Display a picture, graph, or other OLE object that is stored in an Access database table
	Line	Display a horizontal, vertical, or diagonal line
	Rectangle	Display a rectangle
	Page Break	Mark the start of a new screen or printed page
	Command Button	Display a command button that runs a macro or calls an Access Basic event procedure when the button is clicked; can use Control Wizards to create
	Control Wizards	When selected, activates Control Wizards for certain other toolbox tools
	Tool Lock	Keeps a toolbox tool selected when clicked after target tool is selected; clicking another toolbox tool deactivates

Figure 5-25
Summary of tools available in the toolbox for a form or a report

To open and close the property sheet for a selected control, a section of the form, or the entire form, click the toolbar **Properties button**. You use the **property sheet** to modify the appearance, behavior, and other characteristics of the overall form, a section of a form, or the controls on a form. For example, you can change a control's size or position on the form. The properties shown in the property sheet differ depending on the type of control selected.

When you click the toolbar Palette button, you open or close the Palette. You use the **Palette** to change the appearance and color of a form and its controls. **Appearance** options are normal, raised, or sunken. Colors can be chosen for text, background, and borders from a color palette. You can also use the Palette to control the thickness of lines drawn on the form.

The **Detail section**, which appears in white in the Form Design window, is the area in which you place the fields, labels, and most other controls for your form. You can change the default Detail section size, which is 5" wide by 1" high, by dragging the edges. The **grid** consists of the dots that appear in the Detail section. These dots help you to position controls precisely on a form.

You can add four other sections to a form by clicking the Format menu. The other four sections are the Form Header, Form Footer, Page Header, and Page Footer. Use the **Form Header** and **Form Footer sections** for information such as titles, dates, and instructions that you want to appear only at the top or bottom of a form on the screen or in print. Use the **Page Header** and **Page Footer sections** for information such as column headings or page numbers that you want to appear at the top or bottom of each page in a printed form.

Adding Fields to a Form

Elena's first task in the Form Design window is to add bound controls to the form Detail section for all the fields from the Article Type Query. When you add a bound control to a form, Access adds a label and, to its right, a field-value text box. You create a bound control by selecting one or more fields from the field list box and dragging them to the form. You select a single field by clicking the field. You select two or more fields by holding down [Ctrl] and clicking each field, and you select all fields by double-clicking the field-list title bar.

Because Elena wants to place all the fields from the field list box on the form, she adds bound controls to the form Detail section for all the fields in the field list.

To add bound controls for all the fields in the field list:

1. Click the toolbar **Field List button**. The field list box appears.
2. Double-click the **field-list title bar** to select all the fields in the field list. Access highlights the field list box.
3. Click anywhere in the highlighted area of the field list box and drag to the form's Detail section. Release the mouse button when the pointer is positioned at the top of the Detail section and at the 1.25" mark on the horizontal ruler. Access adds bound controls for the five selected fields. Each bound control consists of a text box and, to its left, an attached label. See Figure 5-26.

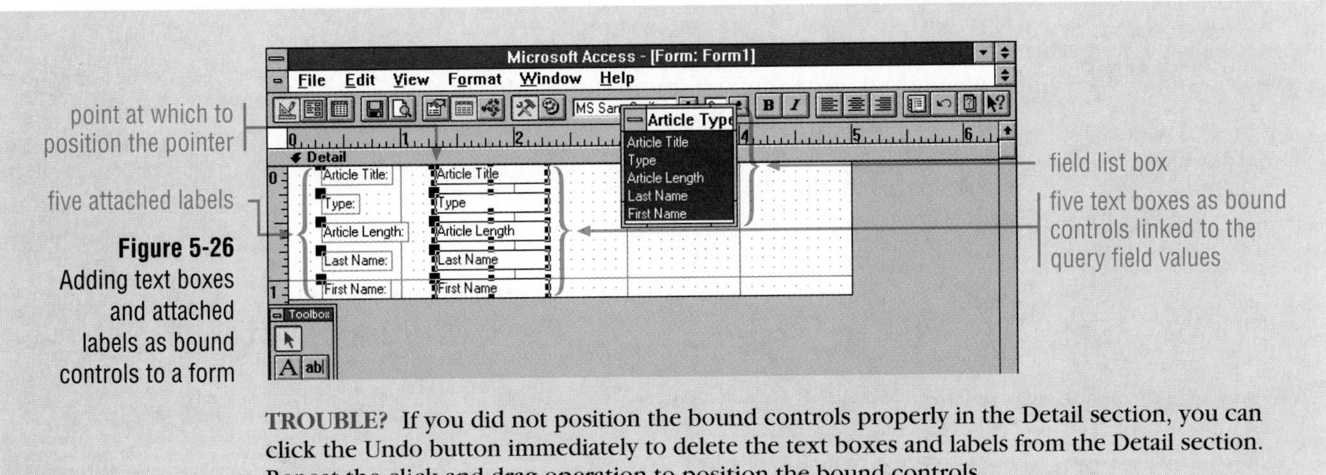

Figure 5-26 Adding text boxes and attached labels as bound controls to a form

TROUBLE? If you did not position the bound controls properly in the Detail section, you can click the Undo button immediately to delete the text boxes and labels from the Detail section. Repeat the click and drag operation to position the bound controls.

Performing operations in the Form Design window might seem awkward for you at first. With practice you will become comfortable with creating a custom form. Remember that you can always click the Undo button immediately after you make a form adjustment that has undesired results.

Selecting, Moving, and Deleting Controls

Five text boxes now appear in a column in the form Detail section. Each text box is a bound control linked to a field in the underlying query and has an attached label box to its left. Because she is done with the field list box, Elena closes it by clicking the Field List button. Elena next compares the form Detail section with her design and arranges the Last Name and First Name text boxes side by side to agree with her form design, as shown in Figure 5-23.

To close the field list box and select a single bound control:

1. Click the toolbar **Field List button** to close the field list box.
2. Two boxes in the Detail section have Last Name inside them. The box on the left is the label box, and the box on the right is the field-value text box. Click in the gray area outside the Detail section to deselect any previous selection and then click the Last Name **field-value text box**. Move handles appear on the field-value text box and its attached label box; in addition, sizing handles appear, but only on the field-value text box. See Figure 5-27.

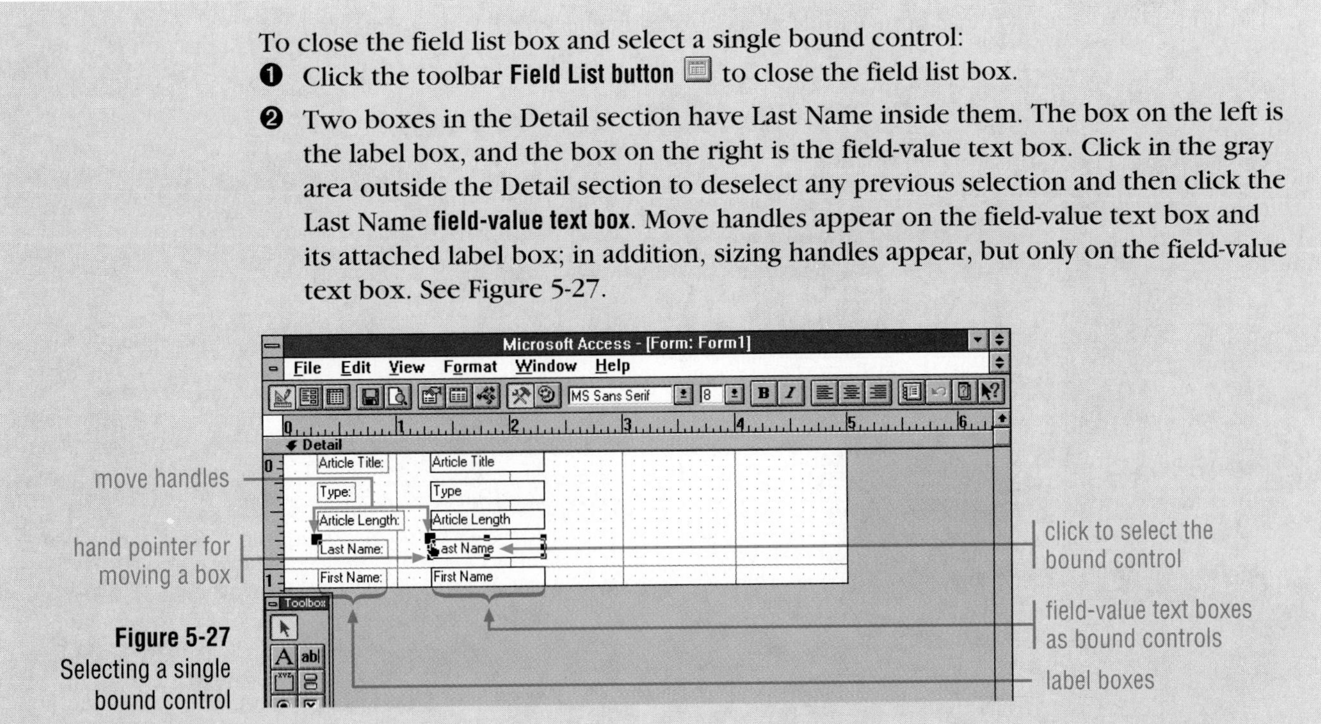

Figure 5-27 Selecting a single bound control

You can move a field-value text box and its attached label box together. To move them, place the pointer anywhere on the border of the field-value text box, but not on a move handle or a sizing handle. When the pointer changes to ✋, drag the field-value text box and its attached label box to the new location. As you move the boxes, their outline moves to show you the changing position.

You can also move either the field-value text box or its label box individually. If you want to move the field-value text box but not its label box, for example, place the pointer on the text box's move handle. When the pointer changes to ☝, drag the field-value text box to the new location. You use the label box's move handle in a similar way to move just the label box.

You can also delete a field-value text box and its attached label box or delete just the label box. To delete both boxes together, click inside the field-value text box to select both boxes, click the right mouse button inside the text box to open its Shortcut menu, and then click Cut on the menu. To delete just the label box, perform the same steps, clicking inside the label box instead of the field-value text box.

Elena moves the Last Name field-value text box to the right without moving its label box. She moves the First Name field-value text box (without its label box) up beside the Last Name box. Then she deletes the First Name label box.

To move field-value text boxes and delete labels:

1. Move the pointer to the Last Name field-value text box move handle. When the mouse pointer changes to ☝, drag the text box horizontally to the right, leaving enough room for the First Name field-value text box to fit in its place. An outline of the box appears as you change its position to guide you in the move operation. Be sure to take advantage of the grid dots in the Detail section to position the box outline.

   TROUBLE? If you move the box incorrectly, click the Undo button immediately and then repeat the step.

2. Click the **field-value text box** for the First Name field and then move the pointer to its move handle. When the mouse pointer changes to ☝, drag the box up to the position previously occupied by the Last Name field-value text box.

3. Click the **label box** for the First Name field to select it. Click the First Name **label box** with the right mouse button to open its Shortcut menu and click **Cut**. The First Name label box disappears. See Figure 5-28.

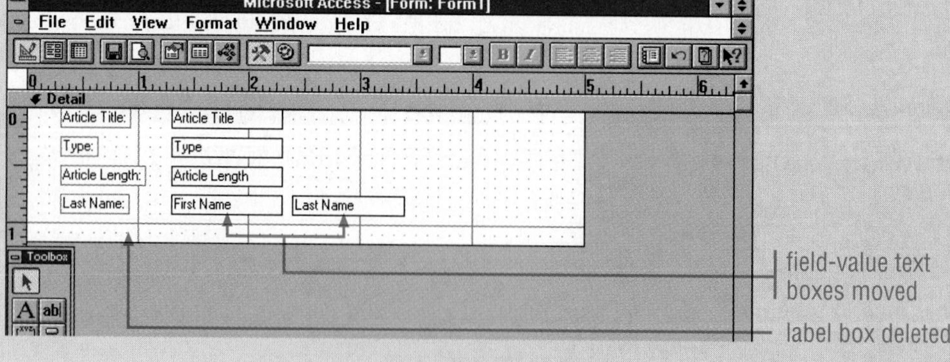

Figure 5-28 Moving field-value text boxes and deleting a label box

Resizing a Control

Elena notices that the Article Title field-value text box is too small to contain long titles, so she resizes it.

You use the seven sizing handles to resize a control. Moving the pointer over a sizing handle changes the pointer to a two-headed arrow; the pointer's direction differs depending on the sizing handle you use. When you drag the sizing handle you resize the control. Thin lines appear, which guide you as you drag the control. You can also resize a label box by selecting the label and using the sizing handles that appear.

Let's resize the Article Title field-value text box by stretching it to the right.

To resize a field-value text box:

❶ Click the **field-value text box** for the Article Title field to select it. Move handles and sizing handles appear.

❷ Move the pointer to the right side of the box over the middle handle. The pointer changes to ↔.

❸ Drag the right border horizontally to the right until the right edge is just past the 3.75" mark on the horizontal ruler. The text box will now accommodate longer Article Title field values.

Changing a Label's Caption and Resizing a Label

Elena now compares the form to her design and notices that she needs to change the name in the Last Name label box to Writer Name. Elena uses the label's property sheet to change the label's Caption property.

To change the Caption property for a label:

❶ Click in an unoccupied area of the grid to deselect all the control boxes.

❷ Click the Last Name **label box** to select it.

❸ Click the toolbar **Properties button** . The property sheet for the Last Name label appears.

❹ Click the **Caption text box** in the property sheet and then press **[F2]** to select the entire value. See Figure 5-29 on the following page.

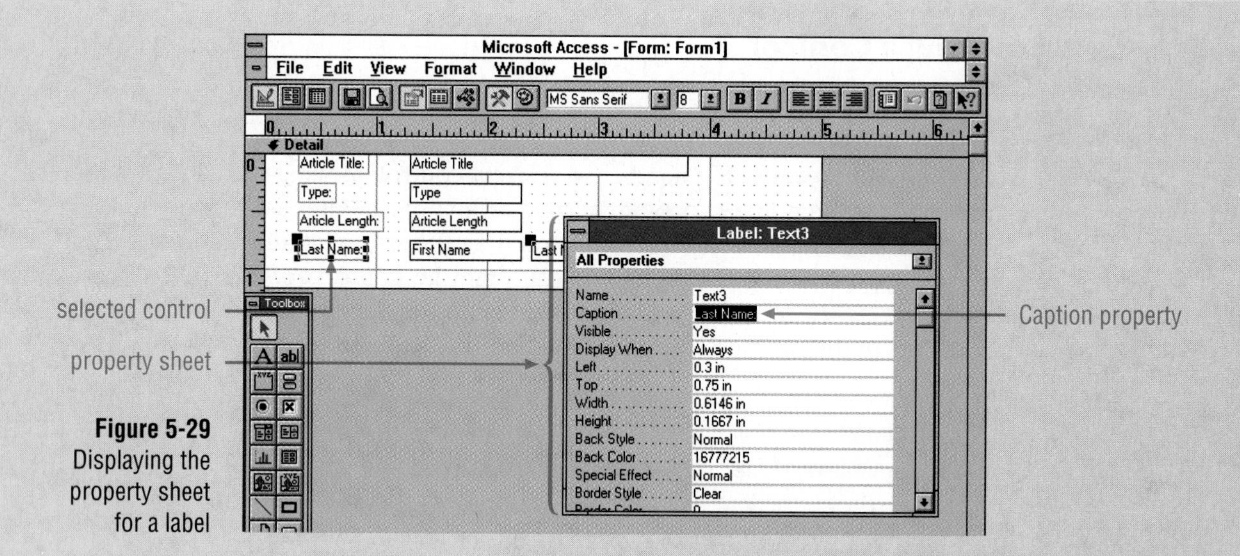

Figure 5-29
Displaying the property sheet for a label

TROUBLE? If the property sheet is not positioned as shown in Figure 5-29, click the title bar of the property sheet and drag the property sheet to the position shown. If some of the property values on your screen differ from those shown in the figure, do not be concerned. Property values will be different if you completed prior operations in a slightly different way.

5. Type **Writer Name:**. Be sure to type a colon at the end of the caption.
6. Click [icon] to close the property sheet. The label box contents change from Last Name: to Writer Name:.

Only part of the new caption is visible in the label box, so Elena resizes the label box.

To resize a label box:

1. The Writer Name **label box** is still the selected control, so move the pointer to the left side of the control over the middle handle. When the pointer changes to ↔, drag the left border horizontally to the left one entire set of grid dots. You might need to try a few times to get it right. If you change the vertical size of the box by mistake, just click the Undo button and try again.

Aligning Labels

Elena next notices that the top three label boxes are left-justified; that is, they are aligned on their left edges. She wants all four label boxes aligned on their right edges. This is an individual preference on her part. Some people prefer left justification for the labels and others prefer right justification. To align several label boxes on the right simultaneously, you must first select all the label boxes by clicking inside each label box while holding down [Shift]. In the following steps be sure you select the label boxes only. If you select the field-value text boxes by mistake, click Undo.

To align all label boxes on the right:

1. While pressing and holding **[Shift]**, click each of the remaining label boxes so that all four are selected, and then release [Shift].

❷ Click any one of the selected label boxes with the right mouse button to display the Shortcut menu.

❸ Click **Align** in the Shortcut menu to open the Align list box, and then click **Right**. Access aligns the label boxes on their right edges. See Figure 5-30.

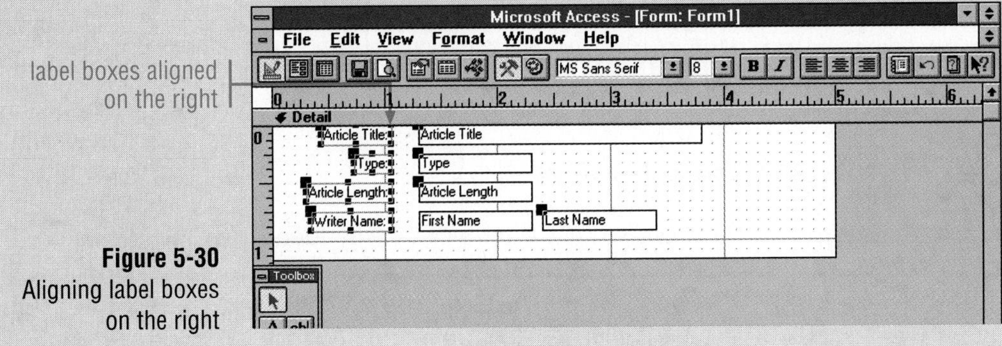

Figure 5-30
Aligning label boxes on the right

Viewing a Form in the Form View Window

Before Elena makes further changes in the Form Design window, she switches to the Form View window to study her results. The first three buttons on the left of the toolbar allow you to switch at any time among the Form Design, Form View, and Datasheet View windows. When you create a form, you should periodically check your progress in the Form View window. You might see adjustments you want to make on your form in the Form Design window.

Let's switch to the Form View window.

To switch to the Form View window:

❶ Click the toolbar **Form View button**. Access closes the Form Design window and opens the Form View window. See Figure 5-31.

Microsoft Access - [Form: Form1]

File Edit View Records Window Help

Article Title:	Advertising Over the Past 25 Years
Type:	ADV
Article Length:	3285
Writer Name:	Thuy Ngo
Article Title:	Cola Advertising War
Type:	ADV
Article Length:	1542
Writer Name:	Chong Kim
Article Title:	AT&T Antitrust Settlement
Type:	BUS
Article Length:	1600
Writer Name:	Chong Kim
Article Title:	The Economy Under Sub-Zero Population Growth
Type:	BUS

first three records

Record: 1 of 27

Form View NUM

Figure 5-31
The Form View window

Your form uses the Article Type Query to sort the records in ascending order by the Type Field. Access displays the first three records from the query and part of the fourth record. You can use the scroll bars and navigation buttons to view other records from the query on the form.

Elena sees some adjustments she wants to make to her design. By default, Access displays as many form records as it can on the screen at one time. Elena wants to display only one record at a time. She also needs to add a form title and add the list box for the article types and descriptions.

Using Form Headers and Footers

Elena next adds a title to the form so that others can easily identify the form when they see it. To do this, she chooses the Form Header/Footer command from the Format menu to add header and footer sections to the form. She then places the title in the Form Header section and deletes the Form Footer section by decreasing its height to zero.

The Form Header and Footer sections allow you to add titles, instructions, command buttons, and other information to your form. You add the Form Header and Footer as a pair. If your form needs one of them but not the other, decrease the height of the unwanted one to zero. This is a way you delete any section on a form.

Elena adds the Form Header and Footer sections to the form.

To add Form Header and Footer sections to a form:

1. Click the toolbar **Design View button**. Access closes the Form View window and opens the Form Design window.
2. Click **Format**, and then click **Form Header/Footer**. Access inserts a Form Header section above the Detail section and a Form Footer section below the Detail section. See Figure 5-32.

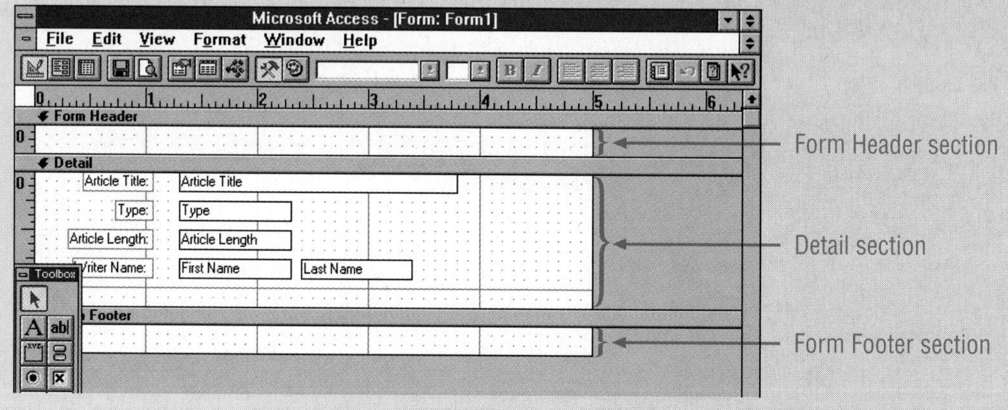

Figure 5-32 Adding the Form Header and Form Footer sections

When you change the width of one section of a form, all sections of the form are affected—the sections all have the same width. Each section, however, can have a different height. You change the width of a form by dragging the right edge of any section, and you change the height of a section by dragging its bottom edge.

Elena deletes the Form Footer section by dragging its bottom edge upward until it disappears.

To delete a Form Footer section:

1. Move the pointer to the bottom edge of the Form Footer section. When the pointer changes to ‡, click and drag the bottom edge upward until it disappears. Even though the words Form Footer remain, the white area defining the section is gone and the section will not appear in the form.

Elena now adds the form title to the Form Header section with the toolbox Label tool. You use the toolbox **Label tool** to add an unbound control to a form or report for the display of text, such as a title or instructions.

To add a label to a form:

1. Click the toolbox **Label tool** A.
2. Move the pointer into the Form Header section. As you move the pointer into the form, the pointer changes to +A. See Figure 5-33. Position the pointer as shown in Figure 5-33.

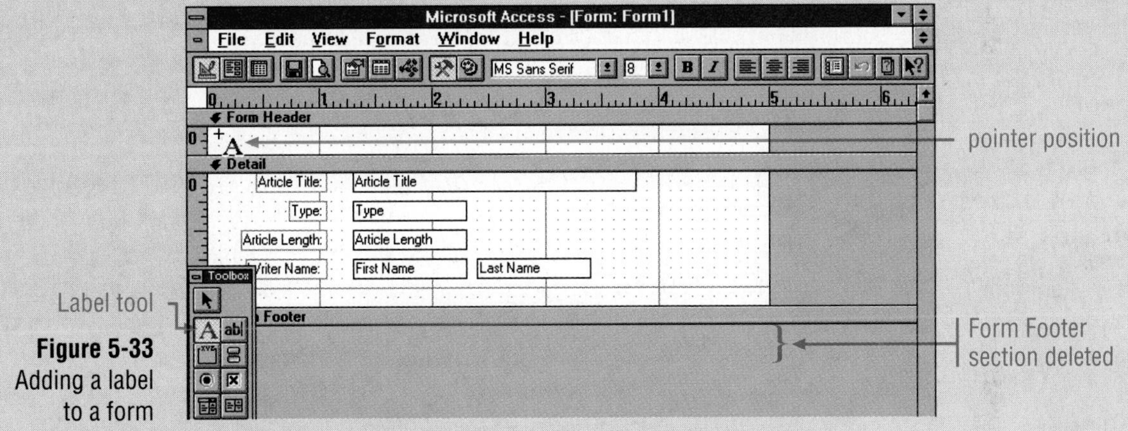

Figure 5-33 Adding a label to a form

3. Click the mouse button when the pointer is correctly positioned. The pointer changes to I.
4. Type **25th-Anniversary Articles** and then press **[Enter]**.

Adding a List Box Using Control Wizards

Because many of her coworkers are unfamiliar with the various article type codes, Elena adds a list box to the form's Detail section. The list box will display all the article types and their full descriptions from the TYPES table. A **list box** is a control that displays a list of values. You can use a list box when a field, such as the Type field, contains a limited set of values. The list box eliminates the need to remember all the Type field values. When you click one of the list box values, Access replaces the form's Type field value with the value you clicked. Thus, you can eliminate the need to keyboard a Type field-value. When you add a list box to a form, Access by default adds a label box to its left.

You use the toolbox List Box tool to add a list box to a form. Depending on whether the toolbox Control Wizards tool is selected, you can add a list box with or without using Control Wizards. A **Control Wizard** is an Access tool that asks you a series of questions and then creates a control on a form or report based on your answers. Access offers Control Wizards for the toolbox Combo Box tool, List Box tool, Option Group tool, and Command Button tool.

Elena will use the List Box Wizard to add the list box for the article types and descriptions. Before she adds the list box, Elena increases the width and the height of the Detail section to make room for the list box. She first moves the toolbox, so that it is out of the way.

To move the toolbox and resize the Detail section:

1. Click the **toolbox title bar** and drag it to the right to the ruler 1" mark.
2. Drag the right edge of the Detail section to the horizontal ruler's 6" mark.
3. Drag the bottom edge of the Detail section to the vertical ruler's 2.25" mark.
4. Drag the **toolbox title bar** to the lower-right corner of the screen. See Figure 5-34.

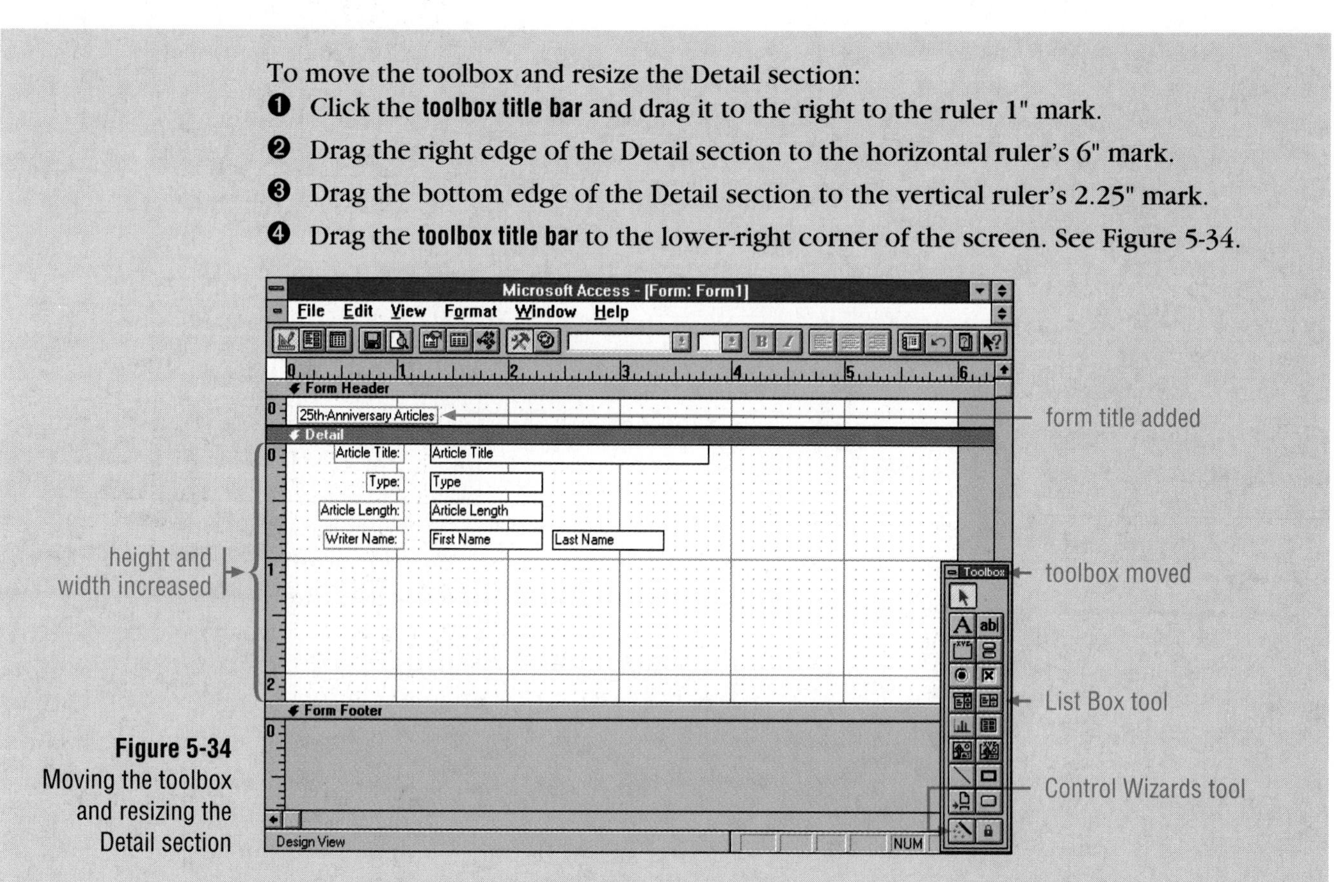

Figure 5-34
Moving the toolbox and resizing the Detail section

Elena adds a list box to the Detail section using the List Box Wizard.

To activate the List Box Wizard:

1. Click the toolbox **Control Wizards tool**.
2. Click the toolbox **List Box tool**. As you move the pointer away from the toolbox, the pointer changes to +. See Figure 5-35.

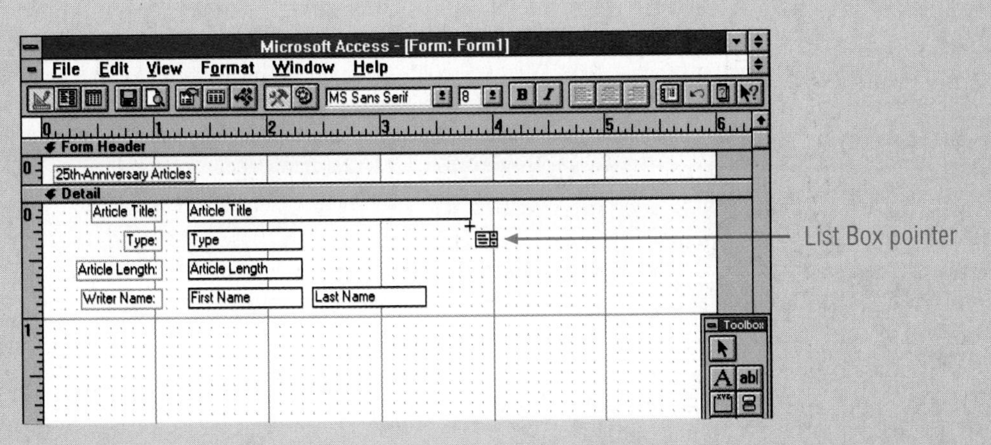

Figure 5-35
Positioning a list box

❸ Click when the list box pointer is positioned as shown in Figure 5-35. After a few seconds, the first List Box Wizard dialog box appears.

Elena tells the List Box Wizard to display two fields from the TYPES table: the Type field and the Description field. She also uses the List Box Wizard dialog box to size the two fields' column widths and to add the label Article Types.

To add a list box using the List Box Wizard:

❶ The TYPES table will supply the values for the list box, so click the **top radio button**, which is labeled "I want the list box to look up the values in a table or query." Then click the **Next > button**. The second List Box Wizard dialog box appears.

❷ Click **TYPES** as the source table for the list box and then click the **Next > button**. The third List Box Wizard dialog box appears.

❸ Because you want both the Type and Description fields to appear in the list box, click the **>> button** to select both fields and then click the **Next > button**. The fourth List Box Wizard dialog box appears.

❹ For both columns, double-click the right edge of each column selector to get the best column fit and then click the **Next > button**. The fifth List Box Wizard dialog box appears.

❺ If Type is not highlighted, click it to select it. Then click the **Next > button**. The sixth List Box Wizard dialog box appears.

❻ Because you want to be able to select a Type field value from the list box and store it in the form's Type field-value text box, click the bottom radio button, which is labeled "Store that value in this field:." Next, click the **down arrow button**, click **Type**, and then click the **Next > button**. The seventh and final List Box Wizard dialog box appears.

7. For a label, type **Article Types:** in the text box and then click the **Finish button**. Access closes the List Box Wizard dialog box and displays the completed list box in the Detail section of the form. See Figure 5-36.

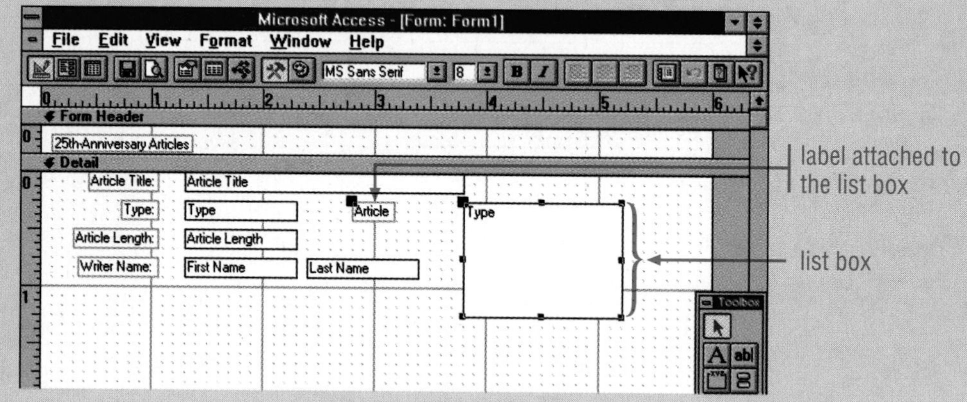

Figure 5-36
Adding a list box to a form

The attached label appears to the left of the list box. Elena resizes the label and then moves it above the list box.

To resize and move a label:

1. Click the label box attached to the list box to select it.
2. Click **Format**, click **Size**, and then click **to Fit**. The label's entire caption is now visible.
3. Click and drag the **label box's move handle** to position the label box above the list box. See Figure 5-37.

Figure 5-37
Resizing and moving a label

Adding Background Colors to a Form

Elena's final tasks are to add background colors to the list box and to the Form Header and Detail sections and to change the form property sheet to display a single record at a time. The Default View property for a form, Continuous Forms, displays as many records as possible on a form. To show a single record on a form, you change the Default View property to Single Form.

To display a single record at a time on a form:

1. Click anywhere in the area below the Form Footer bar. This action makes the form itself the selected control.
2. Click the toolbar **Properties button** to display the property sheet for the form.
3. Click the **Default View box** in the property sheet, click the **down arrow button**, and then click **Single Form**.
4. Click to close the property sheet.

Elena changes the background colors on the form. She changes the list box background to light gray and the background of the Detail and Form Header sections to a darker gray.

REFERENCE WINDOW

Adding Colors to a Form

- Click the control you want to color.
- Click the toolbar Palette button to display the Palette.
- Select the appearance, color, or other special effect from the Palette.
- Click the Palette button to close the Palette.

Let's change the colors of the list box and the two form sections.

To change the colors of a list box and the form sections:

1. Click the list box to select it.
2. Click the toolbar **Palette button** to display the Palette. See Figure 5-38.

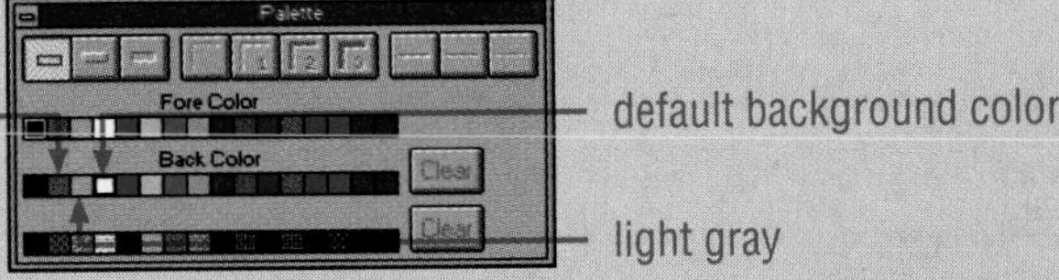

Figure 5-38 The Palette

3. Click the **light gray color box** on the Back Color line. This is the third box from the left.
4. Click the Detail section, but do not click any of the controls in that section. This makes the Detail section the selected control.
5. Click the **dark gray color box** on the Back Color line. This is the second box from the left.
6. Click the Form Header section, but do not click the label box. This makes the Form Header section the selected control.

7. Click the **dark gray color box** on the Back Color line again. See Figure 5-39.

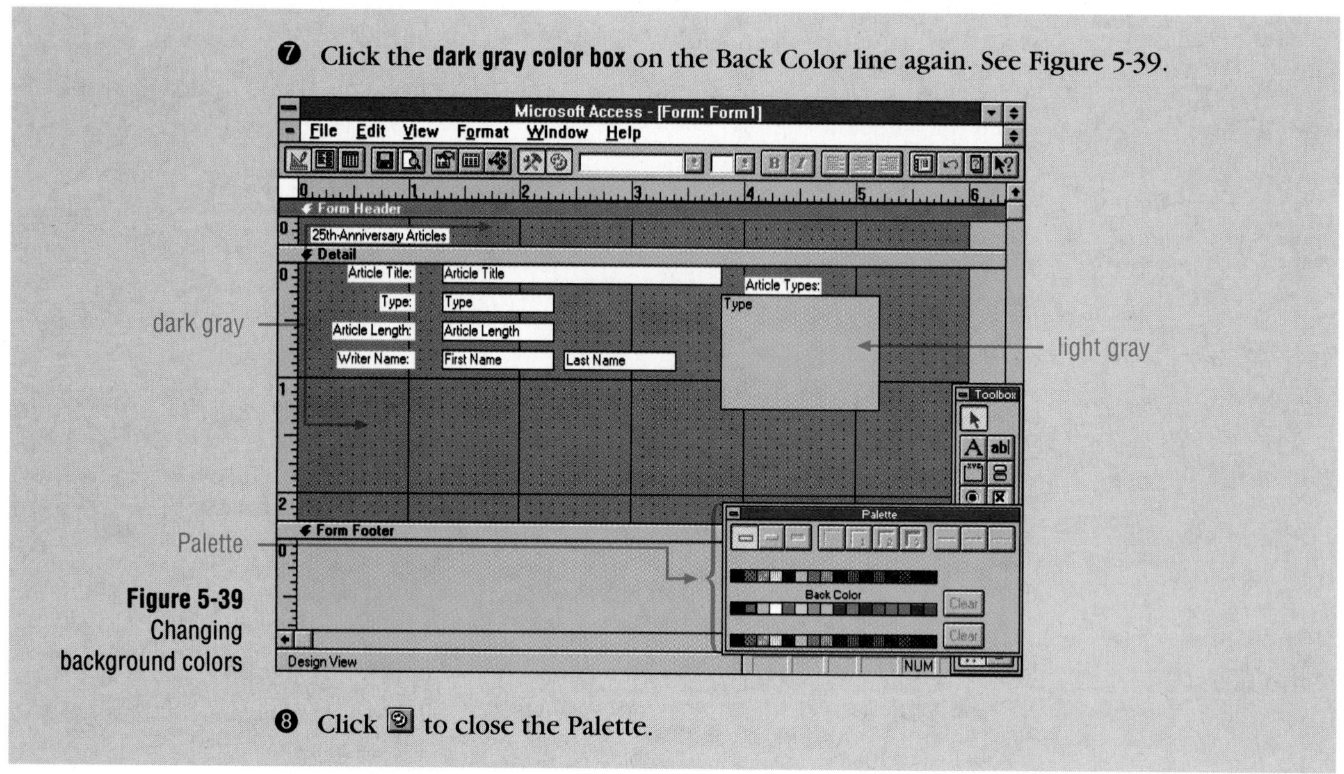

Figure 5-39 Changing background colors

8. Click the close button to close the Palette.

Making Final Revisions to a Custom Form

Elena switches to the Form View window to review the custom form. She wants to see if there are any further changes she needs to make to the form.

To switch to the Form View window to review a custom form:

1. Click the toolbar **Form View button**. Access closes the Form Design window and opens the Form View window. See Figure 5-40.

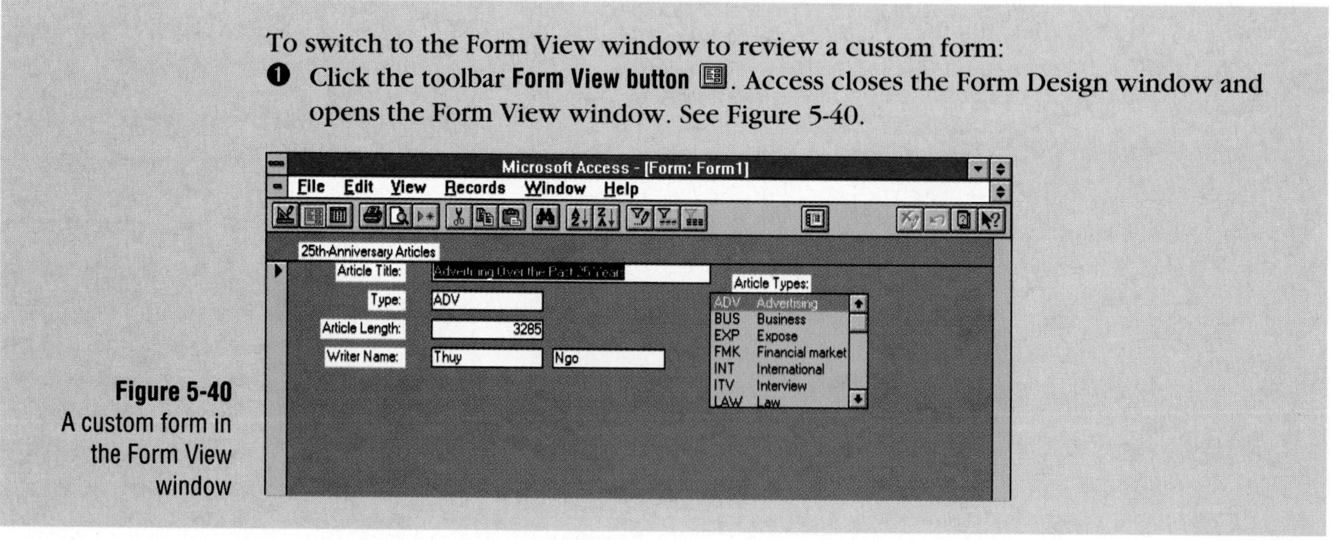

Figure 5-40 A custom form in the Form View window

Elena sees that the list box is not tall enough to show the entire list of article types and descriptions. She switches back to the Form Design window to resize the list box.

To switch to the Form Design window and resize a list box:

1. Click the toolbar **Design View button** . Access closes the Form View window and opens the Form Design window.
2. Click the list box to select it. Drag the middle sizing handle on the bottom border to the 2.00" mark on the vertical ruler to increase the height of the list box. Switch back and forth between the Form View window and the Form Design window until the list box is large enough to show all the article types. See Figure 5-41.

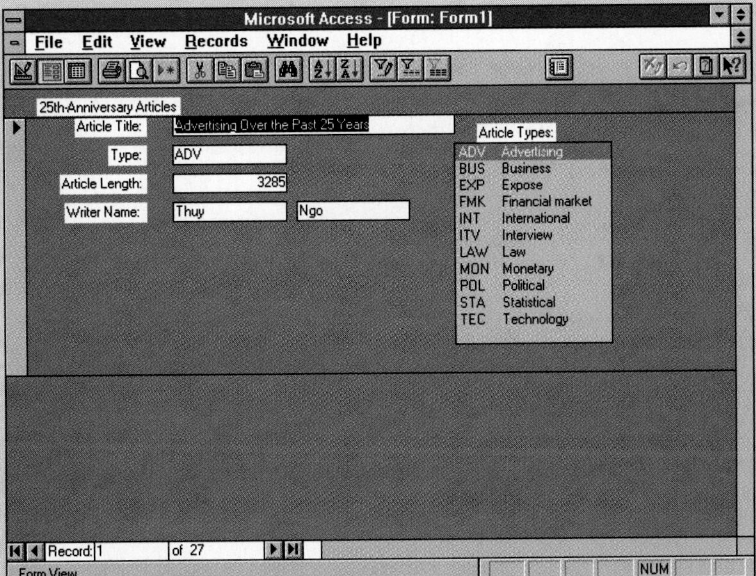

Figure 5-41
The final version of a custom form in the Form View window

3. When you have completed the custom form, switch to the Form Design window to view the form's final design. See Figure 5-42.

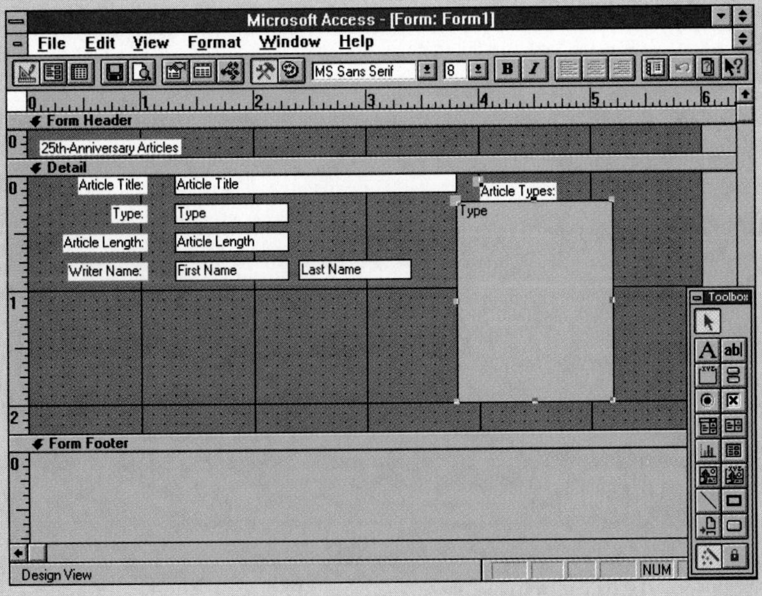

Figure 5-42
The final version of a custom form in the Form Design window

Elena saves the custom form, naming it Article Type form, and closes the Form Design window.

To save a custom form and close the Form Design window:

1. Click the toolbar **Save button**. The Save As dialog box appears.
2. Type **Article Type form** and then press **[Enter]**. Access saves the custom form.
3. Double-click the Form Design window **Control menu box**. Access closes the Form Design window and activates the Database window.

■ ■ ■

Elena now has five forms displayed in the Forms list box. Having completed her work with forms for the Issue25 database, Elena exits Access.

Questions

1. What type of Form Wizard form displays data from two related tables?
2. Which Form Wizard style should you select when you first start working with forms?
3. What is the quickest way to create a form?
4. How does a Form Wizard display the value for a yes/no field?
5. What formats do Form Wizards use to display records in a main/subform form?
6. How many sets of navigation buttons appear in a main/subform form, and what does each set control?
7. When should you use a filter instead of the Find button or the quick sort buttons?
8. If you want to reuse a filter in the future, you save the filter as what type of object?
9. What is the difference between a bound and an unbound control?
10. What five different sections can a form have?
11. How do you move a control and its label together, and how do you move each separately?
12. How do you change a label name?
13. What form property do you change so that Access displays a single record at a time?

Tutorial Assignments

Elena uses a Form Wizard to create a form named PAST ARTICLES form for the Issue25 database. Launch Access, open the Issue25 database on your Student Disk, and do the following:

1. Use Form Wizards to create a single-column form type with the standard style based on the PAST ARTICLES table. Select all the fields from the table in the order in which they are stored in the table, and use the default form title PAST ARTICLES.
2. Open the Form View window and then print the first page.
3. Change the form's design so that the Article Length text box and its attached label box are to the right of, and on the same line as, the Issue field.
4. Move the Writer ID text box and its attached label box up to the position previously occupied by the Article Length bound control.
5. Change the Caption property for the Article Length label box to Length followed by a colon.
6. Resize the Article Title text box so that the field value for each record is completely displayed.

7. Verify your design changes in the Form View window by navigating through all records.
8. Print the first page.
9. Save the form, using the name PAST ARTICLES form, and close the form window on your screen.

Elena next creates a custom form and names it PAST ARTICLES by Issue and Length form. Use the Issue25 database on your Student Disk to do the following:

10. Create a query by selecting the PAST ARTICLES and WRITERS tables and selecting the following fields in the order given here: Article Title, Type, Issue of Business Perspectives, Article Length, Last Name, and First Name. Rename the Issue of Business Perspectives field simply Issue. Then sort the records based on Issue as the primary sort key in descending order and Article Length as the secondary sort key in ascending order. Print the entire dynaset for this query. Finally, save the query, naming it ARTICLES sorted by Issue, Length, and close the active window to activate the Database window.
11. Create a custom form by selecting the query named ARTICLES sorted by Issue, Length and then clicking the Blank Form button.
12. Add all the fields from the query named ARTICLES sorted by Issue, Length to the Detail section and print the first page of the form.
13. Change the Caption property for the Article Length label box to Length, right align all the label boxes, resize the Article Title text box so that the field-value for each record is completely displayed, and print the first page of the form.
14. Move the First Name text box to the right of, and on the same line as, the Last Name text box; delete the First Name label; change the Caption property for the Last Name label to Writer Name; resize the Writer Name label; and print the first page of the form.
15. **E** Use the Format menu's to Fit option under the Size command for the five labels and then right align all the labels. Print the first page of the form.
16. **E** Change the form width to 4.5" and then move the Issue text box and its attached label to the right of, and on the same line as, the Type field. Move all the lines that follow the Type and Issue fields up to eliminate blank lines. If necessary, right align all the labels that appear on the left of the form and then left align the field-value text boxes to their immediate right. Print the first page of the form.
17. **E** Add Form Header and Footer sections; delete the Form Footer section; add to the Form Header section the form title PAST ARTICLES by Issue, Length; change the height of the Detail section to 3"; and print the first page of the form.
18. **E** Use the List Box Wizard to create a list box to display all the article types and their descriptions. Position the list box under all the fields. Use the TYPES table for the list box, and display both table fields. Add the label Types to the form and position it just to the left of the list box. Resize the list box to display all types and descriptions. Finally, change the form's Default View to Single Form, and then print the first and last pages of the form.
19. Save the form as PAST ARTICLES by Issue and Length form.

Case Problems

1. Walkton Daily Press Carriers

Grant Sherman uses a Form Wizard to create a form for his Press database. Launch Access, open the Press database on your Student Disk, and do the following:

1. Use Form Wizards to create a single-column form type with the standard style based on the CARRIERS table. Select all the fields from the table in the order in which they are stored in the table. Use the form title CARRIERS data.
2. Open the Form View window and then print the second page.

3. Save the form with the name CARRIERS form and close the form window on your screen.

Grant creates a custom form named CARRIERS by Name, Route ID form. Use the Press database on your Student Disk to do the following:

4. Create a query by selecting the BILLINGS and CARRIERS tables. Create a join line for the Carrier ID fields and select these fields in the order given here: Carrier Last Name, Carrier First Name, Carrier Phone, Route ID, and Balance Amount. Rename the Balance Amount field simply Balance, and then sort the records based on Carrier Last Name as the primary sort key in ascending order and on Route ID as the secondary sort key in ascending order. Print the entire dynaset for this query. Finally, save the query, naming it CARRIERS sorted by Name, Route ID. Close the active window to activate the Database window.
5. **E** Create a custom form by selecting the query named CARRIERS sorted by Name, Route ID and then clicking the Blank Form button.
6. **E** To the Detail section of the form, add all the fields from the query named CARRIERS sorted by Name, Route ID. Print the first page of the form.
7. **E** Move the Carrier Last Name text box without its attached label to the right on the same line, leaving room to move the Carrier First Name text box from the line below up in front of it. Then move the Carrier First Name text box without its attached label up between the Carrier Last Name label box and the Carrier Last Name text box. Delete the Carrier First Name label box, change the Caption property for the Carrier Last Name label box to Carrier Name, resize the Carrier Name label box to accommodate the shorter caption, and print the first page of the form.
8. **E** Move the Carrier Phone text box and its attached label up one line, and move the Route ID text box and its attached label up one line. Move the Balance text box and its attached label to the right of, and on the same line as, the Route ID bound control. Print the first page of the form.
9. Move the Balance label to the right, so that it is closer to its attached text box.
10. Right align all the labels on the left side of the form.
11. Change the form's Default View to Single Form and change the Detail section background color to blue-green (third color from the right in the Back Color row of the Palette).
12. Add Form Header and Footer sections. Add to the Form Header section the form title CARRIERS by Name and Route ID. Add to the Form Footer section the label Press Database, and print the first page of the form.
13. Save the form as CARRIERS by Name, Route ID form.

2. Lopez Used Cars

Hector Lopez uses a Form Wizard to create a form for his Usedcars database. Launch Access, open the Usedcars database on your Student Disk, and do the following:

1. Use Form Wizards to create a single-column form type with the standard style based on the USED CARS table. Select all the fields from the table in the order in which they are stored in the table. Use the form title USED CARS data.
2. Open the Form View window and then print the first two pages.
3. Save the form with the name USED CARS form and close the form window on your screen.

Maria Lopez creates a custom form, naming it USED CARS by Manufacturer and Model form. Use the Usedcars database on your Student Disk to do the following:

4. Create a query by selecting the CLASSES, LOCATIONS, USED CARS, and TRANSMISSIONS tables. You need join lines between the two Transmission Type fields, between the two Location Code fields, and between Class Type and Class. If any of these join lines are not shown, then create them. Select these fields in the order given here: Manufacturer, Model, Class Description, Transmission Desc, Year, Location Name, Manager Name, Cost, and Selling Price. Sort the records based on Manufacturer as the primary sort key in ascending order and on Model as the secondary sort key in ascending order. Print the entire dynaset for this query. Finally, save the query, naming it USED CARS by Manufacturer, Model.

E 5. Create a custom form by selecting the query named USED CARS by Manufacturer, Model and then clicking the Blank Form button.

E 6. Add to the Detail section all the fields from the query named USED CARS by Manufacturer, Model. Print the fourth page of the form.

E 7. Resize the field-value text boxes, as necessary, so that, in the Form View window, all the field values for each record are completely displayed without unnecessary extra space. Navigate through the records in the Form View window to be sure the box sizes are correct. The Class Description and Transmission Desc text boxes should be widened, for example, and the Year, Cost, and Selling Price text boxes should be narrowed.

E 8. Change the form's Default View to Single Form and then change the width of the Detail section to 5.75" and its height to 3.75".

9. Move the Model text box and its attached label to the right of, and on the same line as, the Manufacturer bound control. Then move the Model text box to the left to be one grid dot away from its related label.
10. Move the Year text box and its attached label to the right of, and on the same line as, the Model bound control. Then move the Year label to the right to be one grid dot away from its related text box.
11. Move the Manager Name text box and its attached label to the right of, and on the same line as, the Location Name bound control.
12. Move the Selling Price text box and its attached label to the right of, and on the same line as, the Cost bound control.
13. Eliminate blank lines by moving text boxes and their attached labels up, and then print the fourth page of the form.
14. Change the Captions properties for these labels: Class Description to Class, Transmission Desc to Trans, and Location Name to Location.

E 15. Apply the Format menu's to Fit option under the Size command for the labels on the left side of the form, right align these labels, and then print the fourth page of the form.

E 16. Use the List Box Wizard to add two list boxes to the form—one for class types and descriptions and one for location codes and names. Position the list boxes side by side below all the control boxes in the Detail Section, placing the one containing class types and descriptions on the left. For the class list box, use the CLASSES table, display both table fields, and enter Classes for the label. For the location list box, use the LOCATIONS table, display the Location Code and Location Name fields, and enter Locations as the label. Resize and move the labels and list boxes to display as much of each record and as many records as possible.

E 17. Print the fourth page of the form.

18. Save the form as USED CARS by Manufacturer and Model form.

3. Tophill University Student Employment

Olivia Tyler uses a Form Wizard to create a form for her Parttime database. Launch Access, open the Parttime database on your Student Disk, and do the following:

1. Use Form Wizards to create a main/subform form type with the standard style based on the EMPLOYERS table as the primary table for the main form and the JOBS table as the related table for the subform. Select all the fields from the EMPLOYERS table in the order in which they are stored in the table. Select all the fields from the JOBS table, except for the Employer ID field, in the order in which they are stored in the table. Use the form title EMPLOYERS and JOBS data.
2. Open the Form View window, save the subform with the name JOBS subform, and then print the first page.
3. Save the form as EMPLOYERS and JOBS form and close the form window on your screen.

Olivia creates a custom form named JOBS by Employer and Job Title form. Use the Parttime database on your Student Disk to do the following:

E 4. Create a query by selecting the EMPLOYERS and JOBS tables and, if necessary, create a join line for the Employer ID fields. Select all the fields from the EMPLOYERS table in the order in which they are stored in the table, and then select these fields from the JOBS table in the order given here: Hours/Week, Job Title, and Wage. Sort the records based on Employer Name as the primary sort key in ascending order and on Job Title as the secondary sort key in ascending order. Print the entire dynaset for this query. Finally, save the query, naming it JOBS sorted by Employer, Job Title.

E 5. Create a custom form by selecting the query named JOBS sorted by Employer, Job Title and then clicking the Blank Form button.

E 6. Add all the fields from the query named JOBS sorted by Employer, Job Title to the Detail section and then print the first page of the form.

E 7. Resize the Employer Name and Job Title text boxes and print the first page of the form.

8. Right align all the labels.
9. Change the form's Default View to Single Form, change the Detail section background color to light gray (third color from the left in the Back Color row on the Palette), and then print the first page of the form.
10. Add Form Header and Footer sections, add to the Form Header section the form title JOBS by Employer and Job Title, add to the Form Footer section the label Parttime Database, and print the first page of the form.
11. Save the form as JOBS by Employer and Job Title form.

4. Rexville Business Licenses

Chester Pearce uses a Form Wizard to create a form for his Buslic database. Launch Access, open the Buslic database on your Student Disk, and do the following:

1. Use Form Wizards to create a single-column form type with the standard style based on the BUSINESSES table. Select all the fields from the table in the order in which they are stored in the table. Use the form title BUSINESSES data.
2. Open the Form View window and then print the first two pages.
3. Save the form as BUSINESSES form and close the form window on your screen.

Chester“creates a custom form, naming it BUSINESSES by License Type and Business Name form. Use the Buslic database on your Student Disk to do the following:

E 4. Create a query by selecting the BUSINESSES, ISSUED LICENSES, and LICENSES tables and, if necessary, create join lines for the Business ID fields and the License Type fields. Select all the fields, except the Business ID field, from the BUSINESSES table in the order in which they are stored in the table; select the License Number, License Type, Amount, and Date Issued fields (in the order given here) from the ISSUED LICENSES table; and then select the License

Description and Basic Cost fields from the LICENSES table. Rename the License Description field simply License. Sort the records based on License Type as the primary sort key in ascending order and on Business Name as the secondary sort key in ascending order, but do not show the License Type field in the dynaset. Print the entire dynaset for this query. Finally, save the query, naming it BUSINESSES sorted by License Type, Business Name.

E 5. Create a custom form by selecting the query named BUSINESSES sorted by License Type, Business Name and then clicking the Blank Form button.

E 6. Add all the fields from the query named BUSINESSES sorted by License Type, Business Name to the Detail section and then print the first page of the form.

7. Resize the Business Name and License text boxes, and print the first page of the form.

8. Right align all the labels.

9. Change the form's Default View to Single Form, change the Detail section background color to blue-green (third color from the right in the Back Color row on the Palette), and then print the first page of the form.

E 10. Add Form Header and Footer sections, add to the Form Header section the form title BUSINESSES by License Type and Business Name, add to the Form Footer section the label Buslic Database, and print the first page of the form.

11. Save the form as BUSINESSES by License Type and Business Name form.

T U T O R I A L 6

Creating Reports

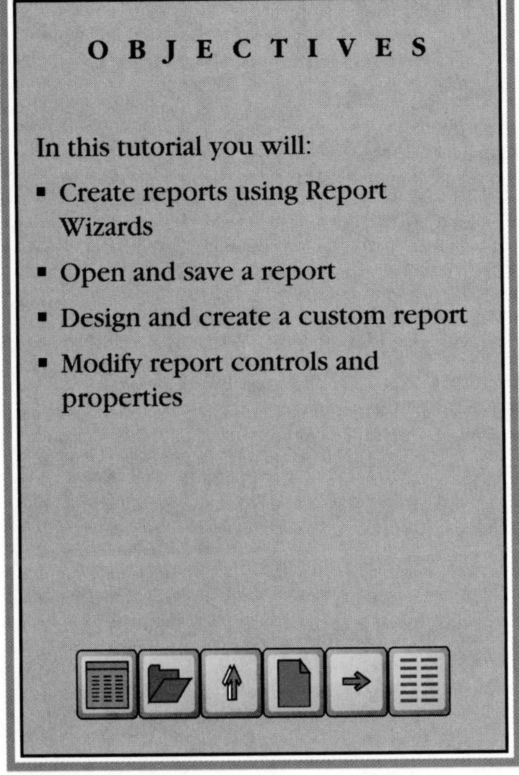

OBJECTIVES

In this tutorial you will:

- Create reports using Report Wizards
- Open and save a report
- Design and create a custom report
- Modify report controls and properties

Creating a Marketing Report at Vision Publishers

CASE

Vision Publishers Harold Larson plans a meeting with several advertisers in New York for the special 25th-anniversary issue of *Business Perspective*. He asks Elena Sanchez to produce a report of all the articles and authors to help him describe their contents to potential advertisers.

Using a Report

A **report** is a formatted hardcopy of the contents of one or more tables from a database. Although you can print data from datasheets, queries, and forms, reports allow you the greatest flexibility for formatting hardcopy output. Reports can be used, for example, to print membership lists, billing statements, and mailing labels.

The Sections of a Report

Figure 6-1 shows a sample report produced from the Issue25 database.

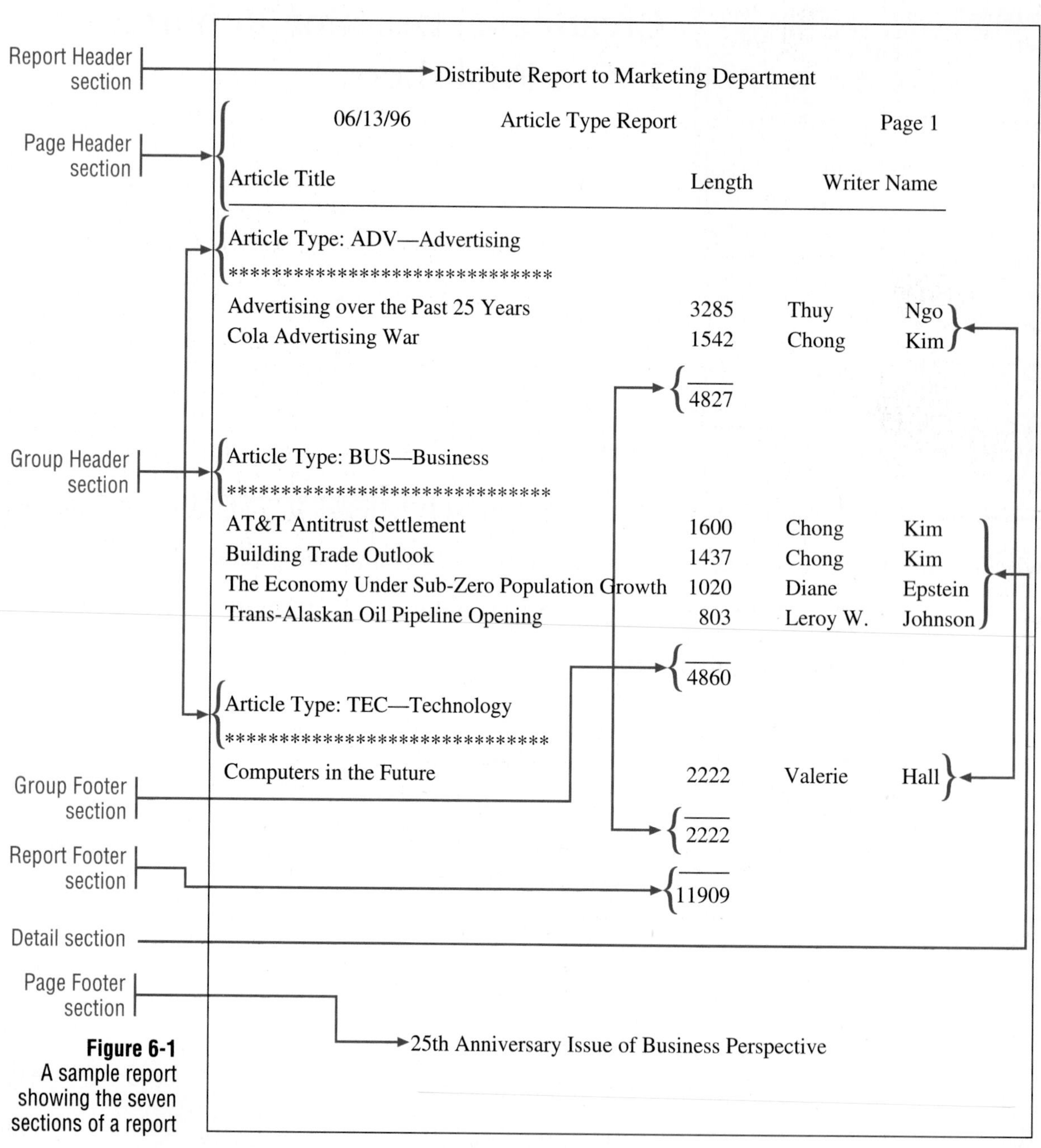

Figure 6-1
A sample report showing the seven sections of a report

The report is divided into **sections**. Each Access report can have seven different sections, which are described in Figure 6-2. You do not need to use all seven report sections in a report. When you design your report, you determine which sections to use and what information to place in each section.

Report Section	Description
Report Header	Appears once at the beginning of a report. Use it for report titles, company logos, report introductions, and cover pages.
Page Header	Appears at the top of each page of a report. Use it for column headings, report titles, page numbers, and report dates. If your report has a Report Header section, it precedes the first Page Header section.
Group Header	Appears once at the beginning of a new group of records. Use it to print the group name and the field value that all records in the group have in common. A report can have up to 10 grouping levels.
Detail	Appears once for each record in the underlying table or query. Use it to print selected fields from the table or query and to print calculated values.
Group Footer	Appears once at the end of a group of records. It is usually used to print totals for the group.
Report Footer	Appears once at the end of the report. Use it for report totals and other summary information.
Page Footer	Appears at the bottom of each page of a report. Use it for page numbers and brief explanations of symbols or abbreviations. If your report has a Report Footer section, it precedes the Page Footer section on the last page of the report.

Figure 6-2
Descriptions of Access report sections

Elena has never created an Access report, so she first familiarizes herself with the Report Wizards tool.

Using Report Wizards

In Access, you can create your own report or use Report Wizards to create one for you. **Report Wizards** ask you a series of questions about your report requirements and then create a report based on your answers. Whether you use Report Wizards or create your own report, you can change a report design after it is created.

Access has seven different Report Wizards. Six of these Report Wizards are shown in Figure 6-3 on the following page.

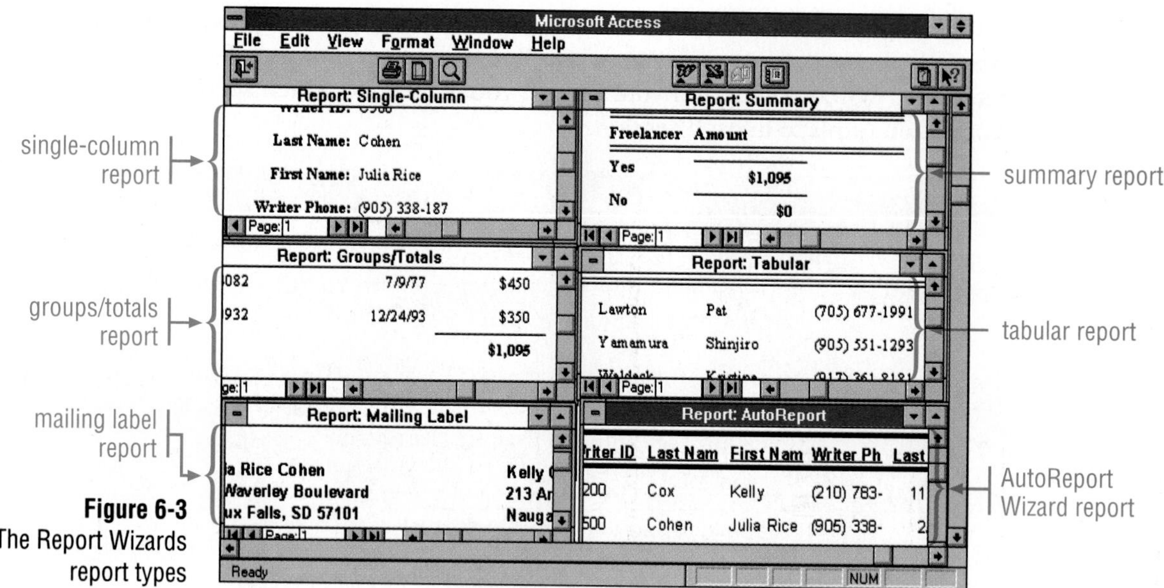

Figure 6-3
The Report Wizards report types

- A **single-column report** prints the fields, one to a line, vertically on the report. Table field names appear as labels to the left of the field values.
- A **groups/totals report** prints record and field values in a row-and-column format with the table field names used as column heads. You can group records according to field values and calculate totals for each group and for all groups. For example, Elena might create a groups/totals report that shows freelancers and then staff writers, with total payment amounts for freelancers, for staff writers, and for all writers.
- A **mailing label report** prints names and addresses that are positioned to fit your company's mailing label forms.
- A **summary report** organizes data into groups and prints both a subtotal for each group and a grand total for all the groups in a tabular format. No detail lines appear in a summary report.
- A **tabular report** prints field values in columns with field names at the top of each column. Each row is a separate record. It is like a groups/totals report, but does not contain totals.
- An **AutoReport Wizard report** is a single-column report of all the fields in the selected table or query. Access automatically produces an AutoReport without asking you questions.
- An **MS Word Mail Merge report** allows you to merge data from a table or query to a Microsoft Word for Windows 6.0 document. You can use the merged data to create form letters or envelopes, for example.

Report Wizards offer you a choice of three different report styles, as shown in Figure 6-4. The main difference between the **executive style** and the **presentation style** is the font in which the report is printed. The executive style uses the serif Times New Roman font, and the presentation style uses the sans serif Arial font. Use either style for the majority of your reports; they both produce easy-to-read text with ample open space. Because it packs more information into a page, the **ledger style** is suitable for long, detailed reports, such as financial reports, especially when they are intended for internal use.

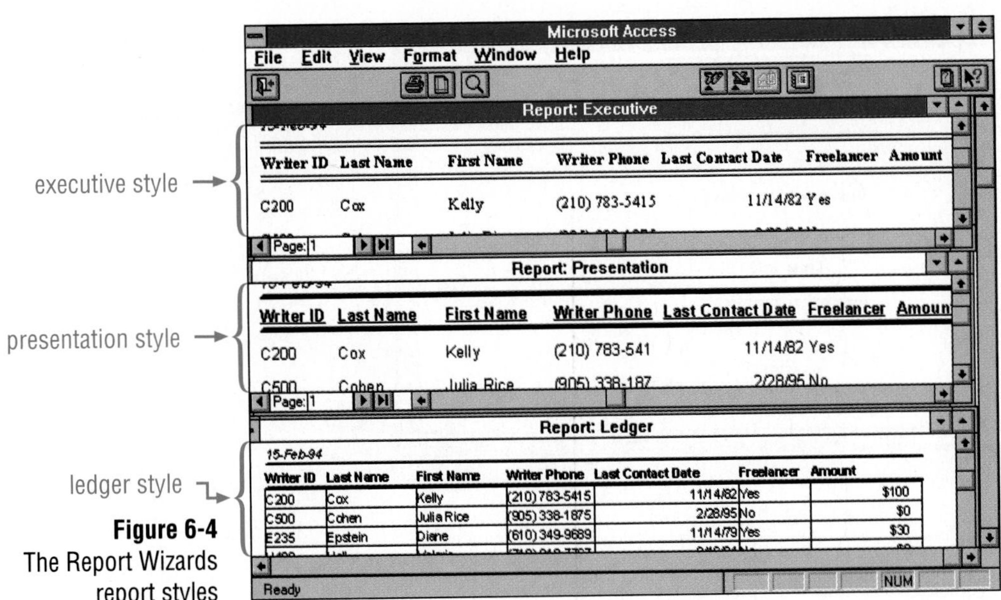

Figure 6-4
The Report Wizards report styles

Access has a set of Cue Cards you can use while working with reports. Although we will not use these Cue Cards in this tutorial, you might find they enhance your understanding of reports. At any time during this tutorial, select Design a Report or Mailing Labels from the Cue Card menu window to launch the appropriate Cue Cards.

Creating a Report Using the AutoReport Wizard

The quickest way to create a report is to use the toolbar AutoReport button, which launches the **AutoReport Wizard**. The AutoReport Wizard selects all the fields from the highlighted table or query in the Database window, creates a single-column report for these fields, and displays the report on the screen in the Print Preview window.

Elena uses the AutoReport Wizard to create a report containing all the fields from the TYPES table. If you have not done so, place your Student Disk in the appropriate drive, launch Access, and open the Issue25 database on your Student Disk.

To create a report using the AutoReport button:

1. Click **TYPES** in the Tables list box. Access will place the fields from the TYPES table, which is now highlighted, into the report it creates when you click the toolbar AutoReport button.
2. Click on the toolbar. Access creates a report that contains the two fields from the TYPES table and displays the report in the Print Preview window.
3. You can use the vertical scroll bar buttons and the navigation buttons on the Print Preview window to view the entire report. See Figure 6-5 on the following page.

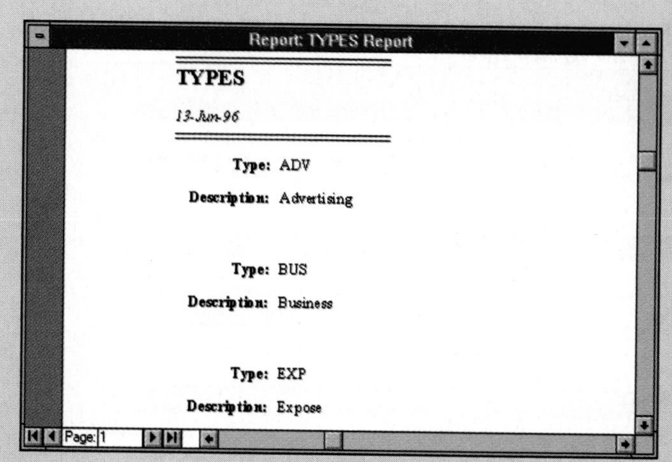

Figure 6-5 An AutoReport Wizard report in the Print Preview window

Saving a Report

After viewing the first several lines of the report based on the TYPES table in the Print Preview screen, Elena saves the report so that she and others can print it whenever they need an updated copy. She saves the report using the name TYPES Report and then closes the Print Preview window.

To save and close a new report:

1. Click **File** and then click **Save As...**. The Save As dialog box appears.
2. Type **TYPES Report** in the Report Name text box and then press **[Enter]**. The Save As dialog box disappears, and Access saves the report.
3. Double-click the Print Preview window **Control menu box**. The report disappears, and the Database window becomes the active window.

Creating Reports Using Report Wizards

Elena next uses Report Wizards to create a report containing all the fields from the WRITERS table. Because she wants space on the report to make notes, she chooses the single-column report type and the presentation style.

Creating Single-Column Reports

Let's use Report Wizards to create a single-column report in the presentation style.

To activate Report Wizards and select a report type:

1. Locate the toolbar New Report button. It is to the right of the New Form button and to the left of the Database Window button.
2. Click. The New Report dialog box appears. Click the Select A Table/Query **down arrow button** to display the list of the Issue25 database tables and queries. Scroll through the list if necessary and click **WRITERS** in the drop-down list box.

❸ Click the **Report Wizards button**. The first Report Wizards dialog box appears. See Figure 6-6. This dialog box displays the list of report types available through Report Wizards.

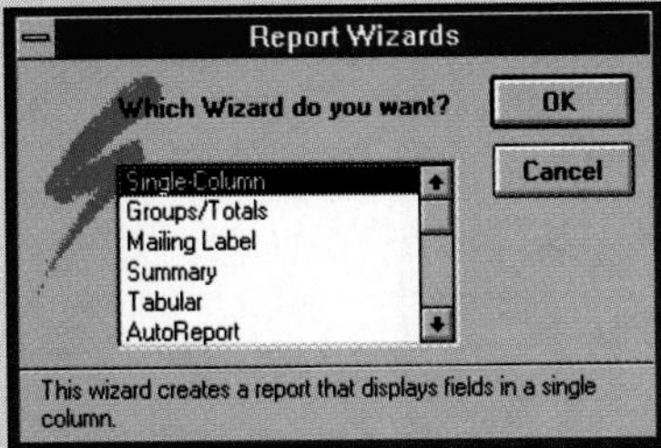

Figure 6-6 Choosing the report type

❹ If it is not already highlighted, click **Single-Column**, and then click the **OK button**. The first Single-Column Report Wizard dialog box appears.

In the first Single-Column Report Wizard dialog box, you select fields in the order you want them to appear on the report. Elena wants the report to contain all the fields in the WRITERS table in the order in which they appear in the table, and she wants Freelancer to be the primary sort key and Last Contact Date to be the secondary sort key. She will include the report title WRITERS by Last Contact Date Within Freelancer.

To finish creating a report using the Single-Column Report Wizard:

❶ Click the **>> button**. Access removes all the fields from the box on the left and places them in the same order in the box on the right.

❷ Click the **Next > button**. The second Single-Column Report Wizard dialog box appears. In this dialog box, you select the primary and secondary sort keys.

❸ Click **Freelancer** and then click the **> button**. Access moves the Freelancer field to the list box on the right, designating the Freelancer field as the primary sort key. Click **Last Contact Date** and then click the **> button**. Access moves the Last Contact Date field under the Freelancer field in the list box on the right, designating it as the secondary sort key. See Figure 6-7.

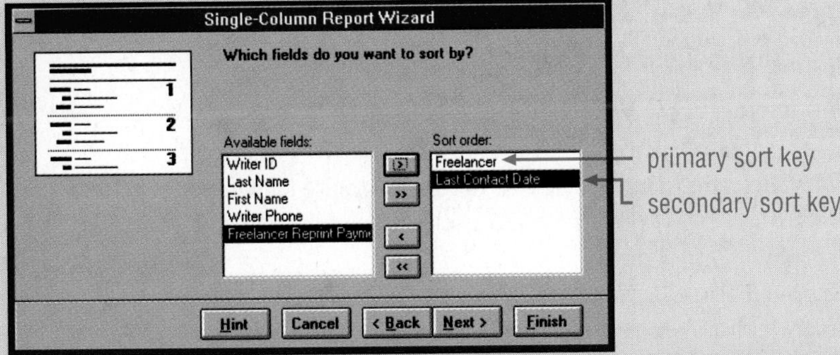

Figure 6-7 Selecting sort keys for a report

❹ Click the **Next > button**. The third Single-Column Report Wizard dialog box appears. In this dialog box, you choose the style for your report.

❺ If it is not already selected, click the **Presentation radio button**; then click the **Next > button**. Access displays the final Single-Column Report Wizard dialog box and shows the table name WRITERS as the default report title.

❻ To change the default report title that will appear at the beginning of the report, type **WRITERS by Last Contact Date Within Freelancer**. See Figure 6-8.

Figure 6-8 The last Single-Column Report Wizard dialog box

The three check boxes in the last Report Wizard dialog box let you do the following:

- Print each record on a new page
- Change the report title that prints once at the beginning of each report to a page title that prints on the top of each page
- Use Cue Cards

Printing the report title on each page is usually preferred, so make sure that the first and third boxes are unchecked and the second box is checked.

Previewing a Report

Now that she has made her report selections, Elena checks the overall report layout. She views the new report in the Print Preview window to see what the report will look like when it's printed.

To view a report in the Print Preview window:

❶ In the last Report Wizard dialog box, be sure that only the middle check box is checked and the top radio button is on.

❷ Click the **Finish button**. The Print Preview window opens, and Access displays the new report.

❸ Click the Print Preview window **maximize button**. See Figure 6-9.

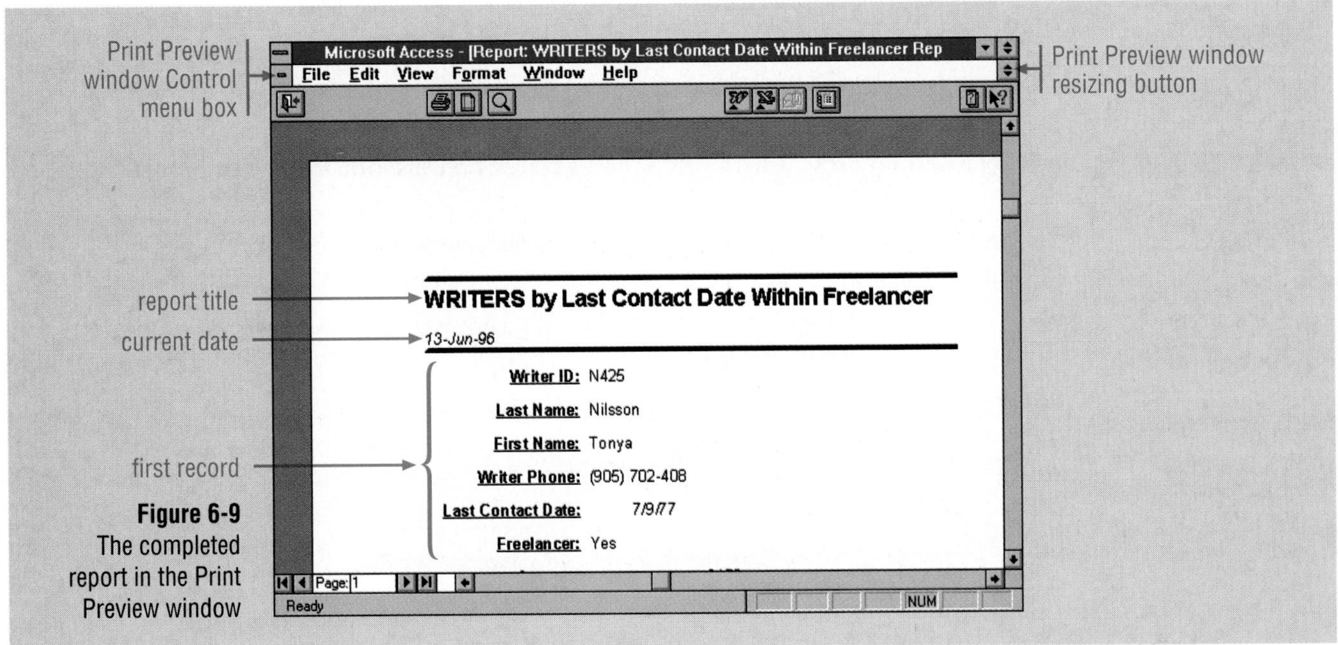

Figure 6-9 The completed report in the Print Preview window

Access displays the report title and current date at the top of the report page. These are preceded and followed by lines that serve to separate this section visually from the rest of the report page.

Below the title section, the record for the freelance writer having the earliest Last Contact Date in the WRITERS table appears as the first record on the report. You can use the vertical scroll bar and the navigation buttons to view the other records in the report.

Printing a Report

Next, Elena prints the first page of the report from the Print Preview window as a sample.

To print the first page of a report from the Print Preview window:

1. Make sure your printer is on line and ready to print. Click the toolbar **Print button** to open the Print dialog box.
2. Check the Printer section of the Print dialog box to make sure your computer's printer is selected.
3. Click the **Pages button** to choose the range of pages to print.
4. Type **1** in the From box, press **[Tab]**, and then type **1** in the To box.
5. Press **[Enter]** to initiate printing. After a printing dialog box appears briefly and then disappears, Access prints the first page of the report and returns you to the Print Preview window.

Elena saves the report as WRITERS by Last Contact Date Within Freelancer Report and then closes the Print Preview window.

To save and close a new report:

1. Click **File**, and then click **Save As...**. The Save As dialog box appears.
2. Type **WRITERS by Last Contact Date Within Freelancer Report** in the Report Name text box and then press **[Enter]**. The Save As dialog box disappears, and Access saves the report.
3. Double-click the Print Preview window **Control menu box**. The report disappears, and the Database window becomes the active window.
4. Click the **Report object button**. Access lists the two reports that have been created and saved. See Figure 6-10.

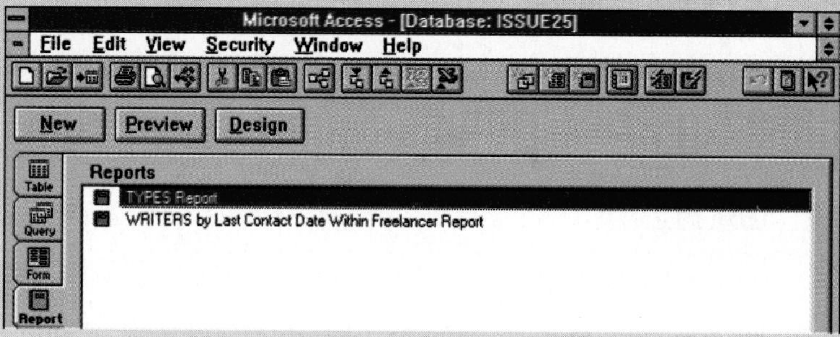

Figure 6-10
List of reports

Creating a Groups/Totals Report

After viewing, printing, and saving the single-column report, Elena decides that a groups/totals report of the same data would be more useful to her and her colleagues. A **group** is a set of records that share common values for one or more fields. Grouping records is a way for you to organize and sequence printed information. When you use a groups/totals report, you can select up to three different grouping fields. The first grouping field is the primary sort key, and any subsequent grouping fields are secondary sort keys.

Elena groups her report using the Freelancer field. This means that all the freelancer records will be printed first, then all the staff writer records. Because Access can print headers before each group and footers after each group, Elena's report includes a **Group Header section** that introduces each group and a **Group Footer section** that concludes each group. The Group Header section prints the value of the Freelancer field, and the Group Footer section prints the total of the Amount field values for the group. Elena's report also has a **Report Footer section** to print the grand total of the Amount field values for both groups.

When you create a groups/totals report, Access asks you to choose a grouping method for each grouping field. A **grouping method** uses either an entire field value or a portion of a field value upon which to base the record grouping process. **Normal grouping** uses the entire field value to group records and is the default grouping method. You can also base groups on a portion of a grouping field. For a date/time field, for example, you can group records based on the year, quarter, month, week, day, hour, or minute portions of the grouping field. For number or currency fields, you can group based on 10s, 50s, 100s, 500s, 1000s, 5000s, or 10000s. For text fields, you can group on the first character, first two characters, first three characters, first four characters, or first five characters. Because yes/no fields have just two values, normal grouping is the only possible option for them.

Elena again uses Report Wizards to create this report. Because the Report object button is selected, Elena can start creating the new report by clicking either the toolbar New Report button or the New command button.

To activate Report Wizards and create a groups/totals report:

❶ Click the **New command button**. The New Report dialog box appears. Click the Select A Table/Query **down arrow button** to display the list of the Issue25 database tables and queries and scroll until WRITERS appears. Click **WRITERS** in the list box.

❷ Click the **Report Wizards button**. Access displays the first Report Wizards dialog box, in which you select the report type.

❸ Click **Groups/Totals** in the list box, and then click the **OK button**. Access displays the first Group/Totals Report Wizard dialog box, in which you select the fields for the report. Elena wants the report to contain all the WRITERS table fields in the order in which they appear in the table.

❹ Click the **>> button**. Access removes all the fields from the box on the left and places them in the same order in the box on the right.

❺ Click the **Next > button**. Access displays the second Group/Totals Report Wizard dialog box, in which you choose the grouping field. Elena groups the records from the WRITERS table by the Freelancer field.

❻ Click **Freelancer** in the Available fields list box, and then click the **> button** to move it to the list box on the right. See Figure 6-11.

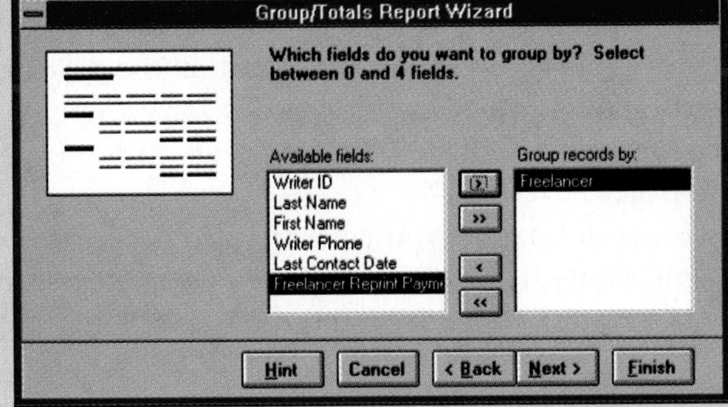

Figure 6-11 Selecting a field on which to group a report

❼ Click the **Next > button**. Access displays the third Group/Totals Report Wizard dialog box, in which you select the grouping method. The only grouping choice for the yes/no Freelancer field is Normal. See Figure 6-12.

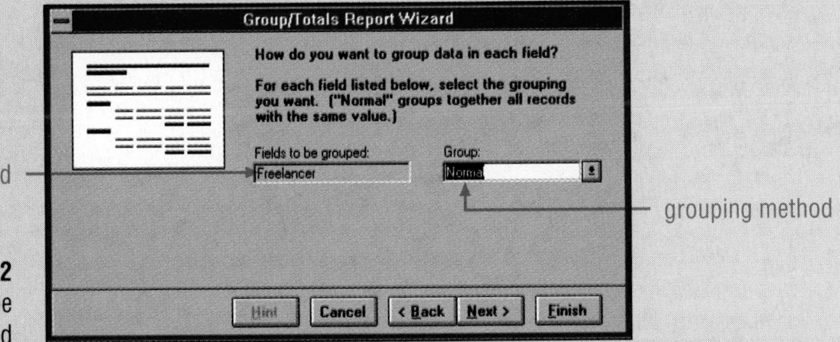

Figure 6-12 Selecting the grouping method

❽ Click the **Next > button**. Access displays the next Group/Totals Report Wizard dialog box, in which you choose the report's sort keys.

Elena chooses Last Contact Date to be a sort key. Because the Freelancer field is a grouping field, Access uses it as the primary sort key and uses Last Contact Date as the secondary sort key.

To choose a report sort key:

1. Click **Last Contact Date** in the Available fields list box, and then click the **> button** to move it to the list box on the right.
2. Click the **Next > button**. Access displays the next Group/Totals Report Wizard dialog box, in which you choose the report style.
3. If it is not already selected, click the **Executive button**, and then click the **Next > button**. Access displays the final Group/Totals Report Wizard dialog box and shows the table name WRITERS as the default title that will appear at the beginning of the report. Elena changes the default report title.
4. Type **WRITERS With Freelancer Group Totals.**

In the final Group/Totals Report Wizard dialog box, Access displays three check boxes. Access uses the first check box, "See all the fields on one page," for reports that have too many columns to fit on one page using the standard column widths. If the box is checked, Access narrows the report columns so that all the fields can fit on one page. If the box is unchecked, Access prints multiple pages for groups of columns. You should check this option box unless you have so many fields that they cannot be read clearly when printed on one page.

Use the other two check boxes if you want to print percentages of the totals for each report group or if you want to use Cue Cards. Elena makes sure that the first box is checked and the other two are unchecked and then opens the Print Preview window to preview the report.

To finish and preview a groups/totals report:

1. Be sure that, in the final Group/Totals Report Wizard dialog box, the first check box is checked and the other two check boxes are unchecked. See Figure 6-13.

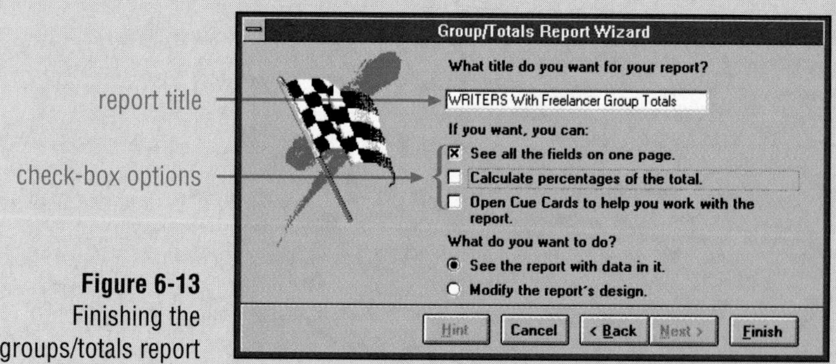

Figure 6-13
Finishing the groups/totals report

2. Click the **Finish button**. The Print Preview window opens, and Access displays the groups/totals report.

❸ Click the Print Preview window **maximize button**, click the **right arrow scroll button** three times, and then click the **down arrow scroll button** three times. See Figure 6-14.

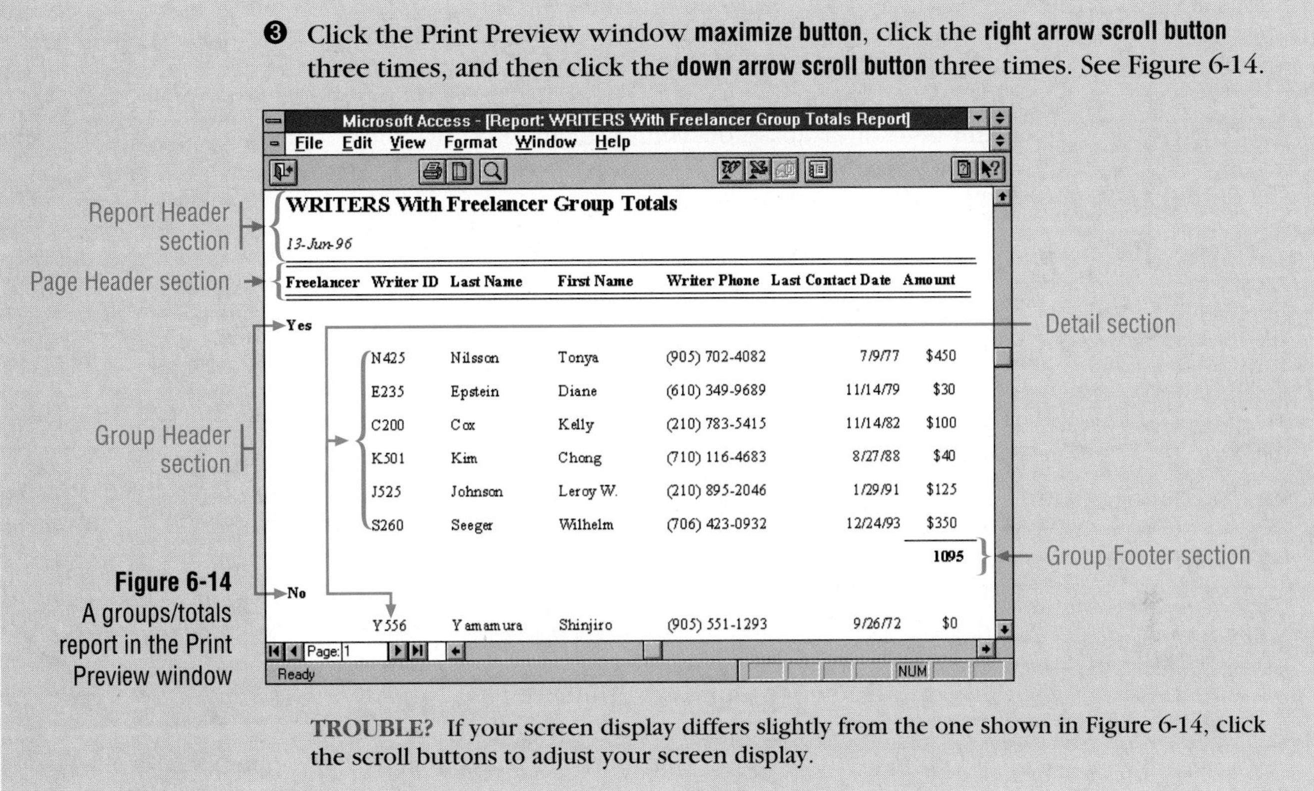

Microsoft Access - [Report: WRITERS With Freelancer Group Totals Report]
File Edit View Format Window Help
WRITERS With Freelancer Group Totals
13-Jun-96
Freelancer Writer ID Last Name First Name Writer Phone Last Contact Date Amount
Yes
N425 Nilsson Tonya (905) 702-4082 7/9/77 $450
E235 Epstein Diane (610) 349-9689 11/14/79 $30
C200 Cox Kelly (210) 783-5415 11/14/82 $100
K501 Kim Chong (710) 116-4683 8/27/88 $40
J525 Johnson Leroy W. (210) 895-2046 1/29/91 $125
S260 Seeger Wilhelm (706) 423-0932 12/24/93 $350
1095
No
Y556 Yamamura Shinjiro (905) 551-1293 9/26/72 $0
Page: 1
Ready
NUM
Report Header section
Page Header section
Group Header section
Detail section
Group Footer section

Figure 6-14
A groups/totals report in the Print Preview window

TROUBLE? If your screen display differs slightly from the one shown in Figure 6-14, click the scroll buttons to adjust your screen display.

Elena previews the rest of the report by using the down arrow scroll button.

To preview the end of a groups/totals report:

❶ Click the **down arrow scroll button** until you see the bottom of the first page of the report. If you do not see the grand totals at the end of the report, click the navigation **Next Record button** ▶ and click the **up arrow scroll button** until the grand totals are in view.

As she previews the report, Elena notices that it contains each of the seven different sections that a report can contain. Elena saves the groups/totals report and closes the Print Preview window.

To save and close a new report:

❶ Double-click the Print Preview window **Control menu box**. The "Save changes to 'Report1'" dialog box appears.

❷ Click the **Yes button**. The Save As dialog box appears.

❸ Type **WRITERS With Freelancer Group Totals Report** and then press **[Enter]**. The Save As dialog box disappears, Access saves the report, and the Database window becomes the active window.

If you want to take a break and resume the tutorial at a later time, you can exit Access by double-clicking the Microsoft Access window Control menu box. When you resume the tutorial, place your Student Disk in the appropriate drive, launch Access, open the Issue25 database on your Student Disk, maximize the Database window, and click the Report object button.

■ ■ ■

Creating a Custom Report

Elena and Harold discuss his report requirements and decide that the report should contain the following:

- A Detail section that lists the title, type, and length of each article, and the name of each writer. Records should appear in ascending order based on Type and in descending order based on Article Length, and the records should be grouped by the Type field value
- A Page Header section that shows the current date, report title, page number, and column headings for each field
- A Group Footer section that prints subtotals of the Article Length field for each Type group
- A Report Footer section that prints the grand total of the Article Length field

From her work with Report Wizards, Elena knows that Access places the report title and date in the Report Header section and the page number in the Page Footer section. Harold prefers all three items at the top of each page, so Elena needs to place that information in the Page Header section. To do this, Elena will create a custom report.

If you modify a report created by Report Wizards or if you design and create your own report, you have produced a **custom report**. You should create a custom report whenever Report Wizards cannot automatically create the specific report you need.

Designing a Custom Report

Before she creates the custom report, Elena designs the report's contents and appearance. Elena's completed design is shown in Figure 6-15.

The report title is Article Type Report. Descriptive column heads appear at the bottom of the Page Header section. The Page Header section also contains the current date and page number on the same line as the report title.

Elena indicates the locations and lengths of the field values by a series of X's. The three X's under the Type field label indicate that the field value will be three characters wide. The Type field value will appear only with the first record of a group.

The subtotals for each group and an overall total will appear in the report. The Article Length is the only field for which totals will appear.

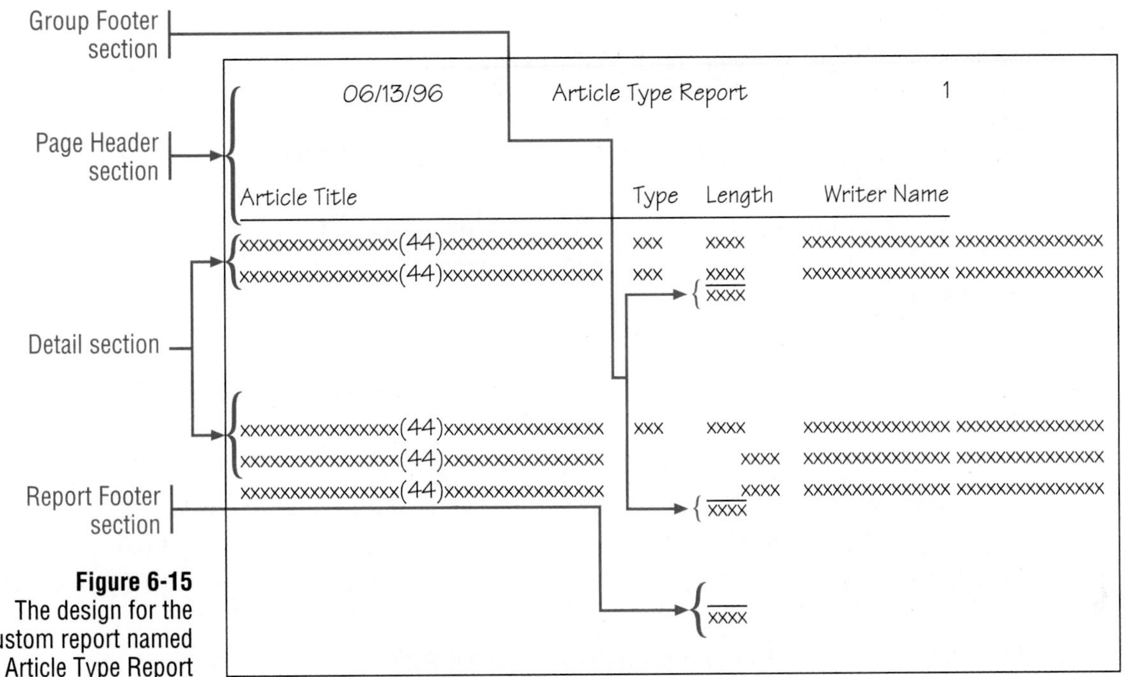

Figure 6-15
The design for the custom report named Article Type Report

Elena's report design contains four different report sections: the Page Header section, the Detail section, the Group Footer section, and the Report Footer section. Her report will not include Report Header, Group Header, or Page Footer sections.

The data for a report can come from either a single table or from a query based on one or more tables. Because Elena's report will contain data from the WRITERS and PAST ARTICLES tables, Elena must use a query for this report. She will use the Article Type Query because it contains the fields she needs from the two tables.

The Report Design Window

Elena could use Report Wizards to create a report based on the Article Type Query and then modify the report to match her report design. Report Wizards would construct the majority of the report, so Elena would save time and reduce the possibility for errors. However, Elena creates her custom report without using Report Wizards so that she can control the precise placement of fields and labels and become more skilled at constructing reports. Elena's first step is to create a blank report in the Report Design window. You use the **Report Design window** to create and modify reports.

REFERENCE WINDOW

Creating a Blank Report

- Click the toolbar New Report button. The New Report dialog box appears.
- Select the table or query you want to use for the new report and then click the Blank Report button. Access opens the Report Design window.

Elena creates a blank report based on the Article Type Query and opens the field list box.

To create a blank report in the Report Design window and open the field list box:

1. Click the toolbar **New Report button** to open the New Report dialog box.
2. Click the Select A Table/Query **down arrow button** to display the list of the Issue25 database tables and queries.
3. Click **Article Type Query** and then click the **Blank Report button**. The Report Design window appears.
4. Click the toolbar **Field List button**. The field list box appears. See Figure 6-16.

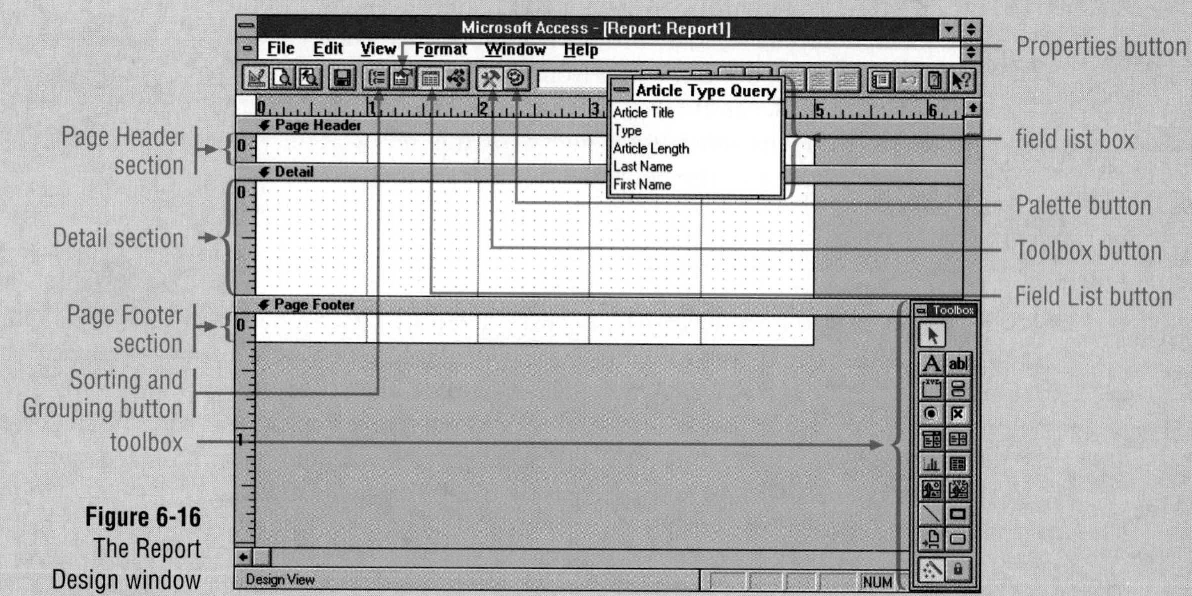

Figure 6-16 The Report Design window

TROUBLE? If the rulers, grid, or toolbox do not appear, click the View menu and then click Ruler, Grid, or Toolbox to display the missing component in the Report Design window. A check mark appears in front of these View menu commands when the components are displayed in the Report Design window. If the grid is still invisible, see your technical support person or instructor for assistance. If the Palette appears, click the View menu and then click Palette to close the Palette.

The Report Design window has several components in common with the Form Design window. The toolbar for both windows has a Properties button, a Field List button, and a Palette button. Both windows also have horizontal and vertical rulers, a grid, and a toolbox.

The Report Design window displays one new toolbar button, the Sorting and Grouping button. Recall that for a form you use a filter to display records in a specific order. In reports, you use the **Sorting and Grouping button** to establish sort keys and grouping fields. A maximum of 10 fields can serve as sort keys, and any number of them can also be grouping fields.

Unlike the Form Design window, which initially displays only the Detail section on a blank form, the Report Design window displays a Page Header section and a Page Footer section in addition to the Detail section. Reports often contain these sections, so Access automatically includes them in a blank report.

Adding Fields to a Report

Elena's first task is to add bound controls to the report Detail section for all the fields from the Article Type Query. You use bound controls to print field values from a table or query on a report. You add bound controls to a report the same way you added them to a form. In fact, every task you accomplished in the Form Design window is done in a similar way in the Report Design window.

To add bound controls for all the fields in the field list:

1. If the toolbox Control Wizards tool is selected, click it to deselect it.
2. Double-click the **field list title bar** to highlight all the fields in the Article Type Query field list.
3. Click anywhere in the highlighted area of the field list and drag to the report Detail section. Release the mouse button when the is positioned at the top of the Detail section and at the 1.25" mark on the horizontal ruler. Access resizes the Detail Section and adds bound controls for the five selected fields. Each bound control consists of a text box and, to its left, an attached label. See Figure 6-17. Notice that the text boxes align at the 1.25" mark.

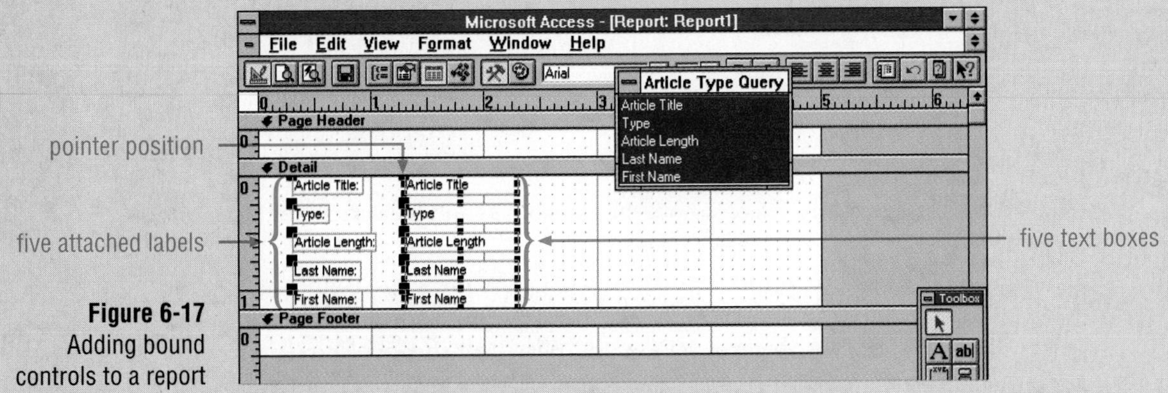

Figure 6-17
Adding bound controls to a report

TROUBLE? If you did not position the bound controls properly in the Detail section, click the Undo button immediately and then repeat the drag operation.

Performing operations in the Report Design window will become easier with practice. Remember, you can always click the Undo button immediately after you make a report design change that has undesired results.

You can also click the toolbar Print Preview button at any time to view your progress on the report and return to the Report Design window by clicking the toolbar Close Window button in the Print Preview window.

Selecting, Moving, Resizing, and Deleting Controls

Five text boxes now appear in a column in the Detail section. Each text box is a bound control linked to a field in the underlying query and has an attached label box to its left. Because she is done with the field list box, Elena closes it by clicking the toolbar Field List button. Elena next compares the report Detail section with her design and moves all the label boxes to the Page Header section. She then repositions the label boxes and text boxes so that they agree with her report design, shown in Figure 6-15.

To close the field list and move all label boxes to the Page Header section:

1. Click the toolbar **Field List button** to close the field list.
2. Click anywhere in the Page Footer section to deselect the five text boxes and their attached label boxes. While pressing and holding **[Shift]**, click each of the five label boxes in the Detail section. This action selects all the label boxes in preparation for cutting them from the Detail section and pasting them in the Page Header section.
3. With the positioned inside any one of the selected label boxes click the right mouse button to display the Shortcut menu.
4. Click **Cut** in the Shortcut menu. Access deletes the label boxes from the Detail section and places them in the Windows Clipboard. See Figure 6-18.

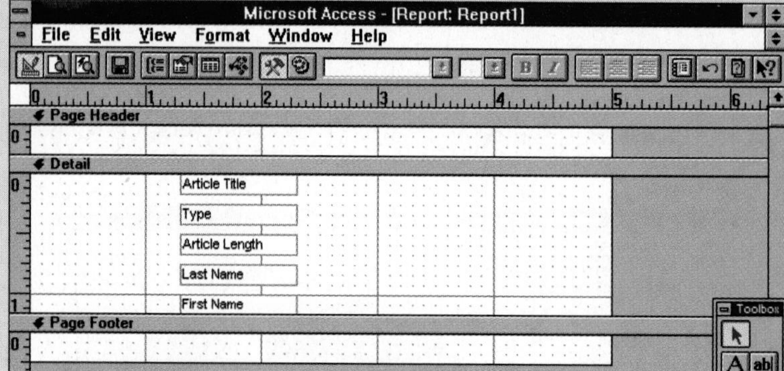

Figure 6-18 Label boxes cut from the Detail Section

TROUBLE? If you selected both the label boxes and the text boxes, click Undo and try again, selecting only the label boxes.

5. Click anywhere in the Page Header section, click the right mouse button in the Page Header section to open the Shortcut menu, and then click **Paste**. Access resizes the Page Header section and pastes all the label boxes from the Windows Clipboard into that section. See Figure 6-19.

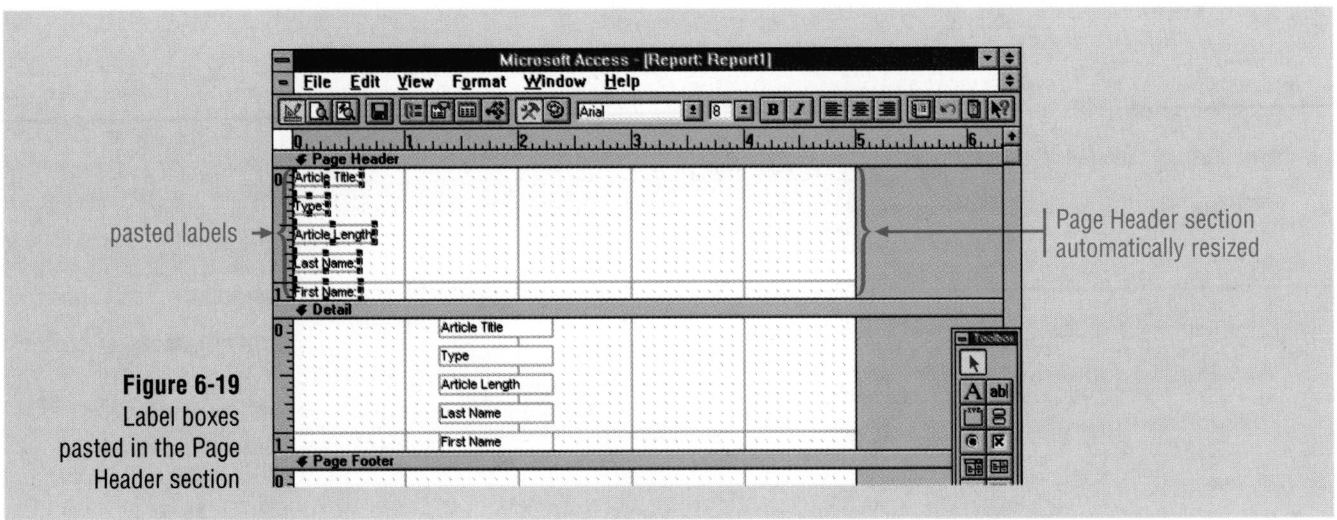

Figure 6-19 Label boxes pasted in the Page Header section

Moving the label boxes has unlinked them from their attached text boxes. You can now select and move either a label box or a text box, but not both at once.

Elena needs to reposition the text boxes and label boxes. She first drags the Article Title text box to the left into the corner of the Detail section and resizes it. She then moves and resizes the other four text boxes and resizes the Detail section.

To move and resize text boxes and resize the Detail section:

1. Click the Article Title field-value **text box** in the Detail section, move the pointer to the move handle in the upper-left corner of the field-value text box, and click and drag the pointer to the upper-left corner of the Detail section.
2. Next, move the pointer to the middle sizing handle on the right side of the Article Title field-value text box. When the pointer changes to ↔, drag the right border horizontally to the right to the 2.5" mark on the horizontal ruler. See Figure 6-20.

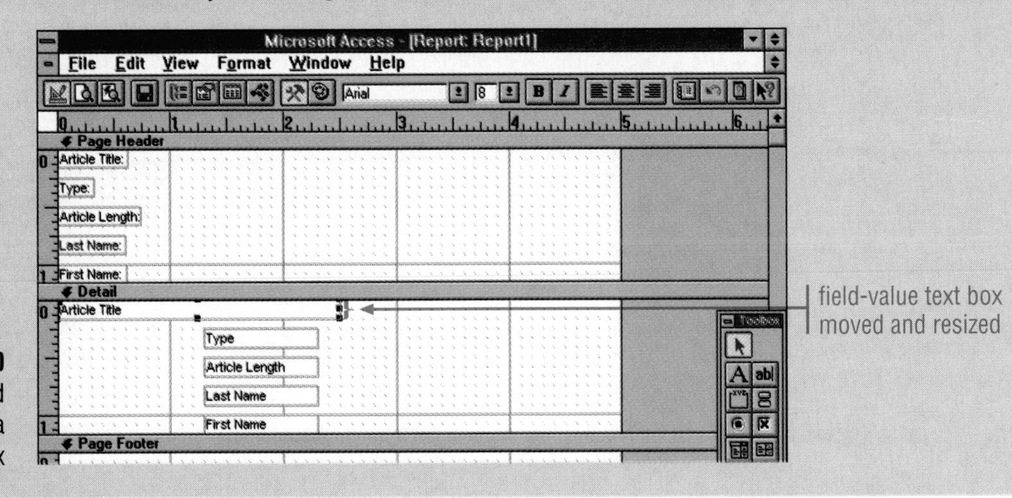

Figure 6-20 Moving and resizing a field-value text box

❸ Select each of the other four field-value text boxes in the Detail section, and move and resize them separately, following the report design. See Figure 6-21.

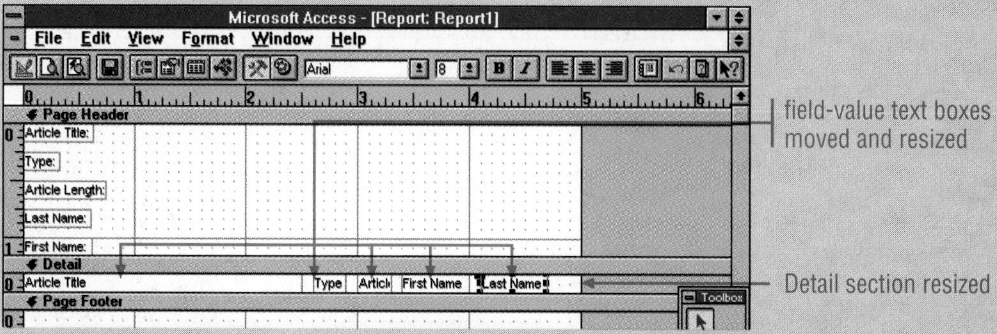

Figure 6-21 After moving and resizing all the field-value text boxes

field-value text boxes moved and resized

Detail section resized

❹ Move the pointer to the bottom edge of the Detail section. When the pointer changes to ✢, drag the bottom edge upward to align with the bottom of the field-value text boxes. See Figure 6-21. When the Detail section height is the same as the text-box height, the lines in the Detail section of the report will be single spaced.

TROUBLE? If Access widens the report too much while you are moving and resizing the text boxes, wait until you are finished with these operations and then reduce the width of the report. To reduce the report's width, start by moving the pointer to the right edge of the Detail section. When the pointer changes to ✢, drag the right edge to the left to narrow the report's width to 5".

Elena deletes the First Name label and changes the Caption property for all other labels in the Page Header section. She changes the Last Name Caption property to Writer Name and the Article Length Caption property to Length. She also deletes the colons in the Caption properties for the Article Title label and the Type label.

To delete a label and change label Caption properties:

❶ Click the First Name **label box** to select it. Click the First Name **label box** with the right mouse button to open the Shortcut menu and then click **Cut**. The First Name **label box** disappears.

❷ Click the Last Name **label box** to select it, and then click the toolbar **Properties button** . The property sheet for the Last Name label appears.

❸ Click the **Caption text box** in the property sheet, press **[F2]** to select the entire value, and then type **Writer Name**.

❹ Click the Article Length **label box** to select it. The property sheet changes to show the properties for the Article Length field. Click the **Caption text box** in the property sheet, press **[F2]**, and then type **Length**.

❺ Click the Type **label box** to select it. Click near the end of the **Caption text box** in the property sheet and press **[Backspace]** to remove the colon from the caption.

❻ Click the Article Title **label box** to select it. Click near the end of the **Caption text box** in the property sheet and press **[Backspace]** to remove the colon from the caption.

❼ Click to close the property sheet.

After checking her report design, Elena resizes the Length and Writer Name label boxes and rearranges the label boxes in the Page Header section.

To resize and move labels:

1. Click in an unoccupied area of the grid to deselect the Article Title **label box**. While holding **[Shift]**, click the Length **label box** and then click the Writer Name **label box** to select them.
2. Click **Format**, click **Size**, and then click **to Fit**. Access resizes the two label boxes to fit around the captions. See Figure 6-22.

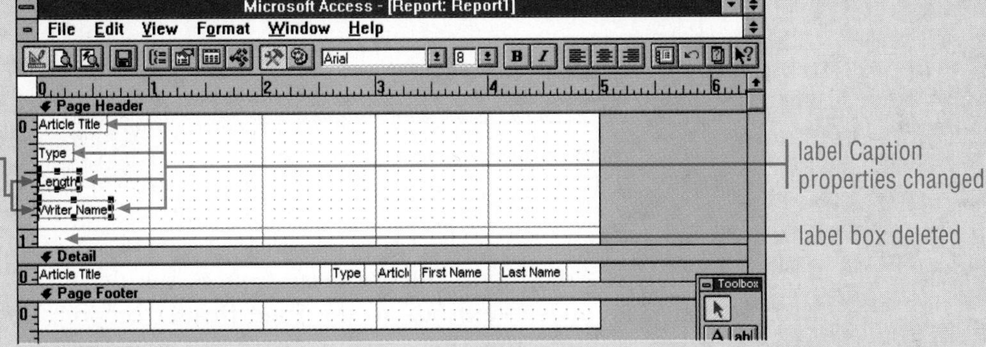

Figure 6-22 Report Design window showing changes made to label boxes

3. Individually select and move each of the label boxes in the Page Header section, following the report design. See Figure 6-23.

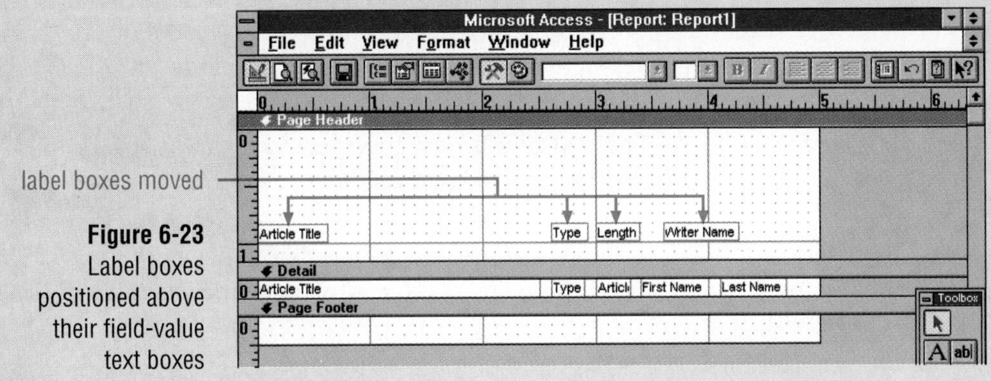

Figure 6-23 Label boxes positioned above their field-value text boxes

Adding a Title, Date, and Page Number to a Report

Elena's report design includes the title Article Type Report. She places this report title in the Page Header section using the toolbox Label tool.

To add a report title to the Page Header section:

1. Click the toolbox **Label tool** [A].
2. Move the pointer into the Page Header section. As you move the pointer into the report, the pointer changes to +A. Click the mouse button when the pointer's plus symbol (+) is positioned at the top of the Page Header section at the 2" mark on the horizontal ruler. The pointer changes to I.

❸ Type **Article Type Report** and then press **[Enter]**. See Figure 6-24.

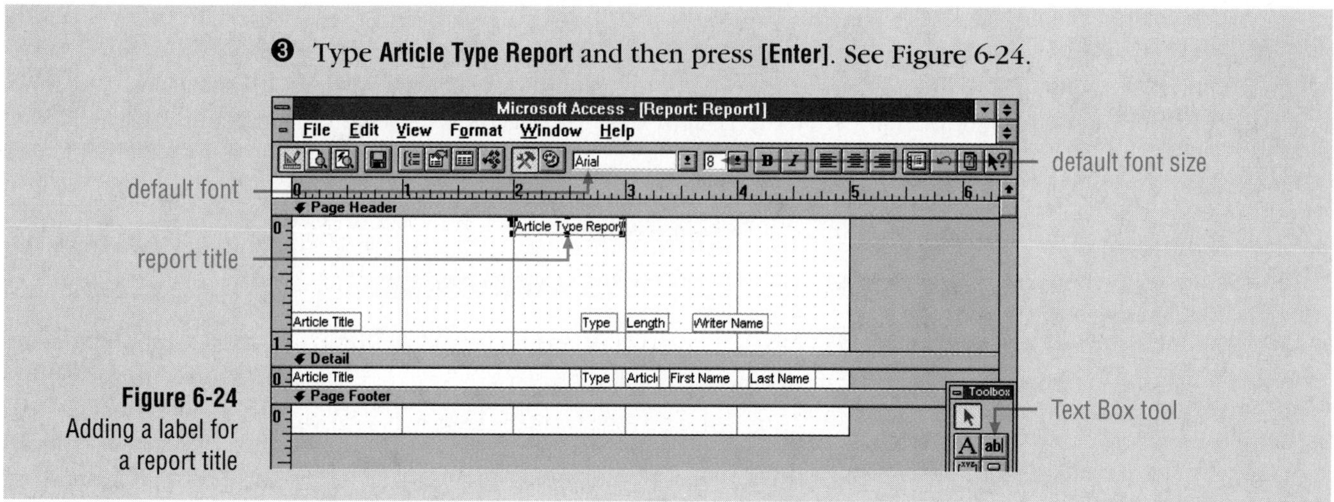

Figure 6-24
Adding a label for a report title

Elena increases the report title font size from 8, the default, to 10 (the default typeface is Arial), and adds a text box to the Page Header section. Here she will insert the Date function. You use the toolbar **Text Box tool** to add a text box with an attached label to a report or form. Text boxes are mostly used to contain bound controls or calculated controls. You use the **Date function**, which is a type of calculated control, to print the current date on a report. Let's do this now.

To change font size and use the Text Box tool to add the Date function:

❶ Click the Font Size **down arrow button** and click **10**. Access changes the font size of the report title from 8 to 10. The text box is now too small to display the entire report title. The text box needs to be resized and recentered in the Page Header section.

❷ Resize the height and width of the report title **text box**, so that the entire report title is visible. Next, move the report title text box one grid mark to the left, so it is centered in the Page Header section.

❸ Click the toolbar **Text Box tool** [abl]. Move the pointer into the Page Header section. As you move the pointer into the report, the pointer changes to [+abl]. Click the mouse button when the pointer's plus symbol is positioned at the top of the Page Header section just to the right of the .75" mark on the horizontal ruler. Access adds a text box with an attached label box to its left. Inside the text box is the description Unbound.

❹ Click the Unbound **text box**, type **=Date()**, and then press **[Enter]**. See Figure 6-25.

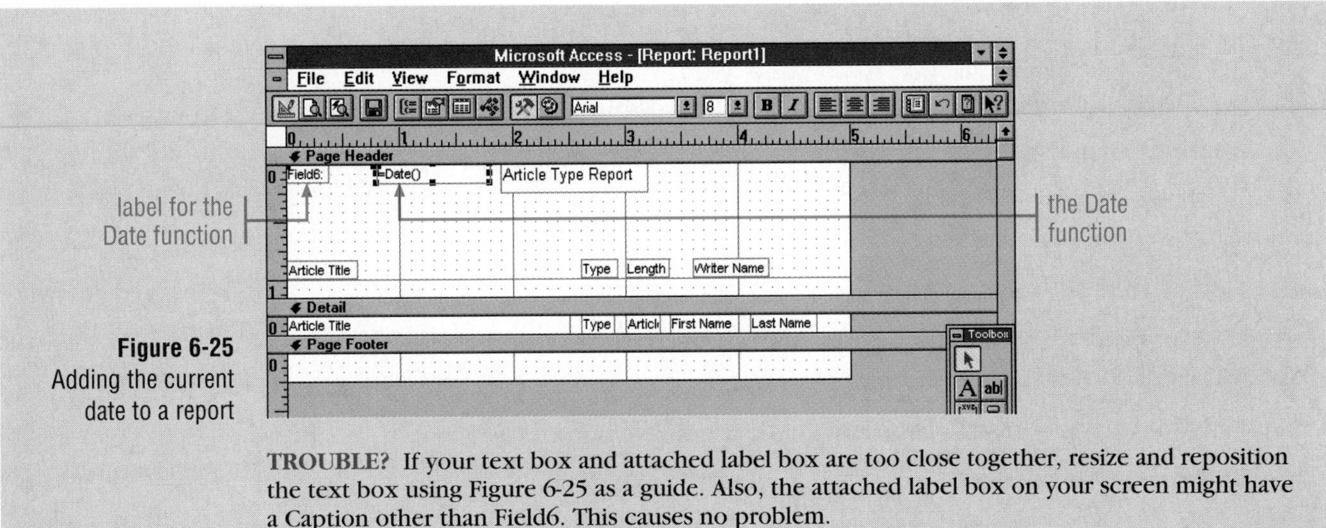

Figure 6-25
Adding the current date to a report

TROUBLE? If your text box and attached label box are too close together, resize and reposition the text box using Figure 6-25 as a guide. Also, the attached label box on your screen might have a Caption other than Field6. This causes no problem.

When Access prints your report, the current date replaces the Date function you entered in the Unbound text box. Because a current date in a Page Header section does not usually need a label, Elena deletes the label box. She then changes the Date text box to font size 10 and moves it to the upper-left corner of the Page Header section. Finally, Elena uses the Text Box tool to add the Page property to the upper-right corner of the Page Header section. The **Page property** automatically prints the correct page number on each page of a report.

To finish formatting the current date and add a page number in the Page Header section:

1. Click the Date **label box**, which is located in the upper-left corner of the Page Header section. Click the Date **label box** with the right mouse button to open the Shortcut menu and then click **Cut** to delete the label.
2. Click the Date **text box** and then drag its move handle to the upper-left corner of the Page Header section.
3. Click the Font Size **down arrow button** and click **10** to change the font size of the Date text box.
4. Click the toolbox **Text Box tool** [abl]. Move the pointer into the Page Header section. The mouse pointer changes to +[abl]. Click the mouse button when the pointer's plus symbol is positioned at the top of the Page Header section at the 4.5" mark on the horizontal ruler. Access adds an Unbound text box with an attached label box to its left.
5. Click the label box with the right mouse button to open the Shortcut menu, and then click **Cut**. The label box disappears.
6. Click the Unbound text box, type **=Page**, press **[Enter]**, click the Font Size **drop-down list box down arrow button**, and then click **10**. See Figure 6-26 on the following page.

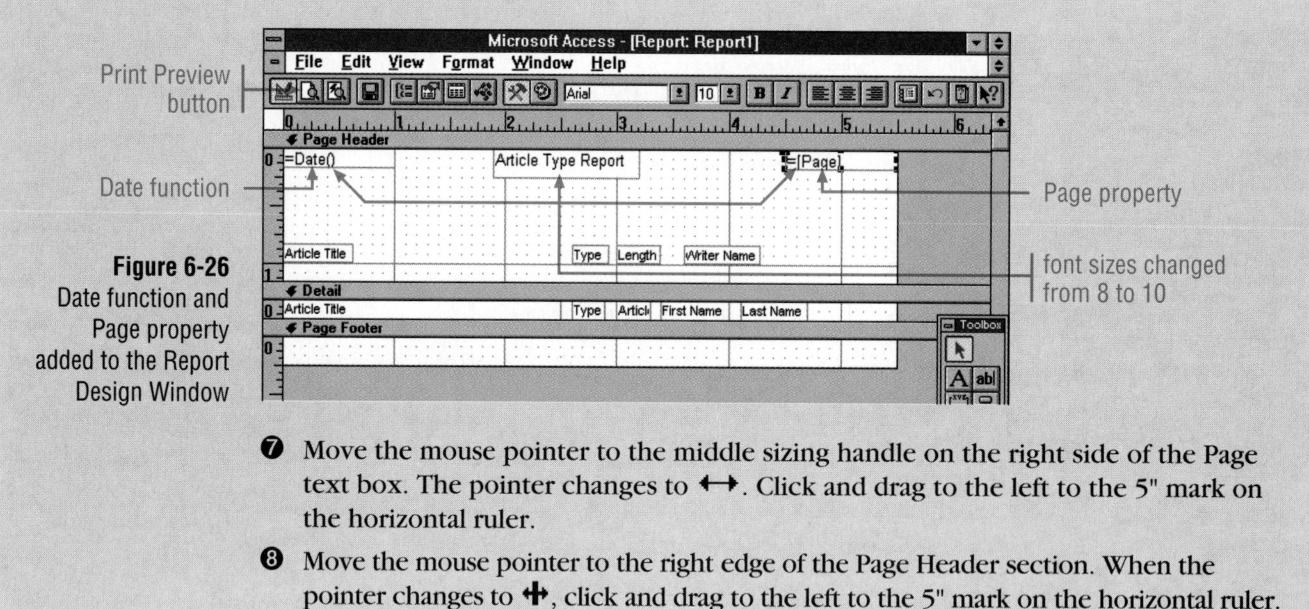

Figure 6-26
Date function and Page property added to the Report Design Window

❼ Move the mouse pointer to the middle sizing handle on the right side of the Page text box. The pointer changes to ↔. Click and drag to the left to the 5" mark on the horizontal ruler.

❽ Move the mouse pointer to the right edge of the Page Header section. When the pointer changes to ✥, click and drag to the left to the 5" mark on the horizontal ruler.

Elena switches to the Print Preview window. She wants to check the report against her design.

To view a report in the Print Preview window:

❶ Click the toolbar **Print Preview button** to open the Print Preview window. See Figure 6-27.

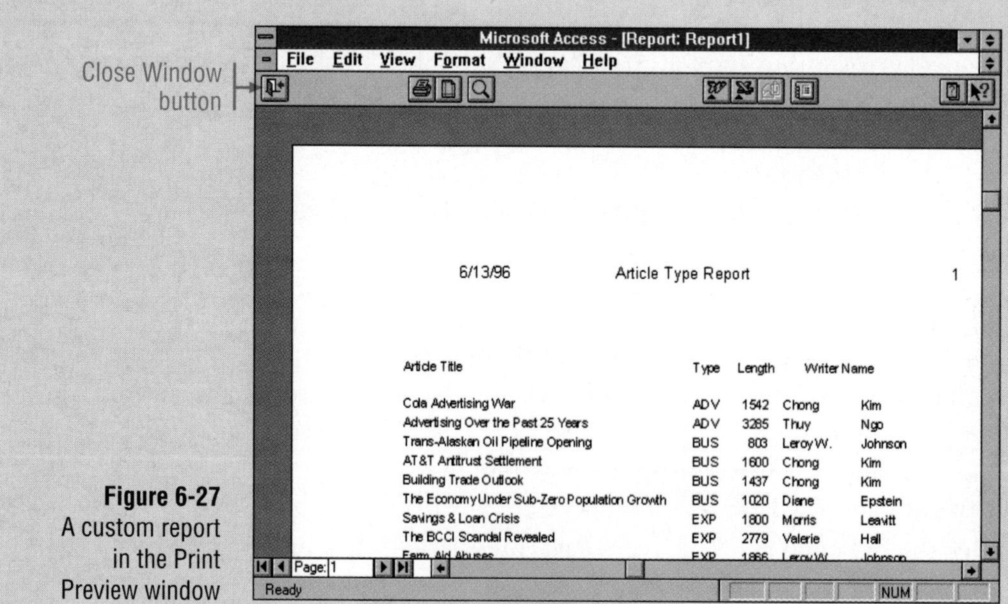

Figure 6-27
A custom report in the Print Preview window

TROUBLE? If your report shows a gap between the first and second records in the Detail section, you need to reduce the height of the Detail section. The bottom of the Detail section should align with the bottom of the text boxes in that section. Reduce the height during the next series of steps.

Adding Lines to a Report

Elena adds a horizontal line to the Page Header section below the column heads. Before doing this, she repositions the column heading labels just below the report title line and decreases the height of the Page Header section.

To move labels and decrease the Page Header section height:

1. Click the toolbar **Close Window button** to return to the Report Design window.
2. While pressing and holding **[Shift]**, click each of the four label boxes in the Page Header section to select them. Click one of the label boxes when the pointer changes to ✋ and drag the label boxes straight up so they are positioned just below the report title. Position the labels so that the top of each label box is at the .25" mark on the vertical ruler.

   TROUBLE? If the label boxes do not move, the Page text box is probably selected along with the label boxes. Click in any unoccupied portion of the Page Header section to deselect all boxes, then repeat Step 2.
3. Move the pointer to the bottom edge of the Page Header section. When the pointer changes to ‡, drag the bottom edge upward to reduce the height of the Page Header section. Align the bottom edge with the grid marks that are just below the .5" mark on the vertical ruler.

Elena now adds a medium-thick horizontal line to the bottom of the Page Header section. You use the **toolbox Line tool** to add a line to a report or form.

To add a line to a report:

1. Click the toolbox **Line tool**. Move the pointer into the Page Header section; the pointer changes to +\. Position the Pointer's plus symbol at the left edge of the Page Header section and at the .5" mark on the vertical ruler.

   TROUBLE? If the toolbox is too low for you to see the Line tool, drag the toolbox title bar straight up until the Line tool is visible.
2. Click and hold the mouse button, drag a horizontal line from left to right ending just after the 4.25" mark on the horizontal ruler, and then release the mouse button.
3. To increase the thickness of the line, click the toolbar **Properties button**. The property sheet appears. The Border Width property controls the line's width, or thickness.
4. Click the **Border Width text box** in the property sheet, click the **down arrow button** that appears, and then click **3 pt**. The line's width increases. See Figure 6-28 on the following page.

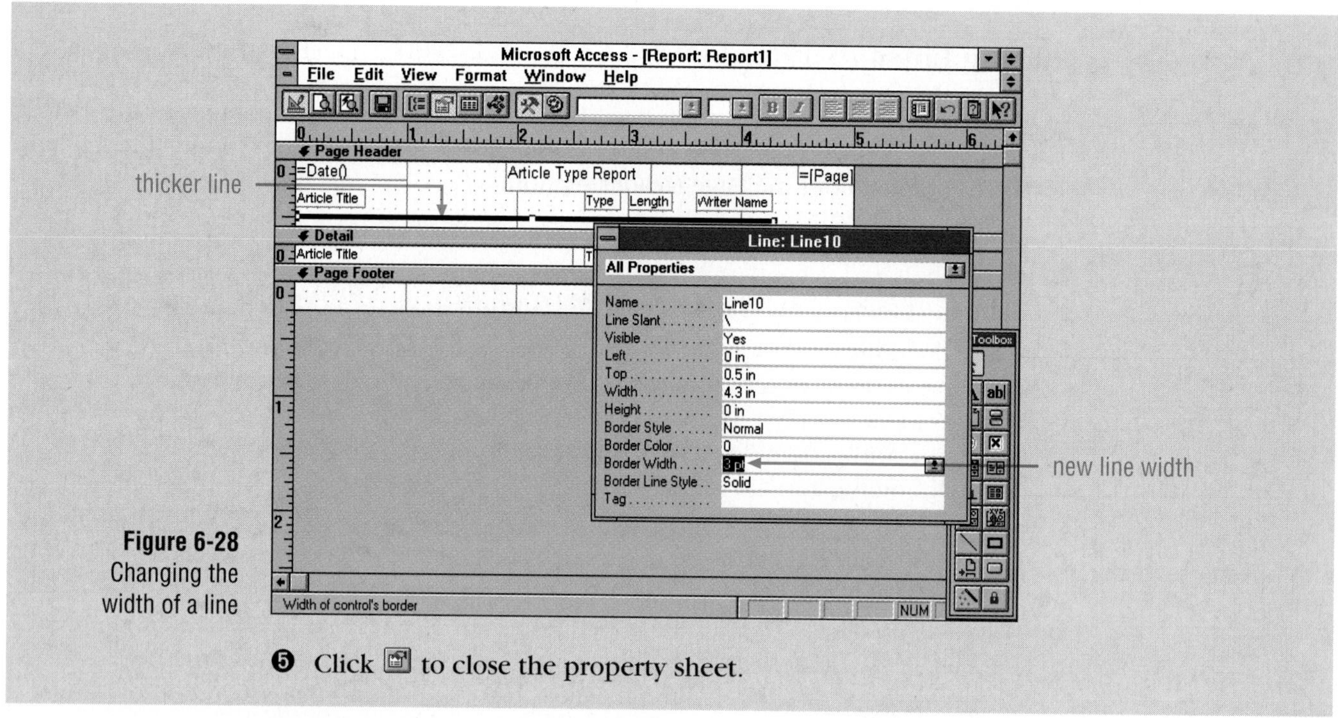

Figure 6-28
Changing the width of a line

❺ Click [property sheet button] to close the property sheet.

Elena has finished her design of the Page Header section. She next chooses the sort fields and the grouping field for the report.

Sorting and Grouping Data in a Report

Elena wants Access to print records in ascending order based on the Type field and to print subtotals for each set of Type field values. Thus, the Type field is both the primary sort key and the grouping field. Elena wants the records within a Type to be printed in descending order based on the Article Length field. This makes Article Length the secondary sort key. Because Elena does not want subtotals for each Article Length value, Article Length is not a grouping field.

You use the toolbar **Sorting and Grouping button** to select sort keys and grouping fields. Each report can have up to 10 sort fields, and any of the 10 sort fields can also be grouping fields.

To select sort keys and grouping fields:

❶ Click the toolbar **Sorting and Grouping button** [Sorting and Grouping button]. The Sorting and Grouping dialog box appears.

❷ Click the **down arrow button** in the first Field/Expression box in the Sorting and Grouping dialog box and then click **Type**. Ascending is the default sort order in the Sort Order box.

❸ Click anywhere in the second Field/Expression box in the Sorting and Grouping dialog box, click the **down arrow button** that appears, and then click **Article Length**. Ascending, the default sort order, needs to be changed to Descending in the Sort Order box.

❹ Click anywhere in the second Sort Order box, click the **down arrow button** that appears, and then click **Descending**. See Figure 6-29.

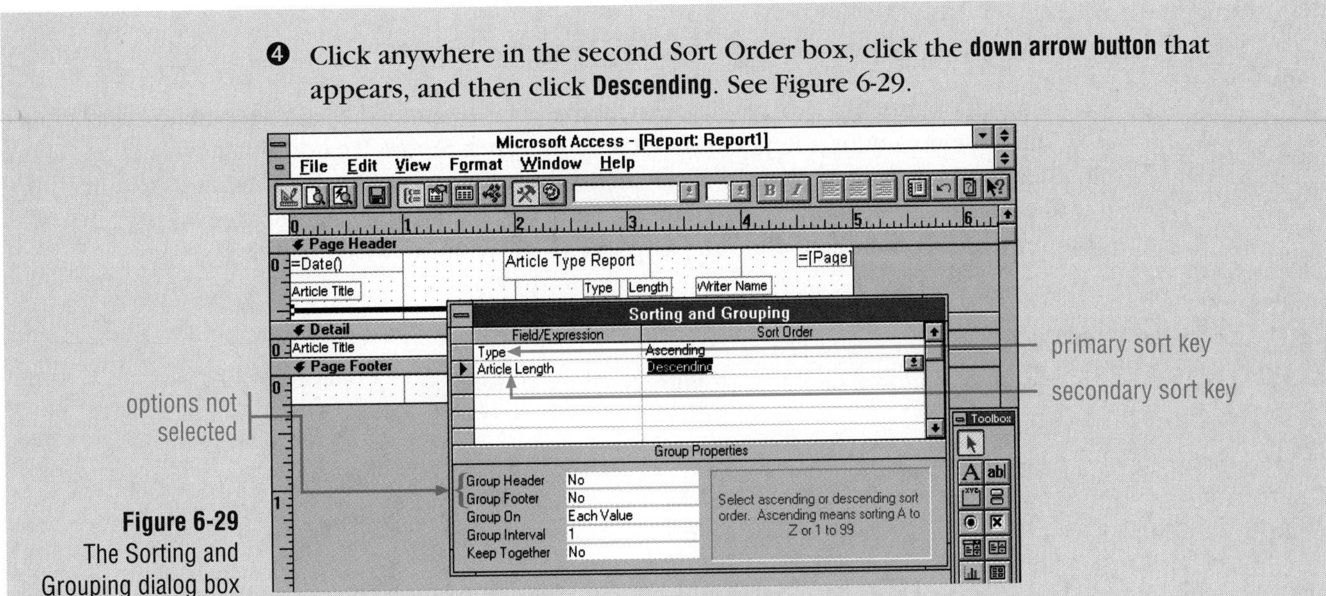

Figure 6-29
The Sorting and Grouping dialog box

Elena notices that adding the two sort keys did not cause any new sections to be added to the report. To add a Group Footer, she must choose the Group Footer option for the Type field in the Sorting and Grouping dialog box.

To add a Group Footer to a report:

❶ Click the **Field/Expression box** for the Type field in the Sorting and Grouping dialog box, click the **Group Footer box**, click the **down arrow button** that appears, and then click **Yes**. Access adds a Group Footer section called Type Footer to the Report Design window. See Figure 6-30.

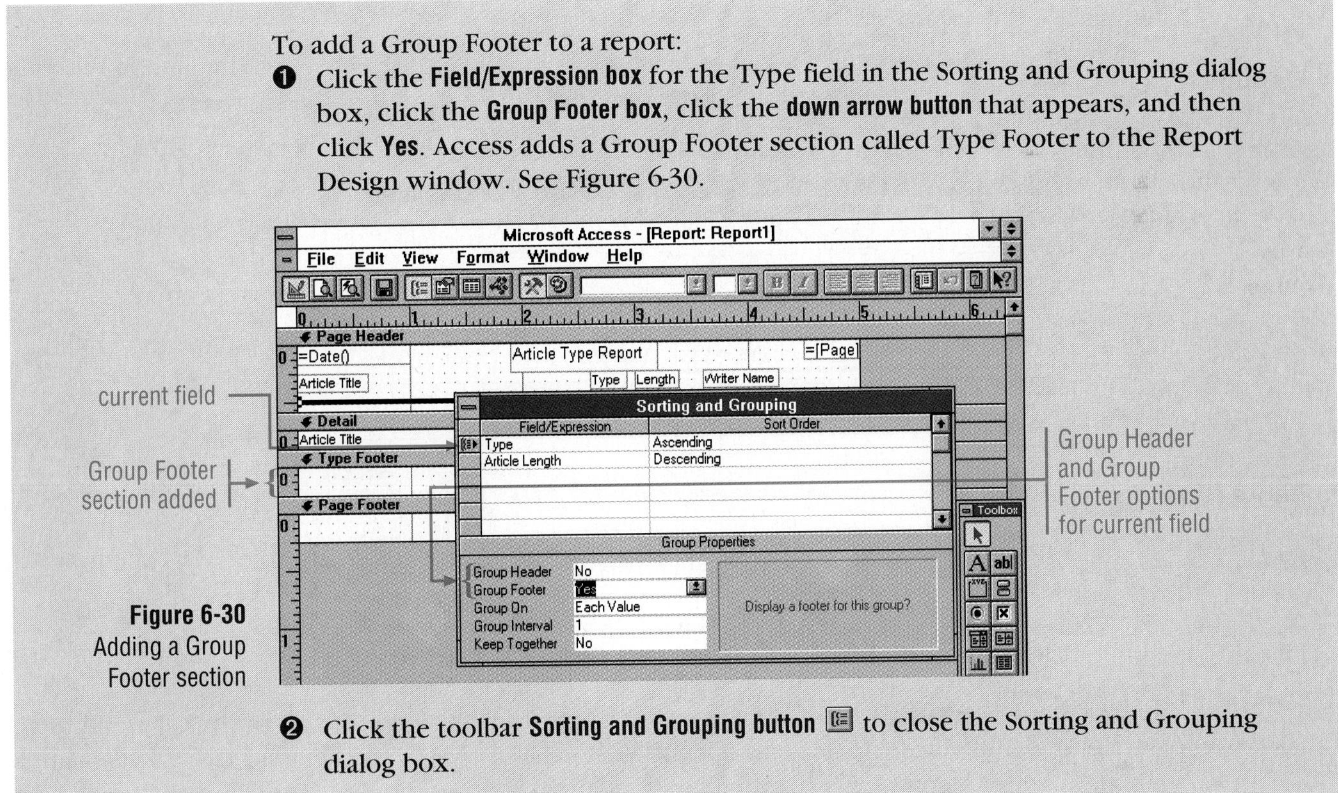

Figure 6-30
Adding a Group Footer section

❷ Click the toolbar **Sorting and Grouping button** to close the Sorting and Grouping dialog box.

Adding a Report Header and Footer

Elena compares her progress against her report design again and sees that she is almost done. She next adds a Report Footer section to her report. To add this new section, Elena adds the Report Header and Footer sections to the report. Because she does not need the Report Header section, she deletes it. She also deletes the Page Footer section that was automatically included when the Report Design window was opened.

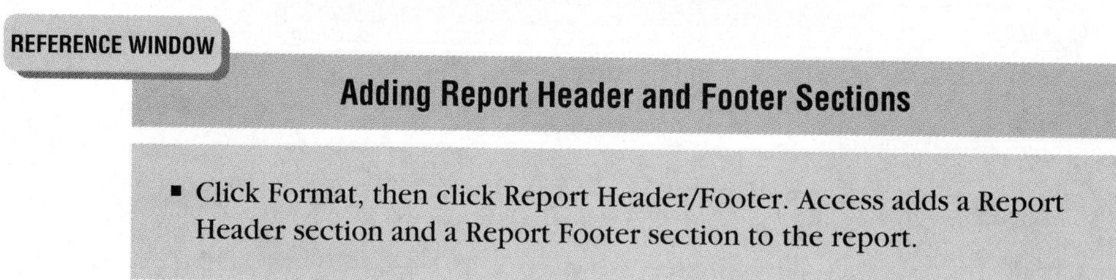

REFERENCE WINDOW

Adding Report Header and Footer Sections

- Click Format, then click Report Header/Footer. Access adds a Report Header section and a Report Footer section to the report.

Let's add Report Header and Footer sections to the report and then delete the Page Footer section.

To add and delete sections from a report:

1. Click **Format** and then click **Report Header/Footer**. Access creates a Report Header section at the top of the report and a Report Footer section at the bottom of the report.
2. Move the pointer to the bottom edge of the Report Header section. When the pointer changes to ‡, drag the bottom edge upward until the section disappears. Repeat this process for the Page Footer section. See Figure 6-31.

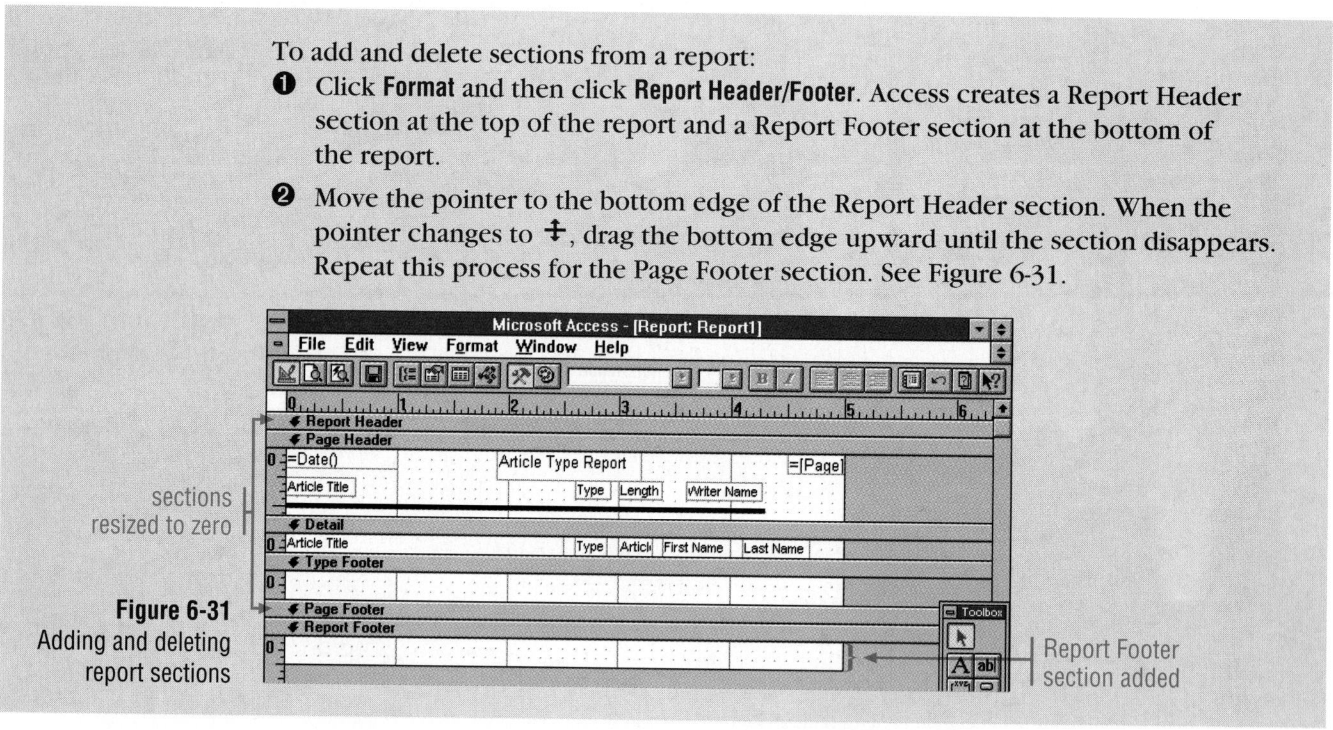

Figure 6-31
Adding and deleting report sections

Calculating Group Totals and Overall Totals

Elena wants the report to print subtotals for each Type group and an overall grand total. She adds calculations to produce these totals for the Article Length field. To calculate a total for a group of records or for all records, you use the **Sum function**. You place the Sum function in a Group Footer section to print a group total and in the Report Footer section to print an overall total. The format for the Sum function is =Sum([field name]). When you enter the function, you replace "field name" with the name of the field you want to sum. Use the toolbox Text Box tool to create appropriate text boxes in the footer sections.

In the Type Footer and Report Footer sections, Elena adds text boxes, deletes the attached labels for both, and adds the Sum function to each text box. She also draws lines above each Sum function so that the totals will be visually separated from the Detail section field values.

To add text boxes to footer sections and delete labels:

1. Increase the height of the Type Footer section so that you see four rows of grid dots, and increase the height of the Report Footer section so that you see three rows of grid dots.
2. Click the toolbox **Text Box tool** [abl]. Move the pointer into the Type Footer section. Click the mouse button when the pointer's plus symbol is positioned in the second row of grid lines and vertically aligned with the right edge of the Type field-value text box. Access adds a text box with an attached label box to its left.
3. Click [abl]. Move the pointer into the Report Footer section. Click the mouse button when the pointer's plus symbol is positioned in the second row of grid lines and vertically aligned with the right edge of the Type field-value text box. Access adds a text box with an attached label box to its left. See Figure 6-32.

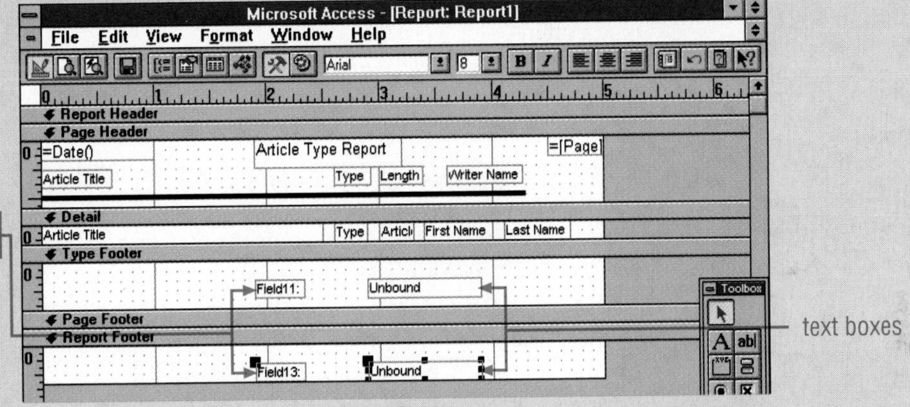

Figure 6-32
Adding text boxes in footer sections

4. Click anywhere in the Type Footer section, outside both boxes to deselect all boxes.
5. While you press and hold **[Shift]**, click the label box in the Type Footer section, and then click the label box in the Report Footer section. You have selected both boxes.
6. Click either label box with the right mouse button to open the Shortcut menu and then click **Cut**. The two label boxes disappear.

Elena now adds the Sum function to the two footer section text boxes.

To add the Sum function to calculate group and overall totals:

1. Click the text box in the Type Footer section, type **=Sum([Article Length])**, and then press **[Enter]**. The text box in the Type Footer section needs to be narrower.
2. Click the middle **sizing handle** on the right side of the text box and drag it to the left until the right edge of the box lines up with the right edge of the Article Length field-value text box in the Detail section.

❸ Click the text box in the Report Footer section, type **=Sum([Article Length])**, and then press **[Enter]**. See Figure 6-33.

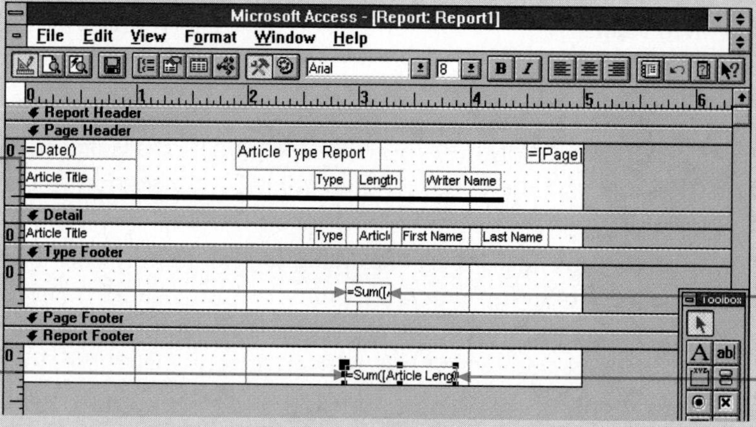

group total

overall total

Sum function added and box resized

Sum function added but box not yet resized

Figure 6-33
Adding a group total and overall total

❹ To resize the text box in the Report Footer section, click the middle **sizing handle** on the right side of the text box and drag it to the left until the right edge of the box lines up with the right edge of the Article Length field-value text box in the Detail section.

Elena next adds lines above each Sum function.

To add lines above totals:

❶ Click the toolbox **Line tool** . Move the pointer into the Type Footer section; the pointer changes to +↘. Position the pointer's plus symbol in the top row of grid lines and vertically align it with the right edge of the Type field-value text box in the Detail section above.

❷ Click and hold the mouse button, and drag a horizontal line to the right until the right end of the line is below the right edge of the Article Length field-value text box.

❸ Repeat Steps 1 and 2 for the Report Footer section. See Figure 6-34.

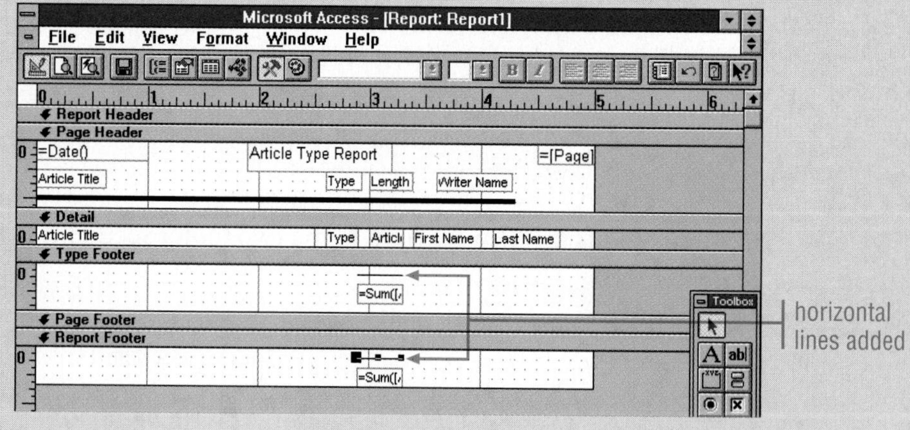

Figure 6-34
Adding horizontal lines above group and overall totals

Elena's report is almost finished. There is, however, still one change she can make to improve its appearance.

Hiding Duplicate Values in a Group Report

Elena's final change is to display the Type value only in the first record in a group. Within a group, all Type field values are the same, so if you display only the first one, you simplify the report and make it easier to read.

To hide duplicate values:

1. Click the Type **text box** in the Detail section and then click the toolbar **Properties button**. The property sheet for the Type field appears.
2. If necessary, scroll through the property sheet, then click the **Hide Duplicates text box** in the property sheet, click the **down arrow button**, and click **Yes**. See Figure 6-35.

the Hide Duplicates property
Text Box: Type
All Properties
Input Mask
Visible Yes
Hide Duplicates Yes
Can Grow No
Can Shrink No
Running Sum No
Left 2.6 in
Top 0 in
Width 0.2917 in
Height 0.1667 in
Back Color 16777215
Special Effect Normal
the property sheet for the Type field

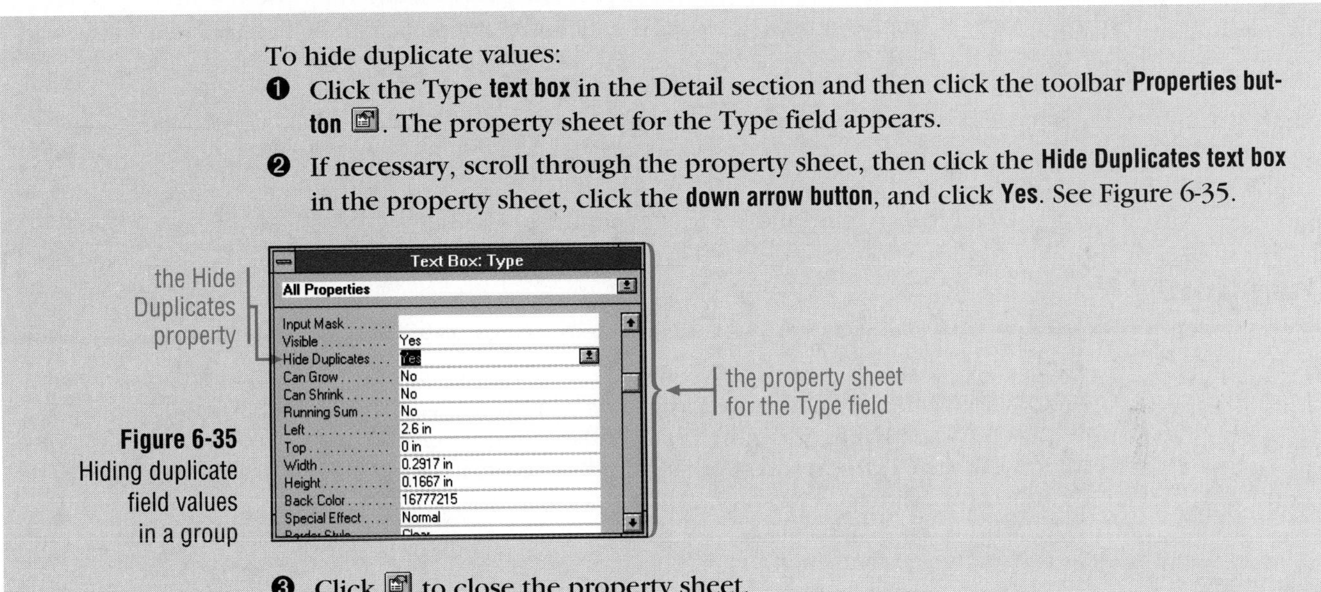

Figure 6-35 Hiding duplicate field values in a group

3. Click to close the property sheet.

Elena views the report in the Print Preview window and then saves the report.

To view and save a report:

1. Click the toolbar **Print Preview button**. Access displays the first page of the report. See Figure 6-36.

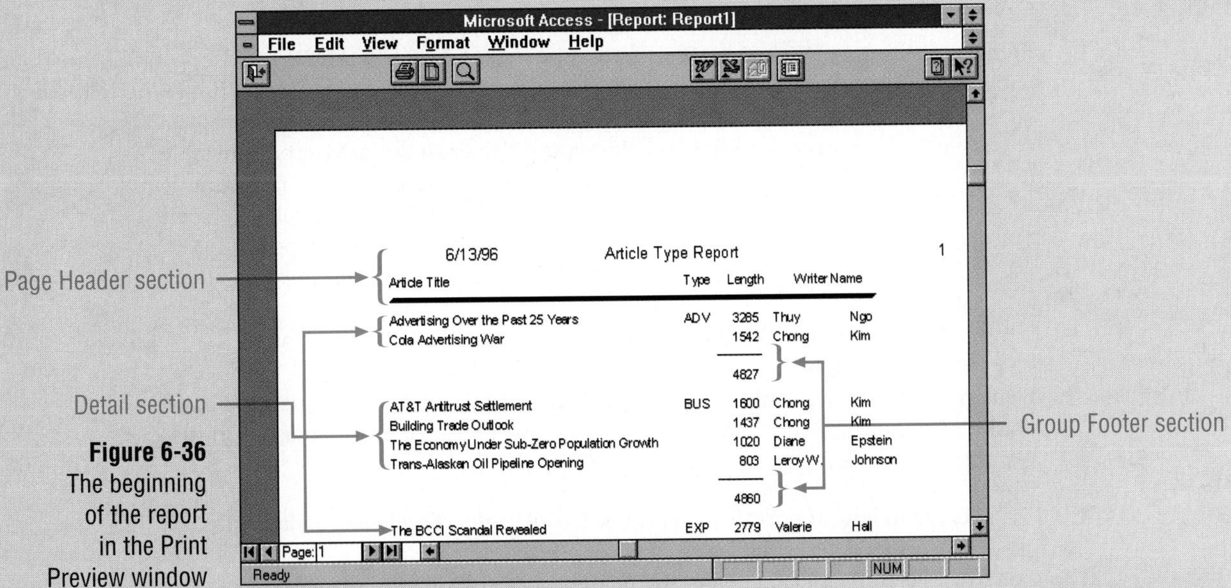

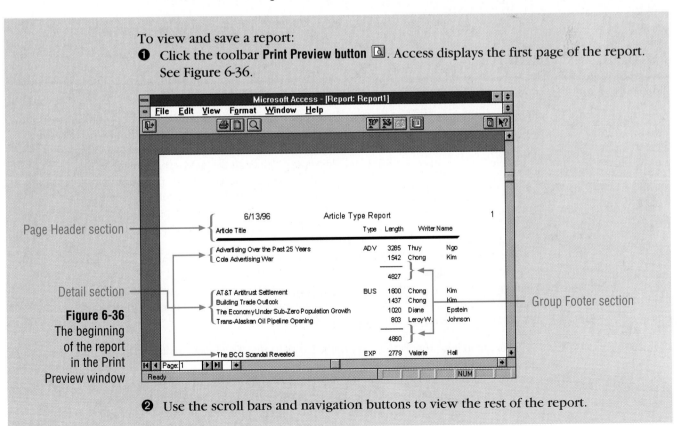

Page Header section
Detail section
Microsoft Access - [Report: Report1]
File Edit View Format Window Help
6/13/96 Article Type Report 1
Article Title Type Length Writer Name
Advertising Over the Past 25 Years ADV 3285 Thuy Ngo
Cola Advertising War 1542 Chong Kim
4827
AT&T Antitrust Settlement BUS 1600 Chong Kim
Building Trade Outlook 1437 Chong Kim
The Economy Under Sub-Zero Population Growth 1020 Diane Epstein
Trans-Alaskan Oil Pipeline Opening 803 Leroy W. Johnson
4860
The BCCI Scandal Revealed EXP 2779 Valerie Hall
Page: 1
Ready
NUM
Group Footer section

Figure 6-36 The beginning of the report in the Print Preview window

2. Use the scroll bars and navigation buttons to view the rest of the report.

3. Double-click the Print Preview window **Control menu box**. The "Save changes to 'Report1'" dialog box appears.
4. Click the **Yes button**. The dialog box disappears, and Access displays the Save As dialog box.
5. Type **Article Type Report** in the Report Name text box and then press **[Enter]**. Access saves the custom report, closes the dialog box, and activates the Database window.

■ ■ ■

Elena exits Access and brings her report to Harold.

Questions

1. What are the seven Access report sections, and when is each printed?
2. What types of reports can the Report Wizards tool create?
3. What three different styles does Report Wizards offer you?
4. What is a group?
5. What is normal grouping?
6. What is a custom report?
7. When do you use the toolbox Text Box tool?
8. What do you type in a text box to tell Access to print the current date?
9. What do you type in a text box to tell Access to print the page number?
10. How do you add a Report Footer section to a report without adding a Report Header section?
11. Why might you want to hide duplicate values in a group report?

Tutorial Assignments

Elena uses Report Wizards to create a report named PAST ARTICLES Report for the Issue25 database. Launch Access, open the Issue25 database on your Student Disk, and do the following:

1. Use Report Wizards to create a groups/totals report based on the PAST ARTICLES table. Use the executive style for the report. Select all the fields from the table in the order in which they are stored in the table, group the records by Writer ID, select Normal grouping, select no sort key fields, check the "Calculate percentages of the total" box, and enter PAST ARTICLES Report as the report title.
2. Display the report in the Print Preview window and then print the last report page.
3. Save the report, naming it PAST ARTICLES Report, and return to the Database window.

Elena next creates a custom report. Use the Issue25 database on your Student Disk to do the following. Use the report shown in Figure 6-14 as a basis for your report design.

E 4. Create a blank report using the WRITERS table.

E 5. Include in your report these sections: Page Header, Freelancer Header, Detail, Freelancer Footer, Page Footer, and Report Footer.

E 6. In the Page Header section at the beginning of the first line, enter Freelancer Group Totals as the report title. Enter the current date at the beginning of the second line. Position the labels under these lines, as shown in Figure 6-14. Add a single line, instead of a double line, below the column heads line. Do not place any lines above the column heads or above the report title.

E 7. Use Freelancer for the grouping field. There are no sorting fields in this report. In the Freelancer Header section, include the Freelancer field value.

E 8. In the Detail section, include the field values, as shown in Figure 6-14.

E 9. In the Freelancer Footer section, include the group total for the Amount field.

E 10. In the Page Footer section, include a page number aligned with the right edge of the Amount field.

E 11. In the Report Footer section, include the overall total for the Amount field.

E 12. When you finish creating the report, print the entire report.

E 13. Save the report, naming it Freelancer Group Totals Report, and then exit Access.

Case Problems

1. Walkton Daily Press Carriers

Grant Sherman uses Report Wizards to create a report for his Press database. Launch Access, open the Press database on your Student Disk, and do the following:

1. Use Report Wizards to create a groups/totals report in the executive style based on the CARRIERS table. Select all the fields from the table in the order in which they are stored in the table. Do not select a grouping field, sort by Carrier ID, do not check the "Calculate percentages of the total" box, and enter CARRIERS Report as the report title.
2. Display the report in the Print Preview window and then print the entire report.
3. Save the report, naming it CARRIERS Report, then close the Print Preview window, and return to the Database window.

Grant next modifies the design of this report. Open the newly created CARRIERS Report in the Report Design window and do the following:

4. In the Report Footer section, delete the two Sum function text boxes, delete the two sets of double lines, and delete the Report Footer section.
5. Click the Print Preview button to display the report and then print the entire report.
6. Save the report, naming it CARRIERS Report #2, and return to the Database window.

Grant next creates a custom report. Use the Press database on your Student Disk to do the following:

E 7. Create a blank report using the query named Carriers sorted by Name, Route ID.

E 8. Sketch a design for the report based on the requirements described in the next five steps, and then create the report following these same steps.

E 9. Include in your report these sections: Page Header, Detail, Group Footer, and Report Footer.

E 10. In the Page Header section at the beginning of the first line, enter CARRIERS sorted by Name, Route ID Report as the report title. Enter the current date at the beginning of the second line and the page number at the end of the second line. Position under these elements a row of column heads with these labels: Last Name, First Name, Carrier Phone, Route ID, and Balance. Add a single horizontal line under the column heads.

E 11. In the Detail section, include the field values for Last Name, First Name, Carrier Phone, Route ID, and Balance. Hide duplicates for the Last Name, First Name, and Carrier Phone fields.

E 12. In the Group Footer section, print the group total for the Balance field. Select Last Name as the primary sort key, and use this field as a grouping field. Select Route ID as the secondary sort key, but do not use it as a grouping field. Choose ascending sort order for each sort key.

E 13. In the Report Footer section, print the overall total for the Balance field.

E 14. When you finish creating the report, print the entire report.

E 15. Save the report, naming it CARRIERS sorted by Name and Route ID Report, and then exit Access.

2. Lopez Used Cars

Maria Lopez uses Report Wizards to create a report for her Usedcars database. Launch Access, open the Usedcars database on your Student Disk, and do the following:

1. Use Report Wizards to create a groups/totals report in the executive style based on the USED CARS table. Select all the fields from the table in the order in which they are stored in the table. Do not select a grouping field, sort by Year, do not check the "Calculate percentages of the total" box, and enter USED CARS by Year as the report title.
2. Display the report in the Print Preview window and then print the entire report.
3. Save the report, naming it USED CARS by Year Report, and return to the Database window.

Maria next modifies the design of this report. Open the newly created report named USED CARS by Year Report in the Report Design window and do the following:

4. In the Report Footer section, delete the Sum function text box for the Year field, and delete its set of double lines.
5. Click the Print Preview button to display the report and then print the entire report.
6. Save the report, naming it USED CARS by Year Report #2, and return to the Database window.

Maria next creates a custom report. Use the Usedcars database on your Student Disk and do the following:

E 7. Create a blank report using the USED CARS table.

E 8. Sketch a design for the report based on the requirements described in the next five steps, and then create the report following these same steps.

E 9. Include in your report these sections: Page Header, Detail, Group Footer, and Report Footer.

E 10. In the Page Header section at the beginning of the first line, enter USED CARS sorted by Manufacturer, Model, Year as the report title. Enter the current date at the beginning of the second line and the page number at the end of the second line. Position under these elements a row of column heads with these labels: Manufacturer, Model, Year, Cost, and Selling Price. Add a single horizontal line under the column heads.

E 11. In the Detail section, include the field values for Manufacturer, Model, Year, Cost, and Selling Price. Hide duplicates for the Manufacturer field.

E 12. In the Group Footer section, print the group total for the Cost and Selling Price fields. Select Manufacturer as the primary sort key and as the grouping field. Select Model, and then Year, as the secondary sort keys, but do not use them as grouping fields. Choose ascending sort order for each sort key.

E 13. In the Report Footer section, print the overall totals for the Cost and Selling Price fields.

E 14. When you finish creating the report, print the entire report.

E 15. Save the report, naming it USED CARS by Manufacturer, Model, and Year Report, and then exit Access.

3. Tophill University Student Employment

Olivia Tyler uses Report Wizards to create a report for her Parttime database. Launch Access, open the Parttime database on your Student Disk, and do the following:

1. Use Report Wizards to create a groups/totals report in the executive style based on the JOBS table. Select all the fields from the table in the order in which they are stored in the table. Do not select a grouping field, sort by Job Order, do not check the "Calculate percentages of the total" box, and enter JOBS as the report title.
2. Display the report in the Print Preview window and then print the entire report.
3. Save the report, naming it JOBS Report, and return to the Database window.

Olivia next modifies the design of this report. Open the newly created JOBS Report in the Report Design window and do the following:

4. In the Report Footer section, delete the three Sum function text boxes, delete the three sets of double lines, and delete the Report Footer section.
5. Click the Print Preview button to display the report and then print the entire report.
6. Save the report, naming it JOBS Report #2, and return to the Database window.

Olivia next creates a custom report. Use the Parttime database on your Student Disk to do the following:

E 7. Create a blank report using the query named JOBS sorted by Employer, Job Title.

E 8. Sketch a design for the report based on the requirements described in the next four steps, and then create the report following these same steps.

E 9. Include in your report a Page Header section and a Detail section.

E 10. In the Page Header section at the beginning of the first line, enter JOBS sorted by Employer, Job Title as the report title. Enter the current date at the beginning of the second line and the page number at the end of the second line. Position under these elements a row of column heads with these labels: Employer Name, Hours/Week, Job Title, and Wages. Add a single horizontal line under the column heads.

E 11. In the Detail section, include the field values for Employer Name, Hours/Week, Job Title, and Wages. Hide duplicates for the Employer Name field.

E 12. Select Employer Name as the primary sort key and Job Title as the secondary sort key. Do not select a grouping field. Choose ascending sort order for each sort key.

E 13. When you finish creating the report, print the entire report.

E 14. Save the report, naming it JOBS sorted by Employer and Job Title Report, and then exit Access.

4. Rexville Business Licenses

Chester Pearce uses Report Wizards to create a report for his Buslic database. Launch Access, open the Buslic database on your Student Disk, and do the following:

1. Use Report Wizards to create a groups/totals report in the executive style based on the BUSINESSES table. Select all the fields from the table in the order in which they are stored in the table. Do not select a grouping field, sort by Business Name, do not check the "Calculate percentages of the total" box, and enter BUSINESSES Report as the report title.

2. Display the report in the Print Preview window and then print the entire report.
3. Save the report, naming it BUSINESSES Report, and return to the Database window.

Chester next modifies the design of this report. Open the newly created BUSINESSES Report in the Report Design window and do the following:

4. In the Report Footer section, delete the Sum function text box for the two fields, delete the two sets of double lines, and delete the Report Footer section.
5. Click the Print Preview button to display the report and then print the entire report.
6. Save the report, naming it BUSINESSES Report #2, and then return to the Database window.

Chester next creates a custom report. Use the Buslic database on your Student Disk to do the following:

E 7. Create a blank report using the query named BUSINESSES sorted by License Type, Business Name.

E 8. Sketch a design for the report based on the requirements described in the next five steps, and then create the report following these same steps.

E 9. Include in your report these sections: Page Header, Detail, Group Footer, and Report Footer.

E 10. In the Page Header section at the beginning of the first line, enter BUSINESSES sorted by License Type, Business Name as the report title. Enter the current date at the beginning of the second line and the page number at the end of the second line. Position under these elements a row of column heads with these labels: License, Basic Cost, Business Name, and Amount. Add a single horizontal line under the column heads.

E 11. In the Detail section, include the field values for License (do not use License Number), Basic Cost, Business Name, and Amount. Hide duplicates for the License and Basic Cost fields.

E 12. In the Group Footer section, print the group total for the Amount field. Select License as the primary sort key and as the grouping field. Select Business Name as the secondary sort key, but do not use it as a grouping field. Choose ascending sort order for each sort key.

E 13. In the Report Footer section, print the overall totals for the Amount field.

E 14. When you finish creating the report, print the entire report.

E 15. Save the report, naming it BUSINESSES sorted by License Type and Business Name Report, and then exit Access.

Index

Special Characters

K

L

M

N

S

T

TASK REFERENCE

ACCESS 2.0 FOR WINDOWS

Italicized page numbers indicate the first discussion of each task.

TASK	MOUSE	MENU	KEYBOARD
Add a field to a table structure, *A 69*	See Reference Window: *Adding a Field to a Table Structure*		
Add a label to a form or report, *A 189*	[A]		
Add a list box to a form, *A 189*	See *Adding a List Box Using Control Wizards*		
Add a record to a table, *A 171*	[▶|], [▶] or [▶*]	Click Records, click Go To, click New	[Ctrl] [+]
Add a text box to a form or report, *(633)*	[ab|]		
Add aggregate functions to a query, *A 138*	See *Using Record Calculations*		
Add all fields to a query's QBE grid, *A 114*	See *The Query Design Window*		
Add an input mask to a field, *A 60*	See *Using Input Mask Wizard*		
Add calculated field to a query, *A 136*	See *Using Calculated Fields*		
Add fields to a form or report, *A 182*	See *Adding Fields to a Form*		
Add Form Header and Footer sections, *A 188*		Click Format, click Form Header/Footer	[Alt] [O], [H]
Add lines to a form or report, *(628)*	[\\]		
Add record group calculations to a query, *A 141*	See *Using Record Group Calculations*		
Add Report Header and Footer sections, *(631)*		Click Format, click Report Header/Footer	[Alt] [O], [H]
Add sort keys and grouping fields to a report, *(630)*	[{≡]		
Align control boxes, *A 186*	See *Aligning Labels*		
Arrange controls on a form or report, *A 183*	See *Selecting, Moving, and Deleting Controls*		
Back up a database, *A 102*	See *Backing Up a Database*		
Change a datasheet's font, *A 86*	See Reference Window: *Changing a Datasheet's Font Properties*		
Change colors on a form, *A 192*	See Reference Window: *Adding Colors to a Form*		
Change the number of decimal places for a field, *A 59*	See *Changing Decimal Places*		

TASK REFERENCE

ACCESS 2.0 FOR WINDOWS

Italicized page numbers indicate the first discussion of each task.

TASK	MOUSE	MENU	KEYBOARD
Close a database, *A 25*	[icon], double-click Database window Control menu box	Click File, click Close, click File, click Close Database	Alt F, C, Alt F, C
Close an object window, *A 22*	Double-click the object window Control menu box	Click File, click Close	Alt F, C
Close Print Preview window, *A 22*	[icon]	Click File, click Close	Alt F, C
Compact a database, *A 103*	See *Compacting a Database*		
Create a custom form, *A 179*	[icon], select table or query, click Blank Form button		
Create a custom report, *(616)*	[icon], select table or query, click Blank Report button		
Create a database, *A 46*	See Reference Window: *Creating a Database*		
Create a filter, *A 174*	See *Using a Filter*		
Create a form with Form Wizards, *A 163*	See *Creating Forms Using Form Wizards*		
Create a multiple-table form, *A 166*	See *Creating Main/Subform Forms*		
Create a multiple-table query, *A 149*	See *Querying More Than One Table*		
Create a new query, *A 113*	Click table name, [icon], click New Query	Click table name, click File, click New..., click Query, click New Query	Alt F, W, Q, N
Create a parameter query, *A 152*	See Reference Window: *Creating a Parameter Query*		
Create a report with Report Wizards, *(606)*	See *Creating Reports Using Report Wizards*		
Create a table, *A 47*	Click the New command button	Click File, click New, click Table	Alt N
Create an AutoForm form, *A 162*	Click the table or query, [icon]		
Create an AutoReport report, *(605)*	Click the table or query, [icon]		
Define a relationship between tables, *A 147*	See *Adding a Relationship Between Two Tables*		
Define fields in a table, *A 50*	See *Changing the Sample Field Properties*		

TASK REFERENCE

ACCESS 2.0 FOR WINDOWS

Italicized page numbers indicate the first discussion of each task.

TASK	MOUSE	MENU	KEYBOARD
Delete a field from a table structure, *A 68*	Right-click the field, click Delete Row	Click Edit, click Delete Row	Alt E, D
Delete a field from the QBE grid, *A 116*	Click field selector, right-click field selector, click Cut	Click field selector, click Edit, click Cut	Click field selector, Del
Delete a form or report section, *A 188*	Drag section's bottom edge to 0" height		
Delete a record in a datasheet, *A 88*	Select record, right-click record selector, click Cut, click OK	Select record, click Edit, click Delete, click OK	Select record, Del, Enter
Delete a table, *A 92*	Right-click table name, click Delete, click OK	Click table name, click Edit, click Delete, click OK	Click table name, Del, Enter
Delete an index, *A 67*	Right-click the index, click Delete Row		
Delete selection criteria from QBE grid, *A 134*	See *The Or Logical Operator*		
Display a single record on a form, *A 192*	[icon], click Default View box, click Single Form		
Display a table's indexes, *A 66*	[icon]	Click View, click Indexes...	Alt V, I
Enter a default value for a field, *A 59*	See *Assigning Default Values*		
Enter record selection criteria in a query, *A 121*	See *Defining Record Selection Criteria*		
Exit Access, *A 12*	Double-click Microsoft Access window Control menu box	Click File, Exit	Alt F, X
Find data in a datasheet, *A 94*	See Reference Window: *Finding Data in a Table*		
Find data in a form, *A 173*	See *Using the Find Command*		
Help screens, *A 27*		Click Help, Contents or Click Help, Search...	Alt H, C or Alt H, S
Hide duplicate values in a group report, *(635)*	See *Hiding Duplicate Values in a Group Report*		
Import an Access table, *A 90*	See Reference Window: *Importing an Access Table*		
Insert a field in the QBE grid, *A 119*	See *Inserting a Field*		
Launch Access, *A 11*	Double-click Microsoft Access icon		

TASK REFERENCE

ACCESS 2.0 FOR WINDOWS

Italicized page numbers indicate the first discussion of each task.

TASK	MOUSE	MENU	KEYBOARD
Move a field or column, *A 117*	See *Moving a Field*		
Move the toolbar, *A 24*	See *Moving the Toolbar*		
Move to first record, *A 18*	[⏮]	Click Records, click Go To, click First	Alt R, G, F
Move to last record, *A 18*	[⏭]	Click Records, click Go To, click Last	Alt R, G, L
Move to next record, *A 18*	[▶]	Click Records, click Go To, click Next	Alt R, G, N
Move to previous record, *A 18*	[◀]	Click Records, click Go To, click Previous	Alt R, G, P
Open a database, *A 13*	See Reference Window: *Opening a Database*		
Open a filter saved as a query, *A 177*		Click File, click Load From Query...	Alt F, L
Open a form, *A 23*	Click Form object button, click the form name, click the Open command button		
Open a saved query, *A 132*	Click Query object button, click query name, click Open		
Open a table datasheet, *A 93*	Click Table object button, double-click the table name		
Open Cue Cards, *A 64*	[Cue Cards button]	Click Help, click Cue Cards	Alt H, U
Print a datasheet, *A 20*	See Reference Window: *Printing a Hardcopy of a Datasheet*		
Print a form, *A 25*	[Print button]	Click File, click Print...	Alt F, P
Print a report, *(609)*	[Print button]	Click File, click Print...	Alt F, P
Print selected records, *A 130*	See *Printing a Dynaset Selection*		
Print table documentation, *A 101*	See *Printing Table Documentation*		
Quick sort records, *A 99*	Click field, then [A↓Z] or [Z↓A]	Click field, click Records, click Quick Sort, click Ascending or Descending	Click field, Alt R, Q, A or D
Remove a filter, *A 176*	[Show All Records button]	Click Records, click Show All Records	Alt R, S
Rename a field in a query, *A 120*	See *Renaming Fields in a Query*		
Rename a table, *A 93*	Right-click table name, click Rename	Click table name, click File, click Rename...	Click table name, Alt F, M
Replace data in a datasheet, *A 97*	See Reference Window: *Replacing Data in a Table*		

TASK REFERENCE

ACCESS 2.0 FOR WINDOWS

Italicized page numbers indicate the first discussion of each task.

TASK	MOUSE	MENU	KEYBOARD
Resize a column, *A 57*	See *Resizing Columns in a Datasheet*		
Resize a control, *A 185*	Click control box, drag sizing handle		
Save a filter as a query, *A 175*	[Save button]	Click File, click Save As Query...	Alt F, A
Save a form, *A 163*		Click File, click Save Form As...	Alt F, A
Save a query, *A 131*		Click File, click Save Query As...	Alt F, A
Save a report, *(606)*		Click File, click Save As...	Alt F, A
Save a table's structure, *A 53*	[Save button]	Click File, click Save	Alt F, S
Select a primary key, *A 63*	See *Selecting the Primary Key*		
Sort records in a query, *A 126*	See *Sorting Data*		
Switch to Datasheet View, *A 53*	[Datasheet View button]	Click View, click Datasheet	Alt V, S
Switch to editing mode from navigation mode, *A 84*			F2
Switch to Form View, *A 187*	[Form View button]	Click View, click Form	Alt V, F
Switch to navigation mode from editing mode, *A 84*			F2
Switch to Table Design View, *A 54*	[Design View button]	Click View, click Table Design	Alt V, D
Undo a field change, *A 55*	[Undo button]	Click Edit, click Undo Typing	Ctrl Z
Undo a quick sort, *A 100*	[Show All Records button]	Click Records, click Show All Records	Alt R, S
View a query dynaset, *A 115*	[Run button] or [Datasheet View button]	Click View, click Datasheet	Alt V, S

Brief PowerPoint 4.0 for Windows Tutorials

Read This Before You Begin

To the Student

To use this book, you must have Student Disks. Your instructor will either provide you with them or ask you to make your own by following the instructions in the section "Your Student Disks" in Tutorial 1. See your instructor or technical support person for further information. If you are going to work through this book using your own computer, you need a computer system running Microsoft Windows 3.1, Microsoft PowerPoint 4.0 for Windows, and Student Disks. *You will not be able to complete the tutorials and exercises in this book using your own computer until you have Student Disks.* You will need three blank, formatted disks. Label each with the appropriate tutorial number(s) based on the following table, which summarizes how the disk creation program will place files on your disks:

Student Disk	Tutorial(s)
1	1+2
2	3
3	4

To the Instructor

Making the Student Disks To complete the tutorials in this book, your students must have a copy of the Student Disks. To relieve you of having to make multiple Student Disks from a single master copy, we provide you with the CTI WinApps Setup Disk, which contains an automatic Student Disk generating program. Once you install the Setup Disk on a network or standalone workstation, students can easily make their own Student Disks by double-clicking the "Make PowerPoint 4.0 Student Disks" icon in the CTI WinApps icon group. Double-clicking this icon transfers all the data files students will need to complete the tutorials, Tutorial Assignments, and Case Problems to high-density disks in drive A or B. If some of your students will use their own computers to complete the tutorials and exercises in this book, they must first get the Student Disks. The section called "Your Student Disks" in Tutorial 1 provides complete instructions on how to make the Student Disks.

Installing the CTI WinApps Setup Disk To install the CTI WinApps icon group from the Setup Disk, follow the instructions on the Setup Disk label. By adopting this book, you are granted a license to install this software on any computer or computer network used by you or your students.

README File A README.TXT file located on the Setup Disk provides complete installation instructions, additional technical notes, troubleshooting advice, and tips for using the CTI WinApps software in your school's computer lab. You can view the README.TXT file using any word processor you choose.

Microsoft PowerPoint Installation

Make sure the Microsoft PowerPoint software has been installed on your computer using the complete setup option, rather than the laptop or typical installation.

System Requirements

The minimum software and hardware requirements for your computer system are as follows:

- Microsoft Windows Version 3.1 or later on a local hard drive or a network drive.
- A 386 or higher processor with a minimum of 4 MB RAM (486 and 8 MB recommended)
- A mouse supported by Windows 3.1.
- A printer supported by Windows 3.1.
- A VGA 64 × 480 16-color display is recommended; an 800 × 600 or 1024 × 768 SVGA, VGA monochrome, or EGA display is acceptable.
- A typical installation requires 22 MB free hard disk space, and a full installation requires 23 MB.
- Student workstations with at least 1 high-density disk drive.
- If you want to install the CTI WinApps Setup Disk on a network drive, your network must support Microsoft Windows.

T U T O R I A L 1

A Tour of PowerPoint 4.0

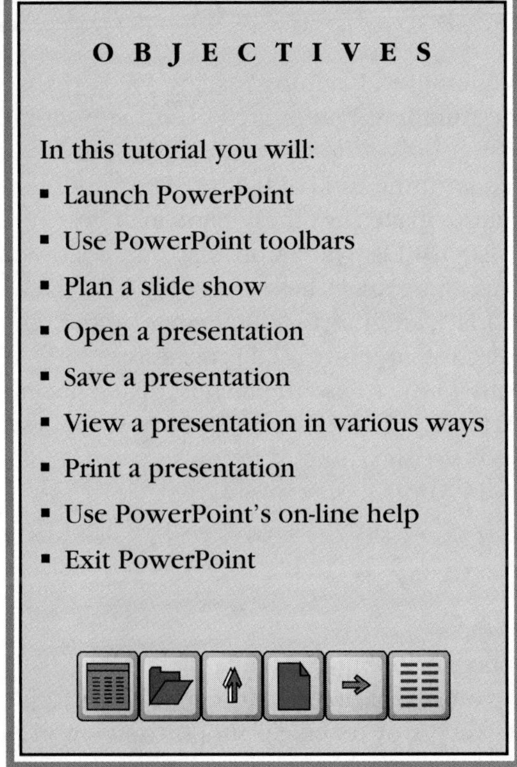

OBJECTIVES

In this tutorial you will:

- Launch PowerPoint
- Use PowerPoint toolbars
- Plan a slide show
- Open a presentation
- Save a presentation
- View a presentation in various ways
- Print a presentation
- Use PowerPoint's on-line help
- Exit PowerPoint

CASE **Inca Imports International** Patricia Cuevas immigrated to the United States of America from San Salvador at the age of 12. After graduating from high school, she began working for Cisco Foods, a distributor to food-services businesses in the Los Angeles area. In the evenings, Patricia attended California State University at Northridge, where she earned a degree in Business Management. After ten years with Cisco Foods, Patricia and another Cisco employee, Angelena Cristenas, began their own small business, Inca Imports International. Working with suppliers in South America, particularly in Ecuador and Peru, Patricia and Angelena imported fresh fruits and vegetables during the winter and spring in North America (which are summer and fall in South America) and sold them to small grocery stores in the Los Angeles area.

After three years in business, Inca Imports International has 34 employees and is healthy and growing. To promote further growth and profits, Patricia wants to establish a permanent distribution facility in Quito, Ecuador. This distribution facility, to include office and warehouse space, would allow Inca Imports International to maintain better quality control, shorten the time to market of the imported fruits and vegetables, and reduce costs.

As one of only three suppliers of imported fruits and vegetables in the entire Southern California area, Inca Imports International is in a position to increase the number and size of the grocery stores and restaurant chains that purchase its goods. Besides building the facility in Ecuador, Patricia plans an aggressive marketing program that would significantly increase the cash flow and value of the rapidly growing company.

In an effort to obtain funding for the new distribution facility and marketing campaign, Patricia has prepared a presentation that introduces Inca Imports International to potential investors. In this tutorial you will see the first few slides of her presentation.

Using the Tutorials Effectively

These tutorials are designed to be used at your computer. Begin by reading the text that explains the concepts. When you come to the numbered steps, read each step completely before you perform it on your computer.

As you work, compare your computer screen with the tutorial figures. The important parts of the screen display are labeled in each figure; make sure these parts match. If you have a problem, follow the procedures in the TROUBLE? paragraph that may follow a step; these paragraphs identify common problems and explain how to get back on track. Reference Windows, located throughout the tutorials, and the Task Reference, at the end of each tutorial, provide you with short summaries of frequently used procedures.

Before you begin the tutorials, you should know how to use the menus, dialog boxes, Help facility, Program Manager, and File Manager in Microsoft Windows. Course Technology, Inc. publishes two excellent texts for learning Windows: *A Guide to Microsoft Windows 3.1* and *An Introduction to Microsoft Windows 3.1*.

Your Student Disks

To complete the tutorials and exercises in this book, you must have Student Disks. The Student Disks contain all of the practice files you need for the tutorials, the Tutorial Assignments, and the Case Problems. If your instructor or technical support person provides you with Student Disks, you can skip this section and go to the section titled "What is PowerPoint?" If your instructor asks you to make your own Student Disks, follow the steps in this section.

To make your Student Disks you will need:

- Blank, formatted, high-density 3.5-inch disks. See the table on the "Read This Before You Begin" page, just before Tutorial 1, for information on the number of disks you'll need, and how to label each one.
- A computer with Microsoft Windows 3.1, PowerPoint 4.0 for Windows, and the CTI WinApps icon group installed on it.

If you're using your own computer, the CTI WinApps icon group will not be installed on it. Before you proceed, you must go to your school's computer lab and find a computer that has the CTI WinApps icon group installed. Once you have made your own Student Disks, you can use them to complete all the tutorials and exercises in this book on any computer you choose.

To make your PowerPoint Student Disks:

1. Launch Windows and make sure the Program Manager window is open.

   TROUBLE? The exact steps you follow to launch Microsoft Windows 3.1 might vary depending on how your computer is set up. On many computer systems, you must type WIN, then press [Enter] to launch Windows. If you don't know how to launch Windows, ask your instructor or technical support person.

2. Place your formatted disk for Tutorials 1–2 in drive A.

TROUBLE? If your computer has more than one disk drive, drive A is usually on top. If your Student Disk doesn't fit into drive A, then place it in drive B and substitute "drive B" anywhere you see "drive A" in the tutorial steps.

❸ Look for an icon labeled "CTI WinApps," like the one in Figure 1-1, or a window labeled "CTI WinApps," like the one in Figure 1-2.

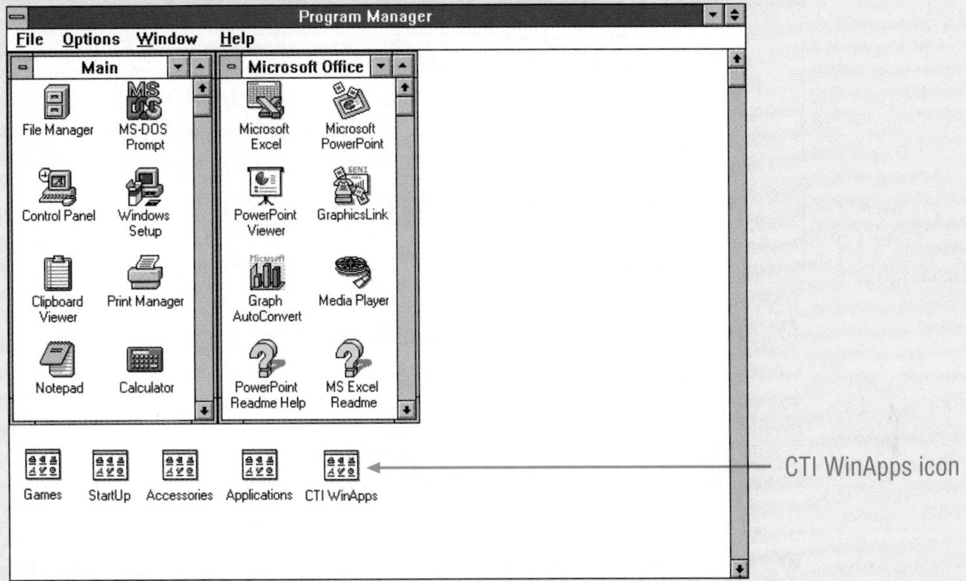

Figure 1-1
CTI WinApps icon

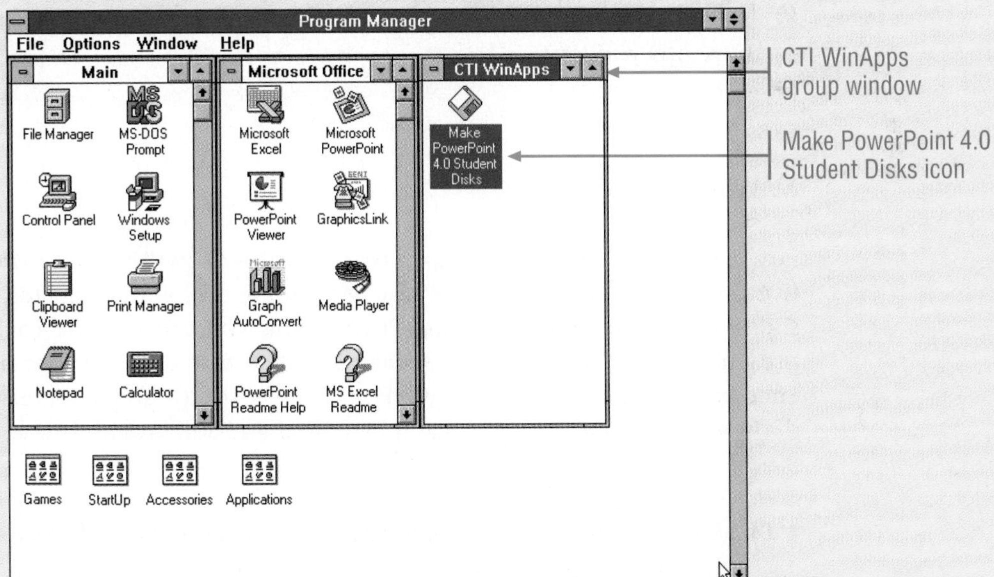

Figure 1-2
Make PowerPoint 4.0 Student Disks icon

TROUBLE? If you can't find anything labeled "CTI WinApps," the CTI software might not be installed on your computer. Ask your instructor or technical support person for assistance.

If you're using your own computer, you won't be able to make your Student Disks. To make them you need to access the CTI WinApps icon group, which is, most likely, installed on your school's lab computers. Ask your instructor or technical support person for further information on where to locate the CTI WinApps icon group. Once you create your Student Disks, you can use them to complete all the tutorials and exercises in this book on any computer you choose.

4. If you see an icon labeled "CTI WinApps," double-click it to open the CTI WinApps group window. If the CTI WinApps window is already open, proceed to Step 5.
5. Double-click the icon labeled "**Make PowerPoint 4.0 Student Disks.**" The Make PowerPoint 4.0 Student Disks window opens. See Figure 1-3.

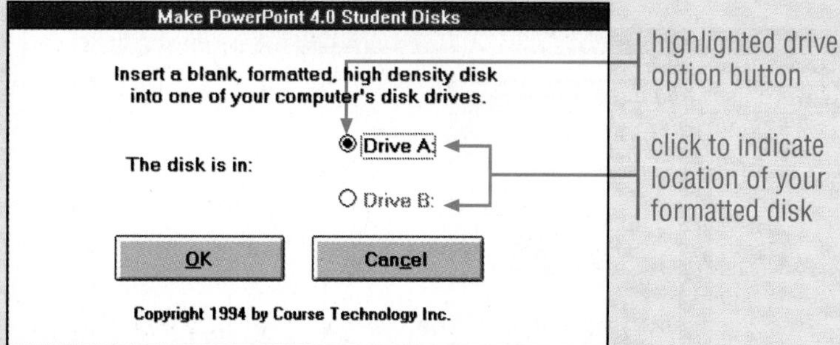

Figure 1-3
Make PowerPoint 4.0 Student Disks window

6. Make sure the drive that contains your formatted disk corresponds to the drive option button that is highlighted in the dialog box on your screen.
7. Click the **OK button**.

   Follow the directions on the screen to create your student disks. Refer to the table on the "Read This Before You Begin" page, just before Tutorial 1, for information about the numbers of disks you'll need and how to label them.
8. When the copying is complete, a message indicates the number of files copied to each disk. Click the **OK button**.
9. To close the CTI WinApps window, double-click the **Control menu box** on the CTI WinApps window.

What Is PowerPoint?

PowerPoint is a powerful program that provides everything you need to produce an effective presentation in the form of black-and-white or color overheads, 35-mm photographic slides, or on-screen slides. Using PowerPoint, you can prepare each component of your presentation: individual slides, speaker's notes, an outline of your presentation, and audience handouts. In addition, PowerPoint allows you to create a consistent format for each of these components, and to manipulate text and add graphics to your presentations.

Presentation Slides, Masters, and Templates

Before you begin this tutorial, you need to understand several key PowerPoint terms: presentation, slide, master, and template. A **presentation** is a collection of slides, handouts, speaker's notes, and an outline, all together in one file. A **slide** is a single image or picture that is part of the your visual presentation. Your presentation could include from one to dozens of slides. A **master** is a slide that contains the text and graphics that will appear on every slide in the presentation. For example, the company name, the date, and graphics such as the company logo can be put on a master so that this information will appear on every slide in the presentation. Using a master allows you to create a consistent overall format for your presentation. A **template** is a predefined format and color scheme provided in PowerPoint that you can apply to your presentation slides. PowerPoint supplies a variety of professionally designed templates.

Planning a Presentation

Planning a presentation before you create it improves the quality of your presentation, makes your presentation more effective and enjoyable, and, in the long run, saves you time and effort. As you plan your presentation, you should answer several questions. What is my purpose or objective for this presentation? What type of presentation is needed? Who is the audience? What is the physical location of my presentation? What information does that audience need? What is the best format for presenting the information contained in this presentation given the presentation location?

In planning her presentation, Patricia Cuevas answered these questions as follows:

- **Purpose for presentation:** To obtain funding
- **Type of presentation:** Sales presentation to sell expansion and marketing campaign ideas
- **Audience:** Potential investors, in their monthly board meeting or in a specially arranged meeting
- **Audience needs:** Company mission, profitability, and growth potential
- **Location of presentation:** A small boardroom with a computer and color monitor and a projection system
- **Format:** Electronic slide show consisting of 7–10 slides and speaker's notes

Having planned her presentation, Patricia used PowerPoint to create it. Let's launch PowerPoint and look at the first few slides of Patricia's presentation.

Launching PowerPoint

To use PowerPoint, you have to start (launch) the PowerPoint program. Let's do that now.

To launch PowerPoint:

❶ Make sure you have your formatted PowerPoint Student Disk.

TROUBLE? If don't have a Student Disk, you need to get one. Your instructor will either give you one or ask you to make your own by following the steps outlined earlier in this tutorial in the section called "Your Student Disk."

❷ If necessary, turn on your computer and start Windows.

The Windows Program Manager should appear on the screen. If it doesn't, consult your instructor or technical support person. Program group windows and group icons appear in the Program Manager window.

The PowerPoint icons appear in the Microsoft Office group window, as shown in Figure 1-4, or in some other window, such as the PowerPoint group window. The arrangement of windows and icons on your computer screen might be different than the one shown in Figure 1-4.

Figure 1-4 Microsoft PowerPoint icon

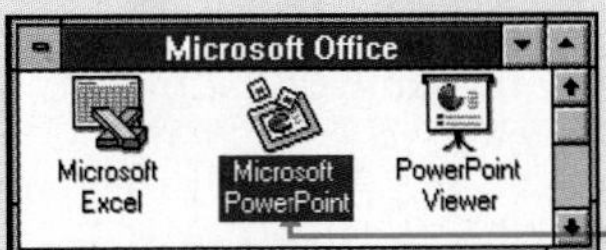

TROUBLE? If the PowerPoint or Microsoft Office group window does not appear on the screen, open it by double-clicking the PowerPoint or Microsoft Office group icon. If you can't locate these program groups or if the PowerPoint icon doesn't appear in the window, consult with your instructor or technical support person.

❸ Double-click the **Microsoft PowerPoint icon**.

TROUBLE? On some computers, the PowerPoint icon may be labeled "PowerPoint 4.0." Double-click that icon to launch PowerPoint.

After a moment or two, the PowerPoint startup dialog box appears on the screen. See Figure 1-5. PowerPoint is now running and ready to use.

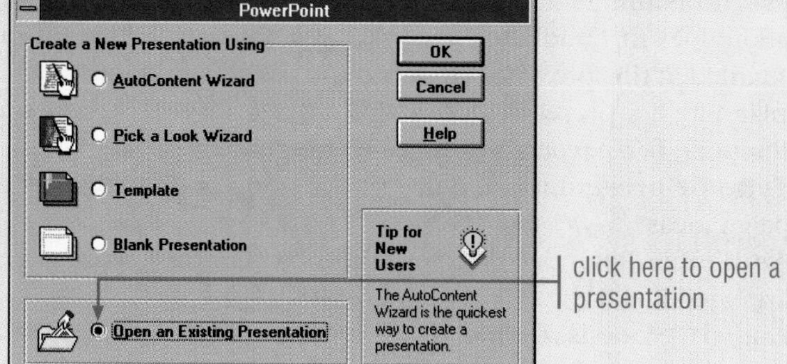

Figure 1-5
PowerPoint startup dialog box

TROUBLE? A "Tip of the Day" dialog box may first appear in the PowerPoint window. If it does, click the OK button. A dialog box asking if you want to run the PowerPoint Quick Preview may also appear. If it does, click the No or Close button.

Opening an Existing Presentation

When you launch PowerPoint, a startup dialog box appears on the screen. This dialog box contains several options. For example, it allows you to create a new presentation or to open an existing one.

REFERENCE WINDOW

Opening an Existing Presentation

- If you have just launched PowerPoint, click the Open an Existing Presentation button in the PowerPoint startup dialog box, then click the OK button or press [Enter].

or

- If PowerPoint is already running, click the Open button on the Standard toolbar, or click File, then click Open.
- From the Open dialog box, choose the disk and directory where the presentation file is located.
- Scroll through the Files list box, and click the filename of the presentation to select it.
- Click the OK button or press [Enter].

Let's open the presentation that Patricia Cuevas created for Inca Imports International.

To open Patricia's presentation:

❶ Click the **Open an Existing Presentation button** in the PowerPoint startup dialog box, then click the **OK button**. PowerPoint displays the Open dialog box. See Figure 1-6.

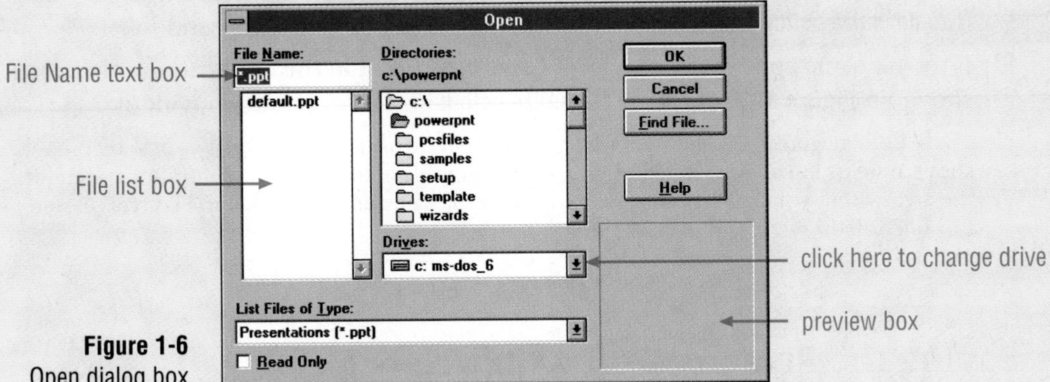

Figure 1-6
Open dialog box

❷ Click the **Down Arrow** to the right of the Drives box, and click **a:** to choose drive A (or click the drive that your Student Disk is in). The list of files on the Student Disk appears in the Files list box.

TROUBLE? If you don't see any files on the disk in drive A or if you get some other error, check to make sure that your Student Disk is in drive A. If you are using drive B, go back to Step 2 and select "b:" instead of "a:".

❸ Click the name of the presentation file **c1file1.ppt** in the Files list box. The name of the document appears in the File Name text box, and the first slide of the selected presentation file appears in the preview box in the lower-right corner of the dialog box.

❹ Click the **OK button** or press **[Enter]**.

You can press [Enter] to execute a command in a dialog box that has a dark border around it. PowerPoint opens the presentation from the disk into the PowerPoint window. See Figure 1-7.

Figure 1-7
PowerPoint window after you open the presentation

TROUBLE? If the presentation window contains text in an outline format instead of the image shown in the presentation window in Figure 1-7, click View on the menu bar near the top of the screen, and then click Slides.

5. If the PowerPoint application window doesn't fill the entire monitor display, click the **Maximize button** in the upper-right corner of the PowerPoint window.
6. If the filename appears in its own title bar instead of in the application title bar as shown in Figure 1-7, click the **Maximize button** in the presentation window.

TROUBLE? Figure 1-7 shows only the top three-fourths of the slide, but your screen could show more or less than this, depending on the graphics mode of your computer system. If the area within your presentation window isn't the same as that shown in Figure 1-7, don't be concerned.

Saving the Presentation with a New Name

To avoid the problem of accidentally overwriting the original disk file C1FILE1.PPT, let's save the document using another filename. Saving the document with another filename creates a copy of the file that you can work with, leaving the original file unchanged.

To save the presentation with a new name:

1. Click **File** on the Menu bar, then click **Save As**. The Save As dialog box appears on the screen with the current filename highlighted in the File Name text box.
2. Type the new filename **s1file1** and press **[Enter]** or click the **OK button**.

   (PowerPoint automatically adds the extension .PPT. You'll learn the convention used in this book for naming files in the next tutorial.) The Save As dialog box closes and the Summary Info dialog box opens. As you create more files with PowerPoint, you will probably decide to use the Summary Info box to help you organize your files. For now, just click the OK button to close this dialog box.
3. Click the **OK button**. The Summary Info dialog box closes and the new filename is displayed in the title bar at the top of the window.

   Slide 1 of Patricia's presentation is displayed in the presentation window.

The PowerPoint Window

Let's examine the PowerPoint window, as shown in Figure 1-8. The PowerPoint window contains features common to all Windows applications, as well as features particular only to PowerPoint.

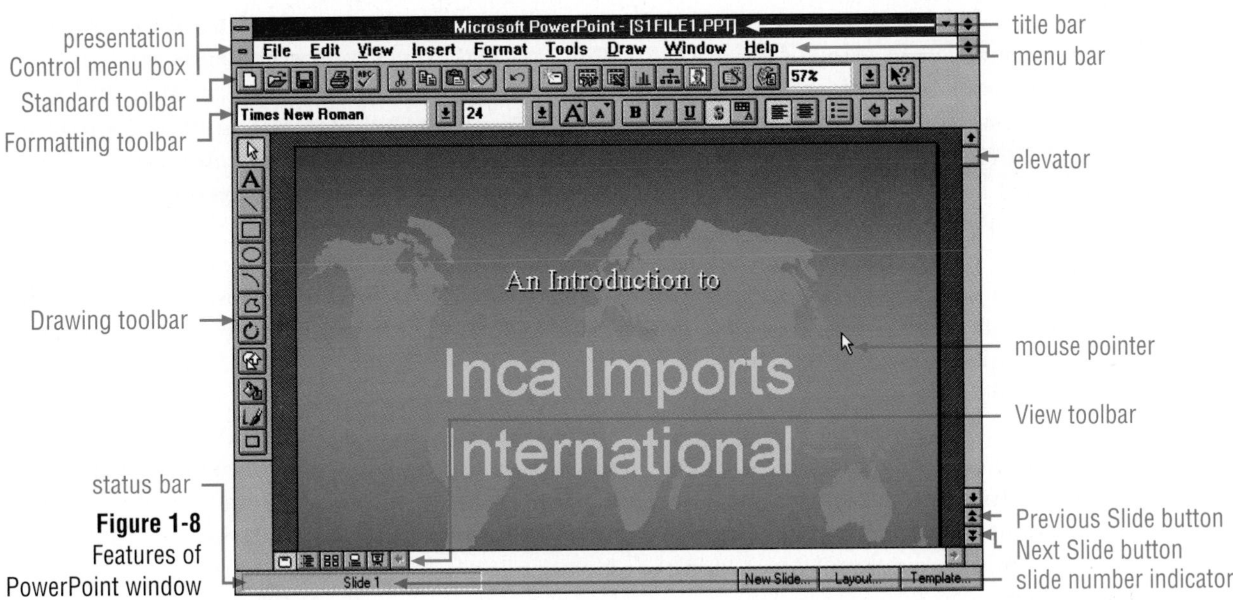

Figure 1-8
Features of PowerPoint window

Common Windows Features

Several features of the PowerPoint window are common to other Windows applications. For example, the application Control menu box allows you to minimize, maximize, and restore the PowerPoint window, to close the PowerPoint window, or to switch to another application running under Windows. In addition, the Minimize, Maximize, and Restore buttons, and the presentation Control menu box function in PowerPoint the same way they do in other Windows applications.

Scroll Bars

In PowerPoint, the vertical and horizontal scroll bars function the same way they do in other Windows applications. The scroll box in the vertical scroll bar is called the **elevator**. At the bottom of the vertical scroll bar are the Previous Slide and Next Slide buttons. Clicking these moves you to the previous or the next slide.

The Status Bar

The bottom line of the screen is called the **status bar**. It tells you which slide you're working on and, when you move the mouse pointer to a command button, provides a description of the command. The status bar also contains three shortcut buttons: the New Slide button, the Layout button, and the Template button. You will use these buttons in later tutorials.

The Toolbars

Like many Windows applications, PowerPoint supplies several toolbars, as shown in Figure 1-8. A **toolbar** is a ribbon of icons that provide menu shortcuts. When you move the mouse pointer over one of the buttons on the toolbar, the **ToolTip** for that button, a yellow square containing the name of the button, appears.

The toolbar immediately below the menu bar is the **Standard toolbar**, which you'll use to select many of the standard Windows and PowerPoint commands, such as opening an existing presentation, saving your current presentation to disk, printing the presentation, and cutting and pasting text and graphics. Below the Standard toolbar is the **Formatting toolbar**, which you'll use to format the text of your presentations. The vertical toolbar on the left edge of the PowerPoint window is the **Drawing toolbar**, which you'll use to draw lines and shapes and enter text on your slides.

Using the Toolbars feature on the View menu, you can turn ToolTips off, display other toolbars such as an additional drawing toolbar or the Microsoft toolbar, hide the toolbars that PowerPoint automatically displays, or create a customized toolbar. You can also hide or add buttons on a toolbar by choosing the Customize feature on the Tools menu.

As with other Windows applications, PowerPoint lets you select commands by using the pull-down menus with the keyboard or the mouse, by using shortcut keys, or by using buttons on a toolbar. Because the buttons on the toolbars are usually the simplest and fastest method of selecting commands, in these tutorials you'll use the toolbars more often than the pull-down menus or keyboard.

The View Toolbar

The small toolbar immediately above the status bar is the **View toolbar**, which contains buttons that allow you to change the way you view a slide presentation. Each way of seeing a presentation is called a **view**. The status bar indicates which view you are in. Clicking the **Slide View button** allows you to see and edit text and graphics on an individual slide. You are in Slide view now. You click the **Outline View button** to see and edit your entire presentation in outline format. Clicking the **Slide Sorter View button** changes the view to miniature images of all the slides at once. You use this view to change the order of the slides or set special features for your slide show. Clicking the **Notes Pages View button** changes the view so that you can see and edit your presentation notes on individual slides. To actually present your slide show, you click the **Slide Show button**. You can also change views by clicking View on the menu bar, then selecting the view you want.

Previewing the Presentation and Changing the Slide Order

Patricia wants to see all of her slides at once to check the order of the slides. Let's use the View toolbar to switch to Slide Sorter view to preview all of Patricia's slides on one screen, and then use the Slide Sorter to change the order of the slides.

To view a slide show in Slide Sorter view:

1. Move the mouse pointer to the **Slide Sorter View button** on the View toolbar, but do not yet click on the mouse button. After a second or two, the ToolTip for this button appears.
2. Click .

Your screen now looks similar to Figure 1-9.

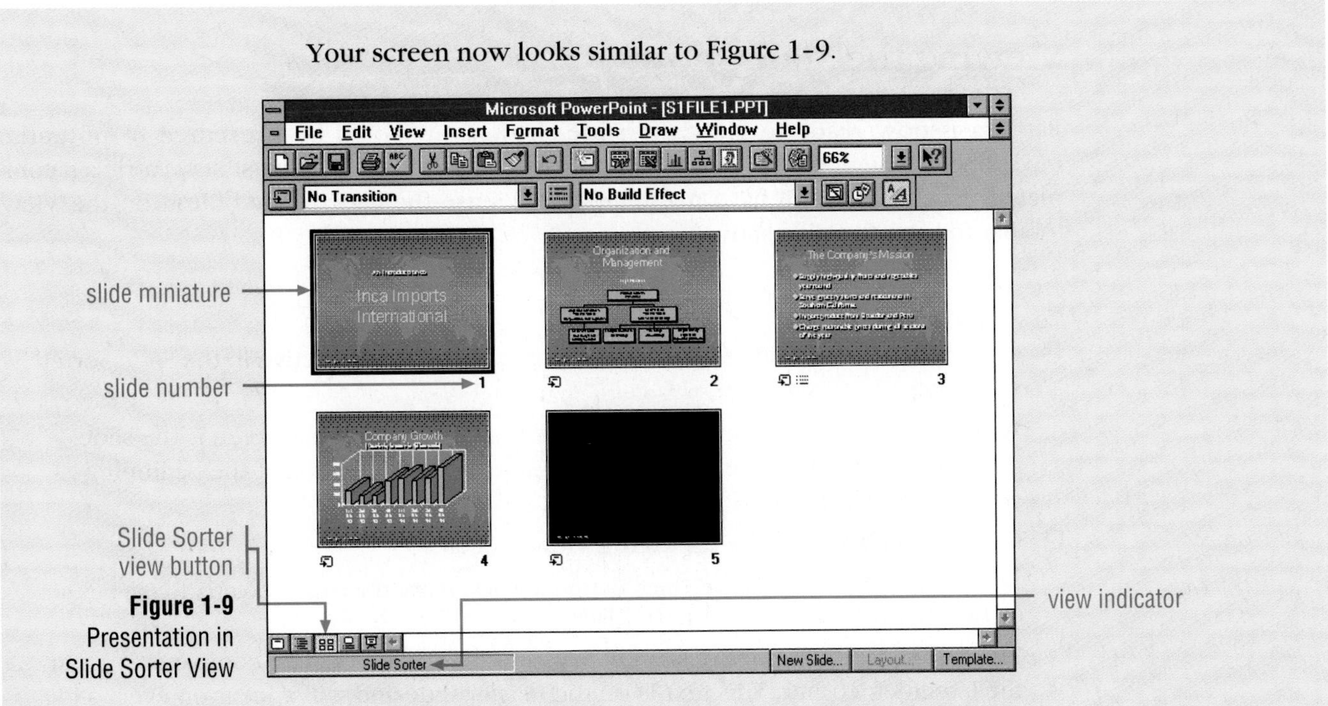

Figure 1-9
Presentation in Slide Sorter View

As you can see, each slide is shown in miniature. In the upper-left corner of the presentation window, you can see slide 1, the title slide of Patricia's presentation. To the right is slide 2, which shows the company management personnel and organizational chart. Slide 3 gives the mission statement of Inca Imports International. Slide 4 presents the company's gross income by quarter over a two-year period. Slide 5 is blank, to mark the end of the slide show. So far Patricia has made only these five slides.

At this point Patricia realizes that slide 3 (company's mission statement) should go before slide 2 (organization and management chart). Let's use the Slide Sorter View to change the order of her slides.

To change the order of the slides:

❶ Click slide 3. A heavy black line appears around slide 3 to show that it is selected.

❷ Drag the mouse pointer between slides 1 and 2, but do not release the mouse button. The mouse pointer changes to ▭. A dotted horizontal line with an arrow at either end shows the slide's new position.

❸ Release the mouse button. The mission statement slide becomes slide 2 and the organizational chart slide becomes slide 3.

Viewing the Slide Show

Patricia is now ready to view the slide show as it would be presented to potential investors. Although the presentation you're looking at has only five slides, Patricia's completed presentation will have many more. Let's use the Slide Show button on the View toolbar to view the slide show.

To view the slide show:

❶ Click slide 1 in the Slide Sorter view to make the first slide active in the Slide Sorter window.

When you run a slide show, the first slide that appears on the screen is the slide that is selected; therefore, if you want to start the presentation at the beginning you have to select slide 1.

❷ Click the **Slide Show button** on the View toolbar.

TROUBLE? If you're not sure which button to click, move the mouse pointer to the buttons on the View toolbar and read the ToolTips.

The first slide fills the entire screen. See Figure 1-10. Notice the company name in the lower-left corner. This text is on the master slide and will appear on every slide in the presentation. To advance to the next slide, click the left mouse button or press [Spacebar]. To go back to the previous slide, click the right mouse button or press [←]. After looking over slide 1, Patricia is ready to advance to slide 2.

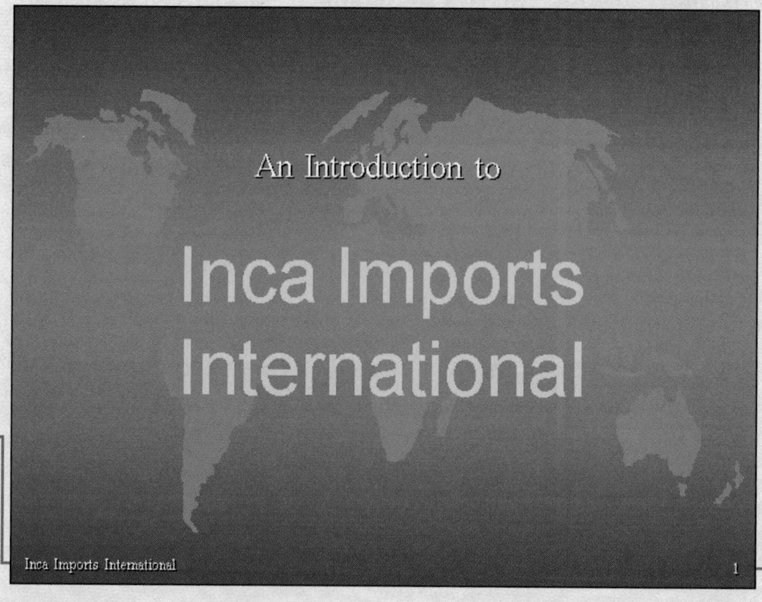

Figure 1-10 Slide 1 of presentation

❸ Click the left mouse button or press **[Spacebar]**. Don't worry about the location of the mouse pointer.

PowerPoint advances from slide 1 to slide 2. This new slide displays only the title "The Company's Mission," not the actual text of the mission. This is because Patricia made this a build slide. A **build slide** is a slide in which a list builds one point at a time as you click the left mouse button or press [Spacebar].

4. Click the left mouse button or press **[Spacebar]**.

   The first item in the bulleted list, "Supply high-quality fruits and vegetables year round," appears on the slide. Patricia has used a build effect called **fly from right**, which, as you can see, causes the item to appear on the screen moving right to left.

5. Click the left mouse button or press **[Spacebar]**.

   Notice that the first item in the list changes color and the second item, "Serve grocery stores and restaurants in Southern California" flies onto the screen. See Figure 1-11.

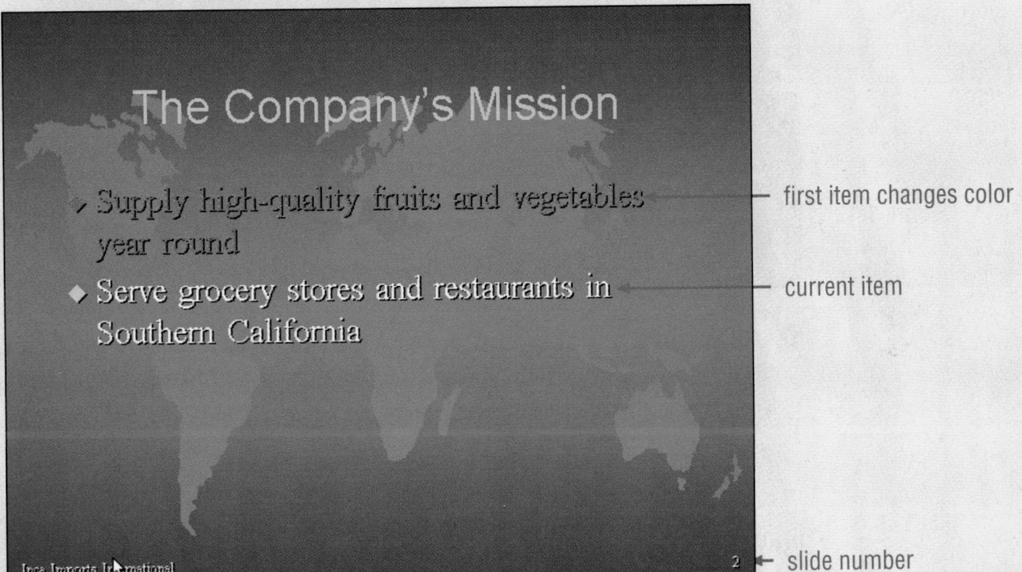

Figure 1-11
Slide 2 of presentation

6. Click the left mouse button twice or press **[Spacebar]** twice, so that the last two items in the list of the company's mission appear on the screen. You're now ready to advance the presentation to slide 3.

7. Click the left mouse button or press **[Spacebar]**.

   PowerPoint now displays the organization and management chart of Inca Imports International. This organizational chart was created using Microsoft Organization Chart, a separate applications program that ships with PowerPoint.

8. Click the left mouse button or press **[Spacebar]**.

   PowerPoint displays slide 4, which is a chart showing Inca Imports' gross income over a two-year period. See Figure 1-12. Patricia created this chart by typing numbers into a table and then letting PowerPoint do the work of formatting and displaying the information in an attractive three-dimensional graph.

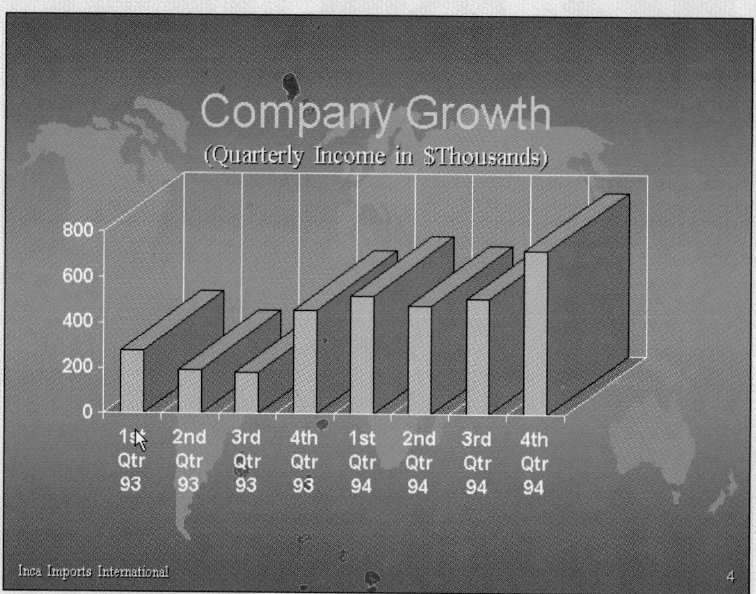

Figure 1-12 Slide 4 of presentation

9. Click the left mouse button twice or press **[Spacebar]** twice, once to display the blank slide that tells Patricia she's at the end of her presentation, and a second time to return to the Slide Sorter view of PowerPoint.

As you can see, Patricia has created an attractive, effective slide presentation. PowerPoint has many features that allow you to create presentations like this one with a minimum of work and a maximum of efficiency.

Viewing the Outline and Speaker's Notes

A presentation includes much more than just slides. It can also include an outline, speaker's notes, and handouts. Let's view the presentation outline and speaker's notes. (**Handouts** are simply printouts of the slides, with two, three, or six slides printed on each page.)

To view the presentation Outline and the Speaker's Notes:

1. Click the **Outline View button** on the View toolbar.

   PowerPoint displays the outline of the presentation and the Outlining toolbar appears. See Figure 1-13.

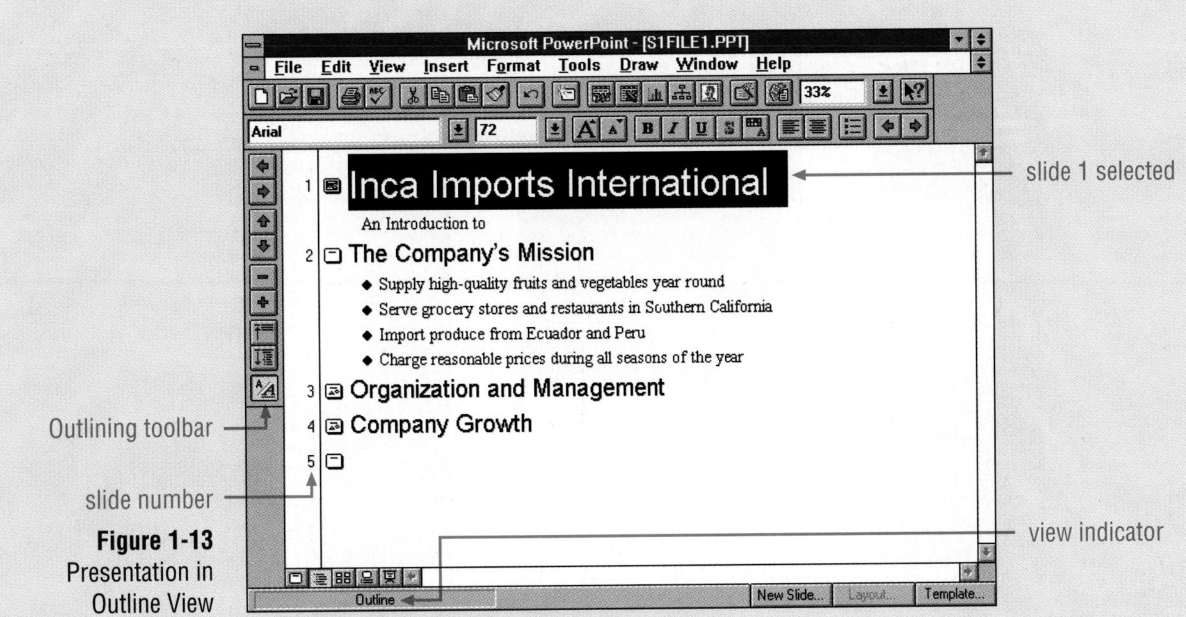

Figure 1-13 Presentation in Outline View

With the outline on the screen, you can edit the text of the slides, just as you would edit text with a word processor. The changes you make to the outline will automatically appear on the slide images. In later tutorials, you'll use Outline View to create text for your slides.

❷ Click the **Note Pages View button** .

PowerPoint displays a note page, which includes a copy of the slide at the top of the page and space for speaker's notes at the bottom of the page. The page is displayed 100% of its size. Let's set the page zoom to 50% so that we can see the entire notes page on the screen at once.

❸ Click **View**, click **Zoom**, then click the **50% button** in the Zoom dialog box, and click the **OK button**.

You should be viewing the notes for slide 1. See Figure 1-14. If you don't see the full slide at the top of the page, drag the elevator up to the top of the scroll bar. If you can't read the text of the speaker's notes, use the Zoom command (as you did in Step 3 above) to increase the zoom to 100%. After you read the notes for slide 1, you are ready to go on to slide 2. Let's use the elevator to select slide 2.

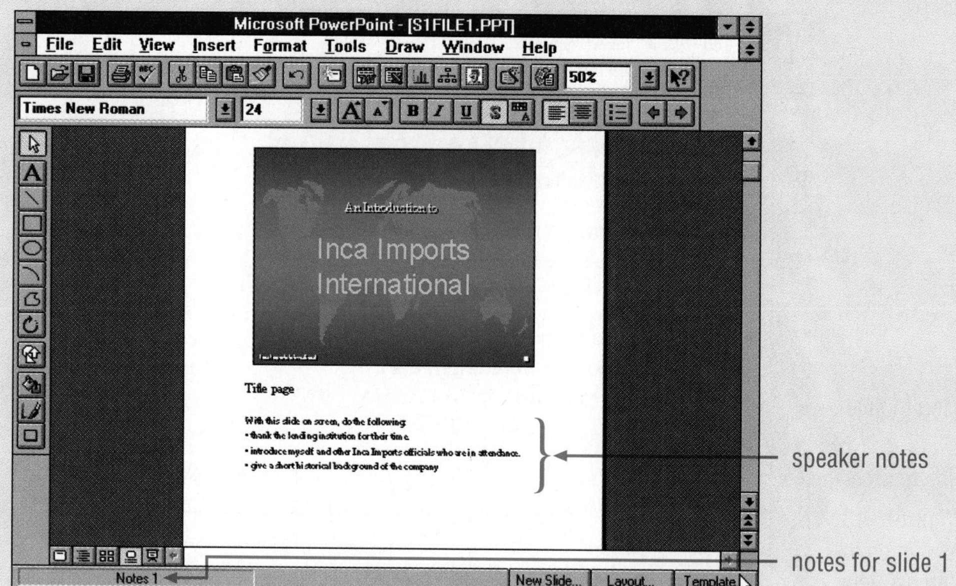

Figure 1-14 Presentation in Notes View with speaker's notes

❹ Drag the **elevator** about a third of the way down the scroll bar, but do not release the mouse button.

As you drag the elevator, PowerPoint displays the current notes number (corresponding to the slide number) next to the mouse pointer on the scroll bar. See Figure 1-15.

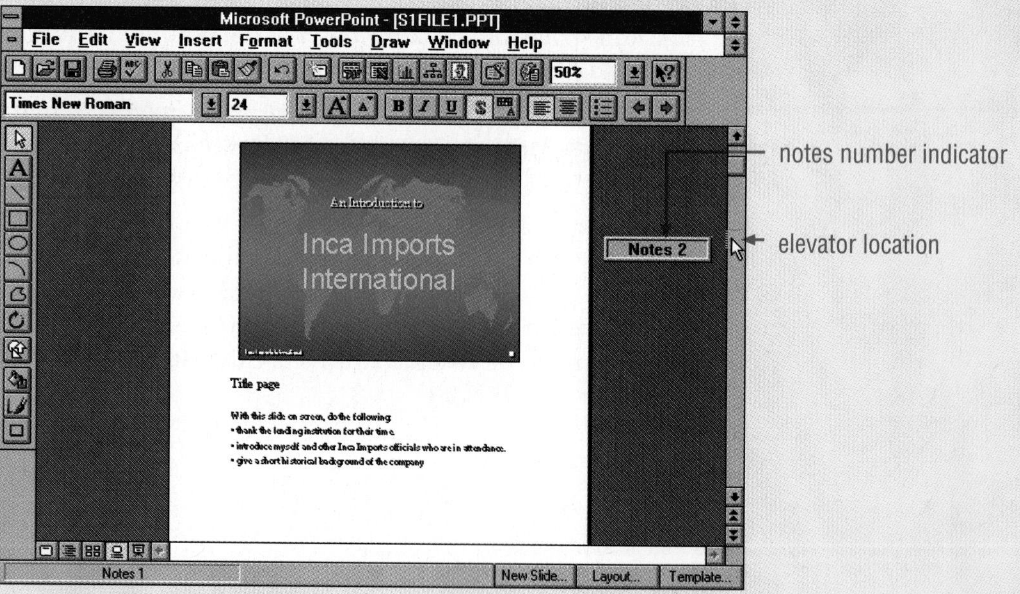

Figure 1-15 Scrolling down to notes for slide 2

❺ Release the mouse button when the elevator reaches "Notes 2."

❻ Click the **Next Slide button** at the bottom of the vertical scroll bar. PowerPoint displays slide 3.

❼ Continue going through the slides, one at a time, reading the speaker's notes.

In a later tutorial you'll learn how to create, edit, and print the speaker's notes.

Saving the Modified Presentation

Having changed the order of the slides and viewed the presentation (slides, outline, and speaker's notes), Patricia is satisfied with the results for now and decides to save the presentation to her disk. She will add more slides at another time. You must remember to save a presentation after you complete it, even if you've saved it one or more times while you were creating it. It's also a good idea to save your presentation before printing it. Let's save the presentation now.

To save a presentation to your disk:

1. Make sure the Student Disk is still in drive A.
2. Click the **Save button** on the Standard toolbar.

   PowerPoint automatically saves the presentation using the current filename, S1FILE1.PPT.

   The new version of the presentation is saved to the Student Disk in drive A.

Printing the Presentation

Patricia decides that she will print her presentation and keep the hard copy for her records. Let's do that now.

To print the presentation:

1. Click **File**, then click **Print**. PowerPoint displays the Print dialog box. See Figure 1-16.

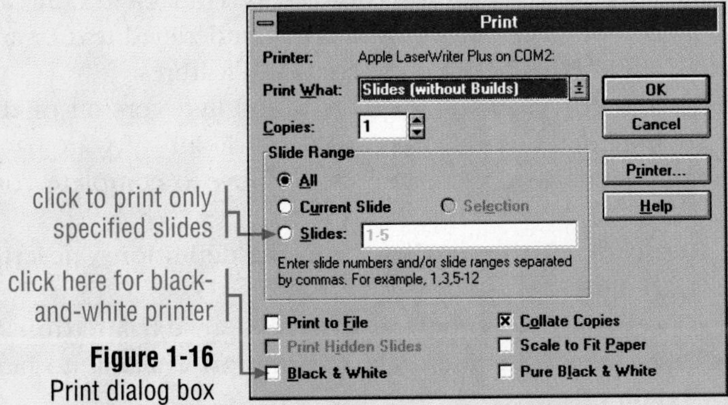

Figure 1-16
Print dialog box

   To print the slides, you can be in any view except Slide Show View.

2. Make sure **Slides (without Builds)** is selected in the Print What box.

Patricia doesn't need the blank slide at the end of the presentation printed.

3. Click the **Slides button** in the Slide Range section of the dialog box, then press **[Del]** three times to delete the information in the Slides text box.
4. Type **1-4** in the Slides text box to print only slides 1 throught 4.
5. If you're using a black-and-white printer, click the **Black & White checkbox** at the lower-left of the dialog box.
6. Click the **OK button** to print the slides.

Be patient. Graphics usually take a long time to print, even on a relatively fast laser printer. The slides are printed one slide per page. Patricia also wants to print the outline.

7. Click **File**, then click **Print**.
8. Click the **Down arrow** in the Print What text box, click **Outline View**, then click the **OK button**.

   Patricia now wants to print her speaker's notes.

9. Repeat Steps 6 and 7, only this time select **Notes Pages** in the Print What text box.

   If you click the Print button on the Standard toolbar, the presentation is printed in whatever view you are in.

Patricia now has a hard copy of her presentation.

Getting Help

When you're using PowerPoint, how do you know which button to click or which menu item to select? The best way is through training and continued experience in using PowerPoint. These tutorials will give you the training and the experience you need to perform the most important PowerPoint operations.

When you need to know something that you didn't learn in your training, PowerPoint provides two ways for you to learn which commands are available and how to execute them: the Help and Wizard features. Let's review some aspects of the Help feature. (We'll discuss the Wizard feature in the next tutorial.)

After you click Help on the menu bar, you can choose several ways of accessing the Help information. If you click Contents, PowerPoint displays the PowerPoint Help Contents window. In the Help Contents window, you can click on the green underlined text or any of the three icons to get information about PowerPoint commands and features:

- Clicking or clicking **Using PowerPoint** displays an on-line version of the printed *PowerPoint User's Guide* that comes with each PowerPoint software package. This choice lets you view step-by-step instructions on how to complete your tasks in PowerPoint.
- Clicking or clicking **Reference Information** provides definitions, descriptions, and tips on using PowerPoint.
- Clicking or clicking **Technical Reference** provides an explanation of Microsoft's support services and describes the technical support available to help you get the most from PowerPoint.

The PowerPoint Help feature also lets you search for specific information by using the "Search for Help on" command. As an example, let's use this command to get help on making an organizational chart.

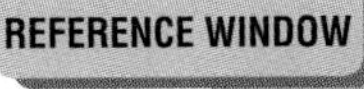

Searching for Help

- Click Help on the Menu bar, then click Search for Help on.
- Type the word or phrase of the topic on which you want help.
- With the desired topic highlighted, click the Show Topics button.
- Click the desired topic to highlight it.
- Click the Go to button to display the help window on the selected topic.

To search for help on a specific topic:

❶ Click **Help** on the Menu bar, then click **Search for Help on**.

PowerPoint displays the Search dialog box. See Figure 1-17.

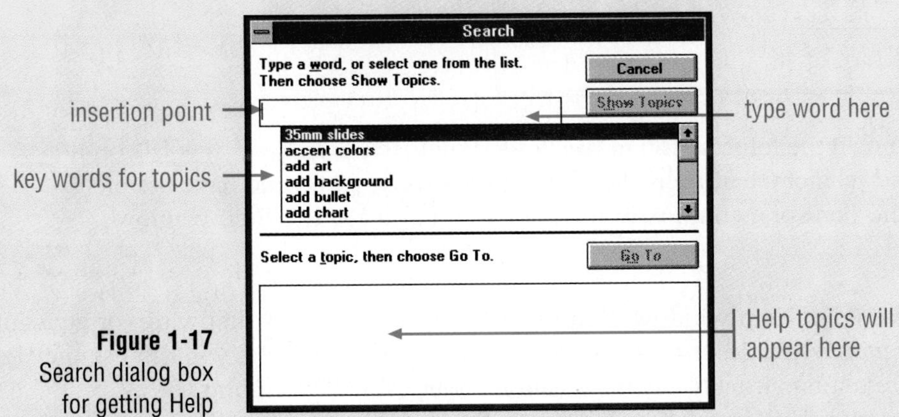

Figure 1-17
Search dialog box for getting Help

❷ With the cursor in the text box at the top of the Search dialog box, type **organiz**, the first few letters of "organizational chart," the topic on which you want help.

Notice that "organizational chart" becomes highlighted in the list of topics.

❸ Click the **Show Topics button** in the Search dialog box.

Now PowerPoint displays a list of Help topics associated with organizational charts.

❹ In the list at the bottom of the dialog box, click **Creating an organizational chart** and then click the **Go To button** to tell Help to show that topic.

The screen now displays a window that describes how to create an organizational chart. See Figure 1-18.

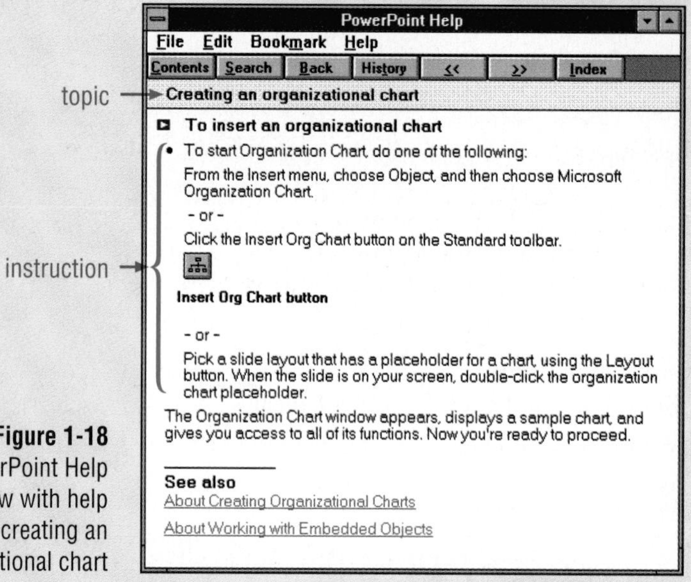

Figure 1-18
PowerPoint Help window with help on creating an organizational chart

❺ After you read the information in the PowerPoint Help window, click **File** on the Help window menu bar, then click **Exit**. Alternatively, you could have double-clicked the Control menu box in the upper-left corner of the Help window.

The PowerPoint Help window disappears from the screen. By knowing (or guessing) one or more words that describe a feature on which you want help, you can use the Help Search feature to find virtually any information about using PowerPoint.

As you work with PowerPoint, you'll want to use other methods for getting help. To access context-sensitive Help, that is, Help about a specific part of the PowerPoint window, use the Help button on the Standard toolbar. When you click that button and then click any feature within the PowerPoint window or click a pull-down menu command, PowerPoint gives you help on the feature or command. You can also use Cue Cards, an on-line coach that walks you through a step-by-step procedure to accomplish tasks in PowerPoint. The Cue Cards feature is on the Help menu on the menu bar. There are other methods for getting help on the Help menu. Feel free to explore these methods now, and then in the future use these methods as necessary for getting help with PowerPoint. For example, you might want to run the Quick Preview option of the Help menu to get a better idea of what you can do in PowerPoint.

Exiting PowerPoint

Patricia has now finished looking at her presentation and is ready to exit PowerPoint. Let's exit PowerPoint.

To exit PowerPoint.

❶ Click **File** on the menu bar, then click **Exit**.

You could also double-click the **Control menu box** on the application window. PowerPoint may display a dialog box with the message "Save changes to **s1file1.ppt**." This message indicates that you have modified the document since last saving it and that you probably need to save it again before exiting.

❷ If the "Save changes" message appeared, click the **Yes button** to save the current version and to exit PowerPoint.

You have now exited PowerPoint. The Program Manager should now be visible on the screen.

■ ■ ■

Questions

1. In three or four sentences, describe the purpose of the PowerPoint program and what you can do with it.
2. How do you launch PowerPoint from the Windows Program Manager?
3. Explain the function of the following items in the PowerPoint window:
   a. the status bar
   b. the Standard toolbar
   c. the Formatting toolbar
   d. ToolTips
   e. the View toolbar
   f. the Next Slide button
   g. the Drawing toolbar
4. How would you find out information about creating charts (graphs) in PowerPoint?
5. What is the easiest way to get information on an item that appears in the PowerPoint window?
6. How would you do the following:
   a. Scroll to a previous slide?
   b. Change the presentation view?
   c. Save the presentation with a new filename?
7. Define the following PowerPoint terms:
   a. presentation
   b. slide
   c. master
   d. template
   e. outline view
8. What are the four components of a PowerPoint presentation?
9. Name and describe the six questions you should ask yourself when planning a presentation.

E 10. Using the Help feature in PowerPoint, define or describe the following:
   a. the Pick a Look Wizard
   b. the Format Painter
   c. transitions

Tutorial Assignments

In the following Tutorial Assignments, make sure you click the Open an Existing File button (or the Open button on the Standard toolbar) when you launch PowerPoint and then open each file.

Open the file T1FILE1.PPT and immediately save it as S1FILE2.PPT, then do the following:

1. Use the View toolbar to switch to Slide Sorter view to preview all the slides on one screen. How many slides are in the presentation?
2. Use the Slide Sorter view to change slide 3 to slide 2.
3. View the slide show. What is the title of the presentation?
4. Switch from Slide Sorter View to Note Pages View.
5. Zoom the notes page to 100%, then view the notes for all the slides. Which slide has speaker's notes that explain what the Basic Care option emphasizes?
6. Drag the elevator to move to slide 7. What is the purpose of this slide?
7. Use the Next Slide button to go to slide 8. Which month is open enrollment for the health care options?

E 8. Delete slide 6. *Hint*: Use the Help feature to find out how to delete a slide.

9. Save the presentation using the current filename S1FILE2.PPT.
10. Print slide 1 only. *Note*: In the Print dialog box, select Slide (without Builds) and, if you don't have a color printer, select Black & White.
11. Print the Notes Page for slide 2 only. In the Print dialog box, select Black & White if you don't have a color printer.

E 12. Using Help, search for help on "build slide." Describe what a build slide is. Which slides in this presentation are build slides?

E 13. Search for help on "transitions." Describe what a transition is. Which slides in this presentation have a transition? List the steps required to create a transition in a slide.

E 14. Using the Help Index, look up ClipArt Gallery. In your own words, what is the ClipArt Gallery? Which slides in this presentation include a clip art image?

E 15. Run the Quick Preview from the Help menu. As you go through the Quick Preview, answer these questions:
   a. List the three types of presentations you can create using PowerPoint.
   b. What features of PowerPoint can you use to organize your thoughts and quickly get you started in making a presentation?
   c. How many AutoLayouts does PowerPoint provide?
   d. List the five items that you can add easily to give your slide "impact."

E 16. From the Help menu, click the Tip of the Day. What does it say?

17. Close the presentation file.

Case Problem

RSVP Consultants, Inc.

Meryl and Albert Szajnberg own RSVP Consultants, Inc., a wedding and special events consulting company. RSVP's goals include building a new reception center, training five new consultants, and winning the bid to host a local Chamber of Commerce summer celebration.

1. What would be the purpose behind an RSVP presentation to each of the following audiences? In your answer, mention the kind of information each audience would need to know.
   a. investors
   b. RSVP's new employees
   c. potential clients

E 2. Select the type of presentation (recommending a strategy, selling a service or product, providing training, and so forth) RSVP would create for each audience listed in question 1. *Hint*: Run the Quick Preview from the Help menu, then look at the items in the AutoContent Wizard.

3. Identify a likely location (boardroom, auditorium, classroom, or other location) for each of the above three presentations.

4. Select a format (overhead, paper, 35mm slides, or on-screen) for each presentation.

Open the file P1RSVP.PPT and immediately save it as S1RSVP.PPT, then do the following:

5. Switch to Slide Sorter view to preview all the slides. How many slides are in the presentation?

6. Move slide 6 to slide 5 in Slide Sorter view.

7. View the slide show from beginning to end.

8. Indicate which slides would be appropriate for training new employees.

9. Indicate which slides would be appropriate for selling RSVP's services to a prospective client.

E 10. Describe how to hide a slide within a presentation. (*Hint*: Use the "Search for Help on" feature to learn about hidden slides.) How would this feature be helpful in using the current presentation for clients only?

11. Switch to Note Pages view and read the speaker's notes for all the slides. Which slide notes have the word "client" or "clients"?

12. Print the Notes Page for slide 9. *Note*: In the Print dialog box, select Black & White if you don't have a color printer.

13. Save the presentation using the current filename S1RSVP.PPT.

14. Print slide 7 only. *Note*: In the Print dialog box, select Slide (without Builds) and if you don't have a color printer, select Black & White.

E 15. What is WordArt? When would you use it? *Hint*: Use the Help Index to look up this topic.

16. Close the presentation.

TUTORIAL 2

Creating a Text Slide Show

OBJECTIVES

In this tutorial you will:

- Use the AutoContent Wizard to create an outline
- Edit a presentation in Outline view and Slide view
- Promote and demote items in an outline
- Insert and delete slides
- Use cut-and-paste and drag-and-drop operations
- Change the font, font size, style, and color of text

CASE

Market Research Following Patricia Cuevas's successful presentation to potential investors, Inca Imports International received a collateral commitment from Commercial Financial Bank of Southern California. The commitment secured debt financing for up to $1.5 million to begin construction of a distribution facility in Quito, Ecuador, and to launch a marketing campaign to allow Inca Imports to position itself for further expansion.

Patricia assigned Carl Vetterli, vice president of sales and marketing, the task of identifying potential customers and developing methods to reach them. Carl has scheduled a meeting with Patricia, Angelena Cristenas (vice president of operations), Enrique Hoffmann (director of marketing), and others at which he will review the results of his market research. His presentation will include a demographic profile of Inca Imports' current customers and the results from a customer satisfaction survey, a vision statement of the company's future growth, a list of options for attracting new clients, and recommendations for a marketing strategy.

In this tutorial, you will help Carl create some of the slides for his presentation.

Planning the Presentation

Before starting PowerPoint, Carl identifies the purpose of and audience for his presentation.

- **Purpose for the presentation**: To identify potential customers and ways to reach them
- **Type of presentation**: Recommend a strategy for completing the new marketing campaign
- **Audience for the presentation**: Pat, Angelena, Enrique, and other key staff members in a weekly executive meeting
- **Audience needs**: To understand who our current clients are, and to determine the best way to reach similar new clients
- **Location of the presentation**: Small boardroom
- **Format**: Oral presentation; electronic slide show of five to seven slides

Having planned his presentation, Carl uses PowerPoint to create it.

Using the AutoContent Wizard to Create an Outline

PowerPoint helps you create effective presentations by means of **wizards**, a series of questions that make it easy to establish an organizational structure and consistent style in a presentation. Using the **Pick a Look Wizard**, you can choose a style or design for the slides. Using the **AutoContent Wizard**, you can choose a presentation category such as "Selling a Product, Service, or an Idea," "Recommending a Strategy," or "General." After you have selected the type of presentation you want, the AutoContent Wizard creates a general outline for you to follow.

If you open a new presentation without using the AutoContent Wizard, you must create your own outline one new slide at a time. You will learn how to do this in the section later in this chapter titled "Adding a New Slide and Choosing a Layout." For now, however, you will adapt an outline that PowerPoint automatically creates for you.

Carl decides to use the AutoContent Wizard to quickly create his slides. The AutoContent Wizard will allow Carl to create a title slide and to select a standard outline to guide him in creating his presentation. Let's launch PowerPoint and help Carl use the AutoContent Wizard.

To use the AutoContent Wizard:

1. If necessary, launch PowerPoint.
2. When the startup dialog box appears, click the **AutoContent Wizard button** in the PowerPoint startup dialog box. See Figure 2-1.

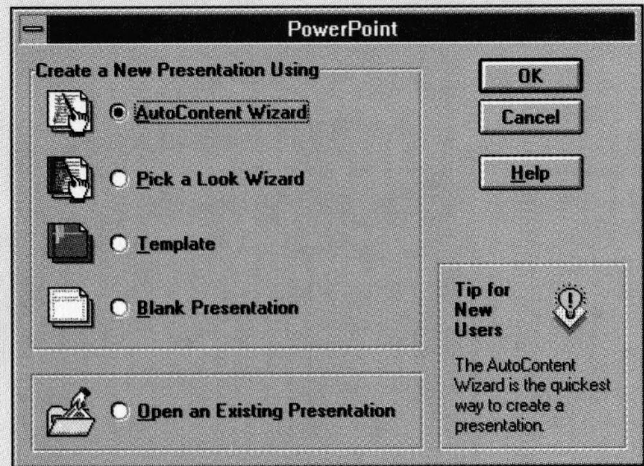

Figure 2-1
PowerPoint startup dialog box

TROUBLE? If the PowerPoint startup dialog box does not appear on your screen, click the New button on the Standard toolbar. When the New Presentation dialog box appears on the screen, click the AutoContent Wizard button.

3. Click the **OK button** or press **[Enter]**.

   PowerPoint displays the first of four AutoContent Wizard dialog boxes. The first dialog box provides information about the function of the AutoContent Wizard.

4. Read the information in the AutoContent Wizard dialog box, then click the **Next button** at the bottom of the dialog box. Step 2 of the AutoContent Wizard appears on the screen. This dialog box creates a title slide for your presentation. The blinking **insertion point** in the text box labeled "What are you going to talk about?" indicates that text will appear at this point when you start typing.

5. Type **Reaching Potential Customers** then press **[Tab]**. The text you typed appears in the first text box, and the text in the second text box, labeled "What is your name?", is highlighted.

6. Type **Carl Vetterli**, press **[Tab]** to move the insertion point to the next text box, labeled "Other information you'd like to include?", and type **Inca Imports International**. Compare your screen to Figure 2-2.

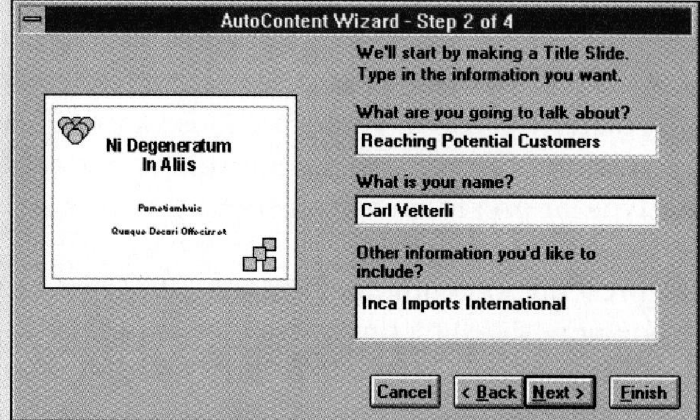

Figure 2-2
AutoContent Wizard, Step 2

TROUBLE? If you accidentally pressed [Enter] before entering all the data, click the Back button in the Step 3 dialog box to return to the Step 2 dialog box, click the mouse pointer in the empty text box, and continue entering the above information.

7. Click the **Next button** to move to Step 3 of the AutoContent Wizard. This dialog box provides six standard formats or outlines for a presentation. Carl wants to recommend a marketing strategy for reaching potential customers.

8. Click the **Recommending a Strategy button**.

   Notice that the list of topics on the left changes to a general outline of presentation ideas for recommending a strategy. See Figure 2-3.

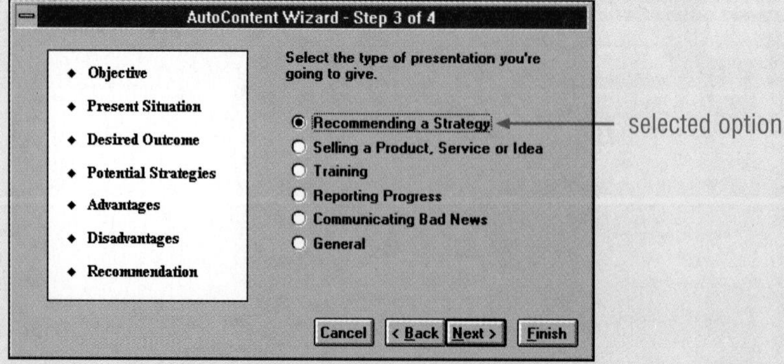

Figure 2-3
AutoContent Wizard, Step 3

⑨ Click the **Next button**, read the information in the Step 4 dialog box, and then click the **Finish button**.

The Outline view appears, with a standard outline of a presentation for recommending a strategy already filled in. A Cue Cards screen with "Tips for Working in PowerPoint" may appear on the right. See Figure 2-4.

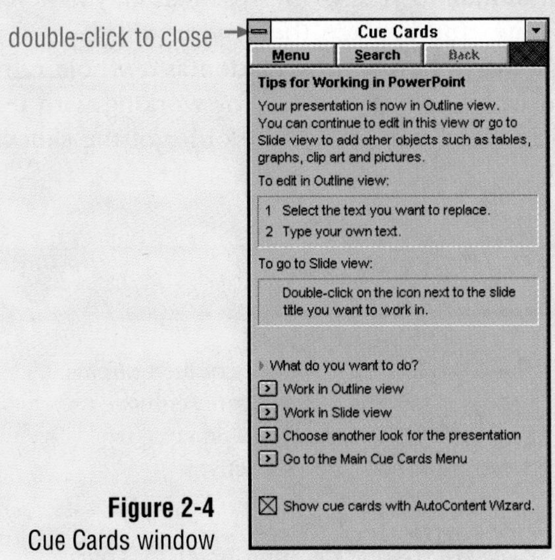

Figure 2-4
Cue Cards window

⑩ If the Cue Cards screen appears, read the information, then remove the screen by double-clicking the **Control menu box** of the Cue Cards window. Your screen should look like Figure 2-5. (If necessary, click the **Maximize button** in the presentation window.)

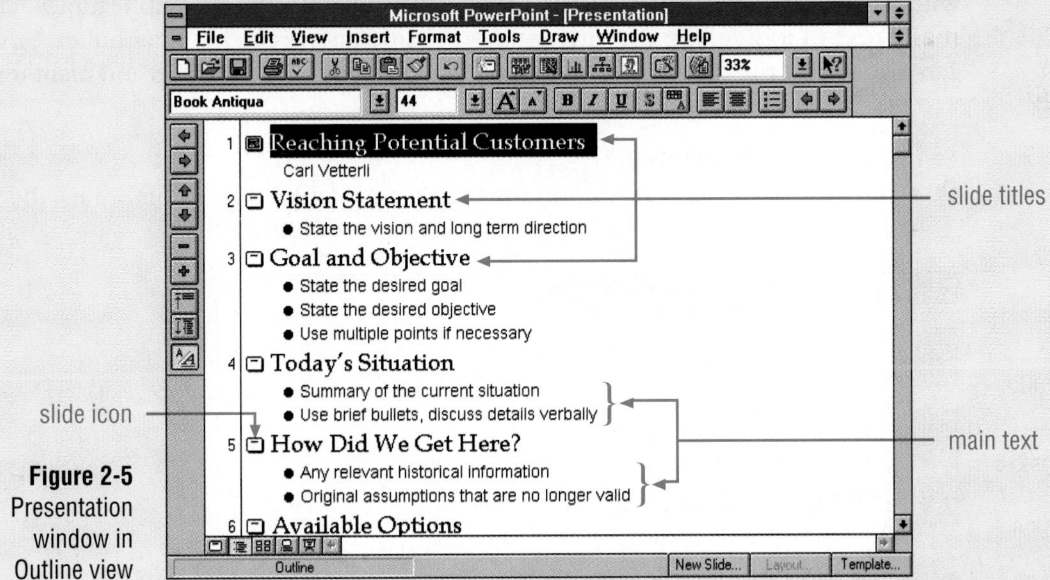

Figure 2-5
Presentation window in Outline view

TROUBLE? If you accidentally click the main Control menu box of PowerPoint, you'll get the message, "Save changes to Presentations?" If this happens, click the Cancel button to cancel the exit from PowerPoint, and then double-click the Control menu box of the Cue Cards window.

Adapting an AutoContent Outline

After completing the AutoContent Wizard, PowerPoint displays an outline consisting of Carl's title slide (Slide 1) and additional slides with text, called placeholders, suggesting ideas for the presentation. A **placeholder** is a region of a window reserved for inserting text or graphics. To adapt the AutoContent outline to your own presentation, you **select**, or highlight, the placeholders, one at a time, and replace them with your own text. Because Outline view allows you to see the text of your presentation as a whole rather than as individual slides, Outline view is usually the easiest view for working with text. You can also apply formatting changes to the text and change the order of the slides in Outline view.

DESIGN PRINCIPLE WINDOW

Principles for Creating Effective Text Presentations

- Think of your presentation as a visual map to your oral presentation.
- Show your organization by using overviews, by making headings larger than subheadings, and by numbering steps to show sequence.
- Follow the **6x6 rule**: Use six or fewer items per screen, and use incomplete sentences of six or fewer words. Omit unnecessary articles, pronouns, and adjectives.
- Keep phrases parallel.
- Make sure your text is appropriate for your purpose and audience.

Each main heading of the outline, called the **title** of a slide, appears at the left, along with a slide icon and slide number, as shown in Figure 2-5. The subheadings, called the **main text** of a slide, are indented under the title and preceded by a bullet. PowerPoint can display just the titles of the slides or the entire outline with titles and main text.

To display the slide titles only:

1. Click the **Show Titles button** on the Outlining toolbar. PowerPoint hides the main text of the outline and displays only the titles. See Figure 2-6.

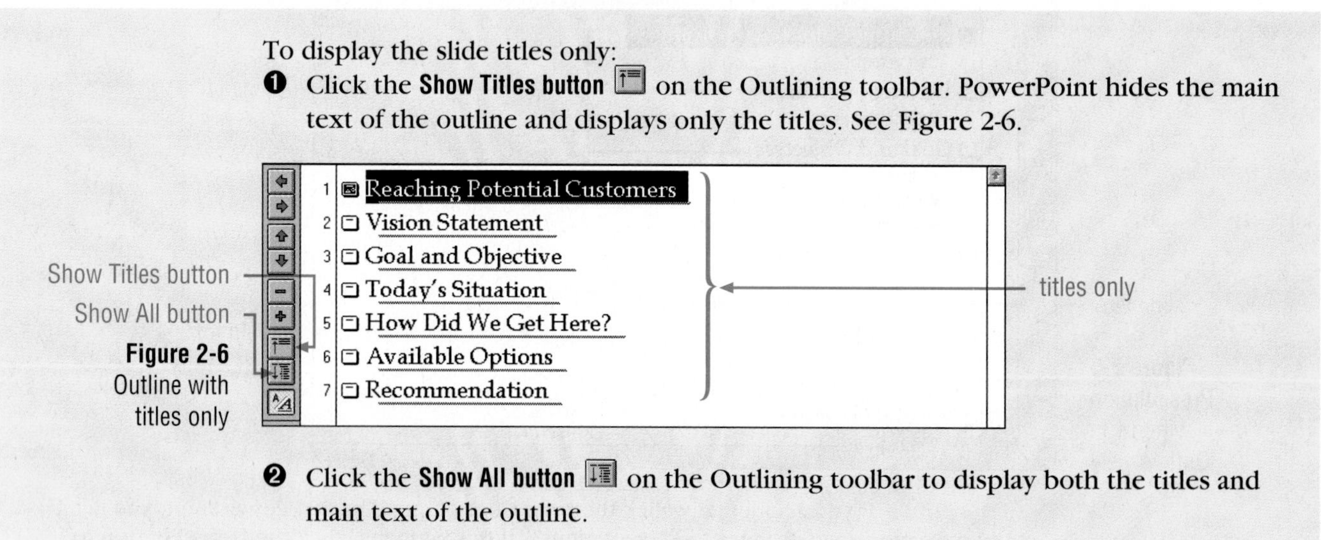

Figure 2-6 Outline with titles only

2. Click the **Show All button** on the Outlining toolbar to display both the titles and main text of the outline.

Carl wants to add his own text to the Vision Statement, which is slide 2. Let's replace the main text in this slide now.

To replace the main text in a slide:

1. Make sure the presentation window is maximized, if necessary, by clicking the **Maximize button** in the upper-right corner of the presentation window. (Your presentation window may already be maximized.) If necessary, drag the horizontal scroll button to the far left so you can see the left edge of the outline text.
2. Position the mouse pointer before the "S" in the sentence "State the vision and long term direction," which is located beneath the title of slide 2. The pointer changes to I.
3. Press and hold the mouse button, drag the pointer to the end of the line, then release the mouse button. Your screen should look similar to Figure 2-7. This method of selecting text is called **dragging**. To replace the selected text, just start typing.

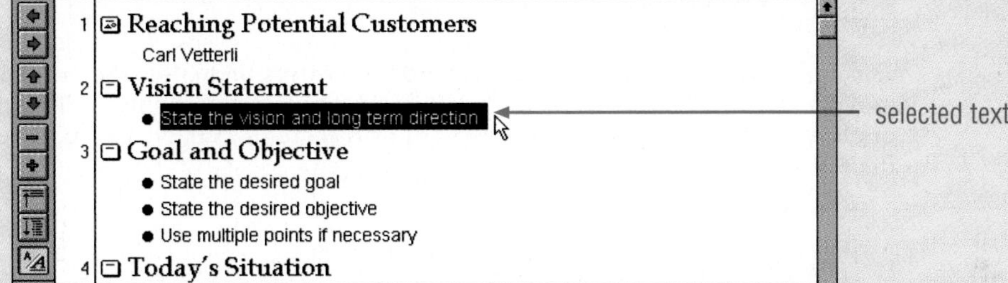

Figure 2-7
Text selected for replacement

4. Type **Inca can improve the quality of its produce**. Your screen should now look like Figure 2-8.

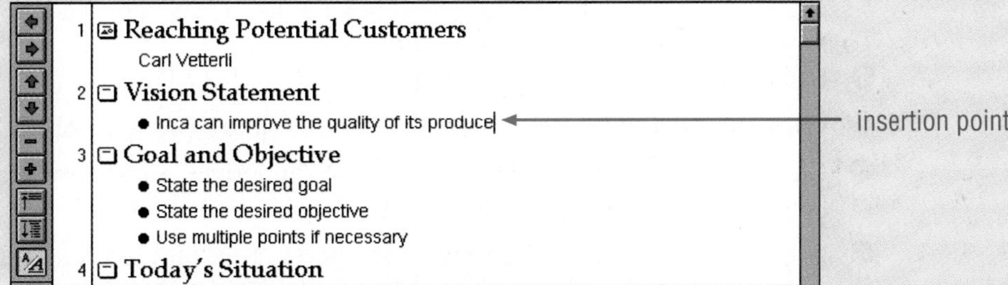

Figure 2-8
New text in slide 2

Notice that as soon as you started typing, the selected text disappeared as the new phrase you typed appeared.

Carl has two more bullets he wants to add to the Vision Statement slide. Let's do that now.

To add new text to the outline:

1. Press **[Enter]**. When you press [Enter], PowerPoint automatically inserts a bullet for the next item in the list, and the insertion point appears to the right of the bullet.
2. Type **Inca can sell more produce to more customers** and press **[Enter]**.
3. Type **Inca can become the clear market leader in Southern California** and press **[Enter]**. Your screen should now look like Figure 2-9.

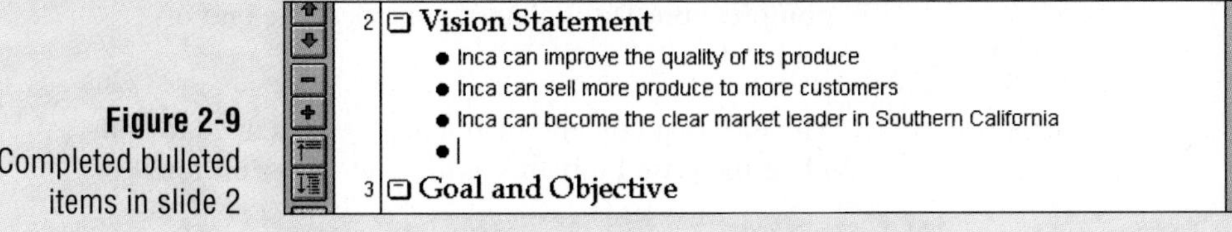

Figure 2-9
Completed bulleted items in slide 2

Carl realizes that he really wants only three items in the list, not four. He deletes the fourth bullet.

4. Press **[Backspace]** to delete the fourth bullet and move the insertion point to the end of the preceding line.

Next Carl wants to replace the placeholder text in slide 3, "Goal and Objective."

5. Make the changes in slide 3 using the text in Figure 2-10.

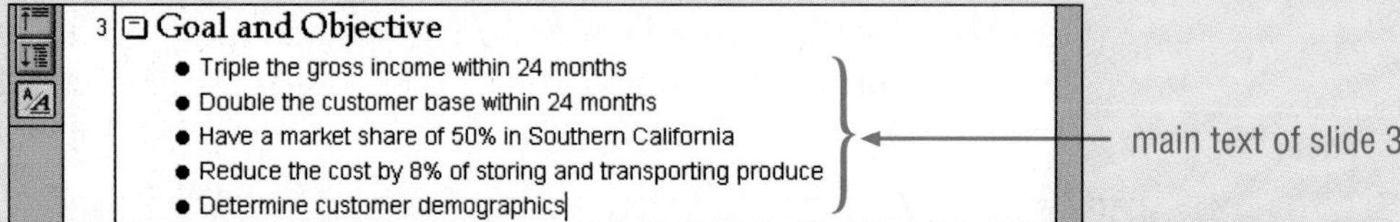

Figure 2-10 Complete text of slide 3

TROUBLE? If you make typographical errors, correct them. Use the normal insertion-point movement keys ([→], [←], [↑], [↓]) to move the insertion point to the location of the mistake or click I at the location; use [Backspace] or [Delete] to remove the mistake, and then retype the text correctly.

Saving the Presentation for the First Time

Carl has made substantial progress on his presentation and he decides to save the changes.

To save a presentation for the first time:

1. Insert the PowerPoint Student Disk into drive A or B.
2. Click the **Save button** on the Standard toolbar. The Save As dialog box appears.
3. Click the **Down arrow** on the right side of the Drives section of the dialog box, then click **a:** (or whichever drive contains your Student Disk).
4. Double-click in the **File Name text box**, then type **s2file1** and click the **OK button** or press **[Enter]**. PowerPoint displays the Summary Info dialog box.
5. Click the **OK button** to close the Summary Info dialog box.

PowerPoint saves the file to the disk using the filename S2FILE1.PPT. That name now appears in the Slide window title bar.

In this book, the four tutorials on PowerPoint involve many files. Therefore, we use filenames that will help you and your instructor recognize the origin and content of the various documents. To name these files so you can recognize their contents, we have categorized them as follows:

File Category	Description
Tutorial Cases	The files you use to work through each tutorial
Tutorial Assignments	The files that contain the documents you need to complete the Tutorial Assignments at the end of each tutorial
Case Problems	The files that contain the documents you need to complete the Case Problems at the end of each tutorial
Saved Document	Any document you have saved

Let's take the filename S1FILE1.PPT, for example. At first glance this filename might appear to have no meaning, but it does contain meaningful abbreviations. The first character of the filename identifies the file as one of the four categories given above, as shown here:

If the first character is:	The file category is:
C	Tutorial **C**ase
T	**T**utorial Assignment
P	Case **P**roblem
S	**S**aved Document

Thus, S1FILE1.PPT is a document that you have saved.

The second character of the document filename identifies the tutorial from which the file comes. Thus, S1FILE1.PPT is a file you saved from Tutorial 1. The remaining six characters of the filename identify the specific file. All documents in the tutorials are named FILE, followed by a number. Each time you save a file, you will increase the number after FILE by 1.

If you want to take a break and resume the tutorial at a later time, you can do so now. If you exit PowerPoint, launch the program again when you want to resume working, open the presentation file S2FILE1.PPT, and select Outline view. Then continue with this tutorial.

Editing the Presentation in Outline View

As Carl reviews the text of the first three slides, he realizes that in a slide presentation, each text item should be as short as possible. It is easier for the audience to read short phrases. In addition, he knows that he will be conveying most of the information orally, so the main text doesn't have to be complete sentences.

Carl decides to apply the "6 x 6 Rule" as much as possible and simplify the text in slide 2. Because the audience will be aware that Carl is talking about Inca Imports International, the company name is unnecessary. Similarly, articles ("the," "a"), many possessive pronouns ("your," "its"), and most adjectives ("high," "clear," "very") can safely be left out of titles and the main text. Therefore, Carl decides to change "Inca can improve the quality of its produce" to "Improve quality of produce." Carl also realizes that by changing the title of slide 3 from "Goal and Objective," to "Two-Year Goals," he can delete the words "within 24 months" from the bulleted list.

To edit the outline:

1. Using Figure 2-11 as a guide, change the text of slides 2 and 3 of Carl's presentation by dragging I to select text and then deleting it or retyping it.

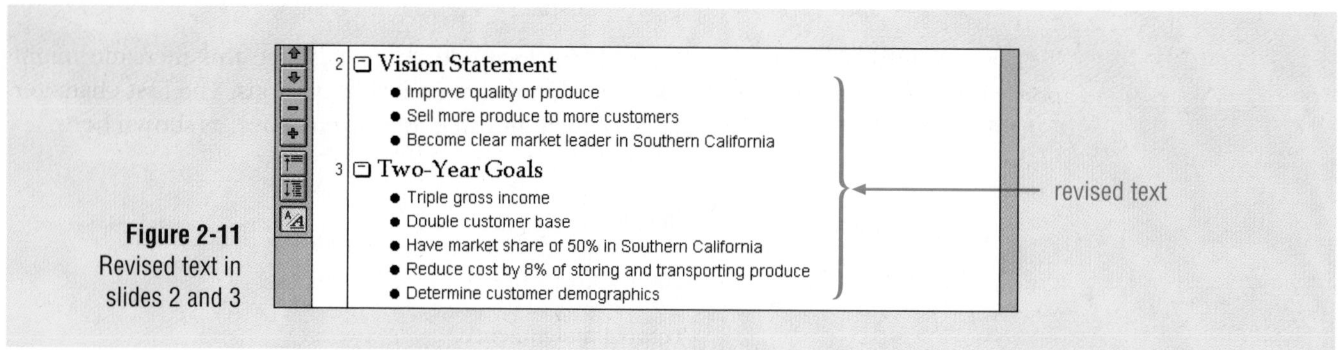

Figure 2-11 Revised text in slides 2 and 3

Moving Text Up and Down in Outline View

As Carl reads through the text of the first three slides, he decides to switch the second and third items under "Two-Year Goals." Let's reverse the order of these items now.

To move an item of text in Outline view:

1. Move the mouse pointer to the left of the text (for example, on the bullet) "Have market share of 50% in Southern California," so that the mouse pointer becomes ✥, and click once.

   PowerPoint highlights the text of that item.

2. Click the **Move Up Arrow button** on the Outlining toolbar.

   PowerPoint moves the highlighted item up one position in the list, so the second and third items are switched. See Figure 2-12.

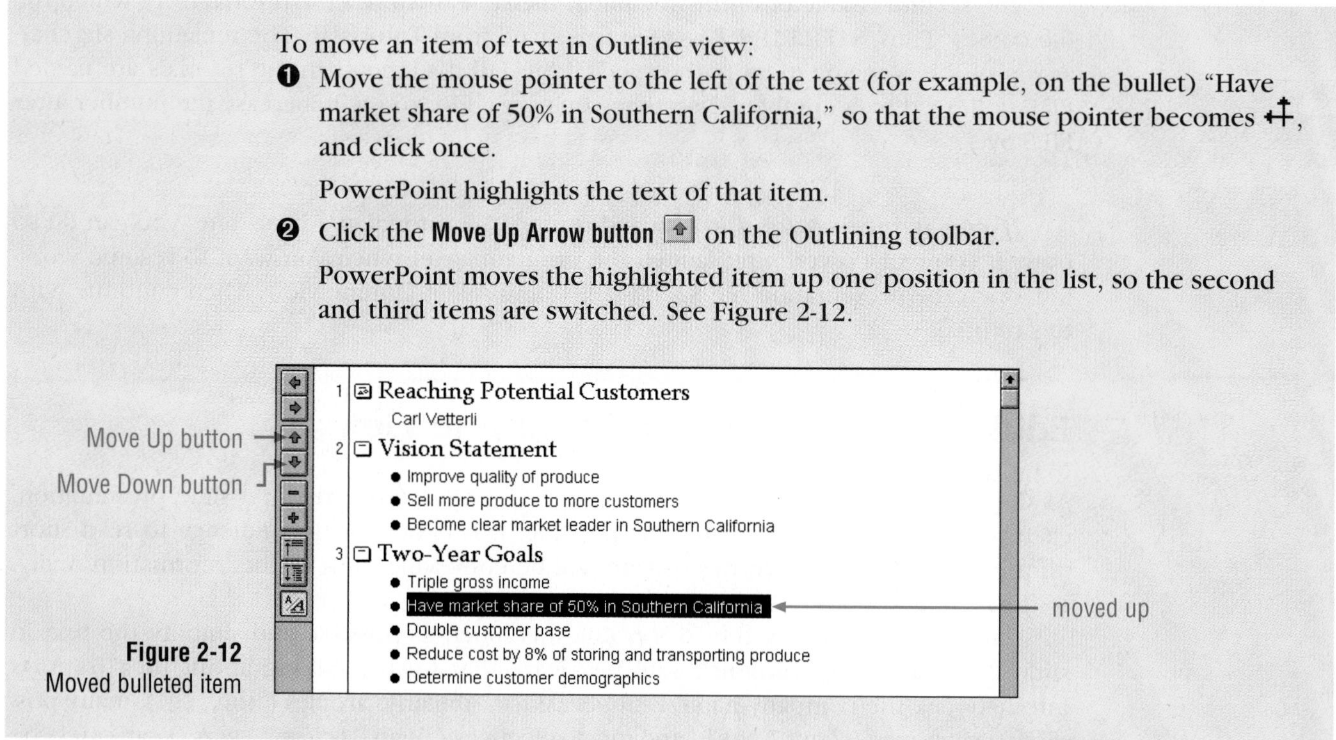

Figure 2-12 Moved bulleted item

You can use this same method to move entire slides. To move a slide, click ✥ on the slide icon of the slide you want to move, then click the Move Up button or the Move Down button on the Outlining toolbar to move the slide.

Promoting and Demoting the Outline Text

While reviewing slide 3, Carl realizes that he needs to present more information on his customer demographic study. Rather than having "Determine customer demographics" as the last item of the main text of slide 3, Carl wants that phrase to be a title of a separate slide. Instead of deleting the bulleted item and then retyping it as a new slide title, Carl will promote the item from main text to slide title. To **promote** an item means to increase the outline level of an item, for example, to change a bulleted item to a slide title. To **demote** an item means to decrease the outline level, for example, to change a slide title to a bulleted item within another slide.

Let's promote the item "Determine customer demographics" in order to create the new slide.

To promote an item:

1. Click I anywhere within the bulleted item "Determine customer demographics" in slide 3.
2. Click the **Promote (Indent less) button** . This button is located in two places: on the Outlining toolbar and on the Formatting toolbar.
   When you click the Promote button, the text moves left and increases in size, and the new slide icon appears to the left of the text. The new slide becomes slide 4, and "Today's Situation" becomes slide 5, as shown in Figure 2-13. Because the title of slide 4 is wordy, Carl decides to edit it.

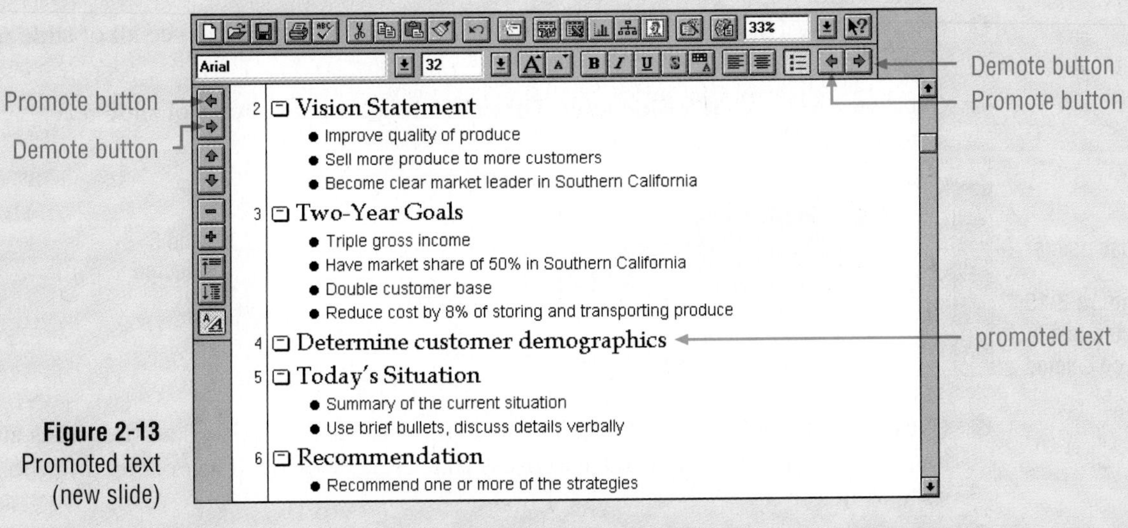

Figure 2-13 Promoted text (new slide)

3. Change the title "**Determine customer demographics**" to "**Customer Demographics.**"

Carl is now ready to add the bulleted items beneath the title of slide 4. However, because the current outline level is a slide title, any text Carl adds will be input at the same level, that is, as a slide title. To add main text, therefore, Carl has to move down a level in the outline. He can do this by using the Demote command.

To demote an item:

1. Click I at the end of the title "Customer Demographics," then press **[Enter]**. PowerPoint creates a new slide 5.
2. Click the **Demote (Indent More) button** on the Outlining or Formatting toolbar to change the outline level from slide title to main text and to indent.
3. Type the main text of slide 4 as shown in Figure 2-14. Carefully check to make sure you have typed the information correctly. Make any necessary corrections.

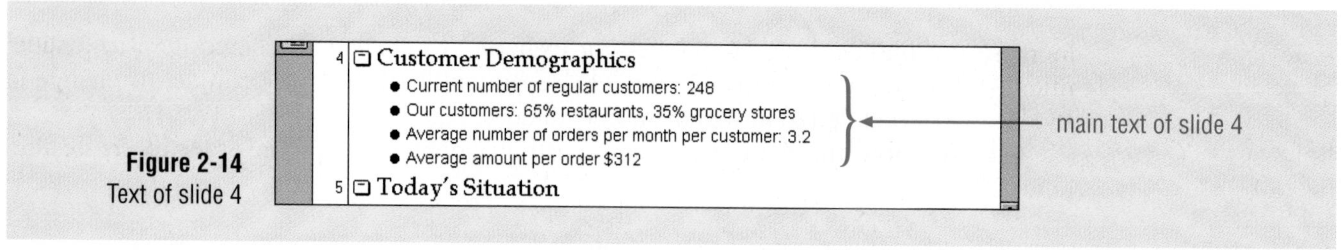

Figure 2-14 Text of slide 4

Deleting a Slide

Carl feels that in his presentation he doesn't need slides on "Today's Situation," "How Did We Get Here?" or "Available Options," which are three of the default titles in the "Recommending a Strategy" outline. You can delete a slide in any view except Slide Show. Carl decides to delete these three slides now.

To delete a slide:

1. Click the **Down Scroll arrow** on the vertical scroll bar until you can see all of slide 5 on the screen.
2. Click ✥ on the slide 5 slide icon. The title and all the main text of slide 5 is selected. See Figure 2-15.

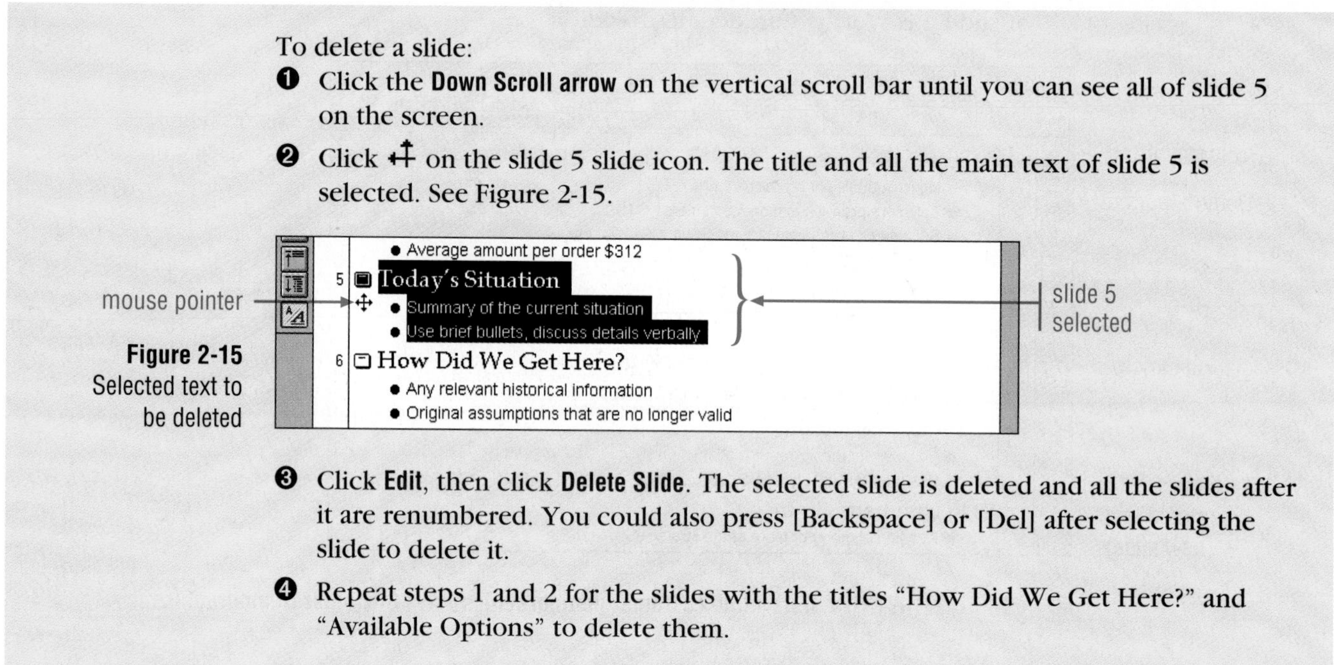

Figure 2-15 Selected text to be deleted

3. Click **Edit**, then click **Delete Slide**. The selected slide is deleted and all the slides after it are renumbered. You could also press [Backspace] or [Del] after selecting the slide to delete it.
4. Repeat steps 1 and 2 for the slides with the titles "How Did We Get Here?" and "Available Options" to delete them.

The last title in Carl's presentation is "Recommendations." Let's create that slide now.

To create the last slide:

1. Edit the title of slide 5 to change "**Recommendation**" to "**Recommendations.**"
2. Edit the main text of slide 5 so that the bulleted items match those in Figure 2-16.

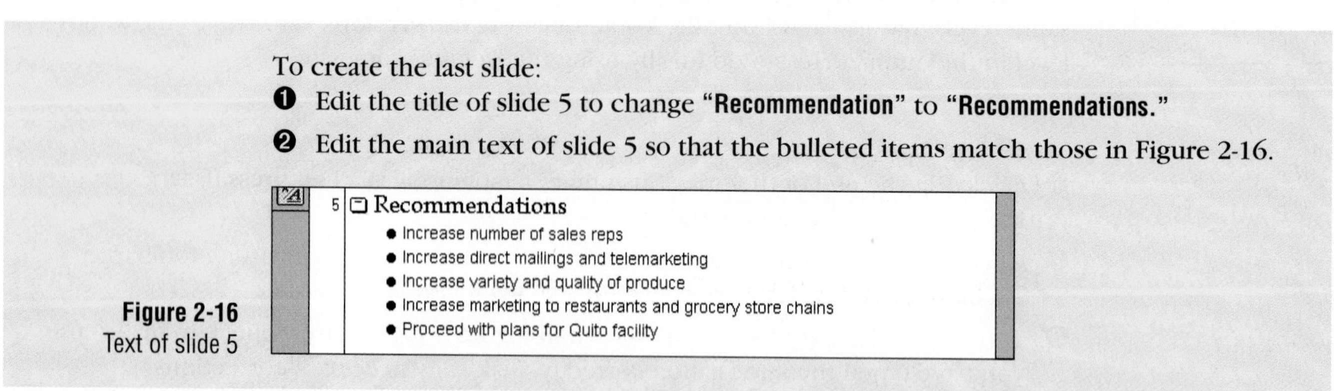

Figure 2-16 Text of slide 5

Carl has adapted and edited his presentation in Outline view and has completed the five slides of his presentation. He decides to use Slide view to see how his presentation looks.

Viewing Slides in Slide View

Viewing your presentation in Outline view doesn't show you how each of your slides will look when you actually make your presentation. To see the slides, you need to change to Slide view. Let's view the first three slides in Slide view.

To show slides in Slide view:

1. Scroll the presentation window so you can see the beginning of the outline, then click the mouse pointer anywhere within the text of slide 1. This makes slide 1 the current slide, so that when you switch to Slide view, slide 1 will appear on the screen.
2. Click the **Slide View button** on the View toolbar.

   You could also click **View**, then click **Slides**. PowerPoint displays slide 1 in the presentation window. After looking over the slide, view the next slide.
3. Click the **Next Slide button** at the bottom of the vertical scroll bar. PowerPoint displays slide 2, "Vision Statement."

   TROUBLE? If PowerPoint doesn't advance to the next slide, you may have clicked the Previous Slide button. Try step 3 again, this time clicking the Next Slide button. If you're not sure which is the Next Slide button, move the mouse pointer to one of the buttons in the lower-right corner of the presentation window and read the ToolTip.

   After looking at slide 2, view slide 3.
4. Drag the **elevator** down until the slide identifier shows that you are on slide 3, as shown in Figure 2-17, then release the mouse button.

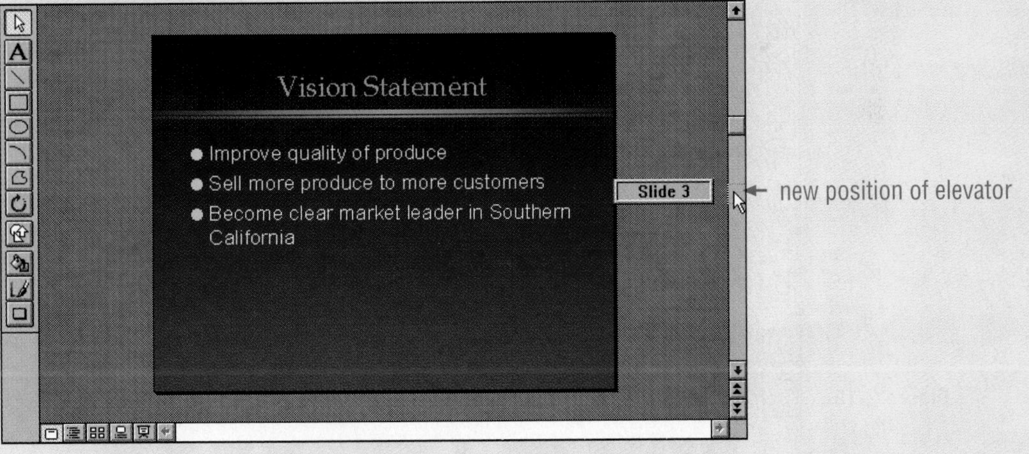

Figure 2-17
Moving elevator to slide 3

As you can see, Slide view allows you to see exactly how the slides will appear during Carl's presentation.

Moving Text Using Cut and Paste

Cut and paste is an important way to move text in PowerPoint. To **cut** means to remove text (or some other item) from the document and place it on the Windows clipboard. The **clipboard** is an area where text and graphics that have been cut or copied are stored until you act on them further. To **paste** means to transfer a copy of the text from the clipboard into the document. To perform a cut-and-paste operation, you simply highlight the text you want to move, cut it, and then paste the text where you want it.

As Carl looks at slide 3, "Two-Year Goals," of his PowerPoint presentation, he decides the fourth bullet sounds a little awkward. He wants to move the phrase "by 8%" to the end of the fourth item, so that it becomes "Reduce cost of storing and transporting produce by 8%."

REFERENCE WINDOW

Cutting and Pasting (Moving) Text

- Select the text you want to move.
- Cut the selected text by clicking the Cut button on the Standard toolbar.
- Move the insertion point to the target location in the presentation.
- Paste the text back into the presentation by clicking the Paste button on the Standard toolbar.

Let's change the text using the cut-and-paste method.

To move text using cut and paste:

1. Make sure slide 3 appears in the PowerPoint window in Slide view, as shown in Figure 2-18.

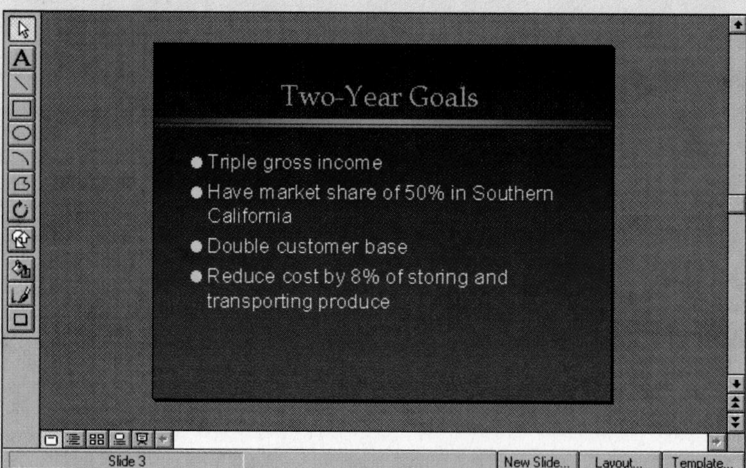

Figure 2-18 Slide 3

2. Click I anywhere on the main text of the slide. A selection box appears around the bulleted items to indicate that the text is selected, and the text is highlighted in color.
3. Select the phrase "by 8%" in the fourth item of slide 3 by dragging the mouse pointer over it. See Figure 2-19.

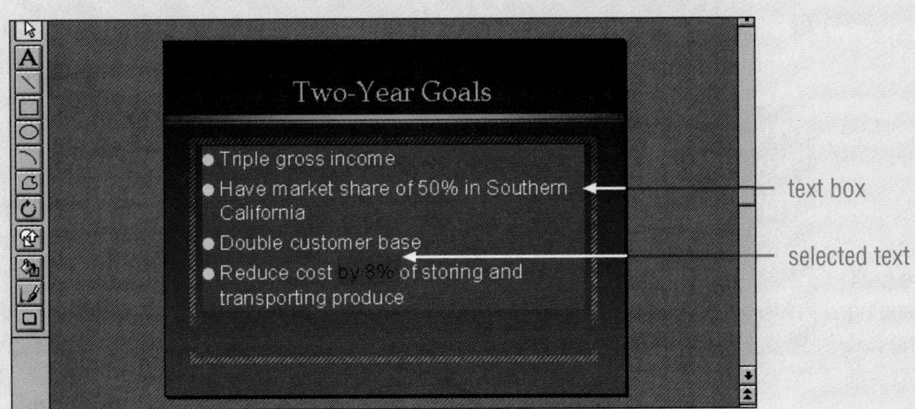

Figure 2-19 Selected text for cut and paste

4. Click the **Cut button** on the Standard toolbar. The phrase disappears from the screen and is pasted onto the clipboard.
5. Click I at the end of the phrase, "Reduce cost of storing and transporting produce." This puts the insertion point at the location where you want to paste the text back into the slide.

   TROUBLE? The insertion point may be hard to see with the PowerPoint default color scheme. If you can't see the insertion point, don't worry about it. Make sure you clicked I in the correct place, then go on to the next step.
6. Click the **Paste button** on the Standard toolbar. The phrase "by 8%" appears again in the slide, but this time at the end of the item. See Figure 2-20.

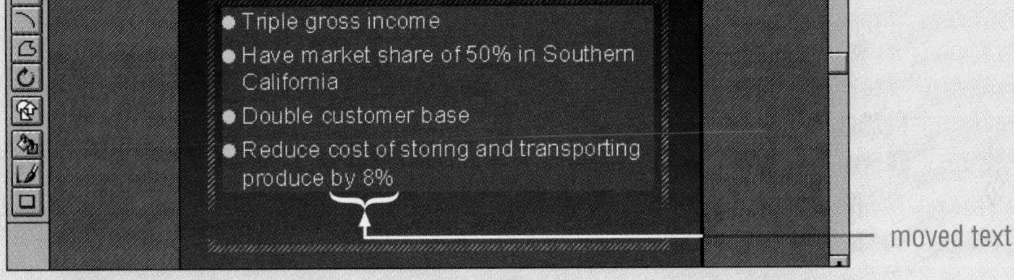

Figure 2-20 Slide after pasting text

To copy selected text rather than move it, click the Copy button on the Standard toolbar instead of the Cut button.

Moving Text Using Drag and Drop

In addition to cut and paste, you can use **drag and drop** to move text in PowerPoint. You simply select the text by dragging the mouse pointer over it, press and hold down the left mouse button while you drag the text, and then release the mouse button.

Carl wants to move the words "of 50%" from the middle to the end of the bulleted item in the main text of slide 3. Let's move the phrase now.

To move text using drag and drop:

1. Select the phrase **"of 50%."**
2. Move the mouse pointer within the region of the selected text, press and hold the mouse button, drag the mouse pointer to the right of the word "California" in the same item of the main text, then release the mouse button.

❸ Click anywhere outside the text area to deselect the text. The phrase "of 50%" moves from the middle of the bulleted item to the end of the item. See Figure 2-21.

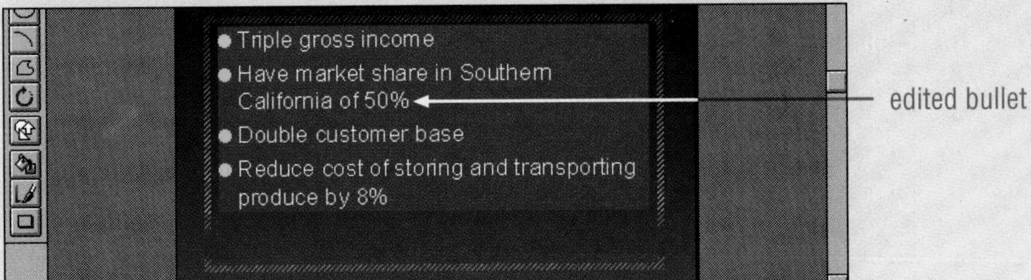

Figure 2-21
Slide after dragging and dropping text

Cut and paste and drag and drop are both effective in moving text from one location to another. You can use both methods in any view except Slide Show.

Adding a New Slide and Choosing a Layout

Carl created his presentation using the AutoContent Wizard, witch gave him a ready-made outline to adapt to his own purpose. However, you don't have to use a wizard to create a presentation. You can create it from scratch using the Blank Presentation button in the PowerPoint startup dialog box. PowerPoint displays blank slides to which you add your own text.

Carl decides his presentation needs a slide that summarizes Inca Import's new marketing plan, so he decides to add a new slide. Let's add the slide in slide view now.

To add a slide in slide view:

❶ With slide 3 still in the presentation window, click the **New Slide button** on the status line. PowerPoint displays the New Slide dialog box. You could also click the **Insert New Slide button** on the Standard toolbar.

The New Slide dialog box appears on the screen. See Figure 2-22.

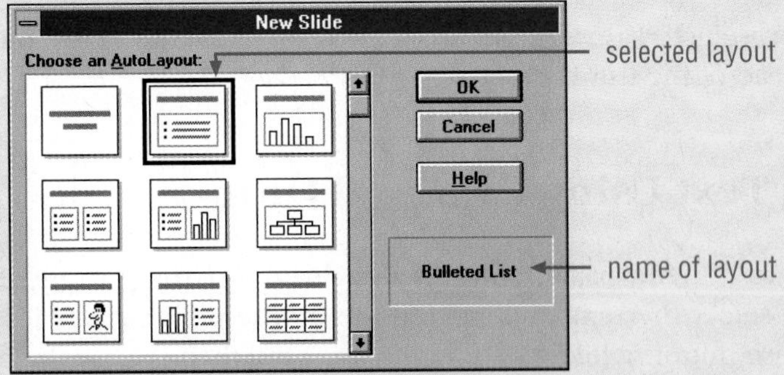

Figure 2-22
New Slide dialog box

When you add a slide, you must decide where you want the placeholders for titles, text, and graphics to go. You do this by choosing an **AutoLayout**, a ready-made format for these placeholders. You can also choose a blank layout.

❷ Drag the **elevator** on the AutoLayout scroll bar to the bottom of the scroll bar.

❸ Click on a few of the AutoLayouts and read the name in the lower-right corner of the dialog box.

4. Click the **Blank slide layout**, which is the last layout in the list. You would click this layout if you wanted to set up your own layout. Carl wants his new slide to be a bulleted list.
5. Drag the **elevator** on the AutoLayout scroll bar to the top of the scroll bar, then click the second layout in the top row, titled "Bulleted List," as shown in Figure 2-22.
6. Click the **OK button**. PowerPoint inserts a new slide containing a title and main text placeholder for the bulleted list.
7. Click the **title placeholder** (where the slide says "Click to add title") and type **Our New Marketing Campaign**.
8. Click the **main text placeholder** and type the three bulleted items shown in Figure 2-23.
9. Click anywhere outside the text areas to deselect the text box. Make sure your slide 4 looks like Figure 2-23.

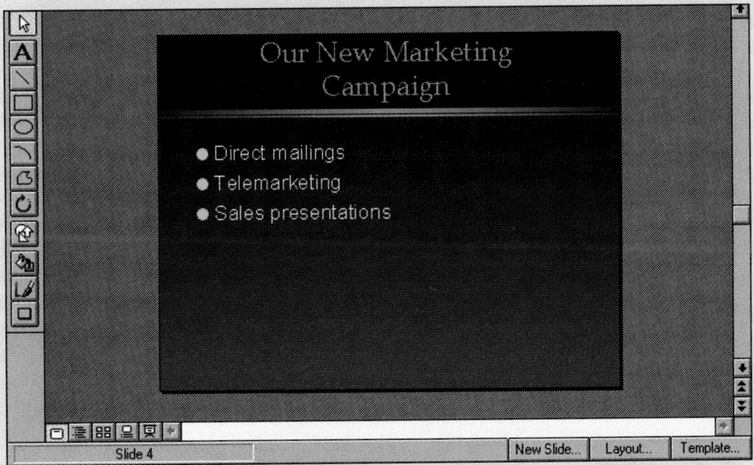

Figure 2-23 Completed new slide 4

Changing the Template

When you use the AutoContent Wizard or open a blank presentation, PowerPoint provides a predetermined **template**, that is, the colors and design on the background of the text, and the type style of the titles, accents, and other text. The default template that PowerPoint uses with the Recommending a Strategy option in the AutoContent Wizard is the double lines (dbllines) template; double lines divide the title from the main text, the background is maroon, the title text is green, and the main text is white. You can change the default template to another one from among more than 100 that PowerPoint provides. To change the template, you either click the Template button in the status bar or you can use the Pick a Look Wizard.

Carl wants to change the template for his presentation. Let's change the template now.

To change the template:

1. Click the **Template button** in the status bar. The Presentation Template dialog box appears. See Figure 2-24.

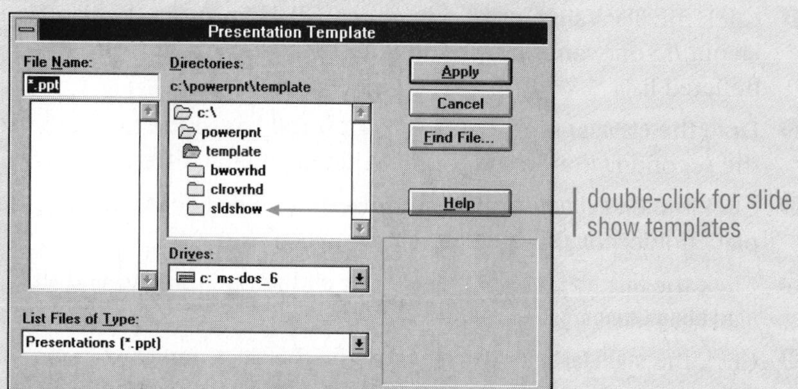

Figure 2-24 Presentation template dialog box

TROUBLE? Your screen may show a list of .ppt template files. If so, skip to step 3.

2. Double-click the sldshow folder in the Directories section of the dialog box.
3. Scroll the template names in the File Name list box until you see **sidebars.ppt**, then click that name. The selected template design appears in the preview box at the lower-right of the dialog box.

   TROUBLE? If you do not have a template SIDEBARS.PPT installed on your computer, choose any other template you like.
4. Click the **Apply button** to change the template for all the slides in the presentation. The new template will appear on all the slides in the presentation. Carl wants to see what the new template looks like in the title slide.
5. Move to slide 1 by dragging the **elevator** to the top of the scroll bar. The title slide appears in the window. See Figure 2-25.

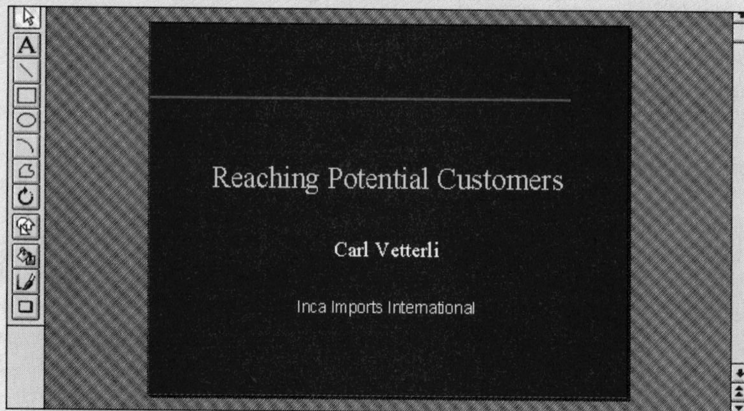

Figure 2-25 Title slide with template

Formatting Text

When Carl created his presentation, he used PowerPoint's default fonts for his slide show. A **font** is a set of characters (letters, digits, and other characters such as !, @, and *) that have a certain design and appearance. Each font has a name, such as Courier, Times Roman, or Univers (Figure 2-26). The current font is listed on the left of the Formatting toolbar. The default font in the SIDEBARS.PPT template is Times New Roman. (Your toolbar might indicate a different font, depending on your printer and on which fonts are installed on your system.) The height of a font is measured in points. A **point** is 1/72 of an inch.

Courier
Times Roman
Univers

Figure 2-26
Example fonts

You can change the font, the font size, the font style (bold, italic, underlined), and the font color. PowerPoint does a good job selecting fonts for the slides; however, there may be times when you want to change the defaults chosen by PowerPoint.

DESIGN PRINCIPLE WINDOW

Typography Guidelines

- The size of the text should reflect the importance level of the text, that is, titles should be larger than main text.
- Use large fonts (24 through 60 points).
- Vary type styles to provide emphasize, but remember that having too much emphasis is the same as having none.
- Words in all uppercase can decrease reading speed. It's easier to read words in mostly lowercase letters because the shapes of the letters help the reader see the words as a unit.
- Bold, italic, and underlining are difficult to distinguish on-screen.

REFERENCE WINDOW

Changing the Font, Font Size, and Font Style

- Select the text that you want to change.
- Click the appropriate button on the Formatting toolbar.

To change the Font, click the Font down arrow and choose the desired font. To change the Font size, click the Font Size down arrow and choose the desired size, or click the Increase/Decrease Font Size buttons. To change the Font style, click the Bold, Italics, Underline, or Text Shadow buttons.

Carl now decides that his name and the company name on the title should be in two different colors rather than the same color text.

DESIGN PRINCIPLE WINDOW

Principles of Using Color on a Slide

- Color can focus the reader's attention.
- Color can establish understanding through associations (for example, red as a warning).
- Color can reveal organization and pattern by using similar colors for related ideas.
- Too much color can be distracting and slow down reading and comprehension.

Carl decides to change the color of the text "Inca Imports International" in slide 1. PowerPoint doesn't allow you to change the color of the text from Outline view, but you can change the color from Slide view.

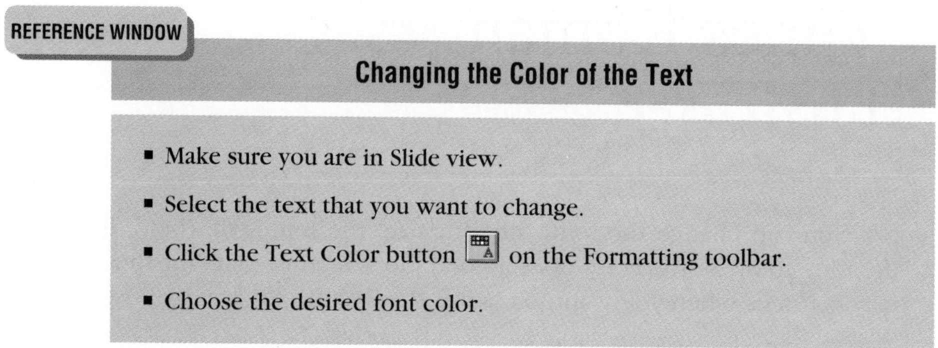

REFERENCE WINDOW

Changing the Color of the Text

- Make sure you are in Slide view.
- Select the text that you want to change.
- Click the Text Color button on the Formatting toolbar.
- Choose the desired font color.

Let's change the color of the company name.

To change the color of the text:

❶ Click anywhere on the company name, then drag I to select the phrase "Inca Imports International."

❷ Click the **Text Color button** on the Formatting toolbar. PowerPoint displays a small grid of colors.

❸ Click the **yellow tile** (small square) on the Text Color menu. PowerPoint changes the color of the company name to yellow, although you can't see that color yet because the text is selected.

❹ Deselect the text by clicking the mouse pointer anywhere in the slide except on text. The title slide now looks like Figure 2-27.

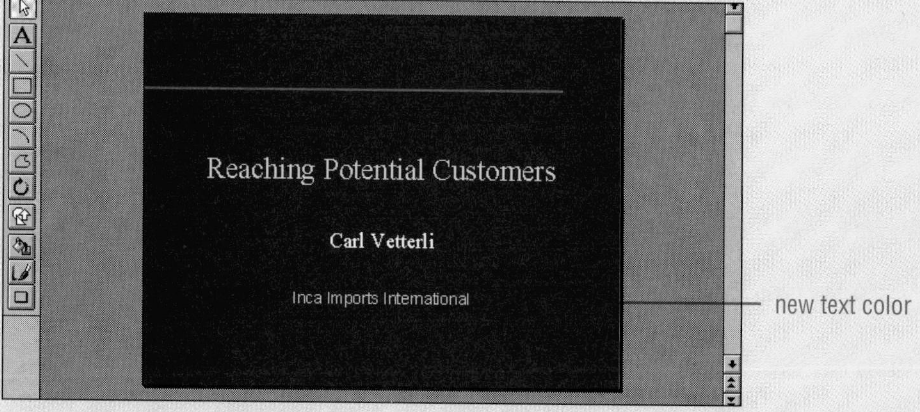

Figure 2-27
Slide 1 after changing text color

By making appropriate changes in the font style and color, you can improve the appearance and readability of the text within your slide show.

Saving the Final Version of the Presentation

Having completed the presentation, Carl is now ready to save the final version. Because he has saved the presentation previously, he can simple click the Save button to save the current version of the file over the now obsolete version.

To save a file that has been saved previously:

1. Make sure your Student Disk is in the disk drive.
2. Click the **Save button** on the Standard toolbar. PowerPoint saves the file using its current filename, S2FILE1.PPT.

A copy of the updated presentation is now on your Student Disk.

Viewing the Completed Slide Show

Carl wants to see his completed slide show.

To view the completed presentation as a slide show:

1. Make sure you're viewing slide 1 in Slide view. If you were in Outline view, the insertion point would need to be somewhere within the text of slide 1. This ensures that when you begin the Slide Show, slide 1 appears on the screen first.
2. Click the **Slide Show button** on the View toolbar.
3. After you read a slide, click the **left mouse button** or press **[Spacebar]** to advance to the next slide. Continue advancing until you've see the entire slide show and PowerPoint returns to Slide view or Outline view.

Printing the Presentation

Carl decides he will print his presentation as handouts in order to have a hard copy for his records. Let's do that now.

To print handouts of the presentation:

1. From Slide view or Outline view, click **File**, then click **Print**. PowerPoint displays the Print dialog box. Don't click the Print button on the Standard toolbar or PowerPoint will immediately start printing without letting you change the print settings.
2. Click the **Down arrow** next to the Print What box, and select **Handouts (2 slides per page)**.
3. If you're using a blank-and-white printer, click the **Black & White** checkbox on the Print dialog box. See Figure 2-28.

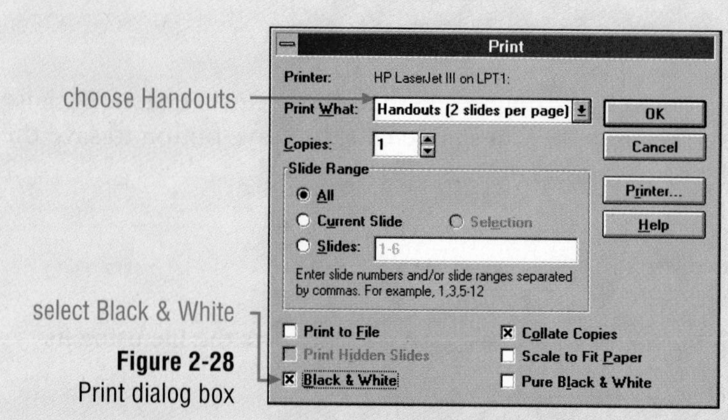

Figure 2-28
Print dialog box

❹ Click the **OK button** to print the slides.
Be patient. Graphics usually take a long time to print, even on a relatively fast laser printer.

❺ To see how the slides look as a group, click the **Slide Sorter View icon** ⊞. You should have three handouts, each containing two slides. Compare your handouts with the six slides shown in Figure 2-29.

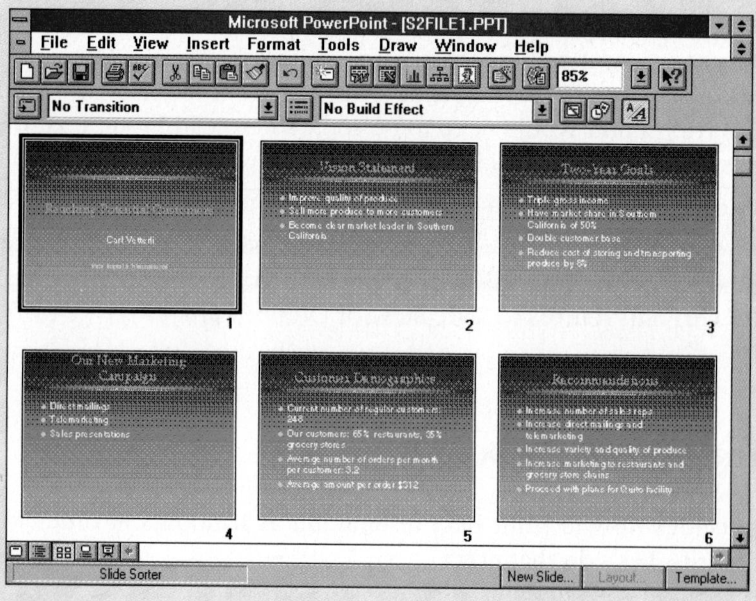

Figure 2-29
Completed presentation in Slide Sorter view

Carl now has a hard copy of his presentation.

Having created, edited, saved, and printed his presentation, Carl is now ready to exit PowerPoint.

To exit PowerPoint:

❶ Click **File**, then click **Exit** (or double-click the **Control menu box** in the upper-left corner of the PowerPoint window).

❷ If PowerPoint asks if you want to save changes to the presentation file, click the **Yes button**.

Your computer screen should now be back to the Program Manager.

■ ■ ■

Questions

1. Describe the purpose of the AutoContent Wizard.
2. Which key(s) do you press or buttons do you click to do the following:
   a. Delete text in Outline view
   b. Move between Outline view and Slide view
   c. Change the color of a font
   d. Increase the size of a font
3. Write a list of steps required to do each of the following:
   a. Promote an item from the main text to a slide title
   b. Change a slide title to a bulleted item within another slide
   c. Delete a slide in Outline view
   d. Add a slide in Outline view
   e. Move text using cut and paste in any view
   f. Move text using drag and drop in any view
   g. Change placeholder text in Outline view
4. Explain the 6 x 6 rule.
5. Explain the meaning of the following terms:
   a. placeholder
   b. title
   c. main text
   d. bullet
   e. promote
   f. demote
   g. font
   h. points
6. Explain the difference between Outline view and Slide view and the benefits of each view.
7. How do you select the text of a placeholder?
8. E After you've made an editing change in PowerPoint, how do you undo it?
9. Give one advantage and one disadvantage of a cut-and-paste operation versus a drag-and-drop operation.
10. Describe how to change the presentation template.

Tutorial Assignments

In the following Tutorial Assignments, make sure you click the Open an Existing File button when you launch PowerPoint (or the Open button on the Standard toolbar) and then open each file. After working with a presentation and saving your changes, close the presentation.

Open the file T2FILE1.PPT, save the file as S2FILE2.PPT and do the following:

1. In Outline view, delete the unnecessary articles "a," "an," and "the" from the main text.
2. In Slide view, change the color of the title of slide 1 from white to red.
3. In Outline view, move the second item in slide 3, "Will develop slide presentation," down so that it becomes the third (last) item in the main text.
4. In slide 4, the third item of the main text is "Step #2. Establishing Contact with Potential Customers." Promote that item to become a slide title (new slide 5).
5. In the current slide 6, demote the second, third, and fourth bulleted items so that they appear indented beneath the first item, "Organize data for our market advantage:".
6. In slides 4 through 7, change the phrases "Step #1," "Step #2," "Step #3," and "Step #4" (but not the text that follows these phrases in the slide titles) to another sans serif font, such as Arial or Futura.
7. Edit the main text of slide 8 so that the phrase "Must hire" becomes simply "Hire."
8. In slide 2, move (through cut and paste or drag and drop) the phrase "by telephone" so it immediately follows the phrase "Follow up" in the same item of the main text.
9. **E** Move the entire slide 9 ("Key Issues") up to become slide 8, so that "Becoming More Effective" is the last slide. Hint: Drag the slide icon in Outline view from one position to another.
10. **E** In slide 2, underline the phrase "New Marketing Campaign" by selecting the phrase and then by clicking the Underline button on the Standard toolbar.
11. **E** Check the spelling within the presentation by using the Spelling button on the Standard toolbar or by clicking Tools, then clicking Spelling. When PowerPoint stops at a word that is misspelled, click the correctly spelled word from within the Suggestions, so that it becomes the "Change To" word, and then click the Change button. If PowerPoint stops at a word that is actually spelled correctly but that it doesn't recognize, click the Ignore button.
12. View the entire presentation in Slide Show mode.
13. Use the Save command to save the presentation to the Student Disk.
14. Print the outline of the presentation.
15. Close the file.

Open the file T2FILE2.PPT, save the file as S2FILE3.PPT, and do the following:

16. Change the template. Choose any template you think looks best.
17. In slide 1, change the text of the name of the author ("Angelena Cristenas") to another color.
18. In the title of slide 2, change "Goal and Objective," to "Objectives".
19. In slide 5, change the title to "Restructuring is Best".
20. **E** Also in slide 5, change the size of the font in the title from 44 to 60 points.

E 21. Insert a new slide between slides 1 and 2 by doing the following: Move the insertion point anywhere within the text of slide 1 in Outline view, then click the Insert New Slide button on the Standard toolbar. (You can also click Insert, then click New Slide.)

22. With the insertion point to the right of the slide icon for the new Slide 2, type the title, "Vision Statement".

23. For the main text in the new slide 2, type the text of the first bulleted item: "Inca Imports can become the premier produce import company in Southern California". Then type the text of the second bulleted item: "Inca Import can triple sales in the next two years".

24. In the new slide 2, change the color of the words "premier" and "triple" to yellow.

25. Edit the main text you added to slide 2 to follow the 6 × 6 rule as closely as possible.

E 26. Check the spelling within the presentation by using the Spelling button on the Standard toolbar or by clicking Tools, then clicking Spelling. When PowerPoint stops at a word that is misspelled, click the correctly spelled word from within the Suggestions, so that it becomes the "Change To" word, and then click the Change button. If PowerPoint stops at a word that is actually spelled correctly but that it doesn't recognize, click the Ignore button.

27. View the entire presentation in Slide Show mode.

28. Use the Save command to save the presentation to the Student Disk.

29. Print a copy of the outline of the presentation.

30. Save the file.

Case Problems

1. New Weave Fashions

Shaunda Shao works for New Weave Fashions, a clothing supplier for specialty retail stores in the northwest. New Weave contracts with wholesale fashion centers to supply New Weave retailers with women's shoes, sports fashions, and boutique merchandise. Shaunda's job is to provide training for New Weave's fledgling retailers.

Open the file P2NWEAVE.PPT, save the file as S2NWEAVE.PPT and do the following:

1. Change the template. Choose the one you think looks best.
2. Increase the font size of the title of slide 1 from 44 to 72 points.
3. In the first bulleted item in slide 2, use cut and paste to move the year ("1993") from the end of the line of text to the beginning, delete the word "in" that now appears at the end of the line, and change "Sales" to "sales".
4. In the second bulleted item in slide 2, use drag and drop to move "increased only 5.5%" from the middle of the line to the end of the line of text.
5. In slide 4, divide the second item into two separate items, and then revise the results so that they become "Obtaining volume discounts," and "Obtaining quick, reliable delivery".
6. Also in slide 4, move the last item ("Competing with well-known stores") so it becomes the second item in the main text of slide 2.
7. In slide 6, promote the phrase "Telephone follow-ups" so that it is on the same level as the bulleted item above it.

E 8. Change the color of title of slide 1 to yellow. Hint: When you click the Text Color button on the Formatting toolbar, yellow might not appear there, so click Other color, then click one of the yellow colored tiles.

E

9. Check the spelling within the presentation by using the Spelling button on the Standard toolbar or by clicking Tools, then clicking Spelling. When PowerPoint stops at a word that is misspelled, click the correctly spelled word from within the Suggestions, so that it becomes the "Change To" word, and then click the Change button. If PowerPoint stops at a word that is actually spelled correctly but that it doesn't recognize, click the Ignore button.
10. Use Slide Show to view all the slides of the presentation.
11. Save the file.
12. Print the outline of the presentation.
13. Print the presentation in black and white.
14. Close the file.

2. InfoTech

Pratt Deitschmann is seeking venture capital in the amount of $2.5 million for his startup company, InfoTech. InfoTech provides mailroom, word processing, in-house printing, and other information-output services for large corporations and law practices. Pratt has created a presentation to give to executives at A.B. O'Dair & Company, a New York City investment banking firm.

Open the file P2INFO.PPT, save the file as S2INFO.PPT, and do the following:

1. Change the font of the title of slide 1 to a sans serif font, such as Arial or Futura.
2. Change the size of the title from 44 to 54 points.
3. Delete "and Objective" from the title of slide 2.
4. Delete the first item of the main text of slide 4.
5. In slide 4, promote the four items that are double-indented to single-indented, so that all items in the main text are at the same level.
6. In slide 4, change the color of the phrase "5% lower" to yellow.
7. In slide 5, move the second item of the main text to become the third (last) item.
8. Move slide 5 so it becomes slide 6.
9. In slide 7, use drag and drop to move the text and make other changes so that the first item becomes "Initial venture capital of $2.5 million".
10. Use Slide Show mode to view the entire presentation.
11. Save the file using the current filename.
12. Print the slides (in black and white) and the outline of the presentation.
13. Close the file.

3. Team One Facilities Management

Virgil Pino works for Team One Facilities Management, a company that manages municipal waste disposal facilities. Virgil must communicate the unfortunate news that escalating travel costs threaten Team One's profitability. Do the following:

1. Close any presentation that might be in the PowerPoint presentation window.

E 2. Begin a new presentation by clicking the New button on the Standard toolbar, clicking Pick a Look wizard, and clicking OK on the New Presentation dialog box. Follow the steps in the Pick a Look Wizard, making the selections as follows:
   a. Step 2: select On-Screen Presentation.
   b. Step 3: select the More button, then select the Travels template (travels.ppt)
   c. Step 4: select all the items.
   d. Step 5 (Slide Options): select Name, company or other text, type the shortened name of the company ("Team One") in place of whatever happens to be in the text box, and select Page Number.
   e. Steps 6–8 (Notes Options, Handout Options, Outline Options): keep the defaults.
   f. Step 9: click the Finish button.

3. Make sure you're in Slide view, then with the new slide 1 on the screen, type the title, "Rescuing Our Road Warriors", and type in the subtitle area the name of the author, "Virgil Pino".

E 4. Virgil has already created some of the text for other slides, so insert the file P2TEAM.PPT into the current presentation. Hint: Click Insert, click Slides from File, and select p2team.ppt from the Student Disk.

5. With slide 2 ("Our Situation") in the presentation window in Slide view, change the word "profitability" in the last bulleted item from black to yellow.

6. In slide 3, add a new bulleted item between the last and the next-to-the-last items. Type the text of the item, "Cost per trip increased by 30%".

E 7. Insert a new slide 4, and from the New Slide dialog box, choose the AutoLayout named "Bulleted list," located on the first row, second column of the AutoLayout box, and click the OK button. Make the title of the slide "Alternatives Considered". Type the following four items in the main text of the slide:
   a. Decrease amount of travel
   b. Decrease travel costs
   c. Increase other means of networking
   d. Increase efficiency of each trip

8. In slide 5, delete the item, "Coordinate trips to visit more clients per trip."

9. Switch to Outline view, and promote the item "Vision for the Future" so that it becomes the title of slide 6.

E 10. Change the fonts of the title and of the main text in slides 2 through 5 so that they are the same as slides 1 and 6. Hint: Click the text in slide 6 and then read the Format toolbar to determine the font and font size in the title and in the main text, then apply those fonts to slides 2 through 4.

11. In slide 6, move the first item in the main text so it becomes the last item.

12. Add a new slide 7, selecting with the title "Summary" and with the bulleted items, "Change to meet growth", "Overcome the efficiency gap", "Manage travel time and money better", and "Rescue our road warriors".

E 13. Create a new slide 8 while still in Outline view. Then go into Slide view and change the Slide Layout to "Blank" (which is the last master style in the Slide Layout dialog box). Hint: To change a slide layout, click Format, click Slide Layout, scroll to the end of the box containing images of layout types and click the very last item, then click the Apply button.

14. Save the presentation using the filename S2TEAM.PPT.
15. Print the slides in black and white.
16. Close the file.

T U T O R I A L 3

Creating Graphics for Your Slides

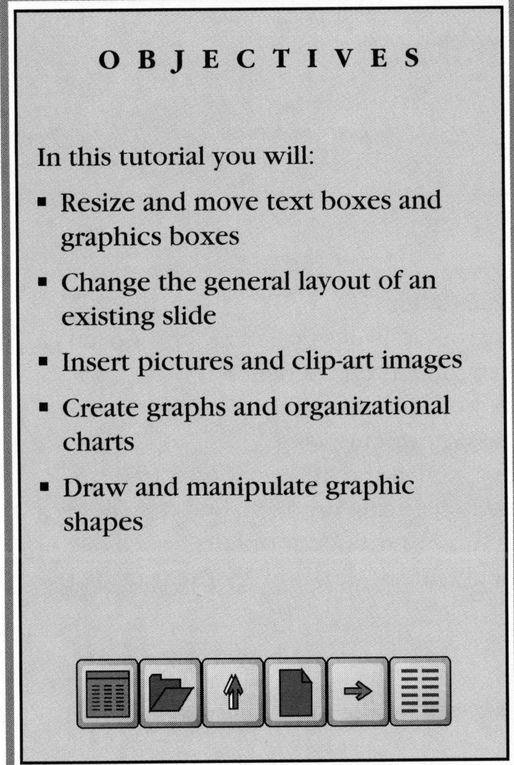

OBJECTIVES

In this tutorial you will:

- Resize and move text boxes and graphics boxes
- Change the general layout of an existing slide
- Insert pictures and clip-art images
- Create graphs and organizational charts
- Draw and manipulate graphic shapes

CASE **Sales Presentation** Using the information gathered previously on customers of Inca Imports International, Enrique Hoffmann, director of marketing, and his staff have identified other businesses in the Southern California area that fit the profile of potential new customers. Enrique and his staff will focus their marketing efforts at these retail customers, who would benefit from having a wide range of fresh produce, year-round availability, and good customer service. Enrique and his staff are ready to prepare a presentation for these prospective clients.

In this tutorial you will create portions of Enrique's presentation, adding graphics to the text that Enrique has already written. A **graphic** is a picture, clip art, graph, chart, or table that you can add to a slide.

USING GRAPHICS EFFECTIVELY

You should use graphics in the following situations:

- To present information that words can't communicate effectively
- To interest and motivate the reader
- To communicate relationships quickly
- To increase understanding and retention

Planning the Presentation

The marketing staff begins by planning their presentation:

- **Purpose for the presentation**: To convince business owners who do not now buy from Inca Imports to start buying our products and services
- **Type of presentation**: A 45-minute sales presentation
- **Audience**: Retail buyers and other business representatives
- **Location of presentation**: A conference room at the offices of Inca Imports
- **Audience needs**: To recognize their need for Inca's products and services and to understand how Inca Imports differs from other produce suppliers
- **Format**: One speaker presenting an electronic slide show consisting of five to seven slides

Manually Changing the Text Layout

After planning the presentation, Enrique and his staff created slides containing only text, knowing that they will need to add graphics to make the presentation more effective. Let's launch PowerPoint and open the current draft of Enrique's presentation.

To open an existing presentation and save it with a new name:

1. Launch PowerPoint and close the Tip of the Day dialog box if necessary. The PowerPoint startup dialog box appears on the screen. You will now retrieve the presentation that Enrique has created using the AutoContent Wizard.
2. Make sure the PowerPoint Student Disk is in drive A or B, then click the **Open Existing Presentation button** in the PowerPoint startup dialog box, and click the **OK Button** or press **[Enter]**. The Open dialog box appears on the screen.

   TROUBLE? If the PowerPoint startup dialog box does not appear on your screen, click the Open button on the Standard toolbar to display the Open dialog box.
3. Click the **Down Arrow** to the right of the Drives box, then click **a:** or **b:** (whichever drive contains your Student Disk).
4. Click **c3file1.ppt** in Files list box, and then click the **OK button**. The file C3FILE1.PPT appears in the presentation window. See Figure 3-1.

As you can see, PowerPoint displays an outline, consisting of Enrique's title slide (slide 1) and six additional slides. Now let's save the presentation using a different filename so that Enrique's original presentation file remains undisturbed.

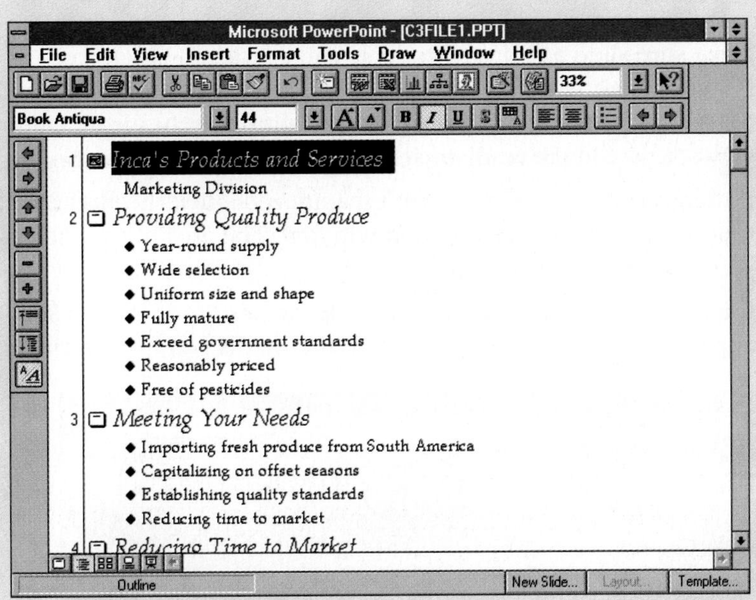

Figure 3-1
Presentation in the presentation window

5. Click **File**, then click **Save As** to open the Save As dialog box.
6. Make sure the drive containing your Student Disk is in the Drives list box, then edit the current filename to become **s3file1** and click the **OK button** or press **[Enter]**.

   The Summary Info dialog box appears on the screen, with the information that Enrique typed previously.
7. Click the **OK button** or press **[Enter]**. PowerPoint saves the presentation to the disk with the new filename.

Enrique is satisfied with his outline, and he is ready to add graphics to the slide. To do this, he will work in Slide view, which allows him to view and modify the position, size, and alignment of text boxes and graphics. **Text boxes** are the regions of the slide that contain text. Text boxes and graphics are objects. An **object** is any item (text box, clip art, graph, organization chart, picture) on a slide that you can move, resize, rotate, or otherwise manipulate.

Enrique first wants to add the company logo to the title slide. A company logo is a visual identification for the company. Enrique needs to make room for the logo by moving the three text boxes on the slide.

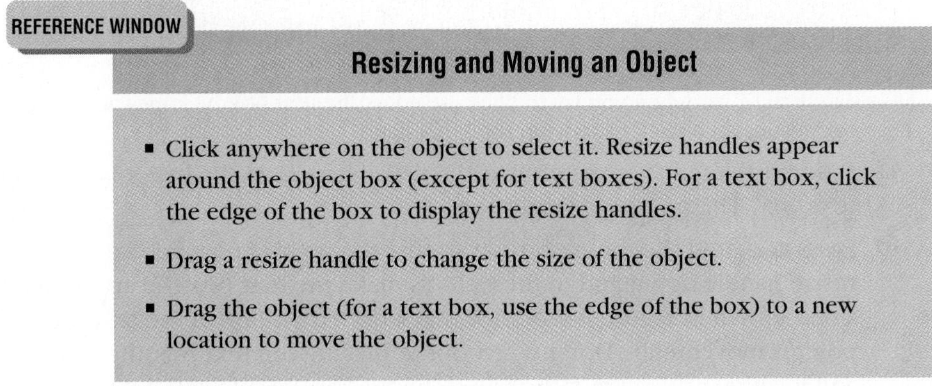
REFERENCE WINDOW

Resizing and Moving an Object

- Click anywhere on the object to select it. Resize handles appear around the object box (except for text boxes). For a text box, click the edge of the box to display the resize handles.
- Drag a resize handle to change the size of the object.
- Drag the object (for a text box, use the edge of the box) to a new location to move the object.

Let's rearrange the text boxes so that the logo will fit on the left side of the slide.

To resize and move text on a slide:

1. Make sure slide 1, "Inca's Products and Services," is selected (or the insertion point is somewhere within the text of slide 1) in Outline view, then click the **Slide View button**, on the View toolbar. PowerPoint switches from Outline view to Slide view. Now you are ready to select and rearrange the text boxes.
2. If the presentation window isn't maximized, click the **Maximize button** in the upper-right corner of the presentation window. The area of the slide is maximized so that you can see the entire slide.
3. Click anywhere in the text of the title "Inca's Products and Services." The text box appears. See Figure 3-2. Notice that the text is centered in the text box.

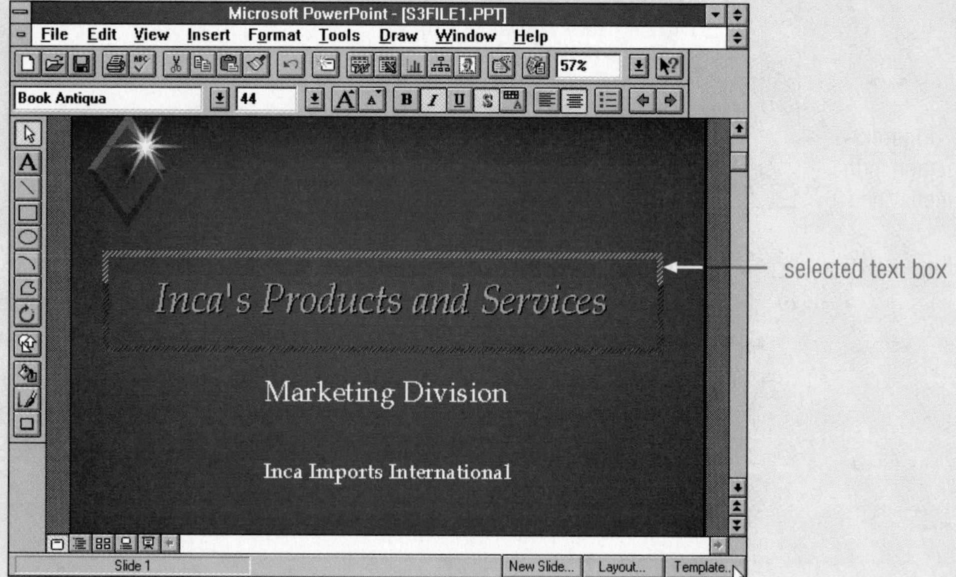

Figure 3-2
Selected text box

4. Click the edge of the text box. PowerPoint displays the resize handles around the text box. See Figure 3-3.

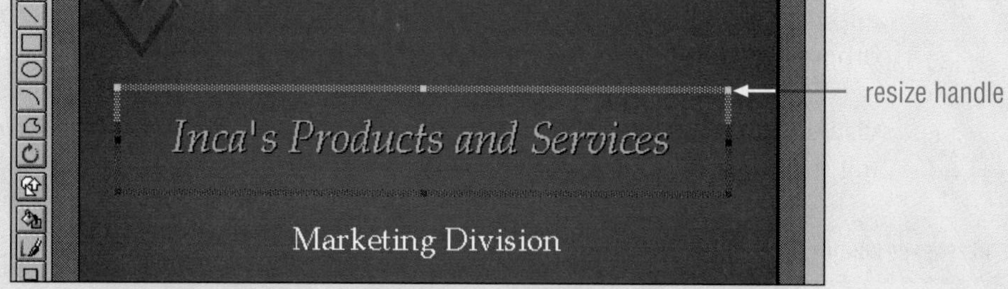

Figure 3-3
Selected text box with resize handles

TROUBLE? If, when you try to click the edge, the text box becomes deselected, click the text again, then click exactly on the box edge.

5. Position the mouse pointer over the resize handle in the lower-left corner of the text box. The pointer changes to ⤢.
6. Press and hold the mouse button so that the pointer changes to +, then drag the resize handle down and to the right to make the text box the approximate dimensions shown in Figure 3-4. Notice that a dotted outline of the text box follows the pointer movements. Don't worry about making the text box the exact same size and location as shown in the figure. Just resize it as closely as you can.

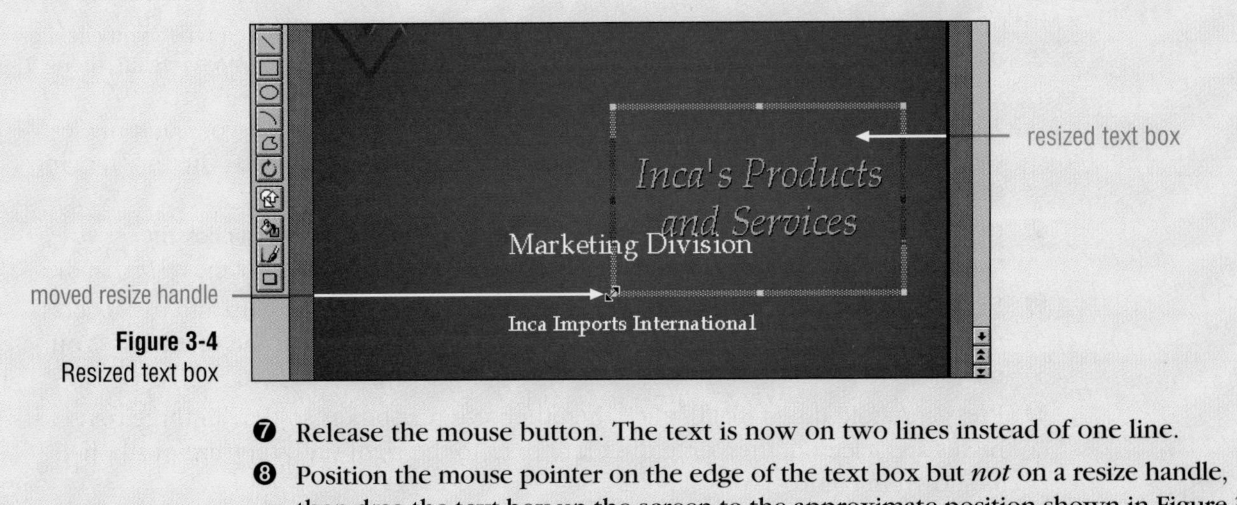

Figure 3-4
Resized text box

❼ Release the mouse button. The text is now on two lines instead of one line.

❽ Position the mouse pointer on the edge of the text box but *not* on a resize handle, then drag the text box up the screen to the approximate position shown in Figure 3-5.

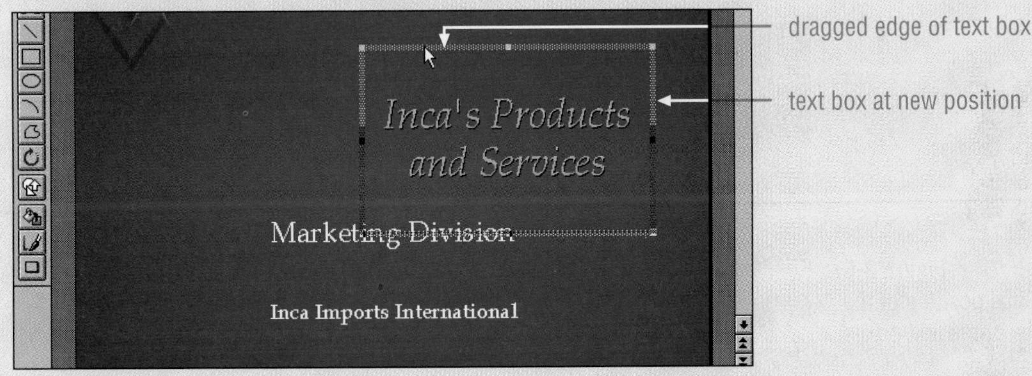

Figure 3-5
Position of text box after dragging

Enrique now wants to align the text in the three boxes along their left margins and then move the text to the right. Let's do that now.

To align and move the text boxes:

❶ With the "Inca's Products" text box still selected, press and hold down **[Shift]**, click the other two text boxes, then release **[Shift]**.

As you can see, by holding down [Shift] while you click text on a slide, you can select more than one text box at a time. Notice that only the resize handles of the three text boxes are visible. You can modify all the selected text at once. First Enrique wants to change the text alignment so that it is aligned on the left side of the text boxes rather than centered, then he wants to align the text boxes themselves.

❷ Click the **Left Alignment button** on the Formatting toolbar. The text in each of the three text boxes becomes aligned on the left edge of its text box. Now you are ready to align the text boxes so their left edges are at the same horizontal position on the slide.

❸ Click **Draw**, click **Align**, and then click **Lefts**. The text boxes become aligned along their left edges.

❹ With all three text boxes still selected, position the mouse pointer on one of the text boxes, then drag the boxes to the right as far as they will go.

TROUBLE? If + appeared and the text boxes resize handles disappeared when you clicked the mouse button, you clicked outside of the text boxes. Select the text boxes again, then repeat Step 4.

As you can see, the "Marketing Division" text box is so large that you can't move the text very far to the right. Let's change the size of that text box, then try moving the slides again.

5. Click anywhere outside the text to deselect the three text boxes, then click the "Marketing Division" text box to select it, and click the edge to display the resize handles.
6. Drag the resize handle in the lower-right corner of the text box up and to the left to decrease the size of the box until it's just a little bigger than the text itself. You may have to scroll down a little to see the bottom of the text box.
7. Press and hold down **[Shift]**, click the other two text boxes so that all three text boxes are selected, then drag the text boxes to the right until they are positioned as shown in Figure 3-6.

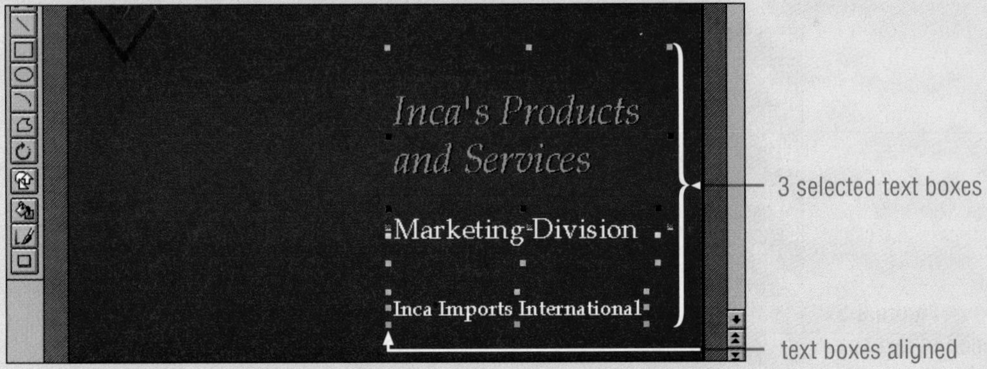

Figure 3-6
Final position of the three text boxes

Having changed the size, position, and alignment of the text boxes, Enrique is ready to insert the company logo into the slide.

Inserting a Picture into a Slide

Enrique now wants to insert the Inca Imports International logo, a computer-generated image of fruit. Enrique wants to insert the logo to the left of the text boxes.

REFERENCE WINDOW

Inserting a Picture into a Slide

- Click Insert, then click Picture to display the Picture dialog box.
- Select the desired picture file from the disk, then click the OK button.
- Move and resize the picture as desired.

Let's insert the logo now.

To insert a picture into a slide:

1. Click **Insert**, then click **Picture**. The Insert Picture dialog box appears on the screen.
2. Make sure the Student Disk is in the disk drive, and select drive **a:** (or whichever drive contains your Student Disk) from the Drives box.

3. Click **iiilogo.bmp** in the File Names list to select the Inca Imports International logo, and then click the **OK button** or press **[Enter]**. The picture appears in the middle of the slide. The picture remains selected, as you can see from the handles around the edge of the graphic.
4. With the logo still selected, drag the graphics box to the left of the text so that the bottom edge of the logo is aligned with the last line of text, as shown in Figure 3-7, then click anywhere outside the slide to deselect the picture.

   TROUBLE? If you accidentally resized the graphic rather than moved it, click Undo in the Edit menu.

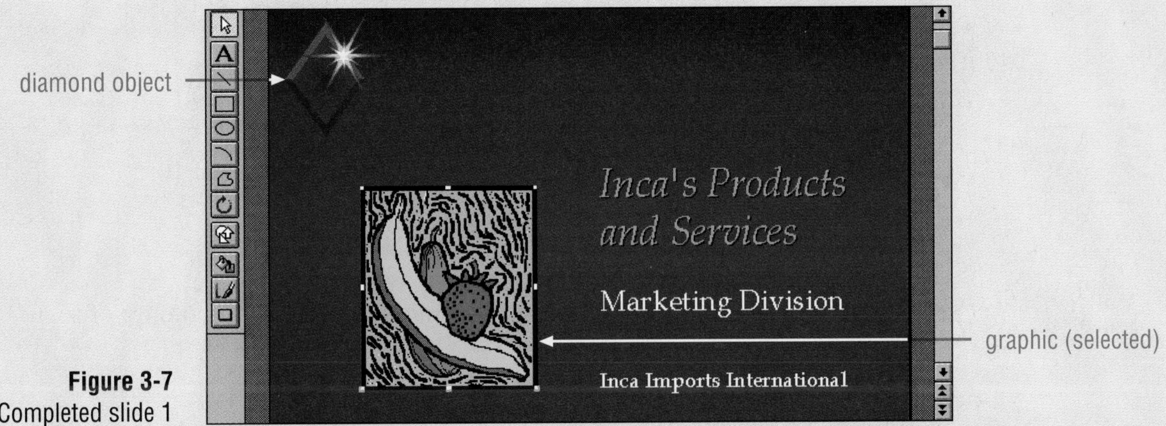

Figure 3-7
Completed slide 1

Enrique looks at his slide and feels that the background diamond shape doesn't go well with the logo, so he decides to eliminate the diamond.

5. Click **Format**, then click **Slide Background**. The Slide Background dialog box appears.
6. Click the **Display Objects on This Slide check box** at the top of the dialog box two times to deselect it. See Figure 3-8. This will delete the object, in this case, the diamond, from the slide background.

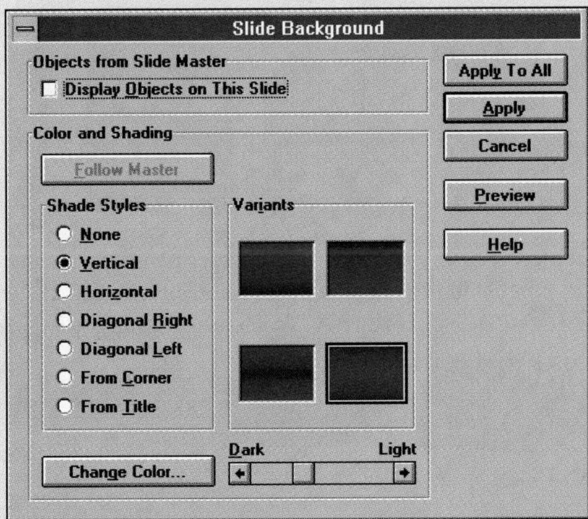

Figure 3-8

7. Click the **Apply button** (*not* the Apply to All button). The diamond no longer appears on the slide. That completes the work on this slide.
8. Click the **Next Slide button** at the bottom of the vertical scroll bar to view slide 2.

You are ready to work on slide 2 of Enrique's presentation.

Changing the Layout Using AutoLayout

Enrique wants to add an item to the bulleted list in slide 2, "Providing Quality Produce." He decides that with the addition of this item, the bulleted list will be too long to fit on the slide. The slide might look better with two columns. He could reformat the slide manually, but he decides to use an AutoLayout.

REFERENCE WINDOW

Changing the Layout of a Slide

- Get into Slide view and then move to (display) the slide whose layout you want to change.
- Click the Layout button in the status bar to display the Slide Layout dialog box.
- Click the layout that corresponds to the desired slide layout, and then click the Reapply button.

Let's change the layout of the slide now to accommodate a second column of text.

To change the layout of an existing slide:

1. Click the **Layout button** in the status bar. PowerPoint displays the Slide Layout dialog box. See Figure 3-9.

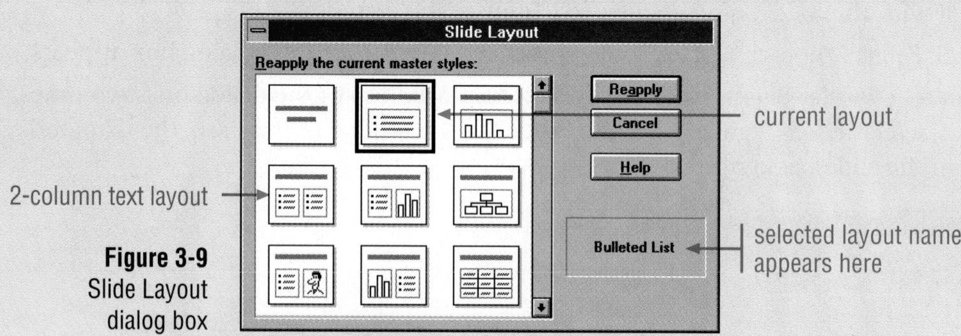

Figure 3-9 Slide Layout dialog box

2. Click the layout with the **2 Column Text** layout.

   TROUBLE? If you're not sure which is the 2 Column Text layout, click each picture until the box at the lower right of the dialog box displays the name "2 Column Text." On most computers, it is the picture in the second row, first column, as shown in Figure 3-9.

3. Click the **Apply button**. PowerPoint reformats the slide, with a new text box on the right. See Figure 3-10.

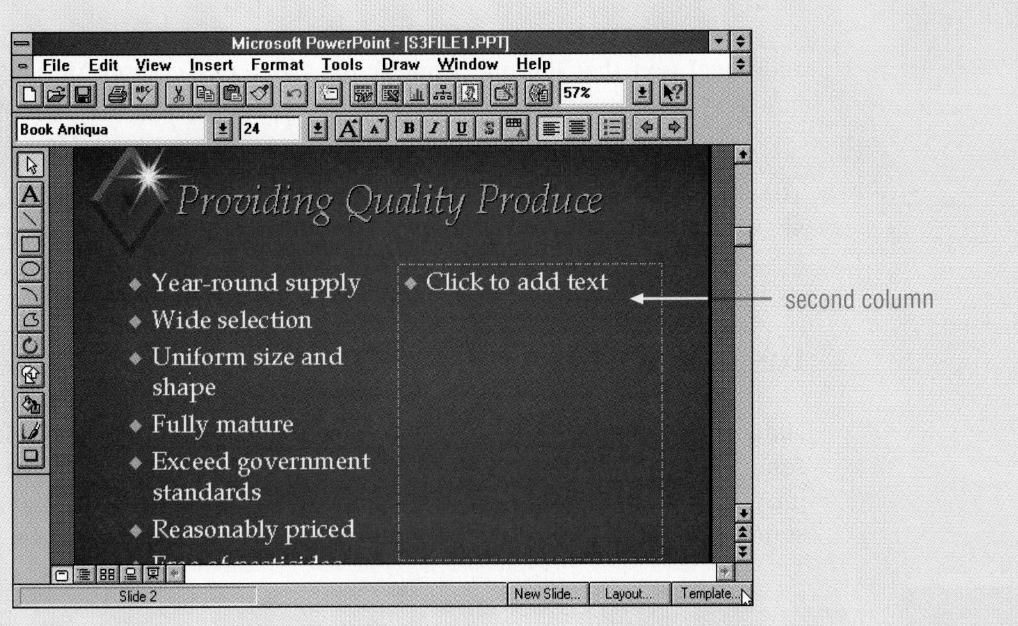

Figure 3-10
New layout of slide 2

Enrique is ready to add the new final item to the bulleted list.

To add text to a new text box:

1. Click anywhere within the text box that says, "**Click to add text.**" PowerPoint removes the message that was in the text box, displays a bullet, and positions the insertion point to the right of the bullet.
2. Type **Hand picked** and press **[Enter]**.

   Now Enrique wants to move the last three items in the first column to the end of the second column so the columns are balanced.
3. Click anywhere on the text in the first column. The text box becomes selected.
4. Scroll down so you can see the last three items in the first column.
5. Position the mouse pointer over the bullet next to "Exceed government standards." The mouse pointer changes to ✥.
6. Click the mouse button, press and hold **[Shift]**, click the bullets next to "Reasonably priced" and "Free of pesticides," then release **[Shift]**.
7. Click the **Cut button** on the Standard toolbar. The text disappears from the screen and is moved to the Clipboard.
8. Press **[Backspace]** to delete the fifth bullet in the first column.
9. Click I just after the second bullet in the second column, then click the **Paste button** on the Standard toolbar. The three cut items appear in the second column. See Figure 3-11.

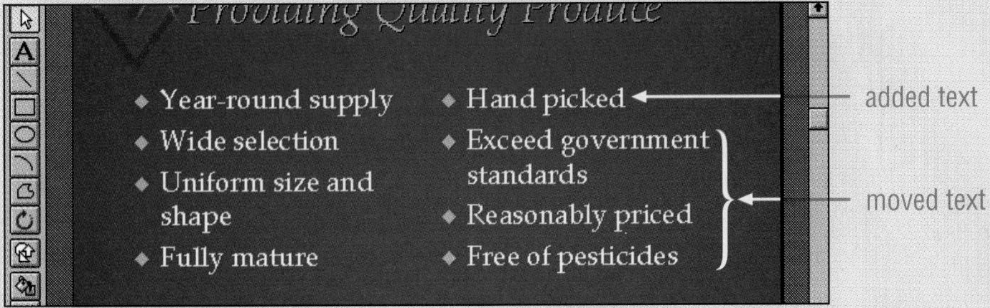

Figure 3-11
Completed slide 2

You have completed slide 2 of Enrique's presentation. The slide now contains the additional text that Enrique wanted and has a two-column design to accommodate the new text in an attractive and readable way. Enrique now wants to look at slide 3.

To move to the next slide:

1. Click the **Next Slide button** at the bottom of the vertical scroll bar.

Inserting Clip Art

Slide 3, "Meeting Your Needs," has four items of information. Enrique wants to include some clip art to add interest to this slide. In PowerPoint, **clip art** specifically refers to images in the Microsoft Clip Art Gallery, whereas **picture** is any image from some other source, including clip-art libraries supplied by other companies.

DESIGN PRINCIPLE WINDOW

Selecting an Appropriate Type of Graphic

- Consider your audience: job, experience, education, culture
- Consider your purpose: to inform, persuade, instruct, identify, interest, motivate
- Consider the type of information on the slide: numerical values, logical relationships, procedures and processes, visual and spatial characteristics

Let's now change the layout of the slide and add clip art to it.

To change the layout of the slide and add clip art:

1. Click the **Layout button** in the status bar to display the Slide Layout dialog box, click the layout with the description of **Text & Clip Art**, then click the **Apply button** to change the layout of the slide. See Figure 3-12.

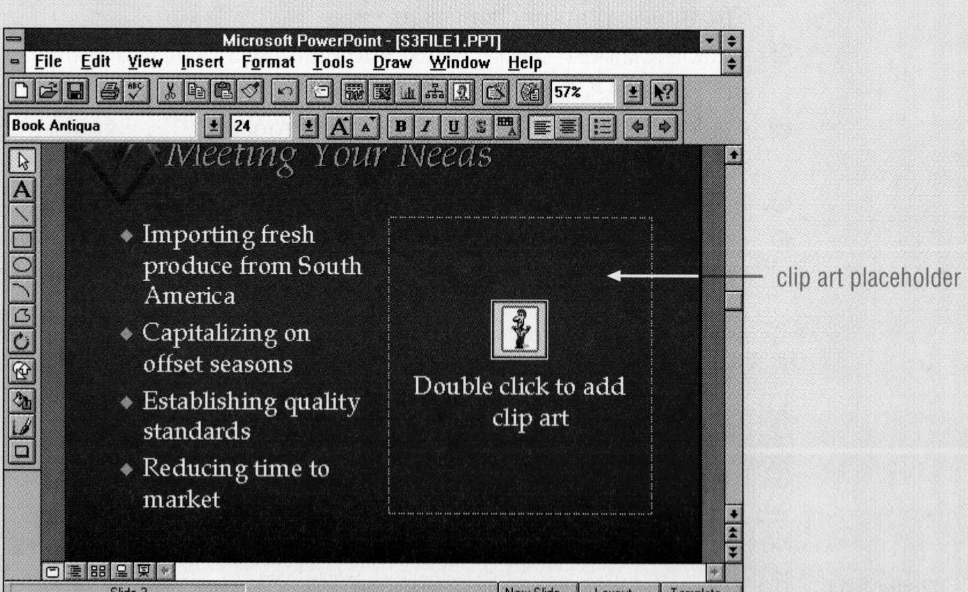

Figure 3-12
New layout of slide 3

❷ Double-click the box labeled "**Double click to add clip art.**" PowerPoint displays the Microsoft Clip Art Gallery dialog box. See Figure 3-13.

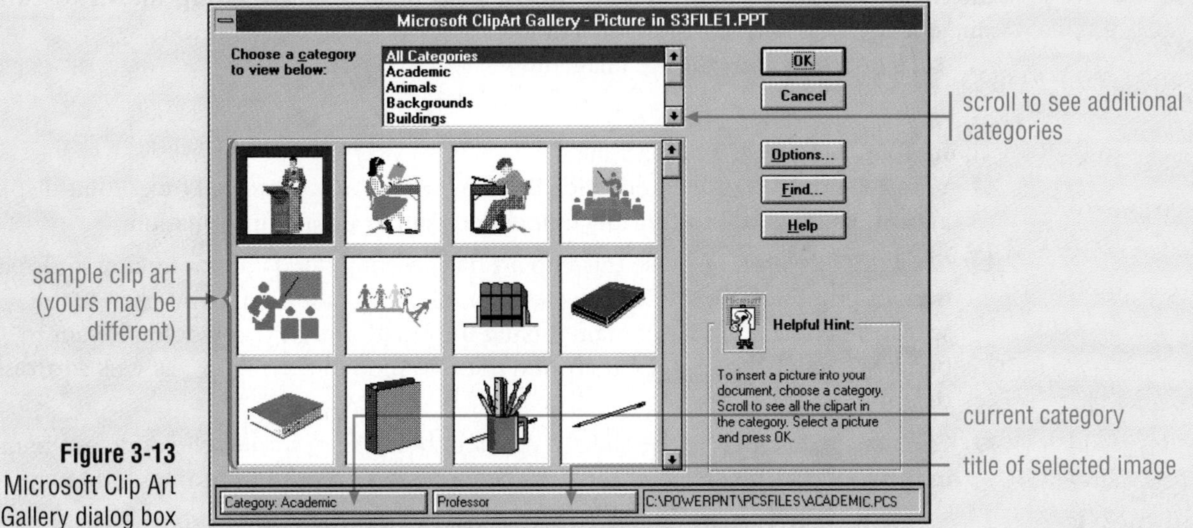

Figure 3-13 Microsoft Clip Art Gallery dialog box

TROUBLE? If PowerPoint displays a dialog box with the question, "Would you like to add clip art from PowerPoint now?," click the Yes button and then wait for PowerPoint to set up its built-in clip-art library.

❸ Scroll the "Choose a category to view below" list box until you see "People," then click **People** to select that category.

TROUBLE? If you don't see a list of categories for the clip-art library, or if the clip art is missing altogether, consult your technical support person or instructor. If you do have clip art to choose from, but you don't have the People category, choose any clip art you prefer in order to complete these steps.

❹ Scroll the clip-art images within the People category until you see the image of two men standing by a world map, then click that image. See Figure 3-14. The clip-art title at the bottom of the dialog box gives the name of the image, "World Map and Men."

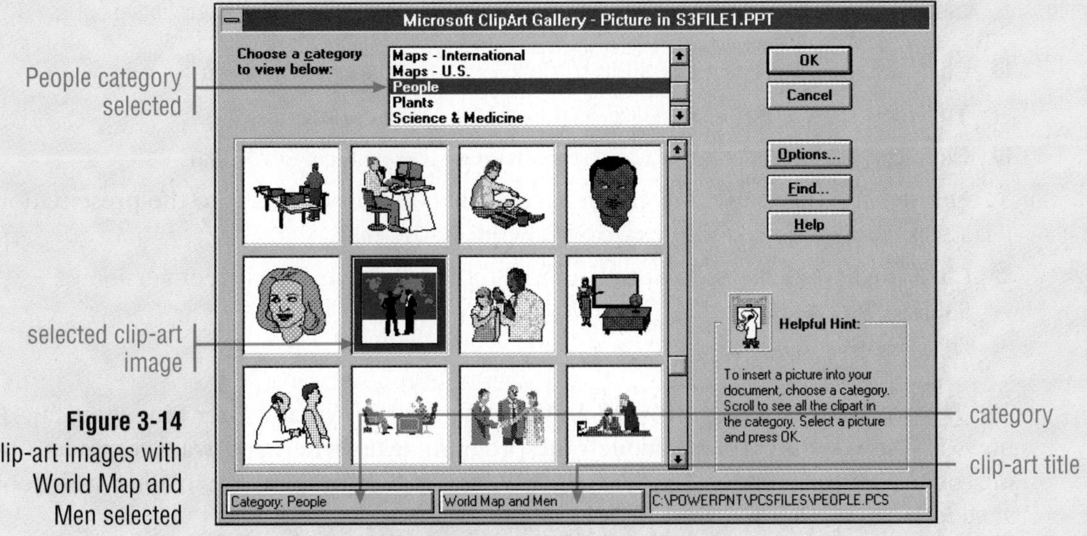

Figure 3-14 Clip-art images with World Map and Men selected

❺ Click the **OK button**. The clip art is inserted into the slide.

Enrique would like the men to point to South America rather than to Africa. To do this, he will ungroup the image into individual objects, then move the object comprising the men to a new location relative to the map object. To **ungroup** means to convert a single image into smaller, individual objects.

Let's ungroup and edit the image now.

To ungroup and edit the clip art image:

1. With the image still selected, click **Draw** and then click **Ungroup**. PowerPoint displays a warning about discarding any embedded data or linking information.
2. Click the **OK button**, because this clip art has no embedded data or linking information. (A graph from a spreadsheet, which might be modified if you change the spreadsheet data, would contain linking information that you wouldn't want to break.) Resize handles appear around the two men in the picture as well as around the world map.
3. Click in a blank area of the slide to deselect both images, then click one of the men in the clip art. The image of the men becomes selected, but not the world map.

   TROUBLE? If you didn't use the World Map and Men clip-art image, your image may not be able to ungroup, or if it does ungroup, you may not be able to individually select one of the items. If this occurs, skip to the next section, "Inserting a Graph."
4. Drag the men to the left and down so that they point to the northern part of South America, as shown in Figure 3-15. To position the selected image more precisely, press [↓], [↑], or [←] to move the image in very small increments.

Figure 3-15 Clip art after ungrouping and moving men

5. Click in a blank area of the slide to deselect the image of the men.

   You have now completed slide 3 of Enrique's presentation.
6. Click the **Next Slide button** at the bottom of the vertical scroll bar.

   Enrique and the marketing group have made considerable edits to the presentation, so they decide they should save their work to the disk.
7. Click the **Save button** on the Standard toolbar to save the current version of S3FILE1.PPT to the disk.

If you want to take a break and resume the tutorial at a later time, you can do so now. If you exit PowerPoint, launch the program again when you want to resume working, open the presentation file S3FILE1.PPT, and make sure you are in Slide view looking at slide 4. Then continue with the next section.

■ ■ ■

Inserting a Graph

On slide 4 of his presentation, Enrique wants to add a column chart that compares Inca Imports International's time to market (that is, the time from picking to customer delivery, in hours) during the past four quarters with the other two major produce import companies in southern California.

REFERENCE WINDOW

Inserting a Column Chart

- Display the desired slide in Slide view.
- If necessary, change the Slide Layout to "Text & Graph" or "Graphic & Text."
- Double-click the area marked "Double click to add graph." PowerPoint displays a data sheet.
- Edit the information in the data sheet for the data that you want to plot.
- Click anywhere outside the data sheet, then click anywhere outside the graph box.

Let's add the graph now.

To add a column chart to the slide:

❶ Click the **Layout button** in the status bar, click the layout with the name **Text & Graph** (it's the picture in the second row in the second column), then click the **Apply button**. The text on the slide becomes formatted into a smaller text box on the left side of the slide, and a graphs box placeholder appears on the right side.

❷ Double-click the **graphs box placeholder**. After a minute or more, PowerPoint inserts a sample graph and displays a data sheet, similar to a spreadsheet such as Microsoft Excel or Lotus 1-2-3 in a window in the center of the screen.

TROUBLE? Don't worry if the colors on the slide become distorted. They'll return to normal once you close the data sheet window.

With the sample graph and data sheet on the screen, you simply change the information in the data sheet to create your own graph. The information on the data sheet is stored in **cells**, which are the little boxes that contain a number, word or phrase. The cells are organized into rows and columns. The rows are numbered 1, 2, 3. . ., whereas the columns are labeled A, B, C. . . . Enrique edits the information in the data sheet to reflect the three companies' times to market. Let's do that now.

To edit the information in the data sheet:

❶ Position the mouse pointer over the cell that contains the word "**East.**" The pointer changes to ✚.

❷ Click the cell that contains the word "**East,**" and type **SCP** (which stands for "Southern California Produce," one of the major competitors of Inca Imports).

❸ Press[↓] to select the cell labeled "**West**," then type **CCF** (which stands for "Central City Foods," the other major competitor of Inca Imports).

❹ Repeat Step 3 to replace "**North**" with **Inca**. See Figure 3-16. Now you're ready to change the actual numbers in the data sheet.

Figure 3-16 Data sheet after changing labels

S3FILE1.PPT - Datasheet

		A	B	C	D
		1st Qtr	2nd Qtr	3rd Qtr	4th Qtr
1	SCP	20.4	27.4	90	20.4
2	CCF	30.6	38.6	34.6	31.6
3	Inca	45.9	46.9	45	43.9
4					

new labels

❺ Click cell **A1**, the cell at which column A and row 1 intersect, then type **18**. This is the average time to market in hours of SCP during the first quarter of the year.

❻ Press **[Tab]** or [→] to select cell **B1**, type **27**, press **[Tab]**, type **22**, press **[Tab]**, then type **20**. This completes the data for SCP.

❼ Using the same procedure as in Steps 5 and 6, replace the current data for CCF and for Inca, using the figures shown in Figure 3-17. Carefully check the data sheet to make sure it matches Figure 3-17. Make any corrections necessary.

Figure 3-17 Completed data sheet

S3FILE1.PPT - Datasheet

		A	B	C	D
		1st Qtr	2nd Qtr	3rd Qtr	4th Qtr
1	SCP	18	27	22	20
2	CCF	30	38	34	32
3	Inca	16	18	17	16
4					

❽ Click anywhere outside the data sheet but still within the graph box (for example, in the lower-right corner of the graph box) to remove the data sheet from the screen. The completed graph appears on the screen.

Now Enrique wants to insert a title to label the vertical axis of his graph. Let's do that now.

To insert a title into a graph:

❶ Click **Insert**, then click **Titles**. PowerPoint displays the Titles dialog box.

❷ Click the **Value (Z Axis check box)**, then click the **OK button**. PowerPoint displays a small text box to the left of the vertical axis with the letter "Z" as its contents.

❸ Double-click one of the resize handles of the **Z-axis title**. The Format Axis Title dialog box appears on the screen. See Figure 3-18.

TROUBLE? If you clicked or double-clicked inside the text box, the resize handles disappear. Click within the graph box but outside of any other object in the box, for example, in the lower-right corner of the graph box, then double-click the Z-axis title. If the Format Plot Area dialog box appears as a result of Step 3, click the cancel button, then follow the steps described in this TROUBLE? paragraph.

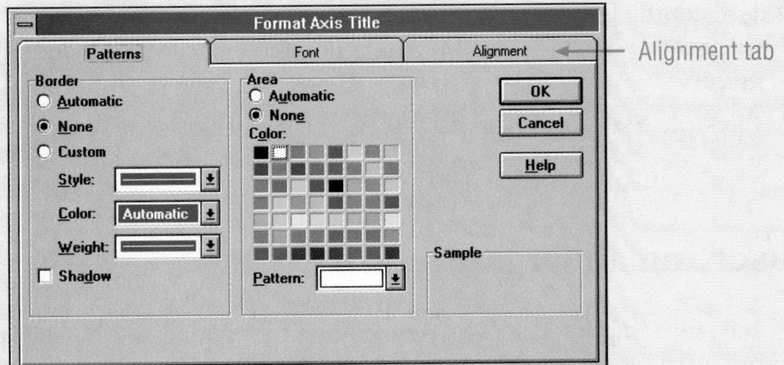

Figure 3-18 Format Axis Title dialog box

4. Click the **Alignment** folder tab at the top of the dialog box, then in the Orientation box, click the "Text" with the vertical orientation (it reads bottom to top). It's the middle box in the row of three boxes.
5. Click the **OK button** to return to the graph on the slide.
6. Click on the **"Z"** in the Z-axis title, delete the Z (for example, by pressing **[Backspace]**), then type **Hours**. This indicates that graphed time from picking to delivery is in hours. Click anywhere within the graph box but outside of other objects to deselect the title.

   Enrique notices that the word "2nd" on the X-axis label is split in two, so he decides to increase the width of the graph to allow more room for the text.
7. Position the mouse pointer over the left center resize handle, wait a moment for the double-arrow pointer to appear, then drag the handle left until the left edge of the graph is near the right edge of the text of the slide. You may have to wait a minute while holding the mouse button before the box will actually resize. See Figure 3-19.

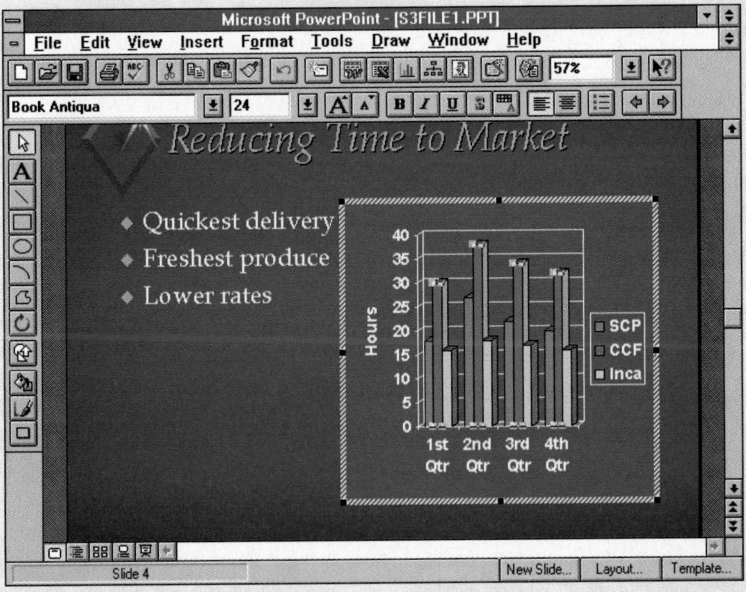

Figure 3-19 Completed graph in slide 4

TROUBLE? If your graph doesn't look like Figure 3-19, click the View Datasheet button in the Graph toolbar to display the data sheet. Make the necessary revisions by comparing your data sheet with Figure 3-17.

You have now completed slide 4 of Enrique's presentation. Let's deselect the graph and go to the next slide.

To deselect the graph and advance to the next slide:

1. Click twice outside the graph area, once to exit the graph and once to deselect the graph.
2. Click the **Next Slide button** on the vertical scroll bar.

Inserting an Organization Chart

Because Inca Imports is a fairly new company, Enrique and his staff feel that it's important for potential clients to understand the high level of experience of Inca employees in the import and produce businesses. Enrique decides that an organization chart will communicate this information better than a bulleted list. Let's create the organization chart now.

To create an organization chart:

1. Click the **Insert Org Chart button** on the Standard toolbar. After a few moments, the Microsoft Organization Chart window appears on the screen with the Organization Chart toolbar across the top.
2. Click the **Maximize button** on the Organization Chart window to make it cover the entire screen. See Figure 3-20. A chart with text placeholders is in the window. The chart has two levels of organization. The first box, at the top of the chart, is already selected, as you can tell from its black background. When you start typing, the text will appear in that selected box.

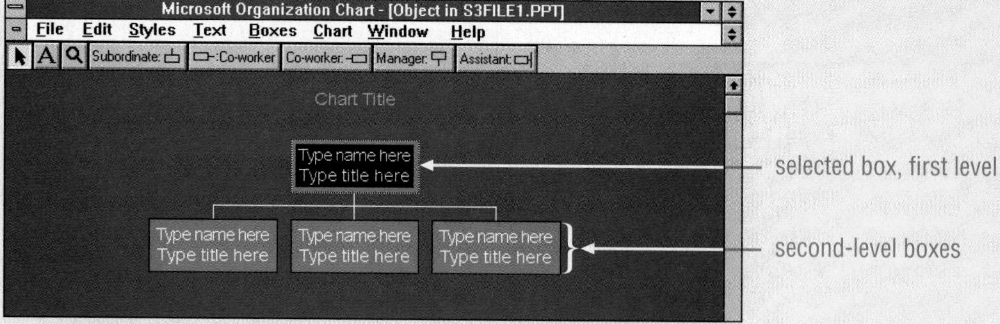

Figure 3-20 Microsoft Organization Chart window

3. Type **Patricia Cuevas.** As soon as you started typing, the box expanded to display four lines.
4. Press **[Tab]** or **[Enter]**. The placeholder text "Type title here" becomes selected.
5. Type **President**, press **[Tab]**, and type **13 years experience**. This completes the first box.
6. Click the second-level box on the left side. The box becomes selected, as shown by its black background.
7. Type **Angelena Cristenas**, press **[Tab]**, type **V.P. of Operations**, press **[Tab]**, and type **13 years experience**. This completes the text of that text box in the organization chart.
8. Using the same procedure as in Steps 6 and 7, complete the other two boxes of the organization chart, so that they contain the text shown in Figure 3-21, then click anywhere within the Microsoft Organization Chart window but outside of any text or organization box.

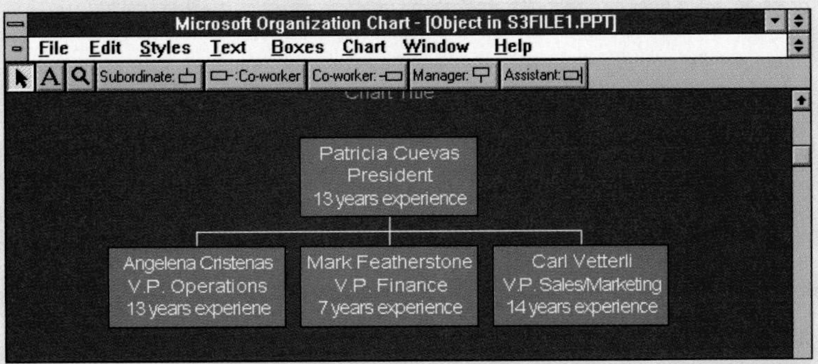

Figure 3-21
First two levels of organization chart

9. If you made any typing errors, click the box containing the error, then press **[Tab]** until the line containing the error is highlighted, then retype that line.

You have completed the first two levels of the organization chart. Enrique also wants to show the experience personnel at Inca Imports have in handling produce and responding to customer delivery needs. The customer service employees work under Angelena Cristenas. Let's add the new levels of organization now.

To add subordinate levels to an organization chart:

1. Click the **Subordinate button** Subordinate: on the Organization Chart toolbar. The mouse pointer changes to .
2. Click the box containing "Angelena Cristenas." A new organization level appears below Angelena's box. See Figure 3-22. The small black box within the new box indicates that the new box is selected and ready for you to type new text.

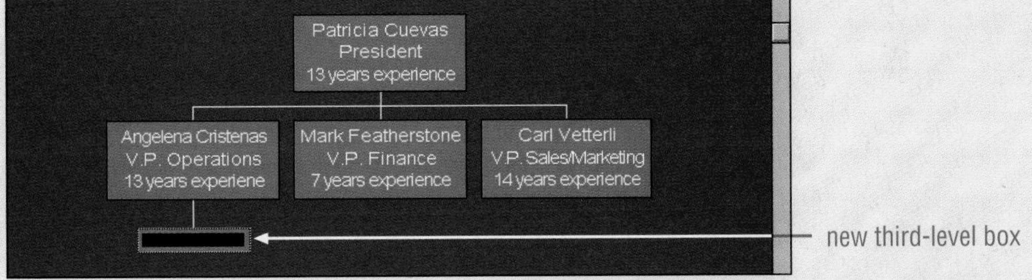

Figure 3-22
New organization level

3. Type **Carlos Becerra**. As soon as you begin to type, the other text placeholders appear in the box.
4. Press **[Tab]**, type **QA Manager**, press **[Tab]**, and type **22 years experience**. This completes the box for Carlos Becerra, QA (quality assurance) manager.
5. Click Subordinate: and click the box containing "Carlos Becerra" to add a subordinate box underneath Carlos.
6. Type **Norma Lopez**, press **[Tab]**, type **Customer Service**, press **[Tab]**, and type **8 years experience**, then click anywhere in the Organization Chart window but outside of any text or box. Your chart should now look like Figure 3-23.

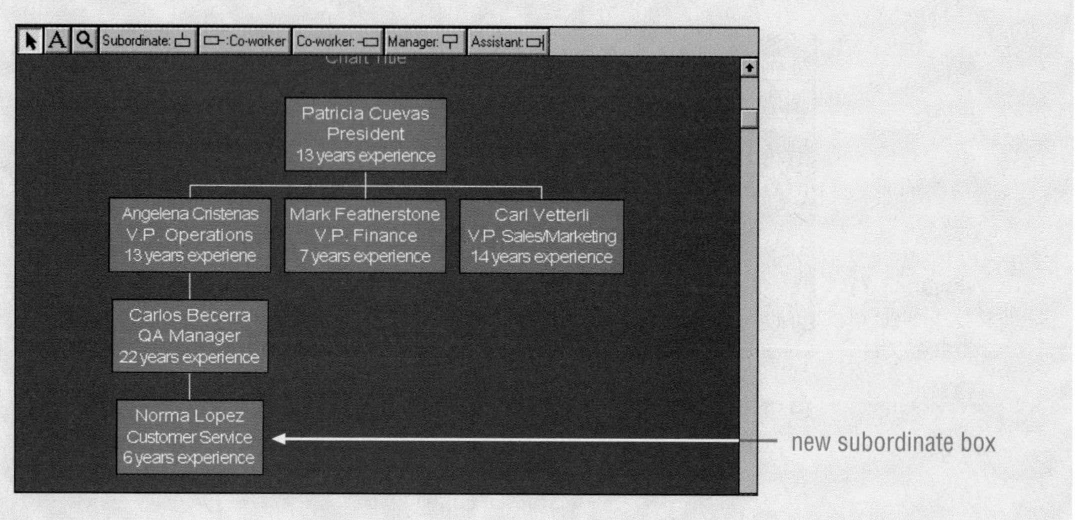

Figure 3-23
Chart after adding a subordinate box

Enrique decides to add a coworker to the chart. Let's do it now.

To add a coworker to an organization chart:

❶ Click the right **Coworker button** Co-worker: on the Organization Chart toolbar. The mouse changes to ⊣▭. This allows you to add a coworker box to the right of an existing box.

❷ Click the box containing **"Norma Lopez"** to add a new box to its right, type **Juanita Rojas**, press **[Tab]**, type **Manager, Quito Center**, press **[Tab]**, type **3 years experience**, and click anywhere in the window but outside of any box or text.

You have completed the organization chart. You now have to exit the Organization Chart window and add the organization chart to the slide.

To exit the Organization Chart window and add the chart to the slide:

❶ Click **File**, then click **Exit and return to S3FILE1.PPT**. A dialog box appears on the screen asking if you want to update the object. The object in this case is the new organizational chart.

❷ Click the **Yes button**. After looking over the organization chart, Enrique thinks it should be bigger.

❸ Drag the resize handle in the upper-left corner up and to the left, and drag the resize handle in the lower-right corner down and to the right until the organization chart is approximately the size shown in Figure 3-24.

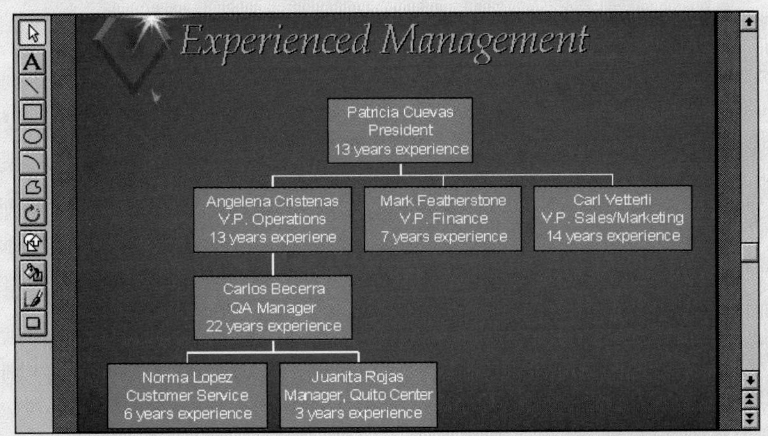

Figure 3-24 Completed organization chart in slide 5

4. Click anywhere outside the selected organization chart to deselect it. Slide 5 now looks like Figure 3-24.

   This completes the five current slides in Enrique's presentation. However, he has decided to add one more slide to the presentation.

5. Click the **Next Slide button** on the vertical scroll bar.

If you want to take a break and resume the tutorial at a later time, you can do so now. If you exit PowerPoint, launch the program again when you want to resume working, open the presentation file S3FILE1.PPT, and make sure you are in Slide view looking at slide 6. Then continue with the next section.

■ ■ ■

Creating and Manipulating a Shape

Enrique wants to add a simple drawing with text to slide 6 to demonstrate the three major benefits of the company. To do this, Enrique wants to insert an inverted triangle onto slide 6. Let's do that now.

To insert a shape onto a slide:

1. Click the **AutoShapes button** on the Drawing toolbar. PowerPoint displays the AutoShapes palette.
2. Click the **Isosceles Triangle Tool button** on the AutoShapes palette. The mouse pointer changes to the cross-bar pointer.
3. Position + an inch below the first "n" in "International" (in the title of the slide), then drag down and to the right. The outline of a triangle appears as you drag.
4. Release the mouse button when your triangle is approximately the same size as the one in Figure 3-25.

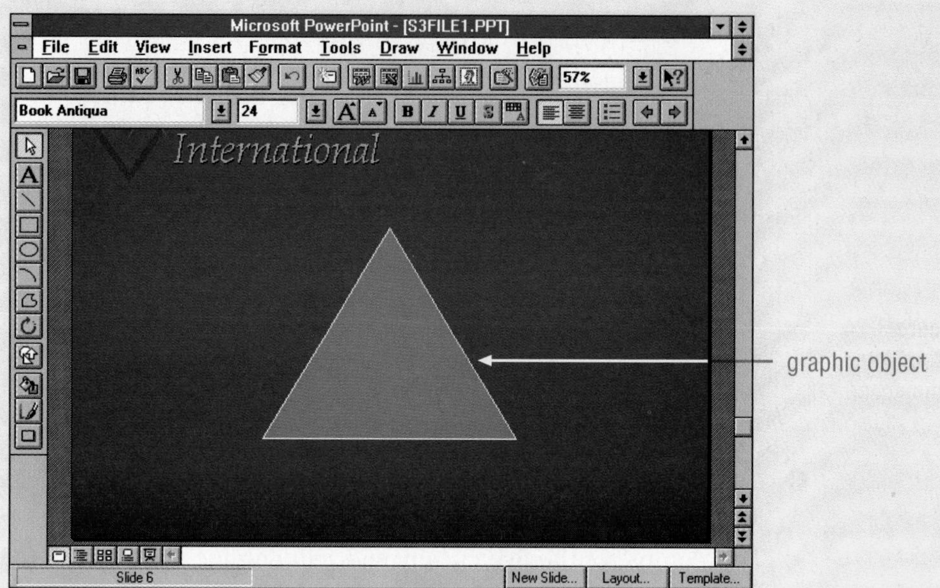

Figure 3-25
Slide with drawn triangle

5. Click the **Control menu box** in the upper-left corner of the AutoShapes palette to close the palette. It disappears from the screen. See Figure 3-25.

   TROUBLE? If your triangle doesn't look similar the one in Figure 3-25, you can move your triangle by dragging it to a new location; you can resize or change the shape of your triangle by dragging one or more of the resize handles; or you can press [Backspace] to completely delete your triangle, then repeat Steps 1 through 5 to redraw the triangle.

   Notice that the default color of the drawn object is pink. Enrique decides that pink is too bright for his presentation, and changes the color of the triangle.

6. Click **Format**, then click **Colors and Lines**. The Colors and Lines dialog box appears on the screen.
7. Click the **Down arrow** in the Fill box, and click the **cyan (blue-green) tile**, then click the **OK button**.

The triangle is the desired size and color, but Enrique decides he wants to flip the triangle so it is pointing down instead of up. Let's flip the triangle now.

To flip an object:

1. Make sure the triangle is still selected.
2. Click **Draw** on the Menu bar, then click **Rotate/Flip**, and click **Flip Vertical**.
3. Click in a blank region of the slide to deselect the triangle.

   Your triangle should be positioned, colored, sized, and oriented similar to the one shown in Figure 3-26.

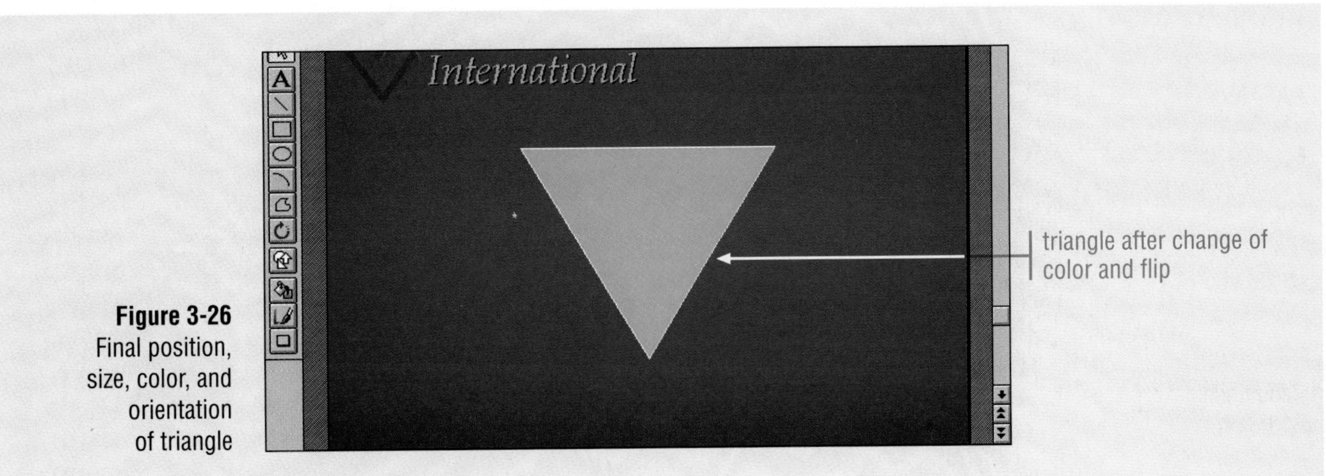

Figure 3-26
Final position, size, color, and orientation of triangle

Adding a Text Box

Enrique is ready to add the text naming the three benefits of Inca Imports on each side of the triangle. Let's do that now.

To add a text box to the slide:

❶ Click the **Text Tool button** A on the Drawing toolbar. The mouse pointer changes to ↓.

❷ Move the mouse pointer so it is just above the upper-left corner of the triangle and click at that position. PowerPoint creates a small empty text box, with the insertion point inside.

❸ Type **Quality Produce**.

❹ Click anywhere on the edge of the text box to select it.

❺ Drag the edge of the text box until it is positioned just above and centered on the upper edge of the triangle, as shown in Figure 3-27.

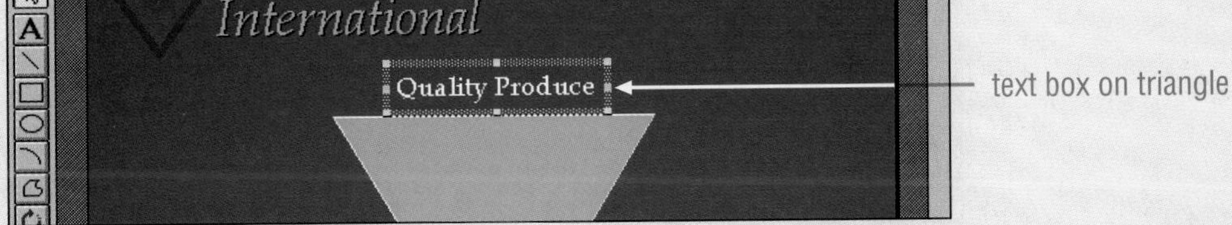

Figure 3-27
Triangle with first text box

❻ Click A, then click ↓ to the right of the triangle and type **Year-round Service**.

❼ Click A, then click ↓ to the left of the triangle and type **Satisfied Customers**. Click in a blank area of the slide to deselect the text box. Your slide should now look similar to Figure 3-28. Don't worry if the text you added to the sides of the triangle is not in the same position as in the figure. You will move it in the next set of steps.

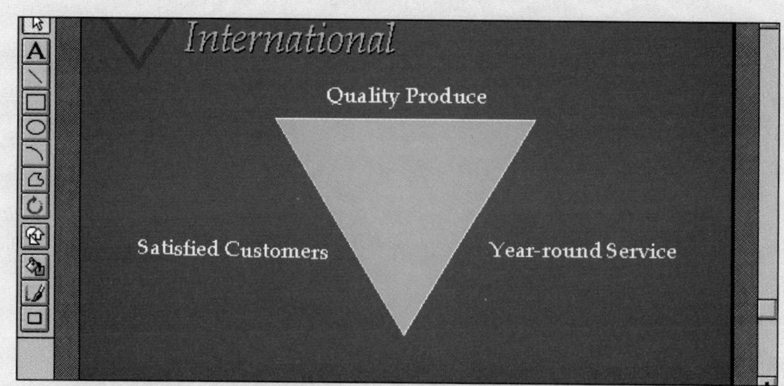

Figure 3-28 Triangle with additional text boxes

Now you'll rotate the text boxes to make them parallel to the sides of the triangle. The method for rotating text is similar to rotating graphics (or rotating any other object).

To rotate and move the text boxes:

1. Select the text box that contains "**Year-round Service**" by clicking anywhere within the box then clicking the edge of the box. The resize handles appear around the box.
2. Click the **Free Rotate Tool button** on the Drawing toolbar. The mouse pointer changes to ↻.
3. Position the ↻ over one of the resize handles (it doesn't matter which). The pointer changes again, this time to ✥.
4. Press and hold the mouse button. The pointer changes a third time, this time to +.
5. Rotate the handle counterclockwise until the status bar indicates that you have rotated the box about 60 degrees or until the top edge of the box is parallel to the lower-right edge of the triangle. See Figure 3-29.

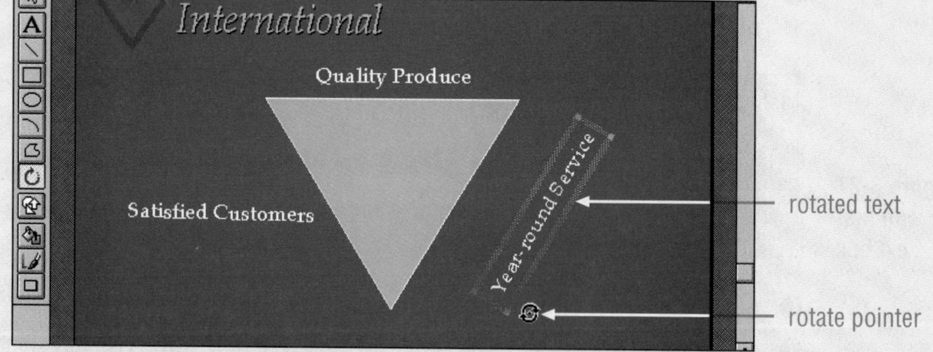

Figure 3-29 Slide after rotating text

6. Click the **Selection Tool button** on the Drawing toolbar, then select the "**Year-round Service**" text box. The first time you click the text, it flips so it is horizontal again. After you click the edge of the text box to select it, the text returns to its rotated position.
7. Drag the edge of the text box until it is close to and centered on the lower-right edge of the triangle.

8. Select the text box that contains "**Satisfied Customers,**" then repeat Steps 2 through 7, except this time rotate the box clockwise to about 300 degrees or until it is parallel to the lower-left edge of the triangle, and then position the text box so it is close to and centered on that edge of the triangle.
9. Deselect the text box. Your slide should look like Figure 3-30.

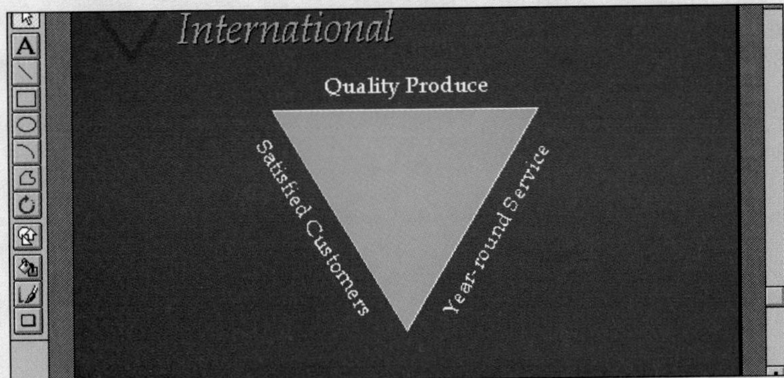

Figure 3-30
Completed slide 6

Enrique and his staff have now completed the entire presentation, so Enrique wants to save the final version to the disk.

10. With the Student Disk still in the disk drive, click the **Save button** on the Standard toolbar. PowerPoint saves the file using its current filename, S3FILE1.PPT.

A copy of the updated presentation is now on your Student Disk.

Viewing and Printing the Completed Slide Show

Enrique wants to view the completed slide show before he prints it.

To view the completed presentation as a slide show:

1. Press **[Ctrl][Home]** or drag the **elevator** to the top of the vertical scroll bar. This ensures that when you begin the Slide Show, slide 1 appears on the screen first.
2. Click the **Slide Show button** on the View toolbar to begin the slide show.
3. After you look at each slide, click the left mouse button or press the space bar to advance to the next slide. Continue advancing until you've seen the entire slide show and PowerPoint returns to Slide view.

Enrique and his staff want a hard copy of their presentation for their files, so they print the entire presentation. Let's print the presentation now.

To print the presentation:

1. Click **File**, then click **Print** to display the Print dialog box, then in the Print What box, select **Slides** if it's not already selected.

2. If you're using a black-and-white printer, click the **Pure Black & White checkbox** on the Print dialog box, and then click the **OK button** to print the slides. The Pure Black & White option speeds up printing because it doesn't print gray-scale objects. All text and graphics appear pure black or pure white.
3. If you desire, you may now exit PowerPoint.

■ ■ ■

Questions

1. Describe how to do the following:
   a. Select a text box so that resize handles appear
   b. Change the size of a text box
   c. Move a text box on a slide
   d. Change the alignment of a text box from center to left alignment
2. Write a list of steps required to do each of the following:
   a. Insert a picture into a slide
   b. Change the Layout of an existing slide
   c. Insert a Graph into a slide
   d. Insert an Organization Chart into a slide
   e. Add a slide to a presentation
   E f. Draw a circle on a slide. Hint: To draw a circle, use the Ellipse Tool while holding down [Shift]
3. List four situations in which you could use graphics effectively.
4. Why would you ungroup a clip-art image?
5. Explain the meaning of the following terms:
   a. Slide Layout
   b. clip art
   c. object
   d. Center Alignment
   e. data sheet
   f. organization chart
   g. subordinate box
   h. resize handles
6. What are two methods (one using the keyboard and the other using the mouse) for moving to (displaying) the first slide in a presentation while in Slide view?
7. How do you rotate an object (text box or graphics box)?
8. List three principles for selecting an appropriate type of graphic.
9. E Explain an advantage and disadvantage of moving a selected object (text box or graphics box) by dragging with the mouse or by pressing the arrow keys.
10. E List and describe the first nine tools (starting with Selection Tool) on the Drawing toolbar.

Tutorial Assignments

In the following Tutorial Assignments, make sure you click the Open an Existing File button when you launch PowerPoint or, if PowerPoint is already running, click the Open button on the Standard toolbar, and then open each file. After working with a presentation and saving your changes, close the presentation.

Open the file T3FILE1.PPT and do the following:

1. Save the file to your student disk as S3FILE2.PPT.
2. Make sure that PowerPoint is in Slide view and that slide 1 appears in the presentation window.
3. Decrease the size of each of the two text boxes so that they fit just around the text contained in each box.
4. Change the text in both text boxes to Left Alignment.
5. Insert the picture file IIILOGO.BMP into slide 1, decrease the size of the logo, then move the picture just to the right of the red bars in the upper-left corner of the slide. Try to align the top of the graphic with the top of the bars.
6. Move the two text boxes so that their left edges are directly beneath the left edge of the picture. Use the Draw, Align, Lefts command to align them precisely.
7. Change the layout of slide 2 to "2 Column Text."
8. In the right-hand column of slide 2, add the following three bulleted items: "Ad in food industry trade magazine," "Sample produce to interested businesses," "Complimentary shipment to large companies."
9. In slide 3 change the layout to "Clip Art & Text," so that the clip art is on the left and the text is on the right.
10. In the placeholder for the clip art in slide 3, add the image from the People category called "Man with Pad," which pictures a man standing up holding a small notepad. If your copy of PowerPoint doesn't have that clip-art image, use another one of your choice.
11. Add an organization chart to slide 4. Put Enrique Hoffmann, Director of Marketing, at the top of the chart. Add Melanie Zapatos and Samuel Clarke, both Marketing Managers, to the second level. Then, on the third level under Melanie Zapatos, add two Sales Representatives, Carlos Anderson and Ana Maria Prado; and under Samuel Clarke add two Sales Representatives, Gina Parker and Jesus Calderon. Hint: To delete an unwanted box on the organization chart, select the box, and then press [Backspace] or [Delete].

E 12. Add a new slide 5. Choose "Title Only" as the slide layout. Make the title of the slide "Marketing Process." Add text and AutoShapes to create a slide that looks like Figure 3-31. You may have to move, resize, and align text and graphics boxes to make the slide look right. Hint: To make the arrows the same size and shape, use AutoShapes to draw one of the arrows and then use the Copy and Paste buttons on the Standard toolbar to create the others. To align the centers of objects vertically (text boxes and graphics boxes), use the Draw, Align, Centers command.

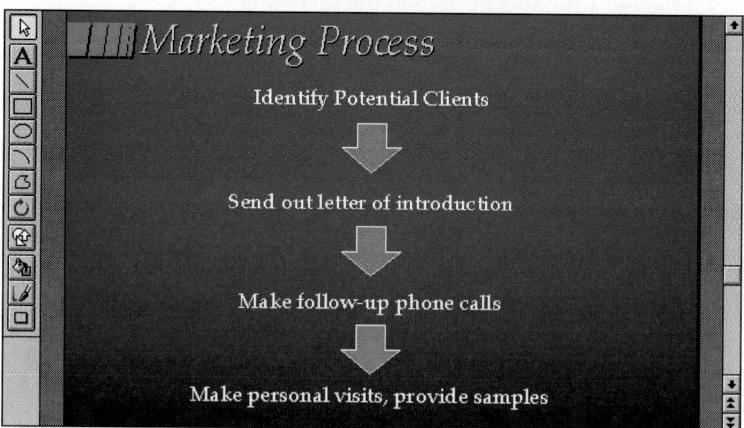

Figure 3-31

E 13. Add a new slide 6. Choose "Graph" as the slide layout. Make the title of the slide "Comparison of 4th Qtr Sales, 1992-95." Double-click the graph icon, and then in the data sheet, delete the second and thirds rows Hint: Click the gray box labeled 2, then click Edit, and click Delete to delete the entire row. Change labels in columns A through D from "1st Qtr," "2nd Qtr," and so forth, to "1992," "1993," "1994," and "1995." Change the label in that row from "East" to "4th Qtr Sales." Make the numbers in cells A1 through D1 the following: $420, $475, $710, $1025. Add the title "Thousands" to the Z-axis; make the title vertical, reading bottom to top. Close the data sheet and then deselect the graph.

E 14. Check the spelling within the presentation by clicking the Spelling button on the Standard toolbar or by clicking Tools, then clicking Spelling.

15. View the entire presentation in Slide Show view.
16. Save your changes, then print a copy of the slides of the presentation. Print them using the Black & White option if you don't have a color printer.
17. Close the file.

Open the file T3FILE2.PPT and do the following:

18. Save it to your Student Disk as S3FILE3.PPT.
19. Make sure that PowerPoint is in Slide view and that slide 1 appears in the presentation window.
20. Insert the picture file T3DESIGN.BMP from the Student Disk into slide 1, then position the picture below the author's name, "Norma Lopez."
21. Remove the Slide Master objects from this title slide.
22. Change the layout of slide 2 to "2 Column Text."
23. In the right-hand column of slide 2, add the following two bulleted items: "Hold customer training" and "Improve product list."

24. Move the fourth item from column 1 to the end of column 2.
25. In slide 3 change the layout to "Clip Art & Text," so that the clip art is on the right and the text is on the left; then in the placeholder for the clip art, add the image named "Group Meeting" from the "People" category, which pictures a woman standing with four others sitting. If your copy of PowerPoint doesn't have that clip-art image, use another one of your choice.
26. Create an organization chart in slide 4. Put Norma Lopez, Customer Service, at the top of the chart, with Delbert Green as her assistant on level 2, and three people—Shirley Alvarez, Daniel Truong, and Whitney Sanders, all Customer Representatives—on level 3 below Delbert Green. Hint: To delete an unwanted box on the organization chart, select the box, then press [Backspace].

E 27. Go to slide 5 and add a square that is about one-fourth the width of the slide. Hint: Use the Rectangle Tool while holding down [Shift]. Add text around the square. Hint: Use the Free Rotate Tool to rotate the text that goes along the left and right sides, but don't rotate the text that goes along the bottom of the square. Type "Quality Products" above the box, "Quick Response" along the right edge (rotated 270 degrees), "Honored Guarantees" along the bottom, and "Regular Follow-up" along the left edge (rotated 90 degrees).

E 28. Go to slide 6 and double-click on the placeholder labeled "Double click to add graph." Click the down arrow immediately to the right of the Chart Type button to display icons of the various chart types. Click the three-dimensional pie chart (on the fifth row, second column). On the data sheet, change the row labels from "1st Qtr," "2nd Qtr," and so forth, to "Extremely satisfied," "Very Satisfied," "Satisfied," and "Unsatisfied." Hint: You may have to change the width of the columns for these labels to fit. To increase or decrease the width of a column, drag the black line located between the gray column buttons along the top of the data sheet to the left or the right. Beneath those labels type the following numbers into cells A1 through D1: 0.31, 0.42, 0.25, and 0.2, respectively. They indicate the percent of costumers in each category. Close the data sheet and deselect the pie chart.

29. View the entire presentation in Slide Show view.
30. Save your changes.
31. Print a copy of the slides of the presentation. Print them using the Black & White option if you don't have a color printer.
32. Close the file.

Case Problems

1. Data Doctor

Enoch Norbert owns a computer-data-backup service in Framingham, MA. His company, Data Doctor, helps small businesses in the greater Boston area back up their disks and recover damaged data. Enoch wants to use PowerPoint to create a presentation for potential customers.

Open the file P3DATA.PPT, save it to your Student Disk as S3DATA.PPT, and then do the following:

1. To slide 1, add the picture P3DATA.BMP. Adjust the position and alignment of the text and the position of the picture to make the slide attractive and readable.
2. In slide 2, change the layout to Text & Clip Art, then add the PowerPoint clip art "Computer Choking Operator" from the Cartoons category.
3. In slide 3, add the PowerPoint clip art "Duck Smashing PC" from the Cartoons category.
4. In slide 4, add to the center of the slide (below the title) the clip art "Man at Computers" from the People category.
5. Also in slide 4, add a text box with the text "Data Doctor." Position the text box in the middle of the clip art across the two computers.
6. Change the slide layout of slide 5 to Clip Art & Text, then add the clip art "Woman at Computer" from the People category.

E 7. Change the layout of slide 6 to Graph & Text. In the graph area, create a graph that compares Restore costs (from backed-up data) and Re-enter costs after losing data. In the data sheet, make the titles of four columns the following: "1 hr," "8 hrs," "20 hrs," and "40 hrs" (the restoration times in hours). Make the titles of two rows "Off-site" and "On-site." Delete any other rows. In the "Off-site" row (cells A1 through D1) type the costs (in dollars) for restoring from an off-site backup: 3, 24, 60, 120. In the "On-site" row (cells A2 through D2) type the cost (in dollars) for restoring from an on-site backup: 10, 80, 200, 400. Add a vertical label to the Z-axis: "Cost in dollars." If the X-axis labels have unattractive wrapping of words, increase the width of the graph. You may then have to change the size of the text box to the right of the graph so the graph doesn't cover up text.

E 8. In slide 7, increase the size of the font in the main text box (below the title) by selecting the text box and dragging I over all the text and then clicking the increase Font Size button five or six times until the longest line of text just fills the width of the text box.

E 9. Use Slide Show to view all the slides of the presentation.

10. Save the file, then print the slides of the presentation in Black & White.

E 11. Close the file.

2. Business Plans Plus

Atu Hemuli helps minority entrepreneurs get funding by preparing business plans for them or by editing their existing plans. Atu wants to create a seminar presentation for other professionals who are interested in becoming business-plan consultants.

Open P3BPLAN.PPT, save it to your Student Disk as S3BPLAN.PPT and do the following:

1. To slide 1, add a PowerPoint clip art of "Woman with Binder—Close-Up View" from the People category. Then rearrange, resize, and move the graphics box and the two text boxes to make the title slide look attractive and readable.
2. Insert a new slide 2 into the presentation. Use the "Bulleted List" slide layout. Make the title read "What does a business plan consultant do?" Then add the following bulleted items to the main text: "Guides clients in writing business plans," "Conducts market research," "Gathers financial information," "Projects growth," and "Projects sales potential."

E 3. In slide 3, change the layout to Text & Graph. Add a pie chart in the graphic box. Hint: After double-clicking the graph icon, click the down arrow to the right of the Chart Type button, and then click pie chart icon (on the fifth row, first column). On the data sheet, change the column labels from "1st Qtr" and "2nd Qtr" to "Formal Business Plan" and "No Business Plan." Delete the labels and information in the other columns. Beneath the column labels, type into cells A1 and B1 the numbers 0.59 and 0.41, respectively. They indicate the percentage in each category. Close the data sheet and deselect the pie chart.

E 4. In slide 4, add a pie chart similar to the one in slide 3, except the numbers in cells A1 and B1 should be 0.42 and 0.58, respectively.

E 5. In slide 5, add a pie chart similar to the one in slide 3, except create three column labels: "No planning," "Some planning," and "Formal planning." Then make the label in row one "Planning." Type into cells A1, B1, and C1 the numbers 30, 45, and 25, respectively.

6. Change the layout of slide 6 to Text & Clip Art, then add the clip art "Three People Shaking Hands" from the People category.
7. Change the layout of slide 7 to Text & Clip Art, then add the clip art "Meeting" from the People category.
8. Change the layout of slide 8 to Text & Clip Art, then add the clip art "Man at Podium" from the People category.
9. Use Slide Show to review the entire presentation.
10. Save the file, then print the slides in Black & White.
11. Close the file.

3. Porter and Cole Ad Agency

Sheri Porter and Sherone Cole have combined their talents to found the Porter and Cole Ad Agency. The partners decide that Sheri should prepare a presentation giving the hourly rates for Porter and Cole services and providing a graph on the cost of preparing a document as a function of the number of pages.

Open P3ADAGE.PPT, save it as S3ADAGE, and do the following:

1. In slide 1, increase the font size of the slide title by selecting the text box and double-clicking the Increase Font Size button.
2. E In slide 2, to the right of the main text, without changing the slide layout, add the PowerPoint clip art "Woman with Books" from the People category. Hint: Use the Insert Clip Art button on the Standard toolbar, and then resize and move the graphic image so that it fits neatly to the right of the text.
3. In slide 3, replace the clip-art placeholder with the "Man at Computer" image from the People category.
4. In slides 4 and 5, add a clip-art picture to the right of the main text. From the People category, use "Man on Phone" in slide 4 and "Artist" in slide 5.
5. E Add a slide 6 with a "Graph" layout. Create a title with the text "Typical Costs of Preparing a Document." Select the graph type by double-clicking the graph placeholder, then clicking the down arrow to the right of the Chart Type button and clicking the line icon (fourth row, first column). Create a graph with the following information:
   a. Column labels (columns A through I, respectively): 0, 5, 10, 15, 20, 25, 30, 35, 40.
   b. First row data (cells A1 through I1, respectively): 0, 300, 250, 200, 175, 150, 125, 125, 125.
   c. Delete other rows and columns.
   d. Z-axis title (make it vertical orientation): "Cost per page"
   e. X-axis title: "Number of pages"
   f. Delete the legend. Hint: Click it, then press [Del].
6. Use Slide Show to review the entire presentation.
7. Save the file, then print the Slides in Black & White.
8. Close the file.

TUTORIAL 4

Presenting a Slide Show

OBJECTIVES

In this tutorial you will:

- Change the slide color scheme and background shading style
- Add text and graphics to the Slide Master
- Modify the color and character of bullets
- Insert slides from another slide presentation
- Apply transitions and builds to slides
- Use the PowerPoint Viewer
- Annotate slides during a slide show
- Create 35mm slides and overhead transparencies

CASE

Report to Investors A year after receiving venture capital from Commercial Financial Bank of Southern California, Patricia Cuevas needs to present her first annual report on Inca Imports International's progress. She will make two presentations: one to the company's board of directors and one to the company stockholders. Patricia decides she can create one slide show for both audiences, and that she should include slides about Inca Imports' successful marketing campaign.

In this tutorial, you will help Patricia create a title slide, gather previously created slides, and arrange and order the slides to create her slide show.

DESIGN PRINCIPLE WINDOW

Preparing for a Presentation Meeting

- Prepare an agenda, including date, time, and place; topics for discussion; names of speakers (and attendees, if it's a small meeting), materials needed (if any).
- Prepare your own presentation. Request help from others, as necessary, and then follow up.
- Check the physical arrangements, including size of room, chairs, tables, podium, and thermostat setting.
- Check the equipment, including microphone, chalkboard (white board), computer with projection system (if you're giving an on-screen presentation), slide projector, overhead projector, VCR and TV (if you're using video).
- Prepare other items, as needed, including beverages, refreshments, pads, pencils, name cards, handouts, and reference materials.

Planning the Presentation

Before starting PowerPoint, Patricia identifies the purpose of and audience for her presentation.

- **Purpose for the presentation:** To present an overview of the progress that Inca Imports has made during the past year
- **Type of presentation:** General presentation
- **Audience for the presentation:** Inca's board of directors; stockholders of Inca Imports at their annual meeting
- **Audience needs:** To quickly gain an overview of Inca's performance over the past year
- **Location of the presentation:** Small boardroom for the board of directors; large conference room at the meeting site for the stockholders
- **Format:** Oral presentation; electronic slide show for the board of directors; 35mm slide show for the stockholders; slide show consisting of five to seven slides

Opening a Blank Presentation

Because she's going to combine previously created slides with new slides, Patricia will open a blank presentation rather than use the AutoContent Wizard. She begins by opening a blank presentation and creating a title slide.

To open a blank presentation:

1. Launch PowerPoint, and from the PowerPoint startup dialog box, click **Blank Presentation**, then click the **OK button**. The New Slide dialog box appears with the AutoLayout selections.

   TROUBLE? If you've already launched PowerPoint, click the New button on the Standard toolbar, then click Blank Presentation and click the OK button.

2. Make sure the Title Slide layout is selected, and click the **OK button**. The placeholders for a title slide appear on the screen in Slide view.
3. If the presentation window is not maximized, click the **Maximize button** of the presentation window. See Figure 4-1.

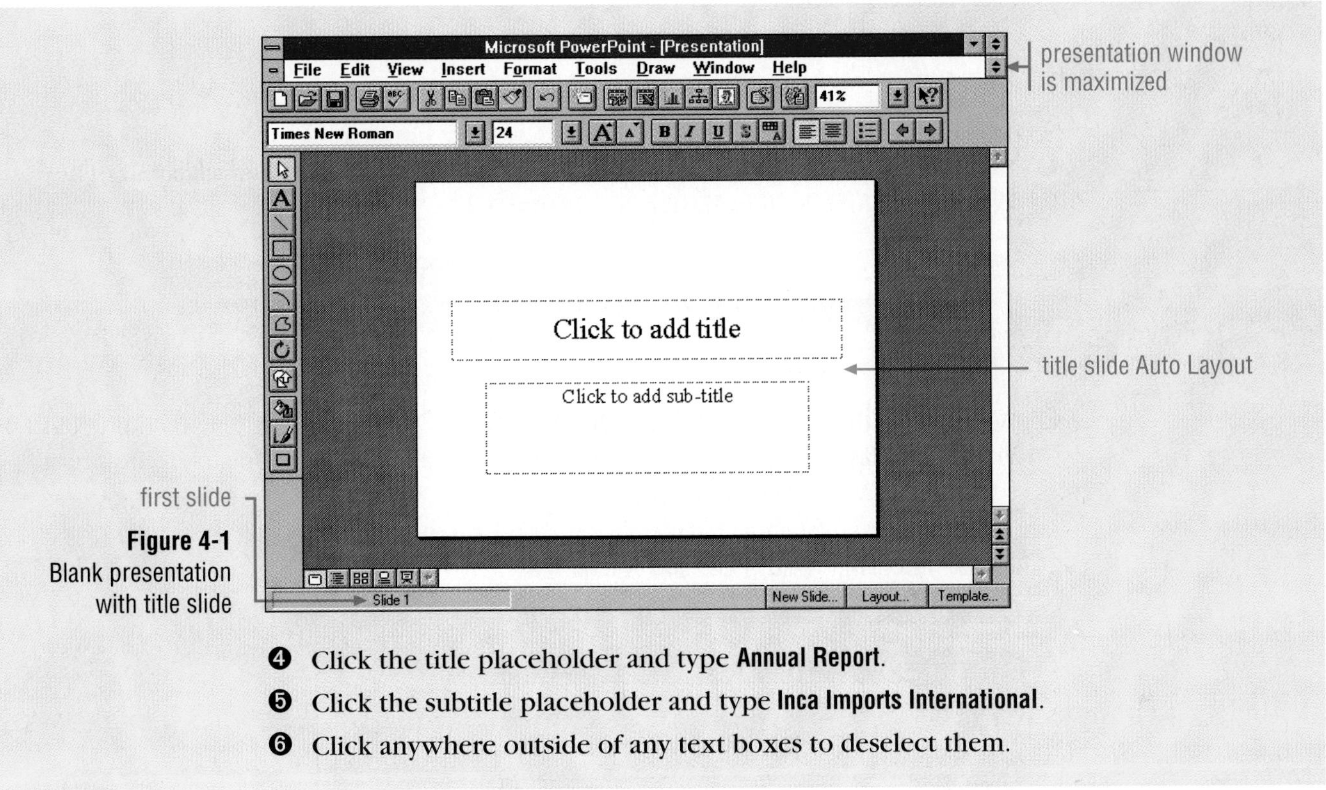

Figure 4-1 Blank presentation with title slide

4. Click the title placeholder and type **Annual Report**.
5. Click the subtitle placeholder and type **Inca Imports International**.
6. Click anywhere outside of any text boxes to deselect them.

Patricia has now created the title slide of the annual report.

Using the Slide Master

When you open a new blank presentation, the default background is white with no design. Patricia wants to select a **color scheme**, that is, an overall color design for the slides in her presentation. When you create a blank presentation, you should choose either a template or a color scheme. Patricia will apply the color scheme to the Slide Master. The **Slide Master** is a slide that contains text and graphics that appear on all of the slides in the presentation and controls the format and color of the text and background on all slides. When you make a change on the master, the change is reflected on all of the slides in the presentation. You can also create a Master for outlines, handouts, and notes.

REFERENCE WINDOW

Modifying a Master

- To display the Master you want, hold down [Shift], then click the appropriate view button. Or you can click View, click Master, then click the desired Master.
- Make changes in color scheme, fonts, bullets, alignment, or in any other formatting feature. Add any desired text, picture, clip art, or other object.
- After modifying the Master, return to another view, such as Slide view or Slide Sorter view by clicking the appropriate view button.

Let's display the Slide Master.

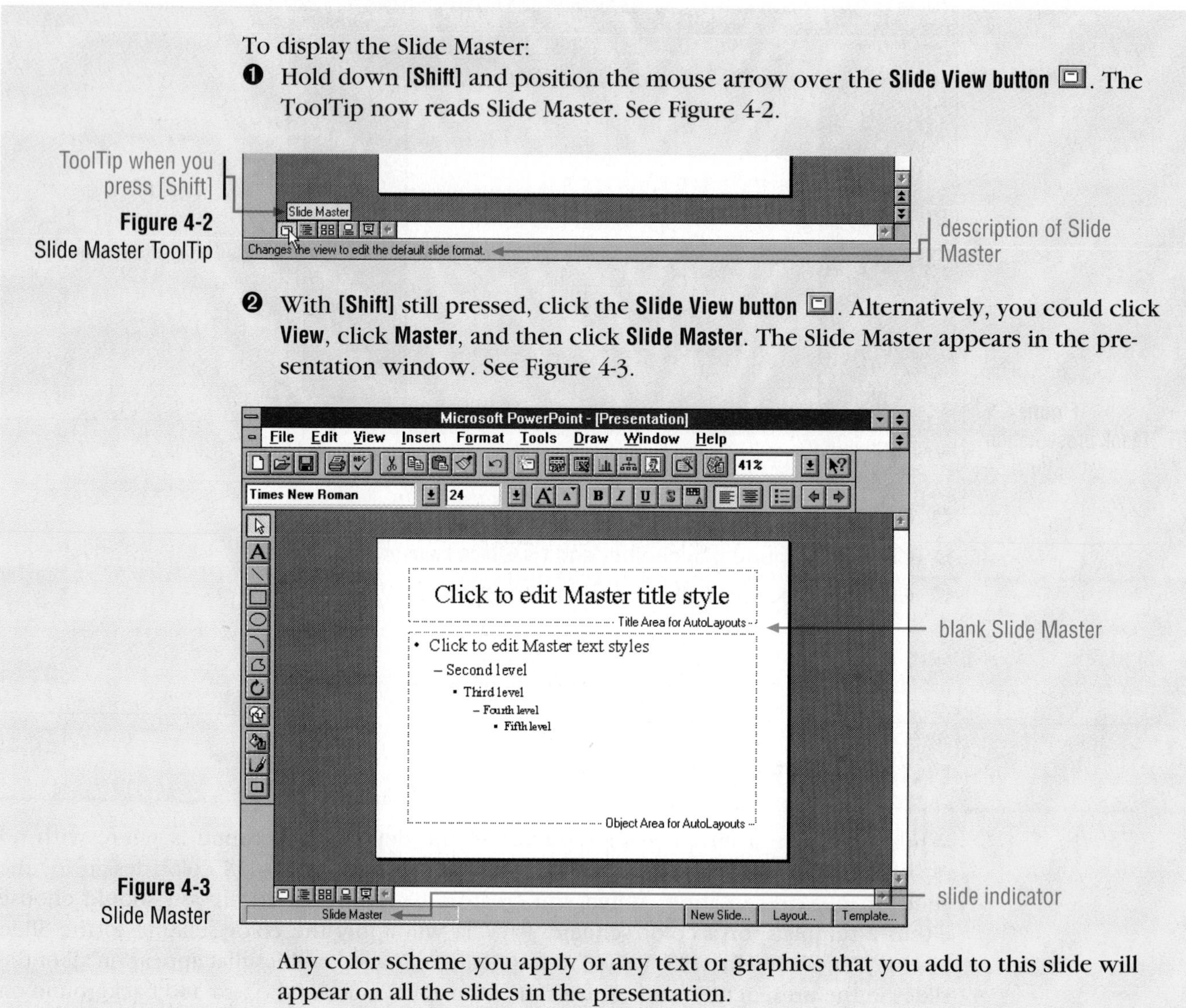

To display the Slide Master:

1. Hold down **[Shift]** and position the mouse arrow over the **Slide View button**. The ToolTip now reads Slide Master. See Figure 4-2.

Figure 4-2
Slide Master ToolTip

2. With **[Shift]** still pressed, click the **Slide View button**. Alternatively, you could click **View**, click **Master**, and then click **Slide Master**. The Slide Master appears in the presentation window. See Figure 4-3.

Figure 4-3
Slide Master

Any color scheme you apply or any text or graphics that you add to this slide will appear on all the slides in the presentation.

With the Slide Master in the PowerPoint presentation window, Patricia is now ready to change the color scheme.

Changing the Slide Color Scheme

Patricia knows she could make changes to individual slides without using the Slide Master, but she also knows that certain changes—like adding text, changing the style of bullets, or inserting a logo—should be made on the Slide Master to take effect on all the slides and promote overall consistency in the presentation. Let's change the color scheme of the slides now.

To change the slide color scheme:

1. Click **Format**, then click **Slide Color Scheme**. The Slide Color Scheme dialog box appears on the screen. See Figure 4-4.

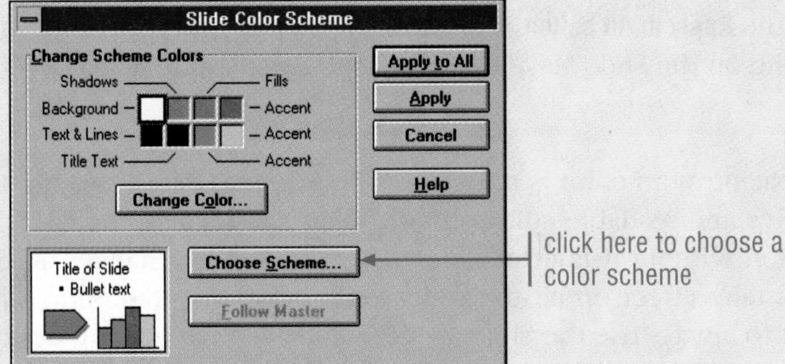

Figure 4-4
Slide Color Scheme dialog box

2. Click the **Choose Scheme button**. The Choose Scheme dialog box appears. See Figure 4-5. Patricia wants to select a conservative background color for her slides because her audience has a business background.

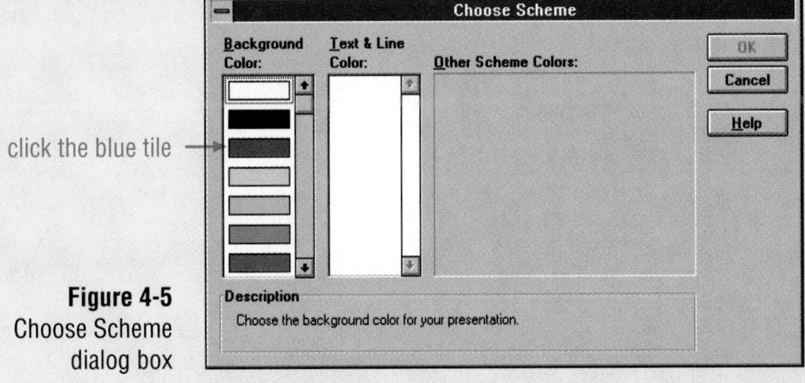

Figure 4-5
Choose Scheme dialog box

3. Click the first blue tile in the Background Color box of the Choose Scheme dialog box, as shown in Figure 4-5. Now let's pick a white text and line color.

4. Click the white tile in the Text & Line Color box. PowerPoint now displays some preset color schemes in the Other Scheme Colors box on the Choose Scheme dialog box. See Figure 4-6. With the blue background and white text selected, you can choose variations on that color scheme.

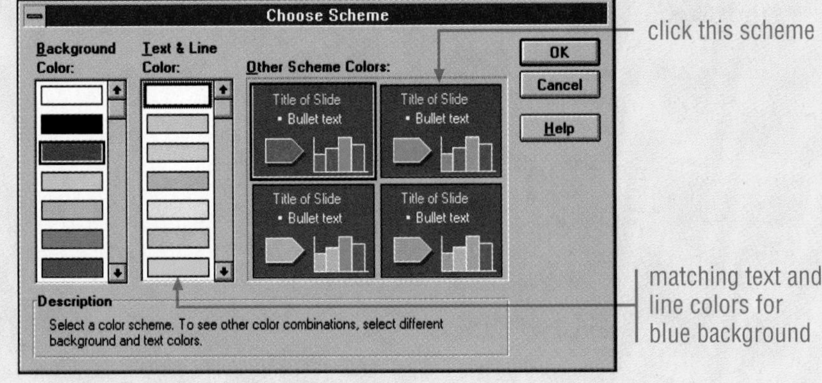

Figure 4-6
Other Scheme Colors box of the Choose Scheme dialog box

5. Click the upper-right tile in the Other Scheme Colors box, as indicated in Figure 4-6, then click the **OK button**. This color scheme keeps the blue background with white letters for the main text as you selected in Steps 3 and 4, but selects yellow as the color for the title on each slide.
6. Click the **Apply to All button**. You could also click the Apply button; because you are working on the Slide Master, any change to this slide will apply to all slides.

The background color is now blue, the title text is yellow, and the main text is white, an attractive and readable color scheme. You can change the color scheme for the entire presentation without using the Slide Master, but other changes, such as modifying bullets and fonts, take effect on all the slides only if you use the Slide Master. Therefore, it's a good idea to always use the Slide Master when you are making design decisions so that all your slides will be consistent.

Although she likes the background color, Patricia decides to change the background from solid blue to a shaded blue. Let's make this change now.

To change the background color to a shade style:

1. Click **Format**, then click **Slide Background**. The Slide Background dialog box appears on the screen. See Figure 4-7.

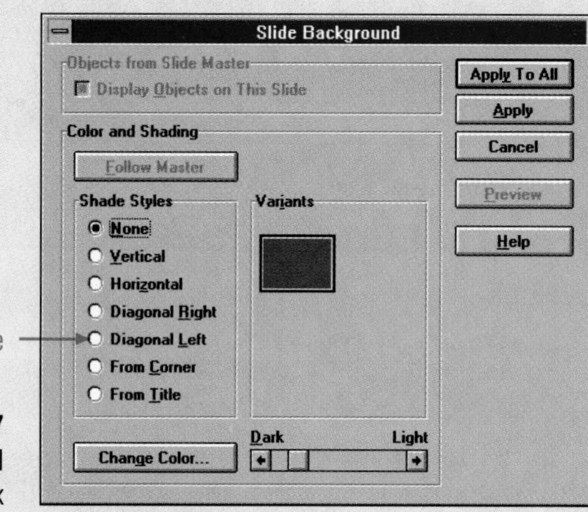

Figure 4-7
Slide Background dialog box

2. In the **Shade Styles box** of the dialog box, click the **Diagonal Left button**; then in the **Variants box**, click the variant that is to the lower right, the style that is lighter along the diagonal and darker in the upper-right and lower-left corners. See Figure 4-8.

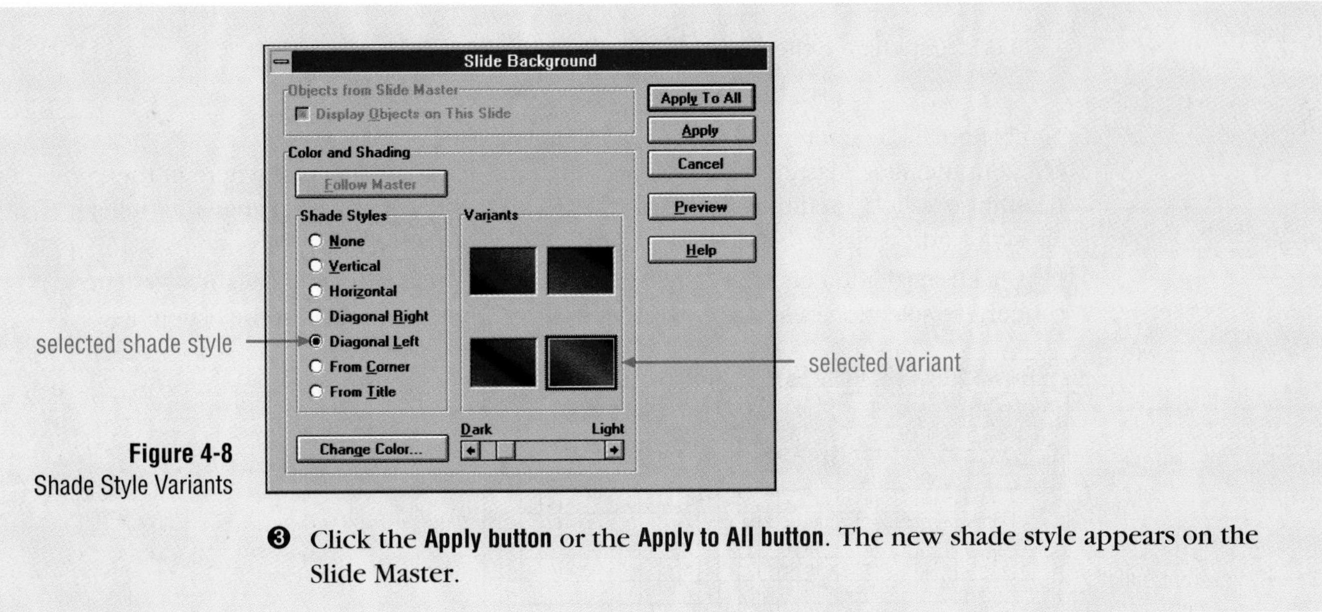

Figure 4-8
Shade Style Variants

❸ Click the **Apply button** or the **Apply to All button**. The new shade style appears on the Slide Master.

You can also change the background color from the Slide Background dialog box. However, by using a preset color scheme from the Slide Color Scheme dialog box, you will always get readable background and font colors in your presentations.

Modifying the Bullets and Font on the Slide Master

Patricia likes the color scheme she has chosen, except that she would like the bullets to be a different color than the main text. She also wants to change the character, or style, used for the bullets. To change the bullets for all the slides in the presentation, she again modifies the Slide Master.

REFERENCE WINDOW

Changing the Bullets

- If you want the change in bullets to affect all slides in the presentation, display the Slide Master by holding down [Shift] and then clicking Slide View. Or click View, click Master, then click Slide Master.
- Click anywhere within the text of the bulleted item.
- Click Format, then click Bullet to display the Bullet dialog box.
- To change the font (so you can select a new bullet character), select a font using the Bullets From list, and then click the desired character.
- To change the color, use the Special Color palette and click the desired color tile.
- Click the OK button.

Let's first change the bullet character and color.

To change the character and color of the bullets:

❶ With the Slide Master still in the presentation window, click anywhere in the phrase "Click to edit Master text styles." Now you're ready to change the bullet style and color.

❷ Click **Format**, then click **Bullet** to display the Bullet dialog box. See Figure 4-9. The current selection of symbols appears in the grid in the middle of the dialog box.

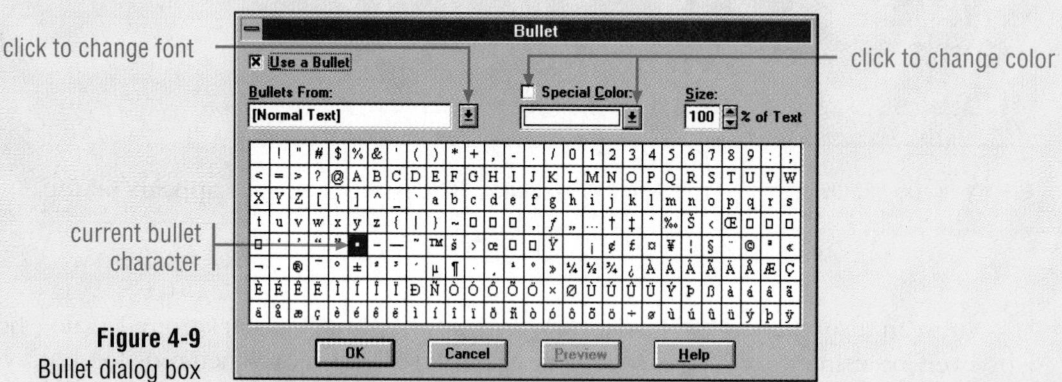

Figure 4-9
Bullet dialog box

❸ Click the **Down arrow button** next to the Bullets From box, then scroll down and click **Wingdings** or some other font that contains a variety of symbols.

TROUBLE? If your Windows system doesn't have a list of fonts available in the Bullets From list, skip Steps 3 and 4 and continue with Step 5, leaving the current bullet symbol as it is.

❹ Click the symbol for a small diamond or for some other symbol that appears in your font. For this presentation, select a simple bullet, like a diamond, square, or circle, that is appropriate for a presentation to stockholders rather than an informal bullet, like a smiley face or a pointing hand. When you click the shapes, the size of the selected shape doubles so you can see it more clearly.

Next, let's change the bullet color.

❺ Click the **Special Color checkbox**. This tells PowerPoint that you want the bullets in your presentation to be a different color from the text color.

❻ Click the **Down arrow button** next to the Special Color box to open the Special Color palette, and click the yellow tile. You have now selected a new bullet character and color. See Figure 4-10.

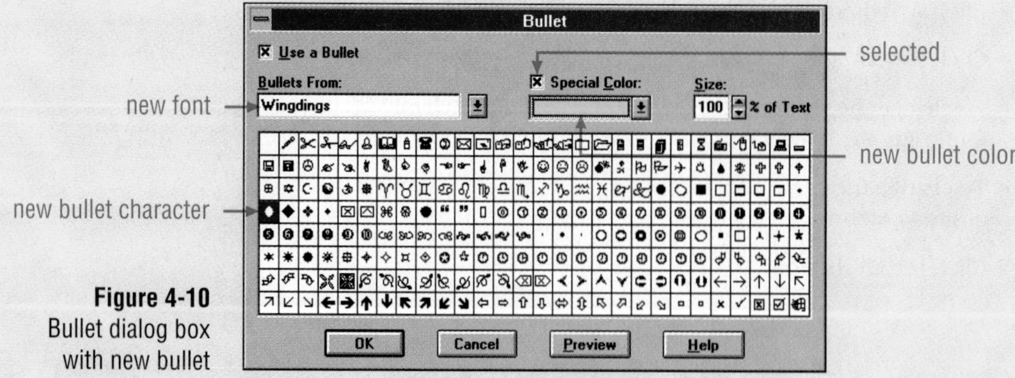

Figure 4-10
Bullet dialog box with new bullet

❼ Click the **OK button** on the Bullet dialog box. The dialog box closes, and the first bulleted item on the Slide Master is a yellow diamond (or whatever shape you chose.)

Having changed the color and style of the bullet, Patricia decides to change the font of the title on the Slide Master to Arial. Let's make that change now.

To change the title font:

1. Click the text box labeled "Click to edit Master title style."
2. Click the **Down arrow button** next to the font box on the Formatting toolbar, then click **Arial**.

   TROUBLE? If your computer system doesn't have Arial, then use another font.

Adding Text to the Slide Master

In addition to changing colors, fonts, and bullets, you can also add text to the Slide Master. The new text will appear on all the slides in the presentation. Patricia wants every slide to contain the company name, so she adds it to the Slide Master.

To add text to the Slide Master:

1. Click the **Text Tool button** on the Drawing Toolbar.
2. Click just below the lower-left corner of the Object Area for AutoLayout box in the Slide Master.
3. Change the Font to **Arial** and the Font Size to **20 point**.
4. Type **Inca Imports International** and then click anywhere outside the slide to deselect the text box. The Slide Master now includes the company name. See Figure 4-11.

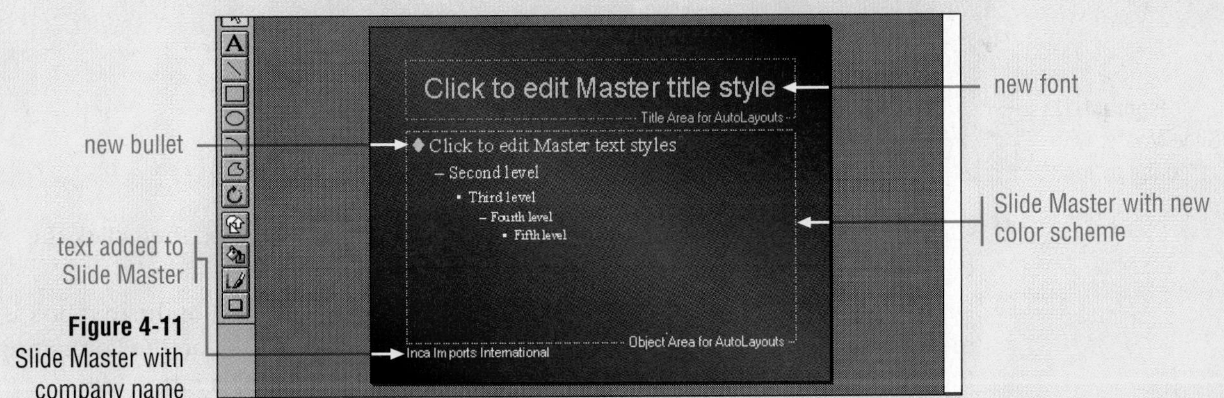

Figure 4-11 Slide Master with company name

TROUBLE? If the position of the company name isn't similar to what you see in Figure 4-11, move the "Inca Imports International" text box to the desired location.

If Patricia had chosen a template, the color scheme, background, font, font style, and font sizes would have been chosen for her. Instead, she decided to make these decisions herself by using the Slide Master.

Adding a Logo to the Slide Master

Finally, Patricia wants to add the Inca Imports International logo to the Slide Master, so that the logo will appear on every slide in the presentation. To add a picture to the Slide Master, you follow the same procedure as adding a picture to a regular slide.

To add a picture to a Slide Master:

1. Click **Insert**, then click **Picture** to display the Insert Picture dialog box.
2. If it's not there already, insert the Student Disk into drive A or B, then make that disk drive the current drive in the Insert Picture dialog box.
3. Click **iiilogo.bmp** to select the logo, then click the **OK button**. PowerPoint inserts the logo into the middle of the Slide Master. Because the logo will be on all the slides, Patricia wants to make it smaller and move it into the upper-left corner of the slide.
4. Drag the logo on top of the box labeled "Title Area for AutoLayout" so its upper-left corner is located at or near the upper-left corner of the title text box.
5. Drag the lower-right resize handle up and to the left so that the height of the image is the same size as the text box. Your Slide Master window should look like Figure 4-12.

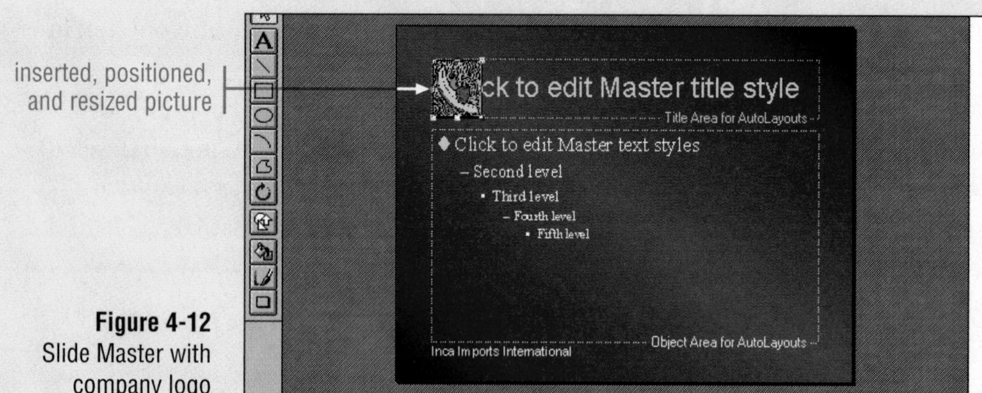

Figure 4-12
Slide Master with company logo

6. Click the **title text box** to the right of the logo to select the title box, then click the edge of the text box to display the resize handles.
7. Drag the lower-left resize handle to the right so that the left edge of the text box is to the right of the logo, and then click the **Left Alignment button** on the Formatting toolbar so that the title is left aligned rather than centered. See Figure 4-13.

   This completes Patricia's changes to the Slide Master, as shown in Figure 4-13. Satisfied with the slide design she has created for her presentation, Patricia changes back to Slide view.

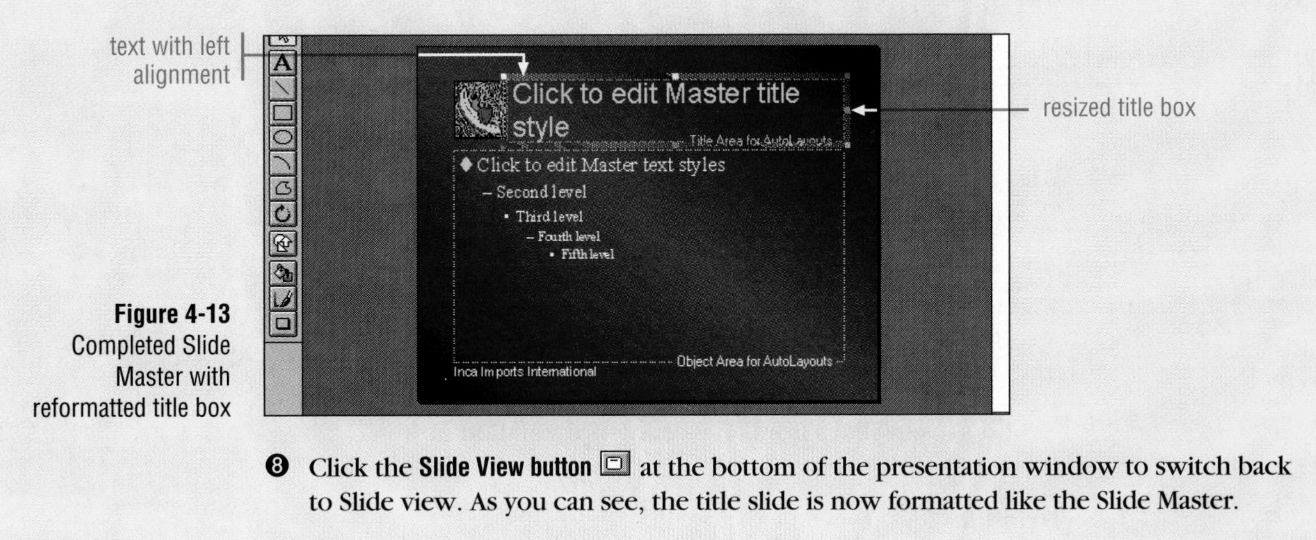

Figure 4-13 Completed Slide Master with reformatted title box

❽ Click the **Slide View button** at the bottom of the presentation window to switch back to Slide view. As you can see, the title slide is now formatted like the Slide Master.

Patricia has worked for about fifteen minutes, so she decides to save the slide presentation changes to this point.

To save the slide presentation:

❶ Click the **Save button** on the Formatting toolbar, then save the presentation to the Student Disk using the filename S4FILE1. The Summary Info dialog box appears on the screen.

❷ Leave the title as Annual Report, and then by clicking in each box or pressing **[Tab]** to move to each box, change the Subject to "Report to Board of Directors and Stockholders," the Author to "Patricia Cuevas," the Keywords to "Annual Report to Stockholders," and leave the Comments blank.

❸ Click the **OK button**. PowerPoint saves the presentation to the disk.

If you want to take a break and resume the tutorial at a later time, you can do so now. If you exit PowerPoint, launch the program again when you want to resume working, and open the presentation file S4FILE1.PPT. Then continue with the next section.

■ ■ ■

Inserting Slides from Another Presentation

Patricia Cuevas's first task in this annual report presentation is to review with her audience the products and services offered by Inca Imports. That information, however, already exists in the presentation developed earlier by Enrique Hoffmann for the marketing division. So Patricia decides to insert slides from Enrique's presentation into the current one.

REFERENCE WINDOW

Inserting Slides from an Existing Presentation

- Get into Slide view, then display the slide after which you want to insert the existing presentation slides.
- Click Insert, then click Slides from File.
- Select the disk and filename that contains the existing presentation, then click the OK button.

Let's insert slides from an existing presentation now.

To insert slides from an existing file:

1. With the title slide of the annual report still in the presentation window in Slide view, click **Insert**, then click **Slides from File**. PowerPoint displays the Insert File dialog box.

   When you insert slides from another presentation, you must insert the entire file, then delete the slides you don't want.

2. With the Drives set to the drive containing the Student Disk, click **c4file1.ppt** in the File Name list, and then click the **OK button**. PowerPoint retrieves the existing presentation and displays a message that the slides from the disk are being updated to match the color scheme on the Slide Master of the current presentation.

Slide 2 appears in the presentation window. This is the title slide from the earlier presentation. You can delete this slide.

To delete a slide:

1. Click **Edit**, then click **Delete Slide** to delete the current slide. The new slide 2 is titled "Providing Quality Produce." See Figure 4-14. The slide has the color scheme of the current slide presentation, not of the original presentation from which it came.

Figure 4-14
New slide 2 with updated design

Patricia now has all the slides she needs from past slide presentations.

Completing the Slide Presentation

Next Patricia needs to change the order of the slides to meet the needs of this presentation, delete unwanted slides, and add new slides as needed. To sort the slides, you'll use Slide Sorter view. You can also change the order of slides in Outline view. Let's sort the slides now.

To change the order of the slides:

1. Click the **Slide Sorter View button** at the bottom of the presentation window. PowerPoint displays the slides of the presentation and the Slide Sorter toolbar appears below the Standard toolbar. Patricia wants to move slide 3, "Meeting Your Needs," so it becomes slide 2.
2. Drag slide 3 to the left, and watch as a vertical line follows the pointer. Release the mouse button when the vertical line is between slides 1 and 2. Patricia decides to delete slide 4, "Reducing Time to Market."
3. Click **slide 4** to make it the current slide, then press **[Del]** or click **Edit**, then click **Delete Slide**. PowerPoint deletes the slide from the presentation. See Figure 4-15.

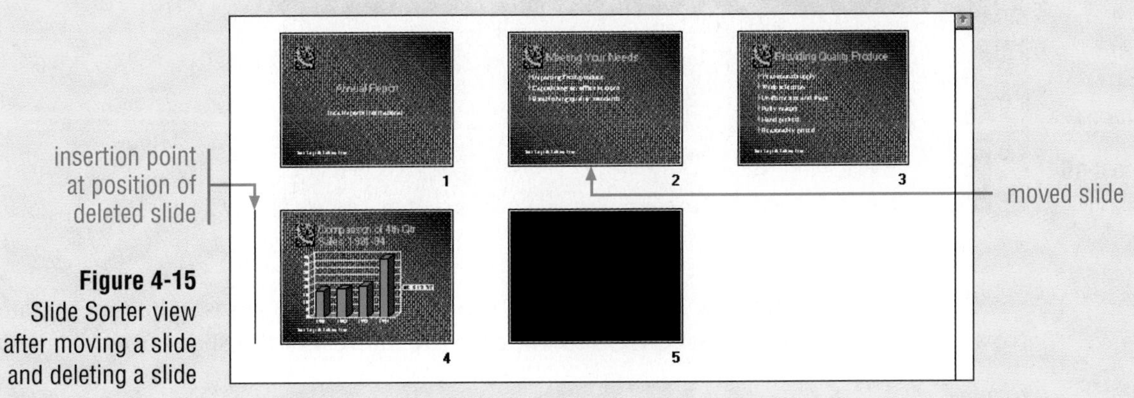

Figure 4-15 Slide Sorter view after moving a slide and deleting a slide

Next, Patricia wants to change the wording in the title of slide 2. You can't change text from within Slide Sorter view. You must be in Slide view or Outline view to edit slide text. Let's change the title of the slide now.

To edit slide text:

1. Click **slide 2**, then click the **Slide View button** at the bottom of the presentation window. PowerPoint displays slide 2 in the presentation window.
2. Using methods you've learned previously, change the title from "Meeting Your Needs" to "Meeting Customer Needs." Then deselect the title text box.

Now Patricia wants to add a slide to the presentation that summarizes the performance of her company.

To add new slides:

1. From within Slide view, move to slide 4 of the presentation.
2. Click the **Insert New Slide button** on the Standard toolbar to insert a new slide into the presentation. PowerPoint displays the New Slide dialog box. You could also have clicked the New Slide button at the bottom of the presentation window.
3. Click the layout titled "Bulleted list," the second slide in the first row, then click the **OK button**.
4. Click the title placeholder and type **Inca's Solid Performance**.
5. Click the main text (bulleted list) text box and type three bulleted items: **Improved products and services**, **Implemented new marketing plan**, and **Increased profitability**.
6. Click outside the text boxes to see the completed slide. See Figure 4-16.

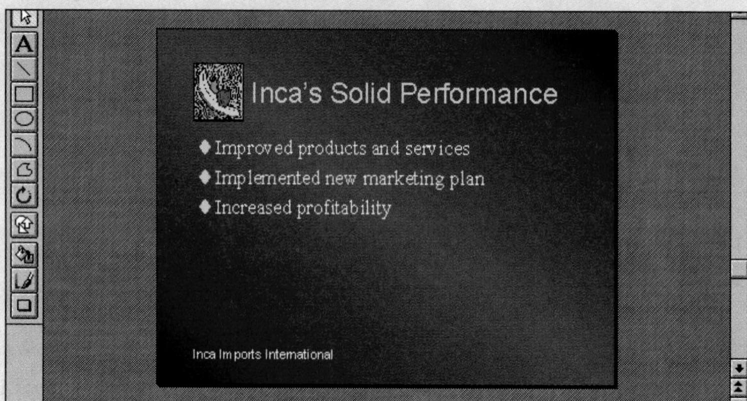

Figure 4-16
Completed new slide

That completes the new slide 5. Patricia is pleased with the slides in her presentation. Now she wants to add special effects to improve the interest of the slide show.

Adding Transition Effects

The first special effect that Patricia wants to add is called a transition. A **transition** is a method of moving one slide off the screen and bringing another slide onto the screen during a slide show. You must be in Slide Sorter view to add transitions.

REFERENCE WINDOW

Adding Transition Effects

- Get into Slide Sorter view and select the slide or slides to which you want to add a transition effect.
- Click the Down arrow button in the Transition Effects box on the Formatting toolbar to display a list of transition effects.
- Click the desired transition effect.

Let's add a transition to all of the slides in the presentation.

To add a transition effect:

❶ Click the **Slide Sorter View button** at the bottom of the presentation window to change to Slide Sorter view.

❷ Click **Edit**, then click **Select All** to select all the slides in the presentation. Now when you apply a slide transition, all the slides will have that transition. Currently, the Formatting toolbar shows "No Transition" in the Transition Effects box. See Figure 4-17.

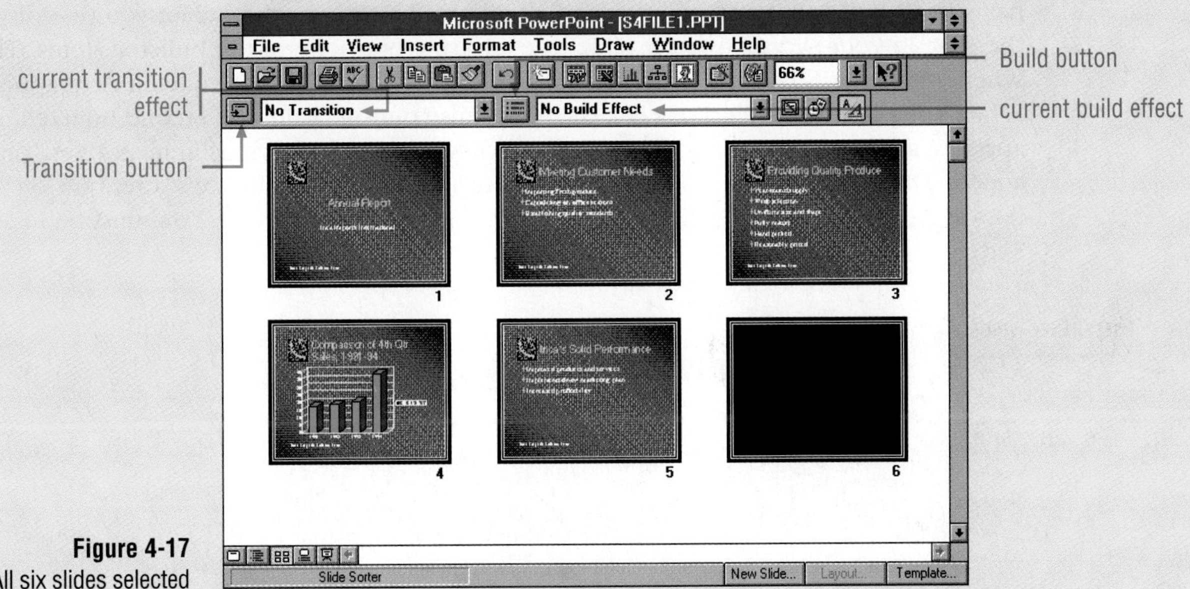

Figure 4-17
All six slides selected

❸ Click the **Down arrow button** in the Transition Effects box in the Slide Sorter toolbar to display the list of transitions.

❹ Scroll through the list until **Dissolve** appears, then click that method of transition. If you watched carefully, you saw PowerPoint demonstrate the dissolve transition with the first slide.

❺ Click anywhere outside of a slide to deselect the slides. PowerPoint has placed a transition icon below the lower-left corner of each slide. See Figure 4-18.

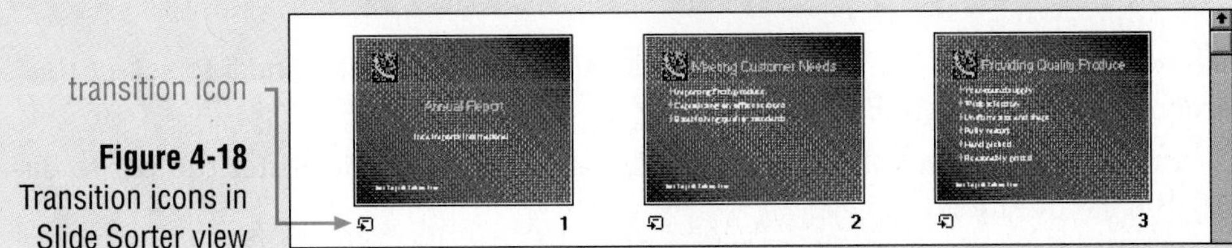

Figure 4-18
Transition icons in Slide Sorter view

You can test the transition of any slide now by clicking on the transition icon. Let's try it.

❻ Click the transition icon below slide 4. As you can see, PowerPoint momentarily displays slide 3 at that location, then performs the transition to slide 4. Click any of the transition icons to see how the transition looks for that slide.

You have now added transitions to the slides. You added the same transition to all six slides, but if you wanted, you could have selected only one slide and created a unique transition for only that slide.

Adding Build Effects

Having added transitions to the slides, Patricia is ready to add another special effect: builds. A **build** (also known as a **progressive disclosure**) is a feature that allows you to progressively display individual bulleted items, one item at a time. For example, if a slide has several bulleted items, you can add a build to the slide so that when you first display the slide in your slide show, the slide title appears, but none of the bulleted items. Then when you press [Spacebar] or click the left mouse button, the first bulleted item appears. When you press [Spacebar] or click the left mouse button again, the second bulleted item appears, and so on. You can also tell PowerPoint to dim the previous item as a new one is added. The advantage of builds is that you can focus your audience's attention on one item at a time, without the distractions of other items on the screen. You must be in Slide Sorter view to add builds.

REFERENCE WINDOW

Adding a Build Effect

- In Slide Sorter view, select the slide or slides to which you want to add a build effect.
- Click the Down arrow button in the Build Effects box on the Formatting toolbar to display a list of transition effects.
- Click the desired build effect.
- To dim previous points in the build, click the Build button to the left of the Build Effects box to display the Build dialog box, select a dim color, and then click the OK button.

Let's add a build effect now.

To add a build effect:

1. Click **slide 2**, then press and hold down **[Shift]**, and click **slides 3** and **5** to select the three slides that have bulleted lists.
2. Click the **Down arrow button** in the Build Effects box in the Slide Sorter toolbar to display the list of builds.
3. Scroll down and click **Wipe Right**. This specifies the type of build effect you want. In this case, the text in each bulleted item appears on the screen from left to right as if someone wiped it onto the screen. Now Patricia wants PowerPoint to dim the old bulleted item, while displaying a new one. This is called "dimming previous points."
4. Click the **Build button** on the Slide Sorter toolbar. PowerPoint displays the Build dialog box.
5. Click the **Dim Previous Points check box**. Below the Dim Previous Points checkbox is a colored bar that represents the color of the dimmed item. Let's change that color to blue-green.

6. Click the **Down arrow button** to the right of the dim-color bar and click the **blue-green (cyan) color tile**. See Figure 4-19.

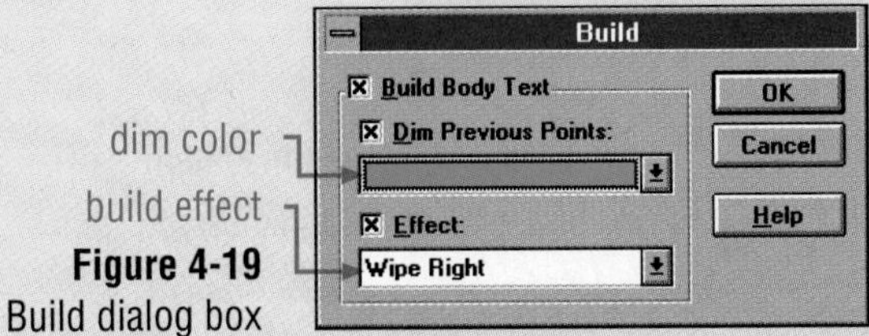

Figure 4-19
Build dialog box

7. Click the **OK button**. PowerPoint adds build effect icons below slides 2, 3, and 5, the three slides to which you have added build effects. See Figure 4-20.

Figure 4-20
Slide with build effect icons

8. Click anywhere outside the slides to deselect them.
   You have now added build effects to the appropriate slides. You could have added different build effects to each slide by selecting each slide individually and then completing Steps 2 through 7 above.

You can't see a build while in Slide Sorter view; you must be in Slide Show view. Let's run the completed slide show to view our special effects—the transitions and builds.

Running the Slide Show

Patricia has completed her slide show, and she's now ready to view it. Let's view the presentation using the Slide Show view.

To view the completed presentation:

1. Click **slide 1** in Slide Sorter view so that your presentation will begin with slide 1.
2. Click the **Slide Show button** at the bottom of the presentation window to begin the slide presentation. The title slide, "Annual Report," appears on the screen.
3. Press **[Spacebar]** to advance to the next slide. (You can also use the arrow keys, the page up and page down keys, or the mouse button.) Only the title of slide 2 appears on the screen, because this is a build slide, which will disclose the bulleted items one at a time as you go through the slide show.
4. Press **[Spacebar]** to display the first bulleted item under "Meeting Customer Needs."
5. Press **[Spacebar]** to display the second bulleted item and dim the first one. See Figure 4-21.

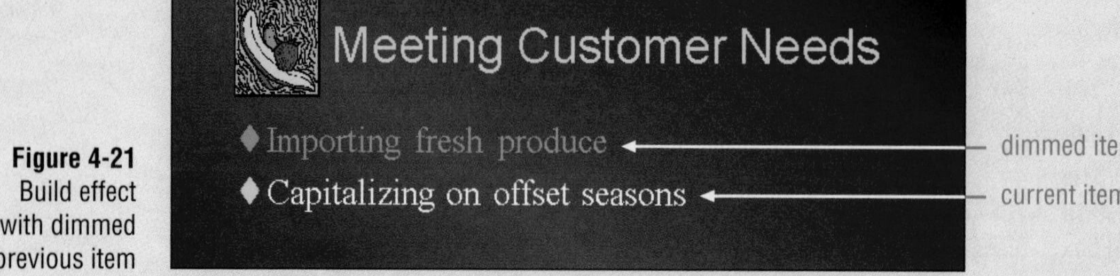

Figure 4-21 Build effect with dimmed previous item

❻ Continue through the slide show, pressing **[Spacebar]** to advance from one slide to the next or, within a build slide, from one point to the next. When you get to the last slide, the one with the black background, stop there.

TROUBLE? If you advanced past the last slide, PowerPoint returned you to the Slide Sorter view. Just click the Slide Show button again, then press [End] to return to the last slide.

At this point, Patricia decides that she wants to look at the "Inca's Solid Performance" slide again.

❼ Click the *right* mouse button. This moves the presentation backwards to the previous slide. Notice that when you go back to the previous slide, all the bulleted items appear and they are in the normal color, not dimmed. If you wanted to return to a previous slide and go backwards through the build effect, you could press [←] multiple times. (This does not work with the right mouse button.)

❽ Press **[Esc]** to return to Slide Sorter view.

Patricia is pleased with the results. She saves the final version of her slide show.

To save the slide show:

❶ Click the **Save button** on the Standard toolbar to save the presentation file using the filename S4FILE1.PPT.

Annotating Slides During a Slide Show

While Patricia rehearses her slide presentation and during the actual presentation to the stockholders, she will annotate certain slides to draw attention to important points. To **annotate** in PowerPoint means to make temporary freehand marks on the slide during a slide presentation. The annotations are not saved to the disk with the presentation itself.

REFERENCE WINDOW

Annotating a Slide

- While running a slide show in Slide Show view or in the PowerPoint Viewer, advance to the slide you wish to annotate.
- Click the Freehand annotation icon in the lower-right corner of the screen.
- Use the pencil mouse pointer to make temporary marks on the slide.

Let's annotate the presentation now.

To annotate a slide:

❶ From Slide Sorter view, click slide 3 to select it.

❷ Click the **Slide Show button** . Slide 3 appears in Slide Show view.

❸ Press **[Spacebar]** six times to see the last bulleted item, "Reasonably priced."

❹ Move the mouse to display the mouse pointer on the screen and to display the Freehand annotation icon in the lower-right corner of the screen. See Figure 4-22.

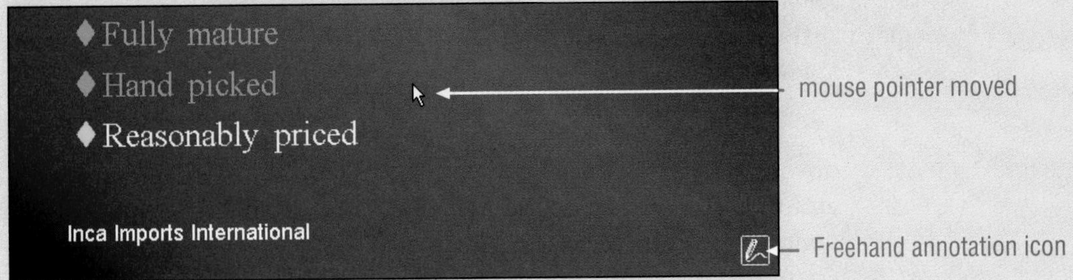

Figure 4-22 Freehand annotation icon

Patricia wants to emphasize that Inca produce is reasonably priced, neither the highest nor the lowest in the industry.

❺ Click the **Freehand annotation icon** in the lower-right corner of the screen. The mouse pointer becomes .

❻ Position under the "R" in "Reasonably," then hold down the left mouse button while you drag the pointer to underline that word. Then release the mouse button. See Figure 4-23. Patricia rehearses what she will say to emphasize the meaning of "reasonably priced."

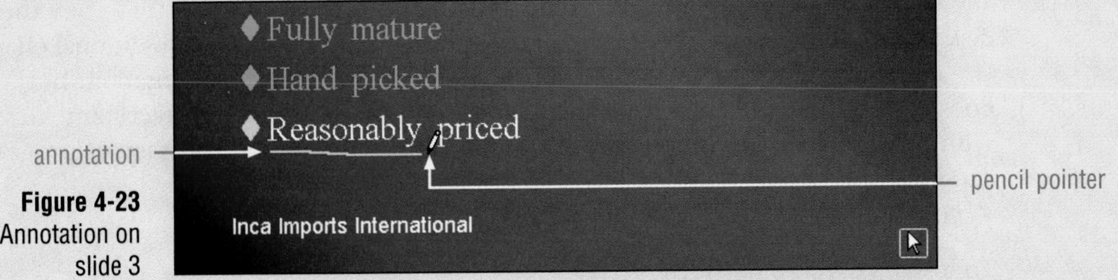

Figure 4-23 Annotation on slide 3

❼ Press **[Spacebar]**. The annotations disappear and the next slide appears on the screen.

❽ Press **[Esc]** to quit the slide show.

❾ Exit PowerPoint.

After rehearsing her presentation several times, Patricia feels confident about making the presentation to the stockholders.

DESIGN PRINCIPLE WINDOW

Tips on Electronic Presentations

- Don't feel that you have to include transitions and builds in your slides. Unnecessary transitions and builds will distract your audience from the message of the presentation.
- If you include transitions, use only one type of transition for all the slides.
- If you include builds, use only one type of build for all the build slides.
- If you are have a tendency to get nervous during a presentation, avoid using the mouse to advance the slides and to make annotations. The audience can see a jittery mouse pointer. Instead, use the [Spacebar] to advance slides.
- Avoid excessive annotations on slides. Annotations can look sloppy if done to excess.

If you want to take a break and resume the tutorial at a later time, you can do so now. When you resume working, make sure the Windows Program Manager is on screen and that your Student Disk with the file S4FILE1.PPT is in the appropriate drive. Then continue with the next section.

■ ■ ■

Using the PowerPoint Viewer

You could run all your presentations from the PowerPoint program, but what if you want to give a presentation on a computer that doesn't have PowerPoint installed? In that case, you could use the PowerPoint Viewer. The **PowerPoint Viewer** is a separate program (shipped by Microsoft on a separate disk) that you can use to show your presentation on any Windows computer. The Microsoft PowerPoint license allow you to copy the Viewer disk and to install the Viewer program on other computers without additional charge.

Patricia wants to get Angelena Cristenas' opinion on her presentation, but Angelena doesn't have PowerPoint on her computer. Patricia brings the PowerPoint Viewer disk with her and runs her presentation from that. Let's first install the Viewer program. You can use your own or someone else's computer.

To install PowerPoint Viewer:

1. Make sure you have a copy of the PowerPoint Viewer disk, which is Disk 11 in the PowerPoint 4.0 package.

   TROUBLE? You might not be allowed to install Viewer on a computer in a lab or on a network. If you don't have the PowerPoint Viewer disk, consult your instructor or technical support person. If they can't provide you with a disk and you don't have your own PowerPoint package, skip this section. Similarly, if PowerPoint Viewer is already installed on your computer, you can skip this section.

2. Launch Windows so that the Program Manager is on the screen.
3. Insert the PowerPoint Viewer disk into a disk drive, click **File**, click **Run**, type **a:vsetup**, and click the **OK button**. Then follow the instructions on your screen to complete the installation.

Patricia is now ready to run her slide presentation using the Viewer.

To use the Viewer:

❶ Double-click the **PowerPoint Viewer icon** in the Windows Program Manager. See Figure 4-24. The Microsoft PowerPoint Viewer dialog box appears on the screen.

Figure 4-24
PowerPoint Viewer icon

❷ From the Microsoft PowerPoint Viewer dialog box, select the disk drive that contains your Student Disk, then select **s4file1.ppt**, and click the **Show button**. Clicking the Show button in the PowerPoint Viewer dialog box is the same as clicking the Slide Show button in the presentation window.

❸ Press **[Spacebar]** or click the left mouse button to run through the presentation. Feel free to press **[Esc]** to stop the slide show whenever you want. When you finish, you will be returned to the PowerPoint Viewer dialog box.

❹ Click the **Quit button** to return to the Windows Program Manager.

Angelena liked Patricia's presentation.

Preparing 35mm Slides

Patricia will present the electronic slide show to the board of directors in a suitably equipped conference room at Inca Imports. The conference room at the stockholders meeting, however, does not have the equipment necessary to run an electronic slide show, so Patricia plans to use 35mm slides. Because the presentation to the stockholders is very important, Patricia also makes black-and-white transparency masters as a back-up to the slides.

Inca Imports International, like most small businesses, lacks the facilities to make 35mm slides or print color output from computer files, but all large U.S. cities have service bureaus that can convert computer files into 35mm slides, provided the files are in the correct format, usually PostScript. You should contact a service bureau near you for details. Check the yellow pages of your telephone book under "Typesetting."

PowerPoint also supports the services of Genigraphics Corporation, a service bureau that handles 35mm slides, color overheads, and posters. With headquarters in Memphis, Tennessee, Genigraphics has facilities in fourteen major cities around the United States. The PowerPoint disks contain the software necessary to prepare and deliver slides to Genigraphics. Patricia therefore decides to use Genigraphics to prepare her slides.

Note: In the following procedure, you will prepare the presentation as if you were going to pay for commercial slide preparation, but you won't actually send the presentation file to Genigraphics.

To prepare 35mm slides in Genigraphics format:

❶ Launch PowerPoint again, and open S4FILE1.PPT.

❷ Click **File**, then click **Slide Setup**. PowerPoint displays the Slide Setup dialog box. See Figure 4-25.

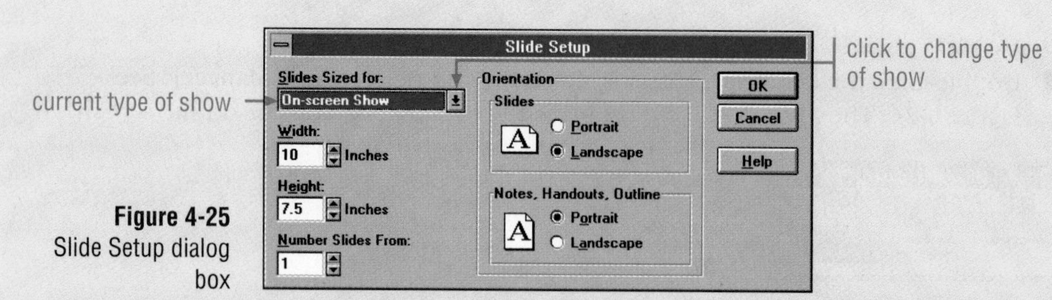

Figure 4-25 Slide Setup dialog box

3. Click the **Down arrow button** next to "Slide Sized for," and select **35mm Slides**. PowerPoint adjusts the width and height of each slide so it is proportioned for 35mm slides. Click the **OK button**.

   Now you will output the presentation to a disk file in the Genigraphics format.

4. Click **File**, click **Print** to display the Print dialog box, then click the **Printer button** to display the Print Setup dialog box.

   Here you will select the printer driver for Genigraphics. A **printer driver** is a disk file that provides information about a printer so that your applications software can prepare output for that printer. Some printer drivers, like the one for Genigraphics, don't actually send the file to a printer but rather create a disk file in a special format. The Genigraphics driver also displays dialog boxes to get additional information when you "print" your presentation to disk.

5. Click **Genigraphics Driver on GENI:**, then click the **OK button**. PowerPoint returns to the Print dialog box. Most of the options in the dialog box are dimmed because the Genigraphics printer driver contains its own set of options.

   TROUBLE? The Genigraphics Driver will only be listed if your computer has the complete PowerPoint installation. If you don't see the driver, see your instructor or technical support person.

You are now prepared to "print" the presentation in Genigraphics format—that is, send the presentation to a disk file. Let's do that now.

To prepare the Genigraphics file:

1. Make sure the Print What text box contains **Slides (With Builds)**. By selecting Slides (With Builds) you are telling Genigraphics to create a separate slide with each of the progressive disclosure items for the build slides. That means Patricia will end up with eighteen 35mm slides, not just six.
2. Click the **OK button** on the Print dialog box. The Genigraphics driver displays a dialog box requesting more information. See Figure 4-26. Patricia knows that she can

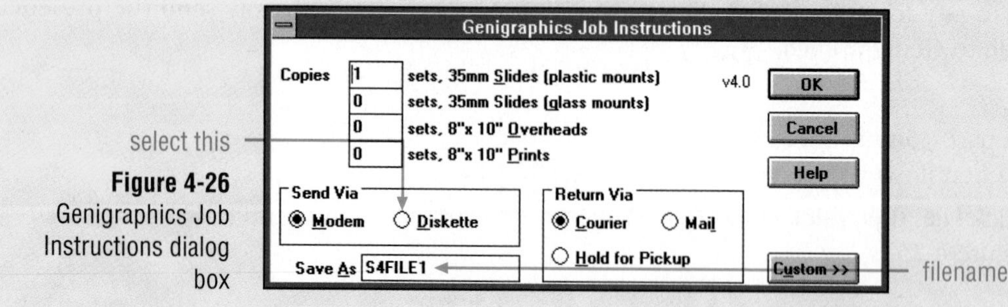

Figure 4-26 Genigraphics Job Instructions dialog box

use her modem to send the file directly to Genigraphics Corporation, or she can save the file on a disk. Patricia decides to save it to a disk, then mail the disk to Genigraphics using an overnight courier service like Federal Express or UPS. You will save the file to your Student Disk.

Notice that at the bottom of the dialog box, the filename in the Save As box is S4FILE1, the file currently in the PowerPoint presentation window.

❸ Click **Diskette** in the Send Via box, make sure **Courier** is selected in the Return Via box, and then click the **OK button**. The Genigraphics dialog box closes and the Save As dialog box appears. Notice the default filename is the same as the one that was in the Genigraphics dialog box, and the Genigraphics driver added the file extension.GNA. You can change the filename, but you must leave the Genigraphics extension so their equipment will recognize the file.

❹ In the Save As dialog box, change the Drives box to display the disk drive where your Student Disk is located, and click the **OK button**. The file S4FILE1.GNA is saved to the disk. Next the Genigraphics driver displays the Genigraphics Billing Information dialog box.

❺ Fill out the information in the dialog box with your name, address, phone number, and so forth. Click the **COD button** so you don't have to fill in a credit card number. Then click the **OK button**. You'll see a message telling you that a file with 18 slides has been saved and that you should send the file to Genigraphics for processing.

❻ After reading the message, click the **OK button**.

Patricia has now prepared the file S4FILE1.GNA to send to Genigraphics.

Preparing Overheads

Patricia's presentation to the stockholders is very important, so she decides to be on the safe side and create black and white overheads of the presentation in case the slide projector doesn't work. With PowerPoint, you can prepare overhead transparency masters quickly and easily. You simply have to change the slide design to overheads. In general, designs that work well for slides might not work as well for black-and-white overheads. PowerPoint provides several templates for black-and-white overheads. Patricia decides to change the slide design to one specifically created for black-and-white overheads. She could do this by choosing a new template or by using the Pick a Look Wizard. You already know how to choose a new template, so let's use the Pick a Look Wizard to change the design to overheads.

To change the design to overheads:

❶ Click the **Pick a Look Wizard button** on the Standard toolbar. PowerPoint displays the Step 1 dialog box of the Pick a Look Wizard.

❷ Read the information on the dialog box, then click the **Next button** to proceed to Step 2. See Figure 4-27. Here the Wizard asks you which type of output you want.

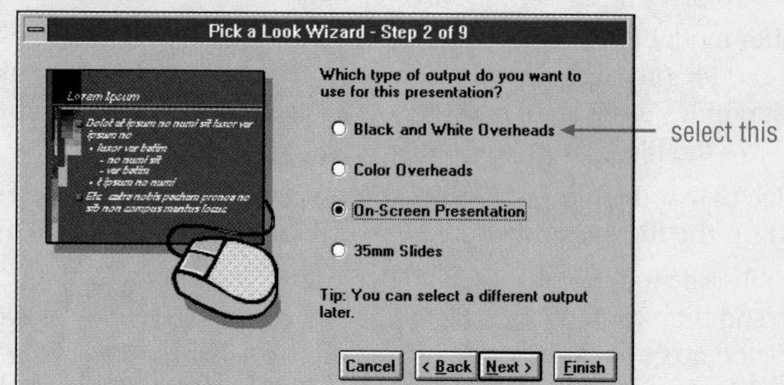

Figure 4-27
Step 2 of Pick a Look Wizard

3. Click **Black and White Overheads**, then click the **Next button**. You can also create color overheads, but that requires a color printer. Step 3 of the Wizard now appears on the screen, where you will select a template design. Only templates specifically designed for black-and-white overheads appear in the list.
4. Click **Double Lines**, a template design with a shaded line across the overhead, then click the **Next button**. PowerPoint displays step 4 of the Wizard. Here Patricia selects the type of material that she wants in her slide presentation. She decides she wants only full-page slides (overheads).
5. Make sure the **Full-Page Slides checkbox** is selected and the other three options are deselected. Then click the **Next button**. Now the Wizard displays the Slide Options. Patricia doesn't want any of these slide options.
6. Make sure none of the slide options is selected, then click the **Next button**. You can now see the final dialog box of the Pick a Look Wizard.
7. Click the **Finish button**. PowerPoint updates the color scheme of the slides. The black-and-white overheads appear in the presentation window.

Patricia observes that when the Pick a Look Wizard added the Double Lines template, it removed the Inca Imports logo from the Slide Master. She decides to add the logo back to the Slide Master. Patricia also realizes that with overheads, you don't need a slide to mark the end of the presentation, so she deletes the final blank slide from the overhead masters. She will then save the overhead presentation file and print the overheads.

To complete the overhead presentation:

1. From slide sorter view, click slide 6, and press **[Del]**. This slide is deleted from the presentation.
2. Add the Inca Imports logo from the file IIILOGO.BMP to the Slide Master in the same position you had it in before, then return to Slide Sorter view. (If you need help, refer back to the section "Adding a Logo to the Slide Master.") See Figure 4-28. The logo appears in color on the screen but will be black and white when you print the overhead masters.

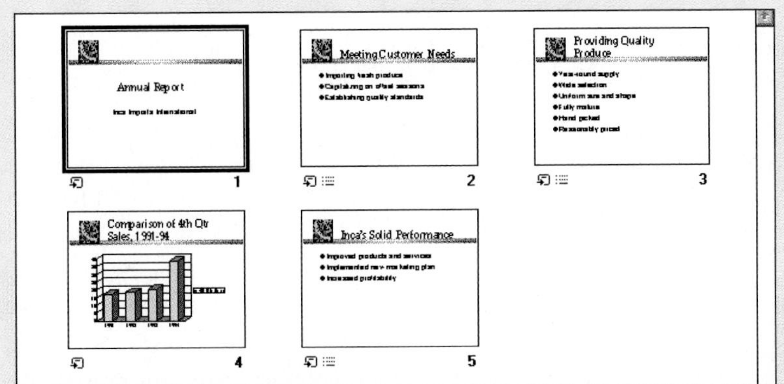

Figure 4-28
Overheads after adding logo

Now Patricia wants to save the overhead presentation using a different filename. She also wants to change the orientation of the printing from landscape, which is wider than it is tall, to portrait, which is taller than it is wide. Overheads fit the projector better if they are in portrait view.

3. Click **File**, click **Slide Setup** to display the Slide Setup dialog box, click **Portrait** in the Slides orientation box, then click the **OK button**. The page orientation now appears in portrait view. See Figure 4-29.

Figure 4-29
Overheads in portrait orientation

4. Click **File**, click **Save As**, and then save the presentation to your Student Disk using the filename S4FILE2.PPT. You will use the same Summary Info as you did earlier, so just click the **OK button**. Patricia now prints the overheads.
5. Click **File**, then click **Print**. PowerPoint displays the Print dialog box. The current printer is listed as Genigraphics Driver on GENI. You'll have to change back to your normal printer.
6. Click the **Printer button** to display the Printer Setup dialog box, click the name of your printer in the Printers box, and then click the **OK button**. PowerPoint returns to the Print dialog box.
7. Make sure that **Slides (without builds)** is selected in the Print What box and that the **Black & White** option and the **Scale to Fit Paper** option are selected.
8. Click the **OK button** to print the overhead presentation. This completes the preparation of the presentation.
9. Save your changes, then if you desire, you may exit PowerPoint.

Patricia is pleased with the appearance of her overhead masters. She asks her secretary to photocopy the transparency masters onto transparency sheets. Within a few days, Patricia receives her 35mm slides from Genigraphics Corporation. She is ready to give her presentation at the stockholders meeting.

DESIGN PRINCIPLE WINDOW

Giving an Effective Slide Show Presentation

- Dress appropriately for the meeting.
- Maintain a proper demeanor at all times.
- Introduce yourself and briefly explain what you'll be showing your audience.
- Look at your audience. Make adequate eye-to-eye contact.
- Speak clearly and audibly.
- If you're using a microphone, adjust it to your height so you won't have to lean down or stretch up to speak into it.
- Keep your language appropriate for the audience and situation. Avoid jargon, slang, and profanity.
- Summarize your presentation, come to a logical conclusion, and field questions courteously.

Questions

1. Define the following terms:
   a. background shade style
   b. variant (of a background shade style)
   c. transition effect
   d. build effect
   e. annotate a slide
2. Describe the purpose of the Slide Master and when you would use it.
3. List the advantages for creating a slide show beginning with a blank slide presentation rather than using the AutoContent Wizard.
4. Write a list of steps required to do the following:
   a. display the Slide Master
   b. change the background color and variant of a slide
   c. change the color scheme of a slide
   d. modify a bullet character and color
   e. insert slides from an existing presentation into the current presentation
   f. adding a transition effect to a slide
   g. add a build effect to a slide
5. What is the PowerPoint Viewer? When would you use it?
6. Describe how to get 35mm slides made from a PowerPoint slide presentation.
7. Describe what you would do to create overhead transparency masters from your PowerPoint slide presentation.
8. **E** List one advantage and disadvantage of adding build effects with dimming of previous points to a slide containing bulleted items.

Tutorial Assignments

In the following Tutorial Assignment, make sure you click the Blank presentation button when you launch PowerPoint or, if PowerPoint is already running, click the New button on the Standard toolbar to create a new presentation. After working with a presentation and saving your changes, close the presentation.

Do the following:

1. Create a new blank presentation.
2. Create a title slide with the title "Employee Benefits" and the subtitle "Inca Imports International."
3. Using the Slide Master, change the color scheme to give a background color of dark blue-green (almost a forest green) and a text and line color of amber (orangish).
4. Change the shade style to From Corner, and the variant with the lightest color in the lower-left corner and the darkest in the upper-right corner.
5. Change the Master title style to a white Arial font.
6. In the Master main text, change the bullet color to red, but don't change the bullet character.

E 7. In the second level text, change the text from black to Yellow #7 and the bullet from a dash to a red plus (+). *Hint*: From the Bullet dialog box, you can change the bullet to almost any color by clicking the down arrow under Special Color, then clicking Other Color to display the Other Color dialog box. When you click a color tile in the Other Color dialog box, the name of the color appears on the status bar.

8. Insert the Inca Imports logo (IIILOGO.BMP) into the Slide Master. Resize it to the approximate height of the Master title style text box. Position the logo in the lower-right corner of the text box of the Slide Master slide text style, near the text "Object Area for AutoLayouts."

E 9. Return to Slide view and remove the Inca logo from the title slide. *Hint*: Use the same procedure you used when you removed the template diamond from the title slide in Tutorial 3.

10. Add a new slide with the Bulleted List AutoLayout.
11. Make the title of the new slide "Basic Benefits." Type the following first-level bulleted list items: "Medical and Dental Insurance," "Group Term Life Insurance," "Disability Insurance," "Occupational Accidental Death & Dismemberment Insurance," and "Master Retirement Plan."
12. Insert the existing presentation file T4FILE1.PPT into the current presentation.
13. In the new slide 3, demote the last two bulleted items, because they are the two types of supplemental retirement savings plans available to Inca Import employees.

E 14. In slide 6, remove the bullets that appear to the left of the address of the benefits office. *Hint*: Display the Bullets menu, then deselect the checkbox labeled "Use a Bullet."

15. To all the slides, add the transition effect called "Random Transition."
16. To slides 2 through 5, add the build effect called "Blinds Horizontal." Select the Dim Previous Points option with gray as the dimmed color.
17. Run the slide show to ensure that the builds and transitions work properly.
18. Save the presentation as S4FILE3.PPT, then print the presentation in Black & White as handouts with four or six slides per page. Close the file.

Do the following:

19. Start a new blank presentation, and on the title slide, type the title "Employee of the Month," and the subtitle "Inca Imports International."
20. Using the Slide Master, change the color scheme to a background color of red and a text and line color of dark blue.
21. Select a background shade style Diagonal Right, and the variant with the lightest color in the upper-left corner and the darkest in the lower-right corner.
22. Change the Master title font size to 60-point Book Antiqua. If your computer doesn't have that font, use a different one.
23. Change the Master text styles so the font is 32-point Arial.

E 24. Draw a large, red star in the middle of the Slide Master to serve as a backdrop for the slides in the presentation. *Hint*: Click the AutoShapes button in the Drawing toolbar, click the Star in the AutoShapes palette, press and hold down [Shift] while you drag from the upper left to the lower right of the slide. (Holding the [Shift] maintains the proportions of the image.) Center the star on the slide.

Change the slide color to Red #3 by clicking Format, clicking Colors and Lines, then selecting the desired color. (The color name appears on the status bar when you click a color tile in the Other Color dialog box.) Put the star behind the text by clicking Draw, then clicking Send to Back.

25. Near the upper-left corner of the Slide Master, insert the text "Employee of the Month." Make the text 24-point, white, Times New Roman (or a similar font).
26. **E** Return to Slide view, and remove the Slide Master text and drawing from the title slide. *Hint*: Follow the procedure you used to remove the template diamond from the title slide in Tutorial 3.
27. Add a new slide with the Title Slide AutoLayout.
28. Make the title of the new slide "Alicia Cardon" and the subtitle "January."
29. Insert the existing presentation file T4FILE2.PPT into the current presentation.
30. **E** To all the slides, add a transition effect and an automatic advance time, using the following method: In Slide Sort View, select all the slides, then click the Transition button on the Formatting toolbar to display the Transition dialog box. Change the Effect to "Cover Right." Set the speed to "Slow." In the Advance box, click Automatically After, then set the time to 4 seconds.
31. **E** Set the slide show to run continuously. *Hint*: Click View, click Slide Show, click Use Slide Timings, and click Run Continuously Until 'Esc'.
32. Start the slide show and watch as the presentation automatically moves from one slide to the next and returns to the first slide after showing the last slide. If the slide show isn't automatic and continuous, you have made a mistake in one of the exercise items above. Review the steps and fix your mistake.
33. Press [Esc] to end the slide show after you've watched the entire presentation at least once.
34. Save the presentation as S4FILE4.PPT, then print the first three slides of the presentation in Black & White. Close the file.

Case Problems

1. Training on Sexual Harassment

Katherine Jaidar is the Director of Human Resources Development for McNeil Manufacturing Company, a large manufacturer of gardening supplies, like rakes, hoes, shovels, hoses, sprinkling systems, and tillers. One of her responsibilities is to provide training to McNeil employees on sexual harassment in the workplace. She prepares a PowerPoint slide presentation for her training classes as well as for a self-training presentation. Do the following:

1. Create a blank presentation with a title slide. Make the title "Sexual Harassment in the Workplace," the first line of the subtitle, "Training for employees of," and the second line of the subtitle " McNeil Manufacturing Company."
2. From the Slide Master, change the color scheme to give a background color of light blue and a text and line color of black.
3. Change the background shade style to Horizontal, and the variant with the darkest color on the left and lightest color on the right.
4. Change the Master title style to Arial font.
5. **E** In the Master text style line (the first level in the bulleted list), change the bullet color to Yellow #8, but don't change the bullet style. *Hint*: The color name appears on the status bar when you click a color tile in the Other Color dialog box.
6. Return to Slide view, and add a new slide with the Bulleted List AutoLayout. Make the title "Definition of Sexual Harassment," and type the following bulleted items: "Promise of career enhancement for sexual favors," "Threats of career jeopardy if sexual demands are rejected," and "Deliberate, repeated, unsolicited comments, gestures, or physical actions of a sexual nature."

7. Insert the file P4HARAS.PPT after slide 2 of the current presentation.
8. On the new slide 3, reduce the size of the text box of the main text, and move the box down on the slide, so the slide appears more balanced top to bottom.
9. To each of the two slides with the titles "Don'ts" and "Do's," add an appropriate clip-art image.
10. Add "Fly from Bottom" build effects to all the slides that have bulleted lists. Include the feature to dim previous points using an appropriate color of your own choosing.

E 11. To all the slides, add the transition effect called "Checkerboard Across" with a slow speed. *Hint*: In Slide Sort View, select all the slides, then click the Transition button on the Formatting toolbar to display the Transition dialog box. Change the Effect to "Checkerboard Across" and set the speed to "Slow."

E 12. Check the spelling in your presentation. *Hint*: Begin by clicking Tools, then click Spelling.

13. Run the slide show to ensure that the builds and transitions work properly, save the presentation as S4HARAS.PPT, then print all the slides of the presentation in Black & White.

2. Report on Using a Presentation Graphics Program

You have agreed to give a presentation to a college fraternity on the benefits of using a presentation graphics program like PowerPoint. As you prepare your presentation using PowerPoint, use proper principles of planning and design as discussed throughout this book. Specifically do the following:

1. Create a blank presentation with a title slide. Choose your own title, but use your name as the subtitle.
2. From the Slide Master, change the background color to Violet #7, the shade style to Vertical, and the variant with the darkest color at the top and lightest color at the bottom.
3. Change the Master title style to Arial font of the color Blue #3, and change all the text in the Master text styles to the color white.
4. In the Master text style line (the first level in the bulleted list), change the bullet color to Yellow #8, but don't change the bullet character.
5. In the Slide Master, insert an appropriate clip art (such as a computer or a diskette). Make sure the clip-art image is simple enough so it can be seen clearly when reduced to a smaller size. Reduce the size so that the image is not more than about an inch in any dimension. Position the image in the lower-right corner of the text box of the Slide Master text style, near the text "Object Area for AutoLayouts."

E 6. Return to Slide view, and remove the graphic image from the title slide. *Hint*: Use the same procedure you used when you removed the template diamond from the title slide in Tutorial 3.

7. Add at least four new slides with the Bulleted List AutoLayout. For example, you might create a slide with the title "Advantages of Presentation Programs" and a list of advantages such as "Easy to use," "Easy to modify," "Professional quality," "Flexible," and so forth. Another example might be a title such as "Weaknesses of Presentation Programs" and a list of disadvantages such as "Requires expensive hardware," "Difficult to get appropriate clip art," "Requires extensive training," and so forth. Other possible titles include "Key Features of Presentation Software," "Possible Uses of Presentation Software," and "Steps in Learning How to use Presentation Software."
8. Add a slide with a graph so your audience can see a sample graph or chart. For example, the title might be "Cost of Presentation Software," with a bar graph

for the cost of PowerPoint, Harvard Graphics, WordPerfect Presentations, and Lotus Persuasion. If you can't easily obtain real numbers, make up some reasonable prices.

9. Add a summary slide with a bulleted list of the most important ideas in your presentation.
10. Add "Dissolve" build effects to all of the slides that have bulleted lists. Include the feature to dim previous points.
11. **E** To all the slides, add the transition effect called "Uncover Right-Down" with a slow speed. *Hint*: In Slide Sort View, select all the slides, then click the Transition button on the Formatting toolbar to display the Transition dialog box. Change the Effect to "Uncover Right-Down" and set the speed to "Slow."
12. Create speaker's notes for all of your slides. Include whatever information you need to help you with your presentation.
13. **E** Check the spelling in your presentation. *Hint*: Begin by clicking Tools, then clicking Spelling.
14. Run the slide show to ensure that the builds and transitions work properly.
15. Save the presentation as S4PRESNT.PPT, print all the slides of the presentation, and then print the speaker's notes in Black & White.
16. Create the file S4PRESNT.GNA that could be sent to Genigraphics for preparation of 35mm slides.
17. Use the Pick a Look Wizard to modify the presentation for creation of black-and-white overhead transparency masters.
18. Save the overhead version of the presentation as S4OVERHD.PPT, then print the overhead transparency masters.

3. Presentation on Personal Interest

Create a presentation on one of your personal interests, hobbies, or college courses. Your presentation might be on such topics as playing the piano, learning Spanish, astronomy, computer games, movies, horseback riding, physical fitness, dating, or cooking—anything that you're interested in and have some knowledge about. Do the following:

1. Choose an appropriate and attractive color scheme, background shading, and fonts. You may use the Pick a Look Wizard if you so desire.
2. Create a presentation of at least seven slides, including a title slide, at least three slides with bulleted lists, at least one slide with a graph or chart, a summary slide, and a blank slide (one with a black background) to signal the end of the presentation.
3. Add clip art or a drawing to the Slide Master.
4. Include speaker's notes on all the slides.
5. **E** Check the spelling of your presentation by clicking Tools, then clicking Spelling, and following the instructions on the Spelling dialog box.
6. Add transition effects for all slides. Add build effects (with dimming of previous points) for all slides with bulleted lists.
7. Save the presentation as S4HOBBY1.PPT, then print the slides as handouts (with 3 or 6 slides per page), and print the speaker's notes in Black & White.
8. Prepare the file S4HOBBY1.GNA for commercial preparation of 35mm slides by Genigraphics Corporation.

Index

Special Characters

A

B

C

D

E

F

Q

R

S

T

U

V

W

X

Z

TASK REFERENCE

POWERPOINT 4.0 FOR WINDOWS

Italicized page numbers indicate the first discussion of each task.

TASK	MOUSE	MENU	KEYBOARD
Add a coworker to an organizational chart, PP 70	Click Co-worker: , click existing box		
Add build effects, PP 98	Click	In Slide Sorter view, click Tools, click Build	
Add subordinate levels to an organizational chart, PP 69	Click Subordinate: , click existing box		
Add transition effects, PP 96	Click	In Slide Sorter view, click Tools, click Transition	
Annotate a slide, PP 100	In Slide Show view, click		
AutoContent Wizard, PP 27	Click , then click AutoContent Wizard	Click File, click New, then click AutoContent Wizard	
Bold text, PP 43	Click B	Click Format, click Font, click Bold, click the OK button	Ctrl B
Center paragraph	Click	Click Format, click Alignment, click Center	Ctrl E
Change background color, PP 88		Click Format, click Slide Background, click Change Color, click the color, click the OK button, click Apply or Apply to All	
Change bullet, PP 89		Click Format, click Bullet, select the bullet character and color, click the OK button	
Change slide layout, PP 60		Click Format, click Slide Layout	
Change slide color scheme, PP 86		Click Format, click Slide Color Scheme	
Change text font, PP 43	Click next to font, click font	Click Format, click Font, click the font, click the OK button	Ctrl Shift F
Change text point size, PP 43	Click next to font size, click size	Click Format, click Font, click the font size, click the OK button	Ctrl Shift P
Change Text Color, PP 44	Click	Click Format, click Font, change the color, click the OK button	
Check Spelling, PP 49	Click	Click Tools, click Spelling	F7 or Alt Ctrl L
Close		Click File, click Close	Ctrl W or Ctrl F4
Copy	Select text, click	Select text, click Edit, click Copy	Ctrl C

TASK REFERENCE

POWERPOINT 4.0 FOR WINDOWS

Italicized page numbers indicate the first discussion of each task.

TASK	MOUSE	MENU	KEYBOARD
Cut, PP 37	Select text, click [Cut button]	Select text, click Edit, click Cut	Ctrl X
Date		Go to Slide Master, click Insert, click Date	Alt Shift D
Decrease text font size	Click [Decrease Font Size button]		Ctrl Shift <
Delete character right, PP 32			Del
Delete character left, PP 32			Backspace
Delete slide, PP 36		In Slide Sorter or Outline view, select slide, click Edit, click Delete Slide	Del
Delete word left			Ctrl Backspace
Delete word right			Ctrl Del
Demote paragraph, PP 34	Click [Demote button]		Alt Shift →
Draw a shape, PP 71	Click [AutoShapes button], click the desired shape, drag the mouse on the slide		
Exit/Quit, PP 22		Click File, click Exit	Ctrl Q or Alt F4
Find		Click Edit, click Find	Ctrl F
Flip an object, PP 72		Click Draw, click Rotate/Flip, click Flip Vertical or Flip Horizontal	
Group		Select objects, click Draw, click Group	Ctrl Shift G
Help, Contents, PP 20		Click Help, click Contents	F1
Help, Search, PP 21		Click Help, click Search for Help on	
Increase text font size	Click [Increase Font Size button]		Ctrl Shift >
Insert a title into a graph, PP 66		Click Insert, click Titles	
Insert a picture, PP 58		Click Insert, click Picture	
Insert clip art, PP 62	Click [Clip Art button]	Click Insert, click Clip Art	
Insert a graph, PP 65	Click [Graph button]	Click Insert, click Object, click Microsoft Graph	
Insert an organizational chart, PP 68	Click [Org Chart button]	Click Insert, click Object, click Microsoft Organizational Chart	
Insert slides from a disk file, PP 93		Click Insert, click Slides from File	

TASK REFERENCE

POWERPOINT 4.0 FOR WINDOWS

Italicized page numbers indicate the first discussion of each task.

TASK	MOUSE	MENU	KEYBOARD
Italicize text, PP 43	Click [I]	Click Format, click Font, click Italic, click the OK button	Ctrl I
Justify paragraph		Click Format, click Alignment, click Justify	Ctrl J
Left-align paragraph, PP 57	Click [Left-align]	Click Format, click Alignment, click Left	Ctrl L
Make text plain		Click Format, click Font, click Regular, click the OK button	Ctrl Shift Z
Move selected paragraph up, PP 34	Click [Move Up]		Alt Shift ↑
Move selected paragraph down, PP 34	Click [Move Down]		Alt Shift ↓
New presentation	Click [New]	Click File, click New	Ctrl N
New slide, PP 40	Click [New Slide]	Click Insert, click New Slide	Ctrl M
Next slide, PP 18	Click [Next Slide]		PgDn
Notes Page View, PP 17	Click [Notes Pages View]	Click View, click Notes Pages	
Open, PP 8	Click [Open]	Click File, click Open	Ctrl O
Outline View, PP 16	Click [Outline View]	Click View, click Outline	Alt Ctrl O
Paste, PP 37	Click [Paste]	Click Edit, click Paste	Ctrl V
Pick a Look Wizard, PP 27	Click [Pick a Look Wizard]	Click Format, click Pick a Look Wizard	
Prepare 35mm slides, PP 103		Click File, click Slide Setup, select Slides Sized for 35mm Slide, click the OK button, click File, click Print, Genigraphics Driver on GENI, follow instructions in dialog boxes	
Previous slide, PP 11	Click [Previous Slide]		PgUp
Print, PP 19	Click [Print]	Click File, click Print	Ctrl P or Ctrl Shift F12
Promote paragraph, PP 34	Click [Promote]		Alt Shift ←
Replace		Click Edit, click Replace	Ctrl H
Right-align paragraph		Click Format, click Alignment, click Right	Ctrl R
Rotate an object, PP 74	Click [Free Rotate]	Click Draw, click Rotate/Flip, click Free Rotate, drag a resize handle	

TASK REFERENCE

POWERPOINT 4.0 FOR WINDOWS

Italicized page numbers indicate the first discussion of each task.

TASK	MOUSE	MENU	KEYBOARD
Save, PP 19	Click	Click File, click Save	Ctrl S or Shift F12
Save As, PP 10		Click File, click Save As	F12
Show all text and headings, PP 30	Click		Alt Shift A
Show titles, PP 30	Click		Alt Shift 1
Slide Master view, PP 85	Hold down Shift and click		
Slide Show View	Click	Click View, click Slide Show, click Show	
Slide Sorter View, PP 12	Click	Click View, click Slide Sorter	Alt Ctrl P
Slide View, PP 37	Click	Click View, click Slides	Alt Ctrl N
Underline text, PP 43	Click	Click Format, click Font, click Underline, click the OK button	Ctrl U
Undo	Click	Click Edit, click Undo	Ctrl Z
Ungroup, PP 64		Select object, click Draw, click Ungroup	Ctrl Shift H

Microsoft® Office Professional for Windows 3.1 Integration Tutorial

Read This Before You Begin

To the Student

To use this tutorial, you must have a Student Disk. Your instructor will either provide you with one or ask you to make your own by following the instructions in the section "Your Student Disk" in this tutorial. See your instructor or technical support person for further information. If you are going to work through this tutorial using your own computer, you need a computer system running Microsoft Windows 3.1, Microsoft Office Professional for Windows, and a Student Disk. *You will not be able to complete this tutorial or its exercises using your own computer until you have a Student Disk.*

To the Instructor

Making the Student Disk To complete this tutorial, your students must have a copy of the Student Disk. To relieve you of having to make multiple Student Disks from a single master copy, we provide you with the CTI WinApps Setup Disk, which contains an automatic Student Disk generating program. Once you install the Setup Disk icon on a network or standalone workstation, students can easily make their own Student Disks by double-clicking the "Make Office Student Disk" icon in the CTI WinApps icon group. Double-clicking this icon transfers all the data files students will need to complete the tutorial, Tutorial Assignments, and Case Problems to a high-density disk in drive A or B. If some of your students will use their own computers to complete this tutorial and its exercises, they must first get the Student Disk. The section called "Your Student Disk" in this tutorial provides complete instructions on how to make the Student Disk.

Installing the CTI WinApps Setup Disk To install the CTI WinApps icon group from the Setup Disk, follow the instructions on the Setup Disk label. By adopting this book, you are granted a license to install this software on any computer or computer network used by you or your students.

README File A README.TXT file located on the Setup Disk provides complete installation instructions, additional technical notes, troubleshooting advice, and tips for using the CTI WinApps software in your school's computer lab. You can view the README.TXT file using any word processor you choose.

System Requirements

The minimum software and hardware requirements to run Microsoft Office Professional on your computer system are as follows:

- Microsoft Windows version 3.1 or later on a local hard drive or a network drive.
- A 386 or higher processor with a minimum of 4 MB of RAM (8 MB or more is strongly recommended when running multiple programs).
- A mouse supported by Windows 3.1.
- A printer supported by Windows 3.1.
- A VGA 640 × 480 16-color display is recommended; an 800 × 600 or 1024 × 768 SVGA, VGA monochrome, or EGA display is also acceptable.
- 82 MB free hard disk space for complete installation.
- Student workstations with at least 1 high-density 3.5-inch disk drive.

OBJECTIVES

In this tutorial you will:

- Launch Office Manager
- Copy spreadsheet information from Excel to Word
- Move spreadsheet information from Word to Excel
- Learn how OLE (Object Linking and Embedding) saves time
- Link spreadsheet information from Excel into Word
- Embed Paintbrush and WordArt objects into a Word document
- Merge an Access mailing list into a Word form letter
- Convert a Word outline to PowerPoint slides

Integrating Microsoft Office Applications

Preparing Integrated Documents for Pet Provisions

CASE

Pet Provisions The "Introducing Microsoft Office Professional" section at the beginning of this book presented Pet Provisions, a company that sells pet food and supplies to pet shops around the world. Started by Manny Cordova in 1991, the company emphasizes excellent customer service and close control of their products' quality and costs. By offering their customers quality products at low prices in a timely manner, Pet Provisions has enjoyed steady annual growth in sales and profits.

Manny holds quarterly sales planning meetings for all sales, marketing, product development, and customer service employees. At these meetings, he aims to help them learn about Pet Provisions' new products and how they are better than the competition. He also tries to generate excitement about their products, because he knows that the staff will in turn transfer that excitement to customers and continue to improve the company's impressive sales record. Manny reviews the company's past performance, explains their new product development plans and strategies for expanding sales territories, and presents financial projections and marketing strategies for the coming quarter.

Before the meeting, he sends all employees a memo to get them thinking about the meeting and to give them a preview of the company's current sales and profit trends. At the meeting, he gives them more detailed financial, product, and sales territory information, using a PowerPoint presentation to illustrate his key points. Following the meeting, Manny launches the Pet Provisions expanded product line by mailing customers a cover letter and a brochure describing the new products and listing all product prices.

Because of the importance of the employee memo, the meeting itself, and the customer product mailing, Manny has spent a lot of time planning their content. He asks his computer analyst, Tami Wells, who knows how to use Microsoft Office, to help him create the documents.

In the Word, Excel, Access, and PowerPoint tutorials in this book, you have learned to create powerful documents, spreadsheets, charts, databases, and presentations, all within the individual applications. And as you learned in the "Introducing Microsoft Office Professional" tutorial, Office Professional (Word, Excel, Access, PowerPoint, and Office Manager) lets you open several applications at one time and switch quickly between them, transferring text, graphics, and numerical information. So now think of the many possibilities available to Manny and Tami, now that Pet Provisions can use Microsoft Office.

You'll see in this tutorial how Office lets them integrate numeric information, text, database information, and presentations from multiple Office applications quickly and automatically. Once Manny learns how to integrate the company information he wants to present, it will be easy for him to prepare for the next planning meeting by merely updating the documents he creates for this meeting with more current information.

Follow along with Tami as she helps Manny prepare the memo, the customer mailing, and finally, his presentation, all using Office.

Your Student Disk

To complete this tutorial, you must have a Student Disk. The Student Disk contains all the practice files you need for the tutorial, the Tutorial Assignments, and the Case Problems. If your instructor or technical support person provides you with a Student Disk, you can skip this section and go to the section "Launching Office Manager." If your instructor asks you to make your own Student Disk, follow the steps in this section.

To make your Student Disk, you need:

- A blank, formatted, high-density 3.5-inch disk
- A computer with Microsoft Windows 3.1, Microsoft Office 4.3, and the CTI WinApps icon group installed on it

If you are using your own computer, the CTI WinApps icon group will not be installed on it. Before you proceed, you must go to your school's computer lab and find a computer with the CTI WinApps icon group installed on it to make your Student Disk. Once you have made your own Student Disk, you can use it to complete this tutorial and its exercises on any computer you choose.

To make your Office Student Disk:

❶ Launch Windows and make sure the Program Manager window is open.

❷ Label your formatted disk "Microsoft Office Student Disk" and place it in the appropriate drive.

❸ Look for an icon labeled "CTI WinApps" or a window labeled "CTI WinApps."

TROUBLE? If you can't find anything labeled "CTI WinApps," the CTI software might not be installed on your computer. Ask your instructor or technical support person for assistance. If you are using your own computer, you will not be able to make your Student Disk. To make it you need access to the CTI WinApps icon group, which is, most likely, installed on your school's lab computers. Ask your instructor or technical support person for further information on where to locate the CTI WinApps icon group. Once you create your Student Disk, you can use it to complete this tutorial and its exercises on any computer you choose.

4. If you see an icon labeled "CTI WinApps," double-click the **CTI WinApps icon** to open the CTI WinApps group window. If the CTI WinApps window is already open, go to Step 5.
5. Double-click the **Make Office Student Disk icon**. The Make Office Student Disk window opens.
6. Make sure the drive that contains your formatted disk corresponds to the drive option button that is highlighted in the dialog box on your screen. Click the **OK button**.
7. When the copying is complete, a message indicates the number of files copied to your disk. Click the **OK button**.
8. To close the CTI WinApps window, double-click the **Control menu box** on the CTI WinApps window.

Launching Office Manager

In previous tutorials you worked with Word, Excel, Access, and PowerPoint, the main applications in Office. As you have learned, Office is a collection of software applications that work alike and share data easily, and the Office Manager lets you move effortlessly among them. Once Tami launches Office Manager, she will have all its software tools—Word, Excel, Access, and PowerPoint—readily available, and will be able to easily integrate information among them.

Tami launches Office Manager to begin her work with Manny on his employee memo, customer letter, and sales meeting presentation.

To launch Office Manager:

1. If the Office Manager toolbar already appears on the screen, skip these steps and go to the next section.
2. Look for an icon or window titled "Microsoft Office."

   TROUBLE? If you don't see anything called "Microsoft Office," click Window on the menu bar and, if you find "Microsoft Office" in the list, click it. If you still can't find anything called "Microsoft Office," ask your instructor or technical support person for help on how to launch Office Manager. If you are using your own computer, make sure the Office Manager software has been installed.

3. If you see the Microsoft Office group icon, double-click the **Microsoft Office group icon** to open the group window. If you see the Microsoft Office *group window* instead of the *group icon*, go to Step 4.
4. Double-click the **Microsoft Office icon** in the Microsoft Office group window. When the Office Manager launch is complete, your screen should look similar to Figure 1-1.

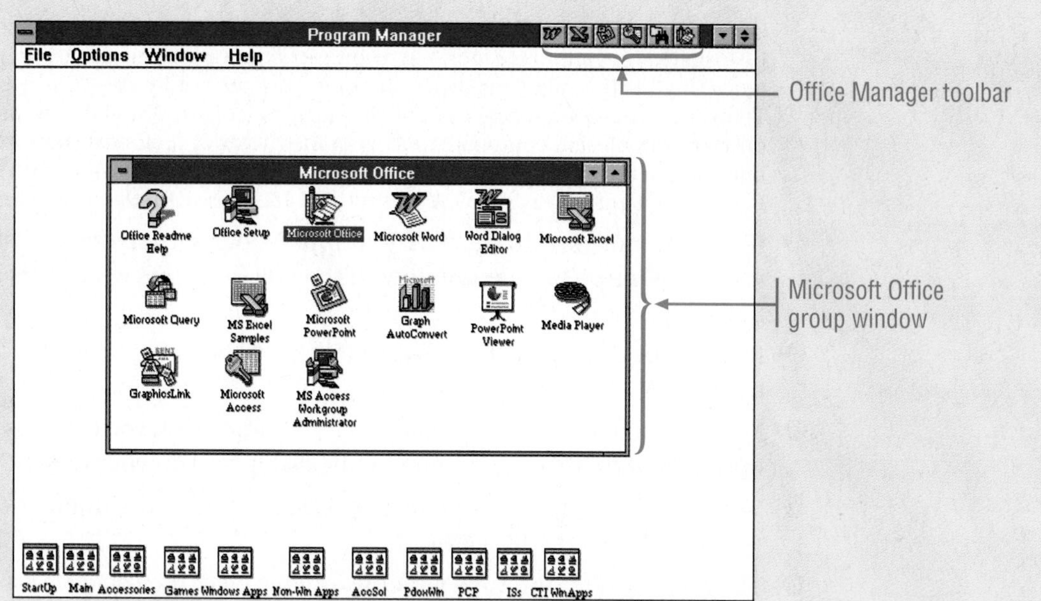

Figure 1-1 The Microsoft Office group window and Office Manager toolbar

TROUBLE? Your Office Manager toolbar may be different from the one shown in Figure 1-1. To change your Office Manager toolbar, see "Customizing the Office Manager Toolbar" in the "Introducing Microsoft Office Professional" tutorial in this book.

❺ Click the **Microsoft Office group window Minimize button**, then if the Program Manager is not already maximized, click the Program Manager's Maximize button.

Copying and Moving Information Between Word and Excel

Before the next quarterly sales meeting, Manny wants to send a memo to all Pet Provisions staff that gives them a preview of the financial data that he will be discussing at the meeting. He has drafted the memo in Word and saved it as PET.DOC. The financial data, which shows sales, cost, and profit information for the last five years, is stored in an Excel spreadsheet file, PET.XLS. He explains to Tami that he wants to present this financial information to his staff in the pre-meeting memo. Tami recommends that he use Office for this task, because Office will not only let him bring in the information quickly and easily but will give him flexibility and speed in updating the information in both documents.

Launching Word and Excel

Tami prepares to transfer Manny's financial information from the Excel workbook, PET.XLS, into the Word memo, PET.DOC. First she launches Word and Excel, and then opens Manny's Word document and Excel workbook.

To launch multiple Office applications:

❶ Insert your Office Student Disk in the appropriate drive.

❷ Click the **Microsoft Word button** on the Office Manager toolbar to launch Word, click the **Open button** on the Standard toolbar, switch to the drive containing your Student Disk, if necessary, then double-click **pet.doc** in the File Name list box. Manny's memo to his staff opens.

3. Click **File**, click **Save As...**, switch to the drive containing your Student Disk if necessary, type **S1PET.DOC** in the File Name text box, then click the **OK button** or press **[Enter]** to save the document under the new filename.
4. Click the **Microsoft Excel button** on the Office Manager toolbar to launch Excel, click , switch to the drive containing your Student Disk if necessary, then double-click **pet.xls** in the File Name list box. Manny's financial summary for 1991–1995 opens.
5. Click **File**, click **Save As...**, switch to the drive containing your Student Disk, if necessary, type **S1PET.XLS** in the File Name text box, then click the **OK button** or press **[Enter]** to save the workbook under the new filename.

Now that she has launched Word and Excel and opened the Word memo and the Excel workbook, Tami is ready to copy the company's financial summary data from the Excel worksheet to Manny's memo in Word, as shown in Figure 1-2.

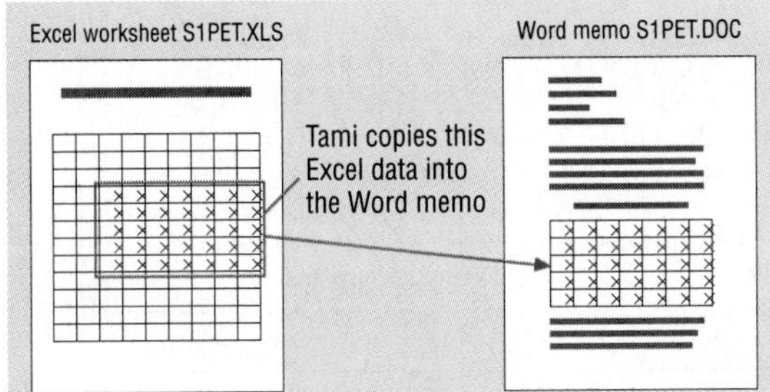

Figure 1-2
Copying data from Excel to Word

Copying Information from Excel to Word

You copy information from one Office application (in this case, Excel) to another (in this case, Word) the same way you copy information within a single application. Tami copies the Excel financial data to the Word memo.

To copy information from one application to another:

1. From the Microsoft Excel window, click the **1991–95 tab** to display the 1991–95 sheet if it is not already displayed. Make sure that the Excel and the workbook windows are maximized.
2. Highlight cells A3 through G6 to select this range, then click the **Copy button** on the toolbar to copy the selected cells' contents to the Clipboard.

❸ Click the **Microsoft Word button** on the Office Manager toolbar, then make sure the Word and the document windows are maximized.

❹ In Manny's memo, locate the paragraph that begins "Congratulations on another outstanding year," and place the insertion pointer before the second blank paragraph marker that follows this paragraph. Click the **Paste button** on the Standard toolbar to copy the cells into a Word table. See Figure 1-3.

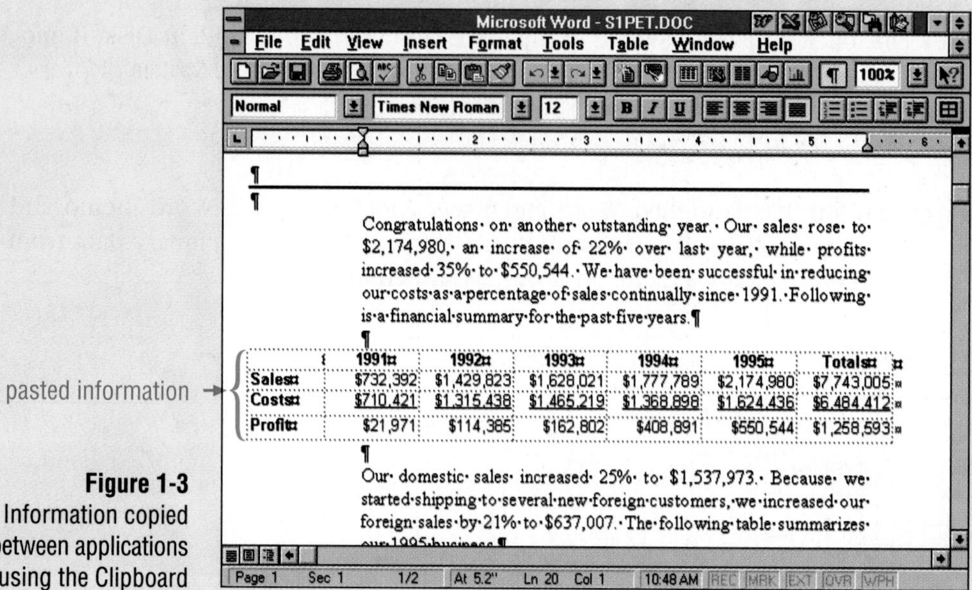

Figure 1-3
Information copied between applications using the Clipboard

Tami notices that she forgot to copy the spreadsheet title, so she uses the drag-and-drop method to copy the spreadsheet title, "Pet Provisions Financial Summary," into the Word document.

❺ Press and hold **[Shift]** then click the **Microsoft Excel button** on the Office Manager toolbar so that the Word and Excel windows appear tiled on the screen. See Figure 1-4.

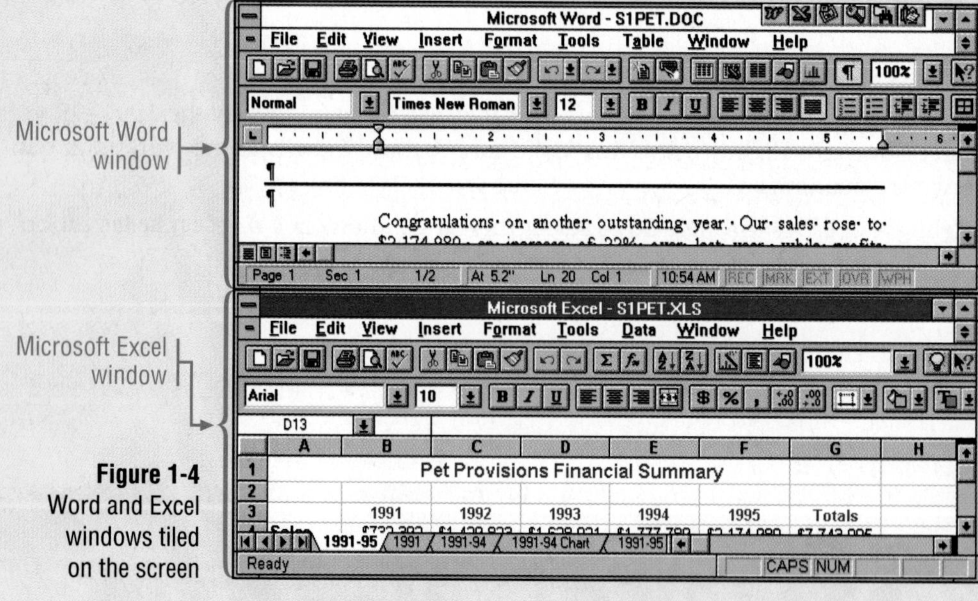

Figure 1-4
Word and Excel windows tiled on the screen

6. Scroll the Word document window until you can see the blank paragraph above the copied table. Make the Excel worksheet the active application, then highlight cells A1 through F1 to select this range in the Excel worksheet.
7. Move the pointer to the edge of the selection until the pointer changes to ↖. While holding down **[Ctrl]**, drag the selection to the blank line before the table in the Word document, release the mouse button, then release [Ctrl]. The selected information is copied to the Word document.
8. Click the **Word window Maximize button**, then click the **Save button** on the Standard toolbar. See Figure 1-5.

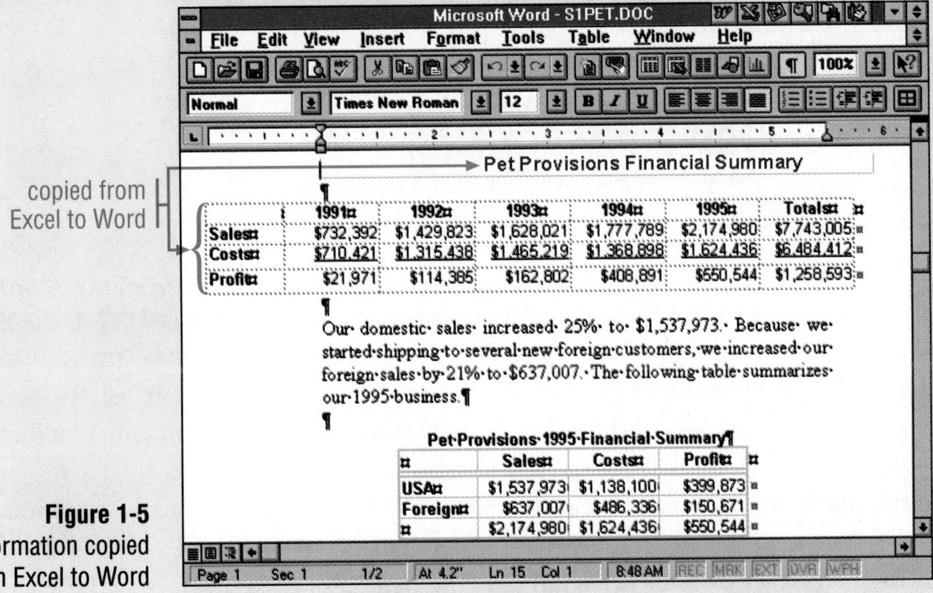

Figure 1-5
Information copied from Excel to Word

Moving Information from Word to Excel

Manny decides that at the quarterly planning meeting he will focus on domestic rather than on international sales. You might have noticed that after the part of his memo discussing the company's successful year, Manny had inserted a Word table containing figures on both foreign and domestic sales. He wants to remove this information from the memo so that it no longer appears, but he realizes it would be useful to have this information in his Excel financial spreadsheet. Tami assures him that it's easy to move the Word table from his Word memo to his Excel spreadsheet, and she proceeds to show him how.

To move information from one application to another:

1. Click the **Microsoft Excel button** on the Office Manager toolbar to switch to Excel, click the **Excel window Maximize button**, then click the **Save button** on the toolbar.
2. From the Excel window, scroll the workbook window until row 10 is the topmost visible row. This is the area you'll use to store the foreign and domestic sales information.
3. Press and hold **[Shift]** then click the **Microsoft Word button** on the Office Manager toolbar. The Word and Excel windows appear tiled on the screen, and row 10 is still visible in the Excel window.
4. Scroll down the Word document window until the table, entitled "Pet Provisions 1995 Financial Summary," is visible and then highlight the rows of the table. See Figure 1-6.

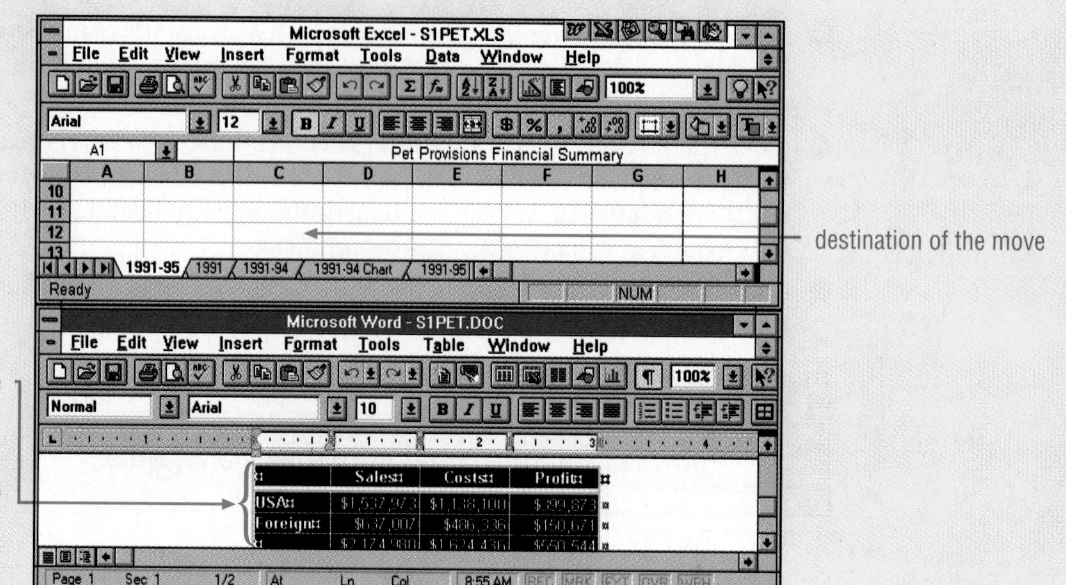

Figure 1-6
A highlighted Word table that you will move to Excel

5. Click the **Cut button** on the Standard toolbar to delete the table from the Word document and to move the table to the Clipboard, click twice in **cell C12** in the Excel worksheet, then click the **Paste button** on the toolbar. The table is copied from the Clipboard to the Excel worksheet. It no longer appears in the Word memo.

Since the title was not part of the table, it remains in the Word document. You'll move this into the Excel document now.

6. Scroll the Word document window until "Pet Provisions 1995 Financial Summary" is visible, then highlight **Pet Provisions 1995 Financial Summary**.
7. Move the pointer over the selection until the pointer changes to ↖. Drag the selection to cell C10 in the Excel window, then release the mouse button. The selected information is moved to the Excel worksheet and is cut from the Word document.
8. Click the **Excel window Maximize button**, then click the **Save button** on the toolbar. If necessary, scroll to the top of the worksheet. See Figure 1-7.

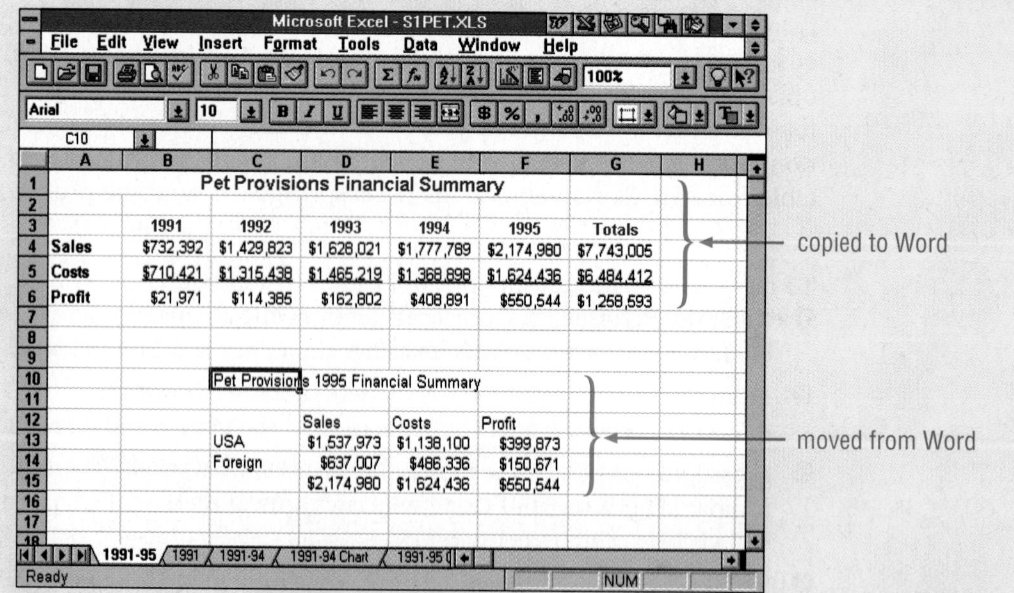

Figure 1-7
Information transferred between Excel and Word

9. Click the **Microsoft Word button** on the Office Manager toolbar to switch to Word, then click the **Word window Maximize button**.
10. Delete the paragraph in the Word memo that begins "Our domestic sales increased by 25%," then click the **Save button** on the Standard toolbar.

Now that Manny has learned to copy and move information between applications, he begins thinking about updating information and the effects updating might have on a copy in another application.

Linking and Embedding Objects

Manny's memo now contains his text and the domestic sales information that Tami copied from Excel. He asks Tami if it's possible to place numbers from an Excel spreadsheet into a Word document without losing the ability to update the figures if necessary.

Tami explains that when you copy information from one application to another, the two copies remain independent. If you change the copied information in one application, the information in the other application does not change.

Object Linking and Embedding (OLE) Concepts

You embed or link objects using Object Linking and Embedding (OLE). An **object** is a chart, graphic, worksheet, or other "package" of data or information. **OLE** (pronounced oh-LAY) lets you embed or link an object from one application into another. For example, you can embed or link a worksheet from Excel and place it in a Word document. The application containing the original object (Excel in this example) is called the **source** application—also called the **server** or **object** application—and the application in which you place the copy (Word in this example) is the **destination** application—also called the **client** or **container** application.

If the object is copied by **embedding**, it exists as a separate object in the destination application. The embedded copy is not linked to the source object, which means that changes to the source are not made to the copy and vice versa. However, you can change the embedded copy using the tools and commands of the source application. This relationship is illustrated in the top half of Figure 1-8.

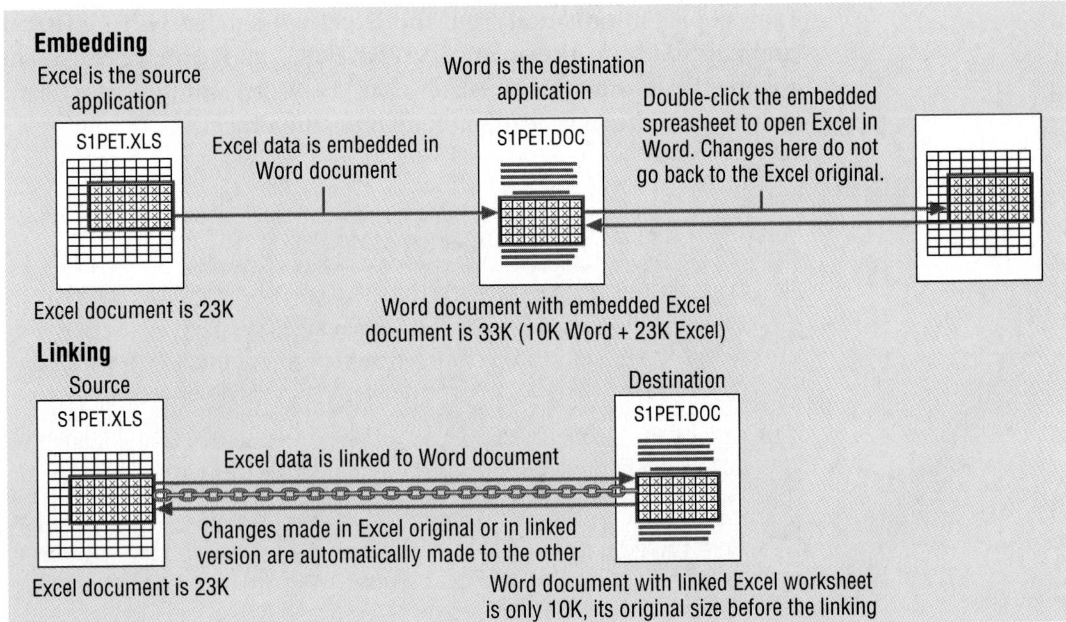

Figure 1-8
Embedding contrasted with linking

To change the embedded copy, double-click the embedded object. The menu and toolbar of the destination application (Word in the example) change to those of the source application (Excel in the example). After changing the embedded object, click outside the object to close the source application and return to the menu and toolbar of the destination application.

You can also use OLE to link objects between two applications. When you **link** an object, changes you make to the object in the source application or the destination application are also made to the object in the other application. See the lower half of Figure 1-8. A linked object does not exist as a copy in the destination application. Instead, OLE creates a connection, or link, between the original in the source application and its linked representation in the destination application. It is this link that allows any changes to the object in either the source or destination application to be reflected in the other. While working in Office, you might see the term DDE in dialog boxes or in the Excel formula bar. **DDE** means **Dynamic Data Exchange**, and, like OLE, is another means of transferring information among applications.

As with an embedded object, you can double-click a linked object to directly access the source application. Because a linked object does not exist as a separate object in the destination application, the size of the document in the destination application is not increased by linking. In contrast, an embedded object increases the size of the file you created in the destination application.

As you use Office in your work, you will have to examine tasks that call for integration among applications and decide whether embedding or linking is the right method for the job. You'll probably want to choose embedding when including a spreadsheet, chart, database, or text object that you expect you'll need to edit quickly in the future but when the object will not have to be updated to match the source. Embedding is also the right choice when file size is not an issue.

You'll want to choose linking when including information that changes on a regular basis, such as a report that contains weekly or monthly sales figures from a spreadsheet or database. If you are working with a large document, linking is often preferable, because the destination document will contain only a link to the source, not a copy of the actual source object, so the document size is not significantly increased.

Linking Objects from Excel to Word

To show Manny how to place Excel data into Word and retain a link between the two, Tami copies information from the Excel worksheet S1PET.XLS, which contains financial summary data, to the memo, S1PET.DOC, in Word. Because she wants to be able to change the information in either Excel or Word and have the change take place automatically in the other application, Tami links the object.

REFERENCE WINDOW

Linking an Object

- Launch the destination application, open the file containing the object to be linked, select the object or information you want to link to the second application, then click the Copy button on the application's toolbar.
- Launch the destination application, open the file that will contain the link to the copied object, position the pointer where you want to establish the link, click Edit, then click Paste Special....
- Click the Paste Link radio button, select the option you want in the As list box, then click the OK button.

Tami links the Excel worksheet information to a Word document.

To link an object between two applications:

1. Make sure that you have launched Excel, opened the S1PET.XLS workbook from your Student Disk, maximized the Excel and the workbook windows, launched Word, opened the S1PET.DOC document from your Student Disk, and maximized the Word and the document windows. Click the **Microsoft Excel button** on the Office Manager toolbar to make Excel the active application if it isn't already. Click the **1991 tab** to display the 1991 sheet.
2. Highlight cells A3 through G6 to select this range of cells, then click the **Copy button** on the toolbar to copy the selected cells' contents to the Clipboard.
3. Click the **Microsoft Word button** on the Office Manager toolbar to switch to Word.
4. Scroll down the document and place the insertion pointer in the first paragraph on the second page, click **Edit**, then click **Paste Special...** to open the Paste Special dialog box.
5. Click the **Paste Link radio button**, then click **Microsoft Excel 5.0 Worksheet Object** in the As list box. See Figure 1-9.

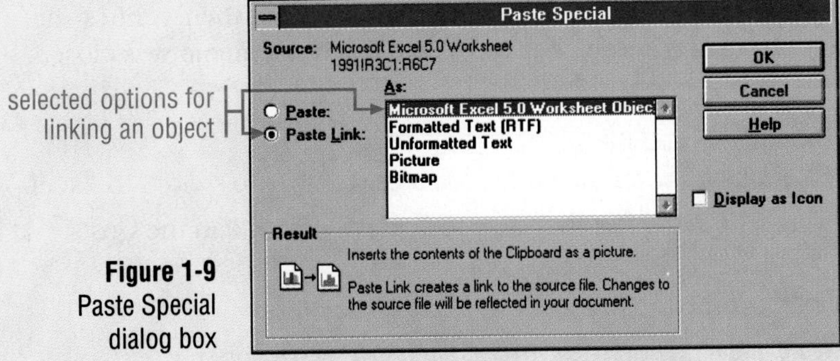

Figure 1-9 Paste Special dialog box

6. Click the **OK button**. After several seconds, the 1991 Financial Summary appears on the second page of Manny's document. See Figure 1-10.

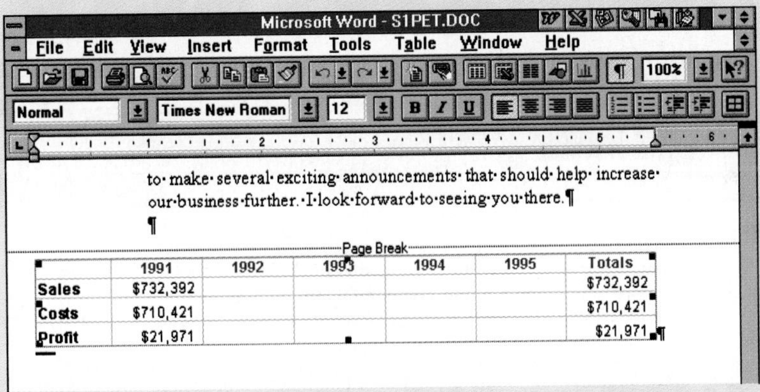

Figure 1-10 An Excel object linked to a Word document

7. Click the **Save button** on the Standard toolbar to save the Word document change.

Now that she has placed the Excel financial summary in Word using Paste Link, Tami proceeds to show Manny how she can add information to the source Excel worksheet, and how it will automatically update in the linked spreadsheet in the Word memo.

To change a linked object in an open file:

1. Click the **Microsoft Excel button** on the Office Manager toolbar to switch to Excel.
2. In the 1992 column, type **1,429,823** in the Sales row, type **1,315,438** in the Costs row, then press [↓]. Formulas in the Profit row and the Totals column show the results of your changes automatically.
3. Click the **Microsoft Word button** on the Office Manager toolbar. The changes you just made in the source spreadsheet for 1992 appear in the linked copy in the memo.
4. Click the **Save button** on the Standard toolbar, click **File**, then click **Close**.

Manny is impressed, but he asks what would happen if he were working on his Excel financial summary worksheet without the Word document open. Would the information still be updated in the memo? Tami answers him by adding the 1993 sales and costs values to the Excel worksheet with the Word document closed. She then verifies that the changes appear in the Word memo automatically, even though the memo was closed.

To change a linked object in a closed file:

1. Click the **Microsoft Excel button** on the Office Manager toolbar to switch to Excel.
2. In the 1993 column, type **1,628,021** in the Sales row, type **1,465,219** in the Costs row, then press [↓].
3. Click the **Save button** on the toolbar, click **File**, then click **Close**.
4. Click the **Microsoft Word button** on the Office Manager toolbar, open the S1PET.DOC file from your Student Disk, then press **[Shift][F5]** to position the pointer at its last saved position. The linked spreadsheet object has been updated with the changes made in Excel. The changes for 1993 appear in the linked spreadsheet on Page 2. See Figure 1-11.

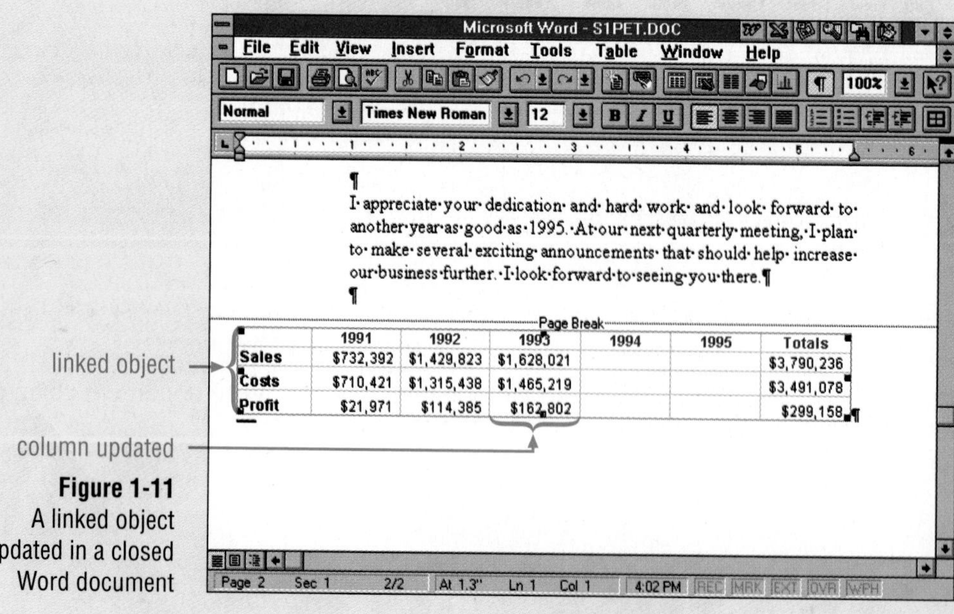

Figure 1-11
A linked object updated in a closed Word document

To show Manny how flexible updating links can be, Tami adds the 1994 sales and costs values to the Excel worksheet, but this time she accesses the worksheet from the Word memo (Figure 1-12).

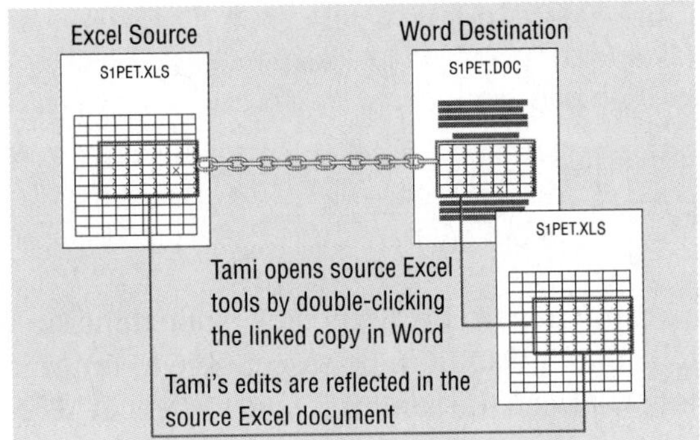

Figure 1-12
Updating the linked source object by editing it from within the destination application

To change a linked object from within the destination application:

❶ Double-click the **linked object** in the Word document. The Excel window appears with the S1PET.XLS workbook open on the screen.

❷ In the 1994 column, type **1,777,789** in the Sales row, type **1,368,898** in the Costs row, then press [↓]. See Figure 1-13.

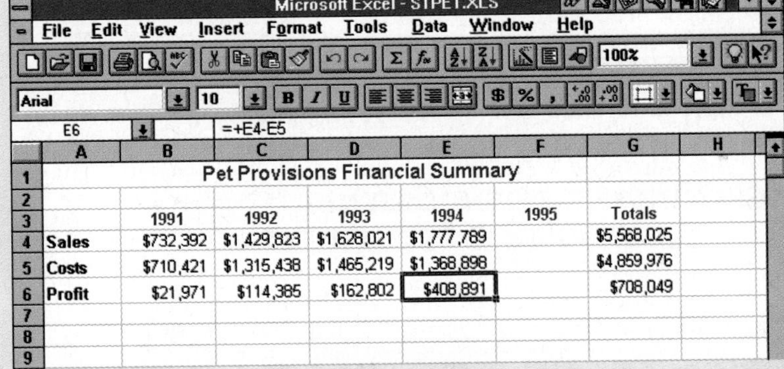

	A	B	C	D	E	F	G	H
1			Pet Provisions Financial Summary					
2								
3		1991	1992	1993	1994	1995	Totals	
4	Sales	$732,392	$1,429,823	$1,628,021	$1,777,789		$5,568,025	
5	Costs	$710,421	$1,315,438	$1,465,219	$1,368,898		$4,859,976	
6	Profit	$21,971	$114,385	$162,802	$408,891		$708,049	
7								
8								
9								

Figure 1-13
Changes made to a linked object from within the source application

❸ Click the **Save button** on the toolbar, click **File**, then click **Close** to save and close the workbook.

❹ Click the **Microsoft Word button** on the Office Manager toolbar. The changes for 1994 appear in the Word document.

❺ Click on the Standard toolbar to save the document.

The only information lacking now is the 1995 data. Tami wants to show one more feature to Manny. You can break the link between applications if you no longer need to have an object linked. Use the Links command on the Edit menu to break a link. Once you break a link, you cannot change the copied object, but you can resize, move, or delete it.

REFERENCE WINDOW

Breaking the Link for a Linked Object

- From the destination application, click Edit, click Links..., select the entry in the Links list box, click the Break Link button, click the OK button, then click the Close button.
- Save the destination application to make sure you retain the break-link action.

Tami wants to show Manny how to break the link, something he would need to do if his memo were finalized and he didn't want it to be susceptible to future changes he might make in Excel. She breaks the link between the summary spreadsheet in Word and its Excel source.

To break the link for a linked object:

1. From the Word window, click **Edit**, then click **Links...** to open the Links dialog box. There should be one entry in the Links list box, and it should be highlighted. If the entry is not highlighted, click it to select it.
2. Click the **Break Link button**. Word opens a dialog box asking, "Are you sure you want to break the selected links?" See Figure 1-14. Your Item entry in the Links dialog box might be different than the one shown in Figure 1-14.

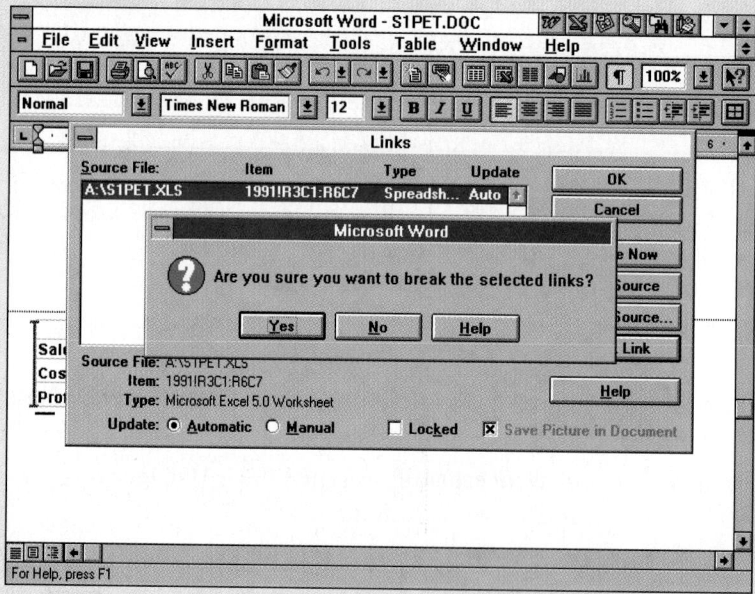

Figure 1-14
Breaking a link to a linked object

3. Click the **Yes button**. The link is broken, the highlighted link disappears from the Links dialog box, and the dialog box closes. *Do not save or close the Word document at this point*, because Tami wants to show Manny how to reestablish the link.
4. Click the **Microsoft Excel button** on the Office Manager toolbar to switch to Excel, open the S1PET.XLS workbook from your Student Disk, then click the **1991 sheet tab**, if necessary, to activate the 1991 sheet.
5. In the 1995 column, type **2,174,980** in the Sales row, type **1,624,436** in the Costs row, then press [↓].

❻ Click the **Save button** on the toolbar to save the workbook.

❼ Click the **Microsoft Word button** on the Office Manager toolbar. The changes for 1995 do not appear in the memo because you have broken the link with the source application.

If you save the Word document, the link to the object remains broken. However, if you close the Word document without saving it, the break-link would not be saved, the link would remain, and the 1995 changes would still appear in the Word document.

Tami now shows Manny how to reestablish the link. *It is important to remember that you can only reestablish a link if you haven't yet saved the document.* She closes the document without saving the break-link change and then reopens the document. Because the last saved version of the Word document contained a link for the object, the 1995 changes will now appear in the document.

To cancel a break-link action:

❶ From the Word window, click **File**, click **Close**, then click the **No button** in the Save Changes dialog box.

❷ Reopen the S1PET.DOC file in Word, then press **[Shift][F5]**. The changes for 1995 appear in the document.

❸ Click the **Save button** on the Standard toolbar to save the document. The object continues to be linked between the two applications.

❹ Click the **Microsoft Excel button** on the Office Manager toolbar to switch to Excel, then double-click the **Excel window Control menu box** to close Excel.

Manny will, of course, want to delete this second table before he prints his memo for his staff members, but for now, he hurries off to a meeting, asking Tami to make this important memo more visually appealing. Tami begins by adding the Pet Provisions logo to the memo.

Embedding an Existing Paintbrush Object

Earlier, you linked information from Manny's Excel spreadsheet into Word using the Paste Link command in the Paste Special dialog box. You can also use the Paste Special dialog box to embed information from another file; you would just click the Paste radio button instead of the Paste Link button. But there are times when you'll want to embed an entire file, not just part of a file, in a destination application. To embed an entire file, you can use the Object command on the Insert menu. Once an object is embedded into a destination document, you can double-click it to bring up the tools of the source application.

The Pet Provisions logo exists by itself in a Paintbrush file. (**Paintbrush** is a Windows graphics application that you can use like any Office application.) Since she wants to embed the entire Paintbrush file, Tami can use the Object command to embed it in the Word document. She can then double-click the embedded logo in Word to open Paintbrush, the source application, to modify it. Because the logo is embedded, not linked, the changes she makes are not made to the source logo.

REFERENCE WINDOW

Embedding an Object with the Object Command

- Launch the destination application, open the file that will contain the embedded object, position the pointer where you want to embed the object, click Insert, then click Object....
- If you are embedding a new object, click the Create New radio button or the Create New tab (depending on the destination application), select the source application name in the Object Type list box, then click the OK button.
- If embedding an existing object, click the Create from File radio button or the Create from File tab; click the Browse... button, if necessary; make appropriate selections in the Drives, Directories, and Source or File Name boxes; then click the OK button.

Tami has created a company logo as a graphic image using the Windows Paintbrush drawing program. Tami now embeds the graphic image into Manny's Word document. Then she makes changes to the Word version of the graphic image using Paintbrush as the source application. Because Tami embeds the graphic image, her changes to the graphic image within Word do not affect the original graphic image.

To embed and change an existing object:

1. From the Word window, press **[Ctrl][Home]**, press **[Enter]**, then press [↑]. The insertion pointer is now at the top of the Word document, S1PET.DOC. This is where you will embed the graphic image.
2. Click **Insert** then click **Object...** to open the Object dialog box.
3. Click the **Create from File tab**, switch to the drive containing your Student Disk, scroll the File Name list box as necessary, and then double-click **petlogo.bmp** in the File Name list box. Word embeds the graphic image at the top of the document.
4. Double-click the **graphic image**. The Paintbrush application is launched with the graphic image open. See Figure 1-15. The size and placement of your Paintbrush window might differ from the figure.

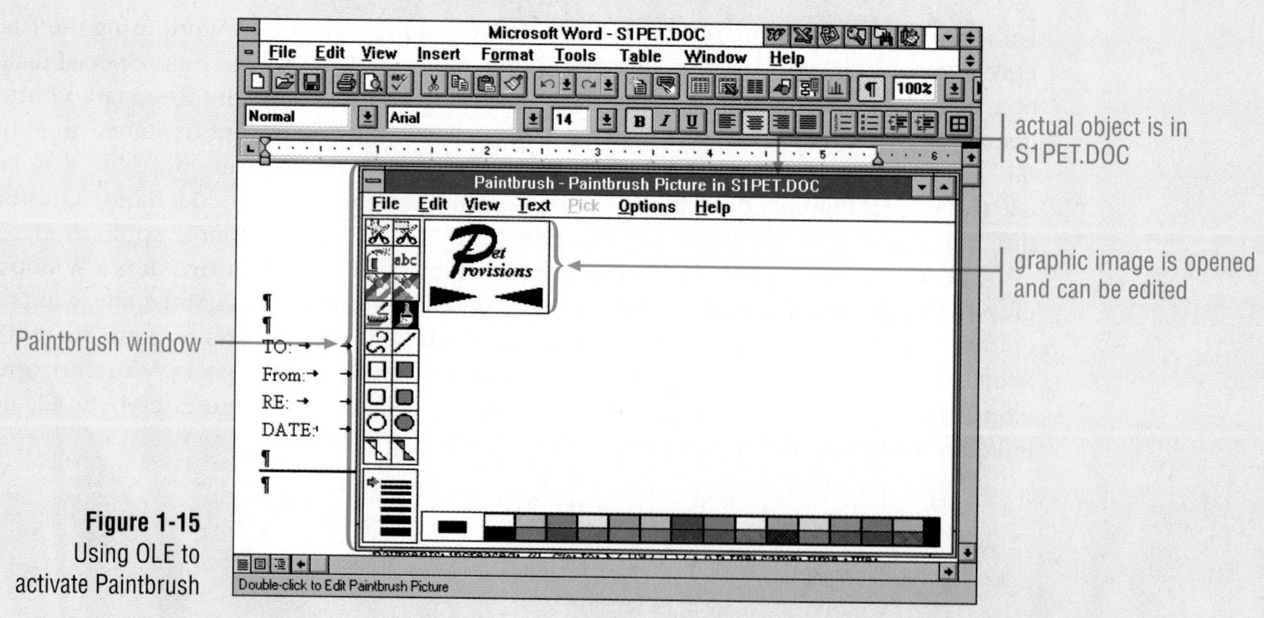

Figure 1-15
Using OLE to activate Paintbrush

5. Click the **red color** in the Palette as the new foreground color, click the **Line tool** in the toolbox, move the pointer above the graphic image "bowtie," draw a horizontal line above the "bowtie" by dragging the pointer, move the pointer below the graphic image "bowtie," and draw a horizontal line below the "bowtie" by dragging the pointer. See Figure 1-16.

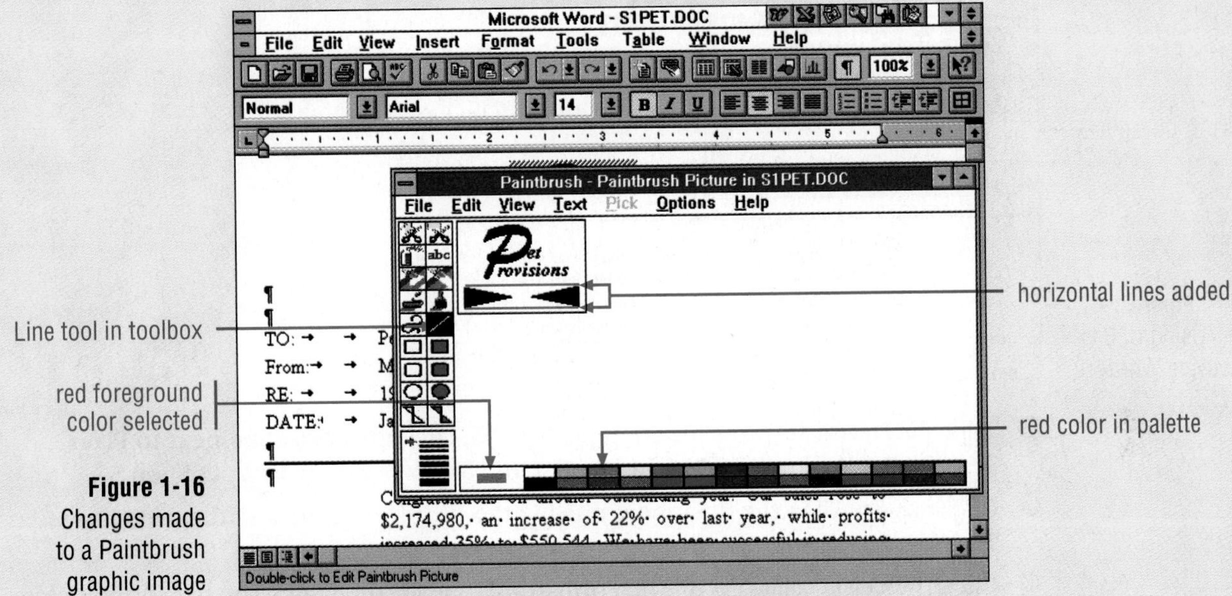

Figure 1-16 Changes made to a Paintbrush graphic image

6. In the Paintbrush menu bar, click **File**, then click **Exit & Return to S1PET.DOC**. If a dialog box with a warning message opens, click the **Yes button** to close the dialog box; this warning tells you that your changes will only affect the version you are embedding in Word; it has no effect on your ability to make further changes to the embedded object.
7. Click the **Save button** on the Standard toolbar to save the document.

Tami has changed the embedded object, but the original object remains unchanged. In the Tutorial Assignments, you will verify that this is true.

Embedding a New WordArt Object

Tami is not satisfied with the finished Word document and decides to try out a different visual effect at the top of the document to see how it looks. She uses WordArt and its special effects to create a new object and embed it in the Word document.

To embed a new object:

1. From the Word window, click the first blank paragraph that follows the MEMORANDUM line. This is where you will embed the WordArt text.
2. Click **Insert** then click **Object...** to open the Object dialog box.
3. Click the **Create New tab** if it's not already selected, click **Microsoft WordArt 2.0** in the Object Type list box (scrolling as necessary), then click the **OK button**. After several seconds, OLE opens the WordArt application. See Figure 1-17.

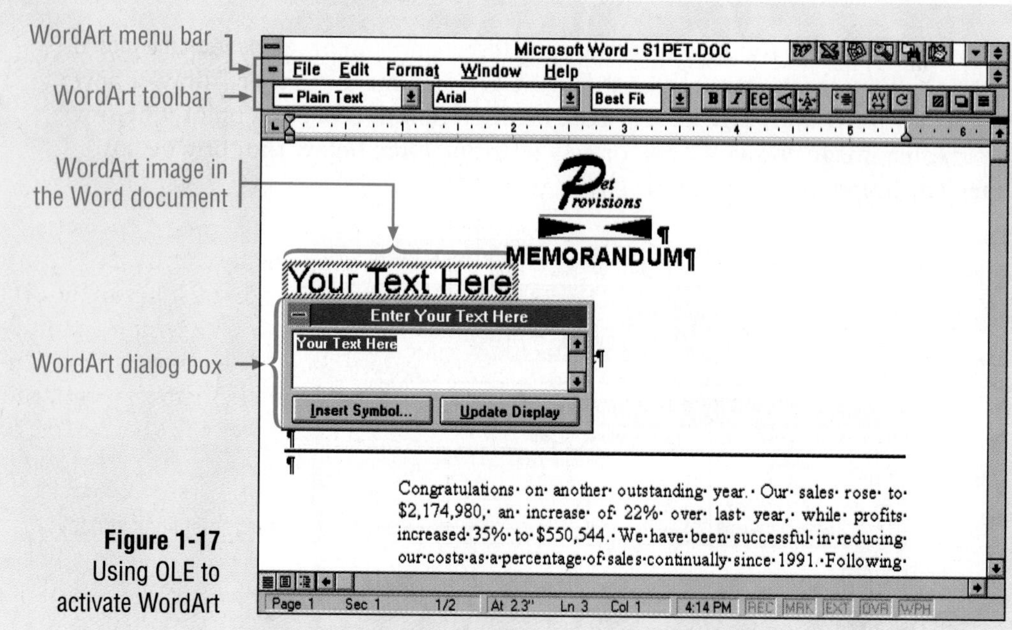

Figure 1-17
Using OLE to activate WordArt

❹ Type **Pet Provisions**, press **[Enter]**, type **1991–95**, click the **down arrow** next to Plain Text on the WordArt toolbar, then click the **Stop Sign style** (row 2, column 5).

❺ Click anywhere in the document outside the WordArt image and the dialog box. The WordArt image appears in the document.

❻ Click the **Center button** on the Formatting toolbar, then click the paragraph below the WordArt image. See Figure 1-18.

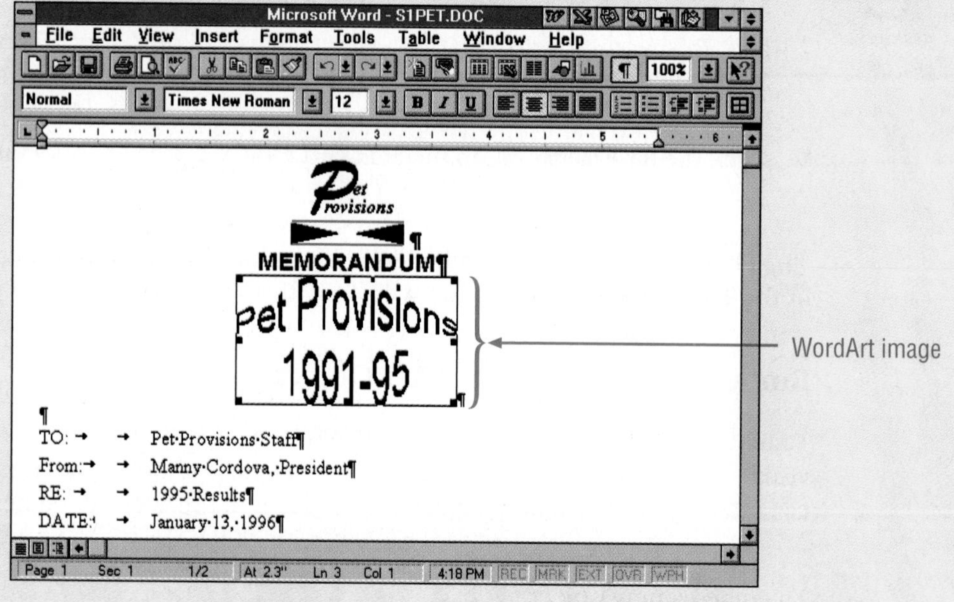

Figure 1-18
WordArt object embedded in a Word document

❼ Click **File**, click **Close**, then click the **Yes button** to save and close the document.

If necessary, Tami can change the embedded object, using WordArt as the source application. She realizes that right now she has both the logo and the WordArt in the memo, and when Manny returns from his meeting, she'll show him her work and he can decide if he'd prefer to use the logo or the WordArt. She needs to get working on her next task.

Now that Tami and Manny have used linking and embedding with Word, Excel, Paintbrush, and WordArt, they use Word and Access to create the mailing to customers.

Specialized Integration Tasks

Each individual Office application lets you accomplish certain specialized tasks. For example, you can use Word's Mail Merge feature to create personalized letters automatically, using mailing addresses stored in an Access database. Mail Merge is actually a form of integration: your letter in Word is the destination document, and the Access database containing names and addresses is the source document. When you **merge** the database with the letter, you combine them, creating a separate letter for each customer in the database. See Figure 1-19.

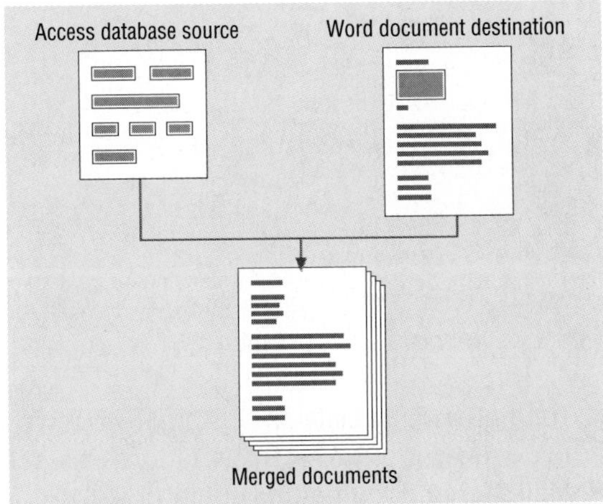

Figure 1-19
Mail Merge is a form of integration

Using Word's Mail Merge Feature with Access

Although Tami and Manny have finished the memo announcing the quarterly sales planning meeting, Manny still has two major tasks: getting out the form letter that announces the company's new products and latest prices to his customers, and preparing his presentation for the meeting. He starts with the form letter.

Manny creates the letter in Word as PETLET.DOC. He wants to mail the letter to Pet Provisions' U.S. customers. The names and addresses of these customers are contained in the tblCustomerUSA table in the Access database called PET.MDB.

REFERENCE WINDOW

Using Word and Access for a Mail Merge

- Create a Word document containing the form letter.
- Create an Access table containing the data to merge into the form letter.
- Open the Word document, click Tools, then click Mail Merge... to open the Mail Merge Helper dialog box. In order, click the Create button, Get Data button, and Merge button, making appropriate responses in the dialog boxes and windows that appear.

Tami uses Word's Mail Merge feature to prepare the letters for mailing to U.S. customers.

To choose the Mail Merge document for a form letter:

1. From the Word window, open the file PETLET.DOC from your Student Disk, then save it as S1PETLET.DOC. This is the main document for the Mail Merge.
2. Click **Tools** then click **Mail Merge...** to open the Mail Merge Helper dialog box. See Figure 1-20. This dialog box contains three command buttons that open list boxes and dialog boxes to help you perform the Mail Merge operation.

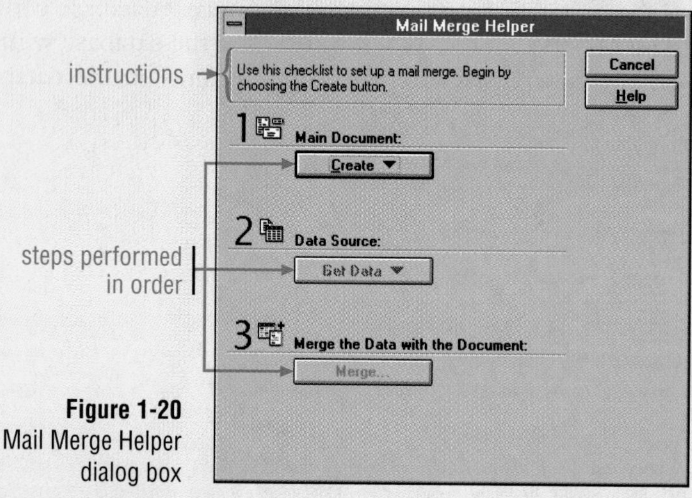

Figure 1-20
Mail Merge Helper dialog box

3. Click the **Create button**, then click **Form Letters...** in the drop-down list box. A dialog box opens, asking if the document in the active window or a new document should be used as the Mail Merge document. See Figure 1-21.

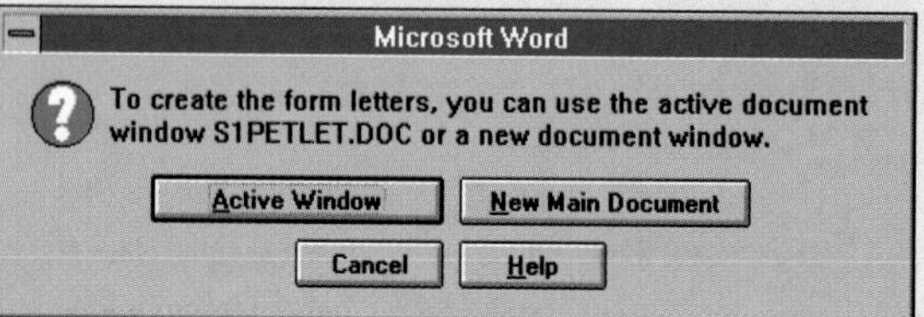

Figure 1-21
Selecting the Mail Merge document

4. Click the **Active Window button** in the dialog box, which then closes. You are returned to the Mail Merge Helper dialog box.

Tami has completed the first of three Mail Merge steps. Next, she selects and opens the tblCustomerUSA table in the PET.MDB Access database as the source of the customer merge data.

To choose the data source for a Mail Merge:

1. Click the **Get Data button**, then click **Open Data Source...** to open the Open Data Source dialog box.
2. Click the **List Files of Type list box down arrow**, click **MS Access Databases (*.mdb)**, click **pet.mdb** in the File Name list box, then click the **OK button**.
3. If a Confirm Data Source dialog box opens, click **MS Access Databases via DDE (*.mdb)**, then click the **OK button**.

4. After several moments, a dialog box opens in which you choose the Access table for the Mail Merge. If necessary, click the **Tables tab**, click **tblCustomerUSA**, then click the **OK button**. Next, a dialog box opens, displaying a warning that no merge fields were found in your Mail Merge document. A merge field identifies a database field that will be merged with the Word document. You need to edit the Word document to add the merge fields to it and will do so in the next set of steps.
5. Click the **Edit Main Document button**. All dialog boxes close and the Word document becomes the active window. See Figure 1-22.

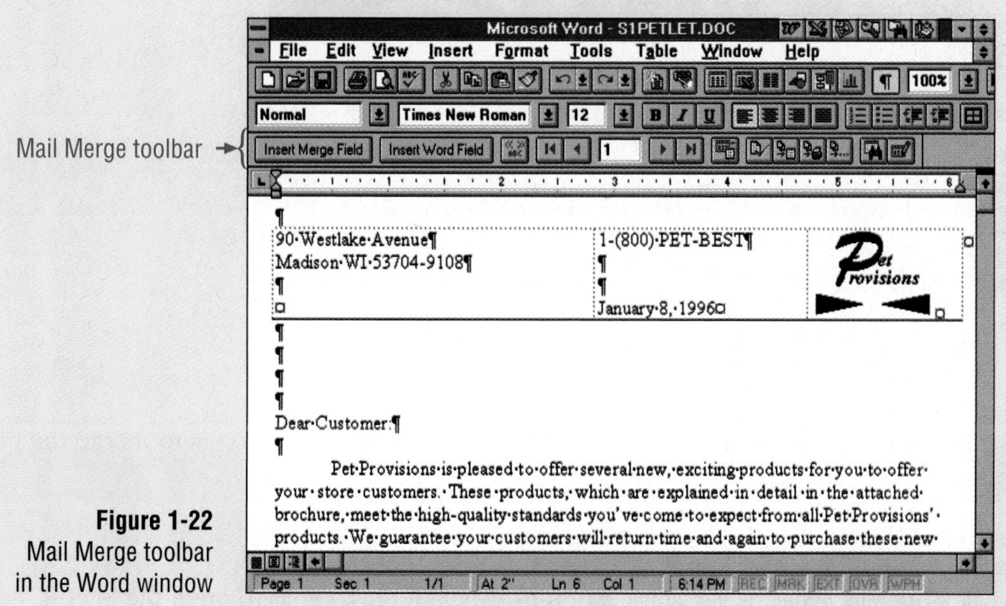

Figure 1-22
Mail Merge toolbar in the Word window

To complete the second Mail Merge step, Tami inserts the merge fields from the Access table into the Mail Merge document.

To insert merge fields into a Mail Merge document from a database table:

1. Position the pointer in the first paragraph below the table, then click the **Insert Merge Field button** on the Mail Merge toolbar. A list of the fields in the Access database table appears. StoreName is the first field to be inserted.
2. Click **StoreName** in the list box. Word inserts the StoreName field between brackets in the selected paragraph.
3. Press [↓], click the **Insert Merge Field button**, click **Street** in the list box, then press [↓]. Word inserts Street between brackets in the Mail Merge document.
4. Click the **Insert Merge Field button**, click **City** in the list box, press **[Spacebar]**, click the **Insert Merge Field button**, click **State** in the list box, press **[Spacebar]**, click the **Insert Merge Field button**, and then click **Zip** in the list box. The customer address block is now complete.
5. Two lines below the address block, highlight **Customer** in "Dear Customer:" and click the **Insert Merge Field button**. Next, click **OwnerName** in the list box. See Figure 1-23.

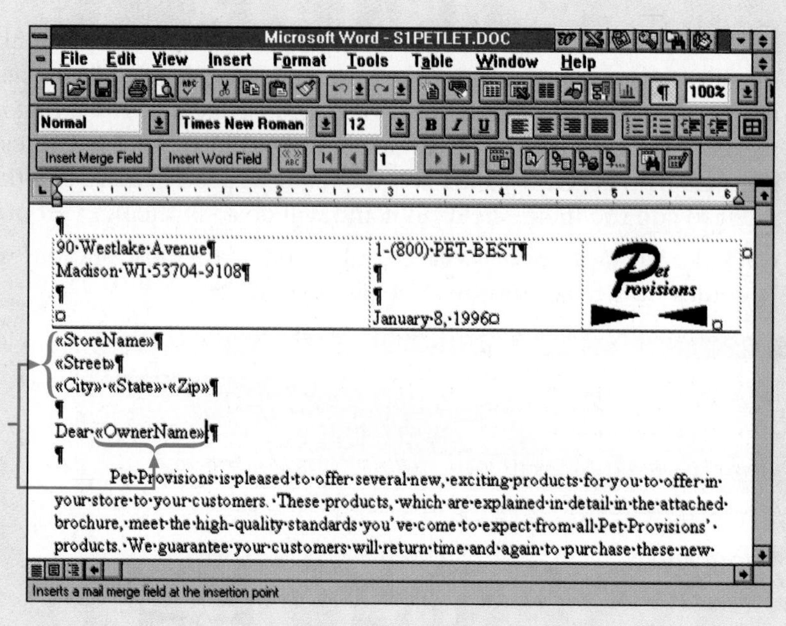

merge fields

Figure 1-23 Merge fields inserted in a Mail Merge document

❻ Click the **Save button** on the Standard toolbar.

Tami has completed the first two Mail Merge steps. Her final step is to merge the customer field values with the Mail Merge document.

To complete a Mail Merge:

❶ Click the **Mail Merge Helper button** on the Mail Merge toolbar to open the Mail Merge Helper dialog box, then click the **Merge button** to open the Merge dialog box. See Figure 1-24.

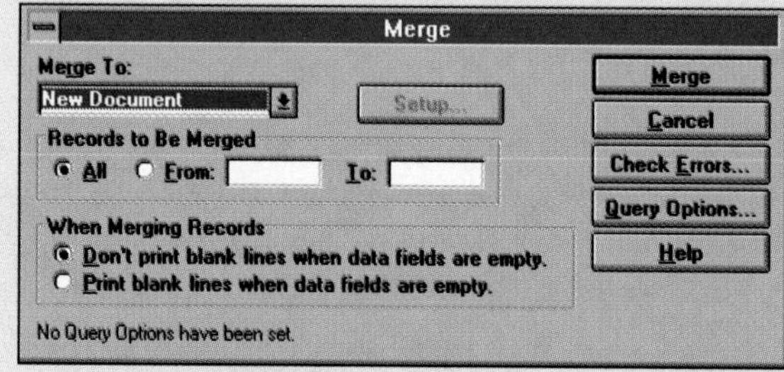

Figure 1-24 Merge dialog box

❷ Click the **Merge button**. Word merges the database table field values and the document. Word creates 20 pages, one page for each customer.

❸ Scroll through several pages of the document and notice that each page contains a copy of the letter for each record in the database.

❹ Click **File**, click **Save As...**, switch to the drive containing your Student Disk, if necessary, type **S1FORM.DOC** in the File Name text box, then press **[Enter]**.

❺ Print the first letter, which is page one of the document. See Figure 1-25.

90 Westlake Avenue
Madison WI 53704-9108

1-(800) PET-BEST

Pet Provisions

January 8, 1996

Animal House
4090 Division Street NW
Fort Lauderdale FL 33302

Dear Ms. Joan Hoffman:

Pet Provisions is pleased to offer several new, exciting products for you to offer in your store to your customers. These products, which are explained in detail in the attached brochure, meet the high-quality standards you've come to expect from all Pet Provisions' products. We guarantee your customers will return time and again to purchase these new products.

To introduce these new products to you, we are offering them at special discount prices for the next 30 days. Please review the brochure and the attached price list and place your order through our 800 number.

If you have questions about our products or have suggestions about future products you would like us to offer, call us any time, any day.

Thank you for your support of our company. We look forward to hearing from you.

Sincerely,

Manny Cordova
President

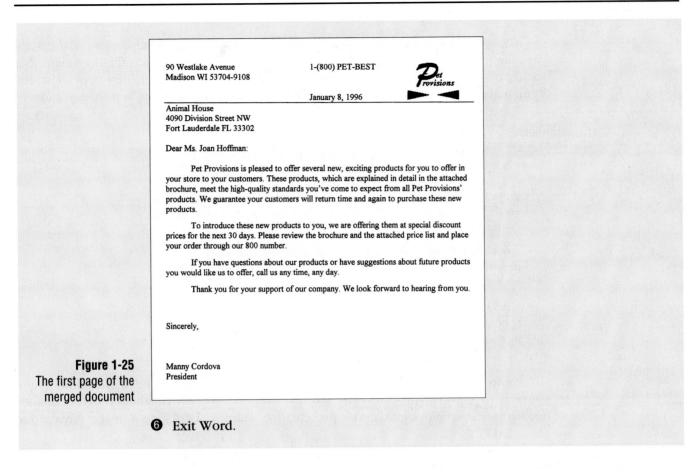

Figure 1-25
The first page of the merged document

❻ Exit Word.

Tami has completed the Mail Merge. All she needs to do now is print the letters, and the mailing is ready to go. Next, she turns her attention to Manny's presentation.

Converting a Word Outline to PowerPoint Slides

Microsoft Word has an **outline** feature that lets you create a topic outline using heading levels for a document, with level 1 headings being the broadest topics, and levels 2 through 9 being the increasingly subordinate topics. If you have a Word document that uses Word's outline feature, you can convert it to PowerPoint slides with a single PowerPoint command. Each level 1 heading in the Word outline becomes a new slide in the PowerPoint presentation. Each Heading 2 through Heading 9 becomes a separate bulleted item. See Figure 1-26.

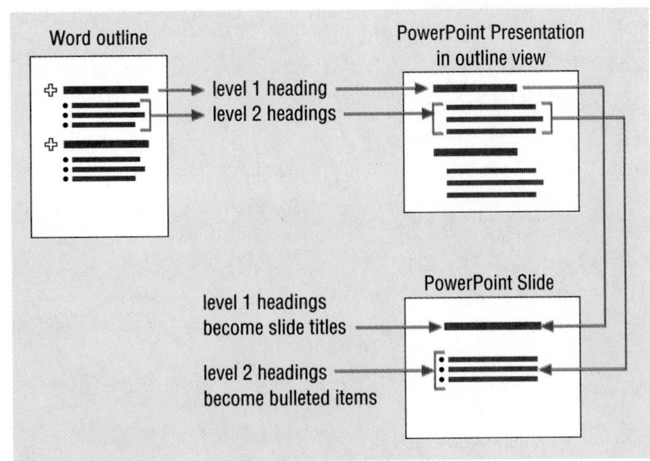

Figure 1-26
A Word outline converts to PowerPoint slides

Manny has a Word document containing an outline of his presentation for the quarterly planning meeting. He is delighted to hear that Tami can easily convert the document to a set of PowerPoint slides, because it means he won't have to reenter the information. His Word outline is the source document, and the PowerPoint presentation is the destination.

REFERENCE WINDOW

Converting a Word Outline to PowerPoint Slides

- Prepare a Word document that outlines the presentation you want to create. In Word, choose Outline from the View menu to view the document in outline view.
- From PowerPoint, open the presentation file and select a slide on the presentation. The Word outline will be converted to slides starting with the slide that follows the selected slide.
- From PowerPoint, click Insert; click Slides from Outline...; make appropriate selections in the Drives, Directories, and File Name boxes; then click the OK button.

Manny's Word document file named PETOUT.DOC contains the Word outline Tami converts to PowerPoint slides. His Word document has two Heading 1 styles, so they become separate slides in Manny's presentation, starting with Slide 4 in the PowerPoint file called PET.PPT.

To convert a Word outline to PowerPoint slides:

1. Click the **Microsoft PowerPoint button** on the Office Manager toolbar to launch PowerPoint, open the PET.PPT file from your Student Disk, then save the file as S1PET.PPT on your Student Disk.
2. Click the **Next Slide button** twice to display Slide 3. The converted Word outline will become Slides 4 and 5.
3. Click **Insert** then click **Slides from Outline...** to open the Insert Outline dialog box.
4. Make sure the Drives box contains the drive letter for your Student Disk, scroll the File Name list box as necessary, then double-click **petout.doc** in the File Name list box. PowerPoint converts the Word outline into PowerPoint slide format. The new slides are Slides 4 and 5.
5. Click the **Next Slide button** to display Slide 4. See Figure 1-27.

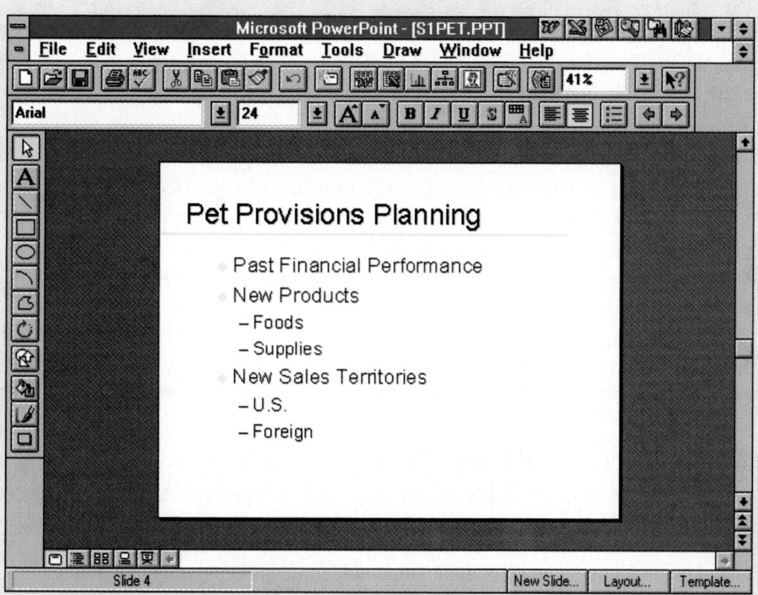

Figure 1-27
A PowerPoint slide created from a Word outline automatically

6. Click the **Next Side button** to display Slide 5.
7. Click the **Save button** on the toolbar, then double-click the **PowerPoint window Control menu box** to save the presentation and exit PowerPoint.

Manny's presentation is off to a good start. In the Tutorial Assignments, you have an opportunity to follow along with Tami as she helps with other aspects of Manny's presentation.

The PowerPoint slides are not linked or embedded to the original Word document outline, so if you change the Word outline or the PowerPoint slides, the changes will not be reflected in the other application's object. Furthermore, you change the new slides in PowerPoint, not in Word. If you want to change the two new PowerPoint slides using Word or have changes occur in both applications automatically, you use the linking and embedding techniques you used earlier in this tutorial.

■ ■ ■

Tami has used the capabilities of Office to begin Manny's employee memo, presentation, and product announcement. Because integrating other types of information and objects among applications is similar to the methods she has already used, Tami is confident she can handle any assignment Manny gives her in the future.

Questions

1. Without using linking or embedding, what are three ways to copy information from one application to another?
2. When using the drag-and-drop method, what determines if the selected information is copied instead of moved?
3. If an Access table is embedded in a Word document, which application is the source application and which application is the destination application?
4. Is the container application or the object application the same as the source application?

5. When an object is linked between two applications, how many copies of the object exist?
6. Is the destination application larger or smaller for a linked object than for an embedded object?
7. If changes are made in the source application to a linked object, do those changes occur to the object in the destination application when it is closed?
8. If you break the link for an object, what operations can you perform on the object in the destination application?
9. What are the three major steps in performing a Mail Merge in Word?

Tutorial Assignments

Tami continues her work on Manny's presentation. She creates a new Word document that Manny will use as a handout for the employees at the quarterly presentation. See Figure 1-28. She also adds slides to Manny's PowerPoint presentation.

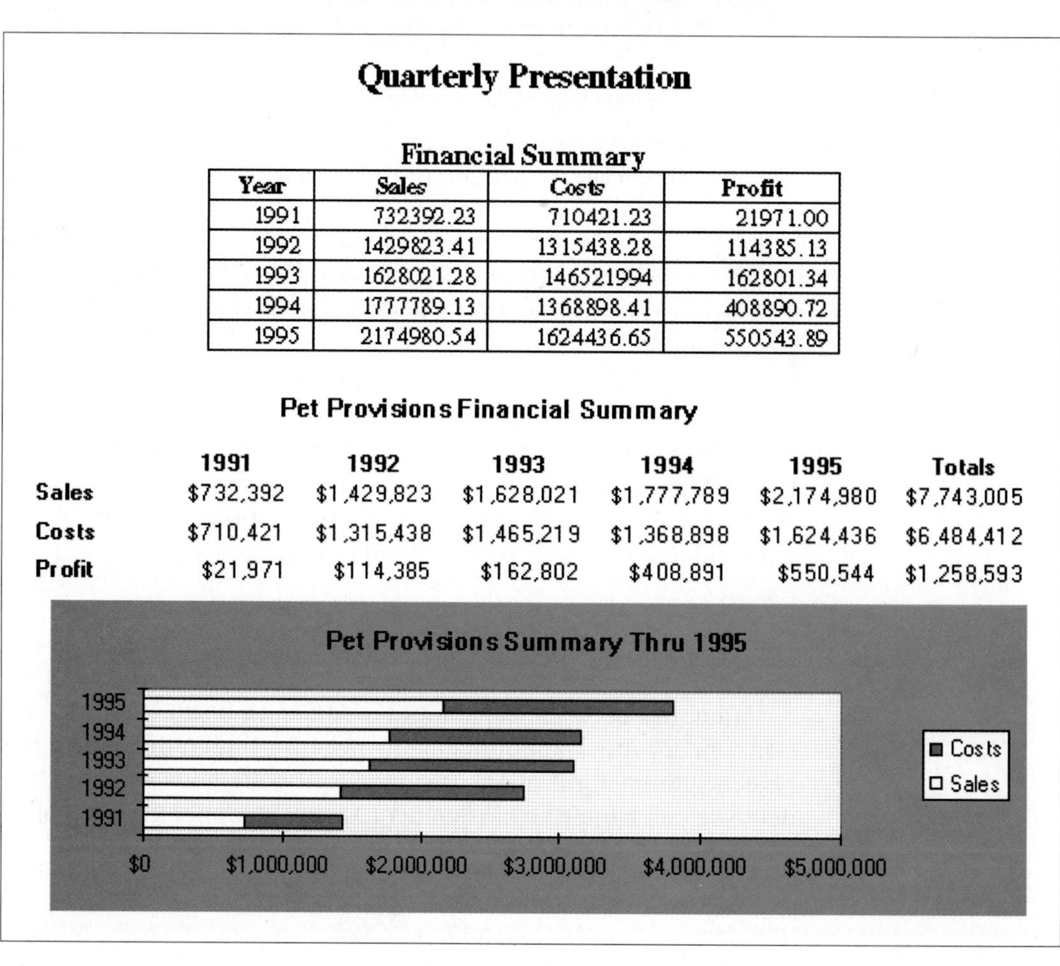

Quarterly Presentation

Financial Summary

Year	Sales	Costs	Profit
1991	732392.23	710421.23	21971.00
1992	1429823.41	1315438.28	114385.13
1993	1628021.28	146521994	162801.34
1994	1777789.13	1368898.41	408890.72
1995	2174980.54	1624436.65	550543.89

Pet Provisions Financial Summary

	1991	1992	1993	1994	1995	Totals
Sales	$732,392	$1,429,823	$1,628,021	$1,777,789	$2,174,980	$7,743,005
Costs	$710,421	$1,315,438	$1,465,219	$1,368,898	$1,624,436	$6,484,412
Profit	$21,971	$114,385	$162,802	$408,891	$550,544	$1,258,593

Figure 1-28